The Shape of Ancient Thought

Comparative Studies in Greek and Indian Philosophies

The Shape of Ancient Thought

Comparative Studies in Greek and Indian Philosophies

THOMAS MCEVILLEY

MOTILAL BANARSIDASS PUBLISHERS
PRIVATE LIMITED • DELHI

First Indian Edition: Delhi, 2008
Earlier published by Allworth Press, An imprint of
Allworth Communications 10, East 23rd Street, New York, NY 10010

ISBN: 978-81-208-3339-5

MOTILAL BANARSIDASS
41 U.A. Bungalow Road, Jawahar Nagar, Delhi 110 007
8 Mahalaxmi Chamber, 22 Bhulabhai Desai Road, Mumbai 400 026
203 Royapettah High Road, Mylapore, Chennai 600 004
236, 9th Main III Block, Jayanagar, Bangalore 560 011
Sanas Plaza, 1302 Baji Rao Road, Pune 411 002
8 Camac Street, Kolkata 700 017
Ashok Rajpath, Patna 800 004
Chowk, Varanasi 221 001

PRINTED IN INDIA

By Jainendra Prakash Jain at Shri Jainendra Press,
A-45 Naraina, Phase-I, New Delhi 110 028
and Published by Narendra Prakash Jain for
Motilal Banarsidass Publishers Private Limited,
Bungalow Road, Delhi 110 007

Table of Contents

EDITOR'S INTRODUCTION
vi

ACKNOWLEDGMENTS
viii

PREFACE
ix

A NOTE ON CITATIONS, TRANSLATIONS, AND TRANSLITERATIONS
x

A NOTE ON SANSKRIT PRONUNCIATION
xi

LIST OF ABBREVIATIONS USED IN THE IN-TEXT REFERENCES AND ENDNOTES
xii

LIST OF ILLUSTRATIONS
xvi

LIST OF MAPS
xviii

Foreword HISTORY: COMPETITION OR COLLABORATION?
xix

Chapter One DIFFUSION CHANNELS IN THE PRE-ALEXANDRIAN PERIOD
1

Chapter Two THE PROBLEM OF THE ONE AND THE MANY
23

Chapter Three THE COSMIC CYCLE
67

Chapter Four THE DOCTRINE OF REINCARNATION
98

Chapter Five PLATONIC MONISM AND INDIAN THOUGHT
157

Chapter Six PLATONIC ETHICS AND INDIAN YOGA
177

Chapter Seven PLATO, ORPHICS, AND JAINS
197

Chapter Eight PLATO AND KUṆḌALINĪ
208

Chapter Nine CYNICS AND PĀŚUPATAS
225

Chapter Ten FIVE QUESTIONS CONCERNING THE ANCIENT NEAR EAST
237

Chapter Eleven THE ELEMENTS
300

Chapter Twelve EARLY PLURALISMS IN GREECE AND INDIA
311

Chapter Thirteen SKEPTICISM, EMPIRICISM, AND NATURALISM
325

Chapter Fourteen DIFFUSION CHANNELS IN THE HELLENISTIC AND ROMAN PERIODS
349

Chapter Fifteen DIALECTIC BEFORE ALEXANDER
403

Chapter Sixteen EARLY GREEK PHILOSOPHY AND MĀDHYAMIKA
419

Chapter Seventeen PYRRHONISM AND MĀDHYAMIKA
450

Chapter Eighteen THE PATH OF THE DIALECTIC
491

Chapter Nineteen THE SYLLOGISM
510

Chapter Twenty PERIPATETICS AND VAIŚEṢIKAS
519

Chapter Twenty-One THE STOICS AND INDIAN THOUGHT
540

Chapter Twenty-Two NEOPLATONISM AND THE UPANIṢADIC-VEDĀNTIC TRADITION
549

Chapter Twenty-Three PLOTINUS AND VIJÑĀNAVĀDA BUDDHISM
568

Chapter Twenty-Four NEOPLATONISM AND TANTRA
585

Chapter Twenty-Five THE ETHICS OF IMPERTURBABILITY
595

Afterword REMARKS TOWARD A CONCLUSION
642

Appendix A THE ARYANS
657

Appendix B THE ARYAN INVASION
663

Appendix C *BLACK ATHENA* AND WESTERN XENOPHOBIA
666

Appendix D THE GOLDEN THIGH
668

Appendix E PHILOSOPHY AND GRAMMAR
672

LIST OF WORKS CITED
678

INDEX
703

Editor's Introduction

by Bill Beckley

Lyotard remarked that post-Modern artists often function as philosophers. They may deal with issues of metaphysics, epistemology, and ethics, as many influential critics today approach art through philosophy.

No critic has unfolded the philosophical aspect of contemporary art like Thomas McEvilley. His fluency, as Classicist and as Indologist, both in ancient and in modern thought, has shone a light on visual objects that we have contemplated for over twenty years. When I first learned that McEvilley's art criticism was adjunct to his studies in ancient philosophy, I was surprised and intrigued. Then when I saw his five-volume manuscript, *The Shape of Ancient Thought*, stacked in the middle of his apartment like a sculpture—this work that he began in the early seventies, his magnum opus, tracing currents of ancient philosophy that are of interest to me as an artist, now—it seemed quite natural, even an honor, to include it here within this series, Aesthetics Today. For the bottom line of this book is the beauty of ideas, or what McEvilley has called "the aesthetics of thought." That was reason enough.

But more recently, events have leant an unexpected urgency to the project by focusing the world's attention on Afghanistan (ancient Bactria), where much of the story unfolds in this volume, and where the difficult karma of cross-cultural contacts is still alive.

I first conceived this series as a way of opening aesthetics to a variety of discourses, including the then neglected creatures of beauty and the contemporary sublime. In doing so, I knew it was impossible to have protected language, an ivory tower of anything—whether it be aesthetics or philosophy. We have seen what happens to ivory towers when the world gets in the way. It is precisely this world, with its ancient and ongoing collision of eastern and western ideologies that confronts us today. I thought *The Shape of Ancient Thought* would be relevant in this series. I could not have imagined then, how relevant it soon would become.

Many thanks to David Rhodes, president of the School of Visual Arts, and to Tad Crawford, publisher of Allworth Press, for their foresight in supporting this project.

–Bill Beckley, Series Editor
November 12, 2001
New York City

Acknowledgments

Several people need to be acknowledged for the generous help they gave to the author.

Through much of the 1970s, when no part of this work had yet been published and virtually no one knew of it, Edward Conze graciously read the first drafts of several chapters and offered caustic, insightful, learned comments. Late in the 1970s Frederick Streng kindly read selections, which he greeted with eager enthusiasm.

For several years in the 1980s, Dominique DeMenil contributed toward my sustenance in order to free some time from teaching for this work; her belief in the project was unwavering, in part because she saw it as contributing to the cause of ecumenism that lay behind the Rothko Chapel and others of her projects.

My warm thanks go also to Katherine Harper and Christopher Chapple, of Loyola Marymount University, both of whom have read an earlier version of this manuscript in its entirety and made useful and insightful comments on it. Juan Echeverri's work with the manuscript at an earlier stage was valuable and much appreciated. Bill Beckley, the editor of this series, has been unfailingly sympathetic and supportive. Tad Crawford and his staff at Allworth Press have given generously of their time and have seemed to care intensely about the text, which made working with them an altogether positive experience.

Very special thanks must go, posthumously, both to Eric Orr, who said he would read this book if he lived long enough to see it finished (he didn't), and to James Lee Byars, who for several years cherished a copy of the manuscript of this book, which he carried about with him in two large shopping bags.

Preface

Chapters 1 through 25–the substance of the book–were written between 1970 and 2000; they deal with the subject matter indicated by the title–*Comparative Studies in Greek and Indian Philosophies*. The foreword and afterword were added more recently, as an afterthought; they treat various issues surrounding the subject matter in the contemporary postcolonial world. Depending on what he or she wants from this book, the reader may wish to skip them altogether or to treat them as appendixes and read them at the end, as the afterthought they are.

My title derives in part from B. N. Seal's pioneering *Comparative Studies in Vaishnavism and Christianity* (Calcutta, 1899), which seems to be the first book about philosophy to bear the word "comparative" in its title, and the work which declared the basic principle: "Historical comparison implies that the objects compared are of co-ordinate rank."

A Note on Citations, Translations, and Transliterations

All references to the pre-Socratics follow the numeration of H. Diels and W. Kranz, *Die Fragmente der Vorsokratiker*. The A fragments are testimonia from other authors; the B fragments are actual quotations from the pre-Socratics. In this book "fr. A1" means an A fragment, while "fr. 1" is a B fragment; if the identity of the author is not obvious from the context. the Diels-Kranz chapter number will be included also—say, DK 1A1 or DK 1B1.

In general I have kept to one source for the reference numbers of a philosopher or group of philosophers, like Diels-Kranz for the pre-Socratics. Similarly I refer to the Upaniṣads in the numeration of Sarvepalli Radhakrishnan's translation, *The Principal Upaniṣads*, and so on, as noted here and there in the text.

Though all Greek, Latin, Sanskrit, and Pali texts have been consulted in their own languages, they are quoted in existing scholarly translations. This way, it is felt, there can be no sense that the translations have been made to serve an agenda. Thus, unless otherwise noted, the pre-Socratics are translated either as by G. S. Kirk, J. E. Raven, and M. Schofield (*The Presocratic Philosophers*), or as by Kathleen Freeman (*Ancilla to the Presocratics*); the Upaniṣads as by Radhakrishnan (*The Principal Upaniṣads*—with occasional changes to eliminate Elizabethan forms), the *Ṛg Veda* as by Ralph T. H. Griffiths (*The Hymns of the Ṛg-Veda*), Plotinus as by Stephen MacKenna (*Plotinus, The Enneads*), and so on. In some cases, such as Plato and Aristotle, a variety of translations have been used, as noted.

Common Greek names will be transliterated into the forms familiar to the general reading public: not Herakleitos but Heraclitus. Sanskrit and Pali are transliterated into the Latin alphabet with diacritical marks.

A Note on Sanskrit Pronunciation

Vowels should be pronounced as in Italian; *c* like *ch* in "church," *ṣ* or *ś* like *sh* in "ship," *ñ* like *ny* (as in Spanish *señor*), *ṛ* like *ri* in "river."

List of Abbreviations Used in the In-Text References and Endnotes

Ad Marc.	Porphyry, *Ad Marcellam* (To Marcella)
Adv. Col.	Plutarch, *Adversus Colotem* (Against Colotes)
Adv. Haer.	Epiphanius, *Adversus Haereticos* (Against the Heretics)
AL	Sextus Empiricus, *Against the Logicians*
Alex. Aph.	Alexander of Aphrodisias
AM	Sextus Empiricus, *Against the Professors*
AN	*Anguttara Nikāya*
Anab.	Xenophon, *Anabasis*
An. Post.	Aristotle, *Analytica Posteriora* (Posterior Analytics)
An. Pr.	Aristotle, *Analytica Priora* (Prior Analytics)
AP	*Anthologia Palatina* (Palatine Anthology)
Ap.	*Apud* (found in or quoted by)
APh	Sextus Empiricus, *Against the Physicists*
Apol.	Plato, *Apologia*
Ap. Rh.	Apollonius Rhodius
AS	*Ākārāṅga Sūtra*
Ath.	Athenaeus
AU	*Aitareya Upaniṣad*
AV	*Atharva Veda*
BCA	*Bodhicaryāvatāra* (The Way of the Bodhisattva)
BU	*Bṛhadāranyaka Upaniṣad*
Cat.	Aristotle, *Categoriae* (Categories)
Choeph.	Aeschylus, *Choephorai* (Libation Bearers)
CU	*Chāndogya Upaniṣad*
Charm.	Plato, *Charmides*
CQ	*Classical Quarterly*
Crat.	Plato, *Cratylus*
CS	Aryadeva, *Catuḥ-śataka*
Curt.	Quintus Curtius Rufus, *Historia Alexandri Magni (History of Alexander)*
D	*Digha Nikāya*

De Abst.	Porphyry, *De Abstinentia* (On Abstinence)
De An.	Aristotle, *De Anima* (On the Soul)
De Div.	Cicero, *De Divinatione* (On Divination)
De Fin.	Cicero, *De Finibus Bonorum et Malorum* (About the Ends of Goods and Evils)
De Gen. Animal.	Aristotle, *De Generatione Animalium* (On the Generation of Animals)
De Gen. et Corr.	Aristotle, *De Generatione et Corruptione* (On Generation and Corruption)
De Interp.	Aristotle, *De Interpretatione* (On Interpretation)
Deip.	Athenaeus, *Deipnosophistae* (Doctors at Dinner)
De Is. et Osir.	Plutarch, *De Iside et Osiride* (On Isis and Osiris)
De Morb. Sacr.	Hippocrates, *De Morbo Sacro* (On the Sacred Disease)
De Motu Animal.	Aristotle, *De Motu Animalium* (On the Motion of Animals)
De Nat. Anim.	Aelian, *De Natura Animalium* (On the Nature of Animals)
De Nat. Deor.	Cicero, *De Natura Deorum* (On the Nature of the Gods)
De Partis Animal.	Aristotle, *De Partis Animalium* (On the Parts of Animals)
De Prim. Frig.	Plutarch, *De Primo Frigido* (On the Principle of Cold)
De Resp.	Aristotle, *De Respiratione* (On Respiration)
De Stoic Repugn.	Plutarch, *De Stoicorum Repugnantiis* (On the Contradictions of the Stoics)
Diod.	Diodorus Siculus
Disc.	Arrian, *Discourses of Epictetus*
DK	Hermann Diels, *Die Fragmente der Vorsokratiker.* Rev. by W. Kranz
D.L.	Diogenes Laertius, *De Clarorum Philosophorum Vitis, Dogmatibus et Apophthegmatibus Libri Decem* (The Lives and Teachings of the Famous Philosophers in Ten Books)
EE	Aristotle, *Ethica Eudemia* (Eudemian Ethics)
EN	Aristotle, *Ethica Nicomachea* (Nicomachean Ethics)
Ench.	Epictetus, *Enchiridion* (Handbook)
Enn.	Plotinus, *Enneads* (Discourses in Groups of Nine)
Ep.	*Epistula* (Letter)
Ep. Ind.	*Epigraphia Indica*
Ep. Men.	Epicurus, *Epistula ad Menoeceum* (Letter to Menoeceus)
Epist. Mor.	Seneca, *Ad Lucilium Epistulae Morales* (Moral Letters to Lucilius)
Erga	Hesiod, *Erga* (Works and Days)
Flor.	Stobaeus, *Florilegium*
FrGrHist	F. Jacoby, ed., *Die Fragmenta der Griechischen Historiker*
Geog.	Ptolemy, *Geographia*
Hdt.	Herodotus
Hec.	Euripides, *Hecabe*
Hell.	Xenophon, *Hellenica*
IHQ	*Indian Historical Quarterly*
In An. Pr.	Alexander of Aphrodisias, *Commentary on Aristotle's Prior Analytics*
Iambl.	Iamblichus

In Phys.	Simplicius, *Commentary on Aristotle's Physics*
JHS	*Journal of Hellenic Studies*
JIES	*Journal of Indo-European Studies*
JNES	*Journal of Near Eastern Studies*
JRAS	*Journal of the Royal Asiatic Society*
Katha	*Kaṭha Upaniṣad*
Kaus. Br.	*Kauṣītaki Brāhmaṇa*
KD	Epicurus, *Kuriai Doxai* (Leading Doctrines)
Kena	*Kena Upaniṣad*
KU	*Kauṣītaki Upaniṣad*
L.P.	Edgar Lobel and Denys Page, eds., *Poetarum Lesbiorum Fragment*
Lanka.	*Laṅkāvatāra Sūtra*
Lucr.	Lucretius
M	*Majjhima Nikāya*
Maitrī	*Maitrī Upaniṣad*
Mā. U.	*Māṇḍūkya Upaniṣad*
Med.	Descartes, *Philosophical Meditations*
Mem.	Xenophon, *Memorabilia*
Met.	Aristotle, *Metaphysica* (Metaphysics)
Meteor.	Aristotle, *Meteorologia* (Meteorology)
Mhv.	*Māhavaṃsa* (The Great Chronicle of Ceylon)
MK	Nāgārjuna, *Mādhyamika Kārikās* (Treatise on the Middle Way)
MKV	Candrakīrtī, *Mādhyamakavṛtti* (Commentary on the *Mādhyamikakārikās* of Nāgārjuna)
Mln.	*Milindapañha* (The Questions of King Milinda)
Mor.	Plutarch, *Moralia* (Moral Essays)
MS	*Manu-smṛti or Manavadharmaśastra* (The Sacred Laws According to Manu)
MU	*Muṇḍaka Upaniṣad*
NA	Aulus Gellius, *Noctes Atticae* (Attic Nights)
NH	Pliny, *Natural History*
NS	*Nyāya Sūtras*
OF	O. Kern, ed., *Orphicorum Fragmenta* (Orphic Fragments)
O.	Pindar, *Olympic Odes*
OP	Sextus Empiricus, *Outlines of Pyrrhonsim*
Or.	*Oratio*
Ox. Pap.	B.P Grenfell, A.S. Hunt, and others, *The Oxyrhynchus Papyri*
Panar.	*Panarion*
Paus.	Pausanias
Pericl.	Plutarch, *Life of Pericles*
Perist.	Prudentius, *Peristephanon*
Pers.	Ctesias, *Persica*
PEW	*Philosophy East and West*
Phaedr.	Plato, *Phaedrus*
Phil.	Plato, *Philebus*
Phys.	Aristotle, *Physica* (Physics)
Plu.	Plutarch
PMG	Denys Page, ed., *Poetae Melici Graeci.*

Pol.	Aristotle, *Politica* (Politics)
Porph.	Porphyry
Praśna Up.	*Praśna Upaniṣad*
Prep. Ev.	Eusebius, *Preparatio Evangelica* (Evangelical Preparation)
Prooem.	*Prooemium* (Introduction)
Prot.	Plato, *Protagoras*
PS	*Pāśupata Sūtra*
Ps.-Plato	Pseudo-Plato
RE	A. Pauly, G. Wissowa, and W. Kroll, eds., *Real-Encyclopadie der Harrisen Altertumevissenssehalf*
Ref.	Hippolytus, *Refutatio Omnium* (Refutation of All Heresics)
Rep.	Plato, *The Republic*
Rbet.	Aristotle, *Rbetorica* (Rbetoric)
RV	*Ṛg Veda*
S	*Samyutta Nikāya*
SB	*Śatapatha Brābmaṇa*
Sent. Vat.	Epicurus, *Sententiae Vaticanae* (Epicurean Aphorisms from a Vatican Manuscript)
SVF	H. Von Arnim, ed., *Steicorum Veterum Fragmenta.*
Skt.	Sanskrit
SN	*Sutta Nipāta*
Sol.	Plutorch, *Life of Solon*
Soph.	Plato, *Sophisticus* (Sophist)
Stromat.	Pseudo-Plutarch (ap. Eusebius), *Stromaties* (Miscellany)
SU	*Śverāśvatara Upaniṣad*
Symp.	Plato, *Symposium*
Taitt. Br.	*Taittirīya Brahmaṇa*
Theat.	Plato, *Theatetus*
Them.	*Life of Themistocles* (by either Plutarch or Cornelius Nepos)
Theog.	Hesiod, *Theogony*
Tim.	Plato, *Timaeus*
TGF	A. Nauck, eḍ, *Tragicorum craccorum Fragmenta*
TU	*Taittirīya Upaniṣad*
Tust.	Cicero, *Tusculan Disputations*
Us.	H. Usener, ed., *Epicurea*
VA	Philostratus, *Vita Apollonii* (Life of Apollonius of Tyana)
VH	Aelian, *Varia Historita* (Historical Miscellany)
Vit. Pyth.	*Vita Pythagorae* (Life of Pythagoras)
VP	*Viṣṇu Puraṇa*
VS	*Vaiśeṣika Sútras*
VV	Nāgārjuna, *Vigraha Vyavartani* (Averting the Arguments)
YS	Patañjali, *Yoga Sūtras*

List of Illustrations

Figure 1: Line drawing of Sumerian stone vase (the "Gudea Vase"), c.2050 B.C., showing two serpents entwined around central axis in caduceus form, their bodies touching at seven points. 216

Figure 2: Tantric portrayal of central nervous system, mid-twentieth century A.D., showing two channels that carry the serpent power entwined around central axis within the yogi's body in caduceus form, the channels touching at seven points. 217

Figure 3: "Snake-stones," fertility icons from South India, early twentieth century A.D. each showing two serpents entwind in caduceus form. 217

Figure 4: Babylonian seal impression,c. 2000 B.C., showing upright figure surrounded by caduceus of entwined serpents, their heads rising above his shoulders. 218

Figure 5: Neo-Sumerian stele fragment showing male figure with serpents' heads rising from his shoulders, their bodies evidently entwined inside him. 219

Figure 6: Sumerian seal impression, third millennium B.C., showing "Gilgamesh" figure holding two lions in symmetrically flanking "dompteur" position. 246

Figure 7: Sumerian seal impression, Uruk period, fourth to third millennium B.C., showing central mountain-and-tree symmetrically flanked by goats with their forehooves raised and placed upon it. 247

Figure 8: Indus Valley seal impression, Mohenjo Daro, third to second millennium B.C., showing central mountain-and-tree symmetrically flanked by goats with their fore hooves raised and placed upon it. 247

Figure 9: Indus Valley seal impression, Mohenjo Daro, third to second millennium B.C., showing "Gilgamesh" figure holding two lions in symmetrically flanking "dompteur" position. 248

Figure 10: Achaemenian seal, c. sixth century B.C., showing "Gilgamesh" figure holding two winged lions or griffins in symmetrically flanking "dompteur" position. 248

Figure 11: Indus Valley seal impression, Mohenjo Daro, third to second millennium B.C., showing "Gilgamesh" figure holding two lions in symmetrically flanking "dompteur" position. 249

Figure 12: Sumerian seal impression, third millennium B.C., showing goddess in tree with god bull below, detail. 250
Figure 13: Indus Valley seal impression, Mohenjo Daro, third to second millennium B.C., showing goddess in tree with bull-god and seven sprout-headed figures below. 251
Figure 14: Akkadian seal impression, third millennium B.C., showing seated tree-goddess with sprout-headed youngster on her lap. 252
Figure 15: Sumerian seal impression, Uruk period, fourth to third millennium B.C., showing bull associated with vegetation being attacked by lion from behind. 252
Figure 16: Painted pottery fragment, Mohenjo Daro, third to second millennium B.C., showing bull associated with vegetation being attacked by lion or other feline from behind. 253
Figure 17: Indus Valley objects, Kunal, third to second millennium B.C., eight-petalled rosette on upper left. 253
Figure 18: Offering stand from Ur, detail. 254
Figure 19: Sumerian ivory figurine, third millennium B.C., showing bull-man. 255
Figure 20: Indus Valley plaques, third to second millennium B.C., showing bull-man. 255
Figure 21: Proto-Elamite seal impression, third millennium B.C., showing three-headed bull and three-headed bull-man. 256
Figure 22: Indus Valley seal impressions, Mohenjo Daro, third to second millennium B.C., showing three-headed bulls or bull-like creatures. 256
Figure 23: Syrian seal impression, c. 1700 B.C., showing four entwined male human figures suggesting swastika form. 257
Figure 24: Indus Valley seal impressions, Mohenjo Daro, third to second millennium B.C., showing four entwined lions suggesting swastika form. 258
Figure 25: Babylonian seal impression, c. 2000 B.C., showing deity and ritualists heraldically flanked by upright caducei. 272
Figure 26: Indus Valley seal impressions, Mohenjo Daro, third to second millennium B.C., showing figure in *mūlabandhāsana* symmetrically flanked by upright serpents. 273
Figure 27: Gandhāran sculpture, Hadda, Pakistan, c. second century A.D., head of "Antinous" figure. 365
Figure 28: Gandhāran sculpture, Peshawar, Pakistan, c. second century A.D., head of ascetic. 369
Figure 29: Head of Gandhāran Buddha with hairstyle of Apollo Belvedere, Peshawar, Pakistan, c. second century A.D. 373
Figure 30: Kushan coin, c. second century A.D., spelling out name Buddha (Boddo) in Greek characters. 375
Figure 31: Corinthian capital from Gandhāra, c. second century A.D., showing Buddha meditating among the acanthus leaves (cf. dustjacket). 377

List of Maps

Map 1: The Persian Empire 3
Map 2: The Bronze Age 239
Map 3: The Alexandrian and Mauryan Periods 353
Map 4: The Roman Period 381

Foreword

History: Competition or Collaboration?

When I was a student at the University of Cincinnati (after the digs at Troy and Pylos were over but while seminars on Linear B were still heavily attended), the British scholar W. K. C. Guthrie, who was at the time writing his ambitious *History of Greek Philosophy*,[1] spoke at the school. Among other comments, he facetiously mentioned the cliché that everyone is born either a Platonist or an Aristotelian. He implied something like William James's distinction between tender-minded and tough-minded, or, in European philosophical terms, idealist and empiricist. He declared himself to be an Aristotelian.

Later I was introduced to him as a student who had recently read both Guthrie's own book on Orphism and also Ivan Linforth's highly critical treatment of the subject.[2] He remarked cordially that I must have heard the seductive chords of Orpheus's lyre.

Not long after, I did seem to hear the chords of Orpheus's lyre—but from an unexpected direction: namely, from what at that time was called "the Orient." In reading E. R. Dodds's *Greeks and the Irrational*,[3] I encountered what seemed to be a parallel to Guthrie's dichotomy in Dodds's distinction between rational Greeks and irrational Orientals. Conflation of the two distinctions suggests that the Greeks (like both Guthrie and his fellow British scholar) were Aristotelians; the "Orientals" were Platonists.

The point in overlaying Guthrie's dichotomy on Dodds's is not to question Plato's Greek credentials. The aporetic quality of his early dialogues and the attempt at logical rigor in his late ones render these tough- rather than tender-minded texts. Considering only the beginning and end of his writings, then, one might say that, in terms of Guthrie's dichotomy, Plato himself was born an Aristotelian. But surely that couldn't be right. Rather, what is implied in the application of Guthrie's dichotomy to Dodds's, and indeed what is assumed in saying that Plato represents tender-mindedness, is not about either the early or the late dialogues at all. What is at issue is the fact that in Plato's *middle* dialogues elements which might be called tender-minded appear with startling frequency and prominence. These are the ideas that are loosely gathered in the category of Orphic: reincarnationism based on ethical accounting, the soul's recollection of the universals, the ambition of having the soul escape the body and its round of incarnations, asceticism as a means toward this end, and so on. These are ideas that, although they are among the most prominent elements in Greek thought, have struck Dodds and many others as somehow essentially non-Greek—as "a drop of alien blood in Greek veins," as Erwin Rohde put it.[4] So the identification of (supposedly non-Greek) irrationalism with Plato in contrast to Aristotle's (Greek) rationalism is based on the belief that Plato, in his middle years, succumbed to the temptation of "Oriental" ideas—something which Aristotle never did.

At the time Dodds was writing, one prominent thesis about the origin of Orphism was that it came into Greece from Asia Minor.[5] Dodds preferred to derive it from Thrace and to trace a larger "line of spiritual descent," of which Orphism was a part, "which starts in Scythia, crosses the Hellespont into Asian Greece . . . emigrates to the Far West with Pythagoras, and has its last outstanding representative in the Sicilian Empedocles."[6] Dodds was not dogmatically dualistic about differences between the Greek and the "barbarian" psyches, but still it was implied in his classic study that one could identify things Greek by their rationality, things non-Greek by their primitive-esque (shamanic, as Dodds would have it) appeals to the irrational. It soon became an unquestioned consensus that Orphism was "so very foreign to the Greek mentality."[7]

And India?

It was easy enough to distance thought-elements which seemed antirational by relegating their origin to Asia Minor—as Dodds did with Orphism. How much more irrational must be things that lie still farther east! This is the general attitude that lies in the background of Guthrie's dismissal of Indian philosophy in his *History*:

> The motives and methods of the Indian schools, and the theological and mystical background of their thought, are so utterly different from those of the Greeks that there is little profit in the comparison.[8]

After spending thirty years investigating this statement, I have concluded that it is deeply and glaringly false. (The glaring part of its falseness is that it was proclaimed by a scholar who had already written sympathetically about Orphism!) In the following twenty-five chapters I will take the readers through the relevant evidence on this question, and will lead them through the byways of the argumentation. Now, before embarking on that sea of evidence, I want to investigate some of the historical and ideological resonances of Guthrie's dismissal—why it seems so overstated, and why it is so brusque.

A Philological Explosion

The Christian millennium, as Enlightenment *philosophes* called it, gave ground to a resurgence of the Greco-Roman impulse in the period from the Renaissance through the Enlightenment. Many turned outside of Western civilization in search of an Other which could be used to unseat and overturn it. It was in this spirit that Voltaire, in the eighteenth century, declared India, about which he knew little, to be the birthplace not only of religion but of civilization itself.[9] "Religion in general," he claimed, "is derived, and has degenerated from, the pure natural revelation of which the Indians were the first possessors."[10]

The time was the so-called Oriental Renaissance, when it seemed briefly that India might replace Greece as the putative source of civilization. Though Voltaire promoted the idea, others were offended by it. Diderot, for example (following Pierre Bayle), dismissed India as a place of "incredible extravagances," not to be taken seriously.[11]

Western authors of this period, when colonialism was not yet in full swing, had little information about distant cultures and were essentially expressing attitudes toward Western civilization through assertions about unknown Asia. Denigration of India went along with chauvinistic support for Western civilization; extravagant praise of India, with disgust for some aspect of the West, usually what was conceived to be its overemphasis on rationalism. Already the situation was in place which Edward Said two centuries later would call "Orientalism"—the West's use of Asia as a projected Other against which to define itself.[12]

As colonialism grew, so did knowledge of the non-Western world. The situation reached explosive volatility in 1786, two years after the founding of the Asiatic Society of Bengal (later the Royal Asiatic Society). The bombshell was Sir William Jones's historic assertion to a meeting of the Society "that no philologer could examine them all three [the Latin, Greek, and Sanskrit languages] without believing them to have sprung from some common source."[13]

Partly as a result of this insight, in the late eighteenth and the nineteenth centuries Europe experienced an intoxication with the discipline of philology—which, if not actually new (since it had been practiced in Greco-Roman antiquity), was newly rediscovered. Comparative philology especially was received as a major new science, impressively confirmed by early discoveries such as language families and Grimm's Law.

The realization that Sanskrit was cognate with most European languages both ancient and modern, arising as it did in the midst of the historic moment of white-on-nonwhite colonialism, aroused troubling questions. What might seem a purely linguistic matter was interpreted as involving issues of race, which in turn involved power and domination. In western Europe, the enormous wealth-source of colonialism was justified by a racial argument that went back to Aristotle's assertion in the *Nicomachean Ethics* that some human communities are naturally meant to dominate others. Aristotle did not state this in terms of skin color but, for whatever reasons, that became the principle defining property of civilized humanity in the discourse of the Enlightenment.

As David Hume put it in the mid-eighteenth century, "I am apt to suspect the Negroes to be naturally inferior to the Whites."[14] The opinion proved durable. About fifty years after Hume's observation, the French naturalist Georges Leopold Cuvier wrote, "The Caucasian race has given rise to the most civilized nations, to those which have generally held the rest in subjection."[15] By Caucasian he seems to mean both Indo-European-speaking and white-skinned—the two traits are identified. A century later the British historian Hugh Trevor-Roper agreed; speaking in a common Hegelian vein, he said: "It is European techniques, European examples, European ideas which have shaken the non-European world out of its past—out of barbarism . . ."[16]

The racial justification for imperialism had to deal with the question of language—specifically, the problem of the Indo-European categorization of Sanskrit, and with it of many other Indian languages including Hindi, the legal language of the post-colonial Indian state. In the nineteenth century and well into the twentieth, language was regarded as connected with race—as virtually a racial characteristic. And if the language of classical Indian literature is of the same family as the literatures of the white-skinned colonizers, then an ambiguity has entered into the equation: Does the racial justification for colonialism apply to India, or doesn't it?

Two very different solutions to the problem arose. According to the linkage of language and race, if Sanskrit was an Indo-European language, its original speakers—the "Aryans" as they had come to be called—must have been more or less white people. To Romantic Orientalists such as Friedrich Schlegel and Arthur Schopenhauer this meant that the leading cultures of East and West were brothers, and the historic meaning of that fact included the idea that Indo-Europeans had dominated the development of civilization both East and West. But to another group the inference that the Indo-Aryans were more or less white people had a different and more ominous implication: It meant that the racial justification for imperialism did not apply to India.

Linguistic Hierarchization

Nineteenth-century studies of cultures tended to involve hierarchization, and in philology the hierarchy placed the languages of the western colonizers—all Indo-European—at the top. These were regarded as the languages of natural conquerors. The languages of the colonized peoples, in contrast, were the languages of naturally slavish peoples who were born to be conquered. The discovery that Sanskrit was Indo-European controverted that assumption shockingly. The supposed language of slaves turned out to be a language of masters after all.

In his modern manual of descriptive linguistics Gleason claims: "The largest and most important language family, from the point of view of both the social importance of the major languages in the group and their interest to linguists, is the Indo-European."[17] The revealing statement that the Indo-European languages are of special "social importance" means that now, factoring in Jones's discovery, Sanskrit culture also has that special "social importance." In fact, as Gleason explicitly states, "The Vedas . . . are the oldest documents in any Indo-European languages."[18] So though India was admitted belatedly to the ranks of the masters, it actually had a claim to priority there. Since, in the nineteenth century, Western scholarship saw a close linkage between language, ethnicity, and culture, Jones's discovery raised India into a potentially hegemonic position, at least on the level of cultural ideology, and implicitly questioned the justification for British domination there.

At about the time of Jones's discovery—roughly the moment when the Late Enlightenment was giving way to the Romantic era—Western scholars undertook a quest for the absolute source of civilization, which was to be discovered by means such as philology and, later, archeology. As Raymond Schwab has argued, the discovery of the linguistic cognateness of India to the West occurred at the perfect moment to intersect with that other search. For a brief period of about thirty-five years—about 1785–1820—the leading candidate for the Ur-civilization was India.

In that heady Indocentric phase, on the heels of Jones's epochal pronouncement, it seemed that the western world's search for its origin—that is, its true self—would be fulfilled by plumbing the mystery of far-off and little-known India. India somehow held the key to the West's quest for ultimate self-knowledge. Schlegel declared enthusiastically: "Everything, yes, everything without exception has its origin in India."[19] This conviction led him to respond to Jones's discovery by declaring that Sanskrit was not only cognate with, that is, a sibling of, Greek and Latin; in fact it was the "mother language of Greek, Latin, Persian, and German."[20] Not dissimilarly Schopenhauer, in line with his belief in "the underlying unity of all things,"[21] thought that both Christianity and the ancient Egyptian religion had originated in India. In a somewhat similar spirit, the poet Novalis "imagined the Garden of Eden to be tucked away somewhere in the Himalayas."[22] Not much later, the French scholar Edgar Quinet, in his *Du genie des religions* (1841), wrote that "in the first ardor of their discoveries, the orientalists proclaimed that, in its entirety, an antiquity more profound, more philosophical, more poetical than that of Greece and Rome was emerging from the depths of Asia."[23] The idea floated abroad that Jones's discovery and its consequences would constitute an "Oriental Renaissance" that would replace the Greek Renaissance of the fifteenth century, reforming European culture yet again—or at least overlaying the Hellenized layer with a layer of Indianization. Schopenhauer and others had high expectations of how far this "Oriental Renaissance" would go. "Sanskrit literature," Schopenhauer wrote, "will be no less influential for our time than Greek literature was in the fifteenth century for the Renaissance."[24] Schlegel agreed, in *Über die Sprache und Weisheit der Indier,* saying that ". . . the effects of Indic studies, if taken up and introduced into learned circles with the same attention today [as Greek studies had been earlier], would be no less great and far-reaching."[25]

The anticipated long period of Indian influence did not in fact materialize; India did not supersede Greece as the guiding spirit of Western culture. When Schlegel and others wrote, the end of India's brief hegemony in the mind of Western Romantics had already been planted by Napoleon's expedition to Egypt in 1798–1801.When Champollion deciphered the Rosetta Stone in 1821, it seemed an even more stunning breakthrough than Jones's perception of the cognateness of Sanskrit, Greek, and Latin. Philology, it seemed, was turning out to be a semimagical "science" through which ultimate facts about history could be concretely discovered. India was replaced for a while by Egypt as the presumed source of "everything." The excitement of this apparent insight led to Grafton Elliot-Smith's overstated diffusionist theory that accounted for more or less everything impressive in world culture by ultimate derivation from Egypt. This overapplication of the idea of diffusion came to be perceived, somewhat prematurely, as an actual disproof of the idea; it amounted to a setback that forestalled diffusionist studies for generations. Nor did the claim of Egypt's supporters that Egypt was the Mother of All Civilizations last long. As the nineteenth century advanced, Europe returned to the comfortable veneration of the "Greek Miracle." "We are all Greeks," Percy Bysshe Shelley wrote in 1822.[26]

In time an account was worked out that dissipated the problem of the Indo-Europeanness of Sanskrit by asserting that the Aryans had indeed been white people, but they had been absorbed into a nonwhite matrix, leaving their language intact while their skin color—and with it their cultural identity—was mostly lost. Modern Indians, then, are not really white people, though they use a language left behind by earlier white conquerors, and the racial justification for colonization does apply after all: The British were going in to finish up the job the Aryans had begun long ago. The Greek colonization of India had reinforced the original Aryan input, but it too had been dissolved and absorbed by the larger brown body of humanity. The Greek infusion of whiteness, coming after the Aryan, constituted a tradition which the British could honorably carry on. As one British imperialist author wrote: "Ex Occidente Imperium; the genius of Empire in India has come to her from the West; and can be maintained only by constant infusions of fresh blood from the same source."[27] James Mill's idea, from the same period, that "the Indian civilization never prospered except under foreign domination" seemed a clear justification for imperialism as a civilizing mission.[28]

Two Types of Comparative Studies

The scholarly excitement stimulated by Jones's discovery led to extensive comparative studies of Indian and Greek classical civilizations, often involving a sense of competition between the two cultures. In the minds of many, both eastern and western, it came to seem that there was a rivalry between ancient Greece and ancient India as to which was not only the highest of ancient civilizations but also the font from which others had flowed.

Certain of these scholarly investigations emphasized the common Indo-European background. This trend culminated in the work of Georges Dumezil and others who have articulated parallelisms in the social structures of different Indo-European-speaking cultures.[29] Why, for example, are there such close parallels between the Hindu caste system as enunciated by the *Manavadharmaśastra*, the caste system fantasized by Plato in the *Republic*, and the social organization of early Latin peoples? Dumezil and others presumed that such parallelisms, like parallelisms in word roots or inflected endings, indicate cognate derivations, and have looked to the Proto-Indo-European culture as their source.

Such studies do not obstruct the Modernist or Hegelian conception of history, since they are restricted to prehistory and do not posit historical diffusion. But in order to account for striking comparative details, such studies must be supplemented by postulates of historical influences—and that is the problem. An admission that Indian philosophers had something to teach Greek philosophers, and that Greek philosophers acknowledged this fact, would add up to an admission that the classical culture of India was equal to that of Greece, not merely that they had shared linguistic roots. It would mean that the ancient Indians could *think* as clearly as the ancient Greeks—and that confuted the rational West/irrational East dichotomy that was firmly fixed in the colonizing mentality.

Other disciplines, such as art history, are less intimately involved in the superiority claims of the West than the history of philosophy, but still contribute to it. "The Gandhāra bias," for example, is a term that has been used by Indian scholars for modern Western attitudes about the so-called Gandhāran Buddhist sculpture. This art form, which is the first nonminiature figurative sculpture in either South or East Asia, seems likely to many to have been made by Greek colonists or under their influence. In fact, virtually no scholar, Indian nationalist or otherwise, denies the Greek connection here. The "bias," starting from the claim that Greek sculptors introduced figurative art to Asia in general and India in particular, proceeds to the value judgment that the realization of *humanness* had not dawned in India, or at least not in Indian art, until the arrival of the Greeks. The Greeks' clarity about the representation of the human body represented their realization of humanness as rationality—seemingly unknown theretofore in the vastness of all Asia beyond the Zagros Mountains.

The bias dwells on the claim that "[t]he anthropomorphic representation of the Buddha was due to the power of Greek civilization." These images were seen as "not only the first representations of the Buddha but the most perfect, with all subsequent Buddha images regarded as poor imitations, the products of a process of degeneration from the origin." This connection, if established, was of global significance: "Once set in motion, Greek influence moved eastward like the inexorable wheel of the cakravartin . . ."[30] "Western progress" replaced "Indian regression."[31] The art-historical issue generated wide ripples; it applied, for example, to the history of philosophy, since the satisfaction the art-historical claim gave to the colonizing powers would have been compromised by an admission that India was philosophically as advanced as Greece.

The word "barbarian" derives from the Greek onomatopoeic utterance *barbar*, which represents an indistinguishable vocalization made by primitives in vain imitation of language. In terms of the present issue, "language" is "thinking." Greeks supposedly could "think," while *barbaroi* could not. And this made comparative studies of Greek and Indian philosophies problematic unless they posited *only* Greek influence on Indians, not the other way around.

Paideia

The issue goes back to Pericles' Funeral Oration as paraphrased in the second book of Thucydides' *History of the Peloponnesian War*. There Pericles says that the essence of the Athenian democracy is that any citizen, regardless of class or profession, should be able to take over any governmental office and execute it properly and wisely with the good of his fellow citizens in mind. The reason *any* citizen would have the necessary ability had nothing to do with family lineage; it was simply the universal dispensation to citizens, in childhood, of *paideia*, the Hellenic education. *Paideia* was an ideology based on democracy, an attitude that was recovered and reconstructed in Europe from the Renaissance to the eighteenth-century Enlightenment. Education was supposed to transform one from a child unthinkingly submissive to autocracy into an adult capable of guiding one's own destiny and that of one's fellows. In terms of the Greek/barbarian dichotomy, the idea was that barbarians, not having been formed by *paideia*, were still childlike; like children in thrall to their parents, they were accustomed to autocracy. Not only would they submit unmanfully to autocratic rule, but, given the chance to take over the reins of government, those formerly oppressed would become new oppressors. It was for this reason—at least in their self-justifying propaganda—that Greeks felt that *paideia* had to be disseminated abroad, and it was for this reason that the Greeks arrogated to themselves the duty of intruding into foreign polities until the latter should gain the requisite maturity to take over their own destiny. This ancient attitude parallels not only the attitude of the British colonizers in India, but the attitude that much of the Western world still holds toward the non-Western.

Two Types of Colonization

"Our history still begins with the Greeks," stated Werner Jaeger in *Paideia*, his study of ancient Greek educational theory. "I have therefore called our group of nations Hellenocentric."[32] The "Hellenocentric" category includes all the modern European colonizing nations—and it may not be merely coincidental that ancient Greece was also a colonizing nation, especially in India.

But although the Alexandrian colonization of northwest India was used as a justification for British colonization, the Greek type of colonization was very different from the modern European type. First, it was not commercial but settler colonies that the Greeks made. In a commercial colony the colonizer comes in through conquest and exercises control until the local resources have been exhausted, or until access to them has successfully been blocked by local resistance, then moves on; in a settler colony, the colonizers intend to stay, have families, and establish communities. The British established settler colonies in the United States, Australia, and Canada; yet in each of these cases, rather than assimilate to their new human environment, they committed genocide of the indigenous nonwhite peoples. In order for them to sink roots the ground first had to be cleared and, as it were, sterilized. In India, on the contrary, they established a commercial colony without the ambition of sinking roots. There they erected strong social barriers against intermingling ("going native"), but did not eradicate the indigenous peoples, who in time would receive their land back, though in deeply altered circumstances.

Greek colonies were a different matter. They were all settler colonies, and they were based not on genocide but on controlled, partial assimilation. In India during the Alexandrian phase, discharged Greek soldiers would be given plots of conquered land on the basis of which they would marry into the community and, in time, join an Indian religion; the evidence is that it was not long—no longer than till Aśoka's time, the mid-third century B.C.—before they were accepted as legitimate and important parts of the community. Later, the Greek merchant colonies of the Roman period were, according to Tamil accounts, prosperous, and the trade to the Red Sea ports which fed Indian goods into the Mediterranean remained strong for centuries. But these Greco-Roman colonists were not simply draining wealth from a community in which they themselves had no lasting investment; the Indo-Greeks were permanent immigrants, often converts to Buddhism, participating constructively in the economic and cultural life of the community.

Another basic difference is that the discourse of racism is not present anywhere in the Greek accounts of colonization. Modern colonialism and imperialism were accompanied by the work of authors such as Joseph-Arthur de Gobineau (1816–1882), early proponent of the theory of Nordic superiority, whose main work was *Essai sur l'inegalité des race humaines.* Such works elevated white over nonwhite peoples as a justification for colonialism. In such racial hierarchies the Greeks were tacitly elevated to the top. An English author writing in 1813, for example, opined that the ancient Greeks "were the most noble tribe of the human race"; the Greek miracle was a result of the "superior natural endowments of the race."[33] The English poet Shelley declared simply that "the human form and the human mind attained to a perfection in Greece."[34]

But nowhere in the ancient Greek texts is there any sign of such overt racism. The African-American classical scholar Frank Snowden has argued that color prejudice did not exist in the Greco-Roman world.[35] "In the Mediterranean world," he notes, "the black man was seldom a strange, unknown being." Further, "in antiquity slavery was independent of race or class," so the stereotype of the black human as inherently slavish never developed as it did in the era of the middle passage.[36] The governing principle of the Alexandrian expansion to the East was the idea that *paideia* was needed there, but this alleged need was not articulated on racial grounds.

As a modern scholar says of Alexander's motives in setting out to conquer Asia: "His ideals were high—to bring to his subjects religious freedom, racial tolerance, political concord, economic prosperity, and peaceful conditions of life."[37] The idea that Alexander's expedition was a "civilizing mission" promoting a kind of marriage of East and West, a synthesis as it were, has been associated with Alexander's conquests at least since Plutarch.[38] No doubt there was more to it. But a certain willingness to give up something of oneself in a merging with another can be seen in several fields, including philosophy.

In modern times Western scholars of the history of philosophy have for the most part excluded India from it. But as Edward Zeller wrote, "The Greeks themselves were inclined from early times . . . to grant the peoples of the Orient . . . that they had a share in the origination of their philosophy."[39] Zeller probably intends to refer to the nations of the ancient Near East, but, as another modern scholar notes, in the Alexandrian period the Greeks similarly displayed "the readiness to accept the possibility of a philosophical partnership, of debate and instruction, in what is foreign, specifically Indian."[40]

On several grounds, then, it seems that the modern colonizing nations wrongly appropriated the Greek tradition into their support system. They trace their own spirituality as conquerors back to the Greeks, although the Greeks seem to have had different motives. Jaeger, the modern German self-appointed spokesperson for *paideia*, goes on about the debt that "Hellenocentric" nations have to the Greeks, whom he sees as "the *archē*, the spiritual source to which, as we reach every new stage of development, we must constantly revert in order to reorient ourselves. . . . Our kinship with Greece," he goes on, "is not merely racial, however important the racial factor may be in understanding the nature of a people."[41] Racial and spiritual empathy, it seems, are interpenetrated: For natives of the "Hellenocentric" nations the fact that they are spiritual descendants of the Greeks depends in part on the fact that they are "racial" descendants. Yet it seems that the ancient Greeks, as they did not have the color prejudice, did not think in terms of the whole linkage of language, culture, ethnicity, and soil. They would not have acknowledged this justification. To them the difference between a Greek and a barbarian was not race but a certain brand of education, or *paideia*, and ethnic differences did not enter into the question of readiness for *paideia*.

So there is a distinct ideological difference between the ancient Greek and the modern British colonizations of India—the one nonracially based, the other racist; the one a settler colony designed to participate in rather than destabilize and exploit the indigenous community, the other a commercial colony bent on exploiting then leaving. In other words, though Indian scholars may have good reason to resent the "Gandhāra bias," it should be blamed on the British, not on the Greeks.

There is something paradigmatic about the Gandhāra bias. With this one masterful stroke, Western scholars reached deep into Indian cultural history and claimed one of its signature elements as their own; the image of the Buddha could hardly be surpassed for its concise effectiveness in this use.

But in terms of the Greek presence in that part of the world, the Gandhāran Buddhas have a different meaning; they show how deeply the Indo-Greek descendants of Alexandrian colonists entered into the Indian community, not only economically but spiritually and artistically; the Gandhāran Buddhas, and many other signs, such as the Aśokan epigraphs published in Greek, would seem to show how willingly the Greek colonists had assimilated, while still not renouncing the cultural inheritance they brought with them. As a modern scholar notes, "Although [the Greek colonists] continued to build shrines to Greek gods, and amphitheaters in which to perform Greek plays, they did so out of attachment to their Hellenic identity rather than as a means of impressing a superior creed on a subservient race."[42] Greek willingness to assimilate culturally is revealingly different from the British dread of "going native"; the difference is the absence of racism. It is difficult to defend colonization, especially when it is militarily executed; still, it must be pointed out that there are different types and degrees of it.

Colonial Indology

Something like the Gandhāra bias on an all-pervasive scale characterizes what Indian archeologist Dilip Chakrabarti has called "colonial indology."[43] "One of the underlying assumptions of Western Indology," he says, "is a feeling of superiority in relation to India, especially modern India and Indians."[44] A western scholar notes more moderately but with a similar underlying thought that "the academic study of Buddhism in Europe and America [emerged] within the context of the ideologies of empire."[45]

According to Chakrabarti, "archaeology has been used"—even beyond the Gandhāra bias—"as a tool for intellectually dominating the subjugated nations and minorities."[46] One of the key tactics has involved "recurrent attempts to link all fundamental changes in Indian society and history to Western intervention in some form."[47] So strong is the reaction against this practice in postcolonial India that recent books by Indian scholars have argued—sometimes with a mixture of outrage and passion—against various Western views about Indian history, above all, the tradition of the so-called Aryan Invasion which most scholars of a generation ago posited.[48] Chakrabarti, for example, says, "We consider, the hypothesis of Aryan invasions of India to be a racist myth."[49] Similar feelings rise against the supposed influence of Alexander's empire on the Mauryan Empire, against the hypothesis that the Gandhāra sculptures were actually formative on the art history of Indian and Central Asian Buddhism, and so on. The most extreme anticolonial reaction is the pan-Indianism espoused by Paramesh Chowdury and others,[50] which allows for virtually no foreign intervention at any time in Indian history and further argues that the Indus Valley culture was the origin of all the world's civilizations.[51] For scholars unwilling to go that far, the question is where to draw the line.

Critics of the Western view of Indian chronologies object to Hegel's opinion that India was "ahistorical." Yet in seeking fixed points in Indian history Chakrabarti lists "the Achaemenid annexation of the Indus valley and the region to its West towards the end of the sixth century B.C., Alexander's invasion in 326 B.C., the identification of Candragupta Maurya with Sandrakottas of the Classical sources, the mention of some Hellenistic kings in the Aśokan inscriptions, and so on"—each point recording a foreign conquest from the West or the consequences of one.

Understandably unhappy with an Indian chronology that depends on foreign conquests, Chakrabarti discusses various attempts by Indian scholars to establish chronology from a combination of Indian texts and archeology without reference to the chronologies of foreign invaders. He concludes that the Bharata War—which would be the key date in pre-Achaemenid historiography, as the Trojan War is in pre-Herodotean—is hopelessly undateable, unlinked as it is to any archeological evidence which might yield rough absolute dates by carbon 14 or other such methods.[52] He concludes that it is "futility" to attempt "to link Puranic genealogies with Indian protohistoric archeological data."

Yet on the Greek side such linkage has been made and is widely accepted. With some adjustments, Carl Blegen's analysis of the mound at Hissarlik has been widely accepted as, more or less, a solution to the "Homeric problem." While archeologists cannot conclude absolutely that Hissarlik was ancient Troy, and thus that there was *some* historicity to the *Iliad*, the linkage is accepted as establishing a probability which is strong enough to induce a provisional consensus.[53] It has often been noted that there is a general similarity in subject matter between the *Iliad* and the *Mahābhārata*, both narrating community-defining ancestral wars, and between the *Odyssey* and the *Rāmāyana*, each telling of a distant war to recover an abducted royal bride. Yet the *Iliad*, supposedly, has its link with history (by way of archeology)—but the *Mahābhārata* does not. Though traditional Indian scholars have tended to date the Bharata War anywhere from 3000–1400 B.C.,[54] the dates lack archeological support and have been rejected by most Western, and many Indian, scholars.

To other Indian scholars, however, there seems something unfair about this, just as the model of Indian history as a series of foreign conquests has been experienced by some as insulting.[55] Discussing the theory of the Aryan Invasion—a hypothesis developed by Western scholars—Chakrabarti writes: "In whatever form or mode of expression we wish to consider the model which is generally accepted as valid even today[, it is] a racist model, visualized as a triumph of a dominant race over the other weaker/inferior/decadent/degenerate races."[56] On this view, the Aryan Invasion in particular, a narrative which was embraced by British archeologists, was a ploy to support British imperialism: "The British," writes Chakrabarti, wanted to appear "at the end of a long line of invaders of the land, beginning with the Aryans."[57]

It is out of this predicament in previously colonized cultures that the so-called autonomist or minimalist position arose in archeological theory, holding that a specific tradition should be studied inwardly—or autonomously—minimizing the impact of foreign contacts. On this view archeologists and cultural historians have been too eager to find diffusions and influences and have tended to exaggerate the importance of foreign conquests as against the inner inertia of a tradition with its tendency to reject foreign influences and maintain its inner balance.[58] It is easy to imagine an autonomist philology as well, and an autonomist approach to the history of philosophy. In these cases, instead of searching for outside influences and the disjunctions that may have been caused by them, the scholar will be more interested in the continuities of a tradition and its tendency to remain self-identical. The autonomist approach was a reaction against the obsession with diffusion that has characterized much archeological theory. Still, it does seem undeniable that outside intervention is a principal cause of disruption and change in sociocultural systems, and Andrew Sherrat speaks for the old view when he says, "It would be wrong to ignore the postcolonial background to the genesis of minimalism"; minimalism, in other words, is a palliative to a particular problem, not necessarily a valid approach in general; that which was "once a useful astringent and corrective," Sherrat says, "now is an embarrassing anachronism."[59]

Colonial Comparative Philosophy?

Any comparative study of Indian and Western cultures must play itself out against this rancorously contested backdrop as the bitterness of postcolonial argumentation swirls around the comparative project. Issues such as the identity of the Aryans and the likelihood and nature of an Aryan Invasion[60] pertain to what Chakrabarti calls "colonial archaeology," but colonial archeology is not the only form that colonial Indology can take; it is merely the one that has been most prominent to date. Philological argument can be used in the same way, as in what Chakrabarti calls "the politics of recent attempts to pull down the date of the Buddha,"[61] which he sees as a tilt of the playing field in favor of Greece over India. If the Buddha's death date is brought down first from 544 to 480 B.C., finally all the way to 371, then "[t]he Buddha becomes younger than Pericles (c. 492–420 B.C.), Socrates (461–399 B.C.) and Pythagoras. Vaiśali, the ancient republic, becomes younger than Athens . . ."[62] Through such chronological manipulations the threat that the Indian past presents to the Greek miracle is defused by chronology.

So the project of truly investigating the relationship between Indian and Greek philosophies has formidable obstacles in its way. First, there is the racist imperialist projection put upon this material by scholars from the colonizing nations beginning in the eighteenth century, and the bad reputation the whole enterprise has been saddled with as a result, and second, the nationalistic and somewhat xenophobic reaction by Indian scholars in the late and postcolonial periods.[63]

Comparisons of Indian and Greek Philosophies

Under these circumstances it is not surprising that the story of the relationship between Greek and Indian philosophies has remained a closed book to this day. Eighteenth- and nineteenth-century scholars, lacking adequate source materials for the Indian side of the relationship, were feeling their way in the dark. Jones himself began the comparison, simplistically proclaiming parallels between Gautama and Aristotle, Kanada and Thales, Jaimini and Socrates, Kapila and Pythagoras, Patañjali and Zeno, and so on.[64] His style of scattershot comparisons not based on analytic readings of accurate texts persisted until very recently, as witnessed, say, by Sylvain Levi's statement early in this century: "Plotinus, Porphyry, and the entire school of Neoplatonists reflect the metaphysics of Kapila and Patañjali. Mani and the Gnostics introduced the Brahman and Buddhist spirit into Christianity"—and so on.[65]

The inadequacy of claims so lightly stated and so unsupported by argument created a situation in which a premature dismissal of the subject was easy. A conviction spread that if these scholars were not producing impressive arguments based on evidence, it must be because no such arguments were available. The temptation to accept this presumption and let the subject go by without really looking into it was supported by the fact that the subject was inconvenient in the extreme. If the Greek miracle were to remain a miracle, its proponents must maintain that it happened by a kind of parthenogenesis, not by a fertilization from outside. So the whole Hegelian view of history and civilization, with its emphasis on cultural purity and its disapproval of hybridity, brushed aside the question of possible influences passing between Indian and Greek philosophers. For scholars like Guthrie, who grew up in the era of the British Empire, it seemed self-evident that no significant comparisons could be made. As part of what Hegel had called "the ahistorical," India was a part of nature, and comparisons between nature and culture were not the point of the humanities.

When enough time had elapsed it became clear to the few who had looked closely that the topic had not yet really been addressed and that it was necessary to reapproach it and start over again. This second approach started in the post–World War II period (which is also the beginning of the postcolonial period), and it has unfolded with extreme slowness. One promising development was the founding of the journal *Philosophy East and West* in 1951. But even though it would seem that the relationship between Indian and Greek philosophies is an absolutely foundational topic of the comparative field, remarkably little on that topic has appeared in this or any journal. In 1952, one year after the founding of the journal, George P. Conger's "Did India Influence Early Greek Philosophy?"[66] appeared in it. This article was roughly along the same lines as Jones's 1799 typological comparisons which lacked philological analysis, archeological grounding, and historical context. Jones's comparison of Patañjali and Zeno, for example, was bizarre—but he admitted that he had read little of Indian philosophical texts before writing. Conger's comparisons are more accurate, being based on better texts, but his methodology is the same—merely noting, for example, that Heraclitus and Siddhārtha Gautama both emphasized the idea of flux. Like Jones, Conger seems to assume that typological similarities are adequate by themselves, without philological and archeological context. In noting, for example, that, in his opinion, Parmenides' arguments go against the thrust of both Zoroastrian and Sāṇkhya dualisms, he seems to assume that this means that Parmenides was aware of those other currents of thought.[67]

In the same journal in the following year Helmuth von Glasenapp extended and refined the range of typological similarities,[68] and in the following year A. N. Marlowe extended it further.[69] Like Guthrie, Dodds, and other British scholars of that generation, Marlowe associates the Greek character with "rationalist humanism" and a "healthy unreflecting extraversion," and believes that irrational and mystical ideas, such as those professed by the Orphics and Pythagoreans, were un-Greek in flavor and thus, in his opinion, probably came from India. Still sounding like Jones a century and a half earlier, Marlowe notes that in comparing Greek and Indian ideas he is focusing on "their affinity of type"[70] without much attention to historical, archeological, and philological evidence.

In the last generation or so the investigation has grown more rigorous in method through a handful of texts—such as Daniel H. H. Ingalls's study of the relationship between Cynics and Pāśupatas, M. L. West's *Early Greek Philosophy and the Orient* (and some previously published parts of this book). [71] Ingalls's argument of 1962 went beyond a focus on surface similarities into a combining of typological and historical/archeological factors. In addition he attends with some meticulousness to details, as opposed to the sweeping and vague comparisons previously made. West's work, even more significantly, seems to have established a single specific connection between Heraclitus and an Upaniṣadic doctrine. This single instance of a rigorous scholarly proof demonstrates that philosophical doctrines *were* in fact traveling between India and Greece in the pre-Socratic period. Prior to West's book that premise, however plausible, remained hypothetical, but it now must be taken as established—at least until the state of the evidence changes.

West's eccentricity was in how he reconstructed the channels of communication. Marlowe notes that he himself "fall[s] back with others on Persia as the intermediary."[72] West, however, regarded Persia not as the intermediary between India and Greece but as the source from which the array of related ideas passed into both those traditions. No doubt he was seeking an easier diffusion pattern; still, he seems to have been seriously mistaken in this decision.[73]

I will not telegraph now what my own methods and conclusions are. In the following twenty-five chapters of argument from evidence I will make a measured attempt to establish significant intrusions first from India to Greece in the pre-Socratic period, then from Greece back to India in the Hellenistic period. In addition I will continue to extend and refine the typological comparisons that scholars have been making since Jones in 1799. Perhaps other scholars will correct me on one point or another, an event which would be welcome, for this is a shared human project that deserves the involvement of many minds. Surely the relationship between ancient Greek and Indian traditions of thought is the foundational level of comparative philosophy. These two ancient peoples were the first to recognize philosophy as a defining trait of humanity, as in the following doggerel (which a philosopher once told to me):

Fish gotta swim
Bird gotta fly
Man gotta sit and say
Why why why

Notes to Foreword

1. W. K. C. Guthrie, *A History of Greek Philosophy*, 6 vols. (Cambridge and New York: Cambridge University Press, 1962–1981).

2. W. K. C. Guthrie, *Orpheus and Greek Religion: A Study of the Orphic Movement* (New York: W. W. Norton, 1966); Ivan Linforth, *The Arts of Orpheus* (Berkeley, California, and Los Angeles: University of California Press, 1941).

3. E. R. Dodds, *The Greeks and the Irrational*, Sather Classical Lectures 25 (Berkeley, California: University of California Press, 1951).

4. Erwin Rohde, "Die Religion der Griechen," in *Kleine Schriften*, vol. 2 (Hildesheim: Georg Olms Verlag, 1969), p. 338.

5. See, for example, R. Keydell and K. Ziegler, "Orphische Dichtung," in Pauly-Wissowa, *Realencyclopädie*, 1385.

6. Dodds, *The Greeks and the Irrational*, p. 146–147.

7. Jocelyn Godwin, *Mystery Religions in the Ancient World* (San Francisco: Harper and Row, 1981), p. 145.

8. Guthrie, *A History of Greek Philosophy*, vol. 2, p. 53.

9. See D. S. Hawley, "L'Inde de Voltaire," *Studies on Voltaire and the Eighteenth Century*, (Banbury: The Voltaire Foundation, 1974), vol. 120, pp. 166f.

10. Wilhelm Halbfass, *India and Europe: An Essay in Understanding* (Albany, New York: State University of New York Press, 1988), p. 58.

11. Ibid., p. 59.

12. Edward W. Said, *Orientalism* (New York: Random House, 1979).

13. Garland Cannon, *Oriental Jones* (London: Asia Publishing House, 1964), p. 141. Though Jones's famous talk was the explosive beginning of a movement, it was not the first observation of the fact. Cf. Batchelor: "[I]n 1767 Pons' colleague Father Couerdoux became the first European to recognize 'that Sanskrit belonged to the same family as the languages of Europe'—although this had already been intuited fifty years earlier by the philosopher Leibnitz." Stephen Batchelor, *The Awakening of the West: The Encounter of Buddhism and Western Culture* (Berkeley, California: Parallax Press, 1994), p. 230. Nathaniel Halhed, in his *Grammar of the Bengal Language* (1778), had remarked on "The similitude of Sanskrit words with those of Persian and Arabic, and even of Latin and Greek" (pp. iii–iv). In fact, as early as 1587 Filippo Sassetti, a Florentine merchant resident in Goa, had perceived the connection.

14. David Hume, *Essays and Treatises on Several Subjects*, vol. 1 (Edinburgh: Bell and Bradfute, 1817), p. 521.

15. George Leopold Cuvier, *Cuvier's Animal Kingdom* (London: Wm. S. Orr, 1811), p. 50.

16. Hugh Trevor-Roper, *The Rise of Christian Europe* (London: Thames and Hudson, 1965), p. 11. This was a common Western sentiment at the time. Compare, for example, Bertrand Russell: "It is to the European races, in Europe or out of it, that the world owes most of what it possesses in thought, in science, in art, in ideas of government, in hope for the future." Bertrand Russell, *The Autobiography of Bertrand Russell: The Middle Years, 1914–1944* (New York: Bantam Books, 1969), p. 24.

17. H. A. Gleason Jr., *An Introduction to Descriptive Linguistics*, revised edition (New York: Holt, Rinehart and Winston, 1961), p. 457.

18. Ibid., p. 462. But it seems the Linear B tablets are as old—in fact, much older, if one thinks specifically of *written* documents.

19. Quoted by Raymond Schwab, *The Oriental Renaissance: Europe's Rediscovery of India and the East, 1680–1880*, trans. Gene Patterson-Black and Victor Reinking (New York: Columbia University Press, 1984), p. 71. Voltaire had spoken similarly, as quoted by Dilip K. Chakrabarti, *Colonial Indology: Sociopolitics of the Ancient Indian Past* (Delhi: Munshiram Monoharlal, 1997), p. 29.

20. Friedrich Schlegel, *Über die Sprache und Weisheit der Indier*, in *History of Linguistics Series*, vol. 4, *18th and 19th Century German Linguistics* (London: Routledge/Thoemmes Press, 1995), p. xii.

21. DeWitt H. Parker, in the introduction to *Schopenhauer: Selections* (New York: Charles Scribner's Sons, 1956), p. xx. Parker also refers to Schopenhauer as "the first important European philosopher to be influenced by Hindu thought" (ibid.). The judgment can only be maintained, as will become clear, by regarding "European" philosophy as a different category from Greek.

22. Batchelor, *The Awakening of the West*, pp. 252, 257.

23. Trans. Schwab, *The Oriental Renaissance*, p. 11.

24. Preface to *Die Welt als Wille und Vorstellung*; quoted by Schwab, *The Oriental Renaissance*, p. 13.

25. Quoted ibid.

26. Percy Bysshe Shelley, preface to *Hellas* (London: Reeves and Turner, 1886), p. ix; quoted by Stanley K. Abe, "Inside the Wonder House: Buddhist Art and the West," in *Curators of the Buddha: The Study of Buddhism under Colonialism*, ed. Donald S. Lopez Jr. (Chicago and London: University of Chicago Press, 1995), p. 84.

27. Risley, in 1908; quoted by Chakrabarti, *Colonial Indology*, p. 128.

28. Quoted ibid., p. 94.

29. See, for example, C. S. Littleton, *The New Comparative Mythology* (Berkeley, California, and Los Angeles: University of California Press, 1982).

30. Donald S. Lopez Jr., "Introduction," in Lopez, ed., *Curators of the Buddha*, p. 14.

31. Stanley K. Abe, "Inside the Wonder House: Buddhist Art and the West," in ibid., p. 83.

32. Werner Jaeger, *Paideia: The Ideals of Greek Culture*, vol. 1, trans. Gilbert Highet (New York: Oxford University Press, 1965), p. xv.

33. Quoted by Chakrabarti in *Colonial Indology*, p. 76.

34. Quoted by Abe in Lopez, ed., *Curators of the Buddha*, p. 77.

35. Frank M. Snowden Jr., *Before Color Prejudice: The Ancient View of Blacks* (Cambridge, Massachusetts: Harvard University Press, 1983).

36. Ibid., pp. 68, 70.

37. N. G. L. Hammond, *A History of Greece to 322 B.C.* (Oxford: The Clarendon Press, 1959), p. 639.

38. Plutarch in his work *On the Fortune or Virtue of Alexander* presents Alexander's invasion of India as a "civilizing mission," but it seems he was influenced by Roman justifications of their own conquests, and perhaps reading back anachronistically into Alexander's time.

39. Edward Zeller, *Die Philosophie der Griechen in ihrer geschichtlichen Entwicklung*, vol. 1 (Hildesheim: Georg Olms Verlag, 1963), pp. 20f.

40. Halbfass, *India and Europe*, p. 12.

41. Jaeger, *Paideia*, vol. 1, p. xv.

42. Batchelor, *The Awakening of the West*, p. 13.

43. Chakrabarti, *Colonial Indology*.

44. Ibid., p. 1.

45. Lopez, "Introduction," in Lopez, ed., *Curators of the Buddha*, p. 2.

46. Chakrabarti, *Colonial Indology*, p. 43.

47. Ibid, p. 1.

48. See the discussions in B. B. Lal and S. P. Gupta, editors, *Frontiers of the Indus Civilization* (Delhi: Books and Books, 1984), especially Dilip Chakrabarti, "Origin of the Indus Civilization: Theories and Problems," pp. 43–50. Also, Georg Feuerstein, Subhash Kak, and David Frawley, *In Search of the Cradle of Civilization: New Light on Ancient India* (Wheaton, Illinois, and Madras: Quest Books, 1995).

49. Chakrabarti, *Colonial Indology*, p. 158.

50. Paramesh Chowdury, *Indian Origin of the Chinese Nation: An Unconventional Challenging Theory about the Origin of the Chinese* (Calcutta: Dasgupta and Co., 1990). See also A. Kalyanaraman, *Aryatarangini: The Saga of the Indo-Aryans*, 2 vols. (Bombay: Asia Publishing House, 1969 and 1970); Navaratna S. Rajaram and David Frawley, *Vedic 'Aryans' and the Origins of Civilization* (Quebec: W. H. Press, 1995); Shrikant G. Talageri, *The Aryan Invasion Theory: A Reappraisal* (New Delhi: Aditya Prakashan, 1993), and so on.

51. This extreme position seems to represent a type of postcolonial reversal that is found commonly in the wake of colonialism. For more on this see Thomas McEvilley, *Fusion: West African Artists at the Venice Biennale* (New York: The Museum for African Art, and Munich: Prestel, 1993); and "Here Comes Everybody," in *From Beyond the Pale: Art and Artists at the Edge of Consensus* (Dublin: Irish Museum of Modern Art, 1994); reprinted in various places.

52. Chakrabarti, *Colonial Indology*, pp. 156–157.

53. Compare Neil Asher Silberman, *Between Past and Present: Archaeology, Ideology, and Nationalism in the Modern Middle East* (New York: Henry Holt and Company, 1989), p. 43: "On one point all scholars seemed to be in agreement: The mound of Hissarlik was the most likely location for ancient Troy."

54. See N. Jaganandha Rao, *The Age of the Mahābhārata War* (Varanasi: Bharat–Bharati, 1978) for the date of 3000; Chakrabarti, *Colonial Indology*, p. 156 for 1400.

55. Gayatri Spivak seems almost to renounce her Indianness on the grounds that Indianness is a British imperialist construct with Greek imperialism in its background: "'India', for people like me, is not really a place with which they can form a national identity because it has always been an artificial construct. 'India' is a bit like saying 'Europe' . . . 'Indianness' is not a thing that exists . . . The name India was given by Alexander the Great by mistake." *The Post-colonial Critic: Interviews, Strategies, Dialogues*, ed. Sarah Harasym (New York and London: Routledge, 1990), p. 39.

56. Chakrabarti, *Colonial Indology*, pp. 149–150.

57. Ibid., p. 99.

58. The autonomist theory has become a staple of Indian nationalist scholars; Rajaram and Frawley, for example, in *Vedic 'Aryans' and the Origins of Civilization* (p. 19) remark (without argument): "Migration and invasion theories ignore the fact that most cultural changes result from internal developments."

59. Andrew Sherrat, "Fata Morgana: Illusion and Reality in Greek-Barbarian Relations," *Cambridge Archeological Journal* 5, no. 1 (1995): 152.

60. See appendices A and B.

61. Chakrabarti, *Colonial Indology*, p. x.

62. B. P. Sinha, *Man and Environment* 20, no. 1 (1995): 20; quoted by Chakrabarti, *Colonial Indology*, p. x.

63. For the additional factor of Western xenophobia see appendix C.

64. Sir William Jones, *The Collected Works of Sir William Jones* (London: J. Hatchard, 1807), vol. 1, pp. 360–361.

65. Quoted by Schwab, *The Oriental Renaissance*, p. 3.

66. George P. Conger, "Did India Influence Greek Philosophy?" *Philosophy East and West* 2 (1952): 102–128.

67. Ibid., p. 122–123.

68. Helmuth von Glasenapp, "Indian and Western Metaphysics," *Philosophy East and West* 3 (1953): 225.

69. A. N. Marlowe, "Hinduism and Buddhism in Greek Philosophy," *Philosophy East and West* 4 (1954): 3–38.

70. Ibid., p. 35.

71. Daniel H. H. Ingalls, "Cynics and Pāśupatas: The Seeking of Dishonor," *Harvard Theological Review* 55 (1962): 281–298; M. L. West, *Early Greek Philosophy and the Orient* (Oxford: The Clarendon Press, 1971); Thomas McEvilley, "Plotinus and Vijñānavāda Buddhism," *Philosophy East and West* 30 (1980): 181–193; "Early Greek Philosophy and Mādhyamika," *Philosophy East and West* 31 (1981): 141–164; "Pyrrhonism and Mādhyamika," *Philosophy East and West* 32 (1982): 3–35; "The Spinal Serpent," *Res: Anthropology and Aesthetics* 24 (Autumn 1993): 68–77.

72. Marlowe, "Hinduism and Buddhism in Greek Philosophy," p. 45.

73. See chapter 4, "The Doctrine of Reincarnation."

Chapter One

Diffusion Channels in the Pre-Alexandrian Period

Ancient cultures from the eastern Mediterranean to the Indian Ocean were shaped through a continuous interplay with one another, an interplay only dimly seen, which is the hidden map of ancient history. It is a map of caravan routes and sea voyages, of travels and commerce—and of their consequences. For an island village in the Aegean Sea in the third millennium B.C., the beginning of the Bronze Age meant the arrival of a single ship with newfangled wares. The establishing of a new school of philosophy in Hellenistic Afghanistan meant the arrival of a single teacher with his books in his pack. The records of caravan routes are like the philological stemmata of history, the trails of oral discourses moving through communities, of texts copied from texts, with accretions, scribal errors, and incorporated glosses and scholia. What they reveal is not a structure of parallel straight lines—one labeled "Greece," another "Persia," another "India"—but a tangled web in which an element in one culture often leads to elements in others.

Indo-Europeans

"For a period of about a thousand years," said H. G. Rawlinson in 1926, "from the invasion of Darius to the sack of Rome by the Goths, India was in more or less constant communication with the West."[1] In fact, the Greeks who settled in the lower end of the Balkan Peninsula in the first half of the second millennium B.C. and the Indo-Aryans who seem to many to have moved into northwest India in the same epoch were linked with one another before their journeys began. Both were once speakers of Proto-Indo-European, probably inhabiting different areas of some culturally and linguistically unified homeland. The traditional idea that they dropped down into the stream of history—meaning the ancient Near East—toward the end of the late third millennium B.C. has recently been challenged by various attempts to reposition the event, usually at an earlier date. Gimbutas's identification of the Indo-Europeans with the Kurgan peoples pushes them back toward the fifth millennium B.C.; Renfrew's association of them with the spread of agriculture locates them in the seventh.[2]

As long as the hypothetical Proto-Indo-European homeland was regarded as occupying the Eurasian steppe north of the Black and Caspian Seas, such loose or vague dates seemed appropriate; the Proto-Indo-Europeans seemed to live in a timeless world in which they were imagined as racing horses over vast treeless terrains much as the Mongols would be envisioned thousands of years later. From such an ahistorical region of the world the moment when they dropped down southward into history could be inserted nearly anywhere.

But recent scholarly revisions have not all tended toward an earlier date; some have wanted to lower it. Drews, for example, has relocated the Indo-Europeans south of the Caucasus, in Cappadocia in eastern Anatolia or in adjacent Armenia, right smack in the middle of the area where history began, early in the second millennium B.C. Drews's synoptic review—and reinterpretation—has the various Indo-European groups setting off on charioteering conquests from someplace around Armenia about 1600 B.C.[3] According to this view the Indo-Europeans who entered Greece and those who entered India were not separated by vast times and distances on the immeasurable steppe but lived in one culture in specific and partly visible historical circumstances.

In any case, the Greek and most of the Indian philosophical texts were written in Indo-European languages and the relation between the traditions can be seen as one aspect of "the Indo-European Problem"[4] in scholarship about antiquity. For the history of philosophy little can be said beyond the observation that the Indo-European languages' emphasis on the noun and on the being verb may have been conducive to the separation of experience into categories and their analysis into discrete ontological states.

Near-Eastern Influence

In addition to Indo-European linguistic forms and mythological legacies such as the Heavenly Twins—the Dioscuri in Greece, the Aśvins among the Vedic Aryans—both groups also show Mesopotamian and other Near Eastern influences. These may have been picked up while passing through the Near East or later through trade. The first regular international maritime trade that is known was carried on "by Mesopotamians and Indians who sailed between the Persian Gulf and the northwestern coast of India."[5] "As early as the middle of the fourth millennium B.C., Babylonian merchants were either sailing these waters themselves or dealing directly with traders who were."[6] From the East the trade brought mainly copper and timber, both in short supply in the Near East, but also featured luxuries such as ivory, precious stones, and rare woods. In third-millennium Mesopotamian sites "excavators have unearthed certain large conchs with a snow-white shell . . . examples of the Indian chank, which is found only in the coastal waters of India and Ceylon."[7]

By 2500–2000 B.C. the presence of cylinder seals and "Persian Gulf" type seals in Mohenjo Daro, Chanhu Daro, Lothal, and elsewhere in the Indus Valley indicates that these cities were in trade contact with Sumerian and Babylonian centers.[8] The Near East, situated where Asia, Africa, and Europe meet, was already becoming international and multicultural. By the middle of the third millennium carnelian beads from the Indus Valley were reaching Sumer, and silver from the mines at Laurium in Attica was being imported into Egypt.[9] Those Proto-Indo-European speakers who became the Greeks, and those who became the Vedic Aryans were both about to enter areas where they would be subjected to a saturation of Near Eastern influences. As West says, "[T]he Aegean world into which the first 'Greek' speakers penetrated . . . had

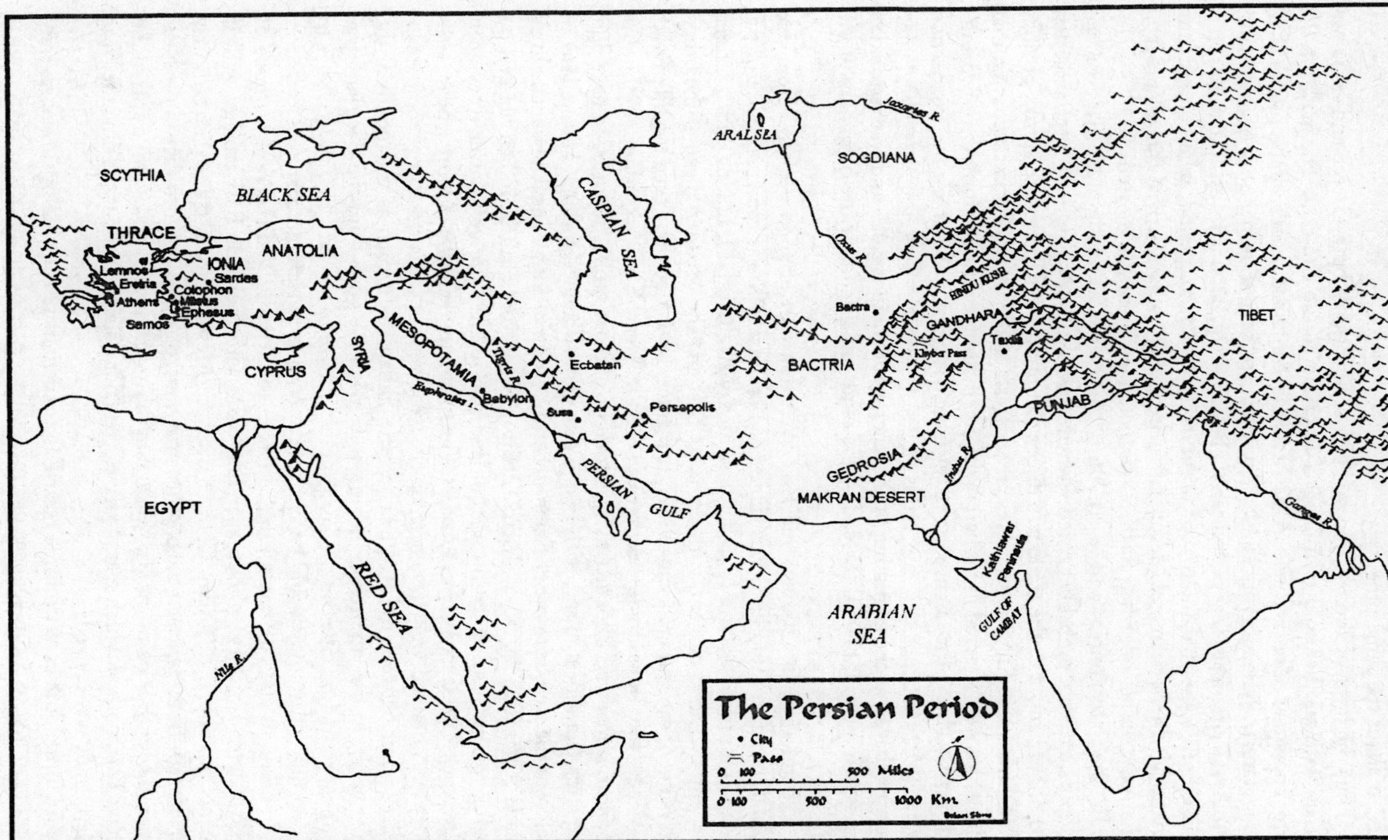

Map 1 The Persian Empire.

already absorbed many cultural elements of West Asiatic origin."[10] And the same could be said of the northwest Indian world into which the first "Sanskrit" speakers penetrated at about the same time.

Thus the layer of Indo-European cultural likeness in both Greece and India was overlaid with another layer of influences from the Fertile Crescent. The graves in the group known as Grave Circle A at Mycenae contained goods that originated in Mesopotamia, Syria, Egypt, Nubia, Anatolia, northern Europe, and Afghanistan.[11] Vedic Aryan sites from that period cannot be identified, but northwest India also seems to have been somewhat internationalized in the Akkadian period, when goods from both the Mediterranean and Mesopotamia are known to have arrived there,[12] and later in the Assyrian period, when further Mesopotamian input is indicated.

In the late fourth and early third millennia Indian goods that reached Mesopotamia were probably carried—whether overland or by sea—by intermediaries. After about 2400 B.C. the trade was direct; the Sumerian Ur-Nanshe speaks of ships from Dilmun bringing timber to his city, Lagash, and Sargon of Akkad boasted that Indian ships were moored in his harbor.[13] This situation continued for four or five hundred years. Then, the archeological evidence suggests, the maritime connection between Mesopotamia and the Indus Valley was lost during the first Babylonian dynasty—that is, at the beginning of the second millennium B.C.—and was restored in the Assyrian period, toward the end of the same millennium or the beginning of the next.[14]

Around 1500 to 1300 B.C. full East-West transport of goods—almost from one end of Eurasia to the other—was achieved. The final link was the appearance of the caravan emporia of Bactria (roughly present-day Afghanistan), linking India, China, and Central Asia at one end with the Near East and the Mediterranean at the other; this system of caravanserais and wholesale markets would later be called the Silk Road.

When the India trade was revived in the Near East, according to the *Old Testament*, it involved Phoenicians. Solomon (c. 965–922 B.C.) is reported to have outfitted a merchant fleet to sail, with Phoenician crews obtained through Hiram, king of Tyre, from the Red Sea port of Ezion-geber to "Ophir"—long believed by many to be India (I *Kings* X.26–28, X.22). Merchants from Tyre would sail to Indian markets on coasting voyages, staying within sight of land, and return with "gold, silver, ivory, apes, and peacocks" for sale to western traders. The Indian market called Ophir, whence such goods were obtained, may have been on the west coast of India itself or at some intermediary point between the Red Sea and the Indian coast, such as the mouth of the Persian Gulf. In the latter case, Indian goods may have gone from the Bactrian caravan towns to trading cities on the Persian Gulf, thence to be taken by Tyrian traders to the Red Sea, where they would be available to Mediterranean merchants.

In India in the late second millennium—the Middle Vedic period in terms of Sanskrit literary history—the reexpanding trade with the Near East brought with it elements of cultural diffusion. Contact with the Mesopotamian cultural stream may have left significant traces in the pantheistic hymns, of a type found widely in the Near East, in the tenth book of the *Ṛg Veda* and in the appearance of Akkadian words in the *Atharva Veda*, both of which seem to have been taking shape at about the time the Near Eastern trade was revived.

In Greece, influence from the Near Eastern centers terminated or slowed severely around 1200 B.C., as a consequence of a mysterious series of urban destructions known as "the catastrophe." In this generation or two the Mycenaean centers, as well as about forty other major cities of Anatolia, Syria, and the southern Levant, were destroyed. Even Egypt and Mesopotamia were threatened.[15] "These upheavals," says West, "destroyed the momentum of east-west trade."[16] This was the beginning of the Greek Dark Age, which lasted for about three centuries. By about 900 B.C., Greek trade with the East was reviving, encouraged partly by the success of Phoenician merchants, some of whom seem to have taken up residence in the reawakening Greece.[17]

Meanwhile, cultural exchanges with India occurred by way of the Phoenician route through the Red Sea. In Mesopotamia the obelisk of Shalmaneser III (around 860 B.C.) shows imported Indian elephants, and the palace of Nebuchadnezzar (around 600 B.C.) shows logs of India teak. The trade between India and the West was to remain a trade in luxury items; it was a trade between leisure classes, and involved cultural delicacies as well as material goods.

The Orientalizing Period

At about the time the Phoenician trade was flourishing, the Greeks were undergoing a new period of intense Near Eastern influence, the "Orientalizing Period" (roughly the seventh century B.C.), when Greek merchants, mercenary soldiers, and tourists were traveling widely again after centuries of sedentary isolation. Increased mixing, both familial and cultural, marked the period. Thales of Miletus, for example, was the son of Examyes, evidently a Carian, and is said by Herodotus and others to have been ultimately of Phoenician lineage; similarly, Pherecydes of Syros was the son of one Babys —again an Anatolian name. Both, true to these Asian lineages, introduced "exotic eastern motifs into Greek mythical philosophy."[18]

Greeks traveled extensively at this time, revisiting cultures which had been important to their ancestors half a millennium earlier but had since been forgotten. Greeks were common in the Assyrian empire, as mercenaries, traders, and craftsmen. There were so many Greek merchants in Egypt during this period that a colony was established for them by the pharaoh Amasis in the second half of the seventh century at Naukratis on the Nile delta; another Greek colony was set aside by Psammatichus I near Buto on the delta. Still other Greek settlements in Egypt followed, and by the time of Herodotus "the number of Greeks living in Egypt was considerable."[19] Many of the Greek merchant captains in the Egyptian trade were literate, and some were aristocrats from highly cultured backgrounds. Charaxus of Lesbos, the brother of the poet Sappho, took shipments of wine to Naukratis (Hdt. II.135; Strabo 808; Ath. 569b), and Solon of Athens is said by no less an authority than Aristotle to have traveled to Egypt "on business" (*Constitution of the Athenians*, XI.1; cf. Plu. *Sol.* V.25). In 591 B.C. some Greek visitors—perhaps mercenary soldiers—surveying the most distant Egyptian temples and sculptures scratched their names on the monumental statue of Rameses II at Abu Simbel in Nubia.[20]

In the Orientalizing period Greek mercenaries became scattered throughout the eastern kingdoms, where they were especially valued for their adaptability and discipline. They are known to have been in the army of Psammatichus I in the mid-seventh century, and in the Judaean and Babylonian armies in the same period.[21] The poet Alcaeus's brother Antimenidas served in the army of Nebuchadnezzar II as a mercenary (Alcaeus fr. 350 L. P.). The example of Xenophon of Athens, a mercenary of Plato's day who wrote a book on Socrates and another on the Persian king Cyrus, shows that a man of this profession could be a medium for significant cultural exchange.

Greek artists also traveled widely at this time, importing influences from relatively distant places such as Egypt and Ur Artu. Artistic motifs and techniques from the Near East had poured into the centers of the Mycenaean age, and in the seventh century the event repeated itself; Greece was "Orientalized" for a second time. Many Semitic loan words entered the Greek language at this time, mostly for commodities and the mercantile process which dealt with them.

In literature also, in the same period, a vast array of Near Eastern myths, poetic motifs, and *topoi* appeared in Homer, Hesiod, and the archaic lyric poets. A review of such linkages underscores the fact that Greece was an eastern Mediterranean culture that had not yet differentiated itself from the others. Countless elements of Greek life and thought in the preclassical period derived from the Near East—from weights and measures to constellation names to time reckoning to musical instruments—and on and on.

In terms of the birth of philosophy, the most crucial thread in this vast weave is the fact that at this time Babylonian mathematical and astronomical lore seems to have been spreading widely among Greek literati.[22] The Lydian court at Sardes may have been an intermediary in this process. Herodotus (I.29) says that all the sages of Greece came to Sardes in its heyday. Thales did military engineering for King Croesus there. It is a reasonable inference that Anaximander was influenced by Babylonian astronomy and map-making, though where he encountered this influence and through what intermediaries is a matter of conjecture. Burkert notes that "there was no transmission of cuneiform script anywhere in the West"; still, he feels that Greeks living in the East may have learned it.[23] All these and many other mutual influences, interminglings, and cultural layerings were in effect before the Persian empire stepped decisively into the middle of Greek and Indian affairs.

The Persian Empire

In the sixth century B.C. direct Greek-Indian contacts occurred in the Persian Empire, which was erected on the ruins of the Assyrian Empire. Cyrus conquered the Median capital of Ecbatan in 550, the Lydian capital of Sardes in 546, and, finally, Babylon itself in 539. In 525 Cyrus's son and successor, Cambyses II, took Egypt.

Almost at once the Persian kings, desirous of extending their realm in both directions, mounted wars of conquest against the Greek border on the West and the Indian border on the Southeast. At the time of Cyrus's conquest of Sardes all the Greek cities of Asia Minor and many of the nearby islands—the very city-states, Miletus, Colophon, Ephesus, Samos, where the pre-Socratic philosophers would very soon be active—were brought under Persian rule. In virtually the same years, Bactria, the area just north of the Hindu Kush, and Gandhāra, the area just south of it, were annexed to the Persian Empire; about 515 this area was expanded by Darius I and constituted as a satrapy. For about a generation and a half after Cyrus's conquests the most advanced parts of Greece and India were in the same political entity, and for a generation after Darius's, when the imperial court scene got fully underway, this relationship was even closer.

During these years Greek and Indian functionaries of various types sat down together at the Persian court, where there was a growing multicultural milieu that promoted diffusion contacts. As Burkert says, it is possible that some Greeks in the East may have learned to read cuneiform versions of Akkadian texts such as the *Enuma Elish*.[24] As Huxley wrote about astronomical lore:

> How such knowledge reached the Aegean from Babylonia is a matter for speculation, but late in the sixth century B.C. the Babylonians and the Asiatic Greeks were both subjects of the Persians and ideas must have travelled far and fast in their unified empire along the Royal Road.[25]

The Royal Road had initially been opened up from Sardes to Nineveh during the Assyrian Empire. The Persians took it over and extended it to Susa, as they generally took over the Assyrian system of roads and maintained quick and efficient transportation throughout the Empire (a tradition that is immortalized in Herodotus's encomium of the Persian postal system), a feature that would encourage and promote the meetings of distant peoples.

Residences of educated Greeks and Indians at the Persian court—Ecbatan during Cyrus's day, Susa during Darius's—were not uncommon. On the Greek side, which has left records of the period while the Indian side has not, "the sources provide testimony for the fact that there were many Greeks who, for various reasons, were in Iran during Achaemenid times. There is no doubt the Greek physicians, scholars and masters of the arts made a definite contribution to the culture of the upper strata of Persian society."[26] Indians, some of whose names are known, were also present in the Persian courts in a variety of functions.

More is known about Persian relations with the Greeks under Darius (d. 486) than under either Cyrus (d. 529) or Cambyses (d. 521), and overall more is known about Persian relations with Greeks than with Indians, primarily since the Greeks wrote a great deal about it and the Indians, who basically did not write history in antiquity, did not. Darius depended, for example, on an east Greek fleet for his forays into Europe, and Histiaeus of Miletus—who brought an entourage of Greeks to the Persian court at Susa from the very city where pre-Socratic philosophy began and at roughly the same time—became his regular advisor for over a dozen years. In addition, Darius sheltered Greek refugees, including such prominent figures as Demaratas of Sparta and the Pesistratids, who no doubt also came with retinues of attendants. The Persian court became a place of sanctuary for statesmen ruined in the revolution-plagued politics of the Greek city-states. In 505 the tyrant Hippias, expelled from Athens, fled to the Persian court. Themistocles later did the same and is reported to have married a Persian woman, to have learned Persian to the extent that he dispensed with an interpreter, and even to have taught the doctrines of the Magi (Plu. *Them.* 29; Diod. XI.57.6; Nepos, *Them.* X.1). Metiochus, a son of Cimon's son Miltiades, Greek ruler of the Thracian Chersonese, Lemnos, and Imbros, also married a Persian woman and produced children with her who were officially listed as Persians (Hdt. VI.41). Alcibiades, Pausanias, and others, when their fortunes were ruined in Greece, made new destinies in Persian employ.

For several years Darius held at his court one Syloson, the brother of Polycrates, the tyrant of Samos, the island city where Pythagoras was born and raised. When Polycrates fell out of favor with the Persian court, Darius returned Syloson to Samos as ruler; Syloson returned with a Persian retinue. Random diffusion events like this must have happened frequently throughout the archaic age, a period when international trade was thriving in the eastern Mediterranean and the Ionian Greeks were bi- or multilingual, speaking Greek and whatever Anatolian language they were contiguous with—and sometimes Persian too.

Workers Imported and Deported

In the late years of the sixth century the Carian Scylax of Caryanda was commissioned by Darius to sail down the Indus River and through the Arabian Sea to Suez (Hdt.

IV.44). The intention was to explore the possibility of sea-trade between India and Persia, presumably to determine whether northwest India was worth securing as part of Darius's empire. Scylax made the voyage in 517 and wrote a book about it, in Greek. The book is lost, but it seems to have been used in 514 B.C. by Hekataeus, in whose few fragments eight Indian place-names occur, and by Herodotus a generation or so later. Scylax's book, along with the later work of Ctesias of Cnidus, who was himself in Persian service in the late fifth century B.C., was one of "the two standard descriptions of India before Alexander the Great."[27]

Some real information got through by such channels. Even though Herodotus's information about India is scanty, it is not worthless. He knew, for example, that northern Indians were lighter skinned than southern Indians, whom he calls Ethiopians; that cannibalism was practiced in some tribal groups, and, most interestingly, that there were people who ate nothing that had animal life and who lived out of doors, eating only wild grains. This last can only refer to the ascetic (or "yogic") communities of India, with whom Skylax and his associates evidently had contact.

About three years after Skylax's expedition of 517, encouraged by the Carian's demonstration that there was a sea route from the Indus to the Red Sea, Darius expanded the Persian area of India to the East, to include the Indus River. Indeed, not long thereafter he built a canal connecting the Mediterranean with the Red Sea, unwittingly preparing for both ends of the later Indo-Greek trade.

In the same period many Greeks entered Persian employ in imperial building projects and other functions, as professional ambitions of various types were stimulated by the developing intercourse between nations. The Persian kings imported Greeks as engineers and artists to build their palace centers, and as mercenary soldiers, generals, and admirals. So widespread were Greek mercenaries, in fact, that in Cambyses' conquest of Egypt, says Herodotus, Greeks fought on both sides.

During the imperial period the Persians reoriented their production system for the use of foreign workers. Called *kurtash*, these were sometimes slaves, sometimes free people working for wages, and sometimes indentured servants. Slave or not, they received wages in proportion to the work they performed.[28] Sometimes these were prisoners of war, sometimes populations driven off their ancestral lands in punishment for rebellion. Among the *kurtash* were individuals from conquered populations, including both Ionians and Bactrians.[29] "Diodorus (XVII.69) and Curtius Rufus (V.5) relate that when Alexander the Great approached Persepolis, 4,000 imprisoned Greek craftsmen came out to meet him."[30] In addition to the ambiguous status of the *kurtash*, the normal ancient Near East–Eastern Mediterranean slave trade contributed to mixing populations; Darius's inscriptions mention Bactrian and Gandhāran women who were brought back after the suppression of uprisings and sold as slaves in Babylon.[31]

Finally, the Persians seem to have adopted from the Assyrians the strategy of deporting troublesome communities to areas where their rebellious attitudes would find no purchase. "By Assyrian conquests and mass deportations," says Frye, "the peoples of the Near East were mixed as they had never been before . . . syncretism in most phases of culture followed."[32] "To some extent," as Cook notes, "the odd community of Greeks deported . . . by the Achaemenids may have contributed to the cultural synthesis."[33] Herodotus tells of Greeks sent to Susa (VI.20) and Khuzistan (VI.119), and in fact "the Achaemenians established settlements of Asiatic Greeks in Bactria."[34] Among the Greeks settled in Bactria were the citizens of Miletus who were relocated after the destruction of that city for its fomenting of the Ionian revolution in 499. It was not just any Greeks, in other words, but Greeks from the very heartland of pre-Socratic philosophy who were settled at the eastern end of the Iranian plateau, providing a potential channel for philosophical contacts and influences between Greece and India.

Multiculturalism

The archeological remains of the Persian palace centers suggest an easy-going, multicultural milieu. At Persepolis twenty-three nations are portrayed in the reliefs. The tablets indicate specialized craftsmen and artists from numerous nations, including Greeks. At the secondary palace at Madaktu there was a "centre for Babylonian, Indian and Egyptian workers."[35] "Darius was at pains to record that many different peoples of empire contributed labour and materials to the construction and decoration of his Apadana at Susa . . . some twenty-six or twenty-seven peoples are mentioned."[36] At Susa "by a gigantic effort at international co-operation artistic elements from many parts of the subject lands were fused . . ."[37]

At Persepolis this polyglot workforce was even more pronounced: "[T]he majority were of foreign origin. Egyptian stonemasons were used in very large numbers, well over 500 at a time. Indians and eastern Iranians seem to be found, and also Babylonians, Cappadocians, and Carians. Yauna (Ionians Greeks) are mentioned, along with more numerous people who may be Hatti from northern Syria; and we know that Greek masons worked in the quarries near Persepolis."[38] "We have here," notes Frye, "probably the most cosmopolitan crew of workers ever assembled up to that time."[39] "Greek sculptors undoubtedly worked at Persepolis,"[40] where drapery, for example, is rendered in a sixth-century archaic Greek style. The sculptor Telephanes of Phocaea, who, the elder Pliny says (*N.H.* XXXIV.68), "was on a par with the greatest of Greek sculptors . . . was little known because . . . he spent his time in the workshops of Xerxes and Darius . . ."[41]

Art and Diffusion

It was first through the Persian Empire that Greek artistic styles began to be imprinted on cultures throughout Asia. This was the beginning of the stunning development in which, later, "along the Silk Road . . . trade and religion carried Greco-Roman art with them,"[42] so its stylistic signatures were to be seen as far away as Tun Huang. Already at this earlier stage, the Persians had a special interest in Greek art. Xerxes brought the famous statue of Harmodius and Aristogeiton from Athens to Susa. Artworks that are purely Greek, making no attempt to synthesize a partly Asian style, have been found at Persepolis, implying that some Persians collected them. Greek artists created portraits of the satraps Tissaphernes and Pharnabazos for coins. The architecture of Persepolis is similarly synthetic and international, and appropriately so as it was known as a "Palace of All Nations," stressing the international cooperation that went into its design and execution. The gate later erected there by Xerxes was called the "Gate of All Nations."

The milieu of the Persian court was one in which intellectual and artistic intercourse between representatives of the various satrapies flourished. The Persians themselves "clearly . . . were not a people that we should call intellectual. They do not themselves seem to have had an inclination towards literature, medicine, or philosophical and scientific speculation."[43] Still, they provided a setting in which such speculation could be freely pursued.

Their attitude toward religion is illustrative. Despite the fierce dogmatism later associated with Zoroastrian monotheism, the Achaemenian government was tolerant toward religions not its own. In general, Darius protected religious institutions, such as the priesthood of Apollo at Magnesia on the Maeander or the medical school connected with the temple at Egyptian Sais (the connection of medicine with religion was not unusual). He constructed "temples of Amon Ra in the Khargeh oasis and other temples at Edfu, Busiris and Elkab."[44] "Babylonian, Egyptian and Hebrew deities were honoured . . . by both (Cyrus and Cambyses)."[45] As Frye notes,

> Hand in hand with the idea of empire went the process of mixture and syncretism; members of distant tribes and nations were brought into contact with each other under the umbrella of the Persian peace and there must have been much give and take . . . Greek doctors, Phoenician explorers and Babylonian astronomers were welcome at the court of the king of kings, and if we believe Greek sources, the Persian monarchs sought to lure, usually unsuccessfully, numbers of prominent Greek scientists or thinkers to their courts with promises of great rewards.[46]

Finally, "what resulted from the 'Pax Persica,'" says Cook, "was syncretism and cultural assimilation on a scale that had not previously been thinkable."[47]

Subsequent Relations with Greece

Soon after expanding his Indian holdings Darius entered Europe and—with the help of Histiaeus—made inroads into Scythia and Thrace. From these holding places, relations with mainland Greece were opened, solemnized by the marriage of a Macedonian princess to a Persian general.

In 500 B.C. the Asian Greek cities, at the instigation of Miletus, revolted from the Persian Empire with the help of two powerful mainland cities, Athens and Eretria. By 493 they had been reconquered, Miletus was burned and the Milesians either slain or deported (some of them to Bactria), and Persia was determined to punish their mainland allies. In 490 and again in 480 Persian armies—with large contingents of light-armed Indian cavalry—arrived in Greece. Both times they lost. For the rest of the fifth century, relations between the Greek communities and the Persian Empire were wary, and contacts between Greeks and Indians were sporadic.

Still, the Persian employment of Greek mercenary soldiers continued in the fourth century, as Xenophon's story makes clear; and trade also seems to have continued through the fifth and into the fourth century by a route that went from Central Asia by a series of waterways and portages—Oxus River, Caspian Sea, Kyros River, Black Sea. There is some reason to believe that Indian ascetics traveled this route and interacted at the northern end of it with Black Sea shamans, ultimately influencing Greek philosophy through Diogenes of Sinope, who seems to have brought Indian-derived ascetic practices into the Athenian philosophical milieu.[48] It is perhaps through this route that an Indian yogi came to Athens to talk with Socrates, according to a story told by Aristoxenus and thus extant at least as early as the fourth century B.C. (*ap.* Eusebius, *Prep. Ev.* XI.3.8).

The Indian Side

Most of what is known about Persia comes from Greek sources; much less is known about the details of the relationship between India and Persia. Indeed, the tradition is garbled about the very beginning of that relationship. Arrian says that the Indians in the region of the Indus River "were in ancient times subject to the Assyrians, afterward to the Medes, and finally they submitted to the Persians" (*Indica* 1). No other source asserts that the Assyrians ventured across the Hindu Kush, but it is not entirely unbelievable. The Assyrians were certainly expansive, the first Mesopotamian polity to extend their rule to the Mediterranean, and they moved people around in great numbers to accommodate their reinvention of the world. As they looked around for places profitable to conquer, they might have been drawn toward northwest India, whose Bronze Age culture was known to have been a wealthy trading partner of some of their predecessors, both Sumerian and Akkadian. If the Assyrians did in fact enter northwest India or even make overtures toward such an act this would provide a channel whereby the Akkadian words in the *Atharva Veda* could have traveled to India in the Middle Vedic period.

The Medes may have lost whatever foothold in India the Assyrians had obtained; still, they are said by both Ctesias and Herodotus (I.153) to have ruled Bactria as far as the Oxus, and possibly Punjab inside the Kush. The Bactrians supposedly rebelled against Cyrus after he had brought about the downfall of the Median dynasty, but before taking on Babylon in 539 he had established, or reestablished, control as far east as the Jaxartes River and Gandhāra at the northwest entrance to India. Darius, in 515, extended Persian control southeast to the Indus, creating the new satrapy of Hindush. Indeed, Bactria and Gandhāra are both mentioned in Darius's foundation inscription for Persepolis as sources of precious materials—teak from Gandhāra and gold from Bactria.

Under Darius and later, Indians served as mercenaries and would be paid off at the end of their term of service by being settled on land somewhere in the empire; such a colony of Indians was located near the old Sumerian city of Nippur in the fifth century B.C.[49] Though there are no Indian records of the period, Persian and Greek sources provide surprisingly intimate glimpses of these Indians resident in the Near East. Recent work on the Persepolis documents has provided for the first time actual names to fill in the blanks of the picture a little on the Indian side, at least *exempli gratia*, as, on the Greek side, they are rudimentarily filled in by such names as Scylax, Syloson, Menochus, and so on.

> The Persepolis documents . . . contain data concerning civil servants who had traveled to Persepolis and Susa on state business. . . . Texts from the time of Darius I frequently mention Indians. In 499 B.C. the Indian Abbatema set out from India to Susa accompanied by 20 men, but after a month he returned back to his homeland. In the year 498 the Indian Karabba was sent by the king to India accompanied by 180 men.[50]

A fragment yields a glimpse of "an Indian woman . . . by the name of Busasa [who] maintained an inn in the city of Kish."[51] Thus there are actual names—and rough dates—giving assurance that in the very heart of the pre-Socratic period there were Indians resident at the Persian court and others whom various opportunities attracted from India to the court. Ctesias reports of a slightly later period that "it was possible to see Indian elephants and their drivers in Babylon at the end of the fifth and the beginning of the fourth centuries B.C."[52] Near Eastern cities, which for centuries—in some cases millennia—had been multiethnic, were not xenophobic toward such arrivals. "Foreigners were gradually assimilated by the local population; they adopted Babylonian names [and] spoke the Aramaic language . . ."[53] Not only were armies multilingual, then, but the cities that lay between Greece and India were polyglot.

Meeting Grounds

Greeks such as (say) Polycrates and Telephanes must have met Indians such as Abbatema and Karabba at the Persian court during the pre-Socratic/Upaniṣadic period. But the circumstances of such meetings must be conjectured. According to Herodotus (III.129-132), one Greek (the physician Democedes, of whom more later) was so honored for his services to the king that he was "accepted into the ranks of the royal table companions and presented with a huge house in Susa."[54]

It is not clear what it meant to be a royal table companion. Greek sources report that fifteen thousand people were fed daily at the king's expense. Some ate outside the palace, some inside, but the king ate in a separate curtained room from which he could glimpse his guests. "Sometimes he would invite a dozen nobles to come up to him; these nobles, however, had to sit on the floor, in contrast to the king, who dined on a couch . . ."[55] Were Greeks and/or Indians among those who sat on the floor in the king's presence? In any case they were not likely to have enjoyed much intimate conversation with the king, as "the Persians . . . kept aloof even from those Greeks whom they received . . ."[56]

Language Questions

As part of an ambience that encouraged cultural exchange, much was done to reduce language barriers. When he was establishing the Lydian satrapy in 546 B.C., Cyrus already was accompanied by Greek interpreters. As their empire developed, the Persian kings provided

> translators who knew several languages at the courts of the king and satraps, and in the army . . . [In addition] there were representatives of many peoples in Persepolis, and numerous translators were required for coordinating their work. Similarly a large staff of translators at the royal court in Susa was required to provide the necessary clarifications to civil servants who had arrived there from all parts of the state . . . when the Greek Syloson from Samos appeared in the palace of Darius I, translators were immediately found at the court and addressed him with questions in Greek.[57]

Letters to the Greek cities were also written in Greek. That the translators knew Indian languages also seems clear even without the assurance of the *Old Testament* that the Achaemenids wrote "to each region in its own script and to each people in their own language" (*Esther* 1:22; 3:12; 8:9). It seems that Greeks in particular—widely traveled merchants and soldiers—were employed as interpreters at the courts of the Persian satraps. "Xenophon (*Anab.* II.4.24) speaks of 'the Greeks who were at (the court) of Tissaphernes.' Cyrus the Younger, satrap in Asia Minor, spoke Greek fluently. He was acquainted with Greek culture and he named one of his concubines, a Greek woman from Phocaea, Aspasiya, after the name of the mistress of the illustrious Athenian political figure Pericles (Plu. *Pericl.* 24)."[58] Datis the Mede, one of the commanders of Darius's second expedition into Europe, actually visited Athens and warned the Athenians to submit before it was too late—speaking a Greek that Aristophanes (*Peace* 292 ff.) ridiculed; and near the end of that period Darius III, who was conquered by Alexander the Great, spoke, evidently, an acceptable Greek. Much communication can be assumed. Herodotus refers to Persian *logioi* ("literati," Burn translates)[59] who, supposedly, wanted "to make a synthesis of Greek and Persian history out of Greek (and perhaps Persian) mythology . . ."[60] Indeed, many Persians spoke Greek, and many Greeks resided either at the Persian court or elsewhere in the Empire. Cultural syntheses such as those Herodotus attributes to Persian "literati" could well have touched on matters that today are called philosophical. One such *logios* was Ostanes, whom Pliny cites (*N. H.* XXX.1.8) as his earliest source for

Zoroaster; he lived in the West and may have been a source for Herodotus too. Another was Zopyros, the son of Megabyxos, who defected to Athens and whom many suspect as Herodotus's primary source for internal affairs within the Persian milieu.

On the other side of the question, the Indians had a head start in knowledge of Persian. "In the sixth and fifth centuries the languages of . . . the Iranians and Indians were still close and . . . hundreds of common words were retained along both sides of the linguistic border."[61] Inhabitants of these border regions seem to have understood one another to some extent. Furthermore, Indian languages borrowed lexical elements from Iranian, and Sanskrit underwent changes under Iranian influence.[62] It seems, finally, that the Empire was sufficiently polyglot that communication between Greeks and Indians in Susa or elsewhere would not have been a problem; the Greeks, as a people who produced interpreters, may be presumed to have known Persian, and the Indians, whose language was so close, to have picked it up easily. It is possible that the two groups communicated in Aramaic, but also possible that they spoke Persian to one another. It was, after all, a time "of ethnic mixing and syncretism of the cultures and religious concepts of various peoples."[63]

Religion must have been a subject of learned conversation, as it was an area in which mixing occurred. The Persian name Megabyxos became the title of a Greek priest at the temple of Artemis in Ephesis. At Sardes, a temple was erected to Ahuramazda under the name "Zeus the Lawgiver." Artaxerxes III set up statues of Aphrodite in his capitals.[64]

Politics also must have been a common topic. Various treaties were signed between Sparta and Persia, united by their enmity to Athens, and Persian satraps occasionally assisted in attempts to break free of the Athenian alliance. Until the time of Alexander the Great, Persia was involved in the politics of the Greek states, and Greeks were similarly involved in Persian affairs. In 393 the satrap Pharnabazus, "a Persian with uniquely strong Greek connections,"[65] addressed the allied Greek council at Corinth. Five years later he married a Greek woman, Apame, by whom he had several half-Greek sons probably destined for political careers. In 368 the Persian Ariobarzanes sent an agent to convene a peace conference at Delphi, where both he and his agent were granted Athenian citizenship. In dealing with rebellions of the Greek cities of Asia Minor or of Egypt, Persian commanders were apt to use armies composed primarily of Greek mercenaries. Greeks in political trouble were apt to flee to Persia, and Persians in a similar plight took up residence in Sparta or elsewhere in the Greek world. On the Greek side, clearly, there was not much, if any, language problem in communicating within the Persian Empire.

In addition to contacts at court, Persian influence penetrated deeply into northwest India in the Achaemenid period. "The Kharoṣṭhī alphabet which became widespread in northwest India owed its origin to Aramaic, the *lingua franca* of the Achaemenid empire. Maurya art, too, little though we know of it, shows Persian influence in the capitals of columns like inverted bells or with animals. So Indian contacts with the West undoubtedly existed before Alexander the Great."[66]

Diffusion Channels?

West, in his study of the influences of Near Eastern poetry on that of Greece in the Geometric and Archaic periods, summarizes his view of what would constitute acceptable diffusion channels for that subject matter:

> The Greek poets' debts to Near Eastern traditions go far beyond what can be accounted for from casual commercial contacts, even over many centuries. They presuppose situations in which Greeks and peoples of the East lived side by side for extended periods and communicated fluently in a shared language.[67]

West points out a variety of situations in which Greeks and Near Easterners were thrown together in such a way as to fulfill those criteria. But whether these criteria were met during early contacts between Greeks and Indians in the Persian Empire is another question. West stresses situations in which one party to the conversation lived in the culture of the other. Both in the period of the Roman Empire, when there were prosperous Roman trading colonies in India, and in the Hellenistic era, when Alexandrian colonies still survived as well as the Greek dynasty in Bactria, those conditions were met. But in the pre-Alexandrian period—especially the pre-Socratic period—there are problems with envisioning a situation that meets these conditions.

Though numerous cases of Asian immigrants living in Greece are known, none mentioned explicitly comes from as far away as India; they are Thracians, Colchians, Lydians, Persians, and Levantines. Nor are specific cases known of Greeks resident in India during this period, though indeed there may have been some (perhaps from Persian relocations), and semilegendary traditions, like the story that Alexander's army came upon a Greek village in India called Nysa which had been founded by Dionysus, support the idea.[68] From the beginning of the Persian Empire we know of the Greek Scylax who spent some time in India, but he is not known to have been living side by side with Indians or communicating fluently with them.

Instead of Greeks living in India or Indians living in Greece, the evidence indicates contacts taking place between them in the intermediary culture of Persia. There, surely, Greeks and Indians lived side by side over extended periods of time and could communicate. The physician and historian Ctesias of Cnidus, who wrote both a *Persica* and an *Indica*, is said to have spent seventeen years in Persia at the end of the fifth century.[69] Demaratas, the exiled Spartan king, lived in Persian territory for many years as a guest of Xerxes (Hdt. VI.70, Xen. *Hell.* III.1.6). Two Eretrians—Gongylos and Gorgion—expelled for their friendly relations with Persia, the former tyrant Histiaeus of Miletus, Pitharcus of Cyzicus, and the Athenian Alcibiades, all received lifelong grants of domains in the Persian empire as rewards for favors done. In general, mercenaries, experts such as Scylax, ambassadors, and physicians can be assumed to have resided in the vicinity of the Persian court where they would have lived side by side with equivalent functionaries from northwest India and elsewhere. Due to the lack of Indian records very little is known about that side of it—but the Indian Karabba had evidently already been resident in the Persian court when sent back to India on a mission by Darius I.

Is that type of contact enough to allow diffusion events that may be said to have radically changed the course of cultural history? The supposed problem is with the meeting in a third territory rather than in the homeland of one interlocutor or the other. Why didn't the Greeks and Indians resident at the Persian court go home full of Persian lore? Is it likely that they would choose to learn the lore carried by other resident aliens rather than the lore of the host nation? The host nation was, to repeat, both aloof and unintellectual—and Burkert mentions structural parallels.[70] In the eighth and seventh centuries, for example, both Greeks and Assyrians were in Cyprus on business, and through such meetings in a third culture, he feels, significant artistic and literary influence took place.

The Medical Profession

In antiquity the custom of the "'market place,' a neutral territory, in which the parties coming from various regions . . . exchange or sell the products of their countries,"[71] extended to other than material goods. Both medical lore and religious lore were considered "products" of this type. The Persian kings were eager to collect physicians to protect the health of the royal family. Herodotus tells us (III.1) that on one occasion before 530 B.C. the pharaoh Amasis sent an Egyptian eye specialist to tend to Cyrus. Egyptian doctors had long been prominent, but in the archaic period the Greeks were also becoming well known in the medical profession. The names of several Greek physicians who resided at different times at the Persian court are known: Democedes, who spend two years there as "personal physician to Darius I";[72] Apollonides, an Asklepiad of Cos, who was there a generation later as physician to Artaxerxes I and seduced the king's sister, for which he was buried alive (Ctesias, *Pers.* 72–73); Ctesias, an Asklepiad of Cnidos, who spent seventeen years there at the end of the fifth century as doctor to Artaxerxes II; and Polykritos of Mende, who was at the Persian court in the same role when Ctesias left. Though the Indian tradition that would later be known as Ayurvedic medicine may already have been underway, it is not clear whether Indian physicians were summoned to court. Nevertheless, the fact that an Indian tradition of physiology was diffused into Greece by the time of Plato at the latest suggests that they might have been.[73]

But there is more involved than medical lore. The specialized profession of "physician" had not yet separated itself out from the larger profession of shaman or "medicine man," which included functions of magic, mythmaking, protophilosophy, and song or poetry, along with healing. Some of those whom we now regard as Greek philosophers would have appeared in the eyes of the Persian kings as "physicians."

Empedocles, for example, was a philosopher to whom monumental achievements of pure thought are attributed; at the same time, he was a magician who claimed the ability to control winds and storms, and, perhaps most famously in his own day, a healer or "physician." He himself said that some came to him "seeking prophecies, while others, for many a day stabbed by grievous pains, beg to hear the word that heals all manner of illness" (DK 31B112, 10–12). As wild, by repute at least, as any shape-changing shaman, he is reported to have died by leaping into the active volcano of Mount Aetna, believing that he would thus pass from the human to the divine realm. A believer in reincarnation, Empedocles said that a nearly perfected soul, in the last incarnation before it returns to godhood, may be a prophet, a poet, a physician, or a prince. Somewhere in the combination of these four categories lay the protoprofession of philosopher.

In a famous passage of Homer's *Odyssey* (17.382–386) the swineherd Eumaeus discusses the categories of foreigners that communities would invite to join them:

> Who ever goes and calls a stranger from abroad? Unless indeed the stranger is a master of some craft, a prophet, healer of disease, or builder, or else a wondrous bard who pleases by his song; for these are welcomed by mankind the wide world through.[74]

Prophet, healer, poet: the philosopher Empedocles would have qualified in three of the four categories. So would others of the pre-Socratics and members of comparable professions from India and elsewhere.

"There is," as Burkert says, "evidence of the mobility of magic-wielding seers already in the ancient Orient"[75] — meaning not that they could roam freely but that they were sent from one country to another at a government's request. About 1500 B.C. a king of Cyprus who previously had bought from Egypt such luxuries as "a bed of rare wood all goldplated, women's dresses [and] jars of oil of fine quality . . . requests an Egyptian specialty . . . a sorcerer [who] had to be an expert with eagles."[76] Similarly, "King Muwatallis of Hattusas ordered a conjuror from Babylon."[77] A famous Greek case occurred in 600 B.C. when Athens sent for Epimenides of Crete to purify the city from a plague brought about by the sacrilege associated with Cylon (*FrGrHist* 475).[78] Burkert adds that "we find religious practice directly imported [into Greece] from the East along with the skilled craft of foreign specialists."[79] This tradition lasted at least until the Mauryan dynasty, when king Bindusāra wrote to Antiochus I asking to be sent several commodities including a philosopher. The philosopher, in other words, was among the "craftsmen of the sacred," as Burkert calls them,[80] alongside "seers and doctors," professions which were "closely connected."[81]

The ancient physician had not only remedies and therapies to purvey but also doctrines and spells. People came to Empedocles, he said, for "the *word* that heals all manner of illness." The "physicians" of all nations whom the Persian kings gathered at their courts must have been carriers of pre- and protophilosophical doctrines, and no doubt had their presentations of them professionally worked out, rehearsed, and ready to expound.[82] A story in Herodotus (III.125, 129 ff.) shows the type of diffusion event that could have brought Indian traditions through the Persian court and into the center of a Greek philosophical school with lightning-like speed and suddenness. The Greek "physician" Democedes, who had been the doctor to Polycrates, the tyrant of Samos, was taken back to the Persian court in about 520, when that tyrant was eliminated by the Persians. He became, according to Herodotus, a favorite (in fact a dinner companion) of the Persian king Darius after he treated Darius's dislocated ankle, and was not allowed to leave the Persian court, where he remained for two years. In this period it was common for skilled craftspeople to be kept under control by Near Eastern rulers and not allowed to move about at will. "A Hittite treaty expressly stipulates that fugitive craftsmen are to be extradited."[83] The same may have applied to medical practitioners such as Democedes, who was not permitted to leave the Persian court.

After curing Queen Atossa's swollen bosom, however, Democedes obtained from her the favor of being sent on a sailing mission to reconnoitre Greece and coastal South Italy. There he escaped with a Persian entourage and went to Croton, where Pythagoras had recently founded his school. The Pythagoreans were "physicians" themselves, and the school at Croton was a center of medical research. Democedes was a member of the Crotonian medical school and may have been a Pythagorean.[84] In any case, he must have been in communication with the Pythagorean medical school in his own town. "Perhaps Pythagoras knew Polycrates' physician Democedes, a member of the famous Crotoniate 'school' of doctors," a modern notes.[85] A seemingly Indian physiology which Plato knew was also known to Pythagoreans, and was exactly the type of thing they sought after. Democedes—or someone else in a roughly comparable situation—may have brought it back with him.[86]

Wandering Seers from India

Burkert, referring to the Homeric passage in the *Odyssey*, speaks of "craftsmen of the sacred"[87] who brought rituals and associated lore into Greece in the Orientalizing period from Mesopotamia and elsewhere. He refers to them also as "migrant seers and healers," "charismatic specialists,"[88] and, speaking of hepatoscopy, holds that through them occurred "the transmission of a 'school' from Babylon to Etruria."[89] Similarly he speaks of "the spread of a Mesopotamian practice . . . across the Aegean linked to the emigration of craftsmen to Crete around 800."[90] Through such channels a variety of divination and purification techniques came from the Old World of the Near East into the emerging world of post–Dark Age Greece.

The Apollonian priestly lineage of the Branchidae seems to go back to Mesopotamian sources, as do elements in the cult of Asclepius, where one finds "the most direct proof of the infiltration of charismatic practitioners of the eastern tradition into archaic Greece."[91] In such phenomena, as Burkert says, "The borderlines between the eastern and the Greek are seen to melt away."[92]

Wandering seers such as the Vratyas were active in the Middle Vedic period in India and, like the Greek cults mentioned, seem to have carried some traditional Mesopotamian elements.[93] Both the Jain and the Ājīvika traditions involved extensive periods of wandering in other cultures by initiates—wanderings which, according to a speculation by Daniélou,[94] may have led into the Orphic tradition in Greece. The assortment of characters who gathered in the milieu of ancient temples in the Near East and eastern Mediterranean displayed a mixed array of strange practices such as browzing (cattle imitation), a common ascetic vow in India known to have been practiced in Mesopotamia in antiquity also.[95] The most plausible account of the origin of Diogenian cynicism involves Saivite practitioners migrating in the practice of their cultic specialties from India to the eastern end of the Black Sea over the trade route beginning with the Oxus River and ending at Phasis.[96]

Not until Aśoka, who was awakened to the Hellenistic world, does an Indian source speak of these foreign wanderings. Rock Edict II refers to the establishment of Indian medical institutions "in the territories of the Yavana king Antiochus." Rock Edict V indicates that Mahamatras, or wandering disseminators of Buddhist teaching, were dispatched "even among the Yavanas, Kambojas and Gandhāras . . . dwelling on the western boundaries."[97] Above all, Rock Edict XIII proclaims that Aśoka's missionaries went as far as "six hundred yojanas, where the Yavana king named Antiyoka [Antiochus] is ruling and where beyond the kingdom of the said Antiyoka four other kings named Turamaya [Ptolemy], Antikini [Antigonus], Maka [Magas of Cyrene] and Alikasundara [Alexander of Epirus] are also ruling."[98] At least one of the most famous of the missionaries sent out by Aśoka was actually a Greek, Dharmarakṣita.[99]

That the information of Rock Edict XIII should be taken seriously is suggested by several facts. First, the five Greek kings who seem clearly to be named—Antiochus (II Theos of the Seleucid kingdom), Ptolemy (II Philadelphus of Egypt), Antigonus (Gonatas of Macedonia), Magas (of Cyrene), and Alexander (of Epirus)—were actually all contemporaries of Aśoka; they are not a random list of names merely meant to impress his subjects, nor are they names collected loosely from Greek history. That Aśoka would have known accurately who five of his contemporary monarchs in the Greek world were indicates some channels of communication. The figure of six hundred yojanas does not seem random, either. "Taking a yojana to be about seven miles, this turns out to be the exact distance from Pāṭaliputra to Macedonia, Epirus and Cyrene as the crow flies . . . This precision in distance, which is verifiable, shows at least that contact with these distant lands was based on actual travel." Granted these confirmatory evidences, "Aśoka's claim to have sent envoys to them," according to one modern scholar, "can hardly be doubted." Furthermore: "A more significant proof comes from the fact that the edicts bearing this information were found in places like Kandahar in Afghanistan and Mansehra and Shahbazgarhi in Pakistan in areas abutting Greek territories and inhabited by Greeks. In fact, the adaptation of RE XIII which was found as far west as Kandahar was in Greek."[100] The missionary Maharakkita seems to have been sent to the kingdom of Antiochus Theos, the epigonid empire of Syria and West Asia which was the immediate western neighbor of Aśoka's kingdom. One of the acts of at least some of Aśoka's missionaries was the planting in foreign nations of certain medicinal herbs.

Two general probabilities can be drawn from this evidence. First, religiomedical missions, involving the simultaneous spreading of doctrine and of medicinal plants, are just the type of thing the Persian kings might have invited or attracted to their courts along with the seemingly regular succession of Greek philosopher-physicians who went there. Second, Aśoka's missions seem to have drawn on an older tradition of "migrant seers" carrying doctrines, rituals, and sacred plants which seems likely to have gone back at least to the early archaic period and thus to have intermingled with pre-Socratics, especially perhaps, as in the cases of Democedes and Pherecydes, with Orphics and Pythagoreans.

Conclusions

The period of unimpeded contact through the medium of Persia lasted approximately from 545 till 490. These dates include the heart of the brief moment of pre-Socratic philosophy. The work of Pythagoras, Heraclitus, Empedocles, Parmenides, and others falls between them. Only the work of Thales seems clearly to have preceded this period, and even before the conquest trade routes between Greece and India were open and in use. Due to these circumstances, there is a relationship between early Greek philosophy and early Indian philosophy as clear as that between, say, early Greek sculpture and Egyptian sculpture.

Notes to Chapter One

1. H. G. Rawlinson, *Intercourse Between India and the Western World from the Earliest Times to the Fall of Rome*, 2nd ed. (Cambridge: Cambridge University Press, 1926), p. 155.

2. Maria Gimbutas, "The Beginning of the Bronze Age in Europe and the Indo-Europeans: 3500–2500 BC," *JIES* 1 (1973):163–214; "The First Wave of Eurasian Steppe Pastoralists into Copper Age Europe," *JIES* 5 (1977): 277–338; "Primary and Secondary Homeland of the Indo-Europeans," *JIES* 13 (1985): 185–202; Colin Renfrew, *Archeology and Language: The Puzzle of Indo-European Origins* (New York: Cambridge University Press, 1990).

3. Robert Drews, *The Coming of the Greeks: Indo-European Conquests in the Aegean and the Near East* (Princeton, New Jersey: Princeton University Press, 1988), especially pp. 158–196.

4. In *Interpreting Early India* (Delhi: Oxford University Press, 1993, p. 5), Romila Thapar speaks of "the Āryan Problem, namely, the historical role of the Indo-Aryan speaking people and their identification in early Indian sources." But the term has taken on a broader meaning than that, as she herself recognizes in the same essay, saying, "The distinction between *aryan* and non-*aryan*, and the polarity of Aryan and Dravidian suggested by them for the Indian scene, echoes to a degree which can hardly be regarded as coincidental, the aryan-non-aryan distinction and the Aryan-Semitic dichotomy based on language and race, in the European context," p. 4.

5. Lionel Casson, *The Ancient Mariners: Seafarers and Sea Fighters of the Mediterranean in Ancient Times* (Princeton, New Jersey: Princeton University Press, 1991), p. 4.

6. Ibid., p. 8.

7. Ibid.

8. Some Mesopotamian-style cylinder seals and "Persian Gulf"-style seals are illustrated in Gregory L. Possehl, *Indus Age: The Writing System* (New Delhi and Calcutta: Oxford and IBH Publishing Co., 1996), pp. 37–41.

9. M. L. West, *The East Face of Helicon: West Asiatic Elements in Greek Poetry and Myth* (Oxford: Clarendon Press, 1997), pp. 4–5.

10. Ibid., p. 5.

11. Ibid.

12. Walter A. Fairservis Jr., *The Roots of Ancient India: The Archaeology of Early Indian Civilization* (New York: Macmillan, 1971), p. 283.

13. Samuel Noah Kramer, "The Indus Civilization and Dilmun: the Sumerian Paradise Land," in *Ancient Cities of the Indus*, ed. Gregory Possehl (New Delhi: Vikas Publishing House, 1979), p. 171; Possehl, "Editor's Introduction," ibid., p. 153.

14. Possehl, ibid., p. 161. And see Casson (*The Ancient Mariners*, p. 9): "For some reason this amazingly far-flung and highly developed trade died out shortly after 1750 B.C. and did not come to life again until almost a thousand years later."

15. For a detailed account of "the catastrophe" see Robert Drews, *The End of the Bronze Age: Changes in Warfare and the Catastrophe ca. 1200 B.C.* (Princeton, New Jersey: Princeton University Press, 1993), especially chapter 2.

16. West, *East Face of Helicon*, p. 8.

17. See Walter Burkert, *The Orientalizing Revolution: Near Eastern Influence on Greek Culture in the Early Archaic Age*, trans. Margaret E. Pinder and Walter Burkert, Revealing Antiquity Series, vol. 5 (Cambridge, Massachusetts: Harvard University Press, 1992), pp. 29–30 and elsewhere.

18. West, *The East Face of Helicon*, p. 620.

19. Ibid., p. 610.

20. Ibid., p. 617, n. 102. See also Muhammad A. Dandamaev and Vladimir G. Lukonin, *The Culture and Social Institutions of Ancient Iran*, trans. Philip L. Kohl (Cambridge: Cambridge University Press, 1989), pp. 313–314.

21. West, *The East Face of Helicon*, p. 617.

22. Huxley has commented on the spread of Babylonian astronomical lore into Greece: "Even before the Persian conquest of Ionia, intelligent Greeks may have learnt much in the emporia of Syria, Palestine and Egypt, and perhaps also at the court of Croesus in Sardes, which had ties with the high civilization of Mesopotamia." George Huxley, *The Interaction of Greek and Babylonian Astronomy* (Belfast: The Queen's University, 1964), pp. 4–5.

23. Burkert, *Orientalizing Revolution*, pp. 50, 95.

24. Ibid., p. 95.

25. Huxley, *Interaction of Greek and Babylonian Astronomy*, p. 5.

26. Dandamaev and Lukonin, *Culture and Social Institutions of Ancient Iran*, p. 294.

27. Wilhelm Halbfass, *India and Europe: An Essay in Understanding* (Albany, New York: State University of New York Press, 1988), p. 11. Halbfass goes on to say that "Scylax . . . is the first recorded European traveller in India"—but Scylax was from Caria in Asia Minor. In any case, Ctesias's *Persica*, which was originally in twenty-three books, is now preserved only in citations in other authors, including Diodorus Siculus, Pompeius Trogus, Polyaenus, Plutarch, and Nicolaus of Damascus; the lengthiest excerpts are from Photius, a ninth-century Byzantine.

28. Dandamaev and Lukonin, *Culture and Social Institutions of Ancient Iran*, pp. 174–175.

29. Ibid., p. 159.

30. Ibid., p. 171. Actually Diodorus (XVII.69.3) and Justin (XI.14.11) give the number as 800. The captives are described as "subjected to various kinds of torture. Some had their feet cut off, some their hands and ears" (Curtius V.5). According to Waldemar Heckel, "The story is probably fictitious." Quintus Curtius Rufus, *The History of Alexander*, trans. John Yardley with an introduction and notes by Waldemar Heckel (London: Penguin, 1984), p. 281, n. 55.

31. Dandamaev and Lukonin, *Culture and Social Institutions of Ancient Iran*, p. 305.

32. Richard N. Frye, *The Heritage of Persia* (London: Wiedenfeld and Nicolson, 1962), p. 58.

33. J. M. Cook, *The Persian Empire* (New York: Schocken Books, 1983), p. 193.

34. A. L. Basham, "The Background to the Rise of Buddhism," in *Studies in History of Buddhism*, ed. A. K. Narain (Delhi: B. R. Publishing Corporation, 1980), p. 23.

35. Cook, *The Persian Empire*, p. 88.

36. Ibid., p. 162.

37. William Culican, *The Medes and the Persians*, Ancient People and Places Series 42 (London: Thames and Hudson, 1965), p. 103.

38. Cook, *The Persian Empire*, p. 87.

39. Frye, *Heritage of Persia*, p. 101.

40. Ibid., p. 105.

41. Cook, *The Persian Empire*, p. 163.

42. Rene Grousset, *The Empire of the Steppes: A History of Central Asia*, trans. Naomi Walford (New Brunswick, New Jersey: Rutgers University Press, 1970), p. 48.

43. Cook, *The Persian Empire*, p. 230.

44. Culican, *The Medes and the Persians*, p. 71.

45. Frye, *Heritage of Persia*, p. 93.

46. Ibid., pp. 125, 126.

47. Cook, *The Persian Empire*, p. 204.

48. See chapter 9, "Cynics and Pāśupatas."

49. Dandamaev and Lukonin, *Culture and Social Institutions of Ancient Iran*, p. 311. This colony might have been there for a while by the time it appears in our records. The leaders are listed by names which appear to have been Babylonian or Persian, suggesting that they had assimilated considerably.

50. Ibid., p. 293.

51. Ibid., p. 311.

52. Ibid.

53. Ibid., p. 312.

54. Ibid., p. 296.

55. Ibid., p. 145.

56. Pericles, Georges, *Barbarian Asia and the Greek Experience: From the Archaic Period to the Age of Xenophon* (Baltimore, Maryland: The Johns Hopkins University Press, 1994), p. 49.

57. Dandamaev and Lukonin, *Culture and Social Institutions of Ancient Iran*, p. 114, citing Xen. *Anab.* I.8.12, II.5.35, IV.2.18, IV.4.5; Plu. *Them.* 6; Curtius V.13.7; Hdt. III.140.

58. Dandamaev and Lukonin, ibid., p. 296.

59. A. R. Burn, "Persia and the Greeks," in *The Cambridge History of Iran*, vol. 2, *The Median and Achaemenian Periods*, ed. Ilya Gershevitch (Cambridge: Cambridge University Press, 1985), p. 339.

60. Ibid., pp. 339–340.

61. Dandamaev and Lukonin, *Culture and Social Institutions of Ancient Iran*, p. 297.

62. Ibid., pp. 297–298.

63. Ibid., pp. 292–293.

64. Ibid., p. 341.

65. Ibid., p. 382.

66. Frye, *Heritage of Persia*, p. 127.

67. West, *The East Face of Helicon*, p. 624.

68. The accounts of Alexander's invasion of India tell that he came upon a Greek city in Gandhāra called Nysa (Arrian, *Campaign of Alexander*, V.1–3; Curtius, VIII.10.11). There was a tradition among the Greeks that Dionysus had invaded and conquered India in prehistoric times. Nysa was presumed to have been founded by him then. The foundation myth aside, several accounts are in agreement on the existence of the town, and there is a plausible mechanism by which it, or some community like it, could have gotten there. Many Greek mercenaries, after their years of service with the Persian king, settled where they had served, because they were awarded a share of the conquered land. Small communities of discharged Greek mercenaries, paid off in conquered land, may have arisen throughout northwest India and Bactria, forming the foundation for the later, more ambitious, settlements left by Alexander.

69. Cook, *The Persian Empire*, p. 21. The number 17 may be inflated; see Dandamaev and Lukonin, *Culture and Social Institutions of Ancient Iran*, p. 391.

70. Burkert, *Orientalizing Revolution*, pp. 103–104.

71. A. Leo Oppenheim, "The Seafaring Merchants of Ur," in Possehl, ed., *Ancient Cities of the Indus*, p. 155.

72. Dandamaev and Lukonin, *Culture and Social Institutions of Ancient Iran*, p. 295.

73. See chapter 8, "Plato and Kuṇḍalinī."

74. *The Odyssey of Homer*, trans. George Herbert Palmer (Cambridge, Massachusetts: Houghton Mifflin Company, 1949), p. 269. Both West (*The East Face of Helicon*, p. 611 and elsewhere) and Burkert (*Orientalizing Revolution*, chapter titles and elsewhere) structure their diffusion arguments around this passage.

75. Burkert, *Orientalizing Revolution*, p. 42.

76. Casson, *The Ancient Mariners*, p. 15.

77. Burkert, *Orientalizing Revolution*, p. 42.

78. Ibid., pp. 42, 178 n. 10.

79. Ibid., p. 54.

80. Ibid., p. 41.

81. Ibid.

82. The connection of medicine and philosophy may survive from the days of shamanic healing; it endures till the time of Sextus Empiricus and Galen and recurs after the Middle Ages in figures like Cornelius Agrippa. See R. J. Hankinson, *The Sceptics* (London and New York: Routledge, 1995), pp. 7–9, 225 ff., and Martha Nussbaum, *Therapy of Desire: Theory and Practice in Hellenistic Ethics* (Princeton, New Jersey: Princeton University Press, 1994), pp. 13–53.

83. Burkert, *Orientalizing Revolution*, p. 24.

84. Cf. Benjamin Farrington, *Greek Science: Its Meaning for Us* (Baltimore: Penguin Books, 1961), p. 69, on the school at Croton: "its founder was possibly the Pythagorean Alcmaeon . . ."

85. G. S. Kirk, J. E. Raven, and M. Schofield, *The Presocratic Philosophers: A Critical History with a Selection of Texts*, 2nd ed. (Cambridge: Cambridge University Press, 1983), p. 224.

86. See chapter 8, "Plato and Kuṇḍalinī."

87. Burkert, *Orientalizing Revolution*, p. 41.

88. Ibid., p. 42

89. Ibid., p. 46.

90. Ibid., p. 55.

91. Ibid., pp. 61, 75–79, 78.

92. Ibid., p. 73.

93. See Thomas McEvilley, "An Archeology of Yoga," *Res: Anthropology and Aesthetics* 1 (1991), pp. 44–77.

94. Alain Daniélou, *Śiva and Dionysus*, trans. K. F. Hurry (London and the Hague: East-West Publications, 1982), p. 28.

95. Violet MacDermot, *The Cult of the Seer in the Ancient Middle East* (London: Wellcome Institute of the History of Medicine, 1971), p. 33: "Some hermits carried their desire for independence of the material world to the extent of casting off their clothing and, like animals, eating the wild vegetation . . . [In the Bible] Nebuchadnezzar lived with the beasts of the field and ate grass until 'seven times' had passed over him, as a prelude to the return of his 'understanding.'"

96. See chapter 9, "Cynics and Pāśupatas."

97. For discussion of these texts and the whole phenomenon of Aśoka's foreign missions see *King Aśoka and Buddhism: Historical and Literary Studies*, ed. Anuradha Seneviratna, (Kandy, Sri Lanka: Buddhist Publication Society, 1994), pp. 51–57.

98. Ibid., p. 53.

99. *Mbv.* XII.5, 34.

100. Seneviratna, *King Aśoka and Buddhism*, p. 56.

Chapter Two

The Problem of the One and the Many

The Greeks, emerging from a Dark Age into literacy again about 800–700 B.C., renewed the contact with Egypt and Mesopotamia that they had conducted, perhaps indirectly, in the Mycenaean period of the Bronze Age. Again, this contact was in large part indirect at first; Asian Greek cities, for example, may have entered into a close relationship with the Lydian court at Sardes, which in turn had direct ties to Mesopotamian courts. Under such influences, the emerging life-form of the Greeks began to take upon itself the questions under the weight of which the older civilizations had first thrived, then wearied. The question of cosmogony for example—how the world began—was transmitted from the older civilizations of the Near East to Hesiod and other early Greek thinkers; their contemplation of such inherited questions prepared the way for philosophy. From the cosmogonical question "What is the *origin* of the universe?" the first philosophical question—"What is the *foundation* or *principle* of the universe, or the *reasoning* behind it?"—derived.

In the late seventh or early sixth century, astronomical ideas derived from Mesopotamian records and handbooks somehow began to enter Greece. This transmission may have occurred in Ionian cities like Miletus, in Sardes, or in Near Eastern centers. However Mesopotamian astronomy entered the Greek world, it took it by storm. In the sixth century the Greek Cleostratus of Tenedos wrote a book called *Astrology*; the Hesiodic school produced a work called *Astronomy*; to Thales himself was attributed a *Nautical Star Guide*.

From Egypt other formative influences came. The Greco-Egyptian settlement at Naukratis was a colony of Miletus, a city which was steeped in the thought and culture of both Egypt, by way of Naukratis itself, and Mesopotamia, by way of its ties with Sardes. Egyptian methods of measurement, which are said to have influenced Thales, lie behind the Greek obsession with geometry that, along with the Mesopotamian-derived obsession with astronomy, became pillars of an emerging cultural synthesis.

In Miletus on the Asian coast of Greece, in the sixth century B.C., Thales and Anaximander—no doubt along with others whose names are no longer known—devoted their lives to assimilating and creatively transforming these older traditions. Astronomy and geometry, in combination, seemed to offer a way to bring things together into a whole through a mathematically ordered system for conceiving both time—through astronomy—and space—through geometry. Both men were primarily known as astronomers during their lifetimes, and both were credited with inventing devices or techniques which in fact had been imported from Mesopotamia or elsewhere.

The first philosophical question, "The Problem of the One and the Many," expresses the same ordering impulse that fueled the obsession with astronomy and geometry—the desire to find unifying principles behind apparent diversity. It is also an attempt to justify the claims for certainty of knowledge that the mathematically based sciences inspired. If things are different and separate, then the universe at large is unknowable, since only specific things may be "known," one at a time. The preoccupation with the Problem of the One and the Many expressed a desire to know the universe in some larger sense than that, by finding principles which would render every situation knowable with or without direct experience of it. Superficial diversity was to be tamed and made knowable by apprehension of underlying unity.

This concern, like the interest in astronomy or geometry, was bequeathed to the pre-Socratics from Mesopotamian and Egyptian thought. In the Bronze Age, under the influence of the increasing unification and organization of states, Near Eastern thinkers became increasingly concerned with questions of universal order. They approached the Problem of the One and the Many through mythological means, exploring it through concrete imagery and narrative. By the Late Bronze Age, mythology was straining at the limits of its expressiveness; the composers of myth seem to have been increasingly seeking abstract propositions and generalizations, and this urge had cost cogency, bursting the seams of imagery and narrative. What would emerge from the dissolution of myth was the birth of philosophy—and its first great topic was Oneness.

The Cosmic Person in Ancient Egypt

Bronze Age mythology ended when the pantheons of separate gods and goddesses, each with his or her special attributes, adventures, and cults, dissolved into pantheism—the deification of the universe as a single vast metadeity or "everything-god" (*pantheos*). This preoccupation was in part a by-product of political amalgamations. When power shifted, the priests of the newly dominant group would compose a theology which elevated their god over those of the dominated groups. At such a moment, a Mesopotamian priesthood would imitate the model of the state, declaring that its god was king of the other gods; by contrast, the more metaphysically inclined Egyptians were apt to declare that the newly dominant deity had absorbed the other gods into himself or become them. Already in the Old Kingdom, the priesthood of Heliopolis portrayed its god Atum as declaring himself to be identical with each of the other great gods.[1] After a shift of power, the priesthood of Memphis declared the various gods and goddesses to be parts of their own metadeity, Ptah, who is conceived anthropomorphically, as a Macranthropus, or Cosmic Person. Atum is declared to be the heart and tongue of Ptah; the nine gods of Heliopolis are declared to be "before him as his tongue and lips." Other gods are declared to become Ptah in their different ways.

A monistic tendency of thought, gathering momentum, creates a meltdown in a polytheistic mythology. Toward the end of the New Kingdom this tendency reached the breaking point in the theology of Amon-Re. The priests of this school, at the great temple of Karnak, were on the verge of the abstract conception of monism. Their sacred discourse had gone beyond narrative, as they declared Amon-Re to be "the solitary sole one,"[2] "the one only," the "one who has no second," the "one one"[3]—all ideas that are essentially antinarrative. Amon-Re was elevated beyond discursive reach, including the reach of mythological narrative and imagery, through a series of paradoxes—the first series of studied and carefully refined paradoxes on record.

In the *Hymn to Amon-Re*, it is said that the god's names are countless, yet his name is hidden from everyone, even the other gods. He is, in other words, both immanent and transcendent; he takes all the forms of the universe, yet his own form is inconceivable in its otherness.[4] He is described as "the marvelous god of many forms" and simultaneously as "hiding himself . . . so that his very color is unknown."[5] Stanza 200 of the hymn strains openly against the limits of mythological expression. First a series of affirmations absorbs everything in the universe into Amon-Re: All gods are parts of him; all places are occupied by him; he is in heaven, the underworld, the East, and the West. At once, a parallel series of negations nullifies these declarations of immanence in favor of a doctrine of a formless transcendent absolute beyond space-time: Amon is hidden; he is far from heaven and also far from the underworld, neither in the above nor in the below; even the gods don't know what he looks like. "His image is not displayed in writings. No one bears witness to him . . . He is too mysterious that his majesty should be disclosed . . . too powerful that he might be known." This transcendent Amon-Re beyond form and cognition could serve as the direct ancestor of primal philosophical conceptions such as Parmenides' formless Being and the featureless absolute *brahman* of Yājñavalkya. The idea of the immanent-transcendent absolute, which would become a central conception of the early stage of metaphysics in both Greece and India, is first recorded in this late mythological context.

The Cosmic Person in Ancient Mesopotamia

In Mesopotamian mythology and theology a similar meltdown was occurring. The discourse of macranthropy—of the universe as a single huge anthropomorphic being—appeared there as early as 2000 B.C., in a poem relating a myth of the goddess Inanna. When her father Enki gives her kingship, Inanna uses the imagery of the cosmic being to describe her newly expanded state: "The heavens he set as a crown on my head," she says, "the earth he set as sandals on my feet."[6] By the Late Bronze Age this mode of imagery in which the elements of the universe are assigned to parts of an anthropomorphic body had virtually replaced the old narrative mode in which individual deities or heroes clashed about specific willed projects. Perhaps, through shifts of political power, the pantheon of Mesopotamia had undergone so much rearrangement that its inner boundaries lacked conviction. In any case, the gods and goddesses began merging into a single cosmic being who bore within himself or herself the old deities as aspects or parts. Egyptian pantheism, which seems to have been articulated somewhat earlier, may have exerted an influence.

A Babylonian hymn from around 1000 B.C. absorbs the pantheon into Marduk as his attributes or aspects:

> Ninurta is Marduk of the hoe,
> Nergal is Marduk of the attack,
> Zababa Marduk of the hand-to-hand fight,
> Enlil is Marduk of lordship and counsel,
> Nabium is Marduk of accounting,

Sin is Marduk, the illuminator of the night,
Shamash is Marduk of justice,
Adad is Marduk of rains . . .[7]

Other Late Bronze Age Mesopotamian hymns identify various gods as parts, rather than aspects, of a single metagod, while homologizing the universe to the human body:

O lord, your face is the sun god, your hair, Aya,
your eyes, O lord, are Enlil and Ninlil.
The pupils of your eyes are Gula and Belit-ili
the irises of your eyes are the twins, Sin and Shamash,
the lashes of your eyes are the rays of the sun god . . .
The appearance of your mouth, O lord, is Ishtar of the stars
Anu and Antum are your lips, your command . . .
your tongue (?) is Pabilsag of the above . . .
The roof of your mouth, O lord, is the vault of heaven and earth
your divine abode,
your teeth are the seven gods who lay low the evil ones.[8]

This hymn moves down the body of the *pantheos*, as does a similar hymn to Nergal:

> His eyes are Enlil and Ninlil, Sin is the pupil of his eyes, Anu and Entu are his lips, his teeth are the Sibittu (the seven gods), his ears are Ea and Damkina, his skull is Adad, his neck is Marduk, and his breast is Nebo.[9]

In terms of Mesopotamian cultural history, macranthropy is an aspect of the idea of a correspondence between macrocosm and microcosm. As early as the third millennium B.C. the state seems to have been conceived in correspondence with the astronomical heavens; the extension of this concept to the human body, and consequent expansion of the human body scale to include the universe, was a major element of late Mesopotamian influence that seems to have extended into both India and Greece at formative stages of their thought.

The Cosmic Person in Ancient India

In India macranthropic hymns begin to appear in the tenth book of the *Ṛg Veda*, in the Middle Vedic period (roughly 1000 B.C.). At the same time, the *Atharva Veda* shows Akkadian loan-words and remnants of Akkadian mythological names. In the *Puruṣasūkta*, or *Hymn to the Cosmic Person*, in the tenth book of the *Ṛg Veda* (X.90), the universe is described as a giant human body. The structure of the hymn parallels Akkadian examples in its tendency to allegorize the body of the *pantheos* from the top down:

> The Brahman (priestly caste) was his mouth; his two arms became the Rajanya (warrior caste); his two thighs are the Vaiśya (artisan caste); from his two feet the Sudra (serf caste) was produced.
>
> The moon sprang from his thought-organ; the sun was produced from his eye; from his mouth Indra . . . and Agni . . . ; from his breath Vāyu . . . was produced.[10]

This cosmic being is said to be the entire universe but also to extend beyond the universe; it is, in other words, simultaneously immanent and transcendent, as was Amon-Re.

The *pantheos* was enunciated many times in India, where archaic concepts were not discarded but continued to exist, with the force of traditional validation, alongside new ones. The Upaniṣadic *ātman*, or Universal Subject, for example, is described as a *pantheos* in terms that mix the imagery of the *Puruṣasūkta* with new more abstract elements:

> Of this Universal Self, the head indeed is the good light, the eye is the universal form, breath is (the air) of varied courses, the body is the full, the bladder is wealth, the feet are the earth, the chest indeed is the sacrificial area, the hair is the sacred grass, the heart is the gārhapatya fire, the mind is the anvāhārya-pacana fire, and the mouth is the āhavanīya fire. (*CU* V.19.2)[11]

The *Aitareya Upaniṣad* (III.1.3) shows the full development of this motif:

> He, the Self (ātman), is Brahmā, he is Indra, he is Prajāpati, he is all these gods; and these five great elements, namely earth, air, ether, water, light; these things and those which are mingled of the fire as it were, the seeds of one sort and another; those born from an egg, and those born from a womb, and those born from sweat, and those born from a sprout; horses, cows, persons, and elephants, whatever breathing thing there is, whether moving or flying or what is stationary. (*AU* III.1.3)

The theme of macranthropy, with its background theme of macrocosm-microcosm correspondence, became basic to that area of Indian thought known as tantric, where the homologization of the human body to the astronomical universe is a pervasive feature of iconography and thought.

The Cosmic Person in Ancient Greece

The idea of the Cosmic Person (Macranthropus) or the god who *is* the universe (*pantheos*) spread also into Greece, where it shows up first (it seems) in the Orphic literature. The Orphics were a protophilosophical group who seem to have exerted a strong presence in what was called Magna Graecia, "greater Greece" as it were, the Greek part of South Italy and Sicily, in the sixth and fifth centuries B.C. They were voluntary ascetics committed to wandering, poverty, celibacy, vegetarianism, purification rites, and the doctrine of reincarnation. The central Orphic doctrine is a simple monism which declares that the One is the source and goal of the Many: "All things are born from the One and all things are resolved back into it" (D.L. *Proem.* 3). The Orphic One was a primitive *pantheos* created by elevating one member of a polytheistic pantheon a metastep above the rest. The tragedian Aeschylus seems to have been expressing Orphic doctrine when he wrote (fr. 43): "Zeus is the air, Zeus the earth, Zeus the sky. Zeus is everything—and something else besides." Zeus is both immanent and transcendent; as Amon-Re in Egypt and the Cosmic Person (Puruṣa) in India are conceived as, in one aspect, everywhere in the universe and in another aspect, completely other than the universe, so Zeus is both everything and something other than everything. An Orphic poem of uncertain date (but unlikely to be as old as the sixth century B.C.) describes the macranthropic Zeus in terms which go back ultimately to Old Kingdom Egyptian texts and which parallel the passage quoted above from the *Aitareya Upaniṣad* in their incorporation of the list of elements:

> Zeus is first and last, one royal body, containing the fire, water, earth, and air, night and day, Metus and Eros. The sky is his head, the stars his hair, the sun and moon his eyes, the air his intelligence, whereby he hears and marks all things; no sound or voice escapes his ears. (*OF 168*)

In Greece as in India, this macranthropic concept appears again and again, from Plato's *Timaeus* to Stoic thought and after.

The concept of the simultaneously immanent and transcendent *pantheos* is a transitional concept between mythology, which it compacts beyond recognition, and philosophy, which will unfold from it. When Thales and other Greek thinkers investigated the traditions of Egypt and Mesopotamia, it was this end-of-an-age, dissolving mythology that they encountered, a mythology undergoing meltdown.

In terms of the Problem of the One and the Many, Late Bronze Age mythology had been characterized by an emphasis on unity over diversity, an assertion that diversity is contained within a higher unity, that of the Cosmic Person. The early period of philosophy in both Greece and India would continue the final preoccupation of Bronze Age mythology: the Problem of the One and the Many, with solutions that emphasize the One over the Many, and the investigation of the relationship between immanence and transcendence, or form and formlessness. Early philosophical efforts translated the insights of the dissolving mythology into terms that go beyond the image, or at least reduce its distracting presence. Abstraction, logic, and mathematical philosophy would ultimately emerge from this difficult and epochal transition from concrete to abstract diction.

Thales and Indian Thought

Of partly Phoenician background, Thales lived in Miletus from c. 624 to c. 545 B.C. During his early and middle life, Miletus was a part of the Lydian empire, ruled from the court at Sardes. Thales was a member of the power structure, living with the ruler of Miletus at the local court. At one time he acted as military engineer to Croesus, the king of Lydia, and probably lived for a while at Sardes. He is credited with spending two years in Egypt studying techniques of measuring from distances—a channel into geometry. He was an advocate of amalgamating the Ionian Greek cities—advice they might have done well to follow, but didn't.

Thales had a considerable reputation in antiquity as an astronomer. Eudemus, writer of an ancient history of astronomy, said Thales was the first to study the heavens—meaning, in effect, that he was the first to import Mesopotamian astronomical knowledge into Greece. Thales is said to have written a book about astronomy, and another one about "philosophy," or the inquiry into the basic constitution of things.

What is known of Thales' teachings about nature comes from Aristotle and is ambiguous. At one place Aristotle reports that Thales said the earth floated on water like a piece of wood (*De Caelo* 294a28–31, DK 1A14). At another, while discussing the idea of a material substrate from which things arise, which unites their changing surface qualities while they endure, and into which they return completely when they die, Aristotle remarks: "Thales, the founder of this type of philosophy, says it is water (and therefore declared that the earth is on water)" (*Met.* 983b20–22, DK 1A12). Finally, Aristotle adds, Thales said that all things are full of gods (*De An.* 411a7, DK 1A22)(and connected this observation with the statement that the magnet has a soul because it is a source of motion [*De An.* 405a19–21, DK 1A22]).

Thales seems, from this slight evidence, to have taught not a Cosmic Person, or macranthropic monism, but a material monism, asserting that everything is One because everything is made of the same kind of underlying matter, which somehow has the ability to change its surface qualities and appear variously. Material monism is a type of substrate monism—the claim that some foundational unity, whether material or not, underlies all apparent differences. In the form of material monism which Aristotle attributes to Thales, it may be intended that water changes its appearances by processes like those of evaporation, precipitation, and freezing. If so, then this is a postmythological concept with elements of both natural science and philosophical abstraction coming to the foreground. "Thales," as modern scholars have said, "earned the title of the first Greek philosopher mainly because of his abandonment of mythological formulations."[12] The discourse has gone beyond the storytelling ascription of personality and the use of a complex of images involved in a narrative sequence; it is a move toward abstract terminology and assertions bleached of image, freed from the inherited image-stream.

On the other hand, Thales' formulation retains an element of mythic expressiveness in the concreteness of the image and in his probable reasons for selecting water as the ultimate element. In the Near Eastern mythologies, water often appears as the substance of cosmogony. The universe is conceived as rising from a primal abyss of water, a cosmic womb from which contraries such as male and female, night and day, and so on, separate out by stages. In Egyptian mythology this primal sea that precedes the first sunrise is called Nun; in the abyss of Nun all the gods are mingled together as in a divine soup. Thales may have had a similar idea in mind in saying that all things are somehow of (or from?) water and that all things are full of gods. In any case, Thales' assertion that all things are full of gods recalls many Egyptian texts, such as the following: "So the gods entered into their bodies of every kind of wood, of every kind of stone, of every kind of clay, of anything which might grow upon Ptah, the Earth, in which they had taken form."[13] Thales has, in effect, taken two mythological motifs—the primal ocean and the livingness of nature—and broken them loose from their mythological contexts, leaving them in a state of isolation that serves to make them semiabstract. To say that the water-nature "underlies" all differentiation is not structurally different from saying that the world floats on water. The difference is that in the first of these formulations the concreteness of the image in the Greek word *hypokeimenon*, "lying beneath" (Latin *substratum*), has been metaphoricized and forced to express an abstract meaning.

The earliest form of monism in extant Indian texts seems to have preceded the wave of Akkadian influence which brought the Cosmic Person concept around 1000 B.C. Occurring in the *Ṛg Veda*, it involved the elevation to a universal stature of single deities who corresponded to the material substances that would later be defined as the elements. These passages show the Vedic polytheism undergoing a meltdown similar to that undergone by Mesopotamian and Egyptian polytheisms. In one hymn, Agni, the Vedic god of fire, of central importance in Vedic rite, is elevated a metastep above the polytheistic status and declared to contain, or be identical with, the other great gods: "You, O Agni, are Indra, you are Viṣṇu . . . You, O Agni, are King Varuṇa . . . You are Mitra . . . You are Aryaman . . . You, O Agni, are Rudra" (*RV* II.1.3–7).[14]

One of the late singers of the *Ṛg Veda*, Prājapati Paramestin, focused on the concept of the birth of the world from water—possibly inherited from Near Eastern mythological sources—in a semiabstract isolation not so unlike that of Thales. "In the beginning," he wrote, "an undistinguished ocean was this all" (*RV* X.129.3). "The mighty waters moved, pregnant with the world as embryo" (*RV* X.121.7). Like the Egyptian ocean Nun, the primal waters are described as the place "where the gods all beheld themselves together" (*RV* X.82.5). Two Akkadian words which entered the Vedic literature at this time are the all-important primal ocean terms *apsu* and *tiamat* from the Creation Epic.

In such *Rg Vedic* passages, water is conceived as the source of the universe in a narrative sense; it is temporally prior to the world of form, as in ancient Near Eastern myth. In the early Upaniṣads, by contrast, it is redefined as the inner nature of things. In this redefinition, priority in time or narrative priority—the mode of myth—gives way to an emerging sense of logical or constitutive priority—the mode of metaphysics. In the *Chāndogya Upaniṣad* (VII.10.1–2) Sanatkumara expresses much the same doctrine of material monism that Aristotle attributed to Thales. A single substance is universalized and said to undergo a process of transformation while still remaining fundamentally itself: "It is just water," says the Upaniṣad, "that assumes different forms of this earth, this atmosphere, this sky, the mountains, gods, and men, beasts and birds, grass and trees, animals, together with worms, flies and ants. Water indeed is all these forms."

Substrate monism diminishes the transient superficial configurations of reality in favor of an underlying foundation which, by being unchangeable, can validate noumenal judgments. The use of a particular entity, such as water, to image forth that is in part self-defeating. If everything is A, then A itself is nothing in particular. Without a not-A to define it by establishing boundaries for it, A becomes a kind of verbal blank. Thus in the statement "Everything is water," water loses its specific meaning and becomes simply "matter" or "same stuff." One might as well have said, "Everything is in some way the same," or, "Everything is made of some indefinite stuff that changes form, now water, now fire, now air, and so on."

The Upaniṣadic teacher Sanaktumara, in saying "Everything is water," did not teach this concrete material monism as an exclusive doctrine, but as part of a staged approach to the concept of *brahman*, or featureless being, as the substrate. Another Upaniṣadic teacher of great importance, Uddālaka, taught substrate monism without any particular material bias, through a series of examples that, by their very difference, point toward a substrate beyond any specific name:

> Just as, my dear, by one clod of clay all that is made of clay becomes known, the modifications being only a name arising from speech, while the truth is that it is just clay. Just as, my dear, by one nugget of gold, all that is made of gold becomes known, the modification being only a name arising from speech, while the truth is that it is just gold. (*CU* VI.1.4–6)

Uddālaka extends his simile through several substances, preventing the mind from fixing definitively on any one. His conclusion is that the unity underlying things is Being-in-itself, or Sanskrit *brahman*, a neuter noun whose meaning or usage has passed beyond mythological modes of conception. In Greece at about the same time, a similar linguistic development took place in the work of Anaximander.

Anaximander and Indian Monism

Anaximander was a younger contemporary of Thales and, like him, a citizen of Miletus. He may have been at his height (or "flourished" as the ancient texts say, conventionally meaning "was forty years old") in about 540 B.C. Lydian, Greek, Egyptian, and Persian merchants were active in the urban milieu of Miletus; travel to Sardes, Naukratis, and elsewhere was easy, and papyrus books were available. Publication was expanding in the Greek world, where, two or three generations before Anaximander's book, the poems of Sappho, for example, had undergone some form of publication that sooner or later spread them all over Greece.

Anaximander, like Thales, was involved in the task and opportunity of bringing into awakening Greece the cultural legacy of the ancient civilizations of the Near East. He was an ambitious and challenging personality who, according to one ancient source, "cultivated a vain theatricality and adopted imposing costumes" (D.L. VIII.70). Like Thales', his primary interest seems to have lain in Mesopotamian astronomy and related pursuits. As Thales had learned the Babylonian cycle for years in which eclipses are most likely to occur, and had been credited by the Greeks with figuring it out for himself, so Anaximander borrowed from the East the gnomon, or astronomical measuring rod, and was credited with having invented it. He is also credited with drawing a map of the world, based probably on Mesopotamian maps of earlier date which involve the circular conformation with surrounding river and other elements which Anaximander passed on. The attribution to Anaximander of a celestial globe again indicates how closely he was associated with astronomy and hence with the East.

Around 550 B.C. Anaximander wrote a book, of which only a single fragment is extant. In it he went beyond Thales to a more abstract formulation of the substrate, which he called the *apeirōn*, a word that can be translated "infinite," "unlimited," "undefined," "indefinite," and so on.[15] The fragment of Anaximander occurs at the end of a paraphrase by Simplicius:

> Anaximander said that the principle [*archē*] and element [*stoicheion*] of existing things was the indefinite [*apeirōn*]; he was the first to use this name for it. He says that it is neither water nor any other of the so-called elements, but some other infinite/indefinite nature, from which all the heavens and the worlds within them come into being. And the source of coming-into-being for existing things is also that into which perishing takes place, "according to necessity; for they pay penalty and retribution to each other for their injustice according to the assessment of Time," as he describes it in rather poetic terms. (D.L. II.1.2 = DK 12A1)

The phrase in quotation marks is widely regarded as Anaximander's own words. Simplicius, expressing the point of view of a later age, criticizes Anaximander's diction as poetic—meaning mythological—rather than philosophical, because its references to punishments, justice, and so on, imply narrative. Anaximander's language in the quoted passage is complex in its references. In addition to the mythological tinge, there is an allusion to the language of the court of law, suggesting natural law within the infinite, and also to the language of Hippocrates and the Hippocrateans, who speak similarly of the body as desiring penalty or retribution in one quality (such as heat or cold) after an overdose of its contrary. The implication is that, for Anaximander, the body of the Unlimited is still a kind of Cosmic Organism with inner health and self-regulatory mechanisms to maintain it. And in fact Anaximander goes on to refer to it by terms applicable to godhead—calling it (according to Aristotle) "divine, immortal, and indestructible" (*Phys.* 203b7).

Aristotle considers whether Anaximander's *apeirōn* is an intermediate nature falling between two elements or qualities or pairs of opposites (hot/cold, wet/dry, and so on), or a mixture of them all together (*De Gen. et Corr.* 332a19; *Phys.* 187a12). A common modern view is that the Indefinite was either a mixture of all the elements or a stage prior to their differentiation from one another, like Egyptian Nun, Aristotelian Prime Matter, or Ovidian chaos. The mode of generation of the infinite, then, is that the pairs of opposites unfold themselves out from it into separate polarities and recombine with one another to make the variety of forms. The *apeirōn* is evidently a material entity, though prior to the specific differentiations by which matter becomes knowable or perceivable. As such it is halfway between the Sumero-Akkadian mythic concept of the oceanic mixture, Apsu-Tiamat, from which things are separated out in unsystematic streams of polarities and singularities, and the completely featureless Being of Parmenides.

Anaximander's Infinite may relate to his Mesopotamian-based astronomical interests by being spherical or circular; in addition to its meaning as "indefinite," *apeirōn* in Greek also has the meaning "ring" or "circle," since the circle is an unlimited line, a line without beginning or end. Anaximander's map of the world was circular, too, as were its probable Mesopotamian models. The common ancient view that the totality of things is best represented by a circle may be a part of the Sumerian package of influences.

The *Ṛg Veda*'s Aditi, "the Unlimited," "the Unbounded," has often been compared with Anaximander's Infinite. Aditi, the "Mother of the Gods," is regarded as the source of all things (*RV* I.89.19, X.72). "Aditi is the heaven," says the Vedic singer in a formulation remarkably like Aeschylus's lines to cosmic Zeus; "Aditi is mid-air, Aditi is the mother and the father and the son. Aditi is all gods, all classes of people, all that has been born and shall be born" (*RV* I.89.19). Aditi is quasi-abstract, "a personified idea,"[16] with no independent hymns and no parts in the Vedic stories.

Still, a goddess who appears in the *Ṛg Veda* as a cow is more mythological than Anaximander's Infinite. "The mother of seven gods of light," she brings with her the tradition of mother goddesses as universal source or cosmic womb.[17] Aditi is a feminine noun whereas Anaximander's Infinite is neuter, essentially postmythological, like Uddālaka's *brahman*.

The neuter conception of deity actually dawned in India earlier than Uddālaka. The Indian sources are much fuller on this point than the Greek, and the process can be seen in more detail. Several hymns of the Akkadian-influenced *Atharva Veda* are addressed to an abstract and neuter deity called Skambha, the Support, or the Substrate, or the Frame, or the Cosmic Pillar;[18] in these hymns the *pantheos* concept is expanded to include mental qualities and at the same time is referred to by the abstract noun *brahman*, "being." Both Anaximander and the poets of the Skambha hymns, in their use of the neuter abstraction, show awareness of the difference between mythology and the emerging sensibility which would come to be called philosophy. It is an important addition to the techniques (such as Thales' isolation of a single image, and the Amon-Re priests' affirmation of contradictory qualities) for getting beyond mythological thought and discourse, which, though they continue to be hiddenly present in early philosophical modes of expression, are increasingly moved into the background.

One hymn (*AV* X.7) to Skambha, the Substrate, involves a critique of the mythological concept of the Cosmic Being. Couched as a series of questions, it seems to express a struggle to get beyond the visual image to an abstract concept of metaphysical substrateness. "In what member of it is the earth located?" the singer-philosopher inquires, evidently parodying models like that of the *Hymn to the Cosmic Person*, which locates the earth in the feet. A series of questions leads to a reduction of such imagery to absurdity: "In what member of it is the atmosphere located? In what member does the sky remain set? In what member is located what is above the sky?" The poet points out the difficulty of imaging time with spatial metaphors: "With how much of itself did the Substrate enter into the past? How much of itself stretches over the future?" Another stanza reveals the difficulty of imaging mental qualities in spatial formats: "In what member of it is fervor located, in what member of it is right deposited? . . . In what member of it is Truth established?" Another stanza points toward the transcendent aspect, as if to quiet the use of concrete imagery: "That in which earth and atmosphere and sky are fixed, in which fire, moon, sun, wind, remain fastened, identify that Substrate. Which of the things that are, pray, is it?" Another stanza suggests awareness of the difference between temporal and logical priority—the modes of myth and philosophy, respectively. "When the substrate, generating, evolved the original cosmos, the original cosmos was recognized as a member of the Substrate."

In another *Hymn to the Substrate* (*AV* X.8) the term "ātman," Cosmic Self or Universal Subject, is used. The poet reflects on the immanence-transcendence relationship and attributes to the abstract Substrate terms traditionally applied to personal deity. "With half of himself," the poet writes, "he created the whole world; the other half of him, what is the distinguishing mark of it? The One [neuter] is finer than a hair . . . yet more embracing than this universe . . . Nearby though it is, one cannot see it." Despite the neuter and abstract nature of the Substrate, the Vedic poet addresses it religiously: "Behold the artistry of the god! It does not die, it does not grow old"—much as Anaximander addressed his neuter indefinite as "divine, immortal, and indestructible."

Many passages in the early Upaniṣads describe *brahman*, or Being, in terms virtually identical to those with which Anaximander described the Infinite. "That from which these things are born, that by which, when born, they live, that into which, when departing, they enter. That, seek to know. That is Brahman" (*TU* III.1.1). As Anaximander's Infinite is declared by him to be neither one element nor another, the *brahman* is declared to be "neither gross nor fine, neither short nor long, neither glowing red like fire nor adhesive like water" (*BU* III.8.8). As Anaximander's Infinite is said by Aristotle (*Phys.* 203b7 = DK 12B3) to "surround all things and steer them," so the *brahman* is said in the early Upaniṣads to contain all things and to be their "inner controller" (*BU* III.7.1). As Anaximander's Infinite is said by Aristotle to be divine and immortal, so the *brahman* "transcends hunger and thirst, sorrow and delusion, old age and death" (*BU* III.5.1). As the ground of being, both of these concepts, *apeirōn* and *brahman*, precede all specific qualities except that of existing; the source of the pairs of opposites, each is itself beyond them.

This concept of a state of being which is beyond qualities, or prior to them, is the first purely philosophical idea. It was obtained through a progressive stripping away of concrete imagery. It is one of the great and characteristic products of ancient thought—both Greek and Indian—and has retained force as an expression of both philosophical and mystical insights into modern times. It was to undergo much criticism, as time passed, on the grounds that being-without-qualities is a contradiction in terms: *To be* means precisely *to have qualities*. But its force, both as an expression of primal wonder and as a first daring incursion into the realm of the abstract, remains undiminished.

Anaximines and Indian Monism

By the time of the third of the great Milesian philosophers, Anaximenes, an established tradition was in place, which he consciously expressed. Virtually nothing is known of his life except that he lived in Miletus, was probably somewhat younger than Anaximander, was either the latter's pupil or anyway under his influence, and wrote a book. This book, like Anaximander's, seems to have contained, along with a version of material monism, a protoscientific description of the universe and its workings.

Philosophically, Anaximenes' work, like Anaximander's, is represented by only one extant fragment in his own words or something close to them; these words are contained within a passage by the late author Aëtius:

> Anaximenes, son of Eurystratus, of Miletus, declared that air is the principle [*archē*] of existing things; for from it all things come-to-be and into it they are again dissolved. As our soul, he says, being air, holds us together and controls us, so does wind (or breath) and air enclose the whole world. (DK 13B2)

At first sight Anaximenes seems to have taken a step back from the more abstract conception of Anaximander toward the more concrete and myth-based conception of Thales. But he was not without his reasons. According to Cicero (*De Nat. Deor.* I.10.26), Anaximenes called air "the divine," and he may have been influenced by the traditional belief that air, or breath, is soul-stuff, that it is the carrier of consciousness. The universe, on that account, is a *pantheos* which has the divine air element as its breath-soul. The Pythagoreans, not long after, would teach similarly that the universe is a living organism which breathes one vast breath. The concept of the *pantheos*, in other words, outlasted the specifically anthropomorphic descriptions of the Macranthropus; even when viewed as a contraption of wheels and gears, the universe was regarded as a living god.

The most important aspect of Anaximenes' innovation was his theory that changes in the one substance are produced by a process of condensation and rarefaction. Thales' watery One may have produced on the analogy with chemical changes of state; Anaximander's One, by separating out opposites in balanced and balancing procedures. Anaximenes' air-substrate produces the variety of forms by condensing and rarefying itself. Air rarefied becomes fire, and produces the fiery objects, sun and stars; air condensed becomes mist or cloud, then precipitates out of the cloud state into the water state as rain, then becomes further condensed as earth, then finally becomes compressed into minerals. The conception is of great importance in several ways. First of all it tacitly contains the message, which Heraclitus would derive from it, that the unity of the world is the unity of a vast process happening; it is not primarily a type of matter that is the substrate, it is the process by which matter is being transformed through various appearances. Air is declared the essential type (or stage) of matter because, as the soul, it is somehow the ruling principle, from which the motive force arises. In addition, Anaximenes' model is based to a certain extent on the observation of cyclical processes in nature such as precipitation and evaporation. Such a basis in natural science may have been present already in Thales, but was definitely present in Anaximenes. Finally, the concept of condensation and rarefaction contains implicitly the seeds of atomism because it posits material change at an infrasensory level.

In India as early as the *Atharva Veda* (X.7.34) the wind was regarded as the breath of Skambha, the "Substrate," which supports the entire universe. Indeed, the "*prāṇa* theory," or theory that air is the material substrate, is prominent in early Indian thought. *Prāṇa* , the Sanskrit equivalent of Greek *pneuma*, "breath, air, soul," appeared in the *Atharva Veda* as a ruling cosmic principle. "Air, in whose power is this All, who is the Lord of all, on whom all is based . . . in air is what has been and what is to be; everything is based on air" (*AV* II.4).[19]

The *Chāndogya Upaniṣad* develops a model still closer to that of Anaximenes. As he called air "the encompassing," the Upaniṣad says: "Air is the absorbent, for when a fire goes out, it goes into the air. When the sun sets, it goes into the air, and when the moon sets it goes into the air. When water dries up it goes into the air. For air, indeed, absorbs them all" (*CU* IV.3.1–2).[20] The *Bṛhadāraṇyaka Upaniṣad* states that "from *prāṇa* the sun rises and in *prāṇa* it sets" (*BU* I.5.21). Similarly the *Kauṣitaki Upaniṣad*, also an early one, declares that all things die into the wind and rise up from it again (*KU* II.12). Yājñavalkya teaches a close analogue to the doctrine of a universal breath that contains all individual breaths: "Air," he says, "is the separate individuals, and air is the totality of all individuals" (*BU* III.3.2).

The description of the world process on the analogy of condensation and rarefaction also seems to be enunciated in the Upaniṣads. The mechanism is not specifically identified, but the series of transformations of matter seems based, as in Anaximenes, on increasing density. In both the *Chāndogya* and *Bṛhadāraṇyaka Upaniṣads*, in what is called the Doctrine of the Five Fires, the process from element to element or state to state proceeds "from space into air, from air into rain, from rain into the earth" (*BU* VI.2.16), much as Anaximenes' progression goes from air to mist to rain to earth.

Finally, it seems that all the metaphysical elements of Milesian monism were present in Indian thought, many of them at a considerably earlier age than their appearance in Greece. An important difference must be observed, however, between the Greek and Indian modes of thought about One and Many. In the Upaniṣads the concept of *brahman* stands more or less as the beginning and the end of thought. Insofar as its ramifications are spelled out, they are ethical ones. But Anaximander's book is known to have included, alongside its elucidation of the Infinite, a complex nuts-and-bolts description of the working of the cosmic mechanisms, in line with his study of astronomy and his use of visual models such as the map and the celestial globe. His description of the cosmos was an eclectic synthesis of elements borrowed from Mesopotamian, Egyptian, and Persian sources.[21] His statement, for example, that the earth is concave like a bowl is associated with the Mesopotamian world-map in which the circular earth is surrounded by seven mountains, and with the related Egyptian belief in the "surrounding mountain" that rings the earth. His vision of wheels within wheels is echoed in the vision of his contemporary Ezekiel, who saw cherubs turning on concentric wheels about the throne of god in the sky; it represents a general Near Eastern conception of the heavens, probably Mesopotamian in origin, that would recur in both Parmenides' and Plato's visions of the cosmic workings. The order in which Anaximander places the celestial bodies—with the stars nearest the earth, then the moon, then the sun—is eccentric in either Babylon or Greece but normal in the Persian *Avesta*, which, at some remove, may be its source.

Indian thinkers of the Middle Vedic and Upaniṣadic periods may have had access to similar sources, but they did not produce from them mechanical models of world process. The Milesians, more so than their Indian peers, are regarded as protoscientists —people who wanted to believe that the world was certifiably knowable and to devise a systematic method with which to know it. In keeping with the intuitionist background to their emerging profession, they approached the project also as quasi-mystics expressing primal wonder at the existence of the universe. Their attempt to go beyond mythological ways of explaining the universe, expressed as it was in mechanical models as well as metaphysical insights, bore as much significance for the development of science as of philosophy.

Heraclitean Monism and Indian Thought

The Ionian tradition in philosophy culminated with Heraclitus, who, since antiquity, has been regarded as the most difficult of the pre-Socratics. Timon of Phlius called him "the Riddler" (D.L. IX.6), a sobriquet that may have led to the more common title, "the Obscure." He was born into an aristocratic family in the Asian Greek city of Ephesus. "He grew up," says Diogenes Laertius, "to be exceptionally haughty and supercilious." As a sign of his arrogance, it is recorded that he resigned to his brother a hereditary "kingship" (or residual ritual kingship). He wrote a book which, says Diogenes Laertius, was deliberately couched in a difficult style so that only the most educated classes could read it. His book seems to have begun with an insistence that no one at all would understand it. It featured scornful criticism of major Greek cultural figures including Hesiod, Pythagoras, Xenophanes, and Hecataeus.

Heraclitus is said not to have formed a school or taken disciples, but to have dedicated his book as an offering in the Temple of Ephesian Artemis. This tradition, like that which holds that Pythagoras's home was dedicated after his death as a temple of Demeter, shows the strange symbiosis of goddess religion and protophilosophy that prevailed at that time and place. Heraclitus's book—by its own force and by circumstantial channels not known—later produced a line of disciples, or advocates, or interpreters, who called themselves Heracliteans. It is not known whether any of them was ever a face-to-face student of Heraclitus.

Late in life Heraclitus is said to have withdrawn from human society, living as a mountain hermit on wild grasses and plants—much like a forest yogi in India. An outrageous story records that he died buried in bovine excrement, trying to draw excess liquid from his body by that means. He may have died in about 480 B.C. or not long after.

Heraclitus's educational background is not known, but it is clear that he was influenced by Milesian monism, especially in the process-oriented version of Anaximenes, and by Xenophanes, who may have worked out his doctrine before leaving Colophon for the west. Responding to these influences and others from abroad, Heraclitus ushered in a new age in thinking of the Problem of the One and the Many. In line with his Milesian heritage, he was fundamentally a monist:

> Listening not to me but to my account it is wise to agree that everything is One. (Fr. 51)

But exclusive emphasis on the One had gone beyond the point of attributing underlying order to the Many and had ended by subordinating the Many to the One, preparing for Parmenides' annihilation of it. Heraclitus sought to rectify this situation by restoring balance between the One and the Many:

> The One is made up of the Many and the Many are made up of the One. (Fr. 10)

And Plato confirms that, according to Heraclitus, reality was both One and Many (*Soph.* 242d). Mediating between the One and the Many along lines suggested by Anaximenes' hints of process-monism, Heraclitus developed the position that the permanent element in nature is change: The unity of things is the unity of an ongoing process, not the unity of a static Other.

The emphasis on process-as-unity leads, in the context of a metaphysics of being, to elusive and paradoxical modes of expression. The metaphysics of pure Being would be consummated in the next generation by Parmenides, whose solution involves a kind of metaphysical projection onto the universe of principles which would in time come to be called the "Laws of Thought": the Law of Identity (that A is A and A is not not-A), the Law of Contradiction (that nothing can be both A and not-A at the same time), and the Law of the Excluded Middle (that every entity in the universe is either A or not-A). Parmenides' universe is the embodiment of these principles; Heraclitus's is the deliberate negation of them all. It features antilogical assertions that breach in one way or another all three of the so-called Laws of Thought, though the emphasis is on paradoxes which reject the Law of Contradiction, for example:

> We both are and are not. (Fr. 49a)

According to Aristotle, Heraclitus generalized this point, saying that all things both are and are not (*Met.* 1012a24). This style was characteristic of him, as in the following:

> That which is in opposition is in concert, and from things which differ comes the most beautiful harmony. (Fr. 8)
>
> The way up and the way down are one and the same. (Fr. 60)

In terms of metaphysics, Heraclitus's central postulate is his emphasis on change, not on things themselves. Things that are constantly changing are not susceptible of definition, since a definition which applies one moment will not apply the next. Since things lack definition, every kind of metaphysical declaration is compromised. (As Aristotle said, "Nothing is true of what is changing" [*Met.* 1010a7–8].)

Following the tradition of his Milesian predecessors Thales and Anaximenes, Heraclitus chose to image forth the Oneness of things through the universalization of one element which seemed to have an analogue of cosmic process built into it:

> This cosmos . . . always was and is and will be one everlasting Fire, kindled in measure and in measure quenched. (Fr. 30)

The process—fire—retains its identity, while the matter undergoing it—the fuel—is constantly changing. In expressing this dualism of the One, Heraclitus echoed the sentiment which Aristotle found paradoxical in Xenophanes:

> While moving, it is at rest. (Fr. 84a)

The combination of sameness of overall structure and constant change of substance is also the point of the famous observation:

> It is impossible to step into the same river twice. (Fr. 49a)

Heraclitus provides an ultimate image of instantaneous and irresistible change as the inmost essence of "things":

> The lightning bolt steers all things. (Fr. 64)

Similar ways of thought had been explored in India also, perhaps earlier. Heraclitus's response to Xenophanic monism is remarkably parallel to the early Buddhist response to Upaniṣadic monism. The early Buddhists, like Heraclitus, presented process and lack of fixed essence as counterarguments to the monistic rejection of experience. Comparisons between Heraclitus and early Buddhism have been made before, as early as the eighteenth century. A more recent author than that points out that in the *Mahavagga* (I.121) the Buddha "compares the existence of beings to the candle-flame that is renewed every instant," and also employs (I.123) "the analogy of the river which is never the same for two moments."[22] The Buddhist doctrine of *anātman* or not-self (Pali *anatta*) confronted the Upaniṣadic emphasis on *ātman* or self, as did such statements of Heraclitus as "We both are and are not," which occupied the position that Parmenides would, presumably later, denounce as "that on which mortals wander knowing nothing" (fr. 6.4–5). In fact, Heraclitus's thought bears close resemblance not only to the flux philosophy of early Buddhism but to the "middle position" —between yes and no—expounded later in the Buddhist tradition in the *Prajñāpāramitā Sūtras* and the Mādhyamika school.

Heraclitus describes reality with a concept that was to become standard in Mahāyāna Buddhist terminology: Plenum-Void. "Fulness and emptiness," says Heraclitus, "are the same thing" (fr. 65). "God is . . . fulness/emptiness" (fr. 67). Elsewhere he foreshadows the *Avatamasaka Sūtra*'s doctrine of the infinite interpenetration of entities:

> The wise is one thing: to understand the Intention which drives all things through all things. (Fr. 31)

It is not only in Buddhism that one finds rich Indian parallels to Heraclitus. In the Vedas and Upaniṣads the images that Heraclitus features recur typically. The *Ṛg Veda*, for example, teaches the ultimacy of fire as a symbol of the One:

> That which is One the seers speak of in various terms: they call it [among other things] Fire. (*RV* I.164.46)

Elsewhere fire is said to contain all gods (i.e., all parts of nature) and to manifest each of them in turn as its process unfolds (*RV* V.3.1). In the *Muṇḍaka Upaniṣad* (II.1.1) fire is seen as the source and goal of all things. Heraclitus's image of the lightning bolt as the force behind the process of change, creating and annihilating identities instantaneously and ceaselessly, also has strong Upaniṣadic parallels. The *Kauṣitaki Upaniṣad* declares, "in the lightning flash is truth" (IV.2). The *Kaṭha Upaniṣad* says that all things in the universe are set in motion by "the great fear of the upraised thunderbolt" (II.3.2–3).

In fact, parallels between Heraclitean fragments and Upaniṣadic passages are uncannily easy to find. In explaining, for example, where his philosophy came from, Heraclitus announced: "I searched myself," or "I investigated myself" (fr. 101). The *Kaṭha Upaniṣad* accounts for its teaching on the Self (*ātman*) in a phraseology that sounds similar: "Some wise man, seeking life eternal, with his eyes turned inward saw the Self" (II.1.1).Another passage suggests that Heraclitus sees the human self in terms of the Mesopotamian idea of macrocosm-microcosm correspondence:

> You could not in all your going find the ends of the soul, though you travelled every road, so deep is its meaning (*logos*). (Fr. 45)

Countless Upaniṣadic passages parallel this remark. The *Chāndogya Upaniṣad*, for example, says:

> As far as the space of the universe extends, so far extends the space within the heart. Within it are contained both heaven and earth, both fire and air, both sun and moon, lightning and the stars. (*CU* VIII.1.3)

This discourse resembles that of pantheistic hymns. The description of the god who contains the whole universe is applied to the individual human self. It expresses the Mesopotamian idea, based on astronomy, that the microcosm is a duplicate in miniature of the macrocosm; this idea in turn may lie behind the correspondence theme of Hinduism which would become dominant in the symbolism of the tantric schools.

Another striking parallel is the image of the cosmic child-god. The Orphics describe Dionysus as a child playing with a ball, a mirror, and a pair of dice, and randomly arbitrating world events as he does so. Heraclitus echoed this, saying:

> Time is a child playing a game of draughts; the kingship is in the hands of a child. (Fr. 52)

A very similar image is found in a later Hindu book, the *Viṣṇu Purāṇa*, where we read:

> Viṣṇu, being thus manifest and unmanifest substance, spirit and time, sports like a playful boy. (*VP* I.2)

The *Viṣṇu Purāṇa* does not belong to the early period that would be most relevant to Heraclitus, but there are signs of an earlier stage of this imagery in India which likely predates both Heraclitus and the Orphics. In the *Chāndogya Upaniṣad* the winning throw at dice is called *krita*, and the commentators add that the sides of a die are marked with the numbers 4, 3, 2, and 1, and are called, respectively, *krita*, *tretā*, *dvāpara*, and *kālī*. These four terms are the names of the four recurring ages in the Hindu myth of cycling time; the correspondence suggests traces of a myth in which historical ages proceeded from a dice game played by a time-god.

Overall, the general ambience of Heraclitus's fragments could not be more receptive to comparisons with India. Scholars have multiplied out-of-context parallels endlessly:

Upaniṣads	Heraclitus
He, on becoming asleep, transcends this world and the forms of death. (*BU* IV.3.7)	All that we see when we have wakened is death. (Fr. 21)
There are two forms of Brahman, the formed and the formless. That which is formed is unreal, that which is formless is the real. (*Maitrī Up.* VI.3)	The hidden harmony is greater than the visible. (Fr. 54)
That self is not this, not that . . . It is unattached, for it does not attach itself. (*BU* III.9.28)	. . . that which is wise is apart from all things. (Fr. 108)
The self, though hidden in all being, does not shine forth. (*Kaṭha* I.3.2)	Nature loves to hide. (Fr. 123)

These and other parallels between Heraclitus and various Indian texts, while they embody many of the repeated themes and motifs of ancient thought, do not constitute an argument for diffusion. One serious argument for diffusion has been presented, however, by M. L. West in his book *Early Greek Philosophy and the Orient*. "The Bṛhadāraṇyaka Upaniṣad alone," West declares, "throws more light on what Heraclitus was talking about than all the remains of the other Pre-Socratics together."[23] This claim rests primarily on a correspondence in the respective treatments of the process of transformation in nature and the afterlife. Anaximenes had described the process as one of rarefaction and condensation. Air thickens to mist, mist thickens to rain, rain thickens to earth, earth thickens to stone—then back again. Heraclitus is in the tradition of Anaximines, yet his description of the transformation sequence is quite different and, in terms of Greek evidence, unaccountable.

Heraclitus's view of the patterns that natural transformations follow is known primarily from a long passage in Diogenes Laertius (IX.9) that probably goes back to a book by Theophrastus, Aristotle's successor, who often wrote with the actual pre-Socratic books on his desk. According to this source, Heraclitus's view of natural change was that the process goes from fire to water to earth to water to fire. Other evidence tells us that, for Heraclitus, the fire state represents soul, so the sequence can be read as: soul to water to earth to water to soul. It is, in other words, not merely interchange of material elements that is involved; the fate of the human soul, its destiny after death, is also regulated somehow by this process.

As Heraclitus puts it, each elements is said to "die into" the next stage of the process.

> To souls it is death to become water; to water it is death to become earth. From earth comes water, and from water soul (again). (Fr. 36)

One other Greek document contains a similar system, and it is an Orphic fragment (*OF* 226):

> Water is the death of soul . . . and from water comes earth, from earth again water, and from it the soul restored leaps to the aether.

In both the Heraclitean and Orphic fragments the sequence from fire to water to earth to water to fire is anomalous in terms of the Greek tradition, which is characterized by Anaximenes' condensation-rarefaction principle leading from air to mist to cloud to water to earth to stone. The intimate involvement of the soul in this process of natural interchange is also anomalous in the Greek tradition, and seems to suggest a doctrine of reincarnation in the process of nature.

But in the Upaniṣads this description of the process is commonly found. In the *Bṛhadāraṇyaka Upaniṣad*, for example, Yājñavalkya expounds a system of elemental transformations in which fire is considered the prime element and is declared to change directly into water (*BU* III.2.10). The *Kauṣītaki Upaniṣad* also teaches a cyclic interchange of elements with fire leading off the cycle and each element described, as in Heraclitus, as "dying into" the next; this the Upaniṣad calls the "dying around of the gods" (*KU* II.12). In the *Chāndogya Upaniṣad* also, Uddālaka, who may have taught at Taxila in the northwest of India, describes the process from fire to water to earth:

> [The One] "thought: May I be many, may I grow forth. It sent forth fire. That fire thought, May I be many, may I grow forth. It sent forth water . . . That water thought, May I be many, may I grow forth. It sent forth food [plant food—earth element]. (*CU* VI.2.3–4)

In the Upaniṣads, as in Heraclitus, the fate of the soul is bound up with this process. The *Chāndogya Upaniṣad* explains this linkage in what is called the Doctrine of the Five Fires, though it might more accurately be called the Doctrine of the Five Stages of Fire—fire being seen, as it was seen by Heraclitus, as the basis or ground for the system as a whole. The five stages of the process are twofold in application; as cosmology they describe the processes of nature, including the change of seasons and the flux of forms; as eschatology they describe the path taken by the soul which is to be reincarnated after the death of its previous body. When a soul (representing the fire element) is ready to be reincarnated, it is said to change into rain and rain down into the earth, then grow out of the earth transformed into plant food, which represents, in ancient Indian philosophical discourse, the earth element; the food, being eaten, is transformed into semen, which is traditionally understood in this context as representing the water element; being sown in a womb, the semen becomes a person, or soul, again. The sequence, as in Heraclitus and the Orphic fragment, is from soul to water to earth to water to soul.

That the Orphics held a doctrine of reincarnation at some time is certain; that Heraclitus did so is likely on the basis of certain fragments and, even more so, on the basis of this Indian comparison. Both the Orphics and Heraclitus seem in fact to have held a doctrine of the process of reincarnation that was spelled out in the early Upaniṣads.

In both Heraclitus and the Upaniṣads the process from fire to water to earth to water to fire is only part of a larger system. In the Upaniṣads it is involved in a system of two "paths": the Path of the Gods (*devayāna*) and the Path of the Fathers (*pitṛyāna*), or the path of the sun and the path of the moon. In Heraclitus the transformation of elements is bound up with a doctrine of two "exhalations" rising from earth to heaven.

Heraclitus's doctrine is told in a somewhat confused form in a passage of Diogenes Laertius, who begins with an attempt to interpret Heraclitus in terms of Milesian condensation process, inserting Anaximenes' mist phase to force the comparison to work:

> For fire by contracting turns into moisture, and this condensing turns into water; water again when congealed turns into earth. This process he calls the downward path. (D.L. IX.9)

Heraclitus's downward path then is the same that Uddālaka described in the *Chāndogya Upaniṣad.* It is in the process of return from the earth phase to the soul phase that the exhalations and paths enter:

> He [Heraclitus] reduces nearly everything to exhalation from the sea. This process is the upward path. Exhalations arise from earth as well as from sea; those from sea are bright and pure, those from earth dark. Fire is fed by the bright exhalations, the moist element by the others.

The bright and dark exhalations seem involved with the sun and moon respectively, as Diogenes Laertius proceeds, without clear connection, to speak of the places occupied by these luminaries—which are probably the destinations of the two exhalations:

> The moon, which is nearer to the earth, traverses a region that is not pure. The sun, however, moves in a clear and untroubled region and keeps a proportionate distance from us.

The doctrine of exhalations, like that of transformations, concerns the fate of the soul after death. Aristotle tells us that the exhalation is a stream of soul-stuff rising from earth to sky. The solar/lunar distinction seems to have something to do, then, with different destinations that the soul may rise to when "exhaled" from its body at death. The exhalations also seem to demarcate some cosmic stations:

> Day and night, months, seasons and years, rains and winds and other similar phenomena are accounted for by the various exhalations. Thus the bright exhalation, set aflame in the hollow orb of the sun, produces day, the opposite exhalation when it has got the mastery causes night; the increase of warmth due to the bright exhalation produces summer, whereas the preponderance of moisture due to the dark exhalation brings about winter. (D.L. IX.10–11)

The bright exhalation of souls goes to the sun and produces day and summer and dryness; the dark exhalation of souls goes to the moon and produces night and winter and wetness.

This very doctrine—or one uncannily similar—is expounded in both the *Chāndogya* and the *Bṛhadāraṇyaka Upaniṣads* (*CU* V.10.3–8, *BU* VI.2.9–12[24]) by a teacher of the Kshatriya, or secular ruling class, named Pravāhaṇa Jaivali; in both cases the doctrine is taught by the Kshatriya teacher to a member of the Brahmanical or religious ruling caste. Deussen described it as the "chief text that sets forth the doctrine of transmigration, on which all subsequent texts are dependent."[25] In terms of the history of religion, it represents a rejection, by Kṣatriya intellectuals, of the ritual-dominated religious practice of the Vedic Brahmins.

In terms of the overall development of Hinduism, this is not only a chief text of "transmigration" but also marks a crucial stage in the development of meditation practice. It has been powerfully argued that the distinction between those who will go into the afterlife by way of the fire (the Path of the Gods) and those who will go by way of the smoke (the Path of the Fathers) involves the pre- or protomeditational practice known as "interiorization of the sacrifice." In the early Vedic period the figure known as the *brahman*-priest "watched silently over the entire drama to make sure that everything was done correctly,"[26] meanwhile running through the ritual mentally, motionlessly imagining the actions and silently reciting the text, while the other priests were performing it physically. If he perceived errors or omissions in the performance, he corrected or compensated for them ("healing" the rite) in his mental rendition. Without a *brahman*-priest's mental performance, the rite was regarded as deficient.[27]

In the age of the *Brāhmaṇas* (say, 1000–800 B.C.), this interior performance was extended to other worshippers. It is here that the distinction between the two paths arises. In the case of a wealthy devotee endowing a rite, the question arose how he would gain for himself the reward, since it is not he but the priests he has hired who actually perform it. "According to Brahmanic ritual theory, the sacrificer ransoms the merit of the sacrifice through the giving of sacrificial gifts (*dakṣiṇā*) to the priests who perform the ritual. . . . Through the agency of the *dakṣiṇā*, the sacrificer [or sponsor] acquires the fruit of his sacrifice . . ."[28] This approach, "where," as Oldenberg put it, "the motif of heavenly reward for generous patrons of the priests stands in the foreground,"[29] is said to lead to the less meritorious but still desirable Path of the Fathers.

He who attains to the far more valuable Path of the Gods, on the other hand, practices the interiorization of the sacrifice rather than, or in addition to, endowing its performance by others; sitting separate from the officiating priests he performs the sacrifice mentally, like the *brahman*-priest, motionlessly imagining the actions and silently reciting the words. This "interior" performance attained the same merit as the dramaturgical performance done by the priests.

The distinction may have begun as a kind of legalism, but it acquired deep religious meaning. The interiorization practice has been suggested as an origin, or early stage, of meditation, which was about to become the center of religious life and thought in the Upaniṣads. "Vedic ideologies centered on the interiorization of the sacrifice," says one scholar, "... [led to] the [Upanisadic] idea that the sacred flame burns within ..."[30] The interior sacrifice became known as "the fire [ceremony] that leads to heaven" (*Kaṭha* I.13)[31]. Interiorization thus led to an overall revision of the Vedic doctrine of sacrifice: "To these priests and others, the true sacrifice took place not only in the outer world, but also within the individual human spirit itself." "[T]he individual person's own inner being was the true sacrificial arena ..."[32]

In the early Upaniṣadic communities the concept of interior sacrifice was generalized to the entire life of the spiritual seeker. "What people call the 'sacrifice,'" according to the *Chāndogya Upaniṣad*, "is really the disciplined life of a seeker of sacred knowledge."[33] As the trend toward interiorization gained momentum, "such a mental sacrifice is said to bring even more desirable results than does the performance of the large public rite." Specifically, the interior sacrifice produces at least three times as much merit as the traditional exterior sacrifice.[34] In time the rite performed within the mind (*manasayajna*) could be practiced by any contemplative; the age of meditation had arrived.

Those who have not imbibed this doctrine and who believe that Brahmanical ritual practice, rather than a special kind of "knowledge," is the center of religious life, will, after death, enter not the Path of the Gods but the Path of the Fathers, on which they will rise to the level of the moon, but not higher, and in time rain down again, become food, be eaten and transformed into semen, be implanted in a womb, and be reborn. Here is the version of the *devayāna*, or Path of the Gods, given in the *Bṛhadāraṇyaka Upaniṣad* by Pravāhaṇa Jaivali:

> People here on departing from this life separate in different directions ... (*BU* VI.2.2). When someone dies they carry him to be offered in the funeral fire ... Those who know this (doctrine) as such and those too who meditate with faith in the forest on the truth, pass into the light (of the fire), from the light into the day, from the day into the half-month of the waxing moon, then from the half-month of the waxing moon into the six months during which the sun travels northward (summer), from these months into the world of the gods, from the world of the gods to the sun, from the sun into the lightning (fire). Then a person consisting (born) of mind goes to those regions of lightning and leads them to the worlds of Brahmā where they live for long periods. Of these there is no return. (*BU* VI.13–15)

Heraclitus's bright exhalation corresponds closely to this Path of the Gods. In Heraclitus's version it is bright and made of soul; in the Upaniṣadic version it is made up of soul and light. Heraclitus's bright exhalation produces day and summer and goes to the sun; the Upaniṣadic version produces day, the fortnight of the waxing moon, and summer, then goes to the world of the gods and the sun. The Upaniṣadic path has more stages listed than the Theophrastean summary of Heraclitus's doctrine, but the two versions need no special pleadings or adjustments to make them agree with each other.

The situation with the dark exhalation and the Path of the Fathers is similar. The Upaniṣadic author writes:

> But those who by sacrificial offerings, charity, and austerity conquer the worlds, they pass into the smoke (of the funeral fire), from the smoke into the night, from the night into the half-month of the waning moon, from the half-month of the waning moon into the six months during which the sun travels southward (winter), from these months into the world of the fathers, from the world of the fathers into the moon. Reaching the moon they become food. There the gods, as they say to king Soma,

> increase, decrease, even so feed upon them there. When that passes away from them, they pass forth into this space, from space into air, from air into rain, from rain into the earth. Reaching the earth they become food. Again, they are offered into the fire of man (sexuality). Thence they are born in the fire of woman (birth) with a view to going to other worlds. Thus, do they rotate. (*BU* VI.2.16)

As Heraclitus's dark exhalation is dark, so the Path of the Fathers enters not the light but the smoke of the fire. Heraclitus's dark exhalation produces night and winter, and probably goes to the moon; the Path of the Fathers proceeds from night to the fortnight of the waning moon to winter; from winter, it goes to the world of the fathers and from there to the moon. Heraclitus's version omits two stages (waning moon, world of fathers) but is otherwise in agreement. From the moon, of course, the soul enters the process from soul, to water, to earth (food), to water (semen), to soul again.

Heraclitus's bright exhalation seems to be a version of the Vedic-Upaniṣadic Path of the Gods, his dark exhalation, of the Path of the Fathers. It seems that "the Riddler" had some contact with the Doctrine of the Five Fires. Assuming that he would not have incorporated a doctrine that he did not understand, he may be presumed to have had some familiarity with the central doctrines of Upaniṣadic Hinduism. The Doctrine of the Five Fires connects intimately to the doctrines of reincarnation and *karma*, and to the practice of meditation. Indeed, this connection resonates not only through the center of the Upaniṣadic religion but also through the center of Heraclitus's cosmology.[35]

This extraordinary parallelism is a strong and clear link between a pre-Socratic thinker and an Upaniṣad. It amounts to a scholarly "proof"—meaning the most reasonable interpretation of the evidence as it currently stands. The Heraclitean system of five transformations and two exhalations has not been accounted for historically by any other approach. Until the evidence changes, it should stand that elements of Heraclitus and of the Upaniṣads came either from each other or from an unknown common source.

Why is this stunning piece of evidence ignored by Western scholars of the pre-Socratics? Sometimes in their confrontations with Heraclitus they seem to be begging for something like this to clarify problems in the corpus. Is the scholars' refusal to look at non-Western evidence the reason Heraclitus is known as such an enigmatic and "riddling" thinker? One scholar observes that Heraclitus's thesis about fire "has a traditional Milesian ring," and that Heraclitus's "physical science [is] of a standard Milesian type." So far, it seems, Heraclitus would be no problem. But "he also advanced an idiosyncratic theory of man and of the human soul; and the fragments contain the remnants of an unusual theology."[36] It is the "idiosyncratic" theory of the soul and "unusual" theology which make him difficult. And the intrusion of Indian elements into these areas of his thought can account for them.

Pythagorean Monism and Indian Thought

The name "Pythagoras" became semilegendary either during or very soon after the lifetime of the historical figure whom the legends are partially based on. The name, in other words, does signify a single historical person—like the name "Sappho," say, as opposed to the name "Homer." The historical Pythagoras seems to have lived from about 572 until about 512 B.C. He was born and grew up on the Ionian Greek island of Samos, which is virtually within sight of the city of Miletus. When Pythagoras was perhaps forty years old, the tyrant Polycrates took over Samos; for unknown reasons, perhaps involving family connections, Pythagoras felt unable to live under Polycrates' government and emigrated from Samos to the small city of Croton in South Italy. There he set up a private "brotherhood," a closed society whose members participated in various activities including religious cult, scientific experimentation in medicine, acoustics, and other fields, mathematics, and South Italian politics. The nature of the Pythagorean involvement in politics is not clearly known, but it seems to have transcended city-state lines (not unlike the Freemasons in the seventeenth and eighteenth centuries A.D. in Europe). For reasons still unclear, but probably at least partly political, the Crotoniates rose up against Pythagoras and his associates late in his life. He went into exile at Metapontum, where he died. His house in Metapontum is said to have been dedicated after his death as a temple to Demeter (D.L. VIII.15).

Pythagoras fused the Ionian and Italian branches of pre-Socratic philosophy. Like his Milesian predecessors he was scientifically oriented and interested in explaining natural phenomena; like the Eleatics who would follow him in the western branch of the tradition, he was involved with systematic thought (mathematics rather than logic); and like Empedocles in Sicily, he, or his lineage, was somehow involved with Orphic cult.

The Pythagorean brotherhood involved a vow of secrecy which was sufficiently effective that much about their activities has remained shrouded in mystery. The exact nature, for example, of the cult which the brotherhood practiced is not known. It seems to have involved a special definition of Apollo along with familiar elements of Apollonian cult. Pythagoras himself, described in the tradition as a charismatic and mysterious teacher claiming special powers and dressing distinctively in a gold crown, a white robe, and trousers, seems to have claimed to be, or to have been designated as, the Hyperborean Apollo. These Apollonian elements mingled with elements adopted from, or designated as from, the Orphics.

South Italy was the center of Orphic activity, and Pythagoreanism had some kind of relationship with it. Like some Orphics, the Pythagoreans practiced religious vegetarianism and believed in reincarnation. Pythagoras himself was later rumored to have written some of the books that went under the name of Orpheus, which may mean that he presented some of his teachings as more traditional than they were by interpolating them into a traditional format that was sufficiently loose to receive them, and sufficiently cognate—as, for example, in the belief in reincarnation—to merge harmoniously with them. Whether Pythagoras adopted beliefs and practices from the Orphics upon his arrival in South Italy or whether, on the contrary, some of the so-called Orphic texts were actually Pythagorean in origin is an open question. Some sources say that Pythagoras wrote nothing, but that so-called Orphic books were written by his early disciples Brontinus, Zopyrus, and Cecrops. The sects have been described as "distinct religious movements which borrowed ideas and practices extensively from each other."[37]

Pythagoras is reported to have been the student of Anaximander, who also dressed flamboyantly and attributed a degree of order to the world that approached the mathematical. The two shared an interest in Babylonian astronomy; in fact, Pythagoras is also said to have studied under a Babylonian teacher, Zaratas, and under Pherecydes of Syros, whose book contained elements borrowed from Iranian cosmology. Some of the ancient sources say that Pherecydes was the first Greek to teach reincarnation; others, that it was Pythagoras.

A leading question is how much of the scientific endeavor of the Pythagoreans should be attributed to the founder. On the one hand, he is reported as an inventor of mathematical philosophy and an innovator in scientific experimentation. On the other hand, he is associated with a variety of mythical motifs that connect him with the realm of the shaman and, behind that, of the fertility deity.[38] Some scholars have chosen to attribute Pythagorean mathematical achievements to Pythagoras's students, such as Hippasus of Metapontum.[39] Others attribute at least the rudimentary beginnings of the mathematical philosophy to the still-shamanic Pythagoras.[40]

Pythagoras, like the Milesian philosophers, was interested in the order and knowability of the universe, and chose to perceive order as a form of underlying unity. He was, to that extent, a monist, though not a material monist. His monism was in part cultic; the Pythagoreans, like the ancient Egyptians, regarded the number 1 as the symbol of god. The nature of the substrate involved in this monism is singularly different from the material substrates of the Milesians. It was a prototype of the modern modes of thought which have been called formalism or structuralism, rather than a metaphor of natural science. In effect, Pythagoras declared that the substrate that unifies everything is—not water, not air, not fire, not an indeterminate Prime Matter—but "number," by which he seems primarily to have meant ratio or arithmetical proportion. As Aristotle put it:

> Since all other things seemed in their whole nature to be modelled on numbers, and numbers seemed to be the first things in the whole of nature, they supposed the elements of numbers to be the elements of all things, and the whole heaven to be a harmonia and a number . . . Number proceeds from the One, and the whole heaven, as has been said, is number. (*Met.* 985b23–986a21)[41]

Pythagoras seems to have interposed numbers between the One and the Many, formulating for seemingly the first time the One-Few-Many which Empedocles would transpose into his theory of elements and Plato would expand into his Theory of Ideas. This doctrine is expressed in a range of ways which embody the transition from mythology to philosophy. There is a more imagistic mythological mode of expression, in which the idea of the Cosmic Person is used, perhaps under Orphic influence, and a more abstract structuralist mode, in which mathematics takes the place of myth. Of the imagistic aspect, Epiphanius says:

> He speaks of the god, that is, the heaven, as a body, and of the sun and moon and the other stars as his eyes and so forth as in a human being. (*Adv. Haer.* 1.7)

This cosmic personification, derived ultimately from Late Bronze Age Near Eastern sources, is conflated with a number-mysticism which seems to have come from the same general source, and with a system of correspondences involving a mystical correlation of shapes, colors, numbers, musical ratios, and astronomical processes. In the system of the Pythagorean Philolaus, for example, the Cosmic Person is correlated to a shape and to the astronomical totality: "The dodecagon, which corresponds to Zeus, is the whole zodiac with its twelve signs."[42]

Pythagoras, like Anaximenes, seems to have taught that the atmosphere was the breath of this cosmic organism. According to Aristotle, the world begins to take shape, on the Pythagorean view, when the primeval One breathes in some void or air; this void then enters in and separates the numbers (which previously, it seems, were mingled together like the gods in the primeval ocean) (*Phys.* 213b23 ff.). The numbers being "separated" from one another, the "things" of the world begin to appear through a spontaneous "imitation" of the structural relationships, that is, the ratios, between them.

There is extensive Mesopotamian background to this doctrine of ratio worship and of the mathematical underpinnings of the universe. Aristotle's statement that all things exist by "imitation" of numbers may be a reference to the Mesopotamian concept of the correspondence between microcosm and macrocosm, a theory based on the astrological assumption that the mathematics of the heavens reproduces itself everywhere. Aristotle says twice in his brief exposition of the Pythagorean number religion that the cosmic numbers are those of the heavens—that is, that they are numbers from astronomical tradition, very likely Near Eastern in origin. Plato, in the Pythagorean dialogue *Timaeus*, attributes all human learning to this source:

> The vision of the day and night and of months and circling years has created the art of number. It has given us not only the notion of time, but also the means of studying the nature of the universe, from which has emerged philosophy in all its ranges. (*Tim.* 47b)

One recent study of the mysterious numerologies found in ancient religious texts has deciphered them as hidden echoes of the arithmetic of musical tuning.[43] These numbers have generally received astronomical interpretations in the past. Remarkably, the two interpretive approaches can exist side by side. The number 720, for example, is important in the arithmetic of the musical octave and is also found in Plato and in the following *Ṛg Vedic* line: "Of Agni, there stand seven times a hundred and a score of sons in pairs" (*RV* I.164.11–12). The 360 pairs in the Vedic passage have traditionally been interpreted as signifying a year—that is, 360 days and 360 nights. The acoustical reading, on the other hand, recognizes 720 as a number involved prominently in musical ratios. There are many such double entendres in the ancient literature. Both astronomy and music have in common the fact that they are outstandingly based on number. Tuning theory and its connection with mathematics are known to have been preoccupations of the Pythagoreans, alongside their preoccupation with astronomy and its connection with mathematics. Plato remarks that music and astronomy are "sister sciences, as the Pythagoreans say and we agree" (*Rep.* 530d).

The triple correspondence of astronomy, music, and number is crystallized in the doctrine of the Music of the Spheres, symbolized by the image of the seven-stringed lyre, whose invention is attributed to the poet Terpander. The seven-stringed lyre is regarded as not only an earthly instrument but a cosmic one: It is associated with the music made by the turning of the planetary spheres, of which one tradition, seemingly Sumerian in origin, says that there were seven, one for each of the planets visible to the naked eye. An alternate tradition, which holds that there are ten planets, is expressed with a musical metaphor in the system of the Pythagorean Philolaus, in which the ten heavenly bodies are said to "dance a roundelay" about the sky.[44] This metaphor is an early expression of the idea of the cosmic dancer that would find continued expression in Plato, in Plotinus, and, in India, in the tradition of the dance of Śiva and elsewhere.

The concept of an intimate interrelationship among tuning theory, sacred or ritually efficacious song, astronomical specifications of ritual occasions, and emerging reverence for the mathematical sense of order, seems already to have been present in Sumerian culture. A Sumerian myth, for example, from a tablet inscribed around 2000 B.C., lists among the ultimate principles of civilization a number of musical instruments, each of which probably embodied a different mode of tuning—that is, of mathematical configuration—regarded as of specific ritual efficacy. The idea that numbers —especially ratios—interwove and permeated all life was implicitly present in these convolutions.

To the Pythagoreans the intimate relationship between astronomy and acoustics suggested the underlying unity of all things. As Aristotle said:

> They thought the principles [of mathematics] were the principles of all things. Since of these principles numbers are by nature the first, and in numbers they seemed to see many resemblances to the things that exist and come into being—more than in fire and earth and water . . . since, again, they saw that the modifications and the ratios of the musical scales were expressible in numbers;—since, then, all other things seemed in their whole nature to be modelled on numbers, and numbers seemed to be the first things in the whole of nature, they supposed the elements of numbers to be the elements of all things, and the whole heaven to be a musical scale and a number. And all the properties of numbers and scales which they could show to agree with the attributes and parts and the whole arrangement of the heavens, they collected and fitted into their scheme. (*Met.* 985b–986a)[45]

Pythagoras's use of pebble drawings whereby shapes were equated with numbers, based on the number of points needed to delineate their structures, may have been derived from "the Babylonian view that each constellation had two chief characteristics —the number of stars composing it and the geometrical figure they form."[46] Indeed, Pythagoras's famous tuning experiments may have represented not the discovery of basic harmonic ratios but the importation into Greece of a Near Eastern demonstration of them. As the Sumerian calendar, the Precessional cycle, and the tuning of the octave were all diffused to Greece and elsewhere, Pythagorean harmonics brought with it a tradition of correspondences which permeated the Mesopotamian worldview and included number, astronomy, sound, and color. The colors which Plato, for example, assigned to the various planets in the *Republic* (616e) are derived from Mesopotamian sources.[47]

Whether the Indian tradition also contained a mathematical monism of this type remains an open question. But the cumulative force of a number of astronomical-acoustic numerological double entendres found in Vedic literature suggests that the idea of a mathematically defined cosmos may have occurred in India as well as in Greece, possibly from a Near Eastern source. If the correspondences between these two sets of numbers—astronomical and acoustic—were more fully understood, they might resolve more passages of ancient numerology than any other single hypothesis; but that has only begun to be demonstrated from the evidence. (The details of this correspondence will be discussed in the next chapter.)

Xenophanean Monism and Indian Thought

Xenophanes of Colophon seems to have lived from about 570 to about 470 B.C. Probably a member of the aristocratic class that produced Pythagoras and Heraclitus also, he was forced, at twenty-five years of age, to leave Colophon, when it was conquered by the Medes in about 545. Like Pythagoras, in other words, he grew up in Ionia and carried what he had learned there to the West. For perhaps seventy years after leaving Colophon he lived what he himself describes as a wandering life in Magna Graecia; tradition connects him with the Sicilian cities of Messana, Catana, and Syracuse, and with the South Italian city of Elea, for the founding of which he is said to have written a poem. It is not certain that he wrote a separate work of philosophy (or "on nature," as Anaximander's and perhaps some other Milesian books were called), but the fragments of his poems contain important thoughts on several philosophical themes, including skeptical proto-empiricism, cultural relativism, and the Problem of the One and the Many.[48]

Xenophanes prepared the way for his monistic theorizing by a critique of the theology of the traditional polytheism which in itself was of enormous importance, constituting, as it does, the earliest extant expression of cultural relativism.

> Mortals [Xenophanes wrote] consider that the gods are born, and that they have clothes and speech and bodies like their own. (Fr. 14)
>
> The Ethiopians say that their gods are snub-nosed and black, the Thracians that theirs have light blue eyes and red hair. (Fr. 16)
>
> But if cattle and horses or lions had hands, or were able to draw with their hands and do the works that people can do, horses would draw the forms of the gods like horses and cattle like cattle, and they would make their bodies such as they each had themselves. (Fr. 15)

Xenophanes pursues the relativity of points of view beyond the range of cultural and into that of species relativism. Anthropomorphism is criticized as an ego-projection of human identity onto the universe. Having dismissed the anthropomorphic polytheism, Xenophanes offers in its place a religious version of philosophical monism.

Xenophanes is regarded as the founder of the western branch of Greek monism, called Eleatic after the city of Elea. As Plato said: "The Eleatics, back to Xenophanes or even earlier, say that what we call 'all things' are really only one" (*Soph.* 242cd). Aristotle adds: "Looking at the whole world, he said that the One is god" (*Met.* 986b18 f.).[49] The One god is coextensive with the universe, that is, it is a *pantheos*. But Xenophanes went significantly beyond the limits of pantheistic monism as known in Miletus. Anaximenes' choice of air, the carrier of consciousness, as the substrate, constituted a sort of primitive turn toward the subject. Xenophanes made this turn explicit by shifting emphasis from the idea of the One as universal object (Everything you see is the One) to the One as universal subject (Everything that sees is the One). The concept that the One is both universal object and universal subject is basic to the early Upaniṣads, too, where the central message of many key passages is the sameness of the One as object, called *brahman* or Being, and the One as subject, called *ātman* or Self.

As against the traditional anthropomorphic view that the gods had eyes and ears, Xenophanes declared that "the One sees as a whole, thinks as a whole, hears as a whole" (fr. 14). This is commonly taken to mean that his entire being sees, and so on, rather than just part of it. Schofield, for example, translates, "All of him sees, all thinks, and all hears."[50] But it makes more sense that the fragment emphasizes that every place is a part of the god's body, so he does not merely see what is before his eyes; whatever happens anywhere in the universe is happening directly to his own body so that he perceives it with a kind of same-body awareness of all things, as one is directly aware of the sensations of one's foot. At the same time it seems clear that the world's combined activities of seeing, thinking, and hearing, are all parts of the sight, thought, and hearing of the One. The same doctrine is found in the *Bṛhadāraṇyaka Upaniṣad*, where Yājñavalkya says:

> [The imperishable] is without eyes, without ears, without speech, without mind . . . and yet there is no other seer but it, no other hearer but it, no other perceiver but it, no other thinker but it. (*BU* III.8.8–11)[51]

The first occurrence of this doctrine—which might be called subjectivist monism—is found in Bronze Age Egypt, where, in the *Hymn to Amon as the Sole God*, it is declared, in the closest thing to abstract thought anywhere in Bronze Age literature,

"He is perception." Indian and Greek thinkers paralleled each other in working out their more developed formulations of this idea. In the Upaniṣads, for example, the *ātman*, or universal subject, is declared to be the "inner controller" that "steers all things." Xenophanes similarly says:

> Apart from toil he moves all things with the thought of his mind. (Fr. 25)

The idea of divine telekinesis became a part of the Greek vocabulary of thought; Aeschylus, for example, adopted it, saying:

> Everything of the gods is without toil. Sitting, Zeus somehow works his will immediately, from his holy resting place. (*Supplices* 96–103)

The darkly beautiful *Kaṭha Upaniṣad* echoes this thought:

> Sitting he moves far; lying down he goes everywhere. (I.2.21)

An Upaniṣadic comparison offers insight into a problem in the interpretation of Xenophanes. In a key fragment Xenophanes describes the One as an unchanging absolute not unlike that of Parmenides (who is reported to have been his student):[52]

> It always remains in the same place, never moving, never going toward anything, for that would be inappropriate to it. (Fr. 26)

But if the One is without motion, then it cannot unequivocally be coextensive with the universe of experience.

In India this dilemma was the source of the *māyāvāda*, or illusion doctrine, which holds that, due to the exclusive reality of the One, the Many must be regarded as illusory. The One, by virtue of being One, is necessarily alone; it is the only thing that exists. Therefore the things that move and change, expressing plurality, must not really exist. The world of movement and change must be an illusion or misunderstanding.

This doctrine was implicit in early Upaniṣadic thought, though not specifically formulated with the word *māyā* until about 200 B.C. Yājñavalkya, the great philosopher of the *Bṛhadāraṇyaka Upaniṣad*, compacted this insight into two "great sayings" (Skt. *mahāvacya*). "*Neti, neti*" ("Not this, not that") points to the inference that the One, by virtue of being One, must be other than every member of the Many. Yet the One, again by virtue of being One alone, must be identical with the totality, which happens to include the Many. This aspect of the question Yājñavalkya stated in the responding *mahāvacya*: "*Iti, iti*" ("Yes, this; yes, that") pointing to the complementary inference that each member of the Many must be only the One again.

Xenophanes seems to have been the first Greek thinker to directly confront this ramification of monism: If only the One is real, then our senses lie, by reporting on a Many; the possibility of a true knowledge of the Many is ruled out: Since they do not really exist they cannot really be known. Xenophanes expressed this as a protoskeptical thought: "Even if someone should happen to be almost right, he could never be sure, for *dokos* is upon all things." The Greek word *dokos* means "seeming" as opposed to really being: The One *is*; the Many merely *seem to be*. This doctrine is substantially the same as the Hindu doctrine of *māyā*, which similarly holds that since only the One is real, the Many must be a kind of seeming. This is the point where Xenophanes has seemed to some Western thinkers to have contradicted himself.

Aristotle complains that if the One "moves all things," and is all things, then it must move itself; and in that case how can it be still? The Upaniṣads resolved this dilemma by compromising the oneness of the One, saying that being has two modes, the formed and the formless—which is much the same as saying that the One is two; the integrity of the One beyond form is then restated or emphatically declared by the insistence that of these two modes the formed mode is unreal, the formless real. The thought that if it is unreal it doesn't exist, and therefore needn't be counted, fell into the interstices between an ontology and an epistemology not yet separated out from one another.

Later Indian terminology would call the two aspects of the one the *nirguṇa brahman* (being without form) and the *saguṇa brahman* (being with form). The *nirguṇa brahman* is transcendent and absolute; it is (as Heraclitus said in his related doctrine) not attached to anything. The *saguṇa brahman* is the formed aspect of being—the teeming universe as opposed to the stillness of eternity. What Aristotle complained of in Xenophanes' thought is that the formed and the formless being were declared to be one. God was declared to be both total inaction and changelessness and at the same time the changing world of "seeming" (Skt. *māyā*, Grk. *dokos*). Yājñavalkya wrestled with this primeval thought in the *Bṛhadāraṇyaka Upaniṣad* by combining the contradictory "great sayings" "*neti, neti,*" "Not this; not that," and "*iti, iti,*" "Yes, this; yes, that."

Substrate monism more or less culminates in this paradoxical assertion that the universal substance is both every existent thing and also the negation—even the annihilation—of all existing things. Among Greek thinkers it seems to have been Xenophanes who first formulated this distinction, found everywhere in the thought of India, between absolute and relative being. Like the Upaniṣadic teachers, he places a higher value on absolute being and relegates the relative and changing world of experience to the diminished integrity of mere "seeming," like a reflection or a representation.

In both Greece and India, when the distinction between absolute and relative being arose, it brought with it the question of which kind of being the gods of the inherited polytheistic mythologies possessed. The answer was obvious. Like all changing and relative things, they lived mortal lives in the realm of *māyā*. The Upaniṣads portray the old gods as bewildered and uncomprehending before the new doctrine of a formless absolute. They do not cease to exist but exist henceforth in a realm of *māyā*, or diminished being. Xenophanes also focuses on this distinction. "There is one God," he says, "who is the greatest among gods and men, and who is not at all like men in either body or mind" (fr. 23). The old gods still exist in a relative way, as do humans, but similarly diminished by the emphasis on the transcendent One. Combining this with Xenophanes' analysis of relativism, one could say that "gods and men" exist through some kind of psychological projection of themselves: They are their own delusion. This idea, common in Hindu and Buddhist thought, occupies a position somewhere between philosophy and mythology; its philosophical status consists in the fact that it does not posit a beginning, but a moment-to-moment indwelling principle. Logical priority has replaced temporal priority; structure has replaced narrative—though the mythical subject is still present.

A remnant of the Bronze Age is found in the assertion, made by many ancient commentators, that the One of Xenophanes was spherical. One of them declares that the "all," that is, the universe, was spherical.[53] The world model of Anaximander seems to have been spherical, too—as that of Parmenides would later be, and those of Plato, Aristotle, and others. The postulate of cosmic sphericity, in terms of cultural history, may have Mesopotamian roots derived from astronomy. Similarly, the Mesopotamian macrocosm-microcosm relationship underlies the relationship between the two aspects of the One, the universal and the particular, or absolute and relative being.[54]

Xenophanes, on this account, seems very much a proto-Eleatic; some modern scholars have criticized this identification as Aristotle's projection combined with an overinterpretation of the fact that Xenophanes wrote a poem for the founding of Elea. But there is a deep and serious continuity between the thought of Xenophanes and that of Parmenides. Xenophanes, as the extant tradition represents him, was both an Ionian-style material monist—when speaking of the world of *dokos*, the apparent Many, and a proto-Eleatic transcendental monist—when speaking of the One in and as itself.

Parmenidean Monism and Indian Thought

Parmenides was a native of the South Italian city of Elea, for the founding of which Xenophanes had written a poem. According to Apollodorus his dates were about 540–480 B.C.[55] He is said to have been a member of a noble and wealthy family and to have either governed Elea or made laws for it which were maintained for a long time (DK 28A12; Plu. *Adv. Col.* 32,1126A; D.L. IX.21). This story is not inherently implausible; many of the pre-Socratic philosophers were involved in government, and not least the Pythagoreans, with whom Parmenides had some form of association. He is said to have been a student of Xenophanes but, says Diogenes Laertius (IX.21), "no follower of him, for he also associated with Ameinias the Pythagorean, a worthy gentleman, though poor. This Ameinias he was more inclined to follow, and on his death, being himself of noble birth and great wealth, he built a shrine to him. It was Ameinias, not Xenophanes, through whom he attained peace."

The relationship between Parmenides' Pythagoreanism and his Xenophanic monism is unclear. Pythagoreanism contained prominent dualistic elements along with prominent monistic ones, and by Parmenides' day Pythagoreans seem to have favored the dualistic aspect. For them, "the contraries," as Aristotle said, "are the principles of things" (*Met.* 986b2). The contraries were formulated in a list of ten pairs of opposites. Parmenides may have been initiated into philosophy among the Pythagoreans, but he seems at some time to have been converted from Pythagorean dualism by encountering the teaching of Xenophanes and becoming convinced that there must be one primal element, not two. In seeking to give more rigorous definition to the motionless absolute of Xenophanes, he seems to have consciously adopted one side of the Pythagorean table of opposites and renounced the other. Thus his Being has the qualities of Limit, Unity, and Motionlessness, which are among the ten "positive" qualities in the Pythagorean list, but it lacks the contraries Indefiniteness, Multiplicity, and Change, which are among the ten "negative" qualities. A plausible view, then, is that Parmenides was first a Pythagorean, then encountered the teaching of Xenophanes—but this is not the way Diogenes Laertius reports it.

In any case, Parmenides' importance for the history of philosophy is not as a Pythagorean but as a monist in the tradition of Xenophanes. He attempted to put into rigorous order and inescapable argument the insight into monism expressed more loosely and imagistically by Xenophanes; with his work the traditions of both dialectic and logic began to emerge and articulate themselves. I will summarize the Parmenidean position through a loose paraphrase/parody of the Eleatic discourse rather than through a line-by-line analysis of the obscure and difficult fragments.

Xenophanes asserted that the ultimate Being must be motionless and static. For later Greek thinkers, and probably for Xenophanes too, the concept of motion includes any kind of transition from one state to another; any change at all, such as change of temperature or of color, is a type of motion. A belief in change of any kind requires a belief in plurality, since the state before and the state after the change are separate; for two or more different states to exist in temporal succession is a type of plurality and breaches the absoluteness of the One. On the ground that change implies plurality, therefore, the One must be unchanging.

Seemingly convinced by Xenophanes' insight that absolute Being must be unchanging and static, Parmenides rigorously accepted the consequences, namely that the world of everyday experience must not exist. Experience involves change, and absolute Being cannot change, for then it would no longer be itself. Experience, then, must be something other than Being; but to *be* other than *being* is absurd. The conclusion is that the objects and events of experience *are not*. Xenophanes had seen that the reality of the One diminishes the reality of the Many; Parmenides saw more radically that it annihilates it. Being *is*, Parmenides pointed out, and non-Being *is not*. Thus there can be no admixture of them, for if Being were to contain some admixture of non-Being, then to that extent it would not be; but that Being should not be is a contradiction in terms. Thus, by an implicit appeal to the Law of Contradiction, the exclusive and total reality of Being is established.

It is as if Parmenides has descended to the bottom-most foundation of the structure of thought, before any myth, before any image—starting over at the beginning. The rugged simplicity of this style of thought is relentlessly unfolded: With no admixture of non-Being to create rifts in it, Being must be a single continuous One.[56] And with no admixture of non-Being to create different textures or densities in it, it must be exactly alike everywhere. Since it must now be, and forever remain, exactly alike (exactly and unchangingly itself), then differentiations such as human senses seem to tell of cannot be involved in it; it is featureless and undifferentiated in a more radical sense even than was Anaximander's Infinite. Whereas the Infinite contains all qualities but refuses to make them explicit, Parmenides' Being simply contains no qualities at all.

This lack of qualities continues to unfold its implications. Since, lacking admixture of non-Being, Being is completely full everywhere, there is no room for anything to move in it. There is no place for Being to go except Being, where it already is. Lacking change, by which differences in time are defined, Being lacks time distinction also; for it there is no past or future, only: *Being Is*. This tautology was the closest approximation yet, in its day, to a pure abstraction.

The dawning of a thought without even hidden metaphors of visual picturing is a truly monumental cultural moment, which came about not all at once but by stages, and Parmenides' text was not the final stage of the process. One seemingly adventitious element of picturing (not mentioned just above) was still retained. Parmenides, following a pre-Socratic tradition observed by Anaximander, Xenophanes, and Pythagoras, described his otherwise featureless Being as spherical. The image may reflect, at however great a distance, the influence of Mesopotamian astronomy, or of some related but currently unknown cultural source which taught that cyclicity and circular motion were characteristics of cosmic entities, such as planets and seasons. It survives as a constant in the Greek metaphysical tradition: For Plato and Aristotle also, all perfect things move in circles.

The form of Parmenides' argument is as remarkable and historic as its content.[57] The Western tradition of systematic thought flowed out of it like a vine growing from a seed. To paraphrase the central point: "It is impossible," Parmenides reasoned, "for anything to come into existence, for it must either come from something, in which case it already existed, or from nothing, which is impossible, since nothing does not exist. Similarly, it is impossible for anything to go out of existence, because it must either go somewhere, in which case it still exists, or nowhere, which is impossible, because nowhere does not exist. Therefore," Parmenides concluded, "nothing can either come into or go out of Being, which means that everything must stay just as it is; change is impossible."

This argument, rugged in its simplicity, perfect in the refinement of its thought, and staggering in the boldness of its reach, is massively significant in two ways. For one, it is "the first systematic metaphysics,"[58] focusing on the concept of absolute Being and its surprising, even alarming, ramifications. In addition, it is the first fully formulated logical structure in any extant human document—the first argument whose elements have been more or less fully unpacked in terms of what has since come to be known as logic. It first demonstrated the enormous persuasive power of a systematically applied logical method, its almost ontogenetic way of positing. By using logic to eradicate the whole world of sense and experience, Parmenides demonstrated the potential power of philosophy as possessing a magic even beyond that of religion and mythology. Parmenides' willingness to sacrifice the realm of human experience for a hyperexperiential absolute demonstrates and embodies the passion that abstraction and logic, the new ways of thought, exercised as soon as they appeared on the stage of consciousness.

Timon of Phlius accurately characterized Parmenides' achievement as introducing actual systematic thought rather than the deceitful intuitions of the imagination. The observation points toward the fact that Parmenides' system contains, implicitly but as its basic structure, the principles that Aristotle would later formulate as the three Laws of Thought. The Law of Identity—that A is A and is not not-A—is embodied in Parmenides' relentless insistence on the self-nature of Being. The Law of the Excluded Middle—the denial that X can be neither A nor Not-A—is embodied in his denial that there is any other path of thought besides Being or non-Being, and in the rigorously applied dichotomic method. The Law of Contradiction—that no X can be both A and Not-A at the same time—is embodied in his rejection of the formulation that it both is and is not, and in the disproofs of the limbs of the dichotomy. His ontology is an embodiment, in almost completely abstract form, of these three assumptions. Logic is projected outward as ontology.

Heraclitus did just the opposite. His ontology is the embodiment of a systematic rejection of the three Laws of Thought. The Law of Identity is rejected along with the permanent selfhood of "things," which, according to Heraclitus (fr. 31), are driven through one another, that is, through one another's identity boundaries, breaching them. Both the Law of Contradiction and the Law of the Excluded Middle are rejected in formulations such as fr. 49a: "We both are and are not." Parmenides renounces the world of sense in favor of the principles of logic; Heraclitus renounces the principles of logic in favor of the world of sense.

While Parmenides denounces the world of sense as nonexistent, he also gives an account of why, though it does not exist, it appears to. He uses the word *hapatē* ("deceit" or "trick") to describe the world of sense experience. (Similarly the Sanskrit word *māyā* means "illusion" in the sense of magical trick.) Elsewhere he uses the word *doxa*, a noun form of the verb *dokein*—"to seem"—from which Xenophanes had adopted the form *dokos. Dokein* has both a subjective and an objective aspect: On the one hand, it means "to seem, to appear, to pretend to be"; on the other hand, it refers to the mind to which the appearance is appearing, in which case it means "to think, to believe, to hold the opinion that." The realm of *doxa* is, on the one hand, the realm of seeming to be, and, on the other, the realm of believing to be. It is further both an individual and a general term, meaning the overall illusoriness of the world as a kind of cosmic principle, and the individual delusions or belief-systems of people. The reciprocity of the appearance and the subjectivity to which it appears is central to the concept which the term signifies: Parmenides seems to have meant that false beliefs arise from false believing. The process of falsely believing, in turn, was set in motion by a primordial misconception:

> People made up their minds [Parmenides claims] to name two forms, of which one should not have been named — that was their mistake; and they determined these two forms as different in form and assigned to them marks or characteristics different from one another. (Fr. 8.50 ff.)

This primordial perception of duality or difference is a semimythical scenario of the Original Moment. In that moment, "people" distinguished wrongly between Being and non-Being, believing these both to somehow contribute to existence. And, at that moment, it began in fact to be so—at least in terms of human experience, or subjectivity, which was now living in its own *doxa*—a word which also has the meaning "dream, fancy, vision."

The Philosophical Goddess

The concept *doxa* corresponds closely to the Sanskrit concept *māyā*, which also is conceived as either a cosmic force or an individual delusion. Both concepts connect to Goddess-religions. Like Parmenides' goddess of *doxa*—Ananke, or Necessity, who sits within the wheels and gears of the illusion and manipulates them—*māyā* is conceived as performing a philosophical version of the mother goddess role. Parmenides' Ananke has been compared with Sumero-Akkadian Inanna-Ishtar, who, at the New Year's Festival, was "decked with the starry mantle of cosmic rulership,"[59] and equated with Hesiod's Themis, Hekate, and Oracle of the Night "concentrated in one figure."[60] As she tells Parmenides that she will teach him first perfect truth and then "opinions in which there is no true conviction," she echoes Hesiod's Heliconian Muses who introduce themselves as "able to speak many false things as though they were true, but also, when we wish, to utter true things" (*Theog.* 27–28).

Still, despite the fact that she has roots and antecedents, this goddess is a chief example of the new philosophical or allegorized deities. She is on a different ontological level from the Homeric and Hesiodic gods. As Xenophanes had said, the gods of the polytheism are creatures of *doxa*, living within the illusion; but Ananke makes the illusion work, and is outside and above it. She is a metagoddess in relation to the deities of the polytheism, whose conditions of being she establishes and maintains. Mediating between One and Many, she echoes ancient goddesses both of fertility, who bring the Many into being, and of destruction, who return the Many into the One. Her association with both truth and opinion is a new type of embodiment of the ancient Double Goddess, queen of both the realms of life and of death. Plutarch calls her Aphrodite, no doubt rightly, considering that Parmenides says of her:

She it is who has charge of all the business of hateful birth, and of sexual union, sending female to mix with male and again conversely male to female. (Fr. 12.4 ff.)

And:

First of all gods she made Eros. (Fr. 13)

Poetically these passages are in a long tradition that will still hold true in Lucretius's verse, as when (near the beginning of *De Rerum Natura*) he says to Aphrodite, "You alone steer the nature of things, and without you nothing is born and comes into the light." Aphrodite had a negative or deathly aspect balancing her erotic aspect under various names such as Epitymbios, Aphrodite of the Tomb. This duality is expressed in Plato's distinction, in the *Symposium*, between the terrestrial Aphrodite, goddess of animal matings, and the celestial Aphrodite, who wears the starry sky—the zodiac of astrological determinism or Necessity—as her crown. In monistic readings, the life aspect of the goddess can equate with the flow of forms, that is, the Many, and the death aspect with the absolute—the "lifeless solitary One," as Hegel would call it (echoing Plotinus, who called it "the alone"). But this correspondence can as easily be reversed, as Plato does, regarding the relative life of the terrestrial Aphrodite as equivalent to death, and the absolute life offered by the Celestial Aphrodite as her true birth-giving function. The association of monistic philosophy with goddess-worship was common. It has already been mentioned that Pythagoras's house, after his death, was devoted as a temple to Demeter, Earth Mother, and that Heraclitus devoted his book as an offering on the altar of Ephesian Artemis.

Indian monistic schools also favored goddess imagery—*māyā*, the bewitching cosmic dancer whose dance *is* the stream of events; Kālī, the devourer with necklaces of skulls around her neck, simultaneously engaged in sexual intercourse with Śiva and in drinking brains from human skulls, and others. Śaṅkara, the unqualified monist and "Indian Parmenides," as one scholar called him,[61] was a worshipper of Kālī and wrote a famous devotional poem to her. He addresses her in ancient Double Goddess terms: "You whose hands hold both delight and pain . . . Both the shade of death and the elixir of immortality are thy grace, O Mother."[62] She is worshipped as the principle which "gives birth to and protects the world, and at the time of dissolution withdraws into Herself the earth and all things."[63] Both Greek and Indian philosophers were evidently sensitive to the fact that the iconography of goddess religions, in a tradition flowing from the Paleolithic, Neolithic, and Bronze Ages, foreshadows in various ways the monistic view of the universe. These ontological goddesses are related to very primitive concepts, such as the Gorgon, whose left breast gives poison and whose right breast nectar. But, like the Indian goddess when she is called Shakti, "Energy," and worshipped by philosophers, Parmenides' goddess has been abstracted from the literal duties of child-bearing and laying-out and has been made to serve the corresponding philosophical concepts: On the one hand, she is the mother of Eros, the spirit of life, and the source of the world illusion through her bewitching dance; on the other, she is the wielder of the sword of reason (the Eleatic *elenchus*, or trial by reason), enforcer of the law of pure being, which devours all forms. It is this same goddess, compounded of both Aphrodite and Artemis, who sits at the center of Plato's universe in the *Republic* (616c–617b), spinning out time like a thread upon her spindle. In Greek contexts the philosophical goddess is more overtly connected to astronomy than in India. The Pythagorean Philolaus, probably an older contemporary of Plato, called Hestia, the central fire of the universe, Mother of the Gods, and placed her out in cosmic space. As Euripides said, "Earth, the Mother . . . but the wise call you Hestia, seated in the sky" (*TGF* 944). In later Pythagorean sources this goddess is Rhea, and the Great and Little Bears are her hands as she turns the rudder of nature; she is also Persephone with the planets as her pack of hounds, following at her heels. The Neopythagorean Nicomachus (second century A.D.) calls her "Lady of the Girdle," "Holder of the Girdle," and "Steadfast Axis"—all astronomical titles.

In his poem "On Being" Parmenides, after a flight away from earth, meets the goddess at the "gates of night and day." The goddess, who was evidently seated on the other side of the gates, opens them and greets him.

> The maidens, daughters of the Sun, leaving the home of Night, hastened their driving toward the light, pushing back the veils from their heads with their hands. There are the Gates of the Paths of Night and Day, and a lintel and a stone threshold hold them. The ethereal gates are filled with great doors, and of these Justice-With-Many-Punishments (*Dikē polypoinos*) holds the alternate keys. (Fr. 1.8 ff)

In terms of the iconographies of goddess religions, the gateway represents the transition between Being and non-Being, or One and Many, the birth gate from which the forms of the Many arise, and at the same time the cosmic drain through which they return to the zero point of pure Being. Poetically, Parmenides' gates, like much else in his poem, seem based on Hesiod's *Theogony* (744 ff.):

> There stands the awful house of murky Night, wrapped in dark clouds . . . where Night and Day draw near and greet one another as they pass the great threshold of bronze: while one is about to go down into the house, the other comes out at the door.

Though Hesiod's gate seems to be Parmenides' poetic forebear, the correspondence is far from exact. Hesiod's gate seems to have Night on one side and Day on the other; at dawn and dusk they pass each other going in opposite directions through the gate. Parmenides may mean something different. His basic poetic/philosophic dichotomy is between Light and Night, primal opposites. There are several points which suggest that Parmenides meant, by the Gate of Day and Night, the gate through which the primal opposites emerge from oneness. On the far side of the gate is the One; on this side are the countless offspring of the union of Light and Night. The two sides of the gate represent the two aspects of the ontological goddess, Being and non-Being, the right hand conferring unity and peace, the left plurality and war.

The Original Mistake

Through this gate duality arises out of unity. The primal moment in which two things are first distinguished (like the separation of heaven and earth in traditional cosmogonic myth) is, according to Parmenides, the birth of language. From an original or first moment of "naming" two things rather than one only, the world of the Many flows out as a complexly ramified mistake. This mistake is enshrined in, and subsequently maintained in place by, linguistic reification. Parmenides refers to the differences people see between things as "only names" (fr. 8.38–39, 53). The original distinction, also, was only a matter of "naming." The world of everyday human experience, in other words, is created by a mental error, constituted enduringly by belief in that error, and maintained in place by language-based ways of thinking.

In the Upaniṣads, similarly, the realm of plurality is known as *nāmarūpa*, name-and-form. Parmenides had spoken of "naming forms" as the constituting process of the world. The *Bṛhadāraṇyaka Upaniṣad* says: "In the beginning the universe was not differentiated. It became differentiated by name-and-form" (*BU* I.4.7). To say that name-and-form was created by name-and-form is the same circularity we find in Parmenides' idea that believing causes belief. The message is the same: It is because name-and-form are perceived that they continue to appear to exist. The processes of sense-perception and linguistic reification constitute name-and-form, or *māyā*, as they do the world of *doxa* for Parmenides.

In the *Chāndogya Upaniṣad* there is a passage that has often been compared with Parmenides. The philosopher Uddālaka seems to express an insight virtually identical to Parmenides': that non-Being does not exist, and hence cannot be brought into causal accounts. He makes clear the mutual exclusiveness of A and not-A, or Being and not-Being, and denies that there can be any intercourse between them.

> Some people say, "In the beginning this was non-Being alone, one only, without a second; from that non-Being Being was produced." But how could this be, my dear? How could Being be produced from non-Being? On the contrary, my dear, in the beginning this world was Being alone, one only, without a second. (*CU* VI.2.1–2)

Uddālaka is pressing toward the same metaphysical absolutism as Parmenides: that nothing can come into existence or go out of existence, and that reality therefore must be a motionless blank, a metaphysical sublime, altogether lacking the features of everyday experience. But Uddālaka, unlike Parmenides, has not produced a logical account of this view; he states it with a rhetorical appeal to its obviousness. Though Indian philosophy was older than Greek in some ways, the development of logical methods was not one of them.

In the same passage of the *Chāndogya Upaniṣad,* Uddālaka, having made Parmenides' first point, proceeds, in a remarkable correspondence, to make his second also. The world of the Many, he declares, is rooted in linguistic practice and sense experience, not in metaphysical reality. As all things made of clay are just clay, he explains, the differences between them being only names, so all things whatever are one same "stuff," namely, Being, and the differences between them are only names.[64]

The doctrine of absolute Being, one without a second, was received from the Eleatic school by Empedocles, Anaxagoras, Leucippus, Plato, and other Greek metaphysicians as an unavoidable condition for their own thought. Uddālaka's denial that Being could have any admixture of non-Being left a similar imprint on that part of Indian thought which was committed to the metaphysics of presence. In the *Bhagavad Gītā*, for example, one reads: "of the non existent there is no coming to be, of the existent there is no ceasing to be" (II.16). And in the *Viṣṇu Purāṇa*: "How can that which was nothing in the beginning and is nothing in the end be anything in the middle?" Centuries later this reasoning became the cornerstone of the school known as the Advaita Vedānta. One scholar has written of Śaṅkara, the most prominent philosopher of this school, that he "comes to the very position of Parmenides."[65]

Śaṅkara, of course, lived many centuries after Parmenides; but his thought was rooted in the *brahman-ātman* doctrine of the Upaniṣads, which was probably in place at some date before Parmenides. The closeness of the parallels between these two bodies of thought should not obscure the difference in the rate of systematization in Greece and in India. Parmenides clarified and systematized an idea-complex that, though it probably preexisted him in India, would wait many centuries before being as adequately systematized there. The rate of philosophical development may have been much faster in Greece than in India because the Greek schools were not committed to a religious orthodoxy whose texts and tenets were slow to evolve.

Chronological Considerations

The early periods of philosophy in Greece and India contained many shared elements: the Problem of the One and the Many as the originative philosophical topic; the meltdown of polytheistic pantheons into the Cosmic Person; the merging of cosmogony into natural inquiry; material substrate monism as a first solution beyond myth; the emergence (anticipated in Egypt) of a category of formlessness beside that of form; their union in an immanent-transcendent absolute; the struggle to escape from the concrete image; the development of devices to empty words of their concrete significations by (1) contradicting them ("We both are and are not"), (2) rendering them absurd (Purusa's thousand feet), (3) isolating and universalizing them ("Everything is water"); the increasingly abstract and systematic modeling of world process; the definition of an ontological absolute; the rejection of the world of experience in favor of that absolute—and more.

What isn't clear yet is how to account for this shared intellectual experience. Are quasi-Jungian intellectual archetypes to be evoked, linked by something like Jung's so-called principle of synchronicity? Were there certain ideas, in other words, that had a metaphysical existence independent of any mind thinking them, that were in place, waiting as it were, for the moment when certain minds, no matter how far apart geographically, should become ready for their dawning? This concept sounds like a religious revelation—even a scholar's *deus ex machina*. Is it, in a more down-to-earth spirit, that in any cultural period there are just so many avenues of thought available and these are bound to generate and regenerate each other in similar shifting constellations? This proposal sounds like an only slightly cleaned up version of the last one: Parmenides and Yājñavalkya *may* have lived in the same historical period—but thousands of miles apart! Surely some concrete mediating factor is needed to cross that distance. Only two seem available. First, what is common to both Greece and India in "the same historical period" is the long-term effect of Near Eastern ideas; if one starts from Babylonian or Egyptian macranthropy, the distance to the Eleatic-Upaniṣadic One is not unimaginably far. Or is there a more concrete historical causation between these thought sequences in Greece and India? It is certain that at least one philosophical convergence between Greece and India in the pre-Socratic period occurred by diffusion, since Heraclitus purveyed an Upaniṣadic doctrine in considerable detail. And it is highly likely that other convergences occurred by way of diffusion, including elements in the theory of monism. What is uncertain is the route via which such transmissions occurred—though obviously Persia was involved during the last half of the sixth century B.C. Any attempt to be more specific on this question faces chronological problems which at present seem insuperable.

On the Greek side, the Milesian chronology depends on the story that Thales predicted an eclipse in the year 585. The ancient writers who, long after the pre-Socratic period, attempted to establish its chronology, assigned 585 as Thales' prime of life (about his fortieth year), then extrapolated dates for his death, and for Anaximander and Anaximenes. But it has been influentially argued[66] that this chronology is based on the date for the fall of Sardes to the Medes combined with Apollodorus's principle of forty-year intervals between master and student. The Milesian dates, on this view, are manufactured; if that is the case, then everything depends on the story of the predicted eclipse—and it too has been seriously attacked. The eclipse is generally accepted by historians of philosophy and rejected by historians of science.[67] If the Milesian chronology is broken loose from the eclipse, it is possible that all three Milesians were active in the years 545–490 B.C., when both Miletus and Taxila were in the Persian Empire.

Even less is known about the chronologies and biographies of Indian thinkers such as Uddālaka and Yājñavalkya than of Heraclitus and Parmenides. Uddālaka, who isolated the concept of pure Being as a substrate, was associated with Gandhāra in northwest India, which was within the Persian empire after 545 or so. In fact, he seems to have been educated in the Gandhāran capital, Taxila, which was later to be a great center of Indo-Greek culture.[68] Taxila was probably a center of Upanisadic thought by the pre-Socratic period, and it is from this area that Indian influence flowed westward to the Persian court and elsewhere.

There are no certain dates for Uddālaka's presence in Taxila, or indeed for the early Upaniṣads in general. In fact, there are no dates for ancient Indian philosophy at all except relative dates; plausible sequences for texts can be worked out—for example, that the *Ṛg Veda* precedes the *Atharva Veda* which in turn precedes the early Upaniṣads—but absolute dates cannot be assigned to these events except by a loose intuitive sensing of how long such development might have taken. Acting on this basis, experts have proposed dates for the early Upaniṣads which vary by as much as a thousand years. The estimates which are accepted so widely today as often to be treated as facts are ultimately derived from Max Müller's. He assigns 800–600 B.C. for the early Upaniṣads, including the *Chāndogya* and *Bṛhadāraṇyaka*, putting them earlier than the Milesian dates and earlier than the fall of Media to the Persians. Dasgupta, on the other hand, gives 700–600 in one place[69] and, in another, says: "The earliest Upaniṣads were compiled by 500 B.C.,"[70] bringing them not only into the pre-Socratic period but into that part of it over which the Persian Empire presided.

So chronology is not going to help much at figuring out this relationship. The alternative tool for the early period is development. The various types of monism, for example, seem to develop in India, beginning in the Middle Vedic period, with a progression so plausible as to make importation unlikely—after the initial probable importation of the Macranthropus concept from the Near East. In Greece, on the other hand, where the so-called Orphic Zeus cannot securely be dated prior to Aeschylus, there seems something of a jumble to the way things developed. Here there is room for intrusive influences. This, however, may be only a random gap in our evidence: If the Orphic (Cosmic) Zeus, as even a rudimentary concept, could be dated to, say, the seventh century B.C., the sequence from Cosmic Person to material substrate monism would be much the same as that in India.

These questions have not been dealt with in recent scholarly literature in part because they have been regarded as unanswerable. The question is what constitutes an answer. No one yet has proven anything at all with absolute certainty. Answers are based on probabilities, and as we continue our peregrinations through ancient thought we will find the probabilities consistently and impressively accumulating in a certain way. Rather than rush to this goal we will let it emerge naturally from a larger picture that will be gradually sketched in.

The chronology of Greek literature is in certain ways roughly similar to that of Indian literature: a body of polytheistic texts with roots in the Bronze Age (Homer and

Hesiod on the one hand, the *Ṛg Veda* on the other), followed by a body of Iron Age literature that immediately effects a change from mythological polytheism to philosophical monism. But there is a crucial difference. In the early body of Greek literature there is no hint of monism or of any leaning toward it; the polytheism has not yet shown a tendency to dissolve into a pantheistic Oneness; if anything, the other tendency, that toward monotheism, is detectable. Homer's Zeus is much closer to Yahweh than to the pantheistic Zeus of Aeschylus.

The Homeric texts were still being composed until about 700 B.C. and still being altered for some time thereafter. They seem to have been followed by Orphic texts which had a more philosophical flavor and did not accept the conventional pantheon. Then, perhaps as early as 580, the first philosophical text, that of Thales, appeared and seems to have expressed material monism. The process from polytheism through Orphic pantheism to philosophical monism seems to have taken a century or so. In India the process took perhaps five to seven centuries. In Greece then, if not in India, there is some reason to look for a special cause that might have precipitated and nourished such a fast-paced development.

In India a combination of factors in the history of religion had disrupted the inner unity of the Vedic polytheism. The Middle Vedic period, when the monistic impulse takes ascendency, is the age when non-Aryan influences were allowed to penetrate Vedic priesthoods and texts; the loss of a sacramental substance has been suggested as a contributing cause for this;[71] the isolation of the Aryans within the vastness of India may also partially account for it; so, it seems, may the importation of late Akkadian texts involving the concept of a Cosmic Person. In Greece, where the transition is more abrupt and discontinuous than in India, even more attention should be paid to external forces that may have upset the internal balance of Greek mythology and tumbled it into a new form overnight.

Another difference is equally suggestive. In India the whole tenor of literature changed when the polytheism decayed, or was absorbed, into the monistic framework. All subsequent Indian literature is saturated with the monistic view. Yet in Greece, literature in general continued the polytheistic view of Homer and Hesiod as if the monistic revisions of Xenophanes and others had never occurred. The monistic attitude became a small enduring philosophical cult as it were, kept alive by special sheltering from society as a whole. It would seem that, if any diffusion claims are to be made as a result of this thorough and detailed parallelism, it is diffusion from India or elsewhere into Greece that is most likely to be its form, not the other way around.

Notes to Chapter Two

1. James B. Pritchard, *Ancient Near Eastern Texts Relating to the Old Testament* (Princeton, New Jersey: Princeton University Press, 1955), pp. 3–4.

2. Ibid., p. 366

3. E. A. Wallis Budge, trans., *The Egyptian Book of the Dead (The Papyrus of Ani)* (New York: Dover, 1967), pp. 108 ff., 195 ff.

4. Pritchard, *Ancient Near Eastern Texts*, pp. 365–367.

5. Ibid., pp. 368–369.

6. See Thorkild Jacobsen, *Treasures of Darkness* (New Haven, Connecticut: Yale University Press, 1975), p. 138.

7. Ibid., p. 235.

8. Ibid.

9. Sidney H. Hooke, *Babylonian and Assyrian Religion* (Norman, Oklahoma: University of Oklahoma Press, 1963), p. 27.

10. Franklin Edgerton, *The Beginnings of Indian Philosophy* (Cambridge, Massachusetts: Harvard University Press, 1970), p. 68.

11. I follow Radhakrishnan's English translations of the Upaniṣads (Sarvepalli Radhakrishnan, ed. and trans., *The Principal Upaniṣads* [London: George Allen and Unwin, 1969]), with minor changes to eliminate archaic diction and occasionally to clarify.

12. G. S. Kirk, J. E. Raven, and M. Schofield, *The Presocratic Philosophers: A Critical History with a Selection of Texts*, 2nd ed. (Cambridge: Cambridge University Press, 1983), p. 101.

13. Pritchard, *Ancient Near Eastern Texts*, p. 5.

14. Edgerton, *The Beginnings of Indian Philosophy*, p. 52.

15. A different etymology derives it not from *peras* ("limit"), but *perao* ("traverse"): untraversable. See C. H. Kahn, *Anaximander and the Origins of Greek Cosmology* (New York: Columbia University Press, 1960), pp. 231–233; Jonathon Barnes, *The Presocratic Philosophers* (London and New York: Routledge, 1982), p. 36.

16. Hermann Oldenberg, *The Religion of the Veda*, trans. Shridhar B. Shroti (Delhi: Motilal Banarsidass, 1988), p. 105.

17. Ibid., pp. 121, 38.

18. For Frame and Cosmic Pillar see Sukumari Bhattacharjee, *Literature in the Vedic Age*, vol. 1, *The Saṁhitās*, Bagchi Indological Series 3 (Calcutta: K. P. Bagchi and Company, 1984), pp. 303, 312.

19. Ibid.

20. Trans. Paul Deussen, *The Philosophy of the Upaniṣads* (New York: Dover Publications, 1966), p. 404.

21. See M. L. West, *Early Greek Philosophy and the Orient* (Oxford: Clarendon Press, 1971), ch. 3.

22. A. N. Marlow, "Hinduism and Buddhism in Greek Philosophy," *Philosophy East and West* 4 (1954): 37–38.

23. West, *Early Greek Philosophy and the Orient*, p. 201.

24. It is also expounded in the *Śatapatha Brāhmaṇa* (XI.6.1.6–10) and the *Jaiminīya Brāhmaṇa* (I.45–46). Tull points out the closeness of these texts to the *Bṛhadāraṇyaka* and *Chāndogya Upaniṣads*. These four massively important texts belonged to the same substream of the already complex tradition—a stream which somehow contacted Heraclitus through another of its texts. See Herman W. Tull, *The Vedic Origins of Karma: Cosmos as Man in Ancient Indian Myth and Ritual*, SUNY series in Hindu Studies (Albany, New York: State University of New York Press, 1989), p. 135–136, n. 120.

25. Deussen, *Philosophy of the Upaniṣads*, p. 328.

26. William K. Mahoney, *The Artful Universe: An Introduction to the Vedic Religious Imagination*, SUNY series in Hindu Studies (Albany, New York: State University of New York Press, 1998), p. 120.

27. Ibid., p. 150.

28. Tull, *The Vedic Origins of Karma*, p. 35

29. Oldenberg, *The Religion of the Veda*, p. 314.

30. Mahoney, *The Artful Universe*, p. 161.

31. For translation see ibid.

32. Ibid., p. 142, 144, 145.

33. Ibid.

34. Ibid., p. 148.

35. As a result, it involves shared themes such as the theme of fire, where there are numerous parallels. In one curious detail, for example, Vedic texts about Agni repeatedly mention his movement, which parallels Heraclitus's fragment 60, "The way up and down is one and the same." "Agni . . . moves in both directions through the three regions of the Vedic universe," says a modern scholar. "He comes down, and he goes up." "Ṛg Veda 7.7.2 . . . mentions Agni's descent from the heavens, and 10.98.11 . . . notes his ascent into the divine heights" (ibid., p. 264, n. 77).

36. Barnes, *The Presocratic Philosophers*, p. 61.

37. Kirk, Raven, and Schofield, *The Presocratic Philosophers*, p. 221.

38. See appendix D.

39. For example, Burkert, *Lore and Science in Ancient Pythagoreanism*, pp. 197–198, 205–206, 215–217.

40. For example, West, *Early Greek Philosophy and the Orient*, pp. 216–217; West does not, however, give him much.

41. Translated after W. D. Ross, *Basic Works of Aristotle*, ed. Richard McKeon (New York: Random House, 1941).

42. Burkert, *Lore and Science in Ancient Pythagoreanism*, p. 349.

43. See Ernest G. McClain, *The Myth of Invariance: The Origins of the Gods, Mathematics and Music from the Ṛg Veda to Plato* (New York: Nicolas Hays Ltd., 1976), p. 111.

44. Ibid., p. 340.

45. Trans. Ross, *Basic Works of Aristotle.*

46. Edward A. Maziarz and Thomas Greenwood, *Greek Mathematical Philosophy* (New York: Frederick Ungar Publishing Co., 1968), p. 13.

47. Burkert, *Lore and Science in Ancient Pythagoreanism*, p. 301.

48. There is a disagreement among scholars as to whether Xenophanes should be understood as a monist or a monotheist. The fragments would serve either view with modest adjustments, and the ancient testimonia are mixed. On record as believing that Xenophanes was a monist, and that his work was the beginning of the Eleatic tradition of philosophical monism, were Plato, Aristotle, Theophrastus, Simplicius, Cicero, Pseudo-Galen, and the *Melissus, Xenophanes, Gorgias*; but Plato's remark may not have been serious ("jesting," Barnes calls it), and "the doxographers slavishly follow their master" (Barnes, *The Presocratic Philosophers*, p. 84; and see Schofield, in Kirk, Raven, and Schofield, *The Presocratic Philosophers*, p. 165). On the other side are Hippolytus, Simplicius, Cicero, Pseudo-Galen, and the *Melissus, Xenophanes, Gorgias*—the last four on different interpretations than for the monistic thesis. (It seems a rather gross overstatement by Barnes to say, "The doxographical tradition generally makes Xenophanes a monotheist" [*The Presocratic Philosophers*, p. 89]).

In terms of modern scholars the issue seems generational. Scholars of a somewhat earlier generation tend to regard him as a monist; Zeller, for example, says, "The basic idea of this philosophy was the unity of everything, that is of the All-One. . . . This All-One . . . is not beyond the world but organically inseparable from it" (Eduard Zeller, *Outlines of the History of Greek Philosophy*, 13th ed. [New York: Dover, 1980], p. 58). Armstrong agreed to the extent of saying that Xenophanes "preached a sort of pan-animism . . . an immanent all-pervading world-soul" (A. H. Armstrong, *An Introduction to Ancient Philosophy* [n.c.: Littlefield: Adams and Company, 1983], p. 12). More recent scholarly books show the other tendency. Barnes argues intently and at length that "Xenophanes . . . was a monotheist" (Barnes, *The Presocratic Philosophers*, p. 92, and see p. 602, n. 6). Yet toward the end of his treatment of the issue Barnes seems to shift position, twice referring as if credulously to Xenophanes' "pantheism" (p. 99). Pantheism is a form of monism, usually regarded as the early, still-residually-mythological form, which would be right in line with Aristotle's description of Xenophanes as (to use Schofield's term) "a primitive Eleatic." Schofield, though less certain than Barnes, seems to lean in the same direction; Aristotle, he says, "clearly implies that [in Xenophanes' system] god is identical with the world . . . but Aristotle must be wrong here . . . Aristotle, by treating him as a primitive Eleatic, misled the whole ancient tradition on this point." He proceeds to agree with Aristotle's complaint that Xenophanes "made nothing clear," conjecturing that "Xenophanes did not produce a discursive elaboration of his theological views, which might not, indeed, have gone very far beyond the extant fragments on the subject" (in Kirk, Raven, Schofield, *The Presocratic Philosophers*, pp. 171–172). Aristotle, on this account, knew no more about it than we do, and simply chose one plausible interpretation—but not the only one—and followed it. In deference to the testimonia of Plato, Aristotle, and Theophrastus, the monistic aspect of Xenophanes' thought will be emphasized here.

49. The text literally says "looking at the whole heaven, or sky (*ouranos*)"; I have followed Schofield's translation "the whole world" (Kirk, Raven, Schofield, *The Presocratic Philosophers*, p. 172).

50. Ibid., p. 170.

51. I have changed Radhakrishnan's "he" to "it."

52. Barnes's caveat should be borne in mind: "Xenophanes is often thought to have influenced Parmenides; but the opposite influence is chronologically possible" (*The Presocratic Philosophers*, p. 83).

53. The passages are gathered at W. K. C. Guthrie, *A History of Greek Philosophy*, vol. 1 (Cambridge: Cambridge University Press, 1962–1981), pp. 367–77.

54. More than one ancient source interprets Xenophanes as a Milesian-style material monist rounding out the list of the four elements. On their view, Xenophanes was saying that "Everything is made of earth," or, alternatively, "Everything comes from the earth," with an intentionality like the Milesian. Yet Aristotle observed, in discussing material monism, that although water, air, and fire had been proposed as material substrates, earth had not been (*Met.* 989a5). He could hardly have been unaware of Xenophanes' poem; but he must have chosen the second of the two translations given just above.

Other ancients clearly believed that Xenophanes had proposed the earth as material substrate in the familiar Milesian sense. A fragment of Xenophanes' own poetry speaks of earth as Anaximander had spoken of the Infinite: "From earth come all things, and all things end in earth" (fr. 27). Alongside this is the apparent contradiction that, unlike the Milesians, Xenophanes denied coming-into-being and passing-away (frs. A32, 33, 36). One ancient commentator (fr. A36) said simply that Xenophanes "forgot" the one statement when he made the other. Modern "solutions" have not been much more convincing. But the Upanisadic parallel, with its implication that Xenophanes is intentionally describing two aspects of one being, makes sense of the discussion.

55. The account in Plato's *Parmenides* suggests about 515–445 B.C., but is not widely credited. Schofield inclines toward it, however, in Kirk, Raven, and Schofield, *The Presocratic Philosophers*, p. 240.

56. Barnes rejects the monism of Parmenides, as he did with Xenophanes. "I incline to believe that Parmenides' poem was not monistic. . . . I suspect that Parmenides was not a monist. . . . Real monism was an invention of Melissos" (*The Presocratic Philosophers*, pp. 206–207). Parts of fragment 8 (ll. 1–6, 25) seem to assert monism—though with less than all possible clarity—and what's more, Aristotle said, "he thinks that what is is one and there is nothing else" (*Met* 986b29 = DK 28A24). But Barnes feels that Aristotle here overstates his interpretation of certain Parmenidean lines.

57. The following paraphrase is based on Aristotle *Phys.* 191a27 and Simplicius *In Phys.* 78.24.

58. Barnes, *The Presocratic Philosophers*, p. 176.

59. Giorgio de Santillana, *Prologue to Parmenides* (Cincinnati, Ohio: University of Cincinnati, 1964), p. 44.

60. Ibid., p. 7.

61. R. D. Ranada, "Presocratics," in *History of Philosophy: Eastern and Western*, vol. 2, ed. Sarvepalli Radhakrishnan (London: George Allen and Unwin, 1952–1953), p. 37.

62. Trans. Heinrich Zimmer, *Myths and Symbols in Indian Art and Civilization* (New York: Harper and Row, 1962), p. 212.

63. Arthur Avalon, pseud. (Sir John G. Woodroffe), trans., *Hymn to Kālī* (Madras: Ganesh and Co., 1965), p. 78.

64. This passage has been compared to Parmenides before, by J. Fritz Staal, "Parmenides and Indian Thought," *Philosophical Quarterly* (India) 28, no. 2 (1955): 81–106.

65. Ranada, "Presocratics," p. 37.

66. John Burnet, *Early Greek Philosophy* (Cleveland and New York: World Publishing Company, 1964), pp. 44, n. 2; 51.

67. There is no reason to regard it as "undoubted fact" (Kirk and Raven, *The Presocratic Philosophers*, p. 80). Against the eclipse: Otto Neugebauer, *The Exact Sciences in Antiquity* (Providence, Rhode Island: Brown University Press, 1957), p. 142; Huxley, *The Interaction of Greek and Babylonian Astronomy*, p. 5.

68. At *CU* VI.14.1–2 Uddālaka shows awareness of the Gandhārans; in the Buddhist *Uddālaka Jātaka* (*Jātaka* VI.298) he is said to have been educated in Taxila.

69. Surendranathi Dasgupta, *A History of Indian Philosphy* (Delhi: Motilal Banarsidass, 1975), vol. 1, p. 28.

70. Ibid., p. 39.

71. See R. Gordon Wasson, *Soma: Divine Mushroom of Immortality* (n.c.: Harcourt, Brace, Jovanovich, n.d.), pp. 13–14.

Chapter Three

The Cosmic Cycle

Empedocles was a late pre-Socratic, a mid-fifth-century thinker whose career seems to have taken place after the Persian Wars and to have overlapped those of Parmenides and Democritus. His maturity seems to have been roughly 470–430 B.C.[1] But though a late pre-Socratic, he has come down in the biographical and doxographical records as in some ways the most primitive of them, a wonder-worker like the Seven Sophoi, for whom flying on an arrow or riding on the wind might not have seemed unlikely. He may have deliberately conformed himself to a typology based on religious lore or may have had such a type projected on him by later writers such as Heraclides Ponticus, a learned but somewhat uncritical author of the fourth century B.C. who preserved the fantastic story of his death by voluntarily descending into the live volcano of Mount Aetna (Heraclides *ap.* D.L. VIII.67–68, 71–72). The story was understandably popular, and after the second century B.C. it displaced all other accounts of Empedocles' death. In addition to the sensationalism of the demographic record, the fragments of Empedocles' poems contain claims of special abilities at healing and the control of natural forces, so he himself seems to have participated in the mythologizing of his own career.

A member of an aristocratic family of Acragas in Sicily (D.L. VIII.51–52), Empedocles, like Parmenides, was involved in the Orphic and Pythagorean tendencies of that part of the Greek world. Perhaps he was influenced by wandering Orphic wonder-workers. In any case, of all the pre-Socratics he has been reported as the most perfect example of the cultural transition from shamanic to philosophical activities. In this respect, the tradition about him was close to those about some of the early philosophers of India whose activity was understood as belonging within a religious milieu of asceticism and wonder-working. He is credited in late sources with accomplishments such as controlling the wind (D.L. VIII.60), raising the dead and, like Orpheus, soothing violent passions by playing the lyre (Iambl., *Vit. Pyth.* 113). Heraclides Ponticus relates that Empedocles revived a woman who had been in a trance without pulse or respiration for thirty days (D.L. VIII.60–61, 67). According to Diodorus of Ephesus (D.L. VIII.70) he modeled his public persona on that of Anaximander, affecting a "theatrical arrogance," wearing stately robes (gold with purple ribbons) like a priest, bronze shoes, and a wreath of laurel like a newly crowned victor at Apollo's games. When the citizens met him in the streets he looked like a king (D.L. VIII.69–70, 72). Still, like Heraclitus (D.L. IX.6) he is associated with the motif of the refusal of a kingship (D.L. VIII.63); when Acragan democracy was wobbling, he entered politics in some way, supposedly on the popular side despite his aristocratic background (D.L. VIII.64–66). A bronze statue, which Hippobotos saw in Agrigentum, portrayed him with his head mysteriously covered.

It is remarkable that such a flamboyant personality should, in addition to acting out a spectacular personal drama, produce philosophical thought both rigorous and orderly. Empedocles wrote two such works, both in heroic hexameters. In one, called *Purifications* (*Katharmoi*), he purveyed, under Orphic and Pythagorean influence, a doctrine of reincarnation, purification, and release. In the other, called, as Parmenides' poem may have been, *On Nature* (*Peri Physeos*), he wrote under pressure of the Eleatic *elenchus*, attempting to mediate between Parmenides' Ways of Truth and Deception—that is, between the rigorous logical conception of the One and the common sense or ordinary-consciousness experience of the Many. In the *Purifications* he speaks as a cultist or prophet, but in the poem *On Nature* he speaks from outside the cultic stance, addressing broader questions of philosophy. The two texts have often been viewed as contradictory, perhaps as representing different stages of the author's life.[2]

In his role as natural philosopher, Empedocles proposed a solution to the Eleatic impasse, introducing two mediating devices to join the realms of the One and the Many. First, the One and the Many were separated and mediated metaphysically by the interposition between them of a realm that might be called the Few. This structure—One, Few, Many—would reappear in Plato's Theory of Ideas. In Empedocles' system the Few were four substances that have come to be known as the Four Elements (so the structure One-Few-Many is, in actual embodiment, One-Four-Many, echoing the Near Eastern Bronze Age emphasis on cosmic quaternity). Secondly, the One and the Many were separated temporally and declared to be not different realities but recurring phases of a single cyclical process. They do not function as two poles of a paradox, for they do not exist at the same time. Each has a time of dominance, then retreats as the dominance of the other returns. This process will be considered in the present chapter; the four elements will be discussed in a later one.

Empedocles' system of cyclical time is based on quaternity, as is the material or spatial system of four elements. The cosmos is said to evolve through four stages which are repeated infinitely, as the hand of a clock circles continually through the four compass points. In the Age of Love, or of the One, Love melts all things together into an undifferentiated unity which, not unlike the Being of Parmenides, is called the Sphere. In mythological terms, this is a Golden Age, an age before strife and separate ego-identities. In the following age, the counterforce—Hate, or Strife, or Separation—gradually disrupts this unity, separating things out into different forms. The next or third age is the Age of Hate proper, the opposite of the Age of Love; the unifying force of Love has been driven altogether from sight and the universe is a hell of Hate and Strife. In the fourth age, the force of Love reappears and gradually expands again as Strife gradually recedes, restoring unity for a new Age of Love.[3]

The General Parallelism

Close parallels to this model are common in the Indian traditions. The Hindu, Jain, and Buddhist views of time are all cyclical. The Buddhist version set forth in the *Abhidharmakośa* is the closest to Empedocles' in its general outlines.[4] It reproduces very closely his system of four ages in which the pure presence of each of two states (Love and

Hate, or Being and non-Being) alternates with two transitional periods. Each of these periods is designated as one *kalpa* long, that is, an immeasurable length that is defined in Indian tradition primarily through similes or metaphors; much as in Empedocles' *On Nature*, the *kalpa* of the existence of the world (i.e., Empedocles' Age of Love) is followed by a *kalpa* of dissolution, then by a *kalpa* of Nothingness (Hate) then by a *kalpa* of refilling the nothingness with Being, then by the first *kalpa*, the fullness of Being, again. The Hindu view, as presented, for example, in the *Manavadharmaśastra*, arranges the four ages more as they appear in Hesiod, as a steady process of degeneration followed by a return to the beginning without any transitional phase. The One, or *brahman*, exists for an age in a state of complete Oneness or nonmanifestation, then produces from itself, or manifests, a world; this world goes through a series of four ages of degeneration, the first being a Golden Age, the last a period of hellish strife at the end of which the golden condition begins again. In this case the general parallel with Empedocles includes not only cyclicity, but also the structure of four ages punctuating a transition from Oneness to Manyness, and the value judgment which regards Oneness as a state of perfection and Manyness as a fall from it. The Jain model is again closer to Empedocles', showing degeneration occupying half the cycle and regeneration occupying the other half.[5]

This circular view of time is part of the shape of ancient thought and one of the major differences between ancient and modern attitudes. Most Indian and Greek philosophers taught such a view. In the early stages of the Greek tradition, versions of it are either found in the works of or attributed to Hesiod, Pythagoras, Anaximander, Anaximenes, Heraclitus, Diogenes of Apollonia, Xenophanes, and Plato—not to mention later schools like the Stoics. In India, it was the standard view of Hindu, Buddhist, and Jain philosophers. It was the most widespread, indeed the normal or ordinary, view of time among ancient philosophers in both Greece and India.

Judeo-Christian-Islamic tradition has featured a linear view of time: While the seasonal cyclicity of the fertility calendar is echoed in the recurrence of holy days, time overall is conceived as a straight-line segment which began at a certain time (Creation) and will end at a certain time (the Last Judgment). This view of time seems to have originated with Zoroaster and has since come to dominate the three western religions whose view of time grew essentially from Zoroastrian origins: Judaism, Christianity, and Islam. In the secularized West, a linear view still holds—usually as an expression of the idea of ongoing scientific progress—but without clear enunciation of its beginning and end.

Most cultures have held the view that time is better described by a circling or spiralling line in which the repetition of some events is emphasized rather than the difference of others. In Greece, for example, both the Orphics and Empedocles (fr. 26) and in India both the Buddhists and Jains described time as a revolving wheel. Such a view may posit many creations and last judgments, within many world-ages, each occupying one revolution of the wheel. The custom of world-renewing rituals around the time of the winter solstice, familiar in many ancient cultures, including those of the ancient Near East, seems to have undergone, at some uncertain time, a macrocosmic expansion into a conviction that there is also, in the nature of things, a Great Year which circles through its own seasons, ends, and is renewed; this Great Year was the lifespan of a world or world-age, usually marked, near its ending, by cataclysmic events not unlike the death of fertility in winter or, in hot climates, in the heat of the summer. The end of the world-age was often viewed, on analogy with these agricultural events, as either occurring in wintry inundation or in summery fire. It is uncertain when this expansion of the concept "year" into the concept "Great Year" occurred, but it must have been deeply influenced by astronomy, and the numbers that are commonly involved may point to ancient Sumer and beyond. In any case, it either diffused widely or sprang up in many different places, since it has appeared in Greece, India, Mesopotamia, Iceland, and elsewhere.

Reviewing the Traditions

In both Greece and India it is difficult to ascertain the origin of this idea—suggesting that perhaps it did not originate in either place. In India, attempts to trace it inevitably look back to the *Ṛg Veda.* There it seems to be intimated in a mysterious and difficult hymn (I.164) called the "Creation Hymn," attributed to a semilegendary blind poet Dīrghatamas, whose name seems to mean "vision in long darkness." Some scholars have disregarded this hymn, feeling that it is unintelligible; others have made it the mainstay of their interpretations of Vedic cosmology. It contains what may be the earliest known passages of wheel symbolism:

> Formed with twelve spokes, by length of time awakened, rolls round the heaven this wheel of during Order.
>
> Herein established, joined in pairs together, seven hundred Sons and twenty stand. (I.164.11)

The twelve-spoked wheel has commonly been interpreted as representing the year of twelve lunar months and 360 days (12 × 30); the 720 sons may then be 360 days plus 360 nights.[6] This interpretation goes back to the Middle Vedic period, when the *Aitareya Āraṇyaka* (III.2.1.4) establishes a correspondence between the numerologies of the human body and the lunar calendar: "Of bones, marrow, and joints there are 360 (parts) on (the right) side and 360 (parts) on (the left) side. They make 720 together, and 720 are the days and nights of the year."[7]

Another *Ṛg Vedic* hymn expresses a related idea:

> He (Viṣṇu) like a rounded wheel, hath in swift motion
> Set his ninety racing steeds together with the four.
> (I.155.6)

The passage may refer to four seasons of ninety days each—though six is more common as the tally of seasons in ancient India. In any case, these passages emphasize the circular nature of time as embodied in the ordinary year; they say nothing yet of a Great Year. This is first hinted in the *Atharva Veda*:

> When between heaven and earth Fire went burning, all consuming, in the place where the monogamous women stood afar, where was Mātariśvan then? Mātariśvan had entered into the waters; the gods had entered into the seas . . . (*AV* X.8.39–40)[8]

The passage is mysterious, but clearly there is a suggestion of a world-destruction by fire, followed by the dissolution of all beings into the primal ocean whence a renewed world would eventually be born. This suggestion is not certain, however, for if the doctrine of the periodic destruction and renewal of the universe existed in the *Atharva Veda*, it would be expected in the early Upaniṣads also, and it is not found there. A related doctrine—that the universe proceeds from and later returns to the state of Oneness—is first found in the *Śvetāśvatara Upaniṣad*, which is dated to about 200 B.C.:

> He, the protector, after creating all worlds, withdraws them at the end of time . . . into him in the beginning and at the end of time the universe is gathered. (*SU* III.2, IV.1)[9]

It is not certain that the process is conceived here as recurring periodically, but this is implied by the word "again" in the following (slightly simplified) passage:

> That God, after spreading out his nets, then gathering them in, having again created the gods, exercises lordship over them. (*SU* V.3)

Absolutely clear statements of the Great Year myth are not found until the so-called Epic period. The main loci include the *Manu Smṛti* or *Manavadharmaśastra*, or the *Laws of Manu*, a compilation of Hindu lore which arose piecemeal between about 300 B.C. and 300 A.D., and the massive epic *Mahābhārata*, the *Great Bhārata War*, which developed over a period from perhaps 400 B.C. to 400 A.D. In these texts the version involving four ages (*yugas*) successively declining in both duration and quality of life is found. When the shortest and worst age ends, the longest and best begins again. When the cycle has taken place a thousand times, a yet bigger cycle is completed, a yet Greater Year called the *kalpa*; the world process then is retracted into complete Oneness and nonmanifestation for the length of another *kalpa*, whereupon it starts up again. This rather complex myth, furnished with an elaborate numerology, appears in the Epic age with only the scantiest hints of a myth of cycling time prior to it, as the Buddhist and Jain versions are attested in later texts.

The Jain version is not divided into four but into twelve stages. There, as in the Dīrghatamas hymn of the *Ṛg Veda*, time is presented as a wheel of twelve spokes, presumably months of the Great Year. As in Empedocles' version, life gets steadily worse for the first half of the cycle—for the first six spokes or ages—then gets steadily better for the second half, then starts declining again. (This structure is echoed again in the cycle myth of Plato's *Politicus*.)

In early Buddhist texts, as in the Hindu versions, the Great Year is divided into four degenerating ages; in later Buddhist texts it is subdivided in different ways: into three, six, seven or nine ages. The image of the six or twelve-spoked wheel occurs commonly in connection with the doctrine of reincarnation. Overall, the Indian evidence does not constitute a continuum of development; on the contrary, there are great gaps in the developmental process (as far as it is visible) that offer room for external input.

In Greece, evidences of the Great Year are found in various forms, including the image of the circle—but the circle can also refer to the solar year. "Time itself," said Aristotle, "is thought to be a circle" (*Phys.* 223b28), and it is uncertain what he means. For Hermippus, an older contemporary of Aristophanes, it clearly meant the solar year:

> He is round to look at, and revolves in a circle, containing all things in himself; and as he runs round the whole earth he brings us humans to birth. His name is Year (*Eniautos*); being round he has neither beginning nor end and will never stop wheeling his body around all day every day.

The circle image leads easily to the wheel. The Orphics, for example, symbolized time as a wheel, used wheels in rituals, and hoped to escape from the wheel of time. "I have flown out of the sorrowful weary wheel," says an Orphic grave inscription. The wheel may have signified not merely rebirth but also the endless cycling of worlds; the symbolism is echoed by Empedocles, a deeply Orphic author, who referred to the cycling of the ages of Love and Hate as a "turning wheel" (fr. 26).

A more detailed myth of cycling ages is found in Hesiod's *Works and Days*, about 700 B.C. There (109 ff.) the poet described a system of four ages in which the quality of life steadily deteriorates. First,

> A golden race of humans . . . lived in the time of Cronos . . . and they lived like gods without sorrow of heart, remote and free from toil and grief . . . the fruitful earth unforced bare them fruit abundantly and without stint.

This Edenic age corresponds to the first age, or *kṛta yuga,* in the Hindu version, in which, Manu says, people "are free from disease, accomplish all their aims, and live four hundred years" (*MS* I.85). After the Golden Age, according to Hesiod, came a second race, called "silver," which initiated wrongdoing, and a third, called "bronze," which "loved the lamentable works of Ares and deeds of violence" (*Erga*, 145–146). Finally an "Age of Iron," which is the present age—as in the Hindu myth the present age is the last, or worst—in which humans have no rest from sorrow and labor, and life is not worth living. That Hesiod is describing a cyclical process which he expects to recur is indicated when he says: "Would that I either had died before (the Iron Age) or been born after it." Since the Iron Age is the last age, to be born after it would presumably mean to be born at the beginning of a new cycle.

The general outline of Hesiod's version is like that of the Hindu myth of the four *yugas*—sufficiently like it, in fact, to promote curiosity about the possibilities of a common ancestry. It seems likely that this myth of ages was imported into Greece, rather than natively developed, because of an alteration Hesiod makes in it. After discussing the third, or Bronze Age, Hesiod deviates from the pattern of deteriorating ages with names of metals and inserts an "Age of Heroes" that does not fit the pattern. This age provides a space which can accommodate the native chronology of the heroic expeditions against Troy and Thebes. These events were not regarded as so long ago as to fit into the Golden Age; yet their world is like a recreation of the Golden Age and could not fit into the Bronze or Iron:

> Happy heroes for whom the grain-giving earth bears honey-sweet fruit flourishing thrice a year . . . and Cronos rules over them.

This account does not fit the context and is an interpolation. Hesiod has taken the four-age structure from somewhere else and inserted into it the Greek tradition of the Age of Heroes.

Among the earliest of the Greek philosophers, as in Hesiod, we find evidence for the myth of cyclical time. Either Pythagoras or his school after him held an extreme form of the doctrine. "He held," says Porphyry in his *Life of Pythagoras* (19), "that past events repeat themselves in a cyclic process and nothing is new in an absolute sense." That the repetition of events was meant to be complete and exact is attested by Aristotle's pupil Eudemus: "If one may believe the Pythagoreans, the same things will recur exactly, and I shall be holding my pointer and talking to you as you sit there, and everything else will be exactly as it is now . . ." (*Phys.* fr. 27 = DK 58B34). The idea of exact repetition was later adopted and developed by the Stoics.

About Thales' view of time we have no information. But the late doxographer Aëtius says of Anaximander:

> Innumerable worlds are both brought to birth and again dissolved into that out of which they came. (Fr. A14)

The question whether these worlds appear successively or simultaneously may be answered by Cicero, who says:

> It is Anaximander's opinion that the gods are born at long intervals of rising and setting and that they are innumerable worlds. (*De Nat. Deor.* I.25)

This idea too was common in both Greece and India. Hindu texts tell of innumerable Indras, or gods, conceived as world-systems. Plutarch remarks that Anaximander's worlds rise from the Infinite "in endless cycling." Anaximander himself wrote that things rise and fall "according to the arrangement of Time." Anaximander also believed that the world was progressively being dried up by the sun (fr. A27), which implies something like Aristotle's concept of the Great Year, which cycles through a Great Summer of extreme drought and a Great Winter of rain and flood (*Meteor.* A143, 352a17). Similar views were held by Xenophanes, and by Democritus, who said that when the sea dried up the world would end. Both Plato and the late Babylonian author Berossus expressed the view that the world would end in drought in the Great Summer of the Great Year and in flood in the Great Winter. This view may have been widely spread among Eastern-influenced Greeks as early as Anaximander and Xenophanes; it was believed that the cycle at that time was approaching the summer solstice of the Great Year. That the other Ionian thinkers held a similar view is indicated by Aristotle:

> Those who say that the world exists forever do not mean the same world forever, but that one world follows after another at certain intervals of time—as Anaximenes said, and Heraclitus, and Diogenes [of Apollonia]. (*Phys.* 1121.12 = DK 13A11)

According to Theophrastus and the Stoics, Heraclitus taught a doctrine of *ekpyrōsis*—the periodic destruction of the world by fire—and later authors (Aëtius and Censorinus) attribute to him an astronomically determined Great Year.[10] Aristotle also seems to implicitly attribute this view to Heraclitus, when he criticizes him for saying that all things will become fire *at the same time* (*Phys.* 204b35). Diogenes Laertius says that Heraclitus thought that:

> Of the opposites, that which tends to birth or creation is called war and strife, and that which tends to destruction by fire is called peace and concord. (D.L. IX.8)

If the attribution is correct, then this teaching of Heraclitus may lie behind Empedocles' system, in which Strife begins the process of change (birth) and Love brings it to a halt. In Heraclitus's system this doctrine relates to the doctrine of the transformation of the elements, particularly the stages in which the substance undergoing the process becomes sea and fire. A simple version of the same idea was taught by Xenophanes (fr. A33):

> A mingling of earth with sea takes place and in course of time the earth is dissolved into the wet element. All people are destroyed when the earth is carried down into the sea and turns to mud—then a new generation begins.

Alternating periods of extreme dryness (the summer of the Great Year) and extreme wetness (the winter of the Great Year), with partial destructions of the universe at one or both extremes, are implied fragmentarily.

Plato presents several versions of the idea: an astronomical version in the *Timaeus* (39d) involving a universal conjunction among the eight planets; another in the *Politicus*

(269c ff.), which, like the Jain myth of six descending and six ascending stages, involves a periodic reversal of fortunes, which deteriorate for an age, then improve for an age, only to deteriorate again, and so on. Aristotle also seems to have taught some version of the Great Year, since in the *Meteorology* (352a30) he refers to a "great period of time (in which) there is a Great Winter and excess of rains." In many of these references it is not the ultimate destruction of the universe that is referred to but either a partial destruction (of all or most humans, usually) or a general reversal of some kind. Others, like Anaximander, Anaximenes, and probably Heraclitus, taught the destruction of the universe of form into some unified matrix, such as water or fire, and its reconstitution or rebirth out of that element at some subsequent time.

Hindu tradition used similar imagery for the destruction. Often the universe is said to dissolve into the ocean, as it does in Xenophanes' version, or to be turned into fire, as in Heraclitus's. The fire-of-universal-destruction (*vaiśvānara-agni*) is an aspect of Śīva, and relates to the parching summer of the Great Year; the Ocean of Creation, into which the world dissolves and from which it is born again, is an aspect of Viṣṇu and relates to the rainy winter of the Great Year. This Hindu version of the myth is most fully paralleled in the Greek tradition by the version of the Stoics, who borrowed from various earlier sources. On this model, the world is periodically destroyed by fire, after which Zeus absorbs it into himself for long periods of quiescence, like the *kalpa* of stillness after the *kalpa* of process in the Hindu myth.

The Sumerian Background

The myth of cycling time is found in closely related forms throughout the classical texts of both Greece and India. In neither tradition is there strong sequential evidence for native development of the doctrine. There is, however, strong evidence which points toward a more ancient common source from which both these cultures might have inherited the doctrine. This evidence consists of numbers. It begins with the fact that the numbers with which the cosmic cycle was defined in both these cultures were not native numbers—which in both cases were decimal—but an imported sexagesimal system.

In sexagesimal arithmetic the number 60 takes on the functions performed in decimal arithmetic by the number 10. Thus the second place to the left of the sexagesimal point represents units of 60^1, the next place to the left 60^2, and so on; in one modern notation,[11] 60 is written 1,0. Then 120 = 2,0; 3,600 (60^2) = 1,0,0; etc. In this system the world will tend to organize itself in units involving 60 or factors of 60 or products of 60. The sexagesimal arithmetic had appeared in Sumer by around 3000 B.C. and left its marks on later cultures. In the system for measuring time, which is currently in more or less global use, sixty-minute hours, sixty-second minutes, and other related notions, are sexagesimal in origin, as are spatial conventions such as the 360 degrees of the circle or compass. The traditional or ancient system for measuring everyday time in India is also sexagesimal, though different in one major detail from the western style. Instead of twenty-four sixty-minute hours, the system recognizes thirty "hours" (*muhūrtas*) of thirty longer "minutes" (*lavas*) each about one and a half western minutes. Thus, the whole system involves sexagesimal numbers; the one step in which the western system lacks it, the 24, is eliminated.[12]

Important "round" numbers in the sexagesimal system include the base of 60; its square, 3,600 (60^2), which the Sumerians called *sar* or universe; and its fourth power,

12,960,000 ($3,600^2$ or 60^4), which has been called "The greatest sacred number in Babylonia . . . the *sar* squared."[13]

This system was founded, Neugebauer says, on a "decimal substrate"; the decimal system, in other words, had been invented first, and interacted with the emerging sexagesimality. Thus we find sexagesimal units like 30 or 60 interacting with decimal units such as 5 or 10. Sixty twice, for example, is 120, which times ten is 1,200, a common number in the texts that flow from this tradition. Six gets special prominence as the decimal reduction of 60; from this interplay arise 36 (6 × 6) and 360 (6 × 60), which also have other connections with the system: 360 × 12 = 4,320, and so on. These numbers interact with calendrical units:

60 / 5 (days in Babylonian week) = 12 (months—lunations—in a year)
12 × 6 (decimal contraction of 60) = 72 (weeks in a Babylonian year)
5 × 72 = 360 (days in a Babylonian year)
6 × 72 = 432 (a common round number in the tradition)

The Babylonian calendar (and to a lesser extent those based on it, such as the one in present use in the western world) has the sexagesimal numbers woven into it, as if they were the ritually right numbers for this all-important cultic device on which the year-long liturgy was based.

At this point in surveying the state of the evidence, it seems that the key fact about the origin of the myth of the Great Year is that in both the Greek and the Indian traditions, when a Great Year is defined by numbers, these numbers are from the sexagesimal arithmetic. Censorinus, for example, says that Heraclitus' Great Year consisted of 10,800 solar years; 10,800 = 30 (half the sexagesimal unit) × 360, or 3 × 3,600 (the *sar*). This yields a Great Year in which each of the 360 days consists of one human generation (30 years). Aëtius, on the other hand, says Heraclitus's Great Year consisted of 18,000 solar years, which equals 50 × 360, or 5 × 3,600 (the *sar*), a factoring that echoes the mingling of decimal and sexagesimal systems in the Mesopotamian mathematical tradition. Similarly, Plato, in the passage called the "Muses' Jest" (*Rep.* VIII.546bc) presents, in an enigmatic code, a pair of numbers which relate the human gestation period to the Great Year of the universe. A fairly broad consensus supports the solution presented early in the twentieth century by Adam,[14] that the first of these numbers is 216 and the second 12,960,000. The number 216 is 6 × 36, or half of 432, a frequent number in Mesopotamian arithmetic (i.e., 6 × 72 [which = 6 × 12], or 12 × 36, and so on). The figure 12,960,000 is the *sar* squared ($3,600^2$). The numbers are linked in several ways; for example, 30 (half the sexagesimal unit) × 432 = 12,960, and 12 × 360 = 4,320.

The same pattern is found in the Indian tradition. In the myth of cycling time presented by Manu, for example—which is the classic Hindu version[15]—the numbers are consistently sexagesimal. The four ages consist of 1, 2, 3, and 4 units of 432,000 years each:

	Years of the Gods (360 solar years each)		Human Years (solar years)	
Krita age	4,800	(× 360 =)	1,728,000	(4 × 432,000)
Tretā age	3,600	(× 360 =)	1,296,000	(3 × 432,000)
Dvapara age	2,400	(× 360 =)	864,000	(2 × 432,000)
Kāli age	1,200	(× 360 =)	432,000	(1 × 432,000)
Totals:	12,000	(× 360 =)	4,320,000	(10 × 432,000)

The basic units are 12 and 432, which are linked by the factor 36, a decimal contraction of the *sar*: 12 × 36 = 432. The *sar* itself occurs, as does a decimal cousin of the "greatest sacred number in Babylonia," 12,960,000. Other cycles in Hindu mythology occupy 3,600 years and 216,000 years. These numbers go back to the same source that Heraclitus's and Plato's numbers came from.

Furthermore, Greece and India are not the only places where these numbers are found in connection with myths of time. They constitute a secret set of numbers that infiltrated the myths of the world at some early period, usually in connection with the themes of cosmic ages and their cycles. The Babylonian priest Berossus—who lived in the third century B.C. and is said to have been the last priest of Marduk, the god of the Old Babylonians—presented a chronology in which 432,000 years elapsed between the descent of kingship from the gods and the great flood—that is, between a world-beginning and a world-destruction.[16] Other examples of the decimal-sexagesimal mix include Berossus's list of ten kings whose reigns totaled 432,000 and the Hindu Great Year, which is made up of 10 units of 432,000. Berossus gives the first extant explicit definition of the Great Year: It lasts 432,000 human years and ends in fire when all the planets are conjunct in Capricorn (an astronomical definition of the Great Winter).

The key fact is that Berossus's numerology seems not to have entered Mesopotamia in or near his period, but to have survived there from an age far earlier than it is attested anywhere else. Not only is the sexagesimal arithmetic a signature of Early Bronze Age Sumerian culture, but specific numbers recur. Many of Berossus's reign numbers from his list of ten kings duplicate reign numbers from the Sumerian king lists made more than two thousand years earlier. Both contain 36,000, 28,000, 64,800, and 43,200, all factors of the holy number 12,960,000. This number system, then, either originated in Sumerian culture or in some earlier and presently unknown setting from which it passed into Sumer. From Mesopotamia it evidently passed not only into Greece and India, but far and wide.

In the *Book of Genesis* a complex hidden code weaves these numbers into the text in a harmonization of the Sumerian and Hebrew myths of the flood. Ten patriarchs are said to have ruled between Adam and Noah (like the ten kings between the descent and the flood in Berossus's list); their reigns, however, total not 432,000 years but 1,656. In 1,656 years of 365 days (the year which the Jewish calendar used, which was derived from Egypt) there are 86,400 Jewish seven-day weeks and 86,400 is twice 43,200. Furthermore, if Berossus's 432,000 years are treated as each equivalent to a day (in a year of the gods), we find that in 432,000 days there are 86,400 Babylonian five-day weeks. At an occult level this numerology is an attempt to harmonize the two chronologies—Babylonian and Hebrew—of the period from the creation to the (first) flood: Each period equals, in a certain way, 86,400 weeks.

The two figures, 432,000 and 1,656, also share as factor the number 72, which leads in many related directions. For one thing, it is a common sexagesimal figure (6 × 12), and is also the number of five-day weeks in the Babylonian 360-day year. Further, 432,000 / 72 = 6,000, and 1,656 / 72 = 23. The number 6,000 is significant as a decimal expansion of the basic number 60 and as an expanded half-form of 1,200, the basic unit of the Hindu *yuga* system. The number 23 signifies in several ways. In 23 years of 365 days, for example, plus the five leap days involved, there are 8,400 days, which equal 1,200 seven-day weeks; 1,200 in turn, multiplied by 72, brings us back to 86,400, twice 43,200. The figures run around in circles, but their significance in a general way is clear: The authors of this passage of *Genesis* went to considerable trouble to conceal within their supposedly decimal chronology a group of sexagesimal figures that would, through a sort of numerical sympathetic magic, reconcile the Egyptian and Babylonian calendars and the Hebrew and Babylonian flood myths. The authors of *Genesis*, quite like Plato and Manu, seem to have received this tradition—by whatever diffusion route—ultimately from the religious centers of Egypt and Mesopotamia.

Farther afield, this subterranean tradition flowed out from the Near Eastern center both westward and eastward. The number 1,260 (60 × 21) occurs five times in prophetic passages in the *Book of Revelations*.[17] The Greek mathematician Claudius Ptolemy used the number 432,000 as the totality of the "Great circle" of the table of chords with which he calculated musical frequencies.[18] In the *Poetic Edda*, composed in Iceland between 800 and 1270 A.D. it is said that at the end of the world—when the world will dissolve into the sea (as it does also in Xenophanes and Hindu Vaiṣṇava myth)—800 warriors will go out to the final battle through each of the 540 doors of Odin's palace (800 × 540 = 432,000). The number 432 is also concealed repeatedly in the ratio-system of the sacred architecture of Angkor Wat in Cambodia (twelfth century A.D.).[19] And the traditional date for St. Patrick's mission to Ireland—ushering in the Christian age—is 432 A.D.

Many Hindu numbers involve 108 (i.e., 1/4 × 432) in various decimal expansions, e.g., the 10,800 stanzas in the *Ṛg Veda* and the 10,800 bricks in the Hindu fire altar. The numbers have multiple readings built into them. The number 108, for example, is 1/4 of 432; 10,800 = 30 × 360. The *Śatapatha Brāhmaṇa* (X.4.3.14–20) says the total number of "ordinary" (*lokamprna*) bricks in a soma sacrifice arrangement of altars is 10,800 and that the altars in such an arrangement are to be surrounded by 360 enclosing stones. To establish a cosmic correspondence, the *Śatapatha Brāhmaṇa* (X.4.4.2) also says that the stars in the sky are 10,800,000 (i.e., 1000 × 360 × 30). Clearly, the fire altar is supposed—by the authors of the *Śatapatha Brāhmaṇa*, anyway—to be in numerical correspondence with the Mesopotamian cosmos. But most of the numerology of the altars—for example in the *Sulva Sūtras*—does not correspond. They seem to have been conceived with one numerology in mind and to have had the sexagesimal numerology superimposed on them later—much as it was imposed on a preexistent decimal system in Sumer. Similarly the *Śatapatha Brāhmaṇa* says the *Ṛg Veda* has 432,000 syllables, but the number does not match the text as we have it. Again Mesopotamian numerology seems to have been imposed on a system that originally lacked it. The believer is left with the consolation of thinking that "the number 432,000 is the ideal number of syllables," and the missing syllables are in a sense really there but "unmanifest."[20]

The Astronomical Account

As soon as written tablets appeared in Mesopotamia, shortly before 3000 B.C., the sexagesimal system appeared on them, in the company of decimal arithmetic. The decimal system is simpler, and, in relation to the human anatomy and its ten counting digits, has at times been regarded as more natural: Virtually all the world's cultures have developed decimal methods of counting. "Among primitive tribes," one scholar says,[21] "5 is referred to as hand, 10 as two hands; 20 is a man." Sumerian arithmetic during the earliest period of Sumerian writing was already a hybrid; the decimal system was "supplemented by the sexagesimal system,"[22] which was the primary focus. There is a question, then, why the sexagesimal system was ever devised in the first place, after the decimal system was already in place, and even more, why the Mesopotamians chose the sexagesimal system to develop to the fullest extent rather than the decimal.

The first answer offered to this question is based on astronomy. "It is only in strictly mathematical or astronomical contexts," says Neugebager, "that the sexagesimal system is consistently applied."[23] "The sexagesimal system," he adds, "was adopted for all astronomical computations not only by the Greek astronomers but also by their followers in India and by the Islamic and European astronomers."[24] "Copernicus often used consistently written sexagesimal numbers,"[25] as did the fifteenth-century Islamic astronomer Al-Kashi.[26] The other area on which the sexagesimal imprint has been left is that of myths of cyclical time, the ends of world ages, and so on. The implication is that the myths of cyclical time are based on the observed cycles of celestial events. And it is here that an account of sexagesimality has been sought.

In 1906 H. V. Hilprecht observed that the number 12,960, a decimal contraction of "the greatest sacred number of Babylonia," was exactly half of 25,920, which is the number of solar years in one Precessional Year—the length of time that the Precession of the Equinoxes takes to complete a cycle.[27] Others have ramified this observation. The Sumerian calendar, for example, consists of 72 five-day weeks plus five intercalated days ($5 \times 72 = 360$ and $360 \times 72 = 25{,}920$). The number of the Great Year, or Precessional Cycle, in other words, was woven into the calendar of the Little Year, illustrating the Sumerian doctrine of the correspondence of microcosm and macrocosm.

The Precession of the Equinoxes is the longest astronomical cycle observable with the naked eye. It results from the fact that there is an obliquity of 23 1/2 degrees between the Earth's equator and the ecliptic. Thus the Earth's axis performs a slow wobbling rotation in relation to the stellar constellations; this rotation takes 25,920 years. It is called the Precession of the Equinoxes because, in relation to the zodiac, the place of the rising of the sun keeps moving backward through the signs. The sunrise on the morning of the vernal equinox is treated as the beginning of the cycle. Between roughly 4000 and roughly 2000 B.C., the spring sun rose in the sign Taurus; from about 2000 to 1 B.C. it rose in Aries; from 1 A.D. to the present it has risen in Pisces; the popular term "Aquarian Age" refers to the fact that in a few years the spring sunrise will have "precessed" or moved backward through the zodiac into the sign Aquarius, where it will rise for the next 2,160 years. The Precessional cycle is reported to have been figured out roughly by the Greek astronomer Hipparchus in about 150 B.C. and to have been worked out more precisely, to the exact value 25,920, by Copernicus in the sixteenth century A.D. Yet there is considerable circumstantial evidence that Sumerian astronomers had worked it out precisely before the development of the sexagesimal system—that is, before the development of writing.

The Precessional movement is sufficiently rapid to be visible to careful observation by the naked eye within a few years, though several centuries of records (not necessarily written down) would be required to calculate it precisely. It moves 50 seconds in one year; 1 degree in 72 years; 30 degrees in 2,160 years; 60 degrees in 4,320 years; 120 degrees in 8,640 years; 180 degrees in 12,960 years; 240 degrees in 17,820 years; and a full 360 degrees in 25,920 years. These numbers are already familiar. The figures at 60-degree intervals (60, 120, 180, 240, 360 degrees) give us the numbers of the Hindu *yugas*. The 180-degree position gives us Plato's Great Number as well as "the greatest sacred number of Babylonia," 12,960,000. The number 432, found as a telltale clue in time-oriented myths around the world, when multiplied by 60, the basic sexagesimal unit, yields the exact Precessional figure, 25,920.

In this analysis, the Sumero-Babylonian sexagesimal arithmetic, the Sumerian calendar, the Sumerian king lists, and myths of time found in Greece, India, Babylon,

Iceland, and Ireland, all involve numbers derived from the arithmetic of the Precession of the Equinoxes. The Precession, as the vastest of observable temporal cycles—still sometimes known among astronomers as the Great Year, or the Platonic Year—holds sway in myths of cosmic cyclicity. This would seem to account for sexagesimality: It was adopted because it was the most convenient notation for the arithmetic of the Precession of the Equinoxes, which in turn was seen, with a religious feeling, as a Master Code controlling (and, by way of the adjusted calendar, uniting) events on earth and in heaven.

Unwritten Evidence

There is no palpable evidence of a systematic mathematical astronomy in Mesopotamia until about 300 B.C.[28]—not even evidence for the complete zodiac of signs (as opposed to constellations).[29] Even in the Alexandrian period there is no direct evidence for knowledge of the Precession. Extant articulation of the exact Precessional figure, 25,920, supposedly waited for Copernicus in the sixteenth century A.D. Yet the burden of the evidence asks us to wonder whether, in fact, it might have been calculated accurately at least five thousand years earlier, while leaving only an indirect imprint on the record.

What the evidence just reviewed suggests is that the Sumerians, in the fourth millennium B.C., working with decimal arithmetic, and with memorized equinoctial sunrise positions—the data having been orally transmitted or otherwise recorded in some perishable fashion for centuries—had correctly calculated the Precessional number, then, still before the invention of writing, had developed an alternative arithmetical method—the sexagesimal—which would magically plug into the Precessional cycle and thus give greater force to human reckonings by harmonizing them with cosmic fact, and finally that they subsequently devised a myth of cycling time, since lost, which diffused secretly from one priestly caste to another, giving rise to variant myths with interrelated numerologies from Cambodia to Iceland. The alternative is that these steps were taken by some earlier culture or cultures and inherited by the Sumerians.[30]

Two points are necessary to render the apparently difficult thesis of early scientific knowledge plausible: (1) a different relationship to memory, and (2) secret, or nonpublic, channels of transmission.

It seems that preliterate groups had a different relationship to language than literate groups. The Yugoslavian oral bards researched by A. B. Lord in his investigations of the sources of the Homeric poems had tales that took weeks to recite. Oral cultures round the world have exhibited extensive and precise traditions stored entirely in living memories. The invention of writing does not signify the moment when people began thinking; it only means that they began writing down bits and pieces of traditions that had already been worked on and partly developed. The invention of writing caught in midstream the flow of cultures which had already been moving along.

One result of the oral maintenance of traditions is that they are not accessible to the unlearned except directly from one of the learned. There are no books to mediate. Within the shamanic milieu oral "texts" were very private property: They were an important part of a shaman's stock in trade. They were a basis of his magic, and for another to know them would compromise him in a number of ways, leaving both him and his clients vulnerable to misfires of his work and to hostile interferences with it. In so-called primitive societies, as a musicologist has noted, "one must not sing thoughtlessly to oneself, for every note summons up a spirit." "Some songs must be sung only by a certain individual."[31] Similar considerations apply to the oral texts that were sung or chanted by those whose business it was to keep them in memory. To commit such texts to writing—a form in which they could be stolen, transported, and read by those from whom they should be hidden—was not a welcome thought to ancient preliterate learned groups. This is perhaps one reason why 97 percent of known Sumerian tablets are economic records, having nothing to do with sacred learning. Julius Caesar tells us that the Druids of Gaul refused to commit their lore to writing even after they had the ability to do so (*Commentaries on the Gaulic Wars* VI.14). And a scholar writing of the still-unpublished *Śāivagamas*—texts which may in part be several thousand years old—says: "Their handing down by oral means is still regarded as being the only valid method. The written form is, in many cases, if not forbidden, at least considered dangerous, as certain teachings must not be imparted except to those who are worthy. Writing has no value in transmitting magical formulae."[32]

The idea of secret doctrines may be dismaying to scholars who would like to believe that the available evidence can be relied upon. But it is plain that ancient traditions did involve channels of transmission that were rigorously kept secret. To this day no one knows what was said and done in the initiations at Eleusis. Pythagoras's school had a strict vow of secrecy, as did Plato's, in its inner circles. The Greeks may have adopted this custom from the Babylonian and Egyptian schools, where such taboos on publication were a common means to protect a priestly or scholarly monopoly of learning. Mesopotamian tablets sometimes contain explicit designations of the allowed readership—for example:

> This prayer is the secret of Esagila. No one save the urigallu of E-kuya shall see it.[33]

Another text advises:

> The young priest may see these rites which you perform, but the stranger who does not possess the hereditary knowledge of the rites shall not see them, unless he wishes his days to be shortened. The initiated shall reveal them to the initiated; the uninitiated shall not see them. It is among the forbidden things of Anu, Enlil, and Ea, the great gods.[34]

An Egyptian text from Edfu Commands: "Reveal nothing that you see in any secret matter of the sanctuaries."[35]

De Santillana and von Dechend have made a special study of ancient knowledge regarding the Precession of the Equinoxes. "The main source of myth . . ." they argue, "was astronomy," and "it all had its origin in the Near East."[36] Ancient scientists, in their view, sought the invariances of nature, as the power points to work from in their constructions. There are two types of apparent natural invariances perceptible by human senses: astronomical recurrences and harmonic intervals. These then were the subjects of ancient research and the hidden armatures of myth. But sometime in the Neolithic age astronomers became aware of the slippage of the equinoctial sunrise, which threw the invariance of the solar year awry and, in time, invalidated ritual devices, such as Stonehenge, which were based on it. This realization affected them with something like the exigency that primitive groups have felt when faced with eclipses. In a world whose lease had to be ritually renewed annually (as in the Babylonian New Year's Festival), such an imbalance in the mechanisms of the universe could seem threatening. Through research on this problem the Precession of the Equinoxes was discovered. The universe was conceived as an armature or frame with four fixed points: the equinoxes (where the ecliptic intersected the equator) and the solstices (where the ecliptic was farthest from the equator). "The sliding of the sun along the equinoctial point affected the frame of the cosmos."[37] This slippage of the frame was "a kind of cosmogonic 'original sin' whereby the circle of the ecliptic (with the zodiac) was tilted up at an angle with respect to the equator, and the cycle of change came into being."[38] The passage of the seasons, which is to say the year, would not occur if the equator and the ecliptic had not slipped apart; this was, in effect, the beginning of time as history, or time as change.

This, de Santillana and von Dechend propose, was the underlying substance of most cosmogonic myths. The mythic motif of the Separation of the Parents of the World, for example, "stands for the establishing of the obliquity of the ecliptic: the beginning of measurable time."[39] Every two thousand years or so the "original sin" is repeated, when the equinoctial sunrise enters a new sign, having passed through thirty degrees of the zodiac. From this arises the myth of periodic destructions and re-creations of the world: At the end of every age the world frame slips, accompanied by disasters such as floods which destroy mankind. For this reason the Sumero-Babylonian texts speak of a series of floods—three are known—instead of just one. These world- or epoch-ending disasters mark the watery end of the cycle, the end of a 2,160 year period in which the equinoctial sunrise has been in one sign. "For those who know," the authors say, "the origin of the world was only a point in the Precessional cycle, like the 0=24 of our dials."[40]

When the frame shifts and the established world order is ended, a cosmogonic hero is needed to readjust it. Thus Marduk, when he sets the heavens in order in the Babylonian *Creation Epic*, Gilgamesh, even Odysseus, are regarded as heroes who initiated new Precessional months (thirty-degree periods) by adjusting the universal frame to its new bearings. This view of the world frame and its periodic convulsions the authors call a "great world-wide archaic construction"[41] which diffused from a Near Eastern origin at sometime in the Neolithic or Bronze Age.

The Argonauts, for example, carrying the fleece of a ram through supernatural perils, were inaugurating the Age of Aries (2000 B.C.).[42] Similarly, the Fall of Troy originally designated the end of an age; the constellations of Ursa Major and the Pleiades, featured on the Shield of Achilles, the destroyer of Troy, signify, as in other mythic contexts, this cosmic disaster. Odysseus then, by a path not unlike that of the Argonauts and an allegorical reorganization of the palace (universe), and so on, must adjust the new age and set it on its course.[43] Both the partial destructions anticipated by Xenophanes and Plato and the complete destructions anticipated by Manu and the Stoics are, according to this view, references to this periodic shaking of the world frame through the Precession. This model accounts for many mythic elements that previously had appeared silly or chaotic. And it offers a strong foundation for the view that the Precession of the Equinoxes was known prior to the invention of writing, and that the arithmetic involved in it has conditioned myths of time ever since.

The Acoustical Account

De Santillana and von Dechend, in defending their form of the Precessional hypothesis, also broached dimly another model. They remarked, as mentioned above, that the only invariances that nature offers to the senses in a human lifespan are (1) the solar year and (2) the harmonic intervals. These invariances were joined in the concept of the Music of the Spheres—a doctrine attributed to Pythagoras but quite possibly known in Mesopotamia thousands of years before his time. This theme—backgrounded by de Santillana and von Dechend while they explored the astronomical model in the foreground—was taken up by de Nicolas in his *Meditations Through the Ṛg Veda: Four-Dimensional Man.* De Nicholas altered the emphases, stressing the harmonic invariance: "In the beginning was tone."[44] McClain in turn took up this subject from de Nicolas and developed a detailed interpretation of the numbers in ancient myths by relating them not to astronomy but to the mathematics of acoustics and tuning theory.

In *The Myth of Invariance* (a title based on de Santillana and von Dechend's book) McClain notes that "[n]obody knows how or why the sexagesimal system was ever invented in the first place" (either implicitly rejecting the astronomical explanation with no argument, or unaware of it), then asserts: "The sexagesimal system [is] probably the most convenient language for acoustical arithmetic the world ever knew until the system of logarithmic cents was introduced late in the nineteenth century."[45] He proceeds to demonstrate that the various myth-prone numbers in question—216, 432, 30, 60, 360, etc., the sexagesimal/Precessional numbers—were as uniquely and specially fitted to acoustical arithmetic as to Precessional arithmetic.

McClain's argument is, in effect, an adaptation of the structure of de Santillana and von Dechend's argument to another content. It starts from the musicological concept of the comma, which is a small difference between definitions of a tone—a difference which arises from inherent problems in tuning. The most basic example is the so-called Pythagorean comma, a disagreement in note-definition that arises between the octave and perfect fifth.

In working with a vibrating string, one obtains octaves by powers of two: To halve the length of a string produces a tone an octave higher, to double it, an octave lower. The fifth is produced by powers of three: A string one-third the length will produce the perfect fifth an octave above. With these two operations alone, it should be possible, say, to tune a piano, producing every one of the eight notes of the diatonic scale (and from them the three remaining to the chromatic scale). But, in fact, it doesn't work out that way. If a piano tuner tunes the bottom, or longest, string to the pitch C, then derives from it a series of eleven octaves by repeatedly halving the string, each of these octaves is perfect. Next, the piano tuner goes back to the string at the bottom and derives from it the G an octave higher—the perfect fifth. From that in turn he produces the D an octave higher and so on through a series of seven derived fifths. At that point the eleventh octave and the seventh fifth should fall on the same C note; but in fact they produce different tones, separated from one another by the so-called Pythagorean comma, which is worth 24 cents an octave and, in the eleven-octave example, would amount to two whole semitones. (There are 100 cents to a semitone.)

McClain's thesis requires us to believe that ancient peoples as early as the Neolithic or at the latest the Early Bronze Age knew about the Pythagorean comma and indeed about other commas that arise from other approaches to tuning. "We are crediting these early thinkers," McClain says, "with understanding 'tuning theory' as well as any people in history."[46] Again, as in the astronomical hypothesis, a degree of specialized scientific knowledge must be postulated at an early date for which historians of science have no direct written evidence. In both cases, the age to which this hidden discovery is attributed is the Neolithic—though McClain specifies the Late Neolithic and de Santillana and von Dechend seem to look to the Early Neolithic.

On McClain's harmonic model the Pythagorean comma performs the same dislocating effect on the (desired) invariant base of reality that the Precession of the

Equinoxes performs in the astronomical model. In both cases the crack or gap in the mathematical system is seen as a source of strife, chaos, and disorder, and ultimately as a threat to the state, which is an orderly system based on the presumption that cosmic order sustains the power of the temple—a presumption undermined by problems with the claimed invariances of which the temple is custodian. No method of tuning avoids such problems. If the octaves are perfect, the fifths will not be, and vice versa.[47] Aristoxenus had learned this, presumably, through experimenting with many tunings; and probably every culture that came deeply under Mesopotamian influence became involved in such research.

Unlike most western scholars, McClain uses not Greek, Egyptian, or Mesopotamian texts as his basic reference point for ancient thought, but the *Ṛg Veda.* "The numbers Ṛg Vedic man cared about," he says, "define alternate tunings for the musical scale."[48] Alternate tunings, after all, even if they don't eliminate "original sin," are alternate strategies to deal with it. McClain's first point is the double relevance of the frequency ratios of various tunings of the scale on base D in the smallest integers. "The smallest integers which can define a diatonic scale with two similar tetrachords—occupy a 'space' of thirty units in the 'octave double' 30:60."[49] The frequency ratios of this fundamental scale, then, lead to the sexagesimal base, 60. Secondly, "The smallest integers which can define the eleven tones [of the chromatic scale] lie within the octave double 720:360."[50] The 360 degrees in a circle and so forth, in other words, could arise from treating the scale as what de Nicolas calls a "tone-mandala,"[51] aligning the circle with the full or chromatic scale—an activity that Claudius Ptolemy is known to have engaged in. In this series the number 432 is present at the fourth-scale degree. Thirdly, "The eleven invariances can be arranged as reciprocal diatonic scales in the basic Hindu-Greek mode within the octave double 384–768, familiar to Plato scholars as the *Timaeus* model of the 'World-Soul.'"[52] Here again 432 is present, this time at the second scale-degree. Finally, the Greek Phrygian Mode (what Plain Chant calls Modus Primus) is bounded by the octave double 432–864.[53]

To sum up: If the Sumerians (or the Babylonians or, as McClain has it, the *Ṛg Vedic* poets) understood tuning of the diatonic scale, the chromatic scale, and the Phrygian mode, then they naturally had encountered, without any astronomical activity necessary, the sexagesimal base and products of it such as 360, 432, and 864. (The last two are *yuga* numbers, and it is not unreasonable to think of the different ages as retunings of the world instrument.)[54] From these, others can be derived by mating them with twelve (the chromatic octave), thirty (the diatonic base), and so on: 12 × 360, e.g. = 4,320, reinforcing that number; 30 × 432 = 12,960. And so on. The Platonic marriage number can be accounted for as easily through this approach as through that of the Precessional Year, as can the numbers of the cryptic Vedic passages touched on earlier in this chapter.

That difficult *Ṛg Vedic* text, Dīrghatamas's "Creation Hymn," for example, can be read acoustically or astronomically through the same numerology.

> Twelve spokes, one wheel, navels three. Who can comprehend this? On it are placed together three hundred and sixty like pegs; They shake not in the least. (I.164.48)

The twelve spokes of Dīrghatamas's wheel are either the twelve semitone intervals in the chromatic scale which, like a wheel, ends where it began, or the twelve lunations in a solar year, or the twelve signs of the zodiac (though these may not have been fully developed yet even in Babylon).

"The 360 'like pegs' which 'shake not in the least' would seem to be the 360 subdivisions within the 720:360 octave matrix."[55] Or, on the other hand, they are the 360 days in twelve lunar months. And so on. A point against the tonal interpretation is offered by the *Praśna Upaniṣad* (I.11), where the wheel and spoke imagery of this hymn is quoted in a context of months and days—implying that the Upaniṣadic authors interpreted this hymn as calendrical. The point, finally and in brief, is that the numerologies in the myths of time in question can be accounted for either by the astronomical hypothesis, or by the harmonic hypothesis, or by a conflation of the two—an activity which Ptolemy actually devised.

The interpenetration of calendar and scale seems, on the present state of the evidence, to revert to Early Bronze Age Mesopotamian sources. Through this arithmetic, the year and the ritual chant that sustained it were made one and the same. The obvious presumption is that the two correlations were made together. As Joseph Campbell asked (even unaware of the harmonic aspect), "should [we] marvel the more at the sexagesimal system or at the Sumerians who invented it?"[56]

McClain applies similar analyses to other classic passages involving the sexagesimal numbers: various numbers in Hindu mythology after the *Ṛg Veda*, the description of Atlantis in Plato's *Critias*, the *Book of Revelations*, and so on. Plato's genetic theory in the *Republic* is seen to be "a theory of tuning."[57] The facts that in the Pythagorean tradition number theory and music theory were one and the same, and that numbers and harmonic ratios were regarded as having ethical properties (as in ancient Babylonia) make such ideas plausible.

But Pythagorean readings are not only applicable to Plato's day. Pythagoras was said in the ancient texts to have studied in both Egypt and Mesopotamia, and whether or not he went to those places in person, clearly their influence had made its way into his world. In his day the great temple centers in Egypt and the Near East were in a decline of power, but not of intellectual and artistic prestige. Like Athens after the waning of its power, they subsisted as university towns, schools to the world, purveying to the "younger" nations of the world (as the Egyptian priests are said by Herodotus to have conceived it) the ancient sciences of their cultures—sciences which seem to have had their origin in the Paleolithic Age, and subsequently, in the wealthy and sedentary cultures of the Near Eastern Neolithic and Early Bronze Ages, to have been brought to a kind of perfection sufficiently awesome to attract converts from surrounding cultures. Though there are many lacunae in the reconstruction, and the stemma of diffusion may be changed by new evidence, at present it seems that when the Hittites, say, or the people of the Indus Valley culture, or the Greeks of the Orientalizing period, began trade with Mesopotamia and/or Egypt they also began a wholesale adoption of iconography, cosmology, myths of time, artistic codes, and so on. To the priests of these cultures studying in the temple centers of Ur or Erech, where (as Akkadian words in the *Atharva Veda* suggest) some of them must have learned first Sumerian and later Babylonian (which, like Church Latin in its time, remained the liturgical language), the rigorous science of the knowledge of the Precession may have conveyed a binding conviction. The translation of this knowledge into a numerology, a calendrical analogue, and an equally rigorous knowledge of acoustical number theory—these achievements merged together with systems of myth, art, and architecture to create a unified cultural construction of overpowering coherence and range. When the political power of Egypt and Mesopotamia waned, the secret weapon of their occult multiscience remained. For another thousand years it attracted seekers—including "Pythagoras" or some other-named person or persons whose study in Babylon stands behind the body of thought known as Pythagorean.

It requires a leap of horizon to understand the intensity with which such things mattered to ancient thinkers. The Pythagorean comma, for example, was known to Aristoxenus, and possibly to Pythagoras as well. The issue which made it so pressingly important was nothing less than the question (not yet a dead issue in a science which has confronted the Uncertainty Principle) whether reality is mathematical or not.

When Pythagoras discovered (or learned) the so-called Pythagorean Theorem, about the relation between the squares built on the short and long sides of a right triangle, it is said that he hastened to sacrifice oxen (D.L. VIII.12). He felt that he had touched on a power center in the mathematical fabric of the universe. The story is almost certainly in some part or aspect spurious, because Pythagoras did not discover the Pythagorean Theorem, which, as Neugebauer said, "was known more than a thousand years before Pythagoras . . . during the whole duration of Babylonian mathematics."[58]

The Pythagorean Theorem is the threshold to the discovery of irrational numbers and incommensurable lengths—a discovery which Hellenists attribute to Hippasus of Tarentum, a renegade Pythagorean whom, according to one account, Pythagoras pushed off a boat for revealing to outsiders the tragic secret of the Pythagorean Theorem, which was irrationality or incommensurability. But this knowledge, too, is likely to be an importation from the older centers of the Near East rather than a Greek discovery. Babylonian mathematicians were familiar with irrationals, and had worked out the square root of two to five decimal places. The power of such knowledge in this archaic pure science was immense. The discovery that the side and diagonal of a square will always be incommensurable produced an ideological convulsion in the Pythagorean order comparable to the shock conveyed by the discovery of the Precession or the Pythagorean comma. Incommensurable lines can be accurately drawn in geometry, but the irrational numbers that represent the relationship between them can never be fully grasped because they are too dynamic: They run away or keep redefining themselves. "It was found, indeed," says de Santillana, "that such a number, if it existed, would have to be both odd and even."[59] This paradoxical breach sets mathematics and geometry at variance as if they described different worlds. Like the Precessional drift and the Pythagorean comma, this apparent crack or gap in the mathematical fabric of the universe seemed ominous, as if such cracks lead through the membrane of order to chaos: They deny that the universe is orderly and hence that it is cognizable, and thereby remove credibility from all human thought. The Precession threatens the calendar and all that depends on it, and through the Pythagorean comma, as through a crack to chaos, the plethora of untuned sounds that could disrupt the harmony of the universe flows in.

"In the Solomon Islands," a musicologist writes, "when an invitation is sent to a neighboring tribe it is customary to send the measurements of the tribal panpipes so that the guests can tune theirs beforehand, thus ensuring the greatest agreement in the mutual musical greeting."[60] Ritual efficacy can depend on tuning, sensitive, as it is, to the exact proper sound for the exact nuance of the event. "A primitive melody is always the musical expression of an idea."[61] The melody is defined in part by the tuning of the instrument. By different tunings the idea is changed:

The extant visual representations of Sumerian culture in the third millenium B.C. show a great variety of stringed musical instruments (over thirty types) and pipes. In an early Sumerian myth in which Enki transfers the values of civilization to Inanna's care, when he lists the ultimate symbols of civilization in Sumerian society, music itself and five different musical instruments are named. Different instruments represented not only different timbres but different tunings. It was not merely their sound and workmanship but the principles of harmony and number embodied in them which made them of metaphysical status. It may also be, as it was in Greece, that different instruments were associated with different deities. A whole realm of meanings and associations was regarded as *in* the instrument, among its personal powers, along with an array of ēthos- or mood-qualities that its tuning system magically commanded. To pick one up and strum it casually would be, in our terms, somewhat like playing with a loaded gun.

Something like this is found in a Greek context when the archaic lyric poet Terpander is praised for introducing the seven-stringed lyre to Greece as if this were a major accomplishment of civilization. It was not merely a matter of adding a string or two: It was the mathematics of the new tuning system that was at issue. When a Greco-Roman text says that someone was wise in "music," what is meant is "music theory," which is more or less the same as number theory, and equally of metaphysical import. Like sounds, numbers had specific efficacies and powers; in a sense they governed the universe. Musical instruments, embodying different tuning theories, represented different ways to deal with the original sin of the comma, each appropriate to different ritual purposes. This tradition leads into Plato's views on the different moods of the modes.

"All the cities of the Mesopotamian plains had their temples in the fourth millennium B.C.," writes a historian of music. "Here, priests and liturgists, mathematicians and astrologers, passed their lives in quiet seclusion."[62] Here, as in the temple communities in contemporaneous Egypt, sung and chanted language was reified, for magical purposes, into an archetypal structure of ontology. "Mesopotamian temple music was *cantus* in its primitive significance."[63] "*Cantus*," with its essential connection to the real, equates with the Hindu idea of *mantra*. The idea that language is a reifying power with ontological force is most thoroughly enunciated in India (in the *Mimamsaka* texts and elsewhere).[64] Both Sumerian and *Rg Vedic* priest-poet-musicians felt that actual metaphysical energy inhered in sound and syllable. In such a context the comma would be as troubling as an eclipse, or as the Precession, or as the discovery of irrational numbers.

The study of the two invariances, that of the solar calendar and that of the harmonic scale, evidently extends into the earliest mists of human prehistory. The search for the origin of the idea of the harmony of the spheres becomes lost in ever more ancient variations or paraphrases. Correspondences among musical, astronomical, calendrical, and other elements may have been rudimentarily known in the Paleolithic era, and awareness of them seems to have jumped in complexity first in the Neolithic, then again in Sumero-Babylonian times. Babylonian mathematicians treated ratios as entities and assigned ratios both to musical intervals and to planets. The Pythagorean Music of the Spheres, and Plato's tunings of the planetary spheres in the *Timaeus*, were already present there, in a seminal form. Plutarch (commenting on the *Timaeus*) seems to realize this, bringing in the information that "[t]he Chaldeans connected musical intervals with the seasons, that is, the fourth (3:4) = Autumn, the fifth (2:3) = Winter, the octave (1:2) = Summer, while the tonic (1:1) = Spring."[65] The year unfolds as a harmonic progression of the four intervals which nowadays are known as the perfect consonances, associated with the four seasons.

The later period which saw the birth of philosophy in both Greece and India was another intense cauldron of Mesopotamian development. "The time of Persian dominion," say two modern scholars, "particularly from the last quarter of the fifth century B.C. until the conquest of the country by the troops of Alexander the Great, was the most creative period for Babylonian mathematical astronomy. There existed at this time astronomical schools in Uruk, Sippar, Babylon, and Borsippa. From the reports of Pliny the Elder and Strabo we know the name of the great Babylonian astronomer Naburianus, to whom is attributed the working out of a system for determining lunar phases . . . Another Babylonian astronomer . . . Cidenas from Sippar . . . distinguished the solar year from the lunar year and computed the duration of the former . . . to 7 minutes and 41 seconds less than the actual duration . . ."[66]

Egypt also was said to be involved in this tradition. Plato in the *Timaeus* (22d) speaks of periodic destructions by fire and others by water, and ascribes the doctrine to Egyptian priests. Evidence seems to point to Mesopotamia, not to Egypt, as the source of that idea; but many Mesopotamian ideas found a home in Egypt. By the end of the fourth millennium B.C., for example, "Egyptian musical instruments were identical with those of Sumer."[67] This suggests shared discourse about tuning theory. Egyptian mythology is shot through with sexagesimal numbers, perhaps diffused from Sumer. And Egyptian astronomy exhibits the mixture of decimal and sexagesimal arithmetics characteristic of Mesopotamia. The heavens were divided, for example, into thirty-six 10-degree "decans" which together comprise 360 degrees. In Egypt also, the fabric of the state was seen as reliant in part on *cantus*, the life-supporting chant that went on more or less constantly in the temples. "A modal system . . . was approved by the temples and so became a fixed and immutable law."[68] Musical definitions became theological. The gods in Egypt, says Dio Cassius, were tones separated by fourths: E was Saturn, A the Sun, and so on.[69]

Some scholars feel that Pythagoras learned, during his reported twelve years of study in Babylonia, the key "Pythagorean" ideas: (1) the harmony of the spheres, (2) the principle of *ēthos*, or the governing powers of different musical modes, (3) the belief in the efficacy of numbers, that is, in the idea that specific numbers have specific powers and together rule the cosmos. In Babylonian religious thought the gods are represented by numbers. The number 1 represented the High God. The god of music, Enki, was represented by the number 40 which, in the sexagesimal system, means 40/60, that is 2/3, or the musical perfect fifth—the same ratio applied to the winter solstice (the New Year). One cannot regain the whole system, only edges of it here and there—a "great worldwide archaic construction" which was "preserved almost intact in the later thought of the Pythagoreans and Plato."[70]

"The Pythagorean string-length ratios," says a musicologist, "were recognized by both Mesopotamia and Egypt at least two millennia before the time of the Greek civilization."[71] The Near East in general, but, it seems, Mesopotamia in particular, constitutes what de Santillana and von Dechend call "that great proto-Pythagorean mint . . . that once coined the technical language and delivered it to the Pythagoreans."[72] Elsewhere de Santillana speaks of the many formulas which were "available in the arithmetical and engineering data which had reached Greece from the great reservoir of Babylonian civilization."[73] "The shades of Babylon, 'learned and wise,' may be discerned over the shoulders of many of these reputed founders of the arts and sciences in Greece."[74] Surely it was from the influence of those "shades learned and wise" that, as Hippolytus says, Pythagoras "in his studies of nature mingled astronomy and geometry and music and arithmetic . . . He first proved the motion of the seven stars to be rhythm and melody . . ."[75]

The dual astronomical/harmonic reading of the various ancient mythological numbers implies a far greater achievement by Neolithic and Bronze Age Mesopotamian thinkers than previously envisioned by scholars. A hypothetical chronology of these events might suggest that: (1) a decimal arithmetic coexisted with musical studies involving string lengths, perhaps as early as 5000–4000 B.C.; (2) the Precession was worked out, perhaps in the period 4000–3500 B.C.; (3) a sexagesimal arithmetic, with a "decimal substrate" (Neugebauer), was worked out to incorporate cosmic cycles into human events in perhaps 3500–3000 B.C.; (4) the 30:60 and 432:864 octave doubles were worked out and selected as correlates of the precessional/sexagesimal arithmetic, by perhaps 3200 B.C.

Both Greek and Indian philosophers, when they spoke of the cyclicity of the cosmos and its eternal recurrence, were passing on a piece of an archaic worldwide construction already thousands of years old, which thousands of years later would attract such European thinkers as Siger of Brabant and Bruno of Nola, and which still exerts force in orthodox Hindu and Buddhist and, in the West, theosophical settings.

More Numbers

The numerology of the cosmic cycle was tight and systematic in Manu and in the Indian tradition in general. In addition to it, there are other, looser and less systematic, intrusions of Mesopotamian power numbers into Indian lore. As a part of basic time-space modeling, Sumerian numerology was diffused throughout Indian religious literature. The sexagesimal arithmetic of the myth of time is only the leading example of this process. Elsewhere too, Sumerian power-numbers were so deeply imbibed as to become naturalized. These tend to be involved with measurements of time and space, but can occur almost anywhere.

The cosmic emphasis on the number 4 seems to rise ultimately from the pre-Sumerian Halaf culture, of the late fourth millennium B.C., with its distinctive ceramic ware involving cosmograms based on center-and-quaternity, a pattern which is equally the basis of the Indian cosmology of Sumeru and of the modern compass. Halaf culture (perhaps indirectly by way of the later Ubaid culture, or somewhat later by way of Ur) had some special relationship with the Indus Valley. The concept of a four-headed god, first found in Sumerian Usmu, and perhaps present on the Indus seals,[76] recurs in Hindu deities like Brahmā. The Mesopotamian concept of four quarters, each indicated by a sacred animal, is found on the Sarnath column and is a basic part of Indian cosmology. The four-faces motif relates to the four-quarters motif: The god of this icon, it asserts, sees everything. So the theme of quaternity links the realms of subjectivity and objectivity: It is one of the channels through which knowledge can happen.

In some late examples of the Paleolithic lunar notation engravings analyzed by Marshack, there may be a tilt toward seven as the fourth of the lunar cycle number twenty-eight. But seven seems to have been especially enshrined in astronomy somewhat later, when Sumerian astronomers focused on the fact that there are seven planets visible to the eye. Due to this astronomical significance, the number seven came to signify totality: The whole cosmos was made up of seven levels. The seven-leveled ziggurat (*Entem enanki* at Babylon) signified ascent through the cosmos, made up of the seven planetary levels; the related idea of the seven levels of hell—which is both Sumerian and Indian—keeps the universe numerically symmetrical. The sacredness of the number seven worldwide is "of Mesopotamian origin,"[77] and it occurs frequently, indeed in almost chaotic profusion, in the sacred literature of the Indian sects.

The Vratya ascetic of the *Atharva Veda* is said to have seven *prāṇas* (breaths in the upper body), seven *apānas* (breaths in the lower body), and seven *vyānas* (breaths pervading the whole body)(*AV* XV 15.1.2). The *Ṛg Vedic rishis*, or wise men, are seven in number (as are the seven sages of archaic Greece). The reincarnation doctrine of Makkhali Gosāla, the Ājīvika teacher, climaxed in seven divine births, seven human births, and seven reanimations.[78] The seven *cakras* of the microcosm in *kuṇḍalinī* physiology, like the seven levels of initiation in Mithraism, or the seven stages of Patañjali's yoga, seem likely to derive ultimately from the seven planetary levels of Sumerian astronomy. Another important image in Indian occult physiology—the central pole with copulating serpents twined round it, their bodies meeting at certain points, typically seven in number—is first seen in late third millennium Sumer. Known as the "caduceus" in the Roman Empire, this icon was somewhat later regarded in India as a map of the three *nāḍīs*, or occult channels, of the body, through which the seven "breaths" proceed. This ancient number of totality yields the seven *cakras*; the seven breaths; the seven heavens and seven hells of the yogic cosmology;[79] the seven steps of the Buddha, which represent the ascending of the seven planetary levels—that is, the surveying of the universe as a whole (*M.* III.123); the seven heads of the cobra hoods of Pārśva, Buddha, and others; the fact that Indra is called "killer of the seven"; the seven *rishis*; and so on.

The Sumerian king list ends with the statement that "twenty-three kings ruled for 24,510 years, three months, and three and a half days."[80] Distinctive echoes of this numerology recur in Indian records of lineages. The Jain tradition, for example, holds that there were twenty-three *tīrthankaras* before Mahāvīra, who, by being the twenty-fourth, started a new age. In a related passage, the *Buddhavamsa* lists twenty-four prior Buddhas who had prophesied the enlightenment of Siddhārtha Gautama.[81] The numbers take on a new cultural life in their new environment and may slip this way or that slightly, but the relationship is still detectable.

The number 108 is also present throughout Indian religious literature, as, for example, the 108 pieces in which Sati's body is torn in the Śaiva myth, the tradition that there are 108 Upaniṣads, and so on. This number, too, comes from the Sumerian king list or an associated source; it derives from Precessional arithmetic as the fourth part of 432, and from sexagesimal arithmetic as the product of 3 and 36.

The number seventy-two, as in the 72,000 *nāḍīs*, or channels, of the occult physiology of India, as mentioned, for example, in the *Dhyanabindu Upanisad*, also derives from Sumer. It both occurs in the king lists and arises in the sexagesimal arithmetic, where it represents 6×12, and in the mixed sexagesimal-Precessional arithmetic, where it is 432 divided by 6. Astronomically, it is the number of years that the Precessional movement takes to traverse one degree.

In addition to these "sub-Sumerian" numbers, both the Greek and Indian traditions involve mathematical investigations that do not conspicuously overlap the sexagesimal system. Hippolytus (as quoted above) says Pythagoras mixed the practices of astronomy, music, mathematics, and geometry. The three fields of astronomy, music, and mathematics seem to have been linked by the sexagesimal number system, but geometry lies somewhat outside this linkage. Except in Plato's *Timaeus*, there is little sign of attempts to generate a geometrical parallel to the other realms. Nevertheless, geometry, famously, was the leading mathematical investigation among the Greeks, involving Egyptian influence as well as the Mesopotamian inheritance coming in through various channels down to and including the school of Berossus, a Babylonian priest who fled into exile in Cos around 280 B.C. and founded a school there.

In India also, geometrical study went on without close linkage to the symbolically weighted complex of astronomy, music, and arithmetic. The texts called *Sulva Sūtras*, or "texts of the cord," which contain instructions for the construction of Vedic altars, are the leading candidates for extant carriers of geometrical knowledge from the ancient period in India. Bricks made with specific properties of shape and measurement (with allowance for shrinkage in baking) were precisely assembled into the intricate five layer structures called *agnis* or fire altars.[82] The so-called Pythagorean Theorem and such other classic ancient problems as Squaring the Circle seem to have been featured. It is in the *Sulva Sūtras* that, according to Thibaut, "we must search whether there are not any traces left pointing to a purely Indian origin of these sciences."[83] Thibaut refers to the quest for an Indian mathematics that is without Greek influence, as he was writing before the discovery of the Indus Valley culture or the possibility of Mesopotamian influence. The *Sulva Sūtras* do reflect the Mesopotamian sexagesimal imprint, though less conspicuously than the astronomical and acoustical accounts. To begin with, the basic measuring unit, the *puruṣa*, which was "equal to . . . the height of a man with uplifted arms,"[84] seems to have been established with sexigesimality in mind, as it is divided into 120 smaller units, and 60 and 30 are common in the texts about its use.[85] Throughout the *Baudhyayana Sulva Sūtras*, there is a sprinkling of sexagesimally based numbers which may or may not exceed ordinary probability.[86]

There is considerable controversy about the dating of these Sutras. On the one hand, philologists have tended to assign them to the period 600–300 B.C. with "the usually accepted view that the mathematics embodied in the texts was created by Vedic priests."[87] On the other hand, there has been a recent tendency to trace them (or the lore they contain) back to the period of the Indus Valley or even earlier.[88]

Mesopotamian texts of the period that was in contact with the Indus cities emphasize the problem of the making of bricks for ritual construction to certain dimensions and shapes, as in the dream of King Gudea of Lagash recorded on the Gudea Cylinders. One wonders if the same source might account for the Greek attention to the geometry of ritual altar construction, as in the case when the solution of "the 'problem of Delos' or duplication of the cube . . . had been requested by the Delian Apollo, through the oracle, for his cubic altar."[89] In so doing, de Santillana notes, "Apollo had been acting clearly in his capacity as god of music . . . the symbolic interest of the cube lies in its being, itself, a 'geometrical harmony.'" "The duplication of the cube, this seemingly out-of-the-way problem, was really part of the enterprise of discovering the 'bonds' of the cosmos."[90]

Scholarly Reservations

The sexagesimal arithmetic is unmistakable and so is its tracing back to Mesopotamia. The implications of this simple fact are too awesome for some scholars who refuse to believe in the undocumented scientific discoveries of the Neolithic age and in the complexity and precision of the Sumero-Babylonian tradition of mathematics. Yet it is commonly understood that Greek mathematics is a continuation of Sumerian mathematics: They are in effect one tradition, the Sumero-Greek, with the Greeks representing the later extension of it.[91]

As so often, the Indian side of the diffusion equation is touchier. Ancient Mesopotamian culture, since it is hailed by western scholars as the pre-Greek root of the western tradition, and since the tradition of imperialism began with Sargon of Akkad, may seem particularly suspect from the Indian point of view. That some elements of the Indus Valley culture and much else in later Indian tradition should be attributed to borrowings from Sumer seems somehow underhanded, that is, it may seem to be serving a political agenda—especially since it is an idea imported into India by western scholars of the colonial period, not one that originated among Indian scholars themselves. At the present time there is no problem in acknowledging that the Greeks borrowed so openly and massively from the Sumerian treasury of knowledge as to be virtually a late stage of the Sumerian tradition—much as de Santillana and von Dechend imply by calling Sumer "that great proto-Pythagorean mint." Yet India, at least in part, surely, because it has been colonized in ancient, medieval, and modern times, is especially sensitive to the idea that its culture is somehow not really its own.

A different reservation, found commonly among western scholars, has to do with the history of science. Ancient cultures seem to have been obsessed with numbers, or, as a Pythagorean might have put it, with Number. Yet there are radically different views of how far they got in working out this obsession. West, for example, takes a conservative view about Pythagorean mathematics, saying that it is not even clear "that he [Pythagoras] knew that the basic musical intervals involve numerical relationships."[92] West is readier to attribute knowledge of the arithmetic of musical tuning to Pythagoras's disciple Hippasus. The point is that what is at issue is not a question of pure scientific discoveries made within Greek schools. From Thales to Pythagoras and beyond, Greek mathematicians in the early period knew essentially what they had learned from Mesopotamia. To say that Pythagoras didn't know something but Hippasus did is simply to say that the knowledge came over from Mesopotamia in between the two. It is not really to say that such knowledge did not exist in Pythagoras's day.

But few western scholars are willing to accept the full implications of ancient numerologies derived from Mesopotamia, which include Neolithic knowledge of the Precession of the Equinoxes and Early Bronze Age knowledge of arithmetical problems in tuning theory such as the Pythagorean comma. In part this reluctance must be attributed to the accident of the invention of writing in between the Neolithic and Early Bronze Ages. That scientific knowledge existed before writing may seem phantasmal and hard to believe. The problem of secrecy enters here also. De Santillana and others seem to be sorting the meager remains of what Daniélou has called an earlier, now more or less lost, civilization.

Shape

What shape is ancient thought? Round. At least in the Mesopotamian lineage, which includes Greece and India, it was round. The spherical cosmos rolling in cyclical time—wheels within wheels, as Parmenides showed with his goddess—the Great Wheel of the Precessional Year, united with the pitch wheel of the song that reaches back to the beginning—the twelve-tone chromatic scale like a twelve-spoked wheel—these round constructions of the real gave birth to others, greater and smaller wheels, some inside them, some outside them, some linked axially, some touched and spun peripherally. The wheel of cycling time sets going a smaller wheel within itself: the wheel of the transmigration of souls. How these two wheels relate to one another—

what the gear ratio is, one might say—is another part of that great archaic construction.

Some have thought that the myth of cyclical time was inherently bound up with the reincarnationist view of human destiny—that the two doctrines form a syntactical complex. Aristotle, for whom all perfect motion was circular, thought the same about this archaic gear construction of the cosmic machine: "In the movement of the heavens and of each star," he wrote, "there is a circle; so why shouldn't the birth and death of people be circular too, so that they are born and destroyed again (and again)" (*Problemata* 17.3).

Notes to Chapter Three

1. More discussion of this at M. R. Wright, *Empedocles: The Extant Fragments* (New Haven and London: Yale University Press, 1981), pp. 3–6.

2. See, for example, Erwin Rohde, *Psyche: The Cult of Souls and Belief in Immortality among the Greeks*, trans. W. B. Hillis (London: Kegan, Paul, Trench, Trubner and Co., 1925), pp. 382–383; John Burnet, *Early Greek Philosophy* (Cleveland, Ohio, and New York: World Publishing Company, 1964), p. 250; Werner Jaeger, *The Theology of the Early Greek Philosophers*, trans. Edward S. Robinson, Gifford Lectures 1936 (Oxford: Clarendon Press, 1947), pp. 132–135. For an attempt to reconcile the two poems see Wright, *Empedocles*, pp. 57–63, and for more bibliography on the question, ibid., p. 57, n. 1.

3. A review of the major problems in the fragments of Empedocles can be found in A. A. Long, "Empedocles' Cosmic Cycle in the 'Sixties,'" in *The Presocratics: A Collection of Critical Essays*, ed. Alexander P. D. Mourelatos (Garden City, New York: Doubleday/Anchor, 1974), pp. 397–425.

4. *Abhidharmakośabhāṣyam by Louis de la Vallee Poussin*, 4 vols., trans. Leo M. Pruden (Berkeley, California: Asian Humanities Press, 1988–90). See also Akira Sadakata, *Buddhist Cosmology, Philosophy and Origins*, trans. Gaynor Sekimori with foreword by Hajime Nakamura (Tokyo: Kosei Publishing Co., 1997), pp. 99–105.

5. See, for example, Padmanabh S. Jaini, *The Jaina Path of Purification* (Delhi: Motilal Banarsidass, 1998), pp. 30–32.

6. Another passage of the same hymn expands the wheel into a chariot, with many unresolved questions about the numbers involved:

> They call him in the farther half of heaven the Sire five-footed of twelve forms, wealthy in watery store.
>
> These others say that he, God with far-seeing eyes, is mounted on the lower seven-wheeled, six-spoked car.
>
> Upon this five-spoked wheel revolving ever all living creatures rest, and are dependent.
>
> Its axle, heavy-laden, is not heated; the nave from ancient time remains unbroken. (I.164.12–13)

7. Quoted by Subhash Kak, *The Astronomical Code of the Ṛg Veda* (New Delhi: Aditya Prakashan, 1994), p. 78.

8. Trans. Franklin Edgerton, *The Beginnings of Indian Philosophy* (Cambridge, Massachusetts: Harvard University Press, 1970), p. 100.

9. Unless otherwise noted, translations of the Upaniṣads will follow S. Radhakrishnan, *The Principal Upaniṣads* (London: George Allen and Unwin, 1969).

10. There is controversy about this attribution; see, e.g., *Heraclitus: The Cosmic Fragments*, ed. Geoffrey S. Kirk (Cambridge: Cambridge University Press, 1954), pp. 311–317; W. K. C. Guthrie, *A History of Greek Philosophy*, vol. 1 (Cambridge: Cambridge University Press, 1962–1981), pp. 454 ff.

11. This is the notation used by Otto Neugebauer, *The Exact Sciences in Antiquity* (Providence, Rhode Island: Brown University Press, 1957), in which commas separate the positions, since each may be occupied by more than one digit.

12. Sadakata, *Buddhist Cosmology*, p. 95–97.

13. E. A. Wallis Budge, *Amulets and Talismans* (New York: Collier Books, 1970), p. 427.

14. J. Adam, *The Republic of Plato*, 2 vols. (Cambridge: Cambridge University Press, 1926 and 1929).

15. Georg Bühler, trans. and comm., *The Laws of Manu* (New York: Dover, 1969), pp. 20–21.

16. S. Burstein, *The Babyloniaca of Berossus*, Sources from the Ancient Near East 1 (Malibu, California: Udena, 1978).

17. *Revelations* 11.3; 11.2; 13.5; 12.14; 12.6. See Ernest G. McClain, *The Myth of Invariance: The Origins of the Gods, Mathematics and Music from the Ṛg Veda to Plato* (New York: Nicolas Hays, 1976), p. 118.

18. Ibid., p. 100; Neugebauer, *The Exact Sciences in Antiquity*, pp. 10–13.

19. Eleanor Moron, *Angkor Wat: Meaning Through Measurement* (Ann Arbor, 1974 [fascimile]).

20. Kak, *The Astronomical Code of the Ṛg Veda*, pp. 93, 91.

21. Vincent Hopper, *Medieval Number Symbolism* (New York: Columbia University Press, 1938), p. 9.

22. Thomas L. Heath, *A Manual of Greek Mathematics* (New York: Dover, 1963), pp. 12–13.

23. Neugebauer, *The Exact Sciences in Antiquity*, p. 17.

24. Ibid., p. 22.

25. Ibid.

26. Ibid., p. 23.

27. H. V. Hilprecht, *The Babylonian Expedition of the University of Pennsylvania: Series A, Cuneiform Texts*, vol. 20, part 1 (Philadelphia: University of Pennsylvania, University Museum, 1906), p. 31.

28. Ibid., pp. 15, 20.

29. Ibid., p. 140; and see Rupert Gladow, *Origin of the Zodiac* (New York: Castle Books, 1968), p. 162.

30. Alain Daniélou, *While the Gods Play* (Rochester, Vermont: Inner Traditions International, 1987), says a great deal about this hypothesis.

31. Marius Schneider, "Primitive Music," in *New Oxford History of Music*, vol. 1, *Ancient and Oriental Music*, ed. Egon Wellesz (London and New York: Oxford University Press, 1969), p. 3.

32. Alain Daniélou, *Śiva and Dionysus*, trans. K. F. Hurry (London and The Hague: East-West Publications, 1982), p. 44.

33. Sidney H. Hooke, *Babylonian and Assyrian Religion* (Norman: University of Oklahoma Press, 1963), p. 104.

34. Ibid., p. 125.

35. Serge Sauneron, *The Priests of Ancient Egypt*, trans. Ann Morrissett (New York: Grove Press, 1980), p. 25.

36. Giorgio de Santillana and Hertha von Dechend, *Hamlet's Mill* (Boston: David R. Godine, 1977), p. 3.

37. Ibid., p. 67.

38. Ibid., p. 5.

39. Ibid., p. 135.

40. Ibid., p. 145.

41. Ibid., p. 4.

42. Ibid., p. 318.

43. Ibid., p. 385.

44. Antonio T. de Nicolas, *Meditations through the Ṛg Veda: Four-Dimensional Man* (Boulder, Colorado, and London: Shambhala, 1978), p. 55.

45. Ernest G. McClain, *The Myth of Invariance: The Origin of the Gods, Mathematics and Music from the Ṛg Veda to Plato* (New York: Nicolas Hays, 1976), p. 131.

46. Ibid., p. 4.

47. In the modern method of equal temperament the octaves are perfect but all intermediary notes share equally the loose change.

48. McClain, *Myth of Invariance*, p. 3.

49. Ibid., p. 12.

50. Ibid., p. 33.

51. See, for example, Antonio T. de Nicolas, *Avatara: The Humanization of Philosophy through the Bhagavad Gīta* (New York: Nicolas Hays, Ltd., 1976), pp. 288, 291, 330–333, etc.

52. McClain, *Myth of Invariance*, p. 89.

53. Ibid., pp. 61, 112.

54. De Nicolas, *Avatara*, p. 294 and elsewhere.

55. McClain, *Myth of Invariance*, p. 35.

56. Joseph Campbell, *The Masks of God: Oriental Mythology* (New York: Viking Press, 1962), p. 118.

57. McClain, *Myth of Invariance*, p. 19.

58. Neugebauer, *The Exact Sciences in Antiquity*, p. 36.

59. Giorgio di Santillana, *The Origins of Scientific Thought from Anaximander to Proclus, 600 B.C.–500 A.D.* (New York; New American Library, 1961), p. 70.

60. Schneider, "Primitive Music," p. 3.

61. Ibid., p. 2.

62. Henry G. Farmer, "The Music of Ancient Mesopotamia," in Wellesz, ed., *Ancient and Oriental Music*, p. 231.

63. Ibid., p. 235.

64. McClain presumes without argumentation that the Vedic poets taught the Sumerians rather than the other way around. Similarly, his tendency to regard the acoustical model as prior to the astronomical one is undefended. The importance of the number 12, which governs the subdivisions of the pitch continuum, may have been first known through the ratio of lunations to solar years. This research was going on as early as 15,000 B.C. (Alexander Marshack, *Roots of Civilization*

[New York: McGraw Hill, 1972]). Anthropological questions remain, too. McClain must presume that the requisite research into harmonic intervals was carried out in early societies by means of string lengths and pipe lengths. But Schneider says that modern primitive groups arrive at their scales not by instruments but by singing (Schneider, "Primitive Music," p. 14).

65. Farmer, "The Music of Ancient Mesopotamia," p. 253.

66. Muhammad A. Dandamaev and Vladimir G. Lukonin, *The Culture and Social Institutions of Ancient Iran*, trans. Philip L. Kohl (Cambridge: Cambridge University Press, 1989), p. 287. It would seem that by this time the inheritors of Sumero-Babylonian astronomy and mathematics were rediscovering some of the elements that seem to have been known in the period before the Sumerian king-lists but were sealed off from public knowledge by priestly secrecy: "As early as before Hipparchus, Cidenas discovered solar precessions" (ibid).

67. Farmer, "The Music of Ancient Mesopotamia," p. 175.

68. Ibid., p. 276.

69. Ibid., p. 277.

70. De Santillana and von Dechend, *Hamlet's Mill*, p. 311.

71. Farmer, "The Music of Ancient Egypt," p. 275.

72. De Santillana and von Dechend, *Hamlet's Mill*, p. 311.

73. De Santillana, *The Origins of Scientific Thought from Anaximander to Proclus*, p. 70.

74. Farmer, "The Music of Ancient Mesopotamia," p. 250.

75. De Santillana, *The Origins of Scientific Thought from Anaximander to Proclus*, p. 53.

76. Meaning the so-called Śiva seals. See McEvilley, "An Archeology of Yoga," *Res: Anthropology and Aesthetics* 1 (1981).

77. Mircea Eliade, *Shamanism*, Bollingen Series 76 (Princeton, New Jersey: Princeton University Press, 1964), p. 274.

78. See A. L. Basham, *History and Doctrine of the Ājīvikas: A Vanished Indian Religion* (London: Luzac, 1951), p. 219.

79. See Shashi Busan Dasgupta, *Obscure Religious Cults* (Calcutta: Firma KLM, 1976), p. 237.

80. James B. Pritchard, ed. *Ancient Near Eastern Texts Relating to the Old Testament* (Princeton, New Jersey: Princeton University Press, 1955), p. 265.

81. See, e.g., Edward J. Thomas, *The Life of Buddha as Legend and History* (London: Routledge and Kegan Paul, 1949), p. 27.

82. See, for example, G. Thibaut, *Mathematics in the Making in Ancient India* (reprints of *On the Sulvasūtra* and *Baudhyayana Sulva-sūtra*), ed. with intro. by Debiprasad Chattopadhyaya (Delhi: K. P. Bagchi and Co., 1984).

83. Ibid., p. 4.

84. Ibid., p. 8.

85. Ibid., pp. 37–40.

86. See, for example, ibid., pp. 129–131, or any pages of the translation of the *Baudhayana Sulva Sūtra* in part 2.

87. Chattopadhyaya, in ibid., p. iv.

88. Chattopadhyaya focuses on the lack of a brick-baking culture in the period from the end of the Indus Valley to the second urbanization about the time of Aśoka, and concludes that "the presumption ... is that geometrical science which we find eventually codified in the Sulva-Sūtras could have come down from the Harappan period," along with "the ritual [that] was borrowed

by the Vedic people from the Harappan survival" (ibid., pp. xviii, xv). Considering the prominence of the fire altar in the closely related Indo-Aryan groups north of the Khyber Pass—especially the Persians—it is difficult not to attribute the Vedic rite to the Aryans themselves. Still, some authors, such as George Feuerstein, Subhash Kak, and David Frawley (*In Search of the Cradle of Civilization* [Wheaton, Illinois: Quest Books, 1995]) want to place the *Sulva Sūtras*, and the rite they refer to, still earlier than the Harappan period. An interesting question is whether the altar shape called *pra-uga*, "the forepart of the poles of a chariot" (Thibaut, *Mathematics in the Making*, p. 6) could have existed in the pre-chariot age of the Indus Valley; it would have been most characteristic of the Vedic Aryan culture.

89. De Santillana, *The Origins of Scientific Thought from Anaximander to Proclus*, p. 70.

90. Ibid., p. 78.

91. In fact, the roots of this tradition may go back not only to the Neolithic Age but to the Paleolithic, when active investigation of the mathematics of lunar cycles was already underway. See Alexander Marshack, *The Roots of Civilization* (London: Weidenfeld and Nicolson, 1972).

92. M. L. West, *Early Greek Philosophy and the Orient* (Oxford: Clarendon Press, 1971), pp. 216–217.

Chapter Four

The Doctrine of Reincarnation

The conviction that there were mutually formative contacts between the Greek and the Indian philosophical traditions goes back to antiquity—Porphyry, for example, felt convinced of it. There were many clues from which this conviction could arise, but the most conspicuous one, without which the very question might not have been raised, is the doctrine of reincarnation: Though it is especially associated with India, reincarnation was also a standard teaching of most Greek philosophers.

This correspondence has been neglected by scholars. Despite its possibly monumental importance, it has been deemed either insignificant or unprofitable, on various grounds: that reincarnationism might be found in two places without inviting interpretation; that it might have entered Indian and Greek religions from various shamanic or tribal groups in their neighborhoods; and that it is, fundamentally, a peripheral issue, even a red herring which threatens to lead beyond the bounds of Greek, and western, rationalism.

Such arguments don't address the main point, which is that the doctrine was held in both Greece and India in a distinctive form not known among shamanic and tribal groups, not found anywhere else in the world, in fact, except places that seem to have adopted it either from India or from Greece. Noticing this, some eighty years ago Theodor Gomperz wrote:

> From what people or creed did the sage who was famous above all for this far-reaching "inquiry" borrow the doctrines of *metempsychōsis*? Herodotus replies by a reference to Egypt . . . [but] there is a far closer agreement between Pythagorism and the Indian doctrine, not merely in their general features, but even in certain details, such as vegetarianism; and it may be added that the formulae which summarize the whole creed of the "circle and wheel" of rebirths are likewise the same in both. It is almost impossible for us to refer this identity to mere chance.[1]

The "formulae" Gomperz refers to are (1) the process of reincarnation (Sanskrit *saṃsāra*, Greek *metempsychōsis*), (2) moral and cognitive laws governing the process (Sanskrit *karma*, Greek *katharsis*), (3) the goal of escape from the process (Sanskrit *mokṣa*, Greek *lusis*).

This tripartite form of the doctrine is very different from the types of reincarnationism found among traditional peoples here and there around the world. Those characteristically involve either familial relationships (a dying grandparent, for example, being reborn in the next grandchild of his or her line) or an animistic relationship to nature (the dead being randomly reborn in animal or vegetable forms), or a totemic context (an archetypal representative of a species instantiating itself in successive instances). In such systems there is no ethical imperative for the reincarnating unit; neither reward nor punishment is involved in the assignment of the next life. Rebirth occurs by chance, in an impersonal process which individual efforts do not affect.

According to the form of the doctrine which is found in both Greece and India, in contrast, it is not chance but the moral quality of one's past behavior that determines the type of rebirth one will have. Plato, for example, says (*Laws* X.903d) that the process of *katharsis*—purification through successive reincarnations—shifts "the character that is becoming better to a better incarnation, and that which is growing worse to a worser, each according to its due." The *Chândogya Upaniṣad* (V.10.7) similarly says, "Those whose conduct here has been good will quickly attain a good birth . . . But those whose conduct here has been evil will quickly attain an evil birth . . ." Plato and the Upaniṣadic teacher may mean different things by good, but in any case the idea of karmic accumulation with positive-negative polarity is in effect in both texts. Elsewhere Plato says (*Phaedo* 81e sq.) that "those who have cultivated gluttony or selfishness or drunkenness . . . are likely to assume the form of donkeys and other perverse animals . . . [while] those who have preferred a life of lawlessness and violence become wolves and hawks and kites . . ." Similarly an Upaniṣadic teacher says (*CU* V.10.7) that those who have lived wickedly may be reborn as dogs or hogs.

Another special feature of the Greek and Indian doctrine is that the return to life in a new body is regarded as a negative outcome. Rebirth is to be dreaded, not welcomed. The desideratum is not to be reborn—either for better or for worse—but to disengage one's gear altogether from the machine of birth and death—to escape, as the Orphics put it, "from the sorrowful weary wheel." This reversed valuation on death and life also is found, in context of a doctrine of reincarnation, only in Greece and India—and, again, in cultures which have learned it from them. It is the occurrence of this identical array of "formulae" in both Greece and India and nowhere else that waits to be accounted for.

The Path to Escape

As rebirth is conditioned by one's behavior, the route to escape from it is so conditioned also. In Greece, Empedocles (frs. 136–137) preached to meat-eaters:

> Do you not see that you are devouring each other in the thoughtlessness of your minds? The father, in his folly, lifts up the son and slaughters him . . . Son takes father, children their mother and, tearing out the life, eat the flesh of their own kin.

In India, Manu (*MS* V.55) expresses a similar concept, somewhat more concisely:

> He whose flesh I eat in this life, will devour mine in the next.[2]

It was believed that vegetarianism (as Gomperz noted), celibacy, and other so-called purifying practices would disengage one from the birth-death linkage. As a character commonly supposed to be an Orphic says in a fragment of Euripides' *Cretans* (*ap.* Porph., *De Abst.* 4.19):

All white are the clothes I wear and I shun human birth, touch not urn of the dead and their tombs, and have been on guard to all taste of meat.

Orphism was connected somehow with Pythagoreanism, and the anecdotal tradition presents Pythagoras as comparably extreme in this respect to the most scrupulous Indian exponents of nonviolence, the Jains. As the Jain monk would sit gently so as not to hurt the grass, so Pythagoras is said to have been killed by pursuing soldiers when he refused to run across a field of bean sprouts. "He not only abstained from animal food," says Eudoxus, "but would have nothing to do with cooks or hunters" (*ap.* Porph. *Vit. Pyth.* 7 = DK 14.9). Similar injunctions, to avoid the company of butchers or hunters, are common in Indian texts on nonviolence. In addition to abjuring violence, Jain monks, under Mahāvīra's regimen, adopted the vow of permanent celibacy. The Pythagoreans similarly were said to "keep clear of births as well as deaths," and Pythagoras is said to have counseled against sexual intercourse (D.L. VIII.33).

Indian terms for a life devoted to such special practices include yoga, "the yoke" (the lifestyle that will yoke one with *brahman*), and *sādhana*, or "special way of life." The concept of a way of life based on nonviolence and vegetarianism was already in effect in India by 517 B.C., for Scylax tells of people who ate nothing that had animal life, lived out of doors, and ate only wild grains. In Greece, the word philosophy—*philosophia*, "love of knowledge," or desire for the knowledge that frees the soul from the wheel (which is what this word, coined, they say, by Pythagoras, must have meant to him)—is the closest equivalent of yoga; *sādhana* finds a very close equivalent in *bios*, meaning a specially adopted lifestyle, such as the Orphic *bios*, the Pythagorean *bios*, and so on.

The Knowledge that Frees

At some point in both Greece and India the path of purification was reconceived to insist on mysterious cognitive breakthroughs in addition to such ascetic practices. In the Upaniṣadic tradition, as Deussen said, "Every man, as soon as he is in possession of the knowledge of the *ātman*, is *jīvanmukta*"—that is, freed from further incarnations.[3] "Knowledge of the ātman" means a sense of realization that one's individuated self (*ātman*) is a part of a Cosmic Self (*brahman*). The *Bṛhadāraṇyaka Upaniṣad* says, "Whoever knows thus, 'I am Brahman,' becomes this all. Even the gods cannot prevent his becoming thus, for he becomes their self" (*BU* I.4.10). The attainment of this "knowledge" of oneself as *brahman* is associated with claims to omniscience on the ground that if one knows the substrate one knows all manifestations even before they are manifest. The substrate is described as lacking any finite qualities whatever. "He who knows the shadowless, bodiless, colourless, pure, undecaying self attains verily the Supreme Undecaying [self]. He who, O dear, knows thus, becomes omniscient, becomes all" (*Praśna Up.* IV.10–11).[4]

Many passages make clear that this knowledge is not the ordinary discursive kind, but rather a kind "by which the unhearable becomes heard, the unperceivable becomes perceived, the unknowable becomes known" (*CU* VI.1.3). This knowledge of underlying unity, or of the featureless substrate as oneself, terminates the illusion of individuation and constitutes release from the wheel of incarnations. As Yājñavalkya, court philosopher of Janaka of Videha,[5] said, "In it (Brahman) there is no diversity. He goes from death to death who sees in it, as it were, diversity" (*BU* IV.4.19).

The realization of one's cosmic nature is held to render the human nature trivial or even repulsive. The consequence is a state of desirelessness resulting from a disengagement from the impulses and activities of individuated life. This state of desirelessness is to be cultivated through programs of abstinence and discipline, but especially through the special knowledge of the unreality of ordinary selfhood. "Because they know this," said Yājñavalkya, "the ancient [sages] . . . have risen above the desire for sons, the desire for wealth, the desire for worlds . . . these are . . . desires only. This Self is . . . not this, not this" (*BU* IV.4.22). The state of desirelessness is sometimes seen as a prerequisite for knowing *brahman*, sometimes as a consequence of that knowledge. "When all the desires that dwell in the heart are cast away, then does the mortal become immortal" (*BU* IV.4.7). Desire is the mechanism that drives the souls onward through further revolutions of the wheel. "The man who does not desire is satisfied, he whose desire is the self, his breaths do not depart to be reborn. Being Brahman, he goes to Brahman" (*BU* IV.4.6).

In the Greek tradition, too, the requirement for release is seen less as physical asceticism than as a nonordinary kind of knowledge. The Orphics held that release is obtained through recollection of one's own god-nature, and Plato's doctrine of recollection implies that for him this means that one must, in effect, become omniscient. In Platonic passages which preserve the Orphic strain it is said (as it is so often said in the Upaniṣads) that the knowledge in question is nondiscursive and cannot be communicated by words. As in India, ethical emphasis is on loss of the ordinary desire habits. In the *Cratylus* (493e), speaking in Orphic terms, Plato says that it is desire which turns the soul "upside down" for its downward plunge into matter; it is the soul's forgetful desire which keeps it embodied, and this desire must be corrected by recollection of its true nature, which will lead to the realization that ordinary desires are inappropriate to it.

The emphasis on knowledge assumes the shared theory that in order to know something, it is necessary for the knowing apparatus to contain some of that thing already. Like is known only by like. To know the god who infuses the universe with life one must have some of that god inside. We may understand the cosmos not by merely beholding it, but by tuning ourselves to its tuning. As Plato puts it in the *Timaeus* (90c–d):

> The motions akin to the divine part in us are the thoughts and revolutions of the universe; these, therefore, every man should follow, and correcting those circuits in the head that were deranged at birth, by learning to know the harmonies and revolutions of the world, he should bring the intelligent part, according to its pristine nature, into the likeness of that which intelligence discerns.[6]

This doctrine very likely goes back in some sense and to some degree to Bronze Age Mesopotamia where the trail of the idea of macrocosm/microcosm correspondence leads. The Upaniṣadic doctrine that the *ātman is* the whole world in miniature inside oneself is another resonance of this idea. In the space within the heart, the *Chāndogya Upaniṣad* says (e.g. VIII.1.3), the whole universe in its full extent is found.

In addition to abstinence, the Orphic *bios* involved rites (*teletai*) which, according to Plato, were supposed to "free us from the troubles of the other worlds" (*Republic* 364b). Plato looked down on these rites as inadequate, calling those who preached that "sacrifices and incantations" were sufficient to remedy the problems of death "charlatans" (ibid.). In India, too, the representatives of the new tripartite doctrine regarded the ritualism of the old Vedic priesthood as inadequate. Upaniṣadic, Buddhist, and Jain teachers, like the Pythagoreans and Platonists of Greece, held that only "knowledge" would constitute release; ritualism would at most win a favorable reincarnation or a happy intermediate afterlife period.

The Released Soul

Through a combination of abstinences, the cultivation of desirelessness, and a raised or expanded notion of the self, the soul is believed to become purer in each successive life until at last, in its final incarnation, it is what the Hindus call a *jīvanmukta*—a human who will not be reborn again after the death of his or her present body-habitation. Both the Greek and the Indian traditions recognized this category of human. Empedocles outspokenly declared himself to be of this group. "I surpass," he said, "mortal men, who are subject to many deaths . . . I walk among men as a god, no longer a mortal—I have been set free" (fr. 113). Something similar may be meant in the Pythagorean tradition when Pythagoras is declared to belong to a class between gods and humans (Iambl. *Vit. Pyth.* 30)—that is, he will not be born again as a mortal, but as an immortal; he is in the transitional incarnation. In India, Upaniṣadic sages such as Yājñavalkya are traditionally regarded as in this category. Before passing out of the body forever, the freed souls use their last incarnation to teach others how to attain that happy outcome.

Special powers may appear to substantiate claims to this status, and in both Greece and India the doctrine was disseminated in a milieu in which such powers were widely believed in. In Greece the lore about the early protophilosophers called *theologoi*, and about the Orphic movement in general, with its extensions into Pythagoreanism and Platonism, is full of stories of teaching masters who worked in part through superpowers. Abaris, who wrote a religious poem that is not extant but that fed into the Orphic stream, was reported to live altogether without eating. He also was said to have the ability to fly and to predict the future. Isteas, a dim figure from the sixth century B.C., was credited with the powers of trance, bilocation, and out-of-body travel. Hermotimus also traveled psychically. These ascriptions of superpowers were remnants of shamanic power claims—such as the claim to fly to other worlds. As the emerging discipline of philosophy defined itself, "legendary masters like Epimenides and Pythagoras appear . . . as taking on the traditional figure of the initiatic teacher, but intent on transforming and reinterpreting the ancient rites."[7]

In the culture of reincarnationism the category of the released soul became a new focus for the myth of the sorcerer-hero. Like shamans, the released souls were credited with special abilities often including retrocognition of past incarnations. Pythagoras prophesied the future and, according to Heraclides Ponticus, could "retain through life and through death a memory of his experiences," specifically, his last four incarnations (*ap.* D.L. VIII.4–5). Empedocles credits him with memory of more than four, in a passage which Porphyry, who preserves it, says is about Pythagoras:

> When he strained with all his mind [says Empedocles], he could easily see everything there is in ten, yes even twenty human lifetimes. (DK 31B129)

Empedocles himself claimed the abilities of retrocognition of his past incarnations, raising the dead, and controlling the winds. From the fifth century B.C. until the early Roman Empire claims of this sort recede in the Greek philosophical milieu; then, in the era of the mystery religions, Neopythagoreanism, and Neoplatonism, they recur in connection with figures such as Apollonius of Tyana.

In India such claims may go back to the Indus Valley culture, from which some of the techniques of yoga evolved, and beyond, to the proto-Australoid stratum of Indian culture, where early forms of some of the practices of yoga may have developed. These practices aim at the accumulation of "heat" (*tapas*) in the body, with the belief that it can then be converted to directed activity. These heat-developing practices are the seedbed from which superpowers (Skt. *siddhis*) arise. It is commonly supposed that they descended from the Indus Valley period through various non-Aryan lineages into the Middle Vedic period, when they began to be appropriated into the Vedic context. In the late Vedic, or Upaniṣadic period, they became increasingly associated with the reform movements, both the Upaniṣadic and the *nāstika* (non-Vedic), and especially with the claim of liberation from reincarnation, which may originally have been more a power claim than an ethical claim, conferring a status beyond ordinary ethical limits. Once release had been attained, "the moral acts of the person . . . were indifferent."[8] A special mythos built up about the liberated one, who has a kind of royal status. He is said to become a *kāmadeva*, or love-god, whom no woman can resist. Garlands, perfumes, music, and women are said to be his lot. He has knowledge of things that are beyond normal ken.[9]

Extrasensory perceptual powers, along with outright magical powers—are believed to arise naturally through advanced *karma* or to be developed deliberately through combinations of austerity and meditation (the exact recipe varying from teacher to teacher). Claims of possessing *siddhis* were normal parts of the philosopher's reputation, as of the yogic master's. The Jain teacher Mahāvīra, for example, was credited with a wide variety of superpowers and, like Empedocles, may have perpetrated the claims himself and believed them. He was said to exercise clairvoyance, clairaudience, and telepathy (the first two of which Pythagoras also claimed).[10] He attributed his powers to the performance of austerities, and occasionally engaged in sorcerers' duels.[11] At times the Jain texts credit him with outright omniscience (*kevala*).[12] In the tradition about the Indian doctrine of *siddhis*, omniscience was defined as a medley of psychic powers including unlimited retrocognition, precognition, clairvoyance, and clairaudience. At least two Ājīvika teachers in the Buddha's day were credited by their followers with omniscience.[13]

The ability to remember his past lives was the first *siddhi* which Siddhārtha attained under the enlightenment-tree. Once, in claiming victory in a debate about how *karma* works, he argued that his opponent could not see as many past incarnations as he could.[14] In various passages of the Buddhist canon, Siddhārtha is credited with either three or six psychic powers, the six being psychokinesis (including levitation, or flying), clairaudience, clairvoyance, retrocognition of his own past incarnations, telepathy, and knowledge of the stage of other people's *karma* (that is, of what someone's next birth would be).[15] The scale of such claims is generally greater in India than in Greece, but the doctrinal framework containing them is the same in both cultures.

The Appearance of the Reincarnation Doctrine in Greece

The *Suda*, a Byzantine encyclopedia that preserves much ancient lore, says the doctrine of reincarnation was introduced into Greece by Pherecydes of Syros, a "bizarre figure" (as one modern calls him)[16] whom Porphyry credits with the ability to remember his past incarnations. This tradition is obliquely supported by Cicero's statement (*Tusc.* I.38) that Pherecydes was the first of the Greeks to teach the immortality of the soul. Pherecydes was one of the semilegendary Seven Sages of the archaic period of Greek culture. He may have lived about 650 B.C. (according to Theopompus) or about a century later (according to Apollodorus). He "was almost certainly a generation younger than Thales," says a modern scholar,[17] and this later date would locate him in the period when Greece and India were linked by the Persian Empire. He wrote a book called the *Theology* (*An Account of Sacred Things*, or *of the Gods*), the fragments of which show traces of doctrines found in the Greek poems called the *Orphic Theogonies*—Zeus, for example, changing into Eros in order to create the world. Pherecydes may have borrowed from books attributed to Orpheus, or he himself, as an author from whom Orphics borrowed, may have contributed to them unwittingly. His sources are variously reported, though it is widely agreed that he imported non-Greek ideas. Josephus said, "Pherecydes and others learned from the Egyptians and Chaldeans."[18] The *Suda* says he used the "secret books of the Phoenicians."[19]

Among the pre-Socratics, Pherecydes' only significant connection is rumored to have been with Pythagoras, whose teacher he is said to have been. An unlikely account preserved by Diogenes Laertius (VIII.56) further states that Pythagoras was for a while a teacher of Empedocles, suggesting a lineage—Pherecydes, Pythagoras, Empedocles—for the doctrine of reincarnation in Greece. In any case "Pythagoras" was already, in the pre-Socratic period, a charismatic name around which rumors tended to cluster; both Empedocles and Xenophanes wrote remarks about him which still exist, though no other pre-Socratic philosopher is known to have been written about by his fellows. The earliest testimonium is the fragment of Xenophanes (fr. 7) (writing probably about 525 B.C.):

> What he [Xenophanes] says about Pythagoras runs thus: "Once they say that he was passing by when a puppy was being whipped and he took pity and said: 'Stop—don't beat that animal; it is the soul of a friend; I recognized its voice when it cried out.'" (D.L. VII.36)

This voice-recognition has resonances in shamanic traditions round the world, as well as in the yogic traditions of India; in both cases the spiritually or magically advanced personality is believed to understand the "speech" of animals and birds. The story attests that Pythagoras, in addition to being able to understand some nonhuman speech, was indeed a reincarnationist—a view which virtually no expert rejects.[20] Many ancient authors regarded him, rather than Pherecydes, as the first Greek to teach the doctrine. Porphyry wrote:

> The following became universally known: first, he maintains that the soul is immortal; next, that it changes into other kinds of living things; also that events recur in certain cycles, and that nothing is ever absolutely new; and finally that all living things should be regarded as akin. Pythagoras seems to have been the first to bring these beliefs into Greece. (*Vit. Pyth.* 19 = DK 14.8a)[21]

Orphism

There is a confusion between Pythagoreans and Orphics in the ancient literature, suggesting a close relationship about which the facts are not known anymore.[22] Herodotus (II.81), for example, refers to certain ritual practices as "Orphic and Pythagorean," and Ion of Chios (DK 36A6) says the Orphic texts were really written by Pythagoras. Yet the two categories are very different. Pythagoras was a historical figure who founded a "brotherhood" in Croton in South Italy—an ancestor of groups like the Rosicrucians and Freemasons which, while pursuing researches into occult and scientific subjects, became involved in politics as well, usually in a hidden and conspiratorial way. Often made up of aristocrats, such associations could be perceived as a threat to the state. Pythagoras's group became so embroiled in politics that the populist party (it seems) burned their buildings and drove them out.

Orpheus is a far less substantial figure even than Pythagoras, a figure who seems primarily out of legend. Strabo remarks that Orpheus went to study in Egypt—and then adds that he went with the Argonauts to Colchis, too. It is widely believed that he represents in part Greek contact with a tradition of Thraco-Scythian shamanism; his famous descent to the underworld to bring Eurydice back, for example, answers to the shaman's role as psychopomp, and various ancient texts connect him with Thrace. Vague as the available understanding of what it meant to be a "Pythagorean" is, the sense of what it meant to be an "Orphic" is vaguer still. We know of no specific Orphic brotherhood or roll of initiates. "Orphic" simply designates those who attached the name of Orpheus to their texts and rituals.[23] "Orphic" groups, defined in this way, were disparate and not bound together by any authoritative body of doctrine or myth. Some texts going under the name of Orpheus were Pythagorean—such as the Orphic *Hymn to Number* known to Neoplatonist authors;[24] others were Eleusinian.[25] Some of the Orphic *Theogonies* taught reincarnation; some did not.[26] There were self-styled "Orphics" who, like some ascetic groups in India, wandered, eschewed property, and performed rituals for a living. Their magic related not only to the present life but to the afterlife. Those citizens who had undergone (and paid for) certain rituals would expect a more pleasant afterlife, a more sybaritic heaven, than those who did not. Orpheus was the attributed author of the ritual texts used by these wandering magicians or "priests."

From a variety of sources—including Plato, the gold plates which were buried with some Orphic initiates in Magna Graecia, and the *Orphic Theogonies*—a view which has come to be called "Orphic" has been reconstructed, though it was not held by all of those who went under that name. In this view, life in a human body is regarded as a punishment for a crime performed by the soul before it was embodied, or when it was in a divine rather than a mortal body. The punishment for the errant soul is to be confined in a series of mortal bodies, subject to pain, decay, and death not only once but over and over again. According to Plato:

> [The Orphics] say that the body (*soma*) is the tomb (*sema*) of the soul . . . as if it (the soul) were dead in its present existence (or buried alive) . . . The followers of Orpheus hold that the soul is undergoing punishment for some reason or other and has this husk around it like a prison, to keep it from running away. (*Cratylus* 400c)[27]

The soul does, however, try to run away, choosing for its attempt the moment of death, when the body is letting go of the soul but its next incarnation or imprisonment has not yet taken hold of it. What it needs to make good its escape is something to refresh its memory. In this mythology the soul is a god who has been exiled, for some wrongdoing, from the banquet table of heaven, and imprisoned in a series of suffering human bodies as punishment. The condition of its punishment is forgetfulness. During the brief crucial period when it is between bodies, it must remember its true identity and demonstrate the recollection by uttering certain formulaic lines. For this purpose the Orphic initiate is sometimes buried with a small gold plate engraved with the necessary words, rolled into a cylinder and suspended from a gold chain around his neck, to be consulted in the afterlife if necessary.[28]

The texts on these gold plates indicate that the soul, on awakening from its sleep in the body, will find a spring of cold water flowing from the Lake of Memory, with guardians standing before it; this is the Spring of Memory, or Recollection. If it drinks from the Spring of Memory, the soul will recall its true identity and will be ready to reclaim its place at the heavenly table. But before it can be allowed to drink from the spring the soul must perform a preliminary or partial demonstration of memory, by carrying over the confusing threshold of death certain lines. In one version the soul, approaching the guardians of the spring, is to declare:

> I am a child of earth and of starry heaven, but my real nature is of heaven alone. You know me yourselves. How I am parched with thirst and perishing! Let me drink quickly from the spring that flows out from the Lake of Memory. (*OF* 32b)

Sometimes the formula involves declaring the names of the guardians, as a sign that one has known them in the past and hence belongs to their company, and claiming that one's ancient wrongdoing has been paid off in punishment:

> I come from the pure, pure Queen of those below, and Eukles and Eubuleus, and other Gods and Daimons: For I swear that I too am of your blessed race. And I have paid the penalty for deeds unrighteous. . . . (*OF* 32de)

Having said this, the soul is allowed to drink and, passing back into the company of the gods, is not reborn again. The formula "born of Earth and the starry sky" occurs also in Hesiod's definition of the immortal gods (*Theog.* 106), and is especially connected with the Titans, offspring of Gaia and Uranus; the primal crime for which the soul claims to have paid may have been the Titans' ancient rebellion against the gods.

Orphism and Empedocles

Some of the gold plates (including the oldest) were found in South Italy, and the Orphic myth seems to have been especially influential there and in nearby Sicily. Empedocles, too, purveyed the myth of an act of wrongdoing in the community of the gods for which the soul was exiled into human life, ambiguously identifying it as either violence or perjury:

> When one of the long-living gods wrongfully stains his limbs with bloodshed, or when one, moved by Hate, has sworn a false oath, they must then wander for three-times ten thousand seasons far from the blessed company of gods, and throughout this period they must be born into all kinds of shapes which are doomed to die, exchanging one hard way of life for another. For the mighty air chases them into the sea, and the sea spews them forth onto the dry land, and the earth drives them toward the rays of the blazing sun; and the sun hurls them into the eddies of the ether. One element receives them from the other and all hate them. Of this number am I too now, a fugitive from heaven and a wanderer, because I put my trust in raging hate. (Fr. 115)[29]

The Greeks at the time of Empedocles recognized three seasons in a year, so three times ten thousand seasons may mean ten thousand years. For this period, the soul which has fallen into matter must be processed through the physical universe, incarnated first in one element, then in another, as if it could not fall into matter without experiencing every possible material state before making its escape. It is uncertain whether there was any possibility of winning early escape, as on the gold plates, by special exertions such as vegetarianism, but it is likely enough, since Empedocles seems to have recommended such exertions. It is possible that thrice ten thousand seasons was the length of his cosmic cycle, and that the soul which does not attain early release must reincarnate through all the parts of nature for one complete cycle, becoming universalized a step at a time, through seeing all forms of matter from the inside.[30]

When after three times ten thousand seasons the last incarnation comes round, "They become prophets, and poets, and healers, and princes among earth-dwelling humans—

from this life they blossom forth as gods highest in honor" (fr. 146). Empedocles himself was a prophet, a poet, and a healer, and dressed, according to the ancient sources, so that the people in the street took him for a prince—perhaps because the doctrine he had received held that the liberated soul must be a prince (as indeed were Heraclitus, Pythagoras, and Siddhārtha). "It is probable," as Wright says, "that E. supposed all four types of life to be united in himself."[31] In any case, Empedocles announced himself to the general population as "an immortal god among you" (fr. 112)—that is to say, one who at the death of his present body will resume his seat among the gods. He demonstrated the ability to remember some (at least five) of his past incarnations, saying that he had previously been born "as a boy, a girl, a plant, a bird, and a mute fish in the sea" (fr. 117).[32] In light of the belief that the reincarnating soul must pass through all the elements, this fragment may represent Empedocles' belief that he had passed through the earth, air, and water stages—leaving only the fire.

In the famous and popular account of his death first found in Heraclides Ponticus (*ap.* D. L. VIII.67–68), Empedocles moved aggressively to rectify this lack. Confident that if he went through fire he would not be incarnated again, he led a group of followers to the top of the active volcano Mount Aetna and leapt in, "to show," as Diogenes Laertius said, "that he was a god."[33]

The custom of religious suicide was practiced in various ascetic groups in India—especially the Jains and Ājīvikas. In these contexts it could be called for by a variety of signs—perhaps that the religious practitioner felt his karmic situation was momentarily at its height, or perhaps that it was about to enter a slump through illness or old age. Often the subject would do away with himself in a prescribed ritual way under the eyes of his fellows and/or disciples. Common methods included starvation, entering water, and entering fire. Empedocles, entering fire, may have been motivated by a tradition of this type, making his death a spectacular demonstration of his detachment from the body and its desires.

Clearly the myth in which Empedocles presents himself is the same in outline as that intimated by the gold plates. Empedocles' association with Orphism became so strong that at some time his second poem, which Aristotle knows by another title (*Rhet.* 1373b14), was renamed *Katharmoi* ("Purifications"), a title that Plato used for Orphic rites and books (*Rep.* 364e).

Orphism and Pindar

About the time Empedocles was writing the *Purifications* (roughly 450 B.C.), the poet Pindar spent time in Sicily and encountered reincarnationist beliefs. In several poems he speaks somewhat obliquely about reincarnation. He says (fr. 131) that there is an "image of life" which "remains alive" when the body dies—perhaps a reference to the doctrine that Cicero attributed to Pythagoras, the immortality of the soul. "Yet," says Pindar, "while the limbs are active this image of life is asleep." The idea seems parallel to the Orphic belief referred to by Plato that while the body is alive the soul is dead (or buried alive).

In Pindar's version, the souls have various experiences between incarnations, probably including periods of reward and punishment for the last incarnation. After a certain period (perhaps the thirty thousand seasons of Empedocles, or some variant of it) the soul is born into its last incarnation. As in Empedocles, the final incarnation is a grand one, involving kingship, near to godhood.

> In the ninth year [says Pindar] Persephone sends their souls to the upper sun-light and they become august monarchs, swift, strong men pre-eminent in wisdom; and for all future time men call them sainted heroes.[34]

Another passage introduces the possibility of gaining early escape from the process through especially virtuous behavior:

> Those who are sufficiently bold to hold back their soul from all injustices while living three times on each side pass by the road of Zeus to the Tower of Kronos, where ocean breezes blow around the isles of the blessed and golden blossoms blaze. (*O.* II.56 ff)

After the third just life, according to one influential interpretation of the passage,[35] the soul will remain in Hades for nine years, then will be sent back to earth for a last life as a king or hero, returning to the god-realm—the Age of Kronos—after this incarnation. Here, as in the Orphic texts and Empedocles, is a myth of a soul which, through purifications carried out over several lifetimes, will be admitted (or readmitted) to the company of the gods, which is conceived as the Golden Age.[36]

Orphism, Hesiod, and Plato

The *Rhapsodic Theogony*, an Orphic poem of the Hellenistic period but preserving much earlier material,[37] also posits intermediary afterlives between incarnations. When a human dies, it says, the soul is led by Hermes to the underworld for judging, after which those judged to be good go to a pleasant meadow by Lake Acheron, and those judged to be wicked go to a less pleasant life in Tartarus. After three hundred years in these reward or punishment afterlives, they are reborn upon the earth. The terms governing this rebirth are unclear. Since the soul has already received its reward or punishment for the last life, the karmic account is balanced and the soul might be reborn with a clean slate. There are other signs, however, that its position in life in its new birth might be determined by its behavior in the last life, in which case there is a kind of double paying in the system, since the period of reward or punishment has already, supposedly, paid off the last life.

Plato, in the *Phaedrus*, presents a more detailed version of what seems to be the same afterlife myth. He describes matter as a contamination into which some souls have fallen through an undefined primal accident or misadventure. Those who have not fallen into matter are the beings whom we call gods. The destiny of souls which have fallen is to struggle to regain the state of godhood, in which the soul dwells pure and uncontaminated. In order to be readmitted to the god state, souls which have fallen must live through a series of ten incarnations, each followed by a period of about a thousand years of intermediate reward or punishment allotted on the basis of one's behavior in the last incarnation.

Again the question of double paying arises. Plato says in the *Phaedo* that those who lived lawlessly may be reborn as wolves or hawks, and so on. The new life, in other words, is determined by the account from the last life. Yet in the *Phaedrus* he says that the account from the last life is paid off in an intermediate period of reward or punishment, and that the new life is partly assigned by lot, implying randomness, and partly selected by the soul according to its own desire. It may be true that the soul's desire will represent its karmic situation and arise from its past behavior—but Plato does not specifically say in the *Phaedrus* that the new incarnation is determined by past behavior. The soul is said to "choose" its next life on the basis of the amount of the vision of truth it had on the other side of the world (248c-e), and that in turn seems to be determined by the amount of "philosophy" the soul practiced in its last life—though this is not explicitly stated. If this is in fact how the system is supposed to work, then the "choice" is not exactly voluntary; it is indirectly determined by one's behavior in the last life, even though this behavior has already been rewarded or punished. Plato presents slightly different models of reincarnationism in different dialogues; in the *Phaedo* (80e–81a), for example, the soul escapes after one life devoted to philosophy, in the *Phaedrus* (249a), after three. In any case, having lived through ten incarnations with their intermediate periods, the soul is released and ascends out of the world of matter, regaining its place among the gods. The cycle of about ten thousand years allotted in Plato's version recalls Empedocles' three times ten thousand seasons.

In the works of Hesiod, some of the background of this myth can be seen. He had both of Empedocles' great themes already; as he taught (or assumed) a myth of cyclical time in the *Works and Days*, in the *Theogony* he purveys the myth of the god who is exiled from the company of the gods for a Great Year. Both these ideas, then, assuming Hesiod's date to have been the seventh century, were current in Greece as early as that time. Both have connections with Bronze Age sources, the cycle seemingly from Mesopotamia and the myth of the soul's crime and exile (as will be seen) from Egypt.

Hesiod unambiguously defines the god's crime as perjury. Any god, he writes, who swears falsely by the water of the river Styx "lies breathless until a Great Year is done" (*Theogony* 793). The state in which the god "lies breathless" seems to echo Pindar's idea that the soul sleeps while the limbs are awake: The god lying breathless, then, is a soul stunned into forgetfulness of its divine nature by the trauma of imprisonment in flesh. The Orphic *Rhapsodies* also speak of the oath by the river Styx, saying that a god who swore falsely by it would be punished in Tartarus for nine thousand years.[38] This figure is echoed in Hesiod, who says that for nine years the exiled god lies "in a heavy trance," but in the tenth he comes again to the assemblies of the gods. The nine years' punishment is the same prescribed by Pindar. Hesiod's years, however, may be years of the gods, each equaling a thousand human years. In that case, his ten-thousand-year exile is the same figure which Plato gives for the period of reincarnations and which Empedocles and the Orphic *Rhapsodies* may also have taught. The idea occurs in Hesiod, however, without any specific reference to reincarnation. Whether the heavy trance in which the exiled god is held for nine thousand years is the same as the Orphic image of the soul asleep in a human body is unknown. In any case, Hesiod's nine years of sleep or trance, read as nine thousand, agrees with the *Rhapsodic Theogony*, and Pindar's "nine years" may similarly represent the nine thousand years that will pass before the final incarnation.

A trace of this myth comes up again in Plutarch's *In Defense of Oracles* (422bc); the souls of men who have lived well, says Plutarch, see once every ten thousand years the sacred realities that are dimly hinted by mystical ceremonies performed here below. Plutarch must be referring to the doctrine of recollection, which Plato expressed by saying, in the *Phaedrus* and elsewhere, that the soul, before becoming embodied, receives a primal vision of reality which, when it enters a body, it forgets—and which the Orphics hope to regain with a drink from the Spring of Memory.

But Plato in the *Phaedrus* does not present just the ten-thousand-year cycle; he, like Pindar, allows early release for good behavior. Pindar had said that three just lives in a row send one to the Tower of Kronos, that is, to the feasting hall of the gods. Plato in the *Phaedrus* similarly says that if one has chosen a "philosophical" life three times in a row he will be set free at the end of three thousand years—that is, after three incarnations with their intermediary excarnate periods—which may be what Pindar's "three times on both sides" means. Plato's "philosophical life" involved various abstinences and disciplines, akin to yogic practices or Orphic vows, designed to loosen the bonds of matter rather than strengthen them, as an ordinary indulgence of the appetites was held to do.

Elsewhere Plato writes of a doctrine "heard from men and women wise in sacred knowledge" (*Meno* 80e ff.). "Those who tell it," says Plato, "are priests and priestesses of the type who make it their business to be able to give an account of what they are up to." An imported or revised doctrine is implied, as in Pindar's remark that he sings for "those who understand," that is, those who have been instructed in the new doctrine.[39] Greek priests and priestesses in general do not seem to have given much of an "account" of what they did; they performed ceremonies involving the manipulation of symbols, and their "accounts" were usually variations on myths. The various myths of Apollo, for example, probably came, over the ages, from various establishments of Apolline priesthoods who promulgated them as doctrine. It is not clear in what way the idea that Apollo slew Python, or that the Centaurs raped the Lapith women, or that Dionysus turned into a leopard on shipboard were meant as "teachings." An intuitive quasi-aesthetic and quasi-religious feeling seems to have been evoked by such images, as in the Eleusinian Mysteries there were "teachings" that were wordlessly acted out. This imagistic communication, in both rite and story, seems to have been a principal means of priestly expressiveness in the Bronze and Early Iron Ages.

But as the Iron Age advanced, and the movement toward abstract thought and philosophical discourse developed, another way of dealing with myth arose, which was to allegorize it intellectually. By the late sixth century the allegorical interpretation of poetry was underway. In Plato's day, the traditional priesthoods, such as those of Apollo at Delphi or Delos, or of Athena in the Parthenon at Athens, still expressed their "teachings" through myth and rite. But some other groups had begun "giving an account" of what they did, that is, allegorizing myths, conflating mythic motifs to create specific allegorical possibilities, and so on. These new priesthoods presumably included some Orphics who not only told myths but also explained their doctrinal significance.

These new doctrines were embodied in poetry, often with attributions to Orpheus or other legendary poets. Plato regards inspired poets as equal revelatory sources with priests and priestesses; indeed, as mythmakers, the professions were the same:

> Pindar tells it too, and many other of the divinely inspired poets . . . that the human soul is immortal, and that one day it comes to its end—which they like everyone else call dying—and at another time it is reborn, and it is never fully annihilated. For this reason it is necessary to live as sinless a life as possible. (*Meno* 81ab)

Orphism and Heraclitus

Several fragments of Heraclitus suggest reincarnationism of this type—for example:

> Immortals are mortal, mortals immortal: each lives the death of the other and dies the other's life. (Fr. 62)[40]

Heraclitus may be referring to the idea behind Pindar's "image of life" which lives while the limbs sleep and Hesiod's slumbering immortal exile. He recalls this doctrine again, saying:

> And what is in us is the same thing: living and dead, awake and sleeping, as well as young and old; for the latter (of each pair of opposites) having changed becomes the former, and this again having changed becomes the latter. (Fr. 88)

The parallel pairs living/dead and awake/asleep are implicit in Hesiod's passage, too, as well as in many Upaniṣadic texts; the young/old dichotomy refers to the repetitiveness of rebirth. Other fragments of Heraclitus seem to describe the transmigration of the soul through all the realms of nature (as in Empedocles) and the Orphic doctrine of its return to the god-realm after its release from nature. It is likely that Anaximander held a version of this general view also, and if he did, then so, probably, did Anaximenes.

Orphism and Parmenides

Parmenides may at one time have been a Pythagorean, and a passage in Simplicius strongly suggests that he taught the doctrine of reincarnation. Speaking of Parmenides' goddess of Necessity, Anankē, who "steers all things" in the realm of experience, Simplicius says: "She sends souls at one time from the visible to the unseen and at another time back again" (*In Phys.* 39.19–20). In other passages of Parmenides, darkness means the earth and light means heaven; if this is what the "unseen" and the "visible" mean in this passage, then the goddess, when causing souls to be born, sends them from their heavenly abode into darkness (sleep, death, matter, individuation), from which in time she releases them and restores them to heaven. This is structurally parallel to the Orphic myth of the primal fall and exile. It is the only evidence we have about Parmenides' eschatology, and it suggests an Orphic-Pythagorean type of view.[41]

Parmenides' book was a religious utterance, and its tone suggests influences from the Orphic-Pythagorean milieu. The only story that we have about his life is that he "was inclined to follow Ameinias the Pythagorean, and when Ameinias died he built a shrine to him . . . It was Ameinias, not Xenophanes, who led him to peace" (D.L. IX.21). Proclus says that both Parmenides and Zeno were Pythagoreans (DK 28A4). The Goddess Dikē Polypoinos, "Justice with Many Punishments," adopted by Parmenides, is otherwise known only as an Orphic goddess (who may have had to do with enforcing karmic consequences in the arrangement of rebirths). If Parmenides held a variant of the tripartite doctrine of reincarnation, then the "peace" for which he thanked Ameinias could only be release from reincarnation—the state of *jivanmukta*.

Reincarnation, to sum up, seems to have entered Greece in the seventh or sixth century. Along with it came a myth of the soul as an exiled god who wanders through the four elements of nature seeking to return to the company of the gods. Either he will wander through all the forms of nature (*pantoĭa eidea thnētōn*, says Empedocles [fr. 115.7]) and then be released, or he will hasten, through asceticism and philosophy, to an early release. The outlines of the doctrine and the accompanying myth seem to have been roughly the same for the Orphics, Empedocles, Pindar, Hesiod, Plato, and others. There is no alternative version (only nuanced variations on this one), nor are there earlier stages in which the doctrine is still unformed in some respect and later ones in which it is more formed. This rough uniformity suggests that the doctrine-and-myth entered Greece already formed and did not undergo its stages of development there. A brief review of the Indian material will show a significantly different picture.

Afterlife Doctrines in the Vedas

The *Ṛg Veda*, like Homer, does not teach reincarnation.[42] On its view, the individual human survives death as the same individual, in another world which is, like this one, conceived as in space-time. The burning of the body transports it to the next world, where the soul, flying temporarily out of the flesh, has to make efforts to rejoin it. Some of the dead, according to this myth, go to hell; what happens to them we are not told. Others go to heaven, which is located on the moon, and there drink the water of life and become immortal (*RV* IX.113.7 ff.) in a hedonistic paradise of flute girls and wishing-cows. There are Persian parallels to the *Ṛg Vedic* eschatology which suggest that it goes back to the Indo-Iranian period before the two peoples separated. The motifs of the water of life and the thirst of the dead are found also in the Orphic plates, and occurred earlier in both Mesopotamian and Egyptian afterlife myths. Perhaps they represent Near Eastern influence from the period before the entry into India, as the Vedic creation myth is also clearly based on Near Eastern antecedents.

"When we examine the eschatology of the *Ṛg* Veda," says Obeyesekere, "we are confronted with an unethicized religion."[43] "There is no notion of ethical compensation or reward, that is, sin and merit."[44] "The idea of a judgement of any sort is as foreign to the Ṛg Veda as to early Iran," according to Keith.[45] With the tenth book of the *Ṛg Veda,* this situation begins slowly to change; ethicization itself does not appear, but an afterlife process of cosmicization that may be seen as a kind of preparation for it through fomenting the individual's sense of participation and sharing in the universe.

Beginning with *Ṛg Veda* X and continuing through the *Atharva Veda*, the *Śatapatha Brāhmaṇa*, and the *Bṛhadāraṇyaka Upaniṣad*, Indian religion and thought were in a state of meltdown in which earlier cultural elements from various proveniences were rendered molten and remodeled in revolutionary ways. (The *Chāndogya Upaniṣad* is also a molten work, though slightly more congealed than the others mentioned.) In this era, on the prevailing consensus, the Aryan establishment admitted tribal influences from Munda and Dravidian peoples along with renewed Near Eastern influences. *Ṛg Veda* X introduces the Near Eastern concept of universalization, or macrocosm-microcosm correspondence, in two complementary ways. In the *Puruṣasūkta* the universe is homologized to the body parts of a Cosmic Person, as it had been in recent Mesopotamian mythology. In addition, one hymn (*RV* X.16) applies the theme of cosmicization to the dead soul as the sun receives his eye, the wind his breath, and so on.[46] This is strongly reminiscent of Egyptian afterlife myth, where also the dead soul expands throughout the universe. Also in *Ṛg Veda* X, the older eschatology of a sensual heaven was deepened with touches of mysticism. The soul, when it enters heaven, is now said to "return to its true home" (*RV* X.8), and to "the pasturage which it will not lose again" (X.14.2). These phrases suggest a myth of exile and return as among the Orphics, but with no mention of reincarnationism.

The *Atharva Veda*, seemingly of about the same date as *Ṛg Veda* X, has Akkadian religious terms, such as the name of the goddess Tiamat, alongside newly introduced ideas and images from Indian tribal groups. In one passage the ancestors waiting in the next world are beseeched to put back together the bones of the dead man, which have become disarranged (XIV.2.24),[47] a motif which may reflect additional Egyptian input as, in the Egyptian *Book of the Dead*, the deceased must gather and rejoin his bones.[48] Alongside these and other signs of fresh Near Eastern input, various primitive types of reincarnationism make an appearance, presumably from non-Aryan sources: the idea that the ancestor can be recognized in birds or insects crawling about the roots of plants and "the practice of using an insect or other animal, which alighted on a garment spread out with an invocation to the soul of the dead, when his bones cannot be found, to serve in place of his mortal relics."[49] These primitive forms of the doctrine of reincarnation may go back to indigenous animists of the Ganges Valley,[50] or even earlier, to the pre-Indus culture of "Austric proto-Australoids."[51] These were what Obeyesekere refers to as unethicized forms of reincarnation, which have the doctrine of rebirth, but not yet the doctrine of *karma.* Finally the tripartite version began to unfold itself in stages, in the texts called *Āraṇyakas* and *Brāhmaṇas*, perhaps about 800 B.C., "through the operation of the crucial causal variable known as ethicization."[52]

The Āraṇyakas and Brāhmaṇas

The *Taittirīya Āraṇyaka* stresses the theme of judgment, already present in the *Ṛg Veda*—that after death the truthful and untruthful will be separated from one another. As in Hesiod and Empedocles, the focus of the judgment is on perjury—as it was in the weighing of the soul in the Osirian afterlife in Egypt, possibly the prototype of the other instances. The *Śatapatha Brāhmaṇa* (XI.2.7.33) images the judgment as a weighing of the good and bad deeds of the deceased, a type of weighing which is found in the Persian afterlife myth, too, and may represent Egyptian influences received in the Indo-Iranian period.[53]

In the *Śatapatha Brāhmaṇa,* the belief appears that some souls will need food again, even in the afterlife, whether after a few weeks or after years; for others it will never be needed (*SB* X.1.5.4). A crucial ramification of this teaching is the belief that some souls, not receiving the food they need, will be caused "to die again and again in the afterlife," whereas others will have become immortal (*SB* II.3.3.8). Dying again and again in the afterlife requires being born again and again in the afterlife, too. "Some souls the god of death causes to be born again from out of the immortal womb" (*SB* XII.9.3.12), so that they may then be forced to die again.

According to the *Śatapatha Brāhmaṇa,* the avoidance of redeath in the afterlife requires both the performance of appropriate rituals to forestall it and an understanding of the process itself—an early version of the double path of both knowledge and works. The requirement of understanding the doctrine suggests that it is a secret or new doctrine which is being disseminated along with certain new rites. One passage (*SB* X.4.3.10) says that either knowledge of the process or performance of the rituals will suffice to avoid "becoming the food of death again and again." The doctrine of renewed death in the afterlife is taught by other Brāhmaṇas, also.[54] This doctrine, apparently new in India, seems to be one of the early stages of the emergent tripartite form of reincarnationism.

Since, on this view, the renewed deaths are seen as a kind of torture or punishment, nothing is heard of the duration or quality of the experiences that intervene between the soul's forced rebirth in the afterlife and its forced redeath. It seems clear, however, that the period of renewed existence in the afterlife was not regarded as desirable. Escape from the process of rebirth and redeath in the afterlife was a positive value. If the doctrine is transposed into the terms of *this* world, it contains the raw essence of the tripartite schema: that undesirable rebirths and redeaths are inevitable unless certain steps—either involving instructions from priests or rituals or both—are taken to escape from the process.[55]

The Vedic emphasis on ritual underlies and pervades these texts to the extent that the doctrine of *karma* is conceived in its terms. "[T]he almost purely ritual character of goodness in the view of the *Brāhmaṇas*," says Keith, "is [shown by the fact that] their concept of torment is inextricably bound up with the correct practice . . . of the ritual."[56] "[A]t death," says Obeyesekere, "a man is weighed in a balance to test the good and the bad, but this is not based on a social morality . . . It is based on violations of taboo and on ritual interdictions."[57] "Good [is] equated with the correct performance of the rite, bad with the incorrect performance."[58] The afterlife, in other words, works out "the merit (the 'good') or demerit (the 'bad') accumulated through a lifetime of sacrificial activity."[59] For instance: "When the Agnihotra is being offered, what he does mistakenly, either by word or deed, that cuts off his vigor, his own self, or his children" (*SB* II.3.4.18).[60] *"Le bien,"* says Sylvain Levi, *"est l'exactitude rituelle."*[61] "Clearly," says one author, "we are dealing with taboo violation rather than with religious ethics or morality."[62] But in fact, the matter is not that clear. The ritual emphasis does not mean that the system in question was still unethicized, but that it used a different understanding of what types of behavior lead to reward and punishment; as Tull puts it: "Although the idea . . . may not reflect morality in a general sense, within the limits of a well-defined system it yet expresses a notion of ethics."[63] The point is that the idea of karmic accumulation with a positive or negative polarity based on past behavior—the structural framework—is in place regardless.[64]

The Upaniṣads: Yājñavalkya and Uddālaka

Two limbs of the tripartite doctrine are articulated explicitly in the discourse of Yājñavalkya (*Yājñavalkya-kāṇḍa*) in the *Bṛhadāraṇayaka Upaniṣad.* The engaging figure of this sage looms large in the history of Indian thought—indeed of world thought, though this is not widely recognized. Yājñavalkya comes down in tradition as the greatest exponent of the path of knowledge in the Upaniṣads, and at the same time, in the *Śatapatha Brāhmaṇa*, is presented as the greatest authority on the path of works or sacrifice. The dates of the texts do not seem to match up, and it has been proposed that a "device employed by the compilers of the Upaniṣads was the attribution of many of their teachings to the same sages that appear in the Brāhmaṇas . . . ,"[65] in which case the discourse we have is actually of a nameless pseudo-Yājñavalkya. In any case, he is recorded to have been a *kṣatriya*, or nonpriestly teacher, who introduced doctrines from outside the Brahmanic community as part of a movement to form a religious teaching establishment that would be alternative, or supplemental, to the sacrificial cult of the Brahmins. In the passage in question ("widely considered to be the earliest formulation of the *karma* doctrine in the Upaniṣads")[66], Ārtabāgha, Yājñavalkya's interlocutor, has already been imbued with "new" doctrines, that is, the Middle Vedic doctrines of cosmicization that replaced the Early Vedic paradise. Ārtabāgha's question expresses the feeling that there is something to selfhood left over after the dispersion to the various parts of nature described in the tenth book of the *Ṛg Veda.*

> Yājñavalkya [Ārtabāgha said], when the voice of the dead person enters into the fire, the breath into air, the eye into the sun, the mind into the moon, the hearing into the quarters, the self into the ether, the hairs on the body into the herbs, the hair on the head into the trees, and the blood and semen are deposited in water—what then becomes of that person? (*BU* III.2.13)

Yājñavalkya's answer shows that he is about to introduce an even newer doctrine: "Ārtabāgha, my dear," he says, "take my hand. We two alone shall know of this. This is not for us to speak of in public." The two go away and deliberate. "After one dies," says

Yājñavalkya, "his knowledge and his work take hold of him as also his past experience." Knowledge and work (or ritual) are the alternative ways to escape from redeath in the afterlife which were prescribed by the *Śatapatha Brāhmaṇa*. "When his work takes hold of him," says Yājñavalkya, "he becomes good by good action, bad by bad action"—meaning that good action will produce a desirable reincarnation, bad action an undesirable one.

The next and crucial passage is one in which Yājñavalkya, who had studied, it seems, under Dravidian as well as some foreign or foreign-influenced teachers, incorporates the primitive notion of the soul creeping about the roots of plants or entering into an insect.

> "Just as a caterpillar, when it has come to the end of a blade of grass, makes an approach to another blade of grass, then draws itself up and moves toward it, so does this self, after having thrown away this body, and dispelled ignorance, after having another approach to another body, draw itself together for making the transition to another body."

Yājñavalkya says that the soul, having shed its body, has also dispelled ignorance: The body, or matter, in other words, *is* ignorance—as according to Pindar it is like sleep.

> "As a goldsmith [Yājñavalkya goes on], taking a piece of gold, turns it into another newer and more beautiful shape, even so does this self, after having thrown away this body and dispelled its ignorance, make unto himself another, newer and more beautiful shape . . . According as one acts, according as one behaves, so does he become. The doer of good becomes good, the doer of evil becomes evil."

Two limbs of the tripartite doctrine—reincarnation and *karma*—may be present here; the third, release (*mokṣa*) is not mentioned.

Another great *kṣatriya* teacher, Uddālaka, taught a version of the third limb, the doctrine of *mokṣa*, in the *Chāndogya Upaniṣad*. The essential distinction which, he suggests, determines whether one is reincarnated or released is a kind of knowledge; works, or ritual observances, which were the center of the Vedic religion, are no longer sufficient. One who knows this new doctrine, he says, will "be released" and will have everything, or the all, for its self (*ātmyam idaṁ sarvam*)—that is, will become cosmicized (*CU* VI.16.1–3). The negative valuation of human life, which no doubt involves social factors of the time, may also proceed from this grandiose expectation of the next world, the state of cosmicization dwarfing the parameters of an individual existence. The new doctrine combines the Dravidian idea of rebirth in insect or animal form, the doctrine of ethical judgment determining afterlife (perhaps derived ultimately from Egypt), and the *Atharva Veda*'s concept (also ultimately Near Eastern) of cosmicization in the afterlife. The development is staged, and the stages seem triggered in part by successive inputs from various sources outside the Aryan tradition.

Hindu Synthesis

The version that would go down into mature Hinduism synthesizes the *Rg Vedic* afterlife with the new Upaniṣadic teaching in the so-called Doctrine of the Five Fires and the Two Paths. One path, that of knowledge, will lead to escape from the wheel of rebirth and redeath; the other, that of works, will lead instead to intermediary afterlife periods of reward or punishment—heaven or hell—followed by rebirth into a form which, even though one has already been rewarded or punished, will still result from past actions. There is a discordance in this syncretic doctrine. Although one's karmic account has been paid off by the time spent in an intermediary heaven or hell, still, somehow, one's old karmic account from before the payoff determines one's subsequent rebirth. There is double payment.[67] The system of heavens and hells, in other words, does not fit the system of karmic reward and punishment, whose ethical imperative it reduplicates redundantly; their conflation into a single system suggests an attempt to synthesize doctrines from different ages, that is, to connect a new and unfamiliar doctrine onto an old familiar one in order to normalize it.

The idea of a double path is given full articulation. Those dead souls who, because of their "knowledge," are to be released from rebirth, travel upward in the smoke of the funeral pyre by the Path of the Gods and are set free among them, as in the Orphic belief the freed soul regains entrance to the company of the gods; they will not be reborn again. Those who have devoted themselves to rituals rather than knowledge, who have stuck with the old Vedic religion and have not delved into the Middle and Late Vedic attitudes, will ascend in the smoke of the funeral pyre by the Path of the Fathers to the moon, where they will remain in a Vedic-style heaven until the good *karma* attained by their ritual piety is used up, then will reenter the process of nature, descending to earth in the rain to be reborn (*CU* V.3–10). Another path, which somehow seems outside a system already complete, leads the wicked to the "joyless regions" for punishment (*BU* IV.11).

In practice, however, the two paths of the afterlife tend to mix, so the enlightened soul that gains release does not thereby forgo its chance at heaven. "The state of liberation . . . does not at all mean the extinction of individual self . . . The liberated self can actualize his desires by mere will . . . The liberated self is without a lord (*adhipati*), for he himself is his own lord and anything he wishes he can realize (*BS* IV.4.8–9)." "The individual which has attained such a liberation experiences infinite blessings and joys . . . the liberated one's lordly powers are equal to [Īśvara's] . . . in the sphere of enjoyment. . . ."[68]

It is in this stage of the development of the system that the influence of primitive cultures can clearly be seen. The doctrine of reincarnation underwent so much spiritualization in later ages that it is easy to lose sight of the probability that it arose from an encounter between a synthesizing impulse in the Aryan community and the tribal peoples of India. There is a speculative distinction in the history of religion between early peoples who assume that the soul of the dead remains close to its body and to the earth, and hence must be propitiated with offerings or kept off by apotropaic rites, and a supposedly later stage of religious thought in which it is believed that the soul, departing from the body, ascends to the sky after death. The primitive idea that the soul stays close to earth, creeping around the roots of plants (*SB* XIII.8.1.20) or entering birds or insects who pass by, seems to have been a basic element in the early stages of the formation of the doctrine of reincarnation in India. The idea of ascent to the sky and an eternity of glory provided the motive of escape from the earth and its limited forms—the negative valuation of human life.

In the *Śatapatha Brāhmaṇa* this stage of conflation is clearly seen. Alongside the doctrine that the souls creep around the roots of plants—evidently in order to reenter the food chain and be reborn through it—is found the idea that the stars are the abode of the dead. The question, in a sense, is whether the soul has an existence separate from the body, whether it can abandon the body and have a life of its own. This idea, like so much in early afterlife systems, is first extant in Egyptian texts. In pyramid texts, for example, one reads, "Soul to heaven, body to earth." "Thy essence is in heaven, thy body to earth." "Heaven hath thy soul, earth hath thy body." And so on.[69] These statements foreshadow both the Orphic's claim, "I am a child of Earth and Starry Heaven, but Heaven alone is my true abode," and the Indian synthesis in the Doctrine of the Two Paths.

In this doctrine, after an intermediate afterlife on the moon, the souls reenter the realm of nature by raining down from the sky and entering into the roots and sprouts of plants, whence they grow up as food; then, eaten as plant food by a male, the soul is converted into semen, deposited in the womb of a female, and reborn (see, e.g., *CU* V.106). The extreme physicality of the doctrine suggests primitive roots not yet mentalized and spiritualized.[70]

Having reentered the stream of nature through the food chain, those souls with good *karma* (even though they have already been rewarded for it with years of flute-girls and wishing-cows) will be reborn into higher-caste human lives. Those with karmic debt (even though they have already been punished in an intermediary hell) will "attain an evil birth—the birth of a dog, the birth of a hog, or the birth of a low caste person" (*CU* V.10.7). Those who at death have neither knowledge of the new doctrine nor accumulation of karmic credit from the performance or endowing of rites are immediately reborn—it is unclear through what process.

This doctrine—probably in place by the seventh century B.C.—shows all the major features of the tripartite doctrine as it occurred in Greece: reincarnation based upon ethical and/or cognitive evolution, with rebirths defined by one's progress in past lives; intermediate periods in heavens or hells; rebirths into animal, plant, or human forms; and an ultimate goal of release from the wheel and return to the soul's "true home." In Greece this doctrine seems to have appeared in the seventh or sixth century with little or no sign of development. In India, on the other hand, it seems to have crystallized in the seventh century, after a series of developmental stages involving the progressive synthesis of a number of elements from different sources. If the doctrine passed from one of these cultures to the other, then, it must have passed from India into Greece.[71]

A Drop of Alien Blood?

Western scholars have never been comfortable with reincarnationism, perhaps because of underlying Judeo-Christian feelings against the propriety of even discussing it. This discomfort is much stronger in regard to the Greeks than the Indians. Reincarnation goes most comfortably with a cyclical view of time, characteristic of the nonlinear, antiprogressive, ahistorical condition that Hegel saw prevalent throughout Asia. In his tradition of historical thought, then, it seems acceptable for Indians to hold what seems to westerners in general a primitive view. But for the Greeks—who in the pre-Socratic period were already passing out of the cyclical view of time into the linear and progressive one—to hold it seems a problem. Still, despite such misgivings, it remains a fact that, overall, the tripartite doctrine of reincarnation is the most widespread eschatological-ethical attitude of the Greek philosophical lineages. Dominant in the pre-Socratic period, it survived in a variety of forms through the Roman Empire and was consistently posited by such major lineages as the Platonic and the Stoic. Still it is widely ignored in discussion of Greek philosophy. There is a kind of denial, a pretense that it is not there, like the rhinoceros in the room. One major tactic has been to assume that the view was not Greek in origin but entered the tradition from without, preferably from a primitive source.

Thus it is that Rohde describes reincarnationism as "a drop of alien blood in the veins of the Greeks."[72] The image implies the view that culture follows ethnicity, and involves the idea that the Greeks represented rationality and the rest of the world was barbaric. "The whole [Dionysian-Orphic] movement," Rohde says, "wherever it came to their notice must have struck the Greeks of Homer as something strange and barbaric, attractive only through the interest ever attached to the unknown."[73] The Greeks themselves presumed that they had imported the doctrine from some foreign source. Indeed, the evidence does seem to support this assumption. The doctrine seems to appear in Greece abruptly, without developmental stages; though it appears only in fragments, these are clearly fragments of a finished whole, an articulated doctrine, not a rudimentary beginning. Where did they come from? For some generations the search has been on.

The Thracian Hypothesis

One widely influential hypothesis broached about sixty years ago proposes Thrace as the source.[74] It involves two beliefs: that the cult of Dionysus came from Thrace, and therefore Orphism came from Thrace; and that the doctrine of reincarnation occurs in Thrace in the cult of Zalmoxis, which various sources link with Pythagoras. Both of these assumptions are seen now as problematic. To begin with, though various ancient authors connect Dionysus with Thrace, the significance of the connection is unclear. The decipherment of Linear B, which took place after the formulation of the Thracian hypothesis, has led to the recognition of the name Dionysus in the Pylos tablets,[75] suggesting that he was a Greek god as early as the Late Bronze Age, which would rule out the idea that his cult entered Greece from outside at the beginning of the period when signs of Orphism first turn up.

Another explanation for the various passages connecting Dionysus with Thrace is that they may result from cultic syncretizing. One ancient source says, for example, "The Thracians call Dionysus 'Sabazius.'"[76] What is suggested may not be that the Thracians natively had the cult of Dionysus, but that the Greek cult of Dionysus was imported into Thrace and there assimilated by being identified with the Thracian cult of Sabazius.[77] The name "Orpheus" does seem to represent a shamanic influence whose introduction into Greece in the sixth century brought Thraco-Scythian elements with it; but these elements do not seem to include the tripartite doctrine of reincarnation, purification, and release.

The idea that the doctrine of reincarnation is found in the Zalmoxis cult is equally problematic. Herodotus (IV.94) and Plato (*Charm.* 156d) refer to Zalmoxis, a god of the tribe of Getae, as a conferrer of immortality; neither mentions a reincarnation doctrine. Hellanicus refers to two other Thracian tribes, the Terizai and the Krobyzi, of whom he says, "the dead are believed to return," "when someone dies they rejoice at the thought that he will return," and that they bring offerings to induce his return.[78] It is this "return of the dead," though it is not specifically attributed to the Getae, that is taken as a reference to reincarnation. But even if this "return of the dead" does refer to reincarnation, it does not refer to the tripartite doctrine of reincarnation that is found in Greece. The desire for release, the belief in moral evolution from one incarnation to the next, and the attainment of release as a reward for good actions—all these elements are missing. They are all ruled out by the fact that the Thracians "rejoiced" at the return of the dead, an attitude directly contrary to the Greek view that it is supposed to account for—that incarnation is a punishment or purgation to be escaped from as soon as possible.

In fact, as various authors have noted, the passages in question are not really credible as references to reincarnation at all.[79] Herodotus says that Zalmoxis, having been a slave of Pythagoras and later being freed, returned to Thrace and acted out some "Ionian practices" which he had learned from Pythagoras and other Greeks:

> He made himself a hall, where he entertained and feasted the chief among his countrymen, and taught them that neither he nor his guests nor any of their descendants should ever die, but that they should go to a place where they would live for ever and have all good things. While he was doing as I have said and teaching this doctrine, he was all the while making him an underground chamber. When this was finished, he vanished from the sight of the Thracians and descended into the underground chamber, where he lived for three years, the Thracians wishing him back and mourning him for dead; then in the fourth year he appeared to the Thracians, and thus they came to believe what Zalmoxis had told them. (IV.95)

What seems to be commemorated here is the establishing by Zalmoxis of a mystery cult promising immortality to those who undergo an initiatory death-and-rebirth rite—a cult somewhat of the type that the Mysteries at Eleusis seem to have been. Ritual and ascetic *katabases*, or descents, like Zalmoxis's descent into his underground chamber, were a common practice among the many ancient religious cults involving incubation and rebirth symbolism. Such practices are attributed to Pythagoras (Porph. *Vit. Pyth.* 16–17, D.L. VIII.3), Epimenides (D.L. VIII.3), Apollonius of Tyana (Philostr. *VA* VIII.19), and others in the Greek tradition. They signal a widespread initiatory motif not involving the idea of reincarnationism but of spiritual rebirth in the same body, as in baptism. Zalmoxis reappeared in the fourth year as the same person he had previously been, not as a new person in a new body,[80] which would have been that of a young child. The "return of the dead," then, may describe the reemergence from the initiation chamber of one who had symbolically died, the moment signifying that one has ritually obtained a happy afterlife.[81] Finally, the idea that Zalmoxis taught reincarnationism contradicts the afterlife doctrine which Herodotus ascribes to him, "that neither he nor his guests nor any of their descendants should ever die, but that they should go to a place where they would live forever and have all good things." This seems a reference to a one-time attainment of a permanent heaven, not to a cyclical peregrination through many species.

The other key passage in the Thracian argument is from Euripides' *Hecabe*, when Polymestor is prophesying Hecabe's death (*Hec.* 1259 ff.):

> Polymestor: Hear my prediction. *I foretell that you—*
> Hecabe: Shall be carried on ship across the sea to Hellas?
> P.: *—shall drown at sea. You shall climb to the masthead and fall—*
> H.: Pushed by force?
> P.: You shall climb the mast of your own free will—
> H.: Climb the mast? With wings?
> P.: *—changed to a dog, a bitch with blazing eyes.*
> H.: How could you know of this transformation?
> P.: Because our Thracian prophet, Dionysus, told me so.
> H.: He neglected, I see, to foretell your own fate.
> P.: Had he told my future then, I never would have stumbled in your trap.
> H.: Shall I live or die?
> P.: Die. *And when you die your tomb shall be called—*
> H.: In memory of my change?
> P.: *—Cynosema, the bitch's grave, a landmark to sailors.*[82]

Poymestor's prophecy is interrupted by Hecabe's question ("Pushed by force?") and by his own answer and her retort. Then he resumes the syntax of the second sentence of his prophecy, to complete that sentence as follows: "I foretell that you shall drown at sea. You shall climb to the masthead and fall, changed into a dog, a bitch with blazing eyes." He seems to mean that when she has climbed to the top of the masthead she will turn into a dog there, lose her prehensile grip, fall into the sea, and drown. She is not to be reincarnated as a dog, but to change her shape before death. This is confirmed by Polymestor's assertion that the area where she drowns will be known as "the bitch's grave." She will be buried as a bitch, not reborn as one. The "Thracian prophet" Dionysus, then, is not talking about reincarnation but about shape-changing and sorcery.[83] Finally, though certain elements relating to Orpheus and Dionysus—the myths of Orpheus' shamanic descent to the underworld and of the dismemberment of Dionysus, and so on—may show Thracian influence, the Thracian hypothesis has nothing to do with the tripartite doctrine of reincarnation, purification, and release found in various early Greek sources.

A related hypothesis proposes that the Greeks learned reincarnationism not from a Thracian mystery cult but from Thracian and Scythian shamans in the area of the Black Sea, in the seventh century B.C., when the Black Sea was opened to Greek trade and colonization.[84] Along with reincarnation doctrine, on this view, came belief in the array of supernatural powers attributed to mysterious figures like Hermotimus, Epimenides, Abaris, and Aristeas. Since both Pythagoras and Empedocles belong to this group, shamanic influence, on this view, flowed smoothly into the mainstream of Greek philosophy, bringing with it the doctrine of reincarnation. This and similar views have been widely accepted, one scholar, for example, attributing the doctrine of reincarnation to "the primitive belief in the kinship of men and beasts,"[85] another to the "primitive idea of universal kinship."[86]

There are two great weaknesses to this approach. First (and the lesser), there is no evidence that Thracian or Scythian shamans had a doctrine of reincarnation, and in terms of what is known of shamanism in general it is unlikely. It is proposed then, that the Greeks derived or extrapolated the idea from "the northern belief that the 'soul' or 'guardian spirit' of a former shaman may enter into a living shaman to reinforce his power and knowledge"—a belief which it is agreed "need not involve any *general* theory of reincarnation."[87] But the word "general" is misleading here: In fact this belief does not involve any theory of reincarnation *at all*, surely not the tripartite form with its distinctive doctrines of purification and release.

A more serious problem with the Thracian hypothesis is that it doesn't involve India. This and similar explanations, offered on the assumption that the Greek doctrine is to be explained by itself, do not address the central problem of the extensive and nearly exact correspondence between the Greek and Indian versions. No parallel development argument has accounted for the correspondence, and neither the Zalmoxis cult nor Thracian-Scythian shamanism can be called on to account for Upaniṣadic doctrines. If shamanism in a more general sense is called on to account for separate but similar traditions in Greece and India—Scythian shamans, say, working on Greek tradition, while related Central Asian shamans influenced the Indian—then an account will have to be given of why shamanic lineages should be presumed to have disseminated a doctrine which they have never been observed to hold.[88] It is specifically the fact that the distinctive tripartite doctrine, including highly unusual elements such as the negative valuation of human life, appears in two places and nowhere else that needs to be accounted for, and there is no primitive or shamanic evidence which is relevant to such an account.

The Magian Hypothesis

An argument which is more fully conscious of the type of account that has to be given proposes that the doctrines that are shared in Greece and India were diffused into both from Persia in the middle. This is a central thesis of M. L. West's *Early Greek Philosophy and the Orient* of a generation ago. The hypothesis is tantalizing in its simplicity and convenient in terms of both geography and chronology. Greeks were in close contact with Persia from at least 545 till 479 B.C., and during much of that period significant centers of Greek culture like Miletus were actually in the Persian Empire. Northwest India, at another corner of the proposed triangulation, was made part of the Bactrian satrapy of the Persian Empire at some time during the reign of Cyrus (560–529) and at some time before 513 was made an independent satrapy, with an annual tribute and a regular sea-trade with the Persian Gulf. Clearly, Persia was in the ideal position, in the sixth century and after, to influence both Greek and Indian cultures directly, and such influence surely did take place. On the Indian side Persian influence has been recognized in key Upaniṣads and, in Greece, on Pherecydes, Anaximander, Anaximenes, and Heraclitus, among the pre-Socratics—not to mention the questionable tradition that Pythagoras was a student of Zoroaster (Aristoxenus fr. 13), that Democritus and Empedocles visited Persia (Pliny *NH* XXX.1.9), and so on.

The evidence for this influence consists of glimpsed fragments of doctrines. Anaximander, for example, virtually alone among the Greeks, believed the stars were closest to the earth, then the sun, last the moon—an odd conception among the Greeks, but "the standard Persian conception."[89] As for Anaximenes, "it can hardly be a coincidence . . . that his explanation of eclipses as being caused by dark bodies circulating below the sun and moon is identical with the belief of the Persians."[90] Heraclitus's choice of fire as his great symbol, his description of the sun as a bowl, his conception of god as an unsleeping and attentive mind, his prescription to throw corpses out rather than burn or bury them, his belief in the resurrection of the "guardians," his tone of censorious moralizing, and the bizarre story of his death—all these elements seem to involve some Iranian influence.[91] But whether these are the right influences to account for the broad correspondences between the early forms of philosophy in Greece and India, including the tripartite doctrine of reincarnation, is another matter.

West's is the only serious proposal about the relationship between Greek and Indian philosophy made in generations. It is remarkable how little attention has been paid to his important book.[92] One of the book's significant accomplishments, from the point of view of one interested primarily in the Greece-India relationship, is West's insight into the connection between Heraclitus's doctrine of the transformation of the elements and the Upaniṣadic Doctrine of the Five Fires and the Two Paths.[93] This constitutes a scholarly "proof" (meaning the most reasonable explanation until the state of the evidence changes) that a pre-Socratic was influenced by an Upaniṣad. This small matter becomes large, because, as Burkert says in another connection: "Once the historical link . . . has been established, then further connections . . . become more likely . . ."[94]

In West's view, some Median Magi must have taken up residence, either permanently or at least for a period of exile, in northeast Greek and northwest Indian cities and in time must have taught their inherited doctrines to selected natives. Since no historical situation exists before Alexander in which learned Greeks lived in India or Indians in Greece, no other scenario is available in which the conversants lived side by side and spoke to one another fluently. The only situation in which Greeks and Indians are known to have lived side by side in the period in question is the Persian court, home to neither, where diplomats, interpreters, physicians, courtesans, artisans, merchants, and mercenary soldiers, were gathered from around the empire. West's proposal removes the need to explain why Greeks and Indians living in Persia should have been more influenced by one another's ideas than by the culture which was a living presence all around them and whose language they may have been speaking. On the principle of simplicity the Persian hypothesis has a lot to recommend it. The danger is that West may have been so attracted by this comfortable diffusion situation that he forced some of his conclusions.

Monism and Dualism

To begin with, the tripartite doctrine of reincarnation is extremely unlikely to have come from Zoroastrianism, the historical religion of the Persian Empire, for the extant evidence about that tradition contains no hint of the teaching.[95] In fact, Zoroastrianism is deeply out of sympathy with the monism complex that is the matrix within which the tripartite doctrine is encountered. Zoroastrianism "repudiates monism," as one scholar had said,[96] and is the most perfectly dualistic of the world's major religions. It also repudiates immanentalism, that is, the idea of the universe as a living being with deity permeating it; this is a trademark of monism and a basic feature of both Upaniṣadic and pre-Socratic thought. Zoroaster's god does not animate from within a world which is consubstantial with himself; he directs from without a world that has no substantial relation to him. Further, "Zoroaster's god creates *ex nihilo* . . . Both the Greeks and the Indians, however, accepted it as axiomatic that nothing can arise out of nothing."[97] The gap between god and the world in Zoroastrianism is bridged by "the principle of revelation," a canon of dogmatic books which constitute the primary step god has taken to make his presence felt in the world. So unquestioned was this dogmatism that the devout Zoroastrian publicly avows, "I believe in whatever this religion says or thinks"[98]—an approach foreign to the dynamic speculations of both Greek and Indian thinkers. Again contrary to the tripartite doctrine, "life in this world is, for the Zoroastrian, not an exile in a valley of tears but a thoroughly satisfactory and enjoyable condition."[99]

In Zoroastrianism, time was conceived not as infinite and cyclical but as finite and extended in a straight line from a beginning to an end. There is no room in such a system for the indefinite duration of ethical reincarnationism. God made the world one day; he will one day destroy it. Judgment will follow, than an unchanging eternity of either reward or punishment. Nothing could be farther from the spirit of the Greek and Indian views of unending cyclical time in which, through chains of myriad lives, the soul gradually purifies itself until at last it can recognize its identity with the immanent absolute, the One. The Greek and Indian views of the afterlife cannot be adapted to noncyclical views of time. If souls reincarnated and worked on their *karma* in a world with finite, linear time, for example, those souls who had not worked out their *karma* by the time the world ended would be unaccounted for; there would be no place prepared for them.

Finally it seems clear that the required stream of influences could not have come from Zoroastrianism itself. West acknowledges this, saying, "Zoroastrianism had no place for metempsychōsis."[100] He suggests that it came instead from the pre-Zoroastrian religion of Persia, the religion that Zoroaster reformed. The whole package of the monism complex, including cyclicity, reincarnation, and so on, West calls the "gift of the Magi." He sums his conclusion up as follows:

> In some ways one might say that it was the very extravagance of oriental fancy that freed the Greeks from the limitations of what they could see with their own eyes: led them to think of ten-thousand year *cycles instead of human generations, of an infinity beyond the visible sky and below the foundations of the earth, of a life not bounded by womb and tomb but renewed in different bodies aeon after aeon.* It was now that they learned to think that good men and bad have different destinations after death; that the fortunate soul ascends to the luminaries of heaven; that god is intelligence; *that the cosmos is one living creature; that the material world can be analysed in terms of a few basic constituents such as fire, water, earth, metal; that there is a world of Being beyond perception, beyond time.* These were conceptions of enduring importance for ancient philosophy. This was the gift of the Magi. [emphasis added][101]

The problem is that the items that are emphasized in this list—cyclicity, infinity, reincarnation, monism, four elements, pure Being—seem to have been alien not only to Zoroastrianism but to the early phase associated with the Magi also. The concepts of cyclical time and infinity seem to have arisen in Persia only in the later Zurvanite sect.[102] Reincarnationism has no place in classical Persian eschatology, though again it may have existed in later mystery-influenced sects such as Mithraism. The view "that the cosmos is one living creature" is also associated only with the late Mithraic and Zurvanite sects. The idea of the four elements does not appear in Persian thought until a later period and then is attributed to the influence of "Greco-Indian writings."[103] In sum, the Persian religion was dominated by doctrines that are irreconcilable with the monism complex: cosmic dualism, resurrection and immortalization of the body, a once-only linear view of time, final judgment followed by permanent heaven or hell, and more. Clearly this is not the same body of ideas that West finds in India and Greece. A closer look at the pre-Zoroastrian phase of Persian religion will confirm this impression.

Persian Religion before Zoroaster

Most of the Magian religion has vanished, but something is known from the relics of its texts which have found their way into the *Zendavesta*, especially the twenty-four hymns called *yashts*, which comprise the central section of that book. "Although all these hymns are used in the Zoroastrian services many of them basically date back to the pre-Zoroastrian period."[104] Another source is the evidence of the "repaganization" that followed the Zoroastrian reform;[105] ritual practices presumably of Magian origin were reintroduced, including cattle sacrifice, *haoma* intoxication, and worship of the Mother Goddess Anahita, all of which Zoroaster had denounced. The pre-Zoroastrian religion of Persia appears, on the basis of the evidence from this repaganization, to have been not an early mystery cult, but a polytheism similar to that of books I–IX of the *Ṛg Veda*,[106] to which it is directly related. The Magi in general seem to have been ritualists not primarily interested in doctrine, much like the Vedic priesthood in India. "Our sources," notes Cook, "do not present the Magi as theologians. They functioned as officiating clergy and were essential above all to the fire cult."[107] Pre-Zoroastrian Persian religion and pre-Upaniṣadic Indian religion seem to have been very close. "I assume with most scholars," says Tull, "that the type of religion characteristic of the Ṛg Veda also extended to Iran. It was also the religion that was subject to the Zoroastrian reform."[108] "In the *Ṛg -Veda* we meet with Mitra, Aryaman, Vāyu, Vata, and Yama, and in the *Yashts* we have Mithra, Airyaman, Vāyu, Vata, and Yima."[109] "The Indo-Iranian religion can be seen as belonging to a single tradition."[110] Thus, if the *Ṛg Veda* purveyed the doctrine of reincarnation there would be an implication that this doctrine belonged in the pre-Zoroastrian religion of Persia too. But except for the late tenth book (which seems to have received Mesopotamian influence), the *Ṛg Veda* itself does not involve any of the doctrines which West's hypothesis attributes to the Magi. Nor do the Zoroastrian texts imply the supercession of such doctrines by denouncing them. They do not denounce a doctrine of reincarnation, or of immanence, or of *māyā*, or of *karma*.[111] Zoroastrianism does not seem to be a reaction against an earlier monism, but against an earlier polytheism of Vedic type.[112]

Date of the Dispersion

The diffusion mechanism West proposes was a dispersion of the priesthood of the earlier religion fleeing persecution by the new Zoroastrian establishment, which had gained the support of the government. On this view, pre- or non-Zoroastrian members of the dominant priestly caste, the Median Magi, being expelled from Persia by political events, migrated both northwest into Greece and southeast into India, taking with them the monism complex and within it the tripartite doctrine of reincarnation, the two paths, and the other elements of the correspondence. Thus the pre-Zoroastrian religion of Persia would be the ancestor of the central themes in both Greek and Indian philosophy in the pre-Socratic and Upaniṣadic period. Behind the powerful, indeed seductive, simplicity of this view (a single diffusion event, with a historical date, operating through migration of refugees, and killing two birds with one stone) lurks a nest of problems.

In addition to the lack of doctrinal agreement, there are deep chronological issues. The articulation of tripartite reincarnationism in India in the early Upaniṣads indicates—unless the consensus dating of these texts is radically wrong—that its Indian form predated both the period of Persian dominance in northwest India and the possible dates of any dispersion of Magi. West agrees that the developed Upaniṣadic doctrine "must go back to the seventh century,"[113] but does not address the fact that the available occasions for possible dispersions of Magi are all significantly later than that.

The most obvious occasion for a dispersion would have been persecution associated with the spread and enforcement of the Zoroastrian reform. It was during the reign of Darius I (521–485 B.C.), many believe, that "the Religion spread from its sources in the East over the whole of Iran and, under the general favor, was being generally adopted."[114] The sign of this transition was the reform of the calendar: "It was under Darius I that in B.C. 505 the Iranian calendar was reformed, the Mazdean months and feasts being adopted in place of the old."[115] But the dates do not match up. If the dispersion of the Magi was prompted by the ascendancy of Zoroastrianism as indicated by the reform of the calendar, it seems to have come too late to have influenced either Pherecydes or Yājñavalkya.

West also considers an earlier occasion for a dispersion of Magi, the "defeat and annexation of Media by Cyrus in 549 or slightly earlier. The Magi were Medes, and remembered it . . . Upon the fall of their country, many of them may have sought refuge abroad, in India and in the West."[116] This date might look at first just barely early enough to have influenced the pre-Socratics, but in fact it is not so: "If Cyrus had annexed Media in 549 B.C.," one scholar reflects, "and Anaximander (at an age of 64) wrote his treatise already in 547/6 (Apollodrus *ap.* D.L. 2,2), where is the time-span necessary for the Magi to emigrate and settle down in Ionia and to teach Anaximander?"[117] In any case, it still does not get the diffusion back into the seventh century, which a consensus of scholars, including West, regard as the latest plausible date for the early Upaniṣads. It is true that the date of these texts is not firmly fixed. Wayman, for one, believes that Yājñavalkya of the *Bṛhadāraṇyaka Upaniṣad* was roughly a contemporary of the Buddha, which makes him, for Wayman, a figure of the sixth century.[118] Unfortunately, even if one is willing to revise the dates of the early Upaniṣads, a dispersion of Magi under Cyrus remains purely guesswork, as much as a dispersion under Darius. "There is no historical evidence whatsoever for such an emigration of the Magi."[119]

Achaemenid Religious Policy

Several other problems about the Magian hypothesis are just as serious. Even after the new calendar was in effect, for example, it does not seem that Darius persecuted the old religion and its priesthood. "The Great Kings of historical Persia—Cyrus, Darius, Xerxes, and Artaxerxes—though Mazdeans, do not seem to have been very keen Zarathushtrians . . . ," "nor did the Great Kings encourage it [the new faith] to the exclusion of others." "In the third century AD . . . for the first time it [Zoroastrianism] became the State Religion all over Iran."[120] More generally, religious persecution was simply not the Achaemenids' style. "The Achaemenid state was the first world empire in history to proclaim a completely tolerant and benevolent treatment of the cultural traditions of dozens of peoples and tribes."[121] Darius's policy of religious toleration was the forerunner of Alexander's and was based in turn on Cyrus's. "Although the Achaemenids considered their own Ahuramazda to be the most powerful god, they also believed in the gods of the vanquished peoples, worshipped them, and sought support from them."[122] "According to a statement by Strabo (XI.13.9), it was accepted practice among the Persians to worship the gods of peoples who were subject to them."[123] As their empire grew, the Achaemenids became worshippers of the Egyptian, Babylonian, Greek, Jewish, and other foreign gods,[124] and there is ample evidence that they carried out the same policy with regard to the religion of the Medes.

To begin with, the Magi retained religious supremacy for some time after the conquest of Media, so it is unclear why they would turn their backs on the new regime and emigrate.[125] Indeed, the Magi do not seem to have been opposed to Zoroastrianism at first. "According to the unanimous statements of the authors of antiquity, the Magi were disciples and followers of Zoroaster."[126] But West's theory requires that they fled Persia because the Achaemenids adopted Zoroastrianism and persecuted them. Not only is there no record of a dispersion of Magi under Persian persecution, there is also no record of such persecution. In fact, the Zoroastrian reform, which might have provided the conditions for persecution, seems not to have gone into effect for some time after the period in question. "At the end of the sixth and beginning of the fifth centuries B.C. Zoroastrianism was just beginning to gain a foothold in Persia, and the Achaemenid kings . . . did not repudiate the cults of the ancient tribal gods . . . Zoroastrianism had still not yet become a dogmatic religion with firmly established norms . . ."[127] Herodotus, who traveled in the area around 460–447 B.C., "does not seem to have heard of Zarathushtra," "and describes the religion of Iran as purely Magian."[128] The Magi, in other words, had not lost power by Herodotus's time.

"Much of the literature on the subject," say Dandamaev and Lukonin, "promulgates the view that the Magi were persecuted under Darius I, but this opinion is unfounded . . . Since the publication of the Persepolis tablets in the Elamite language, there has been no doubt whatsoever that the Magi, from the time of Darius I onwards, played an important role at the royal court and enjoyed great influence."[129] "[T]he material of the Persepolis texts suggests that, at the end of the sixth century B.C., the Magi were priests of the Zoroastrian cult, regardless of whether they had become Zoroastrians immediately after the appearance of the new teaching or had only later accepted it."[130] "Under Xerxes the influence and role of the Magi was strengthened even further."[131]

Robbing India to Pay Persia

Even worse, the Magian hypothesis leaves nothing to India. Everything that the world has regarded as valuable in the Indian religious and philosophical traditions is to be regarded as brought in by the Magi. Nothing, supposedly, was created or realized in India itself. Further, the non-Aryan tradition is brushed aside as if it contributed nothing. In the doctrines of *saṃsāra*, *karma*, and *mokṣa* there is, supposedly, nothing from the Indus Valley culture, nothing from the Dravidian tradition, nothing from Jainism or Saivism, and so on. Everything came from the Aryan stream. The elements italicized in West's passage above are usually assigned to the Dravidian tradition, not the Vedic. Yet West proposes that they existed in the Magian religion which was ethnically kindred to the Vedic.

The mention of Dravidian input into the Aryan tradition points to another problem with West's view: the fact that the various themes in question show development in India, but not in Greece. If they had come by the same diffusion path—from Persia into both India and Greece—and at the same time, they would presumably have come at the same stage of development. But in fact these ideas seem to appear in India earlier than in Greece and then undergo development there under the impetus of Aryan-Dravidian interaction. The fact that they show development in India but not in Greece suggests that they developed in India and were then transplanted into Greece, with some accruing of Near Eastern elements along the way, perhaps mostly in Persia. The Magian hypothesis brushes aside the evidence for the history of Indian religions. Finally, as attractive as the simplicity of the Magian hypothesis is in its geographic and chronological fit, the impression remains that Persia was not an originator in matters of philosophy but, as Halbfass says, "became a mediator between Greece and India."[132]

The Egyptian Question

That the tripartite doctrine of reincarnation developed in India and diffused thence into Greece by way of Persia seems most likely. Still, this seems not to have been the whole story. The earliest Greek author who addresses the question whence the doctrine of reincarnation came into Greece is Herodotus, who says (II.123):

> The Egyptians say that Demeter and Dionysus are the chief powers in the underworld; and they also were the first people to put forward the doctrine of the immortality of the soul, and to maintain that after death it enters another creature at the moment of that creature's birth. It then makes the round of all living things—animals, birds, and fish—until finally it passes once again, at birth, into the body of a man. The whole period of transmigration occupies three thousand years. This theory has been

> adopted by certain Greek writers, some earlier, some later, who have put it forward as their own. Their names are known to me, but I refrain from mentioning them.[133]

Herodotus does not mention whether the system he is reporting on contained the possibility of early release from the process or its desirability. There are, however, clear overlaps with the "Orphic" tradition of reincarnationism. Herodotus's description of the soul proceeding through all the forms of nature, for example, is the same doctrine Empedocles purveys, saying the soul must move through "all the types [forms, species] of mortal beings" (*pantoīa eidea thnētōn)*; in addition Empedocles' description of the soul going from one element to another is much like Herodotus's specification of "the dry land . . . the sea and the air," and something like it may also have been held by Heraclitus. Empedocles' three-thousand-year cycle occurs as the period for early release in Plato's *Phaedrus* and probably also in Pindar. Herodotus has the figure too, and may have mistakenly reported the period for early release as the duration of the whole cycle. There is an unresolved ambiguity, in his brief account, between ethically neutral mechanistic reincarnation and ethically engaged striving for early release. In any case, the version of the doctrine Herodotus reports does fit in several major respects among the various other Greek ones extant. The accuracy of his attribution of this doctrine to the Egyptians, however, has been severely doubted.

Herodotus and Reincarnation

At one time Herodotus's testimony was widely accepted.[134] But for the last couple of generations, despite the facts that Herodotus seems genuinely to have traveled and studied in Egypt and that he was a leading authority on that culture among the Greeks of that time, his claim that the doctrine came from there has been widely discredited by scholars. They have been, in fact, somewhat curt and authoritarian on this point, almost disapproving, as if the question should never have been raised in the first place. One says, "The Egyptians had no such theory," without arguing the point.[135] Another says, also without argumentation, "The Egyptians never had such a doctrine," and "This is regarded as a closed question."[136] And another: "[W]e now know that Herodotus is totally wrong. Metempsychōsis is foreign to the Egyptians' way of thinking . . ."[137] And another: "Herodotus is wrong about the Egyptian origins of metempsychosis."[138] Another: "H. is certainly mistaken in attributing the Greek doctrine of *palingenesia* to the Egyptians," and "This is certainly incorrect. Not only is there no evidence of this idea in Egypt, but it is fundamentally opposed to the Egyptian mentality."[139] An occasional scholar is willing to give Egypt a place in the reincarnationist tradition, but not as its source. "Herodotus' evidence," one points out, "relates to an epoch not far removed (on a large view of history) from that at which metempsychōsis came to India and to Greece."[140] "We should accept that it [reincarnationism] was maintained at least for a short period by some Egyptian theologians."[141] This view is a ramification of the Magian hypothesis, holding that reincarnationism may have entered Egypt from Persia at about the same time it entered Greece. But virtually no expert is prepared to allow reincarnationism in Old, Middle, or New Kingdom Egypt.

So complete is the consensus on this important point, and so authoritarian in its declaration of a "closed question" (*are* there any "closed questions" in scholarship?) that it is hard to believe how meager the argumentation is. In the article that led to the almost universal rejection of Herodotus II.123 by western classicists, Louis Zakbar argued that in Egyptian culture there was no idea to correspond directly to the Greek idea of the soul (*psychē*), so there could be no doctrine of reincarnation of the Orphic-Pythagorean-Platonic type, since these were based on a body-soul dichotomy. In fact, Zakbar points out, Egyptian afterlife texts show anxiety to reunite the *ba* with the body of the deceased. For the Egyptians, he says, "man is not a composite of the body and soul, and death does not mean a separation of the soul from the body."[142] The various passages that say, "the *ba* to heaven, the body to the underworld" do not really refer to such a separation since "it is impossible to identify the *ba*, *ka*, or *akh* with the spiritual element, in opposition to the body as its material or physical element."[143] That is about it for evidence and argumentation. Some later scholars echo Zakbar; Lloyd, for example, declares that body and soul "can never be permanently separated . . . hence mummification . . . There is not the slightest trace of an Orphico-Pythagorean dualism and without it the Greek doctrine of *palingenesia* is impossible."[144] Others fall in line with their denials without citing any source or reason, seemingly just glad to wash their hands of the question.

The curious point is that the serious replies that cry out to be made to this simplistic argument have not been made. Above all is the fact that Buddhism flatly denies the existence of either a self or a soul, yet still insists on reincarnation—that is, it has reincarnationism without mind-body dualism, a situation that, according to Zakbar and Lloyd, is impossible yet, plainly, is not.[145] Zakbar further confuses the situation through a misleading use of the words "spiritual" and "soul." He says, for example, "the expression 'the *ba* to heaven' does not indicate that the *ba* as 'the spiritual element' goes to heaven as the permanent abode of the 'soul' upon the 'separation' from the body, but merely reveals an aspiration on the part of the deceased that his *ba* may enjoy unlimited freedom of movement in the sky in the company of the sun-god . . ."[146] Evidently the idea of flying around in the heavens with the sun god is not "spiritual" in the sense that Zakbar associates with the word—seemingly a Platonic-Christian sense, from a much later age than the Egyptian texts. But Buddhism also posits reincarnation without using "soul" and "spiritual" in that sense, or indeed at all. The fact that the *ba* leaves the body to fly on high with the sun god obviously does indicate liberation attained through separation from the body, and may be regarded as an Egyptian way to express the ambition that Zakbar calls "spiritual." Ancient religions often expressed through images of participation in nature what in the Platonic-Christian tradition has been regarded as immaterial spirit. According to Heraclitus, West says, "Superior souls, being drier, rise to the pure region of sun and stars and survive there indefinitely . . ."[147] The activity of these released souls, then, is not unlike that of the *ba* flying with the sun; if the one can be accepted as signifying "spiritual" liberation, so can the other. The Upaniṣads also speak of the soul rising to the realm of the sun god forever, but one does not hear them called non-"spiritual." Words such as "spiritual" and "soul" do not really belong in an argument about Bronze Age religion, and without them Zakbar's argument becomes emptily tautological: "the expression 'the *ba* to heaven' does not indicate that the *ba*. . . goes to heaven as [its] permanent abode . . . upon the 'separation' from the body, but merely reveals an aspiration on the part of the deceased that his *ba* may enjoy unlimited freedom of movement in the sky in the company of the sun-god"? The word "but" in the sentence quoted creates the misimpression that the phrase before it and the phrase after it are in contradiction—but such is not the case; the conjunction 'and' would be more appropriate: "the ba goes to heaven as its permanent home . . . [and] enjoys unlimited freedom of movement in the sky in the company of the sun-god."

Zakbar's argumentation repeatedly uses such terminology, as when he says "it is impossible to identify the *ba*, *ka*, or *akh* with the spiritual element, in opposition to the body as its material or physical element." He is denying that the Egyptians had soul-body dualism in the terms that one finds in, say, Plato's *Phaedo*, and that seems acceptable. But that there is a dualism between the *ba* and the body, and that the *ba* in certain circumstances separates from the body and ascends to the sky on the death of the body seems undeniably true; the dualism is there, as long as one doesn't insist on calling it a dualism between a "spiritual" "soul" and a "physical" "body." The Egyptians' way of conceptualizing the parts of the person was different from the Greeks', but it does indeed involve a dualism and a separation of parts, one invisible part (call it spiritual if you will) ascending to the sky, the other visible part (call it physical if you will) remaining on or in the earth. The structure of the Egyptian belief thus far does indeed parallel that of the Greeks, though the terminology is somewhat skewed, as should not be surprising between two very different traditions from different cultural ages.

Western scholars, with their Christian orientation, have accepted this flawed argument without cavil. Lloyd, for example, following Zakbar, argues that without mind-body dualism you cannot have reincarnation, and that the Egyptians lacked this dualism. But the fact that a "soul" conceived as the metaphysical "essence" of the person is not available to enter a new body does not mean reincarnation cannot be in force. There are various kinds of reincarnationism. The "Orphico-Pythagorean" form may not be the only form the doctrine took in Greece, anymore than the Upaniṣadic form was the only one in India, where the soul-less Buddhist form arises also. The Egyptians may not have had a doctrine exactly "Orphico-Pythagorean"—no one says they had. Still, they had a number of traits in their religious lore that should be called "reincarnationistic" and some of them seem to have entered the Greek milieu. As Jane Ellen Harrison said: "They [the Greeks] need not have borrowed it from Egypt, and yet it is probable that the influence of Egypt . . . helped out the doctrine . . ."[148]

The Book of the Dead

The Egyptian Pyramid Texts and Books of the Dead contain numerous elements which may have formed part of the background for the development of the doctrine of reincarnation. One of these is the shape-changing which the deceased goes through in the afterlife. In this process there is a reincarnating entity (an entity that changes from one body to another, which can be called the "soul" in a looser, pre-Platonic sense), and in its afterlife adventures, this entity has the power to go through many transformations, passing into human and animal and other forms. Chapter titles in the Papyrus of Ani include (according to Budge's translation), "The Chapter of Changing into a Golden Hawk," "The Chapter of Changing into a Lotus," "The Chapter of Changing into a Crocodile," "The Chapter of Changing into a Heron," and others of the same type. In his more recent, but less complete, translation (which is provided here in endnotes) Faulkner renders the verb in these titles "Being Transformed Into."[149]

The view that these "changing" or "transforming" activities might be considered rebirths that occur *in the afterlife* was held early in the century by Schayer, who argued that the Egyptian verb in question has an ordinary meaning of "be born." "[T]he spells of the *Book of the Dead* were supposed to make it possible for the dead to be reborn in any form he desired in the hereafter."[150] When the reincarnating entity changes its form or species, in other words, the event could be described as a redeath-and-rebirth-in-the-afterlife. In India the doctrine of reincarnation, in an early stage of its development, posited rebirths and redeaths in the afterlife (*SB* II.3.3.8), emphasizing a desire to avoid the redeaths. Similarly in the *Book of the Dead*, Papyrus of Ani, one chapter is entitled "The Chapter of Not Dying a Second Time in Neter-khert," another "The Chapter of Not Dying a Second Time."[151]

Shamanism and Primitive Magic

The Spells of the *Book of the Dead* have been associated with the "shape-changing" common in the realms of shamanism and primitive magic. The powers that the shaman had once exercised in his excursions out of the body into the afterlife realm were preserved as motifs in the afterlife ritual of the deceased, who was, in effect, to act as his own shamanic guide in the other world, aided by the instructions in his *Book of the Dead*. This way of conceptualizing, however, does not eliminate the Egyptians as a source of elements in the Greek doctrine of reincarnation. The idea that shape-changing is an earlier motif that later was recast as an element of reincarnationism has focused attention on the Thraco-Scythian shamanic milieu, but is even more applicable to the Egyptian.

In fact, Egyptian afterlife mythology shows a deep shamanic imprint. The soul, for example, is repeatedly said in the pyramid texts to "mount to heaven by means of a ladder,"[152] an almost universal shamanic ritual practice. "When Teta hath purified himself on the borders of this earth where Ra hath purified himself, he prayeth and setteth up the ladder, and those who dwell in the great place press Teta forward with their hands."[153] The story of Osiris has even stronger shamanic elements than the story of Thracian Dionysus. Osiris is dismembered and reconstituted—a standard element in shamanic myth and rite. (Dionysus is dismembered but not clearly reconstituted.) Osiris ascends to heaven by means of a ladder: "Ra setteth upright the ladder for Osiris and Horus raiseth up the ladder for his father Osiris, when Osiris goeth to [find] his soul."[154] The shamanic performance is relocated into the afterlife, where the deceased is regarded, as it takes up the role of Osiris, as having been dismembered and needing to be reconstituted to climb the ladder to heaven: "Pepi has gathered together his bones, he hath collected his flesh, and Pepi hath gone straightway into heaven by means of the two fingers of the god who is Lord of the Ladder."[155] The shamanic performance, with its dismemberment-initiation, its shape-changing, and its symbolic ascents of ladders to other worlds, seems to have been one of the central formative structures underlying the *Book of the Dead*.

Pharaoh and Avatarism

Many of the powers of primitive magic entered the priest-kings of the Bronze Age. In Egypt the afterlife of the pharaoh was in a sense the only important one, on which the very existence of the state may have depended. Some passages show his "soul," hovering ambiguously between reincarnationism and rebirth-in-the-afterlife. In one passage, for example, Osiris, or the dead soul called Osiris, declares: "I am yesterday, today, and tomorrow, and I have the power to be born a second time." Elsewhere we read: "Homage to thee, Osiris, who maketh mortals to be born again." Both Osiris's second birth and those of "mortals" may be rebirths in the afterlife rather than into new earthly bodies. Similar ambiguities hover around certain pharaonic names which imply something like reincarnationism. Setekhy (19th dynasty), for example, means "repeater of births"; Amonemhat and Senusret (20th dynasty) mean "he who repeats births" and "he whose births live."[156] In the case of the pharaoh more than others, these references may be to a rebirth in the here-and-now world rather than in the afterlife—a rebirth of a particular type known as an avatar.

This aspect of the pharaonic afterlife is the second element of Egyptian religion (after the shape-changing spells) which may have "helped out" the Greek doctrine of reincarnation. The cosmic principle known as Osiris is successively incarnated in the pharaohs (who, as the "avatars of Osiris" are theologically somewhat comparable to the avatars of Viṣṇu in Hinduism). In the afterlife the deceased pharaoh, in whom Osiris has already lived in some way, is treated at times like Osiris, at times like Osiris's son, Horus, the avenger of his father, who will ascend to the throne and become Osiris. A complex web of identity-shifts and ambiguous rebirths surrounds the entity. In popular tales also the doctrines of shape-changing, reincarnationism, and messianic avatarism mix.

The Myth Called Orphic

Still other passages dwell on the soul's eternality in ways that seem to suggest both the idea reported by Herodotus as Egyptian, that the soul is processed through all nature, and the idea, not mentioned by Herodotus, that a karmic purification takes place in that process. The deceased being asks: "How long . . . have I to live?" The answer comes: "It is decreed that you shall live for millions of millions of years." The continuation of the passage foreshadows the Orphic myth of the soul's return, after expiating its crime, to the company of the gods. The deceased being asks: "May it be granted to me that I pass on to the holy princes, for indeed I am doing away with all the wrong which I did, from the time when this earth came into being."[157] In this passage it may seem that the millions of millions of years refer to the afterlife in eternity attained after "doing away with all the wrong which I did." This clearly is the meaning when it is said of Osiris Ani in the Papyrus of Ani, "he shall do whatsover pleaseth him, as [do] the gods who are in the underworld, for everlasting millions of ages, world without end."[158] But other passages place the millions of millions of years in the soul's past rather than its future. Typically the soul, its memory expanded somehow, realizes that it has lived for countless ages rather than for a single, finite lifetime. Ani says, "I am Shu [the god] of unformed matter,"[159] claiming that he had existed prior to the formation of the material world. Again, Ani declares:

> . . . before Isis was, and when Horus was not yet, I had waxed strong and flourished. I had grown old, and I had become greater than they who were among the shining ones who had come into being with him . . .

Here Ani declares himself to have existed before the generation of gods that includes Isis and Horus, that is, in the time of the more primeval gods Re (Sun), Shu (Sky), Geb (Earth), Nun (Primeval Ocean), and so on. He continues:

> . . . and I, even I, arose in the form of a sacred hawk, and Horus made me worthy in the form of his own soul, to take possession of all that belongeth unto Osiris in the underworld. The double Lion-god the warder of the things that belong to the house of the *nemmes* crown which is in his hiding place, saith unto me, "Get thee back to the heights of heaven, seeing that through Horus thou hast become glorified in thy form."[160]

To rise up as a hawk means to seek to enter heaven. The Lion-god guardian declares that Ani, having done away with his past wrongs, is ready to enter there, and hastens him on his way. The exhortation, "Get thee *back* to the heights of heaven" suggests that the soul has been there before, that he started his life of countless ages there, and has now returned—as in the myth called Orphic.

The soul's recognition of its own primeval nature, its recollection that it has lived since before time and will live endless ages more, seems a part of the "glorification" in form that indicates he is ready to "get thee to the heights of heaven" and "pass on to the holy princes." The idea is substantially the same as Plato's belief that the soul, in the afterlife, recalls its true nature as eternal and universal, and is also substantially the same as the Hindu idea that the soul can recognize its own identity with the Universal Self and by this recognition pass into the Self forever.

But what was the soul doing for these millions of millions of years before it was ready to return to heaven? Although there is no overt mention of reincarnation, it seems that the soul has been purified somehow through living for millions of years; whether it is automatically purified by time or purifies itself by special efforts is not made clear. It is also unclear whether the soul (like the *fravashi* in Mazdaism) has waited in heaven for those millions of years before its descent upon earth, or whether the descent itself took place millions of years ago.

In an especially suggestive passage, Osiris says:

> . . . my soul is eternity. I am the creator of darkness, and I appoint unto it a resting place in the uttermost parts of heaven. I am the prince of eternity, I am the exalted one [in] Nebu. I grow young in [my] city, I grow young in my homestead. My name is "Never failing." My name is "Soul, Creator of Nu, who maketh his abode in the underworld." My nest is not seen, and I have not broken my egg. I am lord of millions of years. I have made my nest in the uttermost parts of heaven. I have come down unto the earth of Seb. I have done away with my faults.[161]

The soul has lived forever, according to this passage since even before the primeval ocean, and its descent upon the earth was in order to "do away with its faults." As in both Orphic and Upaniṣadic contexts, the descent to earth (i.e., into a mortal body) is seen as a punishment or purificatory austerity after which the soul may reclaim its place in heaven. Its possession of the kingship seems a sign of this readiness. Empedocles' doctrine that those in their final incarnations are princes and other mighty figures in the community may derive from this pharaonic tradition: To be reborn at last as pharaoh is to be at the end of the cycle, to have access to the Osiris principle again.

If, as happened in the New Kingdom, it was a wealthy commoner like Ani the scribe who was to become Osiris, then he must be ritually declared a king or pharaoh. This is a common theme of the *Book of the Dead*: The deceased must somehow be regarded as a king or prince before he is eligible to "get thee back to the heights of heaven." Thus Ani declares, "I am crowned like unto the king of the gods, and I shall not die a second time in the underworld."[162] Again, the prayer is made, "May Osiris, the scribe Ani, be a prince . . . and may the meat offerings and the drink offerings of Osiris Ani, triumphant, be apportioned unto him."[163] "I am crowned," Ani claims, "I am become a shining one, I am mighty, I am become holy among the gods."[164] "I am the prince of eternity."[165] "May it be granted that I pass on among the holy princes," Ani prays, and he is reassured: "The god Tmu hath decreed that [Ani's] course shall be among the holy princes."[166] "Horus," the *Book of the Dead* says, "was like unto a prince of the sacred bark, and the throne of his father was given unto him."[167]

Something very like the doctrine of Empedocles is suggested, and possibly related to it as forerunner. The *ba*, which was once a god among the other gods, descends to earth, that is, into a body, in order to right some wrong it has done in the past; either it descended as a pharaoh or it has somehow been processed through nature for long ages until it has purified itself sufficiently to be reborn as a pharaoh; after its purification it is ready to return to the company of the gods in heaven, and this is signified by the status as pharaoh. Empedocles said the final incarnation was as a prince, a poet, or a healer. Plato said the last reincarnation was as a philosopher—but he meant philosophers to be kings. They both may be echoing an Egyptian idea either that gods are incarnated only as pharaohs or that the last incarnation is as a pharaoh. A parallel is found in the Hindu caste system, in the idea that only *brahmans* can attain *mokṣa*—that is, "become Osiris"; the soul must reincarnate upward through the castes before it is in position to get off the wheel.

The nature of the primal crime or ancient wrong which the soul "descended on to the earth" to set right is not clearly stated, as it is not in the Greek versions of the myth, where it is either left undefined or ambiguously declared to be either perjury or bloodshed.[168] The Egyptian texts dwell repeatedly on this subject, but with an ambiguity not unlike that of the Greek texts. Various clues in the Greek tradition indicate that the crime which the Orphic was attempting to expiate was either the ancient war of the Titans against the gods, for which they were exiled from heaven and imprisoned in Tartarus, or their rending and devouring of Dionysus Zagreus, or both. (In the Greek tradition, as West says, "The Titans are by definition the banished gods, the gods who have gone out of this world.")[169] The Egyptian texts may foreshadow the Greek myth of the Titans when they refer to a primal rebellion of one group of gods against another. "O ye gods of the underworld," Osiris Ani says, "who set yourselves up against me, and who resist the mighty ones . . ."[170] Again, he says:

> Hail, Thoth! What is it that hath happened unto the holy children of Nut? They have done battle, they have upheld strife, they have done evil, they have created the fiends, they have made slaughter, they have caused trouble; in truth, in all their doings the mighty have worked against the weak . . . I am not one of those who work iniquity in their secret places; let not evil happen unto me.[171]

The children of Nut include Osiris, Horus, Set, Isis, and Nephthys. When Ani claimed "before Isis I was," he was dissociating himself from this contentious generation of deities in which the primal murder of Osiris by Set occurred, and claiming to have been one among the earlier generation, the "gods of the first time." But there are also suggestions that the crime might be Set's dismemberment of Osiris, whom Ani, in his role as Horus, avenger of his father, has to reconstitute to make reparation. Ani, in other words, might be expiating either or both of the Egyptian versions of the crimes of the Titans, and part of his strategy in doing so is to claim that he belongs to the earlier generation of gods.

Despite its roots in the substrate of primitive and shamanic belief, the Egyptian doctrine of the afterlife was not a primitive one, as is indicated by its stress on ethical merit as credential for the opportunity to become Osiris. In the *Book of the Dead*, when the soul arrives at the "Hall of Double Truth and Right" in Osiris's palace, it faces a jury of gods and makes to each one a declaration of its innocence of a specific crime, in a ritual known as the Negative Confession:

> I have not committed evil against men. I have not mistreated cattle. I have not blasphemed a god. I have not done violence to a poor man. I have not killed. I have given no order to a killer. I have not caused anyone suffering.[172]

And so on. The so-called confession seems to operate as a spell, since it is unlikely to be literally true. After the declaration of its guiltlessness the heart of the deceased is weighed against a feather representing truth—presumably to determine whether the negative confession was truthful. As in the Greek versions of the crime of the exiled god, the center of the judgment is the question of whether the soul has committed perjury.

The Hall of Double Right and Truth is the site where not only the weighing and judgment but also the act of recollection of the divine self-nature occurs. The afterlife is sometimes described as specifically tending toward this experience:

> Osiris Ani, triumphant, shall not tarry, nor shall he rest without motion in the earth for ever. Clearly, clearly, shall he see with his two eyes, and with his two ears shall he hear what is right and true.[173]

In the "Chapter of Entering into the Hall of Double Right and Truth" Ani says:

> I have entered in unto the place of secret and hidden things, I have held converse with the god Sut . . . Osiris, the scribe Ani, hath entered into the House of Osiris, and he hath seen the hidden and secret things which are therein.[174]

The hidden and secret things seem to pertain to the soul's primal nature as an existent which predates the separation of the gods; after this realization the soul is homologized to the primal metaphysical principle:

> I am the eldest and the first-born son of matter . . . I live for ever, the lord of years, and the prince of eternity . . . I am the Soul, the creator of Nu.[175]
>
> My nest is not seen, and I have not broken my egg. I am the lord of millions of years.[176]

Entering into eternal life, the soul sees the things of life on the earth as illusory and dreamlike, as in the later Indian and Greek doctrines of *māyā* and *doxa*:

> As for the duration of what is done on earth, it is a kind of dream, but they say, "Welcome, safe and sound!" to him who reaches the court of Osiris in the West.[177]

"Welcome, safe and sound," could be the greeting to the freed Orphic soul when he rejoins the gods.

This dramatic scenario of the soul as a separate immortal individual entering the heavenly banquet hall is balanced in other passages by a belief that the dead soul is cosmicized, or made one with the universe. When the gods of the polytheism see the purified soul ascending toward them they are frightened. "The Lords of Forms are in terror. The gods are afraid of him, for he is older than the Great One . . ." The soul proceeds to become one with the entire universe (which is to say, with all the gods) by the primitive ritual-mythic device of eating it: "He eats their magic and swallows their lordliness. The great ones are for his morning meal, the middle sized ones for his evening meal, and the little ones for his night meal." By this means the soul extends throughout the universe. "He encloses the two entire skies." "He flourishes and their magic is in his belly . . . He has swallowed the understanding of every god. [Now] his duration is eternity and his boundary everlastingness."[178] Finally the soul of the deceased has become the *pantheos*, or all-god, like Ptah or Amon-Re (or like the deceased in *Ṛg Veda* X.16.3), who has as his parts or aspects the other gods, or domains of the universe. By containing them he contains the universe. His hair is Nut, the sky-goddess; his face is Ra, the solar disk; his eyes are Hathor, the cow-goddess; his neck is the neck of Isis, and so on, through his hands, throat, forearms, spine, flesh, back, buttocks, penis, legs, feet, fingers, and bones. He is the Universal Being who manifests himself in every form. "I came into being from unformed matter," the universalized soul declares. "I created myself . . . I am formed out of the atoms of all the gods."[179] "My soul is god, my soul is eternity."[180] "I am the great one . . . I am Osiris the lord of eternity."[181] "I am lord of millions of years."[182] "I am a shining one and a dweller in light."[183] "I am fate."[184]

This Osirian afterlife doctrine parallels the Orphic myth in overall structure. The basic myth of each portrays the embodied soul as an exile from the world of the gods who must return there. The Egyptian version has elements of reincarnationism, though in an unclear form overlapping with shape-changing, identity-merging, and avatarism; it has the idea of a part or aspect of the self that can operate out of the body; the need for purification to do away with faults or expiate a primal crime; the eventual recollection of one's past lives and one's true identity as a god; and, finally, simultaneous beatification as one of the immortal gods, and universalization as the *pantheos* containing them all. The idea of early release is not mentioned, as it is not in Empedocles, but neither addresses the question. There are indications in the Egyptian version that the soul is to be processed through nature—beginning before the primeval ocean, as unformed matter, and culminating in a form on top of a universal hierarchy, as a human, probably a king or other leading figure—as in the doctrine which Herodotus later attributes to Egyptian sources, which Empedocles seems also to have done.

One Myth in Three Places

In addition to these overall structural parallels, there are duplications of detail among Egyptian, Orphic, and Upaniṣadic texts which strongly implicate Egypt as one formative influence on the tripartite doctrine. In the *Kauṣītaki Upaniṣad* (perhaps sixth century B.C.), the dead soul finds itself at the moon, which is the staging place for the afterlife paths. For the Orphics too the soul's drama in the afterlife takes place in the sky, as in Plato's myth in the *Timaeus* of each soul "mounted" in its star for the ride across the sky. In Orphic burial texts the Spring of Memory represents the Milky Way.[185] The same is true of the Egyptian afterlife belief, where the river of the "underworld" flows across the sky and the banqueting gods are the northern circumpolar stars. In the three versions the soul of the deceased is ultimately identified with a star.[186]

In both the Orphic and Upaniṣadic systems the question is whether the deceased soul will be cast down to the earth, into the realm of matter, for another life of punishment, or will be allowed to stay among the stars, that is gods, who dwell in felicity forever. In Egyptian afterlife myth also the point of the afterlife adventure is to be allowed to dwell among the northern circumpolar stars—those stars which never set—which comprise the court of Osiris, where the deities have bodies of light. Plato, who is said to have studied in Egypt, says in the *Timaeus* (41de) that the number of stars is identical with the number of souls. Each soul at the beginning is "in" its star, mounted in it as in a chariot, before they are "sown into the instruments of time," that is, into bodies. While the souls were "in" their stars, says the *Timaeus*, "he [the demiurge] showed them the nature of the universe and declared to them the Laws of Destiny"—as Ani perceived the hidden things in the Double Hall of the northern stars. After becoming free from further incarnations the soul "journeys back to the habitation of its consort star and there lives a happy and congenial life" (42b)—as Ani becomes one among the circumpolar stars.[187]

In a prominent section of the complex, layered, and syncretic myth of the *Book of the Dead* the deceased soul wakes in the "underworld" in the sky and wanders into an area called the Field of Reeds. There he seeks and finds either a tree with a goddess in it, who offers him a drink from her breasts or from a vase, or a pool of fresh water from which he drinks, or both. In the Papyrus of Ani, the vignette of the 59th chapter shows "Ani kneeling beside a pool of water where grows a sycamore tree; in the tree appears the goddess Nut pouring water into Ani's hands from a vessel."[188] Ani says, "Hail, sycamore tree of the goddess Nut! Grant thou to me of the water . . ."[189] and is granted it.

In the Orphic myth of the gold plates, also, the deceased must find a certain body of water to drink from:

> Thou shalt find to the left of the House of Hades a spring,
> And by the side thereof standing a white cypress.
> To this spring approach not near.
> But thou shalt find another, from the Lake of Memory
> Cold water flowing forth, and there are guardians before it.
> Say, "I am a child of Earth and starry Heaven;
> But my race is of heaven (alone). This ye know yourselves.
> But I am parched with thirst and I perish. Give me quickly
> The cold water flowing forth from the Lake of Memory."
> And of themselves they will give thee to drink of the holy spring,
> And thereafter among the other heroes thou shalt have lordship.[190]

A similar motif appears in the *Chāndogya Upaniṣad*, where the deceased, as he progresses on the afterlife adventure, comes to the Brahmā-world in the third heaven and finds there a lake with a tree showering soma (*CU* VIII.5.3).[191]

In the *Book of the Dead*, in a chapter whose vignette portrays Ani and his wife drinking from a pool with their right hands, Ani drinks, then cries out to the guardian of the threshold, "Open to me!" The guardian replies, "Who art thou then, and whither dost thou fare?" Ani replies: "I am one of you." And he is allowed to pass on to the "temple of the divine beings."[192] In the Orphic plates, the guardians of the spring do not specifically ask, "Who are you?" but the question is implicit in the soul's assertion, "I am a child of Earth and starry Heaven, but my race is of heaven alone." The soul came from heaven—from the realm of the gods/stars—down to earth for its exile; that is the sense in which it is child of both earth and starry heaven; but since he sees himself as having originated in heaven before the fall to earth, he declares heaven his true place, as does Ani, saying, "I am one of you," meaning the heavenly beings.

The theme of memory is crucial to the regaining of one's true primal nature. The soul's act of declaring its identity is based on an implicit claim to accurately remember that identity. In the Orphic myth represented by the gold plates, the soul drinks from the spring which flows from the Lake of Memory, and avoids the spring which flows from beneath the white cypress tree; the latter would seem to be the same that Plato in the *Republic* (620a) calls the Water of Forgetfulness, which the souls drink to blur the memory of their last incarnation before entering a new body.[193] Drinking from the Spring of Memory, on the other hand, the soul will recall its divine nature and will not descend into a mortal body again.

The papyrus of Ani preserves traces of the same myth. In, for example, a "Chapter of Causing the Deceased to Remember His Name in Neter-khert," Ani prays, "May my name be given unto me in the great Double House, and may I remember my name in the House of Fire on the night of counting the years and of telling the number of months." In the Egyptian texts, the connection between drinking from the spring or lake and remembering one's true identity is not explicitly stated, but in one short chapter both motifs are found, apparently connected causally:

> Chapter of Drinking Water and of Not Being Burned in the Fire: Vignette: The deceased drinking water from a running stream. [The deceased] saith: "... I have made my name to flourish, and I have delivered [it], that I may make myself to live [in remembrance] on this day."[194]

It is said in the legend of Ra and Isis, in which the goddess finds out Ra's secret name, that "he shall live whose name shall be revealed."[195] In the *Book of the Dead* the requirement of remembering the name extends to the names of the gods. Ani says: "If any god advanceth unto me, forthwith I proclaim his name."[196] When he enters the Hall of Double Truth Ani says, "Homage to you, O ye gods, I know you, and I know your names ... I pray you declare me right and true."[197] He then addresses each of the seated deities by name, to bolster his claim that he is one of them, a former familiar. In the papyrus of Ani, when the jackal god Anubis certifies Ani to the gods, he says: "He knoweth our paths and our cities . . . and the smell of him is to me even as the smell of one of you." Then he addresses Ani: "Pass thou, for thou knowest [the names]."[198] In another version, after the interrogation which begins with the question "Who art thou and what is thy name?" the god, satisfied with Ani's replies, says, "Come, then, pass through the door of this Hall of two-fold Maati, for thou knowest us."[199] Similarly, when the Orphic initiate of the gold plates approaches the guardians of the spring, he addresses them familiarly by name, as one formerly of their company: "I come from the pure, pure Queen of those below, and Eukles and Eubuleus and other Gods and Daemons."

In both contexts recollection of the divine nature is connected to a loss of mortal flaws. In the Egyptian version, the soul, arriving at the assembly of the gods, declares to them, "I have done away with my faults," or "I am doing away with all the wrong I did from the time when this earth came into being." Similarly the Orphic, in a gold plate, declares to the gods:

> I come from the pure, pure Queen of those below,
> And Eukles and Eubuleus, and other Gods and Daemons:
> For I also avow that I am of your blessed race.
> And I have paid the penalty for deeds unrighteous.[200]

As the Orphic tells the gods that he is "from the pure" (that is, from their family), Ani declares to them, "I am glorious, I am pure," and, in another version, "I am pure, I am pure, I am pure."[201]

The same general structure, with many of the same elements, is found in the first chapter of the *Kauṣitaki Upaniṣad.* There the soul of the deceased, arriving at the moon "which is the door of the world of heaven,"[202] is similarly confronted by an inquisitor who blocks the way till his questions shall be answered. "Whoever answers properly, him it sets free to go to the higher worlds"—the worlds of the gods, that is, which are superlunary (i.e., stars). But whoever does not answer rightly descends to earth in the rain and is reborn according to his *karma.* Confronting the soul, the guardian of the moon (like the guardians of the Spring of Memory addressing the Orphic soul or the threshold guardian addressing Ani) asks simply: "Who are you?" And the Upaniṣad says he should answer that the seed that made him was gathered "from the far-shining," that is, from the stars/gods, and, with the agency of a man, was placed in a womb.

He is, in other words, like the Orphic, child of both Earth and starry Heaven, but originally from Heaven alone. Then the guardian of the Moon asks again: "Who are you?" The soul replies simply, "I am you," much as the Orphic soul says, "I am one of your blessed race," and the Egyptian scribe Ani says, "I am one of you." And the guardian of the moon sets him free to go on to the world of the gods.[203]

Being allowed to pass on, according to the Upaniṣad, the soul arrives finally at the world of Brahmā (where again the lake with tree is found), is admitted to the hall of Brahmā, and Brahmā asks him "Who are you?" At this point the Indian author refocuses the Egyptian scenario to make of it an expression of the doctrine of the *ātman*. The soul replies, as before, that it is one of the gods, though made "a seed for a wife," then continues with the greater claim to be "the self of every single being. You are the self of every single being. What you are, that am I." Then Brahmā reverses the direction of the questioning and asks "Who am I?" as Ani was obliged to declare the names of the gods who questioned him. The soul replies, "That which is true, the true." Brahmā then asks, "What is the true?" The soul replies, "[A]ll this whatever there is. All this thou art." Brahmā then asks about the knowledge of names: "How do you obtain my male names?" He should answer: "By breath." Brahmā asks, "How my female names?" He should reply, "By speech." Brahmā asks, "How my neuter names?" He should answer, "By mind." Brahmā continues the questioning a while and then, apparently satisfied with the answers, declares, "The whole Brahmā world now is thine," as Ani became one with Osiris, king of the gods.

This seems to be the same myth found in different states of completeness in the lacunary records of three ancient cultures. If the Egyptian myth did not itself involve an explicit belief in reincarnation, it anyway seems to have provided a vehicle or framework for that doctrine in both Greece and India. It seems to have entered India in the sixth century, the same century when it appeared in Greece, and to have been synthesized with the tripartite doctrine developed by Yājñavalkya and Uddālaka a century or so earlier. Clearly, if this myth came from one of these three cultures to the other two, it could only have traveled from Egypt, which had it five hundred to a thousand years before it is attested elsewhere, into the others.[204]

The Mechanistic Form of the Doctrine

Herodotus seems partly confirmed. Certain elements of the Greek doctrine of reincarnation—especially those pertaining to the mythic framework—seem to have derived from Egyptian influence.[205] He is not, however, confirmed in his doctrinal claim—that the "soul" "makes the round of all living things . . . until finally it passes once again, at birth, into the body of a man." That form of the doctrine, which he describes as Egyptian, cannot be found in extant Egyptian texts. Furthermore, if that version is not meant to contain provisions for early release, then there is no parallel in the Greek record either. A possibly significant parallel is found, however, in India. The context is the doctrinal dispute which led to the schism between Gosāla and Mahāvīra.

One point of disagreement between these primal *nāstika* gurus was the doctrine of reincarnation. Gosāla proposed that beings had to live for 8,400,000 incarnations before being born as human in the final incarnation.[206] This figure survives in the doctrine of the Nath Siddhas in the middle ages, and is echoed in the *Maitrayani Upaniṣad*, which mentions both 84 and 84,000 forms of life. In the Nath tradition Goraksa taught that there were 84,000,000 species of incarnation and 84,000,000 yogic *āsanas* or postures, one for each.[207] Though the numbers involved have different decimal placements, the point seems to be that the reincarnating unit would be processed through all of nature, one species at a time. The soul is thus gradually universalized, obtaining knowledge of every mode of existence from inside. In Gosālā's view, no effort could hasten the end of the process. The ethical value of one's behavior meant nothing; the step-by-step initiation into universality would have its effect regardless. Mahāvīra felt that this mechanistic version of reincarnationism deprived religious effort and asceticism of meaning; he insisted on the possibility of early release from the cycle to be achieved through special efforts.

Like Gosāla, Herodotus says that the soul makes the entire round of nature, being reborn into each species of thing, before it ends the process in a human incarnation. Traces of this doctrine are also found in the language of Empedocles, who speaks of the soul being thrown from one element to another, and Heraclitus, where also the soul appears to be caught up in a current that will carry it through the entire cycle of nature. Pythagoras's reported belief in repeating cycles of events also suggests deterministic reincarnationism. It is worth quoting Herodotus's description of the doctrine again:

> The Egyptians are the first to have maintained the doctrine that the soul of man is immortal, and that, when the body perishes, it enters into another animal that is being born at the time, and when it has been the complete round of the creatures of the dry land and of the sea and of the air it enters again into the body of a man at birth; and its cycle is completed in 3,000 years.

The *Bhāgavati Sūtra* says this about Gosāla:

> He declared that his soul had travelled through all the eighty-four lakhs of great kalpas, which must necessarily elapse before it could end its journey, and had occupied all forms of body in determined order. It had attained its final birth as Udai, an auspicius and beautiful infant.[208]

Herodotus and the *Bhāgavati Sūtra* seem to be describing the same doctrine, though the numbers are different.[209] Gosāla is making the same claim that Empedocles made—to have completed the cycle of the elements and be in the final incarnation.

On the Trail of a Number

The number 84 is common in Indian sacred numerology, occurring in a dizzying array of instances. The *tīrthankara* before Pārśva, for example, is said to have died 840,000 years before Mahāvīra's nirvāṇa. According to the *Mahābhārata* (I.1098) Mount Meru is 84,000 *yojanas* high. Tantras and Purāṇas mention 84 *lacs* of rebirth. The Buddhadharma is traditionally said to be divided into either 84 or 84,000 branches. When Maitreya, the future Buddha, renounces the world, it is said that he will be attended by 84,000 followers. The *Skandha Purāṇa* describes 84 Śīva lingas. The Nath tradition records 84 *siddhas*.[210] Yogic and tantric texts refer to the chief *āsanas*, or yogic postures, as 84, or 84 million. And so on.

"The number 84," says Eliade, "corresponds to no historical reality; it is a mystical number, attested in all Indian traditions, whether Hindu, Buddhist, Ājīvika, or Jain."[211] "It probably," he adds, "expresses completeness, totality." Another scholar says, "The figure of 84 or . . . its plurals[212] frequently appear[s] with the Jains and elsewhere to indicate a large but imprecise number."[213] According to another scholar, 84 is a "purely mystic" number in India.[214]

What has not been remarked upon is the fact that 84 is another of the distinctive Sumerian numbers. In the Sumerian king lists 840 appears repeatedly, along with 420, as regnum lengths.[215] In terms of the astronomy-based numerology of Sumer, 84 represents the product of 7 (the number of known planets) and 12 (the number of lunations in a year). Thus it comprehends time and space in an intimate totality with a distinctive cultural signature. The number 84 in connection with the mechanistic form of reincarnation implies Mesopotamian input of some kind; Herodotus associates the mechanistic form with Egypt. Egypt and Mesopotamia of course influenced each other greatly, and by the Late Bronze Age their traditions moved out into the surrounding world in conflated and eclectic mixtures.

Cultural interchange in the area bounded by Greece on the West and India on the East was complex, elements combining and recombining as they flowed in a variety of directions. The multicultural, layered formation of Orphism contains elements possibly derived from Thrace, Scythia, Egypt, Crete, Lydia, India, and Persia. In the widespread culture-mixing, Mesopotamian influence was pervasive. A number associated with the king lists, which contain veiled allusions to the precessional arithmetic, would be associated with the myth of cyclical time that seems to have diffused from Mesopotamia, and would be quite appropriate for the view that the soul reincarnated through all of nature for a single great cycle.

Though they accepted the innovation of early release, both the pre-Socratic and the Upaniṣadic versions of the doctrine of reincarnation still involve rendering the transmigrating entity from the status of individual to that of universal. For Empedocles, the reincarnating soul is tossed from the realm of one element to that of another till it has viewed things from inside the point of view of each; Herodotus and Heraclitus also seem to have the idea that the individual soul is made quasi-universal by transmigrating throughout the world of species. So does the Ājīvika version, but so also does the version in the Upaniṣads. As Tull said, "the rebirth process entails the individual's integration into the constituents of the cosmos."[216] Again: "this view . . . homologizes the body of the deceased with the spheres of the cosmos."[217] The process involves "becoming integrated into the cosmos as a whole."[218]

There Must Be an Escape

It was probably the mechanistic form of the doctrine of reincarnation that Yājñavalkya, Mahāvīra, and Siddhārtha all reformed in various ways which shifted emphasis to the insistence that the process was not mechanistic but dependent on free will: Not only is one's next incarnation established by one's actions rather than automatically predetermined, but special effort can even gain early release from the process. An early Buddhist text preserves memory of this doctrinal revision. The introduction to the *Jātaka* states that Sumedha, an earlier incarnation of the Buddha, inherited a tradition which did not teach voluntary escape from the process of reincarnation but rather, like Gosāla's and that which Herodotus called Egyptian, taught that one had to wait till one's thread was unwound all the way by itself. Sumedha, before setting out on the path to enlightenment, grasps at early release as a revolutionary and unprecedented idea:

> There is, there must be, an escape!
> Impossible there should not be!
> I'll make the search and find the way
> Which from existence shall release.[219]

It seems that no one was advertising an escape route yet in Sumedha's day. The escape itself may have been the revolutionary idea that caused the religious movements of Buddhism, Jainism, and the Upaniṣads to distinguish themselves with such intensity from both Vedism and the Dravidian substrate.

A Soup of Beliefs

As the Bronze Age turned into the Iron Age, many common assumptions about life were revised—among them, views of the afterlife. In the Early Iron Age, by about the seventh or the sixth century B.C., a kind of soup of afterlife beliefs—including rebirth in the afterlife, transcendent rebirth, redeath in the afterlife, rebirth in this life, redeath in this life, permanent heavens and hells, temporary heavens and hells, and various combinations of these elements—swirled around Egypt, Mesopotamia, Persia, Greece, India, and elsewhere. Out of this soup the Tripartite Doctrine of Reincarnation emerged as one more or less permanent solution, the Zoroastrian belief in permanent heavens and hells as another. The evidence suggests that the tripartite doctrine developed in India and diffused thence to Greece. It also points to the Egyptian Osiris cult as an influence at some fairly early stage.

One early type of reincarnation doctrine—perhaps connected with a myth of cyclical time—that seems to have been known in India, in Egypt, and perhaps in Greece (to Herodotus, at least), involved the necessary reembodiment of the soul in every available life-form before it is reborn as a human and returns to the company of the gods. Reincarnation as a process of being reborn throughout all of nature may be an earlier form—perhaps a Bronze Age form—that was displaced in the Early Iron Age by different cultic versions of the new idea of early escape. This development would be part of a general trend in which Bronze Age communalism was replaced by Iron Age individualism.

In the version in which the reincarnating entity is processed through all of nature, its purification consists in a relentless one-step-at-a-time universalization which gradually wears away all particular points of view. In the later doctrine featuring the goal of early release, an additional type of purification is required that consists in individual ascetic and moral exertions taken on in addition to the step-by-step universalization and having the ability to speed it up and finish ahead of schedule. The first type of doctrine, it seems, entered India from without and was redefined there, into versions of the second type featuring individual exertions, by several thinkers at about the same time—Yājñavalkya, Uddālaka, Mahāvīra, Siddhārtha, and others; meanwhile the more archaic or primitive Ājīvika teacher Gosāla still purveyed an evolute of the earlier version (which Herodotus also inherited).

Under the stress of the breakdown of the Vedic worldview the reforming religious teachers developed new doctrines from a combination of Near Eastern and Dravidian influences conflated and reshaped by the innovative ethical thought of kṣatriya teachers: Reincarnation was seen as able to be affected or even cut short by special ascetic and moral exertions. By the new ethicized approach, the individual soul has the ability to developmentally force its universalization and thus can skip some incarnations. It seems probable that individual *karma* and early release were the revolutionary doctrines introduced in this formative period in India.

When these doctrines emerged in India, the various *nāstika* religions were in seedling forms and shared many points while differing on others. The probably older Ājīvika doctrine emphasizing cosmic process and dismissing individual ethical choices coexisted with the new ethicized form of the doctrine, with its reduplicated reward-and-punishment system and its ultimate reward of early release for good behavior. *Kṣatriya* teachers rebelling against Brahminical control as the Aryan state began to emerge modified Vedic sacrificialism in different ways. Some made it into a transcendental doctrine, as in the Upaniṣads; some broke away from it altogether, as in Jainism and Buddhism, both apparently *kṣatriya* defections to modified forms of Dravidian Ājīvikism. In the late Vedic period, these various doctrines were mingling and interacting in constantly changing ways, until the new set of orthodoxies was firmly in place (which was probably not before c. 400 B.C. and possibly a good deal later).

It is from this "molten" period that a mingled and still inwardly shifting set of Indian doctrines passed into Greek awareness through the imperial Persian "mediator" at the time of the *theologoi* and early Orphism. This revised version, perhaps carried by Jain missionaries among others, surfaced in the Greek world as the doctrine of Orpheus. The myth of the exiled god who must make certain correct answers to the guardians of the afterlife realm or god-world seems to have descended from Egyptian sources—or possibly some related but presently unknown source, and possibly through intermediaries—into both Greece and India, at a date somewhat later than the earliest Upaniṣadic formulation of the tripartite doctrine. These elements passed through Persia on their way and show marks of the transit, such as numerological shifts, but were for the most part isolated from the Persian belief system, whose dualistic eschatology could not accommodate them.

Finally it should be pointed out that the reincarnation doctrine does not exist in a void; it is part of a much broader set of correspondences which holds together with the force of inner syntax. Only part of this set of correspondences has yet been discussed here; still, the array is already massive enough to merit a brief recapitulation. Features of the comparison for the early period (not all of which have been discussed thus far) include:

(1) The development of abstract rather than mythic conceptualization
(2) Philosophical monism, including the concept of an absolute and formless reality which is somehow "higher" than contingent and formed reality
(3) A doctrine that the realm of change and form is an illusion, essentially nonexistent
(4) Within this illusion, human life is governed by a burdensome cycle of reincarnations following
(5) A law of moral and cognitive evolution from one incarnation to the next, which can be escaped through
(6) The practice of nonviolence, including religious vegetarianism, which, along with other practices, will lead to
(7) A kind of absolute knowledge or transcendent state of mind which constitutes
(8) Release from the cycle of reincarnations and
(9) Merging into the overall oneness which transcends specific form
(10) Time is a cyclical process in which the universe periodically flows from unity to multiplicity and back again
(11) In the material realm, the Four Elements—earth, air, fire, water—act as mediators between the One and the Many
(12) Materialistic atomism arises, as if reflexively, as an alternative to monism, with the intention of redeeming the reality of the Many

(13) The process of condensation and rarefaction offers a mechanism of transition between One and Many
(14) A theory of universal flux leads to a conviction of
(15) The impossibility of knowledge and the inadequacy of language
(16) Reality is defined through a paradoxical discourse, for example, that it is characterized by both being and nonbeing.

Finally, the early schools of Greek and Indian philosophy seem to have had more or less the same contents, though presented in different styles and combinations, like different branches of a single tradition.

Notes To Chapter Four

1. Theodor Gomperz, *The Greek Thinkers: A History of Ancient Philosophy*, vol. 1 (London: John Murray, 1920), pp. 126–127.

2. *The Laws of Manu*, trans. Georg Bühler, with extracts from seven commentaries, Sacred Books of the East 25 (New York: Dover, 1969).

3. Paul Deussen, *The Philosophy of the Upaniṣads* (New York: Dover, 1966), p. 356.

4. Unless otherwise indicated, translations from the Upaniṣads follow *The Principal Upaniṣads*, trans. and ed. Sarvepalli Radhakrishnan (London: George Allen and Unwin, 1969).

5. Swami Brahmananda, *The Philosophy of Sage Yājñavalkya* (Rishikesh: Divine Life Society, 1981), p. 361.

6. F. M. Cornford, trans. and comm., *Plato's Cosmology: The Timaeus of Plato*, International Library of Psychology, Philosophy and Scientific Method (London: K. Paul, Trench, Trubner and Co.; New York: Harcourt Brace Jovanovich, 1973), p. 354.

7. Giorgio de Santillana, *The Origins of Scientific Thought from Anaximander to Proclus, 600 B.C.–500 A.D.* (New York: New American Library, 1961), p. 53.

8. Arthur B. Keith, *The Religion and Philosophy of the Veda and Upaniṣads*, Harvard Oriental Series 31 and 32 (Cambridge, Massachusetts: Harvard University Press, 1925), p. 594.

9. Ibid.

10. K. N. Jayatilleke, *Early Buddhist Theory of Knowledge* (London: George Allen and Unwin, 1963), p. 167.

11. See A. L. Basham, *History and Doctrines of the Ājīvikas: A Vanished Indian Religion* (London: Luzac and Company, 1951), pp. 47–50.

12. See, e.g., Padmanabh S. Jaini, "On the *Sarvajñātva* of Mahāvīra and the Buddha," in *Buddhist Studies in Honour of I. B. Horner*, ed. L. Cousins, A. Kunst, and K. R. Norman (Dordrecht: D. Reidel, 1974), pp. 71–90.

13. Jayatilleke, *Early Buddhist Theory of Knowledge*, pp. 152–153, 250.

14. Ibid., pp. 462–463.

15. Ibid., pp. 438, 440, 466, 468, 422, 399; David J. Kalupahana, *Causality: The Central Philosophy of Buddhism* (Honolulu: University of Hawaii Press, 1975), pp. 104–106.

16. Jonathon Barnes, *The Presocratic Philosophers* (London and New York: Routledge, 1982), p. 12.

17. Ibid.

18. Quoted by M. L. West, *Early Greek Philosophy and the Orient* (Oxford: The Clarendon Press, 1971), p. 3, n. 5.

19. Ibid., p. 3.

20. Burkert, for example, writes: "That Pythagoras taught the doctrine of metempsychosis is generally regarded, and rightly, as the one most certain fact in the history of early Pythagoreanism" (Walter Burkert, *Lore and Science in Ancient Pythagoreanism* [Cambridge, Massachusetts: Harvard University Press, 1972], p. 120). And Cornelia J. de Vogel: "That he taught a doctrine of metempsychosis is a fact so solidly attested that it cannot be denied" (*Philosophia*, vol. 1, Philosophical Texts and Studies 19 [Assen: van Gorcum, 1970], p. 91). See also Aristotle, *De Anima* 407b20 = DK 58B39, and 414b22.

21. Trans. G. S. Kirk and J. E. Raven, *The Presocratic Philosophers: A Critical History with a Selection of Texts* (Cambridge: Cambridge University Press, 1957), p. 223.

22. Some modern scholars have been skeptical about whether Orphism really existed as a distinct body of doctrines and a society with a distinct membership (see Ivan M. Linforth, *The Arts of Orpheus* [Berkeley, California, and Los Angeles: University of California Press, 1941]). Even granted the existence of Orphism, its relationship with Pythagoreanism is unclear. Proclus, for example, says that Plato's doctrine is from "those who with Orpheus as their patron are initiated to Dionysus and Kore, for 'Release from the wheel and rest from suffering'" (*OF* 229). Simplicius also submits to the authority of Orpheus such matters as the wheel of birth and release from it (*OF* 230). One scholar argues, on the other hand, that the tripartite doctrine of reincarnation went from Pythagorean circles into the Orphic milieu, rather than the other way around. "It is," he says, "the Pythagorean variant of Orphism that is manifest in Pindar, Empedocles, Herodotus, and Plato" (Burkert, *Lore and Science in Ancient Pythagoreanism*, p. 133). I will follow the custom of calling this myth in its Greek form "Orphic," without intending any dogmatic implications.

23. See M. L. West, *The Orphic Poems* (Oxford: Clarendon Press, 1983), pp. 2–3.

24. Ibid., p. 29.

25. Ibid., p. 23.

26. Ibid.

27. Trans. W. K. C. Guthrie, *Orpheus and Greek Religion: A Study of the Orphic Movement* (New York: W. W. Norton, 1966), p. 157.

28. West seems perhaps overly severe when he says, "We have no warrant for calling the gold leaves themselves Orphic" (*The Orphic Poems*, p. 26). Though Orpheus's name does not occur in them, the other evidences are in place, and there is no other known context into which they might fit.

29. Trans. Kathleen Freeman, *Ancilla to the Presocratic Philosophers* (Cambridge, Massachusetts: Harvard University Press, 1970).

30. Cf. Kirk and Raven, *The Presocratic Philosophers*, pp. 352–354.

31. M. R. Wright, *Empedocles: The Extant Fragments* (New Haven and London: Yale University Press, 1981), p. 291.

32. Wright asserts that "this fragment does not imply a remembrance of the previous lives described, but it is an inference from the decree that the daimon be born in different elements as different kinds of living things" (Wright, *Empedocles*, p. 276). It is possible that he is right, but he sounds much too sure of it. In the tradition of reincarnationism in general, advanced reincarnators like Empedocles are generally held to be able to remember past incarnations. If Empedocles were merely drawing inferences from a doctrine, his stage of advancement would seem rudimentary in comparison.

33. This version of his death story was dominant from the second century B.C. onward, but seems not to have been in the earlier period. See Wright, *Empedocles*, pp. 15–17.

34. Trans. Sir John E. Sandys (*The Odes of Pindar, Including the Principal Fragments*, Loeb Classical Library [Cambridge, Massachusetts: Harvard University Press; London: W. Heinemann, 1919]) slightly altered. I am following Rohde's interpretation of this passage as referring to a final incarnation (Erwin Rohde, *Psyche: The Cult of Souls and Belief in Immortality among the Greeks*, trans. B. Hillis [London: Kegan, Paul, Trench, Trubner and Co., Ltd., 1925], pp. 417–444).

35. Ibid.

36. See Giorgio De Santillana and Hertha von Dechend, *Hamlet's Mill* (Boston: David R. Godine, 1977), pp. 134–135, that Cronos = Kronos.

37. See West, *The Orphic Poems*, p. 69.

38. A connection between the water of Styx and the Spring of Memory in the Orphic version is also possible.

39. Cf. West, *The Orphic Poems*, p. 110 and n.

40. See also frs. 32, 52, and 88.

41. Leonardo Taran, *Parmenides* (Princeton, New Jersey: Princeton University Press, 1965), claims that "the visible" means the earth, "the unseen" means Hades, and compares Aeschylus:

> Earth, who bears all things and, when she has raised them up, receives them again. (*Cheoph.* 127–128)

But the order of events in the two passages is not the same. Simplicius says not that the goddess sends souls from death to life and then claims them back into death again; but that she sends souls from life to death *and then back to life.*

42. One early Vedic hymn has been interpreted as showing the recollection of past lives:

> I was aforetime Manu, I was Surya (the sun); I am the sage Kakshivan, holy singer. Kutsa the son of Arjuni I master. I am the sapient Usana, behold me. I have bestowed the earth upon the Arya, and rain upon the man who brings oblation. I guided forth the loudly-roaring waters, and the gods moved according to my pleasure. In the wild joy of Soma I demolished Sambara's forts, ninety and nine together . . . (RV IV.26)

These lines may have been written by about 1000 B.C., in the Middle Vedic period. In the late Vedic, or Upaniṣadic, period, starting around 700 B.C., when the doctrine of reincarnation was established, the passage was interpreted as a recollection of his former lives by the legendary sage Vamadeva (*BU* I.4.10). But this interpretation may have been forced upon the material. The later lines of the passage are spoken by Indra in reference to his cosmogonic battle with Vritra; there is no good reason to suppose that the earlier lines are not his, too. The passage may represent the Vedic priest, under the influence of Soma, declaring his oneness with a series of cosmogonic forces, especially Indra.

43. Gananath Obeyesekere, "The Rebirth Eschatology and Its Transformations: A Contribution to the Sociology of Early Buddhism," in *Karma and Rebirth in Classical Indian Traditions*, ed. Wendy Doniger O'Flaherty (Berkeley, California: University of California Press, 1980), p. 156.

44. Ibid., p. 146.

45. Keith, *The Religion and Philosophy of the Veda and Upaniṣads*, p. 409.

46. Ibid., p. 405.

47. Cited ibid.

48. See, e.g., E. A. Wallis Budge, trans., *The Egyptian Book of the Dead (The Papyrus of Ani)* (New York: Dover, 1967), p. 294 (". . . gathering his bones and bringing together all his limbs"), p. 317 ("I have knit together my bones").

49. Keith, *The Religion and Philosophy of the Veda and Upaniṣads*, p. 571.

50. Etienne Lamotte, *Histoire du Bouddhisme Indien* (Louvain: Université Catholique de Louvain, 1958), pp. 6–7; Obeyesekere, "The Rebirth Eschatology and Its Transformations," p. 138: "In all likelihood, rebirth theories were found in ancient Indian tribal religions, probably in the Gangetic region, where the great 'heterodox' religions flourished."

51. S. K. Chatterji, "Race Movements and Prehistoric Culture," in *The Vedic Age*, ed. by R. C. Majumdar (London: George Allen and Unwin, 1951), p. 151.

52. Obeyesekere, "The Rebirth Eschatology and Its Transformation," p. 139.

53. See, for example, Robert Zaehner, *Teachings of the Magi* (New York: Oxford University Press, 1976), pp. 133–134.

54. *Taitt. Br.* III.11.8.6; *Kauṣ. Br.* XXV.1.

55. For this theory cf. Deussen, *The Philosophy of the Upaniṣads*, p. 327. The motif of redeath in the afterlife may have existed in ancient Egypt also. Chapter 175 in the *Book of the Dead* is entitled "The Chapter of Not Dying a Second Time" (Budge's trans., p. clii; cf. Faulkner's trans.: "Spell for Not Dying Again" [spell 175]); its contents, however, do not shed light on the question.

56. Keith, *The Religion and Philosophy of the Veda and Upaniṣads*, p. 407.

57. Obeyesekere, "The Rebirth Eschatology and Its Transformations," p. 157.

58. Herman W. Tull, *The Vedic Origins of Karma: Cosmos as Man in Ancient Indian Myth and Ritual*, SUNY Series in Hindu Studies (Albany, New York: State University of New York Press, 1989), p. 2.

59. Ibid., p. 31

60. Quoted ibid., p. 29.

61. Sylvain Levi, *La Doctrine du Sacrifice dans les Brāhmaṇas*, 2nd ed., Bibliotheque de l'École des Hautes Études, Section des Sciences Religieuses, vol. 73 (Paris: Presses Universitaires de France, 1966), p. 10.

62. Obeyesekere, "The Rebirth Eschatology and Its Transformations," p. 157.

63. Tull, *The Vedic Origins of Karma*, p. 29.

64. Chapple quotes Agehananda Bharati to the effect that the *karma*-reincarnation linkage "is a recent use, probably originating with the theosophists and Madama Blavatsky . . . This is not the traditional Indian use in any statistical sense, since in most places it means ritualistic action and only that . . ." ("Speaking About 'That Which Shows Itself': The Language of Mysticism and the Mystics," pp. 234–235, in *Religious Experience and Scientific Paradigms*, comp. Christopher Chapple [Stony Brook, New York: The Institute for Advanced Studies of World Religions, 1985, pp. 210–243]; cited in Chapple, *Karma and Creativity* [Albany, New York: State University of New York Press, 1986], p. 115, n. 1.) Bharati, in other words, feels that the purely ritual meaning of *karma* obtained not only in the Vedic period but throughout Hindu textual history. Chapple himself takes a broader view and emphasizes the positive incentive offered by *karma*: "the doctrine of bondage due to past actions was for many a call for action in the present" (Chapple, ibid., p. 4). He demonstrates through analysis of several Hindu and Buddhist texts that "*karma* and creativity may work in tandem in order to produce a world that is not dissonant with liberation" (ibid., p. 81). "Through the mode of creativity, one is allowed to continue leading an active life without the bondage of attachment" (ibid., p. 82).

65. Tull, *The Vedic Origins of Karma*, p. 23.

66. Ibid., p. 105.

67. Compare Nakamura: "Thus, the effects of the good and bad deeds performed in this life would first be experienced in the lunar world, and then they would determine the type of birth after descent to this world; the concept is therefore of a two-stage effectuality of *Karma*." (Hajime Nakamura, *A History of Early Vedānta Philosophy* [Delhi: Motilal Banarsidass, 1989], p. 526). So Nakamura would, it seems, revise my phrase "double payment" to "two-staged payment"; the problem with this solution is that the *Chāndogya Upaniṣad* says (*CU* V.10.5) that the deceased soul being rewarded for good *karma* in the afterlife will not be born again till the meritorious *karma* has all been used up.

68. Nakamura, *Early Vedānta* pp. 529–530.

69. Budge, *Book of the Dead*, p. lvii-lviii.

70. The idea that souls reenter nature through plants seems echoed in the prohibition about beans, as channels for the return of souls, held by the Pythagoreans (and mentioned in the *Chāndogya Upaniṣad* also); beans in a similarly physical view, seem to have been regarded as carriers of souls due to their causing flatulence, that is, the escape of breath or soul from the body.

(For some remarks on this see Keith, *The Religion and Philosophy of the Veda and Upaniṣads*, p. 608.)

71. This conclusion is in line with the fact that the Greek text in which the doctrine is reported by some to have first appeared—the *Theology* of Pherecydes of Syros—is dominated by concepts borrowed from Oriental literature, including definite signs of Upaniṣadic influence. The same conclusion is indicated by the seemingly redundant element of intermediate heavens and hells which are followed by morally determined rebirths; this element cannot be accounted for in the Greek tradition (where it is found in Pindar and Plato); in the early sixth century B.C., the reward-punishment afterlife seems to have been as foreign to Greece as the doctrine of reincarnation. In India, however, the system of reincarnation developed on top of an existing system of rewards and punishments in heavens and hells; the conflation of elements was a necessary theological synthesis there.

72. Virtually no one has disagreed with Rohde on this point; a lonely voice of protest is provided by Alan B. Lloyd in *Herodotus Book II—Commentary* (Leiden: Brill, 1988): "There is no reason to believe that it is a foreign import into Greece" (vol. 3, p. 59).

73. Erwin Rohde, *Psychē: The Cult of Souls and Belief in Immortality among the Greeks*, translated by W. B. Hillis (New York: Harper and Row, 1966), vol. 2, p. 260.

74. Ibid., pp. 253–282; Dodds, *Greeks and the Irrational*, pp. 140 ff.

75. See, for example, John Chadwick, *The Decipherment of Linear B* (New York: Random House, 1958), p. 124.

76. Rohde, *Psyche*, vol. 2, p. 256, n. 10.

77. The links here are weak. Other ancient authors call Sabazius a Phrygian god, and still others identify him with Zeus rather than with Dionysus. See Rohde, ibid.

78. The passages are gathered by Mircea Eliade, *Zalmoxis: The Vanishing God*, trans. Willard R. Trask (Chicago: University of Chicago Press, 1972), pp. 30 ff.

79. Eliade, for example, says the return of the dead "nowhere implies metempsychosis as has sometimes been maintained" (*Zalmoxis*, p. 32). Others who have argued the same position include Herbert Strainge Long, "A Study of the Doctrine of Metempsychōsis in Greece from Pythagoras to Plato" (unpublished Ph.D. dissertation, Princeton University, 1943), p. 8, and J. A. Philip, *Pythagoras and Early Pythagoreanism* (Toronto: University of Toronto Press, 1966), p. 153.

80. On this basis Long ("A Study of the Doctrine of Metempsychōsis," p. 8) rejects the Thracian hypothesis.

81. Eliade (*Zalmoxis*, p. 32) sees it as "a funerary ritual intended to bring about the periodic return of the dead," a ritual "documented in the Mediterranean, Greek and Balkan areas as well as elsewhere."

82. Trans. William Arrowsmith in *The Complete Greek Tragedies*, vol. 6, *Euripides II*, ed. David Grene and Richmond Lattimore (New York: Random House, n.d.), pp. 149–150.

83. Rohde, *Psyche*, p. 280, n. 70. The remaining evidence for the Thracian hypothesis is slight. Strabo (VII.3.3) reports, after Posidonius, that a Thracian people other than the Getae, the Mysians, abstained from animal food in obedience to their religion. Elsewhere (VII.3.5), speaking of the Thrace of his own day, Strabo says that "the Pythagorean command to abstain from eating living beings still existed as it had been taught by Zalmoxis." Finally, he adds (VII.3.3) that among the Thracians there were sacred hermits who lived apart from women, that is, presumably celibate. Strabo was writing in the age of Augustus. Herodotus does not mention vegetarianism or celibacy among the Thracians of his day.

84. Karl Meuli, "Scythica," *Hermes* 70 (1935), pp. 121–176; Dodds, *The Greeks and the Irrational*, ch. V. See Burkert, *Lore and Science in Ancient Pythagoreanism*, pp. 161 ff., for a brief review of this hypothesis.

85. John Burnet, *Early Greek Philosophy* (Cleveland, Ohio, and New York: The World Publishing Company, 1957), p. 93.

86. W. K. C. Guthrie, *A History of Greek Philosophy*, vol. 1 (Cambridge: Cambridge University Press, 1962–1981), p. 205.

87. Dodds, *The Greeks and the Irrational*, p. 144.

88. Central Asian influence on archaic Greece has also been proposed, "but it is doubtful," as Kirk, Raven, and Schofield note, "how far a historical case can be made for an influence upon Archaic Greece from Central Asian shamanistic cultures . . ." *(The Presocratic Philosophers*, p. 229.) "[T]he evidence for a shamanistic tradition in early Greece is doubtful" (p. 243).

89. West, *Early Greek Philosophy and the Orient*, p. 89.

90. Ibid., p. 107.

91. Ibid., pp. 170–201. Afnán goes much farther in attributing Greek culture to Persian influence (see Ruhi M. Afnán, *Zoroaster's Influence on Greek Thought* [New York: Philosophical Library, 1965]; *Zoroaster's Influence on Anaxagoras, the Greek Tragedians, and Socrates* [New York: Philosophical Library, 1969]).

92. *Early Greek Philosophy and the Orient* has received unenthusiastic reviews from western classicists, most of whom ignore the Indian material West discusses and focus on the Persian. One scholar who granted some credence to his Indian discussions was Kahn, saying, "I happen to believe that West's thesis is correct in at least one case (namely the Eastern, ultimately Indian origin of the doctrine of transmigration) . . ." (Charles H. Kahn, *The Art and Thought of Heraclitus: An Edition of the Fragments with Translation and Commentary* [Cambridge: Cambridge University Press, 1979], p. 298.) Still, Kahn's discussion of the question does little more than distance the Greeks from the "drop of alien blood." In general he dismisses West's links as chance convergences based on either universal human nature or similar social situations. Then he tosses this one concession in—relegating the offensive concepts to a parenthesis as if they were incidental—and has nothing more to say about the matter. He does not acknowledge a momentous significance to such an admission—to the fact that virtually all the pre-Socratics, Pythagoras, Plato, and the entire Pythagorean-Platonic tradition down to and including Plotinus, the Stoics, and others, held this "ultimately Indian" doctrine that was not about incidental things but fundamental to the whole sense of the meaning of life. If this one link alone were acknowledged, already India would have had a major impact on Greek philosophy—and a central doctrine such as this one is not apt to have come alone, but to have brought a cluster of other ideas with it (the monism complex).

93. West, *Early Greek Philosophy and the Orient*, pp. 186–188, 123, 130–133.

94. Burkert, *Orientalizing Revolution*, p. 88.

95. Porphyry (*De Abst.* IV, p. 16) asserts that the Magi (by which he seems to intend the Zoroastrian priesthood) taught the transmigration of souls. But he is paraphrasing Eubalus's book on Mithraism, and Mithraism can tell us little or nothing about classical Zoroastrian doctrines. It was in effect the mystery religion associated peripherally with Mazdaism, as Kabbala was to Judaism and Rosicrucianism to Christianity. In all these cases the mystery doctrine was a deliberate inversion of the doctrine of the host religion—the most striking inversion being the substitution of transmigration for the doctrine of last judgment and permanent heaven or hell: While it is true that Manes, the founder of Manicheism, taught reincarnation in the third century A.D., it is also true that he was denounced by the Magi, who persuaded the Persian king to execute him.

96. Afnán, *Zoroaster's Influence on Greek Thought*, p. 21.

97. Robert C. Zaehner, *The Dawn and Twilight of Zoroastrianism* (London: Weidenfeld and Nicholson, 1961), p. 199.

98. Zaehner, *Teachings of the Magi*, p. 123.

99. Ibid., p. 100.

100. West, *Early Greek Philosophy and the Orient*, p. 67.

101. Ibid., p. 242.

102. Zaehner, *The Dawn and Twilight of Zoroastrianism*, pp. 181–182.

103. Ibid., p. 202.

104. John R. Hinnels, *Persian Mythology* (London: Hamlyn, 1973), p. 20.

105. Zaehner, *Teachings of the Magi*, p. 15.

106. Zaehner, *The Dawn and Twilight of Zoroastrianism*, p. 66.

107. Cook, *Persian Empire*, p. 155.

108. Tull, *The Vedic Origins of Karma*, pp. 158–159.

109. Zaehner, *Teachings of the Magi*, p. 14.

110. Tull, *The Vedic Origins of Karma*, p. 159.

111. See, e.g., Abraham V. W. Jackson, *Zoroastrian Studies: The Iranian Religion and Various Monographs* (New York: AMS Press, 1965), p. 8; and Zaehner, *The Dawn and Twilight of Zoroastrianism*, pp. 37–40.

The extant Persian texts do seem to have influenced doctrines passing through their territory somewhat. In India, for example, the doctrine of reincarnation comes equipped with a Sumerian-based numerology rooted in the sexagesimal arithmetic of the cosmic cycle. In Greece, on the other hand, though the Sumerian numerology persists in Plato's "marriage number" and elsewhere, the numerology of reincarnationism features the figure ten thousand, a characteristically Persian number found frequently in the Zend texts (which do not show as deep a Mesopotamian imprint as either Greek or Indian texts). This discrepancy could indicate the transmission of the doctrine through Persian intermediaries, or its recasting by Persian-influenced Greeks—perhaps even in Persia itself.

112. A passage of the *Vendidad* seems to show a trace of the Upaniṣadic-Heraclitean doctrine of the two paths, but garbled like a foreign doctrine that is only half understood:

> As the sea Vouni-hascha is the gathering place of waters, rise up, go up the aerial way and go down on the earth; go down on the earth and go up the aerial way. Rise up and roll along! Thou in whose rising and growing Ahura Mazda made the aerial way.
>
> Up! rise up and roll along! Thou swift-horsed sun, above Hara Berezaiti, and produce light for the world (and mayst thou [O man!] rise up there, if thou art to abide in Garo Muanem), along the path made by Mazda, along the way made by the gods, the watery way they opened.
>
> As the sea Vouni-hascha is the gathering place of waters, rise up, go up the aerial way and go down on the earth; go down on the earth and go up the aerial way. Rise up and roll along! Thou in whose rising and growing Ahura Mazda made the aerial way . . .
>
> Up! rise up, thou moon that dost keep in thee the seed of the bull, rise up above Hara Berezaiti, and produce light for the world (and mayst thou [O man!] rise up there, if thou art to abide in Garo Muanem, along the path made by the gods, the watery way they opened.

(James Darmesteter, trans., *The Zend-Avesta*, part I: *The Vendidad*, Sacred Books of the East 4 [Delhi: Motilal Banarsidas, 1980], pp. 225–227.) The passage seems to echo the Upaniṣadic doctrine of the two paths— the path of the sun leading to release, the path of the moon leading to reincarnation—but without understanding it. The watery way from earth to sky and back to earth relates to the path of the moon from which the soul rains down into matter; but in this *Vendidad* passage the watery way is not connected to the soul, but is simply a description of the process of rainfall and evaporation; both the solar and lunar paths are called the "watery way," conflating rather than distinguishing them, and both are held to lead to heaven, neither being involved in reincarnation. The text does not show the transformations of matter, as in the Upaniṣads, Heraclitus, and Anaximenes, but only the watery stage which represents the dissolution of the soul. It does not preserve the doctrine intact, but an isolated and magnified fragment of it. While there are traces here of an Indian doctrine that may have been encountered as it passed through Persia, it would require special pleading to find here the source of that doctrine. The doctrine may have been received whole in Greece and not in Persia because the Persian eschatology was inimical to reincarnationism and edited it out.

113. West, *Early Greek Philosophy and the Orient*, p. 62. He must mean "at least to the seventh century."

114. Duncan Greenlees, *The Gospel of Zarathushtra* (Adyar, Madras: Theosophical Publishing House, 1951), p. lxxvi.

115. Ibid., p. lxxvii.

116. West, *Early Greek Philosophy and the Orient*, pp. 240–241.

117. M. Marcovich, review of West, *Early Greek Philosophy and the Orient*, *Gnomon* 47 (1975), pp. 324–325.

118. Alex Wayman, *Untying the Knots in Buddhism: Selected Essays*, Buddhist Tradition Series 28 (Delhi: Motilal Banarsidass, 1997), pp. 46–50.

119. Marcovich, review of West, *Early Greek Philosophy and the Orient*, pp. 324–325.

120. Greenless, *The Gospel of Zarathustra*, p. 89.

121. Muhammad A. Dandamaev, and Vladimir G. Lukonin, *The Culture and Social Institutions of Ancient Iran*, trans. Philip L. Kohl (Cambridge: Cambridge University Press, 1989) p. 367.

122. Ibid., p. 358.

123. Ibid., p. 357.

124. Ibid., p. 355.

125. Compare A. T. Olmstead: "Media ceased to be an independent nation and became the first satrapy, Mada. Nevertheless, the close relationship between Persians and Medes was never forgotten. Plundered Ecbatan remained a favorite royal residence. Medes were honored equally with Persians; they were employed in high office and were chosen to lead Persian armies. Foreigners spoke regularly of the Medes and Persians; when they used a single term, it was 'the Mede'" (*History of the Persian Empire* [Chicago: University of Chicago Press, 1948], p. 37).

126. Dandamaev and Lukonin, *The Culture and Social Institutions of Ancient Iran*, p. 327.

127. Ibid., p. 347.

128. Ibid., p. lxxvii.

129. Ibid., pp. 330–331.

130. Ibid., p. 336.

131. Ibid., p. 352.

Yet another problem is that the Magian hypothesis reverses the overall historical shape of Persian religious tradition. The monism complex, the belief in the universe as a living god, and so on, arose in a later phase of Persian religion, in the era of the mystery cults, which included Mithraism and Zurvanism. These cults belong to the Hellenistic and Roman periods; there is no evidential basis for reading them back into the Magian period except the unsupported assumption that Mithraism and Zurvanism represent resurgences of a monistic spirit which Zoroaster had repressed.

In fact these mystery cults seem to have had very little to do with Magian religion. "Mithraism was," as one scholar has said, "the Freemasonry of the Roman world. Whatever its ancestry in the ancient religion of Persia, it became something very different as soon as it left its native soil and took root in Republican Rome" (Jocelyn Godwin, *Mystery Religions in the Ancient World* [San Francisco: Harper and Row, 1981], p. 98). There it became part of the second monistic age of Greek philosophy, the age of the Neopythagoreans, Middle Platonists, and Neoplatonists, in which a variety of earlier religious forms, such as the Egyptian cult of Isis, were redefined as mystical, monistic, initiation sects, the antecedents both of Freemasonry and of Theosophy.

132. Wilhelm Halbfass, *India and Europe: An Essay in Understanding* (Albany: State University of New York Press, 1988), p. 11.

133. Trans. Aubrey de Selincourt, *Herodotus: The Histories* (Baltimore, Maryland: Penguin Books, 1954), pp. 150–151.

134. For example: Sir John G. Wilkinson, *The Manners and Customs of the Ancient Egyptians*, vol. 3, new ed. rev. and cor. by Samuel Birch (London: J. Murray, 1878), p. 462; Sir William M. F.

Petrie, *Personal Religion in Egypt Before Christianity* (London: Harper and Brothers, 1909), pp. 43, 47; Margaret Murray, *The Splendour that Was Egypt* (New York: Philosophical Library, 1949), pp. 210–211; James Bonwick, *Egyptian Belief and Modern Thought* (London: C. K. Paul and Co., 1878).

135. Dodds, *The Greeks and the Irrational*, p. 160, n. 29.

136. Burkert, *Lore and Science in Ancient Pythagoreanism*, p. 126 and n. 36.

137. Lionel Casson, *Travel in the Ancient World*, p. 105.

138. Barnes, *The Presocratic Philosophers*, p. 103.

139. Lloyd, *Herodotus Book II—Commentary*, vol. 3, p. 59 and vol. 1, pp. 57–58

140. West, *Early Greek Philosophy and the Orient*, p. 62.

141. Ibid.

142. Louis V. Zakbar, "Herodotus and the Egyptian Idea of Immortality," *JNES* 22, no. 1 (1963): 60.

143. Ibid., p. 62.

144. Lloyd, *Herodotus, Book II—Commentary*, vol. 1, pp. 57–58.

145. On the question how there can be reincarnation without a self, one Buddhist scholar declares that the relationship between a person in one life and the "same" person as reborn in another life "is a purely serial relationship—an 'identity' of a certain kind which can only be described in terms of a causal continuum" (Francis Story, *Rebirth as Doctrine and Experience: Essays and Case Studies*, introduction by Ian Stevenson [Kandy, Sri Lanka: Buddhist Publication Society, 1975], p. 31). The elements are "like beads strung on the connecting thread of . . . the unconscious life continuum" (ibid., p. 32). "They are connected only by a causal relationship . . ." (ibid, p. 54). As another author puts it: "No transmigration of consciousness is . . . posited [in Buddhism], but rather a causally linked stream (*sota*) of discrete moments of consciousness" (James P. McDermott, "Karma and Rebirth in Early Buddhism," in O'Flaherty, ed., *Karma and Rebirth in Classical Indian Traditions*, p. 169).

The question whether reincarnationism is a necessary and fundamental part of Buddhism is occasionally still debated in the Buddhist community, as in "Reincarnation: A Debate between Stephen Batchelor and Robert A. F. Thurman" (*Tricycle: The Buddhist Review*, vol. 4, number 4 [summer 1997], pp. 24 ff.). For the opinion that reincarnation is absolutely essential to Buddhism see Martin Willson, *Rebirth and the Western Buddhist* (London: Wisdom Publications, 1987).

146. Zakbar, "Herodotus and the Egyptian Idea of Immortality," p. 61.

147. West, *Early Greek Philosophy and the Orient*, p. 188.

148. Jane Ellen Harrison, *Prolegomena to the Study of Greek Religion* (New York: Meridian Books, 1957), p. 589. Harrison's whole sentence reads: "They need not have borrowed it from Egypt, and yet it is probable that the influence of Egypt, the home of animal worship, helped out the doctrine by emphasizing the sanctity of animal life."

149. See Budge, *Book of the Dead*, p. cl. Cf. Faulkner's translation: "For Being Transformed Into a Falcon of Gold," "For Being Transformed Into a Lotus," "For Being Transformed Into a Crocodile," and "For Being Transformed Into a Heron" (Raymond O. Faulkner, trans., *The Ancient Egyptian Book of the Dead*, ed. Carol Andrews [New York: Macmillan, 1985], pp. 19–20). For various reasons I prefer Budge's currently out-of-fashion translation, but I have used it here primarily when it is confirmed by Faulkner's.

150. Zakbar ("Herodotus and the Egyptian Idea of Immortality," p. 59) paraphrasing the position of Schayer in 1914.

151. Budge, *Book of the Dead*, chapters XLIV and CLXXV. Cf. Faulkner's translation: "For Not Dying Again in the Realm of the Dead," and "For Not Dying Again" (Faulkner, *Ancient Egyptian Book of the Dead*, pp. 18, 22).

152. Budge, *Book of the Dead*, p. lxx.

153. Ibid.

154. Ibid., lxxi.

155. Ibid.

156. Joseph Head and S. L. Cranston, *Reincarnation in World Thought* (New York: Julian Press, 1977), p. 70.

157. Ibid., p. 71.

158. Budge, *Book of the Dead*, p. 275. Cf. Faulkner's translation: ". . . he shall do what he wishes like those nine gods who are in the Netherworld. A matter a million times true" (*Ancient Egyptian Book of the Dead*, p. 73).

159. Budge, *Book of the Dead*, p. 340 (not in Faulkner's translation).

160. Ibid., p. 334. Cf. Faulkner's translation:

> I have made my appearance as a divine falcon, Horus has invested me with his shape in order that I might take his affairs to Osiris, to the Netherworld.
>
> THE DOUBLE LION RAISES AN OBJECTION: The Double Lion who is in his cavern, warden of the House of the Royal Wig-cover, said to me: How can you reach the confines of the sky? Indeed you are equipped with the form of Horus, but you do not possess the Wig-cover. Do you speak on the confines of the sky? (*Ancient Egyptian Book of the Dead*, p. 76).

161. Budge, *Book of the Dead*, p. 340 (not in Faulkner's translation).

162. Ibid., p. 315. Cf. Faulkner's translation: "I have appeared as King of the Gods, and I will not die again in the realm of the dead" (*Ancient Egyptian Book of the Dead*, p. 64).

163. Budge, *Book of the Dead*, p. 328. Cf. Faulkner's translation: ". . . for N is a great one . . . and reckons up his needs" (*Ancient Egyptian Book of the Dead*, p. 122).

164. Budge, *Book of the Dead*, p. 339. Cf. Faulkner's translation: "I have come on the day when I appear in glory with the strides of the gods" (*Ancient Egyptian Book of the Dead*, pp. 80–81).

165. Budge, *Book of the Dead*, p. 340 (not in Faulkner's translation).

166. Ibid., p. 342. Cf. Faulkner's translation: ". . . so says Atum—and *he* [Horus] will despatch the Elders" (*Ancient Egyptian Book of the Dead*, p. 175, Faulkner's emphasis).

167. Budge, *Book of the Dead*, p. 331. Cf. Faulkner's translation: "Horus is in command of the Sacred Bark, and the throne of his father Osiris has been given to him" (*Ancient Egyptian Book of the Dead*, p. 83).

168. On the "crime," see Giorgio de Santillana and Hertha von Dechend, *Hamlet's Mill* (Boston: David R. Godine, 1977), pp. 149–154.

169. West, *The Orphic Poems*, p. 164,

170. Budge, *Book of the Dead*, p. 335. Cf. Faulkner's translation: "Down on your faces, you gods of the Netherworld, whose faces are . . . whose necks are outstretched, and who hide the face of the Great Demolisher!" (*Ancient Egyptian Book of the Dead*, pp. 76–77).

171. Budge, *Book of the Dead*, p. 341–342. Cf. Faulkner's translation:

> O Thoth, what is it that has come about through the Children of Nut? They have made war, they have raised up tumult, they have done wrong, they have created rebellion, they have done slaughter, they have created imprisonment, they have reduced what was great to what is little in all that we have made . . . I am not among those who have done hidden damage, and none will work harm on me (*Ancient Egyptian Book of the Dead*, p. 175).

172. James B. Pritchard, ed., *Ancient Near Eastern Texts Relating to the Old Testament* (Princeton, New Jersey: Princeton University Press, 1955), p. 34.

173. Ibid., p. 328.

174. Budge, *Book of the Dead*, p. 344. Faulkner translates a different version of the introduction to Spell 125 (*Ancient Egyptian Book of the Dead*, pp. 29–31).

175. Budge, *Book of the Dead*, pp. 338–39. Cf. Faulkner's translation:

> I am the eldest of the primeval gods, . . . I am the soul of the souls of the eternal gods, my body is everlasting, . . . I am the soul who created the Abyss . . . (*Ancient Egyptian Book of the Dead*, pp. 82–83).

176. Budge, *Book of the Dead*, p. 340 (not in Faulkner's translation).

177. Pritchard, *Ancient Near Eastern Texts*, p. 34

178. Adolf Erman, ed. and trans., *The Ancient Egyptians: A Sourcebook of Their Writings* (New York: Harper and Row, 1966), pp. 5–7.

179. Budge, *Book of the Dead*, p. 339–340, 342. Cf. Faulkner's translation: "I have flown up like the primeval ones, . . . I am the essence of every god . . ." (*Ancient Egyptian Book of the Dead*, p. 80).

180. Budge, *Book of the Dead*, p. 340.

181. Ibid., p. 317.

182. Ibid., p. 340.

183. Ibid., p. 332.

184. Ibid., p. 342.

185. De Santillana and von Dechend, *Hamlet's Mill*, p. 242.

186. Posidonius has a picture of the afterlife that is closely related to the Upaniṣadic doctrine of the paths of the sun and moon: "[T]he soul comes from the sun and after the death of the body it returns first to the moon where it enjoys a kind of pure contemplative life, and then to the sun." See R. Miller-Jones, "Posidonius and Solar Eschatology," *CQ* 27 (1932), pp. 113ff. Giovanni Reale says the testimonium may be wrongly attributed to Posidonius (*The Systems of the Hellenistic Age*, trans. John R. Catan [Albany, New York: State University of New York Press, 1985], p. 303).

187. What has been called "the astral element in Plato's religion" (R. Hackforth, trans. and comm., *Plato's Phaedrus* [Cambridge: Cambridge University Press, 1952], p. 73), derived in part from Egyptian or some other Near Eastern prototype, entered the occult or spiritualistic level of Greek philosophy. "Heraclides conceived the soul . . . as made up of sidereal and luminous material. Souls, before entering the body, reside in the Milky Way and form the innumerable points of light that we see" (Reale, *A History of Ancient Philosophy*, vol. 3, *The Systems of the Hellenistic Age*, p. 66).

188. Budge, *Book of the Dead*, p. 314. Cf. Faulkner: "Ani kneels beside a pool and receives water and food from a tree goddess" (*Ancient Egyptian Book of the Dead*, p. 67).

189. Budge, *Book of the Dead*, p. 315. Cf. Faulkner's translation: "O you sycamore of the sky, may there be given to me the air . . ." (*Ancient Egyptian Book of the Dead*, p. 68).

190. Trans. Guthrie, *Orpheus and Greek Religion*, pp. 172–173. The motif survives in Greco-Egyptian grave steles with the inscription, "May Osiris give you cold water" (see ibid., p. 177).

191. Cf. *RV* X.135.1; *AV* V.413; *K. U.* I.3.

192. Budge, *Book of the Dead*, p. 314. Cf. Faulkner's translation:

> Open to me!
> Who are you? What are you? Where did you grow up?
> I am one of you.
> . . .
> . . . the Mansion of Him who finds faces . . . (*Ancient Egyptian Book of the Dead*, p. 68).

193. The Springs of Lethe and Mnemosyne may relate to the Mesopotamian Water of Life and Water of Death that appear in the myth of Adapa (Pritchard, *Ancient Near Eastern Texts*, p. 101). To drink from the Spring of Lethe is to descend into another body, which to the Orphic is death; to drink the Spring of Memory ensures immortal life, as does the Water of Life in the

Akkadian myth. The images form parts of a Bronze and Early Iron Age package that cannot be fully seen. Zuntz (*Persephone*) points toward it.

194. Budge, *Book of the Dead*, p. 310. Cf. Faulkner's translation:

> Spell for drinking water and not being burnt by fire. . . . my name will be strong for me, and assuredly you will live daily through me (Spell 63A).
>
> [Vignette:] Nakht stands in a pool cupping water to his lips, while a tree-goddess offers food and pours a stream of water over him (Spell 63A, pl.).
>
> (*Ancient Egyptian Book of the Dead*, pp. 68–69, 70.)

195. Quoted by Budge, *Book of the Dead*, p. xci.

196. Ibid., p. 307. Cf. Faulkner's translation: "As for any god who shall not come following after me, I will declare his name to those who are yet to be" (*Ancient Egyptian Book of the Dead*, p. 52).

197. Budge, *Book of the Dead*, p. 351. Cf. Faulkner's translation: "Hail to you, you gods who are in this Hall of Justice! I know you and I know your names, . . . you shall tell the truth about me . . ." (*Ancient Egyptian Book of the Dead*, p. 32).

198. Budge, *Book of the Dead*, pp. 344–345. Faulkner translates a different version of the introduction to Spell 125 (*Ancient Egyptian Book of the Dead*, pp. 29–31).

199. Budge, *Book of the Dead*, p. 352. Cf. Faulkner's translation: "Come and enter by this door of the Hall of Justice, for you know us" (*Ancient Egyptian Book of the Dead*, p. 33).

200. Trans. Guthrie, *Orpheus and Greek Religion*, p. 173.

201. Quoted by Jane E. Harrison, *Prolegomena to the Study of Greek Religion*, 3rd. ed. (New York: Meridian Books, 1966), p. 588.

202. As in Aristotle the sublunary is mortal and the superlunary is heavenly or immortal.

203. West (*Early Greek Philosophy and the Orient*, pp. 62–66) compares these same passages, though our attentions alighted on them independently.

204. In the Orphic *Cosmogonies* one encounters the deity Protogonos, the "bright god who first sprang into the aither from the egg made by Unaging Time," then created the world. Similarly in the *Atharva Veda*, Kāla, Time, has a firstborn, whose name, Prajāpati, is cognate with Protogonos, who is born from an egg, and proceeds to generate earth, sea, and sky. Both images derive from the Egyptian mythology of Re, the firstborn of the gods, who was born from an egg. The deification of Time derives in general from the Re-Osiris mythology. Re-Osiris says, "I am yesterday, today, and tomorrow," much as the *Kena Upaniṣad* (IV.13) speaks of the "lord of what has been and what will be, he is both today and tomorrow." The sixth-century diffusion wave that brought this image into Greece and India may have brought the myth of the soul as an exiled god, too.

205. Herodotus is also to a degree confirmed in his assertions of other connections between Egypt and Orphic and Pythagorean practices. In Orphic initiation rites, for example, it seems that the "initiate actually mounted a ladder in order to ensure his entrance on the Elysian soul-path" (see Guthrie, *Orpheus and Greek Religion*, pp. 207–209). This is astonishingly close to a central element in the so-called shamanic performance, the ascent of the ladder to other realms. A possible forerunner in the historical context is the New Kingdom Egyptian *Coronation Drama*, where, prior to the coronation of the new pharaoh, the soul of the recently dead pharaoh ascended a ladder to heaven. Rituals involving wheels are another shared Egyptian and Orphic practice (see Harrison, *Prolegomena to the Study of Greek Religion*, pp. 590 ff.). The wheel, of course, is a common symbol for the process of reincarnation. Diogenes Laertius says that "Pythagoras first asserted that the soul went round in a changing wheel of necessity, being bound down now in this, now in that animal" (VII.112). An ancient source says that there were wheels in Egyptian temples which the worshippers set in motion to purify themselves (ibid.).

Herodotus says "the so-called Orphic or Bacchic rites . . . are really Egyptian and Pythagorean, for in these rites too if a man have a share it is not lawful for him to be buried in woolen garments" (II.81). The famous prohibition against eating beans that seems to have prevailed among Pythagoreans was also shared, according to Herodotus, by the Egyptian priests who "cannot even bear to look at beans" (II.37).

206. Shashi Bhusan Dasgupta, *Obscure Religious Cults* (Calcuta: Firma KLM, 1976), p. 204.

207. Ibid., p. 205.

208. Basham, *History and Doctrine of the Ājīvikas*, p. 31.

209. It is possible to suppose that this doctrine, which Herodotus heard from an Egyptian source, was Mesopotamian in origin. It is the only form of reincarnationism that an ancient text explicitly connects with a Bronze Age Near Eastern culture. The Sumerians seem to have had a doctrine of cyclical time (see chapter 3), and their belief in astrology suggests either determinism or something very close to it. These elements are perfectly in line with a doctrine of mechanistic reincarnation.

210. These and other examples are recorded by Dasgupta, *Obscure Religious Cults*, pp. 204 ff.

211. Mircea Eliade, *Yoga: Immortality and Freedom,* translated by Willard R. Trask, Bollingen Series 56 (New York: Princeton University Press, 1969), p. 304.

212. Does he mean its decimal multiples?

213. Walter Schubring, *The Doctrine of the Jainas* (Delhi: Motilal Banarsidass, 1962), p. 28.

214. Dasgupta, *Obscure Religious Cults*, p. 204.

215. Pritchard, *Ancient Near Eastern Texts*, p. 265.

216. Tull, *The Vedic Origins of Karma*, p. 25

217. Ibid., p. 26.

218. Ibid., p. 36.

219. Henry C. Warren, *Buddhism in Translation* (New York: Atheneum, 1977), p. 6.

Chapter Five

Platonic Monism and Indian Thought

Plato was born after the Persian Wars temporarily constricted the channels of contact with Indian thought. Still, from earlier stages of his own tradition, he inherited the monism complex—the Indian-influenced Mesopotamian-and-Egyptian legacy including the cycle of time based on Precessional numbers, the tripartite doctrine of reincarnation, the Orphic-Jain myth of the lost god being punished on the Wheel, and the four elements and their transformations.

Guthrie speaks of a moment when Greek philosophy had to "abandon monism" for the sake of "preserving and explaining the sensible world,"[1] and refers to Diogenes of Apollonia's "attempt to revive monism," and his "return to monism" in the generation of Anaxagoras.[2] But this was not the whole story of Greek monism. It persisted throughout the thousand-year history of Greek philosophy in various forms such as the neo-Eleatic, the Stoic, and the Neoplatonist. And as far as Plato himself goes, as another scholar has noted, "the true trend of Platonic thought is monistic."[3] And as an ancient commentator remarked, Plato "made unity the universal principle of everything."[4] Plotinus's interpretation of Plato highlights the monistic aspect of his system, while Aristotle's highlights its tendencies toward pluralism.

Aspects of pluralism in Plato's thought arise from his attempt to mediate the Problem of the One and the Many through an extended use of the One-Few-Many structure pioneered before him by Empedocles and Pythagoras. Between the absolute One and the phenomenal Many, Empedocles had posited the four elements; Pythagoras had situated there the primal numbers. Plato interposed the expanded hierarchical realm of Forms or Ideas, which included both the elements and the numbers, along with other metaphysical entities. Speaking ontologically, then, "his view was," as Vlastos puts it, "a Degrees-of-Reality theory," in which some entities are positioned "between the purely real and the totally unreal (*Rep*. 478d),"[5] or, as Runciman put it, a "gradational ontology" in which "some things could exist more than others."[6] Still, as Aristotle pointed out, despite the plurality of the Forms or Ideas, Plato's attitude remained fundamentally monistic; for him it was the One alone that was real, as for Parmenides. "Essential reality [for Plato] is the One," says Aristotle; "the Forms are the essential cause of all other things, and the One is the essential cause of the Forms" (*Met*. 987b14–988a15).

Unwritten Doctrines

Many of the details of this area of Plato's thought are obscure today since they were, as Aristotle reports (*Phys.* 209b14), reserved for oral teaching within Plato's school and were never fully presented in his published dialogues. In the *Phaedrus* (275c–277a), and again in the *Seventh Letter* (341c–342a), Plato says that he distrusts written philosophy and teaches his real doctrines only orally and in private—following in the footsteps both of Socrates, who did not write, and of the Pythagoreans, who kept their most-valued doctrines secret. In Plato's day (and for centuries after) reading and writing were not fully established tools of culture, and ultimately, behind this practice (and especially in the *Seventh Letter*'s simile of knowledge passing from teacher to student like flame from a leaping spark [341c-d]), one might hear a distant resonance of the idea of the shamanic lineage—the necessity of learning a tradition from one who directly incarnates it.

Plato's dubiety about the effectiveness of written philosophy serves as an admonition not to expect to find his true system of thought (if such there was) presented wholly and clearly in his writings. Among the unwritten doctrines were some that, according to Aristotle (*Phys.* 209b11–17), were different from (or additional to) the written teachings. Aristotle gives some details about them; other authors, mostly later than Aristotle, give additional testimonia.[7] From the written teachings and the traces of the unwritten ones, Plato's brand of monism seems to have been a complexly qualified encyclopedic kind, with different layers of inherited contents ramifying into an intricate implied pluralism. "The 'unwritten teachings,'" as one scholar says, "seem to articulate the path of dialectical inquiry on the way down," and "the task on the downward path is to disclose the causal power by which forms are constitutive for things . . ."[8] The articulation of "the way down" constitutes "Plato's striving to overcome dualism," meaning the Parmenidean dichotomy between absolute Being and absolute non-Being.[9]

At the same time, "the way down" allows Plato to perform the homage of incorporating pre-Socratic elements into his system. In the intermediate ontological realm of the Ideas, Plato attempts to integrate the various types of pre-Socratic thought into a vast, all-embracing network of metaphysical forces. His system contains, in its different levels, elements of Cosmic Person monism, substrate monism, the monism of absolute Being, mathematical monism, and so on. It is a carefully conceived ladder of qualified monisms in which the universe, while One at every level and in every way, remains challengingly complex and hierarchical.

(Father) Parmenides and (Mother) Heraclitus

From the Heraclitean Cratylus, Plato imbibed the doctrine of the impossibility of knowing phenomena (Ar. *Met.* 987a32, D.L. III.5). If all things are in flux, as Heraclitus said they were, then one has no sooner defined something than it changes and no longer fits the definition. The lack of an unchanging essence renders every entity undefinable and hence unknowable. As Guthrie says, in order to be known, "whatever exists, in spite of apparent changes, must remain essentially what it was . . ." To be knowable, an entity needs "an unchangeable essence which could be the object of reason."[10] Thus Being, says Vlastos, "had one, and just one, sense, whose cardinal feature was changelessness."[11] As Plato said:

> What exists fully [i.e., unchangingly] can be known fully; what does not exist [unchangingly] cannot be known. (*Rep.* 477)

Conversely, what can be known, must exist; what cannot be known, must not exist. The world of Heraclitean flux, with its shifting kind of being—its Being with an admixture of non-Being—cannot be truly known; it is, as Plato put it, "between Being and non-Being" (*Rep.* 478d).

According to Diogenes Laertius (III.6) Plato studied also under Hermogenes the Parmenidean. Indeed, Plato refers to Parmenides as his "father" (*Soph.* 241d) and portrays Socrates as saying he respects Parmenides more than anyone else (*Theat.* 183e). From Parmenides' lineage Plato imbibed the doctrine of unchanging Being, the opposite of Heraclitean flux. Accepting the Parmenidean distinction between knowledge and opinion, he equated knowledge with Parmenidean Being and opinion with Heraclitean flux. On the basis both of the Heraclitean doctrine of flux and of the Parmenidean rejection of the senses, Plato came to view the commonsense world as unreal or at least seriously deficient in reality.

Still, Parmenides himself, after first denying the existence of the phenomenal world, had proceeded to write a cosmological description of it; he was evidently not completely at peace with his own unqualified rejection of the world of sense-experience and of the thoughts which are based on sense-experience. Neither was Plato. The Parmenidean doctrine left the world of phenomena unconnected with the realm of Being, due to its recognition of only two ontological states, either absolute Being or absolute non-Being. Plato's solution to the problem was the "articulation of the way down"—the introduction of a hierarchy of levels of reality to bridge the gap between the absolute "it is" and the absolute "it is not."

The ontological upper limit in this system is absolute Unity, or the One. It is a concept which is beyond the direct grasp of a finite consciousness and as a result it must be approached from a variety of points of view, sometimes contradictory (as Plato demonstrates in the *Parmenides*). The most important of these points of view have been called the contracted and expanded aspects of the One,[12] based, respectively, on the first and second hypotheses of the *Parmenides*. In its contracted aspect, Unity is absolutely pure and unalloyed; no other trait (in addition to unity) can be attributed to it. It is even beyond the duality of existence and nonexistence; it cannot be said that it is, much less that it is A, or B, or C.

The One can also be conceived as possessing a less pure or expanded aspect in which it becomes involved in a dual predication and reveals a hidden plurality. In this case, in addition to "it is one," the proposition "it exists" is also recognized as valid. The One bifurcates itself into a pair—Unity and Being. Each of these is also a pair, since its Unity Exists, and its Being is One, and so on, *ad infinitum*. This expanded aspect of the One has the potential of, or hiddenly contains, infinite multiplicity.

The possession of two aspects seems to compromise the Oneness of the One, making it Other than itself. Plato argues differently, however, in the unwritten doctrines. If the One is regarded in only its pure uncompromised aspect, beyond both being and knowledge, then, in order to produce multiplicity, it must be joined by a second outside itself. But there can be no second if there is only the One and it does not allow any division of itself. Therefore this second principle, Plato argues, should be conceived not as an actual, but as a potential or implied, entity. It is not a separate entity outside of and different from the One. It is the negative implication of the One, the other which the One, by its self-identity, implies—the potentiality of indefinite multiplicity.

It is between the One and this formless other (which the Pythagoreans called the Indefinite Dyad) that the generation of apparent multiplicity occurs. At this point in the narrative, already the four principles or beginnings (*archai*) are involved: first the coextensive and coeval Ideas of Being and Mind (or consciousness), and at once (since each of them is the same as itself and different from the other) the "brother and sister" pair, Sameness and Difference.[13] Sameness, or self-identity, since it is a case of Unity, is associated with the One; difference, a principle of multiplicity, is associated with the dyad or other. In a quasi-mythological gender association which derives from the number religion of the Pythagoreans, these are known respectively as the father and the mother. Plato says, in the *Sophist* (251a–259d), that these four principles pervade all the Ideas, including one another. None of them can be prior to the others, for, as one scholar put it, "Each is a principle of one aspect of the other[s]."[14] Through these four, the one converts itself into power (*dynamis*)—the power to exist, to have identity, and to be known.

Offspring of the One and the Other

Being and Mind, defined and arranged by Sameness and Difference, are the conditions under which existence is possible; from them the Ideal realm proceeds to flow out of unity. According to Aristotle, the highest of the differentiated Ideas are the divine numbers of the Pythagoreans, and their geometrical correlates. In the study of Pythagorean mathematics Plato found a group of entities which are neither the changing and illusory Many of Heraclitus nor the One with no distinguishing marks of Parmenides. Such an entity is the triangle, for example, as it is found in propositions such as "the interior angles of a triangle equal 180 degrees." The triangle which is referred to in such a proposition is not one that can be perceived by the senses, since no physical triangle is perfect; nor does it change, since by definition its interior angles *always* equal 180 degrees. It is not, therefore, a part of the Heraclitean flux. On the other hand, it has distinguishable parts (angles and sides) and is therefore not the indivisible Parmenidean One; furthermore, it does not exist equally everywhere, so it is not pure or absolute Being. Neither the Heraclitean nor the Parmenidean view can account for it, yet clearly it exists in some sense, because it can be known. Evidently, then, it possesses an intermediate type of being, purer than that possessed by the Heraclitean flux, but less pure than that of the Parmenidean One. The mathematical entities posited by the Pythagoreans as underlying the reality of experience were all of this intermediate type. "Mathematical numbers and geometrical figures . . . are transformed into metaphysical entities."[15] Thus the hierarchy of degrees of reality is, as Findlay puts it, "nothing but a vast prolongation and complication of the simple processes through which the Number-series was generated."[16]

Aristotle implies (*Phys.* 206b27–33) that the natural numbers 1 to 10, the *decad*, are the first metaphysical principles; some other ancient authors imply that these are the natural numbers 1 to 4, the *tetractys*, which, by addition of its members, produces the *decad* and thus is regarded as prior to it. In any case, within the *decad* the *tetractys* was given special significance as generator of four pairs of linked geometrical and cognitive states. In this system, geometrically, the number 1 represents the point; cognitively, it is associated with unitive intellection beyond the subject-object distinction. The number 2 is associated geometrically with the line (two points connected) or one-dimensional space, and epistemologically with discursive reasoning which involves subject and object and proceeds from one point to the next. The number 3 is the triangle (three points connected), the first two-dimensional entity, and the type of intellection which the Greeks, after Parmenides, called *doxa*, "opinion" or "seeming." The number 4 is the tetrahedron (four points connected), the first three-dimensional entity. Ontologically, it represents physical existence; epistemologically, sensation, or physical knowledge (*De An.* 404b18–27).

The *tetractys* symbolizes the logical evolution of a solid physical world out of invisible unity, along with a mind attuned to cognize each level in turn. The farther it departs from unity, the lower the process sinks in the ontological scale. At each stage of evolution or descent, Mind degenerates in parallel with the progressive ontological dilution, passing from the unitive knowledge which Plato regarded as wisdom to the pure sense-perception which he regarded as ignorance. From the *tetractys* the *decad* was generated by addition, and from each member of the *decad* stemmata of descending categories may have proceeded, as Plato fused numbers with concepts in unknown ways.

Beneath the primal numbers are the Ideas of the type that the middle dialogues had been concerned with: the Idea of beauty, the Idea of mankind, the Idea of a table, and so forth. Theophrastus says that the One, "acting upon" the Indefinite Dyad, produces the primal numbers. The numbers, then, "acting upon" the Indefinite Dyad, produce the conceptual Ideas. Then the conceptual Ideas, "acting upon" the Indefinite Dyad, produce the particulars. The Indefinite Dyad cannot properly be said to exist; still, though it cannot itself be categorized ontologically, it serves as a negative matrix of generation at all ontological levels.

In the *Timaeus*, where the process of ontogeny is presented more mythologically than in some of the other dialogues, the moment of transition between One and Many is specially presided over by a pseudomythological deity called the Demiurge. This cosmic craftsperson gazes upward at the realm of the pure Ideas and then downward into the realm of matter, and transposes, through his creative or formative act, the pattern of the above into the passive matter of the below. The Demiurge, thus, presides over the imprint of the Ideas on the ontologically null receptacle of the dyad. His activity is "the leading from disorder to order, the conducting of the unformed to form, [the] guiding [of] sensible matter to accept structure from the intelligible."[17]

The *Sophist* and *Philebus* indicate that the conceptual Ideas are arranged in a vast system of genera and species. Once the process of defining and multiplying forms has begun, the levels of reality flow down and down, each level more complex and differentiated than the one above it, containing narrower categories progressively farther removed from ultimate unitive reality.

A passage in the *Seventh Letter* (342d3–8) suggests that the Ideas included: (1) moral Ideas such as those that Socrates was concerned with, the Good, the Beautiful, the Just, and so on; (2) Ideas for ordering space, such as the Straight, the Curved, the Colored; (3) Ideas of the physical elements (earth, air, fire and water); (4) Ideas for every type of natural body (plants, crystals, and so on); (5) Ideas for every type of manufactured body (bed, wheel, and so on); (6) Ideas for every species of animal; (7) Ideas for every disposition of soul; and (8) Ideas for every type of active-passive relationship. A more syncretic account, combining evidence from the dialogues with testimonia about the unwritten doctrines, suggests that the realm of Ideas contains—at the least—eleven levels of decreasing intensities of being:

1. The One (or Idea of the Good) (This level could be two if the contracted and expanded aspects of the One were counted separately)
2. The Principles of the Ideas (Being, Mind, Sameness, and Difference—these could be counted as four except that they are all prior to each other)

3. The Primal Numbers (with their geometric and cognitive correlates, countable in various ways)
4. The Conceptual or Generic Ideas (indefinite in number)
5. The Objects of Mathematics (the regular solids and so on)
6. The World Soul (including its instrumentality as the Demiurge)
7. The Gods (of the polytheism)
8. Human Souls
9. Particulars
10. Shadows, Reflections, etc. of Particulars
11. The Dyad (other or receptacle)

One-and-Many Groupings

As the Ideas are the Many with regard to the One of ultimate unity, so each of the Ideas is the One with regard to its own instantiations. The central One-Many relationship spawns numerous subsidiary One-Many relationships which cluster around it in orbits of decreasing ontological intensity. These are infinite in multiplicity, since at each ontological level the residual imprints of the Ideas re-reproduce themselves through once again "acting on" the indefinite other—a process that has no end.

Within this interpenetrated infinity of metaphysical chains, the soul's overall progress inward from the outermost many toward the absolutely central One proceeds step by step from a many to a one which is then seen to be part of a more powerful many, and, repeating this process, works steadily inward through increasing ontological intensities to the ultimate One. The entire vast and intricate system is controlled by the concept of unity and its perversion into illusory multiplicity.

Kaleidoscopic Synthesis

Plato's elaborately developed and aesthetically sumptuous version of the One-Few-Many structure involves following several leads at once. As Diogenes Laertius said (III.8), "He made a synthesis of the doctrines of Heraclitus, Pythagoras, and Socrates." Parmenides, Anaximander, and Empedocles entered into his synthesis, too. Plato combined and overlaid various ideas of ontological absolutes and intermediaries in order to create a system that would account for the widest possible range of phenomena. His circuit- or machine-like system incorporates most major elements of pre-Socratic thought: the Parmenidean One, the Pythagorean dualism of limit and unlimited, the Socratic/Platonic universal definitions, the Pythagorean divine numbers, Anaxagorean mind, Empedocles' exiled god, the Pythagorean harmony of the universe, the Pythagorean mathematical mysticism, the epic and Orphic polytheisms, the Heraclitean flux, the Anaximinean condensation/rarefaction process, the Heraclitean up/down path, the Parmenidean idea of spherical being, the Empedoclean four elements, the Heraclitean and Empedoclean idea of cosmic strife, Protagorean subjectivism, Ionian substrate monism, the Parmenidean distinction between knowledge and opinion, the Parmenidean rejection of sense data, the Empedoclean cycle of good and bad ages, the Orphic and Pythagorean doctrine of reincarnation, the Orphic doctrine of purification, the Orphic Spring of Mnemosyne (which appears as the doctrine of recollection). Each of these motifs appears as a gear in the vast workings of it all.

The absolute or formless being of the One, gaining elementary form in the Few, is passed through them as lenses into a complex and unstable kind of flickering existence in the Many. The metaphor of the kaleidoscope expresses it for today perhaps more clearly than its ancient forebear, the image of shadows on a cavern wall. A single ultimate principle refracts its radiance through a plurality of separate but unchanging powers which in turn, by the mingling and separation of their influences, produce a shadow world of many changing appearances.

The Imprisoned God

Meanwhile the immortal soul is caught in the tumult of shifting reflections inside the kaleidoscope. In its original state *in potentia*, in the darkness of pure Being, it was beyond the reach of imagistic change; but once it has been confined within the body it becomes vulnerable to violent attacks from without. The seemingly chaotic and yet seemingly orderly stream of kaleidoscopic appearances finds access, through the open senses and their need for nourishment, to that which formerly was beyond its reach. Stimulated by the flow of nourishment through the flickering of appearances, the appetites and ambitions take control. Desire and confusion run amuck. The higher part of the soul is first obscured, then forgotten, as its attention descends into its lower part and turns outward through the senses. Its higher eye is covered with mud.

Plato's essentially narrative concept of soul is a refined and abstracted version of the eschatological myth of the exiled god. Like Empedocles' *daimon*, the soul is of one substance with the gods, but bound within a world of shadows, and struggling to shake free from them; like the Orphic *daimon* which declares itself to be "child of both earth and heaven," it is a mixture of non-Being and Being. The *daimon*, or divine part of the soul, dragged by the lower parts, flows helplessly from life to life in the stream of change, sloughing one shadowy body for another in the grip of appetite and ambition. So it continues until, through philosophical discipline, the lower parts are stilled and reason is set again upon the throne of the self. Then the *daimon* realizes that both the lower soul and the stream of appearances with which it deals are mere shadows or reflections of true being. Remembering its true nature, the soul returns through the kaleidoscope and reclaims its true home in the universal mind. The world below has functioned as a field in which the soul could purge itself of its appetitive and ambitious parts (*Tim.* 41d–44c).

Approaching the Indian Parallels

A broad web of parallels links the Orphic-Pythagorean-Platonic traditions on the one hand and the Jain-Hindu-Buddhist traditions on the other. Certain parallels of detail, especially those in the Jain-Orphic interplay, will be considered in a separate chapter. Here the focus will be on the broad structural similarities between Plato's syncretic synthesis of pre-Socratic thought and the syncretic synthesis of earlier Indian traditions that constituted mature Hinduism—meaning roughly the Hinduism of the Epics, the books collectively known as Dharma Śāstra, and the Purāṇas.

In terms of the myth of cyclicity, the range of solutions of the One-Many problem, the tripartite view of reincarnationism, and other crucial characteristics of this period of thought, all these schools, whether Indian or Greek, are embroiled together. The Hinduism of the Purāṇas—those "collections of myths, philosophical dialogues, ritual prescriptions [and] genealogies"[18]—fitted together elements from many earlier schools, as Plato fitted together the various pre-Socratic tendencies into a syncretic whole. Puranic Hinduism was in turn later syncretized with the various Vedāntic tendencies, especially those of Śaṅkara and Ramānuja. The Purāṇas "probably attained their final shape in the Age of the Guptas"[19]—approximately a millennium after Plato—though their roots go back in part at least to his time or earlier. Here the issue of different rates of development arises, as Plato's derivation of a full syncretic system out of the various pre-Socratic threads, although it seems to have emerged, ultimately, out of Indian prototypes, nevertheless took shape much earlier than the parallel syncretism in India. The process of syncretizing many of the branches of Indian thought into a single vast system of qualified monisms continued well into what in the West is called the Medieval period. Plato's system, rising from the same or related roots, anticipated the full system of syncretic Hinduism in miniature, and far earlier. This relationship could fill a book, and will be treated here briefly.

Hindu Parallels

The Hindu metaphysical system is rooted in the idea of a One which has both formless and formed aspects (*nirguṇa* and *saguṇa brahman*, respectively), like the contracted and expanded aspects of the One in Plato. In the Hindu system, as in Plato's, the universe of the Many proceeds from this One through a series of intermediate stages presided over by a quasi-abstract deity (*Īśvara*) who acts in the role of Plato's Demiurge; unlike transcendent creator deities, Īśvara and the Demiurge manufacture particulars from a position inside the system. In one Hindu formulation, the Many proceed from the One through the interaction of the Purush, active absolute or spirit or Being, and the Prākrit, passive absolute or matter or non-Being, a relationship which closely parallels the action of the One upon the dyad or Receptacle in Plato's system; in both systems, this action is conceived quasi-mythologically as a sexual union.

As part of the dual functioning of the formless-formed One, Plato shares with the Upaniṣads a conception of the One-beyond-Being. At the same time, in the *Timaeus* he describes the world as a vast living creature, a formulation which has resonances in macranthropic passages throughout the Hindu tradition, from Vedic Purush to Vedāntic Virat to Vaiśṅavism. Plato's description of the living world-being as a self-contained process, "designed to feed itself on its own waste, and to act and be acted upon entirely by itself and within itself" (*Tim.* 33c-d), is echoed in the Upaniṣadic definition of the *brahman* as "the food that eats." The relationship of the Demiurge to the world-as-living-being, that of "the god who is forever and the god who is sometime to be," is paralleled in Hindu thought by the relationship between Īśvara and Hiraṇyagarbha. The conception, in the *Timaeus*, of the world god made up of two aspects, world soul (containing reason) and world body, is more or less the same as the Viśiṣṭādvaita (or qualifiedly non-dual) conception of Ramānuja, who taught that god is the world's soul, and the world is god's body. Indeed, Plato is most like the later Vedānta, that is, the Viśiṣṭādvaita. His doctrine, again in the *Timaeus*, that the phenomenal world is composed of Sameness, which tends toward Being and Unity, and Difference, which tends toward non-Being and multiplicity, is close in spirit and formulation to the Bhedābheda school of Viśiṣṭādvaita Vedānta, which holds that the relationship between the world and god, or between the Many and the One, is that of difference/nondifference. Again in the *Timaeus*, Plato's monism of all phenomena in the receptacle, which is specifically defined as space (52ab), parallels the concept of unity which the Upaniṣads call *ākāśa*.

Plato is again most like the Vedānta in his analysis of the consequences for phenomena which follow from the unity principle. At times he teaches a radical rejection of phenomenal reality, as when, in the *Republic*, he likens phenomena to shadows in a cave, or, in the *Timaeus*, to reflections in a mirror. He is at these moments close in spirit to the Advaita, or nondualistic, Vedānta. At other times he seeks to preserve phenomena to a limited extent, not as independent realities but as entities which are validated to some extent by the fact that they are modes or reflexes of that which truly is. At these times he is closer in spirit to the early Vedānta (*Purva Mimamsa*) or the later, qualified nondualistic (Viśiṣṭādvaita) Vedānta.

Plato and the Vedāntins work out some of the difficult details of the One-Many relationship in similar ways. For both, for example, the gods of the old polytheism are considered to exist, but on a relatively low level of the One-Many framework as a whole. The universe, in both systems, is conceived, following in the Sumerian tradition of macrocosm-microcosm correspondence, as a mathematically tuned living being characterized by correspondence of individual souls and world soul. In both systems, there are moments of implication that the individual soul, once freed from the bondage of ignorance or materiality, will reenter the World Soul, which it was a miniature replica of to begin with. The Sumerian astronomy-based worldview is reflected not only in the psychology and eschatology of each system but also in their structures or cosmologies. The universe of the Hindu system is composed spatially of concentric spheres, as Plato's is also spherical and characterized by concentric rings and spheres turning within one another. In the Hindu system as in Plato's, the evolution of phenomenality from the One is represented through a series of increasingly complex geometrical forms, the *bindu* or point, the line, the triangle, the circle, the hexagon, and so on; Plato's use of the *tetractys* is structurally similar, though it differs in details.

In addition to the manifold parallels in the treatment of the Problem of the One and the Many, the three branches of this tradition in Greece—Orphism, Pythagoreanism, Platonism—share with the three Indian branches—Jainism, Hinduism, Buddhism—a whole complex of doctrines about the self, its nature and its destiny, featuring the belief in reincarnation based on moral and cognitive development and culminating in a divine knowledge which entails moral perfection and which, making the individual like god, restores the soul to unity and breaks it loose from the machine of birth and death. All shared the belief that immortality is a kind of knowledge. The *Chāndogya Upaniṣad*'s teaching that the soul about to be incarnated descends to the earth from "outer space," and after death ascends again to moon or sun, should be compared with Plato's doctrine (*Tim.* 41d–42e) that the souls are "sown" first in stars, then in planets, then on the earth, and after death may reascend to the stars to be rewarded.

Max Müller, in rejecting the possibility of connection between Greek and Indian philosophies, asked, "Where is there a trace of such a philosophical theory as the absolute identity of Ātman (the Self) and Brahman (the absolute being), to be found in Greek philosophy?"[20] The question reflects a strange blindness about the meaning of Plato's thought, a blindness which has characterized the reception of his work in Christian cultures, with their belief in the eternal integrity of the individual soul. Even without the *Timaeus*, the doctrine of recollection as expounded in the *Meno* would provide a sufficient parallel to the Upaniṣadic teaching. According to the doctrine of recollection the rational part of the soul contains knowledge of the realm of Ideas, which means, of everything; this knowledge, according to the *Phaedrus*, has been within it since before its birth into a body. "There is *nothing* that the soul has not learned," says Socrates in the *Meno* (81c). The pre-Socratic doctrine of knowledge, which Plato still held, is that to *know* something is to *be* it—true knowledge passes beyond the duality of subject and object. The inner self of each individual being, then, is one with the whole realm of Ideas, at least cognitively, and cognition brings ontology along with it. Like is known by like; one can know the Ideas only by containing the Ideas. As Philoponus said, "The Ideas exist actually in the soul, not potentially, the soul is the place of the Ideas."[21] Within each human soul the whole realm of Ideas opens out. As the *Chāndogya Upaniṣad* says: "The little space within the heart is as great as this vast universe" (*CU* VIII.1). The *Timaeus* (43d) similarly teaches that each soul is a microcosm of the World Soul, and that each soul, like the realm of Ideas, contains pure Being, Sameness, and Difference. Plotinus was only being more explicit when he wrote (*Enn.* V.8.4), "Everyone has all things in himself and again sees in another all things, so that all things are everywhere and all is all and each is all and the splendor is infinite." A Buddhist text similarly says: "Each contains complete within itself all the Ten Thousand forms."[22]

In both Platonism and Hinduism, the adventure of the soul takes place within the framework of a doctrine of cyclical time which proceeds by a series of degenerating ages, culminates in destructions, and begins again. Plato's myth in the *Politicus* is very like the later Vaiṣṇava myth of an age (*kalpa*) in which Viṣṇu projects a world from himself, followed by an age when he draws it back into himself and sleeps; in each instance, an age in which god is active is followed by an age in which he is inactive (*otiosus*).[23]

Plato's conception of the philosopher seeking release from the wheel of cycling time is very much like the Hindu idea of the yogin. He practices asceticism, observes an especially restrictive moral code which sets him apart from the masses, withdraws from the senses, and seeks to extend his consciousness to that part of his soul which is held to be divine. The process parallels Patanjali's three-staged system of morality (*yamniyam*), withdrawal from the senses (*pratyāhāra*), and concentration (*samādhi*).

The parallelism that obtains in the discussion of the soul extends to the discussion of the soul's temporary home, society. The similarity between Plato's classes in the *Republic* and the Indian caste system as set forth in traditional Hindu works like the *Manavadharmaśastra* has been noted in the past.[24] In each system, the class division is justified on the grounds of innate qualities. Each has the priestly caste on top, the warrior caste in second place, and the tradesmen and farmers and so forth at the bottom. The position of the Brāhmins and philosophers at the top is justified by the claim that they alone can attain divine knowledge and thus know how to direct society. The *Māhanirvāṇa Tantra*'s description of the duties of Brahmin and *ksatriya* (in Plato's terms "guardian" and "auxiliary," respectively) is very much in the spirit of Plato:

> The Brahmin, void of hate and attachment [to property], self controlled, truthful, the conqueror of his senses, free of envy and of all guile, should pursue his own avocations. He should ever be the same to, and the well-wisher of, all men, and teach his well-behaved pupils as if they were his own sons. He should ever avoid falsehood, detraction, and vicious habits, arrogance, friendship for low persons, the pursuit of low objects, and the use of language which gives offense . . . For the Rajanya [Kṣatriya] it should be either death or victory in battle . . . He should not in battle kill one who is stunned, who has surrendered his arms, or is a fugitive, nor those of his enemies whom he has captured nor their wives or children. Whatever is acquired either by victory or treaty should be distributed amongst the soldiers in shares according to merit.[25]

Plato's concept of the tripartite soul—made up of reason, aggressiveness, and appetite—forms the basis for his caste divisions; the highest (philosophers') caste is dominated by reason; the second, warrior caste, is dominated by aggressiveness or love of victory; the lowest, laboring caste, is dominated by appetite. The same doctrine of three qualities (Skt. *gunas*) forms the basis of the Indian caste system: *sattva*, reason or purity, characterizes the Brahmins; *rajas*, aggressiveness or honor—which, like Plato's ambition faculty (*thymos)* is considered basically a noble trait, though unenlightened—characterizes the *kṣatriya* or warrior caste; *tamas*, passivity or appetite, characterizes the lower castes.[26]

Buddhist Parallels

The parallels between Plato and the brahmanical Hindu tradition are extraordinary both in breadth and in detail; the treatment of them here has been far from exhaustive. There are also many parallels, both general and detailed, between Plato's thought and Buddhist doctrines, though they seem less likely to reflect historical connections than the Hindu parallels. The Buddhist parallels mostly involve later, post-Platonic developments in India. There is, to begin with, an overall structural resemblance between the theory of Ideas and the earliest known Buddhist philosophy, the *abhidharma* of the Sarvāstavādin school. In both traditions, phenomena are not regarded as ultimately real but as compounded of constituents which are ultimately real, called Ideas in the one case, *dharmas* in the other. Both schools had lists of these constituents, though the Platonic lists have not survived; the Sarvāstavādin *dharma*-list recognized seventy-five impersonal "elements" or ultimate constituent of phenomena.[27] Both schools taught their students to analyze phenomena into their constituents, in order to free the mind from the belief that phenomena are real as themselves, and to accustom it to dealing with unchanging impersonal realities. Socrates said: "We must be able to discern the presence of the Ideas themselves and also of their images in anything that contains them . . ." (*Rep*. 402a). From the Buddhist point of view: "Wisdom requires first of all that we should get the dharmas . . . into view," that we should break up "the apparent unity of persons and things into a conglomeration of elementary dharmic events."[28] In both cases the practice of "discerning Ideas" or "reviewing dharmas" is said to prepare the mind for unconditioned knowledge.

A modern scholar gives a simplified example of abhidharmic analysis: "The reality of a jar is the reality of a patch of color (one thing), of a shape (another thing), of something hard (a third thing), of an image (a thing again), etc.; but there is absolutely no such real thing as their unity in a jar. The jar is imagination."[29] Plato's late dialogues strongly suggest that a very similar kind of training went on in the Academy. A Platonist, if asked to analyze a jar, would likely have invoked the Ideas that contribute to its shape, the Idea of its color, the Idea of hardness, along with more primal Ideas such as Sameness and Difference, while denying that there is any such real thing as the jar. The jar, in both traditions, is regarded as an appearance arising from misapprehension of the temporary conjunction of several factors.[30]

Further, behind the *dharmas*, as behind the Ideas, there lies a yet higher and more ultimate reality: the one and single *dharma*, or *dharmatā*, which is "the essential unity underlying them,"[31] and Plato's Idea of the Good or, in the terms preferred in the later dialogues, the One, which, likewise, is the essential unity underlying the various Ideas. The structural parallelism holds through the three-level systems: ultimate Dharma-

dharmas-phenomena/One-Ideas-phenomena. In early Platonism, it seems, the multiplicity of Ideas was emphasized; in later Platonism, emphasis shifted to the One behind them. As so often, this development is spread over centuries in India. In the early abhidharmic schools of Buddhism, for example, the plurality of *dharmas* was stressed, while in the Mādhyamika and Yogācāra schools of the Mahāyāna period, on the other hand, the ultimate unity underlying the multiplicity of *dharmas* came to the fore.

The study of *dharmas* inculcates in the Buddhist an awareness that phenomena are characterized by the three "marks": impermanence (*anicca*), lack of substantial reality (*anatta*), and suffering (*duḥkha*). The same threefold ontological critique is expressed through Plato's theory of Ideas. The awareness of the first member of the formula, impermanence, is perhaps the central teaching of early Buddhism. According to the Pali *Mahaparinibbana Sutta*, the Buddha's last words were "Dissolution is inevitable for all compound things" (viz. for all things made up of *dharmas*, which is all things period). In the *Milindapañha* (I.31) the first opening of the Wisdom Eye is the perception that "whatever has beginning, that has the inherent quality of passing away." Plato, with his strongly Heraclitean attitude toward phenomena, accepts the same law; even the perfect state envisioned in the *Republic* would not last, he says, because "for everything that has come into being destruction is appointed" (*Rep*. 246a).

According to the second "mark," *duḥkha*, phenomena lack reality and hence dealing with them, for people whose souls long for the real, produces suffering. Similarly, for Plato, phenomena are mere shadows and reflections: Due to their impermanence, attachment to them leads to suffering; the human being in a state of attachment to phenomena is a mere puppet, pulled here and there with no purpose (*Laws* 644d). Buddhist texts similarly declare that phenomena are "like air or a mass of foam, unsubstantial and weak in themselves . . . like a mock show which deludes the mind, like an empty fist with which a child is teased";[32] the human being, while involved in the world of conditioned things, is a puppet which asks only to be disconnected from its strings, so that its suffering will stop.[33]

This attitude is summed up in Buddhism by the third term, *anatta*, or not-self, which denies that phenomena or the phenomenal beings which experience them are real entities or selves, that is, that they have essences. Training in the *anatta* way of thinking undermines the belief in the individual personality, with a consequent freeing of the mind from individual needs, desires, and delusions. Plato's theory of Ideas is also an attack on belief in the individual personality and the ontological integrity of the individual self. Humans are all instantiations of the same Archetype, and only that, which is the same in all, is real. The belief in separately existing individuals with separate and potentially conflicting interests is based on an elementary misunderstanding.

Bodhisattvas and Philosophers

Those who have gone beyond that misunderstanding are given special attention both in Platonism and in Buddhism. In Mahāyāna Buddhism, a bodhisattva, when he is in position to attain escape from *saṃsāra* at will, still, "in order to help suffering creatures, selflessly postpones his entrance into the bliss of *Nirvāṇa* and his escape from this world of birth and death."[34] What Plato requires of his philosopher in the *Republic* (519–520) is much the same. When the philosopher has managed to turn his eyes away from the "mock-show" of shadows on the wall of the cave of ignorance, has cleansed and turned inward his wisdom-eye and has attained the vision of the Good, he must not "linger there," in the presence of the Real, "and refuse to go down again among the bondsmen" in the cave; rather, for the good of the human endeavor as a whole, "down they must go again, each in his turn . . . [to places] ruled darkly as in a dream by men who fight one another for shadows." Whether, in Platonism, this commitment lasts only for one lifetime, or as in Buddhism, for an indefinite number, is unknown. Plato's philosophers, like the Mahāyāna bodhisattvas, are fit to receive religious worship, not merely as heroes, but as gods (*daimones*) (*Rep.* 468e–469b, *Crat.* 398c) and this not only after death, but during their bodily lifetimes as well, if their status of philosopher-set-free is regarded as beyond question.

Platonism and Buddhism also share certain basic approaches to the concept of universal mind. In the *Timaeus* the World Soul, which interpenetrates everything everywhere and is coextensive with space and coeval with time, possesses a mind or consciousness which also is extended throughout the phenomenal universe. This Mind knows everything and is everywhere; it knows every word in every book in every library, every turning of every leaf on every tree, every thought in every human mind, and so forth. The enlightened individual, when freed from personal limitations, becomes one with this Mind and hence actually omniscient. Similarly in the early Buddhist view Nirvāṇa is an "invisible infinite consciousness shining everywhere,"[35] which becomes the consciousness of the enlightened yogi.

Both Plato and the Buddhists are past the simple Parmenidean state of distinguishing two ways: "It is," and "It is not." In both views, the world of phenomena, and the beings who experience it, neither are nor are not in the true senses of the words. Particulars exist in between the "is" and the "is not," as Socrates says in the *Republic.* It is the fact of being impermanent and conditioned that makes them so. Some early Buddhist texts, and many later ones, speak in virtually identical terms:

> Kaccāyana desires to know the nature of the Right View and the Lord tells him that the world is accustomed to rely on a duality, on the "It is" and on the "It is not"; but for one who perceives, in accordance with truth and wisdom, how the things of the world arise and perish, for him there is no "is not" or "is."[36]

Nevertheless, according to Buddhism, "all animate beings have the germ of Buddhahood in them."[37] In Greek thought this Buddha-nature-present-in-all-beings is paralleled by the Orphic *daimon*, the god-nature mythically "defiled," the Wisdom Eye covered with mud, as Socrates says, but still present, alive, and waiting to be cleansed to see again. The theory of recollection, like the more mythic Orphic *daimon*, is also equivalent to the doctrine of the *tathāgatagarbha*, the embryo of enlightenment which resides secretly within each being until that being shall have encountered and awakened it.

The Path of Knowledge

In the Indian yogic tradition, *jñāna yoga* is the yoga of the intellect, the path of philosophy whereby one awakens the embryo of enlightenment and arrives finally at the intellectual intuition of the "hypothesis beyond all hypotheses," as Plato called it. Plato and the Upaniṣadic authors analyzed knowledge into similar levels. At the top for both is absolute knowledge, beyond sense-memory and intellectual conceptualization and hence beyond words. At the bottom is *māyā* or *doxa*, fluctuating sensory cognition which is hardly to be distinguished from the dreams of sleep. In between is the knowledge which is called academic or scientific—in India, knowledge of the Vedas; in Greece, of mathematics; and so forth. The belief in a higher, or transcendent, knowledge—which is virtually omniscience—is encountered in both the Greek and Indian traditions.

For Heraclitus, Parmenides, and Plato, as for Yājñavalkya, Nāgārjuna, and Śaṅkara, what sets the philosopher apart from the majority of mankind is precisely his goal of attaining, or fact of having attained, higher unitive knowledge. *Jñāna yoga* is a formulation of a "course of study" which will lead to this goal. Platonism is a *jñāna yoga*. The Mādhyamika school of Buddhism and the Advaita Vedānta of Hinduism are *jñāna yogas*. They share the beliefs that there are objects of knowledge beyond the empirical and discursive ones; that there is a faculty of the mind which can know them—in fact, that it is the true (but forgotten) nature of the mind to know them and nothing else; that through a long practice, which involves coming to know the unreality of phenomena, one can come to know *noumena*; that having attained this knowledge one is spiritually free, can no longer fall into error, and is exempted from the necessity of being born again—that, in short, one has become like a god. What Murti has said of Mādyamika applies as well to Platonism (with its basis in so-called Socratic irony), that "evil or erratic willing is the consequence of ignorance of the real; the removal of ignorance effectively does away with all forms of evil,"[38] and "to know the real is at once to be free from saṃsāra."[39]

Both philosophies purvey a doctrine of two truths, absolute and relative, without positing two realities to correspond to them. "The Absolute looked at through thought-forms . . . is phenomenon. The latter, freed of the superimposed thought-forms, is the Absolute. The difference is epistemic (subjective) and not ontological."[40] Similarly for Plato, if one looked at what is with the wisdom eye one would see only the Ideas; but since the ordinary soul has chosen to look through the senses rather than the wisdom eye it sees phenomena. It is not a matter of what one is looking *at*, but what one is looking *with*. What is desired, in both traditions, is a revolution in the way of seeing.

The Historical Situation

Plato may have encountered the number religion, the tripartite doctrine of reincarnation, and the doctrine of recollection among the Pythagoreans of South Italy, whom he first visited in 387 B.C. Soon thereafter, according to current, admittedly unsteady, chronologies, he introduced these doctrines to his readers in the *Meno*, where, perhaps in deference to the Pythagorean tradition of secrecy, he attributes them to "certain priests and priestesses." It is not going too far to say that Plato, for all that Parmenides was his "father" and Socrates his teacher, was himself a Pythagorean in the overall drift of his teaching. And the Pythagorean-Platonic line is, as Inge said, "the mainstream of the mystical tradition in Greek religion."[41]

Seeking the pre-Pythagorean sources of the stream, one comes to Pherecydes. Three impressive sources from the fifth and fourth centuries connect Pythagoras with Pherecydes. Aristotle, for example, suggests that Pherecydes may have been Pythagoras's teacher:

> Pythagoras . . . busied himself first with mathematics and the numbers, but later on did not refrain from the magic-making of Pherecydes. (Fr. 191)

Aristoxenus (*ap.* D.L. I.118) adds that Pythagoras supervised Pherecydes' funeral. Ion of Chios says:

> Thus Pherecydes, who was outstanding in manliness and reverence, even after death has a joyful life for his soul, if the wise Pythagoras had insight concerning all men and knew them thoroughly. (DK 36B4)

Pythagoras, with his claimed ability to know other men's *karma* and their afterlife situations, evidently asserted after the death of Pherecydes that the latter had obtained a favorable afterlife. If Pherecydes was indeed Pythagoras's teacher, then Pythagoras, in honoring him after his death, was carrying on a tradition of lineage, not unlike the Indian worship of the guru; in the same tradition we find Parmenides erecting an altar to Ameinias the Pythagorean, who had enlightened him.

It is certain that Pherecydes imported Oriental ideas into the Greek tradition, including some from India. The Indian doctrines he brought entered Greece enmeshed in a net of Persian ideas. It is a plausible hypothesis that Pherecydes called them the teachings of Orpheus in order to naturalize them. In this way he passed them on to Pythagoras, perhaps in Samos, and Pythagoras combined them with elements of number religion, which was derived from other Oriental influences closer to home, and established an organized brotherhood to practice the path to purification.[42] As offshoots of this brotherhood, in later generations, were spawned Parmenides and Plato, and from Plato a host of others culminating (at least in the Greek phase of the tradition) in Plotinus. Thus what Inge called the great "mainstream" of Greek mysticism may go back to India.

Persian Issues: Eudoxus

In the fourth century, contacts between Greeks and Persians were renewed—if indeed they had ever stopped. At least one member of the Socratic circle—the author and mercenary soldier Xenophon—went deep into Persian Asia and spent years there. Plato himself is said to have been curious about Persian thought (D.L. III.7). He had some knowledge of both Zoroastrian dualism and "Chaldean" astronomy.[43] Theopompus (*ap.* Plut. *De Is. et Osir.* 45–47) published, probably during Plato's lifetime, a summary of Zoroastrian doctrines, and Aristotle, while still living at the Academy, also wrote on the subject (D.L. *Prooem.* 8). The *Alcibiades* mentions Zoroaster, and Eudoxus, who for the last twenty years of Plato's life was his close associate at the Academy, wrote about Persian dualism. Three of the four earliest references to Zoroaster in Greek literature come out of the school of Plato in the fourth century. Plato himself must have heard of him, and indeed later Academicians seem to have drawn mythological connections between Zoroaster and Plato, possibly claiming that the latter was a reincarnation of the former.[44] Zoroastrian influence, which may have been imported through Eudoxus, can be seen in the good and bad world souls of the *Laws* and the *Epinomis*, in the fate of the damned souls in the Myth of Er, and elsewhere.

Eudoxus, whose influence on Plato, as on Aristotle, seems to have been very great, was something of an Orientalist. He is reported to have studied astronomy in Egypt, and to have been familiar with "Chaldean" lore, both astrological and religious. According to Cicero (*De Div.* II.42.87) Eudoxus published an explicit denunciation of Chaldean natal horoscopy, saying, "The Chaldeans are the last to be believed in their predictions based on the chart of the natal day." This makes Eudoxus, who was the "official" astronomer of the Academy in Plato's day, the earliest Greek source to mention astrology. An Antonine astrological text cites Eudoxus as its source for a list of Greek gods associated with the different signs of the zodiac.[45] Eudoxus, then, seems not only to have imported knowledge of astrology, but to have taken some steps to Hellenize the astral religion which went with it.

In the *Phaedo*, Socrates specifically advises his friends to seek wisdom, after he is dead, among foreign nations, and the evidence, though slight, suggests that the Academy was in the forefront of those Greek schools actively seeking knowledge of Oriental teachings. Eudoxus may have been a main source of Near Eastern influence in the Academy; he arrived there late in Plato's life, and it is especially in the late dialogues that Plato shows such influence.

The celestial parade of the *Phaedrus*, in which the various unborn souls follow specific gods around the heavens and, when they fall into birth, show the stamp of the god they followed, suggests natal astrology, as does the myth of the *Timaeus* according to which the souls, prior to descending into earthly bodies, are "sown" into the different planets (thus presumably "growing" into the nature of their planetary influences). "Chaldean" influence may also be detected in the outspoken star worship of the *Epinomis* and in the otherwise inexplicable lapse of the *Philebus* in allowing that *some* parts of the realm of becoming (namely, the celestial bodies) are so long-lasting as virtually to partake of true Being. The *Timaeus* says that man will become godlike by studying astronomy; and one could hardly demur from the judgment that "the great fact which dominated Plato's thought in the latter part of his career is the discovery of the planetary order."[46] This great discovery, along with the elements of astral religion, must have come to Plato from the orientalizer Eudoxus.[47]

Notes to Chapter Five

1. W. K. C. Guthrie, *A History of Greek Philosophy*, vol. 2 (Cambridge: Cambridge University Press, 1962–1981), p. 121.

2. Ibid., pp. 362, 368.

3. Cornelia J. de Vogel, *Philosophia*, vol. 1, Philosophical Texts and Studies 19 (Assen: van Gorcum, 1970), p. 414.

4. Alexander, on *Met.* 987b33 ff. Only the least perceptive of the ancient scholars took Plato's One and Dyad as a dualism; Diogenes Laertius, for example, says, "He set forth two universal principles, God and matter" (D.L. III.69).

5. Gregory Vlastos, *Studies in Greek Philosophy*, vol. 2, *Socrates, Plato, and Their Tradition*, ed. Daniel W. Graham (Princeton, New Jersey: Princeton University Press, 1995), p. 179.

6. W. G. Runciman, *Plato's Later Epistemology* (Cambridge: Cambridge University Press, 1962), pp. 66, 21.

7. The important passages are gathered, in Greek, by Konrad Gaiser in *Platons ungeschreibene Lehre; Studien zur systematischen und geschichtlichen Begrundung der Wissenschaften in der platonischen Schule* (Stuttgart: E. Klett, 1963), and a selection of them, in English, by J. N. Findlay in *Plato: The Written and Unwritten Doctrines* (London: Routledge and Kegan Paul, 1974). Also important are Hans J. Krämer, *Arete bei Platon und Aristoteles, zum Wesen und zur Geschichte der platonischen Ontologie* (Heidelberg: C. Winter, 1959); Kurt von Fritz, "The Philosophical Passage in the Seventh Platonic Letter and the Problem of Plato's 'Esoteric Philosophy,'" in *Essays in Ancient Greek Philosophy*, ed. John Peter Anton and George L. Kustas (Albany, New York: State University of New York Press, 1972), pp. 408–447; Harold F. Cherniss, *The Riddle of the Early Academy* (Berkeley and Los Angeles: University of California Press, 1945); *Aristotle's Criticism of Plato and the Academy* (New York: Russell and Russell, 1962).

Though my approach will accept the tradition of the unwritten doctrines, it still does not fall precisely into any of the three categories discussed by Francisco Gonzalez (*The Third Way: New Directions in Platonic Studies* [Lanham, Maryland: Rowman and Littlefield, 1995], preface and introduction). There are other categories of selective neglect in Plato scholarship than those he mentions—for example the fact that all the approaches to Plato he recognizes neglect reincarnationism and its relata—a major element of Plato's teaching which could be paramount to scholars of a different cultural formation.

8. Mitchell Miller, "The Choice Between the Dialogues and the 'Unwritten Teachings': A Scylla and Charybdis for the Interpreter?" in Gonzalez, ed., *The Third Way*, pp. 236–237.

9. Cynthia Hampton, "Overcoming Dualism: The Importance of the Intermediate in Plato's *Philebus*," in *Feminist Interpretations of Plato*, ed. Nancy Tuana (University Park, Pennsylvania: University of Pennsylvania Press, 1994), p. 227.

10. Guthrie, *A History of Greek Philosophy*, vol. 5, p. 146, vol. 2, p. 367.

11. Vlastos, *Studies in Greek Philosophy*, vol. 2, *Socrates, Plato, and Their School*, p. 179.

12. Findlay, *Plato: The Written and Unwritten Doctrines*, p. 251 and elsewhere.

13. The existence of Ideal Mind, doubted by some because it is not mentioned in the crucial pasage of the *Sophist* in which Plato introduces the Principles Being, Sameness, and Difference, is attested by Plotinus: "The primary terms are 'intelligence,' 'being,' 'identity,' 'difference.' And to them must be added 'movement' and 'rest' . . . From these as from originating principles everything else proceeds" (*Enn.* V.1.4, trans. O'Brien). It is also derivable from the dialogues themselves. The *Cratylus* (440ab) speaks of an eternal knowledge and an eternal knower of it, implying an Ideal Mind which knows the realm of Ideas and thus must be prior to it in the hierarchy. In the *Sophist* (248c–e), the discussion of the realm of Ideas commences with the assertion that the real can be known, that is, that there is an eternal knowledge corresponding to the eternal Ideas. At the climax of the discussion, when the Principles Being, Sameness, and Difference have been introduced, knowledge is again mentioned (257cd), in making the point that difference is parceled out among the Ideas in the same way that knowledge is. The implication clearly is that Mind, like Being, Sameness, and Difference, is a principle prior to the hierarchy of Ideas and pervading the other three principles and the hierarchy of Ideas beneath them. Indeed, the very fact that one can know about Being, Sameness, and Difference shows that knowledge must extend that high in the system. Perhaps Mind is not mentioned as a fourth alongside the other three because the discussion began from it and all that follows is based on it; it is taken for granted. In the *Philebus* (28c–30b) Plato states explicitly that there is a Mind which is the ruling Idea (the King of the Ideal Realm). In the *Republic* (508c–509b) Plato says that the Idea of the Good (the One) confers upon all the Ideas both their Being and their Mindness simultaneously. For Plato, in other words, to mention being is to mention knowledge at the same time; they are inseparable concepts.

It is possible that Plato would have wished to discover a hierarchical arrangement even among these highest conditioned principles, but the problems involved seem insoluble. If Sameness and Difference precede Being and Mind, then Sameness and Difference can neither exist nor be known; if Being and Mind precede Sameness and Difference, then Being and Mind cannot each be the same as itself and different from the other.

14. Cherniss, *The Riddle of the Early Academy*, pp. 55–56.

15. Luc Brisson, "Premises, Consequences, and Legacy of an Esotericist Interpretation of Plato," *Ancient Philosophy* 15 (1995), p. 129.

16. Findlay, *Plato: The Written and Unwritten Doctrines*, p. 17.

17. Giovanni Reale, *Toward a New Interpretation of Plato*, trans. John R. Catan (Washington, DC: Catholic University of America Press, 1997), p. 391.

18. Hermann Kulke and Dietmar Rothermund, *A History of India*, 3rd ed. (London and New York: Routledge, 1998), p. 87.

19. Ibid.

20. Friedrich Max Müller, *The Six Systems of Indian Philosophy*, Collected Works 19 (London: Longmans, Green and Co., 1919), p. 60.

21. Quoted by Findlay, *Plato: The Written and Unwritten Doctrines*, p. 450.

22. "On Trust in the Heart," Eduard Conze, *Buddhist Texts through the Ages* (New York: Harper and Row, 1964), p. 296.

23. There are differences. In Plato's myth the destructions at the end of the cycle are not complete: Just as the world is about to fly apart into non-being, god steps back into his active phase and reorganizes things (rather than re-creating them as in the Hindu versions).

24. See Marlow, "Hinduism and Buddhism in Greek Philosophy," *Philosophy East and West* 4 (1954), pp. 35–45.

25. Arthur Avalon (Sir John G. Woodroffe), trans., *Tantra of the Great Liberation (Mahānirvāṇa Tantra)* (New York: Dover, 1972), pp. 171–172.

26. This parallel was noted by Marlow, "Hinduism and Buddhism in Greek Philosophy."

27. See Theodore Stcherbatsky, *The Central Conception of Buddhism* (Delhi: Motilal Banarsidass, 1970), for an exposition of the *abhidharma* philosophy of the Sarvāstavādins.

28. Edward Conze, *Buddhist Thought in India* (London: George Allen and Unwin, 1962), p. 97.

29. Theodore Stcherbatsky, *Buddhist Logic*, vol. 1 (New York: Dover, 1962), p. 507.

30. Edward Conze remarked to me in correspondence about this manuscript in its early stages that there is a basic difference between Ideas and *dharmas* in that *dharmas* are instantaneous and multiple, whereas Ideas are eternal and single; but the Sarvāstavādin *dharma*, like the Platonic Idea, has a permanent real essence apart from its momentary manifestations. (See Stcherbatsky, *The Central Conception of Buddhism*, pp. 41–42.)

31. T. R. V. Murti, *The Central Philosophy of Buddhism* (London: George Allen and Unwin, 1974), p. 5.

32. Edward Conze, *Buddhist Texts through the Ages* (New York: Harper and Row, 1964), p. 158.

33. Ibid., p. 80.

34. Edward Conze, *Thirty Years of Buddhist Studies* (London: Bruno Cassirer, 1967), p. 54.

35. Ibid., p. 10.

36. Murti, *The Central Philosophy of Buddhism*, p. 51.

37. Summary of *Ratnagotravibhāga* I, v. 27, trans. Edward Conze, in Conze, ed. *Buddhist Texts through the Ages*, p. 181.

38. Murti, *The Central Philosophy of Buddhism*, p. 258.

39. Ibid.

40. Ibid., p. 141.

41. William R. Inge, *The Philosophy of Plotinus*, 3rd ed., Gifford Lectures 1917–1918 (New York: Greenwood Press, 1968), vol. 1, p. 82.

42. The origin of the Pythagorean Number Religion is another matter. Some Indian authors argue that the *Sulva Sūtras* (involving elementary geometrical theorems including the Pythagorean theorem) predate Pythagoras. But as always the Indian chronology is obedient to any master. (See C. N. Srinivasiengar [Srinivasa-Aiyangar], *The History of Ancient Indian Mathematics* [Calcutta: World Press, 1967], pp. 8–10.)

43. The subject is covered by Werner W. Jaeger, *Aristoteles, Grundlegund einer Geschichte seiner Entwicklung* (Berlin: Weidman, 1923), pp. 133–138; Richard Reitzenstein and Hans H. Schaeder, *Studien zum antiken Synkretismus*, Studien der Bibliothek Warburg 7 (Leipzig: Teubner, 1926); and Joseph Bidez, *Eos; ou, Platon et l'Orient* (Bruxelles: M. Hayez, imprimeur de l'Academie Royale de Belgique, 1945). André-Marie J. Festugière provides an intelligent and convenient review of the question in "Platon et l'Orient," *Revue de Philologie* 21 (1947), pp. 5–45.

44. See Festugière, ibid., p. 12.

45. Ibid., p. 17.

46. "Le grand fait qui a dominé la pensée de Platon durant la dernière partie de sa carrière, c'est la découverte de l'ordre planétaire" (ibid., p. 19).

47. Compare Franz Cumont, *Astrology and Religion Among the Greeks and Romans* (New York: Dover Publications, 1960), p. 29: "It would appear that Plato in his old age received a 'Chaldean' guest, who was able to instruct him in the discoveries made by his compatriots."

Chapter Six

Platonic Ethics and Indian Yoga

An Indian scholar was expressing a common view when he wrote, "Western philosophical systems, with a few exceptions, are speculative in character. Being mere playthings of imagination, they do not necessarily lead to a spiritual discipline; they can go with any or no path of life. No Indian philosophical system is merely speculative. Each is a darśana, an insight into the real which is at once a path of perfection and cessation of pain."[1] Another eastern scholar, expressing a Zen point of view, feels that western philosophical traditions are based merely on intellectual insight, while Buddhist philosophy is based on a direct mystical apprehension of reality that can only be achieved through years of both hard thought and ascesis.[2]

From a western point of view the same dichotomy has been noticed, but with the values reversed. The crux is the issue of "pure" or autonomous philosophy, which goes back at least to Aristotle's *Protrepticus*. Philosophy, he says there, is not a contributing cause to any good but "a good in the strict sense" or in itself, without any function except to be autonomously good.[3] At the beginning of the *Metaphysics* he insists that the quest for understanding for its own sake is essential to human nature ("all men by nature desire to know"). Philosophy must be "*the pursuit of knowledge for its own sake and not for any further goal* . . . knowledge as the pure contemplation of the truth."[4] From this point of view it is not western philosophy that is deficient in its orientation, but eastern, which subordinates philosophy to practical religious goals, such as release from reincarnation, and never realizes the pure essence of philosophy in and by itself. The view of philosophy as pure and autonomous has come to seem the essentially Greek one, and has been adopted as a foundation by most European philosophers; those involved with eastern philosophies, meanwhile, regard the purely intellectual western commitment as shallow and inadequate. But the dichotomy may not be as secure as spokespeople on both sides of the divide have assumed.

An Indian author, Daya Krishna, argues against the view that Indian philosophy is indissolubly bound up with spiritual practice.[5] "Who does not know that Indian philosophy is spiritual?" he asks rhetorically. "Who has not been told that this is what specifically distinguishes it from western philosophy . . . ?"[6] Against this cliché he opposes the manifold speculative interests of Indian philosophy. Potter and others, he points out, have argued that speculative philosophy arose in the Indian tradition "because of the necessity of meeting the doubts that may assail the seeker after *mokṣa*."[7] But how, he asks, can "the author of the *Vaiśeṣika-sūtra* . . . be taken seriously when he asks us to believe that the knowledge of his various categories such as *dravya* (substance), *guṇa* (quality), *karma* (activity), *sāmānya* (generic qualities), etc., would lead to *mokṣa*?"[8] The only reason to believe in the claimed spirituality, he argues, is because it has been traditional for Indian philosophers to say that the goal of their philosophy is *mokṣa*. But "there is hardly any pursuit or study or discipline," he points out, "which does not make the same claim. Whether it be painting, poetry, music or dance, each is supposed to lead to *mokṣa*. Such is the claim with respect to the sciences of sex, economics, medicine, grammar and politics. This claim . . . is a generalized feature of every systematic study in India."[9] Practitioners of any skill made the claim "to be respectable and draw attention," "especially when the competitors were making the tallest claims for their own paths and pursuits."[10] To take it at face value would be most uncritical. It would be better, he proposes, to think "of Indian philosophy as philosophy proper and not as something radically different from what goes under that name in the western tradition."[11] Otherwise, the naïve claim will "hide the real divergence of pursuits and interests" in Indian philosophy, where "there are many philosophers and many schools of philosophy . . . that have literally nothing to do with *mokṣa* . . . and others which are concerned with *mokṣa* . . . only in certain portions of their work."[12] On the contrary, "the Indian spiritual tradition confirms . . . the essential irrelevance of philosophy to the pursuit of liberation," for which it "would only be a hindrance rather than a help."[13]

On the Greek side, too, there are powerful objections to the view that philosophy was purely speculative. The prominence of the idea of pure philosophy in Aristotle does not extend through most of the Greek schools. Of the Hellenistic schools, with their therapeutic goal orientation, one would not expect it, but neither is it unambiguously present in either the Pythagorean or the Platonic schools, both of which seem to say that for them the practice of philosophy is valued as a means to escape from reincarnation. This of course is the same stated goal many Indian schools—such as the Upaniṣadic, the Buddhist, and the Jain—worked with, and in Greece it must also have included Empedocles' tradition and perhaps Heraclitus's. In those and some other Greek schools, philosophy did in fact involve a *bios*, or way of life, like the Indian *darśana*.

Silence

Aristotle (DK 14.7) and his student Aristoxenus (*ap.* D.L. VIII.15) both say the Pythagorean brotherhood involved some official policy of secrecy. A modern scholar argues that the famous vow of silence applied to mathematical discoveries such as incommensurability, like the silence required from persons who have access to classified information.[14] But a very different view of it appears in some later Greek authors. Philostratus (*VA* I.1), for example, says Pythagoras learned his secret wisdom directly from the gods, and made his pupils keep it in silence "because silence itself is a speaking (*logos*)." The last phrase suggests perhaps a silent inner rumination on the teachings, perhaps the cultivation of a sense of meaning not involving language. Iamblichus (*Vit. Pyth.* 72, 94) claims that new members were required to keep a five-year silence, and Hippolytus asserts that they "remained in silence sometimes three years, sometimes five years."[15] Such a long silence suggests a goal beyond the guarding of information. Palladas (*AP* X.46) says that Pythagoras taught his followers to practice silence because he had discovered "that this potent drug brings tranquillity." The Palatine poet Socrates says that Pythagoras's students were "concentrating deeply upon silence and the eternal discourse of their souls."

Such late authors may have been polluted by influence of the mystery religions or even knowledge of the Indian tradition of *mauna* or vowed silence. But Empedocles, speaking from the Orphic-Pythagorean milieu, suggests the contemplative use of silence in philosophic schools when he exhorts his followers to "press these doctrines deep into your mind, when your mind has been made calm, and contemplate them tranquilly and with pure concentration" (*Phys.* 110). The advice of a modern Buddhist teacher is very similar. "A Mahāyāna Sūtra or a Ch'an text," he writes, "should never be read in a hurry once or twice and then placed in the book-case like a novel or ordinary book. It should be read again and again . . . until the reader understands its profound meaning . . . The more he reads it the more he will comprehend its aim until he will forget all about the printed words and will confront only its deep meaning, which will loom before him to the exclusion of everything else. He will notice his gradual embodiment of the doctrine taught in it, although he may be unprepared for the startling experience."[16]

Withdrawal

Plato, in many passages—including *Phaedo* 66–67, which has been called "the Magna Charta of western mysticism"[17]—advises that the soul should withdraw itself from the senses, concentrate itself by itself, and, becoming still and unchanging, come to know that which is still and unchanging:

> . . . purification [Socrates is saying] . . . consists in separating the soul as much as possible from the body, and accustoming it to withdraw from all contact with the body and concentrate itself by itself, and to have its dwelling, so far as it can, both now and in the future, alone by itself, freed from the shackles of the body. (*Phaedo* 67b ff.)
>
> . . . We have intercourse with real being by means of the soul through reflection. And Real Being . . . is always in the same unchanging state . . . (*Sophist* 248a)

This process of separating the soul from the body and concentrating it in itself is declared to be the special occupation of the philosopher, and furthermore to be a preparation for death (*Phaedo* 67e); this practice, long cultivated, is believed to enable one to escape from the wheel of rebirths after the death of the present body.

A Comparison with Patañjali

Socrates' advice on this issue is similar to that found in Patañjali's *Yoga Sūtras* ("the seminal text on liberative technique in Indian philosophy")[18], which may date from sometime between 200 B.C. and 700 A.D., but which contains materials that go back to the early Upaniṣads and beyond. As Plato advises the aspirant to withdraw the mind from attention to the body, Patañjali calls for "withdrawal from the senses" (*pratyāhāra*). This advice is attested as early as the *Chāndogya Upaniṣad*, which recommends (VII.15) "concentrating all one's senses upon one's self" (rather than upon external objects), much as Plato says the mind should "concentrate itself by itself." In the Upaniṣad, as in the *Phaedo*, the withdrawal of the self from involvement with external objects is considered a preliminary preparation for the unified knowledge which will lead to release from the wheel of reincarnations. Eliade says of Patañjali's *pratyāhāra*, "Thenceforth the yogin will no longer be 'distracted' or 'troubled' by the senses, by sensory activity, by memory, etc. . . . The noninitiate is incapable of gaining this freedom because his mind, instead of being stable, is constantly violated by the activity of the senses."[19] Socrates, in the *Phaedo* (64c ff.) agrees. "The soul," he says, "can best reflect when it is free of all distractions such as hearing or sight or pain or pleasure of any kind—that is, when it ignores the body and becomes as far as possible independent, avoiding all physical contacts and associations as much as it can, in its search for reality . . . The body intrudes . . . into our investigations, interrupting, disturbing, distracting, and preventing us from getting a glimpse of the truth. We are in fact convinced that if we are ever to have pure knowledge of anything, we must get rid of the body and contemplate things by themselves with the soul by itself." As Plato says that the mind, withdrawn from sense objects, "concentrates itself on itself," Bhoja, a classical Indian commentator on the *Yoga Sūtras*, says that in *pratyāhāra* the *citta*, or mind-stuff, having withdrawn from sense objects, "abides in itself."[20]

In the Platonic passage the withdrawal of the mind from the senses is followed by "concentrating itself on itself." Similarly, for Patañjali, *pratyāhāra*—the withdrawal of attention from sense objects and thoughts about them—is to be followed by *dhāraṇā*, concentration. As Plato says that the mind, withdrawn from the senses, should become unchanging and know the unchanging, Patañjali defines the purpose of yoga as "the suppression of fluctuations in the mind" (*YS* I.1). Fluctuations in the mind are due to encountering sense objects and thinking about them. Concentration supplements withdrawal from the senses by holding the mind on a single object or in a single direction, thus removing it from successive involvements in the constantly changing series of sense impressions which distract it and keep it "impure."

A Comparison

Something similar seems intended in these two sets of instructions, something beyond the "rational-theoretic" approach to philosophy.[21] To highlight the similarity it may be useful to contrast related passages from a modern European context. In the *Meditations* Descartes writes:

> I shall now close my eyes, stop up my ears, turn away all my senses, even efface from my thought all images of corporeal things, or at least, because this can hardly be done, I shall consider them as being vain and false; and thus communing only with myself, and examining my inner self, I shall try to make myself, little by little, better known and more familiar to myself. (Med. 3)
>
> I shall now turn my mind away without difficulty from the consideration of sensible or imaginary things, in order to bring it to bear on those which, being disengaged from all matter, are purely intelligible. (*Med.* 4)[22]

Descartes proceeds to "reason with" himself in a discursive way, not in the least having taken leave of his normal consciousness. This is not what the word "meditation" means in relation to Hindu and Buddhist thought. In Patañjali's tradition it is said that when the mind is held immobile for the space of twelve restrained and elongated breaths the state of *dhāraṇā* may be said to begin. *Dhāraṇā* is the first stage of concentration in Patañjali's tradition. *Dhyāna*, meditation, and *samādhi*, trance, are more demanding. One modern authority, Swami Vivekananda, says that *samādhi* begins after the mind has been immobile for half an hour. Even a minute of mental immobility usually takes training and practice. Descartes probably did not get beyond Patañjali's first stage—perhaps he did not even get into it, since his "withdrawal" from the senses was an accompaniment to discursive thinking, which is a fluctuation in the mind. He had not even begun to "meditate" in the yogic sense of the word.

Modern European scholars for the most part assume that when Socrates or Plato "meditated" they did what Descartes was doing rather than what Patañjali spoke of. But stranger things than geometry went on in the Greek philosophical schools. Greek religion in Plato's day still involved ecstatic practices of prophecy, incubation, and so forth, which spilled over into philosophical schools too.

Plato's descriptions of out-of-the-body knowledge have more in common with the practices of Indian yogis than with that of Descartes. Descartes's passages sound like Plato not because the experience was the same, but because he is imitating Plato's language. But Plato, unlike Descartes, surrounds his descriptions of "meditation" with mystical phraseology, speaking of "begetting" wisdom in oneself, of "being wedded" to wisdom, of being flooded with light, of opening the inner eye, and so forth, and he asserts that the knowledge gained by this "meditation" makes the philosopher permanently perfect and virtuous—a claim which would be ridiculous in the Cartesian context, but which in Hindu and Buddhist contexts makes perfect sense.[23] The Upaniṣadic and Vedāntic tradition of Hinduism would agree with Plato that the goal of philosophy is the attainment of a knowledge which permanently and radically transforms the knower, rendering all his or her actions virtuous and freeing him or her from the need for further rebirths. Modern western scholars in general, finding reincarnationism and asceticism both foreign, while Plato they believe to be like themselves (a Cartesian), have simply ignored this level of Plato's thought as if he could not possibly have meant what he plainly says in many passages.[24]

Socrates' Daimon

In the *Symposium*, Socrates, on his way to the party, ducks into a doorway to "listen to his *daimon*" and remains motionless there for hours. Later in the same dialogue he is described as standing motionless and barefoot on the snow for twenty-four hours at Potidea, truly withdrawn from the senses, it seems, as he appeared not to be aware either of the cold or of the jeering soldiers who watched him. The element of either trance or deliberate practice of immobility and withdrawal in the second of these descriptions, and possibly the first also, relates to the Indian, rather than the Cartesian parallels. But what was going on in Socrates' mind when listening to his *daimon* is really unknown. Most moderns have felt that Socrates was doing something like "listening to his own commonsense."[25] One scholar proposes that Socrates at such moments was experiencing a mystical vision of the Forms, that is, an act of Recollection: "The knowledge of the Forms," he says, "was not inferred; it came from experience."[26]

The same scholar has suspected evidence of meditation lessons in Aristophanes' *Clouds* (694 ff.), where Strepsiades, having come to the Thinking House (Meditation Hall?) to learn to think is instructed to lie down on a ram skin (as did those who waited for oracular dreams at the shrine of Amphiaraus [Paus. I.34]) and "ponder."[27] "Isn't this," he asks, "a parody of religious incubation?"[28] He notes that the *Phaedo*'s emphasis on the deathlike quality of the meditation state also relates it to incubation. Such an archaic practice might in fact be found in an ancient Greek philosophical school. According to Hippolytus, Pythagoras "obliged the student to remain quietly in rooms underneath the earth."[29]

Strategies for Escape

That the Pythagorean "silence" meant more than secrecy about doctrines is strongly suggested by evidence from the early Academy, where practices like meditation seem to have been normal enough and were described as "silence." Diogenes Laertius (IV.11) tells us that Plato's second successor, Xenocrates, "would retire into himself more than once a day and would devote, it is said, a whole hour to silence." Similarly we read (D.L. IV.19) that Polemon "would withdraw from society and confine himself to the garden of the Academy."[30] This Pythagorean-Platonic tradition seems to have survived till the time of Plotinus, who spoke of experiences of *samādhi* like those described by Patañjali, and who instructed his students in meditation practices identical to some in the Indian tradition.

Another strategy for escape from rebirth is austerity (*tapas*) which, according to Patañjali, reduces the defilements (*kleśas*) which bind the soul to incarnation (*YS* II.1–3). Fasting and celibacy are common, along with vows of abstention, such as nonspeech (*mauna*) and immobility. Patañjali emphasizes the five restraints (*yamas*) and disciplines (*niyamas*), including not killing (*ahiṃsā*), not lying (*satya*), not stealing (*asteya*), and sexual abstinence (*brahmacarya*). He regards these as conditions without which yogic knowledge cannot be obtained.

Plato similarly feels that ethical abstinences and austerities are essential preconditions for the cleansing and opening of the eye of the soul. In the *Phaedo* (64c ff.) Socrates declares that the philosopher should not "concern himself with the so-called pleasures connected with food and drink . . . [or] sexual pleasures . . . smart clothes and shoes or other bodily ornaments . . . the true philosopher despises them . . . by keeping ourselves uncontaminated by the follies of the body, we shall . . . gain direct knowledge of all that is pure and uncontaminated . . ." On the principle that like knows like, one who is not pure cannot attain to the realm of purity.

Dealing with Faculties

In the *Republic* (439c–441b, 580d ff.) Plato presents a theory of the personality which demonstrates the necessity of austerities and abstinences. He speaks of three faculties, the appetitive, the ambitious, and the rational, which correspond strikingly to the three qualities (*gunas*) of the personality in Hindu tradition: *tamas*, the appetites; *rajas*, desire to dominate; and *sattva*, the rational faculty, or purity.

The most dangerous faculty, Socrates specifies, is the appetitive, for it bonds the soul to the senses and the realm of sense objects and hence to the wheel of rebirths. The appetitive faculty is to be trained through the practice of austerities. His concern about "shackles of the body" parallels Patañjali's concern for the "defilements." Both are outward flows of mental attention distracted by sense input, which defile the true nature of the self and bind it to the wheel of its false appearances. For Plato, the soul's desire for life is its corruption; naïve acceptance of experiences of pleasure and pain leads to attractions and repulsions which shackle the soul to the wheel. Plato feels that these involvements in sense must be attenuated as much as possible while still in a body.

For this purpose Patañjali suggests "austerity and self study" as "preliminary *yoga*" (*YS* II.1); physical pleasures have to be renounced before the knowledge of reality can dawn. This negative connection between pleasure and knowledge (one must, in effect, choose between them) is one of the keys to Plato's ethical stance, too. In order to pursue true knowledge, which is absolute liberation, the soul must first wholeheartedly reject the false "knowledge" which the senses provide, and secondly, free itself from slavery to the pleasures of the appetites, which make the senses credible. "As long as we are alive," Socrates says (*Phaedo* 67a), "we shall continue closest to knowledge if we avoid as much as we can all contact and association with the body." Patañjali is not far from this formulation when he states, "From physical purity (arises) disgust for one's own body and disinclination to come into physical contact with others'" (*YS* II.40).

The Daimon Again

Underlying these concepts in both Plato and Patañjali is the ancient Egyptian-Jain-Orphic myth of the exiled god and the eye of the soul obscured by karmic mud. Socrates refers to "knowledge" as his goal, but (in the middle dialogues at least) this is not knowledge for its own sake; it is that special transformative knowledge which, for Plato as for Yājñavalkya and Patañjali, obtains release from reincarnation. There are still traces, in Patañjali, of the ancient mythic concept of self-remembering in the afterlife, as for example when he says that when the fluctuations of the mind have been stilled "then the Seer is established in his own essential and fundamental nature" (*YS* I.3). The Upaniṣadic injunction to look into one's self, and the afterlife myth of the soul which is required to identify itself as one with the One, seem to lie behind this Sūtra, as the Orphic myth of self-remembering lies behind Plato's desire that the soul should "concentrate itself by itself."

Considering Individual Lives

Many modern scholars have found the asceticism expressed in the *Phaedo* (like the doctrine of reincarnation) unacceptable; it does not sound like the advice of a reasonable man in the Cartesian tradition. One response has been to suggest that the doctrine was never Socrates', but Plato's alone, and even that only for a little while, as he soon rescinded it. This view ignores the evidence of the Cynics, and above all of Antisthenes. He, like Plato, was a member of the Socratic circle who founded, after Socrates' death, a school or tradition which claimed to embody Socrates' lifestyle and teachings. The Socratic way of life as exemplified by Antisthenes was characterized by the same ascetic avoidance of physical pleasures that Plato attributes to it.[31] Xenophon also stresses the famous self-control of Socrates in relation to physical pleasures and indulgences.

> He was in the first place the most self-controlled of men in respect of his sexual and other appetites; then he was most tolerant of cold and heat and hardships of all kinds; and finally he had so trained himself to be moderate in his requirements that he was very easily satisfied with very slight possessions. (*Mem.* I.2)

On this account, Socrates could be living by Patañjali's rules. The emphasis on the polarity "cold and heat" is interestingly like the formulation in the Indian tradition, where the commentator Vyāsa, for example, explains *tapas* as "bearing the 'pairs of opposites,' . . . as for example heat and cold. . . ."[32]

Plato's case is more complicated. One modern view holds that he passed through an ascetic phase, probably in his youth, which coincided with the writing of the *Phaedo*, but that, as other dialogues supposedly show, he later retracted or at least mitigated it. Thereafter he taught and practiced a normal lifestyle characterized by decent, but not unusual, restraint. The focus of the argument varies. Some point to the *Philebus* for the compromise between pleasure and knowledge,[33] others to the *Symposium*.[34] The *Republic* and *Phaedrus* are also mentioned.

"Whereas the *Phaedo*," writes one scholar, ". . . has a message of extreme asceticism . . . the *Symposium* is a vivid picture of warm and genial life."[35] He concludes that Plato wrote the *Symposium* in order to retract or soften the *Phaedo*'s "message of extreme asceticism." But in fact the *Symposium* is filled with incidents that emphasize and reemphasize the asceticism of the Socratic ethic. Of all the dialogues, it is only the *Symposium* that tells of specific acts of asceticism performed by Socrates—for example his withdrawal on the way to the party to commune with his *daimon*; *daimon*, significantly, is the word Empedocles used for the exiled god which is the soul. Socrates' deliberate display of austerity is even more pronounced—walking barefoot in the snow, wearing the same garment he wore in the summer while the warmly clad soldiers shivered; standing immobile for twenty-four hours in the snow, oblivious to the curious yahoos around him. (Aulus Gellius reports a tradition that Socrates had such trances many times [*NA* II.1]). Also in the *Symposium*, Socrates refuses to have sexual relations with a most attractive youth who offers himself in a convenient and forthright way, and, after spending the entire night in conversation at Agathon's house, he goes his way in the morning with no thought of sleeping, and tends his business as usual that day. In this dialogue, and in this dialogue alone, Plato stresses Socrates' trances, his barefootedness, his powers of endurance, his imperviousness to alcohol and sexual temptation. On the view that the *Symposium* renounces asceticism, Plato is held to be saying that "the good man, despite the *Phaedo*, will be ready to participate in the pleasures of this world."[36] But what Plato actually shows us is Socrates emphatically rejecting physical pleasures (comfort, warmth, sex, sleep, drunkenness).

The Ladder

In his long set speech in praise of Eros in the *Symposium*, Socrates presents Eros not as a deity of "the pleasures of this world" but as a sponsor of spiritual growth. He allegorizes this growth in six stages which are similar to many Indian formulations, including the tantric model of seven ascending viewpoints with six steps connecting them. The first or lowest tantric stage is sexual desire or lust; similarly, Socrates' first stage is described as the love of a beautiful body. When one "falls in love" there is an awakening out of oneself which Socrates evidently feels offers an opening for spiritual training; but often the experience leads to jealousy, possessiveness, egotism, and so on, instead.

Socrates' second stage, attacking this problem, involves detaching one's love from its specific object and directing it toward all beautiful bodies alike. The Hindu term *vairāgya*, "detachment, dispassion," is related; it does not mean indifference toward others, so much as not being attached to one object to the exclusion of others. It is, in terms of Indian yoga, a means of overcoming the defilements of *ahaṃkāra*, "I-ness," and *māmata*, "mine-ness"; one must not regard a loved object as "one's own" and other objects as "not one's own." According to Patañjali, *vairāgya*, or detachment, is the "mastery of desires" (*YS* I.15).

The third stage of Socrates' "ladder of love" involves withdrawing one's love from bodily objects altogether, and loving, instead of beautiful bodies, beautiful souls. This is a reformulation of the withdrawal from the senses and is also related to the quest for self-remembering: Socrates says in the *Alcibiades* (133b), "If the soul wants to know itself, then it must look into another soul." As Patañjali says, the self is returned to "awareness of its Real Nature" (*YS* II.24).

Socrates' fourth stage involves the extension of one's now-spiritualized love, through a continuing process of abstraction, from the souls of individual persons to the laws and customs which bind them together harmoniously. The mind is progressively directed away from sensible phenomena to the intelligible patterns which control them; it is gradually being "freed from the body," as Socrates put it in the *Phaedo*. At the fifth stage, one's love is directed away from human institutions and toward the abstract branches of knowledge which reveal not merely the patterns and forces behind human behavior, but those behind all phenomena.

In the sixth and final step the mind turns away from all human sciences and systems and directs its love toward the vision of universal Beauty which is the support of the universe. Totally freed from the body, the mind beholds absolute Beauty, gains ultimate self-knowledge, and is perfected in virtue. There is nothing here that contradicts the *Phaedo*. The "pleasures of this world" are mentioned only as a starting point which one must leave at once and stay permanently separated from by ever-increasing intervals.

Patañjali has a similar staged conception of spiritual growth. "The highest stage of enlightenment," he says, "is reached by seven stages" (*YS* II.27). Socrates' six steps, which lead away from the sense world and toward entities progressively less susceptible to flux, also parallel the prescription of "abstraction" in the *Yoga Sūtras* (II.29).

The Three Qualities

Both Plato, in the *Phaedrus*, and the *Kaṭha Upaniṣad* (I.3.3–9) speak allegorically of the composite person as a chariot and charioteer. Plato regards the charioteer as the wisdom faculty of the soul, the white horse as the ambitious faculty, the black and unruly horse as the appetites. The aim of the journey is to ascend to the vision of the Ideas, but the appetitive horse keeps plunging earthward in pursuit of physical gratification. The Upaniṣadic author is at once more elaborate and less clear. The *ātman* is the owner of the chariot; the chariot is the physical body; the charioteer is the intellect and the mind is the reins; the senses are the horses, the objects of sense the paths they range over. As in Plato's version, the charioteer's aim is to reach knowledge of the real, the *brahman*, but the horses, if not fully controlled, will range at their pleasure over sensory objects instead.

The similarity in imagery is intriguing. "Could this figure," asks Friedlander, "have found its way out of the Far East to Plato?"[37] It may instead bespeak the common Indo-European heritage of Greeks and Indians: The allegory of the self is a development of the Homeric chariot hero on the one hand and the hero of the Bhārata War on the other. The parable of the chariot, with its connection with the concept of yoking, is directly related to the realm of yoga, "the yoke," and especially to the practice of *pratyāhāra*, or withdrawal. "Like that chariot yoked with vicious horses," says the *Śvetāśvatara Upaniṣad* (II.8–13),[38] "his mind the wise man should restrain undistractedly."

Plato's philosopher regards some appetitive pleasures as "pleasures of necessity, since he would have no use for them if necessity were not laid upon him" (*Rep.* 581e). Pleasures of necessity are those which are inescapable and whose satisfaction is beneficial, such as eating in order to stay healthy. The desire for excessive and special foods, on the other hand, is an unnecessary pleasure and "a hindrance to the soul's attainment of intelligence" (*Rep.* 558d ff.). Similar attitudes toward the pleasures are found in many Indian texts. The *Narada Bhakti Sūtras* (14), for example, says, "Activities like taking food may be continued to the measure necessary for the preservation of the health of the body."

In general, chastity, or celibacy, is recommended for both the philosophical and the yogic lives. Life in the Academy, it seems, was one of qualified celibacy, like that of the seers of the Upaniṣads, who had children but mostly abstained. In fact, the Academy seems not unlike early yogic communities in which philosophy was cultivated as a path to release in a milieu of withdrawal from the world.

The Good Horse

The appetitive faculty needs a lot of restraining as it has no natural virtue which can be used to bring it into line. Plato spends much less time on the harmonizing of the ambition faculty, which he holds to be naturally drawn toward honor and to need less persuasion. Also, Plato feels that those drawn to philosophy in the first place will have their ambition faculties already turned in the right direction, presumably because of virtuous activity in former lives (*Rep.* 485a ff.).

If the appetitive faculty is similar to the concept "libido," the ambition faculty is much like the ego, with a drive toward competition and achievement. While noble, it is amoral, and can be turned toward either good or evil. Various abstentions protect the ambition faculty against self-inflation. For example, the philosopher is to own either no property or the barest minimum (*Phaedrus fin.*, *Rep.* 416d) and is to engage in service to others. Between the completion of his mathematical studies and his attempt to gain the highest knowledge, he is to put in fifteen years of public service, working in the administration of the state. After attaining the highest knowledge, the philosopher is once more expected to occupy himself with service of others, presumably of a higher kind. Finally, the soul is to arrive at an inner balance of its three elements in which reason dominates, ambition serves reason, and the appetites are submissive, lacking fuel to fire them up. In this condition the soul is capable of receiving the special knowledge that will restore it to awareness of its true identity and release it from the wheel.

Patañjali's view is remarkably similar. The nature of the mind's activity depends on how the three qualities are interacting. If *tamas*, passivity, dominates, the self is obsessed with passively received sense input and the *kleśas* or defilements accumulate. Austerities and abstinences diminish the power of *tamas* by withholding from it the sense experiences which strengthen it. The opposing qualities—*rajas*, activity, and *tamas*, passivity—are finally brought, through austerities and ethical practices, into a balance in which reason (*sattva*) is the ruling element.

Knowledge

Some have seen the dialectic which Plato mentions so characteristically as some form of logical argumentation—"certainly nothing of the nature of trance or ecstasy," says Cornford.[39] But it is difficult to support this view from the evidence of the texts. As in the rejection of reincarnation and austerity, the taming of the dialectic seems a matter of trying to make Plato "like us," a buttoned-down modern man, by denying the otherness of his cultural stance. Why does Plato require a renunciation of sense pleasures and personal property, and a prolonged period of ascesis, before the dialectic can be attained? These are the types of requirements involved in the knowledge that yogis and religious ascetics are concerned with.

In certain passages (e.g., *Meno* 81cd; *Phaedo* 75cd–79c; *Symposium* 211–212; *Republic* 479, 490a–b, 500b–d, 508d, 514 ff.; *Phaedrus* 249e–250c, 247d; *Timaeus* 41d) it requires special pleading to deny that Plato speaks of a mystical knowledge encountered in trance states. Here are two examples:

> When returning into itself, the soul reflects, then it passes into the other world, the region of purity and eternity and immortality and unchangeableness which are its kindred and with them it ever lives, when it is by itself and is not let or hindered; then it ceases from its erring ways and being in communion with the unchanging is unchanging. And this state of the soul is called knowledge. (*Phaedo* 79c)
>
> But if it were given to man to gaze on beauty's very self—unsullied, unalloyed, and freed from the mortal taint that haunts the frailer loveliness of flesh and blood—if, I say, it were given to man to see the heavenly beauty face to face, would you call this, she asked me, an unenviable life, whose eyes had been opened to the vision, and who had gazed upon it in true contemplation until it became his own forever?
>
> And remember, she said, that it is when he looks upon beauty's visible presentment, and only then, that a man will be quickened with the true, and not the seeming, virtue—for it is virtue's self that quickens him, not virtue's semblance . . . (*Symposium* 211e–212a)

Plato presents this special knowledge as the crux of his philosophy. It is the culminating topic of the *Phaedo*, the *Symposium*, the *Republic*, the *Phaedrus*, and the *Meno*, and is assumed as background in most of the other major dialogues. And it can hardly be regarded as rational conceptualization. If such ecstatic verbiage is only an elevated way of talking about logical thought or academic investigation, then Plato seems a bit simplistically amazed at it all. Does he mean a truth only on the level of concepts and their interactions? He denies this emphatically at several places.

The usual view of modern western scholars is that Plato is merely distinguishing between sense consciousness on the one hand and intelligible cogitations such as those of math or deductive logic on the other. In the *Philebus* (61d–e) Plato distinguishes them like this:

> Knowledge differs from knowledge—one having regard to the things that come into being and perish, the other to those that do not come into being nor perish, but are always unchanged and unaltered. Reviewing them on the score of truth, we concluded that the latter was truer than the former.

Yet sometimes it seems overwhelmingly clear that he is talking about more than this, about three levels in fact, including sensation and reason, but also including a higher intuition that might indeed be called mystical experience, trance, *samādhi*, and so on. Plotinus is said by his biographer to have experienced this type of higher knowledge several times, but Plato has no biographer and does not state this about himself with all possible clarity—as he rarely if ever states anything about himself clearly. It is just possible to read him as if he were only discussing two levels and his ecstatic passages, such as the one just quoted from the *Phaedo*, are not about mystical intuition but are emotionally overwrought descriptions of ordinary reasoning processes. In that case he seems naïvely overimpressed by rather ordinary thought processes:

Another option is to conclude that Plato is in fact talking about three levels but, as far as that ecstatic talk about the highest level goes, "we must see in all this the gesture at a purely unrealizable ideal, or at least at one not realized by him."[40] So those passages where Plato seems to be making his most elevated statements are the ones which he is faking or fantasizing. Here is another example, in which Diotima describes the experience to Socrates in the *Symposium*:

> Whoever has been initiated so far in the mysteries of Love and has viewed all these aspects of the beautiful in due succession is at last drawing near the final revelation. And now, Socrates, there bursts upon him that wondrous vision which is the very soul of the beauty he has toiled so long for. It is an everlasting loveliness which neither comes nor goes, which neither flowers nor fades, for such beauty is the same on every hand, the same then as now, here as there, this way as that way, the same to every worshipper as it is to every other. (210e–211b)

It is hard to believe that this is describing either a concept or a fantasy.

A third option, which is never mentioned but which is the most obvious one, is to take seriously the possibility that Plato, like Plotinus (and perhaps like Socrates), did in fact have that "higher" experience of consciousness at some time or other and is in fact somewhat cryptically referring to it in such passages. Some special knowledge seems to be intended and the description of it is that the mind, "being in communion with the unchanging, is unchanging. And this state of the soul is called knowledge." This special "knowledge," then, is unchangingness—quite as Patañjali says it is the cessation of fluctuations in the mind.

It seems that in the unwritten doctrines rather than the dialogues Plato was more open about the fact that three levels of being and consciousness are involved in his system. The level of the two originary principles, the One and the Indefinite Dyad, is higher than that of the Ideas, which in turn are higher than sense data. A type of cognition is assigned to each ontological sphere. Sense perception belongs to the lowest; next, reason infers the existence of the Ideas; finally, a mystical or unitive cognition corresponds to the highest realm. It would surely make sense of many parts of the dialogues to acknowledge that Plato seems often to be referring to this highest level of consciousness while being, as always in the dialogues, slightly coy about just exactly what he means. In the *Parmenides* he comes closest to being precise about these three levels, which is one reason why "the Neoplatonists found in this dialogue the highest expression of the greatest metaphysical and theological truths."[41] For those who do not acknowledge the legitimacy of the unwritten doctrines, the *Parmenides*, on the other hand, remains a *paignion* or "pure intellectual game."[42]

Plato's distinction between changing and unchanging types of knowledge is paralleled in many passages of the Upaniṣads:

> Ignorance is [knowledge of that which is] perishable, while [true] knowledge is [of that which is] immortal. (*SU* V.2)
>
> To him he said, two kinds of knowledge are to be known, as, indeed, the knowers of Brahman declare—the higher as well as the lower.
>
> Of these the lower is the *Ṛg Veda*, the *Yajur Veda*, the *Sāma Veda*, the *Atharva Veda*. Phonetics, Ritual, Grammar, Etymology, Metrics, and Astrology. And the higher is that by which the undecaying is apprehended. (*MU* I.1.4–5)

But in the Upaniṣads all academic types of study are clearly included along with sense data in the lower knowledge, and by higher knowledge something more than conceptual deduction is intended. The same may be true of Plato, but the longstanding prejudice about Plato being a logician at heart more than a mystic has entered the tradition of translating his works and perpetuated itself there, stifling awareness of other possibilities. This may be seen, *exempli gratia*, in a passage where Plato refers to the distinction, in the *Phaedrus* (247d–e):

> And you say that we have intercourse with Becoming by means of the body through sense, whereas we have intercourse with Real being by means of the soul through reflection. And Real Being, you say, is always in the same unchanging state, whereas Becoming is variable.

The word here translated "reflection" may as easily be translated "intuition." The question is what Plato intends by the "Real Being [which] is always in the same unchanging state." In terms of his system as a whole this would seem to refer to the Ideas, and especially to the Idea of the Good. But the interpretation which dislikes Plato the mystic holds that this is only a reference to mathematical entities and that the distinction made is between changing sense data and unchanging mathematical formulae. Plato writes of this distinction again in the *Politicus* (286a):

> For the existents which have no visible embodiment, the existents which are of highest value and chief importance, are demonstrable only by *phronēsis* and are not to be apprehended by any other means.

The common tendency to translate *phronēsis* as "reason" again begs the question. It can as easily be translated "wisdom" and seems equivalent, in Plato's discourse, to Sanskrit terms such as *prajñā* and *vidyā*, which commonly refer to the so-called "higher" knowledge, which is said to be beyond "reason" as much as beyond sense perception. In the *Timaeus* (27d ff.) Plato writes:

> What is that which is always real and has no becoming, and what is that which is always becoming and is never real? That which is apprehensible by thought with a rational account is the thing that is always unchangeably real; whereas that which is the object of belief together with unreasoning sensation is the thing that becomes and passes away but never has real being.

Again the translation "thought with a rational account" begs many questions. The Greek could be translated in a variety of ways. But Plato, in his cosmology, does not attribute "Real Being" to the mathematical entities, which he places between the Ideas and the sensibles. "Real being" is an attribute of the Ideas alone; furthermore, both the *Republic* and the *Symposium* declare that it is the highest Idea, the Idea of the Good, that is finally to be known. It would seem that this transcendent knowledge, and not mathematical studies, might be what he refers to in these and similar passages.

Socratic Paradoxes?

Reference to some special knowledge seems to be intended again in connection with the so-called Socratic Paradoxes—Socrates' famous assertions that virtue is knowledge (*Meno* 87b, 88c; *Phaedo* 69; and cf. *Prot.* 360cd), and that no one willingly does evil (*Rep.* 589c; *Meno* 78a; *Prot.* 345e; *Tim.* 86d; *Laws* 731c, 860de). Aristotle complained that, "This view plainly contradicts the observed facts" (*NE* 1145b28); it does not allow, he explains, for the fact that many men have weak wills and strong appetites and are unable to abide by what they know to be right. Many modern commentators similarly refer to the Socratic ethic as overintellectual and ineffective. A common resolution suggests that the aim of the Socratic *elenchus*—the trial or ordeal by dialectic—is to awaken people from their dogmatic slumbers into intellectual curiosity. But if that is the case, then again it is a knowledge of concepts that is referred to, and Socrates must have believed that the knowledge which would confer moral perfection and release from the wheel might be the purely intelligible knowledge of, say, mathematics, or the more sense-based knowledge of the history of Zambia or the architecture of the Baroque—or indeed any other knowledge of anything at all as long as it was consistent with the rules of logic.

But Plato puts it otherwise, expressing agreement with the pre-Socratic theory of knowledge that like is known only by like:

> [The true philosopher] will not rest in the multiplicity of individuals which is an appearance only, but will go on—the keen edge will not be blunted, nor the force of his desire abate until he has attained the knowledge of the true nature of every essence by a sympathetic and kindred power in the soul, and by that power drawing near and mingling and becoming one with every being, having begotten mind and truth, then he will have knowledge . . . (*Rep.* 490a–b)

Thus to "know" virtue is in some sense to become it. The distinction between opinion and knowledge is based on the idea that opinion remains something added to the person while knowledge is held to reform the entire being from the inside out. This knowledge is a living process which destroys the old even as it makes the new. It is, as Socrates said, using the Orphic term for the process which prepares one for release from rebirth, "a purification" (*Phaedo* 69c).

Plato describes the knowledge he intends as unlike intellectual knowledge in that it requires a redirecting of the entire being. It is like "an eye that could not be converted to the light from the darkness except by turning the whole body. Even so this organ of knowledge must be turned away from the world of becoming along with the entire soul, like the scene-shifting periactus in the theater, until the soul is able to endure the contemplation of essence and the brightest region of being" (*Rep.* 518c). The Socratic "paradox," like many other Socratic statements in the dialogues, becomes clear on the assumption that Socrates is referring to a knowledge which corresponds to the One.[43] Since only a unified act of knowing can know the One, to know this knowledge is to be it, and hence to know oneself.

Finally Plato's way of talking about this "knowledge" is more or less the way the Upaniṣads (especially the *Kaṭha*) speak of the "knowledge" they are after:

> The Self is not to be sought through the senses. . . . Some wise man, seeking life eternal, with his eyes turned inward, saw the self. (*Kaṭha* II.1.1)
>
> This self cannot be attained by instruction, nor by intellectual power, nor even through much hearing. (*Kaṭha* I.2.23)
>
> Not by speech, not by mind, not by sight can it be apprehended. (*Kaṭha* II.3.12)
>
> By mind alone is this to be obtained. There is nothing of variety here. Whoever perceives anything like variety here, goes from death to death. (*Kaṭha* II.1.11)

Plato speaks similarly in the *Phaedo*:

> The soul, when using the body as an instrument of perception, that is to say when using the sense of sight or hearing or some other sense . . . is then dragged by the body into the region of the changeable and wanders and is confused. But when returning into itself it reflects, then it passes into the other world, the region of purity and eternity and immortality and unchangeableness which are its kindred and with them it ever lives, when it is by itself and is not hindered. (79bd)

The *Kaṭha Upaniṣad* again:

> Not within the field of vision stands this form. No one so ever sees it with the eye.... They who know it become immortal. (*Kaṭha* II.3.9)

And Plato again:

> True being [is] without color or shape, [it] cannot be touched.... All true knowledge is knowledge thereof. (*Phaedrus* 247c)

The *Kaṭha Upaniṣad* again:

> When the five senses, together with the mind, cease from their normal activities and the intellect itself does not stir, that, they say, is the highest state.... This they consider to be Yoga, the steady control of the senses ... (*Kaṭha* II.3.10 ff.)

And Plato:

> When the soul ... ceases from its erring ways and being in communion with the unchanging is unchanging, this is called knowledge. (*Phaedo* 79c)

"When the intellect does not stir," says the Upaniṣad; Plato says, when the mind "ceases from erring ways and ... is unchanging." Says the Upaniṣad: "When the senses have ceased their normal activities ... the steady control of the senses." Says Plato:

> Surely the soul can best reflect when it is free of all distractions such as hearing or sight or pain or pleasure of any kind—that is, when it ignores the body and becomes as far as possible independent (of it), avoiding all physical contacts and associations as much as it can, in its search for reality ... cutting himself off as much as possible from his eyes and ears and virtually all the rest of his body, as an impediment which by its presence prevents the soul from attaining to truth. (*Phaedo* 65b ff.)

These passages are tending in the same direction—perhaps, indeed, arising in the same tradition. An Upaniṣad again:

> There the eye goes not, nor the mind; we know not, we understand not how one can teach this. (*Kena* I.3)

And Plato:

> I certainly have composed no work in regard to it, nor shall I ever do so in future, for there is no way of putting it into words like other studies ... Acquaintance with it must come rather after a long period of attendance on instruction in the subject itself and of close companionship, when, suddenly, like a blaze kindled by a leaping spark, it is generated in the soul and at once becomes self-sustaining. (*Ep.* VII.341c)

And an Upaniṣad:

> Taught by an inferior man He cannot be truly understood, as He is thought of in many ways. Unless taught by one who knows Him as himself, there is no going thither, for it is inconceivable, being subtler than the subtle. Not by reasoning is this apprehension attainable, but dearest, taught by another, is it well understood. (*Kaṭha* I.28)

Plato customarily refers to this knowledge as a type of seeing, or as analogous to the act of seeing, and so does the Indian tradition. In the *Phaedrus* and elsewhere Plato writes of seeing the Ideas, seeing them fully or only catching a glimpse of them, and so forth. In the *Republic* (527d) he writes of an "organ of knowledge" which must be purified because it has become "blind" and which, when purified, "is worth more than ten thousand physical eyes for by it alone is reality seen"; this knowledge organ is the "eye which could not be converted to the light from the darkness except by turning the whole body" (518c). In the same spirit the *Muṇḍaka Upaniṣad* says (III.1.8):

> It is not grasped by the eye nor even by speech nor by other sense-organs, nor by austerity nor by work, but when one's nature is purified by the light of knowledge then alone he, by meditation, sees that which is without parts.

Patañjali refers to the "knowledge" which yoga seeks as "the light of the higher consciousness" (*YS* III.5). Plato similarly speaks of the mind being "flooded with light," and refers to wisdom as "a blaze kindled by a leaping spark" (*Ep.*VII.341c).[44]

Buddhist texts show this same theme of the knowledge which is not known by ordinary means:

> Nirvāṇa is not known directly, as colors, sensations, etc. are known; it is not known indirectly, through its activity, as the sense organs are known. Yet its nature and its activity . . . are objects of knowledge . . . The yogin enters into meditation [and] becomes conscious of nirvaṇa, of its nature, of its activity. (Sanghabhadra)[45]

"*Nirvāṇa*," a modern author explains, "can be 'seen' only with the 'eye of the saints' (*ariya cakku*)—that is, with a transcendent 'organ' which no longer participates in the perishable world."[46] A modern Zen author speaks of the same "organ" when he says, summing up a long tradition, that the goal "is not just an ordinary seeing by means of relative knowledge; it is the seeing by means of a *prajñā*-eye (wisdom eye) which is a special kind of intuition enabling us to penetrate right into the bed rock of Reality itself."[47] As the wisdom-eye of which Plato's Socrates speaks can only be turned to the light by turning the whole body away from the darkness (the world of phenomena), so, "as long as our intellectually analytic eye is hotly pursuing the shadow of Reality by dichotomizing it, there will be no silent stillness of absolute identity where *prajñā* sees itself reflected in itself."[48]

Western scholars have complained that when Socrates says that knowledge is virtue he asserts "the conjunction of two logically distinct things, an intellectual state (knowing . . . something), and an emotional one (one in which there is affective backing for doing the thing one knows one ought to do)."[49] But the special or yogic type of knowledge is held to transcend this distinction. As an Indian teacher wrote: "The experience . . . is one and indivisible. All the powers of the mind are so unified and integrated that it is not possible for the mind to work compartmentally. Intellect, emotion, and will are always in harmony and they never work [so that] the one suppresses the other."[50] The wisdom (*prajñā*) of the Buddhists and Hindus, like Plato's *phronēsis*, is described as both a kind of knowledge and a guarantee of virtue: it means "Wisdom, wisdom as virtue, wisdom as strength [because ignorance cannot dislodge it], the sword of wisdom [which cuts through the defilements] . . ." (*Dhammasaṅgaṇi* 16).[51]

Aristotle's criticism of Socrates' ethics seems to be made in disregard of this distinction between kinds of knowledge. He himself distinguishes between practical knowledge (*sōphia*) and intellectual (theoretical or scientific) knowledge (*epistēmē*), and feels that Socrates is talking about the latter. In the *Eudemian Ethics* (1216b3 ff.) he argues, against Socrates, that the aim is not to find out intellectually what virtue is, but to get virtue, or to act virtuously.[52] Though he acknowledges a kind of absolute knowledge in the self-realization of the Prime Mover, he does not—as had earlier thinkers including Parmenides, and as would later thinkers including Plotinus—regard it as humanly attainable.

No Claim

It remains to ask whether Socrates felt that he had attained the knowledge of which he spoke so often and so lovingly. Parmenides seems to have said that *he* had, and Empedocles that *he* had, and the followers of Pythagoras that *he* had. Indian thinkers commonly claimed that they had. There would have been clear traditional justification for Socrates, if he had wished to claim that he had, also. The passages expressing "Socratic irony" tend to deny any knowledge except the knowledge of his ignorance, and one scholar asserts, "He laid no claim to the knowledge which was virtue, but only a certain insight into the right way to look for it."[53] But this is not quite what Socrates says in the one place where he specifically deals with this question. In the *Phaedo*, when preparing himself for death and reviewing the questions of what the good is, what the knowledge is which provides the good, and whether he has attained it, he says (*Phaedo* 69):

> A system of morality which is based on relative emotional values is a mere illusion, a thoroughly vulgar conception which has nothing sound in it. The true moral ideal . . . is really a kind of purgation from all these emotions, and wisdom itself is a sort of purification . . . You know how the initiation practitioners say, "Many bear the emblems, but the devotees are few"? Well, in my opinion these devotees are simply those who have lived the philosophical life in the right way—a company which, all through my life, I have done my best in every way to join, leaving nothing undone which I could do to attain this end. Whether I was right in this ambition, and whether we have achieved anything, we shall know for certain, if God wills, when we reach the other world, and that, I imagine, will be fairly soon.

Notes to Chapter Six

1. T. R. V. Murti, *The Central Philosophy of Buddhism* (London: George Allen and Unwin, 1974), p. 30.

2. William Barrett, "Zen for the West," in *Zen Buddhism: Selected Writings of D. T. Suzuki*, ed. William Barrett (Garden City, New York: Doubleday Anchor Books, 1956), pp. vii–xx.

3. The long fragment is quoted in Giovanni Reale, *History of Ancient Philosophy*, vol. 1, *From the Origins to Socrates*, trans. John R. Catan (Albany, New York: State University of New York Press, 1985), pp. 316–317.

4. Ibid., p. 315

5. Daya Krishna, *Indian Philosophy: A Counterperspective* (Delhi: Oxford University Press, 1991).

6. Ibid., p. 3.

7. Ibid., p. 18.

8. Ibid., p. 30.

9. Ibid.

10. Ibid., p. 31.

11. Ibid., p. 29.

12. Ibid., p. 31.

13. Ibid., p. 26.

14. Kurt von Fritz, "The Philosophical Passage in the Seventh Platonic Letter and the Problem of Plato's 'Esoteric Philosophy,'" in *Essays in Ancient Greek Philosophy*, ed. John Peter Anton and George L. Kustas (Albany, New York: State University of New York Press, 1972), pp. 408–447.

15. Trans. Milton C. Nahm, *Selections from Early Greek Philosophy* (New York: Appleton–Century Crofts, 1964), p. 53.

16. Charles Luk (Lu K'uan-yü), ed. and trans., *Ch'an and Zen Teaching*, First Series (Berkeley, California: Shambala Publications, 1970), p. 157.

17. Rufus M. Jones, "Liberalism in the Mystical Tradition," in *Liberal Theology, An Appraisal: Essays in Honor of Eugene William Lyman*, ed. David E. Roberts and Henry Pitney van Dusen (New York: C. Scribner's Sons, 1942), p. 124.

18. Christopher Chapple, *Karma and Creativity* (Albany, New York: State University of New York Press, 1986), p. 5.

19. Mircea Eliade, *Yoga: Immortality and Freedom*, trans. Willard R. Trask, Bollingen Series 56 (New York: Princeton University Press, 1969), p. 69.

20. Ibid.

21. Reale, *From the Origins to Socrates*, p. 315.

22. Trans. F. E. Sutcliffe, *Descartes: Discourse on Method and the Meditations* (Harmondsworth and Baltimore: Penguin, 1968), pp. 113, 132.

23. Cf. André-Marie J. Festugière, *Contemplation et vie contemplative selon Platon* (Paris: J. Vrin, 1950), p. 220: "Il semblera a Descartes avoir atteint un point ou la pensée se saisit comme existante, ou elle se saisait dans l'être et, par suite, saisit l'etre même. Il semblera a Platon avoir atteint un point ou toutes les barrières que le separient de l'être se sont enfin evanouis, ou il ne rest plus que l'être seul lequel absorbe en lui même le sujet connaissant."

24. This has been pointed out also by Jeffrey Gold, "Plato in the Light of Yoga," *Philosophy East and West* 46 (1996): 17–18.

25. Hellenist Alister Cameron expressed it that way to me in 1963.

26. "La connaissance des Formes n'est pas inferée, elle résulte d'une expérience." Festugiére, *Contemplation*, p. 215–216. And cf. p. 69: "Socrate avait des extases. Socrate assurement a fait figure de contemplatif"; and, speaking of Plato, p. 219: "la certitude qu'il posséde est du miême ordre que celle des mystiques, laquelle repose sur un fait d'experience, sur une intuition unique et irremplaçable." And he adds, deriving the Platonic philosophy directly from mystical experience: "Ce contact a engendré la philosophie platonicienne."

27. As Benjamin B. Rogers renders it in *Aristophanes*, 3 vols., Loeb Classical Library (Cambridge, Massachusetts: Harvard University Press, 1961–1963).

28. Festugière, *Contemplation*, p. 70: "N'y a-t'il point là comme une parodie de l'incubation religieuse?"

29. Hipp. *Ref.* I.2.18. See Walter Burkert, *Lore and Science in Ancient Pythagoreanism* (Cambridge, Massachusetts: Harvard University Press, 1972), p. 155 n. 197, for more references.

30. In the *Phaedo*, Plato assumed that the Ideas are unchanging and that the mind can enter an unchanging state and, in that state, know them. In the *Sophist* (246–249), however, Plato, as the Stranger, seems to controvert the view that the realm of Ideas is unsusceptible to change. He asks:

> Are we really to be so easily convinced that change, life, soul, understanding have no place in that which is perfectly real—that it has neither life nor thought, but stands immutable in solemn aloofness, devoid of intelligence?

He proceeds at once to conclude, without supporting argument, that the real has intelligence, life, and soul and cannot "rest in complete changelessness," but possesses an element of change as well as an element of changelessness. Plato seems to want to reject the notion, affirmed in the *Phaedo* and *Republic*, that knowledge of the Ideas is an experience of utter mental stillness, beyond change and life. He still believes that one can know the Ideas; but now he feels that this is a dynamic experience, involving a subject/object relationship and hence some degree of change.

The question is whether, as some have proposed, Plato's philosophy was an attempt to conceptualize mystical or meditational experiences, to represent them verbally as a landscape or a still life represents. Other mystics have had both static and dynamic types of experience. Ramakrishna, for example, experienced early in his yogic career the seedless and still *samādhi*, and later grew accustomed to a *samādhi* involving a remnant of subject-object awareness and a sense of dynamic interchange. Plato's earlier descriptions of knowing the Real, similarly, are of a static experience, his later ones of a dynamic one.

31. Antisthenes remarked, for example, "I would rather go mad than feel pleasure" (D.L. VI.3), evidently feeling that the two experiences were of the same order.

32. Quoted by Eliade, *Yoga: Immortality and Freedom*, p. 56.

33. For example, G. M. A. Grube, *Plato's Thought* (Boston: Beacon Press, 1968), pp. 73–75, and Paul Friedlander, *Plato*, vol. 3, *The Dialogues: Second and Third Periods*, trans. Hans Meyerhoff, Bollingen Series 59 (New York: Princeton University Press), chapter 28.

34. For example, J. E. Raven, *Plato's Thought in the Making* (Cambridge: Cambridge University Press, 1965), p. 105.

35. Ibid.

36. Ibid., p. 106.

37. Friedlander, *Plato*, vol. 1, *An Introduction*, p. 193.

38. Trans. Robert E. Hume, *The Thirteen Principal Upaniṣads*, 2nd ed., rev. (Madras: Oxford University Press, 1949).

39. Francis M. Cornford, "Mathematics and Dialectic in the *Republic* VI–VII," *Mind* n.s. 41 (1932), p. 190.

40. Giovanni Reale, *Toward a New Interpretation of Plato*, trans. John R. Catan (Washington, DC: Catholic University of America Press, 1997), p. 107.

41. Ibid., p. 221.

42. Ibid.

43. For a view of Socratic knowledge which anticipates in part the view presented here, see Arthur K. Rogers, *The Socratic Problem* (New York: Russell and Russell, 1971), pp. 134–136.

44. Cf. a later Platonist, Plutarch: "The principle of knowledge . . . flashes through the soul like lightning and offers itself in a single moment's experience to apprehension and vision" (*De Isid. et Osir.*, ch. 77).

45. Quoted by Eliade, *Yoga*, p. 164.

46. Ibid.

47. Daisetz T. Suzuki, "The Basis of Buddhist Philosophy," in *D. T. Suzuki on Indian Mahāyāna Buddhism*, ed. Edward Conze (New York: Harper and Row, 1968), p. 229. The wisdom-eye is an ancient Buddhist concept. See, e.g., Edward Conze, *Selected Sayings from the Perfection of Wisdom*, (London: The Buddhist Society, 1955), p. 80; *Milindapañha*, I.31; Charles Luk (Lu K'uan-yü), trans., *Surangama Sūtra* (London: Rider and Co., 1973), p. 19.

48. Suzuki, "The Basis of Buddhist Philosophy," p. 231.

49. Gregory Vlastos, ed., *Plato, Protagoras*, trans. B. Jowett, revised by M. Ostwald, Library of Liberal Arts 59 (New York: Liberal Arts Press, 1956), p. xliii.

50. Swami Tyagisananda, ed. and comm., *Narada Bhakti Sūtras* (Madras: Sri Ramakrishna Math, 1972), p. 234.

51. Quoted by Edward Conze, *Buddhist Thought in India* (London: George Allen and Unwin, 1962), p. 54. Bracketed passages in original.

52. And cf. *NE* 1103b26–9, 1105b12–18, 1179a35 ff. where the same point is made.

53. W. K. C. Guthrie, *Socrates* (Cambridge: Cambridge University Press, 1971), p. 146.

Chapter Seven

Plato, Orphics, and Jains

Orphism is the great mystery of Greek philosophy. "Without Orphism," a modern scholar claims, "we cannot explain Pythagoras, nor Heraclitus, nor Empedocles, and naturally not Plato and whatever was derived from him."[1] "Whatever was derived from him" is a vast category indeed if one thinks of the famous observation that all western philosophy was a series of footnotes to Plato. The claim seems overstated though, in that Plato's Orphism does not seem to have had much to do with, say, his analytical approach, such as the method of diairesis and synagoge outlined in the *Phaedrus*, otherwise a very Orphic dialogue. Plato's Orphic side coexisted with his logical and analytical side, though they do not seem ideally compatible.

Still, it is true that Plato's mark is everywhere in western thought—and especially in the tradition about the afterlife and the destiny of the soul. He had a particular orientation in this regard. As the same author points out, "Plato began to speak about immortality when he began to speak about the Orphic myths . . . It will be the promptings of the Orphic vision that will move Plato to undertake his 'second voyage,' that is, to undertake the way that will lead to the discovery of the supersensible world."[2] In that case, Orphism stands as the font of the whole western tradition of the soul—with all the ramifications in terms of transcendentalist theories of many kinds.

Among the various scholarly guesses that have been ventured about the source of this mysterious and powerful tradition (Thrace, Scythian shamanism, and so on), one tends to be lost—that is Daniélou's seemingly offhand remark that the doctrine we know as Orphism was seeded in Greece by Jain missionaries from India.[3] "Orphism," says Daniélou, "is derived from the influence of Jainism."[4] The statement, unsupported, as it is presented, by any argumentation, might sound unlikely. Yet this is a conclusion I came to independently from researches into ancient doctrines. Jain thought parallels Orphic doctrine in crucial ways that require special explaining. The most important one, perhaps, involves an uneasy fit, found only in these two traditions, between atomism and mind-body dualism.

Dualism

For the Jains, as for Plato, an animate being is composed of a soul and a body which are absolutely distinct from one another. Souls, which in their own nature are totally immaterial, are eternal; the material body is ephemeral. The unnatural union of the two results from desire. Desires, according to the Jains, "cause the inflow of matter"—that is, they attract matter to the soul, or the other way around—"and prevent the soul from exercising its natural function in full measure. Souls are substances characterized by intelligence, and differences among souls are due to the degree of their connection with matter."[5] Desires plunge the soul ever deeper into matter, driving it onward through a series of incarnations; "the self is never separated from matter until its final release."[6]

For both Plato and the Jains, the soul, as long as it is separate from the body, is perfect and pure. Both "believed that the source of evil lay in the body with its appetites and passions."[7] Once embodied, the soul, bewitched by the instrumentality of the body at satisfying its own desires, forgets itself and plunges deeper and deeper into matter, setting in motion a causal chain that will bind it to the wheel for many incarnations.

Even when the body dies, says Plato, the soul cannot get away; it tries to spread its wings and fly off on high, but it is "saturated with matter when it sets out, and so soon falls back into another body, where it takes root and grows" (*Phaedo* 83d). The puzzling part of this doctrine expounded in the *Phaedo* is the notion that the soul *after it has left the body* is still "saturated with matter;" this seems a contradiction in terms. There is no way to explicate it in terms of Greek thought—but the Jains have the same seemingly contradictory doctrine.

Two Kinds of Atoms

The Jains recognized two classes of material particles or atoms: gross particles that make up physical bodies and very fine or small particles that make their way into the soul and stick or cling there. That particles of matter enter into the immaterial soul and stick to it though it has no physical framework to enter or to stick to, is the same paradoxical teaching as Plato's contention that the immaterial soul, after leaving the body, is still somehow "saturated" and weighed down by matter.[8]

The Jains call this matter, which is conceived as somehow "in" the soul, "karmic matter" or "karmic dirt" (*karma varaṇa*). This karmic matter *is karma* itself. "The passions of the soul . . . act like viscous substances in retaining the inpouring karmic matter."[9] "*Karma* is itself actual *matter*," says a Jain author.[10] It "is an aggregate of material particles which are very fine and are imperceptible to the senses . . . Through the actions of the body, mind, and speech, the finer matter gets into the soul and is tied to it."[11] Jain texts use various images to express the relationship between the supposedly immaterial soul and this karmic matter. The idea of "sticking to" is common, and the image of a dirty or stained cloth is often used.[12] "The soul, disturbed by the activity of mind, speech, or body, attracts the dirt of that substance (*karma*) . . . The passions . . . give direction and intensity to that dirt. The stronger the passions, the longer will the dirt of *karma* last . . . The way to salvation demands a *deliberate* attempt by the soul to purify itself from the karmic dirt by stopping new accumulations and destroying the old."[13] Thus the soul, having been penetrated with karmic matter, and saturated with it as a stained cloth is saturated with the staining material, is still saturated with matter, as Plato said, after it leaves the body. Karmic dirt is also referred to in the Jain texts as a veil, "veiling both knowledge and vision; when the veil is removed, knowledge and vision are already present."[14] The state of the soul veiled with karmic dirt is likened to that of a wanderer in the world, and the path of wandering is symbolized by a wheel.

In Plato's Orphic passages this distinction between two kinds of matter is found, along with the imagery of the dirt, the veil, the wanderer, and the wheel. The matter which makes up the physical body falls away when the body dies; but there is another kind of matter that sticks to the soul in the afterlife and causes it to be reborn. Plato calls this substance *pēlon*, which can be translated "mud, mire, earth, clay, soft soil," or "dirt."[15] Like the Jain "karmic dirt" *(karma varaṇa)*, *pēlon* signifies a state of karmic bondage in which the soul's vision is veiled by the accumulated dirt of activity, which must be wiped away by deliberate effort. In the *Republic* (533d) Socrates says, "It is really true that when the eye of the soul is buried in that barbaric dirt (*pēlon*), dialectic gently draws it forth and guides it upward." The value of the dialectic is that it has the ability to clean *pēlon* away from the soul's eye while the soul is still embodied, thereby decreasing the tendency to reincarnate.

The function of this "barbaric dirt" to cover and blind the eye of the soul is the "veiling of the soul's vision" which in Jain texts is performed by "karmic dirt." In both cases the teaching involves the doctrine of recollection. The spiritual ignorance that is the source of bondage "represents a misunderstanding or lack of awareness of one's 'true nature,'" says a Jain author.[16] To the Jains, as to Plato, the soul inherently possesses not only the knowledge of its true nature but something which is regarded in each cultic context as the knowledge of all things; for Platonists this is knowledge of the Ideas, for Jains it involves knowledge of all empirical facts. Karmic dirt obscures the memory of this knowledge, but once the karmic dirt is cleaned away, the soul will automatically recall its inherent knowledge of everything.[17] Thus, when Mahāvīra or another Jain claimed omniscience (*kevala*), he was claiming to have eradicated all karmic dirt from his soul—as Plato advises his readers to do. In both cases this experience of cleansing and recollecting was a crucial moment in the drama of the destiny of the soul.[18]

Sometimes Plato uses the term *pēlon* in discussing the intermediate heavens and hells where the soul passes time between incarnations, evidently an Orphic reference. In an Orphic afterlife myth, Plato says (*Rep.* 363 ff.), the righteous dead who are in between incarnations recline at an eternal drinking party of the righteous, but "the unrighteous they plunge into a kind of dirt (*pēlon*) in Hades." *Pēlon* is a rare word—this usage, it seems, an Orphic technical term. Jainism also posits temporary heavens and hells between incarnations. In these heavens, as in the Orphic ones described by Plato, some souls "pass the time in luxury and pomp and in the enjoyment of sensual pleasure."[19] In the Jain intermediate hells, as in the Orphic picture, other souls are plunged into karmic dirt, called "darkness matter."[20] As Socrates says, "Whoever arrives uninitiated and unperfected in Hell will lie in mud (*pēlon*), but the cleansed and perfected will dwell with gods" (*Phaedo* 69c). Olympiodorus assures us that in this passage Socrates is expressing an Orphic doctrine (*OF* 235). That these Orphic elements derive from Jainism is suggested not only by the peculiar shared doctrine of matter that clings to the immaterial, but also by an unlikely double coincidence: the fact that both traditions see karmic dirt not only as covering the soul in life but also as the substance in which the defiled soul is plunged in hell.

The Soul's Wandering

The soul wanders in search of its true self (or of its knowledge of its true self), but it is the karmic dirt that obscures this knowledge which keeps it wandering, and its wandering will likely have the effect of picking up more karmic dirt, necessitating more wandering, and so on. Thus in the Jain system the soul continually "attracts" new karmic matter into itself through the effects of living in a body; similarly Plato refers to the continuing accretions of matter to the soul (*Tim.* 42cd). According to the Jains, "while some karmic matter is being purged off, other karmic matter is continually pouring in," forcing the soul to continue its series of transmigrations.[21] Similarly Plato says, "When implanted in bodies they [souls] will always be gaining or losing some part of the bodily substance," so that they "will not cease toils and transformations" (*Tim.* 42ab). The Jains say it is passion that attracts an influx of karmic matter and drives the soul on in its wandering through nature; Plato likewise says that when the soul sees something which it loves, it "admits a flood of particles streaming therefrom" (*Phaedrus* 251c).

The Soul's Destination

In the Jain system the soul which reaches heaven may become a "stellar" (*jyotiṣka*), "residing in the sun, the moon, the constellations and the scattered (*prakīrṇaka*) stars."[22] Similarly Plato says, "He who lived well during his appointed time was to return and dwell in his native star, and there he would have a blessed and congenial existence" (*Tim.* 42b).[23]

The Jain soul which gains complete freedom from the body, when released at the successful end of its wandering, rises to the top of the world, to "the transcendent region of liberated souls,"[24] an immaterial and nonsensual realm above the various heavens, whence it will not again fall into matter. Similarly Plato teaches that, upon the death of the body, if the soul is perfected, it "flies on high" (*Phaedr.* 246c) to "the place beyond the heavens . . . where true Being dwells without color or shape," where it resides in unchanging perfection, no longer subject to falling into a body. Once liberated, according to the Jains, "the soul in its pure state is possessed of infinite perception, infinite knowledge, infinite bliss and infinite power."[25] This knowledge was always in a sense present, but obscured by karmic dirt. "Knowledge arises in the soul from within it, as if by removing a veil which had been covering it before."[26] "All knowledge is in the soul, though it manifests itself [only] when the disturbing media are removed."[27] As Plato said, "The soul, since it is immortal and is often reborn, and since it has seen everything here and in the other world (the afterlife), has learned everything that there is" (*Meno* 80e). Once the soul wipes the dirt from its eyes it becomes, as it was before the fall into matter, "invisible, divine, immortal, and wise" and enjoys perfect bliss and knowledge of transcendent reality (*Phaedo* 81a, *Phaedr.* 247–248). It enjoys, in other words, the infinite perception, knowledge and bliss which the Jains also ascribe to it. In fact, it possesses also the infinite power which the Jains speak of. "When it [the soul] is perfect," says Plato, ". . . it journeys on high and controls the whole world" (*Phaedr.* 246c). In both cases, the imagery of the soul flying on high to control the whole world echoes Osirian myth.

The Path to Escape

Both the Orphic Plato and the Jains believe that the way to free the soul from the dirt which saturates it is detachment from passionate response to fluctuations of the pleasure-pain continuum. For both, an acceptable tactic toward this end is the avoidance or reduction of sense experience in general. Release, for the Jains, involves cessation of both pleasure and pain as they are known in the body. Plato also says that it is pleasure and pain that reduce the soul to its bondage to the body (*Phaedo* 84a). Every moment of pleasure or pain, he says, is a rivet fastening the soul to the body and convincing it that the body's point of view is the true one. The philosopher abstains as far as possible from both pleasures and pains (*Phaedo* 83cd) in order to weaken the soul's link with the body.

In this worldview, the rules of life are governed above all by the principle of nonviolence. "Ahiṃsā," as one scholar says, "[is] . . . the fundamental ethical virtue for Jainism."[28] "Jainas became the primary exponents of vegetarianism in India."[29] And on the Greek side: "The most important Orphic commandment," says another scholar, "[was] the commandment to abstain from meat."[30] Both Empedocles and Plato associate abstention from killing and from meat-eating with the age of Kronos, and in the Jain mythology also the first age of each cycle—the best—involves no killing or meat-eating; those practices enter at a later stage of the degenerative cycle. The Orphic or the Jain monk, then, acts as if he had turned back the clock of the degenerative cycle and were living in the Golden Age. Celibacy and a wandering life of voluntary poverty are found in both settings, too, as is a prohibition against wearing any color but white, an ostentatious sign of purity. Both are religions concerned less with doing than with undoing.

Empedocles

For one who hoped to better himself karmically in his next incarnation, Jains recommended "the Holy Death"—a "controlled death" that would reduce the passionate quality of the experience as much as possible.[31] This death was most commonly by self-starving but could also be induced by "entering" fire. This was to be done with the awareness of one's fellows, so that "his act is in a real sense a public one."[32] There were many examples of such deaths in the Indian record. What is arresting is the fact that they may have occurred in the Greek philosophical tradition too, in Orphic contexts.

When Socrates took the poison from the jail guard's hands to administer it to himself in the company of his friends one might argue that his became a Holy Death.[33] "Jainas believe that the entire spiritual life of a layman (as, to an even greater extent, of a mendicant) is in fact preparation for such a sacred death,"[34] and one might compare Socrates' assertion in the *Phaedo* (64a) that philosophy is rehearsing death.

It is Empedocles above all, in the Greek tradition, who is reported to have had such a death—entering fire in a public act that he declared as an end to his incarnations, quite as a Jain or Ājīvika might have done. The historicity of the story is questionable; what seems to lend an aura of credibility to it is the fact that Empedocles, like Plato, shows a special affinity with the Jain afterlife myth. He framed his reincarnation doctrine as a myth of crime among gods, for which one god is exiled as punishment. Jain texts also describe a society of gods which involves councils, loyalties, rivalries, and punishments—and Jain gods, like those of Empedocles, may be drawn back into the round of incarnations as a punishment for a wrong committed in the society of the gods.[35] (In neither case are the gods immortal, though the Jain gods' lives are very long—as Empedocles said, "Their portion is long life.")

Exiled gods, says Empedocles, "must wander for thrice ten thousand seasons far from the company of the blessed" (fr. 115). Jains feature the same image of the round of incarnations as a "wandering."[36] For Empedocles the soul's wandering proceeds from one element to another, "for the mighty Air chases them into the Sea, and the Sea spews them forth onto the dry land; and the Earth [drives them] towards the rays of the blazing Sun, and the Sun hurls them into the eddies of Ether" (fr. 115). Similarly the Jains classify incarnations as "living beings having earth as their body . . . having water as their bodies . . . having fire as their bodies . . . having air as their bodies . . . and so on.[37] "The Jains regard all the four elements (earth, water, air, fire) as being animated by souls. Thus particles of earth, etc., are the bodies of souls, called earth-lives, etc."[38] This doctrine recalls passages in Herodotus, Empedocles, and Heraclitus about reincarnating systematically through the four elements one by one.

In the Jain system, beings with very good *karma*, but not yet totally purified of matter, are reborn as gods and, after their long lives as gods, may be reborn in another form, usually human. Other humans may have raised themselves from animal incarnations. Unlike the mechanistic view, there are different paths of wandering for each soul. Something similar is hinted at by Empedocles, who may not regard every soul, or even every human, as an exiled god. "Of this number am I too now," he announces to other humans, "a fugitive from heaven and a wanderer, because I trusted in raging Hate" (fr. 115).

Orpheus the Jina?

The image of Orpheus the divine musician is attested as early as the sixth century B.C. It is understood that this has something to do with Apollo, and something to do with Pythagoreanism, too—the Harmony of the Spheres. On a sixth-century mirror, Orpheus strums the harmony, and lion and lamb lie down together. It is interesting, perhaps mere coincidence but perhaps not, that in Jain tradition the Jina "'preaches' by means of a magical 'divine sound,'"[39] a "miraculous sound emanating from his body."[40] This divine sound (*divyadhvani*) is not only pleasing, but full of intellectual content; it "manifests . . . the meaning or import of a Jina's teachings . . . Digambaras imagine the *divyadhvani* as a monotone . . . Svetambaras suggest that the Jina speaks in a human language that is divine in the sense the men of all regions, and animals, can benefit from hearing it."[41] Orpheus too, it seems, strums a chord, or sings a language that all men and animals can understand. Since the message his sound "manifests" is *ahimsā*, the lion and lamb lie down peacefully together when they hear it.

Atlantis and Jambudvipa

In the Jain system, souls which have ascended to heaven and become stars "are characterized by their continuous movement around Mount Meru, which stands at the very center of the loka-ākāśa" ("the inhabited world").[42] In Madhya-loka, the middle tier of the cosmos, are the worlds in which human activity takes places. "These worlds are arranged in countless (*asamkhyāta*) concentric rings of land surrounding a central island (*dvīpa*); each ring is separated by water . . . The land of the second ring from the center of this system is divided into inner and outer halves by a range of huge mountains. It is usually believed that human beings cannot be born anywhere beyond this range . . . The central island is called Jambudvipa, after the Jambu tree which stands, atop Mount Meru, at its very center."[43]

Plato, in the *Critias* (113c–e), which is an extension of the *Timaeus*, the most Orphic (or "Sicilian") of his writings, describes Atlantis somewhat similarly. At the center of the island of Atlantis was a plain ("the most beauteous of all such plains and very fertile") and in the center of this plain a mountain on which lived "one of the original earthborn men of that region, named Evenor, with his wife Leucippe [and their] only daughter Clito, just husband-high . . ."[44] Around this central mountain were "alternate rings of sea and land . . . one within another . . . two such round wheels, as we may call them, of earth and three of sea from the very center of the island, at uniform distances, thus making the spot inaccessible to man."

The structure of elements is much the same: central mountains containing either a sacred tree or an earthborn maiden, surrounding rings of water and earth, the edge of human habitation located at the second ring—though Plato keeps humans out of the inner circles, and the Jain authors keep them in.

The Diffusion Question

A contradiction in the Jain system can be appreciated by comparing two passages of Dasgupta. First he states that, according to the Jains, "The *karmas* are certain sorts of infra-atomic particles of matter (*karma-vargaṇā*). The influx of these *karma* particles into the soul is called āsrava in Jainism." Yet, four pages later, still speaking of Jainism, he asserts, "The smallest indivisible particle of matter is called an atom (*aṇu*)."[45] The contradiction—between atoms as the smallest units of matter and the existence of infra-atomic particles—seems a primitive element from an atomism that was formulated before anything like the Zenonian critique had been applied to it. A similar contradiction is comprised by the "sticking" of material particles to the immaterial soul. Among the many forms of Indian atomism, the occurrence of such contradictions is unique to Jainism and seems to identify it as older than the other forms.[46] It is not just that Jainism seems pre-Buddhistic. In fact, "the Jainas hold that their religion and philosophy are even older than Vedic thought,"[47] and it may be that parts of it can be traced clear back to the Indus Valley culture.[48]

That such a precritical or predialectical motif should be found in Plato needs special interpretation, as, though he was well-aware of the dialectical critique, he did not apply it in this case. It may be that Plato understood *pēlon* as an imported doctrine that had a dogmatic legitimacy in some tradition that he wished to present as itself, without first revising it by his own lights. His teachings on these subjects, after all, are not something he invented, but something he received as part of a religiophilosophical tradition and passed on with a touch of the refined proselytizer.

The general outlines of the Orphic tradition about the soul and its destiny are cut from one mold with the Jain. The special parallels—aside from the general parallel of the tripartite doctrine—include the doctrine of recollection, the nature of the society of the gods, the veiling of omniscience by karmic dirt, and the round of incarnations passing through the elements. Granted this framework of similarity, the ill-fitting conjunction of atomism with mind-body dualism might confirm a special input from Jainism into Orphism. This input somehow involved, at its western end, the Sicilian schools of medicine and philosophy (which will be discussed in the next chapter), at roughly the same time that Upaniṣadic input was entering Heraclitus's thought and other similar transactions were taking place.

The Chronological Situation

Euripides (*Alcestis* 962–972, *Hippolytus* 952–954), Plato (*Rep.* 364e ff.), Herodotus (II.81), and Aristophanes (*Frogs* 1032 ff.) testify for the existence of an Orphic cult with rites and texts in the fifth century B.C. Even earlier, Ibycus of Rhegium (sixth century) speaks of "Orpheus, famous by name" (*PMG* 306), implying a "wide diffusion of the religious movement which goes back to him,"[49] and Aristotle says (*De Philosophia* fr. 7) that Onomacritus (also sixth century) put Orpheus's doctrines into verse.

Were there, as Daniélou says, Jain "missionaries" who might have brought doctrines from far away and purveyed them to strangers in a foreign tongue? Or was Persia somehow the "marketplace"? That the *nāstika* religions of Magadha were in the business of sending out missionaries in Aśoka's time is clear, and Aśoka was probably carrying on an older custom. "We can reasonably postulate a distinct Magadhan religious complex,"[50] as one scholar says, and this may have been a part of it. The pre-Mahāvīran Jains were known as Niganṭhas—"the unattached ones."[51] Missionary zeal is characteristic of therapeutic religions, as later of the Hellenistic religions in the West, and Daniélou says that "like the Buddhists, the Jainas sent missionaries to all parts of the world."[52] A Jain author agrees that the Jains had a "highly developed sense of missionary zeal."[53]

Due to occupational taboos that their code of *ahiṃsā* involved, Jains gravitated to the merchant class. "It has been maintained that more than half the trade of India passed through their hands," said Weber.[54] They were "a merchant communit ,"[55] and thus opportunities for travel were abundant. Religious mendicants and missionaries tend to follow trade, hitching rides along trade routes, and this seems to have been common in ancient India. The Jain ascetic who went back to Babylon with Alexander's army was not the first, nor the last.

Both Ājīvikism and Jainism involved a period of training which had to be carried out in a foreign culture. For the Ājīvika this was a part of the practice called the Seeking of Dishonor: it was easier for a monk to find himself abused among foreigners not familiar with his sect. Mahāvīra, who was closely associated with the Ājīvikas early in his life, is said to have spent twelve years wandering, engaged at least some of the time in the dishonor practice. "At . . . times when he approached a village," says the *Acaranga Sūtra*, "the inhabitants met him outside and attacked him, saying, 'Get away from here.' He was struck with sticks, fists, and lances; he was hit with fruit, clods, and potsherds. Beating him again and again, they raised a huge din" (*Acaranga Sūtra* 502–507).[56] Thereafter Mahāvīra continued to spend two thirds of each year on the road. It is not known whether his wanderings ever took him outside of India; still, Jainism was characteristically "a religion in process of spreading," with a general drift toward the West.[57] The medieval Jain author Hemacandra refers to Jain missionary activities in Telugu and Tamil areas.[58]

Ion of Chios, in the fifth century B.C., attributed some Orphic texts to Pythagoras himself. Others have felt that Pherecydes, who seems to have traveled as far as Persia, wrote some. The transition from Jain missionaries to proto-Orphics such as, perhaps, Pherecydes, is still largely invisible (except for glimpses such as Democedes returning to Croton), though it must have occurred.

Notes to Chapter Seven

1. Giovanni Reale, *A History of Ancient Philosophy*, vol. 1, *From the Origins to Socrates*, trans. John R. Catan (Albany, New York: State University of New York Press, 1987), p. 15.

2. Ibid.

3. Alain Daniélou, *Śiva and Dionysus*, trans. K. F. Hurry (London and The Hague: East-West Publications, 1982), p. 28.

4. Ibid.

5. Sarvepalli Radhakrishnan and Charles A. Moore, *A Sourcebook in Indian Philosophy* (Princeton, New Jersey: Princeton University Press, 1957), p. 250.

6. Ibid.

7. W. K. C. Guthrie, *Orpheus and Greek Religion: A Study of the Orphic Movement* (New York: W. W. Norton, 1966), p. 156.

8. It seems that compromising the strict duality between soul and body would do the more violence to the coherence of the system, but still that is how one Jain author goes about resolving this contradiction. "Jainas themselves are in fact not absolutely rigid in maintaining the immateriality of the soul. They admit, for example, that a defiled soul can actually be 'stained' by *karmas* . . ." (Padmanab S. Jaini, *Jaina Path of Purification* [Delhi: Motilal Banarsidass, 1998], p. 114.)

9. Surendranath Dasgupta, *History of Indian Philosophy*, vol. 1 (Delhi: Motilal Barnarsidas, 1975), p. 191.

10. Jaini, *Jaina Path of Purification*, p. 112.

11. M. L. Mehta, *Outline of Jaina Philosophy* (Bangalore: Jain Mission Society, 1954), pp. 134–135.

12. Walter Schubring, *The Doctrine of the Jainas* (Delhi: Motilal Banarsidass, 1962), pp. 173–174.

13. Indra Chandra Shastri, "Jainism and the Way to Spiritual Realization," in *Aspects of Jainism* (reprints from *The Aryan Path*) (Bangalore: Jain Mission Society, 1955), pp. 1–2 of the article.

14. Schubring, *The Doctrine of the Jainas*, p. 173.

15. Henry G. Liddell, Robert Scott, and Henry S. Jones, *Greek-English Lexicon* (Oxford: Clarendon Press, 1966).

16. Jaini, *Jaina Path of Purification*, p. 134.

17. Buddhism seems to have had such a doctrine. The Buddha says: "Monks, this mind is luminous, but it is defiled by intrusive defilements" (*AN* I.10; quoted by Nyanaponika Thera, *Abhidhamma Studies: Buddhist Explorations of Consciousness and Time*, ed. with intro. by Bhikkhu Bodhi [Boston: Wisdom Publications in collaboration with the Buddhist Publication Society, Kandy, Sri Lanka, 1998], p. 80).

18. Does the recollection of one's true identity include recollection of one's past incarnations? If recollection truly involves omniscience, it must. In the cases of both Pythagoras and Empedocles something like this seems to have happened. Is the soul that declares itself at the gateway of the other world demonstrating that it has attained memory of past incarnations and doesn't need to be incarnated again?

19. Schubring, *The Doctrine of the Jainas*, pp. 243–244.

20. Ibid., p. 212.

21. Dasgupta, *History of Indian Philosophy*, vol. 1, p. 192.

22. Jaini, *Jaina Path of Purification*, p. 129, n. 60.

23. Trans. A. E. Taylor, *Plato: Timaeus and Critias* (Oxford: Clarendon Press, 1929).

24. Jaini, *Jaina Path of Purification*, p. 198.

25. Ibid., p. 189.

26. Ibid., p. 184.

27. Sarvepalli Radhakrishnan, *Indian Philosophy*, vol. 1 (London: George Allen and Unwin, 1971), p. 298.

28. Dasgupta, *History of Indian Philosophy*, vol. 1, p. 200.

29. Jaini, *Jaina Path of Purification*, p. 169.

30. Guthrie, *Orpheus and Greek Religion*, p. 196.

31. Jaini, *Jaina Path of Purification*, pp. 227–228.

32. Ibid., p. 232.

33. This is not to suggest that Socrates was an Orphic, but that the *Phaedo* was written by an Orphic-influenced author who denies the historicity of his account by the declaration that he wasn't there.

34. Jaini, *Jaina Path of Purification*, p. 232.

35. Schubring, *The Doctrine of the Jainas*, pp. 240–244.

36. Shastri, "Jainism and the Way to Spiritual Realization," p. 4.

37. S. C. Rampuria, *The Cult of Ahiṃsā: A Jain View-Point* (Calcutta: Sri Jain Swetamber Terapanthi Mahasabha, 1947), pp. 2–3.

38. Dasgupta, *History of Indian Philosophy*, vol. 1, p. 190.

39. Jaini, *Jaina Path of Purification*, p. 39.

40. Ibid., p. 196.

41. Ibid., p. 42.

42. Ibid., p. 129, n. 60, p. 345.

43. Ibid., p. 29.

44. Trans. A. E. Taylor.

45. Dasgupta, *History of Indian Philosophy*, vol. 1, pp. 192 and 196.

46. See Thomas McEvilley, "Approaches to the Question of the Antiquity of Jainism," *Jinamañjari: International Journal of Contemporary Jaina Reflections* 13, no. 1 (1996): 6–21.

47. I. C. Sharma, *Ethical Philosophies of India*, ed. Stanley M. Duagert (New York: Harper and Row, 1970), p. 121.

48. See McEvilley, "An Archeology of Yoga," *Res: Anthropology and Aesthetics* 1 (1981): 44–77, and "Approaches to the Question of the Antiquity of Jainism."

49. Reale, *From the Origins to Socrates*, p. 294.

50. Jaini, *Jaina Path of Purification*, p. 33.

51. Ibid., p. 3.

52. Daniélou, *Śiva and Dionysus*, p. 28.

53. Jaini, *Jaina Path of Purification*, p. 87.

54. Max Weber, *The Religions of India* (New York: Free Press, 1958), p. 200, quoted by Jaini, *Jaina Path of Purification*, p. 174, n. 39.

55. Jaini, ibid., p. 178.

56. Translated as ibid., p. 26.

57. Schubring, *Doctrine of the Jainas*, p. 53.

58. Ibid., p. 47.

Chapter Eight

Plato and Kuṇḍalinī

In the *Timaeus*, Plato distinguishes between what he calls lower soul—the appetitive part of a personality, obsessed with bodily pleasures—and higher soul—the spiritual part whose ambitions transcend the bodily realm. He does not count sexual desire as among the appetites of the lower soul, but as a degenerate form of higher soul activity. The higher soul desires only to be reunited with the World Soul; this, Plato says, is the true and pure form of *eros*. When, however, the soul is embodied and becomes subject to external influences through the channels of the senses, a degenerate form of desire for the One, and for immortality in the One, arises. Through the bewilderment of existing in time, the soul now mistakenly sees merging with the species as merging with the One, and desires to attain immortality through offspring. Other factors enter also, such as seeing, in a sex object, the shadow of the Idea of Beauty, and mistakenly seeking the Idea in the shadow which stimulated memory of it. Thus the true *eros*, which is desire for supreme knowledge, freedom, and eternality, is temporarily replaced by a false *eros*, which is sexual desire.

Plato proceeds to describe the physiology of sex (*Tim.* 73b ff., 91a ff.). Soul power, he says, resides in a moist substance whose true home is in the brain, the seat of the higher soul. The brain is connected, however, with the penis, and, along the way, with the heart, by a channel which passes through the center of the spine and connects with the urethra. Under the stimulus of false *eros* the soul fluid in the brain is drawn down the spinal passage and ejaculated from the penis in the form of semen, which is able to produce new living creatures precisely because it is soul-stuff. It may be inferred, though Plato does not speak directly to this point, that the practice of philosophy (which requires celibacy except for begetting children) involves keeping the soul-stuff located in the brain, that is, preventing it from flowing downward through the spinal channel. This inference is implicit in the Platonic doctrine, which holds that the philosopher gets beyond false *eros* to the true celestial *eros*. Since the false *eros* draws the seminal fluid down the spinal channel, the transcendence of false *eros* must end this downward flowing.

The Kuṇḍalinī Parallel

What will be obvious at once (though it does not seem to have been previously remarked on in scholarly literature)[1] is that this description of Plato's doctrine in the

Timaeus also applies to the Hindu doctrine of the *kuṇḍalinī*. In the Hindu version, too, the natural or proper place of the *kuṇḍalinī*, or soul-power, is at the very top of the brain; when it is in this position, the yogin is in the state of union with the divine (as Plato said of the philosopher). As in Plato's version, however, the *kuṇḍalinī* power is especially embodied in semen, and in an unpurified person descends in semen from the brain to the penis through the spinal channel. Expressing itself now not as divine union, but as the drive to sexual union, it is expended through the penis during ejaculation. Various practices are recommended for forcing the semen upward through the spinal channel until it resides in the brain again,[2] where its life-giving force can express itself through giving spiritual life rather than physical.[3] There are seven seats, or *cakras*, which the *kuṇḍalinī* may occupy along the way down or up: that at the base of the spine, that at the top of the brain, and five in between, of which Plato mentioned only two, the throat and heart.

The Occult Vascular System

This correspondence is already so remarkable as to invite interpretation; but there is more. The Indian texts distinguish many "subtle" channels (*nāḍīs*) in the body. The foremost is the channel through which the *kuṇḍalinī* passes up and down the spine (*suṣumnā-nāḍī*); nearly as important are two channels which pass along the spine but outside it (*iḍa* and *pingala*). These two surrounding channels conform themselves to the icon of the entwined serpents. Between their origin in the upper brain and their termination at the base of the spine they cross one another five times, that to the right passing to the left, and vice versa; their points of intersection are the five intermediary *cakras*. Plato also, in the *Timaeus* (77c ff.), knows of these two veins (which physical anatomists cannot find) which pass along the sides of the spinal column and which cross one another an unknown number of times (Plato mentions only the crossing at the throat). In Plato as in the Indian texts, these subsidiary veins are secondary carriers of the soul-power.

In both traditions the image of the serpent appears in this context. The spinal marrow was associated with the serpent by Aelian (*De Nat. Anim.* I.51) and others, as in the yogic tradition, where the *kuṇḍalinī* power is described as a serpent which, having been awakened, slithers up the marrow channel in the spine; according to Aelian the spinal marrow of a man slithers out of his body as a serpent when he dies.

That these ideas which, it seem obvious, neither the study of cadavers nor mere theorizing would arrive at, should occur in both Greece and India invites—indeed demands—some explanation.

History of the Doctrine in India

A rudimentary form of this occult physiology is attested in India as early as the *Chāndogya Upaniṣad*, which says (VIII.6.6): "A hundred and one are the arteries of the heart, one of them leads up to the crown of the head. Going upward through that, one becomes immortal." (And compare *Bṛhadāraṇyaka Upaniṣad* IV.2.3.) The somewhat later *Maitrī Upaniṣad* specifies (VI.21) that the name of this channel is *suṣumnā*, and that the goal of yoga is to cause the *prāṇa*, or spirit-energy, to rise through that channel to the crown of the head. (The *Praśna Upaniṣad* III.6–7 has a related teaching.) The much later *Brahmā Upaniṣad* asserts that there are four seats of *prāṇa*, then appears to relate two different traditions, first naming navel, heart, throat, and head; then eye, throat, heart, and head.[4] The *Hansa Upaniṣad* mentions an almost complete list: loins, belly, navel, heart, neck, and eyebrows.[5] It is notable though that none of these Upaniṣadic passages mentions the spine, and those which refer to a channel or vein rising from the heart may mean the heart itself, not the heart level of the spine.

The *Shandilya* and *Dhyanabindu Upaniṣads* describe the central channel and the two subsidiary channels, and mention the anus and navel *cakras*.[6] The *Haṭha Yoga Pradipika* knows of the arrangement of the three channels, and mentions the throat and brain *cakras* (III.50, IV.75, 79).[7] The *Śiva Saṁhitā* spells out the entire system of the three channels and seven *cakras* (V.56–103).[8] Matsyendra, in his *Kaulajñānanirṇaya*, summarizes the system, giving anus, genitals, navel, heart, throat, between the eyebrows, and crown of the head as the *cakra* points.[9]

The relative chronology of these texts is not certain, but may be more or less in the order in which they have been mentioned here. If so, then the pattern with which the system emerges into articulation suggests, though it does not require, that the doctrine either entered India in stages or that it underwent indigenous development in a series of stages there which may have taken well over a millennium to unfold—even, perhaps, two or three millennia. All these texts contain materials sedimented from different ages, so no conclusion on chronology is available at present. It is equally possible that there were different versions of the system extant or that different teachers purveyed it with different emphases.

History of the Doctrine in Greece

The Greek belief in the *Timaeus* can be traced to a period before Plato—and the trail leads primarily to the Sicilian and South Italian schools of medicine, which were connected with the Pythagorean and Orphic communities in the same area. These schools taught that semen comes from the brain and is of one substance with the spinal marrow, by way of which it travels to the genital organ through the spinal channel that Indians call *suṣumṇā* and Greeks called "the holy tube."[10]

This was explicitly taught by Alcmaeon of Croton (DK 14A13) in the Crotonese medical school to which Democedes had returned from the Persian Court a century earlier. Croton was also the center of the Pythagorean brotherhood, and though Alcmaeon may not have been a member, he shared many views with the Pythagoreans.[11] As Aristotle says of another point of doctrine, "Either he [Alcmaeon] got this view from them [the Pythagoreans] or they got it from him" (*Met.* 986a22). In fact, the doctrine of the sperm descending through the spinal channel may have a special connection with the Pythagorean tradition; it is found in Alcmaeon; in Plato's most Pythagorean work, the *Timaeus*; and in Hippo of Samos (DK 38A3 and 10) in the fifth century B.C., probably also a Pythagorean. It is also found in Diogenes of Apollonia, who probably came either from Crete or the Black Sea area, but who lived at the end of the pre-Socratic period, when the vocabulary of such elements was readily available to any Greek thinker.

The association of the spinal marrow with the word *aiōn*, "life" or "life-span," in a fragment of the (at least partly) Orphic poet Pindar, affirms the Orphic, as well as the Pythagorean, associations of the teaching. Pindar was influenced by west Greek mystery cult, and Aiōn, according to later writers, was an Orphic name for Dionysus.[12] Heraclitus, himself very influenced by Orphism, seems also to have taught the retention of semen and a qualified sexual abstinence,[13] and thus probably had the doctrine of the spinal channel with the two surrounding "veins" and of the connection between the spinal channel and the testicles.

Another Greek author whose work contains traces of the doctrine of the *nāḍīs* is Diogenes of Apollonia, who seems to have been a generation or two older than Plato.[14] A long fragment quoted in Aristotle's *Historia Animalium* (DK64B6) speaks of "two veins pre-eminent in magnitude [extending] through the belly along the backbone, one to right, one to left; either one to the leg on its own side, and upwards to the head, past the collar-bones, through the throat. From these, veins extend all over the body, from that on the right hand to the right side and from that on the left hand to the left side . . . one pair runs from each of these through the spinal marrow to the testicles . . ."[15] Though Diogenes has the subsidiary channels beside the spine, he does not picture them crossing one another at special power points in the body as in the configuration of the intertwined serpents. Plato, as we have seen, spoke not only of the three channels but also of the heart and throat *cakras*, which in fact he mentions earlier than does any extant Indian text.[16] Aristotle also had the doctrine of the connection between sperm and spinal fluid, and regarded the testicles not as sources of semen, but as receptacles whose purpose is to retard and "steady" its flow.[17]

Diffusion Possibilities

There would seem to be some connection between the complexes of Indian and Greek doctrines, including the identity of spinal fluid, brain fluid, and sperm; the spinal channel connecting the brain and the penis; the surrounding channels that cross one another; the *cakras* where they cross; the value judgment that prefers the highest *cakra* as the location of the sperm-marrow-soul; the association of the marrow with a serpent, and so on. A concrete hypothesis about the channels of diffusion could take several forms.

Diffusion from India into Greece

One possible account would focus on the diffusion of elements of pre-Socratic lore into Greece from India during the period—roughly the late sixth and early fifth centuries B.C.—when both northwest India and eastern Greece were within the Persian Empire. Heraclitus, who may have known of this doctrine, since he advised the retention of semen, is certain to have expressed ideas learned, directly or indirectly, from an Upaniṣadic source[18]—and in fact doctrines related to those under consideration here. If the tantric physiology was a part of this wave of Indian influence, then it probably entered Greece not long after about 540 B.C. The type of situation that would provide a concrete means of transmission is shown by the story of the physician Democedes of Croton, a contemporary of Pythagoras who spent years practicing medicine at the Persian court and then returned to Greece, no doubt full of foreign medical lore, perhaps including the physiology of the spinal channel. In fact, Democedes returned specifically to Croton, where such ideas would have fed directly into the Pythagorean tradition whence Plato must have gotten them.

Plato traveled to Sicily three times—probably in 387, 367, and 361. The first trip was immediately followed by the appearance of Orphic-Pythagorean themes in the *Meno*, *Phaedo*, and elsewhere, the last by the heavily Pythagorean *Timaeus*. A modern scholar speaks of the great "scale of the influence of 'Sicilian' medicine upon the *Timaeus* . . ."[19] This influence could have included the doctrine of the *nāḍīs*, as at least the central one, the spinal channel, was known to Alcmaeon. In any case, the physician Democedes had returned from Persia in around 500 B.C., perhaps carrying the tripartite doctrine of reincarnation and the physiology of the *nāḍīs* into the medical school at Croton.

In cultural history this may have been no small event: "Herodotus considers that the best physicians in Greece at the time were those of Croton . . . Democedes [he called] 'the most skilled physician of his time . . . It was not least due to him [Democedes] that the Crotoniate doctors were held in high esteem.'"[20] Meanwhile the Orphic, Pythagorean, and medical communities of Acragas, Croton, and later Tarentum were probably in close touch, even in a sense one larger community. Perhaps two generations after Democedes' return, the information about occult physiology brought to Croton by him or someone else passsed from West Greece, perhaps by way of Empedocles and the Sicilian physician Philistion, into Plato's school.

Eudoxus of Cnidus, who came from the milieu of the Sicilian Pythagoreans into Plato's school, had been taught medicine in Sicily by Philistion, who seems to have been medical adviser to Dionysius (Ps.-Plato, *Second Letter* 314d).[21] "It seems likely that it was through Philistion that [Plato] became so deeply influenced by 'Sicilian' medicine." In their medical views, "both Philistion and Plato . . . are . . . demonstrably influenced by Empedocles."[22] Indeed, the whole Sicilian tradition was so influenced. "The most influential ideas in Western Greek medicine . . . were formulated at Acragas in Sicily by Empedocles. Many influential theories characteristic of 'Sicilian' medicine can be traced back to Empedocles . . ."[23] "This influence is most clearly apparent in his [Plato's] cosmological dialogue, the *Timaeus*, which includes a description of the structure and functions of the human body . . ."[24] Guthrie agrees: "The physiology of the *Timaeus* owes much to Empedocles' ideas."[25] Since the description in the *Timaeus* includes both the *nāḍīs* and the *cakras*, it is probable that these came to him from Sicilian medicine, perhaps via Philistion, who was in the tradition that leads back to Empedocles and, behind him, Democedes.

In addition to the physiological details in the *Timaeus*, "for the mythical details of the soul's fall, peregrinations and recovery [in the *Phaedrus*], Plato has relied largely on Pythagorean and Orphic lore, in part by way of Empedocles."[26] Elements of Empedoclean physiology can be identified (for example, at *Phaedrus* 251b1–2); the ten thousand-year cycle (248e6) looks Empedoclean, as do the *daimones* (246e6), and the feasts of gods which the souls may attend (247a-b); the law of Adrasteia (248c2) recalls Empedocles' "Anankēs chrēma," the meadow (248c1) recalls Empedocles fr. 121, the list of prophets, bards, doctors, and princes (*Phaedr.* 248d-e) recalls fragments 146 and 147. Overall, ". . . the basic ideas in Socrates' speech firmly belong within the Pythagorean tradition as we find it represented in Empedocles' *Katharmoi.*"[27] ". . . Plato quite deliberately introduces Empedoclean ideas into his dialogue and . . . wants his readers to realize that he is doing so."[28] A lineage for the transmission of the Indian physiology is suggested, from Democedes to Empedocles to Philistion to Plato.

Chronological Complexity

The main problem with this reconstruction is that Homer already has the idea that the cerebro-spinal fluid (which he calls *engkephalos*) was the container of life power. Whether he equated it with sperm is unknown, but is implied both by the fundamental idea that the *engkephalos* was life-power, and by the fact that at least as early as Democritus (DK 68B32) the *engkephalos* was believed to issue forth in sexual intercourse.[29] The connection of the spinal fluid with sperm seems present in Hesiod too, well before any known opportunity for Indian influence on Greek thought.[30] The importation of this doctrine into the Greek tradition in the sixth century B.C., then, is unlikely, though the form it had already assumed in Greece may have been highlighted and reinforced by material imported from India at that time. The detail of the crossing secondary veins, for example, may have been passed later than the doctrine of the central channel. It appears that in this case, as with reincarnationism, the diffusion even involved a complex set of staged interactions, influences, and cultural exchanges as traditions met and partly merged.

The doctrine of the *engkephalos* is not only present in the Homeric texts but seems well established there, where it is taken for granted, or treated as a given; it may, then, go far back in the Homeric tradition, which is known to contain elements at least as early as the fifteenth century B.C. In fact there is some evidence that the serpent-marrow-seed-soul identity was already in place in the Minoan-Mycenaean period.[31] For this fundamental element of the tradition, then, some additional source may be desired that is earlier than Democedes' stay in Persia, a source which could have influenced both Homer and the early Upaniṣads.

The Indo-European and Semitic Evidence

A second hypothesis, in addition to transmission from India into Greece is that the doctrine may have survived into both the Greek and Indian traditions from proto-Indo-European times. It is indeed widespread among Indo-European traditions. "The head," Onians says, "was believed by the early Romans to contain, to be the source of, the seed,"[32] and Pliny (*N. H.* XI.37.178) describes the spinal marrow as "descending from the brain." There are hints of the doctrine in Germanic and Slavic lore,[33] and remnants of it in Shakespeare's line, "Spending his manly marrow in her arms" (*All's Well That Ends Well*, II.3.298) and in Spenser's assertion that sexuality "rotts the marrow and consumes the brain" (*Faerie Queene*, I.4.26).

But at the same time there are signs of this idea system in Semitic texts of the ancient Near East. In various passages of the *Old Testament* (in *Job*, *Psalms*, *Ezekiel*, and *Isaiah*) and of rabbinic literature, spirit is equated with bone marrow, with brain liquid, and with sperm, implying a system of conduits to carry it among those areas.[34] Elsewhere in the Near East also there are suggestions of the doctrine. It has been proposed, for example, that the priests of Attis and Cybele, who castrated themselves, may have been attempting to interrupt the channel from spine to genitals and thus prevent the sperm from leaving the body and the body, consequently, from aging.[35] Similarly Epiphanius, writing of the Gnostic tradition, says: "They believe the power in both the menstrual fluid and the semen to be the soul, which, gathering up, they eat."[36] These Near Eastern parallels may all be later than the sixth century B.C. and thus may not bear on the Homeric and Hesiodic instances; indeed, they may have derived peripherally from the diffusion stream that carried these ideas through the Achaemenid Empire.

Egypt Again

There is, however, an earlier antecedent for the idea of attaining salvation or enlightenment through a passage up the spine—in the Egyptian myth in which Osiris ascends to heaven over the spinal column of his mother, the goddess Nut, the vertebrae being used as the rungs of a ladder.[37] Onians proposes that the *djed* column, representing the spine of Osiris and worshipped "as an amulet of life," indicates the same idea.[38] The fact that the spine and phallus of Osiris were found together at Mendes in the myth of the dismemberment again implies the channel and the connection. "The vital fluid," Onians notes, "is repeatedly shown [in Egyptian iconography] as transmitted by laying the hand on the top of the spine or passing it down the spine."[39]

It has also been argued that there are hints of the doctrine in Sumerian iconography[40] and in the Indus Valley culture.[41] Finally the fundamental physiological model behind the *kuṇḍalinī* doctrine—the spinal linkage between the brain and the urethra, and the fundamental identity of the brain fluid, the spinal marrow, and the semen—seems to have been extremely widespread in the ancient world, though only the tantric and Platonic texts speak of the two subsidiary channels surrounding the spine.

This distribution does not seem to invite the Proto-Indo-European hypothesis; in fact that hypothesis is very problematic if the Egyptian and Indus Valley occurrences are accepted. In that case it is possible only on the presumption of very early Indo-European migrations, with the corollary of the Indus Valley being regarded as an Indo-European culture.[42]

The Taoist Parallel

The Taoist alchemists of China taught techniques to force the semen up the spine to the brain, where it was expected to nourish fields of cinnabar, leading to the alchemical transformation of the mind. India and China exchanged important diffusion transactions in the early centuries A.D., suggesting the possibility of diffusion in this case too. But chronological circumstances limit the possibilities. On the Chinese side, the general retention of semen was advocated by pre–Han dynasty texts and the specific idea that practices can cause the semen to rise through a channel in the spine to the brain area seems to be mentioned briefly in early Han texts. The text *Uniting Yin and Yang*, for example, advises the practitioner to "suck the *ching*-spirit upward," implying the suction-from-the-bladder technique attested to by Indian yogis at a later date. Another early Han text, the *Shih Wen*, says, "Draw in *ch'i* to fill the brain," and observes, "All the *ching* rises upward."[43] The upwardization theme is barely mentioned in these early texts, and their orientation is specifically toward pleasure, unlike the avowals of tantric alchemists who seek either enlightenment or immortality or both (and Plato). Still, it was present and growing; by the T'ang dynasty the esoteric practices of sexual yoga were used in the hopes of becoming immortal, and by the Sung dynasty the whole system, with the circuit of *ch'i* (in India *prāṇa*) up the *Tu* channel and down the *Jen* had been established.[44] Thus the chronology would allow diffusion of the occult anatomy of *kuṇḍalinī* from China into India—but only if we assume that passages in the early Upaniṣads do not refer to it. On the other side, the chronology as presently understood does not suggest diffusion from India into China. The first Buddhist texts known to have passed from India to China did so between the first and the third centuries A.D.[45]

Accordingly, many scholars have assumed that the sexual elements of tantrism in general came from Chinese Taoism, beginning to show up in India around the third to fifth centuries A.D.[46] One Indian scholar has summed it up: "There can be no doubt that Tantricism in both [Hindu and Buddhist] forms has come from the north, and from that side the only possible source for the sexual aspect of Tantricism can be Taoism." Noting that "Taoism is older than any form of Tantricism known in India," he posits it as the source of tantrism.[47] "Indian Tantra first appeared at points of contact with Taoist China," another scholar observed, "and, in the words of Joseph Needham . . . 'the Taoist department of Buddhism was Tantra.'"[48] Thus it seems plausible that, as the same scholar observed, "a yogic technique of apparent Chinese origin . . . identified with either the practice of urethral suction or that of internally raising semen along the spinal column, would first make its appearance in Indian Mahāyāna sources."[49]

Still, it is questionable whether the dates allow for this conclusion. It is known that "the sea trade between India's southeast coast and Han China . . . [was] already well under way by the beginning of the common era."[50] But if the *Chāndogya Upaniṣad*'s mention of the artery through which the spirit passes to liberation via the heart and the head is accepted as implying the tantric physiology, then it seems at present unlikely that Taoist influence could have come over the mountains or across the sea early enough to account for it. The whole situation is ambiguous because "whatever India exported over the mountains to China seemed to come back, in altered form, to be reappropriated by the Indians a few centuries later."[51]

In any case, it can now be seen that the issue is not simply whether Chinese or Indians began to influence each other first. The introduction of the Greek material into the discussion changes this situation dramatically. An important point involves the Chinese variation in the anatomical model. The Greek and Indian versions both involve the central channel up the spine and the two subsidiary channels which run beside the spine and cross over one another periodically, creating the caduceus configuration which is fundamental to tantric iconography. But the Chinese version lacks this configuration. In that model, the so-called *Tu* channel runs from the perineum up the spine, like *suṣumnā nāḍī*—but, instead of the flanking and criss-crossing *iḍa* and *pingala*, another channel equal to the first (the *Jen* channel) runs down the front of the body, joining with the *Tu* channel at top and bottom, creating a kind of circle or loop. As there are no crossing points, there are no *cakras*, though Taoist texts recognize three "gates" on the *Tu* channel which need to be cleared to allow passage of the *ch'i*. In light of these differences, it does not seem possible that the doctrine went from China into India; if Indians had received it in the Chinese configuration in the early centuries A.D., it is unlikely that they would have independently adapted it into the same configuration that Plato had some centuries earlier—and with the same references to the serpent, which also are lacking in the Chinese version.

A third possibility—diffusion of the doctrine from Greece into India and China (where they adapted the form) or into India alone, whence it passed into China—is chronologically possible and could conceivably turn out to have been the case; it nevertheless seems unlikely to be a popular choice, as the Indian version, at present the most complete of the three, seems to many to express the parent culture most appropriately, while the Greek version is still seen by most classicists as, in Rohde's words a century ago, "a drop of alien blood."[52]

The remaining possibility is that some fourth ancient culture diffused the doctrine into Greece, India, *and* China (or into Greece and India, whence it passed into China). There seems no further possibility. And there *is* in fact an ancient culture which offers most of the elements needed: which has the caduceus icon, which associates it with the serpent motif, and which is known to have diffused other elements into Greece, India and China early enough to qualify.[53]

Mesopotamian Influence on the Indus Valley Culture?

Throughout the 1940s, 1950s, and 1960s, a formidable consensus of Western scholars held that influences from Sumerian culture stimulated the Indus Valley culture to arise out of the village state of the Neolithic Age into the urban-planning stage uncovered at Mohenjo Daro and Harappa. The evidence on this point, which will be discussed in chapter 10 below, will only be briefly reviewed here. It was during the era of this consensus that Zimmer argued that the iconography of the serpent-power complex was diffused from Mesopotamia into India.[54] Not all the motifs involved occurred in the Indian record at the same period, so this diffusion, if it happened, seems to have occurred in a number of waves, perhaps beginning with Sumerian input into the Indus Valley culture and ending with the fall of Persepolis, when many Near Eastern craftsmen carrying Mesopotamian tradition came into India.

Indeed, it cannot be denied that certain Sumerian and Indus Valley icons are the same icons in different instantiations. These icons—the eagle and serpents, the mountain flanked by goats, the hero mastering lions, the lion-bull combat, the goddess and the tree—are among the central icons of Sumerian religion. Their presence in the Indus Valley city of Mohenjo-daro in the strata that indicate Sumerian trade was active suggests that significant cultural exchanges were going on in the Bronze Age between Mesopotamia and the Indus Valley. On generally accepted chronologies, which tend to put the Sumerian flowering of civilization earlier than that in the Indus Valley, it would seem that both iconographical and conceptual elements of Sumerian religion had been

Figure 1 Line drawing of Sumerian stone vase (the "Gudea Vase"), c. 2050 B.C., showing two serpents entwined around central axis in caduceus form, their bodies touching at seven points.

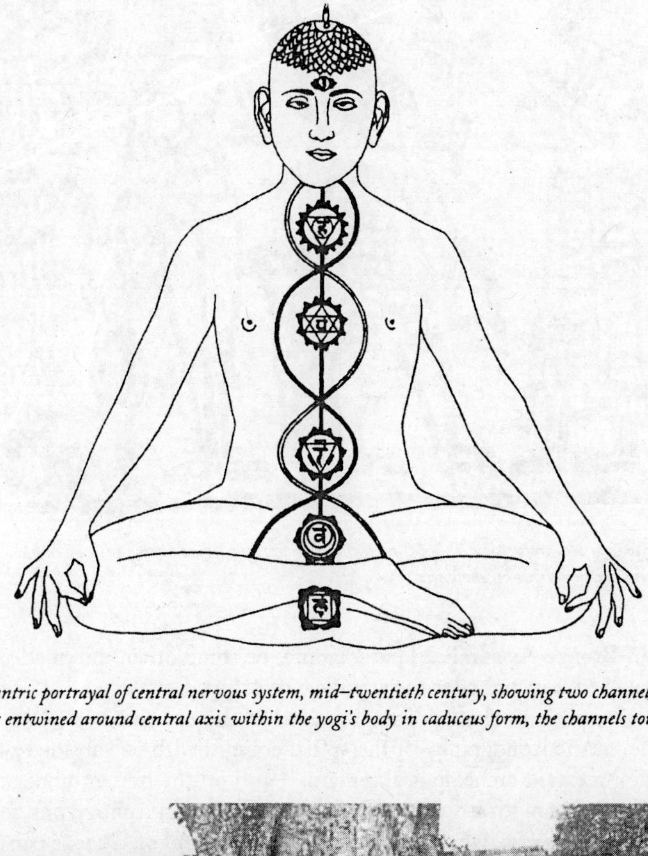

Figure 2 Tantric portrayal of central nervous system, mid–twentieth century, showing two channels that carry the serpent power entwined around central axis within the yogi's body in caduceus form, the channels touching at seven points.

Figure 3 "Snake-stones," fertility icons from South India, early twentieth century A.D.*, each showing two serpents entwined in caduceus form.*

Figure 4 Babylonian seal impression, c. 2000 B.C., showing upright figure surrounded by caduceus of entwined serpents, their heads rising above his shoulders.

assimilated in Bronze Age India. That Elamite, or some other, intermediaries might have been involved does not alter the significance of this fact.

In any case, perhaps the key icon involved is the entwined serpents which are central to the tantric iconography of the spinal column with its subsidiary veins. It is clear that among extant archeological remains—and on the present understanding of the chronology—this motif is first encountered in Sumerian iconography, for example in the famous Gudea Vase, where it seems to be the symbol of Gudea's personal deity, Ningizzida. It is not encountered in the Indus Valley iconography as presently known and in fact is not encountered in India at all until after the fall of Persepolis, more than a thousand years later.[55] In any case, whether this icon came with a certain doctrinal content or as an emptied vessel to be refilled—a form without content—is not known.[56]

Indian versions of the caduceus image which were used in folk or village fertility rites generally show the two serpents symmetrically entwined around a hypothetical central axis which is unseen—as in the image on the Gudea vase. Those which were used in tantric *kuṇḍalinī* iconography, however, portray the serpents/*nāḍīs* entwined around the spine inside the human body. The best known icon of Ningizzida enwrapped by serpents, in contrast, shows the serpents wrapped around his body on the *outside*, from head to foot. The similarity, then, could be much stronger. What has not previously been noted in the literature however, is that there are Mesopotamian examples that indicate the two are intertwined *inside* Ningizzida's body, as their heads emerge into the outside from his shoulders. Whether the portrayal intends the inner caduceus to stop at the bottom of the trunk, as in the *kuṇḍalinī* versions, or to extend downward into the two legs, as in Plato's version of the physiology, cannot be seen. In any case, the important point is that the Sumerian examples do in fact indicate the

Figure 5 Neo-Sumerian stele fragment showing male figure with serpents' heads rising from his shoulders, their bodies evidently entwined inside him.

caduceus existing *inside the human body*. And it cannot be overstressed that the icon on the Gudea vase shows the serpents touching one another at seven points, exactly as do the nāḍīs in the *kuṇḍalinī* physiology. With these points in mind, the similarity seems much stronger.

In any case, it seems clear that again a complex diffusion situation obtained, parts of the tradition descending into Greece, India, and China from some earlier source, other parts being passed from one of these cultures to another at a later time. One detail of this Eurasian-wide diffusion network was a stream that trickled into the Sicilian and South Italian medical schools in the sixth century B.C.

Even Remoter Ages?

The six mysterious Indus Valley seal images often called "Śīvas," all without exception show figures in a position known in *haṭha* yoga as *mūlabandhāsana*, or possibly the closely related *utkaṭāsana* or *bhadda konāsana*, three variants of the same yogic function.[57] The system of yogic ideas and methods that these *āsanas* are involved with consistently throughout their long later history involves the occult physiology discussed here. Specifically, the function of these *āsanas* is, by pressing the heels against the perineum, to drive the sperm-marrow-soul fluid up the spinal channel. There is then some cogency to the view that where this *āsana* is found that physiology may well have been present also. It does not in fact occur in any of the places that have from time to time been suggested as providing analogues of the *āsanas*—in Egyptian sculptures of scribes, for example, or the Gundestrup cauldron,[58] or pre-Columbian seated figures. Some Sumerian cylinder seal impressions of the so-called Displayed Female are close, but the crucial element of the joined heels is never precisely found in them. This posture can, however, be observed in ethnographic photographs of Australian aboriginal rituals.[59] It is possible that this yogic position, perhaps along with certain other protoyogic elements, may have survived from the proto-Australoid stratum of Indian prehistory.

The physiology of the spinal channel seems, in Indian cultural history at least, syntactically related to the heels-joined squatting posture. Whether the connection would hold for earlier cultures is uncertain. But the physiology of the spinal channel may also be extremely ancient and have been diffused widely at an early level of human culture—perhaps even by that hypothetical wave of migration that brought the ancestors of the proto-Australoid peoples out of Africa. The ethnographer Lorna Marshall, in an article on "!Kung Bushmen Religious Beliefs,"[60] writes of an occult physiological power called *ntum* which is aroused by trance dancing, which brings the *ntum* to a boil. "The men," Marshall writes, "say it boils up their spinal columns into their heads, and is so strong when it does this that it overcomes them and they lose their senses." Indeed, when one reflects briefly on the antiquity of marrow cults, known as early as Homo Erectus, this Greek-Indian parallel seems to direct the gaze into the darkest depths of human prehistory.

Notes to Chapter Eight

1. Except in publications of shorter versions of this chapter (Thomas McEvilley, "The Spinal Serpent," *Res: Anthropology and Aesthetics* 24 [Autumn 1993], and, in a slightly different version, in Katherine Harper, ed., *The Roots of Tantra* [Albany, New York: State University of New York Press, 2001]). Filliozat was near to this recognition but did not press onward with his insight (J. Filliozat, *The Classical Doctrine of Indian Medicine: Its Origins and Its Greek Parallels*, trans. Dev Raj Chanana [Delhi: Munshiram Manoharlal, 1964], p. 228).

2. See Thomas McEvilley, "An Archeology of Yoga," *Res: Anthropology and Aesthetics* 1 (Spring 1981), for discussion of these practices.

3. Convenient modern descriptions of the system include Mircea Eliade, *Yoga: Immortality and Freedom*, Bollingen Series 56 (New York: Princeton University Press, 1971), pp. 134, 236–249, and Swami Shivananda, *Kuṇḍalinī Yoga* (Shivanandnagar, India: Yoga-Vedānta Forest Academy, 1971).

4. K. Narayanasvami Aiyar, *Thirty Minor Upaniṣads* (EL Reno, Oklahoma: Santarasa Publications, 1980), p. 107–109.

5. Ibid., p. 213.

6. Ibid., pp. 176–177, 205–206.

7. Pancham Sinh, trans., *The Haṭha Yoga Pradipika* (New Delhi: Munshiram Manoharlal, 1980).

8. Rai Bahadur Srisa Chandra Vasu, trans., *The Śiva Saṁhitā* (New Delhi: Munshiram Manoharlal, 1979).

9. See David Gordon White, *The Alchemical Body: Siddha Traditions in Medieval India* (Chicago: University of Chicago Press, 1996), pp. 134–135.

10. See F. M. Cornford, *Plato's Cosmology: The Timaeus of Plato* (New York: Bobbs Merrill, n.d.), p. 295; R. B. Onians, *The Origins of European Thought about the Body, the Mind, the Soul, the World, Time, and Fate* (Cambridge: Cambridge University Press, 1989), p. 208.

11. See Alister Cameron, *The Pythagorean Background of the Theory of Recollection* (Menasha, Wisconsin: George Banta Publishing Company, 1938), pp. 37–42.

12. W. K. C. Guthrie, *Orpheus and Greek Religion* (New York: W. W. Norton, 1966), p. 228.

13. These points are argued, for example, by M. L. West, *Early Greek Philosophy and the Orient* (Oxford: Clarendon Press, 1971), pp. 151–161.

14. See G. S. Kirk, J. E. Raven, and M. Schofield, *The Presocratic Philosophers*, 2nd ed. (Cambridge: Cambridge University Press, 1983), p. 434.

15. Trans. ibid., p. 451, slightly condensed.

16. Philolaus of Tarentum's four principal organs in the human body—sex organ, navel, heart, brain—may be related to *cakras* in the Pythagorean tradition (Benjamin Farrington, *Greek Science: Its Meaning for Us* [Baltimore, Maryland: Penguin, 1961], p. 69). The possibility that this represents a "spiritual" tradition is suggested by Farrington's observation that "from the point of view of the practical healer it might have been more helpful to assign a less important place to the umbilicus and say something more about the liver and the lungs."

17. *De Partis Animal.* 656a26; *De Gen. Animal.* 717a20 ff.; *Problemata* 879b and 897b23 ff., and see *De Partis Animal.* 651b20 ff. and 652a25 ff.

18. Or from an earlier source that also fed into the Upaniṣads. See West, *Early Greek Philosophy and the Orient*, p. 186 and elsewhere.

19. James Longrigg, *Greek Medicine from the Heroic to the Hellenistic Age: A Source Book* (London: Duckworth, 1998), p. 69.

20. Ibid., p. 61.

21. Ibid., p. 67.

22. Ibid., p. 68.

23. Ibid., p. 62.

24. Ibid., p. 80.

25. W. K. C. Guthrie, *History of Greek Philosophy*, vol. 4 (Cambridge: Cambridge University Press, 1962–1981), p. 36.

26. Ibid., p. 402, n. 2

27. Theodor Ebert, "A Presocratic Philosopher Behind the *Phaedrus*: Empedocles," *Revue de philosophie ancienne* 11 (1993): 221.

28. Ibid. Among Empedocles' identifiable influences is the fact that he "considered [semen] a form of blood," an opinion that survived to be held by Diogenes of Apollonia, by Aristotle, by the Alexandrians, the Stoics, Galen, and others (Longrigg, *Greek Medicine*, p. 65). The semen is supposedly a foamy form of blood, but at the same time it is connected somehow with the spinal marrow by the two veins that bring it from the spine to the testicles. This doctrine is remarkably similar to that found in the *Suśruta Saṁhitā* of ancient Indian medicine, which teaches that "blood is transformed into flesh, flesh into fat, fat into bone, bone into marrow, and marrow into semen" (I.14.10) (Chandra Chakraberty, *An Interpretation of Ancient Hindu Medicine* [Delhi: Low Price Publications, 1997], p. 51). In both traditions blood is regarded as the "agent of nutrition," carrying the value of digested food throughout the body (Chakraberty, *An Interpretation of Ancient Hindu Medicine*, p. 78; Longrigg, *Greek Medicine*, pp. 69–70).

29. There is even a hint of the descent of the brain matter through the spinal channel at *Odyssey* 5.160: "the sweet *aiōn* flowing down."

30. See Onians, *The Origins of European Thought*, pp. 110–111, 177.

31. Nilsson opines that in Minoan-Mycenaean religion "the snake represents the soul of the deceased" (Martin P. Nilsson, *A History of Greek Religion* [New York: W. W. Norton, 1964], p. 13). See also Nilsson, *The Minoan-Mycenaean Religion and Its Survival in Greek Religion* (Lund: C. W. K. Gleerup, 1927), pp. 273 ff., and Jane Ellen Harrison, *Prolegomena to the Study of Greek Religion* (New York: Meridian Books, 1957), pp. 235–237, 325–331.

32. Onians, *The Origins of European Thought*, pp. 124–125.

33. Ibid., pp. 154–155.

34. Some of these passages are assembled by Onians, ibid., pp. 287–288, 492–493.

35. This follows from the fact that the testicles were not regarded as the sources of sperm, but as carriers or waystations for it. Onians argues the point, ibid., pp. 109–110, n. 4.

36. Cf. ibid., p. 110, n.

37. See Theodor Gaster, *Thespis: Ritual, Myth and Drama in the Ancient Near East* (New York: Harper and Row, 1966), p. 396.

38. Onians, *The Origins of European Thought*, p. 208, n. 3.

39. Ibid.

40. See Heinrich Zimmer, *The Art of Indian Asia*, vol. 1, Bollingen Series 39 (Princeton, New Jersey: Princeton University Press, 1955), figure 6, p. 66.

41. See McEvilley, "An Archeology of Yoga," pp. 71–72 and elsewhere.

42. Colin Renfrew (*Archeology and Language: The Puzzle of Indo-European Origins* [New York: Cambridge University Press, 1990]) seems to lean toward an Indo-European Indus Valley (pp. 188–196); others feel more certain. See Subhash Kak, "A Frequency Analysis of the Indus Script," *Cryptologia* 12.3 (July 1988), pp. 129–143; "The Indus Maṇḍala and the Indo-Aryans," *Dr. S. R. Rao's 70th Birthday Felicitation Volume*, 1992; Georg Feuerstein, David Frawley, and Subhash Kak, "A New View of Ancient India," *Yoga Journal* (July/August, 1992): 64–69, 100–102; Jim G. Shaffer, "The Indo-Aryan Invasions: Cultural Myth and Archeological Reality," in *The People of South Asia*, ed. John R. Lukacs (New York: Plenum Books, 1984): 77–90; Harry H. Hicks and Robert N. Anderson, "Analysis of an Indo-European Vedic Aryan Head—4th Millennium B.C.," *JIES* 18 (1990): 425–446. For a recent discussion of the problems of the hypothesis of the Indus Valley as an Indo-European culture see J. P. Mallory, *In Search of the Indo-Europeans: Language, Archaeology and Myth* (London: Thames and Hudson, 1989).

43. Douglas Wile, *Art of the Bedchamber: The Chinese Sexual Yoga Classics Including Women's Solo Meditation Texts* (Albany, New York: State University of New York Press, 1992), pp. 19, 47.

44. Ibid., pp. 19, 41.

45. For the early date see Mircea Eliade, ed., *Encyclopedia of Religion*, vol. 14 (New York: Macmillan, 1987), p. 296.

46. For example: Joseph Needham et al., *Science and Civilization in China*, vol. 2 (Cambridge: Cambridge University Press, 1954–1988), p. 425, and elsewhere; Nagendranath Bhattacharyya, *History of Tantric Religion: A Historical, Ritualistic and Philosophical Study* (Delhi: Munshiram Manoharlal, 1982), p. 97; White, *The Alchemical Body*, p. 63.

47. Nirad C. Chaudhuri, *Hinduism: A Religion to Live By* (Delhi: Oxford University Press; and Calcutta: Chennai Mumbai, 1979), p. 252.

48. White, *The Alchemical Body*, p. 63.

49. Ibid.

50. Ibid., pp. 61–62.

51. Ibid., p. 63.

52. And see Erwin Rohde, *Psyche : The Cult of Souls and Belief in Immortality among the Greeks*, vol. 2, trans. W. B. Hillis (New York: Harper and Row, 1925), p. 260: "The whole movement . . . must have struck the Greeks . . . as something strange and barbaric."

53. Compare Needham, commenting on the beginning of the quest for longevity/immortality in China in the fourth century B.C.: "Something happened at this time to strengthen greatly this belief, perhaps a message from Babylonia, Persia or India about a drug-plant, herb or medicine of immortality" (*Science and Civilization*, vol. 5, part 2, p. 81). For Mahāyāna Buddhist influence on Chinese alchemy see Richard Bertschinger, *The Secret of Everlasting Life: The First Translation of the Ancient Chinese Text on Immortality* (Shaftesbury, Dorset: Element, 1994), p. 19.

54. Zimmer, *The Art of Indian Asia*, vol. 1, pp. 49–50.

55. The evidential record for this diffusion relationship is incomplete, as is shown by the fact that the icon of the entwined serpents is attested in Mesopotamia only until the thirteenth century B.C.—long before the fall of Persepolis. (See Jeremy Black and Anthony Green, *Gods, Demons and Symbols of Ancient Mesopotamia: An Illustrated Dictionary*, [Austin, Texas: University of Texas Press, 1995], p. 168.)

56. See chapter 10.

Onians notes, without mentioning the *kuṇḍalinī* parallels: "The union of the two serpents round the wand might for the Greeks represent the life-power . . . by the union of male *Psychē* (soul; cerebro-spinal fluid) and female *Psychē*" (*The Origins of European Thought*, p. 122, n. 3).

57. McEvilley, "An Archeology of Yoga," pp. 49–51.

58. Timothy Taylor, however, in an article which makes use of my earlier research in "An Archeology of Yoga," notes that the relevant Gundestrup figure does seem to show pressure on the perineum, though only from one heel (Timothy Taylor, "The Gundestrup Cauldron," *Scientific American*, [March, 1992]: 84–89).

59. See, for example, Geza Roheim, *The Eternal Ones of the Dream* (New York: International Universities Press, 1969), plate 7.

60. Lorna Marshall, "!Kung Bushman Religious Beliefs," *Africa* 32 (1962): 221–252.

Chapter Nine

Cynics and Pāśupatas

The cult of Śīva Pāśupata, the horned god who was Lord of the Wild Beasts, seems to have been among the oldest of the sects that would develop in the Middle Ages into first the *Śaivāgamas*, then both Śaiva Tantra and the monistic Śaivism of Kashmir and elsewhere.[1] At a later phase, "the bastions and guardians of Hindu orthodoxy" rejected such literature. "For one thing, the Āgama(s) as a whole rejected the authority of the Vedas,"[2] and the pre-Agamic Pāśupatas already "considered themselves to be independent of the Vedic-Smarta tradition . . ."[3]

The principal extant text of the sect, the *Pāśupata Sūtra*, is attributed to a mysterious figure named Lakulīṣa, who seems to have "really existed," perhaps around the first century A.D. and, despite the anti-Vedic nature of the cult, is described as a Brahmin.[4] This is the source that was used by Mādhavācārya in his fourteenth-century exposition of the system in his *Sarvadarśana-saṃgraha*.[5] The sect had distinct resemblances with both Ājīvikism and Jainism, as well as the other Śaiva cults such as the Kāpālikas, Kālamukhas, and later Kanphat yogis and Aghoris, of some of which it is probably the "parent sect."[6] "The mainstays of these traditions were largely single ascetics, many of whom travelled widely and in so doing spread their cults from one part of India to another."[7] "There were Pāśupata temples in most parts of India" by Gupta times, and "two early seventh century inscriptions registering grants to Pāśupata ascetics have been found as far afield as South-East Asia."[8]

There are also traces of the cult's earlier existence. Lakulīṣa "was regarded as the twenty-eighth or last incarnation of Śīva,"[9] and "we can assume," says one scholar, "that the Pāśupata system existed before the days of Lakulīṣa and that the latter only revitalized the creed."[10] It is mentioned in the *Mahābhārata* in the late centuries B.C.; the connections with Ājīvikism suggest that it may have existed in some form in Makkhali Gosāla's day, probably the sixth century B.C.; and, indeed, many scholars are willing to trace it all the way back to the Bronze Age culture of the Indus Valley.[11] In fact, cults of this general type, involving worship of a horned god by one name or another, had existed for thousands of years by the time of the Indus Valley culture, as the iconographic remains of Çatal Hüyuk in Anatolia—to say nothing of the Magdalenian iconography of Cro-Magnon Europe—demonstrate.[12]

The name of the semimythical founder means "Lord of the Club," and the cult is dedicated to Śiva as Lakulīṣa, or "club-bearer," as well as to Śiva Pāśupata, "Lord of the Beasts." Lakulīṣa is held by the *Vāyu* and *Liṅga Purāṇas* to have been a dead body reanimated by Śiva[13] "at the holy site of Kayavatara, the 'Descent into a Corpse.'"[14] The doctrine of reanimation, as distinct from reincarnation, holds that a sorcerer can inhabit a corpse and act through it. In Ājīvika tradition, Gosāla is a practitioner of reanimation, and the idea is basic to Ājīvikism, where it interacts with the (probably later) doctrine of reincarnation. In the Ājīvika doctrine, each cycling spirit is said to undergo seven reanimations at the end of its cycle of reincarnations.

The Seeking of Dishonor

As one scholar writes, "The spiritual discipline these [sects] prescribe does not involve complex rites or require extensive intellectual development."[15] In the stage of Pāśupata practice known as the "seeking of dishonor," the devotee was to efface his ego through courting contempt and abuse from his fellow humans by actions deliberately feigned but appearing to be forthrightly despicable. "He who is despised," explains the *Pāśupata Sūtra* (III.3), "lies happy, free of all attachment." "Ill-treated, he should wander," says Lakulīṣa, and Kaundinya, his commentator, explicates:

> Ill treatment: the application of sticks and fists, corporal ill-treatment . . . This ill-treatment should be regarded as a coronation to a poor man. It should be to him as the touchstone [is] to gold . . . He should wander under false accusations on the principle that he who is dishonored is on [the path to] acquiring merit and [performing] the religious injunction.[16]

Lakulīṣa prescribes several means of attaining ill-treatment, including (III.15), "He should play the lecher"; (III.16), "He should act improperly;" and (III.17), "He should speak improperly." To quote Kaundinya again:

> He should appear as though mad, like a pauper, his body covered with filth, letting his beard, nails and hair grow long, without any bodily care. Hereby he becomes cut off from the respectable castes and conditions of men, and the power of passionless detachment is produced.[17]

The Pāśupata was instructed to go about among strangers as if he were a madman, and the Pāśupata "scripture is known as *Vātulatantra* which means the tantra of the lunatics."[18] The Pāśupata's seemingly insane behavior is based on that attributed to Śiva himself in texts such as the *Bhagavata Purāṇa* (IV, 2–7):

> Like a madman he haunts horrid cemeteries, surrounded with ghosts and evil spirits. He is naked, his hair in disorder. He laughs, he weeps, he smears himself with ashes and wears as his only ornament a necklace of skulls and human bones. . . . He is mad, adored by madmen, and reigns over the spirits of darkness.[19]

The "seeking of dishonor" was part of that Dravidian substratum which later resurfaced as a dominant force in the tantric movements. It was at one time so widespread that it appears occasionally in Hindu sources, too. Manu, for example, says:

> A Brāhmaṇ should always fear homage as if it were poison; and constantly desire (to suffer) scorn as (he would long for) nectar.

> For he who is scorned (nevertheless may) sleep with an easy mind, awake with an easy mind, and with an easy mind walk here among men; but the scorner utterly perishes. (*MS* II.162–163.)[20]

The *Vaikhānasa Sūtra* (VIII.9) attributes this practice also to the Paramahaṃsas, who "behave like mad persons though they are not so."[21]

Gosāla and Mahāvīra

Religious activity of this kind seems to go back to Ājīvikism, which was evidently an ample enough matrix that Buddhism, Śaivism and, especially, Mahāvīra's Jainism could all derive, at least in part, from it. Mahāvīra's form of Jainism seems to have separated off from Ājīvikism as a reform movement less involved in black magic, but initially Mahāvīra seems to have been a member of Gosāla's sect. Gosāla sought dishonor in his quest for enlightenment, and the practice is also ascribed to Mahāvīra, who devoted the ninth year of his ascetic practice to it, visiting "non-Aryan countries, in order to invite persecution and thus to work off his *karma*."[22] The non-Aryan countries in which he wandered may have been in India, but in any case the example establishes the factuality of the Jain monk wandering abroad.

A textual remnant of this relationship occurs in the account by the Jain author Jinadasa, in which Mahāvīra and Gosāla spent six years of wandering and practice together resulting in a schism between them. According to Jinadasa, Gosāla underwent frequent, indeed constant, humiliations during this period at the hands of strangers, due to his apparent lack of discipline and courtesy. The Jain tradition takes these events at face value as indications of Gosāla's falseness as a teacher and his inferiority to Mahāvīra, who is presented as respected wherever he goes. Modern scholars have tended to ascribe the anecdotes to *odium theologicum* and disregard them as fictions—but they respond better to an interpretation as a deliberate seeking of dishonor along the lines of Pāśupata practice.

Jinadasa relates thirteen events: Once Gosāla spies on lovers and is beaten by the man; three times he is quarrelsome with strangers (twice, these are followers of Pārśva), resulting in his exclusion from group activities; twice he is unkind to children and is beaten by villagers for it; twice he behaves gluttonously in public, the first time he is beaten, the second time the contents of his bowl are poured on his head; falling in with robbers, he is "mercilessly teased, carried pick-a-back, and called 'Grandfather'";[23] twice he is beaten for obscenely insulting an icon in a temple; twice he is beaten for gratuitously mocking groups of strangers. He is presented, in other words, as a classic fool (he has been described as Mahāvīra's Sancho Panza) and moreover as one who is almost invariably beaten for his displays of foolishness.

In the six years of seeking dishonor covered by the narrative of Jinadasa, Gosāla's behavior bears comparison with the ancient Near Eastern ritual of the scapegoat, who wanders seeking abuse among strangers. This theme is found with all possible clarity in the story of Kisa Vaccha, very likely an Ājīvika predecessor of Gosāla, who "obtained the reputation of a scapegoat (*kalākaṇṇi*), who would remove ill-luck when spat upon, and as a result was shamed and insulted by the populace."[24] This motif also hangs over the Jesus myth, which shares with the Gosāla story the scapegoat birth:

> Mankhali [Gosāla's father] left his wife and his luggage in Gabahula's cowshed, and tried to find accommodation in the village. Since he could find no shelter elsewhere the couple continued to live in a corner of the cowshed, and it was there that Bhadda

gave birth to her child. His parents decided to call him Gosāla ["cowshed"], after the place of his birth.[25]

Karmic Transfer

The theory of the Seeking of Dishonor, as formulated in the *Pāśupata Sūtra*, is that through courting the scorn of others, the Seeker "gives his bad *karma* to them," and "takes their good *karma* from them" (*PS* III.8–9). This can be partly understood in terms of the conventional theory of *karma*: One may gain good *karma* by patiently enduring hardship or gain bad *karma* by mistreating another person; the Seeker of Dishonor tries to manipulate these two processes. But the underlying theory goes beyond conventional ideas of karmic process, which would give one bad *karma* for coercing another into acts karmically unfavorable to himself; it posits a magical breach of the usual working of the process.

This karmic transfer is the opposite of a more famous later idea of transferring *karma*, that philanthropic "transfer of the other and the self" (*parātma-parivartana*) formulated by the Mahāyāna Buddhist author Śāntideva in the *Bodhicaryāvatāra*. In that theory, one can transfer one's good *karma* to another and take on the other's bad *karma*, in a saintly act of self-sacrifice (*BCA* VIII.120). In the *Pāśupata Sūtra* the transfer is self-seeking rather than self-sacrificing. The aspirant is told to behave like a vampire, deceptively and deliberately draining off the good *karma* of others and secretly transferring his own bad *karma* to them. While they seem to be mistreating him, he is really mistreating them. Either form of the activity is a violation of the conventional law of *karma*. If, on the one hand, the recipient, in Śāntideva's transfer, has not earned the good *karma* himself, then he must receive it through a mechanism like the Christian concept of grace, contrary to the emphasis on self-reliance in primitive Buddhism; if the recipient, on the other hand, has earned the good *karma*, then there is not really an act of giving, only an illusion of one. As Śāntideva is teaching a doctrine of grace, Lakulīṣa seems to be teaching black magic. In his teaching the stranger's downfall is one's own salvation and one willingly brings it about. Something like the primitive belief in eating one's enemy to obtain his spiritual force for oneself is implied.

Sectarian Connections

The Seeking of Dishonor implies a strong connection between Pāśupatism and Ājīvikism. Śiva, in the *Kūrma Purāṇa*, is represented as singing, dancing, making amorous gestures and loud shouts; this behavior is mimicked by the Pāśupata worshipper, whose practice involves "laughing, dancing [and] singing,"[26] and who "actively encourages censure from the populace by means of several peculiar practices, notably the six so-called Doors . . . snoring or acting as if asleep when one is not . . . shaking one's limbs as if afflicted by 'wind-disease' . . . walking as if crippled . . . making amorous gestures in the presence of women . . . acting as if devoid of judgement . . . and . . . uttering senseless or contradictory words."[27] Gosāla's own behavior just before his death—singing, dancing, and soliciting sexual favors from the potter-woman who had sheltered him—suggests both the Seeking of Dishonor and the miming of Śiva—especially as the tradition tells us that Gosāla did Pāśupata practices before his death.[28] Other cultic elements also point to a connection with Ājīvikism; some Pāśupatas, for example, like the Ājīvikas and Digambara Jains, went naked and pulled out their hair and beards.[29]

Other elements point to connections between Ājīvikism and various Śaiva sects other than the Pāśupata but related to it. Gosāla's own father, for example, seems to have been a Śaiva mendicant.[30] In the *Rāmāyana*, Ravana, the villain, is sometimes disguised as an Ājīvika ascetic, sometimes as a Pāśupata—both unsavory characters and evidently very like one another.[31] The term *ekadaṇḍin* (club-bearer) can be used to denote either an Ājīvika or a Śaiva. The Ājīvikas are reported to have practiced secret bloody rites which find echoes in Śaiva practice, especially among the Kāpālika(s). Both groups featured sexual magic as well as blood rites. Other Śaiva groups, such as the Aghoris, practiced cannibalism and the eating of refuse, common tactics in the "seeking of dishonour." The Aghoris, Kāpālikas, Pāśupatas, Ājīvikas and Jains, all relate to left-hand tantrism,[32] as do the Lokāyatikas.[33] Some ascribe such practices to pre-Aryan fertility rites, assuming that all the above-named groups belong to that stratum, which was submerged from history's gaze by the period of Aryan dominance and reemerged in the Middle Ages in the tantric and *siddha* movements.

There are indications that the Jains also, despite their puritanical overlay of Aryan idealism, participated in this presumably Dravidian stratum of religious practice. The Nath Siddha, or Kanphat yoga tradition—a medieval left-tantra sect involved in the primitive body-practice (*kaya-sādhana*)—specifically conflates its own foundation myth with a Jain foundation myth, and some members of the sect wore mouth cloths like the Jains. The tantrism of Assam and Nepal had a distinctly Jain flavor.[34] The Ājīvikas also shared the extreme doctrine of *ahiṃsā* with the Jains; Gosāla in his most advanced period remained completely silent and immobile for fear of injuring any small beings by the violent expulsion of breath or by the movements of his limbs.

The Kanphat yoga tradition has Ājīvika connections too. Gorakhnāth, the cult hero or master, is said to have created men from horse dung, then burned them alive and revived them seven times. The story seems to echo both the Ājīvika suicide practice of entering a fire of dried horse dung, and the Ājīvika doctrine of the seven reanimations which the *jīva* or reincarnating unit undergoes at the end of its cycle.[35]

Even in the puritanical contexts of Jainism there are records of blood rites, including the ascetic's cutting off pieces of his own flesh and throwing them into the fire. The same rites were performed by the Kāpālika(s).[36] Jain literature also contains at least one sorcerer's duel involving Mahāvīra and "references to the art of entering another's body,"[37] the basic shamanic art and a central feature of Gosāla's doctrine of reanimation. All these cults are rooted in a Dravidian substrate which goes back, in parts, to the Indus Valley culture and beyond, to primeval levels of magic and shamanic belief. They are basically left-handed and in opposition to the Aryan mentalist tradition.

A Greek Parallel

One of the most fascinating attempts to link Greek and Indian traditions was Ingalls's argument that elements of Cynic behavior in Greece replicate the practice of the Seeking of Dishonor and seem to derive from the same source.[38] Ancient sources tell us that "the Cynic exposed himself regularly to scorn; he actively sought dishonor even at the cost of blows" (Dio VIII.16). Cynic methods of exciting censure were various: the wearing of filthy garments, the use of violent and indecent language, the imitation of animals, the performance in public of acts that were ridiculous or obscene or which gave the impression of madness. The Stoic Epictetus preserves this Cynic tradition when he says that in order to be a philosopher "you must keep vigils, work hard, overcome certain desires, abandon your own people, be despised by a paltry slave, be laughed to scorn by those who meet you" (*Disc.* III.15.11–12).

The anecdotal history of the Cynics, especially of Diogenes, is full of such stories. Diogenes repeatedly plays mad and gets beaten for it; when he called himself "Socrates gone mad" he may have been using, in effect, a technical term. "When he was told that many people laughed at him, he said, "'But I am not laughed down'" (D.L. VI.54). Diogenes held to a principle called *parrhēsia*, or shocking freedom of speech, which involved deliberately mocking and offending strangers in the street; Gosāla's practice of public derisiveness to incite censure is not so different.

The tradition of the asceticism of dishonor involves the dishonoring of the corpse through the breaching of traditional funereal taboos and injunctions. Socrates, Diogenes, and Gosāla are all recorded to have wished to avoid any ritual honoring of their corpses. Socrates instructed his friends just to throw his body on the dump. When Diogenes was old and nearing death he refused to make any preparations for it. When asked, "When you die, who will carry you out to burial?" he replied: "Whoever wants my room." The more primitive Gosāla went farther in his karmic black magic. He instructed his disciples to "desecrate his body upon his death. They were to tie a rope to his left foot, to spit thrice into his face, and to drag his body around the streets of Savatthi, proclaiming that he was not a jina (an enlightened one) but a cheat and a murderer, and that Mahāvīra was the only true jina. After this they were to dispose of his body without respect."[39] Even after his death Gosāla was practicing karmic black magic or vampirism, tempting his rival into proud feelings that would drag down his karmic status and give Gosāla one up on him in his next incarnation.

The widespread iconographic category of the club-bearer includes Heracles the club-bearer, "the first teacher, the archegete of the Cynic tradition,"[40] and the Pāśupata teacher Lakulīṣa, the "lord of the Club."[41] Also, Heracles' lion skin recalls Śiva's leopard skin. Heracles, descendant of Sumero-Akkadian Gilgamesh, and at the same time related, perhaps by way of a more ancient stratum, to bull-gods like Śiva, has both the feline skin and the club of the Śiva of the Pāśupatas.[42] On Kushan coins the figure of Heracles is replaced by Śiva, once with a club. The tradition of the madness and shocking behavior of Heracles in Greek mythology relates to the Śaiva practices of behaving like madmen or animals and seeking dishonor.

Animal Imitation

The custom of the "beast-vow" was based on the shaman's ability to transform himself or herself into the shape of an animal ally. The Buddhist texts *Mahānidesa* and *Cūllaniddesa* mention vows to live like an elephant, a horse, a cow, a snake, a dog, and others.[43] Beast ascetics are also mentioned in the Buddhist *Majjhima Nikāya* (I.387 ff.) and the *Dhamma-saṅgaṇi* (261). Bovine ascetics wear a tail and horns and bray like bulls. The Indus Valley figures of therianthropic males with horns and tales (which go back in turn to Mesopotamian representations of bull-men) may have represented persons who had taken such vows. The Pāśupata, in his first stage of training, was obliged to spend a part of every day bellowing like a bull, hoping "to transform himself . . . into the Lord's beast."[44]

Both animal imitation and shocking behavior are encountered in the "bull-vow." "The *Jaiminīya Brāhmaṇa* specifies that the enactor of the bull-vow should have sexual congress in defiance of all human laws, that is, indiscriminately with forbidden members of his family as well as with others."[45] Diogenes similarly advocated incest as a part of an ideal of complete indifference to social and familial customs. Indian texts also mention dog ascetics who sit like dogs, walk and eat like dogs, sleep in the streets like and among dogs, and who eventually are to acquire the very thought patterns and feelings of dogs. Diogenes, "the Cynic," or "the Dog," lived in the streets of Athens among dogs and was called one by the Athenians. In India every Aghori guru was always accompanied by a dog.[46] A Sanskrit drama refers to a madman who delighted in eating the leavings of a dog.[47]

Both Cynics and Pāśupatas, says Ingalls, are "shamans manque's, or if you wish, they were a cult whose shamanism was modified by the mores of a civilized society."[48] Shamans round the world have employed beast-imitations for various purposes. The donning of animal skins, dancing, singing, and imitation of the cries and movements of animals are shamanic practices which go back to the Paleolithic age. "I imagine both the Cynic and Pāśupata cults," says Ingalls, "to have derived from sects of men who performed beast-vows."[49]

Beast initiations with outrageous behavior existed in ancient Dacia and Scythia.[50] Groups of young males who had pledged to behave for a certain period like dogs or wolves would act like "fugitives and outlaws."[51] They would perform cannibalism, an act which Jinadasa ascribes to Goṣāla and which Diogenes Laertius (VI.73) represents Diogenes of Sinope as recommending.[52] In the iconography of some of these cults the club was the common weapon, indeed the common ritual object.[53] Hittites and Spartans, as well as later Germanic peoples, had such cults.

As the state solidified beyond the tribal scale, primitive magicians and their beast-routines, less and less in harmony with the ambient cultural forms, "were driven underground" as Eliade puts it, in the interests of the emerging social order. Sometimes the beast practice was restricted to an initiation society in which boys underwent the shamanic experience in an abbreviated and ritualized form. As time went on these practices were increasingly perceived as eccentric, and membership was increasingly secret. In India such postshamanic societies became orders of ascetics and gradually adopted spiritualistic justifications for their practices. In some cases the shamanic current may have been segregated in certain secret or sheltered priesthoods.

The Ājīvikas were associated with sorcery and goblinism, and had an initiation rite which involved the grasping of a heated iron until the hand was burned.[54] Such practices are common in shamanic contexts, where mastery over fire is one of the most elementary credentials. Samnite wolf-imitators practiced the ordeal of walking on hot coals.[55] Gosāla repeatedly practiced fire magic. He burned a house, a pavilion, and once a whole district, magically.[56] Once he burned two disciples of Mahāvīra to ashes by projecting onto them the inner heat he had accumulated through asceticism.[57] The overlap between Ājīvikism and shamanism is too obvious to need special pleading.

Ājīvikas and Cynics also shared certain cultic practices and paraphernalia. The act of "bearing a staff . . . probably became a regular mark of the Ājīvika order,"[58] as it was of the Cynics. An Ājīvika bodhisattva described in the *Lomahamsa Jātaka* specialized in the austerity of not protecting himself from natural heat and cold. "In winter he would leave his thicket and spend the night exposed to the bitter wind, returning to the shade as soon as the sun rose . . . In summer he reversed the process, and was scorched by the sun all day, while at night the thicket shielded him from the cooling breeze."[59] Diogenes underwent similar heat-practices, standing with his arms around a bronze statue in winter (Plutarch *Sayings of the Spartans* 233.16) and walking barefoot on snow (D.L. VI.34), as Socrates had done before him. In the summer he rolled his tub—a large *pithos*, or earthenware jar—about on hot sand (D.L. VI.23). He did these things, says Diogenes Laertius, "to inure himself to hardship" (ibid.).[60]

Diogenes' Jar and Bowl

The tradition that Diogenes *lived* in an urn is not supported by the ancient testimonia in general. One tradition says that Diogenes used the jar as a temporary shelter while a cottage was being prepared for him (D.L. VI.23). Another says that he rejected a cottage in favor of the urn (*Sixteenth Epistle of "Diogenes"*)[61] which presumably then became his domicile. But usually, "Diogenes is described as sleeping in temples or in gymnasia or on the ground."[62] Teles describes him as sleeping in bath houses in winter and in temples in summer.[63] Dio Chrysostom says that Diogenes lived in public buildings and shrines (IV.13).

Thus they suggest that Diogenes didn't actually live in his urn but *used* it at times for specific practices of austerity. This behavior is unique in the Greek tradition. In India, however, it is recorded. The Jain *Aupapātika Sūtra*, in describing the austerities of the Ājīvikas, says, "The monk is held to have made the highest penance when he entered large earthen pots."[64] A Tamil grammatical commentary of the fourteenth century A.D. speaks of ascetics who performed penances in funerary urns, and these are commonly assumed to have been Ājīvikas.

The tradition of the few possessions officially allowed to a Cynic practitioner also recalls the rules of Indian orders. The Cynic was to possess a staff (which symbolized the club of Heracles), a single cloak (the Buddhist *bhikkhu* was allowed three), a wallet or sack, and a bowl or cup. The anecdotal tradition records that at some point in his career Diogenes, seeing a child drinking from his hands, threw away the cup (D.L. VI.37).[65] Early ascetic groups in India also stressed such issues, discriminating, for example, between those who ate from a bowl and "hand-lickers."[66] A still more advanced vow than that of the hand-licker is that of *Turiyatita*; the ascetic who takes this vow "eats only fruits in the way the cow takes food (i.e. without using hands)."[67] Diogenes' renunciation of the bowl, viewed from the perspective of Indian asceticism, would represent an important moment in his career, a moment at which he advanced from one category of ascetic vow to another: He became a hand-licker.

The hand-lickers followed a tougher regimen than the bowl carriers, developmentally forcing their *karma*. "A monk who collects alms in the hollow of his hand," says a Jain text, "is not allowed to frequent the abodes of a householder, if rain falls down even in the form of a fine spray. But one who collects alms by alms-bowl may collect alms if it rains but a little and if he stops when it rains heavily."[68] The theoretical justification for these distinctions in Jain practice is materialistic, based on *ahiṃsā*: The monk with the bowl is said to run a higher risk of killing microscopic beings than the monk who eats from his hands only; it is considered that rain produces many microscopic beings and hence the monk who is more advanced in *ahiṃsā* will neither eat from a bowl nor go out in even a very fine rain; the monk whose *ahiṃsā* is less advanced will both eat from a bowl and walk about in a shower—but even he will not walk out in a heavy rain, when the air is thick with *animalcula*.

In the iconography of the relationship between these cults, the motif of the ceramic bowl, whether as funeral urn or eating dish, occurs in kaleidoscopic recombinations. Gosāla's headquarters was a potter's shop, and that is one of the sites officially deemed suitable for ascetic practices. The *Acaranga Sūtra* says: "a mendicant may exert himself or stand or sit or lie in a burning place (where corpses are burned), or in an empty house, or in a mountain cave, or in a potter's workshop."[69] Diogenes used a large jar for heat austerities; Ājīvikas entered large jars for austerity. In one anecdote, Diogenes' jar, when broken, was replaced; in another, Gosāla tried to prevent the breaking of a bowl, which had been prophesied by Mahāvīra. Diogenes broke a bowl of soup under a disciple's gown; Gosāla had his gown pulled from him by his master who was chasing him for spilling a bowl of soup. Among Gosāla's prominent lay supporters were potters and bankers; Diogenes' father was a moneychanger. Diogenes tied a rope around the neck of a huge wine jar (a *pithos* such as he was reported to live in or frequent) and spent the afternoon dragging it around the public square (D.L. VI.35).[70]

The Question

The comparative material involving Cynics and Pāśupatas has led to speculation about possible connections between them in the same general period as Upaniṣadic-Ionian and Jain-Orphic connections. Two models have been proposed. One model conjectures that both Cynics and Pāśupatas were influenced by Scythian and Thracian shamans from the Black Sea area.[71] Another proposes that Indian ascetics followed an old overland route from Central Asia that ended at or near Sinope and came into actual contact with Diogenes personally before he left his native city and took the exotic craft he had learned to Athens to convert it, under the influence of Socrates/Antisthenes, into philosophy.[72] The plausibility of the latter view is increased by the fact that, while Diogenes lived in "an entrepot on the ancient trade route between India and Greece," so did Lakulīṣa, whose reputed hometown of Broach "at the time of the author of the *Periplus* (first century A.D.) . . . was the chief trading port in western India [and] seems to have held this position from as early as Mauryan times."[73]

Notes to Chapter Nine

1. See David N. Lorenzen, *The Kāpālikas and Kālamukhas: Two Lost Śaivite Sects* (New Delhi: Thomson Press [India], 1972), especially chapter VI, "Lakulīṣa and the Pāśupatas." For further bibliography see ibid., pp. 173–175, especially notes 5–9.

2. Mark S. G. Dyczkowski, *The Canon of the Śaivāgama and the Kubjika Tantras of the Western Kaula Tradition* (Albany, New York: State University of New York Press, 1988), pp. 8, 9.

3. Ibid., p. 20.

4. Ibid., pp. 20, 23; N. N. Bhattacharyya, *History of the Tantric Religion: A Historical, Ritualistic and Philosophical Study* (New Delhi: Manohar, 1992), p. 200.

5. See Kumar Chakrabarti, ed., *Pāśupata Sūtram with Panchartha-Bhāsya of Kaundinya* (Calcutta: Academie Publishers, 1970), pp. 122–144.

6. Lorenzen, *Kāpālikas and Kālamukhas*, p. 4.

7. Dyczkowski, *Canon of the Śaivāgama*, p. 5.

8. Lorenzen, *Kāpālikas and Kālamukhas*, pp. 182–183.

9. Ibid., pp. 178–179.

10. Bhattacharyya, *History of the Tantric Religion*, p. 200.

11. This question is discussed in McEvilley, "An Archeology of Yoga," *Res: Anthropology and Aesthetics* 1 (Spring 1981): 44–77, and Stella Kramrisch, *The Presence of Śiva* (Princeton, New Jersey: Princeton University Press, 1981), pp. 10–14, 21. And see Alain Daniélou, *Śiva and Dionysus* (Rochester, Vermont: Inner Traditions, 1984), pp. 24, 27.

12. Daniélou, ibid., calls all such early bull-god cults Shivaite; the name seems an anachronism when applied to, say, the sixth millennium B.C., but it is acceptable as a generic designation for a *type* of cult, a category which, strictly speaking, included Shivaite cults and many others.

13. See Lorenzen, *Kāpālikas and Kālamukhas*, p. 176 and notes 15 and 16. Also Haripada Chakraborti, *Asceticism in Ancient India* (Calcutta: Punthi Pustak, 1973), p. 156.

14. Kramrisch, *The Presence of Śiva*, p. 332.

15. Dyczkowski, *Canon of the Śaivāgama*, p. 21.

16. *Pāśupata Sūtra* chapters 3 and 4 have the Seeking Dishonor theme. The quoted passages are trans. Daniel H. H. Ingalls, "Cynics and Pāśupatas: The Seeking of Dishonor," *Harvard Theological Review* 55 (1962): 287.

17. Ibid., p. 289, with the emendation by Lorenzen, *Kāpālikas and Kālamukhas*, p. 118, n. 75.

18. Bhattacharyya, *History of Tantric Religion*, p. 203.

19. Trans. Daniélou, *Śiva and Dionysus*, p. 47.

20. Trans. Georg Buhler, *The Laws of Manu*, with extracts from seven commentaries, Sacred Books of the East 25 (New York: Dover, 1969).

21. Chakraborti, *Asceticism in Ancient India*, pp. 40–41.

22. Basham, *History and Doctrine of the Ājīvikas*, p. 45; Chakraborti, *Asceticism in Ancient India*, p. 345, for more details. The source is *AS* I.8.3.

23. Basham, *History and Doctrine of the Ājīvikas*, p. 44.

24. Ibid., p. 29.

25. Ibid., p. 36.

26. Lorenzen, *Kāpālikas and Kālamukhas*, p. 185; Pranabananda Jash, *History of Śaivism* (Calcutta: Roy and Chaudhury, 1974), p. 36.

27. Lorenzen, *Kāpālikas and Kālamukhas*, p. 185.

28. Chakrabarti, *Pāsupata Sūtram with Panchartha-Bhāsya of Kaundinya*, p. 12.

29. Chakraborti, *Asceticism in Ancient India*, p. 159.

30. Jarl Charpentier, "Ājīvika," *Journal of the Royal Asiatic Society* (1913): 669–673.

31. Basham, *History and Doctrine of the Ājīvikas*, pp. 165–66.

32. Mircea Eliade, *Yoga: Immortality and Freedom*, trans. Willard R. Trask, Bollingen Series 56 (New York: Princeton University Press, 1969), pp. 296–310.

33. Ibid. and Chattopadhyaya, *Lokāyata*, ch. 1.

34. Eliade, *Yoga: Immortality and Freedom*, p. 311.

35. Ibid., p. 312.

36. Kalipada Mitra, "Magic and Miracle in Jaina Literature," *Indian Historical Quarterly* 15 (1939): 180.

37. Ibid., p. 182.

38. Ingalls, "Cynics and Pāśupatas," pp. 281–298.

39. Basham, *History and Doctrine of the Ājīvikas*, p. 64.

40. Ingalls, "Cynics and Pāśupatas," p. 292.

41. Ibid., p. 283.

42. See John F. Fleet, "Śīva as Lakulīṣa," *Journal of the Royal Asiatic Society* (1907): 419–426.

43. M. G. Bhagat, *Ancient Indian Asceticism* (Delhi: Munshiram Manoharlal, 1976), p. 145. See also Chattopadhyaya, *Lokāyata*, ch. 2.

44. Ibid., p. 295.

45. Ibid.

46. Eliade, *Yoga: Immortality and Freedom*, p. 297.

47. Jash, *History of Śaivism*, p. 36.

48. Ingalls, "Cynics and Pāśupatas," p. 296.

49. Ibid., p. 297.

50. Mircea Eliade, *Zalmoxis: The Vanishing God*, trans. Willard R. Trask (Chicago: University of Chicago Press, 1972), pp. 7–16.

51. Ibid., p. 19.

52. Basham, *History and Doctrine of the Ājīvikas*, p. 43.

53. Eliade says, "The club retains its value as a cult instrument when its military use has been supplanted by more modern weapons" (*Zalmoxis*, p. 9).

54. Basham, *History and Doctrine of the Ājīvikas*, pp. 104 ff.

55. Eliade, *Zalmoxis*, p. 3.

56. Basham, *History and Doctrine of the Ājīvikas*, pp. 42–44.

57. Ibid., p. 60.

58. Ibid., p. 99.

59. Ibid., p. 110.

60. Reale writes that "it is beyond doubt that the spirit and the premises of Cynicism are already quite clear in Antisthenes"—abrogating any need for external input on Diogenes (Giovanni Reale, *A History of Ancient Philosophy*, vol. 1, *From the Origins to Socrates*, trans. John R. Catan [Albany, New York: State University of New York Press, 1987], p. 269). But in fact the quasi-shamanic motifs in Diogenes' practice, including his animal imitation, were not present in Antisthenes' practice. It seems that Diogenes, coming from Pontus with his wild, shamanically influenced or Indian-influenced behavior, attached himself to the teacher who seemed most likely to tolerate it since it was closest to his own—this being Antisthenes.

61. See A. J. Malherbe, ed., *The Cynic Epistles: A Study Edition* (Missoula, Montana: Scholars' Press, 1977).

62. Farrand Sayre, *Diogenes of Sinope: A Study of Greek Cynicism* (Baltimore, Maryland: J. H. Furst Co., 1938), p. 101.

63. Ibid.

64. Quoted, without mention of the Cynic parallel, by Chakraborti, *Asceticism in Ancient India*, p. 456; and Basham, *History and Doctrine of the Ājīvikas*, p. 111.

65. See also Seneca, *Epist. Mor.*, 90.14; 6th and 13th *Letters of "Diogenes"* (Malherbe, ed., *The Cynic Epistles*).

66. See, e.g., Chakraborti, *Asceticism in Ancient India*, pp. 40 ff., etc.

67. *Sannyāsa Upaniṣad*; quoted by Chakraborti, *Asceticism in Ancient India*, p. 41.

68. Ibid., p. 383.

69. Ibid., p. 377.

70. The broken-pot stories discussed by Basham (*Ājīvikas*, pp. 37, 42, and 47) are reminiscent of the story of Diogenes at D.L. VI.35 and 37, and of Zeno and Crates at D.L. VII.3.

71. This is Ingalls's view in "Cynics and Pāśupatas."

72. This is Sayre's opinion (*Diogenes of Sinope*). The evidence for and against this route is considered in chapter 14, "Diffusion Channels in the Hellenistic and Roman Periods."

73. Lorenzen, *Kāpālikas and Kālamukhas*, p. 179.

Chapter Ten

Five Questions Concerning the Ancient Near East

Question I: What was the first civilization?

Before the hypothetical "coming of the Greeks" the Aegean area was already peripherally involved in the stream of imagery which blanketed the region from the eastern Mediterranean to northwest India. Subsequently, elements of Near Eastern cult and myth arrived through the Minoan channel. Meanwhile Mycenaean traders were active in Ugarit and elsewhere in the Levant; both Homer and Hesiod show signs of influence from this channel. After the Dark Age in which the great palace centers were abandoned, Greece again experienced a surge of Near Eastern influence. It was at the end of this wave that Indian influence passed, by way of the Persian intermediary, into Greece, becoming implicated with inflowing Near Eastern elements in the early stream of Greek philosophical thought.

Of course, culture is not simply the sum of its influences. One scholar has remarked that "internal factors of socio-economic dynamics [are] pre-eminent, and the external (migratory) factors . . . rather limited from a quantitative point of view."[1] Still, the case of Sumero-Akkadian influence in the Bronze Age and after seems special. Perhaps a dozen different cultures received formative imprints from that source and joined a Sumerian-based cultural consensus that lasted for thousands of years. To deny this in order to affirm some purely self-subsistent cultural urge would be to burden the record with a quasi-theological agenda.

The Near East and India: The Indus Valley

In ancient India also, western scholarship has tended to see Near Eastern influences, with an early wave passing from Mesopotamia into the Indus Valley in the third millennium B.C. It once seemed plausible that this diffusion wave may actually have carried the idea of urbanization across the Himalayas. The cultural similarity between Bronze Age Mesopotamia and the Bronze Age Indus Valley seemed so strong to Henri Frankfort, for example, two or three generations ago, that he opined that "an important element in the population of the two regions belonged originally to a common stock."[2] V. Gordon Childe thought that the Indus Valley culture was created by a colonizing wave from Mesopotamia, as did D. H. Gordon.[3] A generation later this still seemed the plausible option to Sumerologist Samuel Noah Kramer. "There is some reason to surmise," he said, "that the rise of the Indus cities was in the nature of a cultural 'explosion' . . . due to the arrival in India of a new ethnic group which had already attained a high degree of civilization."[4] "Now it is hardly likely," he ruminates, "that this people came to India from anywhere but Mesopotamia . . . [and] if it was a Mesopotamian people who loaded their boats with their families and possessions and abandoned their native homes to start life afresh in distant India—who was this people?" He speculates that it was not the Sumerians, whose script is too different, but some people whom the Sumerians displaced upon their arrival in Mesopotamia, perhaps the Ubaid people, who are otherwise unidentified ethnically.

Mortimer Wheeler proposed "idea diffusion" from both Mesopotamia and Egypt as among the causes of the Indus urbanization.[5] Influenced by the fact that Childe seemed to have established Mesopotamia as the principal source of western civilization, he insisted that "Mesopotamia, and none other, retains her world-priority," meaning priority in "the essential *idea* of civilization. Thanks to Mesopotamia, by the end of the fourth millennium the *idea* of civilization was in the air of the Middle East; and . . . ideas have wings."[6] Thus, borne by its wings, "the *idea* of civilization came to the Indus from the Euphrates and Tigris, and gave the Harappans their initial direction, or at least informed their purpose."[7] Stuart Piggott also doubts that the Indus culture "springs from any separate ultimate origin," and notes that at least in the technology of writing "it is likely to be dependent, in the last resort, on the inventions of late fourth-millennium date in Mesopotamia."[8]

Recently a tendency to reverse this part of the historical model has been gaining momentum. In general, the positing of intercultural diffusion has gone out of fashion, as the pressures of the postcolonial era have confronted scholarship with a demand for special care in matters which might be interpreted as implying cultural hierarchy. Explanations of changes in ancient cultures through migration theory have given way to accounts that stress "indigenous cultural development."[9] An Indian scholar brings out the postcolonial issue: "While most of them [past scholars] broadly belonged, in one way or the other, to the School of Hyper-diffusionism initiated by Elliot Smith, locating the birth of Civilization at one or two places only, such as Egypt and Mesopotamia, some of us totally reject it and call it as [sic] 'hangover' of Imperialism of some European countries with no substance in it."[10] Witzel concurs about the change in scholarly attitude, saying, "There has been, recently, a strong reaction against the invocation of external agents of change, such as migration and diffusion." But he goes on to suggest doubts about this reaction, saying, "However, that such forces [as migration and diffusion] were operating in the past is clear from innumerable historical examples."[11]

The Indus-Mesopotamia Trade

The Indus cities carried out trade with Mesopotamia from around 2500 through c. 1800 B.C., then, after an interval, resumed in the Assyrian period. Mesopotamia, which was poor in natural resources but regularly had bumper crops of wheat and wool, wanted wood, ivory, and above all copper; "highly priced luxury goods which were easily marketable in the emporium"[12] came along with them. In return went barley, silver, wool,

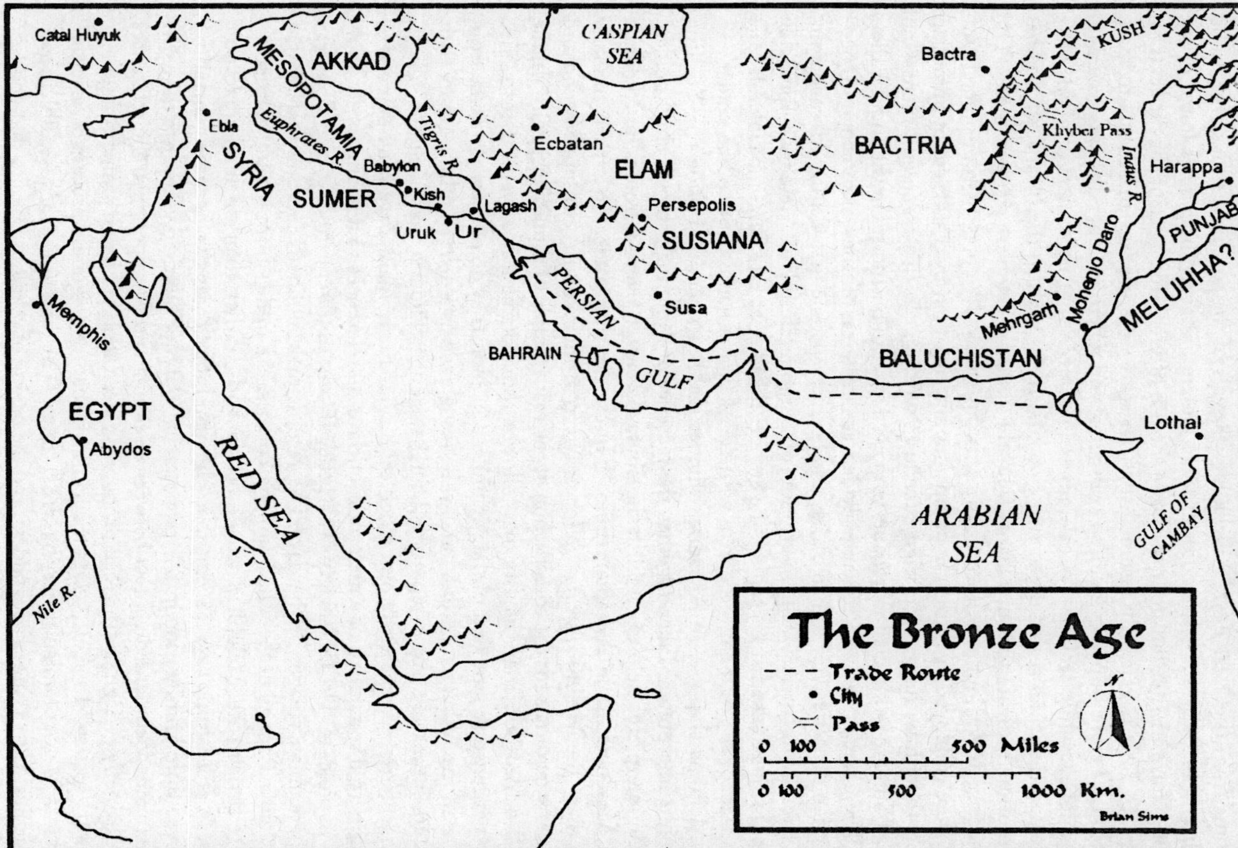

Map 2 The Bronze Age.

textiles, and small luxury items such as perfumed oil and leather goods. The bulk of this trade seems to have been in the Akkadian period, when, as Wheeler put it, "an imperialistic regime had emerged in Akkad and may have influenced . . . contemporary political development on the Indus."[13]

The evidence features "a little over thirty Indus seals [which] have been reported to come from the Near East,"[14] including "18 seals of the so-called Indus type found at Ur and in Babylon."[15] In addition "there are around 25 cylinder seals found at the Indus-Saraswati sites but not one shows the use of Cuneiform script for the texts on them . . . "[16] It is generally assumed that the seals were used by merchants to mark containers before shipping them, so seals are found where merchandise was sealed up and shipped, while sealings or seal-impressions mean that containers of goods were opened, rather than sealed up, at that site. The Indus seals in the Near East, on that assumption, indicate that merchants from the Indus Valley were resident there. The cylinder seals without cuneiform found at Indus sites may represent Indus merchants who were employed by Sumerian companies and had their own seals cut in Sumerian shape, though without the foreign cuneiform writing. On this argument, there is no sign of Sumero-Akkadian merchants who lived and ran businesses in the Indus Valley.

There are, however, concrete evidences, in texts of the Akkadian and neo-Sumerian dynasties,[17] of Indian crafts- and business-people first visiting Mesopotamia and later living in it. "[A]n inscription of Sargon refer[s] to Meluhhan [probably Indian] ships docked at his capital, the city of Akkad . . . a late Sargonic tablet datable to ca. 2200 B.C. . . . mentions a man with an Akkadian name entitled 'the holder' . . . of a Meluhha ship . . . an Akkadian cylinder seal bears the inscription . . . 'Su-ilisu, Meluhha interpreter.' Taken together, the presence of Meluhhan ships, a ship-'holder', and an interpreter help to establish the physical contact, over sea-routes, of Meluhha with Mesopotamia in Akkadian times."[18] Inscriptions of Gudea of Lagash similarly note that "'the Meluhhans *came up* (or *down*) from their country' to supply wood and other raw materials for the construction of the main temple of Gudea's capital."[19] In the Ur III or neo-Sumerian dynasty that followed the Akkadian, however, the texts "give us an entirely different view of the Meluhhans."[20] Now they do not seem to come from afar, as in the Akkadian period, but, "while recognized as a distinct ethnic group, their roles are intimately part of domestic Ur III society."[21] Though the "Meluhha village" that is referred to repeatedly over a half century "may originally have been founded as a commercial settlement or a mercantile enclave, all references to it unanimously imply that its role in Ur III society was little, if any, different from other Southern Mesopotamian villages of the day." The records of Meluhhans indicate that by that time "most if not all of them had Sumerian names."[22] Families from Meluhha, it seems, had settled in the Meluhhan village permanently, rather than on brief mercantile visits. In at least one case it seems that "the man himself was two or more generations removed from immigration into Mesopotamia."[23] "Three hundred years after the earliest textually documented contact between Meluhha and Mesopotamia, the references to a distinctly foreign commercial people have been replaced by an ethnic component of Ur III society." In short, "certain Meluhhans had undergone a process of acculturation into Mesopotamian society by Ur III times." The texts attest to "a Meluhhan garden dedicated to a Sumerian goddess, and the paying of religious taxes to that goddess' temple . . ."[24] Clearly, then, as Kosambi said, "There must have been a small but active settlement of Indian traders in Mesopotamia . . ."[25] And yet, as the same author noted, "The reciprocal settlement seems to have been absent or less prominent in India."

The situation is suggestive but ambiguous. A scholar whose overall orientation is to sever the origin of the Indus civilization from Mesopotamia says: "The balance of trade appears to have been in favor of India; more items were exported from India than imported from the Gulf and Mesopotamia."[26] The term "in favor of" seems to hint that India was the dominant partner in the mercantile relationship. Yet usually, the culture that has imported more is regarded as dominant. That goods from various parts of the world, including India, are found in Bronze Age Mesopotamia, especially in the Akkadian period and the following "Sumerian Renaissance," suggests that Mesopotamia was a dominant center that had agents seeking desired goods from wherever they could find them. Thus, "in his temple-building hymns, Gudea shows off with reports of distant regions he brought the materials from,"[27] including wood and other raw materials imported from "Meluhha." As Snell says, "The . . . Mesopotamians had contact with the periphery mainly to trade for or to seize raw materials, and in that contact they may have influenced the people they confronted."[28] Aside from Sumer itself, the only cultures known to have made cylinder seals were clearly on the receiving end of Sumerian influence, not the other way around.

Some seals of Indian manufacture found in Mesopotamia of the Sargonid period show a mixing of Sumerian and Indus Valley motifs, the Indus-style bull-at-manger, for example, appearing in conjunction with a Mesopotamian scorpion.[29] Other finds indicate that Indian motifs were borrowed by Mesopotamian craftspeople, also; a steatite ritual vase found in Tell Agrab, for example, has been described as "entirely Mesopotamian in execution . . . yet it shows . . . a building which shelters a Brahmanic bull standing in front of its manger."[30] At the same site was found a pot, seemingly dating from the first or second early dynastic period, portraying a Brahmanic bull without manger.

An important issue concerns the pre-Sargonid links—that is, contacts before about 2350 B.C. As Chakrabarty put it, "the basic theoretical significance of Pre-Sargonic contact between the Harappan Civilization and Mesopotamia is that it makes it possible to visualize the growth of urbanization in India at virtually the same time as Sumer."[31] If the Indus cities, in other words, were developed enough by the Early Dynastic period to engage in international trade, then they may have matured too early to have been stimulus-diffused from Sumer. Here the evidence suggests that pre-Sargonid trade with the Indus culture did exist, though perhaps less plentifully than in the following Akkadian period. Seal 420 from Mohenjo-Daro, for example, shows the bull-footed chair which is familiar from both Egypt and early dynastic Mesopotamia.[32] Steatite vessels of probable Indian origin are found in eight cities of Sumer and Elam in early Dynastic contexts.[33] A toilet set from Harappa is the same as one found in the first dynasty cemetery at Ur.[34] In pre-Sargonid graves at Kish were found etched carnelian beads and barrel-shaped stone weights appearing to be Harappan in manufacture, and so on.[35] The cones used for temple wall decoration at Warka are found again so used at Harappa.[36] Both cultures used cockle shells to hold cosmetics.[37] Jewelry has been found in the Indus Valley like that of Queen Pu-Abi of Ur, and ram sculptures very much like the lapis rams and bulls from the Royal Tombs at Ur.[38] The Indus "stamp-seals," which Childe calls "seal amulets," he traces back to the "seal-pendants" of Halaf and Ubaid times.[39] A boat on an Indus seal[40] is extraordinarily like those on Uruk seals and plaques, and the design of the four-wheeled wagon on an Indus seal is like that of the chariot on the Standard of Ur; even the wagon wheels are made in the Mesopotamian fashion. The humpless cattle shown on some Indus seals are unknown in India and may be imitations of Sumerian prototypes. The Sumerian lion swastika[41] is a forerunner of the pinwheel style composite beasts on some Indus seals, and the date of the Sumerian examples is the third early dynastic period.[42] The braid motif and composite beast motif on Indus seals combine Sumerian and other West Asian influences.[43] Clearly, then, although the Akkadian evidence suggests an expansion of the trade, it was already underway somewhat earlier.

New Developments

The belief of Wheeler and others that "the 'idea' of 'city' as a way of life came to India from Mesopotamia"[44] is based on the assumption that the Near Eastern trade occurred either just before or just at the start of "cultural takeoff"[45] in the Indus Valley. Heine-Geldern, for example, "maintained that the civilization of the Indus valley had appeared suddenly, out of the blue as it were, since no traces of earlier development were found in the initial period of excavation."[46] This implies colonization or at least a sudden and very effective stimulus diffusion. But Kenoyer and Meadow's recent claim that they have found Indus writing on potsherds dating back to 3200 or even 3300 B.C. suggests that take-off may have occurred earlier in the Indus Valley than had been thought—perhaps too early to have been stimulated by contact with Mesopotamia. Further, it has been cogently argued that civilizations, even if diffused from elsewhere, do not appear overnight. "This is true of the Chinese civilization and also equally true of the Mesopotamian Civilization. Each one of them took more than a thousand years to crystallize."[47]

In looking over the thousand years prior to the cities of Harappa and Mohenjo-daro in which they could have developed, one finds no sign of major external stimulus, but only the local interaction of Indian communities "at the micro level . . . between 3500 B.C. and 2600 B.C."[48] It was presumably from similar local interaction within a complex settlement system—implying crafts specialization and an emerging mercantile class—that the Mesopotamian cities developed. For Mesopotamia the background of a three- or four-tiered settlement system developed over centuries through the amalgamation of settlements into villages, villages into towns, and, finally, towns into cities.[49] In the case of India, however, "the failure of the early excavations to define an ancestral pre-Harappan period of cultural development indicated to many scholars that the Harappan culture represented yet another western intrusion into South Asia"[50]—a "western intrusion" that might have come from West Asia.

Recent excavations at Mehrgarh in Baluchistan have changed the situation,[51] "making plausible the hypothesis that the domestication of plants and animals and the rise of civilization in the Indus Valley was an indigenous cultural process."[52] The archeological record at the site "begins with the earliest settling by farming peoples, and goes through the middle of the third millennium"; that is, it covers continuously the development from the prepottery Neolithic to the phase immediately preceding the appearance of the Indus Valley cities.[53] A number of scholars feel that this material invalidates the hypothesis of Mesopotamian diffusion. "The new excavations have conclusively disproved the assumption of a sudden appearance of the Indus civilization without any traces of previous development. On the contrary, they have demonstrated that the Harappan civilization should be regarded as a legitimate phase of the evolution of developed village cultures. Urbanization was . . . prepared by the previous stage of the inner development of village cultures which had reached a fairly high level of development."[54] Thus the Indus civilization, like those of Mesopotamia and Egypt, was "the result of deep cultural processes originating in the Neolithic," and was "deeply rooted in local traditions."[55] In that case, input from outside seems unnecessary; supposedly the Indus culture was just about to sprout into urbanism at the same time lower Mesopotamia was. They happened side by side, at the same time, with no stimulus of one upon the other. Their village geographies, that is, happened to come to maturity at the same time. With the earlier dates for Indus Valley urbanization, and the antecedent preparatory stages shown at Mehrgarh, it now appears that "the growth of urbanization in India took place at virtually the same time as Sumer."[56]

Some other new sites offer partial confirmation of the Mehrgarh implications. In terms of the traditional civilizational requisite of monumentality, for example, at Rehman Dheri "monumental public architecture came in vogue much before the emergence of the mature Indus-Saraswati Civilization, the latter only elaborated the efforts of the former."[57] "There was a regular fortified settlement with massive mud-brick structures and houses of the Kot Dijians at Harappa [that] long preceded the mature phases of the Indus Saraswati Civilization."[58] Shaffer and Lichtenstein conclude that "the Mehrgarh data raise serious questions about diffusion as an all-encompassing explanation for major South Asian cultural developments."[59]

But there are several other considerations which must be borne in mind. In the first place, there seem to be exceptions to the idea that it takes a thousand years (more or less) to go from village to city. That period allows time for the development of the four-tiered settlement system, which has been identified as the condition leading to urbanization at Uruk in southern Mesopotamia, with specialization of industry and active trade throughout the system, architectural monumentality, and centralized bureaucracy bringing with it the need for writing. Yet northern Syria produced Ebla, "a community," says Nissen, "that, according to all our criteria, must be called an urban center,"[60] apparently by stimulus diffusion, seemingly without the supposedly requisite systemic preparation having been completed. At the present state of excavation, the site seems to need external stimulus, for it seems that "the complexity of the phase that used writing was the consequence of a very rapid development." The situation of ancient Susa is similar. Susa first adopted cuneiform writing and went into urbanization, then renounced or lost literacy, then after a while readopted it. After the initial urbanization there was a "decline of settlement in Susiana" so that "only very few places were actually inhabited apart from Susa, which, judging from the central terrace uncovered there, was clearly still an important urban center."[61] In other words, it seems that there can indeed be a major urban center without a four-tiered settlement system around it—a city in the middle of nowhere, but still a city. The abandonment of urbanization in Susa after it had once gotten underway suggests that it was initially premature in terms of local preparation. Urbanization was rushed because of stimulus diffusion, the system collapsed, then was revived a century or so later.

There are some signs that the situation in the Indus Valley may have paralleled that of Susa. One such sign involves the system of writing. "Writing first appears, or is first taken over," one scholar notes, "when a city's own development has progressed so far that the introduction of writing solves urgent and already existing problems."[62] These problems are those of conducting a large-scale centralized bureaucracy. But in the Indus civilization, "limited use of writing and a lack of other evidence for bureaucracy suggests, like the absence of monumentality [in architecture], that state level organization was absent." Sumerian writing was, for about six hundred years, used only for lists and as a mnemonic device; it did not develop the ability "not only of bringing to mind known things but also of teaching the unknown"[63] until the Early Dynastic Period, about 2600 B.C. The Indus Valley script, on the contrary, though it was written down for a millennium, does not seem ever to have developed to that stage; the brevity of the inscriptions suggests they did not communicate lengthy texts such as "the long literary and religious works known as 'The Cylinders of Gudea' (dating to around 2130), that were respectively close to 800 lines (Cylinder A) and 550 (Cylinder B) . . ."[64] In other words, it is not certain that the Indus script represents writing in the full sense—writing beyond the mnemonic device. As at Susa, writing may have arisen by stimulus diffusion rather than by the needs of a genuine state-level organization.

A second such sign is the fact that in the Indus Valley the archeological data fail "to confirm a three or four-tiered hierarchy usually associated with ancient states."[65] Just prior to urbanization many of the communities in the Kirthar hills toward the West relocated to the Indus plain, whereupon cities sprang up. The deep-tiered village system was not on the actual site of the cities but nearby. The Indus cities, then, lack the common function of centrality with regard to the inherited village system, which is part of the process as observed elsewhere. As described for Mesopotamia by Nissen, for example, the process involves a "settlement geography" which views "the growth of centrality as the visible expression of hierarchical subordination."[66] Population density in the midst of the thickening tiers of networks is one of the factors that cause the precipitation of a city. Yet the Indus cities were not in fact central to the village network that supposedly produced them. With new settlements on the Indus plain somewhat removed from the Kirthar settlements, it is questionable whether the process would apply. Without some stimulus, the village network in the Kirthar hills might simply have extended itself onto the plain. This too suggests that urbanization may have arisen somewhat prematurely in the Indus Valley, in which case some intrusive or diffusionist input is needed to account for it. Contrary to the excavators' opinion, the archeological sequence at Mehrgarh may even suggest such an event.

Jarrige and Meadow divide the strata at Mehrgarh into seven levels, the sequence being characterized by increasing complexity along with increasing trade contacts with Central Asia. The village system was growing along with foreign trade—but there is no sign of *West* Asian contacts in these seven levels. Then at the end of this period, when the Indus cities arose, evidence of West Asian trade appears. It looks as if the long village-growth process, had partly prepared the area for the transition to urbanization before the Mesopotamian contact, then was tipped over into urbanization by that contact. For most of its long, seven-stage, 4000-year development, though there are signs of gradual complexification, the site of Mehrgarh shows in various ways the static quality of cultures that have not yet experienced cultural takeoff. Stone sickles, for example, remained unchanged from level 2 to level 7, a period measured not in centuries but millennia. Even for so rudimentary a tool, which cannot be expected to change much, the consistency is impressive. The appearance is of a semi-stagnant provincial Chalcolithic culture lacking pretensions to urbanism and cultural complexity, suddenly stimulated into "take-off." Too much of the development is left at the end of the process for the claim that the early stages amounted to a full preparation. Shaffer may be right in claiming that the Mehrgarh material "makes plausible the hypothesis" of indigenous development. But plausible does not mean certain. There is still room for urban stimulation from outside—indeed, perhaps still need for it. Urbanization and Mesopotamian contact seem to appear at about the same time.

Which precipitated the other is an open question. "The Mesopotamian contact . . . ," as the Allchins said, "may well have complemented the internal developments already taking place there."[67]

Sumero-Dravidians?

If there is any mystery of antiquity comparable in importance to the identity of the Indus Valley people, it is the identity of the Sumerians themselves—the question where they came from. These two questions, in fact, have become increasingly embroiled with one another. Recently, as part of a wave of postcolonial corrections in the construction of history, it has been asked not only whether the Indus Valley may have been colonized from Sumer, but also whether Sumer may have been colonized from the Indus Valley. Von Soden observes that "since the discovery of the Indus civilization . . . it has been almost universally accepted that the Sumerians immigrated from the east."[68] The immigrants are regarded as having arrived in lower Mesopotamia either at the beginning of the Ubaid period (c. 5000 B.C.) or at the beginning of the Uruk period (perhaps c. 3500 B.C., but perhaps as late as 3250). In either case, the Sumerians seem to have fitted easily into an advanced Chalcolithic culture where writing was already in the early stages of development. Therefore, the implication is that they must have been from another advanced culture, and that points to the East. Bottero agrees that "the Sumerians must have arrived in Mesopotamia during the fourth millennium, apparently from the southeast."[69]

Von Soden further observes that "this immigration could have succeeded entirely by land if the Sumerians immigrated from somewhere in northern India," and refers suggestively to "the westward migration of the Sumerian groups, whose language may have been related to the Dravidian languages of India."[70] The idea that the Sumerians came from the Indus Valley and originally spoke Dravidian, which like Sumerian is agglutinative, has figured prominently in what have been called "new age" revisions of ancient history—or, less kindly, the "lunatic fringe."[71] It has also been asserted by Daniélou ("the Sumerians, who probably came from the Indus . . .").[72] Nissen notes more conventionally, "Sumerian is an agglutinative language that so far still cannot be linked to any other language in the world."[73]

One major variable is the date at which the Sumerians arrived in Mesopotamia. Snell asks, "Were they Ubaidians?" and answers, "it seems likely that they were because there are no major archeological breaks after the Ubaid."[74] If they arrived at the beginning of the Ubaid Period, an event he dates to 5000 B.C., this would put the Sumerians in Mesopotamia in time to be important in the development of writing, which by that time had not progressed beyond the "tokens" presented by Schmandt-Besserat.[75]

Nissen chooses a later date: "If there is any moment in time to which we can assign the arrival of the Sumerians with a high degree of probability, it is this first period [the Uruk/Warka period] of settlements in large areas of the southern Babylonian plain."[76] Sumerian settlements then marked the beginning of the Uruk period—"the period we designate as the beginning of early high civilization."[77] Von Soden chooses a still later date, placing the Sumerians' arrival "in the last quarter of the fourth millennium."[78] That chronology, however, would leave them little participation in the invention of writing, of which the earliest examples "come not only from the soil of Sumer at Uruk, . . . but also from Akkad, at Kis[h],"[79] and which may therefore have been created by the Semitic predecessors of the Akkadians rather than by Sumerians. By the time the newcomers arrived, the process of "civilization"—urbanization, literacy, monumentality, bronze

Figure 6 Sumerian seal impression, third millennium B.C., showing "Gilgamesh" figure holding two lions in symmetrically flanking "dompteur" position.

metallurgy, and so on—may have already been well underway. But somehow the new arrivals managed to fit in—and even became the leaders, or "pacemakers,"[80] of the urban revolution that was already ongoing. An Ubaid arrival, allowing them to shape that revolution from a fairly early stage, would seem more plausible on this count.

THE DATE OF WRITING

For some time the consensus has been running toward Mesopotamia as the earliest literate culture. It is common to read of "humanity's oldest system of writing, the later cuneiform,"[81] and "the invention of writing in Babylonia around 3100 B.C."[82] But Kennoyer and Meadow may have pushed the date for the Indus script back by five or six hundred years—to 3300–3200 B.C.—and a comparably early date has recently been claimed for Egyptian hieroglyphs.[83] German archeologists have announced new carbon dates for tombs at Abydos that place the hieroglyphics within them as early as 3200, perhaps even 3400 B.C. These new dates are not solid yet, but if they hold up, either Egypt or Harappa, in fact, may have produced "the earliest system of writing in the world, dated to ca. 3300 B.C."[84] The date might allow just barely time enough for colonizers from the Indus valley, proceeding at breakneck speed, to have taken both urbanization and writing to Mesopotamia with them, rather than the other way around. This would be a stunning coup indeed in India's attempt to break into the front rank of Bronze Age high civilizations.

In keeping with the recently dominant indigenous approach to archeology, some suggest that the first writing systems grew up independently but simultaneously.[85] But Wheeler, however discredited he might seem to some,[86] argues that the postulate that "in each of three lands so accessible to one another the immensely complex idea of an evolved civilization [or a writing system] should, within the narrow space of some five or six centuries, have emerged spontaneously and without cross-reference, is too absurd to merit argument."[87]

Finally there seem to be three problems with the view that urbanization was completely indigenous to the Indus Valley. First is the geographical separation of the cities from the village network in which, according to the standard model based primarily on Mesopotamean Uruk, they should have exercised the functions of centrality. Second is the fact that the Indus script might not have developed fully beyond the mnemonic device, so as to perform the complex function of a large bureaucracy. Third is the issue of outside stimulus. The existence of the Mesopotamian trade clearly offers a possible channel for such stimulus, and the archeological sequence at Mehrgarh may be interpreted as suggesting the need for it. While these factors certainly do not eliminate the possibility of indigenous development, they surround it with question marks. In Uruk in southern Mesopotamia, in contrast, the situation allows for no other possibility than indigenous development. The village network was full on all sides of the center where the city would arise, writing went into full bureaucratic development, and no candidates for outside stimulus are available. Wheeler's point about the unlikely coincidence of simultaneous parallel development in the same general area may be counted as a fourth.

Question II: What is the Significance of the Iconographic Issue?

Engrossed by its indigenous reinterpretation of the Indus Valley material, recent scholarship has ceased to discuss the fact that Indus religious iconography is very closely related to that of Mesopotamia. Even if Mehrgarh is accepted as removing the need for external input leading to urbanization, even if the Indus script can be reliably dated to 3300 B.C., still an iconographic parallelism remains that is so extensive as to eliminate mere coincidence and that must be taken into account in assessing the nature of the Indus culture. A generation and more ago, when scholars were discussing this issue, it

Figure 7 Sumerian seal impression, Uruk period, fourth to third millennium B.C., showing central mountain-and-tree symmetrically flanked by goats with their forehooves raised and placed upon it.

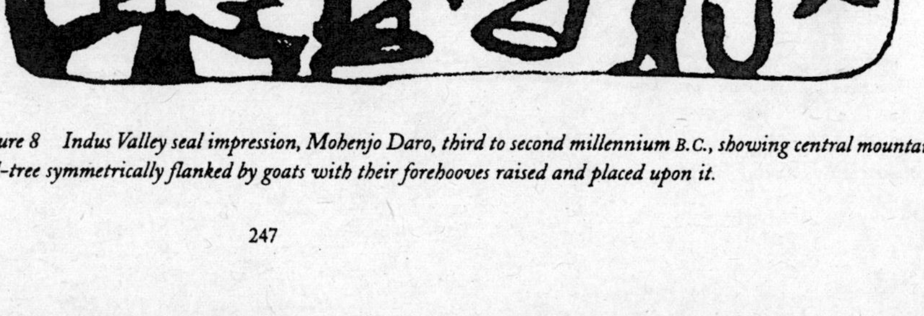

Figure 8 Indus Valley seal impression, Mohenjo Daro, third to second millennium B.C., showing central mountain-and-tree symmetrically flanked by goats with their forehooves raised and placed upon it.

Figure 9 Indus Valley seal impression, Mohenjo Daro, third to second millennium B.C.*, showing "Gilgamesh" figure holding two lions in symmetrically flanking "dompteur" position.*

was generally assumed that Mesopotamian iconography had been transplanted or diffused to India.

A basic structural format in Sumero-Akkadian iconography is the heraldic flanking composition, in which an object on the central axis is symmetrically flanked

Figure 10 Achaemenian seal, c. sixth century B.C.*, showing "Gilgamesh" figure holding two winged lions or griffins in symmetrically flanking "dompteur" position.*

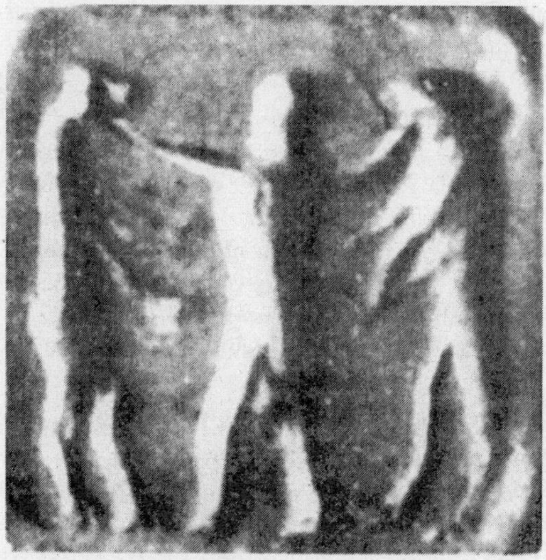

Figure 11 Indus Valley seal impression, Mohenjo Daro, third to second millennium B.C., *showing "Gilgamesh" figure holding two lions in symmetrically flanking "dompteur" position.*

by more or less identical objects on both sides. This format had not previously appeared in the world's iconographies, but is characteristic of all cultures formed on the Sumerian model and is found commonly in the Indus Valley. An Indus seal shows an eagle heraldically flanked by serpents;[88] both the eagle-and-serpent motif and the heraldic flanking format are characteristic Sumero-Akkadian elements. An Indus seal of a ritual of the tree goddess[89] shows clearly, in the lower left-hand corner, the motif, so well-known in Mesopotamia, of a central mountain or hillock flanked by two goats with their front feet on it and a tree or pole of some kind rising from the top. One face of a triangular seal from Mohenjo-daro shows the central tree flanked by goats, identical in form to many Mesopotamian icons.[90] These icons emphasizing centrality seem characteristic of a society which has just evolved through the village-settlement hierarchy into the social centrality of urbanism. Numerous other Indus examples of these types have survived.[91] Some show the Sumerian icon called the *dompteur* or Gilgamesh: a male hero standing between two lions who symmetrically flank him and whom he is holding in a gesture of mastery.[92] A variant of the heraldic flanking structure, the *dompteur* or "master," underlines the sense of dominance that urban centrality seemed to carry in a village-based world. A burial urn from cemetery H at Harappa shows two *dompteurs,* each mastering two bulls. They have long hair and seem to be naked, as the central figure often is in Mesopotamian examples.[93] These motifs—the mountain flanked by goats, the hero mastering lions—are among the central icons of Mesopotamian religion. Since Heinrich Zimmer's writings there has been an odd silence about these and other iconographic parallels, even a willful denial of this material among scholars, Indian and western, who have committed themselves to the ideology of indigenous development.

At a later period the heraldic flanking composition was naturalized and assimilated in India and became (as in Mesopotamia) the most basic iconographic structure. The Buddha meditating, or almost any Indian deity, is shown on a central axis with heraldically flanking figures. One example among many is the Buddhist icon sometimes called the "Bath of Lakshmi," in which the goddess stands on a lotus, heraldically flanked by elephants with their trunks raised, which appears in a railing medallion of the stupa at Bharut. This icon probably passed into the Buddhist milieu from the Jain. It occurs in the *Kalpa Sūtra*'s description of the dream of the (second) mother of the Jain leader Mahāvīra on the night when the embryo was placed in her womb; at that moment, "she sat on the top of Mt. Himavat, reposing on a lotus in the lotus lake, anointed with water from the strong and large trunks of the guardian elephants" (*Kalpa Sūtra* 36). The origins of Jain iconography, as one scholar said, "reach back, like the origins of Jainism itself, to the remotest depths of the unrecorded Indian past."[94] In fact, they may reach back past the Indus Valley into the heart of Sumer.

The Priest-King and Other Figures

The sculptural figure which Marshall called the "priest-king" wears a robe bearing a trefoil pattern which, one scholar said, "to judge from its frequent appearance at Mohenjo-daro and Harappa is obviously a sacred symbol."[95] This design motif does not occur on Indus objects presently published from the era before Mesopotamian contacts. It does occur in sacred contexts in the Near East, in a tradition thousands of years old already by the time of the Indus Valley civilization. It is found, for example, at Çatal Hüyuk c. 6000 B.C. inside the spots of the leopards which represent the goddess in her devouring aspect.[96] Later, in a thematically related use, it marks a sacrificial bull in Uruk.[97] It is also borne by the Egyptian cow-goddess Hathor as she nurses the pharaoh in the afterlife.[98] Similarly contextualized at Mohenjo-daro, it appears on a bull statue,[99] and at both Mohenjo-daro and Harappa on lingams. Perhaps most significantly, it is not only the "priest-king" of the Indus Valley who wears a robe with the trefoil on it but the Akkadian king-god Marduk.[100] The easiest diffusion path which would account for all these occurrences starts in Çatal Hüyuk, drifts southward into Sumer and Egypt, then makes its way oversea to the Indus.

The "Priest-King," furthermore, has his hair worn in what has been called Sumerian fashion, in a bun at the back of his head, and his upper lip is shaved, again in Sumerian fashion. The half-shut eyes (which some have thought a sign of meditation) occur also in early clay figures from Kish and Ur[101]—the latter a city where Indus

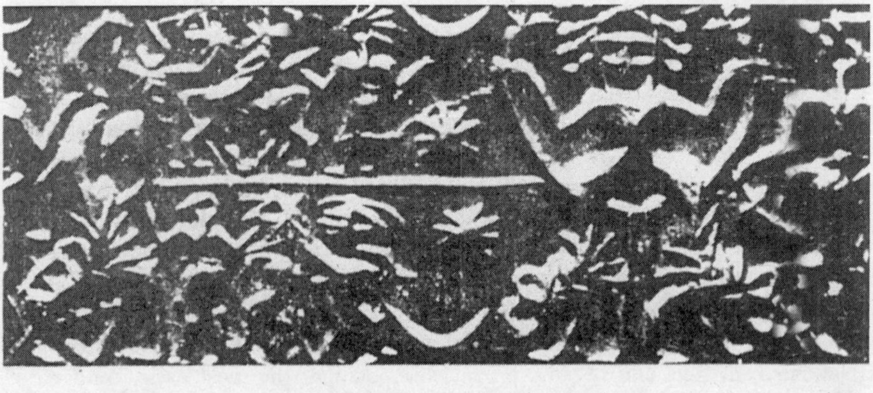

Figure 12 Sumerian seal impression, third millennium B.C., showing goddess in tree with god bull below, detail.

Figure 13 Indus Valley seal impression, Mohenjo Daro, third to second millennium B.C., showing goddess in tree with bull-god and seven sprout-headed figures below.

objects were found, in fact the "port of entry," as Oppenheim says, for the Indus copper trade in the Larsa period.[102] It is possible that some special relationship existed between this Sumerian city and the Indus culture. An Akkadian record is preserved of an official Indian (Meluhhan) interpreter, and of merchants resident at Ur from Dilmun, presumed to be an entrepot, on the island of Bahrain, between Sumer and the Indus.[103]

The complex of shared iconographic motifs includes a goddess represented either as seated in or as identical to a tree (familiar from Bronze Age Egypt and perhaps from Mesopotamia). The Sumerian cylinder seal impression in Figure 12 seems to show a goddess seated solidly in tree and holding on with her hands, while a horned god stands nearby; the composition is uncannily like the Indus configuration in Figure 13, where a goddess sits in a tree and is worshipped from below by a horned male deity behind whom stands his emblem, the bull.[104] Another icon represents Ninhursag as "with a leafy crown on her head, her shoulders covered with sprouting branches, her hair flowing out behind her, and holding the branch of fertility in her hand." Such figures are found not only in Bronze Age Mesopotamia and the Indus Valley, but also in Egypt, where the Sycamore Goddess is frequently seen standing in her tree whence she dispenses food and drink to the *ba* of the deceased in the afterlife. Dompteur, bull-and-lion, and so on, are also found in Egypt. To a meaningful extent these three societies would seem to have occupied the same general cultural zone. Correspondences of detail are sometimes remarkable. In Figure 13, for example, the Indus valley seal impression of ritual worship of a tree goddess by a kneeling male deity and bull, there are seven

Figure 14 Akkadian seal impression, third millennium B.C., *showing seated tree-goddess with sprout-headed youngster on her lap.*

sprout-headed children arrayed in attendance. Figure 14, another Mesopotamian example, shows a tree goddess enthroned before the tree with a similarly drawn sprout-headed child on her lap.

The complex also includes a goddess associated with a lion or tiger, a lion overtaking and leaping on a bull from behind, and a male figure represented as a bull, a phallus, or a serpent. Horns as a sign of divinity (or something like it) "are presumably a Mesopotamian survival," as Rowland notes,[105] as, perhaps, is the eight-petalled rosette like the Mesopotamian "Ishtar rosette," but found at Kunal in the Indus Valley.[106] The most common of the "stamp-seal" motifs—the bull standing at (what seems to be) a manger—relates to the dominant Sumerian motif of Feeding the Temple Herd. Furthermore, the dot-centered circles which tend to ornament these

Figure 15 Sumerian seal impression, Uruk period, fourth to third millennium B.C., *showing bull associated with vegetation being attacked by lion from behind.*

Figure 16 *Painted pottery fragment, Mohenjo Daro, third to second millennium* B.C., *showing bull associated with vegetation being attacked by lion or other feline from behind.*

Figure 17 *Indus Valley objects, Kunal, third to second millennium* B.C., *eight-petalled rosette on upper left.*

Figure 18 Offering stand from Ur, detail.

mangers or altars are found commonly in Sumerian religion in the cult of Ishtar, especially at Brak (with, like the trefoil, an earlier life at Catal Huyuk and a still earlier one in Magdalenian art). The fact that some of these bulls are bearded links them to the Sumerian examples and, again, especially those at Ur. The presence of a deity virtually identical to the Sumerian bull-man motif points in the same direction (Figures 19 and 20).

The Indus Valley stamp seals portraying figures seated in the yogic position *mūlabandhāsana*[107] have several possible Mesopotamian parallels. The motif of three-facedness, for example—or four-facedness if the figures are intended to have another face to the rear—has often been connected with later Hindu many-faced figures. But in the other direction the motif leads to Sumer, where various three- and four-faced figures are known. At Ischali in central Mesopotamia, for example, a four-faced god was worshipped.[108] The closest antecedent to the posture of *mūlabandhāsana* is the so-called Displayed Female motif, in which sometimes the heels are very close together.[109] Further, some Sumerian figures are seated on slightly raised platforms much like those on the Indus seals.[110] Figures seated cross-legged and assuming ritual hand-positions also occur,[111] though not precisely in the heels-joined position. The animals surrounding the "Śīva" figure on the Indus seals answer to the animals floating around the scene in many Sumerian cylinder seals.[112]

Another genre of similarity is composite beast forms. In both cultures, for example, images that combine bull and elephant—the bull's body sporting an elephantine trunk—are found; as Kosambi noted, the motif must be presumed to have diffused from India to the Near East.[113] A three-headed horned beast of some kind is portrayed in one Indus seal and a three-headed bull in another (Figure 22); a Mesopotamian or proto-Elamite cylinder seal impression shows a striding bull with three heads and a kneeling bull-man with three heads (Figure 21).[114] A Persian Gulf–type seal from Mohenjo-daro portrays six animals, perhaps part bull and part tiger, whose bodies merge into a common center, creating a pinwheel shape; several Mesopotamian seal impressions show groups of four, either men or beasts, joined at a center and forming a cross between a pinwheel and swastika effect (Figure 23).[115] An Indus seal showing four tigers merged into a swastika shape is even closer to the Mesopotamian versions (Figure 24).[116]

The possibility of these and other shared motifs having migrated from the Indus to the Euphrates seems less plausible than the other way around, because they show developmental background in Mesopotamia from Samarra and Ubaid sites, and because they are both more common and seem more culturally integrated in Mesopotamia. Another reason why it is easier to imagine these motifs diffusing from Mesopotamia into India than the other way around is that there is no doubt that they did diffuse from Mesopotamia to numerous other ancient cultures including Syrian,

Figure 19 Sumerian ivory figurine, third millennium B.C., *showing bull-man.*

Urartian, Egyptian, Persian, Cretan, and Greek. That this complex of motifs should have arrived in the Indus Valley too is just more business as usual. If indeed it should turn out that the Sumerians came from north India, it nevertheless remains the case that Mesopotamia became the center from which this form of civilization spread outward.

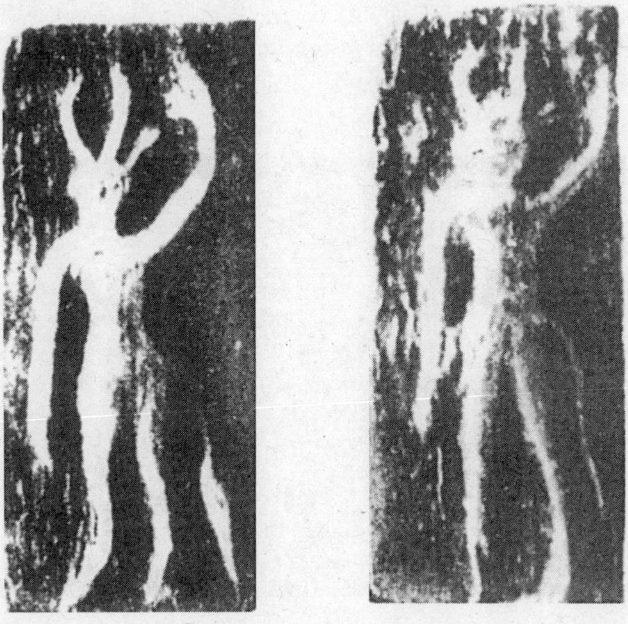

Figure 20 Indus Valley plaques, third to second millennium B.C., *showing bull-man.*

Figure 21 Proto-Elamite seal impression, third millennium B.C., *showing three-headed bull and three-headed bull-man.*

INTO THE ARYAN COMMUNITY

A second wave of relationship consists of influences on the Vedic Aryans, who, on their long path from the Indo-European homeland into northwest India, seem to have passed through the Near East and taken its imprint. Their sacred book, the *Ṛg Veda*, shows the influence of Mesopotamian mythology as conspicuously as does the *Book of Genesis*. The main event in Vedic mythology, the battle between Indra and the serpent demon Vritra, clearly parallels both the battle between Marduk and Tiamat in the *Akkadian Creation Epic* and the related Egyptian myth of the battle of Re and Apophis. In all three cases, a hero figure who represents manifestation, light, or the appearance of the world out of darkness, defeats a giant serpent associated with darkness and hiddenness. Various details coincide. Tiamat-Kingu, for example, the monster destroyed by

Figure 22 Indus Valley seal impressions, Mohenjo Daro, third to second millennium B.C., *showing three-headed bulls or bull-like creatures.*

Figure 23 Syrian seal impression, c. 1700 B.C., showing four entwined male figures suggesting swastika form.

Marduk, has seven heads, and Indra, in the *Ṛg Veda*, is called "Killer of the Seven."[117] Books 1–9 of the *Ṛg Veda*, which are dominated by this subject, may have been composed under Akkadian influence during the period of wandering southward through Central Asia before entering India. Akkadian words found in books 1–9 include a key word from the *Creation Epic*, *apsu*, "the deep."[118]

The *Ṛg Veda* features two types of gods, a roughly "Olympian" group known as *devas*, and their adversaries, known as *asuras*. If the confrontation between the two groups is in fact the entry of the Aryans into India at the time of or shortly after the abandonment of the Indus Valley cities, then the *asuras* were the gods of the Indus culture, at least in part Near Easternized, whom the Aryans, with the help of their *devas*, were replacing. Various scholars have seen the name *asura* as meaning Assyrian.[119] But at *Ṛg Veda* VI.67 the home of the *asuras* is called Hariyupuja, that is, probably Harappa in the Indus Valley. Some have proposed that Assyrian kings ruled parts of the Indus Valley and were conquered by the Aryans, who registered them as the *asuras*. It would seem to be going overboard to postulate Assyrian rulers in India. In any case, the *asuras*' teachings which are opposed to those of the Aryan *devas* may be called the Sumero-Indian tradition. The *Bhagavad Gīta* says that the *asuras*' doctrine is that "the world originated from the union of the male and the female and its force is eros."[120] This, which became the essential doctrine of the Tantras, may be traced not only back to the Indus culture but beyond it to Mesopotamia.

At the next stage of the relationship, the religious innovations of the Middle Vedic literature may have involved both Dravidian elements and others from the Near East. The *Atharva Veda*, it seems, represents the *asura* view as against the *deva*-oriented *Ṛg Veda*. It is in the period of the *Atharva Veda* that the obsession with magic and

Figure 24 Indus Valley seal impressions, Mohenjo Daro, third to second millennium B.C., *showing four entwined lions suggesting swastika form, detail.*

witchcraft enters Vedic culture.[121] The *asuras* are especially connected with magic (*Ṛg Veda* X.124.5, 138.3), and the word *māyā*, magical illusion, is used in connection with them. For whatever reasons, the Aryan community at this time seems to have allowed a controlled inflow of elements from the non-Aryan tradition of ascetic shamanic-yogic body practices and possibly protomeditation. Figures such as the Vratyas, non-Vedic Aryan ascetics and magicians described in the fifteenth book of the *Atharva Veda*, and the Muni, a "pre-Aryan magician"[122] described in the tenth book of the *Ṛg Veda* (X.136) as long-haired, naked, smeared with dust, and "maddened [or ecstatic] with silence [or austerity]" (*unmadita mauneya*), were introduced into the Aryan community and into its religious literature. These figures are usually connected with later Śaiva cults, but there are clear connections between them and the Ājīvika-Jain lineages, too. Ājīvikas as well as Śaiva yogis went naked, smeared themselves with ashes, and vowed silence. "*Keśin*," "long-haired," is a name used not only of the Muni but of the Jain *tīrthankaras* Rishabha and Pārśva.[123]

While these non-Aryan religious leaders were being naturalized in the Aryan community, the Aryan establishment, as part of the same reform, called in a wave of Near Eastern influence that involved the doctrine of macranthropy, or macrocosm/microcosm correspondence—that is, the *ātman* doctrine, or the source of it. The *Puruṣasūkta*, or "Hymn to the Cosmic Person," from *Ṛg Veda* X, with its enormous import for the development of monistic thought, is an example of a type of pantheistic hymn common in New Kingdom Egypt and, at the period in question, diffused from there into Mesopotamia, whence it may have come into India around 1200–1000 B.C.

The *Atharva Veda*, further, has the word *tiamat* (*AV* V.13.6), suggesting renewed acquaintance with the *Akkadian Creation Epic*.[124] The *Atharva Veda* has been described by one Indian scholar as the "Chaldeanization" of the Aryan culture.[125] The goddess Umā (mentioned in the *Kena Upaniṣad*) may derive from the Babylonian word *umma* or *umā*, meaning "other," an epithet of Ishtar. Scholars have often identified the Middle Vedic period as a period when the Aryan community admitted elements of Dravidian culture and religion. It seems that, even beyond this, elements of Mesopotamian culture were imported by some channel, too. Further, it seems that the two were not at odds.

The Brahmanical establishment controlled the inflow of these elements in such a way as to assimilate them to the Vedic sacrificial tradition. This practice of assimilating the attractive elements of the Sumero-Indian tradition by forcing them into a Vedic context went on for a long time, sometimes transparently. The *Ṛgvidhana*, for example, is a late collection of non-Aryan magical practices, all of which have been rationalized as Aryan by connecting them with Vedic verses.

A fourth wave of Near Eastern influence with a strong Persian aspect entered India in about 540–530 B.C., with the conquest of northwest India by Cyrus, and a fifth after the fall of Persepolis to Alexander the Great in about 330 B.C., when a formidable influx of Persian stonecutters and skilled craftsmen of all kinds seems to have entered India seeking work. This last brought with it much visual imagery that had not appeared yet in the Indus or Vedic periods, but would become central to later Hinduism. Specifically, Sumerian iconographs such as the caduceus—the central upright rod entwined by two serpents which became the emblem of the occult physiology of *kuṇḍalinī* yoga—seem to enter at this time.

Egypt and India

One scholar was sufficiently impressed by the apparent affinities between Egyptian and Indian iconographies to suggest "it might be arguable that the Indian development of yoga was colonial to Memphis."[126] The extraordinary similarity is a puzzle, because the evidence to back up a hypothesis of diffusion is meager. Though Tacitus says (*Annals* II.60) that Rameses I conquered Bactria, there is virtually no archeological evidence to support the assertion. Few Egyptian remains are found with the relics of the Indus Valley–Persian Gulf trade. Some beads seemingly of Egyptian manufacture were found in the Indus Valley.[127] One scholar feels that "the discovery of two terracotta mummies from Lothal" amounts to "concrete evidence . . . to prove direct contact with Egypt." He notes that Egyptian mummies are said to have been "wrapped in Indian muslin."[128] Possehl, in addition, observes that "the food supply of the Harappan civilization" around 2000 B.C. involved millets "of African origin." "There is, however, no clear non-biological evidence for contact between India and Africa during or prior to the second millennium."[129] That's about it, at present, for archeological evidence.

But it is questionable whether clear archeological evidence is to be expected in this case. Near Eastern influences tended to move in combinations. The Hittites, for example, received a mixed Mesopotamian and Egyptian culture, as did the Assyrians, the Hebrews, the Persians, the Minoan Cretans, and the Greeks. After the Amarna Age, Egyptian images, tales, myths, and icons were parts of a broad cross-cultural stream of elements flowing out of the Near East. These mixed influences were more likely to be encountered along with Mesopotamian export goods than Egyptian, due to Mesopotamian control of trade and the near-isolationism of Egyptian culture during most of the Bronze Age.

Despite the dearth of archeological evidence the documentary record shows striking parallels. Similarities between Egyptian and Indian mythological styles, for example, include: the way the gods turn into one another and include one another, the extravagant animal and composite forms for them, and the monistic mysticism underlying the polytheistic mythologies. There are also extraordinary similarities of details; the Egyptian myth of the Eye of Re, for example, which he sends out to destroy the world, is echoed in an Indian myth in which Śīva's third eye nearly burns up the universe like a laser. Both Re's and Sīva's power-eyes are in addition to the normal two and are located in the forehead.[130] The Egyptian myth in which Osiris ascends to heaven over the spine of the sky-goddess Nut is echoed by the yogic imagery in which the soul energy must be made to ascend from the base of the spine to the top, and when it arrives at the top, enlightenment occurs.[131] The Vedic myth in which the serpent Vritra traps the ocean inside himself and is forced by Indra to release it is astonishingly similar to the Egyptian myth in which the serpent Apophis drinks up the ocean and, being conquered by Re, vomits it out again.[132] Unusual imagery recurs on both sides. In Egyptian mythology Isis receives from the moon the seed of Horus, and in Indian mythology the moon is thought of as a cupful of sperm.[133] The *Book of Thoth* is described in Egyptian texts as existing under the Sea of Coptos guarded by serpents; Buddhist lore similarly has the image of sacred books guarded by serpents at the bottom of the ocean. Egyptian iconography includes gods "seated on coiled up serpents";[134] the Buddha meditating while seated on the serpent called Mucalinda is much the same, and the Hindu icon of Viṣṇu reclining on the serpent Ananta is closely related. Winged serpent vehicles are common in Egyptian afterlife iconography and in Buddhist and Hindu iconographies as well.

The deification of certain abstractions, such as Speech or Language, is another practice that seems to have begun in Egypt. Speech is first deified in the *Memphite Theology*, where Ptah creates the world by means of heart and tongue, that is, thought and its embodiment in speech; it reappears later in the Amon-Re theology, where every word out of Amon's mouth is considered identical to him, and his speech receives worship as himself. This idea spread far. It is found in Yahweh's creation by speech in the *Old Testament*; in pre-Socratic Greece, where Heraclitus seems to consider the Word (*Logos*) as a divine principle; and in India, where the Word (*Vāc*) is worshipped as the universal creative power. *Vāc* appears in the tenth book of the *Ṛg Veda*, that is, in the Middle Vedic literature (*Ṛg Veda* X.71, X.81, X.125, etc.), and may have entered India as part of the wave of Near Eastern influence that brought the concept of the Cosmic Person with it.

Another element of Egyptian thought that may have entered India in the Middle Vedic period is the deification of time. Re, conceived as the Lord of Eternity, is the first element in the diffusion series. He is set off against the Sumerian Lord and Lady Days of Life by the fact that he is a lone male deity of time; this is the key to the diffusion pattern that follows. In the *Atharva Veda*, the god Kāla (Time) appears in India, and later in the Upaniṣads.[135] The *Maitrī Upaniṣad* says: "From Time do creatures, flowing, issue. From Time they grow and prosper."[136] Among the Jains, Kāla (Time) was worshipped as a substance in which the transformation of things takes place.[137] In the book of Pherecydes of Syros also—an author whose work was clearly influenced either by the early Upaniṣads or by their sources—deified Chronos appears, as he does in Phoenician cosmogonies. The Orphic god Phanes, the Revealer, who manifests the universe out of himself, was created by the god Chronos Ageroas, or Ageless Time.

The Time god is everywhere the same, confirming his single origin; in Pherecydes, in the Phoenician cosmogonies, and in the Indian sources, "he creates out of his own seed, without a consort . . . In each case he is not himself the builder of the material world but the progenitor of a divine demiurge."[138] "[S]omewhere, in about the seventh or sixth century, the old Egyptian myth was refashioned in the more abstract and acceptable form in which it persuaded Iran and India in the East, and in the West Pherecydes."[139] In the iconography, Phanes appears wrapped round by a serpent, as does the Persian deity Zurvan Akarana, also "Ageless Time." Both icons go back to the Sumerian icon of Ningizzida, who is represented as an anthropomorphic male wrapped around by a serpent—a creature commonly associated with myths of cyclical time.[140]

Despite the uneven quality of the archaeological evidence, Egyptian influences seem to have been flowing into both the Greek and the Indian streams of early philosophical thought. Egyptian mythologems, as previously mentioned,[141] control the afterlife myth of the Orphics and of an Upaniṣadic text. Egyptian New Kingdom pantheism is the closest parallel to early Indian monism; the Amon-Re hymns gave birth ultimately to both the pantheistic Orphic hymns and the *Puruṣasūkta*, and something like reincarnationism did in fact exist in Egyptian thought.

Summing Up

It seems, finally, that significant elements of Near Eastern thought and imagery—primarily from Mesopotamia but also from Egypt—are embedded throughout the record of Indian culture, from the Indus Valley on. These include elements in the myth of cycling time (especially Manu's version), in the doctrine of reincarnation as purveyed by Jain texts and Upanisads, and in the occult physiology of enlightenment in *kuṇḍalinī* yoga. These have been dealt with in earlier chapters,[142] and the materials in the present chapter should be regarded in conjunction with them. So massive and crucial is the totality of this input that it would seem ill-advised in the extreme to attempt to account for the formation of Indian civilization without it. Still, it would be an equally egregious mistake to conclude that India lacks a distinctive and world-important character of its own. Nothing, it seems, comes out of nothing, and no culture is born by parthenogenesis. Ancient Greek culture has had at least as much input from the same sources without being denied its own "miraculous" selfhood.

Question III: What happened to the shaman?

Shamanism is practiced primarily in tribal cultures and village-sized communities. It is a one-man operation, scaled to service a small clientele. When this form of social group was replaced by the urban state, adjustments were made. The relatively large urban groups of Mesopotamia were based on irrigation agriculture, an economy requiring an orderly coordination of the community. Such regularity was produced in part by the agricultural calendar and the complex ritual observations connected with it. So fundamental were these that neglect of them would create great unease. The sacred acts of the community not only communicated with the spirits of earth and weather, but also preserved social order and pertained to practical questions which really affected people, such as when to open and shut certain irrigation channels. This business could not be left to independent visionaries each of whom had his own particular access to the cosmic power structure.

The shamanic profession was a one-man operation not only because constituencies were apt to be small. It appealed, Eliade says, to some of those who, in modern societies, would become psychotics.[143] It is in effect a way to mediate their psychosis and society, to turn their psychosis into a profession. The shaman was an independent and isolated worker by definition. His power dreams were his alone; his relationships with the spirit allies were his alone. Powers that rise in part from inner sources are hard to share with colleagues, each of whom is a shaman, too, with his own relationship system in the power realms, and no two systems quite alike.

For the transition to the state this power relationship was externalized to lessen its uncontrollability and generalized to a caste of people to eliminate what Eliade calls the individual shamanic "vocation." This is the moment when shamanic individualism began to give way to the priestly profession. In a priestly college there is a hierarchy, and each individual is not free to assert his or her own model of the whole. A society's transition from shaman to priest involves, therefore, the abandonment of the individual power vision in favor of a doctrine codified by the leaders of the priesthood.

In such a situation the shamanic inheritance could be dealt with in different ways. The shamanic lore of spirit-journeys and encounters could be sublimated into priestly myths and doctrines reoriented to serve the emerging state. Similarly, the drug-taking aspect of shamanic practice could be frozen into a communal ritual. A group of people sitting around in a controlled ritual setting drinking a special concoction (whether *amanita muscaria* or something else) and reciting preordained texts is a far tamer and more socially manageable event than a set of separate shamanic performances. Alternatively, shamanism could be hidden in a special esoteric cult out of public view or, finally, shamanism could be cast out. Eliade says that shamans "go underground"[144] at this time. Presumably he means that vestigial shamanism becomes an asocial stream of activity cut off from the established religions of the emerging states, not unlike the Cynics and Orphics in Greece, the Pāśupatas in India, the Vratya of *Atharva Veda* XV, the modern Gypsies, and so on.

In such groups, vocations and transmissions must have become less clear, since these are matters of social legitimization, which was no longer a possibility. Gradually a free play entered the teaching as the practitioners adopted elements from the official religions and philosophies of the states round which they moved as wanderers and partial outcasts. Thus vestigial shamanic ways could begin to overlap with the birth of philosophy and to exercise influence upon it, like, say, the Orphic influence on the Pythagoreans, or the non-Vedic afterlife views which seem to have stimulated the doctrine of reincarnation in the Upaniṣads. Traditions about early "philosophers" in both Greece and India involve vestigial shamanic traits very prominently—wind and fire magic, raising the dead, sorcerers' duels, flying, bilocation, and so on.

The Mesopotamian Case

The development from the Mesolithic to the Chalcolithic in the ancient Near East was very quick. The spur of agriculture, especially with irrigation, seems to have coupled with an actual sense of cultural takeoff—though that may be a projection from hindsight. Still, that development applied primarily to matters of economic production; cultural matters floated above the change somewhat, slower to adapt. As late as the Uruk or Early Dynastic period of Sumer there would still have been semiprimitive independent religious practitioners, whose hold on their communities might have seemed undesirable to the central authority of an irrigation-based state organization.

It seems that various modes of resolving the problem of residual shamanism—residual Stone Age practices—were employed in ancient Sumer. The group use of narcotics in religious ritual, for example, is suggested. The hundred or so human sacrifices in the Royal Tombs at Ur were buried alive in peaceful postures with cups in their hands which must have contained, in Leonard Woolley's words, "some kind of drug—opium or hashish would serve."[145] Presumably many of the victims had become sedated into unconsciousness before the experience of being buried alive began. Most of the sacrificed were wives and servants to accompany the king, as in Indian suttee in its burial mode, where also, it seems, a victim is often buried alive without losing composure.[146] The hugely dilated pupils of the figures from the Temple of Abu may reflect only the function of "prayer figures," which were supposed to get the god's attention for the petitioner's cause; but they also all hold little cups in their hands, as in the grave-pits at Ur, raising the question whether the religious use of narcotics may at times have been involved in cult practices.

Mesopotamian mythology bears witness to another strategy, that of converting the "primitive magic" accumulated from the Paleolithic and Neolithic eras into a new body of priestly myth that simultaneously tames it and puts it in the service of the state. The *Epic of Gilgamesh*, for example, a work which seems to have served the communal purpose of validating national kingship, involved the classic shamanic motif of the drum which opens access to other worlds.[147] Utnapishtim, in the *Epic of Gilgamesh*, functions as a "father shaman" to whom Gilgamesh comes as novice. Utnapishtim instructs him to keep vigil, a motif that Eliade calls "clearly initiatory in character"—meaning shamanic initiation.[148] Gilgamesh's quest for the plant of immortality may hide an idealized memory of, and nostalgia for, abandoned shamanic drug plants. Gilgamesh's friend Enkidu, who is portrayed as horned and hoofed, may give us a glimpse of the animal imitation practices of the "grazer" ascetics known from later Mesopotamia, who imitated cattle in their movements and means of eating.

Another residual shamanic figure is Atrahasis, the protoguru or father shaman who refuses, in the *Epic of Gilgamesh*, to initiate Utnapishtim. This would seem to be a sign—or a claim on the part of the religious establishment promoting the myth—that the individual shamanic lineage with its private initiations has been terminated; now initiations are rituals of established religion and are under the control of priesthoods. Still, Atrahasis retains his power, displaying the ability to avert plague and bring rain.

Etana was another residual shaman or protoyogin. "A mortal in all respects except that his name may be written with the determinative for 'god,'"[149] he represents the quest of the human for divine status, a mythological surrogate for the shamanic profession. Seeking (like Gilgamesh) the plant of birth, he cannot make the flight to heaven by his own power; he frees the eagle from its combat with the serpent and is flown to heaven on its back. The motif seems shamanic in origin, referring to the shaman's use of animal allies to journey on high to other worlds. The eagle especially is "at the shaman's service"; the shaman "is often carried by an eagle."[150] In this myth the shamanic journey has been redefined for new purposes. It is specifically the continuation of a royal dynasty that is at issue. The old shamanic power has been turned to the service of the state: The king-lists record the offspring of Etana. This myth was written in the Sargonid era, when contact with the Indus culture was at its height. Its myth of flight on an eagle's back occurs in Hindu mythology in the story of Viṣṇu and Gāruda, seemingly another redefined form of the old shamanic journeyer and his ally.

Adapa and Uttanka

Another postshamanic or protoyogic figure in Sumerian literature is Adapa. A special initiate of Enki, the god of wisdom, Adapa "knew the heart of heaven and earth" and was involved in secret practices of which he was the "ointment priest, the observer of rites."[151] "Without him the offering table cannot be cleared."[152] One day the south wind capsized his boat and he cursed it, saying, "South wind, I will break your wing." For seven days the south wind didn't blow. Adapa was called before Anu, the High God, for judgment, and Enki, his sponsor, sent him to heaven with "unkempt hair and mourning garb" like a defendant seeking sympathy in court. The myth has numerous Indian and Greek convergences. The Muni of *Ṛg Veda* X.136 also is master of the wind, flies to heaven, and has long (matted) hair. Empedocles displayed control of the wind as well. The continuation of the myth conceals a shamanic account of flying to heaven and eating the food of heaven. But the motif of the food of heaven has been revised. Anu is about to give Adapa the food of heaven, which will make him immortal, one of the gods. But Enki, not regarding it as proper for a mortal to become immortal, has already secretly told Adapa not to eat or drink anything offered to him, claiming that it would be the food and drink of death. The food of life is freely offered to Adapa and he turns it down. In the *Epic of Gilgamesh*, similarly, a plant of immortality is offered yet not attained. Is the plant they seek, in reality, the drug plant with which their shamanic predecessors had "attained immortality," that is, seen the things of heaven? Such myths seem to signal the end of the free performance of the shamanic rite, the inculcation of a new ethic of subservience to the state.

The *Mahābhārata* (*Aśvamedha Parvan*, XIV.54.12–35) contains a related story. Krishna wants his devotee Uttanka to be given the *amṛta*, or food of immortality. Indra objects that it is improper to give it to a mortal. Bidden to give it anyway, Indra takes the form of an outcaste hunter, urinates in front of Uttanka, and exhorts Uttanka to drink his urine. Uttanka, not knowing he is being offered the food of life (in this case possibly the urine form of the *Amanita muscaria*), refuses it, as Adapa did. This group of myths in general seems to teach the impossibility, or the impropriety, of transcendent experience, perhaps to inculcate the lesson that no individual transcends the claims of the state, the priesthood, and the caste.

Zu

Even closer to the shamanic model is the Sumerian myth of Zu. Sometimes represented as a human, sometimes as a bird, Zu is Etana and the eagle in one. In shamanic contexts the shaman's ability to leave his body and make the flight to the other world is represented either by his bird ally or by his bird form.[153] Magical flight, according to Eliade, is originally a preshamanic motif, belonging to "an ideology of universal magic."[154]

The history of the motif illustrates the process whereby primitive magic survived, somewhat redefined and reorganized, in shamanism, and shamanism in turn was redefined and reorganized as yoga. The Buddha, in the *Jātaka* story of Sumedha, travels in this way:

> Now so it happened at this time
> That I my hermitage had left
> And, barken garments rustling loud,
> Was passing over them through the air.
> Then saw I every one alert,

Well-pleased, delighted, overjoyed;
And, coming downward from the sky,
The multitude I straight-away asked . . .[155]

Flying is mentioned as the first superpower (*siddhi*) in the *Visuddhimagga*, and is cited by Patañjali as a fruit of yoga (*YS* III.45).

There are a number of Mesopotamian myths that show a concern about the inability of human beings to fly, alongside those that show anxiety about the inaccessibility of a plant with special powers. It might be anxiety over the loss of the shamanic performance, and the drug plant used in it, that these myths record. The official story is that nowadays the gods are withholding both plant and flight from humans, though they may have granted these powers to earlier practitioners like Utnapishtim and Atrahasis. The myth of the loss of the drum by Gilgamesh repeats the theme of the loss of the shamanic performance. In the age of the state, such powers are to be used only in the service of the state, as Hammurabi—the king usurping the shaman's function—managed to ascend to Shamash to receive his laws.

The myth of Zu is a poignant story of a power figure from an earlier age who is out of place in the new world of Anu. Zu has stolen the *me,* or tablets of destiny, from Enlil (Enki in the Sumerian version). He is defeated by Ninurta, the storm god, who uses the seven ill winds as his weapons. The myth may conceal an earlier story of a shamanic duel involving control of the wind. The Vratya of the *Atharva Veda* is credited with "seven breaths," like the seven winds of Ninurta. The figure of Zu, the freelance sorcerer who is not in the service of the state, represents disenfranchised holy men who did not make the changeover into the established priesthoods. Ancient Egyptian texts contain memories of fakirs who begged in the temple vicinities and purveyed scraps of magic and doctrine outside the priesthoods.[156] In Mesopotamia, also, there were nonpriestly sorcerers who were outlawed by Gudea and other Sumerian kings.[157] Were they remnants of some ancient initiation no longer reputable? Did they wander, like scapegoats, out of their native countries? Are they the prototypes of the wandering Vratyas and Munis of the Vedas? Of the wandering Orphics?

The Sacred Kingship

The king's magicianly duties included sexual magic, that is, the ritual sex act at the New Year, and substitution magic, that is, becoming the deity during the performance of ritual.[158] Kings in whose time the community had especially prospered were sometimes worshipped after their deaths.[159] These were standard parts of the Near Eastern institution of the sacral kingship. In addition there was another area where vestiges of a more ancient level of religious history survive: those of the shaman. One text, for example, preserves a ritual for the manufacture of the sacred *lilissu* drum of Anu, the king-god. The *lilissu* drum would appear to be a remnant of shamanic performance equipment, here transposed into the equipment of kingship.[160] Sumerian kingship also involves the bull symbol prominently. Anu's sacred animal was the bull; Enlil, who also had a claim to be called the god of kings, is called the Wild Bull.[161] The bull is the most common power animal of shamans, and as such goes back continuously to Çatal Hüyuk and beyond to the Sorcerer of Trois Freres and other Magdalenian icons. By early Sumerian times the bull archetype had been transferred from shamans to kings. The conjunction of sacred kingship with bull image extends down through history, including the Buddha, or Prince Siddhārtha, who was called the "Bull of the Śākyas."

Not only the shaman's symbols and attributed powers, but his duties too, fell upon the king. "The king," as Frankfort says, "became the scapegoat, charged before the gods with all the sins of his community. Hence his time was largely taken up with penitence and prophylactic magic."[162] The king did not, in other words, administer the city or lead the armies so much as he served as a magical talisman and ally for both, much as a professional magician or visionary might. The priests, who in some periods really administered the community, treated the king as a psychic membrane to special knowledge or power. They constantly adjusted his behavior to offset or encourage this or that cosmic force, in response to a constant inspection of omens and astrological events. He was kept by them in a condition which was not meant for administrative work. Once, for example, in a case from the Assyrian period, the moon was ominously covered with clouds. The priests instructed the king to fast. They wrote:

> A day has gone by since the king began fasting and has not eaten a morsel. "Until when?" he asks. Today (also) the king should eat no food. The king is a beggar . . . [163]

In another such document, the king is instructed to spend seven days continuously secluded in a reed hut like those used by the seriously ill, submitting constantly to purification practices. This type of activity—the performance of austerities on behalf of the community as a whole—was once the activity of shamans.

The number of taboos and purification devices that surrounded ancient priest-kings was enormous. Frazer relates that "the Flamen Dialis might not ride or even touch a horse, nor see an army under arms, nor wear a ring that was not broken, nor have a knot on any part of his garments . . . he might not touch wheaten flour or leavened bread; he might not touch or even name a goat, a dog, raw meat, beans, and ivy . . ."[164] There is a distinct similarity between such taboo systems and the lists of taboos practiced, say, by Pythagoreans and by Buddhist monks and yogis.

The conflicting evidence about the Buddha's caste status may be resolved somewhat on the assumption that his "kingship" was not necessarily a *kṣatriya* office but may have been a mythic survival of the sacral shaman-king. Even if the tradition of Buddha's kingship is Aryan in origin, it assumed a rather Near Eastern tinge at some time. The Buddha's royal genealogy is traced back either to the first king of the present cycle (paralleling the Sumerian myth of the repeated descents of Kingship at the beginnings of different eras) or for seven generations.[165] Numerous passages present the Buddha as a Mesopotamian style god-king, Lord of the Four Quarters, traversing the cosmos in seven stages, and so forth:

> As soon as born the Bodhisattva firmly standing with even feet goes towards the North with seven long steps . . . He surveys all the quarters, and in a lordly voice says, "I am the chief in the world, I am the best in the world, I am the first in the world." (*M.* III.118)[166]

The image is not unlike that of Marduk in the *Enuma Elish*, or *Akkadian Creation Epic* (tablet IV), when he "crossed the heavens and surveyed the regions."[167] Royal-birth myths are known to have diffused from Mesopotamia to India at some time, as the Akkadian legend of the birth of Sargon clearly appears in India in the *Mahābhārata's* story of the birth of the hero Karna.[168] Similarly, the legend that Makkhali Gosāla was born in a cowshed may hearken back (like the manger-birth of Jesus) to the

Mesopotamian cult of the byre in which the sacred young calf, symbol of the king, was born. In Jain tradition also, all twenty-four *tīrthankharas* are said to have been kings' sons, echoing the god-king tradition of the Near East. Furthermore, all of them are said to have died (entered nirvāna) on mountaintops—an echo of the motif of the Mesopotamian priest-king or god-king ascending to heaven by way of the ziggurat.[169]

Oneiromancy

In Mesopotamia it was also the king who was primarily responsible for sacred dreaming, a typical shamanic occupation. "Seeing spirits," says Eliade, "in dream or awake, is the determining sign of the shamanic vocation."[170] Dream, rather than trance, seems to have been the primary Mesopotamian way of communicating with the gods.[171]

In one dream king Gudea was ordered to build a new temple; in subsequent dreams he had to get the specifications for brick size and so forth. He was functioning like a medium or shaman who communicates directly with the deity. Gudea's private god was Ningizzida, the god of the entwined serpents; his dreams of Ningizzida sometimes sound like mystical experiences. Once Gudea "dreamt that he saw light coming forth on the horizon. That light, he was told by the goddess Nanshe who interpreted the dream for him, symbolized his personal god Ningizzida, and the dream meant that Ningizzida was able to be present anywhere in the world."[172] In an Assyrian text that, according to Speiser, goes back to the Akkadian period, a king Kumma deliberately induced a dream vision of the underworld; visiting the underworld in dreams is a specifically shamanic activity—indeed perhaps the central shamanic responsibility. In the dream, king Kumma himself visits the underworld and has encounters, for the most part terrifying, with deities there. The tradition of shamanic travel, out of the body, to the land of the dead, could thus be transposed into the social structure of kingship and dreaming. The dream has been retained from the technology of the trance and the drug vision.

The tradition of dream vision and dream interpretation may have been prominent in the Indus Valley culture also, since it survived prominently in the Ājīvika-Jain line that seems to go far back in that stream. The Ājīvika texts are lost, but they are known to have been devoted almost entirely to divination of various kinds, including astrology, ultimately a Sumero-Akkadian export more or less wherever it is found, and dream interpretation. "The Ājīvika mendicant often acted as an astrologer or reader of omens."[173] Jain dream theory recognized "42 normal and 30 major dreams." The mother of a *tīrthankara* will, by the time her pregnancy begins, have experienced fourteen of the major dreams, as has the mother of a *cakravartin*; the mother of a *Vasudeva* has experienced seven.[174] Dreaming was regarded among the Jains "as a special kind of visionary power."[175] This seems a vestigial form of the shamanic practice of seeking special power dreams, which are regarded as qualitatively different from ordinary dreams. The Mesopotamian king seeking divine guidance through dreams is doing a similar thing. The Jain tradition in fact recognized dreaming as a path to enlightenment and nirvāna—echoing the period when the dream was the shaman's access to the heavens and the company of the gods. "14 dreams [from the 30 major ones] immediately lead to true cognition and in most cases to salvation within the same existence."[176] The dreams of one who has attained *samvara,* or stoppage of karmic flow at the five senses, are necessarily true—like those of the Sumerian king when he has properly purified himself. At least one text indicates that major dreams occurred not in true sleep but in a state of semitrance; it is possible that some meditation practices arose in part from attempts to induce special dreams through stillness and balance in the hypnogogic state.

Gosāla

Ājīvikism seems to have been closer to the stream of primitive magic than Jainism; the Ājīvika emphasis on magic and divination may have been one of the elements that Mahāvīra was trying to purge from his branch of the tradition. The *Bhāgavati Sūtra* (ch. 15) portrays Gosāla as expert in reading from omens the good or evil of the people. Mahāvīra, on the other hand, although he sometimes prophesied, did reject divination, and forbade Jain monks to eat food procured by (1) showing pictures, (2) foretelling the future or reading omens, (3) applying medicine, (4) performing magic and spells, or (5) rising in the air.[177] This list seems directed against the tradition of Gosāla, whose father as well as himself made a living by carrying around a holy picture and begging, as well as reading omens and performing spells. "Showing pictures" was not merely piety, but magic; it relates to the tantric use of maṇḍalas and other icons. The power of the god enters directly into the icon, summoned by the proper spells, and is to some extent controlled by the practitioner. The fact that Gosāla's father practiced his same profession suggests lineages whose antiquity can only be guessed at. It has already been remarked that the Tantra is to be regarded as a reemergence into the light of the Sumero-Indian stream which had always been there but was long excluded from the literate milieu. Gosāla and his father give us glimpses of prototantric magical practitioners. Mahāvīra rejected the practice of magic as karmically ineffective, due to his emphasis on personal effort; the Buddha felt similarly. Gosāla on the other hand rejected both personal effort and magic as means to alter (much less terminate) the unfolding of *karma*; granted the framework of unfolding *karma*, however, one could make magical adjustments in details within the frame.

The Empowered Priesthood

When the powers of shamans were being broken up and redistributed in the emerging states, one concern was to create a system of checks and balances on their exercise. The king was the magical center, but as a counterbalance to him the priesthoods also inherited much of the old power, which was either sublimated into new priestly thought or sheltered in temple cults behind vows of secrecy. It must have been through exchanges between priestly communities that intimate transfers of lore and practice occurred. The Bronze Age priesthoods of the ancient Near East were accustomed to receiving visiting inquirers from the provinces. Their facilities and staffs were huge. The Mesopotamian Temple of Bau, a minor goddess, employed 736 persons in about 2600 B.C. Marduk's temple in the neo-Babylonian period employed 7,000.[178] Egyptian temples were even larger. They were the universities of the Bronze Age, and the forerunners of such later institutions as the Library of Alexandria, which was a center of research and study as well as a passive repository of lore. In the time of Ramesses III (c. 1198–1166), the Theban temple of Amon employed about 80,000 people. It was, in other words, a substantial community like a large university today. The temple of Re at Heliopolis employed over 12,000, that of Ptah at Memphis over 3,000.[179]

The ascetic orders of India, whose members were social dropouts, renouncing home and family, bear little resemblance to any Bronze Age priesthood known. The lifestyle of the Egyptian priests, for example, was not based on renunciation. They performed austerities as temporary ritual purifications, not as lifelong vows. Outside of brief ritual periods, they did not renounce sex and offspring or the householder's lifestyle. The scale of austerities was steadily expanded in the yogic stream. The concept of *karma* gave infinite room for purification practices; one was purifying not just for ten days, but for thousands of lifetimes. The Indian practice of *tapas* could have developed out of a set of priestly taboos and purification restraints reinterpreted in the framework of escape from reincarnation. In line with their practice of austerities, Bronze Age priests claimed special powers and magic. Sorcerers' duels are recorded from the Old Kingdom.[180] To the priesthood of the Egyptian temple called the House of Life, Greek texts ascribe the ability to foretell the future and make rain.[181] Such abilities are priestly vestiges of shamanic magic, still closer in intentionality to the shamanic practice—the desire to make adjustments in the quality of life—than to the later yogic redefinition—the desire to escape from life.

Egyptian Yoga?

Yogic *āsanas* or postures, have often been popularly derived from positions seen in Egyptian art, especially the sitting position of the sculptures known as scribes who sit on the floor with the soles of their feet beneath the knees and facing upward.[182] In terms of *āsanas*, their posture relates to both *sukhāsana* and *siddhāsana*, but to neither exactly. Unsupported by other *āsana* parallels, the argument for haṭha yoga in ancient Egypt is weak.

Something like the *ahiṃsā*, or nonviolence doctrine, occurred in ancient Egypt in connection with the priests' obsession with physical "purity." "Twice a day," Herodotus says, "they washed themselves with water, and twice a night" (II.37). Furthermore, "they shave the entire body every other day, so that no impure flea or vermin shall impede them in the practice of their religion."

Similarly the Assyrian king shaved his entire body before entering the temple for an important ritual. The Ājīvikas and Jains also shaved or depilated themselves. The scrupulousness of the Egyptian priest who wished no flea on his body seems at first sight similar to that of the Jains, who meticulously inspected their bodies and clothing for vermin and wore facemasks to keep them out of their mouths. But the motives are different: The Jain wished not to kill any bugs by sitting on them, no matter how unintentionally, whereas the Egyptian priest wished to be sure that he took no uninitiated being into the inner sanctum with him—even a bug should not see secret things.

Still, the Egyptian priest was hemmed in by a great system of taboos on the taking of life, taboos that may be totemic in origin. Various classical authors inform us that they did not eat beef, pork, sheep, fowl, fish, or certain vegetables.[183] This amounts to a form of vegetarianism as among the Orphics and various Indian groups. Such an austere regimen may, however, have been only temporary: the Egyptian priest was on duty in the temple only one month out of four and may have relaxed these rules during the three months of householder's life. Plutarch (*De Is. et Osir.*, 72) makes it clear that such taboos were important in specific localities, perhaps as clan totem taboos originally.

Among the Ājīvikas and Jains *ahiṃsā* was maintained as a taboo or avoidance of pollution, not from a spiritualized yogic intention. Some yogic practices clearly originate in primitive taboos, for example the *Maitrī Upaniṣad*'s statement that an ascetic should not see a menstruating woman. Similarly, *ahiṃsā* may have developed initially as a broadly applied system of totemic food taboos and purification devices, later redefined in various ways by the new wave of religions that inherited it: For Manu it is a means of not being eaten oneself in a future incarnation; for Buddha it is a way of clearly seeing one's own intentions toward other beings; for Mahāvīra it is a way of burning off karmic outflow. All these explanations may be redefinitions, in the late Vedic period, of a practice that initially stood as a purification taboo in a more primitive conceptual framework.

Prolongation of Taboo

Similarly, other prolonged or permanent ascetic practices, such as monastic celibacy, may have developed as generalizations of temporary and occasional purification practices. Celibacy was maintained by the Egyptian priest for a few days before entering the temple for his on-duty month, and probably during his month on-duty.[184] In Greece also, a period of sexual abstinence was required before participation in various rituals. Before Eleusinian initiation, nine days of celibacy were required; before Bacchic initiation, ten. The Vestal Virgins at Rome were celibate for thirty years. The Hellenistic priests of Isis were permanently celibate.

Another practice which is found in India in a different scale than in the ancient Near East is religious silence. While the new temple was being built in Gudea's city of Lagash, prohibitions against noise were in effect throughout the city. In ancient Athens, one did not speak on top of the Acropolis. Both are cases of *euphemia* or ritual silence, the prohibition against speaking when the gods are listening lest something ill-omened might be said. Ritual silence is common enough in religious practice, but it rarely develops into the generalized vow of religious silence (Sanskrit *mauna*). Among the Indian orders such a vow is usually undertaken for a year, sometimes for a lifetime. This practice may have existed as early as the tenth book of the *Ṛg Veda* (X.136), where the Muni is referred to as "ecstatic with silence."

In India, instead of the temporary ritual taboos of ancient Near Eastern religions one finds prolonged feats of abstinence cemented by sacred vows. As Rhys Davids remarked, "Nowhere has the art of pain been more studied."[185] Similarly the Greek *theologoi* and Orphics, like the Jains, Ājīvikas, and others in India, may have generalized such purificatory measures as the period of fasting before the Eleusinian initiation. They wanted, in effect, to be in a state of ritual purity all the time; they made their lives into purification rites. Abaris is said to have traveled completely around the world without eating. Epimenides of Crete was a regular and rigorous faster. Hippocrates (*De Morb. Sacr.*) speaks of the abstinences of the professional purifiers (probably Orphics). Asceticism seems to grow up in a context of pantheism,[186] and perhaps should be regarded as part of the monism complex.

Ningizzida and Kuṇḍalinī Yoga

The iconography of *kuṇḍalinī* yoga is a mix of Mesopotamian and Egyptian models. The icons of copulating serpents entwined around a pole inside the human body, of the central mountain and central tree, the eagle-serpent combat and the flight to heaven on the eagle's back, the eight-petaled lotus or rosette, the seven-headed serpent power, the ascent up the spine, and more, all have clear Bronze Age, Near Eastern antecedents.

Zimmer noted the Sumerian provenience of the icon of two serpents entwined around a central axis, found most famously on the Gudea serpent vase; he connects the symbol with the god Ningizzida, whom he calls "the Mesopotamian deity of healing."[187] Ningizzida was associated with fertility and sacramental cult, as his surname Zid-zi, "meal of life," indicates.[188] In addition to his depiction as the entwined serpent pair, Ningizzida is also portrayed as an anthropomorphic deity seated before an entwined serpent pair, or as a composite deity, human above, serpentine below, or as a double-headed serpent, or as an anthropomorphic deity with snakes protruding from his body at the shoulders. Zimmer regarded this last version as probably the ancestor of the similar icon of the Jain *tīrthankara* Pārśva.[189] Ningizzida's association with the serpent mingles with his association with a tree (memory of which may be preserved in a bowdlerized version in the *Book of Genesis* in the *Old Testament*). Sometimes he is seen in the vicinity of a tree, sometimes with the branches held in his hands as if they were growing from him.

It is primarily on the basis of these and other iconographic parallels that one scholar, E. A. S. Butterworth, has argued for the Temple of Ningizzida as the source from which the serpent power flowed into India. Butterworth confuses iconography with religious practice, assuming that the signifieds which the iconographic signifiers had in India were the same which they had earlier had in Mesopotamia.[190] He assumes, that is, that since the symbolism of Indian yoga came from Mesopotamia, the practices of yoga must have also. On such a faulty assumption, his arguments must be inspired guesses at best.

Yet the Greek knowledge of the *kuṇḍalinī* physiology had not been recognized at the time Butterworth's book appeared. Now, in light of that knowledge, it is appropriate to seek an earlier, non-Indian source for the doctrines of the spinal channel, the surrounding *nāḍīs,* the *cakras,* and the spiritual significance of it all—and Mesopotamia in the Sumero-Akkadian period is the only candidate presently available. Consequently, despite the illogicality of Butterworth's assumptions, the knowledge that this system had diffused from somewhere into both Greece and India makes it necessary to reconsider his argument.

Looking for indications of yogic practice in the Mesopotamian icons Butterworth focuses on the Hydra seal, which shows the conquest of a flaming seven-headed serpent by male figures armed with spears.[191] This seal impression of the Akkadian period, he suggests, is an icon of mastery of the serpent power—that is, of *kuṇḍalinī* "awakening." Each of the serpent's seven heads represents one of the *cakras*; the awakening process has, at the moment portrayed in the picture on the seal, progressed upward as far as the fourth *cakra.* The flames rising from the serpent's back represent the *tapas* or austerity-heat which is associated so prominently with this event. Butterworth does not mention the supportive fact that this seal was found in a temple of Ningizzida.[192] Ningizzida is commonly seen in conjunction with the fire altar,[193] and the conjunction of heat and snake are important for the protoyogic hypothesis. He is "regularly" associated with fire and once appears as a serpent with flames rising from its shoulders.[194] This last image is close to the image of the flaming serpent on the so-called Hydra seal, where it may be Ningizzida who appears as a flaming serpent with seven heads, three of which hang down, having been defeated by a hostile god.

The number seven, in Mesopotamian tradition and others affected by it, is a number of cosmic totality, indicating the seven planetary levels in the universe, which are variously represented. Sometimes they are seven fruits on the central tree which grows from the central mountain, sometimes seven levels of the goddess's mountainlike skirt. On the Hydra seal they are the seven heads of the serpent god Ningizzida. On this reading, there seems to be something here that is related to the *kuṇḍalinī* metaphysics of the serpent power as the moving force of the universe. The Mesopotamian macrocosm/microcosm correspondence could lead to an identification of the seven levels of the planetary universe within the human body, arranged along the spine which corresponds to the central tree or axis (though at the time in question macranthropy is not yet attested in the cuneiform evidence). In the Mesopotamian cylinder seal showing Ningizzida with snakes' heads and throats rising from his shoulders,[195] it is understood that the upright twining of the two snakes is going on inside his body. The Hydra seal was found in Eshnunna (Tel Asmar), one of the Mesopotamian sites where objects

Figure 25 Babylonian seal impression, c. 2000 B.C., showing deity and ritualists heraldically flanked by upright caducei.

from the Indus Valley have been found. The possibility that the milieu in which it arose may stand somehow in the background of certain threads of Indian culture (or vice versa) can by no means be denied.[196]

There is an additional cluster of associations that seem friendly to the hypothesis. Ningizzida is also connected, for example, with the symbol of the tree, which is closely related to that of the serpent. His mother is a cedar tree, and he himself sometimes appears as a tree; his name, according to one authority, means "Lord of the Good Tree."[197] The goddess of the tree, known in both Sumer and Egypt, appears prominently in the Indus Valley iconography, in the period of Sumerian contacts. If the tree goddess who came over is Ningizzida's mother, then he must have come with her. In another form he is the bull-god, Damu;[198] the god in the Indus Valley was also a bull-god. Ningizzida is intimately connected with the sacred kingship. He was incarnated in each of the kings of Sumer, as Osiris was in each of the Pharaohs of Egypt, and was regarded as dwelling in each in turn. (Gudea was, it seems, especially touched by this doctrine.) They are, in effect, his avatars. He is associated with Gilgamesh and also with the snake that stole the plant of immortality from Gilgamesh[199]—a motif that recurs in the *Mahābhārata*.[200] Though Ningizzida is not included in the pantheon of great gods, he is important in lunar and chthonic ways that are slightly hidden. As the chosen personal and state deity of the dreamer king Gudea of Lagash his function as gatekeeper suggests a path of practice.

Ningizzida and the Ājīvika-Jain Tradition

The relationship between Ningizzida imagery and the Ājīvika-Jain tradition is impressive, though unclear in meaning. The Pārśva cult, to which Mahāvīra's parents belonged, abounded with serpent imagery. The *tīrthankara* is called Pārśva ("side") because his mother, when pregnant, sees a serpent by her side one night.[201] The serpent remains a symbol of the saint throughout his life. As a boy, he protects a snake from his cruel brother; this serpent is later reborn as King of the Nāgas (serpent deities) and, called Dhāraṇā, is an attendant of Pārśva while he is becoming enlightened.[202] Like the serpents at the temple of Asclepius in Greece, Dhāraṇā heals by licking the afflicted part with his tongue.[203] Pārśva's head is covered over by seven expanded cobra hoods, his attendants' heads, by five each. In Egypt both these

Figure 26 Indus Valley seal impression, Mohenjo Daro, third to second millennium B.C.*, showing figure in* mūlabandhāsana *symmetrically flanked by upright serpents.*

numerical groupings are found on cobra-hooded icons. In Pārśva lore there is an incident in which a serpent carried in the beak of a bird causes the loss of the plant of immortality to mankind;[204] the story is probably derived from the Gilgamesh epic—or related to it in some other way.

A striking parallel involves the fact that Pārśva is reported to have been protected on both sides by serpents at the moment when he passed into *kevala* or full enlightenment. The motif goes back in the Indian tradition to the Indus Valley *mūlabandhāsana* seal in which the protoyogin is heraldically flanked by upright serpents. Before the Indus seals the motif is found only in certain icons of the Ningizzida cult, in which the god is represented between upright serpents. The Pārśva imagery leads even more directly back to Ningizzida in another icon, in which he is shown with a serpent sprouting from each shoulder. This unusual motif is found in the iconography of Ningizzida, who in at least one extant seal impression appears as an anthropomorphic god with a serpent rising from each shoulder, implying that their intertwining union is going on inside his body. The demon who was attacking Pārśva was called "Cloud-Wrapped"—possibly echoing the Mesopotamian tradition of mythic battles between sky gods and serpent gods.[205]

Minor but striking Near Eastern parallels abound. Ningizzida iconography fed into Jainism as well as into the *kuṇḍalinī* tradition,[206] and, considering the extensive correspondence between Orphism and Jainism,[207] and the presence of the *kuṇḍalinī* physiological doctrine in Orphic-related contexts in Greece, it hardly seems an empty coincidence that Orphism, as well as Jainism, inherited the imagery of Ningizzida. The Orphic deity Phanes, like Ningizzida, for example, is wrapped around by entwining serpents.

The iconograph of an anthropomorphic deity who is wrapped round by a coiling serpent occurs first in the iconography of Ningizzida, then reappears in the Greco-Roman sculptures of the Orphic god Phanes and the Mithraic icons of Zurvan Akarana.[208] With Ningizzida and Pārśva, in another version of the icon, the caduceus is portrayed as if entwined round an inner pole in the anatomy and sprouting upward from the shoulders. The seven-headed serpent is found in Sumer (on the Hydra seal); in Egypt, where it rises above the head of the goddess Isis; in the Mucalinda Buddha icon, where it rises over Buddha's head; in the Hindu iconography of Viṣṇu and the Nāgas; in the myth of Heracles and the Hydra; and in the hairstyle of the Greek Gorgons. The motif of serpents rising from each shoulder occurs in Sumerian Ningizzida, in the Jain images of Pārśva, and in the medieval Persian image of the evil Nanat.[209] The motif of the conquest of the seven-headed serpent occurs in the Hydra seal, in Caananite texts relating to the Biblical Leviathan, in the Hydra fight of the Greek hero Heracles—who has been shown to have been modeled in part on a Mesopotamian hero-god[210]—and in Hindu representations of the god Krishna conquering the serpent Kaliya (whose name relates to the god Kāla, Time). Ritual bowls made in the form of coiled and entwined serpents occur in Sumer, and in the Orphism of the Roman Empire. The serpent twined around a staff figured prominently in the Greek cults of Demeter, Dionysus, Asclepius, and Hygeia (all deities expressive of "vital force"). The caduceus, or icon of copulating serpents, is found virtually worldwide, and everywhere it appears has somehow gotten there from the temple of Ningizzida.

Ningizzida and Nakedness

The figure whom Frankfort calls the Nude Hero was somehow closely associated with Ningizzida. In an icon showing the Nude Hero triumphant over lions, for example, the Ningizzida motif of entwined or copulating serpents hangs over his head as if sponsoring his activity. The Nude Hero is associated with the taming of serpents and conceivably it is he or someone related to him who is portrayed on the Hydra seal. The Nude Hero, indeed, may be a form of Ningizzida, with whom he is sometimes interchangeable. Ningizzida and his symbol the caduceus were the special personal deity and symbol of the dreamer-king, Gudea. Ningizzida acts as Gudea's gatepost holder, and the Nude Hero sometimes performs the same job. He is also associated with Tammuz, the fertility god, and occurs in the immortality myth of Adapa. The Nude Hero characteristically stands upright and naked, like Pārśva in his moment of attaining enlightenment. He occurs in conjunction with the Bull-Man, who is himself quite like some Indus Valley figures. Furthermore, the unidentified object carried by the Nude Hero[211] looks like the "curious kind of bow without a string" that the naked Vratyas wore in the Middle Vedic period.[212] Butterworth argues that in shamanic contexts nakedness is a part of the practice of heat magic, which is to say, the predecessor of the *kuṇḍalinī* awakening process; nakedness is also associated with Pārśva and with the Sky-clad Jains.

Nakedness is common in shamanic performances. Lapp shamans performed entirely naked. The circumpolar shaman, says Eliade, "bares his torso and . . . retains a belt as his only garment."[213] The figures seated in *mūlabandhāsana* on Indus Valley seals appear to be naked or, more precisely, to be wearing only belts, like the circumpolar shamans described by Eliade.

Nakedness is especially common in heat-generating practices, and Butterworth feels that the Mesopotamian nude priests and the Nude Hero imply that such activities may have been carried out in Mesopotamian temples in the third millennium.[214] Frankfort feels that the Nude Hero is not a single figure, but, rather, that a variety of mythological personages, possibly including gods, are represented by the imagery. In any case, it does appear with a variety of yoga-related symbols. In the early dynastic period the Nude Hero is shown grasping snakes, or what is called the "doorpost emblem," or, like the Gilgamesh icon, grasping lions in a conquered position. In the

Akkadian period he is the attendant of Enki/Ea, the water god who is also "the god of wisdom and magic."[215] In the dynasty of Hammurabi he holds the Flowing Vase, a Sumerian symbol which is integral to the whole protoyogic/proto-Orphic/proto-Genesis complex with the tree, spring, snake, fruit, caduceus, and so on.[216] He is not usually but may occasionally appear ithyphallic (like the Indus figures or the Egyptian Min).[217] He is often shown either engaged in or triumphant in battle. One composition, for example, "represents a Nude Hero holding up a reversed feline in each hand; above his head two serpents are entwined, each one biting the tip of its own tail."[218]

Costume also may suggest relationships between cults. Some Egyptian priests wore leopard skins, as Śīva and some Śaiva yogis do.[219] Both the leopard skin and the saffron robe characteristic of the Śaiva yogi and the Buddhist monk are worn in different images by Dionysus, god of the Orphics.[220] Akkadian priests of Ishtar did their duties in the temple while dressed in drag to be like their goddess; so did Ramakrishna and other priests of Kālī in India. The Ājīvika monk went entirely naked, as did the Digambara or Sky-clad Jains. The Svetambara Jains dressed only in white, as did the Orphic of Euripides in *The Cretans*. In the third millennium (when there were Indians in Mesopotamian cities and temples), Sumerian priests at first performed rituals naked. Later they wore only white linen garments.[221] The Jain sectarian split between nakedness and white garments echoes these ritual styles. The Vratyas of the *Atharva Veda* went naked, as did the Muni of the *Ṛg Veda*; both represented a phase of the Sumero-Indian tradition prior to the period of puritanical reforms by Mahāvīra and others.

The Vratyas

The Vratyas may have been either a non-Aryan group or a non-Vedic Aryan group who were admitted to the Brahmin caste in the Middle Vedic period and brought with them ascetic and ecstatic practices from outside. A whole book of the *Atharva Veda* is devoted to this movement, which influenced the Aryan community deeply. The *Atharva Veda* attributes special austerities to them, saying, for example, that "the Vratya" stood erect for a whole year (*AV* XV.3). This feat connects him with the Jain tradition, in which one of the duties of a monk is "the stabilization of the body without the least motion" in "different postures . . . which benefit the soul and which are difficult to perform."[222] The most common of these postures is *kayotsarga*, standing upright and motionless for long periods of time. The Jain *tīrthankaras* Rishabha and Pārśva were both doing this when they became enlightened. It was also a common austerity of the Ājīvikas, and it has tentatively been identified on the Indus Valley seals.[223] The Vratyas were evidently carriers of the Sumero-Indian stream of magico-religious activities that was a part of the Chaldeanization of Brahmanism in the middle Vedic period. They made their living as "traveling magician clans specializing in sex, song, and dance." Their ritual practice may be the source of the tantric ritual of the *pañca-makāra*, or Five *M*s.[224] In the orthodox Hinduism of the *Mahābhārata,* they are regarded as "the trash of society, incendiaries, poisoners, pimps, adulterers, abortionists, drug addicts, and so on."[225]

The importance of the Vratyas evidentially is that knowledge of both *pitṛyāna* (Path of the Fathers) and *devayāna* (Path of the Gods) is said to have come into the tradition by way of them (*Atharva Veda* XV.12.4–5, 8–9). In the early Upaniṣadic period this pair of terms represented the two paths of the afterlife, the one that leads to reincarnation, and the one that doesn't. If the Vratyas taught the doctrines of reincarnation and release, then that doctrine may have been part of a Sumero-Indian complex. Yājñavalkya, in that case, did not originate it, but learned it from some non-Aryan source like the Vratyas. The Vratyas are also associated with the concept of the four quarters of the universe (*Atharva Veda* XV.2.1–4) and with the figure of the *pantheos*, or Cosmic Person (*Atharva Veda* XV.18), both concepts that seem to have come from the Near East into India at this time. The Vratyas may be late arrivals from Western Asia in around the eleventh century B.C. who brought with them the Akkadian words in the *Atharva Veda*, the concept of the *Puruṣasūkta*, and parts of the general change of religious values that followed.

Fertility Cult and Yoga

The enlightenment myths of Iron Age India often employ more ancient—Bronze Age or Neolithic—fertility symbolism. The sculptural decoration of the stupa at Sanchi, for example, is an amalgam of Bronze Age Mesopotamian religious motifs, though they were probably redefined mentalistically to signify not rebirth of the crops but rebirth of consciousness. Indian literature involves the same apparent redefinition of Bronze Age fertility symbolism. When a bodhisattva becomes a Buddha, says the *Jātaka* (I.3.96), "All plants, be they of land or stream, do straightway put their blossoms forth . . . and every tree and every vine is straightway laden down with fruit."[226] This is the language with which the appearance of a fertility deity is ecstatically described by his votaries. Where Dionysus walks, in Euripides' *Bacchae*, flowers spring from the earth and milk gushes out. That Indian enlightenment figures are described in terms of Near Eastern fertility heroes is a basic fact of the history of religion. The Buddha sits on a eight-petaled lotus which is direct descendant of the eight-petaled rosette of Ishtar, symbolic of the womb of the mother goddess and her nourishment. The Buddha, the enlightenment hero, is portrayed iconographically as the favorite son-lover of the earth mother. Further, he sits beneath the tree of life, which is originally of her garden, and is sheltered by the serpent (seven-headed!) which is the guardian or inhabitant of that tree. When the Buddha touches the earth he alludes to his earlier career as a fertility god:

> As when the time of spring has come
> The trees put forth their buds and flowers,
> Likewise dost thou, O Hero Great
> With knowledge of a Buddha bloom.[227]

There seems, finally, to be an interwoven continuity (though it is not entirely visible) from Paleolithic shamanism to the fertility rites of the Neolithic, the state-influenced priesthoods of the Bronze Age and the mentalizing of idealizing philosophers of the Early Iron Age. This continuity can be sporadically glimpsed through the persistence of symbolic motifs that were probably somewhat redefined with each age. Greece and India seem to have occupied roughly parallel branches of this stream as it separated in its flow out of the Near East.

Question IV: How did this inheritance work itself out in India?

Despite an undeniable inner cohesiveness to Indian tradition, aspects of it do indeed seem to have been reshaped periodically by the intrusion of external influences. From the Neolithic– Bronze Age substrate came sexual cults that the Aryans seem originally to have been opposed to, but which they partially accepted in the Middle Vedic period. Aryan culture subsequently underwent a process of mentalization, a conversion to an antimaterialistic and antisensual idealism which arose in part in reaction to the body practices of the ancient cults.[228] In the Sumero-Indian tradition represented by the *asuras*, sexuality was a *numinosum*, whereas for the Aryan Hindu it was closely fenced around with taboos and repressions. At the root of the distinction may be the difference between the matrilineal and the patrilineal situations. The patrilinealist must know the father of the child; puritanism arises in patrilineal communities such as the Aryan as a means of imposing sufficient restrictions on sexual practice to insure knowledge of paternity. In the pre-Aryan cults, on the other hand, presumably matrilineal, only the identity of the mother was important. Sexuality was a primary object of worship and sex acts were prominent elements of ritual practice.

This distinction between sexual and puritanical cults embodies the distinction between *asuras* and *devas*, and is enshrined in the parallel distinction between tantra and Veda, or the left- and right-hand Paths. Tantra seems to represent a later resurgence of the Bronze Age religious attitude of India, perhaps that of the Indus Valley itself, including the elements shared with the ancient Near East. With their emphasis on the homology between the human body and the macrocosm, on sexual union as the primary metaphor of the cosmic process, and on eros as the driving force of the universe, the later texts called Tantras could represent an adaptation of the Mesopotamian fertility religion. The resurgence of the Tantras in the Middle Ages, after the centuries of Aryan cultural prominence, represents the older pre-Aryan view of life reasserting itself in a widespread reaction against the idealistic, puritanical Hinduism developed among the Brahmanical Aryans.

The tantric sects practice the ritual of *pañca-makāra*, the five *M*s, that is, the use of five substances which are taboo in Aryan cult and whose Sanskrit names begin with *M*: *madya* (wine), *māṁsa* (meat), *maithuna* (sexual intercourse), *mudrā* (fried cereals), *matsya* (fish). The left-hand stream is made up of the sects that approve this practice, and the right-hand stream of those that disapprove it. The Lokāyatikas, for example, according to Gunaratna, "drank wines and ate meat and were given to unrestricted sexual indulgence."[229] On one day of each year, they gathered together and mingled sexually without any restrictions of family or marriage. The practice illustrates how close is the relationship between tantric yoga and fertility magic. The Indian sects that share this general inheritance have been called "the Tantric circle."[230] They include Ājīvikism, left-hand tantra, Lokāyata, Sāṇkhya (originally), Śaiva schools like the Kāpālikas and Kālamukhas, the Nāth yogis, and a good deal of unspecified village practice.

Another important dichotomy between tantra and Veda was their attitude toward religious asceticism. In the non-Aryan community, asceticism was practiced with a shamanic intentionality: Ordeal generated inner "heat," which supposedly made possible the practice of wind-fire magic, the obtaining of power dreams and spirit allies, and so on. Various practices of sexual magic were involved, as well as the protoyogic practice of maintaining a bodily posture for a long period of time. In the Early Vedic period asceticism, along with sexual ritual, seems to have been deemphasized in the Aryan community. In the Middle Vedic period these elements were assimilated to some extent,[231] but not without redefinition; Aryan reformers edited out much of the old shamanic intentionality, replacing the bodily emphasis with a mentalist-idealist framework and a puritanical tendency toward celibacy.

Gosāla and Mahāvīra

These contradictory tendencies can be seen at work in the famous schism between Mahāvīra and Gosāla, the Ājīvika leader who is among the six "heretical" teachers discussed in the Buddhist *Sāmaññaphala Sutta*. Gosāla roughly represents the persistence of the left-hand way, while Mahāvīra is a reformer turning his back on the left-hand way in favor of the right.

At first, it seems, they were in the same group. The sayings attributed to Gosāla in the *Sāmaññaphala Sutta* imply Magadhi forms which are not found in the statements of any other "heretics" but which occur regularly in Jain texts. Further, Gosāla is known to have called himself the twenty-fourth *tīrthankara*, or Savior, of the present age—the same title which Mahāvīra claimed for himself. The implication is that they belonged to the same school or tradition and each claimed to be its leader. In fact, Buddhist texts frequently imply such a connection. The *Divyavada* used the words Ājīvika and Nigrantha (i.e., Jain) interchangeably. Further, each school puts the other second in its value categories, suggesting that each saw the other as the closest thing to itself.[232] The Jain *Bhāgavati Sūtra* includes twelve Ājīvikas among those religious figures held up as models for Jains, evidently recalling a time when the two schools shared the same pantheon of saints.

As the record stands, due to the existence of the Jain and not the Ājīvika canon, the Jain school looms larger. But it was not always so. Siddhārtha was more concerned about Ājīvika than Jain rivals. Aśoka placed Ājīvikas before Jains in his Seventh Pillar Edict, and the *Arthaśastra* placed Ājīvikas second behind Buddhists, with Jains third, in its list of *nāstika* religions.[233] "The fact," Basham observes, "that [the Ājīvika] caves [at Lomas Rishi] are the earliest surviving religious edifices in India suggests that the Ājīvikas were the first community to use material more solid than wood for religious purposes."[234]

There are numerous signs that Ājīvikism represents an earlier stage of Indian religion than Jainism, and is "more in keeping with Dravidian [than Aryan] character and tradition."[235] Indeed, its antiquity, though it can only be surmised, seems formidable. Both Jainism and Buddhism reacted against Ājīvikism, which must then have been present before they defined themselves in part by contrast with it. The Ājīvika monk's initiation involved physical ordeals such as grasping a hot iron, a common feature of shamanic lineages. Various points connect Ājīvikism with the Indus Valley culture. Ājīvikas are said, for example, to have performed penances in funeral urns. The Aryans cremated their dead; but the Indus culture performed secondary burials in urns, some of them as much as three feet in height and diameter, that is, adequate for a human body in a contracted foetal-like position.[236] For a monk to take up the posture of the contracted corpse within such an urn suggests an meditation on mortality, not unlike the meditations in graveyards or on rotting corpses that are recommended in later yogic literature.[237]

Ājīvikism, then, seems to be a part of the Bronze Age (pre-Aryan?) substrate, descended from the Indus culture, from which Mahāvīra broke off a splinter group with certain reforms of doctrine and practice. The *Bhāgavati Sūtra* describes Gosāla and Mahāvīra as colleagues who spent six years of wandering penance together prior to their schism. The Jain texts present Gosāla as the disciple of Mahāvīra who broke away;[238] it is widely believed, however, that Mahāvīra was actually the disciple and Gosāla the master.[239] It would seem that Mahāvīra first belonged, by birth, to the clothed proto-Jain religion of Pārśva, the previous *tīrthankara*, to whose religion Mahāvīra's parents belonged. At some point he left this group and associated himself with Gosāla, a naked ascetic possibly in the lineage of the "Muni," whom the tenth book of the *Ṛg Veda* describes as *vātarasana*, wind-clad. Mahāvīra became a naked ascetic like Gosāla, then later broke from him and, partially returning to his earlier affiliation, led a sect of reform Jains who went naked and followed various "rigid rules" which "formed no part of the ancient creed,"[240] that is, the religion of Pārśva. In any case, the origin of the Ājīvika-Jain tradition disappears in prehistory, possibly going back ultimately to the Indus Valley itself, where there are iconographic elements that seem to foreshadow the iconography of Pārśva.[241]

The Schism

The central point of disagreement between Gosāla and Mahāvīra was the issue of free will versus determinism in relation to the possibility of escape from the process of reincarnation. In their case, the issue devolved on questions of the efficacy of divination[242] and the purpose of ascetic practices. On the latter issue, Gosāla, who did not believe that any action could affect the round of eighty-four thousand reincarnations, regarded asceticism as essentially magical in purpose; it gave one special powers for use while in the body, but had no effect on the date of one's issuance from bodily life. For Mahāvīra, however, asceticism has exclusively the goal of early escape from the wheel. The more puritanical Buddhists and Jains regarded the Ājīvikas as immoral for their prototantric advocacy (like the Vratyas') of sexual magic, song, and dance. Mahāvīra ruled that "When found singing, dancing, making music, imitating animal voices, laughing and disguising himself [a monk] is liable to prosecution."[243] Music, dance, and laughter (mockery) are characteristic of the Ājīvika religion which Mahāvīra is "Aryanizing"; imitating animal voices and disguising oneself as an animal are based on beast vows and related shamanic practices. In shamanic practices worldwide, dancing to the drum, chanting while dressed like an animal, and speaking with animal allies in animal tongues are parts of the shamanic performance. Mahāvīra's prohibition constitutes an attempt to edit the remnants of shamanic performance out of his version of Jainism.

Another thematic in which the substrate and the reform can be seen is the practice of religious suicide, which was advocated by both Ājīvikas and Jains, but with different emphases. The Ājīvikas offered a variety of ways, including entering a fire made of dried cow- or horsedung, entering water, self-starving, and others. An Ājīvika ascetic was to end his life in a kind of shamanic show put on before his fellows and designed to magically condition the next incarnation. Jainism seems to represent an attenuated or partially reformed version of this tradition. Mahāvīra's parents, worshippers in the Parsvaite religion, died by the comparatively conservative method of lying on the ground and self-starving, and Mahāvīra himself forbade any method other than self-starving, believing that any other method endangered beings (*animalcula*) other than oneself. The Jain suicide was the culmination of a twelve-year practice which aimed toward it from the beginning. Various vows for the final event could be taken, including the vow of immobility. One Chilatiputta, a Jain, gained fame for lying motionless while his body was eaten by ants.[244] The method practiced by Gosāla was fasting with neither food nor liquid.

The *Jātaka* relates many past incarnations of the Buddha which ended with religious suicides, confirming that this was a part of the primitive substrate which both Mahāvīra and Siddhārtha reformed. Finally, many texts, including the *Yajur Veda*, the

Śatapatha Brāhmaṇa, and the *Mahābhārata*, denounce suicide altogether in their increasing reaction against the shamanic body-practice (*kāyasādhana*).[245]

Aryan Reformers

In the middle Vedic period, when ascetic and magical practices from various sources were being assimilated into the Vedic religion, methods were devised to control them in order to take advantage of their power while limiting their socially disorienting influence. One means of assimilating ascetic practices into the Aryan community without undermining the life patterns of the householder was the expansion of the *aśrama* system, or system of life-stages, to include a life-ending period of austerities to be undertaken only after the performance of one's social and familial duties. This final *aśrama* was defined in great detail and systematized in a set of rules which did not simply depend on the inclination of a single (shamanic) teacher, but was regulated for everybody. This was asceticism as the Brahmanic establishment would have it.

But asceticism (as remarked above) seems to arise characteristically in a context of pantheism, and it does not go well with blood sacrifices and empty ritual forms. Inevitably some members of the *kṣatriya* community saw in the example of the Vratyas, the antinomian Ājīvikas, the Muni, and others, not an old-age retirement plan but a profession, a way to spend one's whole life. A number of *kṣatriya* religious leaders—including, it seems, Mahāvīra and Siddhārtha[246]—dropped out of society and founded separate ascetic communities. These orders were patterned after the systematization of the ascetic *aśrama* by the Brahmins, and contained many of the same rules, but adopted before, rather than after, the duties of a householder.

On this view, the Brahmanical ascetic *aśrama* and the Buddhist and Jain orders are to be regarded as reforms of an earlier ascetic tradition. It seems that Gosāla, Mahāvīra, and Siddhārtha had all engaged in the practices of the older tradition, perhaps in a lineage related to Pārśvaism. Siddhārtha's own words indicate that in his six years of austerities he went naked and shaved his head and attempted to protect even the dew drop; this is an indication either of Jain-Ājīvika practice or of the practice of a tradition which either derived from the same source or served as the source for both of them. Gosāla, who seems to have been non-Aryan, remained an unreformed representative of the ancient tradition descending from the Indus Valley. Mahāvīra and Siddhārtha, on the other hand, reformed this practice in shaping their own sects. Mahāvīra seems to have renounced the use of asceticism (*tapas*) for magical purposes; in his rule asceticism is found useful primarily for purging out bad *karma* by self-sacrifice. Siddhārtha goes a step farther than Mahāvīra into the zone of psychologism, intentional ethics, and the general renunciation of physical austerity (*tapas*) in favor of analysis and guidance of the thought-stream.

Magic

Prominent in the ethical reforms of the era is the question of the meaning and value of magical powers. In the pre-Aryan—or at least now pre-Vedic—tradition religious virtuosos practiced austerities and claimed to receive superpowers from them; the Muni of *Ṛg Veda* X.136, with his claimed ability to travel throughout the universe at will, is one example of many. Such claims made a deep impression on the popular mind. Even when ascetic practices were turned to different purposes within the reform movements, the association of asceticism (*tapas*) with superpowers was ineradicable. All the reform movements accepted to some extent the factuality of superpowers, even while they denied that they were the goal.

The belief in magic was deemphasized in the reform communities because it tended to replace personal responsibility. Magic was a means of overleaping the consequences of one's actions, a kind of alternative to the *karma* doctrine, which held that each being was personally responsible for the consequences of his or her every action. For Mahāvīra, magical powers "have nothing at all to do with the road leading to salvation."[247] Among the early Buddhists they were regarded as actual impediments; one could get so wrapped up in the seeking of *siddhis*, or superpowers, that it became almost impossible to attain basic sanity. Austerity practiced for such rewards is just another goal-oriented ambition, not unlike the ambition for money. Siddhārtha, who focused on the decentering of the self, renounced the ascetic life because he felt that its goal orientation strengthened rather than decreased the dominance of the ego.

Still, the devotees of such teachers as Siddhārtha and Mahāvīra had long believed that sorcerers could provide useful prophecies, blessings, healings, and so on. When they saw monks practicing the same type of austerities, especially in the Jain community, they attributed the same powers to the monks. "To touch them," a Jain book said of its monks, "is considered as beneficial as are their excrements; they procure milk, honey, and butter, and they cause supplies never to run short."[248] Such is the prestige of the fertility hero, compounded of shamanic magic and Neolithic sacrifice, which non-Aryan yogis such as the Nāth Siddhas continued to seek. Stories of the magical powers were inevitably told of Siddhārtha and Mahāvīra by their devotees. They both are said to have engaged in sorcerers' duels or contests with members of other sects. In Mahāvīra's one recorded sorcerers' duel, he "counters the hot missile [viz., the projected *tapas* energy] of his opponent with a cool one of his own, which is contrary to the nature of the subject."[249] Contrary to shamanic practice, which featured control of fire, Mahāvīra responds to a challenge with coolness; his comportment, in other words, even while winning the sorcerers' duel, was antisorcerer. He chose to retain the emphasis on austerity but to link it to nonviolence and release from reincarnation. Siddhārtha chose not to retain the emphasis on austerity at all, and thus the Buddhist monks were mocked by the Ājīvikas as "householders with shaved heads." The Ājīvikas seem to have fully retained the shamanic power emphasis; they continued to make a living by sorcerers' services to the common people, after Mahāvīra had forbidden such practices to his reformed monks.

The Brahmanical tradition, stimulated by the input of primitive magic and asceticism, expanded its purview and enjoyed increasing cultural dominance in the late Vedic and Epic periods. Meanwhile, the tradition of body-emphasizing *sādhana* proceeded in the background as it were, and finally resurfaced in the early centuries A.D. The tantric movement, the various Śaiva sects, the medieval or southern Ājīvikas, the Kanpath yogis, are all manifestations of this resurgence of an earlier, non-Vedic tradition that contains elements from both the Indus Valley (such as the practice of *mūlabandhāsana*) and the ancient Near East (such as the caduceus). In the same period the Jains and Buddhists reestablished their ancient connection with this stratum in their left-hand school. In still later developments the Vedic idealizing tendency struck back again at the revived Bronze Age stream, denouncing and even outlawing tantric practices.

Question V: How is the Sumerian Hypothesis relevant?

About a century ago, Cornford argued that, in terms of their modes of understanding, the Bronze Age was a primarily myth-making, image-using phase of culture, and the Iron Age was primarily a philosophy-making, logic-and-abstraction-using phase.[250] He felt the transition between the two involved the development of monumental abstract ideas like "being" or "nothingness" or "necessity" from mythological images like Brahmā, Humbaba, or the Eumenides. Philosophy, he argued, "the latest of man's great achievements," did not appear suddenly but developed with a smooth continuity out of earlier ages of thought. "If we could survey the whole development of mankind," he writes, "pre-Socratic speculation would no longer strike us as rudimentary and infantile, but as the crowning epoch in a development covering many more ages than history can record . . ."[251] "We must not be misled into . . . imagining that Thales or Anaximander was like Adam on the day of his creation, with no tradition behind him, no inherited scheme of things, opening his innocent eyes on a world of pure sense impressions not as yet coordinated into any conceptual structure."[252]

The Neolithic-Chalcolithic Age was both mythopoeic and protoscientific. Many mythic archetypes were cast into form—and in addition mathematics and observational science seem to have arrived at the precession of the equinoxes and basic tuning theory. In Mesopotamia in the Late Chalcolithic and Early Bronze Age a grand synthesis of this long tradition was worked out by a well-endowed priestly/scholarly community. This complex apparatus was called for by the surrounding social system.

The project of synthesis may have been significantly in place already when—or it may have arisen at just the moment when—writing was developed. In the Uruk and early dynastic periods, the frameworks were fixed for both the western and the eastern ways of conceptualizing time, space, and what happens on the stage they erect.

Combining priestly and philosophical concerns, this Bronze Age synthesis cast all the universe in a mathematical-astronomical-musical unity within which temporal gears generate diversity and articulation. So ample yet so watertight was this synthesis that it overwhelmed the communal cultural minds of other less developed traditions, accumulated momentum, and left a diffusion swathe that circles the globe. Distinctive Mesopotamian icons such as the Gilgamesh or *dompteur* are found on Shang dynasty bronzes, in pre-Columbian Chavin fabrics, and in the metal work of the Sutton Hoo ship burial.

Even if one grants the whole Mehrgarh thesis—that urbanization developed there indigenously with no significant formative influence from outside—and even if one accepts the new dating of Harappan writing as early as 3300 B.C. and the thesis that it also must have developed indigenously with no outside input, still the fact remains that the specifically Mesopotamian-style iconographs remain unexplained by any of this. Even if one were to grant the still-unproven indigenous developments, still, at some point, either before, during, or after these developments, a mass of Sumerian iconography came in. Indeed, so receptive to this material was the Indus Valley culture that it seems to have taken the position of the culture that feels less developed and hence borrows from the one that seems more developed—like the Urartians also borrowing *dompteur* and goats-flanking-tree and so on.

Diffusion Situations

Both Greece and India seem to have felt fairly early impacts of the massive outward-moving cultural wave of civilizational precipitation in Mesopotamia. In the case of ancient Greece there is no longer much resistance to the positing of Near Eastern influence. Indeed, it no longer has to be posited—it's just part of the ordinary landscape of the field. The whole metanarrative of a mathematically and astronomically ordered universe seems to have come from this source, along with corollaries such as the cosmic cycle elaborately worked out in intricate numerology.

The Mesopotamian protoscience, as Bottero says, was "the first serious rough outline of what was later taken over, expanded, deepened, and organized by the Greek thinkers, and developed into the 'scientific mind.'"[253] The cognitive stage on which the Greeks were to perform their startling "miracle"—cracking the code of logic in a clear progression from Parmenides to Aristotle—was set up by Mesopotamian inheritances. During the whole millennium of the Greco-Roman experience Mesopotamia was right there, more or less next-door, as was Egypt. The reality of their presence in the cultural life of the Greeks was too obvious and natural to need insisting on.

> Before ancient Eastern science had disappeared from the historical stage . . . many of its major achievements were borrowed by the Greeks. Greek culture achieved its brilliant flowering to no small degree because Babylonian and Egyptian mathematics, Phoenician writing and many other achievements of the East had preceded it. And the Greeks themselves readily acknowledged that they had learned much from the peoples of the East and that they had borrowed their inventions and scientific achievements. The Greeks considered that they had borrowed their geometry from the Egyptians. According to tradition, Pythagoras made a journey to Egypt and there became acquainted with Egyptian mathematics. The great materialist Democritus spent five years in Egypt, becoming acquainted with local science. The observations of Egyptian physicians were included in the body of works of Hippocrates. Herodotus (II, 109) wrote that the Egyptians were the teachers of the Greeks in astronomy. The works of the Babylonian astronomers (in particular Kidinnu) were translated into Greek. The school organized by the Babylonian scholar Berossos on the island of Cos around the year 270 B.C. played a great role in transmitting Babylonian astronomical knowledge to the Greeks . . . The Greeks had direct access to Babylonian mathematics, the level of which was in many respects not inferior to that of the early Renaissance. The direct development of Babylonian arithmetic methods can be seen in the Greek papyri; Hellenistic science stretched with its roots back into the science of eastern peoples. The achievements of eastern civilizations were thus not lost after the conquests of Alexander the Great, and through the continuity of tradition, they entered the treasure house of universal culture.[254]

Today there would be little or no objection to any part of that statement by classical scholars in general. In India, however, there is still considerable resistance among scholars to the idea of Near Eastern influence on the Indus Valley culture. India is almost three thousand kilometers from the Tigris, and it is unlikely the transit ever became common except for a handful of professional merchant-sailors. Influences from so far away may have been felt more dimly, like waves arriving muffled. Still, it is -

undeniable that the Indian ways of conceiving space and time, as much as the Greek, are involved somehow with the Mesopotamian tradition. In the case of Greece there is no problem in attributing the cosmic cycle to Mesopotamian sources; Greeks themselves would cite Berossus of Babylon as their source. But in the Indian case there are complications.

One such complication is the possibility (unsupported though it is by any evidence other than general language type) that the Mesopotamian synthesis may have been formed in part by north Indian elements brought in during the Ubaid or Uruk periods by Sumero-Dravidian colonizers or settlers. So it is just conceivable that the elements shared by the Indian and Mesopotamian worldviews are in part Indian in origin as well as Near Eastern. On the view that such cultural accomplishments as figuring out the precession of the equinoxes go back all the way to the Neolithic Age, they might possibly have occurred in north India prior to the departure of the hypothetical "Sumero-Dravidian" emigrants to Mesopotamia. There is no comparable opportunity on the Greek side for an attempted appropriation of what has long been seen as the Near Eastern invention of civilization.

Hidden Channels

Still, it remains undeniable that the arithmetic of the cycle in Manu bears a close relationship to Mesopotamian arithmetic; either one came from the other or both survived from an earlier phase of thought which may have taken place either in Mesopotamia, or in India before a hypothetical "Sumero-Dravidian" diaspora, or somewhere else. Along with the myth of time, shared elements of the myth of history must be accounted for, such as the myth of the flood found in the *Śatapatha Brāhmaṇa* along with a key word from the Akkadian Creation Epic, *apsu*, the deep (*SB* I.8.1.1). As Keith said of the flood motif, speaking with the view of his time, "Babylon seems the obvious source."[255]

In fact, in addition to the conceptualizations of time and history, the Hindu conceptions of the spatial universe are also Mesopotamian in type. The central mountain, the four directions or quarters, the vertical stacking of cosmological layers, the watery abyss underlying all—these are the outlines of the Sumero-Akkadian model of the universe. If the diffusion originated in Mesopotamia, it must have entered India in the Indus Valley period itself through the Mesopotamian trade, or in the Middle Vedic wave, or in the wave which followed the Persian conquest of the Northwest, or in a combination of the three.

The channels such influence may have followed are hard to reconstruct. Herodotus (I.9), says that "all the sages of Greece came to Sardes in the bloom of its wealth, among whom was Solon." The impression conveyed is that transmission into Greece from either Mesopotamia or Egypt was fairly immediate and direct, lacking in mystery and strangeness. By the time of Periclean Athens both Mesopotamia and Egypt were understood as great repositories of learning and tradition that were right in the neighborhood; Babylon and Heliopolis were like overpoweringly prestigious university towns. Thereafter—from Alexander the Great till the end of the Roman Empire—Greece, Mesopotamia, and Egypt were usually parts of the same polity.

But the channels through which such Mesopotamian elements as the words *apsu* and *tiamat* might have entered the Middle Vedic culture of Aryan society in India are harder to divine. It is easy enough to say that Pythagoras studied Babylonian mathematics at Sardes—but can one imagine hearing that Yājñavalkhya went to Persepolis to study? Some Jain texts say that Pārśva had already, before Mahāvīra, conceived the overall shape of the cosmos.[256] "Pārśva" here may involve an early contact with the Mesopotamian stream, either in the Indus Valley period or the Middle Vedic period or both. Such a transmission is one possible account for structural elements such as the seven levels of the underworld in the Jain myth of the Cosmic Person, which equate to the seven levels of the underworld in the Sumero-Akkadian myth of the Descent of Ishtar/Inanna, and other such world-ordering frameworks.[257] But "Pārśva" is a far vaguer concept than "Pythagoras" or "Plato," perhaps indicating all earlier phases of Jain and Ājīvika tradition.

SECRET DOCTRINES

Pythagoras was far from the first religious teacher to require a closed mouth of his students. Sumerian cults often involved initiation practices that it was forbidden to divulge to the noninitiate. Certain classical Greek cultic situations, including the Mysteries at Eleusis, seem to have been remnants of this ancient stream of Neolithic and Bronze Age religious practice. The evidence of modern so-called primitives suggests that Paleolithic societies such as those of the Magdalenian period probably had male secret societies, female secret societies, adolescent initiation societies, and so on, each with its secrets. Even within a single culture, secrets were kept from group to group.

Egyptian and Mesopotamian priestly documents frequently contain prescriptions of silence. Sometimes they specify whose eyes they are for, as in this Mesopotamian text:

> This prayer is the secret of Esagila. No one save the urigallu of E-kua shall see it.[258]

Another Mesopotamian text advises:

> The young priest may see these rites which you perform, but the stranger who does not possess the hereditary knowledge of the rites shall not see them, unless he wishes his days to be shortened. The initiated shall reveal them to the initiated; the uninitiated shall not see them. It is among the forbidden things of Anu, Enlil and Ea, the great gods.[259]

An Assyrian ritual text warns:

> If you divulge the teachings of Ishtar, you will not remain vigorous.[260]

In Egypt similar prohibitions are found. A text from Edfu commands:

> Reveal nothing that you see in any secret matter of the sanctuaries.[261]

These were cultures that did not pass all their lore on through the literate tradition. Some parts they passed on only through direct teaching, and among those being taught in the great temple complexes were foreigners—priests or keepers of the sacred lore in their own cultures. It is otherwise impossible to account for the widespread diffusion of Mesopotamian texts and ideas, which do not travel as readily as artistic motifs. It is necessary then to recover a certain amount of ancient Near Eastern culture not from that culture's own written records, for they were censored, but from the effects they produced in other cultures. Sumerian things must often be seen through their aftermaths. The great example of an inferred element is the myth of cyclical time, which is not overtly present in extant Mesopotamian texts but can be inferred to have existed there due to the recognizably Mesopotamian mark it left on many later cultures.[262]

Yoga

In addition to the basic conceptualization of time, history, and space, India shares the anthropomorphizing of the universe with the Mesopotamian culture zone, from which it seems to have come in that Middle Vedic wave that is difficult to concretely picture; the hymn to Ninurta seems to lie in the background, and behind it the basic Mesopotamian idea of macrocosm-microcosm correspondence which seems to underlie the early phases of monism in both Greece and India.[263] Macranthropy seems to have come into India along with Akkadian words from the *Creation Epic*. Insofar as yoga, in the *kuṇḍalinī* /haṭha tradition, homologizes the human body to the universe, it is also formulated on a Sumero-Akkadian basis, or a development of one.

It might not, however, be appropriate to speak of a basis for the formation of yoga rather than of bases. It seems clear that yoga is a layered phenomenon embracing elements of vastly different ages.[264] In India alone, some yogic practices may go back to the proto-Australoid stratum of prehistory,[265] others to the period of the Indus Valley culture, still others to the idealizing assimilations of the Middle and Late Vedic periods. Sometime along the way certain practices of the sorcerers were redefined for adoption into yogic communities—perhaps on more than one occasion. The animal imitation practices common among shamans around the world, for example, seem to have become codified into the various animal-named *āsanas*; shamanic immobility or trance may have evolved in protoyogic communities into practices like the *kayotsarga*, or holding of one position for a long time, and meditation, which also involves prolonged immobility.

While such practices may have remained much the same over ages, the conceptual and ideological frameworks around them changed from age to age, meaning that the reasons that people would have given for practicing them changed. Some forms of protoyogic activity seem to have been practiced as sexual or fertility magic in the Indus Valley cities.[266] The transition from tribal magician to urban priest which apparently took place there would have involved some reinterpreting of practice. The assimilation into the Aryan community in the Middle Vedic period required another reinterpretation, and in the transition to idealist/mentalist philosophy in the Upaniṣads and after, the practices in question were again redefined. The idea that yoga was a path or tool for gaining early release from reincarnation is the most prominent redefinition of an earlier body of practices that had had different shamanic/magical purposes. Patañjali had an altogether different explanation of why the yogi would, say, make a sound like an owl, from the explanation which his primitive magician forebear would have given.

The Mesopotamian hypothesis adds one reinterpretation to this list: the proposal that some elements of the yogic tradition—including at least the iconography of the serpent power, the macrocosm-microcosm correspondence, and the myth of the cosmic cycle—diffused from Mesopotamia into India with a reinterpretation that cannot be reconstructed with any certainty. Finally the Ningizzida cult emerges as a prominent candidate for the source from which the doctrine of the spinal channel, the two side channels, their crossings, and the serpent power inside them, could have diffused, late in the second millennium B.C. or early in the first, into both Greece and India. Renewed interest in the doctrine in Greece in the sixth century B.C. indicates a more complex diffusion sequence. A teaching that came into Greece and India in the Bronze Age or earlier seems to have been reinforced in Greece in the sixth century by a wave of Indian input, which probably originated in the same Bronze Age source but had undergone significant reinterpretation as its context changed. The Mesopotamian doctrine, in other words, if such there was, had traveled into both Greece and India by 1000 B.C.; subsequently it remained inconspicuous and, probably, unchanging in Greece, but in India it underwent further development, associating it with convergent doctrines from the non-Vedic community, and so on; then this developed form of the doctrine in turn was disseminated from India into Greece in the sixth century B.C.

Finally, at least four types of material seem to have flowed into the formation of yoga: (1) the complex of practices involved in primitive magic and/or shamanism, including the so-called proto-Australoid stratum, the Dravidian stratum, Central Asian shamanism, Munda shamanism, etc.; (2) the scapegoat/austerity complex of the fertility religions of western Asia in the Neolithic and Bronze Ages (which were in part a redefinition of (1)); (3) the iconography, cosmology, and mythology of Mesopotamia (including in part a redefinition of (2)), received in a series of successive waves; (4) a redefinition in the direction of idealist thought in the Aryan community, under unknown influences which may, as the discourse grows, have involved factors such as loss-of-the-mushroom and stress of the matrilineal-to-patrilineal shift. The different types of yoga—from the idealist raja yoga of pure mentalism to the sexoyogic practices of village tantrism—have their different specific complexions due to the mixture and proportion of such elements, and to the stage of the overall development in which that particular yoga took form.[267]

Notes to Chapter Ten

1. Mario Liverani, "The Collapse of the Near Eastern Regional System at the End of the Bronze Age: The Case of Syria," in *Centre and Periphery in the Ancient World,* ed. M. Rowlands, M. Larsen, and K. Kristiansen (Cambridge: Cambridge University Press, 1987), p. 69.

2. Henri Frankfort, *Cylinder Seals* (London: Gregg Press, 1965), p. 307.

3. V. Gordon Childe, "The Indus Civilization," in *Antiquity* 11 (1937): 351; D. H. Gordon, *The Prehistoric Background of Indian Culture* (Bombay: Bulabhai Memorial Institute, 1960), p. 60.

4. Samuel Noah Kramer, "The Indus Civilization and Dilmun: The Sumerian Paradise Land," in *Ancient Cities of the Indus*, ed. Gregory L. Possehl (New Delhi: Vikas Publishing House, 1979).

5. Sir Mortimer Wheeler, *Civilizations of the Indus Valley and Beyond* (London: Thames and Hudson, 1966), pp. 61–62.

6. Sir Mortimer Wheeler, *Early India and Pakistan* (London: Thames and Hudson, 1960), p. 104.

7. Sir Mortimer Wheeler, *The Indus Civilization*, 3rd ed., supplement to the *Cambridge History of India* (Cambridge: Cambridge University Press, 1968), p. 135.

8. Stuart Piggot, *Prehistoric India* (Baltimore, Maryland: Penguin, 1950), p. 141.

9. Jim G. Shaffer, "The Indo-Aryan Invasions: Cultural Myth and Archeological Reality," in *The People of South Asia,* ed. John R. Lukacs (New York: Plenum, 1984), p. 77.

10. S. P. Gupta, *The Indus-Saraswati Civilization: Origins, Problems, and Issues* (Delhi: Pratibha Prakashan, 1996), p. 175.

11. Michael Witzel, "Early Indian History: Linguistic and Textual Parameters," in *The Indo-Aryans of South Asia: Language, Material Culture and Ethnicity*, ed. George Erdosy, vol. 1 of *Indian Philology and South Asian Studies*, ed. Albrecht Wezler and Michael Witzel (Berlin and New York: Walter de Gruyter, 1995), p. 88.

12. A. Leo Oppenheim, "The Seafaring Merchants of Ur," in Possehl, ed., *Ancient Cities of the Indus,* p. 158.

13. Wheeler, *Early India and Pakistan*, p. 102.

14. Asko Parpola, "The Problem of the Indus Script," in *Essays in Indian Protohistory,* ed. D. P. Agrawal and Dilip K. Chakrabarti (Delhi: B. R. Publishing Co., 1979), p. 163.

15. Shashi Asthana, "Indus-Mesopotamia Trade: Nature of Trade and Structural Analysis of Operative System," in Agrawal and Chakrabarti, eds., *Essays in Indian Protohistory*, p. 39.

16. Gupta, *The Indus-Saraswati Civilization*, p. 124.

17. Simo Parpola, Asko Parpola, and Robert H. Brunswig Jr., "The Meluhha Village: Evidence of Acculturation of Harappan Traders in Late Third Millennium Mesopotamia," *Journal of the Economic and Social History of the Orient* 20 (1977): 129–165.

18. Ibid., pp. 130–131.

19. Ibid., p. 131.

20. Ibid., p. 150.

21. Ibid.

22. Ibid., p. 151.

23. Ibid., p. 152.

24. Ibid.

25. Damodar Kosambi, *Ancient India: A History of Its Culture and Civilization* (New York: Random House, 1965), p. 59.

26. Gupta, *The Indus-Saraswati Civilization*, pp. iv-v.

27. Hans J. Nissen, *The Early History of the Ancient Near East 9000–2000* B.C. trans. Elizabeth Lutzeier, with Kenneth J. Northcott (Chicago: University of Chicago Press, 1988), p. 186.

28. Daniel C. Snell, *Life in the Ancient Near East, 3100–332* B.C. (New Haven: Yale University Press, 1997), p. 28.

29. Ernest J. H. Mackay, *The Indus Civilization* (London: L. Dickson and Thompson, 1935), p. 192, pl. M: 10, 11; C. J. Gadd, "Seals of Ancient Indian Style Found at Ur," *Proceedings of the British Academy* 18 (1932): pt. I, pp. 191–210, pl. I: 6, 7, pp. 195–196.

30. Ibid.

31. Dilip K. Chakrabarty, "'Long Barrel Cylinder' Beads and the Issue of Pre-Sargonic Contact between the Harappan Civilization and Mesopotamia," in *Harappan Civilization: A Contemporary Perspective,* ed. Gregory Possehl (New Delhi: Oxford and IBH Publishing Co. in collaboration with American Institute of Indian Studies, 1992).

32. K. N. Sastri, *New Light on the Indus Civilization*, vol. 1 (Delhi: Atma Ram and Sons, 1965), p. 77.

33. Ibid., p. 85.

34. Ibid., p. 86.

35. Ibid. On the beads see Dilip K. Chakrabarty, "'Long Barrel Cylinder' Beads."

36. Sastri, *New Light on the Indus Civilization*, p. 87.

37. Mackay, *The Early Indus Civilization*, p. 91.

38. Sastri, *New Light on the Indus Civilization*, p. 182.

39. Ibid., p. 239.

40. Sir John H. Marshall, *Mohenjo-Daro and the Indus Civilization*, vol. 2 (London: A. Probsthain, 1931), pl. LXXIX.

41. Frankfort, *Cylinder Seals*, text fig. 24 and pl. XIV.

42. And see Beatrice M. Goff, *The Symbols of Prehistoric Mesopotamia* (New Haven, Connecticut: Yale University Press, 1963), figs. 530, 602.

43. See Ernest J. H. Mackay, *Further Excavations at Mohenjo-Daro, Carried Out by the Government of India Between 1927 and 1931*, 2 vols. (New Delhi: Indological Book Corporation, 1938), pl. LXXXII, 3; LXXXIII, 24, etc.

44. Gupta, *Indus-Saraswati Civilization*, p. i.

45. Marvin Harris's term, for example, *Our Kind: Who We Are, Where We Came From, Where We Are Going* (New York: Harper and Row, 1989), p. 66.

46. Quoted in B. M. Bongard-Levin, *Ancient Indian Civilization* (Delhi: Gulab Vazirani for Arnold-Heinemann Publishers [India] 1985), p. 23.

47. Gupta, *Indus-Saraswati Civilization*, p. x.

48. Ibid., p. ix.

49. Nissen, *The Early History of the Ancient Near East*, p. 66 and elsewhere.

50. Shaffer, "The Indo-Aryan Invasions," p. 81.

51. Jean-Francois Jarrige and Richard H. Meadow, "The Antecedents of Civilization in the Indus Valley," *Scientific American* (August 1980), pp. 122–133

52. Shaffer, "The Indo-Aryan Invasions," p. 82.

53. Jean-Francois Jarrige, "Excavations at Mehrgarh: Their Significance for Understanding the Background of the Harappan Civilization," in Possehl, ed., *Harappan Civilization*, p. 83.

54. Bongard-Levin, *Ancient Indian Civilization*, p. 27.

55. Jarrige, "Excavations at Mehrgarh," pp. 81, 83.

56. Chakrabarti, "'Long Barrel Cylinder' Beads," pp. 265–270.

57. Gupta, *Indus-Saraswati Civilization*, p. 37.

58. Ibid., pp. 45–46.

59. Jim G. Shaffer and Diana A. Lichtenstein, "The Concepts of 'Cultural Tradition' and 'Paleoethnicity' in South Asian Archeology," in George Erdosy ed., *Indo-Aryans of Ancient South Asia*, p. 131.

60. *Nissen, The Early History of the Ancient North East*, p.158.

61. Ibid., p. 162.

62. Ibid., p. 158.

63. Bottero, *Mesopotamia*, p. 79.

64. Ibid., p. 85.

65. Shaffer and Lichtenstein, "The Concepts of 'Cultural Tradition' and 'Paleoethnicity,'" p. 135.

66. Nissen, *Early History of the Ancient Near East*, pp. 8, 9.

67. Bridget and Raymond Allchin, *The Birth of Indian Civilization* (Baltimore, Maryland: Penguin Books, 1968), p. 322

68. Wolfram von Soden, *The Ancient Orient: An Introduction to the Study of the Ancient Near East*, trans. Donald G. Schley (Grand Rapids, Michigan: William R. Eerdmans, 1994), p. 17.

69. Jean Bottero, *Mesopotamia: Writing, Reasoning, and the Gods*, trans. Zainab Bahrani and Mac Van De Mieroop (Chicago: University of Chicago Press, 1992), p. 68.

70. Von Soden, *The Ancient Orient*, p. 17.

71. Georg Feuerstein, David Frawley, and Subhash Kak, *In Search of the Cradle of Civilization* (Wheaton, Illinois: Quest Books, 1995); Jan E. M. Houden referred to this book and some others as "'new age' anti–Aryan Invasion books." ("Indo-aryan Debate, Sources," on website *www.sarasvati.simplenet*, 10 Feb. 2000.) George Erdosy referred somewhat similarly to the "lunatic fringe" of Indology, "devoid of scholarly value" because of "political motivations (usually connected with Hindu revivalism . . .)" (Erdosy, ed., *The Indo-Aryans of Ancient South Asia*, p. x), including the view that India was the homeland of the Indo-European languages. But recently many scholars, both British and Indian, have emphasized the so-called Aryan presence by pushing back the date of the dispersion from the proto-Indo-European homeland and proposing that the Indus Valley culture was in fact Indo-European. In Renfrew's view, for example, a revised model emerges as follows: First, the Indus Valley culture was itself Indo-European, Indo-Europeans having occupied the area since perhaps 6000 B.C.; second, the Indus culture underwent a complex systems collapse (not a conquest) and the populations dispersed; thirdly, the *Rg Veda* was composed (perhaps as late as 1000 B.C.); fourth, contact with Dravidians brought about the *Atharva Veda*. From the point of view of British scholars such as Renfrew the extension of the arena of Indo-European influence might serve some subcolonial agenda; but it is hard to see how this scenario accrues to the agenda of Indian autonomist scholarship; to escape the invasion by Indo-Europeans, they give the whole Indus culture to them.

72. Alain Daniélou, *Śiva and Dionysus*, trans. K. F. Hurry (London: East-West Publications, 1982), p. 34. See also Paramesh Chowdhury, *Indian Origin of the Chinese Nation: An*

Unconventional Challenging Theory about the Origin of the Chinese (Calcutta: Dasgupta and Co., 1990).

73. Nissen, *The Early History of the Ancient Near East*, p. 13.

74. Snell, *Life in the Ancient Near East*, p. 15.

75. Denise Schmandt-Besserat, "From Tokens to Tablets: A Re-evaluation of the So-called 'Numerical Tablets,'" (*Visible Language* 15 [1981]: 321–344; *Before Writing*, vol. 1, *From Counting to Cuneiform* (Austin, Texas: University of Texas Press, 1992).

76. Nissen, *Early History of the Ancient Near East*, p. 69.

77. Ibid., p. 66. On this point von Soden concurs, calling the Early Sumerian period (around 3200 B.C.) "the time of the earliest high civilization" (*The Ancient Orient*, p. 47).

78. Ibid., p. 17.

79. Bottero, *Mesopotamia*, p. 70.

80. Bottero's term (ibid., p. 69).

81. Von Soden, *The Ancient Orient*, p. 3.

82. Nissen, *Early History of the Ancient Near East*, pp. 2–3.

83. S. P. M. Harrington, "Early Indus Script" *Archeology* (September/October 1999): 15; website *www.sarasvati.simplenet*; John Noble Wilford, "Who Began Writing? Many Theories, Few Answers" (*The New York Times*, April 6, 1999).

84. Website *www.sarasvati.simplenet*; Sarasvati-Sindhu Civilization, 5 Feb. 2000.

85. Mitchell, "Earliest Egyptian Glyphs," p. 29.

86. Gupta, *Indus-Saraswati Civilization*, p. 188, n. 3: "Wheeler knew all about the various pieces of evidence . . . , still he chose to ignore most of them and closed his eyes to the obvious conclusions."

87. Wheeler, *Early India and Pakistan*, pp. 105–106.

88. Sastri, *New Light on the Indus Civilization*, p. 122.

89. Mackay, *Further Excavations at Mohenjo Daro*, pl. XC, 13.

90. Sastri, *New Light on the Indus Civilization*, p. 118.

91. See, e.g., ibid., pl. III, 8; pl V, 4c, 5c, etc.

92. Mackay, *Further Excavations at Mohenjo-Daro*, pl. LXXXIV, 75, 86.

93. Sastri, *New Light on the Indus Civilization*, p. 12, fig. 13. Some consider cemetery H to be post-Harappan, others the final Harappan stratum.

94. Heinrich Zimmer, *Art of Indian Asia*, vol. 2, Bollingen Series 39 (Princeton, New Jersey: Princeton University Press, 1955), p. 134.

95. Mackay, *The Indus Civilization*, p. 52.

96. See, e.g., James Mellaart, *Earliest Civilizations of the Near East* (New York: McGraw-Hill, 1978), fig. 81.

97. Goff, *The Symbols of Prehistoric Mesopotamia*, fig. 437.

98. Kazimierz Michalowski, *Great Sculptures of Ancient Egypt* (New York: William Morrow, 1978), pl. 50.

99. Asko Parpola, *Deciphering the Indus Script* (Cambridge: Cambridge University Press, 1994), p. 213.

100. S. H. Hooke, *Babylonian and Assyrian Religion* (Norman, Oklahoma: University of Oklahoma Press, 1963), p. 6.

101. Mackay, *The Indus Civilization*, p. 53.

102. Oppenheim, "The Seafaring Merchants of Ur," p. 155.

103. Allchin and Allchin, *The Birth of Indian Civilization*, p. 271.

104. I show the seal impression in figure 12 because of its visual similarity to the Indus version in figure 13. The identification of this seal as a goddess in a tree is not certain, however; Frankfort, for example, does not believe in it. Still, regardless of the interpretation of this seal, the tree-goddess type definitely existed in Mesopotamian iconography. Parrot, for example, describes a representation of Ninhursag as "with a leafy crown on her head, her shoulders covered with sprouting branches, her hair flowing out behind her, and holding the branch of fertility in her hand" (*Sumer, The Dawn of Art* [New York: Golden Press, 1961], p. 139). In addition, the many Egyptian examples of the Sycamore Goddess confirm that the type was common in the area in the Bronze Age. "The sycamore became a celestial tree and was regarded as a manifestation of the sky goddess, Nut, who was to 'shield' the dead Osiris and 'rejuvenate his soul among her branches'" (Manfred Lurker, *The Gods and Symbols of Ancient Egypt: An Illustrated Dictionary* [London: Thames and Hudson, 1980], p. 119). The Egyptian goddess is represented as located among the branches of the sycamore tree, much as in figure 13.

105. Benjamin Rowland, *The Art and Architecture of India*, 3rd. ed. (Baltimore, Maryland: Penguin, 1970), p. 38.

106. The eight-petalled rosette associated with Inanna-Ishtar was not merely an ornament. It seems to have been a cosmogram based ultimately on the tradition of the Halaf ware plates of the fourth millennium. In sculptural forms it was attached to the altar in Ishtar temples. In cylinder seals it was the food eaten from the end of a vine or branch by the temple herds. In the Royal Tombs at Ur it occurred in gold (as in the Indus Valley example) both in the jewelry of "Pu-Abi" and at the ends of the branches in the "ram in a thicket" sculptures. It was a central icon of Sumerian religion.

107. See Thomas McEvilley, "An Archaeology of Yoga," *Res: Anthropology and Aesthetics* 1 (Spring 1981), pp. 47–51.

108. Andre Parrot, *Sumer, the Dawn of Art* (New York: Golden Press, 1961), pls. 351, 352.

109. See, e.g., Goff, *The Symbols of Prehistoric Mesopotamia*, fig. 440.

110. Ibid., fig. 352.

111. Parrot, *Sumer*, fig. 252.

112. E.g., Frankfort, *Cylinder Seals*, pl. IV.

113. Damodar Kosambi, *An Introduction to the Study of Indian History* (Bombay: Popular Prakashan, 1975), p. 58. Kosambi does not give the source for the Mesopotamian version, which he identifies as a Jemdet Nasr seal. Two Indus examples are found at Marshall, *Mohenjo-daro*, vol. 3 (London: Arthur Probsthain, 1931), pl. CXII, 380 and 381.

114. Marshall, ibid., CXII, 382; Mackay, *Further Excavations at Mohenjo-daro*, pl. LXXXIII, 24; Jerome M. Eisenberg, "Glyptic Art of the Ancient Near East: 'A Seal upon Thine Heart,'" *Minerva: International Review of Ancient Art and Archeology* (May/24 June 1988), p. 27, fig. 6.

115. Marshall, *Mohenjo-daro*, vol. III, pl. CXII, 383; Eisenberg, "Glyptic Art of the Ancient Near East," part 2, *Minerva*(July/August, 1988), p. 12, fig. 15.

116. Marshall, *Mohenjo-daro*, vol. 3, pl. CXII, 386.

117. See Devadatta Ramakrishna Bhandarkar, *Some Aspects of Ancient Indian Culture*, Sir William Meyer Lectures 1938–1939 (Madras: University of Madras, 1940), p. 32.

118. It is found at *Rg Veda* I.118.11, 139.11; VIII.13.2, 13.12, 36.1, 43.38; IX.106.3, and in the *Śatapatha Brāhmaṇa*. See Keith, *The Religion and Philosophy of the Veda and Upanisads*, Harvard Oriental Series 32 (Delhi: Motilal Banarsidas 1976), p. 81, n. 2 and V. S. Agrawala, "Some Foreign Words in the Ancient Sanskrit Literature," *Indian Historical Quarterly* 27 (1951).

119. Bhandarkar, *Some Aspects of Ancient Indian Culture*, p. 33; Debiprasad Chattopadhyaya, *Lokāyata: A Study in Ancient Indian Materialism* (New Delhi: People's Publishing House, 1959), pp. 55–56.

120. Chattopadhyaya, ibid., p. 49.

121. See *Atharva Veda* IV.16.

122. M. G. Bhagat, *Ancient Indian Asceticism* (Delhi: Munshiram Manoharlal 1976), p. 72.

123. For more on this see McEvilley, "An Archeology of Yoga," and "Approaches to the Question of the Antiquity of Jainism," *Jinamañjari: International Journal of Contemporary Jaina Reflections* (Brahmi Society Publications), vol. 13, no. 1 (1996): 6–21.

124. See Agrawala, "Some Foreign Words in the Ancient Sanskrit Literature."

125. Bhandarkar, *Some Aspects of Ancient Indian Culture*, pp. 36–38.

126. Joseph Campbell, *The Masks of God: Oriental Mythology* (New York: Viking Press, 1962), p. 223.

127. Mackay, *The Indus Civilization*, p. 149–151.

128. M. K. Dhavalikar, *Indian Protohistory* (New Delhi: Books and Books, 1997), p. 48.

129. Gregory L. Possehl, "African Millets in South Asian Prehistory," in *Studies in the Archeology of India and Pakistan*, ed. Jerome Jacobson (New Delhi: Oxford and IBH Publishing Co, and American Institute of Indian Studies, 1986), pp. 249, 250.

130. James B. Pritchard, ed., *Ancient Near Eastern Texts Relating to the Old Testament* (Princeton, New Jersey: Princeton University Press, 1955), p. 6, n. 12; Veronica Ions, *Indian Mythology* (London: Paul Hamlyn, 1967), p. 43.

131. Theodor H. Gaster, *Thespis: Ritual, Myth and Drama in the Ancient Near East* (New York: Harper and Row, 1961) p. 396.

132. Adolf Erman, ed., *The Ancient Egyptians: A Sourcebook of Their Writings* (New York: Harper and Row, 1966), p. 285; Ions, *Indian Mythology*, p. 16.

133. Carl G. Jung, *Symbols of Transformation*, Bollingen Series 20 (Princeton, New Jersey: Princeton University Press, 1956), p. 268; Alain Daniélou, *Hindu Polytheism*, Bollingen Series 73 (New York: Pantheon Books, 1964), p. 98.

134. E. A. Wallis Budge, *Gods of the Egyptians*, 2 vols. (New York: Dover, 1969), p. 251.

135. M. L. West, *Early Greek Philosophy and the Orient* (Oxford: Clarendon Press, 1971), p. 33.

136. Ibid.

137. Surendranath Dasgupta, *History of Indian Philosophy*, vol. 1 (Delhi: Motilal Barnarsidas, 1975), p. 198.

138. West, *Early Greek Philosophy and the Orient*, p. 34.

139. Ibid., p. 36.

140. Zimmer, *The Art of Indian Asia*, vol. 1, p. 66.

141. See chapter 4 above.

142. See chapters 3, 4, and 8.

143. Mircea Eliade, *Shamanism: Archaic Techniques of Ecstasy*, trans. Willard R. Trask, Bollingen Series 76 (Princeton, New Jersey: Princeton University Press, 1964), pp. 23–28.

144. Mircea Eliade, *Zalmoxis: The Vanishing God*, trans. Willard R. Trask (Chicago: University of Chicago Press, 1972), p. 19.

145. C. Leonard Woolley, *Ur of the Chaldees A Record of Seven Years of Excavation* (Harmondsworth: Penguin, 1929), p. 45.

146. See, for example, a case described in Joseph Campbell, *The Masks of God: Oriental Mythology* (New York: Viking Press, 1969), pp. 66–67.

147. But Jacobsen no longer translates *pukku* and *mikku* as drum and drumstick (Thorkild Jacobsen, *Treasures of Darkness* [New Haven: Yale University Press, 1975], p. 212).

148. Eliade, *Shamanism*, p. 313.

149. Pritchard, *Ancient Near Eastern Texts*, p. 114.

150. Eliade, *Shamanism*, pp. 153, 204.

151. Pritchard, *Ancient Near Eastern Texts*, p. 101. Adapa "knew the heart of heaven and earth"; compare the Orphic's claim, in the afterlife, to be "child of earth and starry heaven."

152. Ibid.

153. Eliade, *Shamanism*, pp. 479–481.

154. Ibid., p. 481.

155. Henry C. Warren, *Buddhism in Translation* (New York: Atheneum Press, 1977), p. 12.

156. Serge Sauneron, *The Priests of Ancient Egypt,* trans. Ann Morrissett (New York: Grove Press, 1980), pp. 73–74.

157. Hooke, *Babylonian and Assyrian Religion*, pp. 74–75.

158. Jacobsen, *Treasures of Darkness*, p. 209.

159. Ibid.

160. Ibid., p. 16.

161. Ibid., pp. 16–18.

162. Henri Frankfort, *Kingship and the Gods: A Study of Ancient Near Eastern Religion and the Integration of Society and Nature* (Chicago: University of Chicago Press, 1948), p. 259.

163. Ibid., p. 254.

164. J. G. Frazer, *The Golden Bough: A Study in Magic and Religion*, abridged ed. (New York: Macmillan, 1943), p. 174.

165. See Edward J. Thomas, *The Life of Buddha as Legend and History* (London: Routledge and Kegan Paul, 1949), pp. 5, 28.

166. Ibid., p. 31.

167. Pritchard, *Ancient Near Eastern Texts*, p. 67.

168. See, among others, Otto Rank, *Myth of the Birth of the Hero* (New York: Vintage Books, 1959), pp. 12–13, 15–16.

169. See Asim Kumar Chatterjee, *A Comprehensive History of Jainism* (Calcutta: Firma KLM, 1978), pp. 4–8; Schubring, *The Doctrine of the Jainas*, p. 26.

170. Eliade, *Shamanism*, p. 84.

171. Yet Frankfort feels that certain Assyrian texts indicate "a prophetess in a trance" (*Kingship and the Gods*, p. 264).

172. Jacobsen, *Treasures of Darkness*, p. 156.

173. Basham, *History and Doctrine of the Ājīvikas*, pp. 213–214.

174. Schubring, *The Doctrine of the Jainas*, p. 25.

175. Ibid.

176. Ibid.

177. Chakraborti, *Asceticism in Ancient India*, pp. 389–391.

178. Hooke, *Babylonian and Assyrian Religion*, p. 40.

179. Sauneron, *The Priests of Ancient Egypt*, p. 55.

180. Ibid., p. 64.

181. Ibid.

182. See Michalowski, *Great Sculptures of Ancient Egypt*, frontispiece and pls. 38, 39, 43, 78, and 165.

183. Sauneron, *The Priests of Ancient Egypt*, p. 38.

184. Ibid., p. 40.

185. T. W. Rhys-Davids, "Asceticism," in *Encyclopaedia of Religion and Ethics*, vol. 2, ed. John Hastings (Edinburgh: T. and T. Clark; New York: C. Scribner's Sons, 1908–27), p. 69.

186. As remarked by T. C. Hall, "Asceticism: Introduction," ibid., p. 63.

187. Zimmer, *Art of Indian Asia*, vol. 1, p. 53.

188. Giorgio de Santillana and Hertha von Dechend, *Hamlet's Mill* (Boston: David R. Godine, 1977), p. 367 or index.

189. Zimmer, *Art of Indian Asia*, vol. 1, p. 54.

190. "The conceptions and practices of *kuṇḍalinī* yoga," Butterworth says, "were known ... in ancient Mesopotamia." Edric A. S. Butterworth, *The Tree at the Navel of the Earth* (Berlin: Walter deGruyter, 1970), p. 167.

191. Ibid., pp. 167–170.

192. Frankfort, *Cylinder Seals*, pp. 121–122.

193. Ibid., fig. 34, pl. XXI b and f.

194. Ibid., p. 120.

195. Ibid., p. 143, text-figure 37.

196. It is also in the background of the myth of serpent- and Hydra-slayer Heracles, which has been demonstrated tc be of Asian origin (G. Rachel Levy, "The Oriental Origin of Herakles," *JHS* 54 [1934]). Heracles is the Greek hero who attains heaven, and who was the symbol of spiritual ascesis for the Cynics. His death by self-burning links him to the Indian tradition.

197. Jacobsen, *Treasures of Darkness*, p. 7.

198. Ibid., pp. 69–71.

199. Ibid., p. 229.

200. It has also been traced to Melanesian and Annamese folklore (ibid., p. 214); the point illustrates how extremely widespread are the Sumerian motifs.

201. Maurice Bloomfield, *The Life and Stories of the Jaina Savior Parsvanatha* (Baltimore, Maryland: Johns Hopkins Press, 1919), p. 9.

202. Ibid., pp. 9–10.

203. Ibid., p. 22.

204. Bloomfield, *The Life and Stories of the Jaina Savior Parsvanatha*, pp. 34–35.

205. Campbell, *The Masks of God: Oriental Mythology*, p. 219.

206. Heinrich Zimmer first made this point in *Philosophies of India*, Bollingen Series 26 (Princeton, New Jersey: Princeton University Press, 1969), p. 208; he mistakenly, however, shows a seal impression [plate VIc] of a Syrian example of a Sumerian icon not of the double-serpent god Ningizzida but of the god Ea with streams of water flowing from his shoulders. (See Frankfort, *Cylinder Seals*, p. 124 and pl. XXIe and h.) Still Zimmer's point is correct. Frankfort also illustrates a seal that *does* show a god with snakes rising from both shoulders (ibid., p. 143).

207. See chapter 7 above.

208. These are both time deities: That the angles formed by the serpent's coils have something to do with the ecliptic is likely. If the time symbolism can be read back from Phanes and Zurvan to Ningizzida, then he may be connected with the (lost) Sumerian myth of cycling time, and hence possibly with some doctrine of reincarnation.

209. See Zimmer, *Philosophies of India*, vol. 2, pls. III–VIb.

210. Levy, "The Oriental Origin of Herakles."

211. As in Frankfort, *Cylinder Seals*, pl. XII a, b.

212. Arthur B. Keith, *The Religion and Philosophy of the Veda and Upaniṣads*, Harvard Oriental Series 31 and 32 (Cambridge, Massachusetts: Harvard University Press, 1925), p. 337.

213. Eliade, *Shamanism*, p. 146.

214. Butterworth, *The Tree at the Navel of the Earth*, ch. 4.

215. Ibid., p. 87.

216. Frankfort, *Cylinder Seals*, p. 59.

217. See ibid., pl. XII a.

218. E. Douglas van Buren, *Symbols of the Gods in Mesopotamian Art* (Rome: Pontificium Institutum Biblicum, 1945), p. 41.

219. Sauneron, *The Priests of Ancient Egypt*, pp. 40–41.

220. Daniélou, *Shiva and Dionysus*, p. 75.

221. Hooke, *Babylonian and Assyrian Religion*, p. 48.

222. Chakraborti, *Asceticism in Ancient India*, pp. 368, 437.

223. See Ramaprasad Chanda, "Sind Five Thousand Years Ago," *Modern Review* (Calcutta) (August 1932), pp. 159–169. The best seals in this respect are Marshall, *Mohenjo-daro and the Indus Civilization*, vol. 3, pl. XII, 14, 19.

224. See, for example, Jakob W. Hauer, *Der Yoga, ein indischer Weg zum Selbst; kritisch-positive Dastellung nach den indischen Quellen, mit einer Übersetzung der massgeblichen Texte* (Stuttgart: W. Kohlhammer, 1958), p. 28; Matthias Hermanns, *Schamanen-Pseudoschamanen, Erlöser und Heilbringer: Einer vergleichende Studie religiöser Urphänomene*, vol. 1, (Wiesbaden: Franz Steiner Verlag, 1970), pp. 60–62.

225. *Mahābhārata*, V.35.46.1127.

226. Warren, *Buddhism in Translation*, p. 19.

227. Ibid., p. 31.

228. For more on this, see McEvilley, "An Archeology of Yoga,"pp. 56–59, 64–65, 69.

229. Dasgupta, *History of Indian Philosophy*, vol. 3, p. 533.

230. Chattopadhyaya, *Lokāyata, passim.*

231. On the once-famous view of Gordon Wasson (*Soma: Divine Mushroom of Immortality* [n. c.: Harcourt Brace Jovanovich, n.d.]), their southward migration into India eventually cut the Indo-Aryan community off from the banks of the *amanita muscaria* mushroom, which had long provided experiences of ecstasy and magical travel without asceticism; the reintroduction of ascetic practices from outside their community was a compensatory adjustment. The current of opinion recently runs against the *amanita muscaria* (see Harri Nyberg, "The Problems of the Aryans and Soma: The Botanical Evidence," in Erdosy, ed., *Indo-Aryans of Ancient South Asia*, pp. 390–393).

232. A. L. Basham, *History and Doctrine of the Ājīvikas: A Vanished Indian Religion* (London: Luzac, 1951), pp. 139-140.

233. Ibid., pp. 150, 161.

234. Ibid., p. 156.

235. Ibid, pp. 194.

236. Sastri, *New Light on the Indus Civilization*, vol. 2, p. 148. There were also storage jars large enough for this purpose (Jarrige and Meadows, "The Antecedents of Civilization in the Indus Valley," *Scientific American* [August 1980]: 130).

237. Other details could be arrayed. The *Jātaka*, for example, mentions an Ājīvika ascetic who carried, among other magical objects, a heap of red powder (Basham, *Ājīvikas*, p. 92). Indus Valley corpses were daubed with red ochre (Jarrige and Meadow, "The Antecedents of Civilization in the Indus Valley," p. 124).

238. Stevenson expresses the Jain point of view when she refers to Gosāla as Mahāvīra's "unruly disciple" (Alice M. Stevenson, *The Heart of Jainism*, Religious Quest of India [London: Oxford University Press, 1915], p. 60).

239. See, for example, Benimadhab Barua, *A History of Pre-Buddhistic Indian Philosophy* (Delhi: Motilal Banarsidas, 1981), p. 300.

240. Hermann Jacobi, *Jaina Sūtras*, Sacred Books of the East 22 (Oxford: Clarendon Press, 1884), pt. 2, p. xxxii.

241. See McEvilley, "Approaches to the Question of the Antiquity of Jainism."

242. Three stories from Jain sources record the breakup. First, Gosāla asked Mahāvīra what alms he, Gosāla, would receive while begging one day; Mahāvīra's prophecy was fulfilled. Gosāla derived from this the postulate that what was to be could not be otherwise, that is, a disproof of free will and a proof of determinism, not unlike the controversy between free will and divine omniscience in Christian theology. Secondly, after Mahāvīra prophesied the breaking of a certain pot, Gosāla attempted to prevent the fulfillment of the prophecy and was unsuccessful. The third story, that of the sesamum plant, is most interesting:

> On the way to Kummaragama they passed a flourishing sesamum shrub in full bloom. Looking at it, Gosāla asked Mahāvīra a question, apparently designed to test the latter's intuitive knowledge. "Sir," he asked, "will this sesamum bush bear fruit or not, and what will become of these seven sesamum flowers?" Mahāvīra replied that the shrub would develop, and that the seven sesamum flowers would produce seven seed-pods in one cluster.
>
> This very definite answer displeased Gosāla, and he determined to prove Mahāvīra a liar; so he quietly dropped behind and pulled up the bush. But at that moment a shower of rain fell, the plant took root again, and so the flowers ripened and seven sesamum pods were produced in one cluster, just as Mahāvīra had prophesied.
>
> Soon afterwards the pair returned by the same road. As they drew near the spot where the sesamum plant grew, Gosāla reminded Mahāvīra of his forecast, and declared that he would find that the plant had not ripened and the seeds had not formed. Mahāvīra, on the other hand, stood firm by his prophecy. He declared that he had been aware all the time of what Gosāla had done. The plant had been pulled up, and had temporarily died, but it had been reanimated by the shower and was once more living, while the seven pods had developed in the cluster. Plants, Mahāvīra added, were capable of *paüṭṭaparihāra*, or reanimation without transmigration.
>
> Gosāla would still not believe Mahāvīra's word. But, on approaching the sesamum cluster, he found that it contained the seven seed-pods, just as Mahāvīra had prophesied. The revival of the sesamum plant made such an impression upon him that he became convinced that all living things were likewise capable of reanimation. And on this point he and Mahāvīra parted company, and their association came to an end. (Basham, *Ājīvikas*, p. 48)

This material raises various questions. For one, Gosāla is portrayed in these Jain stories as deriving his doctrine of *niyativàda*, or determinism, from observation of Mahāvīra's omniscience in action. This would suggest that Gosāla's doctrine is the newer or younger, formed in reaction to Mahāvīra, while other evidence suggests that Gosāla's doctrine was the older.

Secondly, the reanimation doctrine would not seem philosophically to have been the schismatic point, but the question of free will versus determinism. Since Mahāvīra was advocating that yogis strive for early release, he had to believe in the efficacy of free will. He would not face the discord between his claim of omniscience and his stress on individual responsibility and free will. The dispute parallels the Greek one over Diodorus Cronus's Master Argument: If a statement about the future is already true or false at the time it is made, then the course of future events is already fixed and, as in "the slogan of the Ājīvika sect" (as Basham calls it [*Ājīvikas*, p. 9]), "N'atthi purisakare," "Human effort [is] ineffectual."

The story of the sesamum bush seems related to Gosāla's doctrine of the seven reanimations that occur at the end of the 84,000 incarnation cycle. The seven seed-pods of the reanimated plant relate somehow to the seven reanimated corpses. (That the number is seven is also not insignificant.)

243. Walter Schubring, *The Doctrine of the Jains* (Delhi: Motilal Banarsidass, 1962), p. 65.

244. Haripada Chakraborti, *Asceticism in Ancient India* (Calcutta: Punthi Pustak, 1973), p. 376.

245. See D. S. Sircar, *Studies in the Religious Life of Ancient and Medieval India* (Delhi: Motilal Banarsidas, 1971), chapter 13, "Religious Suicide," pp. 206–221.

246. Yet there is no decisive evidence for the Aryanism of either Mahāvīra or Siddhārtha. The Pali record has the Buddha marrying a wife whose degree of relationship within the same clan was prohibited among the Aryans. He is on the one hand said to be the son of a king, hence *kṣatriya*, and, on the other, the descendant of an ancient Brahmin rishi, Gotama. The Sākyas, however, never called themselves Brahmins, and several clans claimed a share of the Buddha's relics on the grounds that they too were *kṣatriya*. The fact is that the caste system may not have been fully and clearly in effect at this time. A Marxist argument (by Chattopahyaya in *Lokāyata*) suggests that the Buddha was a tribal Indian whose mission was to establish a sheltered tribe-like group (the *sangha*) that could survive in the midst of the emerging national states—a drop-out commune, in effect. On this view the Buddha's kingship was not a historical but a mythological attribute, a custom inherited from the ancient Near East. The hypothesis may seem supported by the Buddha's association with fertility myth; his mother's name, for example, is Mahāprajāpati, "Rich in Offspring." Mahāvīra's position also is ambiguous. His parents are reported to have been Pārśvaites, and Pārśva may have been non-Aryan. The facts are unclear, but both Buddha and Mahāvīra paralleled significantly in their reforms the idealizing tendency of the Aryan *kṣatriya* movements such as the forest communities of the Upaniṣads.

247. Schubring, *The Doctrine of the Jainas*, p. 316.

248. Ibid., p. 317.

249. Ibid.

250. See F. M. Cornford, *From Religion to Philosophy: A Study in the Origins of Western Speculation* (New York: Harper and Row, 1957); *Principium Sapientiae: the Origins of Greek Philosophical Thought* (Cambridge: Cambridge University Press, 1952); *Before and After Socrates* (Cambridge: Cambridge University Press, 1932).

251. Cornford, *Before and After Socrates*, p. 7.

252. Cornford, *From Religion to Philosophy*, pp. 2–3.

253. Bottero, *Mesopotamia*, p. 5.

254. Muhammad A. Dandamaev and Vladimir G. Lukonin, *The Culture and Social Institutions of Ancient Iran*, trans. Philip L. Kohl (Cambridge: Cambridge University Press, 1989), p. 288.

255. Keith, *Religion and Philosophy of the Veda and Upaniṣads*, p. 26.

256. Ibid., p. 29.

257. See Schubring (*The Doctrine of the Jainas*, p. 210) for a description of the Jain underworld.

258. Hooke, *Babylonian and Assyrian Religion*, p. 104.

259. Ibid., p. 125.

260. Leo A. Oppenheim, "Analysis of an Assyrian Ritual (KAR 139)," *History of Religions* 5 (1965–1966), p. 252.

261. Sauneron, *The Priests of Ancient Egypt*, p. 25.

262. See chapter 3 above.

263. Hooke, *Babylonian and Assyrian Religion*, pp. 26–27; Jacobsen, *Treasures of Darkness*, pp. 234–235.

264. See McEvilley, "An Archeology of Yoga."

265. Proto-Australoid peoples moved through India in the Upper Paleolithic, leaving a pre-Dravidian cultural level on which later strata of India were overlaid. The boomerang is found in India independent of any contacts with Australian cultures. Certain unusual yogic postures, especially the all-important *mūlabandhāsana*, which is found on the Indus seals, are found among Australian aborigines in modern times, and suggest a very early background stage of yogic meditation. (McEvilley, "The Spinal Serpent," *Res: Anthropology and Aesthetics* 24 [Autumn 1993], figure 15.) Something like the Australian practice of immobility in certain postures for the sake of

seeing—though in the aboriginal case seeing the prey of the hunt is meant—may lie in the background of the practice of motionless meditation for "seeing" special realities.

266. McEvilley, "Archeology of Yoga."

267. The doctrine of the spinal channel and the surrounding *nāḍis* seems likely to have descended from Near Eastern sources into India and Greece. The absence of the caduceus in the Indus Valley iconography suggests that a good deal of the Sumerian visual input into the yogic tradition, especially the *kuṇḍalinī* physiological system, did not come in the first wave of Mesopotamian influence. The homologization of the human body to the cosmos is not specifically found in Sumer before the Egyptian-influenced Ninurta hymn of about 1000 B.C., but it seems likely to have existed since the Early Dynastic period at least. It is clear that in the Early Dynastic period the universe was already conceived as a central pole with seven stages; whether this pole was called the spine, and the seven levels of it were called seven nerve centers (or circulation exchanges for serpent energy) is not known. But the fact that the equation of the central pillar with the spine (of the goddess Nut) does occur in Old Kingdom Egypt suggests the possibility that that synthesis was effected at some time in the Sumero-Egyptian syncretic strain of Near Eastern cultural influence.

The possible reconstructions of the channels of influence involved in the formation of yogic icons and doctrines must take into consideration Sumerian origins; Sumerian-Egyptian syncretism; Indus Valley contacts with them; Jain-Orphic relationships; Anatolian, Minoan, and Persian intermediaries; and various shamanic lineages. This complex network of formative elements can be reconstructed in several ways.

Chapter Eleven

The Elements

The monism complex seems to be the central metaphysical statement of the ancient world, but metaphysics wasn't the only type of philosophy being practiced. In both Greece and India the religiously inspirational monism complex was countered by critical or demystifying tendencies almost as soon as it was formulated—in some cases while it was being formulated. Metaphysics' tendency toward absolutism brought with it a denigration of empirical values, which culminated in the *māyā* or *doxa* type of doctrine with a consequent reduction of ordinary life to nothingness or illusion. This impasse produced a countertradition involving skeptical attitudes and arguments, dialectical reductions of metaphysical concepts, and so on. Although history has remembered primarily the constructive arguments of metaphysics, their deconstructivist counterarguments were more or less contemporaneous with them and, in the current post-Modernist skeptical atmosphere, are coming to seem of at least equal importance.

In this countertradition the tendency to denigrate empirical values was rejected in favor of a naturalistic return to the phenomena. In the process another kaleidoscope of stylized motifs arose, complementary to the one that comprised ancient metaphysics.

The history of philosophy transpired in this two-limbed kind of development in both Greece and India, despite the modern idea that Greek thinkers were primarily realistic and logical, while Indian thought was supposedly limited to transcendentalist and intuitive modes. In fact, neither of these ancient cultures was as limited as that. The Greeks quite as much as the Indians had philosophical schools with mystical and transcendentalist orientations; conversely, the various trends of pluralism, naturalism, empiricism, skepticism, and protoscientific rationalism unfolded in the Indian schools as well as in the Greek.

The Influence of Bronze Age Quaternity

The concept of the elements mediates between the monistic and pluralistic trends, or between the illusion doctrine and the data of experience. It is familiar in the West because of its acceptance by Aristotle and through him by western alchemists. It interposes between the doctrine of the One and the experience of the Many the idea that everything in the universe is made up of a combination of a Few basic substances—the One-Few-Many structure already encountered. These substances may be held—as they are by Empedocles—to be unchanging like Parmenides' Being, but the combinations and recombinations they go through are temporary and account for the apparent changes in the world of experience. Thus Being is maintained in its purity while experience also is understood to possess a degree of reality. A compromise is involved. Pure Being is compromised by its loss of unity, as the one unchanging reality of Parmenides becomes four unchanging realities, and the Many are compromised by the fact that experiences themselves are still regarded as illusory on the surface, though comprised of real components underneath.

This shift of attitude involves different trends of thought. On the one hand, the idea of seeking a manageable number of ultimate roots of things expresses a metaphysical desire to appropriate the world into a knowable domain by capturing it in a net of structural projections. On the other hand, the materialism with which the concept of the elements was imbued linked it to naturalistic modes of thought and invited empirical investigation. The idea of a limited or family-sized number of roots of things is a partly demythologized version of the Bronze Age cosmology of a few familially related gods and goddesses who rule and in a sense constitute the universe—even being associated with particular physical substances such as water, earth, or air. It is an Iron Age adjustment of the inherited program of the Bronze Age pantheons.

The Indian model seems to begin as a list of four, then early on assumes a fivefold shape, much as the Greek list first settles on four then expands to five. The element of quaternity again harks back to the Bronze Age. The idea of four elements or categories of matter seems to elaborate the Sargonid image of the four-square universe, the four directions or quarters or pillars of the sky, as well as the four ages or stages of the cycle of time as it is later seen in, for example, Empedocles and Manu. The idea of natural quaternity functioned as an organizing template on the universe, a way of ordering the chaotic disorder of either uncompromised Oneness or unlimited Manyness. It was a last version of the Bronze Age mythological universe before empirical pluralism arose.

Glancing at the Diffusion Question

Deussen said, "[O]n both sides independently of one another the simple observation of nature led to the thought of the five compound states of matter."[1] But it is questionable whether parallel development can account for the fact that the lists of elements in Greece and India are exactly identical: earth, air, fire, and water (with a fifth, *aither* or *ākāśa*, a mysterious element with supernatural properties, sometimes added). This list would not arise inevitably from "simple observation of nature"; the Chinese, for example (in the *Shu Ching*), came up with a different list—water, fire, wood, metal, and earth. The scholarly rejections of diffusion on this point are so casual as to suggest that the subject hasn't really been investigated.[2] Although the details of the cultural transactions which led to the identical lists cannot be recovered, much can be seen by watching the ideas take shape in the two traditions.

The Doctrine of Elements in India

Vedic authors show the same impulse to leap beyond polytheism into abstract thought that was realized by ancient Egyptian theologians: the metastep of declaring one deity to contain or to be all the others. The development of the doctrine of elements began as a transference of this move out of mythic into materialistic terms, by declaring a certain *substance*, without elaboration of the personal details that characterize deities, to be all things. The transition from deities to substances transpires linguistically through the use of god-names that come to designate specific materials. For example, various hymns of the *Ṛg Veda* declare that Agni or Fire is the underlying world-substance:

> You, oh Agni, are Indra, the bull; you are the widestriding Viṣṇu . . . In you, O son of strength, are all gods. (*RV* II.1.3, *V*.3.1)

In the tenth book of the *Ṛg Veda*, water figures prominently as the source of all things, as it had in the Sumero-Akkadian *Creation Epic*, which seems to have influenced it. One couplet may refer to the primal state as described in that myth, when Tiamat and Apsu, fresh and salt waters (both of which names occur in the Vedic texts), lay in one another's embrace, then begat a child.

> When you, oh gods, in yonder deep close-clasping one another stood . . .
> Then you brought Surya forward, who was lying hidden in the sea. (*RV* X.72)

Surya was the Vedic sun god, and this myth about him is of a general Near Eastern, Bronze Age type. It relates not only to the Akkadian *Creation Epic* but also to those Egyptian creation myths that describe a primal state in which the gods are all mixed together in the watery abyss—a state terminated when the sun god rises above the water, setting time in motion. Other *Ṛg Vedic* hymns also know the concept of the waters "wherein the gods were gathered all together" (e.g., *RV* X.82.5–6, X.121.7–8), a Bronze Age concept that is a forebear of Anaximander's Infinite in which opposites lie mingled.

The *Atharva Veda* intensifies the search for the ultimate principle of things. As in the *Ṛg Veda*, both fire and water are accorded that status in different passages; in others, air or breath (*prāṇa*) is treated in this way (e.g., *AV* XI.4). In other words, three of the later four or five elements were already isolated as special roots of things in the Vedas. In the Upaniṣads these rudiments were developed into a mature or fixed system.

The *Bṛhadāraṇyaka Upaniṣad* synthesizes the various primary substances into a single process in a creation scene echoing Egyptian and Mesopotamian images of the primordial deep. A solitary consciousness called The Golden Germ (Hiraṇyagarbha) wanders about in the emptiness of primordial night and creates by the random or intuitive course of his wandering, and by nondeliberate responsive reflections on it.

> There was nothing whatsoever here in the beginning . . . He created the mind, thinking, "Let me have a self" (mind).
>
> Then he moved about, worshipping. From him, thus worshipping, water was produced . . . That which was the froth of the water became solidified; that became the earth. On it he rested. From him thus rested and heated (from the practice of austerity) his essence of brightness came forth as fire . . . (*BU* I.2.2)

The myth is similar to Australian creation myths in which magical heat on the part of a wandering ascetic creates or redefines various features of the world he walks through; perhaps it was brought into the Aryan community from the proto-Australoid stratum of Indian culture. At the same time there are signs of the Aryan trend toward idealism, in that it is the first thought which sets the world going, the primal thought which is the will toward selfhood in a consciousness that drifts aimlessly alone in a void. The myth systematizes creation into a series of steps proceeding from water to earth and from earth to fire, with one suggestion of naturalistic process—the solidification of the froth of water into earth.

In the *Chāndogya Upaniṣad* the sequence suggests solidification as a process that might provide by analogy a naturalistic model of creation. The emphasis on acts of consciousness as real events may show the Aryan trend toward idealism at an early stage.

> It thought, May I be many, may I grow forth. It sent forth fire. That fire thought, May I be many, may I grow forth. It sent forth water . . . That water thought, May I be many, may I grow forth. It sent forth food (i.e., earth). (*CU* VI.2.3–4)

In the somewhat later *Taittirīya Upaniṣad* the list of three stages of matter is enlarged to five by the addition of air and ether (Skt. *ākāśa*), an attenuated substance that exists throughout space and is the medium that carries sound; these five are arranged in a series which is then related to the process of selfhood and reincarnationism:

> From this Self ether arose; from ether air; from air fire; from fire water, from water the earth; from the earth herbs; from herbs food; from food the person. (*TU* II.1.1)

If the last three steps—herbs, food, and the person—are counted, not five but eight stages of matter are distinguished. But the last three are there to provide a linkage into individual human lives; the Indian list assumes a classical stature at five and stays so for the rest of the Indian tradition.

In the *Aitareya Upaniṣad*, the elements receive their official title:

> He is Brahmā, he is Indra; he is Prajāpati, he is all these gods; and these five great elements (*mahābhūtāni*), namely, earth, air, ether, water, light (fire). (*AU* III.1.3)

What will be their normal order appears, in reverse, in the *Śvetāśvatara Upaniṣad*:

> When the fivefold quality of Yoga is produced, as earth, water, fire, air and ether arise . . . (*SU* II.12)
>
> Controlled by Him (this) work (of creation) unfolds itself, that which is regarded as earth, water, fire, air and ether. (*SU* VI.2)

If the usually accepted sequence of these texts is correct, then the doctrine of elements shows a full developmental sequence in India and is unlikely to have been brought in from outside. It may seem that a circularity enters the evidence, since the texts in question have to some extent been dated because of such apparent sequences as these. But there is a certain check on this circularity in the fact that the developmental sequences of various themes, when compared, are found to tend toward the same overall sequence for the texts.

This particular developmental sequence, however, is based on the Upaniṣads alone, and other traditions of Indian textuality seem to suggest the influence of the Near Eastern emphasis on quaternity as a starting point. In the earliest exposition of ancient Indian atomism, in the *Sāmaññaphala Sutta* of the *Digha Nikāya*, the Buddha's contemporary Ajita Keśakambala is said to teach the following doctrine:

> A man consists of four elements. When he dies, the earth goes into the mass of earth, the water into the mass of water, the fire into the mass of fire, the breath into the mass of air, and the sense-organs into space (*ākāśa*). (*D.* II.23)

The passage first asserts four elements, then lists them as earth, water, fire, and air—then adds the fifth element, *ākāśa*, evidently without regarding it as an element, but as the space within which the elements exist. It seems the elements are regarded as independent and immutable, not involved in a process of changing into one another.

Ājīvika theory, which seems to derive from that of the Buddha's contemporary Pakhuda Kaccāyana, posited seven elements: earth, air, fire, water, joy, sorrow, and life. Again, the standard four material substances that the Greeks also recognize are listed; then three ethical concepts are added to them, again to provide a bridge into a human life. Why this foundation of quaternity is not seen in the Upaniṣadic passages, which skip it, leaping from three to five, is not immediately answerable. Judging from the Upaniṣadic passages, we see a native developmental sequence; the apparent foundation in quaternity shown in the other traditions, however, suggests stimulus from the Near East.

The Elements and the Two Fires

The *Chāndogya Upaniṣad* evolves the elements from fire to water to earth, not mentioning air but nevertheless implying a condensation series (*CU* VI.2.3–4). The *Taittirīya Upaniṣad* (*TU* II.1.1) adds the final two elements, ether and air; ether it places at the most rarefied end of the series (where *aither* is placed in the Greek model); but air it places oddly between ether and fire: matter is traced from ether to air to fire to water to earth, whereas the condensation series for the Greeks goes from *aither* to fire to air to water to earth.

> From this Self ether arose; from ether air; from air fire; from fire water, from water the earth; from the earth herbs; from herbs food; from food the person. (*TU* II.1.1 [quoted above])

Here the condensation series is maintained except that fire seems out of place. Two other passages (also quoted above) seem to echo this anomaly; the *Śvetāśvatara Upaniṣad* twice (*SU* II.12 and VI.2) lists the elements in the order earth, water, fire, air, and ether, where again fire occurs between air and water.

There is a relationship between the list of stages of matter and the doctrine of the Five Fires and Two Paths (previously discussed in chapter 4 above). The sequence of the transformations of matter is substantially the same as the path that the soul follows when it returns into incarnation after its intermediate afterlife. In both cases there is a suggestion of a condensation sequence, except that fire seems out of place, occurring between water and air. Both the *Bṛhadāraṇyaka* and the *Chāndogya* Upaniṣads show the condensation sequence, in passages which do not list fire and hence do not show the anomaly under inspection:

> They return again ... from space (*ākāśa*, ether) into air; and after becoming the air they become the smoke; after having become smoke they become mist. After having become mist they become cloud, after having become cloud he rains down. They are born here as rice and barley, herbs and trees. (*CU* V.10.5–6)
>
> They pass forth in this space (*ākāśa*, ether), from space into air, from air into rain, and from rain into the earth. (*BU* VI.2.16)

In these accounts the route the soul traverses involves the principle of increasing density. Ethically the sequence shows the soul becoming more and more deeply embedded in matter as it follows a path from the afterlife area in the sky to an area of human incarnation on the earth.

The other passages, in which fire occurs between air and water, may find an explanation in the imagery of the mythic journey from sky to earth: from space or ether comes air, from air comes the lightning bolt (fire), from the lightning bolt comes rain. The merging of these two lists—the transformations of matter through the elements and the transformations of the soul in its karmic round—suggests a doctrine of karmic transformation through the elements, as found in Herodotus and the Ājīvika-Jain tradition.

The Doctrine of Elements in Greece

The Greek evidence is more jumbled and troublesome. It culminates in Empedocles' formulation of the doctrine of the four great "roots of things," as he called them—earth, air, fire, and water. Some passages of the early poets provide possible sources for his formulation. In the *Iliad* (XV.187 ff.), for example, the universe is divided into four parts: Zeus receives "broad heaven (*ouranos*) in the clear sky (ether) and the clouds"; Poseidon receives the sea, Hades the "misty darkness" (*aer*); the earth is left common to all. The philosophers' list of four elements could be a demythicization of this *dasmos* or division of the universe into provinces. Elsewhere in Homer the four elements seem in place as the first subjects worked into Achilles' shield by Hephaestus: "There he made the earth and there the sky and the sea/and the inexhaustible blazing sun . . ." (*Iliad* XVIII.483).[3] A somewhat similar list is found in Hesiod:

> . . . the holy race of the deathless ones who are forever, those that were born of Earth and starry Heaven and gloomy Night and them that the briny Sea did rear . . . (*Theogony*, 106 ff.)

Again the primary sources of being are four, two of which, earth and sea, correspond to two of Empedocles' elements. For the epic poets *aer* meant not "air" but "mist." Anaximander seems to have used it in this way, whereas Anaximenes used it to mean "air." *Aither* was also redefined from its poetic meaning of light in the sky to the quasi-philosophical meaning of "celestial fire," the stuff of which stars are made; this change had taken place by Anaxagoras's time and perhaps by Parmenides'.[4]

Still, these passages do not fully account for Empedocles' language in announcing the doctrine of the four "roots." In one passage he assigns the names of divinities to fire, air, earth and water, respectively:

> Hear, first, the four roots of things: bright Zeus and life-bearing Hera, and Aidoneus, and Nestis who causes a mortal spring of moisture to flow with her tears. (Fr. 6)

Like the Vedic poet referring to fire by the personal or mythological name Agni, Empedocles presents his four roots of things as if he were describing a pantheon of deities. As one scholar says, "In calling his roots by divine names Empedocles is showing that they are the new gods; he sets them up as worthy, because of their eternal and unchanging nature, of the respect and wonder with which the Olympians were traditionally viewed."[5] But if Empedocles had been thinking of the Homeric passage, the obvious names for the pantheon of four would have been Zeus, Hades, Poseidon, and Gaia.

What is at issue here is the question whether this doctrine developed indigenously within Greece or was brought in from outside. The argument deriving the Empedoclean passage from the epic poets attempts to demonstrate independent Greek development for the doctrine of four elements. Another approach focuses on diffusion from outside the Greek tradition by way of Pherecydes of Syros, an author influenced by both Persian and Indian literature and possibly the earliest Greek thinker on record as clearly referring to a doctrine of elements. Damascius, a countryman of Pherecydes, said (DK 7A8):

> Pherecydes of Syros said that Zeus and Time and Earth, the three first principles, always existed . . . and that Time made from his seed fire and breath and water, and distributed it in five nooks.

Later Greeks identified Zeus in this passage with *aither* and explained that into the five nooks Time placed ether, fire, breath, water, and earth, attributing the doctrine of the five elements to Pherecydes, perhaps anachronistically (DK 7A9). The identification of Zeus with *aither* occurs in Empedocles also, though *aither* seems in his terminology to stand not for ether but for fire. In any case, this passage of Pherecydes provides an alternative source for Empedocles, who shared with Pherecydes a somewhat Orphic orientation. Pherecydes speaks less mythologically than do the poets; he makes the distinction between gods and substances, though he still uses both types of terms. He was a link between the poetic and the philosophic predecessors of Empedocles.

Empedocles was a poet himself, and certainly was influenced by his reading of poets. Most scholars, however, in attempting to explain his derivation of the idea of the four elements, emphasize not the poetic but the philosophical forebears, especially the Milesian materialists.[6] Thales, like the tenth book of the *Ṛg Veda*, echoed Bronze Age myth in calling water the ultimate principle of things. Anaximenes focused on air, Heraclitus on fire, as analogues of an ultimate metaphysical/physical principle. A problem is that Aristotle twice explicitly denies that any of the Milesians declares earth an *archē* (*De An.* 405b8, *Met.* 989a6–9). Otherwise this account is much like that given of the development in India. The elements, or ultimate principles of things, were first isolated one at a time, as in the Vedic literature, each in turn being declared the supreme principle; then they were increasingly synthesized by a series of thinkers culminating in Empedocles. This model, like that of Greek poetic forebears, more or less precludes outside influences.

Possible stages of the proposed synthesis are somewhat visible. Anaximander saw the problem with making one substance the unlimited source of all, namely that, as Aristotle put it, “if one of the elements were unlimited the others would have ceased to exist” (*Phys.* 204b24). He postulated a base which was not associated with one substance more than another, and within it four forces, the so-called opposites—the hot, the cold, the wet, the dry—which produce differentiation while remaining always in balance. This system implies the four-element concept, but its intellectual frameworking of the concept is archaic. Anaximander has erased outright myth from his conception of the Infinite; but his system of symmetrical, four-directional tension echoes the Bronze Age cosmogram of the four directions. A major step in naturalistic modeling was taken when Anaximenes proposed a new type of system emphasizing not a formal cosmogrammic structure but a naturalistic process, arranging the primary substances in a condensation/rarefaction series. Simplicius says:

> Anaximenes . . . also posits a single infinite underlying substance of things, not however indefinite in character like Anaximander's, but determinate, for he calls it air and says that it differs in rarity and density according to the different substances. Rarefied, it becomes fire; condensed, it becomes first wind, then cloud, and when condensed further still, water, then earth, and stones. (*Phys.* 24.26 = DK A5)

Anaximenes' list as reported here is similar to that in the *Taittirīya Upaniṣad*, which also includes the four elements in a list of seven or eight stages. Its basic structure is quite different from the foursquare structure held in shape by opposing tensions proposed by Anaximander. But Plutarch says that Anaximenes correlated his terminology with Anaximander's saying that "what is compacted and dense is cold, but what is rare and loose is hot" (DK 13B1).[7]

This Milesian theory of elements is similar in general outlines to that of the early Upaniṣads, with its transformation series, its varying number that settles into a consistent four, and the later addition of a fifth, defined in both cases as the finest. For Empedocles the four elements would be irreducible; none of them could be converted into another. Yet for the Upaniṣadic thinkers as for the Milesians, the elements proceed from one another by internal changes.

According to Simplicius, Anaximenes said that matter "differs in rarity and density," becoming, in increasing order of density, fire, air, wind, cloud, water, earth, and stone. This pattern more or less holds for the Milesian theory as a whole, which, with its condensation/rarefaction structure, is closely related to the monism complex. It presents reality as an accordion-like continuum able to remain one process while yielding different appearances. Still, to Empedocles, with his Eleatic background, it seemed insufficiently rigorous in its implications about being. He inherited the doctrine of the stages of matter along a condensation/rarefaction continuum and subjected it to the Eleatic *elenchus*, insisting on maintaining the basic Parmenidean distinction between Being and non-Being:

> From what in no way exists it is impossible for anything to come into Being; and for Being to perish completely is incapable of fulfillment and unthinkable. (Fr. 12)

Therefore, changes of one element to another were impossible.

At the same time he altered the concept of elements in order to use it to loosen up the rigor of Eleatic monism. The weak link in Parmenides' argument that reality was an unchanging substance was precisely that there could be as many unchanging substances as one wanted, as long as each independently obeyed the Eleatic signposts. Empedocles was convinced that nothing could exist except on the terms outlined by Parmenides, yet did not want to abandon the empirical realm entirely. He reintroduced ontological integrity to human experience by declaring that there were not one but four unchanging reals which, with their combinatory powers, produce the appearance of the things of experience. Thus the four elements, in his formulation, may combine but cannot be converted into one another.

> There is no creation of substance in any one of mortal existences, nor any end in execrable death, but only mixing and exchange of what has been mixed . . . But men, when the elements have been mixed in the form of a man or in the form of a species of wild animals, or plants, or birds, then say that this has "come into being"; and when they separate, this men call sad fate (or death). (Frs. 8–9)

The Fifth Element

The Pherecydean evidence is one problem facing a parallel-development theory, and another is the parallel between the Heraclitean placement of fire and that of the Upaniṣads. Heraclitus inserts fire into the list not in the characteristically Greek condensation/rarefaction sequence, which would place it before air, but between air and water, where also it appears in Upaniṣadic lists (see, for example, *TU* II.1.1, discussed above). Another problem is the fifth element.

In the Greek experience the fifth element was introduced either in the fifth century (by Philolaus or some other Pythagorean) or in the fourth century (by Aristotle or the anonymous author of the pseudo-Platonic *Epinomis*). In any case the doctrine of the quintessence has a special connection with the Pythagorean tradition. Aëtius attributed it directly to Pythagoras and connected it with the Pythagorean doctrine of the five cosmic solids (DK 44A15). Many read the attribution to Pythagoras as, in effect, an attribution to the fifth-century Pythagorean Philolaus, to whom the following fragment is attributed:

> The bodies of the sphere are five: the fire in the sphere, and the water, and earth and air and fifth the vehicle (or envelope) of the sphere. (DK 44B12)

The sphere is the cosmos. Its vehicle or envelope is a kind of outer air which the world breathes constantly. Plato seems to intend the same doctrine when, in the *Timaeus*, he assigns the four Empedoclean elements to four of the cosmic solids, and calls the fifth the universe as a whole—that is, the outer shape of the universe. In the *Epinomis* the five elements are specifically named for the first time, the fifth being called *aither*. Ether is the space surrounding the cosmos and also dispersed throughout the cosmos; it is space itself but conceived not as empty but as very fine matter. It is the substance that the cosmos, when imagined as an organism, is said to breathe; it makes up the soul of the universe. Aristotle (*De Caelo* book 1) lists five elements and assigns ether to the outer circumference of the spherical universe; he shows its relationship to fire when he says that it is the substance of which stars are made. The Pythagorean-Platonic idea that stars were souls shows *aither* to be the stuff of which the soul is made, also.

This concept is closely related to the Indian concept of the fifth element, *ākāśa*. In the first place, it should be noted that the four elements were adequate to account for phenomena; the addition of a fifth in both traditions invites interpretation. Like *aither*, *ākāśa* is the finest or most rarefied of the elements. It is also the stuff around the periphery of the cosmos, the place where the soul's descent into matter begins. It is a curious state in which the soul is regarded as not yet descended totally into its entanglement in matter. It may have something to do with the Jain and Orphic idea of karmic matter, the very small atoms that attach to the soul. Finally, the Indians regard *ākāśa* as the element through which sound travels, the element which has sound as its inherent sense nature. The fifth-century Pythagorean doctrine of *aither* also involves sound. The Music of the Spheres is the sound of *aither* in its pure state, tuned by the relative distances of the planetary and stellar revolutions. Like *ākāśa* it would seem to be the realm of pure sound.

Tentative Conclusions

The doctrine of the four elements would seem to have arisen in a single source, perhaps in India, where the developmental sequence is clearer than in Greece, and to have entered Greece in different versions, partly conflated with the Doctrine of the Five Fires and Two Paths. Some Near Eastern background, which can only be vaguely discerned, may have been in effect. The doctrines of the fifth elements, *ākāśa* and *aither*, surely are cognate concepts. The comparative dating of the fifth-century Pythagorean Philolaus and the *Taittirīya Upaniṣad* is uncertain—either might have come first. But at that time there is no known Greek influence on India, whereas Indian influence does seem to have arrived in Greece. Most likely the Indian concept was imported into Greece in a later phase of the same general wave of Upaniṣadic influence which brought the transformations of matter.

Notes to Chapter Eleven

1. Paul Deussen, *The Philosophy of the Upaniṣads* (New York: Dover, 1966), p. 189.

2. See, for example, Charles H. Kahn, *Anaximander and the Origins of Greek Cosmology* (New York: Columbia University Press, 1960), p. 151, n. 2.

3. *The Iliad*, trans. Robert Fagles, introduction and notes by Bernard Knox (New York: Penguin, 1990), p. 483.

4. This argument is developed by Kahn, *Anaximander*, p. 151.

5. M. R. Wright, ed., *Empedocles: The Cosmic Fragments*, (New Haven and London: Yale University Press, 1981), p. 22.

6. For example, John Burnet, *Early Greek Philosophy* (Cleveland and New York: World Publishing Company, 1964), p. 228; G. S. Kirk and J. E. Raven, *The Presocratic Philosophers* (Cambridge: Cambridge University Press, 1957), pp. 119, 329; W. K. C. Guthrie, *History of Greek Philosophy*, vol. 2 (Cambridge: Cambridge University Press, 1962–1981), p. 142.

7. Trans. Guthrie, *History of Greek Philosophy*, vol. 1, p. 124.

Chapter Twelve

Early Pluralisms in Greece and India

With Empedocles' multiplication of the Eleatic substances, an attempt was underway to rescue the Many from the smothering embrace of the One—to rescue the apparent plurality of sense experiences from the unifying project of the mind. The reaction against the archaic religious character of the monism complex intensified progressively in the thought of Anaxagoras and the atomists, Leucippus and Democritus.

After Democritus the question shifted. The reaction against the Eleatic appropriation of reality went on, but changed form or stage: Abandoning the Problem of the One and the Many, it took up the Problem of Knowledge; the distinction between noumenal and phenomenal came to seem prior to that between One and Many. A shift from metaphysics to epistemology took place, a turn toward the subject. The pressing question ceased to be "Is reality One or Many?" and became instead "Are we competent to make such a judgment?" Then, quickly, "How could we know if we were competent to make such a judgment?" and "What would it mean to be competent to make such a judgment?" The rejection of Eleatic noumenalism led into Protagoras and Sophistic phenomenalism.

Empedocles' multiplication of Eleatic substances, in other words, contributed to the great countertradition of Greek philosophy to which Zeno's dialectic would also contribute— though neither of these philosophers, perhaps, foresaw or intended that effect of their work. From the time of Democritus, skepticism and materialism would grow in a steady oppositional parallel to the Platonic-Aristotelian metaphysical tradition, the dichotomy culminating, from the point of view of later history anyway, in the second century A.D. antinomy between Sextus Empiricus and Plotinus.[1]

Anaxagoras

Anaxagoras (c. 500–428 B.C.), who was born in Clazomenae during the period when that Greek city-state was a part of the Persian Empire, was a student of Anaximenes. Like his younger contemporary Empedocles, he sought a conception of matter which would conform to the Parmenidean signposts while not disallowing the reality of experience. Again, like Empedocles', his solution was by way of the concept of mixture:

> Nothing comes into being or passes away. Rather, it is mixed together in or separated out from existing things. Thus people would be correct if they called coming into being "mixing" and passing away "separation." (Fr. 17)

Simplicius's explanation emphasizes the Eleatic axiom:

> Taking as a prior axiom that nothing comes to be out of what is not, Anaxagoras seems to have put forward an argument like this: What is generated is generated either from what is or from what is not. It cannot be from what is not, therefore it must be from what is. But if so, it must pre-exist in that out of which it has come . . . Therefore in everything there are flesh, bone, blood, gold, lead, sweet and white, but in quantities too small to be perceived by us, all being in all. For how could everything be seen to be generated from everything (even if through other intermediaries) if everything was not in everything? (*In Phys.* 162.26)

The affirmation that "Nothing comes to be out of what is not"—the essential Eleatic axiom—appears like a leitmotif texturing the philosophical record of ancient Greek consciousness, which found this particular insight, or claim to insight, fundamentally compelling. But Anaxagoras was not the conservative that Empedocles had been in matters of ontology. Empedocles had multiplied the Parmenidean substances; Anaxagoras invented a new conception of substance. "In everything," he said, "there is a portion of everything" (fr. 11), and in addition to the axiom about non-being, he employed an axiom of infinity: "All things (are) . . . infinite in number" (fr. 1). The result, as Simplicius observed, is infinity squared: Each one of the infinite things that are contains the infinity of all the things that are. The concept was revolutionary in pointing toward meta-infinities and ontological interpenetration—motifs which would appear repeatedly as parts of the vocabulary of metaphysics, from ancient into modern times.

In order for something to contain infinite things each of which has magnitude, it must itself be infinite in magnitude. Anaxagoras applied to this problem the Zenonian principle of infinite divisibility. "In the small," he notes, "there is no least, but only a lesser" (fr. 3). The traces of all things that exist together in each thing may be infinitesimally smaller and smaller; there is no problem fitting them into a grain of sand or for that matter into the ten-thousandth part of a grain of sand; in fact, one scale would be as capacious or ample as another. Since all things contain portions of all other things, the differences between one apparent thing and another can only consist in the proportions in which things are mixed in each. Anaxagoras sometimes called his interpenetrated infinity the One (fr. 8).[2]

Radhakrishnan encapsulates Uddālaka's teaching in the *Chāndogya Upaniṣad* somewhat similarly: "Matter is infinitely divisible," and "[t]here is no such thing as the transformation of things into one another. When we get butter from churning curds, curds do not get transformed into butter, but the particles of butter are already in the curds, and the process of churning enables them to rise upwards."[3] Clearly there is a parallel to Anaxagoras here. Uddālaka speaks of creation as combination and perishing as separation. "After separating the parts of things," he said, "the Spirit made new combinations of them." Anaxagoras similarly said, "People would be correct if they called coming into being 'mixing' and passing away 'separation'" (fr. 17). (And compare the Jain *Tartivarta Sūtra* [5.26]: "Aggregates are formed by division and union.")[4]

But a major discrepancy is that the text of Uddālaka's teaching does not show the concept of infinity. Being is asserted to take three forms—fire, water, and earth—from combinations of which all things are made up. Uddālaka next asserts that each of these three was in turn made threefold, and explains:

> That part of fire that is red is fire, the part that is white is water, and the part that is black is earth. (CU VI.4.1)

Each of three elements, in other words, contains parts of the other two. This is related to but not the same as Anaxagoras's position, which is that each thing contains the infinity of all things. There is no evidence that the concept of infinity, or infinite divisibility, had yet been articulated in India.

In Greece the concept of infinity was formulated by Zeno as a set of dialectical practices in the fifth century B.C. It was not formulated in comparably rigorous—meaning logical/mathematical—terms in India until about 200 A.D., in the Mādhyamika school of Buddhism. Anaxagoras's metaphysical (rather than logical/mathematical) concept of infinity squared, or interpenetrated infinity, was not articulated in Indian literature until about 400 A.D., in the Buddhist *Avataṃsaka Sūtra*. There the universe is described not merely as infinity squared, but as infinitely interpenetrated infinities: Each thing (of an infinite number of things) contains each other thing *with each thing's containment of all things*—that is, each thing contains each other thing an infinite number of times: it is infinity to the infinite power.

A similar concept is implied in Anaxagoras's proof that Mind must be separate from matter. If Mind, he argues, were mixed with anything, it would be mixed with everything, since anything contains everything. In other words, it is impossible to imagine containing anything in and by itself but only as an infinite mixture. Each thing is an infinity of infinities.

Anaxagoras's conception of Mind (*Nous*) anticipated Plato's mind-body dualism:

> Other things all contain a part of everything, but Mind is infinite and self-ruling and is mixed with nothing but is alone by itself.

If Mind were a part of matter, he feels, it couldn't control it:

> If it were not by itself, but were mixed with anything else, it would have had a share of all things, if it were mixed with anything; for in everything there is a portion of everything, as I have said before. And the things mixed with Mind would have prevented it, so that it could not rule over anything in the same way as it can being alone by itself. (Fr. 12)

Most thought of the early period had been immanentalist. Thales had said, "Everything is full of gods." Yājñavalkya described the *ātman* as the "inner controller." In ancient thought, the controlling principle of a thing was generally regarded as within it. But Anaxagoras, more like a transcendentalist thinker of a theistic tradition, held that the guiding principle of the universe is not immanent in it but stands over against it as an aloof and independent motive force that causes all motion—that is to say, all life. Traces of mythic imagery still cling to the picture. Anaxagoras's Mind stands over the infinity of matter like Yahweh over the primeval ocean. Something remains of the archetypal Egyptian image that inspired the authors of the J document of the *Book of Genesis*: The story of the primeval ocean with night on its waters when sun or mind or self or will suddenly separates itself out from the mixture in the abyss and rises above the waters in the first dawn.

Anaxagoras's concept of Mind and Matter is another philosophical analogue of the Bronze Age mythologem: At a hypothetical "first moment"—"when the cosmogonic revolution starts," as Guthrie puts it[5]—Mind nudges the limitless oceanlike mass of undifferentiated matter. One spot of the infinity of infinities is set revolving in a whirling vortex. As matter revolves, a centrifugal separation, based on the weights and densities of different substances, takes place; the heavier substances gather toward the middle of the vortex, the lighter move outward in the whirl.

Anaxagoras's view of world process as an orderly sifting vortex conceived on natural models is related to Anaximenes' view of it as a condensation/rarefaction process and to Empedocles' separation of the elements. But Anaxagoras has made a major change. In Empedocles' myth, the separation of the substances from one another is followed by their remixing and the event that is transpiring repeats cyclically forever. This concept of temporal infinity compensates for the spatial finity of the cosmos. But Anaxagoras's Mind moves eternally straight on through the infinity of matter, never circling around or turning back and never coming to an end.

Finite vs. Infinite

Parmenides' insistence that the cosmos—Being—was spatially finite has often been cited as sign of a Greek aversion to the infinite and preference for the specific. This idea, like certain others in the accepted view of Greek culture, may result more from a modern projection of values than from attention to the ancient documents and what they say. The Greeks were, after all, mightily taken by, and given over to, thought about the idea of infinity. Indeed, the concept of infinity is one of the most characteristic products of their culture. An artistic and poetic penchant for clarity of delineation and specificity of imagery need not indicate an aversion to the idea of the infinite. To appreciate the separateness of things is a way to appreciate the mystery of infinity, like the sameness/difference of the countless leaves on the trees. The idea that infinity equals indefiniteness or blurriness, and hence that it is somehow ethically opposed to the precision of actual sense experiences, does not seem to have been a Greek idea. In India, in the Upaniṣads and elsewhere, the concept occurs of the individual melting into the One, and so on—roughly equivalent to the idea of the finite disappearing into the infinite. One finds this idea in Greek thought also, in Anaximander's Justice, in Aristotle's view of the fate of the soul after death, and elsewhere; but in the Greek discourse on infinity this moment is not emphasized. Infinity is not presented as a kind of thing that melted, and in the melting lost clarity of shape and form. For Zeno, infinity was not a thing but a process, and a very precise process; the logico-mathematical precision of Zeno's understanding of infinity is a precise intellectual/aesthetic object.

Those thinkers who pressed for the finity of things—the Pythagoreans, Parmenides, Empedocles—were concerned with knowability, the mind's ability to appropriate Being into its systems of order. To be knowable the universe must have limits or the time that it takes to inspect it and come to know it would be infinite and could not be contained within a human lifetime.

Anaxagoras rejected the cosmic cycle—perhaps regarding it as a mythological element in metaphysics—and he seems also to have rejected reincarnationism, perhaps perceiving that the two suspect doctrines go together, or at least that they are very comfortable with one another. Instead, "in his rationalistic and secular outlook,"[6] he delineated a quasi-materialistic infinity which didn't contain archaic, religiously satisfying elements like the return to Eden, the restoration of the Golden Age, and so on.

Anaxagoras's world process went on forever, the prow of the ship of time cutting through the water always in a perfectly straight line and setting off around it the waves and wakes of froth that are individual lives.

If the elements of the monism complex are archaic, then Anaxagoras was a modernizer. He reduced Empedocles' two motive forces—Love and Hate—to one—Mind. Whereas Empedocles' universe revolves through cycles of expansion and contraction, Anaxagoras's universe only expands. Since it is infinite, its expansion will never reach any limit. The whirling movement merely expands outward forever and its eternally expanding spiral wave *is* the world process. In the opinion of some, Anaxagoras does seem to have expressed some religious feeling toward the concept of Mind, which he describes with the Orphic term *katharos*, "pure," and which is like a transcendent deity in his system.[7] His concept of a universal mind whose wavelike activity constitutes the world process has resonances in later Indian developments such as the *ālayavijñāna* concept of Mahāyāna Buddhism, as his concept of infinitely interpenetrated thingness recurs in the *Avataṃsaka Sūtra*. By rejecting the archaic inheritance of Upaniṣadic–pre-Socratic hylozoic monism, Anaxagoras reached positions which would arise by a similar activity in Mahāyāna Buddhism a half a millennium or more later.

Greek Atomism

The pluralistic solutions to the Eleatic *elenchus* which Empedocles and Anaxagoras had devised prepared the way for the secular materialism of atomism. Leucippus was teaching an atomistic system in his school in Abdera, in Thrace, by perhaps 430 B.C. His student Democritus of Abdera, who was born perhaps 460 B.C., was about a generation younger than Empedocles and Anaxagoras and, like them, was concerned with reconciling human experience with the Eleatic signposts.

The anecdotal tradition associates Democritus with foreign teachers and with travel. "He was a student," says Diogenes Laertius, "of Magians and Chaldeans," through some relationship his father had with King Xerxes, who left Magians in his household. According to fairly early sources (Demetrius and Antisthenes), "he travelled into Egypt to learn geometry from the priests, and to Persia to visit the Chaldeans, as well as to the Red Sea." The seemingly unconnected reference to the Red Sea should perhaps be read in connection with the fact that "some say that he associated with the Gymnosophists in India, and went to Ethiopia" (D.L. IX.34–35).

He is variously said to have been taught by a Pythagorean, perhaps Philolaus, and to have written a treatise on Pythagoras, or to have been taught by Zeno and to have been somehow associated with Parmenides. He was known for his cheerfulness—called the Laughing Philosopher—and for certain disciplines which Antisthenes described as "testing his sense impressions in various ways, sometimes going into solitude, and frequenting tombs" (D.L. IX.38). Some fifty works are ascribed to him, none of which survives. He was in many ways the opposite of Plato philosophically, and Plato's editing him out of the history of Greek philosophy has blurred all later perceptions of his work, which seems to have been comparable in importance to Plato's and not limited to the atomic theory.[8]

In terms of the evolution of Greek thought—as Aristotle and the ancient commentators in general agree—atomism was another attempt to rescue plurality from the signposts of Eleatic monism. Parmenides and his pupils had argued: (1) that nothing can come into Being from non-Being or pass out of Being into non-Being, since non-Being is not; (2) that nothing can move, since non-Being does not exist and there is no empty space, or void, for anything to move into; (3) that a plurality of things cannot exist, since various infinite regress arguments reduce plurality to absurdity. Parmenides had called such points "the mighty bonds of necessity." Both Empedocles and Anaxagoras, in trying to shake the bonds loose, had accepted the principle that nothing comes into being and ceases, but compromised the second and third points in various ways.

Leucippus, on the contrary, chose to compromise the status of the Being/non-Being dichotomy; he rejected the assertion that non-Being is not by declaring the existence of empty space or void. This void is not pure non-Being, since it has a trait, namely spatial extension; but it has no other traits of its own and serves only to separate parts of Being. These parts of Being obey the Parmenidean signposts: Each is full and indivisible with no admixture of non-Being. In place of Parmenides' One full and indivisible Being, Empedocles had offered four; Leucippus offered a multitude, all possessing the traits of fullness and indivisibility, separated from one another by void. Leucippus perceived that the spherical Parmenidean One Being was in effect a huge atom. He multiplied it, perhaps heeding the advice of Melissus of Samos, who had remarked, "If there were a plurality, each of the things that exist would have to be of just the same nature as the One" (fr. 8 *fin.*).

The world then is made up of the movements of atoms through void—not in a semimythological cosmic vortex like that of Anaxagoras, but in a mechanical movement not unlike the modern conception of the movements of gas particles. Atoms of varying shapes and sizes, floating and buffeting one another forever in endless space, combine into compounds and separate out again, producing the sensible masses that make up the world of appearances. In a sense the actual facts of human experience do not really exist, anymore than they did for Parmenides, since the atoms themselves do not inherently possess sense qualities. But in another sense the facts of experience are real, since sense qualities are created by the interaction of our senses with large aggregations of atoms. Sense impressions are intermediary between the mind and the ultimate reality of atoms and void. Democritus's attempt to deal with the breach between atoms and the void on the one hand and human experience on the other is the beginning of phenomenalism in western thought. The qualities of things arise not from the things that really exist, atoms and void, but from our inability to sense directly the things that really exist. Our subjectivity has altered the incoming information. As Democritus put it:

> Sweet exists [only] by convention, bitter [only] by convention, color [only] by convention: in reality there is only atoms and void. (Fr. 9)

Democritus, then, saved plurality from the Eleatic *elenchus*, but he did not save the appearances. The appearances remain as unreal as they were to Parmenides. Between atoms and void on the one hand, and the world of sense experience on the other, there is a gap as huge as that in the *doxa* or *māyā* doctrines. Yet Democritus has drained this fact of the religious feeling it held for philosophers such as Parmenides, Pythagoras and the Upaniṣadic thinkers, for whom the idea of the truth behind appearances was a kind of numinosum. Democritus has reshaded the doctrine so that the difference between truth and appearance becomes not a religious fact but a naturalistic one. The dichotomy involved is not between human and divine points of view but between the evidence of the senses and the deductions of the mind.

Democritus expressed varying attitudes toward this dichotomy. In fr. 11 he says that the senses have only bastard knowledge and the mind takes up where they leave off.

The mind, for example, deduced the existence of eternal unchanging atoms moving through and recombining in empty space, by combining the evidence of the senses with the "mighty bonds of necessity." But at another time, Democritus moved his system very significantly toward phenomenalism. On the brink of the sophistic movement, he recognized that in terms of human life the ultimates, atom and void, were meaningless, and that reality exists for subjects only in terms of their experience, which then is for them the real. "The appearance," he said, "is truth" (DK 68A101). This trend of Democritus's thought had enormous influence on a line of thinkers who focused on relativism, naturalism, skepticism, and phenomenalism, including the Sophists, the Epicurean lineage of atomists, and the Pyrrhonist lineage of Skeptics.

Relationship?

The relationships between the Greek and Indian schools of atomism have been ignored by most scholars and treated with cavalier brevity by others. Guthrie, for example, cites Cyril Bailey's conclusion that no such relationships existed,[9] and Bailey in turn cites Keith's book *Indian Logic and Atomism.*[10] An apparent consensus amounts finally to one, badly out of date, opinion which neither of those who cited it understood, since it applied to only one of the Indian schools of atomism—not, as Bailey and Guthrie assumed, to the topic in general.

Like monism, atomism has been a regular part of the texture of Indian thought since antiquity. It has not been the exclusive domain of one school, but a tool, or a part of a shared vocabulary, available to any theoretician for any gap in his theory that it might fill. Most of the different schools of Indian thought have developed their versions of atomic theory at one time or another: Ājīvika, Jain, Cārvāka, Buddhist, and Nyāya-Vaiśeṣika. The last two mentioned seem to have been formulated after the Greek conquest of northwest India (the Nyāya-Vaiśeṣika system is what Keith was writing about). The Ājīvika, Jain, and Cārvāka brands of atomism, on the other hand, may have been in existence by the sixth century B.C. and are candidates to have influenced the thought of Leucippus and Democritus. The canons of all three schools, however, were systematized and written down centuries after the period in question, a situation which does not make it easy.

Early Atomisms in India

Barua argues that an early form of atomic theory is found in the teachings of Uddālaka Āruni (who has been called "probably the first Indian philosopher")[11] in the *Chāndogya Upaniṣad* (VI.9.1–2, VI.3.2–3, VI.11.3). Without elaboration of details—such as divisibility, relation to elements, and so on—Uddālaka taught that particles too small to be seen mass together into the substances and objects of experience. This suggests that the Upaniṣadic forest communities which are so deeply associated with the Advaita tradition of the *ātman* doctrine were more variegated than that. Since "it is clear that generally the atomic theory was subscribed to and opposed respectively by the realists and the idealists,"[12] protoscientific thinking seems to have been taking place there along with mystical theory. Uddālaka's teaching, however, cannot be regarded as a fully developed atomist theory so much as a seed-form of one. It seems to have involved idealist elements alongside the materialistic.[13]

Basham suggests, perhaps on a solider footing, that "of all the [Indian atomic] theories . . . that of [the Ājīvika] Pakhuda Kaccāyana seems to be the most primitive, the parent of the theories of later times."[14] Later Ājīvika theory, which is attributed to Pakhuda in the *Digha Nikāya* (*Sāmaññaphala Sutta*) and described without mention of his name in the *Sūtrakṛtānga*,[15] posited seven elements: earth, air, fire, water, joy, sorrow, and life. These are declared to be eternal on the Parmenidean ground that "what is does not perish; from nothing nothing comes."[16] The list starts with elementary substances and proceeds to connect them with human ethical attitudes, as do the lists of elements in the *Bṛhadāraṇyaka Upaniṣad* (I.2.2) and the *Taittirīya Upaniṣad* (II.1.1). This connection, which the Indian lists share, is lacking in the Greek lists, which do not include human ethical or emotional attitudes among the material elements—though Empedocles' forces of Hate and Love working upon the physical elements are vaguely similar. The Ājīvika list breaks into two groups of four material and three ethical elements, suggesting a development from an earlier four-element theory.

The parallels between this atomic theory and that of Leucippus and Democritus include the following: (1) the elementary substances are unchanging, unborn, and no more of them can ever come into existence. Thus they mediate between metaphysical permanence and flux, or Being and Becoming: "The atoms, being eternal and immutable, provided for the Being, their conjunctions and dissolutions for the Becoming";[17] (2) like Democritus's atoms, the Ājīvika atoms are said not to contain the sense qualities which are associated with the elements; these qualities emerge only from contacts between sense organs and large atomic aggregations; (3) as with Democritus, the soul is rigorously defined as a material thing; (4) like Democritus, the Ājīvikas recognized as a consequence of their atomism that "all change is illusion."[18] In broad outlines the two systems are profoundly similar. If in fact these outlines can be attributed to the age of Pakhuda Kaccāyana, it is entirely possible that the rudiments of a system much like Democritus's existed in India earlier than in Greece.

The Indian tradition places Jain atomism at least as early as the sixth century B.C.—that is, at least a century before the earliest extant traces of Greek atomism. "[T]he atom has been defined and its qualities have been enumerated," says Gangopadhyaya, "in some of their early texts."[19] Though there is no way at present to check the absolute dates of such texts, there is still reason to believe that Jain atomism is very early. It shows certain archaic forms of thought which even the Ājīvika atomism seems to have gone beyond. The Jains distinguish, for example, between material and immaterial reality and regard the soul as immaterial. Yet fine or subtle atoms known as karmic matter are said to "stick to" the soul—though the soul has no material support for them to stick to. There is a contradiction here. As one author describes the situation: "The soul by its commerce with the outer world becomes literally penetrated with material particles of a very subtle kind."[20] But the spatial image of penetration does not work for an immaterial and hence nonspatial soul anymore than does the image of "sticking to." The Jain thinkers who formulated this doctrine seem to be in a stage of transition from immaterial to material thinking, and not yet to have ironed out the wrinkles. Both Democritus and the Ājīvika atomists as known from Tamil texts make the mind or soul stuff a type of material atom, so that it may plausibly interact with the agglomerations of atoms around it—including atoms of karmic matter. This may suggest that the Jain theory is more primitive than the Ājīvika, which may have corrected it on this point. Plato, like the Jains, has the doctrine that karmic matter adheres to a soul that is itself not made of matter, though Democritus had already enunciated an alternative idea—that the soul is made up of a fine type of atom to which other atoms can bond. This sequence is wrong for the evolution of Greek philosophy in the fifth century—a period of Greek philosophy in which the prevailing sequence is from religious to secular. The religious model is more archaic, the naturalistic more modern in terms of the day. Yet Plato had the naïve or archaic doctrine, and it is one that appears also among the Orphics and the Jains. This sequence supports very strongly the suggestion made in the discussion of Orphism and Jainism, that Orphism, and through Orphism certain areas of Platonism, share traits with Jainism to the point of suggesting they are somehow one in origin. It is also worth noting that this distinction between the material and nonmaterial concepts of the soul was a major polarity between Democritus and Plato. It surely was one of the things Plato had in mind when he defined the differences between Gods and Giants.

A second point is slightly more complex. The Jains distinguished between the gross atoms that make up the body and the fine atoms that stick to the soul. Their doctrine is that innumerable fine or subtle atoms may occupy the space of one gross atom. This implies that the subtle atoms have no magnitude—that is, that they are not really material. The doctrine is parallel to the disputed Pythagorean doctrine of the "point monad."[21] According to Aristotle (*Met.* 1001b7–13) some philosophers declared that the line, the surface, and the solid are built up out of ultimate points. Yet the point was defined as indivisible, with no beginning, middle, or end, allowing of no measurement, that is, having no magnitude. It would seem that nothing could be built up out of such units, no matter how many of them were put together. This doctrine, with its associations of geometrical cosmogony, seems to point to the Pythagoreans, and many scholars think that this was the doctrine attacked so devastatingly by Zeno of Elea, who noted that infinitesimal points may be added to one another forever without causing increase; nothing could ever be built up out of them. In the Jain conception, too, the atom "has no points, beginning, middle or end. It is infinitesimal, eternal and ultimate."[22] The Jain conception of the atom seems susceptible to the same *reductio ad absurdum* to which Zeno subjected the point-monad. The terminology is even similar, as the Jain *Pancastikayasara* declares that the atom (*paramāṇu*) "occupies a single space point."[23] In a later age, the Mādhyamika dialectician Āryadeva employed this Zenonian type of critique against the Nyāya-Vaiśeṣika atomists. The Jain doctrine, in other words, seems to have been formulated in a predialectical age, when such a criticism could not have been leveled at it. This is a point at which the Ājīvika version, with its more thoroughgoing materialism, escapes the criticism, perhaps aware of it—or perhaps of a later age.

In a much later text, of the Nyāya-Vaiśeṣika tradition, this critique also occurred. The Jain doctrine holds that "when [matter] is in the subtle state, innumerable atoms of it occupy the space of one gross atom."[24] But if they are innumerable—that is, if an infinity of them occupies a certain measurable space—then they must have no dimensions and hence be immaterial, not matter at all. Uddyotakara, commenting on *Nyāya Sūtra* IV.1.17, argues that if the atom does not have a specific magnitude, then the smallest possible agglomeration of atoms "would become as immeasurable as a mountain in respect of the number of component parts, magnitude and weight since both would have to be considered as equally composed of an infinite number of parts."[25] This refutation of the Indian version of the point-monad recurs with different imagery in later Nyāya writers. It becomes a *topos*, or formulaic argument. "In some works of the Bhatta school of Mimamsa, the absurdity is put in a slightly different manner. If there is no limit to division [that is, if matter can be divided up infinitely, as Zeno argued], even a mustard seed would have an infinite number of parts, and theoretically, should itself fill up the whole universe."[26] Again the implication is that the Jain system of atomism was predialectical in formulation; it arose before the difficulties of the concept of infinity had been realized and absorbed into the tradition.

In the Jain theory, as in Democritus's, matter is conceived as a homogeneous and eternal substance with no sensible qualities, occurring in ultimate, indivisible units too small to be individually perceived, at least by human senses. These Jain atoms, in other words, like those of Democritus and Pakhuda, fulfill the basic Eleatic signposts: They neither come into being nor perish, and are indivisible. By combination into aggregates of sufficient size they produce the sensible universe. Unlike the atoms of Leucippus and Democritus, which have two inherent qualities, size and shape, the Jain atoms have no inherent qualities, but exhibit secondary qualities of color, taste, smell, and touch. This is an odd formulation in a way. Every atom possesses accidental or adventitious qualities of these four types, but these qualities are not essential to its identity as itself. Furthermore, these qualities are subject to continual change. As atoms combine and separate, they may exchange, take on, or lose qualities. Hence the qualitative surface of things is in continual flux, while its substantial ground is unchanging and eternal. The Buddhist doctrine of perpetual flux, involving denial of any permanent ground, and the Hindu doctrine of the unchanging ground, involving denial of the flow of surface qualities, are wedded, much as Democritean atomism mediated between Heraclitean flux and Parmenidean stasis.

A third branch of early Indian atomism was the school known as Cārvāka ("Materialist") or Lokāyata ("This-Worldly"). Many references in the Buddhist Nikāyas make it clear that this school was earlier than the finalization of the Buddhist canon; yet its ancient texts are all lost, and their doctrines survive only in redactions of more than a millennium later. One late exposition tells that "the chief maxims of the system" are: (1) all that exists is earth, air, fire, and water; (2) objects arise from the combination of these; (3) mind or soul is produced temporarily as a by-product of these combinations. Consciousness arises "like a force of fermenting intoxicant out of yeast"; (4) there is no residue of a person after death and there is no afterlife world.[27] The earliest expositions, in the *Sāmaññaphala Sutta* of the *Digha Nikāya*, indicate that the mixture theory of matter, which requires the movement of unseen bodies and implies atomism, was already articulated at that time. To the Buddha's contemporary Ajita Keśakambala are attributed the following doctrines:

> A man consists of four elements. When he dies, the earth goes into the mass of earth, the water into the mass of water, the fire into the mass of fire, the breath into the mass of air, and the sense-organs into space (ākāśa). (*D.* II.23)

This is substantially the doctrine of Epicurus and Lucretius. Soul or mind is regarded as a temporary by-product of the interaction of the material elements; it arises from their conjunction in certain ways, and when the elements of the body come apart in death the mind or soul simply ceases to exist; its conditions are gone.[28]

The Diffusion Question Again

Chronological problems in the textual traditions make it difficult to appraise the diffusion situation. Three of the Indian atomic systems described (not the Buddhist) may all be earlier than Leucippus; the fact that there were three such systems at an early period suggests a lively interest and discussion and dissemination of atomic doctrines in India, perhaps as a counterforce to the monism complex. The similarities between the Greek and Indian schools should be seen in context of the whole array of relationships, some certain, some likely, some merely possible. Atomism, in several related forms, may have been among the varied philosophical merchandise that contact by way of the Persian Empire carried from East to West or from West to East.

Reading the Shift

In the pre-Socratic age in Greece, and the early Upaniṣadic period of India, similar dissolutions of social order were underway. In Greece, the descendants of Bronze Age aristocrats were being displaced by populist movements amalgamating clannish units into democratic polities; in India, local clan and tribal boundaries were being dissolved and their areas amassed into national states. The upsurge of the monism complex at this time may have resulted in part from the disruption of traditional models, such as the Vedic and the Homeric, and at the same time may have partly compensated for it by providing a powerful new myth of unity.

At the same time, reactions against communal values in favor of individual ones gained strength. While the monistic movements attempted to bind the world to a sense of tribal belonging, skeptical and relativistic movements reversed the hierarchy, acting out the transcending of tribal views and the attaining of etic relativism and subjectivism.

The formation, in both Greece and India at this time, of dropout communities which deliberately created emic bubbles around themselves, further compensated for the dissolution of tradition by providing a matrix of belonging as strong as that of the fading clan and tribe. A communal law, such as the Buddhist *Vinaya* or the rules of the Pythagorean brotherhood, creates a community out of time or history to a degree. Groups such as the forest communities of Upaniṣadic and Buddhist monks or yogis, or the wandering Orphic clans, or models like Plato's *Republic*, in which society is imbued throughout with the archetype of the One, express an impulse to reinstate a tribelike structure in the face of advancing national statism.

Psychological overtones of the issues are not discordant with this view. Parmenides' form of monism, for example, with its insistence both on the exclusive reality of the One and on its finity show simultaneously the ego's tendency to reenter the unconscious, and the ego, through its insistence on finity, making an aggressive move on the unconscious, trying to delimit it, to tame its apparent limitlessness, to make the unconscious over in something like the image of the ego, because the ego stands precisely for limits; its way of conquering is by limiting, and the unconscious's way of conquering is by dissolving the limits and hence the semantic and/or ontological integrity of a thing which now, lacking its limits or definition, is really no longer a thing.

Shifting back to the social model, one sees parallels: the dissolving of ego into tribe, the ego attempting to eternalize its reliance upon the tribe, the individual social will both inflating itself to controller of the tribe and also clinging to the tribal matrix at a poised moment before it takes off into the unknown. As the bonds of the tribe progressively fall away, the monistic impulse keeps stepping in to replace it and is itself progressively countered by pluralistic and relativistic positions. Anaxagoras's crystallization of the idea of Mind as something separate from the whole, rather than permeating it inwardly, suggests a situation in which there is emerging distance from the tribal matrix and growing ability to see society as something manipulable from without by individual will.

Notes to Chapter Twelve

1. This antinomy in the history of Greek philosophy is investigated in more detail in Thomas McEvilley, "Penelope's Night Work: Negative Thinking in Greek Philosophy," *Krisis* 2 (1984): 41–58.

2. This interpretation of Anaxagoras, though widespread and strongly based on the ancient sources, has problems both internal (involving logical consistency) and external (involving the reliability of the sources), many of which are brought out by Gregory Vlastos, "The Physical Theory of Anaxagoras," in Vlastos, *Studies in Greek Philosophy*, vol. 1, *The Presocratics*, ed. Daniel W. Graham (Princeton, New Jersey: Princeton University Press, 1993), pp. 303–327.

3. Sarvepalli Radhakrishnan, *Indian Philosophy*, vol. 1 (London and New York: George Allen and Unwin, 1971), p. 201; see *CU* VI.5–6.

4. The text is given, in both Sanskrit and English, in Mrinalkanti Gangopadhyaya, *Indian Atomism: History and Sources* (Atlantic Highlands, New Jersey: Humanities Press, 1981). The English version of this passage occurs on p. 66.

5. W. K. C. Guthrie, *A History of Greek Philosophy*, vol. 2 (Cambridge: Cambridge University Press, 1962–1981), p. 295.

6. Ibid., p. 320.

7. K. Deichgraber, "Hymnische Elements in der philosophischen Prose der Vorsokratiker," *Philologus* 88 (1933); and Werner W. Jaeger, *The Theology of the Early Greek Philosophers*, trans. Edward S. Robinson, Gifford Lectures 1936 (Oxford: Clarendon Press, 1947), p. 161.

8. For more argumentation on this point see McEvilley, "Penelope's Night Work."

9. See Cyril Bailey, *The Greek Atomists and Epicurus* (Oxford: Clarendon Press, 1928), p. 65.

10. Arthur B. Keith, *Indian Logic and Atomism* (Oxford: Clarendon Press, 1921).

11. Gangopadhyaya, *Indian Atomism*, pp. 40–41.

12. Ibid., p. 40.

13. See ibid., pp. 42–44.

14. A. L. Basham, *History and Doctrine of the Ājīvikas: A Vanished Indian Religion* (London: Luzac, 1951), p. 269. Hermann Jacobi agrees ("The Atomic Theory," in *Studies in the History of Indian Philosophy*, vol. 2, ed. Debiprasad Chattopadhyaya [Calcutta: K. P. Bagchi and Company, 1978], pp. 135, 143); so does H. Ui (*The Vaiśesika Philosophy* [Varanasi: Chowkhamba Sanskrit Series Office, 1962], p. 23–24). For problems with this view see Gangopadhyaya, *Indian Atomism*, pp. 46–47.

15. Hermann Jacobi, *Jaina Sūtra*, Sacred Books of the East 45, part 2 (Oxford: Clarendon Press, 1884–95), p. xxiv.

16. Ibid., pp. 237, 343.

17. Debiprasad Chattopadhyaya, *Indian Philosophy: A Popular Introduction* (Delhi: People's Publishing House, 1972), p. 171.

18. Ibid., p. 262.

19. Gangopadhyaya, *Indian Atomism*, p. 2.

20. Ibid., p. 7.

21. It is disputed for example by J. A. Philip, *Pythagoras and Early Pythagoreanism* (Toronto: University of Toronto Press, 1966), pp. 151 ff.

22. Radhakrishnan, *Indian Philosophy*, vol. 1, pp. 317–318.

23. See the English text in Gangopadhyaya, *Indian Atomism*, p. 58.

24. Ibid., p. 7.

25. Ibid., p. 29; I have omitted the Sanskrit from the sentence.

26. Ibid., p. 30.

27. Erich Frauwallner, *History of Indian Philosophy*, vol. 2, trans. V. M. Bedekar (Delhi: Motilal Banarsidas, 1973), p. 221; for references see vol. 2, p. 258, n. 388.

28. There are other Indian doctrines of atomism, too late to be relevant right here. The Nyāya-Vaiśeṣika school will be discussed (other aspects of it) in chapters 19 ("The Syllogism") and 20 ("Peripatetics and Vaiśeṣikas"). Those Buddhist schools comprised under the heading Sarvastivadin also had one. It is unlikely that it goes back to the Buddha's own teaching, however, as "the terms expressive of the concepts of atoms (*paramāṇu*) or moments (*khana*) [understanding by moments atomic particles of time] are conspicuously absent from the early discourses." Śaṅkara sums the Sarvāstavādin theory up briefly:

> These Buddhists acknowledge the four elements, earth, water, fire and wind . . . The four elements are atomic; the earth atoms have the quality of harshness, the water atoms that of viscidity, the fire atoms that of heat, and the wind atoms that of motion; in combination these atoms form the earthy things etc. (Trans. Gangopadhyaya, *Indian Atomism*, p. 11)

In fact, the occurrence of these ideas in the Buddhist framework may be very late; most of the discourse on Buddhist atomism, such as Śubhagupta's *Bāhyārtasiddhi*, dates from the seventh to the tenth centuries A.D. Sarvāstavāda means the doctrine that the external world perceived by the senses is real—because the atoms that make it up are real. As usual, atomism occurs with realism.

Chapter Thirteen

Skepticism, Empiricism, and Naturalism

In both Greece and India in about the sixth century B.C., emerging national structures were progressively displacing attitudes inherited from either the village or the forest community. A new set of reactions arose. As the monism complex had reacted to an apparent loss of faith in Vedic ritual practices, so reactions to the monism complex followed, in a broad context of skeptical, humanistic, empiricist, and protoscientific elements. These tended to express a naturalistic attitude in which several characteristics came to the fore; one scholar listed them as follows:

1. The naturalist accepts sense experience as the most important avenue of knowledge.
2. The naturalist believes that knowledge is not esoteric, innate, or intuitive (mystical).
3. The naturalist believes that the external world, of which man is an integral part, is objective and hence not "'his idea'" but an existent apart from his, your, or anyone's consciousness.
4. The naturalist believes that the world manifests order and regularity and that, contrary to some opinion, this does not exclude human responsibility. This order cannot be changed merely by thought, magic, sacrifice, or prayer, but requires actual manipulation of the external world in some physical way.
5. The naturalist rejects supernatural teleology. The direction of the world is caused by the world itself.
6. The naturalist is humanistic. Man is not simply a mirror of deity or the absolute but a biological existent whose goal it is to do what is proper to man. What is proper to man is discovered in a naturalistic context by the moral philosopher.[1]

The Beginnings of Secular Humanism in Greece

In Greece, secular attitudes began to be expressed in literature in the seventh century B.C., when the poet Archilochus uttered the first extant denunciation of the religious as opposed to the secular humanist view of life: "All things," he wrote, "are made for mortals by their own toil and care" (fr. 15a, Edmonds). Both the teleological view that the world has some inherent goal and the theistic view that some supernatural force is controlling the world are implicitly renounced; humans are told that they have their destiny in their own hands.

A generation or so later, Mimnermus of Colophon wrote a secular credo rejoicing in the feeling of the independence of human decisions that the lifting of the Bronze Age view promoted; his message is framed as a sequence of allusions to, and revisions of, Homer:

> We are like the leaves that come in the flowery springtime
> And grow so quickly underneath the sun;
> Like them we enjoy the blossoms of youth for just a little while,
> Knowing neither good nor evil from the gods. (Fr. 2)

Homer had said that the generations of humans are like those of the leaves, and he had also said that Zeus has at his feet separate urns of good and evil from which he dispenses to humans. Mimnermus has replied, in effect, that Homer is right about the generations of humans being like those of leaves, but not about the sources of good and evil in human life. He agrees instead with Archilochus, that reward and punishment follow human decision and effort, not divine dispensation. Human experience is described as "knowing neither good nor evil from the gods," which seems to mean roughly: "Independent in a world that has no inherent moral imperative."

The secular materialism expressed by Greek poets in the seventh century B.C. appeared in philosophical contexts in the next century. When the Milesian philosophers "turned their minds to wondering how things worked," as one scholar put it, "they did so in the light of everyday experience without regard to ancient myths."[2] At that time the distinction began to arise between philosophers who emphasized the phenomenal—or the evidence of experience—and those who emphasized the noumenal—or the evidence of thought. For Plato this dichotomy would come to have a dualistic, ethical tinge. He formulated it in two sets of terms, once as the Battle between Gods and Giants—the Gods being noumenalists and the Giants phenomenalists, or materialists—and again as a distinction between *theologoi*, "those who speak about the gods," and *physiologoi*, "those who speak about nature." The *theologoi* were the Orphic lineages extending from the transcendentalist Pythagoreans and Platonists down to Neoplatonism. The *physiologoi* formed the antimetaphysical tradition that expressed itself sometimes as materialism, sometimes as phenomenalism, and was involved increasingly in critical thought, skepticism, and empiricism. In the tenth book of the *Laws* Plato traces this tradition, which extends from Democritus to Sextus Empiricus, back to the Milesians, calling them all *physiologoi*.

Plato attributes three doctrines to the *physiologoi*: that the four elements are the primary existents, that they are moved from within by inherent forces or natural laws, and that the soul is produced as a temporary by-product or epiphenomenon of the interaction of these elements. The antithesis is the view of the *theologoi*, which was Plato's own view: that the soul, not the body, is primary, that it produces the four elements by design and guides them into the process of forming bodies, and that these bodies remain at all times subject to the superior guidance of soul, which is not a transient epiphenomenon but an unchanging essence.

The Milesians

According to Plato's view, the first *physiologos* was Thales. A man of practical experience, Thales was successful at business, studied land measurement, improved methods of navigation by the stars, and is said to have learned how to foretell solar eclipses. His assertion that all things are water may have been a protoscientific utterance arising from observation of the changes of water into ice and steam. It may also show the influence of the quasi-medical belief that (as Aristotle put it) "the seed of all things is wet"—a belief echoed also by Pherecydes' assertion that the elements arose from the seed of Chronos.[3] On the other hand, the idea of the primal status of water may have been adopted from Bronze Age myth. In any case, Thales secularized the mythic image and rendered it materialistic. Thales' assertion that "All things are full of gods" may express a naturalistic attempt to drain the word "god" of religious content.

Anaximander's revision of Thales' substrate from water to an indeterminate potentiality-stuff was an attempt to account for nature on its own terms, in which the elements do not seem eternally separate, but change into one another. First earth, water, mist, and fire were separated out from the primary indeterminate substance and stratified according to density; thereupon fire, by heating the water element and making it evaporate, set the process of natural transformations going. On this view there is no need for divine initiation or interference, nor is there any room for them. Human life is a by-product of the natural process of the transformations of matter, not a special creation with religious or mythological significance. Anaximenes' system employing the processes of condensation and rarefaction seems even more clearly based on the observation of nature, and was influenced by the technology of felting woven materials by pressure.[4]

These Milesian doctrines all contain implications of atomism, that is, of the movements of unseen bodies. If a substance is changing and an observer cannot see the change occurring, then it is inferred to be taking place at an infrasensory level, through rearrangements of material units too small to be seen with the unaided eye.

The Beginnings in India

In Greek philosophy the distinction between Gods and Giants, or *theologoi* and *physiologoi*, is roughly equivalent to the distinction between *astika* and *nāstika* sects in ancient India. The *astika* sects—the "yes" or orthodox sects—are those which affirm the authority of the Vedas; they include the Upaniṣadic communities as well as the rite of the orthodox Vedic priesthood. The *nāstika* sects—those which deny the authority of the Vedas—include the Cārvākas, Ājīvikas, Buddhists, and Jains. The beliefs which Plato attributes to the *physiologoi* of his own tradition can be found among the *nāstika* sects of India, though sometimes mixed, as in Jainism, with the transcendentalist doctrine of the soul and its release.

In Indian thought the first implication of the movements of unseen bodies is in the passages attributed to Uddālaka in the *Chāndogya Upaniṣad*. These descriptions of the curd forming within the milk and so on are, however, religious in motivation, serving as analogues of the presence of *brahman* in the universe. The Ājīvikas went farther in secular explanation; they "appear to have been the first Indian philosophers," says Kalupahana, "to face squarely the philosophical problem of determinism and free will. Like some modern philosophers, they seem to have possessed the courage to openly accept determinism and reject free will."[5] In the Ājīvika system of deterministic atomism, natural elements combine according to their own inalterable inner laws. Nature is presented as its own master, influenced neither from outside, as, say, by gods, nor from inside, as by human effort. They denied the efficacy of *karma* and suspended belief in another world. The problem that others perceived in their position is that the denial of human effort also denied human responsibility and left mankind as tightly controlled by outward circumstances as it had once seemed to be by gods.

The Cārvākas, who represent the ultimate in materialistic naturalism in the Indian tradition, exhibit the full range of doctrines that Plato attributes to the *physiologoi* and in some cases go beyond them in naturalism. They considered "matter to be the ultimate fact of the universe, reducing all phenomena, including the phenomenon of consciousness, to transformations of material elements."[6] Accordingly, they recognized only sense perception as a source of knowledge, rejecting inference—whether inductive or deductive—scripture and testimony. In their attack on religious traditions, they denied any existence after death or any nonmaterial existent such as a consciousness which is not an aspect of the interactions of material elements ("they were the first *anātmavādins* (no-soul theorists) of India").[7] The material elements they described as having indwelling principles—their *svabhāvas* or self-natures—which determine their development without any external causality, and amount to natural laws. The conceptions of religious ethics, such as *karma*, *saṃsāra*, and *mokṣa*, they viewed as deliberate deceptions by the priestly caste which profited economically from them. The *Sarvadarśana-saṃgraha* attributes to the Cārvākas the doctrine (not unlike that of Mimnermus) that "the only purpose of human life is enjoyment produced by sensual pleasures."[8]

Hedonism

In both traditions, hedonism emerged as the ethical stance characteristic of the naturalistic attitude. Mimnermus wrote (fr. 1), "What is life without golden Aphrodite? May I die when I no longer care for secret love and sweet love-gifts and love's couch; these are the flowers of life to be plucked by men and women alike." Among the Cārvākas, heaven and hell were interpreted as present pleasure or pain:

> The enjoyment of heaven consists in partaking of sweet food here, in enjoying the company of damsels of sixteen years of age, and also in enjoying the pleasures that are derivable from the use of fine clothes, sweet scents, flower garlands, sandal, and other such things.[9]

Mokṣa, or salvation, is simply the dissolution of the body.

Pythagoras Theologos

Pythagoras is reported in the ancient tradition as in some ways a practical man in the mold of the Ionian naturalists. He was involved in business and politics and made important contributions to experimental method. His and his school's advances in mathematics were, in the very long run of things, enormously important for science, but in their own day were rather a type of religious activity. Mathematics was understood as suggesting an immaterial level of conscious design as the supreme principle of the universe, in service of which Pythagoras opposed the materialism and natural law posited by the Milesians. He was the primary example of Plato's category of *theologoi* or nonnaturalistic thinkers for whom soul and providence come first, the world of the four elements being produced and controlled by them. Within the framework of ancient empiricism, which recognized more than five senses as sources of evidence, his acceptance of the doctrines of *karma* and transmigration was empirical, since he felt he had observed these processes through extrasensory cognitions.

Emerging Skepticism: Xenophanes

Ionian naturalism was more directly taken up by Xenophanes, who criticized the gods of the polytheism (fr. 15) and rejected dogmatisms on the ground that certainty of knowledge is impossible (fr. 34). He rejected the emerging esoteric (or Indian-style) religions of the *theologoi*, ridiculing Pythagoras's claim to retrocognition (fr. 7). In cosmology, he stays "as close as he can to the immediately given" and attempts "to make unnecessary every explanation of the world's construction and functioning that departed from the realm of naïve sensation."[10] He removed mythological supports from the cosmos by declaring both the earth's depth and the air's height to be unlimited. Observing fossils, he postulated that the sea once covered the earth. He removed heavenly forces from the weather, declaring it to arise from fluctuations of land and sea. He denied heaven and its gods. In his view, "this world of ours is made to seem as familiar, intelligible and present, as this-worldly and free from mystery as possible. All things and appearances are explained in terms of everyday experience . . ."[11] His interest in reality is pragmatic and focuses on questions of utility (frs. 1.23, 2.19 ff., 3.1). He denounced legends as useless and out of date (fr. 1.22), declared omens, oracles, and signs from heaven meaningless (fr. A 52). His example of proper conversation for humans was totally down to earth:

> Who are you among men and where from? How old are you, my friend? What age were you when the Mede came? (Fr. 22)

Xenophanes' rejection of the supernatural was accompanied by advances in the empirical theory of knowledge:

> And as to truth, there never was nor will there be anyone who knew the truth about the gods and the other things I am speaking of. Even if someone should once by chance say what is actually the case, he would not be sure of this. For only illusory opinion is available to anyone. (Fr. 34)[12]

In antiquity the second sentence of this passage was interpreted as meaning: "Even if someone should be speaking the truth he would not really know whether he was or not." The question how one might know whether or not one knew subsequently became a leitmotif of Greek philosophy. Plato alluded to Xenophanes' sentence in the *Meno* (80d):

> If you should chance to come right up against it, how will you know it is this—the thing which you do not know?

The argument recurs seven hundred years later, like a musical refrain, in Sextus Empiricus:

> Even if by chance he should happen to apprehend it, he would not be aware of the fact that he did apprehend it—he is, rather, in a state of belief or opinion. (*AL* 1.51)

A second interpretation[13] emphasizes the crucial Greek verb in the sentence, which is cognate with Latin *video* and like it originally meant "know by seeing." If the word still meant this for Xenophanes, his fr. 34 should mean: "Even if someone should succeed in telling the truth, if he is not speaking from direct personal experience but from conjecture, then his statement is invalid methodologically, regardless of its correspondence or lack of correspondence with the facts."

Both these interpretations of Xenophanes were influential in antiquity. The first— how would we know whether or not we knew?— led into sophistic skepticism and was ultimately the prototype of uroboric statements like Metrocles' "I know nothing, not even whether I know nothing." The empirical interpretation was equally influential. Heraclitus and Empedocles both began their books with declarations of the limitations of human knowledge due, according to Empedocles at least, to the limited amount of direct experience possible in a human lifetime. The Pythagorean Alcmaeon of Croton began his book:

> Concerning non-evident things, concerning things mortal, the gods see clearly but men conjecture.

The author of the Hippocratic treatise *On Ancient Medicine* began similarly:

> I considered that medicine has no need of a novel postulate as do insoluble mysteries, which necessarily require the use of a postulate if an attempt be made to discuss them, for instance the mysteries of heaven and of the regions below. If anyone were to express his opinion about the condition of these, it would not be plain either to the speaker himself or to the audience whether the statements were true or false. For there is no text the application of which would bring certain knowledge.

Xenophanes, on this view, gave expression to an emerging new concept of what makes knowledge certain, namely, that it be empirically grounded and tested. Experimental science was already underway, especially in the area of medical studies; the Pythagorean experimenter Alcmaeon, for example, dissected and vivisected animals, discovered the optic nerve, and identified the brain as the center where sensations are received and organized.

Reactions

This growing empiricism was attacked, a generation later, by Parmenides, who regarded reason alone as the test of a theory:

> Turn your mind away from this path of inquiry! Do not let ordinary experience in its variety force you along the path of allowing the sightless eye, the ringing ear, and the tongue to rule your thought, but test by reason alone the argument which I will present. (Fr. B7)

This was a direct attack on experimental science as it was going on in Parmenides' day. The blind eye, for example, was studying astronomy from an observatory on the island of Tenedos; the ringing ear was carrying out the Pythagorean acoustic experiments; the tongue or taste sense was under study by Alcmaeon and the Hippocratics. Parmenides' own argument was based entirely on reason, without recourse to empirical evidence. The situation was similar to Yājñavalkya's vehement assertion of transcendental idealism against the comparatively observational method of Uddālaka.

Empedocles defended the usefulness of the senses against Parmenides' rejection of them in the name of logic:

> But come, observe with every means, to see by which way each thing is clear, and do not hold any (*percept of*) sight higher in credibility than (*those*) according to hearing, nor (*set*) the loud-sounding hearing above the evidence of the tongue (*taste*); nor refuse credence at all to any of the other limbs where there exists a path for perception, but use whatever way of perception makes each thing clear. (Fr. 3, *fin.*)

He sought to explain nature by observation of techniques, such as bread-making, the use of the sling, and the method of mixing colors for painting—all of which he mentions as sources of his theories. In one case he turned experiment to the service of philosophy. The Milesians had all implied the movements of unseen bodies. Empedocles demonstrated that such movements really exist by proving the corporeality of air. He showed that water will be held in an open-ended tube if the top end is closed off and that if one end of a tube filled with air was closed off, and the other end thrust under water, the water would not enter the tube. As Farrington says: "Empedocles had not merely shown the corporeality of air; he had shown how we can overcome the limitations of our sensuous apprehension and discover, by a process of inference based on observation, truths we cannot directly perceive. He had, by his cautious and critical use of the senses, conquered in the name of science a world that lay beyond the normal range of man's perceptions. He had revealed the existence of an imperceptible physical universe by examining its effects on the perceptible world."[14] The next generation of thinkers could proceed to the explicit formulation of atomism.

Anaxagoras's idea of the interpenetration of the different types of matter was based on inference from the process of digestion: If bread, say, turns into bone, blood, hair, and so on, then these qualities (since nothing can *come into* existence) must already exist in the bread, waiting to be sorted out by the process of digestion. To demonstrate the existence of infrasensory changes in matter he transferred a black liquid, drop by drop, into a container of white liquid. The eye could not apprehend the change till several drops had been transferred, though each drop produced a change. (This experiment or demonstration was a kind of forerunner of the neo-Eleatic conundrum called the Heap.)

The Democritean Lineage

The struggle against the Eleatic *elenchus* continued in the materialistic atomism of Leucippus and Democritus, according to which the world is made up of nonplanned mechanical sequences. Aristotle called this idea "chance," but Democritus called it "necessity." Democritus's cosmogony was based on observation of the behavior of very small bodies, such as sand and pebbles on the beach; the way the waves sift them into groups according to size provided the mechanism for the sorting out of the elements according to density. Once that process was underway all motion was derived from collisions of moving atoms. In this conception there is no room for free will and no place for providence. Men who raise their hands toward the sky to pray are not raising their hands toward Zeus but simply toward air.[15] Religion and mythology result from the projection of irrational emotions onto natural phenomena:

> Men in old days, seeing the occurrences in the sky, such as the thunder and lightning and thunderbolts and the conjunctions of heavenly bodies and the eclipses of sun and moon, dreaded the gods, believing that they were the causes of these things. (Fr. A75)

Consciousness also is corporeal and composed of the finest atoms, so sensation and thought, like everything else, result from nonplanned and mechanical atomic movements. All sensations are reduced to the process of touch, as objects give off effluences of themselves in the form of invisible atomic films which collide with the atoms of the sensing organ.

Democritus's attitude toward sense data looked both backward toward Parmenides and forward toward Protagoras. On the one hand, in his view the senses are fallacious in that they do not reveal atoms and void, the only things that really exist. On the other hand, the qualities which we seem to perceive are an accurate portrayal of the result of the mingling of our senses with those unseen bodies; in terms of ourselves as receivers, they are true. Here Democritus took a fateful turn toward the subjective and made the first western statement of phenomenalism, saying: "The phenomenon, or appearance, is reality" (Aristotle *De An.* 404a27).

Democritus's ethics was an early version of utilitarian hedonism, centered around the concept of *athambia*, "inability to be surprised," or *ataraxia*, "inability to be disturbed." As in the very similar early Buddhist ethics, the concepts of impermanence and moderation were central:

> All who derive their pleasure from the stomach, overstepping the due season in eating or drinking or sexual pleasures, have pleasures that are brief and short-lived, that is, only while they are eating and drinking, but pains that are many. For this desire is always present for the same things, and when people get what they desire, the pleasure passes quickly and they have nothing good for themselves except a brief enjoyment; and then the need for the same returns again. (Fr. 235)

This formulation of the relationship between desire, impermanence, and suffering is very similar to the so-called Four Noble Truths of early Buddhism, which hold that suffering arises from attempts to possess or otherwise control things which, being unstable and impermanent, are inherently unreliable; it will be abated by taking a more detached stance toward externals. The goal in such an ethics is not a penetration through the veils of phenomenality to a transcendent vision of Being, but rather a moment-to-moment attempt to be free of desire-habits, without on the other hand becoming ascetic. Many of Democritus's ethical pronouncements could have been made by Siddhārtha:

> The right-minded man is he who is not grieved by what he has not, but does enjoy what he has. (Fr. 231)
>
> Imperturbable wisdom is worth everything. (Fr. 216)

The Greek and Indian traditions of ethical philosophy both emphasize not the selection of one type of action rather than another, but the state of mind in which an action is performed. For both, the ideal ethical state is conceived as imperturbability or detachment. In the Democritean lineages as much as in the Buddhist schools, the ethical implications of the principle of impermanence was basic. Carneades asserted axiomatically, "nature both constitutes and dissolves" (D.L. IV.64). For Epictetus the basic principle was that "everything that becomes must perish, too" (*Disc.* II.5.12–13). In fact, formulations like the Middle Way, the Three Marks, or the Four Noble Truths of early Buddhism are found throughout Greek philosophy. Plato, for example, teaches in the *Timaeus* (86bc) a rationale for ethics that is identical to the thought underlying the Four Noble Truths:

> Among the gravest disorders for the soul we must rank excessive pleasures and pains. When a man is carried away by enjoyment or distracted by pain, in his immoderate haste to grasp the one or to escape the other he can neither see nor hear aright; he is in a frenzy and his capacity for reasoning is then at its lowest.

With Protagoras, either a pupil or an associate of Democritus, the reaction against the Eleatic *elenchus* entered a new phase. Empedocles, Anaxagoras, and the Atomists had all accepted Parmenides' argument that only absolute Being really Is, or is really real—and attempted to find ways to regard absolute being as pluralistic, in hopes of saving the phenomena. Protagoras's approach (based on Democritus's "the appearance is reality") was breathtakingly bold and different. Confronted with the choice between Being and appearance, he chose appearance, and made no attempt to win for it the attributes of pure Being. The first sentence of his lost book *On Truth*, is justly one of the most famous of Greek utterances:

> Man is the measure of all things, of those that are that they are, and of those that are not that they are not.

According to this doctrine, which has variously been called phenomenalism, relativism, or subjectivism, there is, by definition, nothing accessible to the knowing faculty except experience. Assertions about being, then, must be based on experience, since no other resource is available, nor could any possibly be. If one person says the room is cold and another says it is warm, both are right if they have accurately related their experience. Both appearances truly exist; there is no need to reconcile them, nor indeed any possibility of doing so, since there is no accessible objective criterion to consult. Protagoras had arrived at last at a view directly opposite to that of Parmenides: The sensations and opinions that Parmenides had called non-Being Protagoras declared the only true being; the objectively existent absolute that Parmenides had declared the only Being he perceived as just another subjective opinion. Protagoras, in other words, relinquished the search for objective truth as unreal, as a misunderstanding of the human condition, as not the proper work of philosophy. It was here, really, that western philosophy took its decisive turn toward the subject. In anthropology, Protagoras replaced the myth of the Golden Age followed by a process of degenerative evolution with a positivistic theory of progress. Humans had long ago, he said, lived not in a Golden Age but in a state like that of animals, from which, through long application of technological wit, they had risen to the condition of urban civilization.

Protagorean subjectivism was part of a more general emergence from tribal views that was going on. Herodotus, for example, shows an awareness of cultural relativism that is a part of the emerging awareness of the distinction between *physis*, or nature, and *nomos*, or culture. The awareness that human cultural and social forms are not parts of nature but conventions susceptible to being reshaped by human decision was a sign of the breakdown of religious authority.

The Democritean tradition was the center of Greek atheism and, in Plato's mind, the most harmful influence afield. The direct attack on religion, implicit in Democritus, was prosecuted most vigorously by the Democritean Epicurus, who, according to his own disciple Lucretius, "toppled the gods from their thrones." In his *Letter to Pythocles* (86–87) Epicurus wrote:

> We must not conduct scientific investigation by means of empty axioms or by acts of legislation. Rather we must follow the lead of phenomena. For our life has not now any place for irrational belief and groundless imagining, if we are to live happily.[16]

Concepts of divinity he declared irrelevant to human life:

> The divine nature . . . is neither won by our well-doing nor angered when we do ill. (Lucretius II.646)

His disciple Lucretius, following Democritus and ultimately the Milesian natural philosophers, taught that personality and consciousness are temporary by-products of atomic combinations and that the personality, upon the death of the body, dissolves into the atomic flow of nature.

Back to India

Many events in the Indian tradition relate to these trends of Greek thought. Uddālaka, for example, in the *Chāndogya Upaniṣad*, taught that the soul was corporeal and made up of the smallest or finest grade of particles. In agreement with the naturalistic thread of Greco-Roman thought, he taught that living according to nature will bring satisfaction, while living according to superstition will bring sorrow. The distinction between nature and superstition corresponds to the sophistic distinction between *physis*, or nature, and *nomos*, or convention. The Cārvāka school similarly taught that the soul is produced accidentally by atomic arrangements and will disintegrate and be reprocessed through nature, atom by atom, after the death of the body.

Makkhali Gosāla, the great Ājīvika teacher, taught a deterministic atomism which made human effort ineffectual. Democritus's atomism was also deterministic. For both, the highest ethical value was not placed on acting but on cultivating a state of mind that would remain serene in the face of events which go awry of one's individual hopes and expectations.

Epicurus saw religion not merely as false but as a fraud perpetrated by the priestly class for their own benefit. An early Sanskrit drama, the *Prabodha-Candrodaya*, quotes the Cārvāka teacher Brihaspati as teaching much the same point of view:

> The teacher Brihaspati has declared that the performance of sacrifice, reading the Vedas, penances and rubbing the body with ashes are the means by which ignorant, weak men contrive to support themselves.[17]

A Cārvāka argument against reincarnation asks simply why, if people have gone through past lives, they cannot remember them?[18] Lucretius has the same argument:

> If the spirit is by nature immortal and is slipped into the body at birth, why do we retain no memory of an earlier existence, no impress of antecedent events? (III.670–677)[19]

Jainism

Jainism is a complex interweaving of naturalistic and metaphysical elements. The Jain theory of knowledge is not a phenomenalism but a realistic correspondence view. Democritus held that sense qualities do not inhere in the atoms but arise out of our contact with them; the Jain doctrine was that sense qualities inhere in the atoms, so our perceptions of them really show us what is there. The Jain rejection of deity and of ritual efficacy and emphasis on individual effort show a humanistic naturalistic tendency; yet it is balanced with the most transcendentalist of ambitions regarding the afterlife, and with a heavy emphasis on asceticism.

In the areas of skepticism and relativism, Jain theory made its most important contribution. The Jain relativistic theory of knowledge is popularly represented by the parable of a number of blind men (usually six) touching an elephant and comparing notes; although each is right in what he reports, each makes the mistake of regarding his own partial perspective as the whole truth. Two complementary doctrines are involved, the *syādvāda* or "in a sense doctrine" and the *anekāntavāda*, "doctrine of manifoldness or indeterminacy." Each of these doctrines has received conflicting interpretations emphasizing now empirical naturalism, now metaphysical absolutism.

The *anekāntavāda* is interpreted, on the one hand, as a doctrine of finite manifoldness and, on the other, as a doctrine of infinite manifoldness, or indeterminacy. The theory of finite manifoldness is a form of empirical relativism or "positive relativity," which is regarded as a form of "nonabsolutism";[20] the theory of indeterminacy belongs in the category of metaphysical absolutes. There is a difference between saying that the elephant really has a number of aspects and saying that the elephant either has no determinate nature or has infinite determinate natures, which, as far as the chance of human knowledge goes, amount to the same thing. Many Jain authors hold the infinite view (the view of "absolute inexpressibility," as Samantabhadra calls it)[21], though it seems to conflict with the correspondence theory of knowledge. If reality is indeterminate, then determinate and specific perceptions of it cannot correspond to it even as parts or aspects: It would require an indeterminate perception to correspond to it. If determinate perceptions are misperceptions of an indeterminate real, then they must arise from perceiver rather than perceived, in contradiction of the doctrine that sense qualities inhere in objective reality. Empiricism is forestalled by infinity. The view that, as a Jain author puts it, "every detail in the universe, physical and mental . . . [is] an infinitely diversified fact,"[22] suggests an infinite number of blind men touching the elephant, which means that reality (as infinite) is out of the reach of scientific method.

The *anekāntavāda* is related to the subject, or to epistemology, through the *nayavāda* and the *syādvāda*. A *naya* is a viewpoint which, while legitimate in itself, is not claimed to be complete nor to exclude other viewpoints, even those which may seem to contradict it. According to the infinitist view of *anekāntavāda*, the *nayas*, or "viewpoints from which an object or event can be perceived are not merely numerous but infinite in number because even the humblest fact of existence is infinitely manifold."[23] For practical purposes, however, only seven *nayas* are recognized:

(1) *Naigamanaya* or the teleological point of view: a person lighting a fire doesn't say, "I am lighting a fire," but "I am fixing dinner."

(2) *Saṃgrahanaya*, the class point of view, which emphasizes the universal to the exclusion of the particular; Plato's Theory of Ideas would be criticized by a Jain as an example of overemphasis on the *saṃgrahanaya*, as would much of the thought in the Upaniṣads.

(3) *Vyavahāranaya*, or the standpoint of the particular; any realism which, like the Cārvāka, refuses to go beyond sense-data to inductive generalities embodies the fallacy of exclusively emphasizing this point of view.

(4) *Ṛjsūtranaya*, the standpoint of the moment; this viewpoint takes a thing for what it appears to be at the given moment without regarding past and future. An example is the fallacy of regarding an actor playing a king as a king. The Buddhist doctrine of momentariness is regarded as an overemphasis on this viewpoint.

The last three *nayas* are linguistic and involve errors in thought which arise from misuse of language.

(5) *Śabdanaya*, the viewpoint of synonyms. This involves confusing one meaning or usage of a word with another. It is similar, in Wittgenstein's terms, to using or interpreting a word in a way appropriate to one language game while under the impression that one is playing another language game. It was formulated as a criticism of the *Śabdadvaitavādins*.

(6) *Samabhirudhanaya*, the etymological viewpoint: it consists in regarding synonyms as distinct because one perceives their etymologies to be distinct.

(7) *Evambhūtanaya*, the "suchlike" viewpoint, "calls for a different designation for each of the different attitudes which the same object assumes under different conditions"[24]—somewhat like the overemphasis on the momentary appearance of a thing.

As a type of critical philosophy the *nayavāda* holds that "almost all philosophical disputes arise out of a confusion of standpoints" and that the standpoints we adopt are, though we may not realize it, "the outcome of purposes that we pursue."[25] Since some of the *nayas* are aimed at rather late schools like the Advaita Vedānta's unqualified monism and the Sautrantika Buddhist doctrine of momentariness, it seems that the full system of *nayas* as we have it was probably worked out in the Middle Ages. Its relation to Mahāvīran Jainism is unrecoverable.

The *syādvāda* is the synthetic method balancing the analytic method of the *nayavāda* and may have arisen together with it. It is a systematization of *anekāntavāda* in terms of propositional logic. Here, as in interpretation of the *anekāntavāda*, there are two widely differing approaches, the one declaring that there are a finite number of points of view (the "in a sense" doctrine or "in some respect" doctrine)[26] and the doctrine of infinity or inexpressibility (the "maybe" doctrine). The *syādvāda* proposes seven different approaches to expressing the ontological status of an entity. Either these are seven different points of view, in which case "in a sense it is, in a sense it isn't," and so on, or the seven are meant to convey the idea of indeterminacy, in which case "maybe it is, maybe it isn't," and so on. In the first case, the entity in question is determinate, or determined; one can point precisely to seven different determinants concerning it. In the second case, the entity in question is indeterminate either in terms of the perceiver (he thinks it may or may not have determinations, but can't tell) or in itself (maybe it doesn't have any determined qualities). In either case the *syādvāda* may be taken as an alternate expression of the situation pointed to by the *anekānṭavāda*, the "manysidedness of reality";[27] the question is how many sides: Is there a certain number of determinable sides, or is there an indeterminable number, an infinite number in the sense that a number that is inherently indeterminable lacks boundaries and hence is unlimited?

Generally, Jain authors take the infinitist approach: Since any existent is infinitely manifold, there are an infinite number of correct propositions that may be made about it. For practical purposes, this infinity of possible propositions is systematized into seven: (1) *syād asti*, "in a sense it is" or "maybe it is"; (2) *syād nāsti*, "in a sense it is not," etc.; (3) *syād asti nāsti*, "in a sense it both is and is not"; (4) *syād avaktavya*, "in a sense it is indeterminate"; (5) *syād asti avaktavya*, "in a sense it both is and is indeterminate"; (6) *syād nāsti avaktavya*, "in a sense it both is not and is indeterminate"; (7) *syād asti nāsti avaktavya*, "in a sense it is, is not, and is indeterminate."

The *syādvāda* is a fascinating cultural object, and one of its most fascinating qualities is that there could be so much uncertainty about its meaning, even among Jain scholars, though it has been canonical in Jainism at least since the time of Samantabhadra, probably the second century A.D.; indeed, more than being merely canonical, it is described by a Jain scholar as "a fundamental principle underlying the Jaina philosophy," a principle which in itself constitutes "the whole scope of Jaina philosophy."[28] Yet there is radical disagreement about its meaning.

Hindus and Jains present widely divergent interpretations of it. Hindu scholars, believing the Vedānta to be the central philosophy of India, tend to interpret India's other schools in terms of it, seeing metaphysical absolutes in systems which may not have natively involved them, such as early Buddhism and the Jain *syādvāda*. To absolutist interpreters, the *syādvāda* seems a protokoan indicating that reality is "absolutely inexpressible"[29] or has to be expressed through paradoxical utterances. To western commentators in general this has seemed a satisfying interpretation. But to many Jain scholars the *syādvāda* seems not paradoxical but relativistic. For example, statements (1) and (2)—that it is and that it is not—are interpreted as referring to changes of circumstance. This typewriter *is* in the sense that it is on my desk; it *is not* in the sense that it is not in the street outside my window. Accordingly, assertion (3)—that it both is and is not—does not mean that something is both A and not-A, but that it *is* A and *is not* B. These interpretations embody the difference between the ontological and the predicative uses of the verb "to be"—"be" as a metaphysical statement and "be" as a grammatical copula linking subject and predicate. Confusion of these two uses of the word was common among the pre-Socratics, and even in the fourth century B.C., in Greece, the Megarians showed it in their conundra. Plato, it seems, was aware of the distinction, but for reasons of his own, involving parody of the neo-Eleatic school, at times (in the *Parmenides* especially) pretended not to be.

In terms of Jainism, the dichotomy of interpretations of the *syādvāda* is parallel to that involving the *anekāntavāda*. If the *anekāntavāda* is a doctrine of infinite manifoldness, then the *syādvāda* involves the paradoxical types of ontological formulations that the infinity concept brings with it. The relativistic interpretation would accord better with a reading of the *anekāntavāda* as a doctrine of finite manifoldness, or relativism. Here, as elsewhere, there is an unresolved inner tension in Jain thought between the naturalist and the absolutist approaches. In the Middle Ages, the Jains used the *syādvāda* as a dialectical tool to criticize rival schools. Used thus, it points to the incompleteness of particular dogmas. Opponents replied that the Jains themselves purvey particular dogmas, such as reincarnationism and atomism, and that the *syādvāda*, if it is to discredit another school, must discredit Jainism as well.

Buddhist Naturalism

Within the last generation, several Asian scholars have emphasized a naturalistic strain in early Buddhism, which, it seems, western scholars of the nineteenth and early twentieth centuries had tended to ignore. One scholar recognizes four elements of naturalism in early Buddhism: the existence of uncreated matter, atheism, a humanistic ethic emphasizing personal effort rather than grace or magic, and an ateleological view of the world, that is, the view that the world is not tending inherently toward some moral end.[30] Much can be added to this list.

According to Jayatilleke's reconstruction, the Pali versions of the life of the Buddha indicate that he practiced Jain yoga and abstinence, studied for a time under an Ājīvika teacher, worked with some ritual system, possibly the Vedic, and studied yoga under teachers of a middle Upaniṣadic group before beginning to teach his own *dharma* or doctrine.[31] Jayatilleke emphasizes the influence of the "skeptical movement" of the Ājīvikas and asserts that "Buddhism appears to have been impressed by the epistemology of the Materialists (Cārvākas) and tried to adopt it in its own way."[32] Jain influences or congruences are also apparent in the tradition; Buddhism, for example, uses the parable of the blind men feeling different parts of the elephant (though in the Buddhist version [*Udāna* 69] there are at least ten blind men as against the Jain six).

Siddhārtha Gautama the Buddha, like Epicurus and some other Greek thinkers, was a eudaimonistic teacher, emphasizing the value of happiness rather than knowledge. He did not teach a detailed picture of the universe in terms of ontology and metaphysics, and he "did not worry about discovering strictly logical arguments" in doctrinal debate.[33] In general, his attitude was that "if there are priorities in the accumulation of knowledge, man should first and foremost learn more about his own nature and his destiny in the universe rather than about the nature and origin of the universe."[34] This attitude is like that of Socrates, who also refrained from discussing theories about the universe on the ground that it was more useful to study human nature (*Apol.* 96a ff., *Phaedr.* 230a, *Phil.* 62b). The Buddha characterized metaphysics as "overstatements,"[35] and one scholar has described his philosophical contribution as providing "a pragmatic foundation for . . . radical empiricism."[36] This pragmatic emphasis was conjoined with utilitarian hedonism in a passage of the Pali canon that is known as the "Mirror of the Dharma." When weighing two possible courses of action, the student is instructed to estimate how much suffering this or that course will entail, both for oneself and for everyone else involved—one's own suffering mattering neither more nor less than another's. One's decision was then to opt for the course that would produce the least amount of overall suffering.[37]

Still, despite his humanistic and pragmatic emphases, Siddhārtha did teach a rudimentary ontology which has been interpreted either as realistic or as phenomenalistic—or as something in between the two positions.[38] In the first case, sense data are regarded as reporting accurately on an outside world which actually exists. In the second case, sense data are regarded not as reporting on but as constituting the world of experience, with no presumption of a hyperreality behind or beyond them. In either case, sense data would be regarded as the true content of empirical experience and Siddhārtha's teachings would be seen as occupied with empirical matters—with reality as experienced rather than as deduced or hypothesized. Whether empirical things are regarded as objectively real or phenomenally present, in either case they are the totality. (Compare Democritus: "The phenomenon *is* reality.") The empiricist and phenomenalistic strain is encapsulated in the *Sabba Sutta* or *Discourse on Everything*:

> The exalted one spoke thus: "Monks, I will preach to you 'everything.' Listen to it. What, monks, is 'everything'? Eye and material form, ear and sound, nose and odour, tongue and taste, body and tangibles, mind and concepts. These are called 'everything.' Monks, he who would say, 'I will reject this *everything* and proclaim another *everything*,' he may certainly have a theory (of his own). But when questioned, he would not be able to answer and would, moreover, be subject to vexation. Why? Because it would not be within the realm of experience."[39]

The discourse "purports to reject all the speculative theories which go beyond the data of sensory experience"[40]—a major theme in the early sections of the Pali canon.

In the *Sutta Nipāta*, which has been proposed as possibly the earliest part of that canon, an inquirer asks Siddhārtha about the multiplicity of systems: "What one of them terms 'truth,'" the interlocutor observes, "another says is false, and so they go on." Siddhārtha replies, "There is but one truth, without a second." And when asked what that is, he says: "No truth exists at all apart from what sense-perception offers" (*SN* 885–886). Sense data, whether real or phenomenal, *are* the universe.

Although Siddhārtha, like Socrates, did not teach extensively about the nature of the outside world, he did promulgate four doctrines about it: (1) that all empirical things are impermanent; (2) that, due to their impermanence, they are potential sources of suffering; (3) that they lack self-natures, or essences (*svabhāvas*); (4) that they are subject to certain laws of causation. The latter three points are all ramifications of the first: impermanence entails unreliability and instability and those traits suggest subjection to changing conditions.

Siddhārtha seems to have stated these principles as universal, though empirical (inductive) method does not yield universal propositions. This brings his profession of a purely empirical theory of knowledge into question and accounts for the fact that many authors have called him a rationalist.[41] The rationalist starts from principles which need not be derived from experience—*a priori* principles, like Parmenides' assertion that non-being is not—and proceeds to deduce consequences from them; the empiricist starts from sense data and induces generalizations from them. "The Buddha began his explanation of the process of experience with the sense organ and the sense object . . ."[42] The Buddha of the Suttas does not invoke *a priori* principles, and there is no hint that he was a rationalist. In the *Kālāma Sutta*, he rejects ten sources of knowledge of which four are rationalist and six revelationist. Elsewhere he declares that, "Even that which is well-reflected upon or well thought out is liable to be baseless, unfounded, and false" (*M.* I.171). In the *Sandaka Sutta* he explains:

> It is (sometimes) well-reasoned and (sometimes) ill-reasoned by a teacher who is a reasoner, and it is (sometimes) true and (sometimes) false.

Four categories are implied: (1) well-reasoned and true, (2) well-reasoned and false, (3) ill-reasoned and true, (4) ill-reasoned and false.[43] In other words, the quality of reasoning in a theory has nothing to do with its truth value. Siddhārtha's denunciation of revelation as a source of knowledge is equally direct. In the *Kālāma Sutta* he rejects the authority of scriptures, revelations, teachers, experts, common sense or convention, and hearsay.

Siddhārtha seems to have taught a combination of pragmatism, empiricism, and utilitarian hedonism. His pragmatism varies. In one passage he rejects the premise that what is useful is true, what is useless, false. There are statements, he says, which are true but useless. Again, four categories are implied: (1) true and useful, (2) true and useless (like knowing how many insects there are in the world, to use a later Buddhist example), (3) false and useful, (4) false and useless. In this formulation he said that he himself bothered to teach only what was both true and useful.

Other passages, however, respond well to pragmatic interpretations—above all the famous "Questions that should not be answered" (*ṭhapanīya pañha*), which are listed as either ten or fourteen. The locus classicus is the *Māluṅkyaputta Sutta* (*M.* 63), which lists ten: whether the world is (1) eternal or (2) noneternal; whether it is (3) finite, or (4) infinite; whether the soul is (5) the same as the body or (6) different; whether an enlightened person (7) exists after death or (8) does not or (9) both does and does not or (10) neither does nor does not. These questions "the Blessed One does not elucidate." The Blessed One's motives in not elucidating them are variously reconstructed.

One possibility is that he spoke here as a pragmatist, feeling that these questions, or some of them, are useless and distracting in terms of personal development. Siddhārtha used the parable of the man struck by an arrow who inquires who shot it and where it was made rather than asking to have it removed (*M.* I.429). In the same way, he may have regarded concentrating on questions such as infinity, soul, and the afterlife as useless distractions. Another leading possibility is that he spoke as an empiricist, refusing to answer these questions because some or all of them were beyond the limits of empirical investigation.[44] (This will seem questionable, however, in light of the "extrasensory empiricism" which is attributed to the Buddha by these same authors, and which would seem designed to answer just such questions as these.) It is also suggested that he spoke as an authoritarian—discouraging speculation among his disciples because speculation might lead them to different conclusions than his[45]—and that he spoke as a logical positivist, regarding some questions as logically improper.[46] To some it seems that he spoke as a proto-Mādhyamikin, or transcendental absolutist, meaning either that questions relating to nirvāṇa are not accessible to concepts of any kind, or that no truths at all are accessible to concepts.[47]

In general, the mix of attitudes associated in modern times with Anglo-American philosophy—logical positivism, pragmatism, linguistic criticism, empiricism, and utilitarianism—seems to have been characteristic of early Buddhism. Much of this can be seen in the *Kālāma Sutta*, which recommends a combination of empirical investigation, pragmatic decision-making, and utilitarian hedonist values. It concludes: You should reject those beliefs when you yourself realize that when they are accepted and lived up to they conduce to lack of welfare, and unhappiness.

Siddhārtha's empirical method involved, first, observation or investigation; then, inductive inference based on it. To return to the four universal propositions that he taught, "The statement that 'on account of birth there is decay and death' is an empirical generalization based on the observation (by perception) that all those who are 'known and seen' to be born eventually grow old and die. From the observed cases the inductive inference is made that all those who are born . . . grow old and die."[48] But one does not, even in a traditional society, actually *observe* many deaths; it is more a matter of hearing about them. Siddhārtha's empiricism, in practice, had an intersubjective aspect that, in his rejections of authority and hearsay in the *Kālāma Sutta*, he does not acknowledge.

Siddhārtha's propositions concerning impermanence, nonsubstantiality, suffering, and causality are interpreted, in recent Buddhist scholarship, as empirical inductions. Compare, for example, Kalupahana: "Direct perception . . . provides man with the knowledge of phenomena, and on the basis of this direct knowledge, the Buddha made inductive inferences with regard to the *universality* of (1) causality (*paṭiccasamuppāda*), (2) impermanence (*aniccata*), (3) unsatisfactoriness (*dukkhata*), and (4) non-substantiality (*anattatā*)."[49] But perhaps Siddhārtha's empiricism is pragmatically compromised here. Observation alone cannot rigorously justify the universality of these propositions; for example, the impermanence of things like the earth, the oceans, and the sun and stars cannot be observed in a human lifetime.

Siddhārtha's empiricism included a principle of verification. His rejection of teachers as sources of knowledge is based on the conviction that knowledge is not one's own till it has been verified in the light of one's personal experience. In the *Tevijja Sutta* he criticizes various Brahmins for teaching a reality (the *brahman*) which they have not "seen face to face" (*D.* I.238). He requests that his own teachings be verified in the personal experience of the student before the student should allow conviction to arise in him. Thus Buddhism advertised itself as "an invitation to come and see" (*M.* I.37). It would not be proper for Siddhārtha or anyone else to say anything "if he had not known, seen, experienced, realized and apprehended it with his own insight" (*M.* I.475).

There is, then, a stage in the process when the student must simultaneously suspend judgment and have sufficient faith in a teacher to bother to carry out the process of personal investigation and verification—which can be demanding. The

Vīmaṃsaka Sutta advises withholding faith completely until after the verification process; then and only then can one have "rational faith" (*ākāravatī saddhā*). The irrational—or antirational—type of faith recommended in Christianity and Islam is regarded as an obstacle to enlightenment.

To some scholars this early Buddhist theory of knowledge has seemed meticulously positivistic and empirical. The problem, for others, lies in one element of Siddhārtha's version of the empirical method: "Direct perception [writes Kalupahana], *both sensory and extrasensory*, provides man with the knowledge of phenomena . . ."[50] There are doctrines in the Pali canon that Siddhārtha teaches on the exclusive basis of extrasensory perception. These include his atheism, which consists in a denial of an omnipotent creator god; the assertion of the existence of minor godlings; the doctrine (taught also by Democritus) of a multiplicity or even infinity of worlds, and the doctrines of reincarnation, *karma*, and *mokṣa*.[51] "He was willing," says one scholar, "to accept whatever information was available through such means as long as it possessed any pragmatic value."[52]

Siddhārtha's procedure here has been questioned on the ground that he accepted the inherited doctrines of reincarnation, *karma*, and *mokṣa* simply because he inherited them—that is, that he took them for granted because they were dominant in the culture around him. One scholar suspects that he taught whatever he pleased and concealed his whimsicality under claims of ESP, precisely because the evidence of ESP was unverifiable and had to be accepted on authority alone.[53] On this view, the apparent naturalism of his approach was merely a pretense to cover up his authoritarianism; the claim to ESP allowed him to go beyond naturalistic method without admitting it.[54]

Western scholars have not been sympathetic to expanding the concept of empiricism to include ESP—however accepted it may have been in sixth century B.C. Indian empiricism. Buddhist doctrine portrays the achievement of the necessary empirical evidence as taking multiple lifetimes. Making it unverifiable also makes it unfalsifiable. In Buddhist theory, extrasensory perceptions are obtained as the result of concentration and meditation practices. Yet they cannot be predicted or scheduled, because one's past-life situation is always involved; people who in past lives have already performed the concentration practices required will have ESP experiences more quickly than others. Siddhārtha, who is declared to have been working on such things for thousands of lifetimes, claimed to have developed six extrasensory powers: psychokinesis (the ability to fly), clairaudience (superhearing), telepathic knowledge (mind reading), retrocognition (knowledge of his own and others' past lives), clairvoyance (knowledge of the future deaths and reincarnations of others, himself having none), and, finally, knowledge of the defiling impulses, that is, knowledge of the extent to which an individual's mind is at any moment defiled by the various types of wishful thinking (*M*. I.69).

In the Buddhist tradition, it is held that these powers can be verified intersubjectively. Since meditation practices are held to promote developments based on a pattern of natural causation within the mind, comparing one's experiences with those of other meditators is a valid type of intersubjective empiricism. In western religions, ESP experiences have been called "mystical" and as such put out of the bounds of the natural. One western scholar, for example, says: "The Buddha . . . sees things as they truly are by a mystic potency . . . obviously incapable of verification in any empirical manner."[55] Yet within the Buddhist context the extrasensory perception produced through meditation "is a natural and not a supernatural occurrence."[56] As such, it is subject to causality and to some extent predictable, that is, subject to scientific method. Siddhārtha taught:

> It is in the nature of things that a person in the state of concentration knows and sees what really is . . . (*A.* V.3.313)

In this process the six extrasensory powers claimed by Siddhārtha are supposed to arise naturally, and intersubjective verification can occur. A generation or more ago Jayatilleke appealed to the researches of Rhine and others in parapsychology to bring this aspect of Buddhism down to earth for westerners—though a potential investigator may be deterred by the fact that the verification process may require more than his or her present lifetime!

A significant problem in terms of verification is the fact that the knowledge which Siddhārtha obtained through ESP is often different from that obtained by Jain and Upaniṣadic meditators using related techniques. Siddhārtha himself advises skepticism of rational theories on the grounds that they disagree with one another whereas truth is one; the same criticism could be made of theories based on ESP. The Suttas report several cases in which Siddhārtha disagreed with the extrasensory insights of other yogis. His solution in some cases was not to deny the experience which the other meditator claimed, but to criticize the interpretation which he put on it. In the *Mahākammavibhaṅga Sutta*, Siddhārtha met a yogi, perhaps an Ājīvika, who had extrasensorily perceived a person of very evil life dying and being reborn into a happy condition, whereupon he denied the doctrine of karmic retribution. Siddhārtha replied:

> I am prepared to grant that this yogin has observed a man who has misconducted himself in this life, born at death in a happier and better world, but I do not agree with his conclusion that, therefore, all people, whether they misconduct themselves in this life or not, are born at death into a happier and better world. The knowledge of the Transcendent One with regard to operations of karma is different . . . If a person who has misconducted himself in this life is born at death in a happier and better world, then he has either at some time in his past done good deeds, which have resulted in these experiences, or at the time of his death has changed his ways and adopted the right view of life.[57]

The yogi in question, according to Siddhārtha, should have done more research; if he had observed more cases he would have seen that *karma*, in all its complexity, sometimes ripens in ways that superficially appear irregular. In other cases he criticizes not the research methods of an opposing yogi, but the limitation of his power of ESP. Says Jayatilleke: "Even with regard to the universe . . . the Buddha could observe clusters of galaxies and the vast cosmos, while Anuruddha, the specialist in clairvoyance, could observe only a single galaxy."[58]

The most difficult of the claims to special knowledge characteristically made in the Indian tradition is the claim to literal and complete omniscience. In the Buddhist texts the claim to omniscience first arises in the *Milindapañha*, which comes at the very end of the Pali canon. The claim was not made in the earlier parts of the canon, which are more likely to represent Siddhārtha's own positions, but may result from competition among schools—as "Mahāvīra was the first religious teacher in India to claim such omniscience"[59] and subsequently the claim of omniscience became common among the Jains. The *Kalpa Sūtra*, "the traditional canonical work on the lives of the Jinas,"[60] tells us:

> When the Venerable Ascetic Mahāvīra had become a Gina and Arhat, he was a Kevalin, omniscient and comprehending all objects; he knew and saw all conditions of

the world, of gods, of men, and demons; whence they come, whither they go, whether they are born as men or animals or become gods or hell-beings, the ideas, the thoughts of their minds, the food, doings, desires, the open and secret deeds of all living beings in the whole world; he the Arhat, for whom there is no secret, knew and saw all conditions of all living beings in the world, what they thought, spoke, or did at any moment.[61]

The *Jātaka Nidanakatha*, a Theravādin biography of Siddhārtha, says that at dawn following enlightenment under the bodhi tree, "The great man attained 'omniscience,'"[62] but this is a late Pali text, and the claim of omniscience may be derived from Jain or other sources. Some of the Ājīvikas seem to have claimed omniscience, too—a strange claim for teachers of skepticism.[63]

Earlier works in the Pali canon deal with the question differently. In the *Cūḷa-Sukuludāyi-sutta*, a questioner tells Siddhārtha that, having heard of Mahāvīra's omniscience, he asked Mahāvīra a question about the past, and that Mahāvīra evaded it. Siddhārtha made no comment on Mahāvīra's claim to omniscience, strongly hinted that he himself could answer any and all questions about the past, then, expressing his pragmatic bent, stated that such activity was useless. In the *Tevijja-Vacchagotte-sutta*, an interlocutor tells Siddhārtha that he has heard that Siddhārtha is omniscient in the manner of Mahāvīra. Siddhārtha replies:

> Those who speak thus are misrepresenting me . . . the recluse Gotama (the Buddha) is a threefold knowledge man . . . For I . . . whenever I please to recollect a variety of former habitations, that is to say one birth, two births . . . thus, do I recollect diverse former habitations in all their modes and details. And I . . . whenever I please . . . see beings as they pass hence and come to be . . . according to the consequences of deeds, and I . . . by the destruction of the cankers, having realized here and now by my own superknowledge the freedom of mind and the freedom through wisdom that are cankerless, entering therein, bide therein.[64]

Here the Buddha specifically rejects the claim that he is omniscient, and claims three, not six, types of supercognition.

Some later Buddhists, such as Dharmapāla, puzzled over the questions whether the Buddha was omniscient, and what in fact it would mean to be omniscient.[65] But in time the original pragmatism of early Buddhism reasserted itself somewhat and the question came to be considered irrelevant. Dharmakīrti sounds like Socrates denouncing the study of nature before obtaining self-knowledge, when he says:

> What is the use of . . . wide knowledge pertaining to the number of insects in the whole world? Rather, enquire into his knowledge of that which is to be practised by us.
>
> For us, the most desired authority is not the one who knows everything; rather, we would have a teacher who knows the Truth which leads to prosperity in this world, as well as to the insight into things to be forsaken and things to be cultivated.

Sāṅtarakṣita concurs, with what might be taken as a word of warning for modern scholars:

> When people proceed to prove the existence of the person knowing all the little details of the entire world, they put themselves to the unnecessary trouble of writing treatises on the subject and carrying on discussions on the same.[66]

Early Buddhism seems finally to score high on the six-point list of elements of naturalism: (1) sense data is accepted as the primary source of knowledge;

(2) knowledge is sometimes intuitive, but with the claim that it is available to all on natural grounds and hence susceptible of intersubjective verification; (3) the external world exists apart from any single consciousness, that is, it is the same for all consciousnesses; (4) the world manifests order (causality) which does not exclude human responsibility; (5) supernatural teleology is denied; (6) ethics are generally humanistic, though the ultimate goal of human behavior is sometimes described as an absolute.

Some Greek Parallels

Various early Greek philosophers also recognized ESP as an empirical source of knowledge. Pythagoras and Empedocles, both of whom were important groundbreakers in early science, seem to have justified their teachings of reincarnation by their retrocognitive ability to know past lives. It is unknown what other early teachings were justified in this way. How, for example, did Pythagoras prove the existence of the Music of the Spheres? Did he, like many Indian yogis, claim to hear it through clairaudience? But in Greece the concept of empiricism, as it grew from Xenophanes to Democritus, increasingly excluded ESP evidence. In Buddhism on the other hand, ESP evidence is accepted empirically to this day. This may indicate that such claims initially were imported into Greece, not an enduring part of the native culture. It is notable that the disappearance of ESP claims accompanied the turning away from the monism complex, and that when, in the early Roman Empire, the monism complex made a big comeback, it brought with it again claims of psychokinesis and so on.

The only place in Greek philosophy where a doctrine of complete omniscience is preached is in Plato's doctrine of Recollection. There the doctrine is that knowledge of all things in the universe is innate in the human soul, but obscured at birth by the soul's immersion in matter; when the soul frees itself from matter fully it obtains two new qualities: (1) it will not be reborn again, and (2) its innate knowledge of all things in the universe is once again conscious. The relationship of this doctrine to Jain doctrine is most significant for the whole relationship of Greek and Indian philosophy. In Jain doctrine, the *sarvajñātva* of Mahāvīra, his attaining of complete omniscience—the knowledge of all things which is innate in the human soul but obscured by contact with matter—occurred at the moment when his soul finally freed itself from subjection to matter. The similarity of these Jain and Platonic doctrines is part of a larger parallelism between Jainism and the general aspect of Plato's system which might be called "Orphic."

The *Digha Nikāya* says of nirvāṇa, "Here it is that the conditioned consciousness ceases to be" (*D.* I.223). The state of nirvāṇa is that of the person who has gained "mental freedom"—that is, freedom from conditioning—yet continues to live out his or her life. *Parinirvāṇa*, on the other hand, is the state such a being enters upon the death of the final body. There have always been tendencies toward both naturalistic and absolutistic definitions of these states. In regard to nirvāṇa, the metaphysical attitude stresses the magical powers of the enlightened one; the naturalistic approach deemphasizes that type of cultism. The naturalistic view of *parinirvāṇa* would be simple dissolution of atoms, as for the Cārvākas and Ājīvikas. There is some reason to think this was taught also among early Buddhists; but its lack of ethical inspiration may have discouraged Siddhārtha from dealing with the question if this was in fact his view. The transcendentalist view of *parinirvāṇa* is stated in the *Udāna*:

> There is that sphere wherein is neither earth nor water nor fire nor air; wherein are none of the stages reached by . . . impersonal mystical consciousness, where there is neither this world nor a world beyond nor both together nor sun and moon; this, I say, is free from coming or going, from duration, arising, or passing away; it has no foundation, no beginning, and no object. (*Udāna* 80)

Here *parinirvāṇa* is viewed as the opposite of nature, the negation of it and its constituents such as the four elements. It is virtually identical to Parmenides' concept of Being: spherical, lacking differentiation, to which nothing comes and from which nothing goes, and so on. This transcendentalist version of nirvāṇa conflicts with the predominantly naturalistic texture of Siddhārtha's teachings. It may represent the influence of either Upaniṣadic mysticism or the Jain conception of the *ajīva* world to which the enlightened soul ascends and which is the opposite of life here (the *jīva* realm).

It is worth repeating that Plato's view of the afterlife is similar and probably related. In the *Phaedrus* he says:

> Of that place beyond the heavens none of our earthly poets has yet sung, and none shall sing worthily. But this is the manner of it . . . It is there that true being dwells, without color or shape, that cannot be touched. (247c)

And in the *Phaedo*:

> [When at death the soul is free from reincarnation] it passes into the realm of the pure and everlasting and immortal and changeless, and being of a kindred nature, when it is once independent and free from interference, consorts with it always and strays no longer, but remains in the realm of the absolute, constant and invariable. (79c-d)

In both Greece and India a major dichotomy between the naturalistic and the metaphysical traditions can be seen in the afterlife models; the transcendental models of Plato and the *Udāna* should be contrasted with the models of the Lucretius and Cārvākas, wherein the atoms of the four elements disperse into the flow of nature and the impression of a person simply ceases.

Notes to Chapter Thirteen

1. Dale Riepe, *The Naturalistic Tradition in Indian Thought* (Seattle: University of Washington Press, 1961), pp. 6–7.

2. Benjamin Farrington, *Greek Science* (Baltimore, Maryland: Penguin Books, 1961), p. 35.

3. John Burnet, *Early Greek Philosophy* (New York: Meridian Books, 1957) p. 49, for the first; Richard B. Onians, *The Origins of European Thought* (Cambridge: Cambridge University Press, 1954), pp. 247–248, for the second.

4. Farrington, *Greek Science*, pp. 38–39.

5. David J. Kalupahana, *A History of Buddhist Philosophy: Continuities and Discontinuities* (Honolulu: University of Hawaii Press, 1992), p. 15.

6. Ibid., p. 13.

7. Ibid., p. 14.

8. Sarvepalli Radhakrishnan and Charles A. Moore, eds., *A Source Book in Indian Philosophy* (Princeton, New Jersey: Princeton University Press, 1957), p. 229.

9. *Sarvadarśana-saṃgraha*, quoted by Riepe, *The Naturalistic Tradition*, p. 74.

10. Hermann Fränkel, "Xenophanes' Empiricism and His Critique of Knowledge (B 34)," in *The Presocratics*, ed. Alexander P. D. Mourelatos (Garden City, New York: Doubleday Anchor Books, 1974), p. 118.

11. Ibid., p. 120.

12. Translated as ibid., p. 122.

13. Ibid.

14. Farrington, *Greek Science*, p. 59.

15. See Cyril Bailey, *The Greek Atomists and Epicurus* (Oxford: Clarendon Press, 1928), p. 175.

16. Slightly changed from the translation by Benjamin Farrington in *The Faith of Epicurus* (London: Weidenfeld and Nicolson, 1967), pp. 95–96.

17. Radhakrishnan and Moore, *A Sourcebook in Indian Philosophy*, p. 249.

18. Surendranath Dasgupta, *History of Indian Philosophy*, vol. 3 (Delhi: Motilal Banarsidass, 1975), p. 540.

19. Trans. R. E. Latham, *Lucretius: The Nature of the Universe* (Baltimore, Maryland: Penguin, 1951), p. 116.

20. See Atusi Uno, "A Study of syādvāda," *Jinamañjari* 18, no. 2 (1998): 14.

21. Ibid., p. 16.

22. Y. J. Padmarajiah, *A Comparative Study of the Jaina Theories of Reality and Knowledge* (Bombay: Jain Sahitya Vikas Mandal, 1963), p. 290.

23. Ibid., p. 312.

24. Ibid., p. 324.

25. Sarvapalli Radhakrishnan, *Indian Philosophy*, vol. 1, (London and New York: George Allen and Unwin, 1971), pp. 299 and 301.

26. For this term see Atusi Uno, "A Study of syādvāda," p. 15.

27. This is the term used by Amar Singh Jain, "Path of Moksa According to Kundakunda," *Jinamañjari* 18, no. 2 (1998): 23.

28. Atusi Uno, "A Study of syādvāda," p. 14.

29. Ibid., p. 16.

30. Riepe, *The Naturalistic Tradition in Indian Thought*, p. 176.

31. K. N. Jayatilleke, *Early Buddhist Theory of Knowledge* (London: George Allen and Unwin, 1963), pp. 464–465.

32. Ibid., p. 374.

33. David J. Kalupahana, *Nāgārjuna: The Philosophy of the Middle Way* (Albany, New York: State University of New York Press, 1986), p. 13.

34. K. N. Jayatilleke, *The Message of the Buddha* (New York: Macmillan, 1974), p. 69.

35. Kalupahana, *History of Buddhist Philosophy*, p. 30,

36. Ibid., p. 52.

37. See David J. Kalupahana, *Buddhist Philosophy: A Historical Analysis* (Honolulu: University of Hawaii Press, 1976), p. 62.

38. "[T]he history of Buddhism—beginning with the Buddha himself, through the Abhidharma, especially the *Kathāvatthu*, and the non-idealistic Mahāyāna, represented by the *Vajracchedikā*, Nāgārjuna, and Vasubandhu—represents a gigantic effort to avoid the extreme standpoints of realism and nominalism . . ." Ibid., p. 197.

39. Trans. David J. Kalupahana, "A Buddhist Tract on Empiricism," *Philosophy East and West* 19 (1969): 66.

40. Ibid., p. 67.

41. For example: Radhakrishnan, *Indian Philosophy* vol. 1, p. 359; Vidhushekhara Bhattacarya, *The Basic Conception of Buddhism*, Adharchandra Mookerjee Lectures 1932 (Calcutta: University of Calcutta, 1934), pp. 9 ff.; L. de la Vallèe Poussin, *The Way to Nirvāṇa* (Cambridge: Cambridge University Press, 1917), pp. 30 ff.

42. Kalupahana, *History of Buddhist Philosophy*, p. 189.

43. Jayatilleke, *Early Buddhist Theory of Knowledge*, p. 272.

44. David Kalupahana, *Causality: The Central Philosophy of Buddhism* (Honolulu: University of Hawaii Press, 1975), p. 183; Jayatilleke, *Early Buddhist Theory of Knowledge*, p. 475.

45. Riepe, *The Naturalistic Tradition*, p. 171.

46. Jayatilleke, *Early Buddhist Theory of Knowledge*, p. 475.

47. T. R. V. Murti, *The Central Philosophy of Buddhism* (London: George Allen and Unwin, 1974), pp. 36–54.

48. Jayatilleke, *Early Buddhist Theory of Knowledge*, p. 457.

49. Kalupahana, *Buddhist Philosophy*, p. 22.

50. Ibid.

51. See Jayatilleke, *The Message of the Buddha*, pp. 94, 99–100, 105, 134–135, and *Early Buddhist Theory of Knowledge* pp. 370–372, 375–376; Kalupahana, *Causality*, pp. 104–106, and *History of Buddhist Philosophy*, p. 41, that he came to accept karma and rebirth "on the basis of some of these experiences."

52. Ibid.

53. Riepe, *The Naturalistic Tradition*, p. 171.

54. Ibid., p. 176.

55. Arthur B. Keith, *Buddhist Philosophy* (Oxford: Clarendon Press, 1923), p. 90.

56. Jayatilleke, *Early Buddhist Theory of Knowledge*, p. 420.

57. Trans. Jayatilleke, *The Message of the Buddha*, pp. 145–146.

58. Ibid., p. 146.

59. Kalupahana, *History of Buddhist Philosophy*, p. 19.

60. Padmanabh S. Jaini, "On the *sarvajñātva* of Mahāvīra and the Buddha," in *Buddhist Studies in Honour of I. B. Horner*, ed. L. Cousins, A. Kunst, and K. R. Norman (Dordrecht: D. Reel, 1974), p. 72.

61. Trans. Hermann Jacobi, *Jaina Sūtras*, vol. 1, Sacred Books of the East 22 (Oxford: Clarendon Press, 1884), pp. 263–264.

62. Jaini, "On the *sarvajñātva* of Mahāvīra and the Buddha," p. 76.

63. See A. L. Basham, *History and Doctrine of the Ājīvikas: A Vanished Indian Religion* (London: Luzac, 1951), pp. 56, 79, for Makkhali Gosāla; Jayatilleke, *Early Buddhist Theory of Knowledge*, p. 250, for Nigaṇṭha Nātaputta and Purāṇa Kassapa.

64. Trans. Jaini, "On the *sarvajñātva* of Mahāvīra and the Buddha," pp. 80–81.

65. Kalupahana feels the Buddhist discourse meant something different by terms like *sabaññū*, all-knowing, and *sabbadassāvī*, all-perceiving. When, in the *Sutta Nipāta* (1122) a disciple makes an observation of the Buddha which is conventionally translated as "There is nothing that you have not seen, heard, or conceived," he feels the proper translation, in context of the Buddhist discourse, would be: "You do not recognize anything that is not seen, heard, conceived, or cognized in this world" (*History of Indian Philosophy*, pp. 43–44).

66. Both these passages are quoted by Jaini, "On the *sarvajñātva* of Mahāvīra and the Buddha," p. 87.

Chapter Fourteen

Diffusion Channels in the Hellenistic and Roman Periods

After the Persian Wars, contacts between Greeks and Persians—not to mention Greeks and Indians—diminished for the rest of the fifth century B.C. At the end of the fifth century, Ctesius of Cnidus, when he returned from being a Greek physician attendant on the Persian court, took the trouble to publish trade routes between Ephesus and various centers in Bactria and India, with lengths of travel along them; that there was a readership for such information shows that somebody was traveling these routes, though it is hard to say who. After Alexander the Great, and increasingly until the Neoplatonist period, various authors attributed Asian travels to early philosophers[1]—Democritus, for example, is said (D.L. IX.35) to have traveled widely in Asia, possibly visiting the northwest Indian satrapy—but few, if any, such claims can be considered reliable.

In the fourth century, contacts between Greece and the East increased again. Greek diplomats regularly visited the Persian court, and Greek soldiers were employed in great numbers throughout the East as mercenaries. Among Greeks, the East was coming to be seen increasingly as a beckoning mercantile opportunity. Not only Greek soldiers of fortune, but artists, craftsmen, and hetairai went east to pursue their careers. There was still some traffic in ideas between East and West—indicated, for example, by the presence of Persian ideas in Plato's work.[2]

Greek authors began to write on Persian history, which was understood as including the history of northwest India since its conquest by Cyrus. Geographical features such as the Hindu Kush and the Indus River became commonly known in Greece, along with various wonders that the Greek Indographers testified to. Scylax, the author of the first known Greek book about India, spoke about the *Monophthalmoi*, who had only one eye, the *Enōtikoitoi*, who crept inside their own giant ears to sleep, the *Skiapodes*, whose enormous feet provided shade for them to sleep in, and, as Tzetzes would later put it, "a thousand other wondrous sights" (*Chiliades* 7.629–636). The physician Ctesias, whom one modern author calls "the Marco Polo of his era,"[3] mentions seven races of strange humans including the *Kunēkephaloi*, or dog-headed people, along with nineteen wonders having to do with animals and plants.[4] The Greeks, as the same scholar puts it, "tended to look on their penetration of the Asiatic frontier as a daring assault on the terrors of distant space,"[5] thus promoting a "hypertrophic portrait of India."[6] Herodotus wrote of dog-headed Indians and headless Indians whose eyes were in their chests (IV.191), and so on. Others down to and including Diodorus Siculus contributed to this cataloguing of wonders.

In the later fourth century, Alexander the Great reopened the land channel all the way from Greece to India with an enormous military and cultural expedition which had a long-lasting effect, as it left Greek colonies in Bactria and India in its wake. After Alexander's death his general Seleucus established a kingdom roughly coterminous with the Persian Empire. Overland trade from the Mediterranean passed through the Seleucid kingdom and Central Asia on a route which ran from Zeugma on the Euphrates to either Seleucia or Ctesiphon east of the Tigris, and thence to Artemita; there it branched, one branch running northeast by Ecbatan to various trading centers in Bactria and northwest India, the southern branch passing Susa to Seistan and the lower Indus Valley.[7] In Tashkurgan, at the end of the northern branch (at the caravanserai known as the Stone Tower—*Lithinos Pyrgos*), and Kandahar on the southern, caravans from the Mediterranean would meet both Indian and Chinese traders or their local agents. A second, more northerly route is mentioned by Strabo (II.73, XI.509) and Pliny (VI.52), who say that goods passed from India overland to the Oxus River, down the Oxus to the Caspian Sea, across the Caspian to the mouth of the Cyrus, up the Cyrus, overland to Phasis, and down the Phasis to the Black Sea, unloading at Dioskurias.[8] Around 150 B.C. the Parthian Empire interposed an obstacle along the land route, but overland trade continued nonetheless, either through or around Parthia, though at a reduced rate.

The sea routes from the Red Sea to India were opened shortly after the Parthians made the land routes insecure, perhaps stimulated by this development. By the end of the first century B.C. an enormous trade passed along them between Greek Egypt and various ports in India. Goods to be transported by sea were shipped from Alexandria up the Nile to Coptos, carried overland to Berenike or Myos Hormus on the Red Sea, then shipped either around or across the Arabian Sea (perhaps with a stop at Socotra) to many Indian ports, especially Barygaza and Muziris.[9] This trade was dominated by Greek merchant seamen; *all* the ships' captains whose names are extant from the India trade seem to have been Greek.[10]

This trade may have flagged during the third century A.D. due to wars and generally unsettled conditions in the Roman Empire, but it resurged in the fourth, and in both the second and the fourth centuries whole Greek books are known to have passed along this route to India, to have been translated into Indian languages, and to have exerted a permanent and significant influence there.

Cosmopolitan Tendencies

Although most traffic along both land and sea routes was commercial, cultural influences accompanied it. Both Greece and India—especially, perhaps, Greece—were already, by the fourth century B.C., cosmopolitan and open to foreign influences. Northwest India was in constant contact by way of the Khyber Pass with Iran, Central Asia, and the Silk Road, and various outside cultures (such as the Vedic Aryans and later the Persians, Greeks, Scythians, and Kushans) settled and traded there. The trunk road which started in Bactra ("the obligatory route for any expedition of importance")[11] led through the Khyber Pass and the northwest region into the great Indian market of Mathura on the Jumna, a tributary of the Ganges; from Mathura goods went east into the Ganges plain and the kingdom of Magadha or south via Ujjayini. Even while India as a whole remained remarkably shut in or closed off, this corner was open and somewhat multicultural. In the mid-third century, inscriptions in this region were apt to occur in any of four languages (Persian, Aramaic, Greek, or Prakrit).

In Greece in the archaic and classical periods a xenophobic emphasis on the distinction between Greeks and barbarians had prevailed. The parochial nature of the Olympic games, in which only Greeks could participate, was an instance. The Persian Wars exacerbated it. Isocrates emphasized the difference between Greeks and barbarians, declaring that Greek culture was superior and should be imposed on barbarian nations by conquest. Aristotle, Alexander's teacher, also purveyed the view that "barbarians" were natural slaves (*Pol.* 1) and the Greeks their natural masters.

Yet the countertendency was also prominent. Already in the Sophistic period, Antiphon had taught what would one day be a basic principle of the Enlightenment, that "all people are created alike by nature in all respects, both barbarians and Greeks" (*On Truth*).[12] The Sophistic distinction between nature and culture (*physis* and *nomos*) provided a theoretical foundation for the acceptance of foreign influence: Though nature is beyond human control, culture, or convention, may be remade by human decision; to remake one's own culture, one reasonable course is to model it on another. Socrates actually advised his students to seek out the wisdom of foreign teachers (*Phaedo* 78a).

The invidious distinction had lost much of its force on the Greek scene by the time of Alexander and his Successors. Alexander's concept of *homonoia*, or like-mindedness between Greeks and Persians, echoed Antiphon's view that Greeks and non-Greeks can have a meeting of minds. Eratosthenes of Cyrene, chief librarian of Alexandria under Ptolemy III, extended the liberal view, rejecting ethnic distinctions in favor of distinctions based on merit (Strabo I.66). Contemplating the cultures roundabout, he identified the Romans and Carthaginians as the most civilized non-Greeks in the West, the Iranians and Indians in the East.[13]

Greeks had been extremely active merchants throughout the eastern Mediterranean and Near East since the Orientalizing period, and they knew firsthand that culture moves with trade. Along with an unusual openness to foreign influence came a competitive impulse to disseminate the virtues of Greek culture along with its commodity products. Isocrates defined "Greekness" as a matter of education (*paideia*) rather than race, and proclaimed that the Greeks were "the teachers of the world" (*Panegyricus* 50). Later, in the Alexandrian or Hellenistic period, the dissemination of Greek *paideia*, or cultural education, was carried out as a proselytizing mission. The dissemination of *paideia* involved learning the Greek language, and for this purpose a simplified and easy-to-learn dialect developed called *koinē*, the "common" or international dialect.

Developed primarily from Attic through "processes of simplification and regularization,"[14] the *koinē* reflected Athens's position as "the metropolis of an empire, attracting thousands of foreigners . . ." till the Attic dialect was "enriched (some would say adulterated) by alien borrowings."[15] "The Metropolitan Attic became Imperial Attic,"[16] which was subsequently adopted by Philip of Macedon, the father of Alexander the Great, as his "official language . . . in diplomatic correspondence."[17] Alexander's conquests spread this "Macedonian Koinē" as "the lingua franca of educated men throughout this huge expanse of territory,"[18] and Rome inherited the language with the territory. Various details—such as the change from a pitch to a stress accent, the equalization of long and short vowels, the loss of the optative mood, and the simplification of the declensional system through such details as the gradual disappearance of the dative case—rendered the new dialect easier to learn, while the imperial expansion of the lexicon made it more nearly universal in application.

While the *koinē* grew up as a practical response to "the challenge of empire,"[19] the idea of a language shared by all peoples, transcending national borders and tribal appeals, also had a basis in Greek philosophy. It was in harmony, for example, with the spirit of Theophrastus's claim that all humans are of common ancestry. The Cynics similarly taught that all human societies formed a single, vast culture, the world-community, or *cosmopolis*, and that an enlightened attitude would recognize no distinctions within it (D.L. VI.22). Zeno the Stoic, in his *Republic*, perhaps writing under the influence of Alexander's *homonoia*, called for a world government based on brotherly love and transcending national and other distinctions; the Roman Stoics actually sponsored liberal reforms in the direction of realizing this goal.[20] Similarly, the Epicureans proselytized the barbarians and became the court philosophers of the Seleucid monarch Antiochus IV and his son. Their doctrinal purview, in other words, reached almost to the Indus River and included some of the Bactrian and Indian colonies left by Alexander.

When, toward the end of his campaign, Alexander prayed at Opis for a *homonoia*—a one-mindedness or merging of eastern and western cultures—this was taken by many, both ancient and modern, as a statement of his reason for colonizing Asia. On this view, it seems that the colonies he left were not intended to endure as protected ethnic enclaves; they were specifically intended to bring the Greek mind to the barbarian and to learn from the barbarian in turn. In the wake of his endeavor such idealism became fairly common. Seneca, for example, wrote in the first century A.D.:

> The World is the mother of us all, and the ultimate origin of each one of us can be traced back to her, whether the steps in the ladder of descent be noble or humble. To no one is virtue forbidden; she is accessible to all; she admits everyone, she invites everyone in; free men and freedmen, slaves, kings, and exiles.[21]

With the dissemination of Greek education such attitudes spread to Asian peoples undergoing the process of Hellenization. The Syrian Meleager of Gadara wrote:

> What is the wonder if I am a Syrian? There is one motherland, stranger, in which we all dwell, and that is the Cosmos; there is one Father of whom we are all begotten, and He is the Void.[22]

In India, in the Tamil emporia which were the focus of the Alexandrian sea trade, similar attitudes were taught. A Tamil poet of the first or second century A.D., for example, wrote: "Every country is my country and every man is my kinsman."[23] Neither Buddhist nor Tamil culture recognized the Hindu caste distinctions, and both were open to foreigners, especially rich, prosperous, and cultured foreigners.

Alexander's Expedition into India

Alexander passed into Central Asia in the year 330. The size of his expedition is problematical, the more so because large numbers of reinforcements are known to have

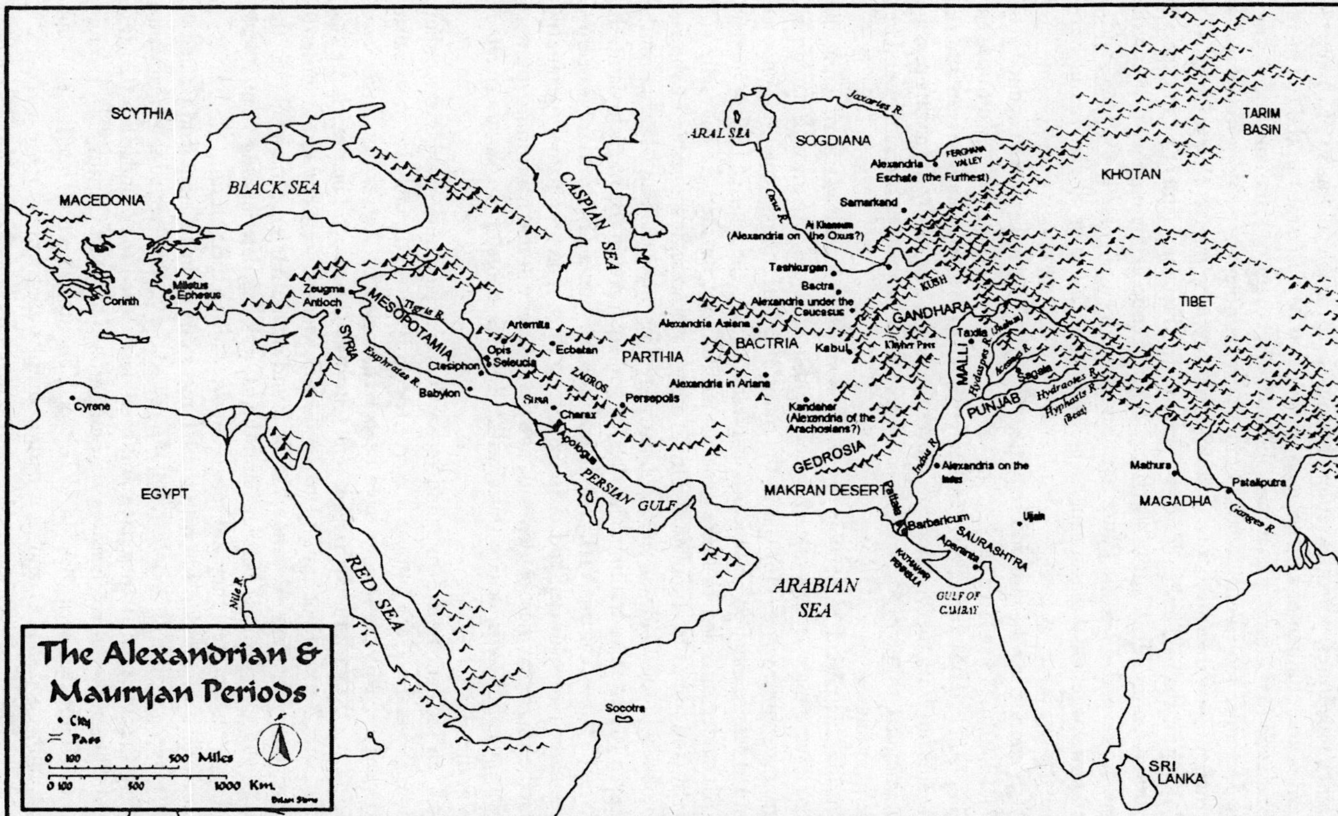

Map 3 The Alexandrian and Mauryan Periods.

joined it on several occasions. But it seems likely that the number of soldiers proper was far surpassed by a great variety of camp followers or noncombatants: artisans, merchants, prostitutes, potential settlers hoping for an arable allotment of conquered land, wives and children of soldiers who expected to be discharged in the conquered territories, and the cultural specialists—philosophers, botanists, historians, and so on—whom Alexander took along to study and report on phenomena along the way. Far more than military maneuvers was at stake, as is shown by the fact that teachers were taken along for the soldiers' children, to preserve the Hellenic element in an expected intercultural community. Curtius (VIII.5.4) gives 120,000 as the number that entered India with Alexander, but the figure has been questioned as possibly too large, and it is not known whether it was meant to include only soldiers or all varieties of camp followers as well.

After conquering the near and central areas of the Persian Empire in about a year, the Macedonian-Greek force reached the eastern Iranian plateau. The expedition spent the winters of 329–328 and 328–327 in Bactra (modern Balkh), where large reinforcements came out from the Mediterranean over the safe routes left by the army's passage and maintained through Alexander's consistent care to protect his supply and reinforcement lines.

During this period he pacified Bactria and fortified it with garrisons along the borders, leaving male settlers in each who would later, if the fort-towns became permanent, take native wives. This was in the tradition of the military colony as opposed to a formal *polis* foundation—as the original settlers of Cyrene married Libyan women. That Alexander intended to make a permanent imprint on the area culturally and politically, and hoped to stimulate a culture-merging process, is suggested by the fact that, probably in the winter of 328–327, he arranged for thirty thousand Persian youths to be given Macedonian training, and dressed and equipped in the Macedonian fashion (Arrian VII.4–5, Curtius VIII.5.1).[24] In addition, he founded in Bactria at least three colonies named after himself and in India at least three more; the name "Alexandria" seems to be a sign that these settlements, like the great city of that name in Egypt, were to be set up as full *poleis*, or city-states, with all the elements of Greek culture represented in them.

Still, an incident near Samarkand in Sogdiana in 329 emits possibly discordant overtones. Several ancient authors preserve the story of the Branchidae, a so-called "sacred gens" of Miletus said to have been transported by Xerxes into inner Asia (Strabo XI.11.4, XIV.1.5; Plutarch, *Mor.* 557b; Curtius VII.5.28–35). The Branchidae had conspired with Xerxes to betray Miletus, and hence were relocated by him in order to protect them. By the time Alexander's army found them, they were bilingual (was the second language Aramaic or Persian?) and their Greek was deteriorating—but at least (according to the sources) they still spoke Greek, assuring their origin.

Alexander's sense of kinship with these Greeks cast up in a distant land yielded to his role as avenger of an ancient betrayal. He sacked the city, massacred the inhabitants (including the unarmed Branchidae), and even demolished the foundations (Curtius VII.5.33). "The guilt of their ancestors was being atoned for," says Curtius, "by descendants who had not even seen Miletus" (VII.5.35).[25] The story has been questioned,[26] but it is relayed by good sources, and "it is hard to dismiss the tradition of the massacre."[27]

In about March of 326 Alexander's army entered India and established headquarters at Taxila for the conquest of the Punjab region. Taxila, situated near the mouth of the Khyber Pass, was a meeting place for traders and travellers from all of Asia, a polyglot culture that exhibited a variety of foreign customs, and "a seat of higher learning in India" already, which would later come to be known both as a center for the development of Buddhist thought (especially the *abhidharma*) and as a center of Greek learning.[28] It was a city long important for religious and philosophical culture, an educational center to which people came to study under experts. The evidence suggests that the Greek expeditionary force stayed about two months in Taxila. During this time, the philosophers Onesicritus and Anaxarchus, and possibly Pyrrhon also, conversed with ascetics who have been variously identified as Jains, Ājīvikas, or followers of Sañjaya.

The expedition remained in India until September of 325, about one year and eight months. During this time Alexander was engaged alternately in contesting areas militarily with local authorities and, having conquered an area, establishing his network of Greek towns and cities in it. His conquests did not extend beyond the Northwest into the Gangetic plain, but stopped at the Beas river—the second easternmost tributary of the Indus—when his soldiers, insisting that the Persian Empire had by now been completely conquered, fulfilling the original purpose of the expedition, refused to go further. By November 30, 325, both Alexander's army and his fleet had left India, three years after entering the Kabul Valley in the winter of 329–328. The evacuating army left behind thousands of their fellows who were settled in communities under various circumstances. Through these communities Alexander evidently intended to hold the region in perpetuity, as the Persians had done insofar as they could.

Motives and Effects

Though this conquest and colonization are widely treated as a turning point in world history, there is considerable disagreement among modern scholars about the motivation behind them. Bosworth has remarked that even though imperialism is no longer in fashion today, still, of all imperialist conquerors, "a positive rose-tinted aura surrounds Alexander . . . He has become divorced from history and elevated into a symbol . . . the culture hero with a mission to propagate Hellenic values world-wide."[29] This elevation into a symbol had already taken place in the ancient world (as the *Alexander Romance* and related texts show), and its classic locus is Plutarch's "bravura portrait of Alexander, the philosopher under arms, with a mission to impose civilization—on the Greek model—on the lesser breeds . . ."[30] Plutarch, paraphrasing a lost work of Eratosthenes, feels that Alexander "was sent by the gods as a mediator and conciliator for the whole world . . . he united all mankind, bringing into one body all men everywhere, uniting and mixing in one great loving-cup, so to speak, men's lives, their characters, their marriages, their very ways of life"[31] (*Mor.* 329 b-c).

Many moderns have accepted this idealized view. Tarn, for example, thinks that Alexander was implementing the Panhellenic program advocated by Isocrates and establishing, by his actions, the model on which Zeno the Stoic derived his idea of the world state and the brotherhood of man.[32] In his *Panegyricus*, c. 380 B.C., Isocrates proposed that Greek culture should seek unity less in genetic relationship than in a shared mental stance (a foreshadowing of Alexander's proclamation of a *homonoia*, "common mind," in the reconciliation speech at Opis). This project should be set going by the Greek states making common cause against Persia to seek revenge for the destructions of Greek cities and temples in the Persian Wars. Some time later Isocrates returned to the theme in his *Philippus*, this time seeing not an alliance of Athens and Sparta against the Great King as the key, but the commitment of Philip of Macedon to the cause. He urged Philip to destroy the Persian Empire, found cities throughout its territory, and send Greek colonists to settle them. The idea was not so much the assimilation of Greek and barbarian as the extension of the cultural boundary of Greece itself to include Asia.

In Plutarch's "bravura portrait" Eratosthenes, his source, condemns (as Strabo, I.4.9, says) those who divide mankind into Greeks and barbarians—that is, Alexander's first teacher, Aristotle, and Philip's self-appointed adviser Isocrates—and praises Alexander for ignoring that distinction. What happened in between Isocrates and Eratosthenes was the development of Cynicism and Stoicism, both of which encouraged such a change of attitude. The figure of Diogenes, who proclaimed himself a citizen of the world (*cosmopolitēs*) and whom the anecdotal tradition associates with Alexander, seems to have been transitional between Isocrates' expanded nationalism and the transnationalistic world-state envisioned by Zeno. In his *Republic* (c. 300 B.C.) Zeno proclaimed all mankind to be one and all men to be brothers, and advised that there are concerns for all humanity which should override local and national interests. Tarn argues that Zeno's revolutionary postnationalistic attitude must have been inspired by Alexander's invocation of *homonoia* at Opis, and by the tenor of his accomplishment as a whole. Most modern scholars regard the speech at Opis as having had a more limited intention; Wilcken, for example, says Alexander was only encouraging "the fraternization of Macedonians and Persians . . . [not] treating all mankind as one brotherhood."[33]

Recently the "rose-tinted aura" has been soiled by a wave of hostile interpretations of Alexander's actions and intentions. According to Plutarch/Eratosthenes, "Alexander desired to render all upon earth subject to a single law of reason" (*Mor.* 330, 8D–9E). Yet others show him as quite bereft of reason himself. O'Brien portrays him as frequently—toward the end, more or less constantly—drunk and irrational, dying finally from alcohol poisoning after the excessive final drinking parties described by the sources.[34] (Plutarch's metaphor of the great loving-cup gains ironic overtones.) Fuller, in contrast, refers to the murder of Cleitas as "the sole occasion on which Alexander is correctly recorded to have been drunk, and to have lost control of his passionate temper."[35] Bosworth's assault on Alexander's reputation seems more serious. Based on "the contrast . . . between the rosy rhetoric of Plutarch and the grim campaign narrative of Arrian," it involves primarily the charge that "massacre regularly marked the major victories of Alexander."[36] Here too there is disagreement; Tarn, for example, says that "among Alexander's campaigns" the small war against the Malli "is unique in its dreadful record of mere slaughter."[37] Fuller goes farther, making the traditional claim that "Alexander's aim was to achieve, as far as it was possible, a bloodless conquest."[38]

It is hard to accept the numbers in ancient accounts of battles, but Bosworth points at numerous events, such as the stoning to death of the pages after the Pages' Conspiracy, that seem to suggest a bloodthirsty nature (though he does grant that "the Macedonian treason law was savage").[39] The incident at Gaza in which Betis was dragged to death behind a chariot (Curtius IV.8.26–29) and another at a town by the river Choes in which, as Arrian says (IV.23), "all prisoners were butchered by the Macedonians in revenge for the wound they had given Alexander" are also cited, and the massacre of the Branchidae might also have been mentioned.

Bosworth's treatment of the battle of the Hydaspes demonstrates his major tactic of diminishing Alexander's opponents and thus the credit he earned in victory over them.

Fuller calls this "the most famous of Alexander's campaigns," and opines that it is "among the most brilliant operations of ancient warfare."[40] Bosworth, however, feels the grandeur of the event has been exaggerated. He notes that Alexander's famous adversary Porus "controlled a territory far smaller than Alexander's Macedonia, and he faced an enemy who had the manpower of an empire at his disposal. He . . . stood virtually alone . . . a small beleaguered prince, who chose to challenge the most professional army of the ancient world . . . It was a forlorn cause from the outset . . ."[41] Finally, in Bosworth's view, Hydaspes "was no epic struggle of heroes, but a stark massacre, the annihilation of a relatively small and inexperienced army fatefully embroiled in a battle it had no chance of winning."[42]

In addition, Bosworth disputes the view that Alexander intended to assimilate Greeks and Persians to one another as the first step in a potentially limitless *homonoia*. He sees Alexander's training of Persian and Iranian youths in the Greek fashion not as an idealistic measure to set cultural fusion going, but as a practical measure necessitated by a shortage of Macedonian soldiers.[43] He notes also that whereas some Macedonians were encouraged to marry Persian women, the reverse was not true.[44]

Frye, who may be described as on the Plutarch/Eratosthenes side of the issue, chooses another detail as the sign of the pursuit of *homonoia*: "The first purpose of Alexander was to bring the Greeks and the Persians together, and he sought to accomplish this by appointing both Persians and Greeks to govern his satrapies."[45] But here too Bosworth objects, noting that Alexander kept Greeks and Macedonians quartered separately; he feels that Alexander intended to have Greeks alone govern the settlements after his departure.

It is possible that the young leader's intention shifted—either matured or degenerated—during the long campaign. It's generally agreed that there was a "breakdown of the lofty purpose behind the expedition" in about 330.[46] Even Tarn acknowledges that a darkness entered the program with the Mallian campaign. Still, there are many signs that Alexander's pro-Persian policy increased significantly in the last two or three years of his life, perhaps leading to his assassination. Fuller attributes this to Alexander's increasing realization, as he moved through literally thousands of miles of conquered territory, that Greek and Macedonian manpower would be inadequate to hold it without help, but does not feel that this invalidates the spiritual goal of *homonoia*. It was that goal, and the implementation of it through the creation of a vast trading network that joined various nations and ethnicities, that has left the young ancient king in the idealized role of an early martyr (if the story of his assassination is true) in the cause of globalization. As Wilcken put it:

> . . . the previous barriers between East and West were removed and in the next generation thousands of Greek traders and artisans entered the new world, to seek their fortunes in the new Greek cities, which shot up out of the ground like mushrooms . . . When the Western Mediterranean was attracted into the orbit of the great revolution that occurred in the East, there was finally created a world commerce, which embraced the whole inhabited world, and extended from Spain to India, and beyond through Central Asia to China. This development was completed only under the Roman Empire, but its basis was the conquest of Asia by Alexander.[47]

The Aftermath

Almost immediately after the departure of Alexander and most of his army, an Indian leader, Candragupta, the founder of the Mauryan Empire, recaptured all the territories conquered by the Greeks inside the Hindu Kush. What happened to the Greek settlements at this time is unknown. Clearly their fate was up in the air. Would they be regained by Candragupta and become part of the Mauryan Empire, or would they become part of the Seleucid recreation of the Persian Empire, or would the Bactrian and Indian settlements left by Alexander become a new dynasty on their own?

At that time the Wars of the Successors were underway, and Greek military leaders, in India as elsewhere, felt involved in them. In 317 B.C. Eudemus, commander of the Greek garrisons in the Punjab, left India to join a coalition of eastern satraps against Seleucus. At that time several thousand Greeks whom Alexander had settled in Bactria and Sogdiana gave up and returned to Greece. It is here that scholarly opinion becomes split somewhat under the influence of late- and postcolonial issues. Some scholars, especially Indians, presume that the Greek settlements in India also disbanded at this time.[48]

One says that Eudemus "left India with all his forces," but this seems to be an exaggeration.[49] Diodorus reports that when Eudemus arrived in Susiana in 317 he had with him only five hundred horse and three hundred foot soldiers (XIX.14.8). In that case he must have left his main forces in India, evidently planning to return there, and taken with him only the elite of the Macedonian soldiers and the 120 elephants—a sure ticket to a high command—which made his fortune in the Wars of the Successors. Diodorus puts the figures in perspective when he says that Alexander settled ten thousand colonists at Alexandria-by-the-Indus (at the junction of the Indus and the Acesines). Typically, about half would have been Greek or Macedonian, the rest Indians, Persians, and others. This number would not have been significantly decreased by the handful who left with Eudemus. Similarly, Pliny says that Alexandria-in-Ariana covered "an area of nearly four miles" (*NH* VI.93), and Curtius adds that Alexandria-under-the-Caucasus was settled with seven thousand Macedonians, three thousand mercenaries, presumably Greek, and as many natives as wished to enroll themselves (VII.3.23). Diodorus has slightly different numbers for this settlement: seven thousand natives, three thousand camp followers, or nonmilitary colonists, and as many Greek mercenaries as wished (XVII.83.2). Curtius and Diodorus, though not in exact agreement, give figures in the same general range, and within that range a defection of a few hundred Macedonians could not have made a significant difference.

In addition to such large foundations as the Alexandrias, there were innumerable small settlements in captured and fortified towns. Pliny says that in India Alexander conquered five thousand towns of more than two thousand population each (*NH* VI.59), and Diodorus says that he left forty armed forts in Bactria, each strongly garrisoned against the more distant barbarians such as the Chinese. On one count, there are mentions of between eight and twelve Bactrian sites in each of which Alexander left settlements of about thirteen thousand.[50] This vast colonial population could not have disappeared with the few hundred soldiers who left with Eudemus, nor could it have failed to exert cultural influence. As Casson says of the earlier Greek age of colonization, "It was like administering injections of Greek culture into the body of barbarism at 250 different points."[51]

The Status of the Greek Settlements: A Dichotomy

There are two conflicting modern views of the situation of the Indo-Greeks—as it is common to call the ancient Greeks who lived in India.[52] The British scholar

W. W. Tarn, writing before the disintegration of the British Empire, views the Greeks as carriers of a higher civilization than others of that time. He delights in the idea of Greek culture spreading beyond the Tigris River. For him the Greek dynasties in Bactria and India were legitimate Hellenistic kingdoms on an equal footing with those of the Seleucids and Ptolemies. Some of the cities planted in India by Alexander were, he argues, full-fledged *poleis*, or Greek city-states, with the full equipment of *paideia*, or Greek cultural education.

An Indian scholar, A. K. Narain, writing soon after independence, in the 1950s, composed a point-by-point rebuttal of Tarn's positions in a book which is virtually a long review of Tarn's work.[53] Narain resents the idea that India was an inferior and passive receptacle into which Greek culture might generously be poured. For him the Greeks in Bactria and India, far from being legitimate Hellenistic dynasties, were a semioutcast group long cut off from Greek culture and soon overwhelmed by the cultures of Asia, into which, on his view, they quickly disappeared without leaving any significant trace. The Indo-Greek communities, he argues, were not independent city-states disseminating *paideia*, but small ethnic ghettoes within larger Asian communities, occasionally growing dominant for a time here and there, but never for long. The Greek conquests in India, regarded by Tarn as very extensive, are reduced by Narain to the minimum that the evidence can be construed to allow. He hardly considers the idea that these conquests may have left an imprint on local cultures.[54]

The first major point of dispute is the origin of the Greek communities in India. Tarn, desiring these communities to be fresh from the Mediterranean with the bloom of their Greekness still upon them, identifies them with the colonies left by Alexander, and assumes that large numbers of additional settlers migrated into them from the Seleucid Kingdom, thereby refreshing and reinforcing their Greekness. Narain, on the other hand, seeing the Greekness of these communities as smothered beneath their Asianness, chooses to trace them back to a period before Alexander's arrival, grasping, for this purpose, at semilegendary communities such as Nysa.[55]

Nysa was a Greek community asserted by Arrian to have been founded by the god Dionysus on the occasion of his visit to India (V.1, 2; VI.1; VIII.1). Curtius describes the experience of Alexander's Greek soldiers there in somewhat mythological terms (they wander like Bacchants, fling themselves down on the grass, and stay drunk for ten days [VIII.10.15–18]). Finally, unlike the unfortunate settlement of the Branchidae in Sogdiana, Nysa was accorded the status of a quasi-independent ally.

The example of the Branchidae also was useful for Narain. He notes that, according to Herodotus (VI.9), "the Greeks of various city-states in Asia Minor were sometimes threatened by the Persians with exile to the far eastern portions of the Achaemenid empire." He invokes the presence of pre-Alexandrian Greek coins in Asia to indicate that this did actually happen. Such exiled Greeks became a part of Indo-Iranian culture, cut off from Greek culture for centuries. To these communities, then, Narain suggested, a few of Alexander's veterans—and later possibly a few Seleucid colonists—were added. Nysa, Narain suggests, may have been a community of this type.

But there are problems in this reconstruction. Herodotus (VI.9) does not actually say that the Persians threatened to move Greek communities; rather, the Persian decree was that:

> they shall be enslaved; their boys shall be made eunuchs, and their maidens transported to Bactria; while their country shall be delivered into the hands of foreigners.[56]

Clearly, if the boys had been made eunuchs, these communities could not have survived as Greek, in Bactria or anywhere else. Further, the pre-Alexandrian Greek coins found in Asia need not have been the result of lasting settlements, but only of trade, which is known to have gone on at different levels of intensity for several centuries.

Finally, the question whether the "Greek way of life" would easily or quickly be smothered among Asians is open; different examples point in different directions. Curtius tells of emigrants from the environs of Miletus who, having been settled in Bactria by the Persians, still followed many Greek customs as late as the 330s B.C., but had gradually fallen out of the habit of using their native language (Curt. VII. 5.29–30). In nearer Asia the environment for the maintenance of the Greek language may have been more favorable. "Darius I settled Eretrian prisoners from Euboea in the village of Arderikka near Susa. They made up a separate community, and when they were visited by Apollonius of Tyana in the first century A.D., they still spoke Greek and remembered their origin."[57]

In any case it must be remembered that the issue of Nysa is not important for its own sake, but for its implications about the settlements that Alexander is said to have left behind him—and the preponderant weight of the evidence as a whole suggests that Alexander settled such great numbers in Bactria and India that it is impossible they could have been merged invisibly into small communities already there—which is what Narain is suggesting.

Arrian comments that the reader may believe in Nysa or not, as he sees fit (V.3), but in fact it is not hard to believe that Greeks might have been settled in northwest India by some happenstance of the Persian Empire, such as a settlement of discharged mercenaries or a community that was relocated, like that of the Branchidae, for some political reason. "There is no warrant for dismissing the story [of Nysa] as late fiction," says Bosworth.[58] But though Nysa itself may be accepted, it has little to say about the thousands of Greeks whom Alexander left behind him.

The Polis Question

On Tarn's side of the debate the evidence seems weightier. Two city-states, or *poleis*, in Bactria and three in India are mentioned by the Alexander historians, and are mentioned again in sources of the first century A.D. and later as still-living cities.[59] There may have been others that survived that long. These were "full-blown cities of the Greek type," says Wheeler, who includes in this category Alexandria-Eschate, or Farthest Alexandria, in Ferghana on the border of China.[60] Such major foundations must be distinguished from others that were "adaptations of, or supplements to, native towns"[61]—the new Greek town being built adjacent to the existing Indian town—and from still others that were "more or less evanescent garrison towns."[62]

There is considerable archeological evidence for the existence and centuries-long survival of these "full-blown cities of the Greek type" in Bactria and India. An extremely important piece of evidence was found in 1958 in Kandahar, once Alexandria-of-the-Arachosians. Ancient Kandahar was "a great meeting place of the highways of Western Asia,"[63] near the Khyber Pass, the entrance to and exit from India which links it with the Central Asian trade routes to both China and the Mediterranean. There an edict of the Buddhist emperor Aśoka Maurya, the successor to Candragupta's successor, was unearthed written in both Greek and Aramaic. The inscription was aimed at the non-Indian population of this border region, and indicates that it was primarily Persian and Greek and further that it was large enough or prominent enough to merit direct royal communications. The larger part of this population seems to have been Greek, as the Greek version of the inscription comes first and is twice as long as the Aramaic. Greeks, it seems, despite their greater distance from "home," had already become prominent in Indian Buddhism—a noncaste religion which welcomed foreigners—by the time of Aśoka in the third century B.C.

The 1958 Kandahar inscription is in good Hellenistic Greek, indicating that it was probably written by a Greek from the local community who was in Aśoka's employ. It is a good-quality, mid-third-century carving, indicating that this Greek community was in touch with the mainstream Greek world, probably through contacts with the Seleucid kingdom that would reflect recent cultural changes in the Mediterranean. The inscription ends with a Greek formula of blessing that is usually appended to oracular utterances, suggesting a conscious effort to merge Greek and Indian cultural forms.[64]

In 1963 another rock-cut Aśokan inscription was found at Kandahar, this one in Greek alone, again a good scholarly Greek of the period, not an outdated or barbaric Greek. "We need then no longer hesitate," says Wheeler, "to accept a full-blown 'Alexandria' upon the site of Old Kandahar. This was no mere tired vestige of a passing army. It was a balanced Greek city with its writers, its philosophers, its teachers."[65] The inscriptions are "new witnesses to a living and sophisticated expatriate Greek society in intelligent liaison with oriental thought."[66]

At Bactra, just north of the Kush in present-day Afghanistan, was a Persian provincial capital which was refounded as another Alexandria, or *polis*. Though it has never been adequately excavated, it has produced a number of Hellenistic objects. Forty miles north, on the opposite side of the Oxus river, is an extensive site at Tarmita which Wheeler identifies as "yet another Alexandria."[67] In addition, both Schlumberger and Wheeler identify Shahri-Kona as a "full-blown Alexandria,"[68] and Frye feels that full-fledged Greek cities on the Iranian plateau also included Raga-Europus near present Teheran, and Alexandria-in-Asia at modern Herat.[69]

The *polis*, as opposed to garrison town, involved several easily recognizable features, above all a centered and rectilinear city-plan along the lines laid out by Hippodamus of Miletus in the fifth century B.C., of which the archeologist's paradigm is Priene, south of Ephesus. In addition, according to Pausanias (X.4.1), a *polis* would have an agora, a theater, a gymnasium, and several temples. A *polis*, in other words, would be able to communicate *paideia* and pass on the "Greek way of life," which is characterized by Aristotle's famous formula for full realization of human nature, that "man is a political animal"—meaning by political, *polis*-dwelling or participating in democracy and, hence, in the individual exercise of reason.

At the site of Aï Khanoum beside the Oxus, where the Kokcha River enters it, French archeologists have uncovered since 1963 parts of "a well-preserved and embattled outpost of the Greek world on a scale worthy . . . of royal enterprise . . . twenty-three centuries ago."[70] Aï Khanoum clearly exhibits the Hellenistic town layout, and archeologists have felt that they could identify the sites of a theater and a stadium.[71] A large public building has been found with "colonnaded porticoes of the Corinthian order" of what Vitruvius called the "Rhodian" type, and adjoining it a "large hypostyle hall . . . with eighteen . . . Corinthian [columns . . . with] typical Attico-Asiatic bases . . . whilst the capitals show features comparable with Seleucid types of the second century B.C."[72] Still another building seems to be a gymnasium. The roofing tiles resemble those from Priene, Olynthus, and other Greek cities, and wall-reliefs were executed in Greek techniques. A bronze Heracles was found at Aï Khanoum, as well as a herm head, a gravestone of a nude youth, and a limestone statue one meter high of a female figure, all in Hellenistic style.[73] Aï Khanoum, judging from its remains, looked something like Dura Europus, a Hellenistic town in Syria, and may have been the Alexandria-on-the-Oxus mentioned in the sources, complete with gymnasium, theater, and a funerary *hērōon*.

From "the overall Hellenism of the scene . . . ," says Wheeler, "Greek priests, philosophers, craftsmen may already be inferred."[74] The correlation of architectural features with "Seleucid types of the second century B.C." indicates that this community remained in contact with the Hellenistic kingdoms of western Asia for centuries. Grid-plan cities were still being laid out by the Indo-Greeks as late as Pushkalavati (modern Charsada) in about 150 B.C. A large Buddhist stupa stands in the center of this Hellenistic city layout, and coin hoards that extend down to about 40 B.C. show Prakrit on the reverse and Greek on the obverse. At Begram in Afghanistan another Hellenistic rectilinear street plan has been found from the same period.

Most revealing of all is the archeological evidence from ancient Taxila, where Alexander is known to have spent about two months in the summer of 326. This city retained its ancient or pre-Greek form until about 180 B.C. In that year Greek forces based in Bactria reconquered much of what Candragupta had taken upon the departure of Alexander's army a century and a half earlier. At this time the city was refounded on a nearby site as "a new and orderly Taxila with a rectilinear street plan of established Hellenistic type."[75] Stupas were common, indicating a prosperous Greek Buddhist community, alongside a large temple of the Ionic order. About a mile away are the remains of another building with Ionic column capitals and Attic bases. This building is dated by a coin hoard to the latter half of the first century B.C.[76] The entire region has yielded an abundance of Greco-Roman objects, including glassware, metalwork, and bronze and stone sculpture, sufficient to indicate continuing trade with the West.

Epigraphic evidence points the same way, and there is a fair amount of it. At the Bactrian site of Surkh Kotal, some fifty fragmentary Greek inscriptions have been found. Some others are more readable. A pre-Aśokan Greek inscription, for example, found on a statue base of the early third century B.C. in Kandahar, was in elegiac couplets in a Greek similar to that of the Aśokan inscriptions from Kandahar—that is, it was written down or inscribed in the same Indo-Greek community.[77]

Another Indo-Greek inscription of the period, also in elegiac distichs, found in the *pronaos* of a *hērōon*, or hero-shrine, on a stone stela base, "states that one Klearchos had transcribed, in the *temenos* of Kineas, certain precepts that had been dedicated in the holy Pytho, that is to say, Delphi, where he [Klearchos] had copied them."[78] Greeks from these far Asian *poleis*, then, would travel to Greece and back. The inscription preserves one of the maxims brought back from Delphi by Klearchos, "exhorting the acquisition of the fundamental qualities of man at each stage of life."[79] The Apolline source of these maxims suggests a connection with the Gandhāran sculptural style soon to emerge. "Their presence on the banks of the Oxus," observes a modern scholar, "more than five thousand kilometres as the crow flies from Delphi, is an astonishing testimony to the fidelity of these Greek settlers of remote Bactria to the most authentic and venerable traditions of Hellenism."[80]

These finds establish Tarn's thesis over Narain's, and they result from merely scratching the surface of a few of many identifiable Indo-Greek sites. As Wheeler summed up their significance: "They demonstrate with astonishing clarity the extent to which the brief transit of Alexander did in fact Hellenize almost instantly vast tracts of Asia populated previously by nomads or semi-nomads and villagers." "Hints at Kandahar and Aï Khanoum have already shown something of the cultural completeness of these new centres of Hellenism *in partibus*; of their immediate concern with moral, philosophical, educational and aesthetic problems, essentially Greek but not unaware of an oriental environment."[81]

None of the three enduring Indian *poleis* which Tarn identified from documentary evidence, and only one of those in Bactria, is among the sites which have been partially excavated. Combined documentary and archeological evidence, then, indicates at least six long-lasting Hellenistic *poleis* in India and at least three in Bactria. And these numbers are almost surely too low. Strabo, who is careful in his use of the term *polis*, says that Alexander founded eight *poleis* in Bactria-Sogdiana alone (XI.11.4). In light of the archeological evidence, such testimony can no longer be brushed aside. It can no longer be maintained that the Greek settlements in India were soon overwhelmed and absorbed by the greater numbers of the Indian population.

Greek Colonial Culture in Asia

The Greek settlements in nearer Asia, about which much more is known than those in Bactria and India, provide models for how such communities interacted with the Asian populations among whom they lived. The *poleis* formed in Egypt, Mesopotamia, and elsewhere by Alexander and his successor Seleucus were parts of Hellenistic kingdoms. Nevertheless, the authority of the state was sometimes compromised with that of the city in order to preserve the spirit of the independent ancient *polis*. Alexander sanctioned the use of democratic constitutions in some of the Alexandrias. Susa, for example, had an elected council, a popular assembly, and magistrates who were proposed by the council and elected by the assembly. These Greek settlers in Asia clung to their Greek forms, both culturally and politically, for centuries. Inscriptional evidence shows that Susa retained well into the Christian period all the usual elements of a *polis*. Even under the Parthians, Susa and Seleucia both remained semiindependent and distinctly Hellenic city-states—and so, thinks Tarn, did the Greek cities in India and Bactria, first under Indo-Greek, later under Śaka and Kushan rule.

When a new city had been fortified, laid out in the Hippodamic manner, and given a constitution, the settlers would tend to its cultural institutions. These would include a theater and a gymnasium, or school. At Susa there were two gymnasia and a stadium, at Greek Babylon a theater and at least one gymnasium. The gymnasium was crucial because it was the purveyor of *paideia*, through which the Greek outlook and way of life could be maintained from generation to generation. The gymnasium was in a sense the center of the community. Education was a part of government functioning, and an establishment of publicly paid teachers was an essential component of a Hellenistic town. Public prizes were given for scholastic excellence. As a part of the publicly maintained gymnasium, a library would be formed, since Hellenistic Greek education consisted primarily of the humanities, that is, in the reading of texts; certain provincial towns, such as Oxyrhynchus in Egypt, had large school libraries. The presence of Hellenically educated non-Greeks such as Meleager of Gadara indicates that non-Greeks were admitted to the gymnasia and that the Greek classics were studied by educated Asians.

Such communities could grow to great wealth and importance. Seleucia on the Tigris became the most important city in Mesopotamia and dominated the trade of all Asia. With its associated Babylonian village, Opis, its population grew to about six hundred thousand. The possibilities which such newly founded *poleis* offered were enormous, and many able and ambitious Greeks emigrated to the new cities. The arts, literature, and philosophy were practiced and taught. "At Ekbatan," says Keith, "there were no fewer than three thousand Greek artists who had come from Greece."[82] In the Parthian period a Stoic teacher named Archedamus founded in Seleucia a Stoic school with succession. Antioch was famous as a school of rhetoric, and Susa for philosophy.

Many of the new cities produced cultural figures of high standing and international importance. "The famous physicist Seleucus belonged to another Seleucia on the Persian Gulf; Crates, the scholarly librarian of Pergamon, came from Cilician Mallus, and the great geometer Apollonius was a Pamphylian of Perge. Famous Hellenistic thinkers and historians came from Phoenician Byblos, Apamea on the Orontes, Amasia in Pontus, Ascalon, Antioch-Nisibis in Kurdestan, Artemita in Babylonia . . . Among the leading literary figures of the age were Aratus of Soli, Meleager of Gadara near the borders of Galilee, Antipater of Sidon, and at a later date Lucian from the barely Hellenized town of Samasota on the upper Euphrates."[83] In the second century B.C. a prominent astronomer, Seleucus "the Chaldean," taught the Aristarchan heliocentric view on the northeast shore of the Persian Gulf. It is to be expected that the Greek cities in Bactria and India also produced their Hellenistic geniuses, whose names are unknown but who can to some extent be known through their works.

In the Near East the implanted Greek cultures seem in many cases to have been attractive to the indigenous communities. "The upper classes . . . welcomed Hellenism with open arms," and, it seems, even "the generality of 'barbarians' did in fact welcome" it.[84] Among educated Near Easterners it seems that Hellenism was received as a world-view that transcended tribal views and revealed their limitations—much as the Greeks themselves, from at least the time of the Sophists, had regarded it. Eastern peoples, says Hadas, "were forced to question [their inherited ways] when they saw amongst themselves gay and witty and attractive people who had superior technology, and who—most exigent argument of all—had proved victorious."[85] Such influence then radiated beyond the walls of the new *poleis*, for the Greek "cities formed the centers of culture and economic life in the new Oriental kingdoms that were carved out of the Seleucid domains."[86]

Frye observes that "the establishment of a Greek *polis* must have had a great influence on the surrounding country . . ."[87] "There must have been a great attraction among the natives to become Hellenic in culture and in time, of course, the Greek and Oriental elements did fuse," Greek colonists "admitting only selected natives into the ranks of citizens, while the majority of natives were admitted into the city as part of a *politeuma*."[88] Frye seems to assume that the exposure to Greek culture would have had a greater effect than any other foreign exposure, such as, say, the Persian. "Merely the external forms of life such as the gymnasia, the city government, the Greek way of life, must have impressed all who came in contact with them,"[89] he says. The implication is that the democratic elements would have been attractive to any human who had lived under either a chieftain type of authority system or a more developed "Oriental despotism." "The Greek model of culture, in the Hellenistic age," Frye feels, "set the pace everywhere in the known world as the American model does today."[90]

This somewhat idyllic picture of harmonious culture-merging seems to have some truth, at least in the Near East, for the Greek communities were powerful centers of trade and brought increased wealth and security to their newly settled areas. But how far this picture describes the situation in India and Bactria is another question. In the Near East the upper classes had already been progressively Hellenized before the conquest—they had been prepared for the view of *paideia* as a transcultural attitude—and such was presumably not the case in farther eastern cultures. Still, it is known that the Greek communities in Bactria and India thrived economically and became important culturally in religion, astronomy, art, and probably other fields. In nearer Asia, says Hadas, "in the

Figure 27 Gandhāran sculpture, Hadda, Pakistan, c. second century A.D., head of "Antinous" figure.

matter of dress all our evidence suggests that Greek forms were universally adopted," and he notes that "on the reliefs of Gandhāra the women present at the birth of the Buddha are dressed like Greek ladies."[91] Furthermore, "the language of the Greek city, and the official language in all the dominions of the Successors, was Greek."[92]

Whether the Greek cities of the Far East possessed all the qualities of those of the Near East is not certain, particularly on the last point. Though the Greek residents of, say, Kandahar, evidently spoke and wrote Greek, it is questionable whether the non-Greek population, which may have been larger, adopted the Greek language; it is possible that an implanted Greek minority lived in a kind of ghetto among people who spoke various Indo-Iranian languages including Persian, and possibly other Central Asian languages as well. Even in the *polis*-foundations which were entirely new cities, such as Alexandria-on-the-Indus, can the Indian residents be imagined to have adopted Greek? The epigraphic remains do not seem to include texts written in halting or foreign Greek. It seems even less likely that the occupants of one of the new East Iranian or Central Asian Alexandrias, such as Alexandria-Eschate on the Jaxartes, adopted Greek in the heart of distant Asia. For their mercantile livelihood they must have depended on relations with Far Eastern traders from China and elsewhere, whereas in the Seleucid kingdom Greek was probably the language of business for all nations, as well as the cultural patois of the educated of any ethnicity. A question that cannot at present be answered is how far east in the Asian Empire of the Greeks the dominance of the Greek language extended. It may have declined, the farther away from its place of origin it got; Greek was the official written language on Parthian coins, but in Kushan coinage in India the Greek alphabet was used not to write Greek but an Iranian language.

Alexander evidently intended the Bactrian and Indian satrapies to function on an agricultural base with a mercantile superstructure which would ultimately supersede it as the communities' chief source of wealth. Bactria had long been irrigated by the Persians, by means of the Oxus River and its tributary system, and was extremely fertile. The town sites chosen there also commanded major commercial routes. Bactra was on the high road between the Near and Far East, commanding virtually all trade from China to the West, and also on the trunk road from North to South, commanding trade from all directions into India. The Indo-Greek cities too were placed in fertile agricultural settings that at the same time offered long-term control of international trade. Alexandria-on-the-Indus commanded trade from across the Khyber Pass into the Gangetic Plain and at the same time provided safe access to a river which fed into the sea, for trade from either the Gangetic Plain or the North with the Near East or Mediterranean as destination. The admiral Nearchus was commanded to investigate the river passage to the sea and the sea route back to the Near East, and Philip, the former satrap of Parthia, was commanded to build large dockyards at Alexandria-on-the-Indus and at the eastern branch of the Indus mouth (Arrian VI.15.2), providing safe access to the "Erythraean" sea and the Persian Gulf. Clearly the overall intention was to make "the Indus a great highway of the world's traffic with a chain of flourishing semi-Greek mercantile cities."[93] Goods from farther Asia could be gathered at Bactra and thence transported by the highroad to the Tigris, or, having been carried over the Kush, could be shipped down the Indus and round to the Persian Gulf. Goods from India and Ceylon would be brought overland to the Indus centers. This master plan seems to have been partially successful. Bactria was converted from a land of villages to a land of walled towns famous in the Mediterranean as the "thousand cities of Bactria," and the *poleis* on major trade routes did indeed survive and flourish for centuries.

The Successors

When Candragupta Maurya regained the areas of northwest India conquered by Alexander and made all of north India into a single state, he may have been imitating the Macedonian's example of empire building. India had not before seen a major native empire. Tarn says that "Alexander indirectly created Aśoka's empire and enabled the spread of Buddhism."[94] This claim—especially, perhaps, in the writings of the British—is anathema to many Indian scholars. One calls Alexander's first Indian ally "the traitor king of Taxila," and elevates Porus, Alexander's great Indian adversary, into the first Indian national hero.[95]

In any case, while the Greeks were occupied with the Wars of the Successors in nearer Asia, Candragupta filled the leadership gap in India and prepared his armies to meet an anticipated Greek attempt at reconquest. His expectation was fulfilled in 305 B.C. when Seleucus Nicator arrived in the Indus Valley. Discouraged by Candragupta's much larger army, and anyway being less interested in India than in his huge holdings in nearer Asia, Seleucus chose to strike a deal. He ceded still more once-Greek territory to Candragupta, who gave him in return five hundred war elephants for use against his Greek rivals.

In addition Seleucus requested a marriage alliance. Since the extensive literary sources on Seleucus do not mention an Indian wife, it is probable that the marriage went the other way: Either Candragupta himself or his son and heir Bindusāra married a Seleucid Greek princess. The custom of marriage alliances between royal dynasties was Greek, and it is possible that through this marriage either Candragupta or his son became an official tributary of the Seleucids and that the Mauryan dynasty remained, in the eyes of the Seleucids, a subdynasty of their line. In any case an official alliance began at this time between the Seleucids and the Mauryas. The Seleucids thereafter maintained an ambassador at the Mauryan court at Pāṭaliputra. Three Greek ambassadors are known by name: Megasthenes, ambassador to Candragupta; Deimachus, ambassador to Candragupta's son Bindusāra; and Dionysius, whom Ptolemy Philadelphus sent to the court of Aśoka, Bindusāra's son. It seems all but certain that Mauryan ambassadors in turn visited or maintained residence at the Seleucid court, and possibly the Ptolemaic.

Throughout the period of the Mauryan dynasty, relations with the Seleucids were open and friendly as between allied kingdoms. A few details are known of what must have been an extensive intercourse. Candragupta sent certain drugs, including aphrodisiacs, to Seleucus I Nicator (Ath. *Deip*. I.32.18d). Candragupta's son Bindusāra wrote to Antiochus I Soter asking to be sent sweet wine, dried figs, and a sophist (Ath. *Deip*. IV.4–6). A certain element of international royal sybaritism obtained between these friendly courts. All their dealings were in luxuries. Ptolemy II exhibited Indian women and Indian spices carried on camelback in his parades, along with other exotica imported from India. The Mauryas in turn imported Greek girls for their harems. Ptolemy Philopator sent to India for a special stone with which to line the saloon of his yacht (Ath. *Deip*. V.25.39). Megasthenes notes that at the court at Pāṭaliputra there was an office in charge of visitors, in parallel with the Greek office of *proxenos* and possibly inspired by it.

Aśoka and the Greeks

Aśoka, the most famous of the many Asian monarchs who have supported Buddhism, may have been either one-half or one-quarter Greek, depending upon whether his father or his grandfather married the Seleucid princess.[96] In any case he had numerous Greek or Indo-Greek connections. Early in his career he was viceroy of Taxila, the Indian city with more Greek associations than any other: Alexander's headquarters, the first Indian city to ally itself with the Greeks, and the capital of the Gandhāran region that later evidence shows to have had a flourishing Greco-Buddhist culture. Probably while in Taxila Aśoka had worked with Greeks in prominent positions. After becoming emperor he appointed Greeks to high government ministries: His viceroy of Saurāṣṭra was a Greek, and he had a Greek governor in Kathiawar.[97] Diodorus tells a story of a Greek named Iamboulos who, being down and out in India, was taken to the palace at Pāṭaliputra where he was received by a king who had a great love for Greeks.[98]

Within Aśoka's domain Greeks may have had special privileges, perhaps ones established by the terms of the Seleucid alliance. Rock Edict Thirteen indicates the existence of a Greek principality in the northwest of Aśoka's empire—perhaps Kandahar, or Alexandria-of-the-Arachosians—which was not ruled by him and for which he troubled to send Buddhist missionaries and published at least some of his edicts in Greek. The speedy prominence of the Greeks in Buddhism may have resulted in part from advantages granted by Aśoka.

In the ninth year of his reign Aśoka was converted to Buddhism and soon became a seriously committed proselytizer by means of his famous edicts, which were published widely on stones and pillars throughout north and central India, even in areas he did not rule, and which comprise the earliest epigraphic record of India.

Three of the Aśokan inscriptions were published in Greek, a Minor Rock Edict[99] and parts of Major Rock Edicts Twelve and Thirteen.[100] Thirteen, the longest and most important of the edicts, contains the claim, seemingly outlandish at first glance, that Aśoka had sent missions to the lands of Greek monarchs—not only those in Asia, such as the Seleucids, but those back in the Mediterranean also. These monarchs' names can be recognized with a high degree of plausibility—notably those of "Antiyoka" (who seems to be Antiochus II Theos of the Seleucid kingdom [261–246]), "Turamaya" (Ptolemy II Philadelphus of Egypt [287–247]), "Antikini" (Antigonus Gonatas of Macedonia [276–239]), "Maka" (Magas of Cyrene [288–258]), and "Alikasundara" (either Alexander of Epirus [272–255] or Alexander of Corinth [252–244]). Aśoka did not send missionaries to other nations, and he may for some reason have felt unusually close to those distant Greek cultures. "When Aśoka," as one scholar has written, "was converted to Buddhism, his first thought was to despatch missionaries to his friends, the Greek monarchs of Egypt, Syria, and Macedonia."[101] The arrival of these missionaries is never mentioned in western sources, but whether or not they in fact arrived at their goals, the sheer interest in the Greeks that it would take to know this breakdown of the political geography of the Successors, as one scholar remarked, "certainly did not exist in India before the establishment of the Mauryan Empire."[102] In Rock Edict Two Aśoka even claims to have established hospitals for men and beasts in the Hellenistic kingdoms.

As outlandish as the claim first sounds, there are two good reasons to believe it. First, Aśoka's list of Greek kings who were his contemporaries is accurate, indicating that his court was in current communication with the Greek world. Second, the figure of six hundred *yojanas*, which is specified as the distance these missions had to travel, is accurate. "Taking a yojana to be about seven miles, this turns out to be the exact distance from Pāṭaliputra to Macedonia, Epirus and Cyrene as the crow flies . . . [which] shows at least that contact with these distant lands was based on actual travel. With the contemporaneity of the five Greek kings among themselves and with Aśoka established by reliable evidence from Greek sources, Aśoka's claim to have sent envoys to them can hardly be doubted."[103] The general credibility of the inscription gains additional confirmation from the fact that several copies of Rock Edict Thirteen "were found in places . . . abutting Greek territories and inhabited by Greeks [and that] . . . the adaptation of RE XIII which was found as far west as Kandahar was in Greek."[104]

In addition to the Aśokan inscriptions, the Pali sources from Śrī Laṅka, such as the *Mahāvaṃsa*, describe missions sent here and there in India in connection with the Third Buddhist Council. This council was run by the Buddhist monk and philosopher Mogaliputta Tissa under Aśoka's sponsorship, and it was Tissa who arranged the mis-

Figure 28 Gandhāran sculpture, Peshawar, Pakistan, c. second century A.D., head of ascetic.

sions at Aśoka's direction. One of the most famous of these missionaries, Dharmarakṣita, who was said to have converted thousands, was a Greek (*Mhv.* XII.5 and 34). Dharmarakṣita was sent to Aparānta, in Saurāṣṭra, the peninsular part of what today is Gujarat, where western traders had been active for centuries, perhaps millennia, and where at that time a Greek was governor. "The combination of two prominent Greeks indicates that a Yavana settlement must have existed already in Saurāṣṭra, a region which later played a considerable role in the history of the Bactrian Greeks, and whose long association with them is still commemorated in the name of its city of Junagadh, originally Yonagadh, which meant Greek-town."[105] It is likely enough, then, that the thousands Dharmarakṣita converted were Greeks too. The entire event, in other words, seems to have been a Greek-to-Greek mission carried out within the inner spaces of a Buddhist orthodoxy where the Indo-Greeks seem to have been both at home and active.

Another famous missionary, Maharakṣita, was sent to the "Yona-country," or Greek area, of the Hindu Kush (*Mhv.* XII.6) and another, Mahyantika, was sent to Gandhāra, which was more or less the Greek homeland in India. Aśoka, it seems, made a major, and successful, effort to proselytize Buddhism among the Greeks in India. The *Mahavamsa* tells that "the celebrated Greek teacher Mahadharmarakṣita in the second century B.C. led a delegation of 30,000 monks from Alexandria-of-the-Caucasus [Alexandria-of-the-Yonas, or of-the-Greeks, the Ceylonese text actually says] to the opening of the great Ruanvalli Stupa at Anuradhapura."[106] "In view of the many conversions among local Yavanas," Woodcock notes, it is probable that "Aśoka sent Greeks from India as his envoys [to western Greek kingdoms]. This would account for the lack of reference to them in the Greek records; the arrival of a group of foreign Greeks would pass unnoticed, whereas a group of Indian Buddhists would be conspicuous and would arouse immediate comment."[107]

THE EUTHYDEMIDS: PĀṬALIPUTRA CONQUERED?

During the reign of Aśoka events occurred in Central Asia which may have spelled the downfall of his dynasty. Parthia and Bactria were at the time two administrative districts of the Seleucid kingdom. Around 250 B.C. both revolted against Antiochus II, Parthia under a native rebel leader named Arsaces (founder of the Arsacid dynasty that followed in Parthia), Bactria under its military governor Diodotus (founder of what came to be called the Euthydemid dynasty). Diodotus was succeeded by his son Diodotus II, who made an alliance with Parthia, hoping to forestall the Seleucid reconquest of both Parthia and Bactria. Like most of the area, Parthia was somewhat Hellenized by this time. Greek was the official written language on Parthian coins, and "surely there were many educated Parthians who knew Greek," says Frye. "We know that Greek drama was cultivated . . . from excavations of theatres and a form for making a comedy mask from Nisa."[108]

In 212 B.C. Euthydemus I of Bactria (accession date unknown) was preparing for the eventual, inevitable Seleucid attempt at reconquest. In 208 B.C. the reconquest was attempted by Antiochus III (223–187), who besieged Bactra for two full years unsuccessfully. Evidently Euthydemus had made Bactra one of the most heavily fortified cities in the Hellenistic world; only one other siege from the third century B.C. lasted so long, the Roman siege of the heavily fortified Syracuse.[109] Furthermore the native Bactrian nobility refused to defect from the Diodoti to Antiochus, suggesting that a strong social and political arrangement was in place. Finally Antiochus III recognized the legitimacy of the Euthydemid dynasty and gave his daughter to Euthydemus's son Demetrius to form another dynastic marriage alliance. The Euthydemids were no longer a subdynasty under the Seleucids.

Euthydemus was a significant presence among Hellenistic monarchs. He seems to have ruled "some of the oases of Central Asia principally in Sogdiana . . . There is a possibility that he led expeditions as far as Kashgar in Chinese Turkestan but rule beyond the Ferghana valley, if it included that, is unlikely."[110] Euthydemus, in other words, went a significant step beyond Farthest Alexandria on the Jaxartes, which marked the limit of Alexander's northeast conquest. This farthest Greek advance led to the first known direct Chinese Near Eastern trade contacts by way of Central Asia.[111]

The Euthydemid dynasty remained a real player, not, it seems, a peripheral outsider, in the history of the Greek East. "We have coins of almost forty Greek rulers in Bactria or north-west India, and some of the earliest are considered the finest specimens of Greek numismatic art."[112] The coins of Heliocles were particularly favored, imitated by non-Greek rulers north of the Oxus and Central Asian (Pahlava-Śaka) rulers south of the Kush. The great influence of the Greek numismatic tradition throughout Central and South Asia was a corollary, as Frye says, to "the long lasting influence of Greek art and culture in north-west India, Afghanistan and Central Asia."[113]

Sometime around 180 B.C., having legitimized and consolidated its kingdom, the Bactrian dynasty turned its attention to the reconquest of those parts of northwest India which had been won from the Greeks by Candragupta and ruled by the Mauryan dynasty. Whereas Seleucus Nicator, in 305, had failed to regain the former Greek holdings, the Euthydemids may have gotten all the way to the Mauryan capital at Pāṭaliputra. That the reconquest happened no one denies, but the extent of it is disputed, Indian scholars sometimes minimizing it while western scholars are apt to read it large.[114] What is certain is that a large portion of northwest India, at the very least, was successfully reconquered by the Euthydemids. Within this reconquered area they founded still more Greek cities of the *polis* type; Ptolemy mentions a Euthydemia in the Punjab and a Demetriaspolis in Arachosia.[115] From about 180 B.C. till at least 30 B.C. the Euthydemid monarchs ruled thriving domains of varying sizes within India.

The alleged Greek conquest of the Mauryan capital of Pāṭaliputra is the key to the question of the extent of the Greek domains at their largest. Both Greek and Indian sources seem to affirm the Greek conquest of Pāṭaliputra in the early second century, probably by either Demetrius or Menander, as these two were the most prominent kings in the records of the invasions. Strabo said that the invaders crossed the Hypanis, or Beas, where Alexander's advance stopped, and went as far as the Imaus, perhaps the Jumna (or Yamuna). Elsewhere (XV.698) he says that "those who came after Alexander went to the Ganges and Pāṭaliputra." On the Indian side of the record, the *Yuga Purāṇa* chapter of the *Gārgī-Saṁhitā* speaks of Greek attacks on Saketa, Panchala, Mathura, and Pāṭaliputra. If these attacks resulted in conquests, then Tarn is right in saying that Demetrius (or Menander) "was monarch of the Mauryan empire."[116] Narain reedits and retranslates the *Yuga Purāṇa* passage to get the Greeks out of Pāṭaliputra. Still, he allows Greek soldiers to lay siege to the city, which is the minimum that the text can be construed to say. In any case, the Bactrian Greek invasion of India lasted about five years, ending in around 175 B.C.

The Bactrian Greek conquests, however, were not only in India. Strabo puts them also at the border of China, and archeological evidence confirms a deep Greek penetration there, at least commercially. Greek coins and Greek words for denominations of money were used in Ferghana and Chinese Turkestan until the third century A.D. Cultural mixing may have been deeper here than mere trade, as Ferghana contained an Alexandria, and art historians have identified Bactrian Greek influence on Chinese art of the Han dynasty.[117] According to Chinese records, Greek trade with China was open by at least 100 B.C. and, as Basham remarks, Greek art styles and motifs flew along with the merchants' coin from the Mediterranean to Central Asia. Tarn concludes that, for a few years at least, Demetrius's empire went from Persia to China to the Gulf of Cambray and the Ganges.

But the Euthydemid Empire was not to last long at this great extent. By about 130 B.C. nomadic peoples from the Jaxartes region had overrun the northern boundary of Bactria itself, and in around 125 B.C. Heliocles abandoned Bactria and moved his capital to the Kabul Valley, thence to rule his Indian holdings. The history of these Indo-Greek monarchs continues for about a century more, till the last recorded king of this line, Hermaeus, died in about 30 B.C. In the interim something like thirty Greek kinglets had ruled reduced areas while participating, it seems, in a continual inter-dynastic struggle which depleted both manpower and morale. Toward the end of this time, the incursions of the Śakas, a Scythian-related group from Central Asia, steadily absorbed the Indo-Greek holdings, and finally the Greek communities lived under Śaka and later Kushan rule. They did not, however, die out or cease to exercise influence for perhaps two more centuries or—if their late history overlapped and channeled into the early history of new Greek populations brought by the Roman trade—as much as another half a millennium.

The Greeks and Buddhism

Gandhāra, the northern area of the Indus Valley, is where the greatest concentration of Greeks lived, in Taxila and elsewhere. The language prevalent there was Gandhāri, one of the many Indo-European languages of north India related to the Vedic form of Sanskrit. A Prākrit dialect (known as Northwest Prākrit), it was related to others such as Pali and Magadhi. Just inside the Khyber Pass, Gandhāra had more foreign contacts than all the rest of India put together and was also an area of intense Buddhist activity. This is where many think the Mahāyāna arose under influences that came from outside the pass. "By the first two centuries of the Christian era Gandhāra had become one of the major centers of Buddhism in India, and it was apparently at some point during this period that Buddhism began to make its way beyond the borders of its Indian homeland and establish footholds in parts of Iran and China."[118]

Gandhāri Buddhism seems to have been a distinctive individual school of the so-called Hīnayāna period. Recent finds of twenty-nine birchbark manuscripts from as early as the first century B.C. contain notations, in the Kharoṣṭhī script, of Gandhāri passages of the Buddha's Suttas, or discourses.[119] Preliminary conclusions from the study of this material posit the likelihood that there was a Gandhāri canon of the Buddhist texts—distinct from, say, the Pali canon—and that it contained some items not otherwise known. "Buddhist texts," in other words, "were . . . translated into, and sometimes also originally composed in, Gandhāri."[120] In fact, these twenty-nine unprepossessing scraps "are likely to be the oldest Buddhist manuscripts, as well as the oldest Indian manuscripts, known to date."[121] They comprise fragments of "a monastic collection or library of the Dharmaguptaka school in or around the first half of the first century A.D."[122] Since this is the area from which Buddhism was transferred into

Figure 29 Head of Gandhāran Buddha with hairstyle of Apollo Belvedere, Peshawar, Pakistan, c. second century A.D.

China and Central Asia, "the collection . . . promises to provide the missing link, or at least one of the missing links, between Indian Buddhism and its early manifestations in central and east Asia."[123]

What needs to be made clear is that Gandhāra had a cultural signature all its own. "The Gandhāran character of the culture of these regions is most clearly attested by their adoption of the distinctive eclectic styles of Gandhāran art and by their use of the Gandhāri language."[124] The most easily identifiable aspect of the Gandhāran cultural signature was visible on its manuscripts: "The fact that it was written in the Kharoṣṭhī script, whereas all the other [Indo-Aryan and Indian languages] have been written, from the earliest times, in the Brahmi script . . ."[125] Kharoṣṭhī goes right to left in the Middle Eastern fashion, implying that it originated across the pass and developed in connection with Aramaic, the lingua franca of the Achaemenid Empire. It was used for the Aśokan edicts in the Northwest; Brahmi was used elsewhere. Thus Gandhāri manuscripts are always immediately recognizable, which is helpful since they spread widely, being at the entrance-exit door of India where the currents of the major Iranian and Central Asian trade routes were liable to pick up cultural influences and carry them along. At some extremely early time in terms of the transmission of Buddhism outside India, "the Gandhāri language and its constant companion, the Kharoṣṭhī script, spread far beyond even the reaches of Greater Gandhāra . . . into the territories of ancient Bactria . . . and the oasis cities of the silk routes around the Tarim Basin in central Asia."[126] The date when this happened is hard to fix; Salomon suggests the second or third centuries A.D., but Puri says, "It was in the first century B.C. that Buddhism was taken to these countries [that is, the Tarim Basin], and peoples from Kashmir and northwest India proceeded to the region of Khotan and Kashgar and set up small colonies."[127] The disagreement about the date is significant, since for much of the first century B.C. Gandhāra was still primarily a Greek culture, but in the following two centuries it was taken over first by the Śakas then by the Kushan dynasty. Even in the Kushan period, however, Greeks were there and Greek influence on the Kushans (philhellenic "heirs" of the Indo-Greeks) was strong.

The elements of Gandhāran culture seem to comprise a coherent complex, which has one additional major element—and that is Greekness. This is more or less the package: the Dharmaguptaka form of Buddhism, the Gandhāri Prākrit canon of it, the Kharoṣṭhī script, the Gandhāran sculpture, and the Indo-Greeks. Wherever some elements of this package are found the others are to be presumed—and that covers a wide area. "Two Buddhist inscriptions in the Kharoṣṭhī script and the Gandhāri language, which must have been written by monks from Gandhāra, have been found near the cities of Lo-yang and Chang-an, which were major centers of Buddhism in China."[128]

The point is that Buddhism flowed on its famous transmission from India to the farthest reaches of northeastern Asia from the distinctive cultural area of Gandhāra, in the distinctively Gandhāran script Kharoṣṭhī, in the distinctively Gandhāran language Northwest Prākrit, along with distinctively Gandhāran artistic motifs—and this whole complex involves Greek cultural presence as part of its signature. It is known that Greeks were sometimes Buddhist missionaries, and some such could have been among those who emigrated from Gandhāra to the Takla Makan. In fact, as Puri says, Buddhism might have been introduced into these countries from Gandhāra "even earlier, in the time of Demetrius and Menander."[129]

At the Jade Gate near Tun Huang were caves used as meeting places for Buddhist scholars from many countries. Some of the twenty thousand manuscripts that have been found at Tun Huang were in Kharoṣṭhī script, hence probably from Gandhāra. And like the Gandhāran art style, the Gandhāran Buddhist style must have had a prominent Hellenic factor. (When Hiuen Tsang came through the area in the seventh century A.D., Bactra, a city that had undergone Hellenic reformation, was a major center of Buddhist learning. How long had it been so?)

Gandhāra was a center of ferment in Buddhist thought, "an important early center of abhidharma studies,"[130] for example. But an oversight seems to mar accounts of

Figure 30 Kushan coin, c. second century A.D., spelling out name Buddha (Boddo) in Greek characters.

this situation. The northwest area had experienced four layers of foreign cultural input, in chronological order Persian, Greek, Indo-Scythian, and Kushan. Salomon gives the Indo-Scythian or Śaka stage the historical importance of possibly having been "formative" on Buddhist doctrine, especially the *abhidharma*. And the next phase, the Kushan, is often given even greater importance, being suspected of harboring the beginnings of the Mahayana. But not much is said about the preceding Indo-Greek phase, though the Indo-Greeks are known to have been specially committed to Buddhism, even active proselytizers of its doctrines, for centuries. The *abhidharma* seems to have developed in the time of Aśoka and Mogaliputta Tissa and after—in other words at the time of the flowering of Indo-Greek Buddhism in the Northwest—and there is an unacknowledged connection there. "After the conversion of Yavana (Greek) country to Buddhism, Mogaliputta Tissa went there and selected an elder, Dharmarakṣita, for missionary work. Dharmarakṣita, it would seem, was probably a Greek. He was then sent to Aparantaka where he made a large number of converts."[131] Aparantaka was another area with a lot of Greeks, and the converts Dharmarakṣita was sent there to make were probably Greek. Tissa, in other words, seems to have been involved directly in Greek Buddhism. He was also the author of the *abhidharma* work *Kattavätthu*. This concatenation of circumstances suggests that if *abhidharma* underwent significant development in Gandhāra this is more likely to have happened among the Greeks there than among the later Śakas and Kushans. The Greeks, after all, had been accustomed to systematic thought for centuries, and both the Śaka and Kushan communities were illiterate until they learned the Greek alphabet. Which group is more likely to have fomented the rigorously disciplined type of systematic thought that the *abhidharma* features? Salomon notes that the Indo-Scythian and Kushan dynasties were very active in promoting Buddhism in various ways, but he does not discuss the fact that the Indo-Greeks had been equally active at an earlier period. Menander, the probable conqueror of Pāṭaliputra, seems to have been a Buddhist, and his name belongs in the list of important royal patrons of Buddhism along with Aśoka and Kanishka. The career of Dharmarakṣita as proselytizer shows Greeks promoting Buddhism—not just living it themselves but exercising a formative influence on it at least in their area. There is even a connection with Kharoṣṭhī: "Two Kharoṣṭhī inscriptions . . . record dedications by a Greek officer named Meridarkh Theodorus who enshrined the relics of the Lord Buddha . . . probably under Menander or his successor."[132]

The deep penetration of Indo-Greeks into the Buddhist establishment is impressively indicated by the fact that they were entrusted with missionary activities by a leading figure such as Mogalliputta Tissa. He was convinced, in other words, that they understood the doctrine—including his specialty, the *abhidharma*—and would communicate it effectively and faithfully. It is striking that the Greeks' association with the promulgation of Buddhist doctrine in the Northwest was a sufficiently well-established part of the history of the church that it was known to the monks in Ceylon who put together the Ceylonese chronicles; they report it matter-of-factly, not seeming to regard the Greek Buddhists as outsiders or intruders (*Mhv.* XXIX 38–39).

Salomon notes that Gandhāri Buddhism seems to have been different in part because it had contact with other cultures—clearly including Greco-Buddhist influence. The diffusion wave that brought the Kharoṣṭhī script into Bactria and to the Tarim Basin was the same cultural flow that brought Greek art motifs and styles eastward along the same route. Due to China and Central Asia receiving their Buddhism from the peculiar area of Gandhāra, "it was this Gandhāran art . . . which . . . travelled over the northern passes with the revolutionary message of Buddhism into Chinese Central Asia."[133] It may, in other words, have been a Greek-influenced and Greek-carried form of Buddhism that passed north and east along the Silk Road.

At several sites in the Takla Makan desert, Aurel Stein found Prakrit manuscripts on wooden panels and leather in Kharoṣṭhī script, indicating a close connection between Gandhāra and the Central Asian Buddhist culture. ("The mountainous tracks which connected India . . . with Kasgaria and Khotan" [began] "to the east of the old Bactra-Taxila artery" around Srinagar in Kashmir.)[134] In Stein's opinion the Kharoṣṭhī texts he found "probably represented official orders or letters," suggesting that the settlements in the Takla Makan were somehow governed or guided from Gandhāra. "Their discovery," says Hopkirk, "lends some credence perhaps to a local tradition, recorded by Hsuan-tsang and also found in ancient Tibetan texts, that the Khotan region was conquered and colonised by Indians from Taxila . . . about two centuries before the birth of Christ."[135] The presence of Gandhāri Buddhism would by itself suggest some Greek involvement, but the evidence is more precise than that. On cleaning the clay seals affixed to the wooden tablets, Stein found on one "the figure of Pallas Athena, with aegis and thunderbolt. Other seals also depicted Greek deities, including a standing and a seated Eros, Heracles and another Athena. A number bore portrait heads of men and women with barbarian features but executed in classical [Greek] style."[136]

Menander: Indo-Greek Arhat?

The *Milindapañha*, or *Questions of King Menander*, is a part of this general cultural phenomenon. It is a Pali text in the form of a conversation about Buddhist doctrine (vaguely like a Platonic dialogue) between the Indo-Greek king Menander (one of the candidates for the conquest of the Mauryan empire) and a Buddhist teacher named Nāgasena. The text as it exists today is in Pali, but may originally have been in Gandhāri, and perhaps in the Kharoṣṭhī script. In addition, "Tarn has put forward the fertile suggestion that the Pali work may actually have been based on a Greek original written shortly after Menander's death; he points to an Alexandrian work, the *Letter of Pseudo-Aristeas*, evidently written in imitation of a Greek version of the *Questions of*

King Milinda, which must have reached the famous Library of Alexandria half a century or so after Menander's death. This is by no means unlikely. Plutarch, who talks of the burial of Menander's relics under monuments or stupas, had obviously read or heard some Buddhist account of the Greek king's death."[137]

Menander was a Bactrian Greek king of the Euthydemid dynasty. His capital at Sagala (Sialkot) in the Punjab, "in the country of the Yonakas (Greeks)," was, according to the *Questions*, "a great centre of trade . . . splendid with hundreds of thousands of magnificent mansions . . . streets filled with elephants, horses, carriages and foot-passengers . . . [It resounded] with cries of welcome to the teachers of every creed and it became the resort of the leading men of each of the differing sects . . ." (*Mln.* I.3). The extent of Menander's prosperous kingdom is not certain, but his coins are common from Kabul to Mathura—one has even been found in Wales! He evidently converted to Buddhism and in time was regarded as an *arhat* (*Mln.* VII.7.21); as Plutarch says, his remains were buried under a stupa. The fact that Plutarch heard about his death from some obviously Indian source suggests that Menander remained in contact with the Mediterranean from Sagala. In addition he clearly participated enthusiastically in Indian culture, being versed in "the Sāṇkhya, Yoga, Nyāya and Vaiśeṣika systems of philosophy; arithmetic; music; medicine; the four Vedas, the Purāṇas, and the Itihasas; astronomy, magic, causation [logic?], and spells; the art of war; poetry; conveyancing—in a word the whole nineteen [arts and sciences]" (*Mln.* I.9). He was an active king, who died in military camp. Strabo (XI.11.1) says he was one of the two Bactrian kings who extended their power farthest into India. He was known for fairness, and several cities in his domain vied for his remains as cult objects after his death. He was trained in philosophical discourse, was fond of visiting learned masters to question them, and complained that, until he met Nāgasena, the Indian wise men he spoke with did not have a sufficiently rigorous and reasoned approach.

It is ordinarily assumed that while King Menander is Greek, his interlocutor, the Buddhist dialectician Nāgasena, was an Indian; but was he? Woodcock points out that "there appears to be no record of Nāgasena's existence except in stories linking him with Menander,"[138] suggesting that he was a part of the Indo-Greek *sangha* of Gandhāra.

Figure 31 Corinthian capital from Gandhāra, c. second century A.D., showing Buddha meditating among the acanthus leaves (cf. dustjacket).

According to the *Questions* (I.32–35) Nāgasena was a student of the Greek monk Dharmarakṣita, the missionary who was sent to Aparānta in Saurāṣṭra by the Third Buddhist Council in Aśoka's time, and he attained enlightenment (as an *arhat*) under Dharmarakṣita. The transmission story is historically possible, if Dharmarakṣita lived past the end of Aśoka's reign and converted Nāgasena, who then lived into old age before meeting Menander; or it may be slightly off in a way that is common in the sources, namely, that Nāgasena may have been converted by a disciple of Dharmarakṣita, perhaps one who had taken the same name. In any case, Dharmarakṣita was a Greek, and he was sent to Saurāṣṭra when it had a Greek governor, and "since he made many conversions, a whole group of Greek bhikkhus doubtless inherited his teachings, and Nāgasena was probably one of these."[139] Nāgasena is described in the prologue of the *Questions* as having gained "perfect knowledge of the seven books of the Abhidharma." Gandhāran Buddhism was a center in which much of the *abhidharma* seems to have been worked out, and Greek Buddhists may have been involved in it. It was the most systematic and analytic part of the Buddhist canon of its time.

Even more than Dharmarakṣita's mission to Saurāṣṭra, this event would have transpired wholly within the special community of Greek Buddhism—a Greek teacher, converted by a Greek teacher, converting a Greek king who arrived at his dwelling to speak with him accompanied by five hundred Bactrian Greeks. It is also likely that the other characters in the dialogue—associates of Menander—were Greeks; as Rhys Davids says, Devamantiya was probably a Pali version of the Greek name Demetrius and Anantakaya might similarly represent Antiochus.[140] The stature of Greek Buddhism, or of Greeks in Indian Buddhism, seems to have been very high. Menander is declared an *arhat*, he is shown "to have a substantial knowledge of the texts,"[141] and the *Questions* is actually included in the Pali canon by the Burmese[142] and functions as "the standard authority" on Theravādin doctrine in Ceylon.[143] Menander is reported in the prologue of the *Questions* as "skilled in debating [so that] no one could resolve his doubts about religious matters."[144] He may have been educated by a representative of one of the Greek schools of Skepticism. Also, Menander's influence on the spread of Buddhism in Bactria may have been considerable—as was Aśoka's influence on its spread in India. Depending on how the dates are worked out, the spread of Gandhāri Buddhism to the north may have been stimulated by Menander's royal patronage, as may the development and spread of the Gandhāran sculpture, which seems to have accompanied it.

Still, the Greek character of the conversation in the *Questions of King Milinda* is not actually very clear; many scholars have compared the form of the work to a Platonic dialogue, but it is hard to see much resemblance, really, except for the question-and-response format. Neither the thinking nor the stylistic nuances it is presented in seem to show much Greek influence. Pesala, for example, says that Nāgasena was "playing the part of Socrates and winning over King Milinda to the Buddhist viewpoint by his sound reasoning and his fitting similes."[145] But persuasion by similes is not really a part of Plato's method; though he does provide some very famous ones, such as the Cave and the Chariot, they are for explanation of an idea rather than for convincing the interlocutor of it.

Menander has been called the only one of the Greek kings of Bactria and India to surely convert to Buddhism, but there may have been others. Euthydemus's son Demetrius was interested in Buddhism and possibly an adherent of it. There is a tradition that he had a partly pious Buddhistic reason for the reconquest of northern India: He "is supposed to have attacked India to punish the Brahmin Sunga ruler for his anti-Buddhist activities and persecution of Buddhist monks . . ."[146]

In any case, the *Questions* clearly demonstrates that catechistic review of Buddhist doctrines through a discourse partly assimilated to Greek tradition was a part of Gandhāran culture. It also suggests that Buddhism received royal sponsorship from within the Greek community. If Menander did indeed conquer Pāṭaliputra and become, as Tarn said, "the monarch of the Mauryan empire," he was truly a successor to Aśoka, and the northern spread of Buddhism, into Bactria, Central Asia, and beyond, may have been carried out in part under his sponsorship.

The Opening of the Sea Trade

Though the Indo-Greek monarchies seem to have ended in the first century B.C., the Greek presence in India and Bactria remained strong. This was partly because of their wealth and their firm control of much international trade, but also because both the Śakas and the Kushans who followed them in positions of rulership were philhellenic peoples who enthusiastically adopted the Hellenized elements of Gandhāran culture. At the same time the Greek presence was renewed by the development of maritime trade that brought new communities of mercantile Greeks into India from the Mediterranean.

The ostensible purpose of Alexander's Asian expedition had been to take revenge on Persia for its repeated invasions of Greece, but its truer purpose was to cement a vast trading network which must have already been partly in place, as Greek coins have been found throughout the Persian Empire. Alexander chose sites for city foundations with trade routes in mind and sponsored work on harbors at Pattala at the top of the Indus delta, Babylon, and elsewhere. At his death he was planning to secure the coastal regions of the Arabian Peninsula. Both the Seleucids and the Ptolemies after him continued the project, the Seleucids by land, the Ptolemies by sea.

The Seleucids founded cities to follow the road from Seleucia to Bactra and brought out more colonists from Ionia for the potentially huge trade with Bactria, India, Central Asia, and China. The overland trade between India and the West thrived through luxury goods, providing Antiochus IV, for example, eight hundred tusks of Indian ivory for his triumphal procession of 166 B.C.

Meanwhile, in the third century B.C. the Ptolemies established the Red Sea ports of Myos Hormos and Berenike to accommodate ships that would coast past Arabia and the Makran desert to the Indus delta and the Kathiawar peninsula. In the second century they appointed a special officer to oversee the trade from those ports, and "by the second century B.C. Indian goods were a regular item in [the] Egyptian part of the royal monopoly of trade of the Ptolemies."[147] The Arabian coast was pacified and involved in the trade, as Alexander had intended. Charax and Apologus were Arabian ports that, along with the island of Socotra in the Gulf of Aden, functioned as "*entrepots* of all intercourse between Egypt on the one side and India on the other."[148] Already by the third century B.C. "Socotra had acquired its cosmopolitan character, with Indians, Arabs, Greeks, and possibly Persians and Africans mingling in its markets."[149]

A staged introduction of navigation on the open sea, rather than coasting, greatly increased this trade. By a moderate use of the southwest monsoon one could sail directly from the Gulf of Aden to ports south of the Indus delta such as Barygaza. Strabo reports (II.5.12) that in the time of Augustus as many as 120 ships a year set sail for India from Myos Hormos alone, whereas, he says, few merchants had attempted the voyage under the Ptolemies, when coasting was the only available method (II.5.12).

Many coins of Augustus have been found in both India and Ceylon. In the reign of Tiberius, c. 50 A.D., the full use of the monsoon was popularized, and at this point three different sea routes were in use for different purposes: By coasting, one could trade at the Arabian, Persian, and Afghani ports along the way and end up at the Indus port of Barbaricum; by making sparing use of the monsoon, one could arrive directly at north Indian ports such as Barbaricum (about 1470 miles from Aden at the mouth of the Red Sea) and Barygaza (about 1700 miles); by fully using the monsoon, one could land directly at south Indian ports such as Muziris on the Malabar Coast. From the South came coveted goods such as the pepper from the Malabar Coast for which Muziris seemed to Pliny (VI.104) "the foremost market of India." Ptolemy describes Muziris as "a port packed with Greek ships" (VII.1.8), and in the Tamil Sangam literature one reads that here "fine vessels, masterpieces of Yavana workmanship, arrive with gold and depart with pepper."[150] From Muziris one could coast around to eastern ports such as Arikamedu on the Coromandel Coast or farther.[151] Ptolemy said, in the second century A.D., that he had personally met merchants who had traveled as far as the mouth of the Ganges, that is, modern Calcutta.[152] Through these sea routes and their linkages with overland trade routes goods could reach anywhere in Asia. Trinkets made by Greek artisans from Naukratis in the Nile delta have been found in Central Asia.[153]

From this time onward the archeological record shows not only Greek influence in India deriving from the Alexandrian conquest, but also Greco-Roman influence from Alexandria by way of the sea. This trade continued throughout the Roman Empire, and Strabo's figure of 120 ships a year, maintained for a total of two to four hundred years, yields the staggering figure of 24,000 to 48,000 Greek sailings to India, from only one of the two Red Sea ports. As Frye says of the Kushan period, "[T]rade connections with the Roman empire were many and ideas, art and culture passed between the two as well as objects of trade."[154] Whole Greek books to be translated into Sanskrit, for example, sometimes traveled on these ships, and residual groups of privileged Greeks in the Kushan kingdom offered the new trading Greeks direct access into Indian Buddhist culture.

As the frequency of trading voyages increased so did the tonnage of the ships. Around 500 B.C. Greek ships averaged 100 tons burden. A ship excavated from the first century B.C. near Toulon was carrying around 300 tons of cargo and another between 500 and 600 tons.[155] "The freighters . . . of the crack grain fleet ran to 1,200 tons."[156]

Still, the trade between India and the Roman Empire remained entirely a luxury trade. There is no record of food staples or practical goods on this route. From India came peacocks, drugs, silks, pearls, ivory, diamonds, sapphires, tortoise shells, perfumes, dyes, agate, carnelian, and Indian girls for the harems of wealthy westerners; into India from the Mediterranean went drugged wine, luxury clothing, vessels of gold and silver, and singing boys and girls for eastern harems.[157] In addition, art works traveled back and forth, such as a Lakṣmi figurine found at Pompeii, a Neptune statue found near Bombay, and a Cupid found in Baroda.[158] Finally, India imported Greek gold coins for use as bullion in sufficient quantity that Pliny (*NH* VI.101) complains about the drain of specie to India. A luxury trade like this is far more likely to result in the exchange of ideas than would a more mundane type of commerce; luxuries are purchased by the rich, who will also in many cases be the educated.

In India a huge native industry grew up to furnish this trade. Ptolemy, c. 150 A.D., lists sixteen *emporia* in India used by western ship captains and shows familiarity with almost thirty other towns of the Tamil district, into all of which Greco-Roman traders

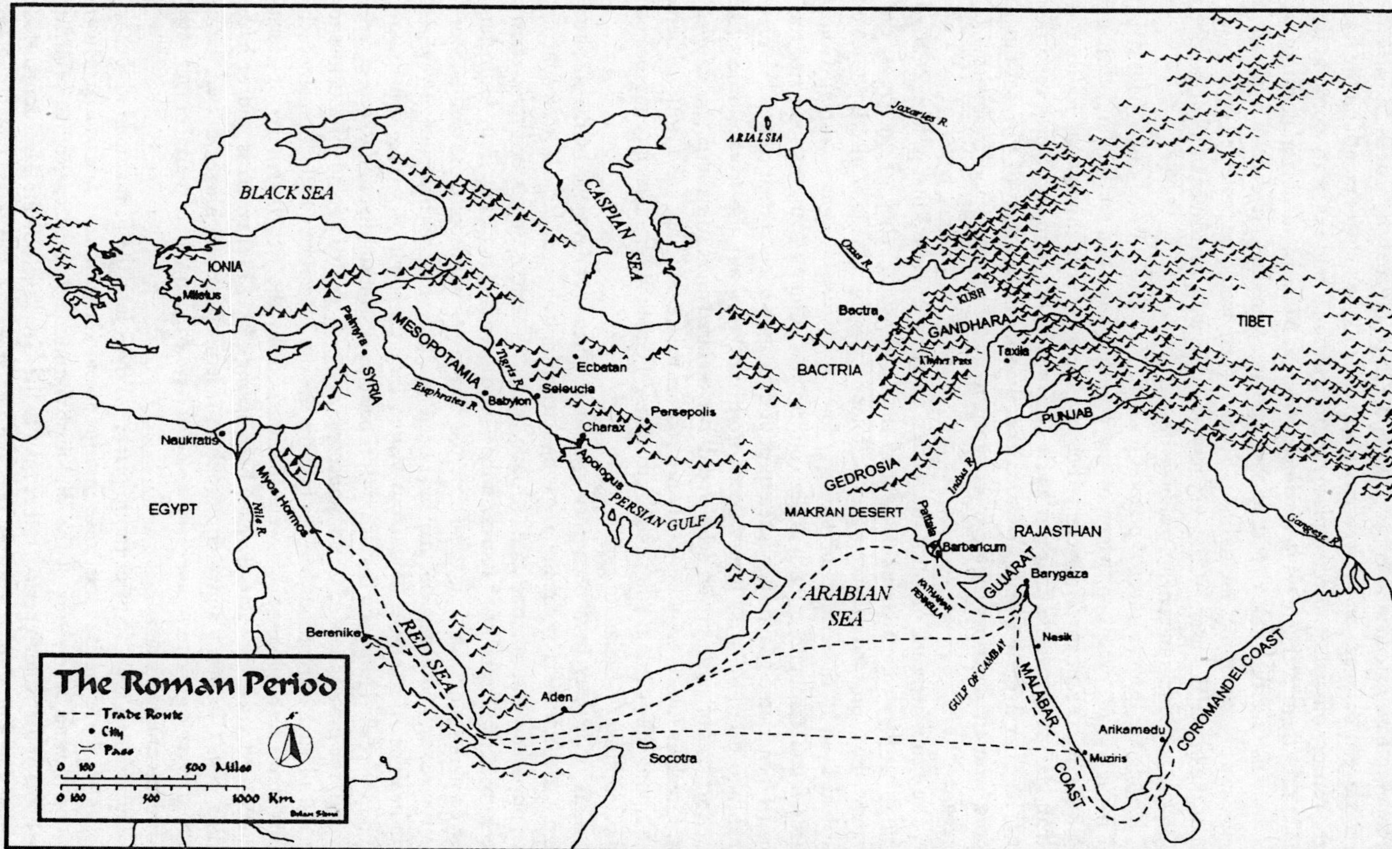

Map 4 The Roman Period.

must have penetrated. The sixteen ports mentioned by Ptolemy were probably an official list established by an imperial agreement. Roman imperial protection of trade is known to have extended as far as Aden and Palmyra,[159] and the sixteen Indian emporia between Barygaza on the west coast of India and the Ganges mouth on the East were probably officially protected places for international trade—"treaty ports" as one scholar calls them.[160] There was a *templum Augusti* at Muziris, possibly indicating that the Romans regarded this as part of their empire, since the presence of a *templum Augusti* usually meant that the rights of Romans there would be protected by the long arm of the imperial power. At the very least its presence "is evidence of a fair number of Greek and Roman merchants residing there."[161]

During the Roman Imperial period Greco-Roman trade thrived throughout Asia, and India was no exception. Many of the ports involved had wealthy and thriving Greek quarters. Roman coin-weights became the standards throughout India, and Roman glass vessels made their way as far as Korea in the third and fourth centuries A.D. The Han dynasty annals of China contain specific mention of Greco-Roman traders, who are described as the most prosperous, well-funded, and trustworthy of merchants.[162]

The Tamil literature of south India often refers to "Yavanas," that is, Greeks, suggesting that they were a common sight in the Tamil world. They are known as "the Yavanas whose prosperity never wanes." Ptolemy (*Geog.* I.17) tells of meeting Greeks who had lived in the district of Madura "for a long time" (*chronon pleiston*). Coins hoards found throughout south India confirm this. Greeks living in such cities as Muziris "penetrated inland and visited most of the native rulers at their courts"[163]—presumably to take orders for luxury goods from the West, but also to take orders for Greek artisans of various types, who would then be hired on at Alexandria and shipped east. Greek architects were especially favored for palace building, and Greek soldiers were among the guards of kings and of city gates.[164] Greek warcraft was much respected and often hired by Indian kings.[165]

This trade may have been very ancient. Eudoxus of Cyzicus, in his ill-fated attempt to reach India by circumnavigating Africa, took along as cargo "Greek dancing girls, physicians and other artisans" (Strabo II.3.4). Wheeler suspects that the western Greeks traded with Aśoka.[166] Aśoka's father, Bindusāra, had requested from Antiochus a Greek philosopher, and it is to be expected that Greek philosophers as well as courtesans, artisans, and physicians may have been on some of those thousands of voyages to India. The Alexandrian Skythianus visited India in about 50 A.D., and his pupil Terebinthus called himself a Buddha.[167] It is perhaps significant that in the second century A.D. the biographers of Greek philosophers began to attribute a visit to India to one and all; such attributions had not occurred before Alexander. No doubt many such claims about early philosophers were spurious, but by the second century A.D. such philosophical visits may actually have been taking place. Pythagoras is said to have studied with Chaldeans and Gymnosophists. Democritus and Pherecydes are both reported to have gone to India. Plato is said to have tried in vain to make contact with the Indians and the Magi.[168]

Curiosity to see distant or exotic places survived into the Roman period. Many scholars attribute the Buddhist cave inscriptions at Karle, Junnar, and Nāsik, which mention Yavana benefactors of the Buddhist community, to Greco-Roman resident merchants of the Roman period, rather than to the Greeks left by the Macedonian-led invasion. On this view it appears that the westerners of this second major phase of Indian experience were as open to the religion and thought of India as were the Indo-Greeks in the time of Menander. It has been suggested that the stupa at Amarāvati, one of the most important of the Mahāyāna Buddhist centers, was architected and engineered by Greeks.[169] Greco-Roman medallions have been found in connection with a Buddhist stupa in Nāgārjunakonda, the supposed home city of Nāgārjuna, the Mādhyamika philosopher.[170]

Archeology has shown that the Greco-Roman trading centers were no more mere transient quarters than the Alexandrian cities were mere garrisons. Two miles south of Pondicherry in the Tamil area one such emporium has been partly excavated at the modern site of Arikamedu. There was a megalithic Indian village on the site, which first gained a foreign quarter, then was rebuilt as a brick town of western type, indicating long habitation and a sense of proprietorship and security on the part of the foreign residents.[171] The town was surrounded by a brick revetment for defense like an autonomous community and may have featured a textile industry in connection with the export trade. International use of the trading facilities begins around 1 A.D. and the main rebuilding of the town dates to the reign of Tiberius, about fifty years later. Similar sites wait to be excavated around Amarāvati.

Indians in the West

At the other end of the East-West sea trade, there is evidence of Indians in the West as of Greeks and Romans in India. Indian ships were sailing to the Persian Gulf for trade before Alexander, and may have penetrated as far as Arabia and even down the African coast to Madagascar; it is possible, indeed, that Indian-African trade of very small volume preceded the opening of the Red Sea trade from Alexandria.[172]

Indian sailors did not display "anything like the same amount of activity as the Graeco-Alexandrian navigators"; still, they "occasionally attempted . . . expeditions westward,"[173] and in the Ptolemaic period they began to focus on the markets at Alexandria. They arrived in some numbers from Potana, the port founded by Alexander on the Indus, to "Arabia Felix" (Aden) and the island of "Dioscurias" (Socotra), and settled there.[174] Aden was "a prosperous and wealthy meeting place of Greeks, Arabians and Indians." Socotra was "inhabited by a mixed population of Arabs, Indians, and Greeks."[175] As the trade increased, Indians began to appear in Greek Egypt itself, especially in Alexandria. Indian women were in the processions of Ptolemy Philadelphus (Ath. *Deip.* IV.4.6, V.25, 3). A Buddhist gravestone from Ptolemaic Alexandria portrays the Buddhist icons of the "three jewels" (*trisula*) and the Wheel of the Law (*dharmacakra*). Indian Buddhists lived and died in some numbers in Alexandria and presumably practiced their religion there.[176] There is no way to estimate the numbers of Indians in Alexandria during the Ptolemaic period, but there is evidence of actual Indian communities there at a later period. Dio Chrysostum, in the second century A.D., reminds the Alexandrians that there are "Indians who view the spectacles with you and are with you on all occasions" (*Or.* XXXII.373). Ptolemy also notes the presence of Indians in Alexandria (*As. Res.* III.53). Bactrians and Indians were known in Asia Minor in Lucian's day.[177]

The information available on these settlements of Indians in the West is very sparse and fragmentary. An inscription near Berenike, from the Ptolemaic period, records the visit of an Indian named Sophon. Several sources refer to a group of shipwrecked Indians living as slaves among the Suevi of Boii and a colony of Indians in Armenia from c. 130

B.C. to C. 300 A.D.[178] Presumably these Indians were involved in the northern route, bypassing the Pārthian empire by way of the Caspian and Black Seas. One scholar feels that there was an Indian "colony" in Memphis, Egypt, in the first century B.C., but the evidence is slight.[179] A story in Posidonius (*ap.* Strabo II.3.4) is worth quoting in part:

> A certain Indian was brought to the king [Ptolemy Physcon, 146–117 B.C.] by the coast-guards of the recess of the Arabian Gulf, who said that they had found him half-dead and alone on a stranded ship, but that they did not know who he was or where he came from, since they did not understand his language; and when the king gave the man into the charge of men who would teach him Greek, he related that on his voyage from India he by a strange mischance mistook his course and reached Egypt in safety, but only after having lost all his companions by starvation.

Ptolemy evidently had interpreters who could mediate between Greek and various Indian languages. A similar story, of a shipwrecked Greek in Ceylon who learned the language, suggests the presence of Greek or bilingual Ceylonese traders there (Pliny *NH* VI.84). As the East-West trade increased from the reign of Augustus on, Indians appeared more often in the West. From 25 B.C. onward, Indian embassies began to arrive fairly frequently at the Roman imperial court, probably to establish and maintain the official relationships necessary for the various treaty ports in Egypt, Arabia, and India itself.[180] The *Res Gesta* states that Indian embassies came to Augustus "frequently." Four can be identified explicitly, one of which brought to Augustus a letter written in Greek (presumably by a Greek resident at an Indian court) and an Indian "sophist," Zarmanochegas, who, in 21 B.C., burned himself alive in Athens (Strabo XV.1.4, 1.73; Suetonius, *Vita Augusti* 21; Dio Cassius LIV.9). Nicolas of Damascus, the source of the story, says the ambassadors brought, as gifts to Caesar Augustus, a youth without arms who could draw and shoot a bow with his feet, a serpent two cubits long, a giant tortoise, and a partridge larger than a vulture—evidently fomenting willingly the "hypertrophic portrait of India" as a place of marvels.

The arrival of ambassadors seeking alliances was not a brief phenomenon that died out. Claudius received an embassy from Ceylon (Pliny VI.84–85), and Trajan, Hadrian, Antoninus Pius, Elogabalus, Aurelian, and Constantine all received Indian embassies. Trajan indeed in the year 99 entertained an Indian embassy royally, giving its members senators' seats to witness the celebration of his recent triumph over the Dacae (Dio Cassius IX.58). Indian embassies came to Justinian in 530 and 532.

It appears, finally, that there was a vast network of Indian-Greek contacts by way of both land and sea routes; details are especially well known from the Roman period, but apparently this network existed in various forms back at least to Alexander. Much important cultural diffusion took place through these contacts, and four topics should be considered, which, though three of them are not directly part of the history of philosophy, will establish the diffusion context of that history: (1) astronomy, (2) literature and drama, (3) Gandhāran art, (4) knowledge of Indian philosophy in the West.

Astronomy

It has long been accepted by both Indian and western scholars that Indian astronomy derived from Greek sources. An Indian work, the *Gārgī-Saṁhitā* , says:

> The Yavanas are barbarians yet the science of astronomy originated with them and for this they must be reverenced like gods.[181]

"Indian astronomy in its scientific form, as in later Sanskrit textbooks," says an Indian scholar, "is derived from the astronomy of the Alexandrian schools and its technical nomenclature is to a large extent Greek, in a slightly disguised form."[182] The *Paulisa Siddhānta*, for example, is directly based on the works of Paul of Alexandria (c. 378 A.D.). The Indian calendar is Greek in origin, the planets and signs of the zodiac, as well as epicycles, tables of chords, and much else.[183]

Recently, an extremely important piece of evidence has come to light. Scholars have for a long time recognized that Greek astronomical texts of the fourth century A.D. somehow arrived in India. But it is now known that a text of the second century A.D. arrived there *in* the second century. A recently translated Indian astronomical text, the *Yavanajātaka* of Sphujidhvaja, "was directly transcribed (with some necessary adjustments) from Roman Egypt to Western India."[184]

The *Yavanajātaka* in its present form is dated to 269/270 A.D., but is "a versified version of a prose translation, made by one Yavaneśvara, 'the lord of the Greeks,'" in the year 149–150 A.D. Yavaneśvara was translating from a Greek text, probably from Alexandria.[185] This text provides "the clearest evidence that has yet come to light of the direct transmission of scientific knowledge from the ancient world of the Mediterranean to the ancient world of India."[186] The *Yavanajātaka* is the earliest surviving Sanskrit text on horoscopy and "constitutes the basis of all later Indian developments in horoscopy" until the Muslim period.[187] This fact has resonances beyond the history of astronomy. If a complex Greek astronomical work could arrive whole in India and there be understood and assimilated, there is no reason to doubt that a complex Greek philosophical work could have the same fate—for example, the lost book of Aenesidemus, or that of Agrippa, or some of Sextus Empiricus's works—a possibility that will be discussed more fully in chapter 18 below.

The *Yavanajātaka* was transmitted in a cultural and political climate that can to an extent be reconstructed. "Yavaneśvara and Sphujidhvaja . . . were 'lords of the Greeks,' that is to say, men exercising some sort of authority over Greeks settled in the domains of the western Kṣatrapas in those areas of India later known as Gujarat, Malwa and Rajasthan."[188] Yavaneśvara lived in the reign of Rudrakaman I, "the greatest of the Western Śakas," of the Karddamaka dynasty. The Karddamaka administration relied heavily on non-Brahmin groups, especially Greeks. Like the more or less independent *poleis* in Aśoka's day, "the Yavanas appear to have had some sort of political organization within the state" in the second century A.D., and "another such organization existed in formerly Śātavāhana territory in the first half of the fourth century. What extraordinary privileges these Greek settlers and merchants may have enjoyed in the kingdom of the western Kṣatrapas is unclear. But it is clear from the cave inscriptions and from the *Yavanajātaka* that, despite their superior station, they tended to accept either Buddhism or Brahmanism."[189] Yavaneśvara and Sphujidhvaja were "Indianized Greeks"; Yavaneśvara, in fact, is the only Greek on record as expressing admiration for yoga.

Several of the Buddhist cave inscriptions recording Yavana dedications date from the first and second centuries A.D. and indicate the cultural context into which Greek science was being inserted. The Greeks of this community may have been merchants who came on the southwest monsoon from Alexandria; in India they formed "trading corporations" that developed into small communities which, perhaps due to imperial arrangements, enjoyed a privileged status within the Indian states.[190] But it is also possible that they had some connection with surviving Indo-Greek communities, which still thrived under Śaka patronage in the first and second centuries A.D., possibly maintaining semiautonomous *poleis* here and there throughout that period. Gujarat and Rajasthan were either partly within or anyway contiguous to the Indo-Greek area in the northwest. It is quite possible that Alexandrian merchants were received and sheltered by these communities and that Indo-Greek political influence or even semi-autonomy may account for the "privileged station" which the Yavana traders seem to have held. The importation of scientific books suggests an interest in Indian culture and in its blending with Greek culture which goes beyond the interest of the merchant. The dynasty of the Kārddamakas was Śaka, hence probably philhellene, and vied with the Kushan dynasty for the Indus Valley, there certainly contacting the remnants of Indo-Graecia. It is, in other words, quite possible that there was a continuity between the two phases. The Yavanas of south India thrived in privileged positions under these dynasties until the Gupta conquest, which indicates a continuity of Greek cultural presence in India from before 300 B.C. till about 400 A.D.

Literature and Drama

A crucial question about Greek lifestyle in India, both in the Alexandrian and Euthydemid cities and in the later Greco-Roman merchant communities, is whether the Greek dramas were performed there. According to Pausanias (X.4.1) a theater is one of the three essential features of a genuine *polis*. Whether in the Near or Far East it seems that "a polis of any pretensions without a theatre is unthinkable."[191] The major Alexandrian and Seleucid foundations in the Near East probably all had theaters; Gadara had two,[192] and Susa, east of the Tigris, had one.[193] So far, in Bactria, a theater has been identified at Aï Khanoum, and others may await the archeologists' efforts. Unfortunately, political and social conditions have interrupted most archeological work in Afghanistan, and the relevant sites in Pakistan are taking a back seat to Indus Valley Bronze Age sites. There is, however, a certain amount of literary evidence on the question.

Alexander the Great was a theater fan; several times on his eastern expedition he relaxed for a dramatic performance. At Salmus in Carmania (east of Susiana), according to Diodorus (XVII.106.4), Alexander held a dramatic competition *in a theater*. At Ecbatan too he held a dramatic festival (Diod. XVII.110.7), but it is not explicitly stated to have occurred in a theater. The account of the performance in Salmus is the only clear documentation of a Greek theater east of the Tigris, but Diodorus is not a historian known for his accuracy of detail, and the question whether there were Greek theaters in the Persian empire prior to Alexander's conquest remains. Some cities that Alexander founded in Asia, however, clearly had them. Pausanias (I.22.1), speaking of the post-Alexandrian age, claims that "the veriest barbarian who has a smattering of Greek knows the story of Phaedra." Several sources claim that the Greek dramas were popular among the Parthian nobility, and Plutarch (*Crassus* 33) tells of a performance of the *Bacchae* at the Armenian court which was attended by the Armenian king Artavasdes and the Parthian king Orodes. It is even reported that Artavasdes wrote histories and tragedies in Greek.[194] In *On the Fortune of Alexander* (328), Plutarch says:

> When Alexander civilized Asia Homer became common reading, and the sons of Persians, Susianians, and Gedrosians learned to intone the tragedies of Sophocles and Euripides.

The inference is that since the kings of Parthia sponsored performances of Greek tragedies, so must the Indo-Greek kings even more. Investment in cultural patronage may have been a part of the Euthydemid dynasty's efforts to establish itself as equal to the other epigonic lineages. A potsherd found at Peshawar seems to show a scene from the *Antigone*, and has been interpreted as indicating that the tragedies were performed there.[195] And it is quite possible, as Rawlinson notes, that "Menander and his courtiers may have enjoyed a Greek comedy at Sagala."[196]

The troubled issue of the relation between the Greek and Indian dramatic traditions depends to an extent on this archeological question. The name Yavana occurs three times in, or in texts relating to, the Sanskrit drama,[197] and scholars have long wondered whether the Indian drama was inspired by the Greek. "It is," as Keith said, "impossible to deny that the Sanskrit drama came into being during the period when Greek influence was present in India."[198] But the typological similarities perceived by some scholars between the Greek and the Indian dramas are not adequate to establish a case for influence.[199]

On the more general question of the interaction of Greek and Indian literary traditions the evidence is not much better. Dio Chrysostom says:

> It is said that the poetry of Homer is sung by the Indians, who had translated it into their own language and modes of expression, so that even the Indians . . . are not unacquainted with the woes of Priam, and the weeping and wailing of Andromache and Hecuba, and the heroic feats of Achilles and Hector, so potent was the influence of what one man had sung. (*Or.* LIII.554–555)

Aelian (*VH* XII.48) agrees with him, but neither of these authors is a strong source for historical fact. It is possible that when Dio says that Homer's poetry was translated into some Indian language, he is speaking of the two Indian epics, which he has mistaken for translations from Homer due to the parallels in subject matter—especially the theme of the war that is fought for the return of an abducted queen. A Gandhāran relief from Pushkalavati-Charsada shows "Laocoon probing the Trojan horse," and Wheeler describes the subject as "unmistakable."[200] The Indo-Greeks had books, and these books must have included Homer and Euripides, two of the most popular authors in Greek Egypt, the primary Hellenistic kingdom from which we have evidence for the reading matter. Some Indo-Greeks knew Indian languages and some Indians knew Greek. The *Mahābhārata* contains Greek words and phrases—*saptantivina* (i.e., *heptatonos phorminx*), III.134.14; *trikona* (i.e., *trigonos*), XIV.88.32; barbarian, III.51.23; it contains references to Yavanas (II.14.4; III.254.18; XII.207.43) and to Romans (II.51.17). At VIII.45.36 it refers to the *sarvajñah yavanah*, "the all knowing Yavanas," which implies a respect for the culture of the Greek communities and a willingness to receive lore from them. That's about all one can say.[201]

A literary phenomenon that arose as a by-product of the Indian-Greek relations was the folkloric corpus about Alexander. The most famous work of this type is the *Alexander Romance*, which seems to have been composed in its rudimentary form in the third century B.C. Many sources contributed, from the fantastical record Onesicritus wrote, involving elements such as Alexander's meeting with the Amazons, to the poetic history of Cleitarchus, various Egyptian tales, influences of the Hebrew prophets, and more.[202] Other texts on this subject matter accumulated in the eastern Mediterranean, such as spurious letters from Alexander to Aristotle and others.[203]

It has been suggested that the fabulous history of Alexander arose in connection with the Mahāyānistic transformation of Buddhism into a messianic religion around the coming Buddha Maitreya, who it was believed would appear, like Alexander, from the West. The god-king concept brought by Alexander from Egypt into India may have fed into the developing bodhisattva concept, which involved the portrayal of the Buddha in Gandhāran art with the face of the sun god, Apollo. The worship of the Roman emperor and the whole tendency toward messianic and apocalyptic texts that occupied religions in that period from the Mediterranean to the Ganges offers a general context.

Gandhāran Art

The Gandhāran sculpture was the earliest figurative sculpture in the Indian tradition after the Indus Valley. It arose in areas of Greek occupation from the Oxus to the Indus sometime in the period from the last centuries B.C. to the second century A.D., and featured sculptural representations of the Buddha, along with other figures and subjects. Marshall and other British scholars of the colonial period identified the Gandhāran art as Greek in facture or inspiration. This claim is provocative since in the eyes of the rest of the world (if not of India itself) the icon of the meditating Buddha is a kind of trademark of India. Shall western art historians give the credit for this icon not to India itself but to the Greeks? In the minds of some Indians the Gandhāran Buddhas have come to represent the presence of colonial outsiders in India and their appropriative intrusions into cultures not their own.

Still, it would be hard to deny that there are Hellenic or Hellenistic features in Gandhāran visual art which do not appear in the art which developed soon after in the more southerly centers such as Mathura. As one Indian scholar says, "the Hellenistic inspiration of this art is undeniable,"[204] and almost no one does overtly and unambiguously deny it. In the art-historical argument stylistic elements such as the measured quality of the faces, the *contrapposto* stance of the upright figures, and the emphasis on drapery, combine with iconographic factors, such as the apparent derivation of the top-knot of the Gandhāran Buddha image from the Belvedere type of Apollo, to establish a complex Hellenic signature. Purely historical details such as the depictions of Corinthian columns are even more telling; they indicate clearly that these sculptures were made in Greek Buddhist communities, whether in Bactria, India, or both. They look like a conflation of the Buddhist with the Apollonian sensibility.

As Wheeler says, "precise dating [of the Gandhāran works] is not . . . available."[205] Some scholars date them to the early first century B.C. "at the latest,"[206] and attribute them to the Greeks who invaded India from Bactria and were not displaced from their hegemonic position in Gandhāra by the Scythians till either the middle or the latter part of the first century B.C.[207] Others, dating the work to the first two centuries A.D., after the waning of Greek autonomy in the Northwest, connect it instead with the Roman Imperial trade, which was just then getting a foothold at sites like Barbaricum at the Indus-mouth.

It has been proposed that one of the embassies from Indian kings to Roman emperors may have brought back a master sculptor to oversee work in the emerging Mahāyāna Buddhist sensibility (in which the Buddha came to be regarded as a kind of deity),[208] and that "bands of foreign workmen from the eastern centers of the Roman empire" were brought into India.[209] The *Apocryphal Acts of the Apostles*, of the third century A.D., suggests an evidential basis for this scenario, with its story that St. Thomas was bought in Syria by an agent of King Gondophares of Taxila (c. 50 A.D.), to be taken to India as a master craftsman. But it was primarily the Tamil centers in the South, not the northwest region, which imported western craftsmen.

Other authors have attempted to connect the Gandhāran school with Kanishka:[210] The philhellenic Kushan king, in passing through Central Asia on his way into India, may have picked up some Greek artists from residual Bactrian Greek communities, or some Persian artists who had been semihellenized, and brought them into India to provide a visual expression for the emerging Mahāyāna Buddhism to which he seems to have been committed. This would account for what has been called the tripartite style of the works—part Greek, part Iranian, and part Indian.[211] Still, the view of Kanishka as mastermind of the emerging artistic and religious synthesis of the Mahāyāna has yet to be firmly established.

A crucial question is whether to dichotomize the Alexandrian Greek settlers from the later Greco-Roman merchants, or whether there may have been a continuity between them. Some of the Indo-Greek cities seem to have survived at least until the reign of Augustus, when, according to Strabo, the sea trade was already enormous. Clearly, then, the two phases of Greek presence in India overlapped chronologically, and their communities must have been aware of one another and interpenetrated somewhat. Two of the three types of sea passages known to have existed—that which coasted, and that which used the monsoon guardedly—would have arrived within the cultural domain of the colonies left by Alexander. It is unlikely that the two waves of Greek migrants would have survived for centuries side by side without mingling. The new Greco-Roman communities occasioned by the sea trade seem, for example, to have followed the example of the old Indo-Greek cities in converting to Buddhism.

The question is still not settled whether Gandhāran art developed from Roman influence at a later date or from Bactrian Greek influence that had been in place on the Iranian plateau since Darius's Persepolis project, but now was supported and promoted by powerful governments reaching clear across Asia from Syria to Chinese Turkestan. Frye points out that the abundance of remarkable coins from the Bactrian Greek kingdoms implies that significant Greek art was being made there, too.[212] One of the relevant historical questions is whether the Bactrian Greek tradition continued through to the Kushan period when it produced the Gandhāran style that is known today, or whether it died out and, after an interval, new input from Roman sources led to the Gandhāran work.

The account which attributes the Gandhāran art to the effects of the Roman sea trade is based on two assumptions: first, that the Indo-Greek communities were short-lived; second, that the Gandhāran sculpture arose in the Kushan period, thus placing a gap between the two phenomena. But recent scholarship has supported the survival of the Indo-Greek communities into the Śaka and Kushan periods, and, as Frye says, "the coinage, and especially the use of the Greek alphabet by the Kushans, does point to continuity . . ."[213] Recent discoveries at sites such as Aï Khanoum have confirmed that there was a Greco-Bactrian sculptural style that could have given birth to the Gandhāran, thus shifting the likelihood of Gandhāran sculptural origins back from the Roman trade to the Greek dynasties.[214]

In either case, the Gandhāran style was carried out of India in the northeastward diffusion wave that brought Buddhism into Central Asia, China, Korea, and Japan. The influence of Greek art, coming as it were from another world thousands of miles away in the Aegean, can be seen in drapery and facial portrayals as far afield as the Chinese paintings and sculptures of Tun Huang.

Greek input into Indian astronomy is known, on hard evidence, to have been serious and major, as was Greek input into Indian Buddhist art. The idea that Greek input into Buddhist philosophy may have been important during the same period flows naturally from these facts. The Gandhāran Buddhas would seem to have been chronologically contemporaneous with the Prajñāparamitā texts, which, according to Lamotte,[215] were prominent in the same region and may have appeared there. The philosophical encounter recorded, however mistily, in the *Milindapañha* also took place in Gandhāra. And in the same period Gandhāran Buddhism was being preserved in the Kharoṣṭhī script. The chronological and geographical linkage of these elements may show the emergence of Greek analytic skepticism into prominence not only in the late Hīnayāna development of *abhidharma* but also in the transition to the Mahāyāna. The speed with which the *abhidharma* was developed and soon thereafter the Prajñāparamitā dialectical reduction of it are characteristic of the onrushing tendency of philosophical history in the Greek tradition.

In the cultural politics of the Indian situation an ethical and ethnic dichotomy has grown up between the Gandhāran and the Gupta versions of the Buddha image. At first, when British dominated the field of Indian art and archeology, the Gandhāran figures were considered supreme; the uncompromising frontality of the Gupta figures seemed insufficiently developed sculpturally, still primitive and two-dimensional. The Greek figures, loaded as they are with the long, highly honed tradition of Greek sculpture back to the measured archaic head and the sinuous fourth-century spine seemed to show a tradition of mastery that was conceivably slightly overripe, but which anyway had achieved a new mode of perfection in its old age. The serenity of the Gandhāran figures and faces combined paradoxically with their look of being realistic everyday humans; they were somewhat idealized in the Apollonian way (the Apollo from the west pediment at Olympia lies behind them, as does the mood of the Charioteer of Delphi), but not so idealized as to seem transcendentalist.

More recently, a preference for the Gupta figures has arisen among many art historians. The Gandhāran figures have been reevaluated as decadent in various ways, whereas the Gupta figures seem to express the newness and fresh potential of a tradition just about to burst into its strength. The Gupta has seemed, above all, truly Asian, whereas the Greek has seemed the work of a foreign invader shallowly posturing in the mode of his adopted domain. From a Modernist point of view, with its emphasis on national or cultural identity, the Gupta seems preferable; but from a post-Modernist point of view with its emphasis on cultural hybridism and nomadism, the Gandhāran mode is more intriguing. The Gandhāran figures do not seem to be thinking about the disciplined pursuit of release from the pain of reincarnation. Many of them seem to be enjoying themselves in a Dionysian sort of way; at the same time they are as idealized as Apollo.

Knowledge of India in the West

In the Greek tradition there is a steady increase in knowledge of geographical matters from Herodotus to Strabo to Ptolemy. Pliny (*NH* VI.60) says that Seneca, in his work on India, mentioned sixty rivers and one hundred eighteen different races—suggesting more than adequate research facilities on India in the library at Alexandria. By Ptolemy's time, "The classical geographers knew of the three Tamil kingdoms . . . their capital cities and the sources of their wealth; they knew other smaller dynasties and clans . . . they knew of Ceylon and the sailings from Ceylon to the South Indian coast, and mention in detail the merchandise which the Romans sought from the Tamil emporia."[216] Ptolemy could even give fairly accurate latitudes and longitudes for certain Indian cities.

Aside from this type of knowledge derived from trade there is little in surviving Greco-Roman literature about Indian culture. Apollodorus and possibly other Hellenistic historians[217] wrote histories of the Greeks in Bactria and India which have been lost except for excerpts in Strabo and elsewhere; Seneca's book on India also is lost; Bardesanes wrote a book on the teachings of the Gymnosophists, or yogis, which was used by Porphyry the Neoplatonist but which also is lost. The few extant references to India show a spotty knowledge of the subject, as when Pliny says that the Indian sophists *always* burned themselves alive (*NH* VI.66), or in the repeated Greek description of India as a semimythic paradise on the edge of the world, or when Greek authors assert that India is a continuation of Egypt—and so on.[218]

In the literature of the Christian polemicists occasional references to Indian religion are found, not for their own sake but as fuel for the Christian attack on paganism. Clement of Alexandria (150–218 A.D.), for example, who has been called "the first [western] author to show any real knowledge of Indian philosophy,"[219] provides the first known western reference to the Buddha, with the admonition to remember that the Greeks "stole their philosophy from the barbarians." St. Jerome also mentions the Buddha (who, he says, was born from the side of a virgin).[220] A fragment of Archelaos of Carrha (278 A.D.) mentions the Buddha's virgin-birth. Clement knew of the practice of stupa worship (*Stromat*. III.194) and describes matters of lifestyle—for example that the Brahmins were vegetarian, drank no wine, and practiced celibacy. He mentions the Indian belief in reincarnation. Most importantly, in the fourth century A.D. the church father Hippolytus, in the *Refutation of All Heresies*, was familiar with the *Maitrī Upaniṣad* or with some other similar source.[221]

The Neoplatonists were very interested in India, perhaps because they had become aware of the similarity between their philosophy and that of the early Advaita Vedānta. Still, they provide inadequate information. Philostratus is hardly worth mentioning. Porphyry preserved a passage of Bardesanes' book on the Gymnosophists, and Stobaeus has another, but they make no mention of technical philosophical teachings or of yoga, meditation, *mokṣa*, and so on.[222] Bardesanes, like Strabo and Megasthenes, concentrates on the lifestyle of the Brahmins and Śramanas, their relationship to the government, and their practice of self-immolation. A passage preserved by Stobaeus seems to be a description of the Śīva temple at Elephanta.

Though no extant Greek work may be said to preserve a detailed technical knowledge of any branch of Indian philosophy, there are several isolated references to yoga. Curtius calls the Indian philosophers "a wild and hideous group" (*unum agreste et horridum genus*) (VIII.8.31), perhaps referring to long-haired, barely clad, forest-dwelling yogis. Aristoboulos knew of the yoga of maintaining uncomfortable postures for a long time. Strabo mentions wonder-workers who wandered about with cymbals and drums (XV.22). Pliny (*NH* VII.23) mentions the practice of gazing at the sun while standing still on one foot, and describes the monasteries of India (*NH* VII.21–30). Priscian also knew of the sun-gazing yoga and its role in meditation, and said that while sun-gazing they would "concentrate their minds on holy themes and through the sun's light would grasp the meaning of the secret signs of what is to be."

The relative silence about Indian thought in our sources from the late Roman Empire may in part be due to the philosophical war, with its attendant book-burnings, that was flaring between the Christian and pagan schools (especially Neoplatonism). The persecution of pagan scholars under Theodosius created an exodus from the Greco-Roman centers by the professional purveyors of pagan thought, many of whom went to the provincial centers of the West, while others took the sea route eastward to India.

Skeletal Conclusions

Archeological and documentary evidence show several things clearly. First, that there was a Greek presence in India continuously from Alexander's arrival or before until toward the end of the Roman Empire—about eight hundred years. Secondly, that the Greeks in India maintained contact with Greeks in the Mediterranean throughout this period. Finally, that the Greeks in India were deeply involved in cultural interaction with Indians, in the fields of art and astronomy surely, and probably in the fields of literature, theater, and philosophy as well. The deep Greek penetration into Buddhism, and the fact that the Mahāyāna forms of Buddhism arose specifically at the period of maximum Greek involvement, suggest Greek influences on Indian culture as profound and historic as the penetration of Indian ideas into Greek thought in the pre-Socratic period.

Notes to Chapter Fourteen

1. Cf. Wilhelm Halbfass, *India and Europe: An Essay in Understanding* (Albany, New York: State University of New York Press, 1988, p. 11): "Reports on travels to India, or other Indian connections, of Greek philosophers are not found in Greek literature before Alexander."

2. See A. Goetze, "Persische Weisheit in Griechischen Gewande," *Zeitschrift für Indologie und Iranistik* 2 (Leipzig, 1923): 60–98 and 167–177; J. Duchesme-Guillemin, "Persische Weisheit in Griechischen Gewande?" *Harvard Theological Review* 49 (1956): 115–122; Joseph Bidez, *Eos; ou, Platon et l'Orient* (Brusells: M. Hayez [imprimeur de la Academie Royale de Belgique], 1945). According to Apuleius, Plato tried in vain to make contact with Indian philosophers. B. Breloer et F. Boemer, eds., *Fontes historiae religionum Indicarum*, Bonn: Ludovicum Röhrschied, 1939 (*Fontes historiae religionum*, fasc. 7), p. 103.

3. James S. Romm, *The Edges of the Earth in Ancient Thought: Geography, Exploration, and Fiction* (Princeton, New Jersey: Princeton University Press, 1992), pp. 85–86.

4. Ibid., pp. 87–88.

5. Ibid., p. 83.

6. Ibid., p. 93.

7. See Martin P. Charlesworth, *Trade Routes and Commerce of the Roman Empire* (Cambridge: Cambridge University Press, 1924), pp. 101–103, and W. W. Tarn, *The Greeks in Bactria and India* (Cambridge: Cambridge University Press, 1951), pp. 44, 54.

8. There is controversy over the existence of this route, which Tarn feels may be derived from an ancient misreading of sources (ibid., app. 14). Still, even Tarn acknowledges that "there must have been an active trade of some sort down the Phasis to the Black Sea, for in the third century B.C. Dioscurias on the Black Sea coast was one of the most polyglot of ports" (ibid., p. 112). In any case, "there was in existence in Strabo's own time (XI.506) a trade-route from the East to the Black Sea which passed *northward* of the Caspian" (ibid., p. 490).

9. The main source is the anonymous *Periplus of the Erythraean Sea* of the first century A.D. See John W. McCrindle, *The Commerce and Navigation of the Erythraean Sea and Ancient India as Described by Ktesias the Knidian* (Amsterdam: Philosophical Press, 1973).

10. George Woodcock, *The Greeks in India* (London: Faber and Faber, 1966), p. 138.

11. Etienne Lamotte, "Early Relations between India and the West, Part I", *Buddhist Studies Review* 5, no. 2 (1988): 117.

12. Bernard P. Grenfell and Arthur S. Hunt, eds., *The Oxyrhynchus Papyri*, vol. 11 (London: Egypt Exploration Fund, 1898–1998), no. 1364.

13. Tarn, *The Greeks in Bactria and India*, p. 387.

14. Leonard R. Palmer, *The Greek Language* (Norman, Oklahoma: University of Oklahoma Press, 1980) p. 185.

15. Ibid., p. 175.

16. Ibid.

17. Ibid.

18. Ibid., p. 176.

19. Ibid.

20. See, for example, Moses Hadas's treatment of this subject (*Hellenistic Culture: Fusion and Diffusion* [New York: W. W. Norton, 1972], pp. 15–17).

21. Trans. X. S. Thani-Nayagam, "Indian Thought and Roman Stoicism," *Tamil Culture* 10, no. 3 (1963): 17.

22. Ibid., p. 16.

23. Ibid., p. 20.

24. W. W. Tarn, *Alexander the Great*, vol. 1 (Cambridge: Cambridge University Press, 1948, 1950), p. 77, says these youths were given Macedonian (i.e., Greek) "educations"—as well as military training. This is not specified in the sources, and Curtius, who feels they were primarily to serve as hostages, suggests the contrary. Still, Arrian notes that Alexander called these youths his "successors" (*epigonoi*), causing some consternation to the Macedonians who had assumed they would be his successors. Even Bosworth notes that this event "may suggest some degree of integration" (A. B. Bosworth, *Conquest and Empire: The Reign of Alexander the Great* [Cambridge: Cambridge University Press, 1988], p. 157).

25. Quintus Curtius Rufus, *The History of Alexander*, trans. John Yardley with an introduction and notes by Waldemar Heckel (London: Penguin Books, 1984), p. 161.

26. For example by Tarn, *Alexander the Great*, vol. 2, pp. 272–275, and, more recently, J. M. Bigwood, "Ctesias as Historian," *Phoenix* 32 (1978): 36–39. Yet as Bosworth notes, "There is no apparent reason for invention" (*Conquest and Empire*, p. 108, n. 251).

27. Bosworth, ibid., p. 108.

28. "Seat of higher learning": John Maxwell O'Brien, *Alexander the Great: The Invisible Enemy* (London and New York: Routledge, 1992), p. 156.

In connection with the cosmopolitanism of Taxila, Strabo reports:

> Aristoboulus mentions some novel and unusual customs at Taxila: those who by reason of poverty are unable to marry off their daughters, lead them forth to the market-place in the flower of their age to the sound of both trumpets and drums . . . thus assembling a crowd; and to any man who comes forward they first expose her rear parts up to the shoulders and then her front parts, and if she pleases him, and at the same time allows herself to be persuaded, on approved terms, he marries her; and the dead are thrown out to be devoured by vultures. . . . (XV.1.62)

The marriage-mart seems to reflect Babylonian influence, and the exposure of the dead to vultures is a Zoroastrian custom, as H. G. Rawlinson pointed out (*India: A Short Cultural History* [London: Cresset Press, 1965], p. 58).

29. A. B. Bosworth, *Alexander and the East: The Tragedy of Triumph* (Oxford: Clarendon Press, 1996), p. 1.

30. Ibid., p. 2.

31. Trans. ibid., pp. 2–3.

32. For example, Tarn, *Alexander the Great*, vol. 2, pp. 437–441.

33. Ulrich Wilcken, *Alexander the Great*, trans. G. C. Richards, notes and introduction E. N. Borza (New York: W. W. Norton, 1967), p. 221.

34. O'Brien, *Alexander the Great: The Invisible Enemy*.

35. J. F. C. Fuller, *The Generalship of Alexander the Great* (Ware, Hertfordshire: Wordsworth Editions, 1998), p. 66.

36. Bosworth, *Alexander and the East*, p. 5 n. 12, 19.

37. Tarn, *Alexander the Great*, vol. 1, p. 103.

38. Fuller, *The Generalship of Alexander the Great*, p. 286.

39. Bosworth, *Alexander and the East*, pp. 21–22.

40. Fuller, *The Generalship of Alexander the Great*, p. 180; he is agreeing with the opinion of Hogarth.

41. Bosworth, *Alexander and the East*, pp. 9, 11.

42. Ibid., p. 21.

43. Bosworth, *Conquest and Empire*, p. 157.

44. Ibid.

45. Richard N. Frye, *The Heritage of Persia* (London: Wiedenfeld and Nicolson, 1962), p. 132.

46. H. W. Parke, "The Massacre of the Branchidae," *JHS* 105 (1985), p. 68.

47. Wilcken, *Alexander the Great*, p. 284.

48. A. K. Narain, *The Indo-Greeks* (Oxford: Clarendon Press, 1957), does so, and see also R. Mookerji, "Chandragupta and the Maurya Empire," in *The Age of Imperial Unity*, 2nd ed., ed. R. C. Majumdar, (Bombay: Bharatiya Vidya Bhavan, 1953), p. 58.

49. Mookerji, ibid.

50. Tarn, *The Greeks in Bactria and India*, p. 72.

51. Lionel Casson, *The Ancient Mariners: Seafarers and Sea Fighters of the Mediterranean in Ancient Times*, 2nd ed. (Princeton, New Jersey: Princeton University Press, 1991), p. 67.

52. On the basis of modern terminology such as Asian-American, Irish-American, French-Canadian, and so on, the first element of the compound should represent the invading or immigrating or influencing group, the second element the community which they are invading, migrating into, or influencing from abroad. On this basis one should refer to the Indianized strain of Greek philosophy as Indo-Greek and to the Greek settlers in India as Greco-Indian. Yet Narain (*The Indo-Greeks*) and others have chosen the term Indo-Greek for the latter group, and Narain has placed it prominently in the title of his well-known work on the subject, so that terminology—whether in some formal sense "correct" or not—is apt to remain in place at least for a while.

53. Narain, *The Indo-Greeks*.

54. "The Greek influence on Hindu culture," says Chaudhuri, "has always been discounted by Indian scholars from purely nationalistic sentiments. But there can be no doubt that this influence was real" (Nirad C. Chaudhuri, *Hinduism: A Religion to Live By* [Delhi: Oxford University Press, 1979], p. 94).

55. A Greek presence in India well before Alexander's conquest is suggested by the linguist Pāṇini's references to the Greeks as "Yavanas." If this is, as commonly supposed, a transliteration of "Ionians" (cf. Assyrian *Iawanu*, Persian *Yauna* or *Yavanu*, Biblical *Yavan* or *Jawan*, Arabic and Turkish *Junan*) then, it is argued, that term must have passed into India at a time before the disappearance of the letter *digamma* from the Greek alphabet—that is, at least as early as the sixth

century B.C., the heyday of pre-Socratic philosophy, and possibly much earlier, as Chadwick has argued that some of the Mycenaeans called themselves Yawones. But Burkert greatly weakens the claim by his argument that "the uncontracted form remained in current use . . . [especially] by non-Ionians . . ." (Walter Burkert, *The Orientalizing Revolution: Near Eastern Influence on Greek Culture in the Early Archaic Age*, trans. Margaret E. Pinder and Walter Burkert, Revealing Antiquity 5 [Cambridge, Massachusetts, and London: Harvard University Press, 1992], p. 160.)

56. Trans. H. G. Rawlinson in *The Greek Historians*, ed. Francis R. B. Godolphin (New York: Random House, 1942).

57. Muhammad A. Dandamaev and Vladimir G. Lukonin, *The Culture and Social Institutions of Ancient Iran*, trans. Philip L. Kohl (Cambridge: Cambridge University Press, 1989), pp. 298, 299.

58. Bosworth, *Conquest and Empire*, p. 121, n. 300.

59. Tarn, *Alexander the Great*, vol. 2, p. 236.

60. Mortimer Wheeler, *Flames over Persepolis* (New York: William Morrow, 1968), p. 65.

61. Ibid.

62. Ibid.

63. Rawlinson, *India: A Short Cultural History*, p. 57.

64. For this inscription see Daniel Schlumberger, Louis Robert, Andre Dupont-Sommer, and Emil Benveniste, "Une bilingue grec-arameénne d'Aśoka," *Journal Asiatique* (1958): 1–48; Wheeler, *Flames over Persepolis*, pp. 66 ff.; Sachhidananda Bhattacharya, *Select Aśokan Epigraphs* (Calcutta: Mukhopadhyay, 1960), pp. 108–110.

65. Wheeler, *Flames over Persepolis*, p. 68.

66. Ibid., p. 71.

67. Ibid., p. 75.

68. Louis Dupree, *Afghanistan* (Karachi: Oxford University Press, 1997), pp. 289, 292.

69. Frye, *Heritage of Persia*, p. 138.

70. Ibid., p. 76.

71. See ibid., p. 79.

72. Ibid.

73. Amelie Kuhrt and Susan Sherwin-White, eds., *Hellenism in the East: The Interaction of Greek and Non-Greek Civilizations from Syria to Central Asia after Alexander* (London: Duckworth, 1987), pp. 153–154, plates VI and IX.

74. Wheeler, *Flames over Persepolis*, p. 84.

75. Ibid., pp. 111–112.

76. This coin hoard has caused some to wonder whether the new Taxila may have been ordered by the Indo-Scythian ruler Azes I, who seems to have replaced the last Greek king of Taxila around the middle of the century. The Indo-Scythians, like the Kushans after them, entered India through the Kush and found themselves in the Hellenized region of Gandhāra, whose culture they adopted with enthusiasm. ("The Kushans perhaps felt themselves the heirs of the Greeks of Bactria," says Frye [*Heritage of Persia*, p. 203].)

77. Romila Thapar, "Epigraphic Evidence and Some Indo-Hellenistic Contacts During the Mauryan Period," in *Indological Studies: Prof. D. C. Sicar Commemoration Volume*, ed. S. K. Maity and Upendra Thakur (New Delhi: Shakti Malik, Abhinav Publications, 1987), and see also P. M. Fraser, "The Son of Aristonax at Kandahar," *Afghan Studies* 2 (1979): 17.

78. Wheeler, *Flames over Persepolis*, p. 82.

79. Ibid.

80. Paul Bernard as quoted by Wheeler, ibid., p. 82.

81. Ibid., pp. 118, 120.

82. Arthur B. Keith, *The Sanskrit Drama: Its Origin, Development, Theory and Practice* (Oxford: Oxford University Press, 1924), p. 59.

83. J. M. Cook, *The Greeks in Ionia and the East* (New York: Praeger Books, 1963), pp. 198–199.

84. Hadas, *Hellenistic Culture*, pp. 30, 32. Tarn goes so far as to claim that "Asiatics were attracted to Greek city forms" (*The Greeks in Bactria and India*, p. 19).

85. Hadas, *Hellenistic Culture*, p. 24.

86. Cook, *Greeks in Ionia and the East*, p. 168.

87. Frye, *Heritage of Persia*, p. 142.

88. Ibid., pp. 142–143.

89. Ibid., p. 152.

90. Ibid., p. 134.

91. Hadas, *Hellenistic Culture*, p. 39.

92. Ibid., p. 34.

93. E. R. Bevan, "Alexander the Great," in Edward J. Rapson, ed., *The Cambridge History of India*, vol. 1, *Ancient India*, (Cambridge: Cambridge University Press, 1922), p. 379.

94. Tarn, *Alexander the Great*, vol. 1, p. 143.

95. Mookerji, *Age of Imperial Unity*, p. 45.

96. Since polygamy was common, Aśoka's lineage cannot be known for certain. For discussion of this question see John Allan, Sir T. Wolseley Haig, and H. H. Dodwell, *The Cambridge Shorter History of India*, ed. H. H. Dodwell (New York: Macmillan; Cambridge: Cambridge University Press, 1934), p. 33; Tarn, *The Greeks in Bactria and India*, pp. 152–153.

97. Mookerji, *Age of Imperial Unity*, pp. 102, 106.

98. McCrindle, *The Commerce and Navigation of the Erythraean Sea and Ancient India*, pp. 204–205.

99. Schlumberger, et al., "Une bilinque greco-araméena d'Aśoka," and see J. Filliozat, "Graeco-Aramaic Inscription of Aśoka near Kandahar," *Ep. Ind.* 34 (1961–62): 1–8.

100. D. Schlumberger, E. Benveniste, "A New Greek Inscription of Aśoka at Kandahar," *Ep. Ind.*, 1965–66, part. V, pp. 193–200. See also H. Humbach, "The Aramaic Aśoka Inscription from Taxila," *Journal of Central Asia*, Dec. 1978, I(2), pp. 87–98; K. R. Norman, "Notes on the Greek Version of Aśoka's Twelfth and Thirteenth Rock Edicts," *JRAS* 1972, 2, pp. 111–118, and Romila Thapar, *Aśoka and the Decline of the Mauryas* (Oxford: Oxford University Press, 1961), pp. 40–41.

101. Rawlinson, *Intercourse between India and the Western World*, p. 39.

102. Woodcock, *The Greeks in India*, p. 56.

103. Ánanda W. P. Guruge, "Buddhist Tradition and Aśokan Inscriptions," in *King Aśoka and Buddhism: Historical and Literary Studies*, ed. Anuradha Seneviratna (Kandy, Sri Lanka: Buddhist Publication Society, 1994), pp. 54, 56.

104. Ibid., p. 56.

105. Woodcock, *Greeks in India*, p. 54.

106. Ibid., p. 55.

107. Ibid.

108. Frye, *Heritage of Persia*, p. 197.

109. See Tarn, *The Greeks in Bactria and India*, p. 82, for remarks on this.

110. Frye, *Heritage of Persia*, p. 169.

111. Ibid., p. 165.

112. Ibid., p. 168.

113. Ibid., p. 174.

114. Strabo described it thus:

> The Greeks who caused Bactria to revolt grew so powerful on account of the fertility of the country that they became masters not only of Ariana, but also of India, as Apollodorus of Artemita says; and more tribes were subdued by them than by Alexander—by Menander in particular (at least if he actually crossed the Hypanis toward the east and advanced as far as the Imaus), for some were subdued by him personally and others by Demetrius, the son of Euthydemus the king of the Bactrians; and they took possession not only of Patalena, but also, on the rest of the coast, of what is called the kingdom of Saraostus and Sigerdis . . . And more than that, they extended their empire even as far as the Seres and the Phryni. (XI.11.1)

Tarn, who believed that the Bactrian Greeks wished to conquer the entire Mauryan empire, not just the parts previously under Greek rule, accepts Apollodorus, as quoted by Strabo, and has Demetrius conquering 900 miles south of Kabul and 1,100 miles east. Narain disagrees, but not thoroughly: He might grant this extent, or nearly it, to Menander, but not to Demetrius (Narain, *The Indo-Greeks*, pp. 34–37). Some of Narain's reductions of the area have since been disproved by archeology. Tarn, for example, said that Demetrius I made a new capital at Taxila, and Narain replied "until now the excavations of Taxila have failed to show any major settlement of the Greeks of a permanent nature" (ibid., p. 31, and see note 8). This is no longer the case.

115. D. C. Sircar, "The Yavanas," in *Age of Imperial Unity*, ed. R. C. Majumdar.

116. Tarn, *The Greeks in Bactria and India*, p. 154.

117. See, for example, C. A. S. Williams, *Outlines of Chinese Symbolism and Art Motives* (Shanghai: Kelly and Walsh, 1932), pp. 272–274.

118. Richard Salomon, *Ancient Buddhist Scrolls from Gandhara: The British Library Kharoṣṭhī Fragments* (Seattle: University of Washington Press, 1999), p. 5.

119. See ibid.

120. Ibid., p. 7.

121. Ibid., p. xv.

122. Ibid., p. 10.

123. Ibid.

124. Ibid., p. 3.

125. Ibid., pp. 3–4.

126. Ibid., p. 4.

127. B. N. Puri, *Buddhism in Central Asia* (Delhi: Motilal Banarsidass, 1987), p. 18.

128. Salomon, *Ancient Buddhist Scrolls from Gandhāra*, p. 5.

129. Puri, *Buddhism in Central Asia*, p. 19.

130. Salomon, *Ancient Buddhist Scrolls from Gandhāra*, p. 12.

131. Puri, *Buddhism in Central Asia*, p. 91, n. 14.

132. Ibid., p. 92

133. Peter Hopkirk, *Foreign Devils on the Silk Road: The Search for the Lost Cities and Treasures of Chinese Central Asia* (Oxford: Oxford University Press, 1980), p. 24.

134. Lamotte, "Early Relations Between India and the West I," pp. 116–117.

135. See Hopkirk, *Foreign Devils on the Silk Road*, p. 93.

136. Ibid., p. 92. Khotan is a big step beyond the farthest eastern advance of the Greeks under Euthydemus, and Stein found Kharoṣṭhī manuscripts still farther east, in Lou Lan.

137. Woodcock, *Greeks in India*, p. 95. Another scholar comments, in regard to the *Questions of King Milinda*: "I presume this debate was conducted in the Bactrian Greek language but was later translated into Pali and Sanskrit." Hammalawa Saddhatissa, "Foreword," in *The Debate of King Milinda*, an abridgement, trans. and ed. Bhikkhu Pesala, Buddhist Traditions Series 14 (Delhi: Motilal Banarsidass, 1991), p. v.

138. Woodcock, *Greeks in India*, p. 95.

139. Ibid., p. 96.

140. Rhys Davids, *The Questions of King Milinda*, Sacred Books of the East 35 and 36 (New York: Dover, 1963), vol. 1, p. xix.

141. Bhikkhu Pesala, *Debate of King Milinda*, p. xiii.

142. Ibid., p. ix.

143. Sarvepalli Radhakrishnan, *Indian Philosophy*, 2nd ed. (London: George Allen and Unwin, 1929), vol. 1, p. 345.

144. Trans. Pesala, *Debate of King Milinda*, p. 1.

145. Ibid., p. ix.

146. Puri, *Buddhism in Central Asia*, p. 91.

147. Thapar, "Epigraphic Evidence and Some Indo-Hellenistic Contacts During the Mauryan Period," p. 17.

148. George F. Hourani, *Arab Seafaring in the Indian Ocean in Ancient and Early Medieval Times*, revised and expanded by John Carswell (Princeton, New Jersey: Princeton University Press, 1995), pp. 15–16, 23.

149. Ibid., p. 22.

150. Etienne Lamotte, "Early Relations between India and the West, Conclusion," *Buddhist Studies Review* 6, no. 1 (1989): 14.

151. See M. Cary and E. H. Warmington, *The Ancient Explorers* (Baltimore, Maryland: Penguin, 1963), pp. 94–98; Casson, *The Ancient Mariners*, p. 205; Lamotte, "Early Relations between India and the West, Conclusion," pp. 5–16.

152. Woodcock, *The Greeks in India*, p. 142.

153. Dandamaev and Lukonin, *Culture and Social Institutions*, p. 214.

154. Frye, *Heritage of Persia*, p. 203.

155. Casson, *Ancient Mariners*, p. 172.

156. Ibid., p. 191.

157. See Charlesworth, *Trade Routes and Commerce of the Roman Empire*, p. 137; Wheeler, *Rome Beyond the Imperial Frontiers*, pp. 120–122.

158. Wheeler, ibid., pp. 151–152.

159. Charlesworth, *Trade Routes and Commerce of the Roman Empire*, pp. 138–139.

160. Wheeler, *Rome Beyond the Imperial Frontiers*, p. 177.

161. Hourani, *Arab Seafaring*, p. 29.

162. Ibid., p. 174.

163. Cary and Warmington, *The Ancient Explorers*, p. 102.

164. Ibid., p. 103.

165. Wheeler, *Rome Beyond the Imperial Frontiers*, p. 133.

166. Ibid., p. 131.

167. Rawlinson, *Intercourse Between India and the Western World*, p. 138.

168. Breloer and Boemer, *Fontes historiae religionum Indicarum*, pp. 102, 103.

169. Woodcock, *The Greeks in India*, p. 147.

170. Wheeler, *Rome Beyond the Imperial Frontiers*, pp. 152–153.

171. See Wheeler, ibid., pp. 146–153; and Mortimer Wheeler, "Arikamedu: An Indo-Roman Trading-Station in the East Coast of India," *Ancient India* 2 (1947), pp. 17–124; R. F. Facheux, *Une vieille cite indienne pres de Pondichery, Virapatnam* (Pondicherry, 1945).

172. See Tarn, *The Greeks in Bactria and India*, p. 367; R. C. Majumdar, "India and the Western World," in *Age of Imperial Unity*, ed. R. C. Majumdar, p. 620.

173. Lamotte, "Early Relations between Indai and the West, Conclusion," pp. 7, 16.

174. Rawlinson, *Intercourse Between India and the Western World*, pp. 94–95; E. H. Warmington, *The Commerce Between the Roman Empire and India* (Cambridge: Cambridge University Press, 1928), p. 25.

175. Ibid.

176. Tarn, *The Greeks in Bactria and India*, p. 370; William Simpson, "The Buddhist Praying Wheel," *Journal of the Royal Asiatic Society* no. 4 (1898), p. 875.

177. John W. McCrindle, *Ancient India as Described in Classical Literature* (Westminster: Archibald Constable and Co., 1901), p. 196.

178. Warmington, *The Commerce Between the Roman Empire and India*, pp. 27–34.

179. Majumdar, "India and the Western World," *Age of Imperial Unity*, ed. R. C. Majumdar, pp. 619, 633.

180. See Osmond de Beauvoir Priaulx, *The Indian Travels of Apollonius of Tyana* and *The Indian Embassies to Rome* (London: Quaritch, Piccadilly, 1873), pp. 63–253.

181. Trans. Woodcock, *The Greeks in India*, p. 155.

182. Quoted ibid.

183. See, e.g., Otto Neugebauer, *The Exact Sciences in Antiquity* (Providence, Rhode Island: Brown University Press, 1957), pp. 7, 82, 186.

184. David Pingree, *The Yavanajātaka of Sphujidhvaja*, 2 vols., Harvard Oriental Series 48 (Cambridge, Massachusetts: Harvard University Press, 1978), p. v.

185. Ibid., p. 3.

186. Ibid. The passage continues, "Doubtless there were many other lines of transmission, running in both directions, between the two cultures."

187. Ibid., p. 5.

188. Ibid.

189. Ibid., p. 4.

190. As Pingree argues, ibid., pp. 7–10.

191. Tarn, *The Greeks in Bactria and India*, p. 382.

192. Hadas, *Hellenistic Culture*, p. 109.

193. Tarn, *The Greeks in Bactria and India*, p. 17.

194. Ibid., pp. 62–63.

195. H. G. Rawlinson, "Foreign Influence in the Civilization of Ancient India, 900 B.C.–400 A.D.," *Journal of the Royal Asiatic Society* (1908–1913), pp. 217–238.

196. Rawlinson, *Intercourse Between India and the Western World*, p. 171.

197. Tarn, *The Greeks in Bactria and India*, p. 383.

198. Keith, *The Sanskrit Drama*, p. 59.

199. For a review of the question see Keith, ibid., pp. 57–69; I. Shekhar, *Sanskrit Drama: Its Origin and Decline* (Leiden: Brill, 1960), pp. 54–59. J. Gonda ("Zur Frage nach dem Ursprung und Wesen des indischen Dramas," *Acta Orientalia, Ediderunt Societates Orientales Batava Danica Norvegica* 19 [1943]: 329–330), remarks on differences which he feels exclude altogether the possibility of Greek influence on Sanskrit drama.

200. Wheeler, *Flames over Persepolis*, pp. 157–158.

201. Tarn infers two lyric poems and a hexameter written in Greek in Menander's kingdom. (*The Greeks in Bactria and India*, pp. 246–249.)

202. See Richard Stoneman, trans., *The Greek Alexander Romance* (London: Penguin, 1991), introductory essay.

203. Richard Stoneman, trans. and ed., *Legends of Alexander the Great*, Everyman Library (London: J. M. Dent, 1994), pp. ix-xiii.

204. Nihar Ranjan Ray, "Sculpture," *Age of Imperial Unity*, ed. R. C. Majumdar, p. 519.

205. Wheeler, *Flames over Persepolis*, p. 150.

206. Tarn, *The Greeks in Bactria and India*, pp. 403–404.

207. This was Alfred Fourcher's view (*La ville route de l'inde, de Bactres à Taxila* [Paris, 1942], pp. 340–341), supported in a modified form by Sir John H. Marshall in *The Buddhist Art of Gandhāra* (Cambridge: Cambridge University Press, 1960), pp. 5–6. More recent discoveries at Aï Khanoum have confirmed that "Gandhāran art descended directly from Hellenized Bactrian art" (Chaibi Nustamandy, "The Impact of Hellenised Bactria on Gandhāra Art," *Gandhāran Art in Context: East-West Exchanges at the Crossraods of Asia*, ed. Raymond Allchin, et al., [New Delhi: Regency, 1997], p. 19).

208. But Hallade regards Gandhāran art as "faithful to the most ancient aspect of Buddhism—the Hīnayāna" (M. Hallade, *Gandhāran Art of North India* [New York: Abrams, 1968], p. 75).

209. Benjamin Rowland, *The Art and Architecture of India*, 3rd ed. (Baltimore, Maryland: Penguin, 1970), p. 121; A. C. Soper, "The Roman Style in Gandhāra" *American Journal of Archeology* 55 (1951), pp. 301–319.

210. See Rawlinson, *Intercourse Between India and the Western World*, p. 163; Woodcock, *The Greeks in India*, p. 171; Wheeler, *Flames over Persepolis*, pp. 167 ff.

211. Doris Srinivasan, for example, has argued for the presence of elements in Indian folk art. See, for example, "Gandhāran Textiles: A Local Craft with Western Connections," *Gandhāran Art in Context*, ed. Allchin et al., pp. 95–117.

212. Frye, *Heritage of Persia*, 175.

213. Ibid.

214. Dupree, *Afghanistan*, p. 295.

215. E. Lamotte, "Sur la formation du Mahāyāna," *Asiatica* (1954), p. 386, n. 49. Edward Conze half agrees with him (*The Prajñāpāramitā Literature* [The Hague: Mouton, 1960], p. 11–12).

216. Thani-Nayagam, "Indian Thought and Roman Stoicism," p. 11.

217. Such as the somewhat hypothetical figure whom Tarn (*The Greeks in Bactria and India*) reconstructs as "Trogus's source."

218. See Romm, *The Edges of the Earth in Ancient Thought*; McCrindle, *Ancient India as Described in Classical Literature*, p. 153.

219. Rawlinson, *Intercourse Between India and the Western World*, p. 174.

220. Convenient collections of such passages are found in McCrindle, *Ancient India as Described in Classical Literature* and Rawlinson, *Intercourse Between India and the Western World.*

221. See J. Filliozat, "La doctrine des brahmanes d'après saint Hippolyte," *Revue de l'Histoire des Religions* 130 (1945), pp. 56–91.

222. See McCrindle, *Ancient India as Described in Classical Literature*, pp. 167–171; Rawlinson, *Intercourse Between India and the Western World*, pp. 142–146.

Chapter Fifteen

Dialectic before Alexander

In both Greece and India there were philosophers who aimed at disproving all philosophical propositions. Rather than constructing with the syllogism, they deconstructed with the *reductio ad absurdum*. Their approach can be called dialectic to differentiate it from the constructive logic of the syllogism. By dialectic is meant reasoning that proceeds by negations and disproofs; by logic, reasoning that proceeds by positions and proofs. Logic has often represented the metaphysical impulse, dialectic the deconstructive. They are in a sense each other's opposites, yet in another sense each other's alter egos, or negative implications.

Logic is based on the assumption that things have essences, or fixed identities—that each entity is exactly what it is and nothing else. Properly formed propositions about such entities will have a clear and indubitable truth value—that is, they will be either true or false in an absolute, not a relative, sense. This clarity is assured by rules (the "Laws of Thought") which prevent entities from merging with one another or otherwise becoming ambiguous in their identities.

The Law of Identity holds that each thing is itself and nothing else: A equals A, and A does not equal not-A.[1] The Law of Contradiction is a restatement of this primal fact, saying that it is impossible for a thing to be both itself and something else—both A and not-A—at the same time. The Law of the Excluded Middle holds that everything must be either A or not-A: There is no "middle" area in between these positions.

In terms of ordinary speech, the Law of Identity is equivalent to Yes, the Law of Contradiction to No, and the Law of the Excluded Middle to the assertion that there is no position in between Yes and No. (This doesn't exclude Maybe, which means not that there is something between Yes and No but that the speaker has not ascertained yet whether Yes or No is the case.) These extraordinarily simple rules of thought (and speech) took ages to articulate because speech is involved in so many motivations besides the simple stating of what is the case.

Ancient dialecticians inhabited a different world from ancient logicians, a world where entities were not so absolutely separate, where the line between self and other was vague and mutable, and where there might well be positions between Yes and No. They often rejected the philosophy of essences by undermining the logical principles which enforced it.

A big problem from the point of view of the deconstructivist dialectician is that the philosophy of essences does not contain a provision for change or process in the world. With such rigid identities, how could things become other things? How could any situation change? Aristotle solved this problem by postulating a realm of potentiality where possibilities for the future resided latently and whence they could be actualized. But in so doing he contradicted the philosophy of essences by recognizing a state in between Being and non-Being, in between Yes and No; this position—or non-position—contravenes the Law of the Excluded Middle, involving the metaphysical and logical aspects of Aristotle's system in contradiction of one another.

The formal elements of logic are the propositions derived from the three Laws of Thought and the syllogisms constructed from them. The formal elements of the ancient dialectic, on the other hand, in both Greece and India, were counterstatements to the syllogism. The most elementary form was the dichotomy-and-dilemma structure. A question is first dichotomized into either A or not-A, then the dichotomy is turned into a dilemma by disproving both alternatives, rather than just one. The Law of the Excluded Middle, which holds that either A or not-A must be true, is implicitly refuted—and there may be an implication that some other alternative than A and not-A exists. This breach of the logical principle has ramifications beyond the merely formal; it implies that the entities in question lack essences which can be constrained by limits. It is implicitly a critique of ontology as well as of speech.

In the dichotomy-and-dilemma structure, the nature of the disproof that is applied to each limb of the dichotomy varies. Sometimes the proposition in question is shown to lead to a conclusion that contradicts ordinary experience. Then either the proposition or belief in the reality of ordinary experience must be abandoned. Sometimes the proposition is involved in a logical rather than an empirical contradiction, so that either the proposition or the Law of Contradiction must be abandoned. Sometimes it is involved in an infinite regress—a formally elegant tactic that is a kind of stylistic signature of the ancient dialectic. When a proposition is involved in infinite regress it is regarded as reduced to absurdity, because infinity melts down identities. When any entity "enters" infinity it loses the identity which formerly differentiated it from other entities; in infinity everything is everything. The proposition which becomes entangled in infinite regress is no longer just itself; it has passed beyond the Law of Identity, and dichotomies such as true and false no longer apply to it.

There is no inherent reason why dialectical forms should be used primarily to negate and logical ones primarily to posit. Dialectic can be used to posit and logic to negate. Parmenides, for example, used the dichotomy-and-dilemma type of *reductio ad absurdum* to construct a positive proof. By disproving the counterthesis of the thesis he wished to posit, he established that thesis through a tacit invocation of the Law of the Excluded Middle. He argued against A, in other words, not primarily in order to disprove A, but in order to establish its contrary, not-A. He used the forms of the dialectic to posit rather than to disprove. In a similar way, the forms of logic, such as the syllogism, may be used to negate rather than to posit, as in the *modus tollens* form of syllogism, which holds that: if A, then B; not B, therefore not A. In fact, the dichotomy-and-dilemma structure of argument can be described as a disjunctive *modus tollens*: If A, then either B or C; not B and not C, therefore not A. Despite this overlap between the uses to which the dialectical and logical forms may be put, the two strains of thought have retained their separate functions with an almost aesthetic and ethical force over millennia—the one positing, the other negating.[2]

Both the Greek and the Indian traditions of dialectic began their criticism of dogmas through demonstrations of subjectivity or relativity. Truth claims were undermined by demonstrations of the subjective elements in judgment. Existing opinions were played against one another so that they seemed to cancel each other out.

The dogmatizing tendency of early metaphysics, which carried a heavy weight of myth and religion, called forth counterpositions that protested and attempted to refute metaphysical propositions. The process seems to reflect social changes going on in both Greece and India. Relativism and skepticism, for example, may be seen as responses to the dissolution of tribal systems in the face of advancing concepts of the national state. The limitations of any inherited tribal point of view are highlighted when the existence of a variety of points of view is seen. The tendency of tribal boundaries to erode in the face of increasing awareness of cultural diversity shifted emphasis from communal solidarity to subjective individualism, including sophistic subjectivism and skepticism in Greece and, in India, Jain relativism and the Buddhist tradition of maintaining a so-called "noble silence" on certain hotly contested issues.

The transition between tribal and national structures led, in one direction, to schools of skeptics and protodialecticians who denied that any point of view could be absolute. In an earlier period, when the tribal lore had been unquestioned, it had not seemed necessary to construct logical proofs in support of it. Thus, when tribal cohesion was breaking down, dialectic arose first, and logic was subsequently developed as a weapon with which to respond at a formal level to the skeptical attacks of the dialectic. In terms of the social situation, then, the development of logic can be seen as an attempt to arrive at an objective truth over and above tribal or partial truths, a truth whose objectivity would override and replace tribal points of view as the state overrode and replaced them, and validate the state by demonstrating that it was founded on a new and greater singleness of truth. The dialectic then participated in the breakdown of tribal belief-systems, or to the breakdown of the idea of truth, and logic in turn arose in the defense of truth at a national scale which would override the loss of tribal identities. In India, this development proceeded over a period of centuries in which the center of civilization shifted from the Northwest, where the number of archeological sites declined in the post-Harappan period, to the Ganges valley, where the number of sites increased, "showing an eastward shift of power that continued up to the time of the Mauryas." Cultural complexity increased as more and more tribal groups were assimilated, and this complexity was mediated by "regional networks" that "were integrated into a wider system."[3] In Greece, these developments can be seen against the smaller but in some ways structurally similar background of the post–Persian War Delian League and the transition to the imperial tenor of the Athenian League.

At the same time the transition from tribal to national organization seems to have led in a contrary direction. While skeptical and protodialectical impulses contributed to breaking down tribal cohesiveness, small extended family- or clanlike communities arose to provide a sheltered setting in which traditions of cohesiveness could be artificially nourished and maintained. Among the Buddhists and Jains in the forests and deer parks of India, or the Pythagoreans and Orphics in Greece, communal rules for living replaced the deteriorating tribal lore of the past. In the one direction the emerging national state, and in the other direction the small, sheltered community with its own rules, replaced the passing unity of the tribal tradition.

The *Nyāya Sūtras*, 1

The chronology of the successive developments of first dialectical then logical forms is pretty clear in Greece. In India it is much less clear. One key problem is the date of the *Nyāya Sūtras*, which includes the earliest extant Indian exposition of the syllogism. The *Nyāya Sūtras* is traditionally attributed to the sage Gotama (not Siddhārtha Gautama, known as the Buddha), who is said to have lived in the sixth century B.C. This date seems to be pious in motive, intended to root the Naiyāyika school in the semi-legendary age of the great teachers and reformers such as Buddha, Mahāvīra, Gosāla, and Sañjaya. Little if any of the text seems really to belong in that legendary century of wise men. Above all, there is nothing in the cultural environment of the sixth century that reflects the presence of formal logic. At a later date the Naiyāyika syllogism incurred the criticism of Mādhyamika and Lokāyatika dialecticians. But in the earlier period Naiyāyika logic is not mentioned anywhere. It could hardly have been present without being remarked on.

Philological evidence suggests that the *Nyāya Sūtras* took form in stages from about 200 B.C. to about 450 A.D. Within this range it seems that the passages on formal logic are rather late. The early Mādhyamika literature—the works of Nāgārjuna and Āryadeva in the second or third centuries A.D.—contains a fully articulated dialectic but no hint of awareness of the syllogism. If the Naiyāyikas already had the syllogism in hand, Nāgārjuna and Āryadeva could not have avoided a dialectical confrontation with it. The external source which first shows awareness of the Naiyāyika syllogism is Asaṅga, about 400 A.D. The syllogism, then, seems to have appeared in the Naiyāyika literature after Nagarjuna and before Asaṅga, that is, between c. 150 and c. 400 A.D.

In addition, certain passages of the *Nyāya Sūtras* show awareness of the dialectical arguments of Nāgārjuna and Āryadeva, which therefore these passages must have come after. These passages occasionally turn the Mādhyamika strategies back against them. At one point, for example, two dialectical arguments against atomism are repeated from the Naiyāyika's opponents, and are countered with a dialectical argument about space (*NS* IV.2.91–93). Again, a dialectical argument (perhaps aimed against the emptiness doctrine of the Perfect Wisdom texts), establishes the reality of things by disproving the counterthesis with an implied dichotomy-and-dilemma argument: The unreality of things is either proven or unproven—if proven, then something is real, namely the proof; if unproven, then there is no reason to believe in it (*NS* IV.2.98 [30]). If the Naiyāyika syllogism had been known, it could have expected similar deconstruction. In India, then, dialectic arose first, to deconstruct traditional ideas of truth, and logic followed, to supply a new criterion of truth.

By the scholarly dating, both the *Nyāya Sūtras* and the Mādhyamika dialectic fall in the period when the Indo-Greek and Greco-Roman presences were still active, and may be possible focuses of Greek influence. This possibility in regard to the development of the Indian syllogism will be investigated in chapter 19 below. The present chapter and the three that follow it will explore relations between the Greek and Indian dialectical traditions, including the question of diffusion. First it will be inquired whether there are signs of the dialectic in India prior to the Alexandrian colonization.

Was There a Pre-Alexandrian Dialectic in India?

Recorded Indian thought until the tenth book of the *Ṛg Veda* seems to express a unified tribal attitude. In *Ṛg Veda* X.129, one of the most famous and unorthodox of the Vedic hymns, signs of skepticism toward received lore appear. The text is attributed to

Prajāpati Parameṣṭhin, one of the legendary early sages of India who were poets and, somewhat like the "Seven Wise Men" of the pre-Socratic period in Greece and some of the pre-Socratics themselves, bridged the gap between mythology and metaphysics. Parameṣṭhin has been called "the Thales of India" because he suggested water as the substance from which all things are formed.[4] He may have been expressing a Chaldean-influenced form of the ancient Near Eastern myth of creation from water, as Thales himself may have done.

But alongside Parameṣṭhin's mythical or metaphysical speculations are skeptical or questioning elements which suggest a discontent with inherited explanations. His hymn ends with doubt that anyone, even the creator god, can know the roots of things:

> Who truly knows? Who shall here proclaim it—whence the gods were produced, whence this creation? The gods arose on this side later, by the creation of this (empiric world, to which the gods belong); then who knows whence it came into being?
>
> This creation, whence it came into being, whether it was established, or whether not—he who is its overseer in the highest heaven, he verily knows, or perchance he knows not.[5]

In this passage there are intimations of the Law of the Excluded Middle in the series of A/not-A dichotomies: "[W]hether it was established . . . or not . . . he verily knows . . . or . . . knows not." But dichotomy as used here does not imply an emerging dichotomy-and-dilemma method, which involves rejection of the Law of the Excluded Middle. Despite the skeptical content, there is formally more protologic here than protodialectic. In either case it does not go very far.

The stage of Hindu literature that follows the *Ṛg Veda* is dominated by an obsession with the Vedic sacrifice, which functioned socially as a guarantee of priestly power. The formulas of sacrifice are contained in the *Yajur Vedas* and the explanations of these formulas are in collections called the Brāhmaṇas. In these works the skeptical streak that appeared in the tenth book of the *Ṛg Veda* has disappeared, and with it the suggestions of a rudimentary formal logic based on dichotomy. Insofar as these texts contain reasoning, it consists of fanciful arguments from analogy which may operate through references to legend or to magical etymologies. Doubt (*vicikitsa*) about ideas of the afterlife is mentioned only in order to be allayed through arguments from sacrificial analogies.[6]

The Brāhmaṇas were followed by the Āraṇyakas and Upaniṣads, compendia of various doctrines and tendencies. These texts also lack a systematic formulation of dialectical thinking, though dialectical patternings may be dimly suggested. Uddālaka Āruni, whose doctrines are compiled in the sixth book of the *Chāndogya Upaniṣad*, seems to carry the speculations of Parameṣṭhin farther. Parameṣṭhin, in *Ṛg Veda* X.129, had asserted that at the beginning there was neither Being nor non-Being, then later, contradictorily, that the cause of the existent was found in the nonexistent. Uddālaka, seemingly attending to the same question, even possibly thinking of that passage, says:

> In the beginning, my dear, this was Being alone, one only without a second. Some people say "in the beginning this was non-being alone, one only; without a second. From that non-being being was produced." But how, indeed, my dear, could it be thus? how could being be produced from non-being? On the contrary, my dear, in the beginning this was being alone, one only, without a second. (*CU* VI.2.1–2)

Uddālaka's assertion that Being could not come from non-Being has often been compared with Parmenides' argument. But the comparison does not hold in terms of formalization. Parmenides employed the dichotomy-and-dilemma method outlined above. First he dichotomized, arguing that if something comes into Being it must come either from Being or from non-Being. He then reduced each limb of the dichotomy to absurdity, rendering the dichotomy into a dilemma: Something cannot, on the one hand, come from Being, for if it comes from being then it was already in Being and cannot be said to have come into Being. It cannot, on the other hand, come from non-Being either, because non-Being does not exist. The conclusion is that there is Being alone, with no transits between Being and non-Being in either direction. The dichotomy-and-dilemma structure is so clearly and economically employed that Parmenides' awareness of it would be hard to doubt. Uddālaka, on the other hand, does not diagram the formal process of his thought. He states a dichotomy, and dogmatically takes a side of it. There is no dilemma; in fact there is no actual reasoning here. Between the argumentation of *Ṛg Veda* X.129 and Uddālaka, there has been no visible advance in terms of formalizing the dialectic.

Like Uddālaka and Parameṣṭhin, Yājñavalkya, a teacher of the *Bṛhadāraṇyaka Upaniṣad* ("who is regarded as the greatest philosopher of the Upaniṣads")[7], shows a tendency to teach in dichotomized terms. His two Great Sayings, or *mahāvākyas*, are a dichotomized pair: *neti, neti* and *iti, iti*, "neither this nor that," and "both this and that" (or, more literally, "not this, not this," and "this, this"). The Great Sayings seem a shorthand for two ontological doctrines, first the denial of the reality of particulars ("not this, not that"), and second the affirmation that all particulars are, in fact, however hiddenly, identical with pure being ("this, that"). The apparent rejection of the Law of Contradiction may show a dialectical impulse, but, as with Parmenides, the impulse serves the cause of a metaphysical absolute, and, as with Uddālaka, there is no sign of dialectical formalization.

The *Nyāya Sūtras*, 2

The *Nyāya Sūtras*, in which the first extant Indian formalization of logic is found, seem to preserve traces of rules of debate, which may have developed over a long period of time into logical forms. The Naiyāyika syllogism, for example, accomplishes in five steps what Aristotle's syllogism accomplishes in three. The two steps which seem logically unnecessary may preserve conventions of debating practice. The debates, in other words, may have been the matrix in which dialectical and/or logical thought developed in India, between the late Vedic period and the age of both the *Nyāya Sūtras* and the dialectical works of Nāgārjuna, that is, over a period of at least six hundred years.

Many scholars have traced the debate back to the Vedic ritual called *brahmodya*, a ceremony involving an exchange of questions and answers that took place within the greater Vedic sacrifice.[8] Sometimes the *brahmodya* took the form of a catechistic practice, involving rote recitation of questions and responses; the questions are riddle-like and the answers are ritually based—for example:

> Q. Who walketh singly?
> A. The sun.
> Q. Whose light is equal to the sun?
> A. A brahman.
>
> (*ŚB* XIII.5.2.11 ff.)

If such ritualized utterances were the material out of which logical and dialectical forms developed, then at some point the ritual nature of the *brahmodya* must have been radically altered to allow new answers to old questions and even, perhaps, individual free-form input on the part of independent thinkers. More than that, serious schools of thought are assumed which, after long preparation of doctrines, would present them in the "debate" form.

At some point the debate seems to have been secularized in contexts such as public assemblies and courts. The secular debates in turn seem to have influenced the ritual debates, which became more free and investigative. In the *Mahābhārata*, which shows a later period than the Upaniṣads, we read that "as the sacrifice progressed eloquent reasoners put forward many theories based on reasoning (*hetuvāda*) with the intention of defeating each other" (*Aśvamedhaparvan* 86.27).[9] From this context, then, what Śaṅkara was to call *tarka-śāstra*, or theory of reasoning, may have developed. How far the debates progressed, however, in either systematic dialectic or formal logic is unknown. There are examples in the Buddhist Nikāyas of the language employed in debates (*M.* II.243, *S.* III.11 *et al.*), such as: (1) "The text is on my side, there is no text on your side"; (2) "You state later what ought to be stated earlier"; and (3) "You state earlier what ought to be stated later."[10] The first is a nondialectical appeal to scriptural authority. The third may or may not be an accusation of the fallacy of petitio principii, that is, using as a premise the proposition that one intends to prove. There seems to be no formal fallacy corresponding to (2). There is no certain evidence of formal logic or dialectic here.

Sources later than the Nikāyas throw only a faint light on the question. One of the schools that seem to have vied in the debates was the Cārvāka or Lokāyata, the "this world" school, a materialistic doctrine whose principal text, the *Brihaspati Sūtra*, from perhaps the sixth century B.C., is not extant. Lokāyatika teachings are now known principally from encyclopedic compendia of the twelfth century A.D. and later, such as the *Compendium of All Doctrines* (*Sarvadarśana-saṃgraha*). The *Compendium* presents the Lokāyata doctrine as a dialectical system involving the formal structures of dichotomy-and-dilemma and infinite regress. These features cannot, on that basis, however, be read back into the pre-Alexandrian period.

The *Compendium* presents the Lokāyatika dialectic as undermining the practice of inference from universal propositions; and the debate over universals does not apply to the early or middle Upaniṣadic periods, but to the much later *Nyāya Sūtras*. Furthermore, a thousand years before the *Compendium* the school of Nāgārjuna employed the same styles of argumentation. Mādhyamika texts may be the source whence medieval Lokāyatikas derived the dichotomy-and-dilemma method. There is no evidence that suggests that the Lokāyata school of the sixth century B.C. possessed even the most primal forms of the dialectic.

There are, however, certain passages of the *Compendium*'s synopsis of Lokāyatika thought which may go back to the *Brihaspati Sūtra*, that is, to the early Upaniṣadic period. These passages are quoted in verse in the generally prose *Compendium* and contain primitive arguments from analogy formed into implied *modus tollens* proofs. For example:

> If a beast slain in the *Jyotiṣṭoma* rite will itself go to heaven, why then does not the sacrificer forthwith offer his own father?[11]

The argument questions the sincerity of the Vedic priests: If the sacrificer really believed that a beast slain in the rite would go to heaven, then he would sacrifice his own father (if A then B); he does not sacrifice his own father (not B), therefore he does not really believe (therefore not A).

Another example from the *Compendium* questions the efficacy of the rite rather than the sincerity behind it:

> If beings in heaven are gratified by our offering the sacrifice, then why not give food below to gratify those standing on the roof?

If food eaten on earth satisfies beings in heaven, then, on the analogy of the above-below relationship, food eaten on the floor should satisfy people on the roof—which manifestly it does not.

In these two examples the possible *modus tollens* structure is only implied, not spelled out; but the arguments are so parallel in formulation as to suggest a rudimentarily formalized practice. Still, they provide no evidence about the development of the dichotomy-and-dilemma and infinite regress arguments; they have more bearing on the rudimentary stages of the syllogism.

Another text which enters into the discussion is *The Refutation of All Theories About Reality* (*Tattvopaplavasiṁha*), attributed to one Jayarāśi Bhaṭṭa. This is the only surviving Lokāyata text, a work of about the seventh century A.D. It employs a systematic dialectic, but subject to the same chronology as the *Compendium*, because it argues against universal propositions and the legitimacy of inferences from them. The discussion of inference is introduced with the question "What is inference?" and this is answered by an immediate quote from the *Nyāya Sūtras*. The fact that the *Refutation* is directed against the Naiyāyika school renders it irrelevant for reconstructing a pre-Greek system of formal dialectic in India.

The Pali Suttas of Buddhism are texts which seem pre- Naiyāyika (though they were not written down till the last century B.C.), and they shed a dim and scattered light on the protodialectical period. The *Samyutta Nikāya* (II.77) and the *Aṅguttara Nikāya* (IV.428) ascribe the following doctrines to Lokāyatikas:

1. Everything exists.
2. Nothing exists.
3. Everything is a unity.
4. Everything is a plurality.[12]

One scholar proposes that these dichotomies represent opposing Lokāyata schools, a "pluralist school of metaphysical materialists" and a "nihilist school of pragmatic materialists."[13] They may, on the other hand, represent a protodialectical rejection of prominent metaphysical positions and the principle of contradiction. But all that can be said with certainty is that the elementary dichotomy structure is being used for some purpose here, as it was in *Ṛg Veda* X.129, in the early Upaniṣadic thought of Yājñavalkya and Uddālaka, and elsewhere in early Indian thought.

The *Brahmajāla Sutta* (*D.* I.12–38) lists several types or schools of Skeptics. They fall into a variety of groups which are difficult to sort out, but, discounting differences in emphases, they shared certain protodialectical insights and principles. The medieval Jain author Śīlāṅka tells us, for example, that early Skeptics emphasized subjectivity and regarded philosophy as a therapeutic activity, arguing that becoming entangled in argumentation or in mistaking subjectivity for objectivity conduces to unease of mind and anxiety, and that the Skeptic adopts the skeptical attitude to avoid this unease.

The most famous of the early Indian Skeptics was Sañjaya Belaṭṭhiputta, who has been called "the Pyrrho of India."[14] He seems to have been an older contemporary of both Siddhārtha and Nigaṇṭha Nāttaputta—that is of the Buddha and Mahāvīra—and an important influence on the formation of both Buddhism and Jainism.[15] If the Nikāyas' account of the doctrines of the "eel-wrigglers" (*D.* I.24–25) is properly attributed to the school of Sañjaya, then he is described as teaching: (1) that one can never know how one's own fears, hopes, prejudices, and so on have shaped one's opinions—better, then, not to trust in opinions; (2) that holding an opinion leads to passionate involvements—either of grasping or aversion—that will destroy peace of mind; (3) that holding an opinion is just asking for an argument, and arguments also destroy peace of mind.

Sañjaya and other early Skeptics may have employed a fourfold formulation in the pattern:

1. It is.
2. It is not.
3. It both is and is not.
4. It neither is nor is not.

This fourfold formula was to be important in different stages of Buddhist thought, and it may have entered Buddhism from Sañjaya or another Skeptic source.[16] The fourfold negation as employed by Sañjaya and, probably, other early Skeptics, may express the protodialectical belief that the conflict of opinions invalidates them all. This radical skepticism is balanced in Jainism by a relativist belief that each of a variety of alternative views may be true in a partial sense.

The central carrier of this relativistic attitude is the Jain doctrine known as the *syādvāda* or the "in-a-sense doctrine." It offers a list of seven propositions, generally seeming to contradict each other, all of which are to be applied to any entity simultaneously in order to get a rounded view of it. The seven propositions are:

1. In a sense it is.
2. In a sense it is not.
3. In a sense it both is and is not.
4. In a sense it is indeterminate (or unpredicable).
5. In a sense it both is and is unpredicable.
6. In a sense it both is not and is unpredicable.
7. In a sense it both is and is not, and is unpredicable.

Attempts have been made to relate this to the fourfold formula found in the teachings of the Skeptics and the Buddhists. Clearly there are formal resemblances; the first four propositions in the Jain list seem more or less equivalent to the fourfold formula. But there are functional differences even stronger than the formal resemblances. The seven Jain propositions are understood as all simultaneously true of the same entity when viewed from different points of view or in different aspects. The idea is illustrated by the Jain parable of the six blind men touching different parts of an elephant, each mistaking his part for the whole.

The fourfold formulation, on the other hand, does not seem to have been relativistic, though it may have had a variety of different uses. Sañjaya's intentions are not clearly known, but the formula may have functioned for him as a fourfold negation; in some cases at least, he denied that any of the four propositions applies, in contrast to the Jain view that all of their list of seven apply. Siddhārtha made a mixed use of the formula. Usually he seems to have regarded the four propositions as a set of logical alternatives, one of which had to be true in any case, the other three false. They are not, in other words, in the context of the Buddhist Nikāyas, dialectical. The third proposition, understood in this way, is not meant to assert a contradiction, nor is the fourth meant to breach the Law of the Excluded Middle. Rather, the third shows the influence of the relativistic thinking of the Jains and means that the entity in question in one sense is and in another sense is not—for example, it is A but it is not B. To achieve this reading, one must interpret the second proposition not as the contradictory of the first but as its contrary, that is, its direct opposite. The fourth, then, recognizes a state in between the two opposites, a state which the Law of the Excluded Middle would disallow if the second were the contradictory rather than the contrary of the first. The four alternatives about happiness illustrate this interpretation; in terms of any human being at any moment, one of them must be true and the others false:

1. The soul is exclusively happy.
2. The soul is exclusively unhappy (not not-happy, the contradictory, but positively unhappy, the contrary or opposite).
3. The soul has mixed feelings of happiness (about some things or in some respects) and unhappiness (about other things or in other respects).
4. The soul is neither happy nor unhappy but in a neutral hedonic state.[17]

In the case of a handful of metaphysical questions about the absolute and the afterlife, on the other hand, Siddhārtha seems to have followed Sañjaya's practice of denying all four alternatives. It is this which constituted his "noble silence," which has been invoked as the source or seed-form of the Buddhist dialectic. At a later stage of Buddhist thought, Nāgārjuna universalized Siddhārtha's application of the fourfold negation, applying it equally to all questions; in doing so, he may have restored Sañjaya's practice, but this is not really known.

Finally, very little is known about the early history of the fourfold formula in India. The attribution of it to Sañjaya or other Skeptics called "eel-wrigglers" depends on passages in the Buddhist canon which do not necessarily predate the third century B.C. It may be that the Buddhist texts are not quoting the Skeptics but formulating skeptical attitudes in their own, Buddhist way. The later sources, such as Śīlāṅka, which similarly seem to ascribe the formula to early Skeptics exhibit the same ambiguity: The words of the Skeptics cannot be authoritatively separated from the later matrix of expression in which they are found. It is, in other words, not certain that the fourfold formulation was pre-Alexandrian in India, though it seems likely, at the least, that materials from which it could have been developed—such as the Lokāyatika antinomies and the Jain sevenfold formulation—were that early.

Other skeptical motifs of the early Buddhist literature may have fed into the Mādhyamika school along with the fourfold negation. In the *Sutta Nipāta* are found exhortations to abstention from opinion, conceptualization, behavioral rules, and value judgments. He who acts rightly is described as "not like those who are entranced by the passion of their views" (*SN* 891d).

> He does not take sides among those who uphold the various assumptions . . . Giving up assumptions, unattached he builds no reliance on knowledge itself . . . he does not rely on any views whatever. (800)
>
> Gone beyond all limits, he does not delight in passion nor does he delight in dispassion. (795)[18]

Clearly the protodialectical attitude has been crystallized here. The Buddha of the *Sutta Nipāta* seems influenced by Sañjayan Skepticism in general.[19] Still, one does not find in the *Sutta Nipāta* any trace of formal dialectical argumentation yet. Alongside the influence of Sañjayan Skepticism it exhibits a relativistic tendency which may be derived from Jain influence; the *Udāna*, in fact, has adopted the Jain parable of the blind men and the elephant.

In addition to protodialectical skepticism and relativism, a phenomenalism arose in the early Buddhist period which attempted to turn attention from inherited lore about reality to the direct evidence of experience. It appears conspicuously in the *Sutta Nipāta*, where we read: "There are not many and various permanent truths in the world apart from conscious experience" (*SN* 886). It is featured as a shorthand for the whole Buddhist teaching in the *Sabbasutta*, where Siddhārtha, being asked about "everything," said:

> Monks, I will teach you "everything." Listen to it. What, monks, is "everything"? Eye and color, ear and sound, nose and odor, tongue and taste, body and tangibles, mind and concepts . . . Monks, he who would say: "I will reject this *everything* and proclaim another *everything*," he may certainly have a theory (of his own). But when questioned, he would not be able to answer and would, moreover, be subject to vexation. Why? Because it would not be within the range of experience.[20]

In this passage Siddhārtha expresses the eudaimonistic view of skepticism attributed to a number of early Skeptics: that to hold unprovable or untestable views about reality is a source of vexation.

The *Dīghanakha Sutta* (*M.* I.498) preserves a conversation between the Buddha and a representative of some Skeptical school. The Buddha deals with three positions which were evidently held by some thinkers or other:

1. I agree with every view.
2. I agree with no view.
3. I agree with some views and disagree with others.

There is an obvious similarity among all these lists of propositions. "I agree with all views," for example, recalls the Lokāyatika position "Everything exists" and is substantially the same as Jain relativism. "I agree with no view" recalls the Lokāyatika "Nothing exists" and is the position of Siddhārtha's interlocutor, Dīghanakha. Siddhārtha, testing Dīghanakha's position, asks: "Do you agree with the view that you hold, namely that you disagree with every view?" And Dīghanakha replies, "Even if I agree with this view, it is all the same" (*M.* I.397). He refuses, in other words, to entertain his nihilism as a passionate position, since it is intended as a rejection of both passionate adherence and denial.

Certain debaters called "hairsplitters" in the Buddhist texts are said to "go about shattering with their intelligence the theories (of others)" (*M.* I.176, II.122, 123).[21] Very little is known of the types of arguments they used, but one scholar has argued that, in effect, they employed the dichotomy-and-dilemma structure. This view is based on three Sutta passages. In the first (from the *Cūḷahatthipadopamasutta* [*M.* I.176, repeated II.122]), these debaters are said to proceed so that "if they questioned thus and he [Siddhārtha] answers thus, we shall join issue with him thus, and if questioned thus he answers thus we shall join issue with him thus."[22] This could be a reference to a partial enumeration of a series of propositions and their refutations; the problem with thinking of it as a description of the dichotomy-and-dilemma method is that the text implies two questions, each answered once, rather than one question with a double (either/or) answer. In addition, two passages from the Suttas have been proposed as examples of dilemmas. In the first (*Abhayarājakumāra Sutta*, *M.* I.392–393) the interlocutor, King Abhaya, involves Siddhārtha in a dilemma: Either the Buddha will make statements that are unpleasant to others or he will not; if he does, he is no different from ordinary people (as he claims to be); if he does not, then presumably he has not said that Devadatta is doomed to hell (which he is known to have said). A problem is that this apparent dichotomy-and-dilemma form has been recovered from a passage of unsystematic conversation in the text. The difference between the text as it stands and this abstracted structure is so great that even the scholar who argues for the dilemma here says, "There is no reason to suppose that the person who framed this question was aware of the logical form of the arguments."[23] It should be noted also that the limbs of the dilemma are voided not through formal procedures but through empirical means, the invocation of the audience's memory of past claims made by Siddhārtha. The second example (*S.* IV.323 ff.) is even less formal than the first. Only half of a possible dilemma is present, and the scholar in question notes that "it is only the fact that it is called a dilemma" (*ubhatokoṭikaṃ*, two-pronged question) "that justifies our reconstruction of it."[24] But it should be noted in this case that the word used here for "two-pronged question" is not the same word meaning "dilemma" in later Indian logical manuals, and may have meant something else.

It is, finally, possible that the "hairsplitters," in the age of the Pali Suttas, were marginally working out a dichotomy-and-dilemma form of debating in which the limbs of the dilemma are voided by empirical methods; but it can hardly be regarded as established or as occupying an important position in the tradition as it is presently known.

The Pali Suttas, then, do not themselves exhibit either dialectical or logical formalization, nor do they reflect the existence of such formalization in other groups with whom the Buddha debated. In the age following the canonization of the Suttas, however, the age in which the *abhidharma* texts were developed, such formalization has been claimed. (It is doubtful that the *abhidharma* formalization preceded the Alexandrian Greek entry into India, but as it is possible the topic will be treated here.)

Warder, in introducing another scholar's book on the development of the *abhidharma* out of the *Nikāyas*, states that "the dialogues attributed to the Buddha himself [in the Suttas] are full of arguments, partly informal and conversational but partly set out in a systematic way embodying logical principles," and, more emphatically, "in the subsequent period of the growth of the Abhidhamma in the various schools we find a new stage of strictly formalized arguments and debates, recorded especially in the Pali *Kathāvattu* and the Chinese translation of the . . . *Vijñānakāya*." He adds a reference to the idea that the "method called *abhidhamma* is itself the early logic of the Buddhists."[25] In discussing the two crucial texts, *Kathāvattu* and *Vijñānakāya*, he says, "Here a truly 'formal logic' is first found in the Buddhist tradition . . . [it] appears to confirm the 3rd century B.C. as the period of the origin of a formal logic out of the practice of a formal debate with strict rules of procedure."[26]

Under close analysis of the text does not seem to live up to this optimistic introduction. The author attributes to the Nikāyas "certain embryonic anticipations of formal logical procedures."[27] In illustration he cites the possible dichotomy-and-dilemma form (from the *Cūlahatthipadopamasutta* [*M*. I.176]) quoted above.[28] In treating the *abhidharma* itself there is even less result. A certain formalization of doctrines from the *Nikāyas* is represented by the *abhidharmic* practices of "classifying *dhammas* into different types . . . [and] arranging *dhammas* in numerical order."[29] But in fact, it appears that the classification and listing of *dhammas* is not made on logical principles but on perceptions of psychological processes, such as the listing of the five *skandhas*. That such *mātikās*, or lists, may have existed in the period of the *Nikāyas* does not really relate to the issues of logic and dialectic, but to the development of Buddhist psychology. While there is, as there was in *Ṛg Veda* X.129, a certain attention to contraries and contradictories,[30] these relationships (found useful for listing by the primitive Pythagoreans in Greece, too) are not developed into constructions for argument, such as the syllogism. The Suttas, for example, distinguish the contraries *sukha*, happiness, and *duḥkha*, unhappiness, and the neutral term *adukkhamasukha*, neither happy nor unhappy. One Sutta text states, in effect, "Whenever one feels item (1), one feels neither item (2) nor item (3). Whenever one feels item (2), one feels neither item (1) nor item (3). Whenever one feels item (3), one feels neither item (1) nor item (2)."[31] Logical relationships between categories are being explored, in elementary set theory; but that is a far more primitive stage than the systematization of either dialectical or logical argumentation. The authors in question are working out the forms of propositions, not yet devising structures of argumentation that involve relationships among propositions.

Finally, the forms of argument known to have been prominent in the pre-Alexandrian period of India are (1) appeals to scriptures, (2) appeals to experience, (3) arguments from analogy which range from fanciful etymologies to primitive *modus tollens* refutations. There is no sign of the formalized logic of the *Nyāya Sūtras* or of the dialectical reductions by logical contradiction, circularity, and infinite regress which were to be basic to Nāgārjuna in the post-Alexandrian period. The conclusion holds that there are no clear signs of the systematic dialectic in what is known about pre-Alexandrian India, but primarily of a protodialectical attitude.

Greek Dialectic in the Early Period—Briefly

Negative thinking developed in Greece from about 500 B.C. on, in two different directions which Plato described as a battle between Gods and Giants (*Soph.* 246). By "Gods" he meant Parmenides, Pythagoras, and others who laid the foundations of the western metaphysics of essence. By "Giants" he meant Democritus, Protagoras, and the Sophists, who began the tradition of critical and skeptical thought. Both these movements utilized dialectical forms. But their negative formulations served different purposes. Sometimes they were absolutistic and metaphysical in intent, sometimes critical and deconstructive. The formalization of dialectic was a project that overlapped this distinction. It had taken place more or less completely not only before Alexander the Great's colonization of northwest India but in fact before Plato's day. (It will be spelled out in more detail in the next chapter.)

Parmenides' primal argument for Being employed dichotomy-and-dilemma form to disprove the ideas of motion and change and to prove, by tacit appeal to the Law of the Excluded Middle, the idea of changeless being. Parmenides' disproof of motion left reality as a static absolute and reduced everyday human experience to illusion. It uttered with a precise formal framework what Uddālaka and Yājñavalkya had uttered with less formal awareness, but probably earlier, in India. Parmenides began by dichotomizing the basic issue of Being, then converted the dichotomy into a dilemma by disproving each limb in turn. Logic has proved, contrary to the senses, that reality is static and unchanging.

Parmenides was among Plato's "Gods" or constructive metaphysicians. He used disproof to prove the counterthesis. By disproving motion he posited a hyperexperiential reality of unchanging Being. His student Zeno provided substructures for the disproof of the two links of the dichotomy, especially the technique of infinite regress featured in his arguments called Paradoxes. Like Parmenides, he exercised dialectical negation to metaphysical or absolutist ends. This use of negative thinking in the service of metaphysical absolutism produced a counterthesis in the skeptical negations of the "Giants."

About 445 B.C., roughly twenty years after the writing of Parmenides' book *On Nature, or On Being*, a reply appeared in the poem *On Nature, or On Non-Being*, by Gorgias of Leontini. This book is the earliest extant example of a total dialectic—one which reduces to absurdity the central questions of ontology, epistemology, and semantics, without implying the establishment of a positive counterthesis. It is a rigorously patterned tour de force of dichotomy-and-dilemma units generating one another until they are terminated by an impasse of infinite regress or contradiction.

By the time of the sophistic movement the formalization of the critique of philosophy had become a major preoccupation of Greek philosophers. Protagoras, Euthydemus, and other "giants" made contributions that will be discussed later.

It was Plato—or Socrates as depicted by Plato—who made the term "dialectic" prominent. At different periods of his life he used it for different purposes, at times metaphysical and absolutist, at times critical and skeptical. His demonstrations of virtuosity with dialectical patterns are among the most advanced displays of formal thought before the nineteenth-century mathematics of the infinite.

From Plato's time until the second century A.D. (the probable century of both Sextus Empiricus and Nāgārjuna) both streams of Greek dialectic were in full flow, the absolutist tradition extending from Plato to Plotinus and the critical-skeptical line extending from Socrates to Sextus Empiricus. In the period before Alexander's invasion of India, the students of Socrates, of whom three in addition to Plato founded philosophical lineages, are the central figures in the continuing development of negative thinking. They were all aggressively involved with the systematization of methodical doubt through the formal properties of the dialectic, which became increasingly honed and elaborated. This tradition of negative arguments survived longest in the Pyrrhonist lineage, which extended from Pyrrhon of Elis (born c. 370 B.C.), who went to India with Alexander, to Sextus Empiricus in the second century A.D.; the Pyrrhonist tradition is the key body of evidence for the relationship between Greek and Indian dialectic.

With Pyrrhon of Elis's trip to India the pre-Alexandrian period ends. In that period Indian and Greek thinkers had developed similar dialectical attitudes. But only in Greece, it seems, had these attitudes equipped themselves with formal methods in this period. After Alexander's colonization of northwest India a five-hundred-year-long period of Greek and Indian cultural intermixing took place. Toward the end of this period, the array of Greek dialectical forms turns up in India, mature, complete, and without evidence of developmental stages, in the school of Buddhist thought called Mādhyamika.

Notes to Chapter Fifteen

1. Sometimes these principles are stated in two parts: the Law of Identity (A equals A) and the Law of Double Negation (A does not equal not-A). In this case there are not three but four Laws of Thought.

2. The foregoing paragraphs explain the way I will use these terms, which is not necessarily the way ancient philosophers used them. "Stoic dialectic," for example, according to a modern scholar, ". . . contains an epistemology . . . a theory of arguments, in particular syllogisms . . . and a treatment of fallacies . . ." (Michael Frede, "Principles of Stoic Grammar," in *Essays in Ancient Philosophy* [Minneapolis: University of Minnesota Press, 1987], p. 315.) So the formal opposition which I posit between the dialectic and the syllogism did not obtain for them. Still, on the level of content it may hold true. As the same author says, "for Zeno the main function of dialectic was avoiding and dissolving fallacies" (ibid., p. 327), implying a general agreement with my use of "logic" to indicate the construction of meanings and "dialectic" to indicate their deconstruction.

3. George Erdosy, "The Prelude of Urbanization: Ethnicity and the Rise of Late Vedic Chiefdoms," in F. R. Allchin, ed., *The Archeology of Early Historic South Asia: The Emergence of Cities and States* (Cambridge: Cambridge University Press, 1995), pp. 81, 78.

4. Benimadhab Barua, *A History of Pre-Buddhistic Indian Philosophy* (Delhi: Motilal Banarsidass, 1981), p. 12.

5. Trans. Franklin Edgerton, *The Beginnings of Indian Philosophy* (Cambridge, Massachusetts: Harvard University Press, 1970), p. 74, slightly altered.

6. Arthur B. Keith, *The Religion and Philosophy of the Veda and Upaniṣads*, Harvard Oriental Series 31 and 32 (Cambridge, Massachusetts: Harvard University Press, 1925), p. 483.

7. Hajime Nakamura, *A History of Early Vedānta Philosophy* (Delhi: Motilal Banarsidass, 1989), p. 274.

8. For example , Keith, *The Religion and Philosophy of the Veda and Upaniṣads*, pp. 344–345; Maurice Bloomfield, *The Religion of the Veda: The Ancient Religion of India (From Ṛg-Veda to Upaniṣads)* (New York: AMS Press, 1969), pp. 216 ff.

9. Quoted by K. N. Jayatilleke, *Early Buddhist Theory of Knowledge* (London: George Allen and Unwin, 1963), p. 45.

10. Ibid., p. 234.

11. Sarvapalli Radhakrishnan and Charles A. Moore, *A Sourcebook in Indian Philosophy* (Princeton, New Jersey: Princeton University Press, 1957), p. 233.

12. Jayatilleke, *Early Buddhist Theory of Knowledge*, p. 50. The later Buddhist *Laṅkāvatāra Sūtra* gives a longer list of dichotomized propositions about reality that seems to be a development of this one.

13. Ibid., p. 91.

14. Barua, *A History of Pre-Buddhistic Indian Philosophy*, p. 326.

15. Sañjaya has even been proposed (Barua, ibid., pp. 328–332) as the forerunner of Greek, and hence European, skepticisms through influence of later members of his school on Pyrrhon.

16. There is so much uncertainty about a third early formalization, associated with the Skeptics generally and particularly with Sañjaya, which has been analyzed as a five-limbed *relatum* of the four-fold formulation, that I will not specifically discuss it here. See chapter 18, "The Path of the Dialectic." For a detailed discussion, see, e.g., Jayatilleke, *Early Buddhist Theory of Knowledge*, pp. 135–140.

17. See ibid., pp. 341–349, which much of this discussion of the *syādvāda* is indebted to.

18. All quotations from the *Sutta Nipāta* are translated as in Luis O. Gomez, "Proto-Mādhyamika in the Pali Canon," *Philosophy East and West* 26 (1976), pp. 137 ff.

19. See H. Saddhatissa, trans., *The Sutta-Nipāta* (London: Curzon Press, 1985).

20. See D. J. Kalupahana, "A Buddhist Tract on Empiricism," *Philosophy East and West* 19 (1969), pp. 65–67; and *Buddhist Philosophy: A Historical Analysis* (Honolulu: University of Hawaii Press, 1976), p. 158.

21. Jayatilleke, *Early Buddhist Theory of Knowledge*, p. 225.

22. Ibid., p. 226.

23. Ibid., p. 227.

24. Ibid., p. 228.

25. A. K. Warder, "Foreword," in Fumimaro Watanabe, *Philosophy and Its Development in the Nikāyas and Abhidhamma* (Delhi: Motilal Banarsidass, 1983), p. vii.

26. Ibid., p. viii.

27. Watanabe, ibid., p. 6.

28. Ibid., p. 30.

29. Ibid., p. 36.

30. Ibid., p. 49.

31. Ibid., p. 52.

Chapter Sixteen

Early Greek Philosophy and Mādhyamika

The Buddhist school called the Mādhyamika, or Middle Way, arose in either the late second or the early third century A.D. in the works of Nāgārjuna, and survived for over a thousand years as a living tradition of thought in India, Tibet, and China. It was the inheritor and systematizer of the protodialectical thought of Sañjaya, Nataputta, and the authors of the *Sutta Nipāta*. More immediately it is traced back to a group of texts called the Perfect Wisdom (Prajñāpāramitā), which originated around 100 B.C.[1] The Perfect Wisdom texts feature somewhat poetic rejections of the reality of passing phenomena, which are said to be like foam or bubbles or smoke or cloud, "empty, false and fleeting," "like a mock show which deludes the mind," like a lightning flash, a dewdrop, a dream, and so on. Like certain Greek texts, including Timon's summary of the teaching of Pyrrhon, they featured formulaic series of negations. The most famous, the *Heart Sūtra*, says:

> . . . there is neither form, nor feeling, nor perception, nor impulse, nor consciousness, no eye, or ear, or nose, or tongue, or body, or mind, no form, nor sound, nor smell, nor taste, or touchable, nor object of mind . . .[2]

It is worth noting that there are Greek texts that speak in a very similar voice, for example the following (probably Pyrrhonist) statement which is quoted by a commentator on Plato's *Theatetus*:

> No form, no words, no object of taste, or smell, or touch, no other object of perception, has any distinctive character.[3]

Yet the Prajñāparamitā texts, like other pre-Mādhyamika Indian texts expressing skeptical or critical attitudes, do not exhibit the formalization of the dialectic that appears at last only with Nāgārjuna's *Verses on the Middle Way* (*Mūlamadhyamikākarikās*).

Nāgārjuna was an approximate contemporary of both the Pyrrhonist author Sextus Empiricus and the Neoplatonist Plotinus. Virtually no biographical information about him can be recovered. His teaching was called the Middle Way, and the Middle Way is the way between Yes and No—the way that the Law of the Excluded Middle says does not exist. Exponents of the Middle Way did not construct a metaphysics of their own, but were content to criticize the metaphysics of rival schools of thought, along with the assumptions of common sense, down to such fundamental concepts as motion and rest, being and non-being, self and not-self, and so on.

Nāgārjuna's attack on the metaphysics of essence was carried out through the *reductio ad absurdum* applied in the dichotomy-and-dilemma pattern, with liberal use of *regressus ad infinitum*, and a battery of arguments against motion, change, potentiality, and so on, which were familiar to Greek dialecticians during the seven hundred years from Parmenides to Sextus. A comparison of the Mādhyamika dialectic with the accumulated layers of the Greek tradition will yield some probable conclusions about the circumstances in which it arose.

The Motives of the Dialectic

In Greece two motives appear. To Parmenides, Plato, and other metaphysicians—to the Gods, that is, of Plato's dichotomy—the dialectic involved the distinction between conditioned and unconditioned being, that is, between the givens of everyday experience and an unchanging and absolute ground of Being. Specifically, the dialectic was used to destroy belief in the reality of conditioned being so that a mystical intuition of unconditioned being might ensue. Reality was to be sought outside of phenomenal experience, through a dialectical negation of it.

For other Greek philosophers, including Democritus, Protagoras, Gorgias, Antisthenes, Pyrrhon, and Sextus, on the other hand—Plato's Giants and their successors—the purpose of the dialectic was to free the mind from the belief that linguistic concepts correspond to reality and that, therefore, it is possible to frame from them propositions or opinions that will be objectively true. The dialectic was conceived as an antilinguistic or anticonceptual force that would blow away what the Cynics called the smoke or mist of opinions and value judgments and restore attention to phenomena in themselves. In the one case, phenomena are considered unreal; in the other case, conceptualization about phenomena is considered unreal.

For the thinkers of the latter, phenomenalistic tendency, the goal of philosophy was not unlike Wittgenstein's desire to "get the fly out of the flybottle"—the flybottle being essentially linguistic categories. Dialectical criticism was meant to cure the mind of opinions, which, functioning like screens or templates, shape parts of experience to one model while repressing others. The study of counterarguments to one's own opinions was meant, according to Sextus, to lead to a general state of *epochē*, "suspension of belief," which would lead in turn to a state of inner freedom from the domination of linguistic categories (*aphasia*), which in turn will steady into an affective balance (*arrepsia*) which is naturally and effortlessly followed by a state of imperturbability (*ataraxia*) (*OP* I.8, 12, 25–30).[4]

The ethics of both the metaphysical and the critical branches of the Greek tradition involves withdrawal from passionate belief and the development of equanimity. The ethical terminology is mostly negative, designating the states of mind to be avoided, and Democritus seems to have been especially important in developing it. The term *ataraxia*, "inability to be perturbed," is attributed by Stobaeus to Democritus (DK 68A167), and the fragments of Democritus also show the term *athambia*, "inability to be astonished, alarmed, etc." ("Pyrrho apparently," says one scholar, "read Democritus with approval.")[5] The central ethical term for the Cynics and Stoics was *apatheia*, "lack of passionate response [to events that are not in one's control]." The Pyrrhonist terms *aphasia*, "lack of passionate involvement in linguistic category projections," and *arrepsia*, "lack of inclination (as of a balance beam)," express the idea that emotions or passions may be set going by words attached to events rather than directly by events themselves—by *nomos* or convention, in other words, rather than by *physis* or nature.

In India the situation is similar. Some early protodialecticians aimed at eradicating belief in ordinary experience in order to clear the way for transcendental experience of the absolute. This is the meaning behind Yājñavalkya's sayings, *neti neti* and *iti iti*. "Not this, not this" negates all phenomena or experience, which get in the way of the proper practice of philosophy; "this, this," posits the universal presence of an unchanging ground of being, knowledge of which is the goal of the practice of philosophy. On the other hand, some of the protodialecticians referred to in the Pali Suttas held that the purpose of the dialectic was to establish peace of mind. Mental turmoil was understood as arising from the conflict of opinions; the quelling of opinions through dialectical criticism was a path to equanimity.

Recent scholarship has presented two views on the question why Mādhyamika thinkers in particular wanted to clear the mind of concepts and beliefs. These two views are more or less the same as the two motives behind the Greek dialectic and behind the early Indian protodialectic. The absolutist or metaphysical view holds that the so-called double truth of the Mādhyamika consists in a rather Parmenidean or Yājñavalkyan distinction between conditioned and unconditioned being. The dialectic, on this view, negates everyday experience in order to posit the exclusive reality of unconditioned being, and to prepare the mind for its incursion or realization.[6]

A phenomenalist view presented by other scholars holds that the double truth does not distinguish between conditioned and unconditioned being but between conditioned being experienced raw or without conceptual and linguistic overlay and conditioned being experienced through a linguistic "partial truth" or interpretive and evaluative model (*vikalpa*) which is superimposed onto the dynamic and noncategorical character of reality.[7] Both views seem accurate for some Mādhyamikins and not for others.

Dialectic and Logic Again

These two modernist views of Nāgārjuna go back to the dichotomy between the Prasaṇgika and the Svātantrika schools of Mādhyamika, the first represented primarily by Candrakīrti, the second by Bhavaviveka. The Prasaṇgikas emphasized dialectical reductions, the Svātantrikas syllogistic constructions. The two positions are commonly held to be absolutist and phenomenalist. Through much of the Indian period, and especially later in Tibet, Candrakīrti's view of Nāgārjuna as a negative thinker dedicated to the dialectical refutation was much preferred to Bhavaviveka's view of him as one who wished to save the appearances without exaggerating their ontological status. In the Tibetan tradition, which was heavily Prasaṇgika, Bhavaviveka actually became a "butt of ridicule" for his alleged vanity in wanting to show off his logical dexterity at the construction of syllogisms.[8] A part of the issue was formal. Candrakīrti's predecessor Buddhapalita, perhaps one generation before Bhavaviveka, "avoided putting forth formal syllogisms in a dogmatic manner, preferring to use consequential [i.e., reductionist] inferences in a dialectical manner to demonstrate the inherent contradictions in the opponent's position."[9] Bhavaviveka, on the other hand, "elaborated the method of proving the [Mādhyamika] position with positive, private, dogmaticist syllogisms."[10] So the conservative or dogmatist Bhavaviveka seems to have presented his conservatism or dogmatism by switching from dialectic to the syllogism; the critical formulations of Bhuddapalita, however, remained dialectical in form. Despite the equivalency of the dichotomy-and-dilemma reduction and the disjunctive *modus tollens* syllogism, the syllogism retained its cultural iconicity as the constructivist mode of reasoning, dialectic as the deconstructivist.

In the later phase of Mādhyamika the Prasaṇgika or deconstructivist branch clearly won out. Candrakīrti, wholeheartedly following Buddhapalita's example, explicitly argued "the incorrectness of using autonomous syllogisms and the correctness of consequences [*prasaṇga*s, or dialectical reductions] for generating in another the view of the middle way."[11] Specifically, the "consequence" was regarded as the most effective way to undermine the opponent's own view; once that has been accomplished, it may be appropriate to follow up with syllogistic reasoning. The formal difference between these two modes of argumentation, then, acquired an ideological value, as it did in the Greek tradition also, the Megarians, for example, opposing their dialectical reductions to Aristotle's syllogistic proofs, and the later Skeptics maintaining this ideological preference for one mode of argumentation for five centuries after Aristotle's *Prior* and *Posterior Analytics*.[12]

A general procedural parallel follows from this dispute. In both traditions the process of breaking down the opinions of the interlocutor (the job of the dialectic) proceeds through accepting, for the sake of the argument, the assumptions and beliefs of the interlocutor himself. From Socrates to Sextus Empiricus this procedure held in Greece. "One crucial feature of this kind of Socratic argument is that all its premises are supplied by the opponent. Socrates does not have to know their truth, he does not even have to have any view as to their truth . . . Since the skeptic wants to see whether his opponent at least by his own standards or canons has knowledge, he in his arguments adheres to these standards. But this does not mean that he himself is committed to them."[13] In India this same rule or procedure was basic to Mādhyamika practice, where "the technique of the dialectic consisted in drawing out the implications of the view of the opponent on the basis of the principles accepted by himself and thus showing the self-contradictory character of that view."[14] "Our arguments," Candrakīrti said, "can have only the result of repudiating the tenets of our opponents, for us they are not valid in themselves."[15]

Eleatics and Mādyamikas

The parallelism between these traditions in Greece and in India is intimate and thoroughgoing. The cumulative heritage of seven hundred years of Greek dialectic was summed up in handbooks in and before the time of Sextus, and the contents of such a handbook, or their equivalent, may all be found in the Mādhyamika texts. A step-by-step review of this cumulative tradition will find constant echoes in Nāgārjuna and his students.[16]

The Ur-argument of dialectical thought was Parmenides' argument about Being, enunciated in his book *On Nature, or On Being*, of about 475 B.C.[17] It is impossible, Parmenides asserted, for anything to come into Being, because it must either come from Being, in which case it already existed, or from non-Being, which is impossible, since non-Being does not exist. Similarly nothing can pass out of existence, for it must pass either into Being, in which case it still exists, or into non-Being, which is impossible. The dichotomy-and-dilemma structure is clearly and consciously present. The proposition (something comes into Being) is dichotomized into A (it comes from Being) and B (it comes from non-Being), and each limb of the dichotomy is shown to have unwelcome consequences. Since, according to the Law of the Excluded Middle, there is no third alternative in addition to A and not-A, the investigation has reached an impasse. The original proposition (that entities come into and pass out of Being) must be abandoned. Its counterthesis, that Being is unchanging and full, is tacitly established.

Parmenides did not use the dialectical forms here primarily to refute, but to posit by disproving the counterthesis. Since process is denied, the unchanging fullness of Being is regarded as established. So there is something of logic here as well as dialectic. The Law of the Excluded Middle, for example, is accepted at two points in the argument. Parmenides' proof is like dichotomy-and-dilemma, but it is also like a *modus tollens* form of hypothetical syllogism: "If A, then either B or C; neither B nor C; therefore not A." The dichotomy-and-dilemma structure has in effect been used as a disguised *modus tollens*: The dichotomy is the first premise, the dilemma the second. In Parmenides' argument the seeds of both formal dialectic and formal logic may be seen, both rather clearly schematized.

The Upaniṣadic teacher Uddālaka, though he may have intended the same absolutist view of Being that Parmenides intended, did not have the formal elements of Parmenides' argument. In the seventh chapter of Nāgārjuna's *Verses on the Middle Way*, however, Parmenides' argument is found, in an extremely terse Sūtra form: "Does the originating thing exist prior to its origination? If so, its origination is no origination; if not, then it must come from nothing [which is absurd]" (*MK* VII.13, 17, 20). Uddālaka, roughly Parmenides' contemporary, did not have the formalized dialectic, but Nāgārjuna, about seven hundred years after Parmenides, did have it. Where did it come from?

The most characteristic form of reduction in the dilemma section is infinite regress, which seems to have been invented by Zeno of Elea in about 460 B.C. Zeno's use of infinite regress can be demonstrated in the argument called the "Dichotomy": One could never traverse a given finite space, since one would first have to get halfway across it, then halfway across the remaining distance, then halfway across what still remains, and so on *ad infinitum*; there would always be a remaining space to cross, no matter how small. It is characteristic of Zeno that the concept of infinity is approached through infinitesimal smallness rather than infinite size. The "Dichotomy's" disproof of motion from one point to another seems to have been designed to support Parmenides' idea of the unchanging fullness of Being, which leaves no slack or empty space in which things might move. The argument is a *reductio* by infinite regress. It demonstrates that since a continuous space is infinitely divisible, it is as impossible to traverse it as if it were infinitely extensive.

Nāgārjuna similarly used the concept of infinite divisibility to disprove the idea that space can be understood as a continuum. If a continuum is infinitely divisible, a discrete point can never be located on it. Searching for a point, we might divide a section of continuous line into ten thousand parts, but we would then be no closer than when we began, for each part could still be divided ten thousand times more, and so on *ad infinitum*. This is the basis of Zeno's "Dichotomy" and "Achilles" paradoxes, and of Nāgārjuna's statement that motion is impossible because one cannot locate a point where it might begin (*MK* II.14, 15). Nāgārjuna also attacked the concept of origination with an adapted form of the argument against motion: "If origination exists, then it must also have origination: infinite regress follows: origination must have origination, and the origination of origination must have origination also, and so forth" (*MK* VII.18–19). Both

Eleatics and Mādhyamikins, it turns out, rejected motion through continuous space through arguments based on the infinite divisibility of a continuum.

It is questionable, however, whether Nāgārjuna turned his dialectic against the other limb of the dichotomy, the conception of space and time as discontinuous, as made up of discrete and indivisible particles (points in space, moments in time).[18] Zeno, possibly more rigorous in following out the dichotomy-and-dilemma method, attacked the particle view in two of his paradoxes. As Aristotle said of the argument called "the Arrow":

> The flying arrow is at rest. This conclusion follows from the assumption that time is composed of instants; for if this is not granted the conclusion cannot be inferred. (*Phys.* 239b30)

To paraphrase: If at any moment the arrow is only in one place (that is, in a space equal to itself), then the arrow is always at rest; in order to be moving, the arrow would have to be in one place during part of the moment and in another place during another part of the moment; but since the moment has been defined as an indivisible particle of time, there is no such thing as a part of a moment; thus motion is impossible if time is made up of separate moments.[19]

Further, one of Zeno's arguments against plurality in general can be turned against the possibility of motion through discontinuous space or change in discontinuous time specifically.

> If many things exist, then things that exist are infinite; for there are always things between the things that exist, and again other things between them and the things that exist (and so on), and thus the existing things are infinite in number.[20] (DK 29B3)

To paraphrase: If there are two things, they must be separated by something, or they would be not two but one. Hence they are in fact three. But this separator, in order to be nonidentical with the things separated, must itself be separated from them on both sides; the two entities have now become five. By infinite regress of separators the original two multiply to infinity.

This argument can be used (as Zeno was probably aware) to deny motion through discontinuous or particulate space or time. In this case we can avoid the problem of the infinitely divisible continuum and can locate a point; the problem arises when we try to move from this point to the next. For this point, in order to exist as a separate entity, must be separated by something from its neighbors. The infinite regress follows, and we find that in order to move from one point to the next we must traverse an infinite series of intermediary separators. Motion, then, is found to be impossible on the assumption of either continuous or discontinuous space. The same arguments, applied to time, prove the impossibility of change. The overall form of Zeno's argumentation, then, was a large dichotomy-and-dilemma structure containing smaller ones as its limbs: Space-time must be either (1) continuous or (2) discontinuous, and in either case change or motion is proven to be impossible (by smaller dichotomy-and-dilemma units). The arguments yield the following conclusions: If time is continuous there can be no present, and if time is discontinuous there can be only the present (no change); if space is continuous there can be no here, and if space is discontinuous there is only here (no motion).

A second Zenonian argument against the existence of a plurality of indivisible units (that is, against atomism) has a very clear Mādhyamika parallel. To paraphrase Zeno, "If a thing exists, it must have size." ("If it did not have size, then no matter how many such particles we added together, the sum would get no bigger, and no matter how many we took away, no smaller. Therefore the units which are being added or taken away must be nothing; but nothing does not exist. Therefore if a thing exists it must have size" [fr. 2]. "Since it has size, it must have distinguishable parts. [If it has size, it is measurable; if it is measurable, it has beginning and end, hence parts.] If it has parts, it is not an indivisible unit. Infinite regress follows: each of the parts must have parts, and so on" [fr. 1].)

Nāgārjuna's student and colleague, Āryadeva, argues very similarly against Vaiśeṣika atomism: When one atom contacts another, it does not contact it with its entire physical being, for then the sum would be no larger than one of its units (this would be like Zeno's particles without magnitude). It must, therefore, contact its neighbor with only part of itself. Therefore it has parts, and is not an atom (*CS* IX). The same argument is found in Aristotle, who probably got it from some Eleatic source. Atoms, he said, must either "coincide and so not make up a magnitude, or they would be in contact part to part, and so they would be divisible after all."[21]

Another form of this argument is found in a Mādhyamika text, the *Bodhicāryavatāra*, or *Entering the Path of Enlightenment*, of Śantideva, who applies it both to the contact of a sense with its object and to the question of the indivisibility of the atom:

> If there is an interval between the sense and its object, how is there a contact between them? If there is no interval, they are a unity; and how then is there a contact? There is no entering into an atom by an atom; it is equal (to the other atom) and without free space. Without entering there is no mingling, there is no contact. (*BCA* IX.94–95)

If an atom can be entered or penetrated, then it has inside and outside, therefore parts. Āryadeva continues, in the passage referred to just above: Since the atoms are said to move, each must have a front (that aspect of it which is "facing" its destination) and back (that which "faces" the place of departure); but front and back are distinguishable parts, and whatever has them cannot be an atom (*CS* IX).

This type of argument, which first appears in India among the Mādhyamikas, became a *topos* and spread to other schools. It occurs in Śantideva (*BCA* IX.87, 95–96), and is known to the authors of the *Nyāya Sūtras*, who refer to it at *NS* IV.II.23–25. "An atom must be composed of parts," say the *Nyāya Sūtras* (IV.II.24), "because the conjunction of one atom with another is possible . . ." The Naiyāyika Vātsyāyana, in his commentary, the *Nyāyabhāṣya* (c. 300 A.D.), explains: "Whatever . . . can be conjoined with something is invariably composed of parts" (IV.II.25). He proceeds to point out that this leads to an infinite regress: Since the parts are conjoined with one another, they too must have parts, and so on.[22] Vasubandhu, in the *Abhidharmakośa*, also has this argument. He says (commentary on verse 43, chapter 1)[23]: "If the atoms would touch one another in their entirety the [resulting] substances would be simply a lump. If the atoms would touch one another through their segments, they would become composite. But the atoms are [conceived to be] partless." That is: If the atoms touch with their entirety, they must simply become one; if they touch with parts, then they have parts, and are not atoms.

There exist, then, extremely close parallels between the fundamental arguments of the Eleatics and Mādhyamikas against origination, destruction, motion, change, and plurality. It is not exaggerating to say that the two traditions comprise a single discourse on this subject. Still, in a broader sense, there is an important difference between the two schools: One does not find, among the Eleatics in general, a rejection of *all* concepts, as among the Mādhyamikas; on the contrary, the Eleatics seem to destroy plurality and process while espousing unity and stasis. At least, this is the case with Parmenides. Zeno's case is less clear and deserves separate attention.

Zeno has been reproached as an inconsistent dialectician for destroying only one side of the unity-plurality and rest-motion pairs.[24] But Zeno's argumentation, though it may have been aimed, as some have argued, at the atomic unit postulated by the Pythagoreans, works just as effectively against the Parmenidean One.[25] Parmenides clearly intended his One to be extended in space, and if it is extended it must have limits and a middle area in between them—in other words, distinguishable parts—which means that it is not (conceptually) One after all. The ancient commentators Eudemus and Alexander of Aphrodisias remarked on this point, Eudemus saying that Zeno, in arguing against the atom, "does away with the One" (*ap.* Simplicius 99.7) and Alexander that he proves "the One is non-existent" (*ap.* Simplicius 138.3).[26] It is hard to imagine that Zeno himself was not aware of this ramification of his argument. Plato, in the *Parmenides* (128c), represents Zeno not as teaching simply that plurality is absurd, but that it is *more* absurd than unity, which also is absurd, and in the *Phaedrus* (261d) he clearly implies that Zeno would argue both sides of a question without resolving the dilemma, "so that the same things appear to his listeners to be both like and unlike, both one and many, both at rest and in motion."[27]

It is hard, finally, to reject the ancient view (espoused by Aristotle [*ap.* D.L. VIII.57]) that Zeno was the originator of the dialectic—at least of the formal dialectic. He seems to have been the first to attempt a "systematisation of a methodical doubt."[28] As one scholar has said, "Zeno's work did not consist of making additions to the Eleatic metaphysics but of developing new operational methods for dialectic."[29] Specifically, he saw the need to expand the negation by dichotomy-and-dilemma into something like a total dialectic, and added to it the *regressus ad infinitum* as an elegant stylistic flourish.

Murti has proposed the Buddha as the first dialectician, but on rather shaky grounds. He first assigns to primitive Buddhism the tradition of the Buddha's Noble Silence—that is, his refusal to answer certain questions; but there is no evidence as to whether the Noble Silence was a part of primitive Buddhism. He then accepts the traditional Pali date for the Buddha's death—again questionable. The Pali date, 543 B.C., is usually regarded by scholars as too early; the modern scholarly date is 480 B.C., and the traditional Sanskrit date is 371 B.C. The event may have occurred at any time over about two hundred years. And, finally, he asserts, without evidence, that the Noble Silence arose from a clear awareness of "dialectical equipollency" (to use Sextus Empiricus's term). Even if these three suppositions were acceptable, they would still establish only a protodialectical attitude, not the "mathematical" (as it has been called) dialectic which Zeno developed, and that much could be posited of a number of thinkers of the time, including Sañjaya and the Buddha's interlocutor Dīghanakha (quoted above).

In any case, the Eleatic tenderness toward one side of an argument was soon enough rectified, in the book *On Nature, or On Non-Being* by Gorgias of Leontini, which appeared in about 445 B.C., roughly twenty years after Parmenides' book. *On Nature, or On Non-Being*, as the title already shows, used the methods of the Eleatic school to controvert their conclusions. Both Parmenides and his follower Melissus, it seems, had named their books *On Nature, or On Being* and had used the dichotomy-and-dilemma in a one-sided way to establish their thesis of unchanging being. In a display of dialectical virtuosity, Gorgias sets himself to champion non-Being, which Parmenides had banished from discourse.

On Non-Being is the earliest extant example of a total dialectic, an argument which reduces all propositions without exception and offers nothing in their place. It contains an uncompromising dialectical rejection of both Being and non-Being, both One and Many, both stasis and change. The argument is a complex stratified *reductio ad absurdum* which echoes Parmenides and Zeno and anticipates with great clarity the total dialectic of the Mādhyamikas. The dichotomy-and-dilemma method, inherited from Parmenides, against whom Gorgias turns it, is applied with diagrammatic clarity, leaving no doubt that Gorgias was fully conscious of it.

Gorgias's text is structured around three propositions, one ontological, one epistemological, and one semantic. The first, ontological proposition parodies Parmenides' assertion that "Nothing comes into being or goes out of being, but everything Is." Gorgias's counterposition to Parmenides' famous "Everything *is*" is to declare that "*Nothing* is." We may compare the contrary positions attributed to early thinkers of the Lokāyata school, that "Everything exists," and "Nothing exists," though in this case the intentions may have been different.

To summarize Gorgias's book, Hypothesis One: That Nothing Exists. This is defended first by arguments against Being and non-Being, then by arguments against monism and pluralism. Against Being and non-Being: If anything exists it must be either Being or non-Being. It cannot be non-Being, for then it would both be and not-be, which is absurd by contradiction. (Gorgias may be implicitly arguing against the Law of Contradiction; the idea that things both are and are not seems necessary, as Plato remarked, to allow the world to work. It is what Aristotle said in an only slightly disguised form in his doctrine of potentiality.) Nor can it be Being: For if it is Being it must be either created or uncreated. It cannot be uncreated, for then it would have no beginning, and if it has no beginning it is infinite; if it is infinite it is nowhere, for it must be either in something, in which case it is not infinite but bounded, or in itself, which is absurd because the container and the contained are not one. Therefore it is nowhere, and what is nowhere does not exist. Therefore, if Being exists, it cannot be uncreated. But neither can it be created: For if it is created it must be created from something, that is, either from non-Being (which is impossible, as Parmenides had shown), or from Being; but Being cannot be created from itself, for then it would be different from itself and would no longer be Being. (Nāgārjuna has this argument at *MK* I.1.) So Being, which, if it exists, must be either created or uncreated, can be neither, and therefore does not exist. Thus neither Being nor non-Being exists. (This conclusion, though oddly put, amounts to the middle position, between Being and non-Being, of the Mādhyamikas.)

The second section of *On Nature, or On Non-Being* modulates out of ontology into epistemology: If anything does in fact exist, it is argued, it can never be known. In this argument Gorgias abandons the "mathematical" dialectic of the Eleatics to introduce an important Sophistic critique of the five senses and mind (or, as Buddhist psychology has it, the six senses). The senses being different from one another, it is argued, they are separate and isolated and the evidence of one cannot be used to confirm or deny or in any way comprehend the evidence of the others. Each of the senses may be perceiving a different universe. Confirmation and denial of sensory perceptions are impossible, so their status as real or unreal can never be established; they can never be known.

The same critique of the senses, based on declaring their isolation from one another, is found in Śantideva, about a thousand years later:

> If form gives birth [to consciousness], then why does it not hear? Because there is no connection with sound? But then it is not consciousness. (*BCA* IX.63)

The argument aims to "tear apart any sense of connection between the forms of sense perception . . . [They] are without relation and [none] can claim to be a principle of consciousness in and of itself."[30]

Gorgias next moves from epistemology to the critique of language, or of the idea of a language-reality isomorphism, a critique which again is basic to Mādhyamika thought. If anything could be known, Gorgias argues, it still could not be communicated to anyone. Words are sounds; they are not identical with the things they seek to express and therefore have no connection with them. Words express only words. Similarly, "Nāgārjuna denies that . . . words gain their meaning by referring to something outside of the language system . . . Nāgārjuna explicitly denies that his argument, or any statement, has validity because of a supposed ontological basis outside the language system."[31] One scholar, speaking of the Mādhyamika school, says that "[t]he Buddhist thinkers had without realizing it stumbled upon the fact that the terms of ordinary language do not express the real facts of experience . . . The contradictions were attributed not to the defects of verbal expression, but to the nature of the experience."[32] Whether in fact the Mādhyamikas felt that they were criticizing experience rather than language is not at all certain, but the distinction is relevant. Parmenides clearly felt that the problem was in reality itself rather than in language. But Gorgias had already, in the fifth century B.C., conceived the possibility that the problem might reside in language, and had extended the Greek dialectic to language criticism as well as criticism of metaphysics.

The Sophistic Movement and Indian Skepticism

Gorgias is sometimes regarded as an Eleatic philosopher, sometimes as a Sophist. The distinction is equivalent to Plato's distinction between Gods and Giants. Sophist means, in effect, a critical philosopher, rather than a metaphysician, specifically those of the fifth century. That the Sophists are popularly known nowadays primarily for accepting money for their teaching is a distant echo of Plato's class prejudice. His Gods represented aristocratic approaches to philosophy, with their postulation of hierarchical ideal realms in which the highest value attached to the fewest; his Giants represented populist approaches, with their leveling of metaphysical hierarchies through skepticism, which cheapens claims of inherent value; relativism, which makes one person's point of view as valid as another's, regardless of social factors; and phenomenalism, which declares plain experience, accessible to all, to be the sole criterion.

The Sophists were critical thinkers of a somewhat different bent than the Eleatic dialecticians. The Eleatics exhibited the deconstructive impulse—but primarily in the service of a metaphysical absolutism. The Sophists counterposed skeptical, relativistic, and phenomenalistic attitudes to the absolutist dialectic of the Eleatics, as the early Indian Skeptics had done to the absolutist protodialecticians of the Upaniṣads. The Sophists—in this also like the early Indian Skeptics—were interested in providing philosophy with a humanistic and experiential basis. Beginning with Democritus, who forms the bridge between Eleatic absolutism and Sophistic relativism, they sought a philosophy which begins from and deals with human experience rather than ideas of a beyond. It was this element in Socrates that was related to the Sophists—though he also displays, at least in Plato's rendition of his views, strong Eleatic tendencies.

The relationship between Eleatics and Sophists is complex and deep. To the Sophists, Zeno's practice of arguing contradictory positions was inspiring, while his formalistic obsession with dialectical virtuosity smelled of dogmatic transcendentalism—like a conceptual version of Pythagoras's Music of the Spheres. In place of the Eleatic and Pythagorean belief in a higher knowledge that was absolute and that could be approached discursively only through mathematics-like conundra, the Sophists redirected attention to everyday life and to arguments from analogy and experience that deliberately avoided dialectical formalism.

Like Democritus, who exhibited a metaphysical impulse, Gorgias is an ambiguous figure in the Sophistic tradition. His concern with the formalism of Eleatic thinking speaks against his apparent desire to bring philosophy down to earth. That he was at pains to satirize the Eleatic formalism while demonstrating his virtuosity at it suggests the complexity of his situation and the precision of his awareness of it.

By the time of the Sophistic movement (mid- to late fifth century B.C.) the critique of speculative philosophy had become a major preoccupation of Greek thinkers. Protagoras, who was a lawyer and a teacher of courtroom argumentation, taught his students to argue both sides of a case and is reported as saying that "of everything two contradictory accounts can be given" (D.L. IX.51), that "Everything is true" (ibid.), and that refutation is impossible (D.L. IX.53)—in other words, that reality is indeterminate in relation to the concept systems embodied in language. He is said to have written two books called *Contradictory Arguments* in which he argued both sides of various questions and left the antinomies unresolved (D.L. IX.55). His arguments were probably not dialectical in the mathematical or Zenonian sense, but relativistic and inductive. Plato portrays him arguing against the idea that there is an absolute good by collecting examples of relative goods: A food which is good for one animal may be poisonous to another, for example, and so on (*Prot.* 334 a–c). Protagoras seems to have been less concerned with dialectical formalism than with basic attitudinal skepticism—something he had in common with the early Indian Skeptics. His declaration that "Everything is true" should be compared with the position, "I agree with all views," discussed in connection with the *Dīghanakha Sutta*, and its various correlates in the philosophy of its time, such as the Lokāyatika position, "Everything exists."

In both the Sophistic period in Greece and the early Skeptical period in India, the breakdown of tribal structures seems to have led to the multiplication of speculative conceptual systems. The resultant skepticism and relativism were accompanied by a return to the phenomenon as the surest grounding of perception. The subjectivism behind such claims as "Everything is true" was ultimately based on phenomenalism—the idea that personal experience is the only criterion and that all experience is real. In Greece this return to the appearances dawned with Democritus's assertion, "The appearance [or the phenomenon] is truth." Siddartha similarly stated, in the *Sabba Sutta*, that sense knowledge is "everything." Aristippus of Cyrene, a student of Socrates, continued the Democritean line when he said, "Only of the sensations can we be certain" (*ap.* Sextus *AL* I.191). Democritean phenomenalism survived also in Timon's assertion that "the phenomenon prevails on all sides" (fr. 69), and in Sextus Empiricus's assurance that "the affection which takes place in us reveals to us nothing more than itself."

During the Sophistic period, critical philosophy elaborated its apparatus. Euthydemus, a Sophist who is known primarily from Plato's dialogue bearing his name, clarified the same/not-same dichotomy, or denial of partial identity, which underlay, somewhat semiconsciously, Gorgias's critiques of the senses and of language and its objects. Gorgias invoked the dichotomy of sameness/difference when he insisted that any two things must either be identical or different—where different is understood as "unrelated." So the senses are unrelated to one another, language is unrelated to its supposed referents, and so on. The dichotomy means that there is no partial identity, which would breach the Law of the Excluded Middle. Again, it may be presumed that it is the Law of the Excluded Middle, with its presumption of definite stable concepts, each of which has its own essence, that is implicitly being criticized. Euthydemus argues: If Socrates knows something, then he is knowing. If he is knowing, he must know everything; otherwise he would be both knowing and not-knowing (both A and not-A) at the same time (contrary to the Law of Contradiction). In other words, either the subject, Socrates, is completely the same as the predicate, knowing, or it is completely different; there can be no partial identity, no middle position between same and not-same, yes and no. This denial of partial identity (as in a Buddhist argument discussed above) seems to assume that the Law of the Excluded Middle deals with a proposition and its contrary rather than its contradictory. The contrary, to repeat, is the absolute opposite of the positive term; the contradictory is the whole field of reference other than that term. The contrary of knowing everything is not knowing anything, whereas the contradictory of all-knowing would include partial-knowing along with complete unknowing.

That the discourse in the *Euthydemus* expresses the dialectical desire to controvert the laws of logic is shown by Dionysiodorus's triumphant conclusion, "Both and neither!" (anticipating the conclusion of Plato's *Parmenides*). "Both" is a rejection of the Law of Contradiction, which says that something cannot be both A and not-A at the same time, whereas Euthydemus has in one sense shown that Socrates is both knowing and not-knowing at the same time. "Neither" is a refutation of the Law of the Excluded Middle, for in another sense Euthydemus has shown that Socrates is neither (completely) knowing nor (completely) not-knowing, that is, neither A nor not-A. These antilogical conclusions in a sense go back to Zeno, who had demonstrated that either two points in space are one and the same or there can be no traversal from one to the other; that is, either they are identical or there is no connection between them. The argument from denial of partial identity became basic to both the Greek and the Indian dialectical practice. It is the basis, for example, of Nāgārjuna's critique of cause and effect at *MK* I: If they are one, the words are meaningless; if they are separate, there is no connection between them.

Other Fifth-Century Thinkers

Several late–fifth-century thinkers not connected with the sophistic movement, and of whom we know very little, seem to have been impressed by the "dialectical equipollency" which Zeno, Gorgias, and Protagoras had revealed, and by the breakdown of predication after the attacks on the Laws of Thought. The most striking example is the neo-Heraclitean Cratylus (a younger contemporary of Socrates).

Heraclitus had taught that in a realm of becoming or flux nothing can be said to exist in and by itself; since all things are continually flowing and interpenetrating, nothing seems to have an essence, an inner principle as a result of which it is what it is and nothing else. The first Law of Thought, then, the Law of Identity, simply does not apply to the world as Heraclitus described it. On the contrary, what we experience is said, in a striking foreshadowing of the middle position of the Mādhyamikas, to be between Being and non-Being. As Heraclitus put it (fr. 49a): "We both are and are not." (In terms of relative existence we are, in terms of absolute existence we are not; or: At one instant we are A, at the next we are not-A—and the "instants" are not clearly separable.) This point of view is very closely related to the Buddhist doctrines of impermanence (*anicca*) and not-self (or non-essence: *anatta*), and to the doctrines that Nāgārjuna emphasized, dependent origination (*prātitya-sāmutpada*) and emptiness of self-nature (*svabhāva-śūnyata*), which similarly teach that since things rise and pass away in dependence on surrounding conditions in the process of flux, they have no essence (*svabhāva*, "own being" or "self-nature"). It is this quality of dependent origination that Nāgārjuna identifies as "emptiness" (*śūnyata*) (*MK* XXIV.19): "Nothing arises that is not dependently co-arisen; therefore nothing arises which is non-empty." Heraclitus used a closely related term, which appears in post-Nāgārjunan Buddhism, "fullness-emptiness" or "plenum-void," to indicate the reality which both is and is not:

> God is . . . fullness/emptiness. (Fr. 67)
>
> Fullness and emptiness are the same thing. (Fr. 65)

Although not formally a dialectician, and thus not treated at length here, Heraclitus seems clearly to have sensed a dialectical tension underlying reality:

> That which is in opposition is in concert and from things that differ comes the most beautiful harmony. (Fr. 8)
>
> Connections whole/not-whole, agreement/disagreement, consonance/dissonance, and from all things one and from one thing all. (Fr. 10)

In the latter half of the fifth century, after the dialectical movement had added formal method to Heraclitus's intuition, the Heraclitean Cratylus was so impressed with the impossibility of making meaningful statements that he abandoned verbal teaching altogether, evidently thinking that "to utter any statement is to commit oneself to the affirmation that something *is*."[33] According to Aristotle, Cratylus "did not think it right to say anything, but only raised his finger" (*Met.* 1010a10 ff.). One cannot help being reminded of the Buddha of Zen legend, who was so impressed with the impossibility of verbal teaching that he only held up a flower and smiled. The later Greek dialectical schools, especially the Cynics and Pyrrhonists, felt themselves to be based ultimately on the attitude of Heraclitus (supported by the method of Parmenides and Zeno), as the Mādhyamikas felt themselves based on the early Buddhist doctrines of impermanence and not-self. In both cases the antecedent philosophy was one critical of essences. Heraclitus, like Siddartha, recognized a middle position, between A and not-A, that would escape the rigorous closure of an exclusively two-valued logic, which the dichotomy-and-dilemma method shows to be inadequate.

There were other late–fifth-century teachers involved in the critique of speculative philosophy, but we know next to nothing about them. Xeniades of Corinth, for example, taught "that everything is false, that every impression and opinion is false" (*ap.* Sextus *AL* I.53). One may compare the words of the modern Zen master Seung Sahn: "The moment you open your mouth you are wrong"[34] and, as their distant Indian antecedent, the position, "I disagree with all views," expressed by Dīghanakha. In all of this the meaning of the "noble silence" is seen to be a generalized withdrawal from passionate adherence to verbal formulations.

Plato and Mādhyamika

It was Plato, or Socrates as presented by Plato, who made the term "dialectic" prominent. Dialectic, of course, was a principal concern of Plato, and at different periods of his life he used it for different purposes—at times metaphysical and absolutist, at times critical and skeptical. Because in some later dialogues Plato tried, more or less unsuccessfully, to develop a positive or constructive logic (laying the groundwork for Aristotle's more successful completion of the task), scholars in general have regarded him as more sympathetic to Aristotelian than to Zenonian types of thinking. Yet in all the early dialogues and several of the most prominent middle and late ones (including the *Republic*, the *Theatetus* and the *Parmenides*), Plato used an essentially Eleatic dialectic. This appears primarily in the conversations of Socrates, a highly ambiguous figure who foreshadowed modern linguistic philosophy in his aporetic or unresolved discussions in which knowledge claims and reality models are criticized by close attention to language usage.

In the famous Socratic *elenchus*, or "trial," a central theme of the early dialogues, Socrates attacks the blind spots of his interlocutors' discourses without offering a teaching of his own. This element of Socratic method was an adaptation of the Eleatic *elenchus*, in which all ordinary opinions about reality—such as that change and motion exist—were reduced to absurdity. In applying the *elenchus* Socrates operates only negatively, deducing from the cherished beliefs of the interlocutor contradictory consequences and then proposing no solution. His purpose in this activity is not altogether clear.

For Protagoras, Pyrrhon, and others in the tradition of Democritus, the purpose of the dialectic was probably the attainment of *ataraxia*, or imperturbability, through withdrawing from the war of opinions to a position of suspended judgment and emotional indifference. In the dialogues of his middle period, such as the *Republic*, Plato spells out in unusual detail the other purpose, inherited from Parmenides, of destroying opinions in order to attain to an absolute which is beyond them. The "mere opinions" which are to be destroyed seem to include the constructive metaphysical parts of what is called Platonism, such as the theory of Ideas, on the grounds that they are not *ultimately* real. In their place a supraconceptual knowledge which transcends both sense impressions and mental concepts is to be induced by a kind of staged preparation.

This staged preparation is outlined in books VI and VII of the *Republic*. First the belief in the reality of sense impressions is attacked. Asceticism is prescribed to withdraw one from passionate involvement in sense impressions, and the study of mathematics and astronomy to lift one's mind above sense data to a more abstract and purely formal world. Finally, belief in and attachment to these systems of abstraction must be destroyed also, for "they merely dream about reality but cannot see it with waking eyes because they use mere hypotheses" (*Rep*. 533b). "Hypothesis" here means more or less what *vikalpa* means to Mādhyamika thinkers—a subjective partial truth arising from a process of personality projection through the mediation of linguistic categories. This moment of rejecting the final tools is the mysterious point at which fallible hypothetical opinion, up to and including mathematics, is to be replaced with an infallible unhypothesized knowledge. The transition, Plato's Socrates says, is to be effected by the dialectic.

This is the point at which Plato habitually pulls down the veil or modulates into myth or metaphor. Only a moment before, Glaucon had asked, "Tell me, what is the nature of this dialectic, what are its ways?" And Socrates replied, "You would not be able, dear Glaucon, to follow me further, though on my part there would be no lack of good will" (532e–533a). The veil is coming down—but before it is lowered completely Plato has made, through the character of Socrates, one statement which alone in all the dialogues seems actually to describe how this transition to perfect wisdom is to be effected.

> Then, said I, the dialectical method alone proceeds by its method of *destroying the hypotheses* back to the very beginning, in order to obtain confirmation. It gently pulls and draws upward the eye of the soul that is literally buried in a sort of Philistine filth, using the sciences we have detailed [i.e., mathematics and astronomy] as its assistants in the conversion. "Knowledge," we often called them owing to custom; but they need another name, clearer than opinion but less clear than "knowledge." (533c-d; emphasis added)

The key phrase is "destroying the hypotheses." Socrates has just finished saying that geometry and such, though higher than sense-impressions, are nevertheless merely "hypothetical." Now, at the final stage of education, the dialectic, which for Plato as for Zeno meant primarily the use of *reductio ad absurdum* refutations, will enter and "destroy the hypotheses," going beyond them back to the unhypothesized beginning. That the dialectical method proceeds "back to the beginning" means, in terms of the general tenor of the thought of Plato's middle period, that the mind ascends the great chain of being to the direct vision of what Plato sometimes calls the Good, at other times the One, which is more or less a correlate of Parmenides' unchanging and absolute Being. The mind is drawn, by the negative dialectic, beyond the hypothetical realms of mathematics and astronomy, which it destroys in passing.

Plato expresses this process with the metaphor of the "wisdom eye" or eye of the soul. The wisdom eye, he feels, at the beginning of philosophical practice, is befouled with beliefs in the reality of sense impressions. Nonsensory tools such as Pythagorean mathematics are brought in to break the belief in the sense world. The mind rises in its study through ever "higher," meaning less sense-related, hypotheses, the number of rejected hypotheses—and with each a multitude of sense-related beliefs—continually increasing. This is a progressive cleaning of the wisdom eye. Finally the eye is befouled only by the tools themselves—the highest known hypotheses of Pythagorean mathematics and astronomy. Now one's teacher takes the sword of dialectic—of dichotomy-and-dilemma refutation—and annihilates these tools too. Now the wisdom eye sees, and the light of knowledge, which, like the sun shining on a shuttered window, had always been right there waiting, shines in. The soul knows its own nature, now that it has dialectically negated everything adventitious to it (including the Ideas). This is the outcome of the *elenchus* or "trial," a sort of savage shamanic initiation of the mind.

Most western scholars have had difficulty with this aspect of Plato, whom they prefer to regard as a constructive metaphysician rather than an absolutist dialectician. Various attempts have been made to read this passage of the *Republic* as a description of some method of additive thought. Some emend the text to remove the key phrase "destroying the hypotheses." Other just reject the obvious meaning of the phrase out of hand. One scholar, for example, said: "Certainly the phrase ['destroying the hypotheses'] cannot have its most obvious meaning of 'refuting.' Plato cannot be thinking of proving an hypothesis to be false (although that is what Aristotle meant by the phrase, *EE* 1222b28) for he implies that dialectic destroys all, or at least all relevant hypotheses, and he surely would not think that every hypothesis mooted would by some strange accident turn out to be false, that we should never hit upon a true one."[35]

But the "strange accident" is at the very center of what Plato means. He has repeatedly told us that the ultimate real, which he calls the Good or the One or the unhypothesized source, is beyond words, which is to say that it is beyond the reach of any and all hypotheses—that it is, like the emptiness (*śūnyata*) of Candrakīrti or the *brahman* of Yājñavalkya, devoid of all qualities of which either sense impressions or intellectual conceptions have the ability to tell us. It is no "strange accident" that we should have to reject *all* our hypotheses; it is the inevitable result of Plato's postulation, or his inheritance from Parmenides, of an absolute reality more ultimate than the Ideas.[36] This passage has resonances in Mādhyamika texts.

Compare, for example, Nāgārjuna: "Negation of all views is the path to enlightenment" (*MK* XIII.8), and these encapsulations of the Chinese Three-Treatise (Mādhyamika) school: "Refutation—and refutation only—can lead to ultimate truth";[37] "Refutation of all erroneous views is essential for and indeed identical with the elucidation of right views."[38] Surely it does not stretch the imagination that this is what the author of the *Parmenides* may actually have meant.

It is, finally, the *Parmenides* which is most problematical to the view of Plato as a constructive metaphysician. In that dialogue Plato offers a more massive demonstration of dialectical virtuosity than that of Gorgias (though probably inspired by it), employing the dichotomy-and-dilemma pattern to turn the contraries Being/non-Being, one/not-one, same/not-same against one another. The argument is put into the mouth of Parmenides, suggesting an absolutist purpose behind it, yet it does not, like Parmenides' own argument, neglect to reduce both sides of its dilemma. Its concluding sentence reads:

> Whether the One is or is not, it and the others, in relation both to themselves and to each other, both are and are not, and both appear and do not appear, everything in every possible way.

Plotinus (and some modern commentators)[39] received the *Parmenides* as a demonstration of the semantic collapse that must necessarily attend any attempt to express the absolute. On this view the *Parmenides*, as summed up by its final sentence, is a kind of grandly expanded version of Dionysiodorus's "Both and neither!" which in turn can be seen as very close to what Yājñavalkya meant by his two "great sayings"—"this, that" and "not this, not that." In terms of the western tradition, the *Parmenides* joins Zeno's perception of the negativity of infinity with the negative theology of Plotinus, which was to become a central expressive method of European thinkers from Aquinas to Eckhardt to Heidegger.[40]

Mādhyamika and the Socratic Schools

The Megarian school was founded by Eucleides, a Socratic disciple who was present at the death scene described in the *Phaedo*. It is sometimes called neo-Eleatic for its specialization in dialectical formalism and its founder's supposed belief in the Parmenidean absolute—a belief not always evident in the dialectical elaborations that seem a kind of art for art's sake. This emphasis gave the members of the school, as time passed, first the name Eristics (one might compare "hairsplitters"), then that of Dialecticians.

Eucleides argued against the analogical proofs used by his teacher, Socrates, through applying the denial of partial identity, or same/not-same dichotomy, which he generalized or universalized beyond the particular application made of it by

Euthydemus. Either the things compared, Eucleides argued, are the same, in which case the comparison is unnecessary and tautological, or they are different, in which case the comparison is invalid and misleading (D.L. II.107). By the Law of the Excluded Middle no third alternative, no partial identity, is recognized. Eucleides always attacked the opponent's conclusions without offering a positive doctrine of his own.

Eucleides's student Eubuleides developed a number of paradoxes (the Liar, the Heap, the Electra, the Horned Man) aimed against Aristotelian and Stoic logics, primarily the former. These are mostly rather simple sophisms aimed at forcing the interlocutor to answer both yes and no to the same question, thus breaching the Law of Contradiction. The most famous is the Liar: "If you say that you are lying and tell the truth, you are lying; if you say that you are lying and lie, you are telling the truth." "Here the speaker concedes both that he is lying and that he is not lying."[41] The Electra: Electra knows her brother Orestes, but does not know him when he appears in disguise; hence she is both knowing him and not knowing him. (This critique of the two-valued logic goes back to Euthydemus's paradox about Socrates.) The Horned Man: "If you never lost something you have it still; but you never lost horns, *ergo* you have horns" (D.L. VII.187). The Heap: The Megarian drops one pebble after another and each time asks if it makes a heap; at some point the interlocutor says Yes and the Megarian asks him, since one pebble has made the difference, whether one pebble makes a heap. He must answer both yes and no. The four alternatives of early Buddhism would reply with the third alternative, namely that it both *is* in a sense and *is not* in a sense. Aristotelian two-valued logic is here treated very simplistically as if it could not make such distinctions, when in fact it can. The Stoic logic seems to have been impelled—in part by the dialectical criticisms of the two-valued logic—into seeking three- and four-valued systems. The dialectical critiques aimed specifically at a particular doctrine of another school recall the Indian debate tradition in which one school would devise a very specifically aimed form of question with which to discomfit the representative of another school, such as the dilemma mentioned before devised by "hairsplitters" for Siddartha.

Stilpo, another Megarian teacher, focused his critique on the theory of Ideas. In that theory, the phenomenon is said to be such and such because of its resemblance to an ideal model. But, Stilpo argues, the ideal vegetable is eternal; therefore this carrot is not a vegetable because it was not here a thousand years ago (D.L. II.113). In general, he seems to have focused on the question of the relation between model and representation. He asked whether the Athena Parthenos by Phidias was a god and when the answer was affirmative he asked if, then, a human, such as Phidias, could make a god. When people flocked to see him an acquaintance said, "Stilpo, they stare at you as if you were some strange creature." "No, indeed," said he, "but as if I were a genuine person."

Aristotle tells us that some Megarian or Megarians had argued against potentiality, an argument he rejects with an appeal to common sense.

> There are some who say, as the Megaric school does, that a thing "can" act only when it is acting, and when it is not acting it "cannot" act, e.g., that he who is not building cannot build, but only he who is building, when he is building; and so in all other cases. It is not hard to see the absurdities that attend this view. For it is clear that on this view a man will not be a builder unless he is building (for to be a builder is to be able to build), and so with the other arts . . .

He proceeds to the weightier ramifications of the denial of potentiality, clearly connecting it with the Eleatic school:

> Again, if that which is deprived of potency is incapable, that which is not happening will be incapable of happening . . . Therefore these views do away with both movement and becoming. For that which stands will always stand and that which sits will always sit . . . it is no small thing they are seeking to annihilate. (*Met.* 1046b29)[42]

This Megarian position amounts to a generalized rejection of potentiality and hence of all process and change. We do not know which of the Megarians Aristotle would attribute the argument to, but we do know from various ancient sources of one ancient argument against potentiality, called the Master Argument (*kurieuōn logos*), formulated by the Megarian Diodorus Cronus, a student of Eubuleides, in the second half of the fourth century B.C.[43] The Master Argument sets Aristotle's doctrines of contradiction and potentiality against one another, that is to say, Diodorus Cronus points at Aristotle's championing of a two-valued logic while he inserts a third value in between them in his metaphysics. To paraphrase the Master Argument: Any (meaningful) statement is necessarily either true or not-true. Therefore any statement about the future is already either true or false at the moment it is made. Thus there is no indeterminacy about the future; there is no event which "can" happen but does not; there are only those which "can" happen and do, and those which "cannot" and do not. Thus there is no difference between potentiality and actuality, which is to say, there is no potentiality: "The possible is that which either is or will be"—that is, the possible is the actual.

Some scholars, ancient and modern, have felt that the Master Argument is aimed against free will and means to demonstrate determinism; others that it is aimed against the logical principles or axioms, the Law of Contradiction and the Law of the Excluded Middle.[44] In either case, we can appreciate the quandary Diodorus has left his Peripatetic opponents in: Either they reject potentiality and find themselves in an Eleatic world with no change or process, or they reject the Laws of Contradiction and Excluded Middle and relinquish their constructive propositional logic.

The argument seems designed to reveal inconsistencies in the philosophy of Aristotle, who held both a doctrine of essences, which is the basis of the laws of propositional logic, and a doctrine of potentiality, of a non-essential reality that is between Being and non-Being, and thus is in breach of the Law of the Excluded Middle. The propagator of the Master Argument would seem to be pointing to the fact that a doctrine of potentiality is out of place in a philosophy of essences. It is the doctrine of essences, it seems, which is discredited.

There are two Indian developments which should be compared with the Master Argument. Jain texts quote the following verse on the Ājīvika doctrine of determinism called *niyativāda*: "That which is not to be will not be, nor does that which is to be perish."[45] This Ājīvika doctrine has been interpreted as a response to Uddālaka's statement that there can be no passage between Being and non-Being. Since Being cannot pass out of Being, what will be cannot be otherwise; since non-Being cannot turn into Being, that which will not be cannot be. "So everything, past, present and future is unalterable and fixed."[46]

If the Master Argument is regarded as an attempt to prove determinism, the Ājīvika comparison is appropriate. But if the Master Argument is regarded as an attack on the philosophy of essences and the propositional logic that embodied it, then an argument devised by Nāgārjuna should be compared. In the passage in question, Nāgārjuna is arguing against the substance-attribute relationship. The substance is a moving object; the attribute, its motion. If the mover and the motion both move, then there are two movers, and hence must be two motions (*MK* II.11). An infinite regress follows, though Nāgārjuna does not specifically mention it. If only the mover moves, and not the motion, then there is an unmoving mover, which is absurd by contradiction. Substance and attribute, then, cannot be conceived either together or separately without leading to contradiction. At this point the idea of motion has been disproved, but the argument goes on to become universal in application. When the mover stops moving, either the attribute of motion must continue to exist *by itself*, that is, with no substance in which to inhere (which is absurd by the definition of attribute), or the mover, by stopping, has lost (annihilated) the attribute of motion and can never commence moving again (which is absurd empirically) (*MK* II.20). This argument is generalized to a rejection of all substance-attribute pairs. It is implicitly based on a rejection of potentiality (a "state" intermediary between Being and non-Being where an attribute can "reside" while it is not being "used," and from which it can be recalled into actuality when its substance chooses to use it again). Nāgārjuna's position, that that which is running will always run and that which is standing still will always stand still, is identical with the position Aristotle attributes to the Megarians, that that which is sitting will always sit and that which is standing will always stand.

The Elean-Eretrian school was founded by Phaedo, for whom Plato's story of Socrates' death was named. Philosophically it seems almost a branch of the Megarian school. Its most important representative was Menedemus, who studied first in Plato's Academy then under Stilpo of Megara, finally joining the school of Phaedo at Elis (D.L. II.125–127). He specialized in negative dialectic of the Megarian sort, learned no doubt from Stilpo, and is especially known for applying dichotomy-and-dilemma to the critique of predication. Take for example the sentence, "The giving of gifts is good." If there are two things, then each is separate or different from the other. Goodness and the giving of gifts are two things, hence different, hence the giving of gifts is not good, or, if it is, then it is identical with goodness and nothing else can be called good (D.L. II.134). The same denial of partial identity, applying the Law of the Excluded Middle to the same/not-same dichotomy, is at the basis of Eucleides's rejection of arguments by analogy. Menedemus has added an emphasis to the same half of the same/not-same dichotomy, in pointing out that if one thing is called good, then nothing else can be called good, since that one thing, if it truly *is* the good, is wholly and fully identical with the good and hence exhausts its nature. (Stilpo had argued similarly that an instance exhausts its universal or is one with it: If there is a man in Megara then there is no man in Athens, since the man in Megara, in order to be a man, must be like the Ideal man, who therefore is a Megarian.)

The dichotomy-and-dilemma method, featuring denial of partial identity, was the basic tool of the Socratic schools in their war against the Peripatetic and other more speculative traditions. The technical criticism that the denial of partial identity involves confusing the contrary with the contradictory, leading to its two-valued structure, was not recognized or formulated. By the fourth century, it had become one of the dominant themes of Greek philosophy (it had not by that time yet appeared in India) and acted as a powerful counterbalance to the Academic quest for a pure mathematical logic and the Peripatetic quest for a constructive propositional logic which would tend to support the claims of common sense.

Among the Socratics, it was the Cynics who provide the clearest parallel not only to the methods but also to the motives of the phenomenalist, as opposed to the absolutist, Mādhyamika. Unlike the Eleatics and, probably, Plato and the Megarians, the

Cynics do not seem to have postulated an unconditioned absolute Being over against conditioned relative being: Like Nāgārjuna himself (according to the phenomenalist interpretation), they sought to cease imposing supposed *svabhāva* concepts, concepts of unchanging essence, on the dynamic flow of experience, which in itself, if lived directly and without assumptions, they regarded as freedom. A hypothetical absolute they saw as no better than other superimposed concepts, and they tended to oppose the direct relationship with present experience to the Eleatic-Platonic rejection of phenomena for noumena; for example, when Diogenes heard the Eleatic disproofs of motion, he got up and walked away (D.L. VI.39).

The Cynic lineage is traced back to Antisthenes, who was first a student of Gorgias and later of Socrates, whose ascetic lifestyle and negative *elenchus* he adopted. He may himself have been the teacher of Diogenes, with whom Cynicism may be said to be in full career. Cynicism was, on the one hand, a destructive or negative philosophy which (as Murti says of the Mādhyamika school) was not involved in "imaginatively constructing the real . . . and deluding itself that this is knowledge,"[47] but in stripping away the unreal, in which it would include all verbal expression; and, on the other hand, an austere ethic stressing indifference to phenomena which even some in antiquity recognized as similar to the life of the yogis of India, and a preference for the animal aspect of life over the spiritual. The combination of these qualities made it "the most anti-cultural of the philosophies that Greece and the West have known."[48]

Antisthenes' great contribution to negative thinking was his critique of predication. Like some modern language critics, he regarded only tautologies as demonstrably true statements, or, to put it in terms evidently closer to those used by Antisthenes, the only true statement that can be made about a thing is to name it or, if it has parts, to name its parts. For this doctrine, Aristotle called Antisthenes "simple-minded" and "uneducated" (*Met.* 1024b32 ff. and 1043b23 ff.).

Antisthenes' argument is essentially linguistic; it is an attack on linguistic reification rather than an attack on the status of the phenomena themselves. It corresponds in this sense to the Mādhyamika and to earlier and vaguer Indian antecedents of it such as the rejection of opinions in the *Sutta Nipāta* and the eudaimonizing early Skepticism. Another argument of Antisthenes went to the same effect—the elimination of belief in language as a model of reality—by asserting that it is impossible to speak falsely, since that would be to say what does not exist, and what does not exist cannot be known. The argument is Eleatic in origin, going back to Parmenides himself, who wrote, "You could neither recognize that which is not nor express it" (fr. 1). It also has sophistic roots, in Protagoras's assertion that everything is true. And it should be compared with the first position ("I agree with all views") attributed to an Indian "hairsplitter" in the *Dīghanakha Sutta*.

Parmenides, Plato, and the Megarians seem to have denied the existence or reality of phenomena; Antisthenes, following the insights of Gorgias and Protagoras, did not deny the existence of phenomena but our ability to make meaningful statements about them, such as that they exist or that they do not exist. It was, in other words, language criticism he was engaged in rather than ontology. He criticized language in order to save the phenomena. His belief that the mind distorts and remakes reality through the veil of language is illustrated by his advice to the Athenians that if they run short of horses they should simply vote that asses are horses (D.L. VI.8), as well as by his nominalist criticism of Plato that the forms are only mental constructs which are projected onto a reality which does not and (because of its exclusive immediacy) cannot correspond to them.

> Being asked what learning is the most necessary he [Antisthenes] said, "Stripping away and unlearning." (D.L. VI.7)

The goal of Cynic teaching was "that it should no longer be difficult for the mind to be silent."[49] (Compare Siddartha's stated goal of "quietude of the heart.")[50]

For the Cynics, as for Mādhyamikas, Zen teachers, and others, phenomena could be dealt with legitimately only in a nonverbal and nonconceptual cognition (*phronēsis)* the same word Plato used for "unhypothesized knowledge")[51], which can result only from the ultimate *elenchus* of stripping the mind of all the conceptions with which it ordinarily tries to deal with them. Each phenomenon, in the Cynic view, is either composite or simple; if composite, it can be analyzed into simples—that is, its parts can be named; if simple, then no conception can apply to it, because a conception would add something to it, destroying its simplicity and making it a composite. It can be known, then, only by a correspondingly simple or postconceptual knower, the mind of the philosopher who has cleared away the mist or smoke of opinions.

The rejection of predication was accepted by the Cynics in general and led to the concept of *typhos*. The word literally means "smoke" or "mist"; it describes the blurring effect that preconceived ideas of reality have on the sharp edges of raw experience. By analogy (and most commonly) it meant "illusion" or "error." Sextus Empiricus tells us (*AL* II.5) that the Cynic Monimus, a student of Diogenes, said, *"Panta typhos"* ("All things are like smoke"). According to Menander (*ap.* D.L. VI.83), he said, *"To hypolēphthen pan esti typhos"* ("All opinions are like smoke," or "All opinions are deluded"). We may compare the continually repeated assertions of the Prajñāpāramitā texts, those probable precursors of Mādhyamika dialectic, that all things are like foam, or bubbles, or smoke, or cloud (cf. *typhos*, mist), "empty, false, and fleeting," "like a mock show which deludes the mind," like a lightning flash, a dewdrop, a dream, and so forth.

From the central conception of *typhos* the Cynics developed an ethic which is remarkably like that of the Buddhist schools which are based on the Mādhyamika. The *sophos* (sage or saint) who seeks to escape from illusion through the *askēsis kai machē* (the discipline and struggle) of philosophy, must first practice *autarkeia* (self-rule), the great principle of Diogenes, derived from the example of Socrates, whereby all material and social habits and all beliefs connected with them are nullified through a realization of the emptiness or smokelike nature of opinions. Cynic sages, like Buddhist monks, renounced home and possessions and took to the streets as wanderers and temple beggars. The closely related concepts *apatheia* (nonreaction, noninvolvement) and *adiaphoria* (nondifferentiation) became central to the Cynic discipline. Certain qualities lead to "virtue" (self-rule and freedom from opinions), others do not. Beyond this, no distinctions are to be made.

The Cynic ethical distinction is paralleled very closely in early Buddhism where, as one scholar put it, "One way of deciding whether an action is right or wrong, good or bad, is by finding out whether it leads to detachment (viraga) or attachment (rāga)."[52] Beyond this distinction, for the Cynics, all things are *adiaphora* (nondifferent from one another), and are alike to be treated with *apatheia* (nonreaction), an attitude which stands above pleasure and pain alike (and which seems closely related to Buddhist *upekṣā*). Similarly in early Buddhism, enlightenment is "the ability to remain unmoved when in contact with the external world or when experiencing happiness and suffering."[53] When we add to this the idea of *philanthropia* (universal loving kindness), which was elevated to great prominence by Diogenes' pupil Crates, we have an attitude remarkably like the Mahāyāna Buddhist linkage of *prajñā* (wisdom) and *karuṇā* (love).

The similarity could be extended through many details, of which I select a few. The Cynic typically gave up his possessions and limited himself to one robe, a bowl, and a wallet. One might compare Śantideva's advice:

> With the exception of the three robes of the monk, one ought to sacrifice all. (*BCA* V.87)[54]

The Cynic's poverty and his practice in general are declared to be "for the salvation of everyone" (*10th Epistle of Diogenes*).[55] Similarly, Śantideva advises the aspiring bodhisattva to "act only for the welfare of sentient beings" (*BCA* V.101).[56] The Cynic lifestyle is based on a perception of suffering which is much like the Buddhist concept of *duḥkha*; first, pain is held to be more prominent in life than pleasure; compare Śantideva:

> Indeed, goodness is weak, but the power of evil is always great and very dreadful. (*BCA* I.6)[57]

There is in fact, in the Cynic view, no avoiding suffering, and the attempt to avoid it is regarded as the surest way to increase it; acceptance is the surest way to mitigate it:

> Suffer, so that you may not suffer; by attempting not to suffer, suffering is not avoided—on the contrary, it is even pursued. (*4th Epistle of Crates*)[58]

We may compare Śantideva again:

> . . . and how difficult it is for happiness to be seized, while sorrow exists without effort. And still, escape is only by means of sorrow: Therefore make firm the mind! (*BCA* VI.12)

Happiness, the goal of Cynic practice, is not defined as pleasure, nor as the avoidance of pain (which is not to be hoped for), but consists of a complete independence (*autarkeia*) which is called virtue:

> Happiness is not pleasure, for which we need externals, but virtue, which is complete without any externals. (*3rd Epistle of Crates*)[59]

The independence from externals restores one to his own mind, which is "the only real thing that belongs to man."[60] As a result, says Crates, "having nothing we have everything" (*7th Epistle of Crates*).[61] This virtue which is self-rule which is wisdom consists precisely in "keeping the mind free from empty fancies,"[62] that is, stripping away *typhos* (*vikalpa, prapañca*) so that the mind becomes silent and equanimous.[63] Mankind is divided into the wise and the foolish, the former being freed from *typhos*, the latter enslaved to it.

All this sounds very much like the yogic paths of India, and specifically like the Buddhist attitude toward mind as expressed in the *Sutta Nipāta* and the Mādhyamika treatises. The Cynic Onesicritus, who accompanied Alexander to India and talked with yogis there, compared their teachings with those of Socrates and Diogenes. According to Strabo the yogis had taught him:

> That nothing that happens to a man is bad or good, opinions being merely dreams,

and that:

> the best philosophy [is] that which liberates the mind from [both] pleasure and grief. (Strabo XV.1.65)

The parallel between the Cynic epistemology and that of the Mādhyamika thinkers is very strong. The Mādhyamika thinker, having stripped away all yes-or-no conceptualizations, does not then proceed to construct, in the cleared space, an alternative system of concepts which he declares to be true. He takes his position in the emptiness resulting from his destruction of concepts (what some Buddhist texts call "standing firmly because he stands nowhere") and declares this emptiness to be the real. No positive statement, he says, can be made about it, such as that it is one or many, permanent or impermanent, that it exists or does not exist. It cannot be conceptualized because it is precisely what is left when concepts are erased. It is apprehended in a direct, nonconceptual cognition (*prajñā*) which can only occur after the layers of conceptual belief are stripped from the mind. Philosophy, then, is a purely negative path; through the exercise of reason the philosopher negates each and every view which he finds arising in his mind. This continuing process of negation leads to the birth of *prajñā*. As Nāgārjuna put it: "The negation of all views is the path to enlightenment" (*MK* XIII.8). Philosophy, on this view, is not a container or discoverer or expresser of truth; it is a tool for clearing the mind, then to be put aside.

The most striking parallels occur between Cynicism and the much later Ch'an and Zen traditions, which are ultimately based on the Mādhyamika. Indeed, Cynicism seems almost a foreshadowing of the "sudden school" of Ch'an founded by Hui Neng in the seventh century A.D. Some similarities may be listed briefly.

(1) The short-cut to enlightenment: The Theravādin Buddhist texts say that the Buddha toiled for thousands of lifetimes to become enlightened; Zen of the sudden school aimed to bypass all unnecessary aspects of practice (including, generally, academic study) and achieve enlightenment in this lifetime. Similarly, Cynicism was called the "shortcut to happiness" (*12th Epistle of Diogenes*), "the short road to happiness" (*13th Epistle of Crates*) (understanding by "happiness" not a state of pleasure, but an attitude of equanimity toward the fluctuations of pleasure and pain).

(2) The nonreliance on scriptures: As Zen is said not to rely on scriptures but to proceed directly to enlightenment through life-practice, so Diogenes wrote:

> Avoid discoursing, for the long road to happiness is through discourses, but that through the daily practice of deeds is the short way. (*21st Epistle*)

As in Zen, the emphasis was always on direct practice rather than on study:

> They also dispense with the ordinary subjects of instruction . . . hence it has been said that Cynicism is a short-cut to virtue. (D.L. VI.104)

And Julian the Apostate:

> It [Cynicism] seems to be in some ways a universal philosophy and the most natural, and to demand no special study whatsoever. (*6th Oration* 187)

As one scholar noted, "The Cynics never had any canon or body of authoritative writings similar to those of the Stoics and Epicureans."[64] We may compare this with another scholar's statement that the Mādhyamikas "commit to the flames matters which have no immediate empirical concern."[65]

(3) Emphasis on the present moment and acceptance of it:

> Teles quotes Crates as saying that a man should live contented with present things, not desiring what is not present and not discontented with chance happenings. (Stobaeus *Flor.* I.5.67)

Acceptance of the present moment seems to be the key to "sudden enlightenment" among the Cynics. Teles said:

> We should not try to change things, but should prepare ourselves to meet and endure them. (Stobaeus *Flor.* I.5.67)

Living from moment to moment dissolves goal-oriented activities and thought processes of regret and anticipation, and frees one from enslavement to a hypothetical future; since concepts are "like smoke," so are the various strivings which they bring with them. We may compare the *Heart Sūtra* (37 ff.): "Because he attains nothing, the bodhisattva lives without thought-coverings [without *typhos*]. . . . Through living without thought-coverings . . . he attains to nirvāṇa." As Crates said, "Having nothing, we have everything." Like the Zen practitioner who "eats when he is hungry and sleeps when he is tired," the Cynic seeks to become *hēmerobios* (one who lives from day to day), responding to the present moment rather than to concepts about the past and the future.

(4) Sudden enlightenment: Plutarch attributes to the Stoics a view which is widely regarded as Cynic in origin (and whose meaning the Stoic thinkers compromised somewhat):

> The wise man in a moment of time changes from the lowest possible depravity to an unsurpassable state of virtue . . .
>
> The man who was the very worst in the morning becomes the very best in the evening . . . (*Progress of Virtue*, 75)

This sudden attainment through nonattainment is connected both with the principle of self-rule and with the bypassing of systems and scriptures, and we may compare Hui Neng:

> Since it is with our own efforts that we realize the Essence of Mind, and since the realization and the practice of the Law are both done instantaneously and not gradually or stage by stage, the formulation of any system of law is unnecessary.[66]

If we look into the anecdotal traditions of these two schools we find again an astonishing number of similarities. It is, for our purposes, a matter of indifference whether the anecdotal traditions are historical or fictional; they are hagiography, and the point is that they show a similar conception of what the wise person is and how he passes on his wisdom. In both traditions the following elements are prominent:

(1) An overwhelming emphasis on teaching by example rather than by discourse.
(2) The frequent use of perverse, irrational, and/or violent examples (Diogenes, like a Zen master, striking his students with his staff to produce sudden insights; Diogenes sitting in the theater gluing together the pages of a book [*33rd Epistle of Diogenes*]).
(3) A requirement of total dedication, and of signs of total dedication, from the student.

The story of Diogenes's application to study under Antisthenes bears comparison with the story of Bodhidharma's student cutting his arm off to show his seriousness:

> On reaching Athens he fell in with Antisthenes. Being repulsed by him, because he never welcomed pupils, by sheer persistence Diogenes wore him out. Once when he [Antisthenes] stretched out his staff against him, the pupil offered his head with the words, "Strike, for you will find no wood hard enough to keep me away from you, so long as I think you've something to say." From that time forward he was his pupil. (D.L. VI.21)

(4) The use of shocking and/or enigmatic verbal formulae as teaching devices (for example, Crates again: "Having nothing we have everything").
(5) An emphasis on hardihood, indifference to phenomena, and extreme simplicity or frugality of physical milieu.
(6) A mirthful attitude which often expresses itself as ridicule of convention.
(7) An extreme self-possession, a mental balance impossible to disturb.
(8) A tendency to reject or at least neglect inherited doctrines such as reincarnation and purification, preferring the emptiness of no-doctrine.

Certain Cynic practices, which have been discussed in chapter 9, seem to have derived from Jain or proto-Jain or Jain-related practices. The Cynics were vegetarians and water drinkers who (like the yogis of India) practiced austerities of heat and cold and were conspicuously scornful of bodily death. Diogenes died by stopping his breath; Metrocles choked himself to death; Peregrinus burned himself alive before the assembled multitudes at the Olympic games (in direct imitation of the Indian yogi Calanus). The art of voluntary death through breath control or self-burning is an integral part of Ajīvikism and early Jainism, and the yogis whom Onesicritus met and compared to Cynics are commonly supposed to have been either Jains or Ājīvikas.

The similarity between Cynics and yogis is so striking that Indian influence on Diogenes has been hypothesized by way of the Asian trade routes to the Black Sea. "It is probable that Indian merchants accompanied their goods as far west as Sinope. Merchants and travellers from Babylon and India no doubt required the services of a money changer and this is said to have been the occupation of the father of Diogenes (D.L. VI.20). It is likely that Diogenes had at Sinope an opportunity to gain a considerable amount of information on the customs and ideas of the Indian people."[67]

The idea is attractive and may even be right but there are weak spots in the evidence. At present there is no record of the Black Sea trade with India till the first century B.C., and Indian cargoes are said at that time to have been dispersed not from Sinope, the home of Diogenes, but from nearby Phasis.[68] Most important, it is difficult to agree with the claim that "there were elements of Cynic teaching for which no Greek antecedents are found."[69] *Apatheia* and *adiaphoria* are clear implications of both Parmenidean monism and Democritean atomism; relativism and the rejection of traditional codes are at the heart of the Sophistic movement; we need look no farther than Socrates for an example of extreme hardihood, and the itinerant Orphic preachers show us a class of "holy beggars" who advocated vegetarianism. The Cynic espousal of cannibalism and other acts shocking to the Greek tradition could arise from a combination of Sophistic relativism with Herodotus III.99.[70]

Most scholars have preferred the occasion of Alexander's visit to India in 326 B.C. for the transmission of yogic ideas into the Greek "philosophies of retreat." But most of the features which might be traced back to India had already appeared in Greece before Alexander's expedition. It is certain, for example, that the Antisthenean-Megarian rejection of conceptualization preceded Alexander's visit to India, and thus we can rule out the frequent but careless suggestion that Pyrrhon of Elis, who accompanied Alexander, brought it back with him from there.[71] The doctrine of *apatheia* goes back in the Greek tradition to Speusippus and Democritus. The available evidence suggests that Diogenes was teaching *autarkeia*, or self-rule, as a means of escape from *typhos* (delusion) in Athens by about 340 B.C.[72] But other elements of the Cynic style are less firmly anchored to a pre-Alexandrian personality. Crates, who may have been the first Cynic to teach *philanthropia* (love for all beings rather than just for those to whom one happens to be connected), was post-Alexandrian. The explicit emphasis on inner silence may be post-Alexandrian. But it at least seems clear that the Greek "philosophies of retreat" were underway before the opening of the East by Alexander, and that there is no problem in deriving them from earlier Greek sources—though those earlier Greek sources might connect in turn with Indianized elements of pre-Socratic thought.

This chapter has shown that the methods used by the Mādhyamika dialectic had appeared in Greece five to seven centuries earlier. Pyrrhonism, which the next chapter will discuss, is the key body of evidence for the relationship between the ancient dialectical traditions.

Notes To Chapter Sixteen

1. See Edward Conze, "The Development of Prajñāparamitā Thought," in Conze, *Thirty Years of Buddhist Studies* (London: Bruno Cassirer, 1967), p. 124.

2. Trans. Edward Conze, *The Short Prajñāparamitā Texts* (London: Luzac and Company, 1973), p. 142.

3. Quoted by Phillip H. DeLacy, "*ou mallon* and the Antecedents of Ancient Skepticism," *Phronesis* 3 (1958), p. 71.

4. Sextus will be quoted in the translation of R. G. Bury (*Sextus Empiricus*, 4 vols., Loeb Classical Library [Cambridge, Massachusetts: Harvard University Press and London: W. Heinemann, 1933–1949]) with occasional slight changes which do not depart from literalness. In Bury's system *OP* refers to *Outlines of Pyrrhonism*, *AL* to *Against the Logicians*, *APh* to *Against the Physicists*, *AE* to *Against the Ethicists*, *AP* to *Against the Professors*. The last four titles refer to sections of Sextus's large work *Adversus Mathematicos* (*Against the Experts*). *AL* = *AM* 7–8, *APh* = *AM* 9–10, *AE* = *AM* 11, *AP* = *AM* 1–6.

5. R. J. Hankinson, *The Sceptics* (London and New York: Routledge, 1997), p. 53.

6. This view has been presented by Theodore Stcherbatsky, *The Conception of Buddhist Nirvāṇa*, Indo-Iranian Reprints 6 (The Hague: Mouton, 1965), pp. 46–48; Radhakrishnan, *Indian Philosophy*, vol. 1, pp. 658–659, 662–669; Edward Conze, ed., *D. T. Suzuki On Indian Mahāyāna Buddhism* (New York: Harper and Row, 1968), pp. 109, 236, 270; Edward Conze, *Buddhist Thought in India* (London: George Allen and Unwin, 1962), pp. 239–243; T. R. V. Murti, *The Central Philosophy of Buddhism* (London: George Allen and Unwin, 1955), pp. 121–126. This seemingly Vedānta-influenced view of Nāgārjuna is commonly believed to go back at least to Buddhapalita in the sixth century and Candrakīrti in the seventh; in terms of modern scholarship it was in general the view of that generation of scholars on whom the recent awareness of Advaita Vedānta had impacted powerfully.

7. This view is expressed by Frederick J. Streng, *Emptiness: A Study in Religious Meaning* (Nashville, Tennessee, and New York: Abingdon Press, 1967); "The Significance of Pratītyasamutpāda for Understanding the Relationship Between Saṃvṛti and Paramārthasatya in Nāgārjuna," in *The Problem of Two Truths in Buddhism and Vedānta*, ed. Mervyn Sprung (Dordrecht and Boston: D. Reidel, 1973), pp. 27–39; "The Process of Ultimate Transformation in Nāgārjuna's Mādhyamika," *The Eastern Buddhist* n.s. 11, no. 2 (October 1978), pp. 12–32; Kenneth K. Inada, *Nāgārjuna: A Translation of His Mūlamadhyamikākarikā with an Introductory Essay* (Tokyo: Hokuseido Press, 1970), pp. 9–11, 18, 21–24. Kalupahana's position (*Nāgārjuna: The Philosophy of the Middle Way* [Albany, New York: State University of New York Press, 1986]), though unique in locating the *Madhyamikākarikās* in terms of the *Kaccāyanagotta Sutta*, belongs

generally to this group. "His primary goal," says Kalupahana, "was to reject substantialist or essentialist thought" (p. 81). And: "That Nāgārjuna was rejecting sense experience *in favor of* a special intuition is not at all evident . . ." (p. 82). What Nāgārjuna is after is "perceptions [that result from] . . . the absence of ignorance . . . or confusion . . . created by one's dispositions or inclinations . . ." (ibid). This view, which might be called phenomenalist, goes back to the *svātantrika* interpretation of the commentator Bhavaviveka in about 500 A.D.; in terms of recent scholarship, it arose later than the absolutist, Vedānta-influenced view.

8. Robert A. F. Thurman, *The Central Philosophy of Tibet: A Study and Translation of Jey Tsong Khapa's* Essence of True Eloquence (Princeton, New Jersey: Princeton University Press, 1984), p. 40.

9. Ibid., p. 39.

10. Ibid., p. 40.

11. Jeffrey Hopkins, *Meditation on Emptiness*, revised edition (Boston: Wisdom Publications, 1996), p. 431.

12. This dispute about forms of argument was most explicit in Tibet; Hopkins (ibid., pp. 443–453) summarizes the positions.

13. Michael Frede, *Essays in Ancient Philosophy* (Minneapolis: University of Minnesota Press, 1987), pp. 203–204.

14. Jaideva Singh, "Introduction," in Stcherbatsky, *The Conception of Buddhist Nirvāna* (Delhi: Motilal Banarsidass, 1978), p. 16.

15. Ibid., p. 123.

16. The *Madhyamikākarikās* will be quoted primarily in the translation of Inada (*Nāgārjuna*), the *Vigraha-vyāvartanī* in the translation of Streng (in *Emptiness*, pp. 221–227) or that of Kamaleswar Bhattacharya (*The Dialectical Method of Nāgārjuna* [Delhi: Motilal Banarsidass, 1978]).

17. The *reductio ad absurdum* may have appeared earlier in the work of Pythagorean mathematicians, who used it in their proof of incommensurability. See W. and M. Kneale, *The Development of Logic* (Oxford: Oxford University Press, 1962), p. 8. For the counterargument—that geometers learned it from Eleatic philosophers—see H. D. P. Lee, *Zeno of Elea*, Cambridge Classical Studies 1 (Cambridge: Cambridge University Press, 1936), p. 112; and A. Szabo, "Eleatica," *Acta Antiqua Academiae Scientiarum Hungaricae* 3 (1955): 67–103, and "Wie is die Mathematik zu einer deduktiven Wissenschaft geworden?" ibid., 4 (1956): 109–152. Szabo regards the *reductio ad absurdum* in Eleatic context as the oldest form of logical argument.

18. Mark Siderits and J. Dervin O'Brien ("Zeno and Nāgārjuna on Motion," *Philosophy East and West* 26 [1976]: 281–301) argue that *MK* II.3 is directed either against the view that both space and time are discontinuous or against the view that time is discontinuous and space continuous. Their interpretation seems overly dependent on Brumbaugh's questionable reading of the tetralemma (Robert Brumbaugh, *The Philosophers of Greece* [New York: Thomas Y. Crowell, 1964], pp. 57–67), which, contrary to Siderits and O'Brien, is far from representing a consensus among Hellenists (see, for example, Michael C. Stokes, *One and Many in Presocratic Philosophy* [Cambridge, Massachusetts: Harvard University Press, Center for Hellenic Studies, 1971], pp. 175–217).

19. As the Arrow undermines the idea of particulate time, the idea of particulate space seems to be reduced to absurdity in the argument called the Stadium. But there is less than complete agreement on the purpose of the Stadium. For the view I am using see Lee, *Zeno of Elea*, pp. 83–102. For a contrary view see Stokes, *One and Many in Presocratic Philosophy*, pp. 184 ff.

20. Trans. Stokes, ibid., p. 202.

21. David J. Furley, *Two Studies in the Greek Atomists* (Princeton, New Jersey: Princeton University Press, 1967), p. 128.

22. The text is given in English translation in Mrinalkanti Gangopadhyaya, *Indian Atomism: History and Sources* (Atlantic Highlands, New Jersey: Humanities Press, 1980); this passage is at pp. 139–141.

23. The text is given in English translation, ibid., p. 85.

24. By Murti, *The Central Philosophy of Buddhism*, p. 178.

25. The idea of Pythagorean atomism has been attacked (see especially Furley, *Two Studies in the Greek Atomists*, pp. 44 ff.); it should be noted that this view of Zeno's motive is not necessary to my analysis of Mādhyamika parallels.

26. Lee (*Zeno of Elea*, p. 26) argues that this is not Zeno's intention; but the fact seems as Simplicius and Alexander stated it, whatever the intention. Vlastos argues that Zeno was in fact pointing to the need to change from Parmenides' corporeal one to an incorporeal one, as his contemporary Melissus tried to do (Gregory Vlastos, "Zeno of Elea," *The Encyclopedia of Philosophy*, vol. 8, ed. Paul Edwards [New York: Macmillan, 1967], p. 377).

27. But Diogenes Laertius says that Protagoras was the first to argue both sides of a question and leave the antinomy unresolved (D.L. IX.51).

28. Theodorus G. Sinnige, *Matter and Infinity in the Presocratic Schools and Plato*, Philosophical Texts and Studies 17 (Assen: van Gorcum, 1971), p. 95.

29. Ibid., p. 109.

30. Marion L. Matics, *Entering the Path of Enlightenment* (New York: Macmillan, 1970), p. 133.

31. Streng, *Emptiness*, pp. 141, 143.

32. Edward J. Thomas, *The History of Buddhist Thought*, 2nd ed. (New York: Barnes and Noble, 1951), p. 218.

33. W. K. C. Guthrie, *A History of Greek Philosophy*, vol. 3 (Cambridge: Cambridge University Press, 1962–1981), p. 201.

34. Stephen Mitchell, ed., *Dropping Ashes on the Buddha: The Teachings of Zen Master Seung Sahn* (New York: Grove Press, 1976), p. 126.

35. Richard Robinson, *Plato's Earlier Dialectic* (Ithaca, New York: Cornell University Press, 1941), p. 166.

36. As Socrates says a little later in the same passage:

> If a man cannot by his account separate and distinguish the idea of the good from all else, and persevere through everything in the battle of refutation, eager to refute in reality and not in appearance, and go through all these things without letting his argument be overthrown, you will not say he knows the good itself or any other good; but, if he is somehow grasping some copy of it, he is grasping it by opinion and not by knowledge; his present life then is a dreaming and dozing, and before he wakes up here he will have gone to Hades and be completely asleep. (534b–d; trans. as in ibid., p. 157)

37. Junjiro Takakusu, *The Essentials of Buddhist Philosophy*, ed. Wing-Tsit Chan and Charles A. Moore, 3rd ed. (Delhi: Motilal Banarsidass, 1975), p. 110.

38. Wing-Tsit Chan, ed., *A Source Book in Chinese Philosophy* (Princeton, New Jersey: Princeton University Press, 1963), p. 359.

39. J. N. Findlay, *Plato: The Written and Unwritten Doctrines* (London, Routledge and Kegan Paul, 1974), pp. 229–254.

40. Yet other scholars, also unwilling to accept the "strange accident" of the "battle of refutations," have seen both Gorgias's book, *On Nature, or On Non-being*, and the *Parmenides* as elaborate quasi-musical games (*paignia*) in which ontological concepts appear, give place, transform, and reappear like philosophical leitmotifs in an otherwise empty virtuoso display. (See, for example, Guthrie, *History of Greek Philosophy*, vol. 5, p. 53.)

41. Emile Brehier, *The Hellenistic and Roman Age* (Chicago: University of Chicago Press, 1965), p. 4.

42. Trans. Richard McKeon, *The Basic Works of Aristotle* (New York: Random House, 1941), p. 823.

43. See Epictetus, *Disc.* 2.19; Plutarch, *De Stoic Repugn.* 46 (1055d); Cicero, *De Fato* 13 and 17; Alex. Aph. *In An. Pr.* (ed. Wallies), 184; Aristotle, *De Interp.* ch. 9.

44. Cf. W. and M. Kneale (*The Development of Logic*, p. 133) on the one hand, and Brehier (*The Hellenistic and Roman Age*, p. 6) on the other.

45. A. L. Basham, *History and Doctrine of the Ājīvikas: A Vanished Indian Religion* (London: Luzac, 1951), p. 221, n. 1; and see K. N. Jayatilleke, *Early Buddhist Theory of Knowledge* (London: George Allen and Unwin, 1963), pp. 142–143.

46. Jayatilleke, ibid., p. 143.

47. Murti, *The Central Philosophy of Buddhism*, p. 295.

48. Giovanni Reale, *A History of Ancient Philosophy*, vol. 3, *The Systems of the Hellenistic Age*, trans. John R. Catan (Albany, New York: State University of New York Press, 1985), p. 22.

49. The *8th Epistle of "Heraclitus"* in *The Cynic Epistles: A Study Edition*, ed. A. J. Malherbe (Missoula, Montana: Scholars Press, 1977), p. 208. I will make sparing use of the Cynic Epistles, the earliest of which are dated to c. 300 B.C., to illustrate teachings which seem already to have been formulated in the generation of Diogenes and his disciples. It is interesting to note that Heraclitus, who of all early Greek thinkers is the closest to primitive Buddhism, was the only pre-Socratic to whom Cynic teachings are attributed in the Epistles.

50. Trans. T. W. Rhys Davids and Hermann Oldenberg, *Vinaya Texts*, vol. 1, Sacred Books of the East 13, p. 84.

51. Cf. Sanskrit *prajñā*, as in *Prajñāpāramitā*.

52. David J. Kalupahana, *Buddhist Philosophy* (Honolulu: University of Hawaii Press, 1976), p. 60.

53. Ibid., p. 75.

54. Matics, *Entering the Path of Enlightenment*, p. 170.

55. In Malherbe, *The Cynic Epistles*, p. 103.

56. Matics, *Entering the Path of Enlightenment*, p. 171.

57. Ibid., p. 43.

58. Malherbe, *The Cynic Epistles*, p. 56.

59. Ibid., p. 54.

60. E. Zeller, *Socrates and the Socratic Schools* (New York: Russell, 1962), p. 304 and n. 1.

61. Malherbe, *The Cynic Epistles*, p. 59.

62. Zeller, *Socrates and the Socratic Schools*, p. 306.

63. Ibid., p. 309 and n. 5.

64. Farrand Sayre, *Diogenes of Sinope: A Study of Greek Cynicism* (Baltimore: J. H. Furst Co., 1938), pp. 34–35.

65. Inada, *Nāgārjuna*, p. 31.

66. Trans. A. F. Price and Wong Mou-Lam, *The Diamond Sūtra and the Sūtra of Hui Neng* (Berkeley, California: Shambhala, 1969), p. 87.

67. Sayre, *Diogenes of Sinope*, p. 40.

68. The existence of this trade route has been disputed. For arguments in favor of it, see George McDonald, "The Hellenic Kingdoms of Syria, Bactria and Parthia," in *Ancient India*, ed. E. J. Rapson, p. 433; for arguments against it, W. W. Tarn, *The Greeks in Bactria and India* (Cambridge: Cambridge University Press, 1951), pp. 112–113, 444, 488–490.

69. Sayre, *Diogenes of Sinope*, p. 38.

70. Ingalls suggests that this aspect of Cynicism originated in Black Sea shamanism (Daniel H. H. Ingalls, "Cynics and Pasupatas: The Seeking of Dishonor," *Harvard Theological Review* 55 [1962]). I do not reject this possibility (see chapter 9, "Cynics and Pasupatas"); my point is that this strain of Cynicism *can* be accounted for from within the Greek tradition. Chrysippus also recommended cannibalism of the dead.

71. The opinion that Pyrrhonism sprang from its founder's experience in India is found in, for example: Edward Conze, *Buddhism: Its Essence and Development* (New York: Peter Smith, 1959), pp. 140–143; George Woodcock, *The Greeks in India* (London: Faber and Faber, 1966), p. 27; Cornelia J. De Vogel, *Philosophia*, Philosophical Texts and Studies 19 (Assen: van Gorcum, 1970), vol. 1, p. 428; Mary M. Patrick, *Greek Skeptics* (New York: Columbia University Press, 1969), p. 57; Leon Robin, *Pyrrhon et le scepticisme grec* (Paris: Presses Universitaires de France, 1944), pp. 6, 8; Everard Flintoff, "Pyrrho and India," *Phronesis* 25 (1980): 88–108.

72. See Donald R. Dudley, *A History of Cynicism* (London: Methuen and Co., 1937), pp. 23 ff.

Chapter Seventeen

Pyrrhonism and Mādhyamika

Pyrrhon of Elis (c. 365–275 B.C.) is said to have first been a painter, then studied philosophy under a Megarian (either Bryson or Stilpo), then under Anaxarchus of Abdera, who was a student either of Democritus himself or of a Democritean. Both Pyrrhon's teachers, in other words, must have been dialecticians, though the Megarian may have been a neo-Eleatic absolutist dialectician, and Anaxarchus a Sophistic relativist. At age thirty-five or so Pyrrhon went with Anaxarchus on Alexander the Great's expedition to India.[1] He spent perhaps eighteen months in India altogether, including time in the philosophically important northwest Indian city of Taxila, and in that time had some contact with yogis—or Gymnosophists, as the Greeks called them: "naked philosophers." Returning to Greece when he was perhaps forty-five or fifty years old, he taught in Athens for about forty years and founded the lineage known as Pyrrhonism or Skepticism. Like Socrates, he wrote nothing, teaching more by personal example. As Diogenes Laertius said, "He had no positive tenet, but a Pyrrhonist is one who in manner and life resembles Pyrrhon" (D.L. IX.70). Two surviving stories about Pyrrhon illustrate the ambiguities in this definition:

> He led a life consistent with this doctrine [of non-discrimination], going out of his way for nothing, taking no precautions, but facing all risks as they came, whether carts, precipices, dogs, or what not, and, generally, leaving nothing to the arbitrament of his senses; but he was kept out of harm's way by his friends, who . . . used to follow close after him. (D.L. IX.62)

It is tempting to compare the stories of those Taoist and Ch'an sages who, while walking into the jungle, would encounter a tiger without diverting their steps or altering their manner. It has been suggested that this story is a parody, a reduction to absurdity of the idea of living in the world without any beliefs or aversions whatever.[2] Another anecdote tells an opposite story:

> When a cur rushed at him and terrified him, he answered a critic that it was not easy entirely to strip oneself of human weaknesses. (D.L. IX.66)

The Pyrrhonist school seems not to have survived continuously from Pyrrhon's day to that of Sextus, but to have lapsed at some time and been revived by Aenesidemus in the first century B.C. Aenesidemus seems to have felt that the reigning Skeptical school of the period, the late Academy under Philo of Larissa, had ceased to be rigorous in its skepticism and, accepting too much as persuasive, had lost the suspended life which for Pyrrhon evidently had been a real imperative. Aenesidemus defected from the Academy and revived a more radical skepticism under the name Pyrrhonism.[3] At a later stage Pyrrhonism became associated with the Empirical school of medicine, who were at pains to argue against rationalist approaches to their science. Sextus Empiricus, the great second-century A.D. encyclopedist of Skeptical arguments, was a medical doctor of this school.

Only two sayings attributed directly to Pyrrhon have survived, both clearly in the tradition of Democritus, who is said to have elicited Pyrrhon's greatest respect. The first is, "Nothing really exists, but human life is governed by convention." In such a context the concept "to exist" means to have distinguishing marks which make an entity itself in contradistinction to other things, which have different distinguishing marks—ultimately, to have an essence (Skt. *svabhāva*). Democritus had asserted the nondifference of things (and hence their nonexistence as separate entities) on the sub-Ionian monistic ground that all things are made up only of atoms and void and hence are not what they seem and are not really different from one another. It was on this basis that Democritus asserted that all human realities are conventions rather than essences. This insight in turn inspired Protagoras's assertion that each person's subjectivity made up reality for him; subjectivity came to the foreground, and the basis in atomic theory was seen to be unnecessary to it. The view that things are without essence and flowing became an independent idea divorced from its atomist source. The legacy of Democritus split in the fourth century B.C., the skeptical, sophistic, relativistic, phenomenalistic aspect entering into Pyrrhonism by way of Pyrrhon's teacher Anaxarchus, while the atomist, metaphysical, monistic, dogmatic, rationalist aspect entered into the Epicurean school.

The statement that things and perceptions lack distinguishing marks is equivalent to the statement that nothing really exists (as itself), and is more or less equivalent to the many parallel assertions in the Prajñāpāramitā texts, with their basis in the early Buddhist ideas of impermanence and lack of self-nature (*svabhāva*).

The second surviving saying of Pyrrhon goes to the same effect, denying that things have essences which keep them separate from one another and self-identical: "Nothing is in itself more this than that" (D.L. IX.61). The statement that nothing is more this than that is attributed by Plutarch to Democritus (*Adv. Col.* 1108 ff. = DK 68B156) and was used by the Democritean Nausiphanes as well as by the Pyrrhonists. Both Plato (*Prot.* 166c) and Plutarch (*Adv. Col.* 1109a) attribute it to Protagoras, too, again pointing to his connection with Democritus.[4] At the other end of this lineage, six hundred years later, the slogan is still central to Sextus Empiricus in the second-to-third century A.D.

These thinkers regarded such statements as both meaningful and useful. Yet in the rationalist tradition, as opposed to the Skeptical, the phrase became, on the contrary, a "formula of refutation."[5] "No more this than that" is an example of an uroboric[6] or self-devouring proposition, for it presumes "no more 'no more this than that' than 'more this than that.'" As Aristotle said, if an affirmation is no more true than its negation, then the affirmation that an affirmation is no more true than its negation is itself no more true than its negation (*Met.* 1062b2–7). For Aristotle, in other words, the "no more" formula cancels itself out. Yet for Sextus and others who were quite aware of the principle of contradiction it seemed to perfect and complete itself by canceling itself along with all other propositions. For Sextus, as for Wittgenstein and Nagarjuna, philosophy itself was uroboric and would complete itself by destroying itself. Philosophy was a macrocosmic uroboric statement.

In the rationalist and absolutist tradition self-canceling or uroboric formulas were excluded from the discourse about experience, where they were seen as invalid by contradiction, and were applied only in discourse about the transcendent and absolute One. The Neopythagorean Moderatus, for example, used the formula "It is neither this nor that" to describe the transcendent One; Plotinus said of the One, "It is the not-this." In this tradition it was considered that Plato had shown (primarily, but not exclusively, in the *Parmenides*) that language must lapse into paradox when it approaches ultimate reality. Meanwhile Pyrrhon and others in the Democritean tradition used such phrases about everyday experience, which, when viewed without linguistic overlays and projections, became a kind of ultimate reality itself. (As Democritus had said, "The phenomenon *is* truth." Pyrrhon's follower Timon, in a passage from his *Images*, agreed: "The phenomenon is always omnipotent wherever it appears" [D.L. IX.105].)

There is in addition a verse which Pyrrhon drew from Homer to illustrate impermanence:

> As leaves on the trees, such are the lives of men. (D.L. VI.146)

Like Democritus and Anaxarchus, Pyrrhon is reported as seeking solitude and developing a tranquil mood unaffected by shifting phenomena; according to Diogenes Laertius, he was influenced by his Indian experience in at least the first point:

> He would withdraw from the world and live in solitude, rarely showing himself to his relatives; this he did because he had heard an Indian reproach Anaxarchus, telling him that he would never be able to teach others what is good while he himself danced attendance on kings in their courts. He would maintain the same composure at all times. (D.L. IX.63)
>
> They say that, when septic salves and surgical and caustic remedies were applied to a wound he had sustained, he did not so much as frown. (D.L. IX.67)

For further knowledge of primitive Pyrrhonism one must rely on later stages of the tradition, which may or may not be closely tied to Pyrrhon himself. One of the earliest accounts of Pyrrhon's critique of the philosophies was written by Timon of Phlius, a first-generation student.[7] Pyrrhon, according to Timon, held happiness to be the goal of philosophy, and recommended that a person who would be happy should consider the following three questions: What is the nature of things? What is our position in relation to them? What, under the circumstances, should we do? The answers appear as a formulaic series of negations in the tradition of Democritean *athambia* and Cynic *apatheia*. Questions one and two are answered by three negative adjectives: Things are *adiaphora*, "nondifferent," or "without distinguishing marks"; *astathmēta*, "nonstable," or "without fixed essence"; and *anepikrita*, "nonjudgeable," or "unable to be reached by concepts." As a result, Timon quotes, "Neither our perceptions nor our opinions are either true or false."

Without assuming a one-to-one correspondence between Greek and Indian philosophical terms, one should nevertheless note that the important Pyrrhonist concepts are expressed in the related areas of the Indian tradition by Sanskrit terms with very similar denotative realms. Indeed, the philosophical terminologies of these two languages included the same concepts, combined and recombined into very similar sentences, for many centuries. *Adiaphora*, "nondifferent from one another," corresponds closely to the meaning of *lakṣaṇa-śūnya*, "empty of distinguishing marks"; *astathmēta*, "unstable or without fixed essence," to Sanskrit *anitya*, "impermanent" or "without self-nature"; *anepikrita*, "unable to be grasped by concepts," corresponds to many common terms in Buddhist philosophy, such as *avyākṛta* ("indeterminable"), *anabhilapya* ("inexpressible"), *atarkāvacara* ("beyond logical argument"), and so on.

Question three is also answered by a series of three negative adjectives, which again have Sanskrit equivalents from related Indian texts: We should be *adoxastoi*, "without opinions" (cf. Sanskrit *aprapañcita*, "undiscriminated"); *aklineis*, "without agitation," or "firmly balanced" (compare Sanskrit *upekṣā*, "indifference"); and *akradantoi*, "without agitation" or "firmly balanced" (compare Sanskrit *śānta*, "tranquil, steady"); and so on. Two negative nouns describe the qualities of one who had reached this state: *aphasia*, "nonspeech," or "cessation of belief in language-reality isomorphism," and *ataraxia* (the Democritean term), "nonagitation" or "imperturbability."

The formulaic series of negative terms with which Timon summarizes Pyrrhonism are in the tradition of Greek *apatheia*, *athambia*, and so on; but they also compare interestingly with Buddhist formulations such as the strings of negations in the *Heart Sūtra*, or in Nāgārjuna's "Verses on the Middle Way," XVIII.11:

> "Non-identity, non-differentiation, non-interruption and non-continuity." These are the immortal teachings of the world's patron *Buddhas*.

This way of speaking is extended in Candrakīrti's eight negations. Finally, Timon's Pyrrhon rejects all possible verbal assertions in a summation of Pyrrhon's teachings that is virtually identical with the Mādhyamika formula called the *catuṣkoṭi* or Fourfold Negation:

> We should say of each thing that it no more is than is not, than both is and is not, than neither is nor is not.

The Fourfold Negation, found in Nāgārjuna at *MK* XVIII.8, says:

> Everything is such as it is, not such as it is, both such as it is and not such as it is, and neither such as it is nor such as it is not.[8]

The relationship between these two passages will be explored in detail later in this chapter.

The Second and Third Academies

In addition to the Pyrrhonic tradition of Skepticism the Academy—the School of Plato—abandoned its dedication to his metaphysics around the end of the fourth century B.C. and began instead to emphasize the skeptical elements of Plato's oeuvre: the early aporetic dialogues, the Socratic profession of ignorance, the contradictions of the *Parmenides*, the denial of the written teachings in the *Seventh Letter*, and so on. This development, which is known as the Second Academy, took place under the leadership of Arcesilaus, who was acting under the influence of Pyrrhonism and purveyed a brand of Skepticism closely related to the Pyrrhonist. He was a contemporary of Timon, who was Pyrrhon's "official" successor and who felt that Arcesilaus was trying to steal that succession from him for the Academy. Numenius called him "a Pyrrhonist except in name; he was not an Academic except that his job-title identified him as one" (Eusebius, *Prep. Ev.* XIV.6.6). As Sextus put it:

> Arcesilaus seems to me to have shared the doctrine of Pyrrhon, so that his way of thinking is almost identical to ours. For one does not find him asserting anything concerning the reality or unreality of anything, nor does he prefer one thing over another in terms of credibility or lack of it, but suspends judgment about everything. He also holds that the end is *epochē* (which is accompanied as we have said by *ataraxia*). (*OP* I.232)

Diogenes Laertius, in fact, says that Arcesilaus "was the first to hold his judgments in suspension because of the contrariety of opinions" (D.L. IV.32). That is, Arcesilaus is said to have originated the concept of *epochē,* which was to become basic to Sextus's Pyrrhonism (though Pyrrhon had already spoken of *adoxia*, opinionlessness, and of withholding assent to propositions). The one significant difference between Academic and Pyrrhonist Skepticism is that the Academics insisted that they were certain about some things, whereas the Pyrrhonist denied certainty about everything. Arcesilaus, for example, according to Sextus, declared "that suspension regarding particular objects is good, but assent regarding particulars is bad" (*OP* I.232 f.). Since the Academic Skeptics were usually certain about negations (for example, as above, negating assent to particulars), the Pyrrhonists called them not true Skeptics but "negative dogmatists." Aside from this point,[9] Arcesilaus shared in the same stream of concepts and terminology that was basic to Pyrrhonism; he also drew from the same accumulated array of forms of argument—and very skillfully, it seems: according to a hostile witness, Numenius, "by preparation and study in the delusive show of his arguments he used to stupefy and juggle . . ." (Eusebius, *Prep. Ev.* XIV.6.2).

In the early first century B.C. Carneades became leader, or *scholarch,* of the Academy and continued the obsessive dialectic against the Stoics begun by Arcesilaus—but this time it was the later Stoicism of Chrysippus, not of Zeno, that was involved. "If we leave out the anti-Stoic polemic," says Reale, "the thought of Carneades appears to be almost non-existent."[10] The final upshot of the two-century–long attack by the Academic Skeptics on the Stoa is that the Stoa won—or outlasted them, anyway; Sextus says (*OP* I.235) that under Antiochus of Ascalon the fifth Academy taught Stoicism.

Neither Arcesilaus's nor Carneades' works have survived except through citation from other authors such as Diogenes Laertius and Cicero (primarily in the *Academica*). Much of Sextus Empiricus's writing, on the other hand, has managed to survive, which is probably posterity's good fortune, since the argumentation of both Arcesilaus and Carneades was designed especially against the Stoics whereas Sextus's is more widely directed at knowledge claims of all kinds and can apply equally to any cultural epoch. Sextus's work is the basic source that has been left to posterity to stand for the whole Greek Skeptical tradition. The following discussion, consequently, will be based on Sextus, though much of it may be taken as indirectly applying to the Academic Skeptics, too.[11]

Pyrrhonism and Mādhyamika

Timon's brief summary of Pyrrhonism could as easily describe the Prajñāpāramitā as the Pyrrhonist point of view. In the generations after Pyrrhon and Timon this central body of teaching was provided with a powerful dialectical support which is in turn remarkably similar to the Mādhyamika dialectic which arose in support of the Prajñāpāramitā point of view.[12] The parallelism between these two dialectical systems will be brought out by a series of comparisons which will prepare us to propose a probable answer to the question of historical connections between them. For the Greek side of the comparison the Pyrrhonist encyclopedist Sextus Empiricus will be the leading source, for the Indian side the *Verses on the Middle Way* and *Refutation of All Contests* of Nāgārjuna.[13] It is worth mentioning that current scholarship among Hellenists places Sextus in the late second and/or early third century A.D., and the current view of Buddhologists places Nāgārjuna in exactly the same time frame.[14] It is, in other words, probable that the two great ancient deconstructivists, East and West, were alive at the same time.

The title of Nāgārjuna's central work is worth pausing over. *Madhya* in Sanskrit means "middle" and *madhyamaka* is the superlative, "the radical middle," so to speak. He seems to have called his main treatise the *Madhyamakaśastra*, *Treatise on the Middle Way*, or *Mūlamadhyamakakārikās*, *Verses on the Middle Way*. (Like the book of Parmenides it is in verse.) "Middle way" seems to be meant here "not in the sense of the middle path but the middle way things are."[15] "By "middle" Nagarjuna seems to have meant to refer to the Law of the Excluded Middle. The middle way is the way between A and not-A. This book title then gave its title to the school which developed from Nāgārjuna's innovations, the *Madhyamaka* or Mādhyamika, that is, the school that takes its position in the exluded middle, the school that is expressly devoted to the controversion of that principle of thought, to the farming, as it were, of the land in the excluded-middle zone.[16] Sextus's Pyrrhonism finds its most comfortable location in the same place. The location is not merely logical but ethical or eudaimonistic as well, the positions, Yes and No, being equivalent to the passions of grasping and fleeing that make life a tumult, the position in between being the calm at the eye of the hurricane, as it were.

Pyrrhonists and Mādhyamikas expressed a very similar stance toward life. To begin with, neither school propagated positive doctrines; by "positive doctrines" I mean doctrines that assume that the entities they refer to have essential existence, that is, that they possess self-nature (Skt. *svabhāva*) or substantiality (Skt. *nairātmya*). Both Sextus and Nāgārjuna regard experiences as real phenomenally—that is, they do not deny that experiences occur—but not real essentially. As one scholar writes of Nāgārjuna: "He does not eradicate existence; he eradicates only the false sense of inherent [essentialist] existence . . . it is possible to realize a sense of valid nominal existence through gaining the understanding that emptiness is an elimination only of inherent existence."[17] Nāgārjuna's "primary objective," says another,[18] "was to reject . . . substantialist or essentialist thought . . ." And another: "[A]ll aspects of everyday experience, both subjective and objective, are emptied of any ontological content, whether defined as 'self' (ātman), or as 'intrinsic being' or 'essence' (*svabhāva*)."[19] "What is negated," says another, ". . . is self, defined as inherent existence."[20] Similarly, Sextus "seeks not to destroy ordinary beliefs in material objects, but only to show that none of the Dogmatists' accounts of them are satisfactory in their own terms [which are essentialist terms]." The Pyrrhonists' conclusions are "non-dogmatic because they make no positive assertion about anything's nature or essence." The Skeptic can affirm "in some suitably relativized sense." Pyrrhonism is "Essential Scepticism," meaning that it is skepticism only about essences.[21]

Instead of offering doctrines of their own, both schools devoted their philosophical activity to undermining the doctrines of other schools without exception. As Diogenes Laertius said of the Pyrrhonists: they "were constantly engaged in overthrowing the dogmas of all schools, but enunciated none themselves; and though they would go so far as to bring forward and expound the dogmas of the others, they themselves laid down nothing definitely, not even the laying down of nothing" (D.L. IX.74).

As for the Mādhyamikas, the Tibetan text *Emptiness in the Prasangika System*, by Jam-yang-shayba, says:

> Because they do not accept autonomous inferences,
> But mainly state consequences
> That contradict the assertions of their opponents,
> They are called Prasangikas.[22]

Candrakīrti defines a Prasaṇgika as:

> A Mādhyamika who mainly states refutations of an opponent's assertion . . . through the expression of a correct contradictory consequence . . . [23]

And Nāgārjuna's own famous statement in the *Refutation*:

> If I would make any proposition whatever, then by that I would have a logical error. But I do not make a proposition; therefore I am not in error. (*VV* 29)

The Goal

Sextus Empiricus states the purpose of this activity from the Pyrrhonist point of view: Through forsaking all opinions about the nature of reality, the Skeptic practitioner is to bring his mind into a state of suspension (*epochē*) wherein the various mind-states are experienced as nondifferent from one another (*adiaphora* [cf. Skt. *lakṣaṇa-śūnya*]). "Experience," in this suspended view, as one modern author described it, "is a simple sequential flow of sense impressions, and all impressions are intrinsically of equal authority."[24] This "suspension" is said to solidify into an inner balance (*arrepsia*) in which the mind neither affirms nor denies, neither grasps at some impressions nor pushes others away. This position between affirmation and negation expresses itself in a withdrawal from commitment to linguistic categories and value judgments (*aphasia*, "nonassertion" or "nonspeech"),[25] which ripens finally into freedom from phenomenal influence (*apatheia*, "nonreactiveness," "noninvolvement") and imperturbability (*ataraxia*), in which the mind is said to experience each moment without either attachment or aversion.

As for the Mādhyamika, "its purpose, as stated by Candrakīrti, is to eradicate the innate tendency of conceptual thought to construct reified notions of being (*bhāva*) and non-being (*abhāva*)."[26] Such reified concepts lead to dispositions (*saṃskāras*) which keep one involved in the tumult of opinions. One who attains a middle position between Being and non-Being "pacifies" these dispositions and "is said to have attained enlightenment and freedom."[27] As the *Sutta Nipāta* (which is often viewed as a text lying in the background of the Mādhyamika attitude) describes the enlightened person:

He has not formed even the slightest opinion or conceptualization about what is here seen, heard, or thought. (*SN* 802)

From this belief in, or desire for, an opinion-freed stance, suspended in the (logically excluded) middle between affirmation and negation, both the Skeptic and Mādhyamika dialectics arose. Some parallel passages will highlight their extraordinary similarity in both basic attitudes and modes of expression. The Greek passages come primarily from Sextus; the Buddhist passages are selected to show the survival of a tradition, from the early Buddhism represented in the *Sutta Nipāta* to its negative enunciation in the Perfect Wisdom texts, to the Mādhyamika formalization, to the later schools which were shaped by their influence.

Skeptic:

[Pyrrhon] denied that anything was honourable or dishonourable, just or unjust . . . for no single thing is in itself any more this than that. (D.L. IX.61)

Nothing is more this than that. (Sextus *OP* I.188)

Buddhist:

In the final wisdom there is neither this nor that. (Tilopa *Vow of Mahamūdra*)[28]

Pure vision has neither limiting periphery nor fixed center. It cannot be shown as this or that . . . It has nothing to do with philosophical systems. (Long-chen-pa)[29]

Things are neither this nor that. (Seng Chao)[30] (With this statement Seng Chao sums up Nāgārjuna's *Verses on the Middle Way.*)

Skeptic:

Let us neither grasp at one thing nor flee from another. (Timon or Aenesidemus, *ap.* D.L. IX.108)

All things are by nature equally indeterminable, admitting of neither measurement nor discrimination. For this reason our sense experiences and beliefs are neither true nor false. Therefore we ought not to put our trust in them, but be without beliefs, disinclined to take a stand one way or the other. (Timon *ap.* Aristocles)

Suspension of judgment brings with it tranquillity [*ataraxia*] like its shadow: so Timon and Aenesidemus declare. (D.L. IX.107)

Non-assertion [*aphasia*] is an avoidance of both affirmation and negation; it is a state of mind because of which we neither affirm nor deny anything. (*OP* I.192)

The term suspension [*epochē*] is derived from the fact of the mind being held up or suspended so that it neither affirms nor denies anything. (*OP* I.196)

I define nothing, [or] I determine nothing. (*OP* I.8)

Everything is undetermined . . . [meaning that] there is no preference among the things that are placed in opposition to one another. (*OP* I.198–99)

I grasp at nothing; I cling to nothing. (*OP* I.201)

"Suspense" [*epochē*] is a state of mental rest owing to which we neither deny nor affirm anything. "Quietude" [*ataraxia*] is an untroubled and tranquil condition of soul. And . . . quietude enters the soul along with suspension of judgment. (*OP* I.10)

Buddhist:

> Let him not think something is better or worse or even the same as another. (*SN* 795)
>
> They [the enlightened ones] do not fancy, they do not prefer. (ibid.)
>
> He . . . has no leanings here to either of the two extremes: being or not being, here or beyond, he has no moorings whatsoever, no clutching while distinguishing between dharmas. (ibid. 801)
>
> Common people take their stand on their own points of view, on their own doctrines and on their own thoughts, and hence there arise all the contentions . . . He who understands that all opinions . . . are in truth of the same nature, has already become free from all these. (*Mahaprajñāpāramitā Śastra* 61A)
>
> The intention of the Buddha is this: my disciples [should be] free from passion for doctrine, free from attachment to doctrine, free from partisanship . . . They do not quarrel about the nature of things. (*Mahaprajñāpāramitā Śastra* 63c)
>
> Perceptions used as a base for building up positive concepts are the origin of all ignorance. (*Surangama Sūtra*)
>
> The Tathāgata is one who has forsaken all reflections and discriminations. (*Aṣṭasāhasrikā Prajñāpāramitā* 137)
>
> Thinking in terms of being and non-being is called wrong thinking, while not thinking in these terms is called right thinking . . . The same applies to all the other categories of thought . . . (Hui Hai)[31]
>
> Develop a mind that clings to nothing. (*Vajracchedikā Prajñāpāramitā* 10)
>
> It is considered perverse to affirm or negate. It is said to be correct only when there is neither affirmation nor negation. (Chi-tsang)[32]
>
> [Right perception] means beholding all sorts of forms but without being stained by them as no thoughts of love or aversion rise in the mind. (Hui Hai)[33]
>
> The Great Way is not difficult for those who have no preferences. When love and hate are both absent everything becomes clear and undisguised . . . If you wish to see the truth, then hold no opinions for or against anything. To set up what you like against what you dislike is the disease of the mind . . . It is due to our choosing to accept or reject that we do not see the true nature of things . . . Do not search for the truth, only cease to cherish opinions . . . If there is even a trace of this and that . . . the mind-essence will be lost in confusion. (*Sūtra of the Third Zen Patriarch*)

These series of passages emphasize the rejection of the Law of the Excluded Middle as an ethical and psychological factor associated with relativity and subjectivity. The doctrine of indeterminacy (Grk. *aoristia*, "lack of boundary or definition"; Skt. *svabhāva-śūnyata*, "lack of self-nature or essence") is simultaneously a critique of ontological claims of absolute Being or non-Being, of epistemological claims for knowledge (here *aoristia* becomes *akatalepsia*, "ungraspableness," "inability to be circumscribed by concepts"; compare Sanskrit *anirvacaniya*, "undefinable" and *nirvikalpa*, "transcending conceptual description"), and of the view that there is a language-reality isomorphism. Things, being of no fixed nature, are outside the distinction between Being and non-Being, which is an essentialist dichotomy, and are similarly outside of the categories of language, which also are rigid and essentialist. The fact that the dialectic functions on three levels—ontological, epistemological, and semantic or language-critical—was first perceived by Gorgias; in India it seems to have dawned with Nāgārjuna and his colleagues, some seven hundred years later. In any case, both schools felt that what is usually called philosophy is a veil of words which cuts the mind off from the reality of experience. For Sextus, *aphasia* was the basis of mental balance; for Candrakīrti "nirvāṇa is 'Quiescence' of all plurality, because . . . there is for the philosopher absolutely no differentiation of existence to which our words (and concepts) could be applied. That . . . is called (Nirvāṇa) the quiescence of Plurality, for which there are no words" (*Prasannapadā* VIII).[34]

The Dialectic against Cause and Effect

The desire to escape from the web of language and confront experience directly neglecting for the moment the question whether this is or is not a realistic ambition led, in both schools, to a radical rejection of concepts, focusing on the central concept pair, being/non-being. This rejection was supported, in both schools, by a complex dialectic of the reducing or destroying type, designed, as one scholar put it, "to redirect energies which were caught in the net of discourse."[35] In both cases the basic dialectical pattern is the dichotomy-and-dilemma type of *reductio ad absurdum*, with liberal use of *regressus ad infinitum* (Skt. *anavastha*), and special emphasis on the denial of partial identity, or same/not-same dichotomy (or disjunctive *modus tollens*). Finally, it should be noted that for Sextus, as for Nāgārjuna, "'Is' refers only to what exists through own-nature . . . ," and "what exists by means of own-nature is permanent, fixed, unproduced, unstopped, and unchanging."[36]

The Sūtra style in which Nāgārjuna wrote the *Karika* calls for the argument to be boiled down to an extremely compressed form which then, in order to be readable, is to be reexpanded to discursive scale through commentaries. In this case, the relationship between the Sextan and Nāgārjunan texts is so close that often one can see Sextus's version as an expansion of Nāgārjuna's—or Nāgārjuna's as a compressed form of Sextus's. In what follows paraphrases addressing primarily the dialectical form of the argument will sometimes be offered in lieu of commentaries.

One of many possible examples of the parallelism in the lines of thought of these two schools is the dialectic against causality. Nāgārjuna's application of the same/not-same dichotomy to the cause-and-effect pair has already been mentioned: If they are the same, then the terms are meaningless; if they are different, then (based on both the denial of partial identity and the argument from infinite regress of separators) there is no relationship between them. Both Sextus and Nāgārjuna have this argument. Nāgārjuna's formulation is, as usual, the more succinct. First he states the principle:

> Any existence which is relational is indeed neither identical to nor different from the related object. (*MK* XVIII.10)

If they are identical there is only one object, not two, hence there cannot be a relationship; if they are truly different, each having independent self-nature, there can be no connection between them, hence no relationship. Then he applies this principle to causality:

> It is not possible indeed for a cause and effect to be identical. But again it is not possible for them to be different.
>
> If the cause and effect were identical, there would be an identity of the producer and the produced. If they were different, however, then the cause would be the same as a non-causal cause (i.e., it would not touch the effect). (*MK* XX.19–20)

In such passages one must remember that the idea of "different," in this type of discourse, means *ontologically* different; it means, in other words, that each of the entities involved has "inherent existence," which, in western terms, means an essence; and an essence is unchangeable, that is, it cannot be affected (which would mean changed) by anything else and hence is independent ("the very words 'inherent existence' . . . imply independence")[37]. Hence if the so-called "cause" and "effect" were really "different" from one another then each would be independent and could not be changed or affected from outside; hence the effect, being independent, could not be "caused" by the "cause," which therefore, in a state of independence, would be a "noncausal cause." So if the entities in question were "different" from one another there could be no cause-and-effect relationship. Hence, in order for the cause-and-effect relationship to exist, the entities involved must be neither the same nor different—which is to say, they cannot have real existence. Nāgārjuna's remark about producer and produced reminds one of Gorgias's argument, quoted above, about container and contained: "The container is not the same as the contained, as the producer is not the same as the produced." An implied dichotomy of agent and patient underlies both passages.

Sextus formulates this argument at greater length, providing meanwhile the fullest explication of the denial of partial identity, and introducing an argument based on the relationship of succession, which cause and effect are premised on. This is one of the cases where Sextus's longer version might almost be an expansion of or commentary on Nāgārjuna's compressed Sūtra form.

> If there exists any cause of anything, either it is separate from the matter affected or it co-exists with it; but neither when separate from it nor when co-existing with it can it be the cause of its being affected, as we shall establish; therefore no cause of anything exists. Now, when separated from its matter obviously it is not a cause, since the matter with respect to which it is termed a cause is not present, nor is the matter affected, since that which affects it is not present with it. But if the one is coupled with the other [then the arguments against contact, based, as in the Mādhyamika, upon the denial of partial identity, apply]: . . . In order that a thing may act or be acted upon, it must touch or be touched; but, as we shall establish, nothing can either touch or be touched; therefore neither that which acts [the cause] nor that which is acted upon [the effect] exists. For if one thing is in contact with another and touches it, it is in contact either as a whole with the whole, or as a part with a part, or as a whole with a part or as a part with the whole . . . Now it is according to reason that a whole does not touch a whole; for if whole touches whole, there will not be contact but the union of both . . . Nor again is it possible for part to touch part. For the part is conceived as a part in respect of its relation to the whole, but in respect of its own limited extent it is a whole, and for this reason again either the whole part will touch the whole part, or a part of it a part. And if the whole touches the whole, they will be unified and both will become one body; while if with a part it touches a part, that part again, being conceived as a whole in respect of its own limited extent, will either touch as a whole the whole part, or touch a part of it with a part—and so on *ad infinitum*. (*APh* I.252–261)

Cause and effect, then, can be neither the same nor different, and according to the Law of the Excluded Middle there is no other possibility. The basis of the critique is the idea that concepts like cause and effect have the Law of the Excluded Middle, the distinction between entities, the Law of Identity, and so on, built into them; that is, they have the naïve realist assumption of inherent or essential existence built into them. It is this that is the object of the critique.

Both Sextus (in an argument that goes clear back to "father" Parmenides) and Nāgārjuna reject the possibility that the cause somehow "contains" the effect, because in this case, as Sextus says, "[the effect] is already in existence and being already in existence it does not become, since becoming is the process toward existence" (*APh* I.226). As Nāgārjuna put it:

> If a cause is a void with respect to an effect, how could it give rise to the effect? If, on the other hand, a cause is not a void with respect to an effect, how could it give rise to the effect? (*MK* XX.16)

That is: If the cause does not contain the effect, the effect cannot arise from it; if it does contain the effect, then the effect already exists and cannot be said to arise from it.

Nor can we get around the problem by saying that the effect is self-produced, or reduplicated, for if the nature of the cause is to reduplicate itself, then the effect, being a duplicate of the cause, will also have that nature, will also reduplicate itself, and so on *ad infinitum*; the world will be filled with identical objects. The Mādhyamika version is found in the first alternative of *MK* I.1: "At nowhere and at no time can entities ever exist by originating out of themselves . . ." along with Candrakīrti's commentary on the passage: "There will be no conceivable limit to the process of reduplication" (*MKV* 14). The Mādhyamika thinkers sound at one moment like Parmenides, at the next like Zeno. Sextus makes the same Eleatic point:

> One thing is not able to become two . . . for if one is able to become two, then each of the two, being one, will produce two, and each of the four, being one, will make two, and similarly each unit of the eight, and so on *ad infinitum*. (*APh* I.220–221)

Another approach to the critique of causality focuses on the problem of time, or succession, and establishes that cause and effect can exist neither simultaneously nor successively, and again, by the Law of the Excluded Middle, there is no other possibility. Sextus and Nāgārjuna not only both have the argument but state it in almost identical terms. First, Sextus:

> If anything is the cause of anything, either the simultaneous is the cause of the simultaneous, or the prior of the posterior or the posterior of the prior . . . Now the simultaneous cannot be the cause of the simultaneous owing to the co-existence of both and the fact that this one is no more capable of generating that one than is that one of this one, since both are equal in point of existence. Nor will the prior be capable of producing that which comes into being later; for if, when the cause exists, that whereof it is cause is not yet existent, neither is the former any longer a cause, as it has not that whereof it is the cause, nor is the latter any longer an effect, since that whereof it is the effect does not co-exist with it. For each of these is a relative thing, and relatives must necessarily co-exist with each other, instead of one preceding and the other following. It only remains for us, then, to say that the posterior is the cause of the prior; but this is a most absurd notion . . . for we shall have to say that the effect is older than what produced it and consequently is not an effect at all since it is without that whereof it is an effect. (*APh* I.232–235)

And Nāgārjuna's boiled-down version:

> If the cause gives to the effect a causal nature before extinguishing itself, then there will be a dual causal form of the given and the extinguished.
>
> If however the cause does not give the effect a causal nature before extinguishing itself, then the effect, rising after the cause extinguishes itself, will have no cause.
>
> If again the effect and the assemblage (inc. cause) appear together, then it would follow that the producer and the produced are contemporaneous. Moreover, if the effect appears prior to the assemblage (of conditions containing the cause), then it, without cause and relational condition, will have a non-causal nature. (*MK* XX.5–8)

In this passage the translator's phrase "give a causal nature to" means "exerts causal efficacy upon." If the cause exerts its causal efficacy before extinguishing itself, then cause and effect are not successive but simultaneous; if the cause extinguishes itself first, then it cannot exert its causal efficacy. Finally, if the effect precedes the cause, no relationship exists; both Sextus and Nāgārjuna treat this option, the priority of the effect, in the last place. Śantideva focuses on the relationality of cause and effect to indicate that each has only dependent existence:

> If there is no father without a son, what is the origin of the son? If there is no son, the father does not exist. Thus the nonreality of both of them. (*BCA* IX.114)

Finally, Sextus and Nāgārjuna use the same exemplum, wood and fire, to sum up some of the difficulties in the concept of causality. Sextus says:

> If fire is the cause of burning, either it is productive of burning by itself and using only its own power, or it needs for this purpose the cooperation of the burning material. And if it produces the burning by itself, being sufficient of its own nature, then, since it always possesses its own nature, it ought to have been continually burning. But it does not burn always, but burns some things and does not burn others; therefore it does not burn by itself and by using its own nature. But if it does so in conjunction with the suitability of the burning wood, how can we assert that it, rather than the suitability of the wood, is the cause of the burning? For just as no burning takes place if the fire is non-existent, so also no burning takes place if the suitability of the wood is absent. Thus also, if it [fire] is the cause because the effect occurs when it is present and does not occur when it is absent, the suitability [of the wood] too will be the cause for both these reasons . . . (*APh* I.241–243)

By this exemplum Sextus argues (1) that a cause produces nothing by itself and thus is not a cause, and (2) that a cause is as much an effect as it is a cause, and an effect is as much a cause as it is an effect—in other words, that it is impossible to distinguish between cause and effect and as impossible to call them one (the same/not-same dilemma again).

Nāgārjuna devotes the tenth chapter of the *Verses on the Middle Way* to the same exemplum, with the same implications evidently in mind:

> If wood is the same as fire, then likewise the doer and his deed will be identical. If fire is distinct from wood, then it will exist without wood.

The same dilemma is invoked: that cause and effect are neither the same nor different, which means they lack ontological "independence" or "inherent existence."

> If there is no cause for burning, then fire should burn constantly. And there will be no purpose in fire to start (i.e., to burn) again and it will then be without a function.

If there is a cause for burning then the removal of that cause will make the fire go out; if there is no cause which can be removed, the fire should burn forever. Further, once the fire has gone out, if there is no cause of burning it will never start again. So fire cannot function without the cause-and-effect relationship, which has been seen to be impossible.

> Being unrelated to an other, it (i.e., fire) will be something without a cause for burning. Moreover, it will follow that a constantly burning fire would have no purpose of starting (i.e., burning) again.

If fire had inherent existence, or ontological independence, it would be unrelated to any other, including any cause. Also, if it had inherent existence it would burn forever, rendering meaningless the empirical fact of starting a fire.

> Thus if it is granted that there is wood in the burning (process) and that only wood is burning, then by what means will it burn?

The fuel cannot be conceived as burning by itself without the fire, as it could if it had inherent existence. The effect cannot exist without the cause, or the patient without the agent—and these relationships have already been shown to be unreal.

> Fire which is distinct from wood will unite with the latter . . . if and only if the two have mutually distinct identities. (*MK* X.1–4)

If they are not distinct to begin with, how can they be said to unite? But if they were in fact distinct, each would have independence and there could be no relationship between them.

> If fire is dependent on wood and wood on fire, then each one must have a prior completed state . . . to which the other depends. (*MK* X.7–8)

Fire must exist before wood in order to be available for the wood to exist by dependency on it, and wood must exist before fire for the same reason; each precedes the other *ad infinitum*.

> Fire does not exist in dependence on wood nor does it exist by non-dependence on wood. Likewise, wood does not exist by dependence on or non-dependence on fire. (*MK* X.12)

This is the QED. Cause and effect are neither the same nor different, neither together nor apart.

Nāgārjuna's argument, in brief, is that the cause cannot exist without the effect, therefore the effect is the cause of the cause and the cause is the effect of the effect; each precedes the other in a logical circularity *ad infinitum*. Finally they can neither be conceived as the same or different, and on the Law of the Excluded Middle there is no third possibility.

Arguments against the World of Change

The arguments against causality would be sufficient in themselves to establish the "nonexistence" of the phenomenal realm, that is, its noncompliance with the verbal categories and logical laws that make such statements as "it exists" or "it does not exist" ontologically meaningful. The causality critique does not, however, bear this burden by itself; it is supported by a variety of arguments against origination, destruction, motion, and rest, which are mostly the same as the arguments already reviewed in chapter 16 in connection with parallels between Eleatic and Mādhyamika dialectics. They can be reviewed more briefly here in the context of Sextus, who inherited them ultimately from the Eleatics.

The Mādhyamika arguments against origination and destruction include:

(1) The argument from relationality: Origination, duration, and cessation cannot be separate or different, because then it would be impossible for them to contact one another (*MK* VII.2).

(2) The argument from infinite regress: If origination, duration, and cessation exist, then each of them must also have origination, duration, and cessation, and so on *ad infinitum*: Origination must have origination, and origination of origination must have origination, and so on (*MK* VII.18–19).
(3) Does the originating thing exist prior to its origination? If so, it already existed and cannot be said to originate. If not, then it must come out of nothing, which is impossible, as nothing does not exist (*MK* VII, XIII, XVII, XXI).
(4) What is it that ceases? An existing entity cannot cease, for its nature is to exist, and a nonexisting entity cannot cease, for it has nothing to cease from (*MK* VII.26–27).

From the multitude of arguments which Sextus compiled on these points, a few examples will suffice to show the parallels with the Mādhyamika arguments.

(1) The argument from relationality (argument 1 above) is identical in form with a Skeptic argument against cause and effect, which Sextus specifically remarks is to be applied to generation and perishing also (*APh* II.322).
(2) The argument from infinite regress (argument 2 above) is identical to Zeno's argument about the infinitely divisible continuum: It is impossible for anything to begin because it is impossible to locate a point at which it might do so—in Nāgārjuna's formulation, it is impossible to locate its first origination among an infinity of them. This type of argument occurs throughout Sextus's books, where it is applied to origination, destruction, time, space, motion, and change. (See, e.g., *AP* III.109 ff.; *OP* III.71 ff.; *APh* II.37 ff., II.320.)
(3) and (4) Argument 3 above is the fundamental argument of Parmenides—the Ur-argument of all Greek philosophy. It involves the rejection of potentiality which is basic to both dialectical traditions. An argument of Sextus's for the rejection of potentiality parallels both arguments 3 and 4 above; the Being/non-Being dilemma brings into focus the fact that the concept of potentiality is a breach of the Law of the Excluded Middle:

> If a thing becomes, either the existent becomes or the non-existent. But the non-existent does not become; for the non-existent has no property, and of that which has no property neither is becoming a property. And again: what becomes is affected, but the non-existent cannot be affected at all; for affection belongs to the existent; therefore the non-existent does not become. Nor yet does the existent; for the existent exists already and has no need of becoming; neither, therefore, is the existent generated. But if neither the existent becomes nor the non-existent, and besides these no third thing can be conceived, nothing is generated. (*APh* II.326 ff.)
>
> Nor, for the same reasons, does anything perish. For if anything perishes, either the existent perishes or the non-existent. But the non-existent does not perish; for what perishes passes into a state of non-existence, but the non-existent, as it is already in a state of non-existence, does not require transference into this state. So then, the non-existent does not perish. Nor yet does the existent. For it perishes either while remaining in existence or while not remaining. And if it does so while remaining, it will be at once existent and non-existent, perished and not perished; but if it does so while not remaining, it is destroyed, and it is no longer the existent but the non-existent which perishes. So that if neither the existent nor the non-existent perishes, and besides these there is nothing, nothing perishes. (*APh* II.344 ff.)

Nāgārjuna's arguments about motion have already been touched on in connection with Zeno's arguments. First, the critique of the continuum: There is, says Nāgārjuna, the path that has been passed and the path which has not been passed, but there is no path which is being passed (*MK* II.1–2, 12–14). The argument is based on the impossibility of locating a point on a continuum. Secondly, the argument against the substance-attribute relationship: If both mover and motion move, then there are two movers, and must be two motions, and so on *ad infinitum.*

His arguments against rest are of the same types: Rest conceived as cessation of motion is impossible, due (again) to the infinite divisibility of the continuum: It is impossible to locate a point at which the cessation might take place. Rest conceived as an attribute added to a substance is impossible because a moving thing cannot receive that attribute, nor can a nonmoving thing, since it already has the attribute and would have to be two substances, requiring two attributes, and so on *ad infinitum* (*MK* II.16–21, and *MKV* 101).

In this area, also, Sextus presents a great number of arguments which are often more or less rewordings of Zeno's paradoxes:

> For if bodies, and also the places and the times in which the bodies are said to move, are divided to infinity, motion will not occur, it being impossible to discover amongst the infinite any first thing wherefrom the object said to move will derive its initial movement. And if the aforesaid objects are reducible to atomic parts, and each of the moving things passed equally in an atomic period of time with its own first atom into the first atomic point of space, then all moving things are of equal velocity . . . which is an absurd result. (*OP* III.77)
>
> In replying to those who declare that the moving thing occupies two places, that wherein it is and that whereto it shifts . . . we shall ask them *when* the moving object shifts from the place wherein it is to the other place—whether while it is in the first place or while it is in the second. But when it is in the first place it does not pass over into the second, for it is still in the first; and when it is not in this, it is not passing from it. (*OP* III.75 ff.)
>
> If a thing moves, it moves either in the place where it is or in that where it is not. But it does not move in the place where it is, for if it is in it, it remains in it; nor yet does it move in the place where it is not; for where a thing is not, there it can neither effect nor suffer anything. Therefore nothing moves. (*OP* III.71)

As for rest, Sextus fills in Zeno's oversight, reducing it equally with motion, by turning the refutation of causality against it.

> What is said to be at rest is, in fact, held to be embraced by the things which surround it, and what is embraced is acted upon; but nothing acted upon exists, since no causal activity exists, as we have shown; therefore nothing is at rest. (*OP* III.116)

It would be possible to extend this topical comparison through other subjects—time, space, change, selfhood, and so on—but the comparisons would show us no new types of arguments; the types of arguments that have been seen already would be found to be varied and reapplied in these contexts. As one scholar said, "Nāgārjuna states explicitly that the form of his arguments may be abstracted from their content, that other proofs may be performed by substituting different terms within the same pattern. This comes rather close to recognition of the principle of variables."[38] Sextus, as we have seen, also works with a few formulaic patterns of argumentation, shifting terms to focus the dialectical thrust now against one area of conceptualization, now against another. It will be more valuable to switch now from a topical survey to a comparison of these abstracted formulaic structures.

Regressus ad Infinitum

Both traditions operate primarily through the *reductio ad absurdum* (though some arguments on both sides imply syllogisms), and in both cases, the reductions are effected through two continually repeated patterns, the *regressus ad infinitum* and the rejection of relational existence.

Nāgārjuna employs the infinite regress against origination, duration, and destruction (*MK* VII.18–19), and against motion through continuous space (*MK* II.1–2, 12–14), and implies, but does not make explicit, an infinite regress in his critique of the substance-attribute relationship. Sextus inherited a rich store of Eleatic arguments from infinite regress (*all* the arguments which can confidently be ascribed to Zeno himself were of this type). Sextus uses the infinite regress reduction against origination, duration, and destruction, and against motion through continuous or discontinuous space, and, in a passage quoted above, makes it clear that the denial of partial identity also rests on an infinite regress. In addition, both Sextus and Nāgārjuna have a critique of proof on the grounds of an infinite regress of premises. Sextus:

> The thing adduced as proof of the matter proposed needs a further proof, and this again another, and so on *ad infinitum* so that the consequence is suspension of judgment as we possess no starting point for our argument. (*OP* I.166–167)

And Nāgārjuna:

> And if, for you, there is a source (of knowledge) of each and every object of proof, then tell how, in turn, for you there is proof of these sources. If by other sources (of knowledge) there would be the proof of a source—that would be an "infinite regress"! In that case neither a beginning, middle, nor an end is proved. (*VV* 31–32)[39]

The argument is the same as the critique of motion through continuous space: A point from which to begin the proof cannot be found.

The Critique of Relational Existence

The arguments based on infinite regress are so sweeping and powerful that they could do the job of throwing all concepts into question by themselves. They receive, however, overwhelming assistance from arguments based on a critique of relational existence (or of *svabhāva*, or essence, claims for relatives), which might be said to be the fundamental content of both the Pyrrhonist and the Mādhyamika schools.

On the Mādhyamika side, the rejection of relational existence (*pratītya-samutpāda*, "dependent coarising") is the "signpost," as Parmenides might have put it, of emptiness. "Neither produced nor maintained by itself," says Conze, "a thing by itself is nothing at all. And this is equivalent to the insight into the emptiness of all dharmas."[40] As Murti says: "Things that derive their being and nature by mutual dependence are nothing in themselves; they are not real . . . What is relative is subjective, unreal . . . No phenomenon, no object of knowledge, escapes this universal relativity."[41] As Nāgārjuna put it, with characteristic invoking of the same/not-same dilemma: "Any existence which is relational is indeed neither identical to nor different from the related object" (*MK* XVIII.10). If they were identical there could not be a relation between them (identicality is not a relationship), and if they were truly, ontologically different, then each would be a *svabhāva* entity, hence completely autonomous, thus not in relation to anything. So a relational "entity" is clearly not a real (*svabhāva*) entity, for if it were, the categories of identity and difference would apply to it. We may compare Chi-tsang, of the Chinese Mādhyamika ("Three-Treatise") school:

> Dharmas are neither existent nor non-existent, because they are produced by causes. If existence is not existence by its own nature but depends on causes to be existent, we know that although it (appears to) exist, it has no true existence. Since it has no true existence, it cannot be called existence in the real sense, although it (appears that it) exists.[42]

And the Tibetan Prasangika Tsong Khapa:

> Whatever depends upon conditions
> Is empty of intrinsic reality . . .
>
> Things' existence with objective status
> Precludes dependence on cause and condition.[43]

We may compare Plato's statement (*Rep.* 477–478) that phenomena are situated "between Being and non-Being" (that is, square in the excluded middle), which goes back in turn to Heraclitus's "we are and are not."

As Sextus Empiricus put it:

> Relatives are only conceived and do not exist. (APh I.208)
>
> Relative terms are in and by themselves unknowable. (Ap. D.L. IX.88)
>
> Since all things are relative, we shall suspend judgment regarding their independent and real essence. (OP I.135)

This point of view is based on a critique of relativity in general and of opposed or dependent pairs in particular. Whatever exists as a real entity must have in itself the power of existence, must be able to exist in and by itself; a thing which is called into existence by conditions, or which exists only in relation to other things, does not have this real existence. In and by itself it would not exist, which is to say, in and by itself it is nonexistent, a nonentity, nothing. Its apparent existence is only an epiphenomenon of a certain set of circumstances or conditions, an appearance created by them. "The own-being of the thing," as Conze says, "is then dissolved into the conditions of its happening."[44] Since dependent things do not really exist, they must simply appear to exist; but to appear means to appear to a mind, and hence they exist only as mental concepts or imaginative constructs (Skt. *vikalpa*, Grk. *typhos*), not as objective substances which have essences and ontological wholeness. "This principle," says Murti, "is enunciated in almost every chapter of the *Mādhyamika Kārikās*,"[45] and the same may be said of Sextus's monumental work, where the denial of relatives, like the infinite regress, is worked into practically every proof.

Both Sextus and Nāgārjuna saw dependent pairs—that is, pairs of concepts which cannot be meaningful except in relation to each other, such as left/right, male/female, yes/no—as a specially clear illustration of the critique of relational existence. Such pairs of concepts are like two sticks leaning against one another; take one away and the other falls, demonstrating that in itself it had no power to stand. Any verbal category can be placed in such a relationship by naming its negation as the other side of the pair. The problem with asserting anything is that an assertion is not meaningful except in a universe where its converse (the other leaning stick) is meaningful too. Thus the danger of grasping at yes or no, being or non-being, good or evil: Assert one and its negation is called up also. As D. T. Suzuki put it:

"A" cannot be itself unless it stands against what is not "A"; "not-A" is needed to make "A" "A," which means that "not-A" is in "A."[46]

Nāgārjuna makes this explicit in the *Ratnāvalī*:

When this exists, that exists, as "long" exists when "short" exists.[47]

Thinking of this, the Ch'an master Huang Po advises:

Beware of clinging to one half of a pair.[48]

And Sextus:

Every assertion is nullified by an equal and opposite assertion. (*OP* I.202)

In addition to annulling all statements, the principle of relationality applies to every act of perception. As Sextus explains:

The statement is twofold, implying firstly relation to the thing which judges (for the external object which is judged appears in relation to that thing), and in a second sense in relation to accompanying percepts, for instance the right side in relation to the left. (*OP* I.135)

Thus anything perceived is unreal, as is any perceiver, for what is perceived "exists" only in relation to the perceiver, and the perceiver only in relation to the perceived; perceiver and perceived then are a dependent pair and neither can be said to have independent existence. Nāgārjuna has the same argument, rejecting seeing and the seen on the ground that they "exist" only in relation to one another, and then, by the system of "variables," applying the same proof to the other senses, including mind (*MK* III.6, 8). Compare Śantideva:

The imagination and the thing imagined are both mutually dependent. (*BCA* IX.109)
If an object is dependent upon knowledge, what has become of the reality of knowledge? Likewise, if knowledge is dependent upon that which is to be known, what has become of the reality of that which is to be known? Because of mutual dependence, the reality of both is nullified. (*BCA* IX.112–113)

Everything that is perceived by the senses or apprehended by the mind is relative, since sense objects "exist" in relation to the perceiving sense, and mind-objects in relation to the mind. Nothing that cannot be perceived or thought of can be known to have any kind of existence at all. "[O]nly if the thought that designates an object exists, can that object be posited as existing . . . Since this applies to all objects, nothing exists inherently."[49] Thus the category of the relative is universal in terms of human experience. Whatever, for example, might be described as spatial involves the left/right dependent pair; whatever temporal, the before/after or simultaneous/successive pair; whatever indeed can be said to exist is at once involved in the existence/nonexistence relation and thus cannot really exist after all. There are countless possible formulations of existence in terms of relative pairs, and no formulation can possibly escape them. Nāgārjuna rejects causality on the grounds that cause and effect are a dependent pair (*MK* I), and so do the Skeptics, as Diogenes Laertius tells us:

Causes too they destroy in this way: a cause is something relative, for it is relative to what can be caused, namely the effect. But things which are relative are merely objects of thought and have no substantial existence. (D.L. IX.97)

The denial of relational existence is fundamental to both traditions. Both Sextus and Nāgārjuna felt that this argument alone was sufficient to undermine any and all assertions about reality. As Murti says, "The entire Buddhist thought revolves on the pivot of Pratītya Samutpāda [conditional or relational existence] as śūnyata."[50] In other words, the denial of relational existence leads to the denial that anything at all can be said to have real existence: It enforces a middle way between existence and nonexistence. Even ultimate reality, since the concepts real and unreal are leaning sticks, is reduced by this approach. Sextus demonstrated that it is impossible to postulate any real being which would not be involved in the flaw of relationality; it is, in other words, impossible to imagine any realm of being in contradistinction to the realm of becoming, any absolute over against the relative: Absolute and relative, after all, are a dependent pair. As Sextus explains:

> Do things which exist "in themselves" differ from relative things, or not? If they do not differ, then they too are relative; but if they differ, then, since everything which differs is relative to something (for it has its name from its relation to that from which it differs), things which exist "in themselves" are relative too. (*OP* I.137)

So much for Parmenidean Being, the Platonic Ideas, and Aristotle's Unmoved Mover! On the Mādhyamika side, Nāgārjuna (*MK* I.19) denied the difference between absolute and phenomenal reality, and Candrakīrti drew attention to "the relation of 'the thing' to its characteristic 'in itself,' since this characteristic has a meaning only if contrasted with or relative to, the thing 'not in itself.'"[51]

The Uroboric Path

The universality of relation (which is perhaps the only positive ontological doctrine taught by either Sextus or Nāgārjuna), combined with the denial of real-being to relatives, effectively disqualifies human experience from any metaphysically definitive verbal description whatever—for the term "unreal" as well as for the term "real." But it would be a mistake to think that the dialectic finally emerges as a kind of triumphant principle in itself. Both Sextus and Nāgārjuna rejected any attempt to find in the dialectic the security which the dialectic itself has removed from other concept-systems. For both, the dialectic is an "uroboric" or self-destroying path: First it wipes out conceptual proliferation (Skt. *prapañca*, Grk. *typhos*), then it erases itself, too. To put it differently: The dialectic disappears at the same moment when opinions disappear. Opinions and the rejection of opinions are a dependent pair: When opinions are gone, it is no longer possible for a rejection of opinions to exist. This is what is known in the Buddhist tradition as *śūnyata*: the emptiness of the emptiness doctrine. As Candrakīrti put it:

> Emptiness is not a property, or universal mark, of entities, because then its substratum would be nonempty, and one would have a fixed conviction (*dṛṣṭi*) about it. In fact, it is a mere medicine, a means of escape from all fixed convictions. It is taught so that we may overcome attachment, and it would be a pity if we were to become attached to it. It is not a positive standpoint, but a mere turning away from all views and thought constructions. To treat it as an object, and to oppose it to non-emptiness, is to miss the point. (*Prasannapadā* 12)[52]

Similarly, Sextus Empiricus says that the various Skeptic mottoes "are confuted by themselves, seeing that they themselves are included in the things to which their doubt applies" (*OP* I.206). Thus the Skeptic motto "Nothing is true" means "Nothing is true including the statement that nothing is true." "Nothing is comprehensible" means "nothing is comprehensible including the statement that nothing is comprehensible."

It is here that we encounter among both Skeptics and Mādhyamikas an insistent tendency to breach the Law of the Excluded Middle. As Streng says, "They do not accept the condition that in refuting one view they must affirm the contrary."[53] Sextus defends his practice exhaustively, offering four different arguments to his hypothetical Stoic opponent, who claims, "If the statement that nothing is true is true, then we must accept its converse, that something is true." First Sextus says in regard to the negative slogans:

> We do not employ them by way of authoritatively explaining the things with reference to which we adopt them, but without precision and, if you like, loosely; for it does not become the Skeptic to wrangle over expressions. (*OP* I.207)[54]

The negative generalizations, in other words, are teaching devices, not assertions about reality. Nāgārjuna likewise says that the emptiness terminology is not meaningful but a teaching device:

> Nothing could be asserted to be *śūnya*, *aśūnya*, both *śūnya* and *aśūnya*, and neither *śūnya* or *aśūnya*. They are asserted only for the purpose of provisional understanding. (*MK* XXII.11)

Second, Sextus upholds by various analogies the validity of a negative generalization which also negates itself:

> [The dialectic] is like fire, which, after consuming the fuel, destroys itself also. (*AL* II.480)
>
> And also it is like aperient drugs, which do not simply eliminate the humours from the body, but also expel themselves along with the humours. (*OP* I.206)
>
> And again, just as it is not impossible for the man who has ascended to a high place by a ladder to overturn the ladder with his foot after his ascent, so also it is not unlikely that the Skeptic, after he has arrived at the demonstration of his thesis by means of the argument proving the nonexistence of proof, as it were by a step-ladder, should then abolish this very argument. (*AL* II.480–481)

Remarkable parallels to these passages are found in the world's dialectical traditions, both absolutist and critical. Candrakīrti, like Sextus, compares the dialectic to a medicine which, having cured the disease, dissolves itself rather than constituting a new ailment, and to a fire which, when the fuel of opinions is used up, dies out (*Prasannapadā* 12). In regard to the latter image, we may also compare the "crypto-Buddhist" Vedāntin, Ramana Maharshi:

> The thought "who am I?" will destroy all other thoughts and, like the stick used for stirring the burning pyre, it will itself in the end get destroyed. Then there will arise self-realization.[55]

And Wittgenstein, in the famous passage at the end of the *Tractatus*, seems to allude to Sextus's ladder analogy:

> My propositions are all elucidatory in this way: he who understands me finally recognizes them as senseless, when he has climbed out through them, on them, over them. (He must, so to speak, throw away the ladder, after he has climbed up on it.) He must surmount these propositions; then he sees the world rightly.[56]

Related also is the common Buddhist imagery of the *dharma* or teaching as a raft to be thrown away once one has reached the other shore, and Nāgārjuna's statement that his refutation is like one phantom destroying another (*VV* 23–24).

In stressing the reflexive nature of their rejection of views, both Sextus and Nāgārjuna attempt to prevent the student from adopting indeterminacy (*aoristia*) or emptiness (*śūnyata*) as a supposedly superior point of view. The dialectic, they say, must not be clung to anymore than the assertions which it has refuted. It does not describe an ultimate reality; it is not a premise or a set of premises, but a method of analysis which can be applied to premises. It is a philosophical discourse designed to eliminate philosophical discourse. Mādhyamika emptiness and Skeptic suspension are not intended to provide a new place to stand, but to make a case that there is no place to stand. Nāgārjuna warns his readers:

> The victors have declared emptiness as the expeller of all views; but those who hold emptiness as a view they have pronounced incurable. (*MK* XIII.8)

"Emptiness," as a modern author explains, "is not a term in the primary system referring to the world, but a term in the descriptive system (meta-system) referring to the primary system. Thus it has no status as an entity, nor as the property of an existent or an inexistent. If anyone considers it so, he turns the key in the descriptive system into the root of all delusions."[57] And another modern author: "The word emptiness . . . is . . . a fruitful fiction which, if reified, leads to confusions which obviate the desirable religious ends for which . . . the concept of emptiness . . . [was] generated . . . It is not a 'thing,' rather it is a relation-word, the function of which is to evaluate and contrast the differences between what-is-happening and the methods and structures by which we recognize and communicate about what-is-happening."[58] And another: "The only 'answer' one can receive from wisdom is silence." (Compare Sextus's *aphasia*.) "Wisdom was not itself an ultimate view, nor was it an assertion about an absolute being. Wisdom was the practice of dissolving the grasping-after-hoped-for-ultimates either in the phenomenal world or the realm of ideas."[59] Here Sextus and Nagarjuna lay claim to the status of practical, rather than theoretical, teachers; their dialectic, both insist, is not an exercise in logic but a functional and experiential learning. Its value, like that of a medicine, is not in itself, but in its ability to do a job.

Sextus proposes in addition a third justification of the reflexive negations which is worth inspecting in detail. He presents a debate with a Stoic opponent (*AL* 453 ff.). First Sextus denies proof, by the critique of relational existence: Relative things do not exist. Proof is relative both to the object proven and to the mind which apprehends the proof. Therefore proof, being relative, does not exist except as an imaginative construct.

The Stoic opponent bases his reply on the apparent circularity of the Skeptic argument. If this argument does not constitute a proof of the nonexistence of proof, then it cannot convince us that proof does not exist; if it does constitute a proof (of the nonexistence of proof), then it demonstrates that proof does in fact exist: It demonstrates the opposite of what it asserts. The Skeptic reply is in parallel, but inverted: If the argument does not constitute a proof (of the nonexistence of proof) then it does not demonstrate the existence of proof; if it does constitute a proof (of the nonexistence of proof), then the nonexistence of proof, having been proven, must be accepted.

This is a conundrum similar to the Megarian one about lying. For Sextus the real point of this circular dispute about proof is that it *demonstrates* (not proves) that, in his terms, proof neither exists nor does not exist: The whole matter about proof simply does not make sense. Sextus concludes: "[One can] no more affirm than deny proof" (*AL* II.472).

Thus far the purely dialectical approach prevails, based on the equipollency of yes and no. But Sextus adds another reply to the Stoics which removes the question from dialectical treatment and seems to avoid the logical difficulties in the self-negating negations too. The Skeptic, says Sextus, cannot really make any statements about reality, such as that proof or anything else does or does not really exist; he can only look at his mind at the present moment and report what is in it:

> Of none of our . . . statements do we positively affirm that the truth is exactly as we state it, but we simply record each fact, like a chronicler, as it appears to us at the moment. (*OP* XI.4)
>
> For this is not a dogmatic assumption, that is to say assent to something non-evident, but an expression indicative of our own mental condition . . . This he says simply by way of announcing undogmatically what appears to himself regarding the matters presented, not making any confident declarations, but just describing his own state of mind. (*OP* I.197)

At the moment of arguing with the Stoic, then, what appeared in the Skeptic's mind was a conviction that proof does not exist; a present state of mind is simply a fact and cannot be affected by argument. One cannot by argument convince a joyful man that he is not joyful, or a hungry man that he is not hungry. From the Skeptic point of view, of course, the Stoic is not justified in making statements about reality either; all he can do, like the Skeptic, is say what is present to his mind at the moment. When the one says that the nonexistence of proof is present to his mind, and the other that the existence of proof is present to his mind, the same situation exists as when one says a room is cool and another that it is warm: Neither has said anything about an external reality, only about how he feels. Thus Sextus, while using the dialectic, remains aware of its emptiness.

In the *Refutation* Nāgārjuna engages in a similar debate. His opponent argues:

> Your statement (viz., that nothing has self-existence), itself being without self-existence, is not able to discard self-existence.
>
> But if that statement has its own self-existence, then your initial proposition is refuted. (*VV* 1–2)

This is precisely the Stoic attack on Sextus. Nāgārjuna's opponent says that his proposition demonstrates the opposite of what it states: If your argument does not exist, it can prove nothing; if it does exist, then existence is demonstrated. Nāgārjuna replies with a simile:

> This statement (viz., that nothing has self-existence) is not self-existent . . .
> Just as a magically formed phantom could deny a phantom . . .
> Just so (is) this negation. (*VV* 24, 23)

The opponent's reply is based on an appeal to the Law of the Excluded Middle. To paraphrase: If the phenomena which your argument negates lack self-existence, then that which lacks self-existence has been negated; consequently, on the principle of the excluded middle, that which has self-existence has been proven. Nāgārjuna replies with an explanation of why he does not feel bound by this fundamental principle of logic. To paraphrase: "The Law of the Excluded Middle only applies to things which exist; in this case, neither the phenomena rejected, nor the argument rejecting them truly exists." (As Murti paraphrases: "If we want to formulate the contradictory of any proposition—'S is P'—it is not only 'S is not-P' but also 'S is not'; i.e., the proposition is contradicted if the subject does not exist.")[60] Nāgārjuna then denies categorically the need to affirm the negative because he has negated the positive:

> If I would make any proposition whatever, then by that I would have a logical error. But I do not make a proposition; therefore I am not in error. (*VV* 29)

Nāgārjuna's concern that he not be conceived as making any proposition whatever is paralleled in the Pyrrhonist tradition, for example in the following summary from Diogenes Laertius:

> The Sceptics, then, were constantly engaged in overthrowing the dogmas of all schools, but enunciated none themselves; and though they would go so far as to bring forward and expound the dogmas of the others, they themselves laid down nothing definitely, not even the laying down of nothing. So much so that they even refuted their laying down of nothing, saying, for instance, "We determine nothing," since otherwise they would have been betrayed into determining . . . (D.L. IX.74)

The rejection of the Law of the Excluded Middle is of central importance to both Skeptic and Mādhyamika thought. The dialectic, as Murti said, means "the consciousness of the antinomical conflict of Reason in the opposition of two 'moments'—'is' and 'not-is'; [and] . . . their resolution by rising to a higher plane of consciousness."[61] The awareness of the antinomical conflict of reason is what Sextus calls the equipollency of the arguments. Sextus speaks of the "interminable conflict of views" as Murti speaks of "the interminable and total conflict in reason."[62] As Sextus says:

> With regard to any object presented, there has arisen both amongst ordinary people and amongst the philosophers an interminable conflict of views because of which we are unable either to choose a thing or to reject it, and so fall back on suspension. (*OP* I.165)

Nonadditive attention to the present mental state is an activity of the condition of *epochē* or suspension and relates to the neglect of the Law of the Excluded Middle. As Murti put it: "Affirmation and negation do not exhaust all attitudes toward an assertum; we may not assert anything at all, but simply entertain a datum without committing ourselves to any one of these modes."[63] The resolution by "rising to a higher plane of consciousness" that Murti refers to may be simply this rejection of either position in favor of a nonconceptual awareness of mind—as opposed to specific mind-objects or positions. Murti, however, with his Vedāntin orientation, may have a more absolutistic "higher plane" in mind.

In any case, what must be emphasized is that neither Pyrrhonist nor Mādhyamika dialecticians regarded their negation as another philosophical position (e.g., nihilism) which could be clung to as another dogmatism. So completely, Sextus says, does the Pyrrhonist refrain from identifying the negative position as *his* that he rejoices when an opponent presents a positive proof as convincing as the negative—for then the necessity of taking the middle position between yes and no becomes the more obvious (*AL* II.476–477).

The Double Truth

The relation between absolute and relative being necessarily involves the doctrine of the double truth, another central theme which is shared by Pyrrhonists and Mādhyamikas. Sextus says (*OP* II.14–18, *AP* VII.29–35, and elsewhere) that there are two criteria: that by which we judge reality and unreality, and that which we use as a guide in everyday life. According to the first criterion, nothing is either true or false, no statements can be made, no opinions have meaning. According to the second, inductive statements based on direct observation of phenomena may be treated as either true or false for the purpose of making everyday practical decisions. The distinction, as Conze has noted,[64] is equivalent to the Mādhyamika distinction between "Absolute truth" (*paramārthasatya*), "the knowledge of the real as it is without any distortion,"[65] and "Truth so-called" (*saṃvṛti satya*), "truth as conventionally believed in common parlance."[66]

Everyday life, according to the doctrine of the double truth in both its versions, is to be carried out on the basis of conventional truth, while the mind remains aware that this conventional truth is in fact neither true nor false. As Sextus said:

> We live according to the normal rules of life, undogmatically, seeing that we cannot remain wholly inactive. (*OP* I.23)

Nāgārjuna agrees:

> We do not speak without accepting, for practical purposes, the work-a-day world. (*VV* 28)

It is interesting, in terms of the duration of the life of a tradition, to compare the words of a modern Buddhist master of southeast Asia:

> Externally we shall behave the same way as others—eat like they eat, work like they work, and speak like they speak . . . The mind however is void . . . For example, outwardly the man of Dhamma may appear to have wealth, a family, honor, and fame. Inside, however, there is nothing. In his mind he possesses nothing . . . Outwardly one may possess all the things that others possess, but the mind possesses nothing.[67]

That the mind possesses nothing refers to its noninclination (*arrepsia*) toward either yes or no; and it also means that the mind is not carrying a burden of opinions, of pseudoknowledge—*vikalpa* or *typhos*. One may compare Crates: "Having nothing, we have everything."

This approach to life, with its mental balance between yes and no, reifies ethically and psychologically the rejection of the Law of the Excluded Middle. The psychological stance between affirmation and negation is the ethical analogue of that rejection. This middle stance toward phenomena, neither accepting nor rejecting predications about them, is articulated in Buddhist texts which denounce the rejection of phenomena as the heresy of nihilism ("is-not"), and their acceptance as the heresy of eternalism ("is"). Hui Hai says:

> The Buddha never rejected anything phenomenal from the moment when he first determined upon his quest up to the time when he achieved Enlightenment beneath the Bodhi Tree and from then up to his entrance into Parinirvāṇa beneath the twin sala trees. This is non-annihilation of the worldly.[68]

It is a common error to believe that the Mādhyamika point of view, with its emphasis on "The Void," consists of the heresy of nihilism. Certain passages in Sextus could give the same impression. This is because of a certain looseness of expression which both authors engage in fairly often. Since the ordinary view of reality consists in the heresy of eternalism or essentialism, that is, belief in the enduring objective selfhood of things as named by language, both Nāgārjuna and Sextus at times express themselves against this view, without bothering to point out that they are equally against the heresy of nihilism (which, after all, practically no one needs to be cured of). Nāgārjuna, for example, often says of some part of conventional reality that it does not exist, when what he means is that, since it resists rational formulation in terms of either "is" or "is-not," it is either outside of or in between such categories. Saying it does not exist is a shorthand for the longer formula set forth in the fourfold negation. Similarly, after arguing that cause and effect are irrational concepts, Sextus says that they do not exist, meaning that they do not have the kind of existence to which two-valued expressions apply; since our opinions about them cannot be either true or false, they effectively do not exist in a two-valued world. (See, e.g., *APh* I.253 ff., II.45–49, II.320; *OP* III.65.)

The ethical endeavor which is recommended is to refrain from entangling experience with verbal concepts, or to disentangle the two, and to focus attention on an aspect of experience which is declared to be more basic. As Conze says, the dialectic "opens the way to a direct approach to the true nature of things (*dharmatā*) by removing all adherence to words, which always detract or abstract from reality instead of disclosing it."[69]

Breaching the Laws of Thought

Both Skeptic and Mādhyamika dialecticians invoked the Laws of Contradiction and Excluded Middle when attacking the contentions of the dogmatists, to show them that their rules do not provide them with adequate range to think in.[70] In their own statements, however, they frequently breach those principles, often with a sense of celebrating their demise. In the Greek tradition the use of deliberate contradiction as a critical inroad into the citadel of logic begins with Zeno's paradoxes ("The flying arrow is at rest"), proceeds through the *Contradictory Arguments* of Protagoras, the *Parmenides* of Plato, the conundra of Eubulides of Miletus designed to force the interlocutor to answer yes and no to the same question, and is enshrined in Cynic slogans such as Crates' "Having nothing we have everything."

In the Indian tradition it is found in certain Upaniṣadic passages that deal with the distinction between absolute and relative. Yājñavalkya's "*Iti, iti*"/"*Neti, neti*" paradox is paralleled by the *Kena Upaniṣad*'s distinction of two opposite types of knowledge: He who knows everything knows nothing, and he who knows nothing knows everything. It appears in the Buddhist literature of the Prajñāpāramitā, such as the *Diamond Sūtra*'s assertion:

> Although innumerable beings have thus been led to Nirvāṇa, no being at all has been led to Nirvāṇa.[71]

Nāgārjuna does not breach the Law of Contradiction in the *Verses on the Middle Way*, which are more focused on the breach of the excluded middle, but he does once in the *Refutation*, in a passage at the very end of the text that parallels Crates' "Having nothing we have everything":

> All things prevail for him for whom emptiness prevails. Nothing whatever prevails for him for whom emptiness prevails.[72]

The Chinese Mādhyamika author Seng Chao used paradoxes that often echoed Zeno, especially "The flying arrow is at rest":

> The raging storm that uproots mountains is always tranquil, rivers rushing to the sea do not flow, the fleeting forces moving in all directions and rushing about do not move.
>
> What people call remaining, I call passing on, whereas what people call passing on, I call remaining. Although passing on and remaining are different, ultimately they are the same. This is why it is said in the scripture, "Straight words seem to be their opposite. Who will believe them?"
>
> Thus things and I sprang from the same root, and right and wrong come out of the same breath.[73]

The Ch'an and Zen masters, whose attitudes were essentially based on the Prajñāpāramitā and Mādhyamika texts, made regular use of it:

> When you understand, you belong to the family. When you do not understand, you are a stranger. Those who do not understand belong to the family. And when they understand they are strangers. (Ummon)[74]

Statements which breach the Law of the Excluded Middle are more common than paradoxes in both traditions, and indeed are central to both. Again the Zen teachers made enthusiastic use of them:

> The path does not belong to the perception world, neither does it belong to the non-perception world . . . If you want to reach the true path beyond doubt, place yourself in the same freedom as sky. You name it neither good nor not-good. (Nansen)[75]

The rejection of the logical principles has both a cognitive function and an ethical one. The most basic of the dialectical arguments, the one that amounts to a positive ontological and ethical doctrine, is the analysis of the relationality of existence and the exhortation against choosing one side of a dependent pair. This theme takes priority in the psychological and ethical stance which emerges from the dialectical *elenchus*. In escaping the web of (two-valued) relationality there are only two paths: either to accept both halves of the pair, which is a breach of the Law of Contradiction, or to reject both, which is a breach of the Law of the Excluded Middle. The dialectic, in other words, *requires* the breach of the logical principles.

The dialectical *elenchus* proposes to show that the most scrupulous application of these principles fails to result in meaningful statements about experience, and that the principles of logic are not consistently and rigidly applied by their advocates for precisely this reason. Nevertheless, they championed these principles while covertly breaching them, because these principles seemed to give them control over reality, to make reality manageable in a certain way. Without the laws of logic, language and discursive thought seem strangely meaningless: If A and not-A are the same, then all words mean the same thing, which is to say, everything and nothing; language is just another silence. Since the application of the Laws has seemed to show them to be meaningless and ineffective, their negation appears to take on a certain meaning and effectiveness. A sense arises that the breach of the discredited principles of logic can free one from them, right square *in* the excluded middle ground, or right *at* the intersection point of a contradiction.

A challenge to groups that adopt this stance is to develop a new way of verbalizing, a way more suitable to a flowing and interpenetrating reality than to a rigid and separated one. The paradoxical formulations of the Megarians were examples, but they may not have affected everyday discourse. Diogenes more publicly reversed the traditional *euphemia* with his principle of *parrhēsia*, free-speaking or counterspeaking. The tactic was in part to speak what society was specifically calculated and shaped and devised to keep unspoken. It seems that he altered form as well as content, but unfortunately little is known of the Cynic style of discourse. In the Buddhist tradition a similar impulse was behind the paradoxical expressions of the Prajñāpāramitā style, which may ultimately lie behind the Zen conventions of discourse, of which the koan is the most well-known.

Neither Sextus nor Nāgārjuna, however, recommends a stance outside of logic. Such a stance does not really escape the principles of formal logic, since to accept the negative because one has disproved the positive is to apply the Law of the Excluded Middle—even though that law was the positive that was disproved. Further, the rejection of noncontradiction and excluded middle means that the usefulness of ordinary language is curtailed; the ordinary purposes of life are put in jeopardy when the language that models them has been discredited. To act as if statements that controvert the Laws of Thought have meaning is to fall back into the fly bottle—the trap of believing that one can say something about reality, albeit in an unaccustomed way. Conze has noted the danger of seeing the paradoxes as new positive principles: "When the paradoxes . . . have succeeded in removing all attachment to logical modes of thinking they again must be left behind."[76] In the fourfold negation both Sextus and Nagarjuna were at pains to reject the language constructions that breached the laws of logic along with those that observed them: Both the principles of logic and the statements which negate them are negated.

Four types of discourse are implied. First is the practical everyday discourse based on conventional truth, what Sextus calls "acquiescing in the appearances or accepting them undogmatically": When one seems to feel hot or cold one reports it. No assertion about the relationship of the appearance to some hypothetical absolute reality is implied. The statement is said to be made on the basis of the present moment alone. There are redemptive overtones to the idea of a mind cleansed of conceptual overlap ("thought coverings"), somewhat like the Orphic idea of cleaning the wisdom eye though aimed at a clear seeing of phenomena rather than noumena.

Second, there is the discourse suitable to the critique of dogmas, where the principles of formal logic are employed because the interlocutor must be disproved in terms whose validity he acknowledges.

Third, there is discourse with students, in which either logical or antilogical formulations may be useful as teaching devices.

And finally there is an inner silence in which the subject does not posit, negate, accept both positive and negative, or reject both. It neither makes nor implies statements about the real but simply entertains experience as a datum. This may be described matter-of-factly, as Sextus tends to do, or with an absolutist religious tinge, as when Conze says, "Words fail, and the spiritual reality communicates directly with itself."[77]

Nirvāṇa

The purpose of the Mādhyamika dialectic is clear up to a point. It aims, Nāgārjuna said, at the pacification of *prapañca*, or conceptual proliferation (*MK* XXV.24). This pacification, says Candrakīrti, *is* nirvāṇa.[78] When the mind no longer grasps at notions of real or unreal entities (*bhāva* or *abhāva*), it is, says Nāgārjuna, in the state of nirvāṇa (*Ratnāvalī* I.42).[79] The texts have difficulty demystifying that moment. A somewhat Vedāntin aura clings to the idea that the Mādhyamika is a "transformational dialectic" which "purports to move consciousness beyond any and all conceptual structures, beyond any form of discourse, beyond any natural or philosophical language, beyond any ontology."[80] The mind's attempt to project linguistic categories ontologically is the source of its suffering; by living "without thought-coverings," as the *Heart Sūtra* puts it, the aspirant "overcomes what can upset, and in the end attains to Nirvāṇa."[81] Again there is something like the Jain or Orphic idea of the cleansed mind, as in the Tibetan text that says, "The View of Mahamūdra is to add nothing to Mind's nature" (*The Vow of Mahamūdra* 8). According to one view "adding nothing to mind's nature" means not conceptualizing about mental states but entertaining them as neutral data. This aspect of the Dharma was prominent in the Ch'an and Zen traditions. Huang Po, for example, says:

> If you would spend all your time—walking, standing, sitting or lying down—learning to halt the concept-forming activities of your mind, you could be sure of ultimately attaining the goal.
>
> To be absolutely without concepts is called the Wisdom of Dispassion . . . You must get away from the doctrines of existence and non-existence . . . This is not something which you can accomplish without effort, but when you reach the point of clinging to nothing whatever, you will be acting as the Buddhas act. This will indeed be acting in accordance with the saying, "Develop a mind which rests on nothing whatever." For this is your pure Dharmakāya, which is called supreme perfect Enlightenment.[82]

So the goal of Mādhyamika dialectic was enlightenment, but in approaching the question what the Pyrrhonist's goal was, one notices a difference in feeling tone. In India the goal of reaching enlightenment was originally a religious goal having to do with the afterlife; detachment from worldly things was a condition for escape from the cycle of reincarnations. Desire for the material realm pulled the soul back there. Dialectically criticizing the opinions which underlie desire could free it. Something of a religious aura surrounded this goal. The difference in feeling tone expresses the more enduring association with religion in the history of Indian philosophy. Sextus does not employ pious invocations of saints; Nāgārjuna does.[83]

Beyond this difference in style is a remarkable parallelism in substance which has often been obscured by scholarly readings of Pyrrhonism. One recent author, for example, wrote:

> The positive side of [Pyrrhonic] skepticism consists in a practical and supposedly beneficial situation which, however, bears on no higher level of illumination or understanding of truth. The simple point of the Skeptic is that once all judgments are withdrawn, we are not to be disturbed by uncertain expectation or vexation about the future, and thus we are able to enjoy the present . . . [84]

This interpretation is very questionable. That the Skeptic's suspension "bears on no higher level of illumination" is an unsupported judgment. It would be easy to amass Zen texts which, with their insistence on "ordinary everyday mind" as the goal, could be interpreted the same way. The condition of being able to enjoy the present without vexation about the future is the state that Hui Hai calls the Buddha state. Countless Buddhist texts in the Theravādin, Mādhyamika, Mahamūdra, and Zen traditions assert that the ability to relate directly to the present moment *is* the "higher state of illumination" that is sought through dialectic and other practices. That this state does not bear on a higher "understanding of the truth" implied dogmatism. The Mādhyamika or Pyrrhonist practitioner attempts to take a stand above or anyway outside of the true/not-true dichotomy, feeling that this in itself constitutes a higher understanding of the truth.

Another recent author questions whether Sextus's method will in fact lead to the lack of vexation (*ataraxia*) which it aims at:

> A true Skeptic, at least as conceived by Sextus, will be engaged in a continuing (and perpetually unresolved) search for a definitive answer to each and every philosophical question that comes before him. He will (and Sextus did) amass a large stock of philosophical arguments . . . from which he may draw to support any side of each philosophical question . . . The so-called quietude of the Skeptic thus begins to resemble the peace of the well-armed man, always on guard and ready for combat, though with a reasonable expectation neither of victory nor defeat. It is not in the least like the quietude of the man who has once and for all renounced contention—the man for whom, in the words of Wittgenstein, "philosophical problems . . . *completely* disappear."[85]

This impression seems to result from overstressing a single passage of Sextus:

> Some have claimed to have discovered the truth, others have asserted that it cannot be apprehended, while others again go on inquiring. Those who believe they have discovered it are the Dogmatists . . . the Academics treat it as inapprehensible; the Skeptics keep on inquiring. (*OP* I.2)

Sextus's statement that the Skeptic "keeps on inquiring" does not mean that he is actively engaged in a search for the truth, but that he has not settled on a position, in contrast to the Dogmatist, who asserts Yes, and the Academic, who asserts No. To go on actively seeking the truth is in opposition to the thrust of Sextus's work as a whole, which has taken a stand outside the true/not-true dichotomy and avoids "combat" over opinions on the grounds that "it does not befit the Skeptic to wrangle" (*OP* I.207).

A third view is more accurate: "It must be remembered that the most important effect of the Skeptic's *epochē* (suspension) is to preserve him from philosophical discussion." "His main non-cognitive motivation for finding the truth is no longer there: the peace of mind which he was seeking is already found." "Although he throws arguments into the discussion, he takes no part in it . . . he does so without accepting any of them as true or valid."[86]

It is not to be imagined that Skeptics in general amassed arguments as Sextus did. Sextus describes the work of collecting and opposing arguments as a therapy used to cure the disease of opinions. He was a medical doctor as well as a philosopher, and his view of philosophy was essentially therapeutic. He was a professional purveyor of Skeptic remedies, a practicing Skeptic doctor, who engaged in philosophy not to seek the truth, but to help people see the limitations of their points of view. Candrakīrti, as quoted above, said the same of the Mādhyamika dialectic, and in fact the Buddhist literature in general regularly attributes this view of teaching to the Buddha himself:

> The mystery of the Tathāgatas etc. is difficult to understand, Sāriputra, because when they explain the laws . . . they do so by means of skillfulness, by the display of knowledge, by arguments, reasons, fundamental ideas, interpretations, and suggestions. By

a variety of skillfulness they are able to release creatures that are attached to one view or another. (*Saddharma-Puṇḍarīka* 2)[87]

Q. Why did the lord decline to decide the question, whether the living being is identical with the body or not?

A. Because he took into consideration the intention of the questioner . . .

Q. Why did not the lord declare that it does not exist at all?

A. Because he took into consideration the questioner's state of mind . . .

Q. Why then did not Buddha declare that the "living being" is a conventional name for a set of constantly changing elements?

A. Because his interlocutor was not capable of grasping the theory of elements. (*Abhidharmakośa-kārikā* V.22)[88]

When the Sage said that things go, he did not mean that they really go; he merely wanted to prevent ordinary thoughts (i.e., that things endure), and when he said that things remain in the same state, he did not mean that they really remain; he merely wanted to discard what ordinary people call the passing (impermanence) of things.

The Tathāgata (Buddha), in accordance with the obstruction in the common people's views, speaks appropriate words to dispel their delusions. He exercises his true mind which transcends any duality and preaches various doctrines which need not be the same. (Seng Chao)[89]

The idea of non-existence is presented primarily to handle the disease of the concept of existence. If the disease disappears, the useless medicine is also discarded. Thus we know that the Way of the Sage has never held to either existence or non-existence. (Chi Tsang)[90]

From the Buddhist point of view, then, there is no disharmony between Sextus's practice of teaching and his claim that he has attained a peace of mind beyond the battle of opinions; the same is said of the Buddha himself.

The last-quoted critic of Sextus continues his criticism as follows:

> The Skeptic's positionless position would in no way affect the ordinary beliefs of anyone moved by his arguments—for it is not the affairs of daily life that Sextus is skeptical about. Rather, he is skeptical about philosophers' claims to have discovered facts about reality.[91]

This again is very far from what Sextus says, as is yet another scholar's claim that Pyrrhonism "is in essence a rudimentary scientific method."[92] Attention to two passages where Sextus explains his sense of his purpose will clarify the situation.

> Skepticism is an ability, or mental attitude, which opposes appearances to judgments in any way whatsoever with the result that, owing to the equipollence of the objects and reasons thus opposed, we are brought firstly to a state of mental suspense [*epochē*] and next to a state of "unperturbedness" or quietude [*ataraxia*]. (*OP* I.12)

> An "End" is "that for which all actions or reasoning are undertaken, while it exists for the sake of none"; or otherwise, "the ultimate object of appetency." We assert still that the Skeptic's End is quietude [*ataraxia*] in respect of matters of opinion and moderate feeling in respect of things unavoidable . . . For the man who opines that anything is by nature good or bad is forever being disquieted: when he is to be tormented by things naturally bad and he pursues after the things which are, as he thinks, good; which when he has obtained he keeps falling into still more perturbations because of his irrational and immoderate elation, and in his dread of a change of fortune he uses every endeavour to avoid losing the things which he deems good. On the other hand, the man who determines nothing as to what is naturally good or bad neither shuns nor pursues any-

> thing eagerly; and, in consequence, he is unperturbed . . . The Skeptics were [once, like other people] in hopes of gaining quietude by means of a decision regarding the disparity of the objects of sense and of thought, and being unable to effect this they suspended judgement; and they found that quietude, as if by chance, followed upon their suspense, even as a shadow follows its substance. We do not, however, suppose that the Skeptic is wholly untroubled; but we say that he is troubled by things unavoidable; for we grant that he is cold at times and thirsty, and suffers various affections of that kind. But even in these cases, whereas ordinary people are afflicted by two circumstances—namely by the affections themselves and, in no less a degree, by the belief that these conditions are evil by nature,—the Skeptic, by his rejection of the added belief in the natural badness of all these conditions, escapes here too with less discomfort. Hence we say that while in regard to matters of opinion the Skeptic's End is quietude, in regard to things unavoidable it is "moderate affection." (*OP* I.25–30)

Sextus does not say that it is only vexation about the future that the suspended mind is free of, but vexation about the present too. He also does not say that he is altering only one's response to philosophical ideas and not to ordinary life; indeed, he suggests a new way to relate to daily discomforts and misfortunes. Nowhere in his statements of purpose does he mention the idea of searching for truth or improving the method of seeking truth; he speaks only about being free from the concepts good and evil and the entanglements of desire and aversion these concepts invite.

There is a strong relationship between Sextus's passages just quoted and Buddhist texts. On Sextus's claim, for example, that once the mind has become suspended imperturbability follows naturally like a shadow, compare Śantideva:

> When neither existence nor non-existence is presented again to the mind, then, through lack of any other possibility, that which is without support becomes tranquil. (*BCA* IX.35)

Sextus's passage should be compared also with the Buddhist doctrine of the Four Noble Truths. In both cases the genesis of suffering is identified as the habit of discriminating between good and bad, which locks one into anxiety about avoiding what one dislikes and getting what one likes and, once one has got it, anxiety about holding on to it. In both cases the path out of suffering is described as freeing oneself from the discrimination that leads to desire and cultivating a moderate involvement in phenomena. Sextus's Skeptic who gets cold or hungry and simply entertains the cold and hunger as data without judging them evil is not unlike the Buddha of the Hīnayāna biography, who died of a stomachache without thinking it an evil.

The path to this concept-freed condition is said to involve the cultivation of a more direct relationship with the present moment; to "live without thought coverings," as the *Heart Sūtra* says, means to live with one's experience without projecting concepts onto it under the prods of desire and aversion. Sextus's emphasis on a direct nonconceptual relationship with the present moment, his "acquiescing in the phenomena" or using the present moment as one's "criterion for action" (*OP* I.21–24), but "without intense goal orientation (*prosklisis*) or intense emotional involvement (*prospatheia*) (*OP* I.230) resembles the simple and nonjudgmental "mindfulness" (Pali *sati*) of Buddhism. Pyrrhonism, like Buddhist mindfulness practice, is "the return" from concept motivation to "life itself as the only guide."[93] The Skeptic, Sextus says, "is guided by thirst to drink and by hunger to food" (*OP* I.24, 238, and elsewhere). Similarly a Zen master is often said to "eat when he is hungry and sleep when he is tired"—acquiescing in the present moment as the guide to conduct.

Here is an example—one of many—of this theme, in a dialogue in which Hui Hai is interrogated by a certain Master Yuan:

> Q. Do you make efforts in your practice of the Way, Master?
> A. Yes, I do.
> Q. How?
> A. When hungry I eat, when tired I sleep.
> Q. And does everybody make the same efforts as you do, Master?
> A. Not in the same way.
> Q. Why not?
> A. When they are eating, they think of a hundred kinds of necessities, and when they are going to sleep they ponder over affairs of a thousand different kinds. That is how they differ from me.[94]

According to many important Buddhist texts, living in the present moment, acquiescing in it as a guide to action without conceptualizing about it, *is* enlightenment. And that is what Sextus says the Skeptic does, when he has achieved suspension and his mind has been put at rest. Sextus's dialectic, then, is, like that of Nāgārjuna, a "transformational dialectic," designed to release the mind from bondage to "some form of consciousness, some ontology, some intelligible or rational structure which it has not seen through or called into question," an "analytical meditation in which the formal conditions of *all* discourse or *any* possible world are themselves shown to be conditioned and not independent, absolute, or self-existent."[95]

Is the Skeptic's use of the immediately present state of consciousness, without adventitious conceptualization or discrimination, equivalent to the practice of moment-to-moment awareness which was taught in the *Mahā-satipaṭṭhāna Sutta*,[96] and which has been called "the foundation stone of Buddhist practice, common to all traditions and sects"?[97] Clearly the two stances overlap, but we cannot say how far, for Sextus, like Nāgārjuna, presented in his writings only the dialectical support for the Skeptic's way of life, not any practical mind-training recommendations which may have gone with it.

The correlation is difficult to assess in part because Buddhist texts use a more flamboyant language to describe their ambitions and attainments than do Greek texts, especially Pyrrhonist. Nevertheless, the substance of what is being said often seems to amount to the same thing. Hui Hai, for example, when asked, "What does right perception mean?" made the flamboyant reply, "It means perceiving that there is nothing to perceive." But when asked further, he replied in language that could have been used by a Pyrrhonist as easily as a Buddhist:

> It means beholding all sorts of forms, but without being stained by them as no thoughts of love or aversion arise in the mind.

Then he returns to the type of poetic imagery which among the relevant Greek authors only Plato used:

> Reaching this state is called obtaining the Buddha-eye, which really means just that and nothing else. Whereas, if the spectacle of various forms produces love or aversion in you, that is called perceiving them as though they had objective existence, which implies having the eye of an ordinary person, for indeed ordinary people have no other sort of eye. It is the same with all the other organs of perception.[98]

Does the Pyrrhonist Skeptic, then, have the Buddha-eye when, being established in suspension and imperturbability, he views things without desire or aversion arising in him and without convictions about their objective existence or lack of it? There is disagreement among Buddhist authors on what constitutes the Buddha-eye, but some clearly have taught that this moment-to-moment awareness without passionate involvement is at the center of it. Two modern Buddhist masters have spoken about it as follows:

> By the questioning and neutralizing influence of detached observation . . . [phenomena] will increasingly lose the sting of irritation, and, thereby, their disturbing effect. This will prove to be an act of true *viraga* ("dispassion"), which literally means "decoloring." This is to say, these experiences will lose their emotional tinge that excites towards lust and aversion, and they will appear as "bare phenomena."[99]
>
> Try to keep your mind in the present. Whatever there is that arises in the mind, just watch it. Let go of it . . . No discriminating between good and bad, hot and cold, fast and slow, no me and no you, no self at all. Just what there is . . . Be mindful and let things take their natural course . . . Eventually your mind will reach its natural balance . . . Problems will arise and you will see through them immediately. This is the happiness of the Buddha.[100]

When the contemporary Zen teacher Seung Sahn Sohn Sa advises his students to "keep don't-know mind," it seems that he means something like Sextus's suspension and Nāgārjuna's empty mind:

> Don't-know mind is empty mind. There are no words, no speech [cf. Grk. *aphasia*]. So there is no one, no God, no nothing, no mind, no emptiness. This don't-know mind is very important . . . This is your true self. So always keep don't-know mind.
>
> Only keep don't-know. Don't be attached to words.
>
> So you must keep only don't-know, always and everywhere. Then you will soon get enlightenment. But be very careful not to want enlightenment. Only keep don't-know mind. Your situation, your condition, your opinions, throw them all away.
>
> I don't know, but when I am thirsty I drink. I don't know, but when I am tired, I rest. Only this.[101]

There is a general congruence with Sextus: By maintaining a suspended or "don't-know" mind and acquiescing in the phenomena (drinking when thirsty, etc.), one naturally and inevitably "attains" peace. The Zen theme of the Great Doubt or Great Questioning is to the same effect. As the Rinzai teacher Hakuin said:

> Underlying great doubt there is great satori; where there is thorough questioning there will be a thoroughgoing experience of awakening.[102]

In both traditions a link between detachment and compassion is posited. Diogenes Laertius says:

> According to some authorities the end proposed by the Skeptics is insensibility (*apatheia*); according to others gentleness (*praotēs*). (IX.109)

A modern Theravādin teacher says:

> Vipassana [attention to the present moment] extricates you from greed, hatred and delusion . . . And this is an end to selfishness . . . Compassion appears in the natural progression of sādhana . . . The natural state of the mind is automatically compassion . . . You don't have to do anything to create it.[103]

It is hard to identify any significant difference between either the methods or the stated purposes of Pyrrhonist and Mādhyamika dialectic. If the pacification of conceptual proliferation (Candrakīrti) and the suppression of belief in real entities or their absence (Nāgārjuna) constitute nirvāṇa for an Indian or a Chinese it is hard to say why they should not conitute nirvāṇa for a Greek as well. And if Conze is right in saying that "The teaching of the sameness of everything cannot fail to promote the virtue of evenmindedness" and "the attitude of non-assertion . . . alone can assure lasting peace"[104] then there can be no reason (beyond cultural prejudice) why his remarks should seem to apply less to Greeks than to Indians and Chinese.

Notes to Chapter Seventeen

1. "[T]here seems no reason to doubt the tradition of his Indian travels," says R. J. Hankinson (*The Sceptics* [London and New York: Routledge, 1995], p. 59).

2. See Michael Frede, "The Skeptic's Beliefs," in *Essays in Ancient Philosophy* (Minneapolis: University of Minnesota Press, 1987), p. 181; Burnyeat similarly calls the suspended life "not, after all, a possible life for a man" (Myles Burnyeat, "Can the Skeptic Live His Skepticism?" in *Doubt and Dogmatism: Studies in Hellenistic Epistemology*, ed. M. Schofield, M. Burnyeat and J. Barnes [Oxford: Clarendon Press, and New York: Oxford University Press, 1979], p. 53).

3. See Burnyeat, ibid., pp. 29–31 and n. 17.

4. Also, Aristotle mentions it in discussing Protagoras at *Met.* 1009b10–11.

5. Phillip H. DeLacy, "*ou mallon* and the Antecedents of Ancient Skepticism," *Phronesis* 3 (1958): 61.

6. For this term see John Visvader, "The Use of Paradox in Uroboric Philosophies," *Philosophy East and West* 28 (1978), pp. 455–467.

7. A fragmentary paraphrase is preserved *ap.* Aristocles; see H. Diels, ed., *Poetarum Philosophorum Fragmenta*, fasc. 3, pt. 1 of Ugo von Wilamowitz, ed., *Poetarum Graecorum Fragmenta* (Berlin, 1901), pp. 175–176. For an English translation, see Burnet in *Encyclopaedia of Religion and Ethics* s.v. "Sceptics." Frede has argued that Timon's account is of dubious value (Michael Frede, "Review of *Greek Skepticism: a Study in Epistemology*, by C. L. Stough," *Journal of Philosophy* 70, no. 21 [1973]: 805–810, 806). For remarks on the problems in the sources on Pyrrhon see Frede, "The Skeptic's Beliefs," p. 183, and Hankinson, *The Sceptics*, pp. 3–12.

8. Trans. J. Fritz Staal, *Exploring Mysticism* (Berkeley, California: University of California Press, 1975), p. 36.

9. Sextus also relays the rumor that, whereas Arcesilaus spoke as a Skeptic in public, inside the Academy "he passed on to those of his companions who were naturally talented the dogmas of Plato" (*OP* I.134 f.). Sextus does not seem to believe this rumor, as he asserts unequivocally that he regards Arcesilaus as a Skeptic. Numenius and Cicero also mention this rumor, which may have been put forth by members of the Academy still loyal to Plato's memory in order to foster an impression of continuity in the school's orientation.

10. Giovanni Reale, *A History of Ancient Philosophy*, Vol. 3: *The Systems of the Hellenistic Age*, trans. John R. Catan (Albany, New York: State University of New York Press, 1985), p. 335. Reale also quotes, in a footnote, the following remarks of Dal Pra: Carneades "struck at the roots of Stoicism till he finally destroyed it; and then? Carneades did not go beyond Stoicism

. . . there is nothing in front of the founder of the new Academy except an empty horizon" (p. 444, note 23).

11. For a summary of Arcesilaus's long dialectical battle with Zeno of Citium about the Stoic theory of the kataleptic impression see Hankinson, *The Sceptics,* pp. 74–91.

12. Or did it? This is the usual view, as when Jeffrey Hopkins says, "Nāgārjuna . . . founded Mādhyamika through his definitive presentation of the explicit meaning of Buddha's Perfection of Wisdom Sūtras . . ." (*Meditation on Emptiness* [Boston: Wisdom Publications, 1996], p. 11). But the conventional interpretation is not the only one. Nāgārjuna's expression is so stripped down as to be ambiguous, while at the same time it is historically so important that it cannot be ignored. This situation has come to invite leaps of interpretation. Candrakīrti, in the opinion of many, began the process by redefining Nāgārjuna as a Vedāntin (he did not use that word). Recently the idea that he was a proto-Wittgensteinian has been popular (but see Kalupahana's negative remarks on the comparison [*Nāgārjuna: The Philosophy of the Middle Way*, Albany, New York: State University of New York Press, 1986, p. 93]). My own idea (about to be expounded in the text) concerning the possibility of Hellenistic dialectical input is another such suggestion. Yet another is Kalupahana's argument that Nāgārjuna was not a Mahāyānist but a Hīnayānist, and specifically that his *Karikas* were an exposition ("a grand commentary") in a new dialectical form of the canonical *Kaccāyanagotta Sutta* (ibid., p. 81). Though most assume Nāgārjuna was a Mahāyānist (it was he who turned the Wheel of the *Dharma* the second time) Kalupahana's view is not really peculiar. Cf. Richard Robinson and Willard Johnson: "Scholars have questioned whether Nāgārjuna was a Mahāyānist," etc. (*The Buddhist Religion: A Historical Introduction* [Belmont, California: Wadsworth Publishing Company, 1997], p. 89, with his following discussion.) A. K. Warder also dealt with the question (*Indian Buddhism*, Delhi: Motilal Banarsidass, 1970, p. 376).

Kalupahana's position is powerfully argued and may well be true. What is unique about it is the attempt by a Theravādin scholar to appropriate *the* great philosophical hero of the Mahāyāna. It is a counterpunch to the sometimes brutal battering that the so-called Hīnayāna has taken from the Mahāyāna over the millennia. In any case, Kalupahana's suggestion does not displace mine but may complement it. *Why* did Nāgārjuna redo the message of the *Kaccāyanagotta Sutta*? He did not revise its content, according to Kalupahana. His point, then, must have been to introduce a new form of argumentation by connecting it with an inherited traditional text whose orthodoxy was unquestioned. That this new and foreign form of argumentation came already focused on the "middle" position only recommended it the more.

13. Sextus will be quoted in the translation of R. G. Bury (*Sextus Empiricus*, Loeb Classical Library [Cambridge, Massachusetts: Harvard University Press, and London: W. Heinemann, 1933–1949]) with occasional slight changes which do not depart from literalness. In Bury's system *OP* refers to *Outlines of Pyrrhonism*, *AL* refers to *Against the Logicians*, *APh* refers to *Against the Physicists*, *AE* refers to *Against the Ethicists*, *AP* refers to *Against the Professors*. The *Mādhyamikakārikās* will be quoted primarily in the translation of Kenneth K. Inada (*Nagarjuna: A Translation of His Mūlamadhyamikakārikā with an Introductory Essay* [Tokyo: Hokuseido Press, 1970]), the *Vigraha-vyāvartanī* in the translation of Streng (in Frederick K. Streng, *Emptiness: A Study in Religious Meaning* [Nashville, Tennessee, and New York: Abingdon Press, 1967], pp. 221–227) or that of Kamaleswar Bhattacharya (*The Dialectical Method of Nāgārjuna* [Delhi: Motilal Banarsidass, 1978]).

14. According to D. K. House ("The Life of Sextus Empiricus," *CQ* 30 [1980]: 227–238) he probably wrote no earlier than the end of the second century and perhaps in the third. Robinson and Johnson (*The Buddhist Religion: An Historical Introduction,* p. 88) give "circa 150–250 c.e." as the time frame in which Nāgārjuna's life fell.

15. Hopkins, *Meditation on Emptiness*, p. 400.

16. Mervyn Sprung has made some of these observations (*Lucid Exposition of the Middle Way: The Essential Chapters from the Prasannapadā of Candrakīrti* [Boulder, Colorado: Prajñā Press, 1979], pp. 1 and 25).

17. Hopkins, *Meditation on Emptiness*, pp. 10–11.

18. Kalupahana, *Nāgārjuna*, p. 81.

19. C. W. Huntington Jr., *The Emptiness of Emptiness: An Introduction to Early Indian Mādhyamika* (Honolulu: University of Hawaii Press, 1989), pp. 17–18.

20. Hopkins, *Meditation on Emptiness*, p. 36.

21. Hankinson, *The Sceptics*, pp. 245, 128.

22. Hopkins, *Meditation on Emptiness*, p. 584.

23. Ibid., p. 585.

24. Charlotte L. Stough, *Greek Skepticism: A Study in Epistemology* (Berkeley, California: University of California Press, 1969), p. 80.

25. Compare Āryadeva that *nirvāṇa* is "the extinction of all words" (*Satasastra*, in Giuseppe Tucci, ed. and trans., *Pre-Dignāga Buddhist Texts on Logic from Chinese Sources*, Gaekwad's Oriental Series 49 [Baroda: Oriental Institute, 1929], p. 82).

26. Huntingon, *Emptiness of Emptiness*, p. 30.

27. Kalupahana, *Nāgārjuna*, p. 92.

28. See Garma C. C. Chang, *Teachings of Tibetan Yoga* (New Hyde Park, New York: University Books, 1963), p. 34.

29. In Long-chen-pa, "Sems-nyid rang-grol (The Natural Freedom of Mind)," trans. Herbert V. Guenther, *Crystal Mirror; Journal of the Tibetan Nyingma Meditation Center* 4 (1975): 117.

30. In Wing-Tsit Chan, comp. and trans. *A Source Book in Chinese Philosophy* (Princeton, New Jersey: Princeton University Press, 1963), p. 356.

31. Trans. John Blofeld, *The Zen Teaching of Hui Hai* (New York: Samuel Weiser, 1972), p. 51.

32. See Chan, *A Source Book in Chinese Philosophy*, p. 367.

33. Blofeld, *Zen Teaching of Hui Hai*, p. 51.

34. Trans. Theodore Stcherbatsky, *The Conception of Buddhist Nirvāṇa* (The Hague: Mouton, 1965), p. 91.

35. Streng, *Emptiness*, p. 87.

36. Richard H. Jones, "The Nature and Function of Nāgārjuna's Arguments," *Philosophy East and West* 28 (1978): 489. Except that in Sextus's case we must accept his disclaimer for a certain looseness in usage: "It is essential to note that here, just as in other cases, we employ the expression 'it is' in place of 'it appears [to be]'; so that in effect [when we say 'all things are relative'] we are saying 'it appears that all things are relative'" (*OP* I.135).

37. Hopkins, *Meditation on Emptiness*, p. 38.

38. Richard H. Robinson, *Early Mādhyamika in India and China* (Delhi: Motilal Banarsidass, 1976), p. 50.

39. Cf. A. J. Ayer, "If the validity of every proof had to be proved in its turn, we should fall into an infinite regress" (*The Problem of Knowledge* [New York: Penguin Books, 1977], p. 43).

40. Conze, *Buddhist Thought in India* (London: George Allen and Unwin, 1962), p. 240.

41. T. R. V. Murti, *The Central Philosophy of Buddhism* (London: George Allen and Unwin, 1974), pp. 138–139.

42. Chan, *A Source Book in Chinese Philosophy*, pp. 354–355.

43. Trans. Robert A. F. Thurman, *The Central Philosophy of Tibet: A Study and Translation of Jey Tsong Khapa's* "Essence of True Eloquence" (Princeton, New Jersey: Princeton University Press, 1984), pp. 178–179.

44. Conze, *Buddhist Thought in India*, p. 240.

45. Murti, *The Central Philosophy of Buddhism*, p. 137.

46. Daisetz T. Suzuki, "Existentialism, Pragmatism and Zen," in *Zen Buddhism: Selected Writings of D. T. Suzuki*, ed. William Barrett (Garden City, New York: Doubleday/Anchor, 1956), p. 269. See also Jones, "The Nature and Function of Nagarjuna's Arguments," pp. 491–492.

47. Quoted by David J. Kalupahana, *Buddhist Philosophy: A Historical Analysis* (Honolulu: University of Hawaii Press, 1976), p. 138.

48. John Blofeld, trans., *The Zen Teaching of Huang Po* (New York: Grove Press, 1958), p. 130.

49. Hopkins, *Meditation on Emptiness*, p. 37.

50. Murti, *The Central Philosophy of Buddhism*, p. 166.

51. Stcherbatsky, *The Conception of Buddhist Nirvāṇa*, p. 162.

52. Trans. Edward Conze, *The Large Sūtra on Perfect Wisdom* by Maitreyanatha (Berkeley, California: University of California Press, 1975), p. 144, n. 4.

53. Streng, *Emptiness*, p. 97. (But it seems that he means not the "contrary" but the "contradictory.")

54. On "wrangling" compare the attitude expressed in the *Sutta Nipāta* (for example, IV.3, 5, 8, 9, 11) and by Hui Neng: "We do not quarrel even in the midst of a hostile crowd" (A. F. Price and Wong Mou-Lam, *The Diamond Sūtra and the Sūtra of Hui Neng* [Berkeley, California: Shambhala, 1969], book 2, p. 41).

55. *The Spiritual Teachings of Ramana Maharshi* (Berkeley, California: Shambhala Publications, 1972), p. 6; and compare Murti, *The Central Philosophy of Buddhism*, p. 353.

56. Ludwig Wittgenstein, *Tractatus Logico-Philosophicus*, German text with an English translation by C. K. Ogden (London: Routledge and Kegan Paul, 1922), p. 189. There are numerous correspondences between Wittgenstein and both Pyrrhonism and Buddhism. The Buddha, when asked where the Tathāgata goes when he dies, replies that the question should be set aside, then gives as an illustration the question where the fire goes when it goes out (*M.* I.487). Wittgenstein (in *The Blue and Brown Books* [Oxford: Basil Blackwell, 1958], p. 108) gives the following example: "It can come about that we aren't able to rid ourselves of the implications of our symbolism, which seems to admit of a question like, 'Where does the flame of a candle go to when it's *blown out*?'"

57. Robinson, *Early Mādhyamika in India and China*, p. 43.

58. Douglas D. Daye, "Major Schools of the Mahāyāna: Mādhyamika," in *Buddhism: A Modern Perspective*, ed. Charles Prebish (University Park, Pennsylvania, and London: Pennsylvania State University Press, 1975), pp. 91–92.

59. Streng, *Emptiness*, pp. 89, 98.

60. Murti, *The Central Philosophy of Buddhism*, p. 148.

61. Ibid., p. 328.

62. Ibid., pp. 124 ff.

63. Ibid., p. 147. Yet it is true, as Robinson pointed out, that "Nowhere does he [Nāgārjuna] acknowledge a third mode of judgment other than affirmation and negation" (*Early Mādhyamika in India and China*, p. 51).

64. Edward Conze, *Buddhism: Its Essence and Development* (New York: Harper and Row, 1959), pp. 140–141.

65. Ibid., p. 244.

66. Ibid.

67. Buddhadāsa, in *Toward the Truth, by Buddhadāsa*, ed. Donald K. Swearer (Philadelphia, Pennsylvania: Westminster Press, 1971), p. 101.

68. Blofeld, trans., *The Zen Teaching of Hui Hai*, p. 68.

69. Conze, *Buddhist Thought in India*, p. 243.

70. It is in connection with Zen uses of the logical breaches that Streng's analysis is most interesting, when he says that the Mādhyamikas at times drifted out of the "dialectical structure of religious apprehension," according to which no meaningful statement about reality can be made, and made temporary use of the "intuitive structure of religious apprehension," which encourages the use of contradictory and excluded-middle statements to stimulate intuition of a position outside of two-valued logic and ontology.

71. Trans. Edward Conze, *Buddhist Wisdom Books* (London: George Allen and Unwin, 1958), p. 25.

72. Bhattacharya, *The Dialectical Method of Nāgārjuna*, reads the text differently here and eliminates the paradox.

73. Chan, *A Source Book in Chinese Philosophy*, pp. 346, 349, 351.

74. From Paul Reps, *Zen Flesh, Zen Bones* (Garden City, New York: Doubleday/Anchor, n.d.), p. 103.

75. Ibid., p. 105.

76. Conze, *Buddhist Thought in India*, p. 249.

77. Ibid.

78. See Stcherbatsky, *The Conception of Buddhist Nirvāṇa*, pp. 187–188.

79. Giuseppe Tucci, trans., "The *Ratnāvalī* of Nāgārjuna," *Journal of the Royal Asiatic Society* (1934): 307–325; (1936): 237–252, 423–435.

80. Ashok Kumar Gangadean, "Formal Ontology and the Dialectical Transformation of Consciousness," *Philosophy East and West* 29 (1979): 22.

81. Trans. Conze, *Buddhist Wisdom Books*, p. 93.

82. Blofeld, trans., *The Zen Teaching of Huang Po*, pp. 61–62.

83. E.g.: *MK* prefatory verse and 27.30; *VV* closing verse. It should be remarked that the Epicurean tradition involved similar pious invocations of the saint.

84. Chung-ying Cheng, "Nature and Function of Skepticism in Chinese Philosophy," *Philosophy East and West* 27 (1977): 138–139.

85. Dick Garner, "Skepticism, Ordinary Language, and Zen Buddhism," *Philosophy East and West* 27 (1977): 167. Burnyeat agrees that "the practice of argumentative enquiry is so considerable a portion of the sceptic's way of life . . ." (Burnyeat, "Can the Sceptic Live His Scepticism?" p. 35).

86. Arne Naess, *Scepticism* (Oslo: Universitetsforlaget, 1968), pp. 4, 6, 38.

87. Trans. H. Kern, *Saddharma-puṇḍarika, or the Lotus of the True Law*, Sacred Books of the East 21 (New York: Dover, 1963), pp. 30–31.

88. Trans. Murti, *The Central Philosophy of Buddhism*, p. 42.

89. Chan, *A Source Book in Chinese Philosophy*, pp. 347–348.

90. Ibid., p. 366.

91. Garner, "Skepticism, Ordinary Language, and Zen Buddhism," p. 168.

92. Stough, *Greek Skepticism*, p. 104.

93. Jean-Paul Dumont, *Le scepticisme et le phènomène: essai sur la signification et les origines du pyrrhonisme* (Paris: J. Vrin, 1972), pp. 212, 215.

94. Blofeld, trans., *The Zen Teaching of Hui Hai*, pp. 95–96.

95. Gangadean, "Formal Ontology and the Dialectical Transformation of Consciousness," pp. 38, 37.

96. For a selection of Pali texts on this subject see Nyanaponika Thera, *The Heart of Buddhist Meditation* (New York: Samuel Weiser, 1973). Many Buddhist texts of Tibet, China, and Japan teach the same practice.

97. Chogyam Trungpa, "Remarks on the Tradition of Mindfulness," *Gāruda* 4 (1976), p. 15.

98. Blofeld, trans., *The Zen Teaching of Hui Hai*, p. 51.

99. Nyanaponika Thera, *The Power of Mindfulness* (San Francisco: Unity Press, 1972), p. 23.

100. Achaan Chaa in *Living Buddhist Masters*, ed. Jack Kornfeld (Śānta Cruz, California: Unity Press, 1977).

101. Trans. Steven Mitchell, *Dropping Ashes on the Buddha*, pp. 35, 45, 45, 210, 78.

102. Isshy Miura and Ruth F. Sasaki, *The Zen Koan* (New York: Harcourt, Brace, and World Inc., 1965), p. 47.

103. Jack Kornfeld, in *The Laughing Man* 2 (1976): 23.

104. Conze, *Buddhist Thought in India*, pp. 242–243.

Chapter Eighteen

The Path of the Dialectic

The overall stance toward life of Mādhyamikas and Pyrrhonists was similar, indeed nearly identical; the dialectic which supported this stance was similar, indeed nearly identical; and the purpose for which this stance was adopted and this dialectic practiced was similar, indeed nearly identical. Did the parallelism arise out of contact and diffusion, or was it a remarkable result of independent, parallel development?

The diffusion hypothesis has two forms—from India to Greece, and from Greece to India. The first form is the one which has been proposed repeatedly and which is still being proposed. It is such an uncritical proposal as to invite interpretation itself. The European reception of Greek philosophy has been dominated by a model in which Plato and Aristotle are seen as the centers and others such as Sextus Empiricus—whose extant works are comparable both in extent and in importance to those of Plato and Aristotle and as representative of the Greek philosophical tradition—are not heard of. In fact, Plato too is censored, in that the *Parmenides*, which Plotinus regarded as the essential Platonic work, is regarded as a joke or a game, and passages such as "destroying the hypotheses" in the *Republic* are either edited out of the text or interpreted out of the commentary. The fact that Greek philosophy from the very beginning was characterized by critical dialectic and by the ethics of retreat that often attends it is not studied in our schools. When attention is occasionally paid to, say, Pyrrhonic skepticism, it is seen as outrageous and inhuman. Greek philosophy has, in effect, been forced into the mold of European philosophy, when in fact it had a great deal more in common with its contemporaneous Indian thought.

On the basis of this partial view it has often been supposed that Skepticism was the expression of an inherently non-Greek frame of mind, and (much as happened with Orphism) scholars have been eager to locate its sources elsewhere. A potential foreign source was readily available. In 326 B.C. Alexander the Great entered the religious center of Taxila in northwest India and remained there for some months. With him were three Greek philosophers: Anaxarchus the Democritean, his student Pyrrhon, and Onesicritus, a disciple of Diogenes. These philosophers were taken along for the purpose of studying local systems of thought, as biologists were brought to study animal and plant specimens. Strabo reports that Onesicritus was sent to converse with

Indian "sophists" (Strabo XV.1.59), and Anaxarchus and Pyrrhon also, in the months in Taxila, are reported to have had contact with some of their Indian counterparts (D.L. IX.63).

Megasthenes, a Greek historian who, about a generation later, spent a decade at Pāṭaliputra in India, wrote a description of Indian philosophy as he knew it and attributed the following, among other teachings, to the "Brachmanes":

> They believe that nothing that happens to mankind is good or bad, for otherwise some would not be grieved and others delighted by the same things, both having dream-like notions.[1]

Pyrrhon must have heard similar things in Taxila, if not from Brahmins then from Buddhists, Ājīvikas, Jains, and possibly descendants of the lineage of Sañjaya. Northwest India has been proposed as the origination point of the Prajñāpāramitā literature, the probable historical forerunner of the Mādhyamika,[2] and there also one can find the doctrine of nondifference and the comparison of human notions to dreams. Diogenes Laertius represents Pyrrhon as teaching, after his return from India, that

> there is nothing good or bad by nature, for if there is anything good or bad by nature, it must be good or bad for all persons alike . . . But there is no good or bad which is such to all persons in common; therefore there are no such things as good or bad by nature. (D.L. IX.101)

There is a great temptation to say that Pyrrhon imported into Greece alien and pessimistic teachings from the East—and many have succumbed to it—including Diogenes Laertius:

> [Pyrrho] even got together with the Indian Gymnosophists and with the Magi. This led him to adopt a most noble philosophy, to quote Ascanius of Abdera, by introducing *akatalepsia* [the incomprehensibility of things] and *epochē* [suspension of judgment]. (D.L. IX.61)[3]

One scholar says that Pyrrhon's contact with Indian culture "revealed to him a type of 'wisdom' totally unknown to the Greeks,"[4] and another even refers to Pyrrhon as "a sort of Buddhist arhat."[5]

But in fact it seems certain, if one attends to the Greek tradition as a whole, that Pyrrhon must have imbibed the main attitudes of his philosophy from Greek teachers, before the visit to India. The position he came to teach was clearly in the Democritean lineage, which Pyrrhon should be regarded as a part of, as his teacher Anaxarchus was a Democritean. Due to Plato's censoring of references to Democritus out of his writings, that lineage has a tendency to be forgotten. Yet the Democritean lineage is of a profound importance, despite the fact that it has been little acknowledged in a world in which Plato—Democritus's great enemy—is seen as the primary philosophical figure. If it were given the proper contextualization, Pyrrhon's teaching would not seem "a type of 'wisdom' totally unknown to the Greeks." Pyrrhon's exposure to the Democritean tradition through study with Anaxarchus preceded his journey to India, and his skeptical-phenomenalistic orientation was probably already in place before the brief contact with Gymnosophists occurred.

Pyrrhon's Teachers

Pyrrhon was educated in the lineages of both the great protoskeptics of the Greek tradition, Socrates and Democritus. From his first, Megarian (hence both Socratic and neo-Eleatic) teacher, he learned the infinite regress reductions of Zeno, the inductive Socratic *elenchus*, and the dichotomy-and-dilemma conundra of the Megarians themselves—in short, the basic apparatus of the dialectic.

Subsequently Pyrrhon became a student of Anaxarchus of Abdera, who in turn was a pupil either of Democritus or of a Democritean (D.L. X.58). According to Diogenes Laertius, "Pyrrho most frequently mentions Democritus" (D.L. IX.67), and according to Philo of Athens (*ap.* D.L. IX.67), "He was most fond of Democritus." Already in the fifth century B.C. Democritus had taught the nondifference of phenomena and the eudaimonistic approach to philosophy—philosophy as a path to a tranquil attitude beyond the effect of phenomenal change—which Pyrrhon is sometimes regarded as having received from an Indian teacher.

> The end of action [according to Democritus] is tranquillity, which is not identical with pleasure, as some by a false interpretation have understood, but a state in which the mind continues calm and strong, undisturbed by any fear or superstition or any other emotion. This he calls well-being, and many other names. (D.L. IX.45)

This "state in which the mind continues calm and strong, undisturbed by . . . any . . . emotion" Democritus called *athambia* (inability to be astonished or frightened) and, according to Stobaeus (DK 68A67), *ataraxia* (inability to become agitated or upset), the term which descended through the two Democritean lineages—the dogmatic or Epicurean and the critical or Pyrrhonist. It is related closely to the *apatheia* (nonemotionality) taught by the Cynics and seems substantially the same as the condition which the Prajñāpāramitā literature attributes to one who knows emptiness:

> One who is convinced of the emptiness of everything is not captivated by worldly dharmas, because he does not lean on them. When he gains something he does not rejoice, when he does not gain it he is not depressed. Fame does not make him proud, lack of fame does not depress him. Pleasure does not attract, pain does not repel him. One who in such a way is not captivated by the worldly dharmas is said to be one who knows emptiness. (*Sikṣāsamuccaya* 264)

In the Prajñāpāramitā-Mādhyamika tradition the basis for this condition is the realization that linguistic categories are unable to contain the shifting and undefinable human experience. In Democritus also we find that imperturbability results from an awareness that linguistic categories don't correspond to externals. As Robin says, for Democritus what we call "knowledge" is "a sort of social habit resulting from a tacit agreement which has the purpose of replacing with a system of words or names, of shared usage and permanent signification, the moving flow of our impressions, always distinct, changing with the state of our body and with their relations to external objects, whose condition and constitution are themselves perpetually changing."[6] Democritus taught:

> The qualities of things exist merely by convention; in nature there is nothing but atoms and the void. (D.L. IX.45)
>
> Opinion says hot or cold, but the reality is atoms and empty space. (D.L. IX.72)

The criticism of the idea of language-reality isomorphism which is expressed by Hermogenes in Plato's *Cratylus* is generally attributed to Democritus himself (whose name Plato seems to have censored out):

> I cannot convince myself that there is any principle of correctness in names other than convention and agreement. Any name which you give, in my opinion, is the right one, and if you change that and give another, the new name is as correct as the old . . . For there is no name given to anything by nature; all is convention and habit of the users. (*Crat.* 384c)

Democritus evidently felt that the idea of truth was an epiphenomenon of the reification of language, and in fact truth is inaccessible:

> Of truth we know nothing, for truth is in a well. (D.L. IX.72)

Democritus's linguistic criticism leads to skepticism, which in turn is said to lead to *ataraxia*—the state in which the distinctions rooted in language are understood to be empty convention. The author who has written the most thoroughly flawed treatment of this topic remarks that for Pyrrhon "the aim of the process [of doubting was] so that a certain tranquillity can supervene. Now the harnessing of doubt to a goal of this sort seems to me to be without precedence in Greek thought."[7] Yet Democritus had taught this in the fifth century B.C., and by Pyrrhon's time it had been taught by many prominent Greek masters. In fact, Democritus's teacher Leucippus already had some or all of this linkage of ideas. He taught that:

> Everything comes to be according to imagination and opinion, not according to truth; it is like the appearance of an oar thrust in water [which appears to be bent though it is not]. (Fr. A 33)

Leucippus and Democritus both taught a double truth (noumenal and phenomenal) as Plato was later to do; what turned Plato against Democritus was that the latter championed not the noumenal but the phenomenal truth:

> Everything is only appearance. (Fr. A 48b)
> The appearance is truth. (Fr. A 101)

Democritus provides an early Greek source for the idea Pyrrhon supposedly learned from yogis in India—that "there is nothing good or bad by nature but only by appearance." Democritus's associate Protagoras declared the relativity of the good which Megasthenes attributes to Indian Brahmins. His student Metrodorus, in turn, emphasized the "acquiescing to the immediate phenomenon" which was basic to both Pyrrhonists and Mādhyamika. "One must trust nothing," he said, "but the bodily sensations" (DK 70B1). Compare the *Sutta Nipāta* (or many other passages in the Buddhist canon): "No truth exists at all apart from what sense-perception offers" (*SN* 886).

Anaxarchus, finally, with whom Pyrrhon traveled to India, was a student either of Democritus or of Metrodorus or of both. He is credited by the ancients with extreme success at the tranquil acceptance of phenomena as nondifferent, comparable, indeed to the more extreme of the *Jātaka* stories:

> When Anaxarchus was forced against his will to land in Cyprus [Nicocreon the tyrant] seized him and, putting him in a mortar, ordered him to be pounded to death with iron pestles. But he, making light of the punishment, made that well-known speech,

> "Pound, pound, the pouch containing Anaxarchus; ye pound not Anaxarchus." And when Nicocreon commanded his tongue to be cut out, they say he bit it off and spat it at him . . . For his fortitude and contentment in life he was called the Happy Man. (D.L. IX.59–60)

It is clear, then, that the essentials of Pyrrhonism were already to be found among the followers of Socrates and Democritus in the late fifth and early fourth centuries B.C., well before Alexander's visit to India. If Pyrrhon encountered such doctrines in India, they must simply have reminded him of doctrines that had been common in Greece for a hundred and fifty years and which his own teachers had taught him. Thus the dialectical, ethical, psychological, and language-critical levels of Pyrrhonism may be said to have been Greek before Alexander. Still it is possible that Pyrrhon brought back from India some bits or pieces of thought or formulation which seemed useful in terms of attitudes he himself already held.

The Fourfold Negation

An extraordinary similarity, that has long been noticed, between Pyrrhonism and Mādhyamika is the formula known in connection with Buddhism as the fourfold negation (*catuṣkoṭi*) and which in Pyrrhonic form might be called the fourfold indeterminacy. Nāgārjuna says:

> One should say of each thing that it neither is, nor is not, nor both is and is not, nor neither is nor is not.

Pyrrhon is reported as saying—and Sextus echoes the formula many times:

> We should . . . [say] of each thing that it no more is than is not, than both is and is not, than neither is nor is not. (Timon *ap.* Aristocles)[8]

The question whether the fourfold negation (*catuṣkoṭi*) was known in Indian philosophy prior to 326 B.C. has been considered above.[9] There is evidence to suggest that it was, but this evidence is more ambiguous than is usually acknowledged. The formula appears several times in the Pali Suttas, but these are not necessarily earlier than Alexander.[10] Further, in the passages of the Pali canon where the formula is associated with a school of Skeptics, possibly that of Sañjaya, it is impossible to separate the wording of the Buddhist authors from that of the Skeptic being reported on. Śīlaṅka, writing on the *Śutrakṛtānga* in the ninth century A.D., seems to associate the *catuṣkoṭi* with different schools of Skeptics supposedly contemporary with the Buddha. But again the passage is ambiguous—where does Śīlaṅka's wording end and the Skeptics' begin?—and the connection is not certain. Attempts to derive the fourfold logic from the fivefold form attributed to early Skeptic schools, or from the sevenfold logic of the Jains are interesting but inconclusive.[11] In fact, the *syādvāda* of the Jains would seem, on purely internal grounds, to be later than the fourfold formula, of which it seems an elaboration: the first four propositions more or less duplicate the fourfold formula and the last three are recombinations of the first four. Nor can the age of the *syādvāda* be known with any clarity at all. It may be a doctrine developed in medieval Jainism on the basis of the Buddhist formula. The fivefold series attributed to "eel-wrigglers" in the Suttas also may be derived from the fourfold formula—a reaction to it, perhaps:

(1) I don't take it thus.

(2) I don't take it the other way.

(3) I advance no third position.

(4) I don't deny your position.

(5) And I don't say, none of the above.[12]

There is, in other words, no absolute certainty that the fourfold formula existed in pre-Alexandrian India or, for that matter, that the materials out of which it would develop did. Still, the preponderance of the evidence at least makes the thesis plausible.

The other side of the question—could Pyrrhon have derived the fourfold negation from elements in the Greek tradition alone?—is in a similar evidential situation. Though scholars in general have thought that this is an element that Pyrrhon surely borrowed from India, the fact is that there are constant suggestions of its presence in the Greek tradition well before Pyrrhon, and one can be sure, at the least, that the materials out of which it was put together were fully present in Greece in the fifth century B.C. Heraclitus anticipated the third branch of the four when he said, "We both are and are not." Democritus first formulated the Skeptic slogan, "No more this than that" (*OP* I.213 and Simplicius *In Phys.* 28.4), and his student Protagoras explicitly denied the principle of contradiction on the basis of indeterminacy (D.L. IX.50–51). Dionysodorus's assertion "Both and neither" in Plato's *Euthydemus* anticipates the third and fourth branches of the *tetralemma*. Plato's *Parmenides* is a mother lode of such sayings: "Both coming to be and ceasing to be and doing neither" (165d); "the non-existent One both comes to be and ceases to be and also does not come to be or cease to be" (163b), and so on. Aristotle (*Met.* 1008a30 ff) complains about some unnamed thinker—perhaps Pyrrhon—that "he says not yes and not no, but both yes and no; and then he denies these, saying neither yes nor no."

There is, in short, considerable precedence in the Greek tradition for the fourfold negation, which Pyrrhon could have put together from materials ready at hand in the Greek schools. Above all, the form in which Pyrrhon cast the four alternatives is strictly Democritean, based on Democritus's "No more this than that":

> We should . . . [say] of each thing that it no more is than is not, than both is and is not, than neither is nor is not. (Timon *ap.* Aristocles)

Pyrrhon seems to have combined Democritus's description of each thing as "no more A than not-A" with a Megaric formula of the type used by Plato in the *Parmenides* ("both A and not-A and neither A nor not-A"). Thus both the Socratic and Democritean traditions may have contributed to the Pyrrhonist form of the fourfold formula.

In addition to the four alternatives in their Democritean form (as a "fourfold indeterminacy"), Sextus has several occurrences of the four alternatives in the form of logical alternatives or *disjuncta*, of which, as in the Buddhist Suttas, one and one only must be true in every case. These seem to be inheritances from the Stoic logicians, who attempted to formulate a multivalued logic as an alternative to Aristotle's logic of two values:

> The "something" which they [the Stoics] declare the highest genus of all is either true or false or neither true nor false or both true and false. (*OP* II.86)
>
> [The highest genus] then is either true or false or at once both true and false or neither true nor false. (*AL* II.32–33)

> In the doctrine of the Stoics . . . some [presentations] are probable, some improbable, some at once both probable and improbable, some neither probable nor improbable. (*AL* I.241–242)
>
> And of the probable presentations some are true, some false, some both true and false, some neither true nor false. (*AL* I.243–244)

All four of these passages occur in discussions of Stoic thought, and indeed Sextus's book *Against the Logicians*, where three of the four cases occur, is aimed primarily against the Stoics. An earlier scholar stated that "the form of the quadrilemma has nothing to do with Stoic philosophy,"[13] but he is clearly mistaken on that point. Aulus Gellius speaks of a Stoic *disjunctum* which contains three of the four alternatives:

> This is of such a sort as "Pleasure is either good or bad or neither good nor bad". . . of all the disjuncts, one ought to be true and the others false. But if none of them is true, or all . . . then that disjunction is false. (*NA* XVI.8.12–24)

This formula, which lacks the third alternative (both A and not-A), probably comes from Chrysippus, who "wrote books against 'those who think that a proposition may be both true and false.'"[14] But the Stoic logic originated two generations before Chrysippus as a continuation of Megarian logic, and Megarian logicians did indeed feature the simultaneous yes and no (as in the conundra of Eubulides). In the pre-Chrysippan phase of Stoic logic, as one scholar has written, "The classes of true and false presentations are neither mutually exclusive nor mutually exhaustive; some presentations are both true and false and some are neither."[15] It is probable, then, that the fourfold negation arose in the line of development that includes Megarian and early Stoic logic, to be controverted by the more conservative Chrysippan logic, which the Pyrrhonists in turn attacked, in part, perhaps, by adopting the Megarian/pre-Chrysippan formula.

It is possible that Indian influence could have intruded somewhere in the long evolution of this formula from Democritus to Pyrrhon. But clearly there is no need to postulate it. Skeptical mottoes verging on the fourfold negation had been common in Greece for centuries, and there is no difficulty whatever in imagining its occurrence in a Socratic-Megarian-Stoic logician whom Pyrrhon, in Democritean fashion, attacked by converting the alternatives to indeterminates, thus casting all the Stoic disjuncts into a limbo between yes and no.

Finally it is worth noting that as Pyrrhon, following Democritus, denies the possibility of affirming any of the alternatives more than the others, and as Sextus rejects each alternative on its own merits, so the Buddha, in the Nikāyas, is sometimes represented as having "set aside and rejected" all four alternatives (e.g., *M.* 63). As Jayatilleke says, "They also rejected all four alternatives when they considered the question meaningless (that is, a thapanīya pañha)."[16] Both Pyrrhon and Nāgārjuna, by declaring the inapplicability of all four alternatives in every case are, in effect, declaring all questions to be *ṭhapanīya pañha.* Among Indian schools associated with the *catuṣkoṭi*, however, Pyrrhon seems closer to the Skeptics than to the Buddhists of the Nikāya, in that he advises suspension of judgment only for the psychological purpose of attaining tranquility, not for the additional and essentially religious purpose of escaping from transmigration.

The redefinition of the four alternatives into a fourfold negation which occurred with the Mādhyamika school had happened considerably earlier in Greece, and even though the four alternatives may not have been planted in India by Greek influence, it is quite plausible that the redefinition of them as negations may have been.

Wood, Smoke, and Fire

Aside from the *catuṣkoṭi*, Indian influence has been suggested for certain of Sextus's philosophical exempla. Sextus and Nāgārjuna, as quoted above,[17] both use the image of wood and fire to exemplify the problem of causation. In addition, both Sextus and various Indian logical traditions use the imagery of smoke and fire to illustrate the process of inference. The image is well known from both Naiyāyika and Buddhist logicians.

> One seeing smoke on a hill infers that there is fire on it. (*Nyāya Sūtras* I.1.5, comm)[18]

This example is used constantly in the Naiyāyika literature, as it is in the later Buddhist logical texts, for example in Dharmakīrti's *Short Treatise on Logic* (2.40):

> Negation of causes is as follows: (Thesis). There is here no smoke. (Reason). Because there is no fire.[19]

In Sextus we find:

> As soon as we see . . . smoke we recall . . . fire. (*AL* II.152–153)
>
> We . . . infer fire from smoke. (*AL* II.157)
>
> When a man sees smoke, fire is signified. (*OP* II.102)
>
> They [the Stoics] term a sign "suggestive" when, being mentally associated with the thing signified, it . . . suggests to us the thing associated with it, which is not clearly perceived at the moment—as for instance in the case of smoke and fire. (*OP* II.100)

The chronological situation is worth mentioning. Sextus derives the image from Stoic and Epicurean logical sources which probably go back to the third century B.C. The earliest known Indian occurrences, which are Naiyāyika, seem to be later; the beginning of Naiyāyika logic is estimated as the last two centuries B.C.[20] As chapter 17 showed, Nāgārjuna's treatment of the wood/fire exemplum in the *Kārikā* is virtually identical in content, and often even in expression, to Sextus's. Kalupahana suggests that Nāgārjuna uses the image because the Buddha (*M.* I.487) used the metaphor of a fire going out to illustrate the *tathāgata*'s evanishment after death. "Nāgārjuna's criticism of the metaphor of 'fire and fuel,'" he says, "seems to follow closely the Buddha's own explanation of the phenomenon of fire."[21] But in fact, Nāgārjuna's treatment of the image is far more extensive than the Buddha's metaphorical analogy, and serves different purposes. Sextus's treatment of the image, however, parallels Nāgārjuna's both in its purpose and in every single point of argumentation.

Ropes and Snakes

Another exemplum found in both Greek and Indian texts is the imagery of rope and snake. The earliest known occurrence is in Demetrius, *De Elocutione* (159):

> Relief from fear provides an occasion for wit, as when a man has been afraid without reason, mistaking a strap for a snake, or a pot for a hole in the ground.[22]

The *De Elocutione* has been dated by one scholar to circa 270 B.C. and by others as late as the first century A.D.[23] Sextus in turn seems to have derived the image from Carneades, who did not himself write but whose views were written up by his student Cleitomachus. Sextus, or his source, has altered the image into the form in which it occurs in India:

> When a rope is lying coiled up in a dark room, to one who enters hurriedly it presents the simply "probable" appearance of being a serpent; but to the man who has looked carefully around and has investigated the conditions—such as its immobility and its color—it appears as a rope, in accordance with an impression that is probable and tested. (*OP* I.227 ff.)

In India the image appears in the book *Cittaviśuddhiprakaraṇa* of Nāgārjuna's student Āryadeva,[24] and subsequently becomes "a classical illustration . . . in Buddhism," "the simile of the fool who sees a rope in the dusk and thinks it to be a snake. A wise man appears and teaches him that he has nothing to fear, for the snake is a mere illusion created by a simple rope."[25] It appears in the *Pràmāṇa-samuccaya* of Dignāga[26] and in Candrakīrti:[27]

> Now, these elements which do not exist there, in the Absolute, really do not exist at all; they are like that kind of terror which is experienced when, in the dark, a rope is mistaken for a snake and which dissipates as soon as a light is brought in . . . Indeed, the rope which in the dark has been mistaken for the serpent, is not really in itself a serpent, since it is not apprehended by sight and touch, whether in the light or in the darkness, as a real serpent would necessarily be.[28]

It is found in the late *Nāḍabinḍu Upaniṣad*:

> As a person through illusion mistakes a rope for a serpent, so the fool not knowing Satya (the eternal truth) sees the world (to be true).[29]

Finally, it is well known from the Mādhyamika-influenced Advaita Vedānta, where the point is made that the connection between *brahman* and the world "is as illusory as the appearance of a snake in a rope."[30]

It must be stressed that this image—which is popularly regarded as a signature of Indian thought—is found in the Greek tradition (the example of Demetrius) perhaps five centuries earlier than any known Indian occurrence. In addition, the fact that Sextus or a predecessor seems to have improved on Demetrius's version suggests that it evolved natively in Greece, whereas in India it appears in a single static form, like something which has been imported. The earliest Indian occurrence may be the one in Āryadeva, suggesting that the image entered the Indian discourse through Nāgārjuna's school in his lifetime, possibly in a skeptical handbook which brought the forms of the Greek dialectic, and from there passed, like the rest of the package, into the vocabulary of Indian thought in general, especially that of the Vedānta.

Finally there is nothing in Pyrrhonism which requires the hypothesis of foreign input. The other possibility, that the Mādhyamika dialectic somehow "came from" Greece, has never been seriously considered, yet there is a good deal to be said for it, not only the abrupt appearance of the dialectic in India and the uncanny similarity in both form and content in Sextus's and Nāgārjuna's writings, but also several explicit philosophical formulae: fourfold negation, wood/fire, and rope/snake, all of which are attested earlier in Greece than in India.

Nāgārjuna in the Lineage of Aenesidemus?

Nāgārjuna seems to have written in either the late second or the early third century A.D. He was, then, roughly a contemporary of Sextus. Virtually all of Sextus's arguments were collected from earlier Greek dialecticians, who had been working steadily at the expansion and formalization of the dialectic since the time of Parmenides. The main body of arguments seems to have been systematized at least by the time of the Pyrrhonist Aenesidemus in the first century B.C. Aenesidemus, in fact, seems to have been the great Pyrrhonist dialectician, and Sextus his redactor. "It is usually assumed," says one scholar, "that his hand lies behind much of Sextus's voluminous argument . . ."[31]

On the Indian side, it is commonly taken for granted by Buddhologists that Nāgārjuna, like Sextus, was the culmination of a long tradition—but there is really no evidence for that tradition as far as the formal aspect of Nāgārjuna's reasoning goes. His argumentation involves "the basic ways of reasoning found in the West."[32] Like Sextus's book, Nāgārjuna's is a compound of empiricism and formal dialectic, with no use of mystical or traditional religious arguments. Although the purpose of pacifying *prapañca* is already in the Prajñāpāramitā texts and the *Sutta Nipāta*, there is inadequate background—almost none whatever—to account for the sudden appearance of the full-blown formal dialectic in Nāgārjuna's *Verses*. Nāgārjuna's work has the whole pattern of the Greek dialectic, with its complex and extensive system of arguments which in Greece developed over a period of centuries; yet it arises suddenly, without evidence of developmental stages, in its own tradition.

One scholar has written: "What was the original contribution of Nāgārjuna? His original contribution was the dialectic that he evolved."[33] But perhaps this is too much to attribute to a single thinker, and altogether too coincidentally like the material that circulated widely in the Greco-Roman world (which included parts of India) in various handbooks of dialectical arguments. Even in Greece, where philosophical developments—especially purely formal ones—generally happened much more quickly than in India, it took four generations—from Parmenides to, say, the students of Socrates to develop the basic dialectical apparatus and several centuries more to elaborate its full system of arguments. The sudden appearance of the whole system in India in the work of a single author suggests input from outside. The situation should lead a historian to look around for channels of diffusion.

One such channel passed through the Hellenized areas of northwest India and neighboring Bactria, areas which purveyed Hellenistic cultural influence from the time of Alexander to that of Kanishka—that is, during the presumed formative period of both the Prajñāpāramitā and the Mādhyamika. The Hellenistic Greeks were passionately interested in the religions and philosophies of other cultures, and the Mediterranean mystery cults show how ready they were to participate in them. As they participated in the rites of Isis, they would participate in those of Śiva. But they penetrated most deeply into Buddhism—a culture zone not requiring Indian parentage and caste-validation—and brought their talents to the service of the Buddhadharma. Four images can suggest the Greco-Buddhist milieu of the Indo-Greek communities discussed in chapter 14: (1) the Buddhist emperor Aśoka issued edicts in good literary Greek; (2) major Buddhist rock-cut monasteries at Karle and Nasik were endowed by wealthy Greeks; (3) Corinthian capitals from Indo-Greek communities show Buddhas sitting in meditation among acanthus leaves; (4) a Kanishkan coin shows the name Buddha written in Greek characters.

Recent archeological work at Kandahar, Aï Khanoum, Charsada, and Taxila has yielded the rectilinear plans of Hellenistic cities far beyond the scope of mere garrison towns. Throughout these sites the impression is of a full and integrated Hellenism (or *polis* culture), in more or less continuous touch with the Mediterranean, and yet sensitively open to Indian thought, especially Buddhist. Wheeler says of Kandahar, "It was a balanced Greek city with its writers, its philosophers, its teachers"; and of Aï

Khanoum, "from the overall Hellenism of the scene . . . Greek priests, philosophers, craftsmen may already be inferred."[34]

Judging from what is known of Hellenistic cities in the ancient Near East, provincial philosophy schools had a primary orientation toward either Stoicism, Epicureanism, or Skepticism—which comprises the tradition of Megarian, Academic, and Pyrrhonist dialectic. Each teacher taught from a selection of books mostly, but not completely, in his own lineage; his own pedagogical identity was bound up with what works or ideas of other lineages he would introduce into his version of his own. It was also a part of the ideology or ethic of the Alexandrian/Roman quasi-imperial dissemination of their culture that in each area it would assimilate some local elements. Among the works which were involved in this process of dissemination and recombination in the last three centuries B.C. are the works of Chrysippus, Epicurus, Eubulides, Diodorus Cronus, Menippus, Cleitomachus, Timon, Aenesidemus, Sextus, and others.

Northwest India, the area so deeply saturated by Greek civilization that Wheeler calls it "Indo-Graecia" (compare "Magna Graecia" for Sicily and South Italy), has been prominently mentioned as the area in which the Prajñāpāramitā developed.[35] It seems likely that there is some historical connection with Greek Skepticism,[36] and the school represents "the origin of dialectical consciousness" in India.[37] The matter awaits further clarification through archeology; but at present, archeology, typology, chronology, and geography are all in line for explosive Greek input into both the Perfect Wisdom (Prajñāpāramitā) and the Middle Way (Mādhyamika), and the current trend of the evidence is to make such input increasingly likely.

Another available diffusion channel is through the Greco-Roman trading centers of southeast India. These settlements were in some cases permanent towns—colonies, really—like Arikamedu near Pondicherry, built or rebuilt in Roman fashion. At least one, Muziris, was equipped with an offical *templum Augusti*, which indicates the presence of a Roman imperial official and an assertion that this city was, in effect, a part of the Roman Empire.[38] Its Greco-Roman communities would be protected; they may have had their own police. The amount of traffic between these towns and the Mediterranean was simply enormous. Strabo (II.5.12) records that before 14 A.D., hundreds of ships set sail yearly from Myos Hormos (one of the two Red Sea ports of Alexandria) for India. This trade continued at high volume from both Red Sea ports till at least 200 A.D., suggesting literally tens of thousands of such voyages. All the ships' captains' names which are extant are Greek, and for the Greeks any occasion could involve the discussion of ideas or the copying of books. Between Gorgias's *On Nature, or On Non-Being* and Sextus's *Outlines of Pyrrhonism* there were scores of Greek dialectical books, no longer extant, at least one of which seems to have made its way to India during or shortly before the time of Nāgārjuna. The fact that no Indian text mentions this is simply not important: No Indian text is known to mention Alexander the Great either, though he left some forty colonies in northwest India and seems to have had a major influence on the development of the Mauryan Empire.[39]

It is clear that there is some other force involved in the development of Mādhyamika in addition to the *Sutta Nipāta* and the Perfect Wisdom texts, and it is from this other factor that the formalization of the dialectic came. The dialectical forms of the Pyrrhonists had clearly been articulated before that event. The possibility of Greek influence on the Buddhist centers of northwest India, where the Perfect Wisdom literature may have originated,[40] is quite open. Further, the area of Amarāvati in South India, where many scholars feel the Perfect Wisdom originated, while not touched directly by the Alexandrian invasion, was soon thereafter opened up for Greek and later Greco-Roman trade, and was a center of Greek influence in India.[41]

It is very suggestive that the areas of India where Mahāyāna Buddhism is most commonly supposed to have arisen—Gandhāra, Kashmir, and Amarāvati—are the areas where Greek culture penetrated most deeply. The points of contact in these areas are many. The area of Amarāvati shows clear signs of Greco-Roman influence in the early centuries A.D., though the main Greco-Roman area of that city awaits excavation still. At nearby Nāgārjunakonda, where Nāgārjuna is traditionally supposed to have spent most of his life, Greco-Roman medallions have been found at a Buddhist stupa from the second century A.D.—suggesting that Greeks were active in the local Buddhist community, as they are known to have been in others, during Nāgārjuna's lifetime or shortly before it.[42] Here, as in the Northwest, there were Greeks who knew Indian languages and Indians who knew Greek. Much circumstantial evidence suggests Stoic influence on Tamil literature, and at the same period some Sanskrit books made their way in Greek translation to the Mediterranean.[43]

The clearest evidence of intellectual diffusion from the Mediterranean to India is in connection with Greek astronomical texts. It has long been recognized that such diffusion took place in the fifth century A.D., and one Indian text, the *Gārgī-Saṁhitā*, explicitly acknowledges it, saying, "The Yavanas [Greeks] are barbarians, yet the science of astronomy originated with them and for this they should be reverenced as gods."[44] It has recently been demonstrated that in 149–150 A.D., shortly before or during the lifetime of Nāgārjuna, a Greek astrological text "was directly transmitted . . . from Roman Egypt to Western India."[45] Its translators were called "Lords of the Greeks, that is to say, men exercising some sort of authority over Greeks settled in the domains of the Western Kṣatrapas."[46] These Greeks "appear to have had some sort of political organization within the state," enjoying "extraordinary privileges" and "superior station."[47] Assuming the accuracy of this description, we may agree that "doubtless there were many other lines of transmission running in both directions between the two cultures,"[48] and one such would seem to have involved the transmission of dialectical works. We know that an appetite for Greek philosophy had existed in India for centuries: the Indian "sophists" at Taxila questioned Onesicritus about Greek philosophy (Strabo XV.1.65), and the Mauryan emperor Bindusāra, in the third century B.C., specially requested a Greek philosopher from Antiochus I (Ath. XIV.652f–653a).

The *Milindapañha*, or *Questions of King Milinda* (or Menander) dramatically shows the stimulus diffusion process in action. Menander was a Greek king of an Indo-Greek kingdom who was elevated to the status of *arhat*, or enlightened one (freed from reincarnation), in the Buddhist tradition. The *Questions of King Milinda* (as he was called in Pali) show a Greek king skilled in eristics who was seeking an Indian sage with whom to engage in dialectical discussion of certain *aporiai*, or traditional dialectical themes. Finding no one who could engage in dialectical discourse, he declared: "Truly India is empty, contains nothing, has no one who can dispute with me." For twelve years he tried one learned Indian after another, always disappointed in their lack of dialectical education. This is strong evidence that India at this time was predialectical. The saints, or *arhats*, in heaven, observing the situation, sent one of their own number, Nāgasena, to discourse with the king. Nāgasena was successful, overcame Menander in disputation, and converted him to Buddhism. The story, when read less as a pious conversion myth than as a resonance of intellectual history, suggests that, stimulated by the presence of Greek dialectic in India, some Buddhist teachers learned that dialectic and incorporated it into the Buddhist tradition. The date, circa 150 B.C., could indicate the moment when the Prajñāpāramitā protodialectical attitude began to develop into the Mādhyamika formalized dialectic.[49]

The question is a delicate one, involved with feelings of both religion and nationalism. The vastness of it is staggering: the influence that seems to have been exercised from India to China and beyond by a dialectical handbook such as are known to have floated around the Hellenistic-Roman world—perhaps the famous one by Aenesidemus (*Pyrrhonic Discourses*), or by Cleitomachus, or Agrippa, or one of those by students of Arcesilaus and Carneades, or countless others, some by nameless authors or compilers—all containing more or less the same accumulated apparatus of arguments, any one capable of accounting for the entire argumentation of the early Mādhyamika thinkers, Nāgārjuna and Āryadeva, and most of the subject matter of their successors down to and including Candrakīrti in around the seventh century and later the Vedāntic argumentation of Śaṅkara, and so on. Aenesidemus's *Pyrrhonic Discourses* has not survived, but Photius, a ninth-century Byzantine scholar, gives a precis of its contents; Book Two, he says, dealt with "principles, causes, affections, motion, generation and destruction," and Book Three with "motion and sense perception and their properties."[50] These lists of topics agree well with Nāgārjuna's contents.

One modern author remarks that "Nāgārjuna had all the help he needed to achieve this task [the *Kārikā*]."[51] He then mentions the Suttas and *abhidharma* as available to Nāgārjuna. But he seems to have forgotten about the revolutionary formal dialectic never before seen in India that Nāgārjuna introduced; neither the Suttas nor the *abhidharma* could have given him any help there (see chapter 15). Hence "all the help he needed" must have included some unacknowledged input from outside. The tradition that Nāgārjuna obtained his teachings from the *nāga* (hence his name, "one who has achieved [his goal] with the aid of the dragons")[52] similarly suggests awareness that something significant must have come in from outside here, and similarly offers no help in identifying the source of this input.

Nāgārjuna (whom some have taken as the historical figure behind the *Milindapañha*'s Nāgasena) may have read the Hellenistic book or a translation or precis of it, or met the teacher who was purveying its doctrines, perhaps one of many Greco-Roman teachers purveying their schools' wares in the expanded imperial range, perhaps an Indian connected with the Indo-Greek community. Perhaps the Greco-Buddhist teacher, or perhaps an Indian student, recast the argumentation to make it relevant to Buddhism. In any case, as Conze has remarked, the effect was virtually like a new religion—Mahāyāna Buddhism—the form of Buddhism which (regardless of how Hinduized its later forms became) seems to have originated in the Greco-Buddhist communities of India, through a conflation of the Greek Democritean-sophistic-skeptical tradition with the rudimentary and unformalized empirical and skeptical elements already present in early Buddhism.

The drastic change in Buddhist thought represented by the Mahāyāna has been traditionally called the Second Turning of the Wheel of the *Dharma*—as Nāgārjuna was called the "second Buddha." The stature accorded to it in Buddhist history can hardly be exaggerated. "Of the great philosophers of Mahāyāna Buddhism," opines one scholar, "Nāgārjuna . . . was undoubtedly the greatest."[53] His system "marks the beginning of Mahāyāna Buddhism's classical philosophical formulation."[54] To attempt to appropriate it into a foreign tradition, or to redescribe the conditions of its coming together as involving a foreign input, brings up complex nationalistic sentiments which Buddhism itself disavows. Is Nāgārjuna really to be called "perhaps the most important Indian scholar of any persuasion"[55] for having borrowed a small part of the equipment of a foreign culture? The introduction to a recent edition of the *Prasannapadā* of Candrakīrti exemplifies the issues involved. "Nāgārjuna," we read, ". . . had, probably in the second century A.D., with a lion's roar second only to that of Buddha, flung the philosophy of the 'middle way' at his receptive, dumbfounded, and outraged contemporaries."[56] The leaven of foreign yeast, introduced into a pious tradition, brings outrage. "*Mādhyamika* thought has been virulently controversial from the beginning, arousing misunderstanding, disbelief, and outrage in roughly equal measure. Classical Indian opponents frequently repudiated it as nihilist."[57] That "classical Indian" teachers repudiated it supports that it was a foreign or imported doctrine. Change from outside influence represents the breakdown of emic or tribal views, and to one conditioned by those views must seem nihilistic. But the impulse to regard a tradition as ethnically pure is inappropriate to the doctrines of the Dharma. "Nāgārjuna," our modern author goes on, "generally agreed, whether grudgingly or admiringly, to be the acutest intellect in Buddhist history, thinks his way relentlessly through to the conclusions he found implicit in Buddha's promise of freedom (*nirvāṇa*) for all beings."[58] That Nāgārjuna was "grudgingly" appreciated again suggests foreign input in his teaching. Is it painful to rewrite: "to the conclusions he found in the foreign book that came into his hands"? The same author continues, in his introduction to Candrakīrti, to note that Nāgārjuna "made it impossible for Buddhist religious and philosophical thinking ever again to turn back to earlier conceptions."[59] Again this change is typical of explosive diffusion events. Diffusion which is suited to the shore on which it washes up causes growth and intensifies change in creative thought.

The scholar continues: "The invocation to the *Prasannapadā*, the body of literature from which quotations are drawn in every chapter, and Buddha's easy coming and going from page to page throughout the work, leave us in no doubt about its cultural origins."[60] This insistence on purity of cultural heritage is inappropriate, since Mahāyāna Buddhism is a polyglot tradition into which other traditions from Pyrrhonism to Bon to Shinto have fed. The Buddhadharma always came with the understanding that it should be adapted everywhere to its new conditions. The pious Indian claim to its patrimony has in this sense no more force than any other. Diffusion is a vast and complex process, and all cultures are made up of manifold influences and borrowed elements.[61] The scholar in question described the *Prasannapadā* as "a bright jewel in the rich crown of Indian philosophy"—as if philosophy were a nationalistic competition. "Those who have penetrated even a short way into Sanskrit and Chinese find that the great questions which frame the religious sense and the intellectual wonder of these cultures are, however different from those of Greece and Europe, still indefeasibly cognate with them so that we can move from one tradition to another without ever leaving the human scene."[62] But it may not be some archetypal humanness that unites these traditions so much as the actual empirical causality of history and historical contact. And indeed the "razor-sharp dialectic" of the "critique of pure reason"[63] of the "second Buddha" may bear the philosophical signature of a far-off culture barely heard of in the India of the Buddhists.[64]

This story offers a sense of the power of books to move through and across cultural barriers. Candrakīrti's *Prasannapadā*, we read on, "arrived in Europe in manuscript form from Nepal about the middle of the nineteenth century."[65] Did the little book of

Aenesidemus (or some other in his tradition) travel, through the lineage of its influence—from the Greek Mediterranean in the early Christian era, either through the Red Sea and Bay of Bengal or overland through Central Asia—to India, thence to create a wave that washed up centuries later in Tibet, Mongolia, China, Korea, and Japan, finally to return to Europe, at about the end of the Christian era?

In fact, the situation is balanced. As the dialectical-logical dichotomy entered India from Greece, so the whole monism complex had entered Greece from India several centuries earlier, and has dominated the monistic and idealistic strands of westrn philosophy from Parmenides, Pythagoras, and Plato, to Spinoza, Hegel, and Heidegger.

Notes to Chapter Eighteen

1. Trans. Horace L. Jones, *The Geography of Strabo*, vol. 7, Loeb Classical Library (Cambridge, Massachusetts: Harvard University Press and London: W. Heinemann, 1917–1933), p. 101.

2. See E. Lamotte, "Sur la formation du Mahāyāna," *Asiatica* (1954).

3. More recent scholars than Diogenes Laertius, who have assumed that Pyrrhon's journey to India in general—and his encounter with Gymnosophists in particular—must have had a significant influence on his later teachings, include: Victor C. L. Brochard, *Les sceptiques grecs* (Paris: Impr. Nationale, 1887), pp. 73 ff.; Benimadhab Barua, *Prolegomena to a History of Buddhist Philosophy* (Calcutta: University of Calcutta Press, 1918), p. 6; Mary Patrick, *Greek Skeptics* (New York: Columbia University Press, 1969), p. 57; Leon Robin, *Pyrrhon et le scepticisme grec* (Paris: Presses Universitaires de France, 1944), pp. 6, 8; A. M. Frenkian, "Sextus Empiricus and Indian Logic," *Philosophical Quarterly* (India) 30 (1957): part 2; Edward Conze, *Buddhism: Its Essence and Development* (New York: Peter Smith, 1959), pp. 140–143; George Woodcock, *The Greeks in India* (London: Faber and Faber, 1966), p. 27; Cornelia J. de Vogel, *Philosophia*, vol. 1, Philosophical Texts and Studies 19 (Assen: van Gorcum, 1970), p. 428; Everard Flintoff, "Pyrrho and India," *Phronēsis* 25 (1980): 88–108, and Giovanni Reale, *A History of Ancient Philosophy*, vol. 3, *Systems of the Hellenistic Age*, ed. and trans. John R. Catan (Albany, New York: State University of New York Press, 1985–87), pp. 310–311. Reale notes that Pyrrhon's thought was "'a philosophy of transition,' that is, a position of thought which shows an unexpected passage from one world to another" (ibid.). But he has positioned Pyrrhon as a witness to and indeed a participant in the end of the world of the *polis*—the Hellenic world—and the beginning of the world of the Hellenistic international monarchy, and this as much as the transition via travel from the West to the East can account for the "philosophy of transition." "Pyrrho was placed at the precise moment in which the Greek awareness lost some truths and as yet did not succeed in finding any to take their place and hence . . . he is situated 'at the zero moment of truth'" (ibid.).

4. Ibid., p. 311.

5. John Burnet, "Sceptics," *Encyclopaedia of Religion and Ethics*.

6. My translation from Robin, *Pyrrhon et le scepticisme grec*, p. 6: "[S]orte d'habitude sociale resultant d'une 'convention' tacite, qui a pour objet de remplacer par un système de noms, d'usage commun et de signification permanente, le flot mouvant de nos impressions, toujours individuelles, changeant avec l'état de notre corps et avec ses relations aux objets exterieurs, dont l'état et la constitution sont eux-memes perpetuellement changeant."

7. Flintoff, "Pyrrho and India," p. 93.

8. Long and Sedley hold that the phrase *ou mallon* ("no more . . . than") refers only to the first construction that follows it: Each thing no more is than is not, or it both is and is not, or it neither is nor is not. The three predicates become not cumulative parts of one option but three alternative options, and the quadrilemma or fourfold negation disappears. (A. A. Long and

D. N. Sedley, ed., *The Hellenistic Philosophers*, vol. 1, [Cambridge: Cambridge University Press, 1987], p. 17.) Hankinson seems to agree with them (*The Sceptics* [London and New York: Routledge, 1995], pp. 63–64). I follow the traditional quadrilemmic interpretation of the passage, not only because it opens the question of Indian influence but also because that interpretation fits better into the relevant environment of Greek philosophy—as will become clear.

9. See chapter 15, "Dialectic before Alexander."

10. See Edward Conze, *Thirty Years of Buddhist Studies* (London: Bruno Cassirer, 1967), pp. 4–10.

11. See K. N. Jayatilleke, *Early Buddhist Theory of Knowledge* (London: George Allen and Unwin, 1963), pp. 121, 134 ff., 336–338.

12. There is no agreement on how to translate this list. This somewhat loose translation is based on both Jayatilleke's discussion (*Early Buddhist Theory of Knowledge*, pp. 135–140) and Barua's (*A History of Pre-Buddhistic Indian Philosophy* [Delhi: Motilal Banarsidass, 1981], p. 329).

13. Frenkian, "Sextus Empiricus and Indian Logic," p. 123.

14. Benson Mates, *Stoic Logic*, University of California Publications in Philosophy (Berkeley, California: University of California Press, 1953), p. 84.

15. Ibid., p. 34.

16. Jayatilleke, *Early Buddhist Theory of Knowledge*, pp. 293, 344–345.

17. See chapter 17, "Pyrrhonism and Mādhyamika."

18. Satis Chandra Vidyabhusana, ed. and trans., *The Nyāya Sūtras of Gotama* (New Delhi: Munshiram Manoharlal, 1975), p. 3.

19. Theodore Stcherbatsky, *Buddhist Logic*, vol. 2 (New York: Dover, 1962), p. 97.

20. The question is more relevant to the relationship between the Greek and Indian syllogisms, and it will come up again in chapter 19, "The Syllogism," which discusses that topic. In dating the beginnings of Naiyāyika logic I follow Innotentius M. Bochenski, *A History of Formal Logic*, trans. and ed. Ivo Thomas (Notre Dame, Indiana: University of Notre Dame Press, 1961). Frenkian absurdly dates it to the sixth century B.C., the cultic date of the sect's hero-founder Gotama (see Frenkian, "Sextus Empiricus and Indian Logic"). (Frenkian's argument overall suffers from inattention to chronological problems, even more so its revival by Flintoff ["Pyrrho and India"] who shows no sense that chronological problems even enter into scholarship.)

21. David J. Kalupahana, *Nāgārjuna: The Philosophy of the Middle Way*, SUNY Series in Buddhist Studies (Albany, New York: State University of New York Press, 1986), p. 197.

22. Georges M. A. Grube, ed. and trans., *A Greek Critic: Demetrius on Style, by Demetrius of Phaleron*, The Phoenix; Journal of the Classical Association of Canada, suppl. 4 (Toronto: University of Toronto Press, 1961), p. 98.

23. Grube settles on 270 (*A Greek Critic*); Schenkeveld favors the first century A.D. (Dick Maria Schenkeveld, *Studies in Demetrius "On Style"* [Amsterdam: A. Hakkert, 1964], p. 147).

24. Quoted by Shashi Bhusan Dasgupta, *Introduction to Tantric Buddhism* (Berkeley, California: Shambala, 1974), p. 40.

25. Alfonzo Verdu, *Dialectical Aspects in Buddhist Thought* (Lawrence, Kansas: Center for East Asian Studies, University of Kansas, 1974), pp. 27–28.

26. Quoted by Frenkian, "Sextus Empiricus and Indian Logic," p. 117.

27. Candrakīrti *Prasannapadā* XXV.3. See Stcherbatsky, *The Conception of Buddhist Nirvāṇa* (Delhi: Motilal Banarsidass, 1978), p. 198; and Mervyn Sprung, trans., *Lucid Exposition of the Middle Way: The Essential Chapters from the Prasannapadā of Candrakīrti* (Boulder, Colorado: Prajñā Press, 1979), p. 250.

28. Quoted by Stcherbatsky, *The Conception of Buddhist Nirvāṇa*, p. 198.

29. Translated by K. Narayanasvami Aiyar, *Thirty Minor Upaniṣads* (El Reno, Oklahoma: Santarasa Publications, 1980), p. 257.

30. Radhakrishnan's paraphrase of Śaṅkara's commentary on *Brahmā Sūtras* II.1.9 (Radhakrishnan, *The Brahmā Sūtra: The Philosophy of Spiritual Life* [London: George Allen and Unwin, 1960], p. 33). Frenkian also cites Gaudapāda (*Māṇḍūkyakārikā* II.17), Śaṅkara (*Māṇḍūkyakārikabhāṣya, passim*) and the Viśiṣṭādvaita Vedāntin Ramānuja (*Śri bhāṣya* I.1.1) (Frenkian, "Sextus Empiricus and Indian Logic"). The image is still used in Tibetan *dharma* discourse (see Jeffrey Hopkins, *Meditation on Emptiness* [Boston: Wisdom Publications, 1996], p. 37).

31. Hankinson, *The Sceptics*, p. 120.

32. Richard H. Jones, "The Nature and Function of Nāgārjuna's Arguments," *Philosophy East and West* 28 (1978): 485–486.

33. Singh, "Introduction," in Stcherbatsky, *The Conception of Buddhist Nirvāṇa* (Delhi: Motilal Banarsidass, 1978), p. 14.

34. Mortimer Wheeler, *Flames over Persepolis* (New York: William Morrow, 1968), pp. 68, 84.

35. E. Lamotte, "Sur la formation du Mahāyāna." *Asiatica* (1954).

36. Edward Conze, *Buddhism: Its Essence and Development* (New York: Harper and Row, 1959), pp. 140–143. In *The Prajñāpāramitā Literature* ('S-Gravenhage: Mouton, 1960), p. 10, he suspects Greek influence on the school.

37. David J. Kalupahana, *Buddhist Philosophy, A Historical Analysis* (Honolulu: University of Hawaii Press, 1976), p. 129. Note the parallelism between Kalupahana's statement that Prajñāpāramitā literature pointed out "the conflict between noumenal reality and phenomenality" (ibid.) and Sextus's remark that the Skeptic "opposes appearances to judgments" (*OP* I.8).

38. Mortimer Wheeler, *Rome Beyond the Imperial Frontiers* (London: Bell, 1954), p. 121.

39. See Sylvain Lévi, "Alexander and Alexandria in Indian Literature," *Indian Historical Quarterly* 12 (1936): 121–133.

40. See Conze, *The Prajñāpāramitā Literature*, p. 11.

41. Ibid., pp. 9–11. For some of the evidence of Greek activity in this part of India see M. Cary and E. H. Warmington, *The Ancient Explorers* (Baltimore, Maryland: Penguin, 1963), pp. 101 ff.; and Mortimer Wheeler, "Arikamedu: An Indo-Roman Trading Station in the East Coast of India," *Ancient India* 2 (1947).

42. Wheeler, *Rome Beyond the Imperial Frontiers*, pp. 152–153.

43. For the influence of Latin poetry, for example Seneca, on Tamil literature, see X. S. Thani-Nayagam, "Indian Thought and Roman Stoicism," *Tamil Culture* 10, no. 3 (1963). E. H. Johnston says ("Two Notes on Ptolemy's Geography of India," *JRAS* [1941]: 222), "An identifiable Sanskrit text [was] available in some form or other at Alexandria," a Puranic text which served as one of Ptolemy's sources in the second century A.D.

44. Quoted by H. G. Rawlinson, *Intercourse Between India and the Western World from the Earliest Times to the Fall of Rome* (Cambridge: Cambridge University Press, 1926), p. 173. Compare O. Neugebauer, *The Exact Sciences in Antiquity*, 2nd ed. (Providence, Rhode Island: Brown University Press, 1957), p. 7.

45. David Pingree, *The Yavanajātaka of Sphujidhvaja*, vol. 1, Harvard Oriental Series 48 (Cambridge, Massachusetts: Harvard University Press, 1978), p. v.

46. Ibid., p. 3.

47. Ibid., p. 4.

48. Ibid., p. 3.

49. André-Marie J. Festugière, "Trois Rencontres entre la Grèce et l'Inde," *Revue de l'histoire des religions* 125 (1942–43): 32–57.

50. Hankinson, *The Sceptics*, pp. 127–128.

51. Kalupahana, *Nāgārjuna*, p. 26.

52. Robert A. F. Thurman, *The Central Philosophy of Tibet: A Study and Translation of Jey Tsong Khapa's* "Essence of True Eloquence," (Princeton, New Jersey: Princeton University Press, 1991), p. 24.

53. Noble Ross Reat, *Buddhism: A History* (Berkeley: Asian Humanities Press, 1994), p. 67.

54. Ibid.

55. C. W. Huntington Jr., *The Emptiness of Emptiness: An Introduction to Early Indian Mādhyamika* (Honolulu: University of Hawaii Press, 1989), p. 32.

56. Sprung, *Lucid Exposition of the Middle Way*, p. 1.

57. Ibid., p. 2.

58. Ibid.

59. Ibid.

60. Ibid, p. 2.

61. For a discussion of the diffusion situation see, for example, the author's "The Common Air: Contemporary Art in India," *Artforum* (Summer 1986).

62. Ibid.

63. Thurman, *Central Philosophy of Tibet*, pp. 30–31.

64. In fact one might think that the adulation of Nāgārjuna in the Mahāyāna tradition is somewhat overblown, considering that most of the *Kārikā* consists simply of the early Buddhist doctrine of dependent arising (*pratītya-samutpāda*) expounded in a mode of reasoning that was unaccustomed in India but is, nonetheless, simple enough to be explained in a page. Hopkins's Tibetan sources argue that "the *Treatise* is not limited to an extensive explanation of emptiness; it also extensively sets forth the suitability of conventional phenomena within an emptiness of inherent existence as well as the four truths, actions and their effects, the Three Jewels, the eight levels of approaching and abiding in the fruits of Stream Enterer, Once Returner, Never Returner, and Foe Destroyer, and so forth . . ." (*Meditation on Emptiness*, p. 403.) Still, he immediately acknowledges that "these varieties are not the principal objects of discourse in the *Treatise*; the profound emptiness is" (ibid., p. 404). And the profound emptiness is "the lack of inherent existence" (ibid.), which is the "Hīnayāna" doctrine of *pratītya-samutpāda*, as set forth (as Kalupahana stressed) in the *Kātyāyana Sūtra*. This—the secret that *śūnyata* is a code word for *pratītya-samutpāda*—is the simple substance of what in the Tibetan tradition is called "the highest system" (ibid., p. 337) and for declaring which Nāgārjuna was hailed in Tibet as "the prophesied upholder of Buddha's deepest teaching."

65. Sprung, *Lucid Exposition of the Middle Way*, p. 2.

Chapter Nineteen

The Syllogism

The Nyāya-Vaiśeṣika school, in which the Indian syllogism arose, was especially susceptible to diffused influences from abroad because its commitment to Vedic orthodoxy was superficial and its relationship to it virtually invisible. One scholar wrote:

> Though in later times it was tenaciously claimed that the Nyāya-Vaiśeṣika was a Vedic philosophy and though our traditional scholars are never tired of tracing its origin to the Upaniṣads and even to the Saṁhitās, the really distinctive peculiarities of this system appear to be quite new in the Indian philosophical tradition.[1]

The author points to the presence in this school not only of atomism, but of universals, syllogisms, and categories, and concludes: "The easy hypothesis . . . [is] that of wholesale borrowing by the Indians from the Greeks."[2] The idea of "wholesale borrowing" cannot be established *in toto*. But if one element could be clearly related to a Greek source—as certain Greek elements from the pre-Socratic period can be tightly linked to Indian sources—then the general hypothesis would have more claim to attention.

The Indian syllogism arose in the Naiyāyika tradition and was further developed by Buddhist thinkers. Some sixty years ago Vidyabhusana attempted to demonstrate Aristotelian influence on the Indian tradition in general and the syllogism in particular.[3] Since the Indian syllogism evolved over a period of half a millennium—from the earliest syllogistic passages of the *Nyāya Sūtras* (perhaps the first century B.C.) until the time of the Buddhist Dignāga (fifth century A.D.)—the thesis is not simple to establish, or even to conceptualize. The problem is further complicated by the fact that the earliest form of the Indian syllogism, that of the *Nyāya Sūtras*, is the least like Aristotle's in form, and the latest, that of Dignāga, the most like it.

To account for this development Vidyabhusana suggested a staged entry of Greek logic into India. First, he suggested, c. 175–30 B.C., a few passages of Aristotle's *Rhetoric* arrived, passages conveying the basic idea of inference but without its formal exposition. A century or two later, the *Prior Analytics* was absorbed into the Indian tradition, and several centuries later still, the *Posterior Analytics*. Given the great differences between the Aristotelian and Naiyāyika syllogisms, this unwieldy model was perhaps the best that could be offered.

Other scholars have referred to such theorizing as a waste of time, pointing to certain differences between the Naiyāyika and Peripatetic syllogisms which render the possibility of influence implausible. The point can be made by comparing standard syllogisms from the two traditions. In the Aristotelian type called "Darii"—which has one universal and one particular premise, both positive—a particular is assigned to a category and then is concluded to have the defining trait of that category:

(Universal premise:) All humans are mortal.

(Particular premise:) Socrates is a human.

(Conclusion:) Therefore Socrates is mortal.

The reasoning is deductive and abstract, passing from a universal to a particular that is subsumed within the universal.

The standard Naiyāyika syllogism, on the other hand, has five or six, not three, members:

(1) (Thesis:) There is fire on the hill.
(2) (Reason:) Because there is smoke on the hill.
(3a) (Positive example:) As in a kitchen.
(3b) (Negative example:) And not in a lake.
(4) (Application:) There is smoke on the hill.
(5) (Conclusion:) Therefore there is fire on the hill.

The Naiyāyika syllogism does not involve a universal proposition. Instead it offers a pair of particular cases or analogues. It is not deductive but inductive. This is the main difference, though differences in form are prominent too.

Though the logic of the *Nyāya Sūtras* is primarily inductive, this is not because deductive awareness was lacking. The *Sūtras* and the commentarial literature on them show deductive tendencies. One commentator, for example, speaks of a "universal connection between the reason and the predicate,"[4] a concept suggested, in texts by "Gotama" and his commentator, Vātsyāyana, by the still-inductive idea of universal concomitance—that the two factors, for example, smoke and fire, occur together in every instance that one can think of.[5] Though the logicians of this school clearly were aware of universals and deduction from them, the form of the syllogism remained inductive and analogical.

In the five-step syllogism illustrated above, the positive example (3a) establishes an inductive concomitance of the two terms which the syllogism seeks to connect—in the classic example, smoke and fire: When there is smoke in the kitchen there is fire in the kitchen. The negative example denies that the terms appear separately: As when in a lake there is no fire, there is also no smoke. From these examples the conclusion, that the two terms share a relationship of mutual concomitance—that is, that one never appears without the other being present—is induced by appeals to analogy rather than to principles of deduction. The reasoning does not proceed from universal to particular but from particular to particular. As a result of this important difference, as well as the formal discrepancy between three- and five-limbed structures, attempts to connect the Peripatetic and Naiyāyika syllogisms have been difficult. "A more useful comparison" for the Naiyāyika syllogism, one scholar suggests, "can perhaps be found with John Stuart Mill's canons of inductive reasoning."[6]

These opinions are all based on the idea that the only Greek form of logic was Aristotle's; thus, to find an inductive logic to refer to, one goes as far afield as Mill. But an even more fruitful comparison may be found among Greek logics that were not exclusively Peripatetic—the Megarian, the Stoic, the Epicurean, and the Neoplatonist. The first three of these are chronologically eligible to have stimulated the Naiyāyika syllogism, quite as much as is the Peripatetic form. In fact, the widespread presence of the Hellenistic schools throughout the eastern Roman Empire makes these variants more likely to have turned up in India than Aristotle's. By the Hellenistic period, interest in both Plato and Aristotle, which was typical of the classical milieu of the *polis*, had waned. There were Stoic and Epicurean teachers active in Afghanistan and quite possibly in northwest India also. The Epicureans especially disseminated their message with a missionary fervor and believed that it was their duty to teach the "barbarians." And the central point is that the very quality that differentiates Naiyāyika logic from Peripatetic renders it similar—indeed nearly identical—to the Epicurean and other Hellenistic varieties.

Epicurean logicians stripped Aristotelian logic of its universals and reshaped it into an empiricist form. Like Naiyāyika logic, the Epicurean form is based on particular-to-particular reasoning employing induction and analogy; it does not acknowledge the legitimacy of the universal proposition and is not involved in a quasi-metaphysical belief in abstract logical necessity. Again like the Naiyāyika, it infers "the nature of unperceived objects by analogy with the objects of our experience."[7] In place of the repudiated universal statement, it substitutes the analogous exemplum. The exemplum is drawn from experience and hence is empirical, whereas the universal proposition, with its pretension of embodying a law of the universe, implies metaphysical ambitions.

The general philosophical frameworks of the Epicurean and Naiyāyika logics are identical. Both, above all, faced up to the problem of induction. In rejecting the quasi-metaphysical implications of deductive logic, both Naiyāyikas and Epicureans were aware that they left themselves open to the ultimate fallibility of empirical generalizations. The Naiyāyikas "viewed the examples as providing evidence for pervasion"—that is, for the formation of a category generalization which, being based on generalizing from examples, only really applies to those examples and hence is less ambitious than the universal proposition—but they generally admit that the statement of pervasion is always fallible—that subsequent examination may show that what seemed to be concomitance between *h* [the sign] and *s* [the inferred nonobserved datum] is not really such."[8] Similarly the Epicurean logician Philodemus (c. 100 B.C.) taught that "the inference from signs is of course not infallible, but if it is based on sufficiently broad empirical observation it will be highly probable."[9] The fact that an inference may have to be reviewed when new evidence arises is, in other words, taken for granted in both traditions. No *a priori* universals are recognized.

The two schools also shared an attitude of semantic realism. Neither Naiyāyikas nor Epicureans taught a completely formalized logic in which free variables could be replaced by any term whatever, as the deductivist Peripatetic and Buddhist logicians did. In both cases, a resistance to complete formalization around variables arose from an empiricist conviction that terms without experiential or existential referents are meaningless. An Aristotelian could syllogize about unicorns. In his view, the fact that one term of the argument lacked existential connection had no effect on the validity of the reasoning, which resided in purely formal matters. Epicureans, on the other hand, felt that the meanings of words are based exclusively on empirical references. In this view, language is based on perception and "any use of words to refer to non-empirical entities . . . should be rejected as lacking cognitive meaning."[10] Among the Indian schools a similar division is found. The Buddhists could syllogize about imaginary entities. But among the Naiyāyikas, if one term in a proposition failed to denote any empirical referent, the proposition was ruled out as "semantically unfit."[11]

Smoke and Fire

An exemplum used consistently in the Indian systems of inductive inference involves the concomitance of smoke and fire (as in the five-limbed Naiyāyika syllogism cited above). Smoke is the *liṅga* or *lakṣaṇa*, that is, the "sign" of fire, or the *hetu*, that is, the evidence which convinces us of the presence of fire. According to Naiyāyika theory, we experience the concomitance of this signifier and signified many times and, when looking at the smoke rising from behind the hill, remember these experiences of smoke/fire concomitance and interpret the present sign on analogy with those remembered events.

The Epicurean Philodemus also used the smoke/fire image to illustrate inductive inference from "signs" (*semeia*). In arguing against the Stoic method of proof by contraposition, he wrote:

> In order to make the contraposition "If there is or has been no fire, there is no smoke," we contend that always in all cases smoke has been observed to be given off by fire.[12]

Even beyond the Epicurean tradition, the empirical-inductive inference from signs was a common subject in the Hellenistic philosophical milieu. Aristotle had recognized the value of induction, but limited its application to the "lower" sciences (*Rhet.* I.1357a32-b36; *An. Pr.* II.70a3–38). But the Democritean Nausiphanes taught a thoroughgoing inductive inference which, along with his atomism, probably influenced Epicurus in his revision of Aristotle, and which may be the foundation of Philodemus's theory. Furthermore, the Greek physicians had been systematic empiricists since Hippocrates in the fifth century B.C., and the specifically Empiricist school of medicine arose in the third century B.C.; its texts shared terminology with Philodemus and other Epicurean inductivists. Indeed, the terms and concepts of empirical-inductive logic were shared among many Hellenistic schools, including the Stoics, Epicureans, Empirical Medical Writers, Pyrrhonists, and a variety of eclectics.

In this common stream, some of which probably washed up on the shores of India in the same way in which Greek astronomy books and Roman coins arrived there, the use of the smoke/fire exemplum was widespread. It is found after Philodemus, for example, in the works of the Pyrrhonist encyclopedist Sextus Empiricus, a member of the Empirical medical school, in terms which suggest that it is the common exemplum for discussion of these issues:

> As soon as we see . . . smoke, we recall . . . fire. (*AL* II.152–153)
>
> We . . . infer fire from smoke. (*AL* II.157)
>
> They [the Stoics] term a sign "suggestive" when, being mentally associated with the thing signified, it . . . suggests to us the thing associated with it, which is not clearly perceived at the moment—as for instance in the case of smoke and fire. (*OP* II.100)
>
> When a man sees smoke, fire is signified. (*OP* II.102)

Sextus's exposition parallels the Naiyāyika not only in the smoke/fire exemplum but in the terminology of "signs" and the use of them to inductively infer a nonperceived datum from past associations. A longer passage will show Sextus's empiricizing tendency wrapped up with the same exemplum and the same terminology of signs; here Sextus is discussing the Epicurean logic, and the tactic which it adopted to arrive at the inference of atoms and void:

> But things naturally non-evident, and things temporarily so, have need of the kind of observation effected by sign—the temporarily non-evident because, in certain circumstances, they are removed from our clear perception, and the naturally non-evident because they are forever nonapparent. As then, there are two distinct classes of things which require sign, sign also has revealed itself as twofold—the "commemorative," which appear to be chiefly of use in the case of things temporarily non-evident, and the "indicative," which is deemed proper for adoption in the case of things naturally non-evident.
>
> Thus the commemorative sign, when observed in conjunction with the thing signified in a clear perception, brings us, as soon as it is present and when the thing signified has become non-evident, to a recollection of the thing observed along with it and now no longer clearly perceived—as in the case of smoke and fire; for as we have often observed these to be connected with each other, as soon as we see the one—that is to say, smoke—we recall the other—that is to say, the unseen fire. (AL II.150–153)

Sextus is engaged, in this passage, in an empiricizing purification of the Epicurean logic, as the latter was of the Aristotelian. He goes on to attack the doctrine of the "indicative" sign by which the Epicureans hoped to use indirect empirical data to establish the truth of propositions which were by nature not available for direct empirical testing—that is, atoms and void. He limits the application of logic to the discovery of data unseen at the time but not naturally and inherently unseeable, that is, to the "commemorative" sign based on memory of actual experience. The "indicative" sign he criticizes on the grounds that it goes beyond actual experience and thus, in Sextus's phenomenalism, is meaningless; the commemorative sign, arising from and applying to everyday experience, is the only criterion.[13] Sextus's "commemorative" sign is the *hetu-liṅga-lakṣaṇa* which the Naiyāyikas also exemplify as smoke in relation to fire. In general, his version of the theory of signs, while adapted from Stoic and Epicurean sources, is closer to "Gotama's" than are the Stoic and Epicurean forms.

It is impossible, on present evidence, to be certain how early the smoke/fire exemplum appeared in either Greek or Indian literature. Though Philodemus used it in countering Stoic logic, it is not found either in Diogenes Laertius's or in Sextus's expositions of Stoic logic. It may be more likely to have arisen in the atomist tradition of Epicurus; not only is it found in an Epicurean author, Philodemus, but it is used by Sextus especially when arguing against Epicurean positions. In extant Indian literature it seems to be first used in the *Nyāya Sūtras* of "Gotama"—a work accumulated over a long period of time—from around 200 B.C. to around 450 A.D., with possible memory traces of a period as early as 500 B.C. But the syllogistic passages are not early in this period. Nāgārjuna and Āryadeva apparently did not know of them, and the first extant author who did is Asaṅga, about 400 A.D. The syllogism, in other words, probably appeared in the Naiyāyika literature after Nāgārjuna and before Asaṅga, that is, between c. 150 and c. 400 A.D.

It is more than plausible that both the Nyāya-Vaiśeṣika and its classical adversary, the Mādhyamika school, were responding to stimulus from Hellenistic Greek schools, especially in the development of their methods. Both the systematic dialectical *reductio ad absurdum* and the logic of the syllogism probably arose at least in part from western sources, and the conflict between them which enlivened Indian philosophical discourse for several centuries may reflect a similar, somewhat earlier moment of the Greco-Roman milieu. These seem to be parts of a new wave of Indian thought ushered in by a mélange of Hellenistic philosophical *koinē* brought by the eclectic professors who taught in Asia and in eclectic compendia not unlike those of Sextus.

The Five-Limbed Structure

The principal problem with this model of the origin of the Indian syllogism is the five-limbed structure of the Naiyāyika syllogism, which does not occur in any extant Greek text. The Stoics, it is true, suggested four-limbed *disjuncta*, but these had much more in common with the dialectical fourfold formula (*catuṣkoṭi*) than with the Naiyāyika syllogism, which is, as Nakamura says, "unnecessarily diffuse, since the members (4) and (5) are, in fact, only repetitions of (2) and (1)."[14] Perhaps a century or more after this form was devised, the Buddhist logician Dignāga "established the three-proposition syllogism . . ." But this is not to imply that "Gotama" could not see that the job could have been done in three steps. "The aim . . . of the founder of the Nyāya system was not in the least to propound the most concise form of syllogism possible; he desired to teach how best to impart to others a conviction reached by an inference."[15] And the rules of debating practice, on which the five-limbed syllogism may have been based, were an appropriate place to look for the best way "to impart to others a conviction."

It has repeatedly been suggested that "Gotama's" five-limbed syllogism was derived from a ten-limbed pattern of debate that was more rhetorical than systematically inferential.[16] This model has been taken as supporting the evolution of the syllogism out of the earlier debate in a purely Indian context, not needing any outside influence.

One problem with this view is that from a philological standpoint the *Nyāya Sūtras* do not seem to preserve a developmental record of a coherent tradition. They do not show a development from a set of debating rules to a set of syllogistic rules so much as a conflation of textual records on these two subjects. They seem to be a compilation from at least three sources, not a single source which was gradually developed and elaborated. Books two and three of the *Sūtras* seem to have been adopted from a Vaiśeṣika source in the period in which the two schools were amalgamating—possibly around 450 A.D. Parts of books one and five preserve a debating textbook whose history goes back at least as far as the age of the Buddhist Nikāyas. Other parts of these books purvey principles of syllogism which have no extant antecedents in the Indian tradition. There is little internal connection among these three elements, which seem to have been adopted as packages from different sources during the formation of this composite school.

The sections on debating rules can be traced back in the Indian tradition to earlier texts that describe these rules in terms recognizably related to the *Nyāya Sūtras*. The atomist source in turn is recognizably Vaiśeṣika (though its ultimate sources are another question). But for the syllogistic sections there is no identifiable source anywhere in the Indian tradition. Only one known source in the world could have provided the input at the time, and that very source is known to have been abundantly present in India during the period in question. The fact that the Nyāya school is widely recognized as nonorthodox, that is, non-Vedic (though it officially calls itself a Vedic tradition), may explain why this school in particular might have been receptive to non-Vedic—and even, perhaps, non-Indian—input.

A hypothetical reconstruction of a diffusion event might suppose that the tradition of debating encountered, in the Greek communities of either or both northwest and south India, a more rigorous form of argument like that of the Epicurean logicians. The new method of argumentation was adapted to the local style by means of the five-membered syllogism based in part on the ten-limbed debating procedure and in part on the imported materials. The Naiyāyikas, in other words, may have tamed the Hellenistic syllogism into assimilable form by rendering it superficially similar to the inherited forms of debate.

Śabda

Śabda means "hearing presented as a source of knowledge" (a *pràmāṇa*). In the Hindu tradition in general, *śabda* refers to the hearing of scriptural authority, that is, the Vedas. The Naiyāyika teacher "Gotama," however, offers a new and bold expansion of the concept to include hearing "the instructive assertion of a reliable person" (*NS* I.1.7). A reliable person, or authority, is "one who has direct knowledge of something and is both desirous and capable of speaking about it."[17] The same doctrine is found in Philodemus and other Hellenistic inductivists, as a means of avoiding empirical solipsism by establishing an intersubjective basis. Philodemus, for example, says:

> We collect [in our empirical investigations] not only the signs appearing to us or tested by our experience, but also the appearances taken from observation by others.[18]

The Naiyāyika interpretation of *śabda* is unusual in the Indian tradition and may in fact represent the memory of the experience of an important cultural transaction. Vātsyāyana, the first great commentator on the *Nyāya Sūtras*, says that the "reliable person" whose testimony is used may be a foreigner.[19]

Notes to Chapter Nineteen

1. Debiprasad Chattopadhyaya, *Indian Philosophy: A Popular Introduction* (Delhi: People's Publishing House, 1964), pp. 160, 162. And compare Gangopadhyaya: "[T]he Nyāya-Vaiśeṣika, of all the schools of Indian philosophy, were unique in not having any religious affiliation. With their serious methodology, invincible logic and strong common sense, they were best suited to follow a scientific line of thought . . . Thus they fought, all along, for the atomic theory and sought to develop it against the relentless tirade of the idealists through the ages for a period extending over about 1500 years" (Mrinalkanti Gangopadhyaya, *Indian Atomism: History and Sources* [Atlantic Highlands, New Jersey: Humanities Press, 1981], p. 54).

2. Chattopadhyaya, *Indian Philosophy: A Popular Introduction*, p. 162.

3. Satis Chandra Vidyabhusana, "Influence of Aristotle on the Development of the Syllogism in Indian Logic," *JRAS* (1918): 469–488.

4. Satis Chandra Vidyabhusana, trans., *The Nyāya Sūtras of Gotama* (Delhi: Munshiram Monoharlal, 1975), p. 142.

5. For example, Kumar Chakrabarti, *The Logic of Gotama*, Monographs of the Society for Asian and Comparative Philosophy 5 (Honolulu: University of Hawaii Press, 1977).

6. Karl H. Potter, *Encyclopedia of Indian Philosophies*, vol. 2, *Indian Metaphysics and Epistemology: The Tradition of Nyāya Vaiśeṣika up to Gangesa* (Princeton, New Jersey: Princeton University Press, 1977), p. 183. The suggestion that Mill was the closer analogue had already been made in 1895 by S. N. Gupta, "The Nature of Inference in Indian Logic," *Mind* 6 (1895): 159–174.

7. Phillip H. and Estelle A. DeLacy, *Philodemus: On Methods of Inference*, Philological Monographs 10 (Philadelphia: American Philological Association, 1941), pp. 13–14. See also Estelle Allen DeLacy, "Meaning and Methodology in Hellenistic Philosophy," *Philosophical Review* 47 (1938): 406–409.

8. Potter, *Indian Metaphysics and Epistemology*, p. 195.

9. DeLacy and DeLacy, *Philodemus*, p. 107.

10. Ibid., p. 140.

11. Potter, *Indian Metaphysics and Epistemology*, pp. 149, 195.

12. DeLacy and DeLacy, *Philodemus*, p. 107.

13. Ibid., pp. 173–174.

14. Hajime Nakamura, *Indian Buddhism: A Survey with Bibliographical Notes* (Delhi: Motilal Banarsidass, 1987), p. 296.

15. Ibid.

16. See, for example, Henry N. Randle, *Indian Logic in the Early Schools* (Oxford: Oxford University Press, 1930), p. 14; Theodore Stcherbatsky, *Buddhist Logic*, vol. 1, (New York: Dover,

1962), pp. 27–28; K. N. Jayatilleke, *Early Buddhist Theory of Knowledge* (London: George Allen and Unwin, 1963), pp. 42 ff.

17. Potter, *Indian Metaphysics and Epistemology*, p. 176.

18. DeLacy and DeLacy, *Philodemus*, pp. 97–99.

19. Potter, *Indian Metaphysics and Epistemology*, p. 176.

Chapter Twenty

Pepripatetics and Vaiśeṣikas

Most scholars agree that the Nyāya and the Vaiśeṣika were once separate schools.[1] After the crystallization of doctrines in the *Nyāya Sūtras* and the *Vaiśeṣika Sūtras*, the two schools seem to have entered a long period of interaction and side-by-side development culminating in a formal synthesis in perhaps the tenth century A.D. During this long period, each openly shared large parts of the other's teachings. The dates of the two Sūtras—not even to mention the pre-Sūtra phases of both schools—are very much in doubt. Both are dated cultically to the sixth century B.C. and may contain some residue from that period, but both seem to have taken something like their present form in about the second century A.D., and most of their development can be assigned to the two or three centuries before that.

The *Vaiśeṣika Sūtras*, attributed to one Kaṇāda, about whom nothing definite is known, are widely considered to have been more ancient in origin than the *Nyāya Sūtras*; they are "the earliest basic text in the whole range of the Nyāya-Vaiśeṣika literature"[2] and are often attributed to the age of the great *nāstika* or non-Vedic systems, Buddhism, Jainism, and Ājīvikism.[3]

One question involved in this dating is the relationship between Jain and Vaiśeṣika atomisms. Some have derived the Jain from the Vaiśeṣika, other the Vaiśeṣika from the Jain. At any rate, certain similarities seem to point to a connection. Several primitive elements in Jain atomism have been mentioned as indications that it may have arisen before dialectical criticism. First, the absolute distinction between *jīva* and *ajīva*, or material and immaterial, brings with it the problem of the adhering of material atoms to a nonmaterial soul. Second, the Jain doctrine that all atoms are exactly alike makes problems at the stage of atomic aggregates that appear to have different qualities. Most serious of all is the Jain assertion that the atoms are infinitesimal, that is, lacking in magnitude, like the point-monads of the Pythagoreans. Zeno pointed out that aggregates of constituents which lack magnitude will also lack magnitude; thus the infinitesimal point-monad cannot account for visible bodies. Jain atomism seems to have been formulated without awareness of its vulnerability to such criticism, and hence to have arisen before it—that is, before Nāgārjuna and Āryadeva.

Vaiśeṣika atomism seems to be a partially revised version of Jain atomism. It defines the atoms of the four elements as possessing different sense qualities. (Air atoms possess tangibility, fire atoms both tangibility and color; water atoms add taste, and earth atoms add smell.) Like the Jain atoms, however, the Vaiśeṣika atoms are said to lack magnitude—to be "extensionless, mathematical points" that do "not 'occupy' space" but become "related to spatial directions."[4] This doctrine, which would seem to have been adopted from the Jains or from their source, is a primitive, or as one scholar put it, a "quaint and archaic" feature of the system.[5] The Vaiśeṣika view, then, like the Jain, seems to have been developed prior to the introduction into the Indian discourse of the Eleatic type of criticism.

In time both Mādhyamika and Advaitin dialecticians put the Vaiśeṣika theory to the test, or *elenchus*. If the atoms are said to have extension, then they have parts and thus are not indivisible units; if they lack extension, then they cannot coalesce into extended aggregates, and so on. By the time the dialectical *elenchus* had appeared in India, the Vaiśeṣika doctrine had evidently hardened to the point where it could not be abandoned but only defended. As time passed, the whole range of criticisms was made. Even the disproof of point-monads on the basis of the incommensurability of the hypotenuse of the right-angled triangle—a criticism which had been made by Hippasus of Metapontum in the fifth century B.C.—was leveled against the Vaiśeṣika doctrine centuries later by the mathematician Kamalakara Bhatta.[6] Nyāya-Vaiśeṣika polemicists like Vātsyāyana and Uddyotakara became masters of dialectical argumentation in response to this barrage of attacks. As one scholar notes, "[T]hey fought, all along, for the atomic theory and sought to develop it against the relentless tirade of the idealists through the ages for a period extending over about 1500 years."[7]

Still, the primitiveness of elements of Jain and Vaiśeṣika atomism does not necessarily indicate a pre-Alexandrian date, only a predialectical date, which is to say, a pre-Mādhyamika date. In fact, there is no certain proof of the existence of atomism in any Indian philosophy until after 326 B.C. Perhaps it is worth mentioning that one of the philosophers who accompanied Alexander, Anaxarchus, was a Democritean. One scholar, noting the lack of pre-Alexandrian evidence for Indian atomism, felt that atomism appeared "suddenly" in India at a time when Greek influence was present and Epicurean atomism a popular and widespread doctrine in the Greco-Roman world.[8] Another has pointed out interesting parallels with Empedocles: the presence of four elements and two forces and the denial of origination and destruction in favor of the mixing and remixing of elements which do not themselves originate or perish.[9] Jayatilleke, perhaps in part attempting to keep the development Indian, has proposed the derivation of Vaiśeṣika from the doctrine of Pakudha Kaccāyana.[10] But this may still point elsewhere, as Keith has pointed out that Pakudha's six elements correspond to Empedocles's six factors, "which means that sukha (pleasure) and duḥkha (pain) are comparable to Empedocles' principles of Harmony and Strife."[11]

Another comparison with Greek philosophy—that between the "categories" of the Vaiśeṣika and Peripatetic schools—has been proposed and not well received.[12] These two systems are the most determined attempts at realist metaphysics in their traditions. The relations between both the equipment and the strategies with which they sought to preserve the integrity of phenomena has not yet been given the attention it deserves. A superficial comparison of the lists of "categories" of the two schools does not go nearly far enough. There are in fact deep and close affinities between the two systems on all metaphysically important points.

Saving the Particulars

Aristotle strove to save the particulars, or commonsense reals, from the realm of *doxa* or illusion to which Parmenides and Plato had relegated them. For Plato, particular existents are really only partially existent and hence are unknowable—since what does not really exist cannot really be known, as Parmenides pointed out (fr. 2). What is knowable, according to this view, is the noumenal structure of primordial abstractions arranged as a hierarchy of ontic genera which do not necessarily touch the commonsense reals. Aristotle, seeking to make particulars knowable again, converted Plato's hierarchy of ontic genera into a naturalistic system of scientific categories for use in classifying the experienced entities of nature. He inverted the value structure of Plato's system by removing primary value from the universal and reassigning it to the particular. "In the main," as one scholar remarked, "he might perhaps be called a naïve realist."[13]

Seen in context of the history of Indian philosophy, the Vaiśeṣika system served a parallel function. Kaṇāda may have been reacting against Buddhist phenomenalism or against the various monistic systems; in either case the Vaiśeṣika tradition, as Radakrishnan said, "takes its stand on the deliverance of the empirical consciousness, which deals first and last with real and separate things."[14] *Viśesa*, from which the school takes its name, means "distinctions" or "differentiations," and refers to the real individuality of empirically experienced things. The objects of experience are viewed as really existing, in their separate individualities, outside of any mind.

Furthermore, the Vaiśeṣika school, like Aristotle, went beyond saving the phenomena to attempting to make them amenable to scientific analysis. It offers "a philosophical base for accommodating scientific insights."[15] Its "standpoint is more scientific than speculative, more analytic than synthetic."[16] Consequently the Vaiśeṣikas valued logical consistency and observed the principle of contradiction quite as much as did Aristotle or indeed any western school. The Nyāya-Vaiśeṣika credo, "Whatever is is knowable and nameable,"[17] is a rejection of the three doubts of Gorgias at one stroke.

Categories

Aristotle and Kaṇāda present lists of topics which are usually translated by the English equivalent of Aristotle's word for them, categories (Grk. *katēgoriai*, Skt. *padārtha*). These lists are not entirely fixed. Aristotle, in the *Categories*,[18] presents ten topics; in another work, the *Posterior Analytics*, only eight. In the Vaiśeṣika tradition Kaṇāda lists six, and later authors make various changes in the list.

Aristotle:	Kaṇāda:
Substance	Substance
Quantity	Quality
Quality	Motion
Relation	Universality or genus
Place	Particularity or species
Date	Inherence
Posture (not in *An. Post.*)	Absence (added after Kaṇāda)
Possession (not in *An. Post.*)	

Action
Passivity

The word *padārtha* literally means "a thing to which a word refers,"[19] and Kaṇāda refers to his categories as "predicables" (*VS* I.4). They have something to do, then, with language analysis, but in addition are described as "the 'reals,' the stuff of which everything else is made."[20] This two-aspected, linguistic-metaphysical nature of the categories suggests a belief in a language-reality isomorphism—a belief, that is, that the categories of language are the categories of reality. Such linguistic reification is characteristic, in the Indian tradition, of the Mimamsa school. In one passage, Kaṇāda argues against this school, asserting that a word does not contact its object and therefore any connection between them is purely by convention (*VS* VII.2.15–24). Yet in another passage the proof of the reality of the self, as against the Buddhist doctrine of not-self, seems based on linguistic reification:

> [The proof of the existence of the self is not solely] from revelation, because of the non-application of the word "I" (to other designates or objects). (*VS* III.2.9)[21]

Since, in other words, the word "I" does not apply to anything else than a self, and since it is assumed that it must apply to something that exists, the self must exist. The argument remained a standard one in Vaiśeṣika thought until at least the time of Śrīdhara (c. 1000 A.D.), who says:

> We find the word "I" used in the Veda as well as in ordinary parlance, by learned persons; and this word could not be without something that it would denote. Its own form could not form its denotation, as that would involve the incongruity of its operation bearing upon itself; as has been well declared—"no word ever denotes itself." And hence that something which is denoted by the word "I" would be the self.[22]

Like Sanskrit *padārtha*, Greek *katēgoria* means essentially "a thing said." In Aristotle, as in Kaṇāda, it means specifically "a predicable." For both Kaṇāda and Aristotle there is considerable reason to believe that the category lists were based on grammatical distinctions.[23] The author of the *Categories*—whether Aristotle or an Aristotelian—begins his work with the statement:

> Things are said to be named "equivocally" when, though they have a common name, the definition corresponding with the name differs for each.

In a properly ordered universe, one may infer, there would be exactly one thing (or type of thing) for each name. The categories are given a linguistic definition: They are "expressions which are in no way composite" (*Cat.* 1b25)—that is, expressions each of which refers to one datum and no other. Primary substances are defined as "things which can be predicated only of themselves" (*Cat.* 3b15 and 3a35).

But nowhere in the *Categories* are there metaphysical assertions based on language quite as baldly as Kaṇāda's proof of the reality of the self by the existence of the word "I." Despite the fact that Aristotle begins his classifications from linguistic principles, his attitude toward language seems to involve less reification than that of the Vaiśeṣikas. In his definition of the category of "quality," for example, he writes:

> In most . . . cases, the name of that which is qualified is derived from that of the quality . . . There are some cases, however, in which, as the quality in consideration has no name, it is impossible that those possessed of it should have a name that is derivative.

> [Nevertheless such qualities are real.] . . . Sometimes, even though a name exists for the quality, that which takes its character from the quality has a name that is not a derivative. [Nevertheless, these qualities also are real.] . . . We may therefore state that those things are said to be possessed of some specific quality which have a name derived from that of the aforesaid quality, or which are in some other way dependent on it. (*Cat.* 10a25 ff.)

Aristotle, aware of the considerable language criticism that had already occurred before him in the Greek tradition, holds the relationship between language and reality to be primary but still limited. He is most comfortable when language and reality seem to coincide, but he does not argue directly from language to reality, as the Vaiśeṣikas occasionally do.

Beyond these basic congruences the two lists of categories have only superficial similarities. Aristotle and Kaṇāda have used different principles to arrive at their lists of topics. The basis of Kaṇāda's categories is that everything there listed is asserted to be partless. The Vaiśeṣika system is an investigation of how these ultimate entities "combine to become facts."[24] "Facts" in this context are commonsense reals, the "things" of everyday life. The minimal "fact" in the Vaiśeṣika view is made up of three metaphysical reals: a substance plus an attribute plus the reified relation which binds them together. The Vaiśeṣika list of categories accepts both reals known by sense-perception and reals known only by inference—such as relations. In this "erector set" or "building code" metaphysics both are simples which may be combined according to, and only according to, certain specified rules.

Aristotle's categories, on the other hand, are not based on a metaphysical concept such as simplicity or partlessness. Some of them seem to reflect the classification of different types of propositions. Qualities, for example, are presented as the basis of judgments of likeness and unlikeness, and the category of quantity is said to be the basis of statements of equality and inequality (*Cat.* 6a27).

Some cases will make these differences clear. In the *Vaiśeṣika Sūtras*, the category of substance is defined as follows:

> There are nine substances, viz., earth, water, fire, air, ākāśa, time, place, self, and mind (*manas*). (*VS* I.1.4)

The list begins, predictably, with the four atomic elements and the infinite and partless element *ākāśa*; then proceeds to the immortal soul ("self"), which is also conceived as infinite and partless; the mind (*manas*) which is material and composed of atoms; and the two Kantian "conditions" of space and time.

Not one of these terms will be found in Aristotle's list of substances. Aristotle's substances are ordinary individuals (*Cat.* 3b10), meaning by "individual" not a simple but a particular, a commonsense real such as *this* man or *this* horse. For Kaṇāda the substances are the primordial elements from which particulars are made and the conditions under which they exist; for Aristotle the primary reality is the particular itself. In this Aristotle is less a materialist and more a naïve realist than the Vaiśeṣikas, more explicitly dedicated to saving the particulars from the universals which, in Plato's thought, had gobbled them up.[25] Aristotle's primary substances are all commonsense particulars, and his secondary substances are the class concepts (species and genera) which include them. For Aristotle, time and place, which Kaṇāda treats as substances, are classed as categories separate from substance, as its conditions; for Kaṇāda, the class concepts, which Aristotle treats as secondary substances, belong to the category of universals. The Vaiśeṣika system goes farther than Aristotle in the practice of reifying abstractions which Aristotle found unsavory in Plato's teachings. When unity and separateness, for example, are reified as real existents (*VS* VII.2.1–2), we are back in the world of Plato's *Sophist,* where (255d3–7) a very similar thought is found. Aristotle avoids the reification of relations which may be construed as draining off reality from the particular entities being related.

Similar differences are found in the structuring principles of the other categories. Kaṇāda treats number and size as qualities, whereas for Aristotle they comprise the category of quantity. Contact and disjunction, remoteness and nearness, which Kaṇāda treats as qualities, would fall in Aristotle's category of relations. Pleasure and pain, which for Kaṇāda are qualities, are affections or passivities for Aristotle.

In short, the lists of categories are sufficiently different that there need be no speculation on their account about borrowing in either direction. Past speculators about affinities or relations between these schools have come to the same conclusion—and then neglected to go beyond this point. But the dissimilarities between their lists of categories does not mean that the two systems as wholes are equally different. The category lists are introductory presentations, ways to get into the systems of which the lists are only abbreviated hints. It is not in these introductory lists that the relationship lies, but in the real stuff of the metaphysics underlying the lists.

Matter

Kaṇāda was an atomist and Aristotle was not. Kaṇāda seems to have written in the period before the dialectical critique of atomism had developed in India. Aristotle, on the other hand, was well aware of the Zenonian critique of atomism, which he summarizes in the *De Caelo* (303a3 ff.) and the *Physics* (231a21 ff.). His own conception of Prime Matter is less a rejection of atomism than an attempt to retain its useful qualities while avoiding the problems pointed out by Zeno. Aristotle accepts the atomist premise that the changes of matter as we experience it must be accounted for by the movements of unseen bodies—that is, matter must be conceived as made up of separable parts which can alter their arrangement at a level below our ability to perceive. Yet Aristotle, aware of the Eleatic *elenchus,* realized that to designate these unseen quantities either as dimensionless points or as extended indivisible atoms can lead to contradictions. He conceived matter as a body that "can be divided anywhere, but not everywhere at once";[26] that is to say, its selfhood could not be taken completely apart as an aggregate of atoms could theoretically be taken apart to the point where the reality of the aggregate, its selfhood, was totally denied.

For the Vaiśeṣikas, the four elements are primary or ultimate; atoms are of four types, each permanent and unchangeable. For Aristotle the division into four elements is not primary; prime or primary matter has no internal distinctions of quality. But since Aristotle's prime matter never occurs, in experience anyway, as itself, but only in conjunction with one of the primary qualities—that is, as one of the four elements—this distinction is not so important. In fact, Aristotle asserts once that there is no body prior to the elements (*Phys.* II.1). Prime matter, in other words, does not exist by itself, but only as actualized by a quality, which at once makes it an element; it is related to Aristotle's concept of potentiality, both being ways to avoid the deconstructive rigors of the Eleatic *elenchus.*

The ultimacy of the four elements in the Vaiśeṣika system means that though they can combine with one another they cannot change into one another. Empedocles had similarly taught that there is no transformation of matter, only its mixing. Aristotle felt certain difficulties in this view. In the first place, he complained that "it makes even growth impossible, unless it be increase by addition . . . but it is not by addition that growing things are believed to increase" (*De Gen. et Cor.* II.6). Addition alone, for example, could not account for the changes of form that an organism displays as it grows; it could only account for changes in quantity or size. Secondly, change by addition cannot account for the uniformity which natural processes, like the changes of organic form, or reproduction, exhibit; random aggregations of atoms should produce all manner of odd entities, rather than the regular production of humans from humans, wheat from wheat, and so on. Finally the question of the changes of the soul seems unaccountable: "How, e.g., is the change from being musical to being unmusical, or how is memory or forgetting, to occur?" (*De Gen. et Cor.* II.6). Aristotle avoided these and other criticisms leveled against the Empedoclean view by declaring that the elements change into one another by exchanging their primary qualities. He conceived the combining or mixing of elements into a fact to occur "through chemical union as opposed to mechanical mixture."[27]

The Vaiśeṣikas seem to be revising the Jain doctrine to accord greater integrity to the particulars. Whereas each atom, in the Jain view, contains all sense qualities *in potentia*, in the *Vaiśeṣika Sūtras* they occur in precise and consistent number:

> Earth possesses color, taste, smell, and touch. Waters possess color, taste, and touch . . . Fire possesses color and touch. Air possesses touch. (*VS* II.1.1–4)

This view was criticized by Śaṅkara for its attribution of multiple qualities to atoms which are asserted to be simple and infinitesimal. Aristotle's elements, being nonatomic, avoid this criticism. Each possesses two of the four primary qualities: Fire is hot and dry, air hot and wet, water cold and wet, earth cold and dry. For Aristotle each type of matter has also a characteristic motion: Fire rises, earth sinks; air rises in earth or water and sinks through fire, and so on. Vaiśeṣika texts hint at a correspondence between certain types of motion and certain elements, but less clearly articulated: Earth and water both have a tendency to sink, though water, earth, and fire all have a tendency to flow. Under the influence of fire, water rises rather than sinks, and so on (*VS* V.2.3–6).[28]

Each system recognizes the quintessence, or fifth element, which has special properties. In both traditions it is defined as rarer than the other four elements and as characterized by sanctity. Aristotle's ether is the substance of which the heavenly bodies are made, entities which are associated, from the Egyptian *Book of the Dead* to Plato, with divinities and souls. Unlike the four elements found in the sublunar realm, ether is eternal and unchangeable. Similarly in the Vaiśeṣika system, "earth, water, fire and air are both eternal and noneternal, while ākāśa is eternal only."[29] In both systems the fifth element is kept carefully separate from the others, in the Vaiśeṣika view by the doctrine that it does not combine with the other elements, in Aristotle's by secluding it in the superlunary realm where the four elements and the process of change they are involved in do not exist. Aristotle's ether moves only in circular motions, and Kaṇāda's *ākāśa* is spherical. In fact, in the Vaiśeṣika view, all eternal things are spherical, as Parmenides' Being was spherical and Aristotle's cosmic entities, especially the heavenly bodies, which are composed of ether alone, are spherical, and move only in circular rotation. Vaiśeṣika authors distinguish two types of sphericity: the infinitesimal sphericity of atoms and the infinite sphericity of *ākāśa*. These concepts both seem predialectical in origin. Sphericity in atoms would give them parts, such as center and circumference; sphericity in an infinite thing would delimit its form, making it finite.

Time and Space

Both Kaṇāda and Aristotle approach the definitions of time and space linguistically, through expressions with which they are referred to. Kaṇāda says:

> "Posterior," "simultaneous," "slow," "quick," such are the marks of time. (*VS* II 2.6)

Aristotle speaks very similarly:

> We apprehend time only when we have noticed motion or change, noticing it by the markers "before" and "after." (*Phys.* 219a22)
>
> When we perceive a "before" and an "after," then we say that there is time. (*Phys.* 219b1)
>
> "Fast" and "slow" are defined by time. (*Phys.* 218b14)

Radhakrishnan says of the Vaiśeṣika view: "Time which is one appears as many on account of its association with the changes that are related to it."[30] And Ross, paraphrasing Aristotle: "There is only one time but there are many movements."[31] Each, in other words, associates time with motion but denies that it simply *is* motion. Aristotle says:

> The movement of each thing is only in the thing which changes and where the thing itself which moves or changes may chance to be. But time is present equally everywhere and to all things . . . Clearly then time is not movement. (*Phys.* 218b)

And Kaṇāda:

> Time is eternal and uniform. However, plurality is ascribed to time because of the difference among its effects. The view that time is nothing other than motion is untenable. (*VS* summ. 24)

Space is treated much like time. Says Kaṇāda:

> That which gives rise to such (conditions and usage) as "This (is remote, etc) from this,"—(the same is) the mark of space. (*VS* II.2.10)

And Aristotle:

> The distinction of "before" and "after" holds primarily then, in place; and there in virtue of relative position. (*Phys.* 219a13)

In regard to the conception of matter, overall, Aristotle is postdialectical, the Vaiśeṣika atomists predialectical. If this were the whole picture, the Vaiśeṣika system would seem closer to that of Empedocles than to that of Aristotle. But it is not the whole picture. We have so far considered some of the building blocks these two realist systems use to put the world together. It is not exaggerating to say they are uncannily similar. But the heart of the two systems, and of the correspondence between them, lies in the way these building blocks are put together to make "facts." Four topics are involved: the relation between substance and attribute; the status of universals; the doctrine of privation or absence; the doctrine of causality.

Substance and Attribute

The Vaiśeṣika view of the substance-attribute relationship may be summarized in six points; first, a double view of the nature of substance:

> (1) Substances are independent existents; qualities are not.

(2) "Substance is the substrate of qualities."[32] In English-language philosophical terminology there is a similar double use of the word substance. It means, as in (1) above, a self-existent entity, and, as in (2), a featureless substrate of being in which a quality can inhere. (Aristotle's prime matter, a special case, is pure substrate, possessing no qualities of its own, but offering embodiment to any quality.)

(3) "The qualities of a substance may change while the substance persists."[33]

(4) "Substrata and qualities are different entities entirely."[34]

(5) Substances do not occur in experience without qualities (like prime matter); qualities absolutely do not occur without substances as substrates (*VS* I.1.16, VII.1.4).

(6) "The minimal form of a fact . . . consists of a substratum connected by a relation to a property."[35]

A similar six points express Aristotle's view of how "facts" are put together:

(1) Substances are independent primary existents (*Met.* 1028a28). Unwilling to posit an inferred entity as prior to an experienced one, Aristotle designates as primary not the qualityless substrate, prime matter, but the ordinary existents, which are already compounds of substrate and qualities. The point is that the members of the category of substances are the substrates for all the other categories; they are the real existents in which the various conditions of existence exist.

(2) Substances are the substrates, or locuses, of qualities, quantities, etc. (*Met.* 1028a10–30)

(3) Substances endure while their qualities change. (*De Gen. et Cor.* I.4)

(4) Substrate and qualities are different entities.

(5) Substrates never occur in experience without qualities; qualities never occur apart from substrates.

(6) The minimal entity is a primary substance including material substrate, quality, and relations linking them.

The two lists of points are virtually identical; the erector sets the two philosophers are using to construct the universe seem to be the same brand. There is more to the two philosophies than those lists of points, however. There is, for example, a problem with the Vaiśeṣika view in the apparent contradiction between the statement that substance and quality are different entities entirely, and the statement that sense qualities inhere in the four classes of atoms. Since the Vaiśeṣikas knew that their atoms had qualities, why did they assert the independent existence of substances apart from qualities? There is a crack or gap here in the fabric of the Vaiśeṣika system which may reflect interchanges among schools. The Vaiśeṣika atomism, with its probable Jain source, may already have been in place when new input brought up a set of questions not quite in harmony with it.

Universals and Particulars

The nature and status of universals is a central question for Vaiśeṣika thought as it is for Plato and Aristotle. Again the two traditions developed virtually identical lines of thought on the question. Kaṇāda's fourth and fifth categories are genus (*sāmānya*) and species (*viśesa*). Kaṇāda further distinguishes the *summum genus*, the genus which is not also a species of a higher genus, and the *infima species*, the species which is not also a genus in relation to any lower species:

> Existence, being the cause of assimilation only, is only a genus. Substantiality, and attributeness and action-ness are both genera and species. (The statement of genus and species has been made with the exception of the final species.) (*VS* I.2.4–6)

Being characterizes all things and thus cannot constitute a category distinct from something else. In class terms, it is only a genus; it is not also a species within a broader genus. It is itself the broadest, or highest, or greatest genus—the *summum genus*. The categories are all species in relation to being and genera in relation to lower species contained or subsumed within them. Substance, for example, has nine subspecies of which six also have subspecies. At the other end of the chain from the *summum genus* are the "facts," the particulars of experience, each of which is an *infima species* (Skt. *antya viśesa*), lowest or final species; these are only species, not also genera. As a result they are not knowable in the direct way of universals. The Vaiśeṣika author Candramati (c. 450 A.D.) proposed that universals are known only by mind, unaided by the senses, whereas particulars are known by mind in cooperation with senses. The Platonic-Aristotelian distinction between noumenal and phenomenal is mirrored here.

In one place Kaṇāda seems to speak as a conceptualist or nominalist: "The notions, genus and species, are relative to the understanding" (*VS* I.2.3). Yet he admits *sâmânya*, the realm of universals, as a real. It seems that he intends "the Aristotelian view of *universalia in re* [universals only in particulars]."[36] On this view, universals are real and are intellectually separable from their instantiations, but they are not posited, as by Plato, as independent of any and all instantiations. Praśastapāda placed more emphasis on the integrity of the universal than Kaṇāda had done, calling it, in a religious style of address, "eternal, one, yet residing in many things."[37] Thus "the Platonic doctrine of *universalia ante rem* [universals prior to their instances] is also true,"[38] because the universal survives the passing of its instances and precedes their appearances. Both *universalia in rebus* (universals in particulars) and *universalia ante res* (universals prior to their particulars) are acceptable Nyāya-Vaiśeṣika concepts. Kaṇāda emphasizes the former, Praśastapāda the latter. But even Praśastapāda at times sounds like a conceptualist or nominalist, saying, for example, that the universals are different from one another both because they reside in different particulars and "also by reason of people having a distinct notion with regard to each of them."[39]

The key question between realists and nominalists is whether a universal could exist without any instantiations at all. Praśastapāda, in calling universals eternal, implies that a universal would continue to exist after becoming an empty genus. Vacaspati (c. 950 A.D.) says further that universals are all-pervasive, implying that a universal is present even where it has no instantiation. Udayana (c. 1000 A.D.) asserts specifically that universals exist regardless of whether or not they have instantiations.

It hardly needs pointing out that this line of thought, with these gradations and positions, was a central concern of the Platonic-Aristotelian tradition, too. But the chronology may seem to be reversed in this sequence, as Kaṇāda's hierarchy of genera and species is essentially Aristotelian in type while Udayana's much later positing of universals independent of particulars is Platonic. In the *Metaphysics*, however, Aristotle includes Socratics in the development, yielding a sequence like that of the Vaiśeṣika school but compressed into a tiny fraction of the time:

> Two things may be fairly ascribed to Socrates—inductive arguments and universal definition, both of which are concerned with the starting-point of science. But Socrates did not make the universals or the definitions exist apart; his successors, however, gave them separate existence, and this was the kind of thing they called Ideas. (1078b28 ff.)
>
> They at the same time treat the Ideas as universal substances, and as separable and individual. That this is not possible has been shown before. The reason why those who say the Ideas are universal combined these two views in one is that they did not make

> the Ideal substances identical with sensible things. They thought that the sensible particulars were in a state of flux and none of them remained, but that the universal was apart from these and different. And Socrates gave the impulse to this theory . . . by means of his definitions, but he did not separate them from the particulars; and in this he thought rightly in not separating them. (1086a32 ff.)

Active among the Naiyāyikas was a Platonic-like tendency "to find an entity to correspond to each legitimate notion."[40] Aparārkadeva (c. 1100 A.D.) proposed that not only the number one but indeed all numbers were universals. One is reminded of the Pythagorean "number religion" and of Plato's so-called unwritten doctrines, in which the numbers one to ten were given special prominence near the top of the hierarchy of universals. Plato's successor Speusippus continued the practice of hypostatizing numbers as eternal substances. Aristotle, on the other hand, shunned this tendency since it resulted in cutting off the world of experience from reality by reifying a possibly endless stream of abstractions in between pure Being and experienced facts. The substrate-attribute relationship shows the difference in emphases. Reacting away from phenomenalists and idealists who virtually made the attribute into a substance, the Vaiśeṣikas emphasized the distinction between substance and attribute. Aristotle, reacting against Plato's extreme separation of substance and attribute, emphasized their universal concomitance.

The cognitive status of particulars unfolds in another parallel sequence of thoughts. Both systems insist that particulars which may seem identical—which in terms of the universals they instantiate *are* identical—are nevertheless separate because of the different matter of which they are comprised. But matter did not give enough purchase to attempts to know the separateness of the particulars. There is a danger that particulars be, as Plato felt, lost in the unknowability of matter. Atoms are imperceptible by smallness, and prime matter is imperceptible because it has no qualities. In both conceptions matter is known only by inference. Both traditions, consequently, flirted with the idea of a separate species for each individual, a separate essence for each thing. The purpose of the essence for each particular is to render each clearly knowable, to give each a purely noumenal element for the mind to perceive.

The positing of an essence of each individual, entirely *sui generis*, multiplies the metaphysical entities of the Vaiśeṣika system enormously. Stcherbatsky felt that the Vaiśeṣikas "demonstrated practically that whosoever resolves to remain a realist to the end must unavoidably people the universe with such a wealth of objective realities that life in such a realistic home must become quite uncomfortable."[41] While Aristotle was less given to separating metaphysical entities from the particulars they reside in, he nevertheless believed in much the same equipment for the realist erector set that the Vaiśeṣika thinkers arrived at. One remarkable entity was what the Vaiśeṣikas call "nonexistence" or "absence," which Aristotle calls "privation" or (in a sense to be explained) "potentiality."

Absence and Potentiality

The entities called absences formed a seventh category in Vaiśeṣika thought after the six proposed by Kaṇāda. Kaṇāda did not posit the category of nonexistence, but he does have the distinction between different types of nonexistence which is at the root of the doctrine of absences (*VS* IX.1.3, 5). He distinguishes non-being into four types: (1) prior nonexistence, or the nonexistence of something before it exists; (2) posterior nonexistence, or the absence of something that has ceased to exist; (3) reciprocal non-being, or mutual exclusion, or nonidentity: A is absent as B and B is absent as A; this is essentially Aristotle's principle of identity (or principles of identity and double negation). Thus both Kaṇāda and Aristotle define darkness as the absence of light (*VS* summm. 51; *Phys.* 418b15 ff.); (4) absolute nonexistence, the absence of something that neither has existed nor ever will exist (a barren woman's son). Absolute nonexistence is included primarily to underscore the nonabsoluteness of prior and posterior nonexistence, which play an important function in the Vaiśeṣika school and also have an important correspondence in Aristotle.

Prior and posterior absence are considered positive entities which relate necessarily to, or cannot exist without, an existent counterpart, or "counterpositive." The absence is not simply a locus which lacks this or that, it is the locus plus a positively real and apprehended absence, as one might say, after a change in the weather, "I don't see the sun anymore." The doctrine that this absence is a positive entity in its own right might seem unnecessary, but it is useful at explaining the world.

Aristotle has it also, in his so-called doctrine of privation, and at *Physics* I.8 he explains it. To paraphrase: A thing does not come into being from absolute non-being—a concept which both traditions regard as unthinkable, a "pseudoidea," like a word that has no referent, or that has nothing as a referent. Rather, a thing comes into being from a qualified non-being, specifically a non-being-as-itself; it is activated specifically from its own prior non-being rather than from non-being in general. Its non-being-as-itself resides in a substratum of being, waiting to be replaced by the specific being-as-itself and by no other. A prior absence is, as it were, an emptiness shaped for the thing that will fill it. When the thing in question passes out of existence it likewise does not pass into unqualified non-existence, but rather, its presence-as itself alters into its absence-as-itself, that is, into its posterior absence.

Through this qualified non-being, both Aristotle and the Vaiśeṣikas hoped to solve the problem of change without breaching the principle that nothing comes from nothing. The postulation of an absolute dichotomy between Being and non-Being had led to the Eleatic impasse; the opposition between Being and non-Being was an improper or meaningless dichotomy since non-Being does not exist and hence can neither oppose nor negate anything. Instead of this false dichotomy, Aristotle and Candramati proposed three principles: the substrate, the form, and the absence of the form. The substrate is at one moment characterized by the absence of a certain thing and at another by its presence. So the doctrine of prior and posterior absences amounts to a doctrine of potentiality. At *Physics* I.8 Aristotle proposes two forms for the solution of the problem of becoming; the first is the passage on privation summarized above, which continues with the second argument. In this case "The difficulty," says Ross, "is removed by the distinction of grades of being—potentiality and actuality; a thing comes from that which is it potentially and not actually."[42] "That which is it potentially" is the conjunction of substratum and privation, or, in Vaiśeṣika terms, its prior absence. The Vaiśeṣika distinction between absolute non-being and non-being-as-a-particular-thing is equivalent to Aristotle's distinction between non-being and potential being.

Potentiality (*śakti*) was the basis of the Sāṇkhya doctrine of causality, which held that the cause contains the effect in a potential state. The Vaiśeṣikas were philosophical opponents of the Sāṇkhya and did not simply adopt their concept. Still, their doctrine of absences is equivalent to a doctrine of potentiality. B cannot come from not-B; but A-not-B (where A is the substrate of the prior absence of B) can be converted into A-B; A-not-B, then, means, in effect, a substrate which implies B by absence, or which has within it the specific power to become B, or, in short, potential-B. The Vaiśeṣika Śrīdhara evidently recognized this when he criticized the Sāñkhyas by asking how a thing which exists "in potentiality" differs from the same thing when it is "not-existent yet." Visvanatha went so far as to declare that when a jar is present on a mat its absence is already there, but hidden; when a jar is absent from a mat its presence is there, but hidden. "Hidden," on this reasoning, is tantamount to "potential." Potter says, "There is no such thing as pure absence—absence of everything or of nothing in particular. Every absence has a counterpositive, something which is absent."[43] Thus the totality of absences is the totality of potential existents; it is Aristotle's realm of potentiality. In it everything that exists has both preexisted itself and will survive itself through the mode of absence.

Parmenides had denied origination and destruction by his argument dichotomizing absolute being and absolute non-being. Since absolute non-being absolutely did not exist, nothing could come from it. Heraclitus attempted a solution by introducing a middle ontological realm, qualified or relative being, in between absolute being and absolute non-being ("We both are and are not"). Aristotle's doctrine of privation or potentiality does not point to the same mode of being that Heraclitus acknowledged; in effect, it adds a fourth level, a qualified non-being to correspond to Heraclitus's qualified being. While the thing exists it has only relative, not absolute existence; and while it non-exists it has only relative, not absolute, nonexistence. Nothing can come from absolute non-being because it absolutely does not exist. But qualified non-being has a sort of existence precisely in that it is qualified: How could it have qualities if it didn't exist? This specific or qualified non-being is the space in being that things not yet born will occupy—the space that is waiting for them. And since they will be specific things the emptiness that awaits each one of them is specific.[44]

Relation?

Kaṇāda's sixth category is "inherence" (*samvaya*), which he held to be the relationship between cause and effect, and between substrate and attribute (*VS* V.2.23; *VS* summ. 7). As it came to be defined, the inherence relation is *necessary*: It relates A and B when neither could subsist without the other; it presumes invariable concomitance of its *relata*. Vātsyāyana extended it to the relationship between whole and parts, and Praśastapāda generalized it into "the relation between two inseparable things related as located to locus,"[45] thus including the relationship between a universal and the particulars in which it inheres. *Samvaya*, inherence, is contrasted with the weaker relationship called *samyoga*, or accidental conjunction. When A and B separate, the relation of accidental conjunction simply ceases to exist. But inherence is held to be an eternal objective entity in its own right—"a kind of glue," as Potter says, which holds the universe together. The concept is similar to Bradley's distinction between internal relations, which relate things from essence to essence so that to change the relation would change the *relata*, and external relations, which relate things from their outer surfaces, as it were, without effecting their identities.

Aristotle recognizes the same entity, though he does not hypostatize it apart from its occurrences in particulars. He calls it the "essential relation," and defines it as a relation which is "true in every instance" of its *relata* (*An. Post.* I.4); it relates things which could not exist as themselves without each other. The definition is virtually identical to that of the Vaiśeṣikas. Praśastapāda says, "Inherence is the relationship between things . . . which stand to one another in the relation of container to contained."[46] Aristotle says that all attributes which are essential are so "either in the sense that their subjects are contained in them, or in the sense that they are contained in their subjects" (*An. Post.* I.4.73b15 ff.). Aristotle also carefully distinguishes the category of "coincidence" or "accidental conjunction":

> In another sense again, a thing which is consequentially connected with anything is essential; one not so connected is "coincidental." An example of the latter is "While he was walking it lightened"; the lightning was not due to his walking; it was, we should say, a coincidence. If, on the other hand, there is a consequential connection, the predication is essential; e.g., if a beast dies when its throat is being cut, then its death is also essentially connected with the cutting, because the cutting was the cause of death, not death a "coincident" of the cutting. (*An. Post.* I.4.73b10 ff.)

Aristotle believed that the essential relation and the coincidental relation are both reals, not merely projections of mental processes; still, he did not reify them as universals, as Plato had done with the same/not-same dichotomy in the *Sophist*. The Vaiśeṣika thinkers, however, did so, and it is here that one encounters examples of what Stcherbatsky, as quoted above, regarded as "quite absurd, but logically unavoidable, consequences" of their dogged realism. Disjunction— that is, the absence of conjunction—is regarded as a real entity that "inheres in a pair of substances when one has just parted from the other."[47]

Praśastapāda distinguishes three kinds of disjunction. Others, however, denied that disjunctions were a separate category of reals, regarding them instead as instances of absences (of conjunctions), that is, as prior and posterior nonexistences. Yet another thinker "argues that disjunction cannot be construed as an absence, since it has a structure different from an absence. A disjunction is the parting of some *x* from some *y*, where both *x* and *y* are positive entities and remain so before and after the rising of the quality called disjunction. An absence, on the other hand, has a counterpositive: An absence is that *x* which occurs when its counterpositive *y* does not occur."[48] The tendency to reify every legitimate notion leads on and on. There is the reification of a contact or conjunction, and of a disjunction, and of an absence; there is even the reification of relations between these, for example, the contact between an absence and the sense-organ which perceives it is held to be a real metaphysical entity in its own right.[49] A relation between two absences is similarly a metaphysical real.

Causality

Kaṇāda explained causality by saying that cause and effect are bound by the inherence relationship. A later Nyāya-Vaiśeṣika doctrine holds that a "collection of causes" (*sàmagrī*) is necessary to the production of an effect: the inherence cause, the noninherence cause, and the instrumental cause. Aristotle similarly held that a collection of causes collaborate to produce an effect; there are striking similarities in the definitions of these collections.

The inherence cause is exemplified in the Vaiśeṣika literature by the relation between the halves of a pot and the whole pot, and by the relation between the threads in a cloth and the cloth itself. The Aristotelian counterpart is the material cause, which is exemplified in the *Physics* (195a ff.) by "the material of artificial products and the parts of a whole."[50]

Second in the Vaiśeṣika collection of causes, the noninherence cause is exemplified by the contact between the two pot halves and, in the analogy of the cloth, by the color of the threads, which causes the color of the cloth and hence its shape. This is equivalent to Aristotle's formal cause, which he defines as "the combination of the parts into a whole, giving it form."

The third, or "instrumental," cause of the Vaiśeṣikas is exemplified by the presence of the potter who fits the pot halves together, or the action of the potter's stick and hand in fitting them together. This conception is identical to Aristotle's third, or "efficient," cause, which he describes as the immediate source of the change, or that which directly makes change take place; the sculptor, for example, is held to be the efficient cause of the statue, as the marble was its material cause.

Aristotle's fourth (and last) type of cause, the "final" cause—that is, the end or purpose for which the effect has been brought about—has no equivalent in the Vaiśeṣika list. Otherwise they are identical. The fact that Kaṇāda has only one cause and Udayana, a thousand years later, has three, implies that the causation systems were developed independently rather than by borrowing.

God and the Soul

Kaṇāda was an atheist—perhaps another suggestion of a Jain origin to his lineage. He invoked the "unseen force" (*adṛṣṭa*) as a Prime Mover to set the atomic motions going again after the period of quiescence (*pralaya*) of the Hindu myth of cycling time, in which they are separated and motionless. By the time of Praśastapāda (c. 500 A.D.), however, the school had affiliated itself with Hindu theism and espoused a Śaiva monotheism. God was conceived as necessary to start the world process going again after the period of cosmic quiescence by pushing one atom into another.[51] There is a similarity here with Anaxagoras's Mind setting the infinity of matter in motion, and with Aristotle's doctrine of the Prime Mover. But Aristotle's Prime Mover is not a physical cause, nor is it bound up with the idea of a first movement in time. Here, as in some other places, the Vaiśeṣika view seems closer to Plato's—that is, somewhat more primitive and myth-influenced than Aristotle's. In the *Politicus* Plato posits a god who does precisely what Praśastapāda's god does: At the end of each cosmic cycle, or Great Year, he momentarily takes hold of the universe and sets it moving again physically.

Later Nyāya-Vaiśeṣika thinkers, after the turn toward theism, worked out what is considered, in Hindu philosophy, the classic treatment of the themes of the proof of god's existence and the description of his nature. This tendency culminated in Udayana (c. 1000 A.D.), whose arguments have been classified into three types:[52]

(1) The world is an effect and an effect needs a cause.
(2) The world is orderly and needs an orderer.
(3) The world is morally governed and needs a dispenser of karmic justice.

Again the argumentation has closer parallels in Plato than in Aristotle. In the *Laws* the "Athenian Stranger" proposes precisely the same three proofs:

(1) The world as an effect needs god as its first mover (888e–900); this passage seems the probable source of Aristotle's concept of the Prime Mover.

(2) The world is orderly and presupposes an orderer (886, 966e).
(3) The world is morally governed and needs a moral governor (906–907c). (But the *astika* argument of Jayanta—that god is necessary as the author of the Vedas—will not be found in Greek philosophy.)

Aristotle felt that the idea of god as a physical source of motion was too mythlike, as was the idea that god would be interested in the world and would want to create it. He postulated god as a nonphysical and nonintending cause—in effect a final cause which functions as an efficient cause: The universe moves by desire for god, not by any direct interference or manipulative action of god itself. The later, theistic, Nyāya-Vaiśeṣika thinkers also sometimes conceived god as a nonphysical and atemporal cause, and rejected the idea that god desired the universe rather than the universe desired god.

The Vaiśeṣika system, like Aristotle's master, Plato, maintained the doctrines of *karma*, purification, and release. The claimed orthodoxy of the school required this. Aristotle regarded this Orphic strain in Plato as archaic and mythological, and left it behind. In the Vaiśeṣika tradition this level of doctrine seems earlier than the level we have already discussed.[53]

A later, more rationalist phase of Vaiśeṣika ethics paralleled Aristotle in many ways. In both cases a knowledge of logic and of the lore of the categories is considered an end in itself. Worldly activities are not despised. There is at once a hedonic tinge and a concern for social welfare. Moral distinctions are seen as applying only to voluntary acts, as in Buddhism and not in Jainism, where ethical prohibition and taboo are undistinguished.

To approach the soteriological doctrines psychology must first be considered. Both schools assume that like can only be perceived by like. For the Vaiśeṣikas each sense organ is made up of the type of atoms which it is designed to perceive. All the senses function by the one method of contact or touch of atoms as in Democritus. It is the common Greek view also that like is known, or sensed, only by like. Aristotle asserts that there is likeness of quality between the sense organ and its appropriate objects. He also asserts that touch is the basic mechanism of sense. Both describe memory as an "impression" left on the brain.

The most important parallel lies in the distinction between self and mind, on the Vaiśeṣika side, and active and passive intellect, on Aristotle's side. Vaiśeṣika mind, or *manas*, is "incapable of any such activity as thought, intrinsically unconscious."[54] When in contact with the activating power of soul, however, mind processes and organizes sense-data, and soul reflects upon them, making inferences and so forth. Vaiśeṣika self, or soul, in turn, also cannot think by itself, because it is intrinsically above involvement in matter and the subject-object relationship. It is defined by Praśastapāda as "neither the doer nor the enjoyer. It is wholly indifferent."[55] But when in contact with material mind, soul has access to sense-impressions and begins its cogitations upon them.

Aristotle's psychology is virtually identical. His "passive intellect," like Vaiśeṣika "mind," is material, a part of the body, innately passive, unable to do anything active like thinking by itself. "Active intellect," on the other hand, like Vaiśeṣika "soul," is held to be "impassible; it takes no impress from the circumstances of life,"[56] because, being immaterial, it exists entirely separate from body. But when in conjunction with passive intellect, active intellect regards and thinks about its sense impressions, making categories of them, forming propositions about them and tests of those propositions, and so on. "Without the passive reason the active reason knows nothing."[57]

In this distinction both traditions seem to show signs of the early Jain-Orphic levels of their traditions. The Vaiśeṣika soul, or self, is bound to the body by its association with the material atoms making up mind, which obscure its true nature, knowledge of which is restored by dissociation from the body. In Aristotle, similarly, the active intellect's "true nature is obscured during its association with the body, but exists in its purity when this association is over."[58]

The crucial difference in the treatment of the Jain-Orphic heritage lies in the Vaiśeṣikas' acceptance of reincarnationism. According to their doctrine, in order to maintain the continuity of the person on which the system of karmic debt depends, the mind (*manas*) must survive the transition between bodies and endure through a series of incarnations. Aristotle's passive intellect is not involved in this process. The eschatology of Vaiśeṣika soul and Aristotelian active intellect, on the other hand, are very similar. The active intellect comes into the body from outside and survives the body's death. After being freed from the body the active intellect is merged "into some wider spiritual unity,"[59] perhaps into the Prime Mover itself. Aristotle is less than clear on this point, and commentators both ancient and modern have differed in their readings of it. If the active intellect still has awareness after leaving the body it is of the infolded self-aware type of the Prime Mover, since "no one can learn or understand anything [outside of oneself] in the absence of sense" (*De An.* 432a5) and "the soul never thinks without an image" (*De An.* 431a15). Similarly the Vaiśeṣika soul, after release from contact with the body, is "inert and unconscious,"[60] "free from all connection with qualities."[61]

Summing Up

There is an extensive and detailed overall parallelism between Vaiśeṣika and Aristotelian metaphysics. The correspondences on the doctrines of (1) the substrate-attribute relationship, (2) the status of universals and particulars, (3) the doctrines of absence or privation, (4) the doctrines of the essential relation, and (5) the different types of causality reveal an almost uncanny similarity in two culturally separate attempts to construct a realist metaphysics.

Earlier attempts to establish parallels between the lists of categories may have been, as one scholar has remarked, "the result of inadequate information or reflection,"[62] but surely the subsequent rejection of the idea of affinities in general has also been open to that charge. Despite formal differences, these two traditions came to identical solutions of all the substantive metaphysical issues they dealt with—with the exceptions of Vaiśeṣika adherence to the archaic traditions of atomism and reincarnationism.

The Historical Aspect of the Relationship

Vaiśeṣika seems to have two perceptible strata. The earlier involves adherence to a pre-dialectical form of atomism with little awareness of implied dilemmas; adherence to the traditional belief in reincarnation, purification, and release; an emphasis on yogic isolation of the spiritual nature from contact with matter, and a belief in the revealed authority of the Vedas. The later stratum seems based on different assumptions and purposes. While retaining much of the earlier stratum it attempts to reform it in the direction of protoscientific realism, making a systematic attempt to provide a metaphysical basis for empirical reality.

It is possible to imagine stimulus diffusion channels whereby this second layer could reflect Greek, and specifically Peripatetic, influence. A suggestion of such diffusion can be seen in the apparent discrepancy between the two levels of Vaiśeṣika thought. Not only is their value structure and purpose different, but some of their details are incompatible and forced together. The basic Vaiśeṣika idea, for example, that substrate and qualities are completely different entities, is out of harmony with the doctrine that individual atoms contain inherent qualities which are eternal and unchanging. The doctrine of the absolute difference of substrate and quality is more compatible with Aristotle's indeterminate prime matter. The discrepancy looks like a crack or gap which reveals an attempt to merge two originally separate systems.

To posit Peripatetic influence on Vaiśeṣika metaphysics, one would have to devise a complex staged model like that which was proposed by Vidyabhusana for Aristotelian influence on Naiyāyika syllogisms. One would have to take into account, for example, the fact that in the *Physics* Aristotle explains change by the doctrine of privation and in the *Metaphysics* by potentiality. When, after 326 B.C., Greek philosophy entered India, it found long-established traditions of philosophy already present which were not about to be discarded wholecloth in favor of imported brands. The assimilation of foreign ideas, then, would have been more like a process of digestion, where new material is transformed into the nature of the ingesting body. If Aristotle came into the Vaiśeṣika zone it could only have been in a messy organic weld producing not a clone but a new child.

Notes to Chapter Twenty

1. Karl H. Potter (*Indian Metaphysics and Epistemology* [Princeton, New Jersey: Princeton University Press, 1977], p. 12), however, questions the view of separate development.

2. Mrinalkanti Gangopadhyaya, *Indian Atomism, History and Sources* (Atlantic Highlands, New Jersey: Humanities Press, 1981), p. 17.

3. Dasgupta regards the *Vaiśeṣika Sūtrās* as probably pre-Buddhistic (Surendranath Dasgupta, *A History of Indian Philosophy*, vol. 1, [Delhi: Motilal Banarsidass, 1975], p. 280).

4. Ibid., pp. 79–80, 81–82.

5. Ibid., p. 1.

6. Umisha Mishra, *Conception of Matter According to Nyāya-Vaiśeṣika* (Allahabad: M. N. Pendeyattre Allahabad Press, 1936), p. 97.

7. Gangopadhyaya, *Indian Atomism, History and Sources*, p. 54.

8. Arthur B. Keith, *Indian Logic and Atomism* (Oxford: Clarendon Press, 1921), pp. 17–18.

9. Dale Riepe, *The Naturalistic Tradition in Indian Thought* (Seattle: University of Washington Press, 1961), pp. 242–243.

10. K. N. Jayatilleke, *Early Buddhist Theory of Knowledge* (London: George Allen and Unwin, 1963), p. 267.

11. A. B. Keith, *The Religion and Philosophy of the Veda and Upanisads*, Harvard Oriental Series 31 and 32 (Cambridge, Massachusetts: Harvard University Press, 1925), p. 611.

12. Proposed by Walter Ruben (*Geschichte der Indischen Philosophie* [Berlin: Deutsches Verlag der Wissenschaften, 1954], p. 191), received ill by Riepe (*The Naturalistic Tradition*, p. 235), and by Potter (*Indian Metaphysics and Epistemology*, p. 16).

13. W. D. Ross, *Aristotle* (London: Methuen, 1964), p. 132.

14. Sarvepalli Radhakrishnan, *Indian Philosophy*, vol. 2 (London and New York: George Allen and Unwin, 1971), p. 183.

15. Potter, *Indian Metaphysics and Epistemology*, p. 1.

16. Radhakrishnan, *Indian Philosophy*, vol. 2, p. 176.

17. Potter, *Indian Metaphysics and Epistemology*, p. 48.

18. The authenticity of this work has been attacked and defended. I follow Ross in regarding it either as a work of Aristotle or at least as an authentic work of his school, representing (with the possible exception of the last six chapters) the teachings of Aristotle (see Ross, *Aristotle*, pp. 9–10).

19. Potter, *Indian Metaphysics and Epistemology*, p. 49.

20. Ibid., p. 43.

21. Sarvepalli Radhakrishnan and Charles A. Moore, eds., *A Source Book in Indian Philosophy* (Princeton, New Jersey: Princeton University Press, 1957), p. 392.

22. Ibid., p. 407.

23. Faddegon has argued that Kaṇāda's list was based on Pāṇini's grammatical studies (Barend Faddegon, *The Vaiśeṣika System Described with the Help of the Oldest Texts*, Nieuwe Reeks, Deel XVIII, no. 2 [Amsterdam: Afdeeling Letterkunde, 1918], pp. 177–180). On Aristotle, Ross says: "Trendelenburg held that the distinctions between the categories are derived from grammatical distinctions. It is easy to see that a study of the forms of language was one of Aristotle's main guides in the formulation of the doctrine; e.g., correlates are distinguished from other things by the fact that the names for them govern a word in the genitive or in the dative case" (Ross, *Aristotle*, p. 22).

24. Potter, *Indian Metaphysics and Epistemology*, pp. 43, 49.

25. Potter says (ibid., pp. 73–74) that entities such as "this man" or "this horse" are recognized as substances in the Vaiśeṣika system—middle-sized substances, between the atomic and the infinite—but Kaṇāda does not state this.

26. Ross, *Aristotle*, p. 100.

27. Ibid., p. 105.

28. And see Potter, *Indian Metaphysics and Epistemology*, pp. 128–129.

29. Radhakrishnan, *Indian Philosophy*, vol. 2, p. 194.

30. Ibid., vol. 2, p. 192.

31. Ross, *Aristotle*, p. 89.

32. Radhakrishnan, *Indian Philosophy*, vol. 2, p. 188.

33. Potter, *Indian Metaphysics and Epistemology*, p. 84. See *VS* I.1.12–13.

34. Potter, *Indian Metaphysics and Epistemology*, p. 49.

35. Ibid., p. 48.

36. Radhakrishnan, *Indian Philosophy*, vol. 2, p. 214. Radhakrishnan, like many authors referring to the Thomistic tradition, uses *universalia* as a nominative singular (hence first declension) noun, which is (as the *OED* notes *ad locum*) "erroneous," as, in classical Latin anyway, it is clearly a neuter nominative or accusative plural.

37. See ibid., p. 209.

38. Ibid., p. 214.

39. Radhakrishnan and Moore, *A Sourcebook in Indian Philosophy*, text 155.

40. Potter, *Indian Metaphysics and Epistemology*, p. 123.

41. Theodore Stcherbatsky, *Buddhist Logic*, vol. 1 (New York: Dover, 1962), pp. 49–50.

42. Ross, *Aristotle*, p. 66.

43. Potter, *Indian Metaphysics and Epistemology*, p. 53.

44. The Vaiśeṣika doctrine of specific absences seems to be the predecessor of the Mādhyamika doctrine of specific emptinesses: Each thing is characterized by emptiness, or lack of inherent being, but this is not a vague nothingness; each thing's emptiness is *its own* particular emptiness, unlike any other. "The emptiness of one thing, though no different in color, shape, and so forth from another emptiness, is not the emptiness of another thing . . . One must understand that emptinesses are divided by way of their bases, that is, the things that are empty." "Emptiness is not a vague negative, but a specific negative of inherent existence in each and every object." (Jeffrey Hopkins, *Meditation on Emptiness* [Boston: Wisdom Publications, 1996], pp. 408, 410.)

45. Potter, *Indian Metaphysics and Epistemology*, p. 51.

46. Radhakrishnan and Moore, *A Sourcebook in Indian Philosophy*, text 157.

47. Potter, *Indian Metaphysics and Epistemology*, p. 122.

48. Ibid., pp. 122–123.

49. See Stcherbatsky, *Buddhist Logic*, vol. 1, p. 50, note 1.

50. Potter (*Indian Metaphysics and Epistemology*, p. 56) denies that the inherence cause as defined by Udayana is equivalent to Aristotle's material cause, and attributes the doctrine of a material cause instead to the Sāṇkhyas, the Vaiśeṣikas' great opponents. But Aristotle's definition of the material cause as the material of artificial products clearly does not resemble the Sāṇkhya doctrine of *satkaryavada*, which holds that the cause contains the effect or that the effect preexists in the cause, but the Nyāya-Vaiśeṣika exemplum of pot-halves and pot.

51. The atoms are nonsentient and thus need some conscious agent to set them going again. Prior to the theistic phase of the school the *adṛṣta* meant "some cause the exact nature of which cannot be determined, but nevertheless its existence has to be postulated to explain certain effects . . ." Praśastapāda says, "[M]ovements for which we cannot find any cause either by sense-perception or by inference . . . should be regarded as produced by *adṛṣta*." Vātsyāyana felt that *adṛṣta* was "a peculiar property of the atoms" themselves. (Gangopadhyaya, *Indian Atomism*, p. 37–38.)

52. By M. Hiriyana, *Outlines of Indian Philosophy* (New York: Macmillan, 1932), p. 243.

53. Some authors emphasize the secular and rational aspect of the Nyāya-Vaiśeṣika tradition and feel that the stated desire for release through yogic practice is more or less a token; others disagree, emphasizing the yogic disengagement of mind from the senses which might be promoted by rationalist thinking. For the first view see, e.g., Riepe, *The Naturalistic Tradition*, pp. 244–245, and Ninian Smart, *Doctrine and Argument in Indian Philosophy* (London: George Allen and Unwin, 1964), p. 96; for the latter see Potter, *Indian Metaphysics and Epistemology*, pp. 31 ff.

54. Potter, ibid., p. 93.

55. Radhakrishnan and Moore, *A Sourcebook in Indian Philosophy*, text 133, p. 417.

56. Ross, *Aristotle*, p. 152.

57. Ibid., p. 152.

58. Ibid., p. 151.

59. Ibid., p. 132.

60. Smart, *Doctrine and Argument in Indian Philosophy*, p. 95.

61. Radhakrishnan, *Indian Philosophy*, vol. 2, p. 225.

62. Potter, *Indian Metaphysics and Epistemology*, p. 16.

Chapter Twenty-One

The Stoics and Indian Thought

The Stoic school was founded about 300 B.C. by Zeno of Citium after he had studied under various teachers in Athens for about a dozen years. His main masters were Crates the Cynic and Stilpo of Megara, from both of whom he imbibed a Cynic/neo-Eleatic approach to life; but he is also said to have studied under Xenocrates and Polemon, both Academicians, from whom he may have received the impulse to constructive thought which he would try to reconcile with the Cynic stance toward life (D.L. VII.2). Not being an Athenian citizen, and hence unable to purchase a building, he opened his school in a stoa, or porch, that had been painted by Polygnotus. Throughout the five-hundred-year-long history of the Stoa, or Porch, it was characterized by an extraordinary freedom of debate and reconception. "[I]t was permitted to discuss the teachings of the founder of the school, and, for this reason, his doctrine was subject to analyses, revisions, and reinterpretations. . . . The philosophy of Zeno was subject to innovations, even important ones, going through . . . considerable development."[1]

Throughout its long history, the Stoic school was dominated by its attempt to harmonize the Cynic emphasis on the percept with the Platonic-Aristotelian emphasis on the concept. The task was not easy, and most of the Stoic masters seem to have represented one side or the other, rather than truly balancing them. Ariston of Chios, for example, a student of Zeno, rejected conceptual "knowledge" (logic, physics, metaphysics, etc.) for the sake of direct spontaneous action without conceptual framework—a point of view which the Stoic philosopher shared with Cynics and Skeptics as well as with other schools farther afield. His near contemporary Chrysippus, on the other hand, wrote hugely and devoted much attention to syllogisms and their uses in metaphysical construction. Later Stoics such as Musonius and Epictetus reverted strongly to the old Cynic (ultimately Socratic) type—the type which Onesicritus had recognized also in the yogis of Northwest India.

Cosmology

The Stoic cosmology is a qualified monism much like those of the Vedāntic and Vaiṣṇava philosophies of India. In both the Greek and Indian traditions, the same basic world-structure is found: a cyclical monism postulating both immanence and transcendence. For the Stoics, god is at once identical with the world and different from it, which is to say, both immanent and transcendent. His original, unmanifest, transcendent state or aspect is pure god, his derivative manifest aspect is the world. This manifest aspect is worshipped as both passive matter and creative power. The creative power aspect is called the World Soul, or god in a more limited and theistic sense; passive matter is the body which is enlivened by this World Soul.

The Cosmic Being which contains both the transcendent and the immanent aspects is called by a variety of more and less theistic names, many of which are allusions to earlier Greek thought: Fire (Heraclitus), Air (Anaximenes), Breath (the Pythagoreans), World Soul (Plato), Aether (the Peripatetics), Universal Mind and Universal Reason (Heraclitus and the Peripatetics), Cosmic Law (Heraclitus), the United-Whole-Containing-the-Germs-of-all-Things (cf. Heraclitus's "Synapse," the Connection), Nature (the Cynics), Destiny, and others. The Olympian name is Zeus, and here we find Orphic resonances, in the cosmic being Zeus who contains the germs of all things within himself and, as the Skilful Fire (cf. Heraclitus's Thunderbolt), produces from himself by an unalterable Law, which is also himself, the world and its creatures, which are also himself. (The Stoics have been called "the first pantheists" in western thought.)[2]

In this production of a world the Stoic Zeus expresses himself through a cyclical process. He becomes manifest for a cosmic year (estimated by Diogenes Laertius as 360 × 18,000 solar years), and then, destroying the world of form in a conflagration, becomes unmanifest again for a timeless time (since when form stops time stops), then manifests himself again. While cyclicity is the most common ancient philosophical view of time, the Stoic version was unusual in its rigor: In each cycle of manifestation, according to the doctrine, events in the world of form are *exactly the same* and will be so in all future cycles also; each "new" age of manifestation is an exact repetition of the last.

At the dissolution of the manifest universe—Hindu *pralaya*—all separate beings are reabsorbed into unity (Zeus), and the distinction between god and the world ends. Zeus is then in his hidden or quiescent state, like Viṣṇu when he sleeps upon the serpent Ananta. Both at the commencement and at the end of each phase of manifestation, the traditional pre-Socratic (and Upaniṣadic) transformation through the lighter to the heavier of the four elements, or back from the heavier to the lighter again, takes place. Some later Stoics (Boethus, Panaetius) replaced this mythological cyclicity with the ontological paradox that the manifest and unmanifest phases of Zeus are in fact not phases but aspects, that is, that they are simultaneous rather than successive.

Hindu Parallels

The Stoic reality-model is a version of the standard pre-Socratic/Upaniṣadic cosmology involving qualified monism with or without theistic tinges, an enclosed polytheism and a cyclical process; another fourth-century Greek version is found in Plato's *Timaeus*. This type of world-model was eventually driven into hiding throughout most of the western world by the dualistic models taught by Zoroastrianism, Judaism, Christianity, and Islam, but it maintained itself in various occult and peripheral traditions. In India it was never displaced from the religious center, and much of it is retained in the still-prevalent Vedāntic and Puranic philosophies which took shape in the middle ages. The broad parallelisms between these schools and Stoicism are remarkable.

Monism and Theism

The fundamental Stoic distinction between the manifest and the unmanifest Zeus is paralleled repeatedly in these Hindu schools. In the Advaita Vedānta the parallel is the distinction between the *brahman* as *saguṇa* (with form) and *nirguṇa* (without form); the Advaitins, like the Panaetian Stoics, taught that the two were simultaneous aspects rather than successive phases. The various Puranic schools present the distinction mostly in mythological imagery: In the Vaiṣṇava version, at the *pralaya*, or dissolution of the world of form, Viṣṇu draws the world of the many back into himself and sleeps (i.e., becomes nonmanifest), then, waking from his sleep, projects the many outward again from their seed-state inside him. Similarly, in Stoicism, Zeus absorbs the world into himself at its dissolution, then, after timeless time, manifests it outwardly again. Śaiva and Shakta Purāṇas have the same idea, with variations in imagery. The Puranic authors in general favor mythological cyclicity over ontological paradox, and thus agree with the earlier form of the Stoic teaching.

There is a particularly striking similarity between the Stoic concept of the active or manifest Zeus and the Vedāntic concept of Īśvara. In both cases the way is opened for introducing theistic touches (such as devotional worship) into an essentially monistic system. For the Stoics, the world is identical with the manifest Zeus, which is simple pantheism; but at the same time he functions as a somewhat separate guiding principle to the world, a Providential Mind which human beings should relate to with awe, submission, and love. This superdeity contains within himself, not as seeds but in their actuality, all beings, including the gods of the Greek polytheism, whose existence and power are (as in Plato's *Timaeus*) considered real but limited. This creative Zeus is conceived at once as an inner law forever sustaining the world, and as an external artisan creating and overseeing it. His vast soul (the Universal Soul) is pure etheric fire-breath, and individual small souls are sparks from this universal fire. Thus the monism allows opportunities for direct personal relating to a deity, whether one of the Olympians or the great Providential Zeus itself.

Similarly, Śaṅkara calls the *saguṇa brahman* by a quasi-theistic title, Īśvara, "Lord" or "Master." This is *brahman* as the creator and sustainer of the finite universe, whose body is the universe, and who has a supermind and superpersonality analogous on a vastly larger scale to human ones. Individual souls are parts of his larger soul. The healthy human relationship to him is *Īśvara praṇidhāna*—submission to the Lord, comparable to the Stoic *amor fati*, love of what is allotted by Zeus. This compromise with theism is found in the Purāṇas also, where, for example, Viṣṇu is a supergod like Zeus, containing within himself as specific channels of dynamism a host of lesser gods, and able to be worshipped in a variety of dualistic ways.

Finally, in both traditions the relationship between the manifest and unmanifest aspects of the cosmic being is described by an analogy from logic: For Chrysippus, god (i.e., unmanifest Zeus) is the first premise of an argument and world (i.e.,the manifest Zeus) is an infinite series of posterior propositions deduced (led out ontologically) from that first premise and thus having existence only as its implications. For the Vedāntin Ramānuja, god is the substance, or ontological substrate, and the world is a shifting set of attributes adventitiously attached to the substance.

Ethics

Within this cosmological framework, the Stoics developed an ethic remarkably similar to that of the *Bhagavad Gīta*, the great classic of *karma yoga*. Since in their view each age of form is precisely the same as the last, the realm of ego-striving is seen as futile; as Cleanthes put it (*ap.* Sen. *Ep.* 107.11), "Fate [or Zeus] leads the willing—the unwilling He drags." The point then is to be willing, to harmonize oneself completely with nature, or Zeus, or destiny. The Stoic system (before Posidonius anyway) featured a macrocosm/microcosm correspondence such that each individual self is in fact a tiny version of the Great Self, Zeus; by harmonizing oneself with fate, one centers one's microcosm on the macrocosmic center and becomes in a sense one with Zeus. Thus the sage, or harmonized being, is seen as radically higher than the ordinary person, not just higher by measurable degrees. The action of a harmonized sage is precisely like the action of the accomplished *karma yogin* as described in the *Bhagavad Gīta*, action not performed for personal ends or with attachment to any particular goal, but simply out of cooperation with the facts of cosmic harmony; one relates always to the infinite Zeus or Krishna while performing one's finite actions.

Religion

Not only were the gods of the polytheisms maintained in both traditions, but in both cases the shifting absolute was treated as capable of receiving emotional projection. The school of Ramānuja interpreted *Īśvara praṇidhāna* less as manly endurance than as tender devotion. Similarly in Stoicism one finds, along with the mood of staunch acceptance, moods of love and tenderness. A key phrase is *amor fati*—love of fate; the Stoic does not merely accept fate, but loves it. This feeling feeds into devotional moods: As Seneca said, "The Cosmos is the mother of us all," and Epictetus: "Nature is wonderful and full of love for all creatures."

Prāṇa

Not only are the general structures of the Stoic and Puranic universes, and their religious and ethical attitudes, very similar, but the force which lies at the basis of both the physical and the ethical spheres (*pneuma* to Stoics, *prāṇa* to Hindus) is described in amazingly close parallel.

In the *Puruṣasūkta* of the *Ṛg Veda* (X.90), *prāṇa* was the breath of the cosmic being, the Macranthropus, Puruṣa, and also functioned as wind in the natural universe. In the late Brāhmaṇas and early Upaniṣads the concept receives further definition. The *Bṛhadāraṇyaka* and *Chāndogya Upaniṣads* repeatedly equate the *prāṇa*, or life-force, with the absolute *brahman-ātman*:

> Breath (*prāṇa*) is the immortal, name and shape are the real. By them this breath (*prāṇa*) is veiled. (*BU* I.6.3)
>
> Life-breath (*prāṇa*) gives life . . . Life-breath is one's father, life breath is one's mother, life-breath is one's brother, life-breath is one's sister, life-breath is one's teacher, life-breath is the Brahman. (*CU* VII.15.1)

As the *brahman*, the fundamental ontological principle or force, the *prāṇa* is conceived as the substrate from which forms arise and into which they return:

> All these divinities, having entered into wind (*prāṇa*), though they die in the wind, do not perish (altogether). Therefrom, indeed, they come forth again. (*KU* II.12)

At the same time, in Yājñavalkya's discourse on the *brahman*, the *prāṇa* is identified as the inner cohesive force running through all phenomena and holding them together:

> By air (*prāṇa*) as by a thread this world, the other world, and all beings are held together. (*BU* III.7.2)

Thus when someone dies his faculties are said to have been loosened, since the inner thread of *prāṇa* is no longer holding them together.

As vital force, then, *prāṇa* functions on both cosmic and personal levels. As Deussen said: "The *prāṇa* is not merely a psychical but also a cosmical principle . . . not only the breath of life in man, but also the universal breath of life which prevails throughout the whole of nature."[3]

Although breath or wind is the most common physical form attributed to *prāṇa*, it is also sometimes identified with fire and *ākāśa* (space or ether). The *Śatapatha Brāhmaṇa* asks:

> What is the fire which is this universe?

And the answer is given:

> In truth *prāṇa* is this fire. (*SB* X.3.3.5–8)

Says the *Chāndogya Upaniṣad*:

> Life (*prāṇa*) is Brahman, Joy is Brahman, Ether is Brahman. (*CU* IV.10.4)

In an even more rarefied and attenuated aspect, the *prāṇa* is consciousness and wisdom is a special relationship with *prāṇa*:

> What the prāṇa is, that is the prajñā [consciousness or wisdom], and what the prajñā is, that is the prāṇa. This prāṇa is the *prajñātman* [the consciousness aspect of the absolute].(*KU* 3 and 4)[4]

In mature post-Upaniṣadic Hinduism *prāṇa* is no less important. It assumes a constant role as "the empirical representative" of the *ātman*,[5] the absolute when conceived as an active vital force engaged in the world of form. As such it is the substance on which the yogi works in his attempts to know and to some extent to manipulate the force of life. Since the *prāṇa* retained its ancient and fundamental identification with the breath, the yogi's attempts to control it begin with *prāṇāyāma*, or breath control. This means much more than controlling the inhalation and exhalation, since other breaths are recognized also, such as the *apāna*, or downward breath, which breathes downward from the navel to the rectum as the *prāṇa* breathes upward from navel to nostrils. Another breath current is conceived as running through the veins. *Prāṇa* as a genus, the basic life energy, flows everywhere in the body through a network of channels centered in the navel, and effects all things. When the mind directs the muscles to act, it is *prāṇa* which carries the impulse from brain to nerves and from nerves to muscles. Thus every action uses up a certain amount of *prāṇic* energy, and it is the yogi's aim to accumulate and manipulate this energy. To give a mild example, the yogi can direct *prāṇa* to an injured part of his body and heal it. As a modern manual of yoga puts it:

> Knowledge and control of *prāṇa* manifested in the individual is called *prāṇāyāma*, which opens to us the door to almost unlimited power. The control of *prāṇa* being the one idea of *prāṇāyāma*, all the training and yogic exercises advocated in Haṭha Yoga are for that one end.[6]

Not only physical powers, but also mental illumination arises from control of *prāṇa*:

> The finest and highest manifestation of all *prāṇa*'s action in the human being is thought. By the trained manipulation of this subtle force or *prāṇa*, the yogi is able to give a push to the mind to go higher up into the superconscious plane and to act from that plane.[7]

Enlightenment, in other words, may be said to consist in a special relationship to the *prāṇa*.

Pneuma

Extant information about the Stoic concept of *pneuma* is more fragmentary, yet is still sufficient to establish an extensive and detailed parallelism in the two traditions. Stoic *pneuma*, like Hindu *prāṇa*, means literally "breath," and very likely came from an earlier semimythological concept of the breath of a cosmic being. The Pythagorean view of the cosmos as a living being which breathes a huge (universal) breath which flows through, enlivens, and interconnects all beings is a possible forebear, or in any case a representative of the same tradition in Greek thought.

While its early history in the Greek context is vague, with Aristotle, who discusses it in *De Motu Animalium* and *De Generatione Animalium*, the concept of *pneuma* becomes more visible.[8] He associates it with heat, with air, and with soul in the sense of vital spirit. It is akin to the fifth element, ether, which makes up the stars. It is involved in the beginnings of movement in the body and plays a complex role in reproduction, which seems to involve transmitting the soul.[9] It was from Aristotle that the Stoics inherited *pneuma*, as they received his influences in psychology and ethics generally. Various medical theorists also employed the concept.

Pythagoras of Cos (fl. c. 300 B.C.) theorized that, since the arteries are found empty in a corpse, blood was carried in the veins alone and something else, which he called *pneuma*, in the arteries. This idea remained active in the medical tradition for several generations and was elaborated. *Pneuma* was distributed into several different types performing different vital functions. From this tradition "the Stoics . . . adopted the idea that *pneuma* is a single, but highly differentiable, vehicle whose workings can explain a wide variety of human functioning."[10]

Pneuma is soul, which is distributed throughout the body by a complex arterial system and makes the body able to move and function. As the Stoic system ramified and extended its account under Chrysippus, *pneuma* took on an elevated position like *prāṇa* in the Hindu system. A mixture of fire and air, as Chrysippus conceived it, *pneuma* was described in part on the model of Heraclitus's universal fire. The *logos*, or ruling part of the human personality, had been composed of fire, according to Zeno and Cleanthes; for Chrysippus it was *pneuma*. For Heraclitus the different constituents of the world were "modifications of fire";[11] for the Chrysippan Stoa the differences among things consisted primarily of different mixtures of air and fire in the *pneuma*. The *pneuma* was an all-pervasive force which both holds things together—from the universe as a totality to an individual body within it—while at the same time straining outward and creating a tension which "makes the universe into a dynamic continuum."[12]

Prāṇa/Pneuma

The parallelisms between *pneuma* and *prāṇa* are thoroughgoing.[13] In the Stoic system, *pneuma* is a synonym for Zeus, the absolute Cosmic Being itself, as *prāṇa* is a synonym for *brahman*; as such, *pneuma*, like *prāṇa*, is the substrate from which all forms arise, of which they are composed, and into which they perish when their inner connection comes loose. *Pneuma*, like *prāṇa*, is conceived as a connecting element which holds all things together from inside and as a unifying breath which penetrates and pervades all things. When a person dies, the cohesive *pneuma* is said to have loosened its grip on the faculties, so that they flowed apart—precisely the function that *prāṇa* performs in death in the Hindu tradition. Further, *pneuma*, like *prāṇa*, is primarily conceived as air, but is at other times identified with the elements of fire and ether and is called the Universal Consciousness, as the Hindu *prāṇa* is called the *prajñātman*.

Thus the *pneuma*, like the *prāṇa*, functions both on a cosmic and a personal level, as the breath or soul or mind of Zeus, the Macranthropus, and as the breath or soul or mind of each individual being contained within the cosmic Zeus as a tiny fragment or manifestation of himself. The Stoic term for soul is *hēgemonikon* (the leading or guiding faculty), and the *hēgemonikon* is identified with the *pneuma* in a particularly sensitive and rarefied state; the *hēgemonikon* is the consciousness aspect of the *pneuma*, paralleling the *prajñā* aspect of the *prāṇa*.

On the personal level, the *pneuma*, like the *prāṇa*, is the bodily breath as well as the consciousness. In a remarkable parallel, the Stoics, like the Hindus, do not limit the bodily breath to the inhalation and exhalation of the lungs. The *pneuma* flows as air currents, or breaths, throughout the body, through a network of channels unknown to modern physiologists, and centered in the area of the breast, as the Hindu network centers on the navel. Thoughts are produced by upward action of rarefied *pneumata* or breath currents. This highest action or form of the *pneuma* constitutes the soul or reasoning faculty, the *hēgemonikon*.

The *hēgemonikon*, like the *prāṇa*, moves vibrationally,[14] and the process of becoming a sage involves controlling this vibration so that it harmonizes with the vibration of the cosmic *pneuma*, the *hēgemonikon* or soul of Zeus. When these vibrations coincide, the individual can think only reasonable thoughts; in other words, he is enlightened. Thus for the Stoic as for the Hindu, enlightenment consists in a special relationship to the *pneuma*.

Whether Stoics, like Hindu yogis, attempted to establish the right inner vibration through direct control of the breath is not known; more probably they worked directly on the *hēgemonikon* rather than on the bodily breath. We cannot be sure, however, for Zeno's death, as related by Diogenes Laertius, sounds like an advanced feat of *prāṇāyāma*:

> The manner of his death was as follows: as he was leaving the school he tripped and fell, breaking a toe. Striking the ground with his fist, he quoted a line from the Niobe: I come I come, why dost thou call for me? and died forthwith, by stopping his breath. (D.L. VII.28)

Enlightenment

The Stoics distinguished between the (small) community of the Wise and the (large) community of fools, with no intermediary classification. Such distinctions are normal in the enlightenment religions of India, like the Southern Buddhist distinction between the enlightened and the "foolish common people." In both traditions enlightenment is conceived as a state radically different from the ordinary, to which access was in some sense instantaneous and from which it was impossible to slip back.

The difference between sage and fool, in the Stoic view, is that the sage accepts what comes, the fool accepts only what he likes and attempts to reject what he does not like; he strives egotistically against Zeus, or Fate. The sage's little personal self has all but disappeared; at the moment when the vibration of his *hēgemonikon* clicked into perfect synchronization with that of Zeus, he ceased to think ego-oriented thoughts. The fool is an egotist; the sage has expanded beyond the limits of ego. There are obvious similarities here with the Buddhist teaching of non-ego, and with the Hindu teaching that the little self (*jīva*) should in some way merge with the great self (*ātman*).

Differences

The Stoic system, like many pre-Christian Greek systems, reveals a way of thought and a constellation of leading ideas which are more or less equivalent to those which are found in most Indian systems. The Stoic system overall is like a miniature version of Brahminical Hinduism. Still, there are differences: The Stoics did not teach reincarnation; their successive cycles of manifestation, unlike those of India, are exact repetitions; they did not teach a period of quiescence exactly equal in length to the period of cosmic activity (for when the cosmos ends, in the Stoic view, there is no longer anything to measure); finally, and most importantly, the Stoics seem no more than other Greek schools to have taught meditation and bodily discipline in anything like the Indian yogic manner.

Notes to Chapter Twenty-One

1. Giovanni Reale, *A History of Ancient Philosophy*, vol. 3, *The Systems of the Hellenistic Age*, trans. John R. Catan (Albany, New York: State University of New York Press, 1985), pp. 215–216.

2. Ibid., p. 214.

3. Paul Deussen, *The Philosophy of the Upaniṣads* (New York: Dover, 1966), p. 106.

4. Ibid., p. 139.

5. Ibid., p. 103.

6. Swami Vishnudevananda, *The Complete Illustrated Book of Yoga* (New York: Julian Press, 1960), p. 223.

7. Ibid.

8. A medical papyrus contains references to *pneuma* in the systems of Philolaus and Hippocrates. It is criticized by Julia Annas (*Hellenistic Philosophy of Mind* [Berkeley: University of California Press, 1992], pp. 26–27, n. 24).

9. See ibid., pp. 17ff.

10. Ibid., p. 25.

11. A. A. Long, *Hellenistic Philosophy: Stoics, Epicureans, Skeptics*, (Berkeley, California: University of California Press, 1986), p. 156.

12. Ibid., p. 157.

13. Filliozat wrote interestingly on this: "The entire Greek literature of pneumatic physiology," he says, " . . . serves as a pendant to Sanskrit literature" (J. Filliozat, *The Classical Doctrine of Indian Medicine: Its Origins and Its Greek Parallels*, trans. Dev Raj Chanana [Delhi: Munshiram Manoharlal, 1964], p. 228).

14. John M. Rist, *Stoic Philosophy* (Cambridge: Cambridge University Press, 1969), pp. 86–87.

Chapter Twenty-Two

Neoplatonism and the Upaniṣadic-Vedāntic Tradition

In both India and Greece philosophical lineages were cumulative; later representatives of a school would continue to teach some of the ideas of their predecessors along with their own additions and adjustments. Plotinus's lineage went back through the Middle Platonists Ammonius and Numenius, then leapt over the skeptical period of the New Academy to the Old Academy of Plato, and before him the pre-Socratics—especially, but not exclusively, Pythagoras and Parmenides. Accordingly, on the Greek side, a comparison of Neoplatonism with Vedānta, which must center on the thought of Plotinus, will also refer to earlier stages of his lineage.

On the Indian side no single figure will form the center. The obvious candidate would have to be Śaṅkara; but his thought—which was regarded by the later Vedāntins Ramānuja and Mādhva as crypto-Buddhist—is a rather extreme position in the Vedāntin lineage. Though Śaṅkara is important in the comparison, the center of the Indian side must be the Upaniṣads, with other later texts, such as the *Brahmā Sūtra*, and thinkers, such as Ramānuja, also in the discussion.

Plotinus and India

Plotinus may have been a somewhat younger contemporary of both Sextus Empiricus and Nāgārjuna. The biography written by his student Porphyry says that he studied in Alexandria from 232 to 243 A.D. These years fell in a period when Indian yogis (whom the Greeks called Gymnosophists, or "naked philosophers") could be found in the streets of that city. If it is correct that "the word Gymnosophist is a version—part translation and part mime—of the Sanskrit words *Jaina Muni*, i.e., 'Jaina monk,'"[1] then the "naked philosophers" were probably Jains.

In addition to the presence of yogis, it has been argued that information about—even, perhaps, texts of—some Upaniṣads were available in Alexandria, though this is not completely established.[2] Plotinus's contemporary, the Christian father Hippolytus (d. 235), in his book *Refutation of All Heresies*, showed an accurate, if elementary, knowledge of Upaniṣadic teachings, with suggestions that he had seen the *Taittiriya* and *Maitrī Upaniṣads*, or some related texts no longer extant.[3] One scholar asserts that "[a] Roman of the third century interested in India, e.g., Plotinus, could have a quite detailed and not inadequate knowledge of Upaniṣadic doctrines."[4]

In Plotinus's case, then, as in that of Pyrrhon, it may be said that it is highly likely—perhaps "virtually certain" would be better—that he had some contact with Indian ideas, though—again as in Pyrrhon's case—it probably wasn't much. This contact may have whetted his appetite for Indian thought, for in the year 243, at the end of his stay in Alexandria, Plotinus joined the emperor Gordian's expedition to the East, hoping, according to Porphyry, "to learn directly the philosophy which is practiced among the Persians and that which is honored in India" (*Vit. Plot.* III.15–17). But Plotinus's desire to go directly to the sources of the philosophies he had contacted in Egypt did not get him to India. Gordian was killed in Mesopotamia, and Plotinus escaped with difficulty first to Antioch, then to Rome, where he stayed for the rest of his life as a teacher of philosophy.

Even though he did not get clear through to India, many scholars have felt that Plotinus's philosophy is so like that of the Upaniṣads and the Vedānta that it must have been influenced by those sources. Even those who dislike Indian influence on Greek thought in most cases find it acceptable to acknowledge that the possibility cannot be excluded for Plotinus.[5] Some have felt that the similarity is enough to establish contact, but ". . . the question which tradition is influencing the other must for the moment remain uncertain and the possibility of influences both ways must be borne in mind."[6]

Still, modern western attitudes toward Plotinus have not been shaped by the widespread acknowledgment of the extraordinary similarity of his teachings to doctrines taught in India in his day, but by the role he unwittingly played after his death as a formative influence on Christian theology. Translations of his work may have a churchy kind of ring. The view of Plotinus as a kind of proto-Christian theologian may express, at least in part, a dread of finding possible Indian origins for the texts whose influence was to contribute to shaping the thought of Thomas Aquinas, Nicholas of Cusa, Meister Eckhardt, and many later western thinkers. So it is not only that "to admit 'oriental infuences' on [Plotinus] was tantamount to besmirching his good name,"[7] but even more it would also besmirch that whole aspect of the western tradition that flowed from him. If Plotinus had passed massive Asian influence into the western tradition, there would be little point to calling it western anymore.

The principal strategy adopted by those who wish to see a Plotinus who has not been besmirched by influence from the East is to argue that his ideas were clearly in the Platonic tradition and that they would have derived coherently from within that tradition with no input from without. "Plotinus's philosophy is an authentic unfolding of Platonism . . ." declares one scholar.[8] Another agrees that "Plotinus's thought can be understood as an organic elaboration of the Platonic philosophy."[9] And another: "Plotinus's mysticism has a character all its own, the character of a genuine Hellenic, in fact Platonic, growth, and is not contaminated by oriental influences."[10] Still another argues that "there is nothing Oriental about Neoplatonism. All its component elements may be traced back to purely Greek thought."[11]

But the phrases "genuine Hellenic . . . growth" and "purely Greek thought" need to be inspected. It can be argued that Plato was already Indianized through Orphic and Pythagorean influences, and on that basis alone some, at least, of his works cannot be regarded as "purely Greek thought." Plotinus, then, may have received the Indian influence from Gymnosophists in Alexandria, or from the works of Plato, or both; it comes to the same thing: He was philosophizing in an Indianized tradition.[12] It is not just a question of whether Plotinus's philosophy was derived from India *by him*. Its major outlines, on the view presented in this book, had been derived from India almost a thousand years earlier and handed down through what might be called the Indianized, or Indian-influenced, strand of Greek philosophy, to which Plotinus emphatically belonged. He could, then, and perhaps would, have come up with his model of things without any additional Indian input in his lifetime, though it seems clear, in any case, that he had some.

Plotinus's Teaching Style

In Rome, Plotinus developed a circle of disciples who were mostly of the senatorial class and mostly, also, of Asian origin.[13] From Tyre came the disciple Malchos, later known as Porphyry, Plotinus's biographer and an important Neoplatonist philosopher himself. Others of his intimate circle came from Alexandria, Scythia, Arabia, and Syria. The small group included three women who were regarded as equal to the men in dedication to philosophy—technically speaking, in dedication to the goal of attaining the knowledge which frees from reincarnation, for that is what Plotinus, like the gurus of India (and like Plato and Pythagoras before him), taught.

Plotinus lived in the house of the noblewoman Gemina and her daughter of the same name. Nothing is known of their personal relationship. In her house he gave talks that were open to the public though mostly attended by the inner circle. Plotinus did not write much, but, like Socrates and Siddhārtha, allowed his discourses to be memorized—and thus made available for commitment to writing—by his disciples. The records of many of those talks are still extant under the title *Enneads*, the "nines," because they are divided into six books of nine discourses each.[14] He would generally take as the subject of his comments a passage of Plato or of a Peripatetic author like Alexander of Aphrodisias or of a later Platonist like Numenius or Plotinus's own teacher Ammonius. After his talk, questions would be asked without limit, so that rational doubts could be allayed. Plotinus seems to have lived an austere and contemplative life such as would be expected in the Platonic lineage. As also would be appropriate to a follower of Plato, he was, according to Porphyry, an all-around intellectual whom "nothing of geometry, arithmetic, mechanics, optics, or music escaped." He was a mystic who three times had experiences like what Patañjali called *nirvikalpa samādhi*, "formless trance." He spelled badly and refused to have his portrait painted.

The Upaniṣadic-Vedāntic Tradition

Plotinus may be placed chronologically about in the middle of the tradition. The oldest of the "old" Upaniṣads predate him considerably, and the great commentators Śaṅkara, Ramānuja, Bhāskara, and so on lie in the future, in relation to Plotinus, about as far as the oldest Upaniṣads lie in the past.[15] Bādarāyana, on whose no-longer-extant writings the fundamental text of the Vedānta schools—the *Brahmā Sūtra*—was based, was closer to Plotinus, perhaps the first century B.C. The Vedāntic tradition was a two-millennia-long unfolding of the implications and intentions of certain passages of the Upaniṣads.

The *Brahmā Sūtra*, "a commentary on and summary of the doctrines in the *Upaniṣads*," is referred to as "the treatise for investigating Brahman."[16] It took its present form c. 400–450 A.D., but seems to have developed in a number of stages over a period of at least five hundred years, and to have been "handed down in secret from master to disciple among a very limited section of Brahmin theologians."[17] Like Plotinus's thought, it took place in a wealthy, upper-class context, and both can be seen as conservative viewpoints that tended to elide social problems.

Unlike the *Enneads*, the *Brahmā Sūtra* was rendered difficult to interpret in order to maintain its secrecy—primarily by a brevity so extreme that it is virtually incomprehensible without at least one commentary. Sometimes a Sūtra, or numbered passage, contains only one word, and the reader needs to have context supplied by a commentator—and sometimes the commentators are in disagreement about what additional words to supply. Whether the text is translatable with any clarity has been questioned. Somewhat expanded paraphrases are useful.

Investigating Oneness

Aside from their location in nests of wealth, the social situations in which Plotinus and the Indian authors worked were very different. Plotinus did not live in a caste system, did not exclude women or foreigners from philosophical discussion, did not practice secrecy for sectarian reasons, did not deal with issues of ritual purity, and did not recognize a body of authoritative scriptures; the author of the *Brahmā Sūtra* and its later commentators, in contrast, all regarded the Upaniṣads as revelation on a footing with the *Ṛg Veda*. Nevertheless, many passages of Plotinus respond well to a comparison with Vedāntin texts.[18] These are the world's two great corpora of intense systematic thought about monism.

In both the Greek and the Indian traditions the question of the relationships that exist between the polar elements of pairs of terms such as Being and non-Being, One and Many, sameness and difference seemed especially revealing of the nature of things. Greek and Indian thinkers worked over the same ground in investigating these questions and came up with similar images and answers, sometimes, it seems, borrowed from one another, sometimes generated separately under influence of the fact that the two groups were working from a common beginning involving ancient Near Eastern inheritances.

The Vedāntic tradition is dominated by Yājñavalkya's *neti, neti*/*iti, iti* dilemma: (1) If only the One is real, then the Many must be unreal; (2) If only the One is real, then the Many must *be* the One. In the first case, unity is a transcendent quality—not actually residing in experiential flux but over and above it; in the second, unity is immanent, residing, however disguised, in the elements of experience.

Like a sleight of hand (*māyā*) these positions flicker into and out of one another, almost as if complementary, in both the Upaniṣadic-Vedāntic and the Platonic/Neoplatonic traditions. In both bodies of texts three types of passages are found: those which stress the world-negating transcendence of the One, those which stress its world-affirming immanence, and those which make an effort to balance the two aspects. Some Upaniṣadic passages, and many texts of the later school known as Advaita or nondualist Vedānta—the school of Śaṅkara—flatly deny the reality of the Many—*neti, neti*. So does Porphyry, Plotinus's student, biographer, and successor. Plotinus himself sometimes takes this position, but at other times takes a position closer to the Viśiṣṭadvaitin or "qualified nondualist" position associated with Ramānuja, who leaned toward the *iti, iti* or immanentalist position, and partly redeemed the Many. The third great Neoplatonist, Iamblichus, similarly qualified his monism, regarding the world of the Many as firmly rooted in and expressive of the One. *Neti, neti* is later called a *māyāvāda*, or "illusion doctrine"—the doctrine that the

Many are an illusion—and *iti, iti* a *parinamavada*, or "transformation doctrine"—the doctrine that the Many are a transformation of the One. The third position which mediates holds (*BS* II.3.43) that the world of the Many is different from the absolute and also not-different from it. *Bhedābheda*—difference/nondifference—was the position of Bhāskara and Nimbarka. Plotinus's system which, like Plato's, is multileveled, accommodates all three views at different levels. When he acts as spokesperson of Oneness, the One is transcendent and the Many are unreal or nonexistent; when he speaks for the Many, the One is immanent and the Many are magically informed by it. On the middle plane of Nous—interpenetrated One and Many—something like difference/nondifference obtains.

The illusion doctrine goes back, in the Greek tradition, to Parmenides, who referred to multiplicity as "non-being," and in the Indian to the early Upaniṣads, such as the *Bṛhadāraṇyaka*, which says, "In it [being] there is no diversity. He goes from death to death, who sees in it, as it were, diversity" (IV.4.19). The rejection of multiplicity leads to a rejection of predication, for as soon as one has substance and attribute, or subject and predicate, one has a plurality. Descriptions of the One must be phrased negatively if at all. The *Brahmā Sūtra* describes *brahman* as without limits (III.2.26), without parts (II.1.26), without form (III.2.13), and without distinction or differentiation (III.2.11). "It is difficult to describe it positively in terms of words; it can be expressed only negatively (III.2.12)."[19] Even to call the One "one" is to breach its unity by implicitly contrasting it with a Many without which it could not be recognized as One. Śaṅkara calls his formulation "nondualism" rather than "monism." He will say that Being (*brahman*) is not Many, but he will not say that it is One. Plotinus expresses himself similarly, saying, "The name One denotes nothing but a negation of multiplicity . . ." (*Enn.* V.5.6).

Since the One is beyond predication, it follows that it has no qualities; it is featureless. "Nothing," said Plotinus, "can be affirmed of the One" (*Enn.* VI.7.41). "It is even for itself nothing" (ibid.). It is "other than all things" (V.3.11). It is "neither thing nor quality nor intellect nor soul; not in motion, not at rest, not in place, not in time" (VI.9.3). It is "neither this nor that" (ibid.). In various places he describes it as beyond being (V.1.8), beyond language (V.3.19), beyond change (V.1.6), beyond affection (I.8.2), beyond partition (IV.1.1), beyond form (V.5.6), beyond limitation (VI.9.6), beyond valuation (I.8.2), and so on. This way of speaking is the background of the so called "negative theology" that was to become basic to medieval philosophy and is still influential.

The negative theology was practiced long before Plotinus in the Upaniṣads. Yājñavalkya said in the *Bṛhadāraṇyaka Upaniṣad*:

> It is neither gross nor fine, neither short nor long, neither glowing red (like fire), nor adhesive (like water). (It is) neither shadow nor darkness, neither air nor space, unattached, without taste, without smell, without eyes, without ears, without voice, without mind, without radiance, without breath, without a mouth, without measure, having no inside and no outside. (III.8.8)

Yājñavalkya introduced the formula *neti neti*, which may be translated either "not this, not this," or "neither this nor that." In various places in the Greek monistic tradition, also, the absolute was called "neither this nor that." Once, paralleling this Upaniṣadic formula directly, Plotinus calls it "the not-this" (*Enn.* V.5.6.13). In a related locution, both Śaṅkara and Plotinus at times refer to the featureless absolute by the neuter demonstrative adjective "that" (Skt. *tat,* Grk. *ekeino*). For Śaṅkara the world is an illusion created by ignorance (*avidyā*), and when the mind attains an understanding (*jñāna*) beyond distinctions the world will simply cease to appear to exist. This was the position of Parmenides and was maintained continuously in some branch or other of the Greek tradition for eight hundred years, till Porphyry, the student of Plotinus, expressed it in his *Sententiae.* In the Indian tradition this idea has maintained itself as a viable philosophical counter until the present.

In both traditions the illusion doctrine was countered by and mingled with the transformation doctrine. While Parmenides proclaimed the illusion doctrine, Heraclitus proposed that the One is constantly being transformed through conditions of multiplicity. Plato incorporated both these views at different levels of his hierarchical universe. For Parmenides, as for Śaṅkara, the universe had only two aspects—Being and Non-Being, or One and Many. The Pythagoreans suggested a more complexly stratified metaphysics, and Plato stabilized it, for the Pythagorean-Platonic lineages, in a three-leveled model—One-Few-Many—inherited by Plotinus. The highest level, the One, he described as "beyond being," as Plato had; the middle level, the realm of the Ideas, occupies a location which Plotinus calls Mind, or Universal Mind; and the lowest level, the Many, occupies a location which he calls Soul or World Soul, which includes as its lower side the realm of Nature, or ordinary experience.[20]

In explaining the level of Mind, or the Ideas, Plotinus employs something like a transformation doctrine with hints of difference/nondifference. Each of the Ideas in Mind is one with the One, yet they are also described as outflows from the One. Plotinus expresses the transformation in much the same ways Vedāntin thinkers expressed it. The *Brahmā Sūtra*, for example, compares the One to a source of light and the Many to its rays or illumination (I.1.24, I.3.40, III.2.15 and 25), and Bhāskara, in about 1000 A.D., used the image of the sun and its rays for the One and the Many.[21] Plotinus also has the image, saying the lower levels of being radiate from the One like the sun's rays. According to Bhāskara's successor, Yādava Prakāśa, the relationship between the One and the Many is *bhedābheda*, "difference/nondifference." The absolute, by exercising its own potential energy (*śakti*), transforms itself into the world, while yet remaining itself.[22] Plotinus had it figured out similarly: By its *dynamis*—a term as close as Greek gets to *śakti*—the One spontaneously radiates the Many. Ramānuja, around 1100 A.D., synthesized the tradition: The power of the One proceeds from it without truly becoming separate from it, as moonbeams proceed from the moon, and constitutes the manifest universe, which is both different from the One and not different from it. Plotinus's own doctrine was more like those of Ramānuja or Bhāskara than like that of Śaṅkara. "Nothing is separate," he said, "which originates from the One—but nothing is identical with it either" (VI.3.12).

Imaging the Many

At the lowest level of the universe, Plotinus often applies a pure illusion doctrine. He usually denies altogether the reality of matter and its appearances (e.g., II.5.5)—that is, of the world of everyday experience—as did Parmenides and, often, Plato, and the *advaitins*, or nondualists, in India. Plotinus expresses the illusion doctrine in terms as close to those of Indian thinkers as to Plato's. The realm of matter is made up, as Plato had taught, of mere "image and imitation" (*Enn.* V.9.3). It is a "phantom" (II.5.5) and a "shadow" (VI.3.8). Through it "ghostly and feeble images" pass with "no thrust and meet none in matter either; they pass through it leaving no cleavage as through water;

they are phantoms projected upon a void" (III.6.7). The reality of matter is denied by Plotinus as radically as it had been by Parmenides some seven hundred years before him: "It is not a being, it is non-being, truly non-being" (II.5.5). "Its every utterance is a lie."

Similarly, in the *Śvetāśvatara Upaniṣad*, "Prakriti [matter] is maya [illusion]" (*SU* IV.10). *Māyā* means an illusion in the sense of a magician's illusion or magic trick, a sleight of hand. Plotinus, who may have come across the *māyāvāda* from Indian sources in Alexandria, uses the same metaphor, describing matter as a "passing trick making trickery of all that seems to be present in it." He describes the flow of appearances of matter as "phantoms within a phantom." "It is like a mirror showing things as in itself when they are really elsewhere" (III.6.7). The similes of the phantom and the mirror are also used in India, and for the same purpose.[23]

The Greek tradition was as fertile as the Indian in producing images of this type (a part of the Greek achievement that the European tradition has tended to overlook). Pindar, in the *Eighth Pythian Ode*, said: "What is it to be, what is it not to be? Man is a dream of a shadow." Plotinus, almost a thousand years later, wrote, "[Matter is] a shadow, and on this shadow is traced a sketch" (*Enn.* VI.3.8). Elsewhere Plotinus describes the World Soul contemplating the infinite splendor of Mind and says that the realm of appearances arises as an "unconscious reflex of its contemplation" (III.8.4). The concept is much like the Hindu image of the world as the dream of the sleeping god Viṣṇu (Ramānuja seems to have been a Vaiṣṇava), or as the side effect of the meditation of the god Śīva. "I gaze," says the World Soul, "and the figures of the material world take being as if they fell from my contemplation." Plotinus even has the image of the universe as the dance of a cosmic deity—and earlier than it appears in any Indian text currently known:

> The limbs of the dancer conform themselves to the dance; they bend themselves to it, one lowering, another rising, one moving, another still, as the different patterns unfold . . . The movements of the cosmos should be compared to those of the dancer . . . The entire cosmos, while living its universal life, so moves and changes its limbs . . . (*Enn.* IV.4.33)

In the imagery of the dance and of the unconscious reflex, Plotinus applies a transformation rather than an illusion doctrine to the realm of Mind. The transformation doctrine, by denying the absolute separation of the world from the One, tends toward a world-affirming position like pantheism. In the Upaniṣads, also, monistic utterance often sounds pantheistic, employing variants of the Vedic and pre-Vedic idea of the *pantheos* or all-god. The *Chāndogya Upaniṣad*, for example, says, "Verily this whole world is pure being (Brahman)" (III.14.1). The *Brahmā Sūtra* agrees, saying that "nothing is distinct from Brahman" (II.3.6). This pantheistic trend is elaborated in the *Chāndogya Upaniṣad* with reference to imagery of the *purush*, or Cosmic Person , of the tenth book of the *Ṛg Veda*: The sun is the *brahman*'s eye, space its body, the earth its feet, and so on (*CU* V.12 ff.). Yājñavalkya, in the *Bṛhadāranyaka Upaniṣad*, equates *brahman* separately with air, earth, water, fire, sky, heaven, the sun and space, the moon and stars, the ether, darkness, and light; it is said to be in all beings, in the breath, in the speech organs, in the eye, in the perceiving mind, in the skin, in the conceptualizing mind and in the semen (*BU* III.7.3). The *Svetāśvatara Upaniṣad* describes the One both theistically and pantheistically. It is the "ruler of all," and "the overlord of the gods," and at the same time the being "in whom the worlds rest . . . the one embracer of everything" (*SU* IV.11–14). The *Brahmā Sūtra* declares that the *brahman* simultaneously controls all things (I.3.11), supports the world (IV.4.18), and resides within all things (III.2.20).

Plotinus has parallels to all these formulations. He inherited from Plato, Posidonius, and others the pantheistic view of the world as a living organism with a single vast soul enlivening all its parts. Plato, however, did not talk this way about the whole of Being, but only about the World Soul. Plotinus also applies this type of imagery to the level of Soul, which contains ordinary experience. "The universe," he says, "exists in the Soul, which contains it; there is nothing which does not participate in that Soul" (IV.3.9). But at the same time, Plotinus says, the upper aspect of Soul, which is rapt in contemplation of Mind, withholds itself from embodiment; just so, the *Kaṭha Upaniṣad* says of the one Self that it "becomes varied according to whatever (it enters) and also exists outside (them all)" (II.2.9). In the Greek tradition this idea goes back to Orphic sources echoed in Aeschylus's line, "Zeus is the earth, the sea, and the sky; he is everything and also something left over." Similarly, Śaṅkara held that "Brahman as the world cause is clearly distinguished from Brahman in itself."[24] Ramānuja, Mādhva, and other Vedāntins taught that the One transforms only a part of itself into the phenomenal world, another part remaining transcendent. Plotinus duplicates this structure of Vedāntic thought, in the concept of the World Soul, which has a lower immanent aspect and a higher transcendent aspect.

In other passages both Plotinus and the Upaniṣadic-Vedāntic authors shift from the imagery of pantheism to that of omnipresence. As the *Śvetāśvatara Upaniṣad* called *brahman* "the one embracer of everything" (IV.14), so Plotinus says "everything is fully held by the divine" (*Enn.* V.5.9).

> We cannot think of something of god here and something else there, nor of all god gathered at some one spot: there is an instantaneous presence everywhere. (*Enn.* V.5.9)
>
> The divine nature is infinite. Therefore it is not limited. That means that it is never absent; and if it is never absent, it is present in all things . . . Conceive it as a power of an everfresh infinity, a principle unfailing, inexhaustible, at no point giving out, brimming over with its own vitality . . . You cannot pass onto where it is not; you will never halt at a dwindling point where it fails at last and can no longer give; you will always be able to move with it—better, to be in its entirety—and so seek no further. (VI.6.12)

At times Plotinus even applies this world-affirming mood to the One, by collapsing the levels upward into it. The body, he says, is contained in Soul, Soul in Mind, and Mind in the One; therefore everything, at whatever remove, is contained in the One. Contrary to his statements of the absolute transcendence of the One, Plotinus states that the One "is not absent from the other things" (V.5.9), much as the *Brahmā Sūtra* says that nothing is distinct from *brahman* (II.3.6).

Paradoxical Formulations

The Upaniṣadic authors and Plotinus were both at pains to unite these two approaches to the One, and both did so by expressions of bipolar contradictions. "It is far and it is near; it is within all this and it is also outside all this," says the *Īśa Upaniṣad* (V). The *Brahmā Sūtra* declares "that the individual self is different . . . from Brahman but at the same time not different" (II.3.43), that the world of the Many is a part of *brahman* (II.3.43), yet that the *brahman* has no parts (II.1.26). And Plotinus: "The One is all things and none of them" (*Enn.* VI.2.1). "It can be none of existing things—yet it is all" (VI.7.32). "It is both present and absent" (V.5.9).

Western scholars have tended to regard this contradictory way of speaking as indicative of something unresolved in Plotinus's thought.[25] But seeing it in context of Indian parallels suggests something else: that it is not an unresolved contradiction but a balanced view of the implications of monistic thought. When Plotinus is thinking in terms of the outward force of emanation or progression by which the Many radiate from the One, he praises the sense realm for its source in the higher realms; when he thinks in terms of the force of regression, or return to the One, he denounces the sense realm for being so far from the higher realms. These two attitudes correspond to the complementarity of *neti, neti* and *iti, iti*. This type of contradictory statement does not represent a loose end, but a positive mode of expression that is a central thematic feature of ancient thought both eastern and western.

This contradiction inherent in monism applies to all particular things, including human selfhood. The individual personality is seen as unreal in itself, yet superreal in the sense that behind or underlying it is the ultimate and universal Self. In the Upaniṣads this takes the form of the doctrine that the *ātman*, or self, *is* the *brahman*, or ultimate principle. Yājñavalkya (*BU* III.7.3) taught that the individual human self is one with the universe as a whole or with each and every part of it. The absolute (*brahman*) is the true self of all beings. According to the *Chāndogya Upaniṣad*:

> This whole world is Brahman . . . this is my self within the heart, smaller than a grain of rice, than a barley corn, than a mustard seed . . . This is myself within the heart, greater than the earth, greater than the atmosphere, greater than the sky, greater than these worlds . . . (III.14.1, 3)

The *Muṇḍaka Upaniṣad* says:

> Vast, divine, of unthinkable form, subtler than the subtle, It shines forth, farther than the far, yet here near at hand, set down in the secret place (of the heart). (III.1.7)

Each finite being, in other words, contains the infinite universe. In the Puranic imagery, Viṣṇu, the great Self of the universe, lies asleep and in his dreams seems to become multitudes of tiny persons who will simply cease to appear to exist when he awakens; and yet the dreamed self contains the self which is dreaming it. In Vedāntic terms, the force of ignorance (*avidyā*) clouds the mind and cuts off perceptions at the boundaries of the little self; when *avidyā* is dispelled by the special knowledge of *brahman*, then the little self simply disappears, since it never really existed anyway, but was a misimpression like a dream or a thing seen in a cloud.

Knowing the One in Vedānta

In certain ways the attitude of the *Brahmā Sūtra* is extremely different from the Advaitin or nondualistic view of Śaṅkara. The *Brahmā Sūtra* clearly seems to favor the position that would later be espoused by the school of Bhāskara and Nimbarka, that the relation between the individual self and the ultimate self or *brahman* is difference/nondifference—*bhedābheda*. Despite its close relationship to the *brahman*, says the *Brahmā Sūtra* (I.1.8, II.3.17, etc.), the individual self never disappears completely into it; even when it has become impossible to distinguish from pure Being, it somehow retains enough semblance of individuality that it may be said to exist—and this remains the case eternally. For Śaṅkara, however, when the individual self experiences knowledge of the One it literally vanishes into the One, becomes unambiguously indistinguishable from it forever; after all, it was only an illusion all along, and knowledge simply dispels the illusion. It is not so much that the self ceases to exist as that it ceases to seem to exist, because it never really existed to begin with.

For Plotinus this point appears differently depending which level of his metaphysics he is referring to. At times he affirms the type of self-annihilating knowledge that Śaṅkara speaks of, which he believed he had occasionally experienced and in which, he says, there is simply no trace of the separate self left. The trick, or *māyā*, of individual consciousness is that, through its feeling of separateness, it seems to disprove the doctrine of the underlying oneness of all things. The goal of religious or philosophical practice, for both Śaṅkara and Plotinus, is to recapture knowledge of underlying oneness. In the Indian tradition, attempts to describe this knowledge first appear in the Upaniṣads.

Before the Upaniṣads, Hinduism had recognized three means of spiritual advancement, two of them from the Vedic culture and one surviving from pre-Vedic times: ritual sacrifices inherited from Vedic cult; the study of sacred scripture, that is, of the Vedas; and asceticism (*tapas*), the old shamanic way of attaining special powers. In the Hindu tradition, where religious formulations were not lightly altered and the Vedic rite, along with Vedic scripture, had absolute authority, the new Upaniṣadic doctrine of knowledge of *brahman* coexisted somewhat uneasily with the old ways. The *Brahmā Sūtra*, for example, though it is committed above all to the theme of *brahman*, still holds that sacrifice is a necessary aid to attaining the knowledge of one's true nature (III.4.26), and the conservative doctrine of the qualified nondualists (*viśiṣṭādvaitin*) advises a combination of works and knowledge. Nevertheless, the *brahman-ātman* doctrine was revolutionary, and was clearly incompatible with the old means: Sacrifice assumes a subject-object relationship; the polytheism of the Vedas was superseded—philosophically anyway—by the monism of the Upaniṣads; and asceticism is transformation-oriented—whereas what is needed, according to the new doctrine, is not to become *brahman* but to come to know that one already *is*.

According to the Upaniṣads, this special knowledge (which is equivalent to the Orphic recollection of its original home among the gods) is to be gained not by austerity or sacrifice but by direct self-seeing, or meditation. The *Muṇḍaka Upaniṣad* expresses this revolution in religious theory and practice:

> He [the *brahman*] is not grasped by the eye nor even by speech, nor by other sense-organs, nor by austerity (*tapas*), nor by work (sacrifice), but when one's (intellectual) nature is purified by the light of knowledge then alone he, by meditation, sees Him who is without parts. (III.1.8)

How did this new method arise? "Previously," says an Upaniṣad, "all men looked outward through the senses; then a wise man looked within, and saw the Self" (*Kaṭha* IV.1–2). The Upaniṣads sometimes say that the older types of religious practice are henceforth to serve only as preparations for the direct intuition of oneness through meditation (*BU* IV.4.22; *CU* II.23.1; *Kena* IV.8, etc.), and the third book of the *Brahmā Sūtra* lists the meditations they suggest.

When through meditation the yogi has perceived the *brahman*, according to the general Upaniṣadic version, he becomes free of karma; his past karma dissolves and no further karma will accrue. Like the Orphic practitioner in Greece, he will have perceived, or remembered, his true nature, and will not be born again. For Śaṅkara it seems that at this point the individual soul disappears into the One. The *Brahmā Sūtra* takes its usual *bhedābheda* position: The soul is now indistinguishable from the *brahman* yet somehow maintains its individuality forever in a condition like a god. "The liberated self can actualize his desires by mere will (*saṃkalpād eva*) . . . [he] is without a lord (*adhipati*), for he himself is his own lord and anything he wishes he can realize . . ."[26] Here the *Brahmā Sūtra* combines the Upaniṣadic *brahman/ātman* doctrine with elements from earlier afterlife myths.

The Upaniṣads, like the Advaitins, are less ambivalent about this. Their underlying epistemological-ontological point is that one is what one knows. As the *Muṇḍaka Upaniṣad* puts it: "He who knows the Supreme Brahman becomes Brahman himself" (III.2.8, 9). This knowledge supersedes the Vedic polytheism, which is based on the separateness of beings: "Whoever knows thus, 'I am Brahman,' becomes this all. Even the gods cannot prevent his becoming thus, for he becomes their self" (*BU* I.4.10); when the soul becomes the all, he also becomes the Vedic gods, who thus no longer have power over him. This "knowledge," since it does not involve a subject-object relationship but rather the annihilation of all difference between subject and object, is not cognitive in the ordinary sense. The *Kaṭha Upaniṣad* presents it as the absolute contradiction of all that is ordinarily regarded as knowledge. "When the five (sense) knowledges together with the mind cease (from their normal activities) and the intellect itself does not stir, that, they say, is the highest state" (II.3.10). The *ātman* is the absolute subject, the knower of all knowledge, and hence its knowledge is completely infolded or nonmanifest:

> For where there is duality as it were, there one smells another, there one sees another, there one hears another, there one speaks to another, there one thinks of another, there one understands another. Where, verily, everything has become the Self, then by what and whom should one smell, then by what and whom should one see, then by what and whom should one hear, then by what and to whom should one speak, then by what and on whom should one think, then by what and whom should one understand? By what should one know that by which all this is known? By what, my dear, should one know the knower? (*BU* II.4.14)

The *brahman* is the knower in all acts of knowing and the senser in all acts of sensing. So the idea of knowing the *brahman* is circular, like Aristotle's thought that thinks itself (*noēsis noēseōs*). This is expressed in a variety of metaphors, as the fingertip trying to touch itself, the knife trying to cut itself, and so on. Still, though the contradiction in terms of ordinary types of knowing is acknowledged, the mind is declared capable of knowing absolute unity. "By mind alone," says the *Kaṭha Upaniṣad*, "is this to be obtained. There is nothing of variety here" (II.1.11). Sometimes the paradox is openly acknowledged: *Brahman* is described as the knowledge "by which the unhearable becomes heard, the unperceivable becomes perceived, the unknowable becomes known" (*CU* VI.1.3). Since *brahman* is everything, knowledge of *brahman* is a kind of omniscience. "[He who] knows Brahman, he knows the worlds, he knows the *Vedas*, he knows beings, he knows the self, he knows everything" (*BU* III.7.1).

This knowledge is not approached by the traditional types of discipline. "Not by learning is the ātman attained, not by genius and much knowledge of books" (*Kaṭha* II.23). In fact, it requires the rejection of ordinary types of knowledge, even a rejection of the whole Vedic-Aryan educational system. It goes beyond both the Vedas and the traditional social responsibilities of the stages of life (*aśramas*). "Let a *Brahmin* renounce learning and become as a child," says the *Bṛhadāraṇyaka Upaniṣad* (III.5.1). The *brahman* is the knowledge object "from which all speech and the mind turn away, unable to reach it" (*TU* II.4). "The eye does not go thither, nor speech, nor mind. We do not know, we do not understand, how anyone can teach it" (*Kena* II.3). Sometimes the two opposed meanings of the word "knowledge" are brought into deliberate contrast: "It is unknown to those who know, and known to those who do not know" (*Kena* II.3). This knowledge of absolute sameness erases all appearance of difference. It is "the abyss of the eternal unity," says a later or "new" Upaniṣad; in it "all distinctions of being and knowing vanish, the entire expanse of the universe is obliterated, and even god is swallowed up in the abyss" (*Nrisimhottara-tāpanīya Up.* 1).[27] It is not the accumulation of many small knowledges, "not a mass of cognition" (*Ma. U.* 7). In fact, it is "not cognitive, not non-cognitive" (ibid.). It is the "non-thought that stands in the midst of thought, the unthinkable, the hidden . . ." (*Maitrī* VI.19).

This concept of knowledge is one part of a three part doctrine that is among the deepest and most characteristic structures of Early Iron Age thought: (1) that the self is the same as the ultimate, but (2) it has forgotten its real nature and needs to regain the knowledge of it although (3) this knowledge is so unlike what is usually called knowledge as to be the annihilation of it. This complex, present as Orphism in Greek philosophy at or near its beginning, was still fully present and alive in Plotinus's day. He seems to speak of the same special "knowledge" which constitutes the evanishment of the small self in the great.[28]

Knowing the One for Plotinus

The act of knowledge that is necessary to reawaken awareness of oneness with the All is described by Plotinus much as by the Upaniṣadic authors. It is an act of knowledge in which "the subject is its own object . . . The intellection is the more profound for this internal possession of the object" (*Enn.* VI.6.1). The type of knowledge in which subject and object are one is the "thought that thinks itself" that Aristotle attributed to the Prime Mover, and Plotinus calls such knowing "primal intellection." When the mind cognizes something external to it the act "cannot be the primally intellective since it does not possess the object as integrally its own or as itself—the condition of true intellection" (VI.6.1). He calls primal knowing "a unity in duality . . . being dual by the fact of intellection and single by the fact that its intellectual object is itself" (VI.6.1). This primal act of knowing, in other words, is simply an ultimate self-awareness. It is absolutely opposed to what is usually called knowledge, which is awareness of an other. It simply annuls all ordinary knowledge. One must turn one's back on all ordinary acts of thinking and knowing in order to know primally. Similarly in the Vedāntic schools, knowledge of *brahman* (*parā vidyā*) is opposed to and in fact annuls all other acts of knowledge (*apara vidyā*) because it is nondual knowledge.

This nondual knowledge is so primal that every sentient being is regarded as already permeated with it at a level so basic and personal that one cannot even see it. "It does not have to come and so be present to you," says Plotinus, "it is you that have turned from it" (VI.6.12). And Śaṅkara: "It only removes the false notion, it does not create anything" (*Commentary on the Bṛhadāraṇyaka Upaniṣad* I.4.10).

Differences between the two doctrines usually result from the fact that Plotinus is using the Platonic three-leveled ontology and the Vedānta is using the older Parmenidean-Upaniṣadic two-leveled model. The act of primal intellection is Plotinus's description of a mind which has realized its identity with the intermediate realm of Universal Mind, not with the ultimate One, whereas Yājñavalkya and Śaṅkara are speaking of oneness with *brahman*, the ultimate One. Plotinus is of two minds about this. In one mood he says that Mind is the highest element in our nature (I.1.8) and warns against the attempt to ascend beyond the infinite splendor of this realm of eternal Ideas (*Treatise Against the Gnostics*). Often, however, he expresses another mood about it. Once he calls the soul "hyperontic," or beyond being, a description that applies only to the One (*Enn.* VI.9.7). Again, he calls the soul explicitly "hypernoetic" or beyond mind (IV.8.1). Once he states that the soul "lays aside all the shape it has taken, even to the Intellectual shape that has informed it [i.e., Mind] . . . so that it may be alone with the alone" (VI.7.34).

This state Plotinus describes from his own experience not as a unity-in-duality, like the oneness with Mind, but as an absolute unity. "It was not a vision compassed," he says, "but a unity apprehended. The man formed by this mingling with the Supreme . . . is become the Unity, nothing within him or without inducing any diversity" (*Enn.* VI.9.11). The system of telescoping emanations does not make any sense without this element. As Plotinus says of the principle of regression, "All things return to the One" (V.2.1). "There is no longer a duality," he says of his own experience, "but two in one; for so long as the presence holds, all distinction fades" (VI.7.34). As an Upaniṣad said, "all distinctions of being and knowing vanish."

Plotinus repeatedly refers to the One as the First or Supreme Self (*autos*) (VI.8.14; V.1.1). The Upaniṣads, of course, use the same terminology when saying the *brahman* is the *ātman*, or self, of all. The point is that the One is characterized by utter simplicity. It is nonrelational, simply itself, self-identical, self-defining, itself as itself and nothing more, nothing added on to a nature which is pure and simple self-sameness. This idea is contradictory inherently in terms of ordinary thinking. To be self-same one must have some quality or other to be the same as; the One is declared to have no qualities except self-sameness, to be, as it were, a blank or void of self-sameness. The One, says Plotinus, is "cause of itself; for itself and of itself, It is what It is, the first self, transcendently the Self" (VI.8.14). Similarly in the Upaniṣads: "That which is the subtle essence, this whole world has for its self. That is the true. That is the self" (*CU* VI.10.4). The concept of the ultimate as pure selfhood or self-identity provides a way to know the self, namely the kind of immediate present intuition with which we know ourselves rather than our objects. "When one beholds the First Principle," Plotinus says, "one does not behold it as different from one's self, but as one with one's self" (VI.9.10). Similarly, in the *Bṛhadāranyaka Upaniṣad*: "Whoever worships another divinity (than his self), thinking that he is one and (Brahman) another, he knows not" (I.4.10).

The two traditions are in agreement about this on every point. Plotinus, for example, emphasizes that in that state "reasoning is in abeyance and all intellect" (VI.9.11). The *Kaṭha Upaniṣad* stresses the same point: "When the five senses together with the mind cease (from their normal activities) and the intellect itself does not stir, that, they say, is the highest state" (II.3.10). Again, both agree that this condition cannot be willed to happen. "We must not run after it," says Plotinus, "but fit ourselves for the vision and then wait tranquilly for its appearance" (V.5.8). And the *Kaṭha Upaniṣad*: "This self cannot be attained by instruction, nor by intellectual power, nor even through much hearing. He is to be attained only by the one whom the (self) chooses" (I.2.23). In a locution that shows how close are the Orphic and the Upaniṣadic discourses, Plotinus defines "acquiring identity with the Divine" as "awakening into myself" (IV.8.6). Since the self is already there, how can it be sought? Since the self is what would seek, how can it be sought?

The Individual and the All in Plotinus

Plotinus's three-leveled universe is more complex than the two-leveled universe of the Vedānta and leaves more options for the fate of the soul once it has gained knowledge of its self and attained release from the "prison" of the body (*soma sema*). In a sense the three realms—World Soul (containing the phenomenal world), Mind (containing the Platonic Ideas), and the One—may be conceived as concentric circles, each level containing the previous; but in another sense the image is inaccurate, as the One would more appropriately be located at the center. Soul, for Plotinus, is a dynamic continuum which is able to adapt to each of these different modes of being. He seems to have had varying moods in regard to which level the soul most inherently belongs to. He always says that the individual soul, if truly known, would be seen to be one with the World Soul—the universal soul of the realm of phenomenality. Sometimes he declares that it would, in addition, expand to the next concentric circle (or rise to the next higher level) and include Mind also, where the Platonic forms reside. Finally, there are a few passages where he says that the individual soul is, in its true nature, one with the ultimate One, the highest level (if one sees the process as a series of three stages of up-and-down emanation and return) or the largest circle, which contains the others—that the soul, upon realization, "becomes the all," understanding the "all" in the largest possible sense.

In another way of picturing it, the soul may be said to have two realities—embodied and disembodied, in "prison" or out. On the one hand, it is an individual embodied self; on the other, it has higher realms within it. This dual human nature, both immanent and transcendent, Plotinus expresses by saying that humans are "amphibious" (IV.8.4.32). The individual soul is made up of a changeable part and an unchangeable part. The former is limited to the embodied state in which it is moved about by incoming sensations; the latter is eternal and belongs in higher realms. Similarly, an Upaniṣad says, "This same breathing spirit," that is, the embodied individual, "is truly . . . ageless, immortal" (*KU* III.8). In Plotinus's system the conditions of this lower embodied soul are much the same as in the Upaniṣads: It is subject to cyclical time and morally directed reincarnation in different bodies until it shall have risen high enough—that is, into a human incarnation for which the study of philosophy is available—to attain release.[29]

Both Plotinus and the Upaniṣads teach that when the soul descends into matter it first puts on a body of thin, almost immaterial stuff, then, as it descends farther and farther, puts on successively heavier layers of consciousness/corporeality (*Enn.* IV.3.15; *TU* 2). These sheaths do not replace one another, but accumulate, so that the soul finally is encased in a series of layers. Plotinus distinguishes five layers of consciousness or soul: the vegetative consciousness, which is the body; the perceptual consciousness, which receives and organizes sense-data; the intellective consciousness, which is the higher aspect of the realm of Soul, where it merges into Mind; and the unified consciousness, which is at one in the One. In one of the more remarkable convergences of detail, the *Taittirīya Upaniṣad* distinguishes exactly the same five levels of consciousness: first matter (*annā*), then vital spirit (*prāṇa*), perceptual mind (*māna*), conceptualizing mind (*vijñāna*), and bliss mind (*ānanda*).

For both Plotinus and the Upaniṣadic teachers, the soul that has remained emotionally identified with its lower, embodied, changeable aspect will go on into further incarnations, perhaps animal or vegetable ones, remaining lost, and wandering on in the abyss of non-being or illusion. But one who realizes his identity with higher soul will transcend change, and hence transcend causality and *karma*. "He does not become great by good actions or small by evil actions" anymore (*KU* III.8). "The one within all beings is not tainted by the sorrow of the world, as He is outside (the world)" (*Kaṭha* II.2.11). For Plotinus, after realizing identity with Higher Soul, a further step of expanded awareness will reveal oneness with Universal Mind, which Higher Soul is always lost in contemplating. But somewhat like the *Brahmā Sūtra*, he usually does not follow the soul right through its annihilation when it disappears completely into the One, because then the soul can no longer be said to exist at all. Instead, it is the intermediate plane of Universal Mind (the realm of the Ideas) which he sees as the soul's natural abode, because there it is both the same as and different from the One; it both exists with the One, and yet exists as itself. "We remain one with ultimate Mind, but by our lower edge we are tied to the world below" (*Enn.* III.4.3).[30] The entire universe, in all its various modes, remains a living continuum. "Every being is in identity with its prior as long as it holds that contact" (*Enn.* V.2.2). Embodied or Lower Soul contacts Higher Soul, which contacts Mind, which contacts the One. The path of regression leads back up the great chain of Being from everywhere.

Plotinus echoes the Orphic model of the Fall and Salvation, which never lost its grip on the Greek—or indeed the European—tradition.[31] Every soul, he says, has an affinity with Mind, because it originally lived there, and though it has descended into lower realms, its home remains on high. He does not say it originally lived in the One, because when it is in the One it does not exist and cannot be said to live anywhere. Man's self, says Plotinus, "came from the Transcendent, and the essential man is [remains] There" (*Enn.* I.2.6.7). Hence the soul "ascends to Mind" and "becomes God" (I.7.6.7), much as the liberated soul is said in the *Brahmā Sūtra* to still retain enough of a separate nature to have the life of a god. When it "becomes god" the soul is not undergoing a transformation, but realizing or remembering the true nature which it possessed all along but forgot about. The reason it forgets (as in Plato's *Phaedo*) is that once it is plunged into the body the meaningless chaos of sensory input distracts and confuses it. The bodily nature—the densest of the sheaths or prison walls—is added on to the original and true Mind nature of the self, as *avidyā* is added on in Vedānta. As the self, in the Upaniṣads, is above *karma* when it is identified with *brahman*, and is not tainted by the sorrow of the world, so, for Plotinus, the soul, when one with Mind, "demonstrates that all evil is accretion, alien, and that in the purged soul the noble things are immanent" (*Enn.* IV.7.10). The soul, insofar as it is One with Mind is god; insofar as it is lower embodied Soul it is a *daimon*—Empedocles' term for the fallen Orphic god. Plotinus preserves not only the Empedoclean-Orphic tone but, at times, the tone of the Egyptian *Book of the Dead* which lay behind it: "Becoming man, he has ceased to be the All; ceasing to be man . . . he soars aloft and administers the Cosmos entire; restored to the All, he is the maker of the All" (*Enn.* V.8.7). As in the Upaniṣads and the *Brahmā Sūtra*, the individual self, when understood in its identity with the higher principle, is seen to be in one sense the entire universe and in another sense the maker or controller or inner essence of the universe. "Restored to the All," Plotinus says, "he is the maker of the all." Says the *Bṛhadāraṇyaka Upaniṣad*, "Whoever has found and awakened to the self that has entered into this perilous inaccessible place (the body), he is the maker of the universe, for he is the maker of all" (*BU* IV.4.13). In the *Brahmā Sūtra* also, the *brahman* from which the soul becomes indistinguishable is not only the universe but also the cause or maker of the universe (I.1.2, II.1.14).

It is worth quoting a passage at some length because it is a model of the interpenetration of the Greek and Indian styles of thought; here the Indian emphasis on transformation interpenetrates with the Parmenidean Greek emphasis on the binary logic of Being. It is a conceptual portrait of the intersection where Indian philosophy and Greek philosophy touch one another at a historical moment.

> In that you have entered into the All, no longer content with the part, you cease to think of yourself as under limit but, laying all such determination aside, you become an All. No doubt you were always that, but there has been an addition, and by that addition you are diminished; for the addition was not from the realm of Being—you can add nothing to Being—but from non-Being. It is not by some admixture of non-Being that one becomes an entire, but by putting non-Being away. By the lessening of the alien in you, you increase. Cast it aside and there is the All within you; engaged in the alien, you will not find the All. Not that it has to come and so be present to you; it is you that have turned from it. And turn though you may, you have not severed yourself; it is there; you are not in some far region; still there before it, you have looked the other way. (*Enn.* VI.6.12)[32]

Having said that the individual soul will become an All, Plotinus hastens to add, "No doubt, you were always that." Here the Orphic doctrine of recollection and the Vedāntic doctrine of *brahmātman*—the oneness of *brahman* and *ātman*—coincide. In his "addition that diminishes," Plotinus indulges the characteristic Greek love of paradox, and especially of paradoxical formulations of the relationship between the concepts Being and non-Being, which go back to Gorgias and Zeno, if not to Father Parmenides himself. The addition of non-Being to the soul refers, in the spirit of Platonic Orphism, to the fall into matter, which is absolute non-Being. It involves a rejection of the value of the embodied self like that in Plato's *Phaedo*. Remove the element of non-Being—which for Plotinus as for Plato, and as for the Upaniṣadic-Vedāntic tradition, if in slightly different terms, is matter or the body—and one is knowingly what one has always unknowingly been—the All, the Totality, the Universal Mind. As in the Vedāntic tradition, the embodied self is seen as *māyā*, or nonreality, and, again as in the Vedānta, the return to one's true nature is not so much transformation as a kind of recollection or realization. One has turned away from the true and unchanging part of oneself, and locked one's gaze as in a dream onto the screen of illusion that is matter—"a sketch upon a shadow," empty images thrown upon the darkness of non-Being by distant reflections of the splendor of Mind filtering the rays of the One. The concept of "what is alien in you" again derives from the Orphic roots of this Greek view of life—the idea that the soul, in entering into matter, has come into a foreign and alien country from which it must find its way back. "Cast it aside," Plotinus exhorts, meaning the involvement in the alien country of matter. No matter how far one has wandered, the All is directly present as soon as one turns toward it. "Right there before it—you look the other way."

Notes to Chapter Twenty-Two

1. I. C. Sharma, "Some Critical Conclusions," *Neoplatonism and Indian Thought*, ed. R. Baine Harris (Norfolk, Virginia: International Society for Neoplatonic Studies, 1982), p. 328.

2. John J. O'Meara expresses skepticism ("Indian Wisdom and Porphyry's Search," in ibid., pp. 11–12.

3. J. Filliozat, "La doctrine des brahmanes d'après saint Hippolyte," *Revue de l'Histoire des Religions* 130 (1945): p. 60; *Les relations exterieures de l'Inde* 1 (Pondichery, 1956), p. 48.

4. J. F. Staal, *Advaita and Neoplatonism* (Madras: University of Madras, 1961), p. 245.

5. See, for the first position, Emile Brehier, *The Philosophy of Plotinus*, trans. Joseph Thomas (Chicago: University of Chicago Press, 1958); for the second, Staal, *Advaita and Neoplatonism*, p. 246.

6. Richard T. Wallis, "Phraseology and Imagery in Plotinus and Indian Thought," *Neoplatonism and Indian Thought*, ed. Harris, p. 115. Wallis remarks: "In light of such parallels I find the hypothesis of cultural contact hard to resist" (ibid.).

7. Albert M. Wolters, "A Survey of Modern Scholarly Opinion on Plotinus and Indian Thought," in *Neoplatonism and Indian Thought*, ed. Harris, p. 295.

8. Jean Trouillard, "Le neoplatonisme," in Encyclopédie de la Pléiade, *Histoire de la philosophie I* (Paris: Gallimard, 1969), p. 891.

9. H. R. Schwyzer "Plotin," *RE* XXI (1951), cols. 580–581, quoted by Wolters in "A Survey of Modern Scholarly Opinion on Plotinus and Indian Thought," p. 297.

10. Vicenzo Cilento, *Antologia plotiniana* (Bari, 1970), p. 17, quoted ibid., p. 296.

11. A. W. Benn, *History of Ancient Philosophy*, London n.d., p. 139, quoted by Wolters, "A Survey of Modern Scholarly Opinion on Plotinus and Indian Thought," p. 296.

12. Compare C. L. Tripathi, "Influence of Indian Philosophy," in *Neoplatonism and Indian Thought*, ed. Harris, pp. 279, 283:

> Those scholars who try to find the hypostases of Plotinus in the 'Trinity' of Plato and the simile of One and the sun in the *Republic* [and so on] and then emphatically assert that Neoplatonism is a legitimate development of Greek thought and Plato's own speculations—forget the fact that these [earlier] philosophers were also influenced by Indian thought through Orphicism and Pythagoreanism. In fact, the philosophy of Plato and even that of his independent disciple Aristotle was a kind of splendid digression from the main current of Greek speculation . . . In Plato's philosophy . . . there is not even a single concept which is in tune with the Greek theology.

13. John M. Rist, *Plotinus: The Road to Reality* (Cambridge: Cambridge University Press, 1967), p. 7.

14. Plotinus will usually be quoted in the translation of Stephen MacKenna: *The Enneads, by Plotinus*, 2nd. ed., revised by B. S. Page (New York: Pantheon Books, 1957), occasionally in that of Elmer O'Brien, *The Essential Plotinus* (New York: New American Library, 1964).

15. Of the thirteen "old" Upaniṣads (*Bṛhadāraṇyaka, Chāndogya, Aitareya, Kauṣītaki, Taittirīya, Kena, Īśa, Kathaka, Muṇḍaka, Praśna, Śvetāśvatara, Maitrī*, and *Māṇḍukya*) the latest, the *Māṇḍukya*, is regarded as having been composed not long before 200 A.D. (Hajime Nakamura, *A History of Early Vedānta Philosophy*, [Delhi: Motilal Banarsidass, 1989], p. 42). Bādarāyana, who has long been regarded as the author of the *Brahmā Sūtra*, is dated by Nakamura to the first century B.C. (ibid., p. 407). I follow Nakamura in regarding him not as the author but rather as one of the anonymous author's main sources: "[I]t is a definite fact that the [*Brahmā*] *Sūtra* is not a work by Bādarāyana" (ibid., p. 406). The *Brahmā Sūtra* was a compilation from various sources of various dates. "[W]e can take it," says Nakamura, "that 400–450 is the period during which the *Brahmā -Sūtra* was compiled in its present form. Nevertheless . . . the great part of the *Sūtra* must have been in existence much earlier than that . . . the sections of the *Sūtra* which deal directly with verses of the *Upaniṣads*. . . can be taken, for the most part, to have been compiled prior to the Christian era" (ibid., p. 436). So in Plotinus's time any one of the older *Upaniṣads* might have found its way to Egypt, as well as the thought of Bādarāyana—but not the *Brahmā Sūtra* in its present form.

16. Ibid., pp. 438, 425.

17. Ibid., p. 434.

18. The Upaniṣads will be quoted in the translation of Sarvepalli Radhakrishnan, *The Principal Upaniṣads* (London: George Allen and Unwin, 1953).

19. Nakamura, *A History of Early Vedānta Philosophy*, p. 485.

20. Staal feels that Plotinus's distinction between the state of Being (the hypostasis of Mind) and the state beyond Being (the One) parallels the Vedāntic distinction between *nirguna brahman* and *saguṇa brahman* (*Advaita and Neoplatonism*, pp. 179ff.). But *saguṇa brahman* is phenomenality or nature, and for Plotinus Mind exists in a much different and metaphysically higher sense than this. The Advaitic terminology is inadequate here because its dualism cannot describe the Plotinian version of the Great Chain of Being, with its three or four ontological levels.

21. Sarvepalli Radhakrishnan, *The Brahmā Sūtra: The Philosophy of Spiritual Life* (London: George Allen and Unwin, 1960), p. 41.

22. Ibid., p. 45.

23. For phantoms see, for example, *Vigraha Vyāvartanī*, II.27 (Frederick J. Streng, *Emptiness: A Study in Religious Meaning* [Nashville, Tennessee: Abingdon Press, 1967], p. 224); for the image of the mirror: Candrakīrti, *Prasannapadā* (see Edward Conze, ed., *Buddhist Texts through the Ages* [New York: Harper and Row, 1964], p. 167).

24. Nakamura, *A History of Early Vedānta Philosophy*, p. 486.

25. See, for example, Rist (*Plotinus*, p. 112): "The two positions may be incompatible, the result of conflicting pressures which Plotinus was never able to resolve."

26. Nakamura, *A History of Early Vedānta Philosophy*, pp. 529–530.

27. Quoted by Paul Deussen, *The Philosophy of the Upaniṣads* (New York: Dover, 1966), p. 179.

28. Some have seen this doctrine of the complete evanishment of the individual into the One in Plotinus, others have denied it. (It is seen by William R. Inge, *Christian Mysticism; Considered in Eight Lectures Delivered Before the University of Oxford*, 6th ed. [London: Methuen, 1925], p. 97; Emile Brehier, *The Philosophy of Plotinus*, trans. Joseph Thomas (Chicago: University of Chicago Press, 1958), chapter 7; Olivier Lacombe, "Note sur Plotin et la pensée indienne," *Annuaire de l'.École Pratique des Hautes Etudes, Section des Sciences Religieuses* [1950–1951]. It is not seen by René Arnou, *Le désir de dieu dans la philosophie de Plotin*, *2éme* ed. revue et corrigée [Rome: Presses de l'Université Gregorienne, 1967], pp. 247 ff.; Rist, *Plotinus*, p. 229; R. T. Wallis, *Neoplatonism* [London: Duckworth, 1972], p. 89; Arthur H. Armstrong, *The Cambridge History of Later Greek and Early Medieval Philosophy* [Cambridge: Cambridge University Press, 1967],

p. 263. But Armstrong expresses himself somewhat differently in *The Architecture of the Intelligible Universe in the Philosophy of Plotinus, An Analytical and Historical Study* [Cambridge: Cambridge University Press, 1940], p. 4: "The boundaries shutting off the self from the universe are largely illusory and disappear in the higher stages of perception.")

The widespread feeling that Greek thinkers shied away from the infinite has prejudiced discussions of this point. Yet Greek thinkers discovered the concept of infinity and formulated it in every important mode discovered before nineteenth-century mathematical formulations. It was a concept they used often and positively. It may be that this view arose from the finity-emphatic Christian view of Greek thought, not from Greek sources themselves.

Plotinus sometimes speaks as if the small self vanishes totally into the macrocosmic or great self in the moment of knowing it, and at other times he is less convinced of the totality of this evanishment; the scholars on both sides of the issue have some justification. In the Vedāntic tradition the same ambiguity of expression occurs. It seems that the old view of the individual self enjoying the afterlife in heaven has not totally disappeared with the appearance of the Upaniṣadic concept of becoming the *ātman* through knowing it. See Nakamura, *A History of Early Vedānta Philosophy*, p. 529.

29. The idea of cyclical time appeared in the Upaniṣadic tradition with the *Śvetāśvatara Upaniṣad* (III.2; IV.1; V.3), became standard in Hindu texts by the age of the Purāṇas, and remained so throughout the Vedāntic centuries. Plotinus (IV.3.12–19; V.7.3.13–18) inherited it from Plato, but with Stoic influence that made it significantly different from the Upaniṣadic-Vedāntic version. For the Vedānta, a soul which has obtained the knowledge of its identity with *brahman* is freed forever from the process of birth and death. If, at the end of a world cycle, one has not obtained this knowledge, one's rebirths simply start again in the next cycle right where they ended in the last; *karma*, in other words, survives cycles and *mokṣa* transcends them. Plotinus saw the relations between cosmic time and the destiny of the soul differently. He adopted the Stoic doctrine of the exact cyclical recurrence of events, so that the soul which has returned to Oneness will redescend in each successive cosmic cycle and undergo its process of rebirths and salvation through knowledge all over again. The doctrine seems strangely out of harmony with both Plotinus's emphasis on free will and his attention to the desire to rise through the spheres. Really, it seems that the salvationist doctrine of escape from reincarnation was never as real to the Greeks as to the Indians. Though it is a standard feature of Greek philosophy almost as much as of Indian, the Greeks seldom express the desire to go beyond this world with the intensity that Indian philosophers seem to have felt about it. This distinction may reflect the importedness of this doctrine in Greece and its indigenous development in India.

30. Trans. Armstrong (*The Architecture of the Intelligible Universe*), slightly altered.

31. For instances of the Orphic view reappearing as a theme of contemporary art see Thomas McEvilley, *Sculpture in the Age of Doubt* (New York: Allworth Press, 1999).

32. MacKenna's translation, slightly altered.

Chapter Twenty-Three

Plotinus and Vijñānavāda Buddhism

The parallels between Neoplatonism and the Upaniṣadic-Vedāntic tradition are basic, extensive, and thorough, applying to structural patterns, to details within them, and, often, even to styles of expression. Yet the Upaniṣadic-Vedāntic tradition differs radically from Neoplatonism in that it recognizes only two aspects or levels of being. (Though the *bhedābheda* approach is a preliminary attempt to address this problem, it was not followed up and carried through.) Structurally, a more complete parallelism is found between Plotinus's model of the universe and that of the "three-level" (*trisvabhāva*) schools of Buddhism.

Three Levels in Plotinus

Plotinus teaches that the universe is made up of three levels, called in Greek *hypostases*, each one corresponding to a different type of being and a different type of consciousness. The highest level Plotinus calls, after Plato, the Good, or the One. It goes back to formulations by Plato such as the form-beyond-forms of the *Republic* and the negatively defined One-Absolute of the first two hypotheses of the *Parmenides*. Plotinus describes the One as completely infolded, undifferentiated, formless, and qualityless. It is called the One, he says (*Enn.* V.5.6), only to indicate that it is not many; in fact, even oneness cannot be predicated of it, since it is beyond predication and beyond dualities, such as the duality between One and Many. In epistemic terms, it is pure subject without object. It produces by a kind of unintentional radiation or emanation a second, lower level called Mind.

Whereas the One is an absolute unity, Mind is a unity-in-plurality made up both of Aristotle's self-knowing mind and Plato's realm of Ideas. It may also be described as a dual unity, since it has two aspects, an "upper" and a "lower." Its upper aspect is in direct contact with the One from which it emanates, and is permeated with unity through and through. It is an ontological-epistemic stage before the alienation of subject and object has taken place. Here it is not a matter of Mind knowing the Ideas. Rather, Mind and Ideas are totally permeated or interpenetrated with one another. Each of the Ideas is itself Mind knowing all the Ideas. Every part, in this realm, is equal to the whole. As Plotinus says: "All is all and each is all and the splendor of it is infinite" (*Enn.* V.8.4).

Two Forces

Following Plato, Plotinus compares the One to the sun and the process of "creation" to irradiation of sunlight outward from the sun. This process, which is called emanation or progression, is balanced by a force of regression which draws separate forms back toward the One. Plotinus sometimes, following Empedocles, calls this force Love, and at other times calls it Contemplation. This force draws back to the One all that the force of progression draws away from it. Distantly behind the formulation lie not only Empedocles' forces of Love and Strife but Heraclitus's Up and Down Paths. As the force of progression proceeds outward from the One, the force of regression increasingly slows its outward flow till it is stabilized at a farthest remove, from which it then flows back.

Soul

This outer edge of the universe, where the force of progression is slowed to a halt and turns around into the force of regression, is the third and lowest level, called Soul. Whereas the One is complete unity, and Mind is interpenetrated unity and multiplicity, Soul is separated unity and multiplicity. Whereas the One is immobile and static, and Mind is immobile and dynamic, Soul is mobile and dynamic. Whereas the One is absolute subject, and Mind is interpenetrated subject and object, Soul is alienated subject and object. Whereas the One corresponds to the *unio mystica*, and mind to direct intuition, Soul corresponds to discursive subject-object cognition.

Plotinus's level of Soul is in turn divided into two sublevels, one rapt in upward contemplation, the other dynamically involved below. The tradition of this distinction in Greek philosophy goes back from Plotinus through Middle Platonist and Neopythagorean sources to Aristotle's distinction between active and passive intellect, and ultimately to Plato's conception of the World Soul in the *Timaeus*. In Plotinus's model, Lower Soul is turned outward from the sunlike center of things toward the darkness of non-Being; onto that darkness as onto a screen it casts an image or reflection of Higher Soul's contemplation of Mind: This image or reflection *is* the cosmos. This image cast onto the darkness-stuff by Lower Soul *is* the world of experience. Plotinus calls this darkness and negativity *hulē*, a word usually, but somewhat misleadingly, translated "matter." "Non-Being" is more what is intended; matter was unreal for Plotinus as for both Plato and Parmenides before him. This "screen" on which empty images are cast might be regarded as a fourth level of the universe except that Plotinus does not wish to grant it that much substantiality.

Ontology or Epistemology?

Plotinus vacillates constantly between an emphasis on the ontic-ontological aspect of his system—the concern with being—and the mentalist-idealist aspect—the concern with consciousness. If one emphasizes the ontic-ontological aspect, the three hypostases mean something like unity, unity-in-multiplicity, and multiplicity. If one emphasizes the consciousness aspect, they are pure subjectivity, interpenetrated subject and object, alienated subject and object.

The tendency to regard ontological states as different configurations of consciousness goes back, in the Greek tradition, to Parmenides, and was common in the Platonic lineage, of which Plotinus felt himself to be a member. Xenocrates, second successor to Plato as head of the Academy, equated the One with Mind. Aristotle described the

Prime Mover as Self-Knowing Mind. Albinus divided the universe into an inward-turned nonactive Mind and an outward-turned, generative Mind. Numenius described absolute and relative realities as "Mind-at-Rest" and "Mind-in-Motion."

Plotinus inherited this tradition and gave it its most explicit formulation. He associated a specific kind of mental activity with each hypostasis, or metaphysical level. Lower Soul, or Nature, which is more or less the realm of phenomenality, is sensation and discursive one-thing-at-a-time reasoning. Higher Soul is a changeless unified vision of Mind. Mind is a complete and unchanging awareness of all reality by direct simultaneous intuition. The One is pure subjectivity with all manifestation of consciousness folded into itself (*Enn.* II.3.17–18; III.8.5, 8; IV.4.10–12; IV.8.3; V.1.12; V.3.3–5; V.4.2; V.6.1; V.8.3–6; VI.2.21; VI.7.9, 12, 15; VI.8.14; VI.9.3).

The levels may be sorted out like this:

One:	unity	totalizing awareness	pure subject
Mind:	unity-in-multiplicity	selective intuition	interpenetrated subject and object
Soul:	unity-and-multiplicity	discursive thought	separated subject and object
Matter:	multiplicity	sense perception	pure object[1]

Plotinus describes the universe as made up of different levels or degrees of subjectivity, which is to say, of pure mental reality (III.4.3; III.8.5, 7; IV.3.9; V.1.1; V.5.9). In his vision, ontology fades into epistemology and loses itself there (V.1.4). Mind *is* its own thoughts (V.9.5). It *is* what it beholds. Nature "*is* a vision of itself" (III.8.4). Creation is not so much a making (*poiēsis*) as a thinking (*theōria*): The act of contemplation *produces* the thing contemplated. "That all things," Plotinus says, "including those that are truly beings, are from consciousness [*theōria*] and are themselves consciousness is clear" (III.8.7).

Plotinus is not always consistent when he speaks about the question whether being or consciousness is prior. That being is produced by contemplation, or consciousness, means that mind is prior to being. But this is denied at *Enneads* V.9.7, and at VI.6.8 Plotinus says that Being is prior to Mind. Elsewhere he says that the two are simultaneous and mutually implicative (VI.7.2). This would seem to be his basic position.

Sometimes Plotinus is concerned that to call the One a kind of knowledge or consciousness would imply a subject-object division within it (V.6.1; V.3.12–13). To avoid this, he calls the One "a self-knowledge which *is* itself" (V.4.2) and a "superknowledge" (VI.8.1). It is "the pure, absolute, single subject, without any relation to external objects."[2] Plotinus does not call the subjective awareness of the One a *noēsis*, or act of knowing with subject and object, but an *epibolē*, literally a kind of hurling of oneself upon the object, an immediate intuition without self-discrimination (VI.7.38–39). Sometimes he calls it a "pre-knowing" (*pronoousa*) (VI.3.10). He notes that he is speaking loosely when he says, "The One, as it were, made itself by an act of looking at itself. This act of looking at itself is, in effect, its being" (VI.8.16). A little later in the same passage he calls the One "a wakefulness and an eternal superknowledge."

The universe is consciousness, or mental activity, at different levels of intensity, from the extremely vague and inert consciousness of stones and vegetables up to the highest contemplation, that of oneness with the One. Consciousness *is* being. The act of contemplation makes what it contemplates. "As I contemplate," says Nature, "the lines which bound bodies come to be as if they fell from my contemplation" (III.8.3–4).

The universe is a continuous medley of mental processes, or a single huge mind with different levels of activity going on in it at once. As awareness descends through these levels, it produces ever more thoughts so that the lower reaches of this mind are noisy and full of chaotic and disharmonious impulses bound together only by the illusory chain of causality; as it reascends, it produces at each higher level fewer, less object-oriented and fragmented thoughts, up to the objectless contemplation of the One.

The Two Forces Again

Contemplation is a force now operating downward through the levels and again upward through them. Descending contemplation and ascending contemplation are the forces binding the universal process together. The outward, downward, form-generating tendency of consciousness Plotinus calls the process of "progression," whereby the dependent levels of being descend or progress outward from the One. That this progress is considered a "descent" (*kathodos*) indicates its mythological background in the Orphic myth of the descent of the God/soul into matter.

The reverse tendency—the inward, upward, form-synthesizing tendency—Plotinus calls "regression" or "reversion." It is the force by which everything returns to the One. Each level is produced by a certain mental activity, consists of that activity, and is transcended in the reversion process by regressing to a more primal type of mental activity. What would seem, in terms of developmental psychology, the most infantile stage is preferred on the same grounds that cause the Upaniṣads sometimes to regard the state of dreamless sleep as preferable. Here again, the ancient Greeks espouse a view common in India and distinctly out of step with later European attitudes. The Piagetian attitude toward stages of cognitive development tends to place greater value on more discrimination and cogitation, as indeed do western attitudes in general. Consciousness is seen as fighting its way out of a swamp of unconsciousness. Yet Plotinus used the word "wakefulness" to describe a state which for Europeans would seem sleep and unconsciousness.[3]

Plotinus's model of the universe is of a bidirectional process: the progressive alienation of subject and object and their progressive reintegration. The One is the still center of the universal mind; matter is the outer surface of its disintegrating thought-activity. "There exist only subjects which are conscious and in which consciousness exists in varying degrees of concentration and purity."[4] Even at the lowest level, the sensory "soul" of the cosmos, there is really no object; rather, the subject, forgetting its exclusive self-identity, projects "bits" of itself "outward" as objects and fastens other bits of itself onto these as accompanying subjects (II.9.2; IV.3.5, 12–13; V.3.3–4; VI.4.3, 16). There is only subjectivity; the world of objectivity is dreamlike, reflection-like, unreal. The universe is made up of subjectivity alone, in differing degrees of concentration.

Parallels

Most modern western commentators have emphasized the ontological aspect of Neoplatonism, which brings Plotinus into line with Plato (and behind him Parmenides). When this emphasis is in place, the parallels between Plotinus and the Upaniṣadic-Vedāntic tradition come to the foreground. But if, on the other hand, the mentalist-idealist aspect is emphasized, then quite a different set of parallels emerges—parallels which are in fact more striking and detailed—those between Plotinus and the consciousness-only (*vijñānavāda*) schools of Buddhism.

The parallelism between the Plotinian and *trisvabhāva* models is deeper and closer than the Upaniṣadic comparison not only in that it involves a tripartite ontology, but also in that it emphasizes the concept of consciousness rather than the concept of being. Both Plotinian Neoplatonism and *trisvabhāva* Buddhism are forms of idealism, which is to say they sometimes posit consciousness as prior to and determinative of being.[5]

The doctrine which is closest to Plotinus is found in the Buddhist schools featuring the Consciousness doctrine, or the Consciousness-Only doctrine (*vijñānavāda*). This doctrine received several formulations, all after the time of Plotinus. The problem this view arose from was the question of how to explain karmic consequence. The *abhidharma* psychology recognized passing states of mind as the only reality, but did not recognize a substrate, an enduring level of consciousness or selfhood, in which present mind-moments could karmically ripen into future ones. Karmic debt was said to persist, but without any medium or matrix for it to persist in.

Three Levels in Buddhism

In the fourth century A.D., a century or a century and a half after Plotinus, the philosopher Vasubandhu sought to remedy this apparent contradiction through the concept of the Storehouse Consciousness (*ālayavijñāna*). The Storehouse is a level underlying all human mental activity and providing a bed in which the seeds of present thoughts can grow to fruition as future states of mind. The Storehouse is pure subjectivity, yet the appearance of objectivity arises out of it as its dream, or aura, or emanation, or fume. It is the dynamic source of everything. Vasubandhu describes it as "flowing like a torrent" (*Trimsikakārikā* 4).[6]

In *Trimsikakārikā*, Vasubandhu set out a doctrine of *trisvabhāva* or three levels. *Trisvabhāva* means three modes of being, but as Suzuki said, "Svabhāva in this case is to be understood as an epistemological term."[7] Vasubandhu was writing about individual psychology, not about the universe at large; but since his view is that the mind creates the world, the effect is the same. Each level of being is described as a level of consciousness. As in Plotinus, the overlap between ontology and epistemology is virtually complete. Each realm of being is created by the next higher one through what Plotinus would call a *poiēsis/theōria*, a making through contemplating. The three levels of being are three levels of consciousness. This system was given further definition in the *Laṅkāvatāra Sūtra* and the *Mahāyānaśradottpāda* or *Awakening of Mahāyāna Faith* (both probably around 400 A.D.), and was elaborated in the *Avatamsaka Sūtra* and in the texts of various Chinese schools based on it into a model virtually identical to Plotinus's.[8]

The fundamental parallelism of the Indian and Greek conceptions of three levels of being/consciousness is as follows:

Svabhāva:	Ontological/Epistemological Status:	Hypostasis:
pariniṣpanna	absolute being/knowledge	The One
paratantra	dependent being/knowledge	Mind
parikalpita	non-being/ignorance	Soul

The three levels represent "three densities in entitative value" or "three degrees of self-being" or self-identity. The lowest realm of being, called *parikalpita*, "signifies mere imagination, 'imagined being' as the shallow and null degree of entitative value that results from the activities of discrimination."[9] It "is the world of false discrimination, for it exhibits a mere manifold of mutually conflicting and deharmonized being . . . It is the realm of . . . mere particularity—the world of delusion."[10] "Its subjective side . . . presents a disconnected plurality of egos . . . (an) essenceless matter-bound subject. Its objective side [presents a] . . . deluded" sensation of feelings "which refer to a mere plurality of illusorily independent and self-standing objects."[11] This realm, says Suzuki, "is the fabrication of one's own imagination or mind."[12] And another scholar: "Objects in the external world are supposed to exist because of an assumption (*upācara*). In reality, they do not exist."[13]

The *Laṅkāvatāra Sūtra* frequently refers to this level as *māyā*, "magical illusion."[14] This level is ordinary phenomenality as experienced by a mind which has not yet begun to recognize its errors. It corresponds precisely to Plotinus's Soul, especially Lower Soul or Nature, the illusory realm of unlimited subjective discrimination which Plotinus describes as "non-being . . . a weak and dim phantom . . . a falsehood . . . a shadow . . . a passing trick [cf. *māyā*] . . . phantasms within a phantasm" (*Enn.* II.5.5; III.6.7; VI.3.8). The concepts are so closely related that Plotinus and the Buddhist authors often use the same metaphors to describe it. The *Awakening of Mahāyāna Faith*, for example, says:

> All things, therefore, are just like the images in a mirror which are devoid of any objectivity that one can get hold of. (3Bc2a)[15]

And Plotinus:

> [Particulars are] nothing but phantoms in a phantom, like something in a mirror . . . like things in a dream or water or a mirror. (*Enn.* III.6.7)

This correspondence holds good throughout the stages of the Buddhist Consciousness schools, from Vasubandhu to the Chinese commentators on the *Avataṃsaka* or *Hua Yen Sūtra*.

One/Mind and Storehouse

The correspondence in conceptions of the highest level arose in part after Vasubandhu. He identified the *pariniṣpanna* or highest level as the Storehouse Consciousness (*ālayavijñāna*). As such it is partly like Plotinus's One and partly like Plotinus's middle realm of Mind. Like the One, it is said to be unaware of all "clinging and sensation . . . indifferent to its associations . . . [and] not affected by the darkness of ignorance" (*Trimsikakarika* 3–4).[16] In this passage Vasubandhu is describing "the pure (*amala*) state" of the Storehouse; this aspect corresponds to Plotinus's One. He goes on, however, to attribute to the Storehouse an impure and differentiated aspect which "is always flowing like a torrent" (*Trimsikakarika* 4) and in which karmic seeds ripen. This aspect of the Storehouse is the active source of the differentiation of the lower realms. Plotinus, on the other hand, while acknowledging that the One must in some way be the ultimate source of differentiation, will not attribute to it any active part in that process (*Enn.* I.7.1; V.1.6). Vasubandhu's impure Storehouse-Consciousness is more like Plotinus's Mind; as Vasubandhu's *ālaya* is "always flowing like a torrent," so Plotinus describes Mind as "boiling with life" (*Enn.* VI.7.12).

In the *Laṅkāvatāra Sūtra* the conception of the highest realm is brought closer to Plotinus's One. Its authors show a scrupulousness about the unity of the Storehouse which is comparable to Plotinus's scrupulousness about the One: The Storehouse Consciousness, on their view, cannot be said to have either knowledge or being, for "that which is perfect is beyond the dualism of being and non-being" or knowledge and ignorance (*Lanka.* II.199).[17] The Storehouse now is regarded as the ultimate Supercognition, or the cognitive aspect of Suchness (*tathatā*), that is, of absolute self-identity or self-sameness. Aristotle's Self-Knowing Mind is a comparable conception. The Storehouse is "absolute knowledge . . . free from all discrimination of signs, names, entities, and marks."[18] In this formulation the Storehouse corresponds very closely to Plotinus's One as pure self-identity/self-awareness with no internal discrimination and no knowledge of the lower realms of being/consciousness which emanate from it and depend on it (*Enn.* V.5.12).

The various Chinese Buddhist schools in the Consciousness lineage brought the conception still closer to Plotinus's. The *She Lun* school, which was based on Vasubandhu's text, designated the highest level "immaculate consciousness" (*amalavijñāna*), or unchanging self-identity/self-awareness; it corresponds both to Plotinus's One as superknowledge without object, and to Vasubandhu's "pure state" of the Storehouse Consciousness.[19] The *She Lun* authors revised Vasubandhu conspicuously on this point. They demoted his concept of the impure aspect of the Storehouse consciousness to the second level, *paratantra*, where it now corresponds directly to Plotinus's Mind. The *Fa Hsiang* school reinstated the Storehouse in the highest level, but only after bringing it close to Plotinus's One by conceiving of it as "primordial unity, purity, and universality," an "absolute, infinitely open and self-related substratum," a "non-evolving . . . static superconsciousness," "a self-abiding, unrelated, empty and totally undifferentiated superconsciousness," "passive, unalterable and quiet," which "does not actively intervene in causative ideation."[20] This absolutism for the highest realm was solidified further in the *T'ien-t'ai* school, with its concept of "Mind of Pure Self-Nature."[21] It was maintained in the most Plotinian formulation of all, the *Hua Yen*, which will be discussed later.

There is a second major difference between Plotinus's One and Vasubandhu's Storehouse Consciousness. Vasubandhu presented his book not as a model of the cosmos but as a model of individual psychology. The Storehouse was like an unconscious mind behind each individual conscious mind. He postulated many Storehouses, one for each subject in the lowest or *parikalpita* realm. Like the other differences between them, this is most evident in Vasubandhu and is eliminated by the later schools. It is probable that the *Laṅkāvatāra Sūtra* meant to teach a single universal and eternal Storehouse; it is certain that the *Fa Hsiang* and *Hua Yen* schools did.

Paratantra and Nous

The most interesting and complex correspondence between levels is that between the middle realms, *paratantra* and *Nous* or Mind. Here, too, the difference is most marked at the Indian stages of the tradition and virtually insignificant at the Hua Yen stage. With regard to the Indian schools, the following similarities hold:

(1) The *paratantra* level, though it has some degree of reality and cognizability, exists only in dependence on the highest level; Plotinus's Mind, similarly, while it has a degree of ontic and noetic reality, exists only in dependence on the One.

(2) "In the Paratantra view of existence there is no (subjective) discrimination" (*Laṅka.* II.183);[22] in Plotinus's Mind realm, also, there is no possible occurrence of personal error or unjustified discrimination.

(3) The entities in the *paratantra* realm, like those in Mind, exist not only in dependence on the absolute, but also in mutual interdependence; in fact, this mutual interdependence is what constitutes them; it is a "leaning-on-each-other-in-order-to-be." The realm as a whole is a "correlational interdependent totality."[23] In Plotinus's intermediate realm of Mind, similarly, the entities exist by correlation with one another and dependence on one another, while the realm as a whole exists in dependence on the One.

(4) The middle, or *paratantra*, realm is the source of phenomenality and provides it with whatever degree of reality it may have; similarly, Mind, in Plotinus's model, is called "the Demiurge" (*Enn.* V.9.3) and, as ideal model or pattern, is the reality which is clouded in the lowest realm by subjective discrimination.

The chief differences between the Neoplatonist and Vijñānavāda conceptions of the middle levels are two:

(1) The *paratantra* realm is the source of delusion and as such is inherently deceptive (*Trimsika.* 6–7). Plotinus's Mind, on the other hand, conforming to the doctrine of Plato, is absolved of all active causative function in relation to the realm of delusion; it serves as a passive model for the phantasms of that realm rather than as an active generator of them.

(2) There is nothing in the *trisvabhāva* texts that corresponds very closely to Plato's Ideas (*eide*), which for Plotinus are the entities in the realm of Mind: They are the Ideas in the Universal Mind, somewhat as Philo called them the thoughts in the mind of God. Their deeply Pythagorean mathematicized nature is an emphasis that Indian thought seems to lack. Still, the *paratantric* entities are the metaphysically real facts of which the *parikalpita* fantasies are subjective misapprehensions or distortions, as the Platonic Forms represent the real factual content of which the phenomenal realm is said to be a distorted reflection. The functions are very similar, though the metaphysical definitions of the correlational entities are slightly at variance.

The Two Forces Again

The *Awakening of Mahāyāna Faith* discusses two forces, or "permeations," as it calls them, which are not limited to one level of being but operate in all three and are the transitional channels between them. These the *Awakening* calls the permeation of enlightenment and the permeation of nonenlightenment.[24] The force of nonenlightenment tends away from Suchness or pure Being and Subjectivity toward multiplicity and the alienation of subject and object; the permeation of enlightenment tends in the other direction. They perform, in other words, precisely the functions performed by Plotinus's forces of progression, or emanation, and regression, or return to the One. The force of nonenlightenment obscures the self-identity of original Mind, fragments it into apparent subject and object, and progressively alienates subject from object until the subject is lost in a nightmare of chaotic multiplicity to which it is bound by its own apparent actions, as Plotinus's individual subject is bound to the realm of Nature by the effects of its own actions. The force of enlightenment involves the reintegration of subject and object until they are once more completely infolded, until object is lost in subject and the appearance of any object has ended. As in Plotinus, these two forces are simultaneous and interlocking; they comprise the one-way-up-and-down of Heraclitus, but operating in Mind-stuff, not in matter. In both systems the universe is viewed as made up of two movements or processes which are definable only in terms of relative concentration or diffusion of subjectivity. The pure subject turns extrovertedly out of its concentration and diffuses itself into realms of scattered and fragmented awareness, progressively losing subjectivity and ending in a dark and meaningless dream next to total oblivion. The reversion process then turns the scattered mind power back toward its source and progressively concentrates it until it disappears in total inwardness again.[25]

Just as Plotinus's One produces stratified emanations, so the Storehouse consciousness "is provided with separational functions and the nature of manifesting itself [by positing the world-object]."[26] In both systems, the first force leads from infinitude to finitude, the second from finitude to infinitude. Through the permeation of ignorance, the Storehouse Consciousness "fades downward" through descending degrees of subjectivity into the world of sensation. Plotinus uses the same image of fading downward when he says that the lower realms emanate from the One like the sun's rays fading away from their source (I.7.1; V.1.6–7; V.3.12). In both systems, the source deteriorates into the world, the world saves itself by returning to the source—the two processes going on simultaneously. These complementary movements—the simultaneous concentration and diffusion of subjectivity—*are* the universe; yet the universe is not basically dualistic: The opposed processes are the positive presence of the One and its negation or absence or negative implication.

The structure would seem to have an Orphic-Jain origin. The descent from outside the visible sky, descending level by level into bondage in matter and forgetfulness; the reascent or return to the soul's true home—these are the outlines of the Orphic myth peeking through the quasi-abstract metaphysical structure.

Infinity/Totality

The full and precise articulation of the doctrine of infinitely interpenetrated totality (*dharmadhātu*) is one of the notable achievements of Mahāyāna Buddhist thought. It is also a characteristic theme of Greek thought. In fact, the Greeks seem to have been the first thinkers to formulate the concept of infinity except as an indefinite mass, the first to give it mathematical and logical formulations. The concept of interpenetrated infinities, that is, an infinity of separate entities in which each one contains all the others, was first articulated by Anaxagoras, in his conception of matter. Of infinite entities, each is conceived to have in it tiny parts of every other. Each separate thing contains, in a microcosmic form, everything else. Each apparent unit is in fact infinity squared—which is to say infinity to the infinite power.

Plotinus applied this concept not to matter but to the realm of Mind, the mediating realm where One and Many, subject and object, universal and particular intersect and fuse their natures. Plotinus's central passage on the subject uses the imagery of transparency, as some Buddhist texts do too:

> [The forms in the realm of Mind] see all things . . . and they see themselves in them; for all things There are transparent, and there is nothing dark or opaque; everything is clear, altogether and to its inmost part, to everything, for light is transparent to light. Each There has everything in itself and sees all things in every other, for all is all and each is all and the splendor of it is infinite: for each of them is great because even the small is great; the sun There is all the stars, and each star is the sun and all the others. One particular kind of being stands out in each, but in each all are manifest. (*Enn.* V.8.4)

This interpenetration of the Platonic Ideas within the Mind realm is extended downward and upward to include both Soul and the One, when Plotinus asserts that every individual subject is represented by a Form in the intelligible realm (V.7.1) and that the intelligible realm, or Mind, is contained whole in each individual subject, as, indeed, though indirectly, is the One itself (I.1.8; II.9.8; III.4.3; V.3.8, 17; VI.6.12; VI.7.34–36).

> The *Nous* which thinks a particular living thing does not cease to be the *Nous* of everything (including, for instance, man), since every part, whichever one you take, is all things, though in a different way from the way in which it is a part. (*Enn.* VI.7.9)

Strictly speaking, the infinite interpenetration of realities occurs in the zone of universal Mind. It is the thought process of the universal Mind going on. But Plotinus includes man in the totality because the nature of Mind is the true hidden essential nature of man and indeed of all phenomenal being, though it is hidden from ordinary perception by the limitations of the phenomenal mind. This is a resonance of Plato's doctrine of recollection, and, behind it, the Orphic myth of the forgetful god. The single soul, when it recalls its true nature, expands and thinks the thoughts of universal mind, thereby becoming one with it. The Orphic origin of this myth seems obvious. But now the soul, when it returns upward on the force of return, carries with it—instead of the claim, "I am a child of earth and of starry heaven, but heaven alone is where I belong," engraved on gold foil and worn about the neck—the concept of interpenetrated infinities of unimpeded being/consciousness.

In Buddhist literature, the *Awakening of Mahāyāna Faith* seems to contain the earliest extant mention of the idea of metaphysical/epistemological interpenetration. It refers to the middle realm as "the place of intersection of the absolute order and of the phenomenal order."[27] The *Avataṃsaka Sūtra* elaborated this concept into a series of image streams, and the Chinese *Hua Yen* (or *Avataṃsaka*) school combined the idea of infinite interpenetration with the three levels as formulated by the *Fa Hsiang* school and the two permeations taught in the *Awakening* to produce an ontological/epistemological system that parallels Plotinus's in every major point. The Greek and Chinese systems offer models of reality rather than analyses of individual psychology, as Vasubandhu does; both also deemphasize, in comparison with Vasubandhu, the unreality of the lowest (*parikalpita*) realm, which is conceived to a degree as a valid part of the universal interpenetration process (*Enn.* III.3.17–18; II.9.16; IV.8.5). For both Plotinus and the *Hua Yen* school, the middle realm is to be described as an infinite interpenetration of intersubjective consciousnesses.

In the *Avataṃsaka* and *Hua Yen* formulations, the *paratantra* realm is very close to Plotinus's Mind realm of Platonic-ideas-as-interreflexive-consciousnesses. *Paratantra* is "an intersubjective net of individual consciousnesses . . . [which] are also termed . . . the 'immaterial subjects' or pure thought subjects; . . . *paratantra* . . . in itself constitutes an 'ideal realm.'"[28] The difference between the plurality of ideal subjects in *paratantra* and that of particular subjects in *parikalpita* is that the "category of *paratantra* implicitly contains the universality of *pariniṣpanna* and thereby includes 'suchness' (*tathatā*) as permeating all [its] determinations" (which thereby retain their unity as an interdependent whole), whereas in *parikalpita* "the 'particular' subjects and objects appear as devoid of their ultimate all-permeating universality, and thus erroneously manifest themselves as independent of one another."[29] Just so, Plotinus taught that the interdependent subject/objects in the realm of Mind are saturated with the direct presence of the One and thereby are made indissoluble from one another, while particulars lack direct contact with the One and therefore falsely appear as separate and independent existents (III.2.2; IV.3.4; V.3.17; VI.2.21–22; VI.4.4, 16; VI.5.12). In *paratantra* "there is identity between the universal and its determinations"; Plotinus similarly says that the Ideas in Mind are both universal and particular. "*Paratantra* . . . represents the true, although ideal, nature of *parikalpita*,"[30] just as Plotinus's realm of Mind is the true and ideal reality of which the realm of particulars is a false copy.

There are a number of famous Buddhist images for conveying the sense of interpenetrated infinities. They include the Golden Lion, the Net of Indra, the Hall of Mirrors, and the Vairocana Tower.

An argument based on substrate monism is found in Fa Tsang's *Golden Lion*, a discourse on the principle of *dharmadhātu*, or infinite interpenetration. The argument's lineage goes back to the early Upaniṣadic argument that all things made of gold are just gold, and so on.

> . . . the gold and the lion both establish and include each other in harmony. [Therefore] there is no obstruction between one and many. [And yet] the one and the many remain in their own positions. This is called the mutual inclusion and differentiation of one and many.
>
> . . . all the parts of the lion, down to the tip of each and every hair, take in the whole lion insofar as they are all gold. Each and every one of them permeates the eyes of the lion. The eyes are the ears, the ears are the nose, the nose is the tongue, the tongue is the body. They all exist in total freedom without obstruction or impediment.
>
> . . . in each of the lion's eyes, in its ears, limbs, and so forth, down to each and every single hair, there is a golden lion. All the lions embraced by each and every hair simultaneously and instantaneously enter into one single hair. Thus in each and every hair there are an infinite number of lions. Furthermore, each and every hair containing infinite lions returns again to a single hair.[31]

A metaphor of reflections within reflections occurs in Fa Tsang's Hall of Mirrors.

> He then led the Empress into a room lined with mirrors. On the ceiling and floor, on all four walls, and even in the four corners of the room were fixed huge mirrors—all facing one another. Then Fa Tsang produced an image of Buddha and placed it in the center of the room with a burning torch beside it. "Oh, how fantastic! How marvellous!" cried the Empress as she gazed at this . . . Fa Tsang addressed her:
>
> "Your majesty, this is a demonstration of Totality in the Dharmadhātu. In each and every mirror within this room you will find the reflections of all the other mirrors with the Buddha's image in them. And in each and every reflection of any mirror you will find all the reflections of all the other mirrors, together with the specific Buddha image in each, without omission or misplacement. The principle of interpenetration and containment is clearly shown by this demonstration . . .
>
> As for the principle of the non-obstruction of space, it can be demonstrated in this manner . . . (saying which, he took a crystal ball from his sleeve and placed it in the palm of his hand). Your Majesty, now we see all the mirrors and their reflections within this small crystal ball. Here we have an example of the small containing the large as well as of the large containing the small. This is a demonstration of the non-obstruction of "sizes," or space.
>
> As for the non-obstruction of times, the past entering the future and the future entering the past cannot be shown in this demonstration . . . "[32]

A related image is the Net of Indra, made up of faceted jewels, each facet of each jewel reflecting all the others, including their reflections of it, *ad infinitum*.

The *Hua Yen* text *On the Meditation of Dharmadhātu*, by Tu Shun, sums up the doctrine in four points:

First, one includes all and enters all.
Second, all includes one and enters one.
Third, one includes one and enters one.
Fourth, all includes all and enters all.[33]

These principles are most clearly expressed in passages of the *Avataṃsaka Sūtra*. A famous passage on the Vairocana Tower employs the metaphor of transparency, as Plotinus had. The Vairocana Tower is the realm of *paratantric* interpenetration. It is the home of enlightenment, which is the same thing. A young pilgrim, Sudhana, finds and enters it. Within it he finds "hundreds of thousands of infinities of towers . . . and all these towers beyond calculation in number stand not at all in one another's way; each preserves its individual existence in perfect harmony with all the rest; there is nothing here that bars one tower being fused with others individually and collectively; there is a state of perfect intermingling and yet of perfect orderliness."[34] Becoming both subject and object, Sudhana sees himself within each of the towers, and from each of them sees himself seeing. He has a long series of visions of infinite intermingling of One and Many and of Many and Many. He sees infinite bodhisattvas and "from every single pore of their skin multitudes of transformation-bodies [issue]." He "now hears all the teachings and doctrines of the Buddha melodiously issuing from every single pore of the skin of all the Bodhisattvas," and so on.[35]

Elsewhere in the *Avataṃsaka Sūtra* the theme recurs in varying forms.

In each dust mote of these worlds
Are countless worlds . . .
The indescribable infinite Lands
All assemble in a hair's tip [of Buddha]
Neither crowding nor pressing
Nor does this hair even slightly expand . . .
In the hair all lands remain as usual
Without altering forms or displacement . . .

When a Bodhisattva obtains the ten wisdoms, he can then perform the ten universal enterings. What are they? They are: To bring all the universes into one hair, and one hair into all the universes; to bring all sentient beings' bodies into one body and one body into all sentient beings' bodies; to bring inconceivable kalpas into one moment, and one moment into inconceivable kalpas; to bring an inconceivable number of places into one place, and one place into an inconceivable number of places . . . to make all thoughts into one thought, and one thought into all thoughts; to make all voices and languages into one voice and language, and one voice and language into all voices and languages; to make all the three times into one time, and one time into all the three times.[36]

The Goal

For both traditions, realizing this interpenetrated infinity in one's own mind is the stated goal. "The way to the mystic union," says Armstrong, "is for Plotinus through the knowledge of the One in Multiplicity"[37]—that is, through attaining the middle level of the universe, *Nous* or Mind. It seems that Plotinus's own experiences of *ekstasis* were sometimes of being at one with the One, sometimes with Mind; the latter he regarded as somehow the more authentic to the nature of things.[38] Theoretically, this relocation would necessarily expand one's mind to think the thoughts of the Universal

Mind, which is the continuous thought of infinite mutually containing yet clear and individual infinities. The bodhisattvas described in the *Avataṃsaka Sūtra* were in the *paratantric* state of mind which enabled them to perform the ten interminglings.

In the Chinese tradition, there are "two opposing interpretations of the *trisvabhāva*," associated with Hsuan Tsang and Fa Tsang. That of Hsuan Tsang (who had spent five years in the Indian Buddhist center of Nalanda), identifies *paratantra*, the middle realm equivalent to Plotinus's realm of Mind, as "the critical member," "the solution."[39] This would seem to be in line with the long Indian Buddhist tradition of "the middle way." Fa Tsang's less Indianized appraisal, however, abandons the middle way and sees the three modes of being/consciousness as a simple hierarchy in which the topmost level, *parispanna*, is the desired ultimate.

Despite Fa Tsang's eminence in the formulation of the Hua Yen school, many Zen and Hua Yen texts seem to deny that the state of mental arrest in which all objects are obliterated, and which is described as the goal of yogic practice in Patañjali's *Yoga Sūtras*, is the proper goal. The obliteration of consciousness is contrasted to the idea of reconstituting total consciousness (*dharmadhātu*). To emphasize the absolute unity and subjectivity of the highest realm is, on this view, as unbalanced as to emphasize the plurality and objectivity of the lowest. The Mādhyamika idea of the middle way seems to point to *paratantra*, where the Vedāntic idea of *bhedābheda*, "identity-in-difference," is at last hypostatized as a separate *svabhāva* or mode of being.

Historical Considerations

Plotinus's system of three hypostases or levels of reality, with two forces binding them together and effecting transitions between them, is structurally parallel to the *vijñānavāda* system of *trisvabhāva* with two permeations. Plotinus's system is more similar to the Chinese reformulations of Vasubandhu than to Vasubandhu himself. The most striking resemblance is the doctrine of interpenetration as found in Plotinus and the Hua Yen school.

Neoplatonism was a culminating synthesis of Greek metaphysics, incorporating elements from most of the known pre-Socratics, from the paradoxical and absolutist passages of Plato, from Aristotle, the Stoics, the Neopythagoreans, and the Middle Platonists—with some touches of Skeptical Pyrrhonist terminology. This is the lineage of the monism complex, the tripartite doctrine of *karma*, reincarnation, and release. Neoplatonism represents the last stage of the Indianized tradition in Greek thought.

Nevertheless, though the lineage that led to Neoplatonism seems to go back in part to Indian origins or influences, there seems to have been little further outside influence between the pre-Socratics and the time of Plotinus. The monistic idea seems to evolve within the Greek tradition independently over that long period. Plato's immediate successor, Speusippus, posited a One that is prior to Mind, "nonexistent," a seed from which the stream of appearances flows. Xenocrates gave a mentalist emphasis to the concept, calling the ultimate principle the *monad-nous* or "unity-mind." Neopythagorean thinkers combined these conceptions in various ways. Eudoros taught a "one cause or principle of all things" that, like Speusippus's One-as-seed is prior to all dualities, and below it a second One which, like the Xenocratean One, actively begets the Ideas. Moderatus subsequently taught a three-leveled One: a highest One beyond Being and predication that was called "neither this nor that," a second One which is changeless eternal Being like that described by Parmenides, and a third, lowest One which is a dynamic generative principle. This is the model adopted by Plotinus through various intermediaries including the Middle Platonist Numenius.

According to Numenius, the highest level, the self-knowing consciousness, does not turn outward toward any object at all, yet radiates a kind of unintentional aura of its self-contemplation. This aura or emanation does not simply stop but continues outward with consequences of its own. It has an upper aspect that remains connected to the First Mind, which it continually contemplates; its lower aspect is called "what is made" (*poiēma*) and constitutes the world of experience, which is produced as a copy or reflection of First Mind, but at two removes from the original. This tradition was infused with the Orphic myth of the soul as a denizen of the above lost here below. In Numenius's view, the soul wanders down through the three levels until, losing its way, it has to confront the problem of how to retrace its steps. Albinus similarly divided reality into a First and a Second Mind. The First Mind, impersonal and noncreative, has the Platonic Ideas as its thoughts; the second is both turned upward in contemplation and turned downward toward its creative task of forming a world of difference and change. The higher level consists in intuitive thought processes, the lower in discursive.

Clearly these thinkers provided Plotinus both with the elements of his thought and with the general structure in which these elements are combined. Furthermore, Vasubandhu's formulation seems to have arisen a century or more after Plotinus's. Plotinus may have had contact with Upaniṣadic-Vedāntic strains of thought in Alexandria, but most of what he used was already present in the Greek tradition—though it may have come over from India at an earlier date.

Similarly, Vasubandhu's system can be derived coherently from Indian tradition alone. "The expedient of the three natures exists already in the *Pañcaviṃśatisāhasrikā-prajñāpāramitā-Sūtra*."[40] The *Awakening of Mahāyāna Faith* points to the *Avataṃsaka Sūtra*. These texts in turn can be seen as reasonable developments from the Mādhyamika school and the *Laṅkāvatāra Sūtra* without positing any input from outside.

It is chronologically possible, in other words, that influences moved in either direction. On the one hand, Indian thought could have influenced Plotinus in Alexandria; on the other, resonances of this type of thought in the Roman Empire could have moved via the Red Sea trade into India before the time of Vasubandhu. But there is at this time—at this state of the evidence and the argument—no crux that seems to call for positing influence in either direction.

The correspondence of these models of reality seems rather to speak not of direct influence but of a thought stream which once set going—such as the Orphic-Jain substrate—has a certain momentum and direction in its unfolding. The synchronicity is remarkable: The idea of mind-only seems to have been fully adumbrated and ramified for the first two times in the world, within about a century of each other. This in itself suggests a vague stimulus diffusion of the type meant when one says that an idea is "in the air."

Notes to Chapter Twenty-Three

1. This scheme is somewhat simplified. Plotinus repeatedly says that Higher Soul is *in* Mind (*Enn*, III.3.5; II.5.3; III.4.3) and that it does not reason discursively (or "seek") but possesses an unchanging eternal "vision" (*theōria*) of Mind (IV.4.10 and 12); Lower Soul, on the other hand, "reaches to the things of this world" (IV.8.7), and thus includes both sensation and the discursive thought based on it (III.8.5). Elsewhere he says, contrariwise, that Soul as a whole is *from* Mind, that is, that it descends from it in the emanation process. Whether one should regard Lower and Higher Soul as two separate hypostases or higher Soul and Mind as one together, or some other view, is a question much discussed by Plotinus specialists. For the present purposes the simplified scheme is adequate.

2. Émile Bréhier, *The Philosophy of Plotinus*, trans. Joseph Thomas (Chicago: University of Chicago Press, 1958), p. 189.

3. There is an interesting and deeply significant difference here between European and ancient Greek values. The things that Europe has feared in the Indian tradition—its cyclical view of time, leading to a denigration of the idea of progress; its preference for unity over multiplicity, and for less active mind-states over more active ones—these traits are all prominent in the Greek philosophical tradition also, but are more or less ignored by European commentators who are not comfortable with them.

4. Bréhier, *The Philosophy of Plotinus*, p. 192.

5. It may be that this aspect of Plotinus's thought has been neglected because of a certain prejudice in the western philosophical tradition against radical Idealism. European thought has not yet produced a fully Idealist philosophy. Both Hegel and Berkeley shy away from the mind-created object and the self-sufficient universal. Hegel wants the universal to be concrete; Berkeley wants the mind's object to have a separate existence of its own. Only Plotinus, in the West, has produced a truly and thoroughly idealist metaphysics that goes as far into radical idealism as do the Buddhist schools known variously as the *yogācāra*, or yoga-oriented; the *vijñānavāda*, or consciousness doctrine; and the *trisvabhāva*, or three-level model.

6. The *Trimsikakārikā* will be referred to in the English translation in Sarvepalli Radhakrishnan and Charles A. Moore, eds., *A Source Book in Indian Philosophy* (Princeton, New Jersey: Princeton University Press, 1957), pp. 333–337.

7. Daisetz T. Suzuki, *Studies in the Laṅkāvatāra Sūtra* (New York: Routledge and Kegan Paul, 1930), p. 158.

8. The authorship and provenience of these works are in doubt, and there exists a good possibility that this tendency in the development of Vasubandhu's tradition was more Chinese than Indian in origin. The *Awakening of Mahāyāna Faith*, a crucial text of Buddhist idealism, was traditionally attributed to Aśvaghoṣa, the author of the *Buddhacarita*, but that attribution is now widely acknowledged as spurious. "[S]cholars today almost unanimously consider it a Chinese creation . . ." (Dan Lusthaus, "Critical Buddhism and Returning to the Sources," in *Pruning the*

Bodhi Tree: The Storm Over Critical Buddhism, ed. Jamie Hubbard and Paul L. Swanson, Nanzan Library of Asian Religion and Culture (Honolulu: University of Hawaii Press, 1997), p. 33). Indian authorship of the *Avataṃsaka Sūtra* is also less than certain. No Sanskrit version of the text is known (Hajima Nakamura, *Indian Buddhism: A Survey with Bibliographical Notes*, Buddhist Tradition Series 1 [Delhi: Motilal Banarsidass, 1996], p. 194) and "the *Hua-yen Sūtra* was transmitted to China largely from Central Asia, not India" (Lusthaus, "Returning to the Sources," p. 49). Fa Tsang, the great champion of the Avataṃsaka (Hua Yen) point of view in China, was instrumental in a "deliberate attempt [in the early T'ang dynasty] to divorce Chinese Buddhism from developments in India" (ibid., p. 38).

9. Alfonzo Verdu, *Dialectical Aspects in Buddhist Thought* (Lawrence, Kansas: University of Kansas, Center for East Asian Studies, 1974), p. 25.

10. Ibid., p. 59.

11. Ibid.

12. Suzuki, *Studies in the Laṅkāvatāra Sūtra*, p. 158.

13. Nakamura, *Indian Buddhism*, p. 273.

14. For example, *Lanka*. II.184 (Daisetz T. Suzuki, trans., *The Laṅkāvatāra Sūtra* [London: Routledge and Kegan Paul, 1932], p. 112).

15. Trans. Y. S. Hakeda, *The Awakening of Faith* (New York: Columbia University Press, 1967), pp. 48–49. I use the more common and more literal translation of the title as *The Awakening of Mahāyāna Faith*.

16. Trans. Radhakrishnan and Moore, *A Sourcebook in Indian Philosophy*, pp. 333–337, and, with selected commentary by Dharmapāla, in Wing-Tsit Chan, *A Source Book in Chinese Philosophy* (Princeton, New Jersey: Princeton University Press, 1963), pp. 374–395. Cf. *Enn.* V.1.6; V.5.12.

17. Suzuki, *The Laṅkāvatāra Sūtra*, p. 114, and *Studies in the Laṅkāvatāra Sūtra*, p. 162.

18. Edward Conze, *Buddhist Thought in India* (London: George Allen and Unwin, 1962), p. 259.

19. Verdu, *Dialectical Aspects in Buddhist Thought*, pp. 30–31.

20. Ibid., pp. 42, 44, 45.

21. Hui-ssu, in Chan, *A Source Book in Chinese Philosophy*, p. 399.

22. Suzuki, *Studies in the Laṅkāvatāra Sūtra*, p. 160.

23. Verdu, *Dialectical Aspects in Buddhist Thought*, p. 26.

24. Hakeda, *The Awakening of Faith*, pp. 37–45.

25. In a larger comparison one might include the *rupajhanas* of the *abhidharma* presentation of meditation, which, like the return process for both Plotinus and Vasubandhu, are staged according to "the increasing simplicity of the act of concentration." (David F. T. Rodier, "Meditative States in the Abhidharma and in Pseudo-Dionysius," *Neoplatonism and Indian Thought*, ed. R. Baine Harris [Norfolk, Virginia: International Society for Neoplatonic Studies, 1982], p. 125.)

26. Hakeda, *Awakening of Faith*, p. 59, with bracketed addition as in Verdù, *Dialectical Aspects in Buddhist Thought*, pp. 22, 72.

27. Hakeda, *The Awakening of Faith*, p. 37.

28. Verdu, *Dialectical Aspects in Buddhist Thought*, p. 58.

29. Ibid., pp. 58–59.

30. Ibid., p. 62.

31. Trans. Garma C. C. Chang, *The Buddhist Teaching of Totality* (University Park, Pennsylvania, and London: The Pennsylvania State University Press, 1974), pp. 225, 228, 229.

32. Ibid., p. 24.

33. Ibid., p. 222.

34. Daisetz T. Suzuki, "The Gandavyuha," in *D. T. Suzuki on Indian Mahāyāna Buddhism*, ed. Edward Conze (New York: Harper and Row, 1968), p. 184.

35. Ibid., p. 186.

36. Chang, *The Buddhist Teaching of Totality*, pp. 5, 6–7.

37. Arthur H. Armstrong, *The Architecture of the Intelligible Universe in the Philosophy of Plotinus, An Analytical and Historical Study* (Cambridge: Cambridge University Press, 1940), p. 46.

38. According to the biography by Porphyry, though Plotinus's meditational experiences of *ekstasis* were of both types—sometimes being oned with the One, sometimes with Mind—he more often spoke of Mind as the goal than of the One; he refers to oneness with the One as a transient and unnecessary, albeit highly exalted, experience (I.2.6; I.4.4; II.3.9; II.9.9; III.4.3; IV.7.10; V.3.4; V.8.7; VI.5.7; etc.).

39. Lusthaus, "Returning to the Sources," p. 45.

40. Stefan Anacker, "Major Schools of the Mahāyāna: Yogācāra," in *Buddhism, a Modern Perspective*, ed. Charles Prebish (University Park, Pennsylvania and London: The Pennsylvania State University Press, 1975), p. 97.

Chapter Twenty-Four

Neoplatonism and Tantra

Plotinus's system of emanations is accordion-like and can be compressed to emphasize unity and the force of regression or expanded to represent multiplicity and the force of progression. The variations arise from whether or not the upper and lower aspects of Mind and Soul are counted separately, and whether matter is recognized as a level. The expanded system emphasizes the alienation of the soul from its true home and the difficulty of its return; the compressed version emphasizes the closeness of the soul to the One. Plotinus sometimes compressed and sometimes expanded the levels. His two great successors, Porphyry and Iamblichus, took these two paths respectively. In terms of Indian thought the two courses correspond to the Advaitic tendency to contract the universe into an overriding unity and the tantric tendency to spin out an expanded and detailed cosmology; the former option is more in line with philosophical economy, the latter leaves more range for magical penetration into and manipulation of the great chain of being.

Porphyry telescoped the lower hypostases into the One and discredited the sensible universe, collapsing the levels of Plotinus's model into something like the two-leveled model of Parmenides and the Advaitic authors, where only absolute Being and absolute non-Being are recognized. He described each of the levels as "everywhere and nowhere," more or less dissolving the boundaries between them.[1] He denied the reality of experience and of the consciousness that seems to perceive it. In his view, as in Advaita or as in the Mahāyāna schools that posit the Buddha-nature (*tathāgata-garbha*, *tathāgata-dhātu*, etc.), all humans are enlightened, only seeming otherwise—just as experience is all really One, only seeming multiple. Thus, at the end of the thousand-year tradition of Greek speculation on the One and the Many, something like the unqualified monism of Parmenides returns to close the system and imply an end to options within the framework of the question, and an inability, with present cultural equipment, to get beyond it.

This return to the absolutism of the beginning of monistic thought in Greece is taken farther in a fragmentary commentary on the *Parmenides* written either by Porphyry or by another Neoplatonist of his tendency.[2] There the lower emanations are dismissed as mind-constructions—what the Advaitins call *avidyā* (ignorance) or the Vijñānāvadins *upācara* (assumption). Only the One and Mind exist in reality, the One being called "Mind at Rest," while Mind is called "Mind in Motion." Here—even more than in Plotinus—is an ontological distinction that parallels the Advaitic distinction between *nirguṇa* and *saguṇa brahman*. Only the ultimate beyond characterization is real, and only the consciousness which has surmounted all internal distinctions and become one with the real knows it. Mind, the formed aspect, is an illusion produced by and constituted by unenlightened forms of thinking. There is no elaborate chain of being and consciousness, but only the real and the unreal: the subject and object in absolute union—and the subject and object absolutely alienated from one another.

Iamblichus of Chalcis dominated the last stage of Neoplatonism, in the first half of the fourth century A.D. Whereas Porphyry compressed the levels, Iamblichus strung out the great chain or hierarchy of being into a complex multileveled structure of various god-realms and such. He was a theurgist who recommended religious magic as the most effective means of obtaining escape from the cycle of reincarnation. He represents what might be called the tantric stage of the school.[3]

Tantra and Theurgy

Tantrism in India and Tibet was a phenomenon of religious synthesis in which either Hindu or Buddhist ideas were synthesized with ritual forms surviving, in the Indian case, either from earlier strata such as the *Atharva Veda* and possibly the Indus Valley culture, or in the indigenous religions of South India, and in the Tibetan case in the inherited forms of the Bon religion. The theurgic movements in Greco-Roman culture were similar syntheses. They involved a syncretism of ritual practices from Egypt and the ancient Near East on the one hand, and, on the other, a popular form of Greek philosophy. This syncretic philosophy grew up in the Roman Imperial period much as a popular form of the Greek language (the *koinè*) had grown up in the Hellenizing of the Mediterranean and the Near East.

The dominant element in this popular philosophy was Platonism, with elements of Aristotelianism, Pythagoreanism, and Stoicism mixed in. It taught a hierarchical universe based on Plato, a magical cosmos based on the Stoics, and an eternal soul based on Aristotle's Active Intellect, which, in Orphic fashion, is regarded as alienated from its true home or nature and faced with the problem of remembering and regaining it. The Orphic idea that the soul needs to regain its true home, when combined with the Stoic emphasis on the magical correspondences in nature, produces the conception of a religious magic through which the soul will effect its return. Elements of Pythagorean and Neopythagorean number magic combine with ritual forms imported with the mystery religions and astrology to produce a vast, eclectic, shifting mass of deities and rituals from many cultures, given overall form by the Platonic hierarchy of levels of being and consciousness.

Social Situations

The social position and function of Roman Imperial theurgy, especially in the Neoplatonic context, was somewhat different from the contemporaneous tantric forms in India. Chattopadhyaya, Bhattacarya and others have emphasized the lower caste or village milieu of the left-hand or tantric path of Hinduism.[4] According to this view, the tantric impulse and practice survived from before the Aryanization of India and was repressed by the Aryan caste establishment till, early in the so-called Christian centuries, it was adopted by some learned individuals and began to undergo Vedāntization.

According to Wayman, the *Guhyasamājatantra* was written in the fourth century A.D.[5] and thus was just about contemporary with Iamblichus and his theurgic revival of the Bronze Age ritual elements that had been pouring into the Roman Empire from its eastern provinces for several centuries. Yet Neoplatonic theurgy does not seem to have carried low-class social connotations, and the adoption of Near Eastern ritual elements which were, in their native locales, of the common people, into a learned philosophical milieu by Neoplatonists and others would roughly equate with the social elevation of Tantrism in India when it became Vedantized.

Variety of Means

In this flexible theological situation, a variety of ethical and salvationist theories prevailed in different times or groups. The Upaniṣadic teachers regarded the special knowledge of *brahman* as the only means of escape from causality, that is, from *karma* and reincarnation. But they recognized scriptural study, ritual practices, austerities, and moral discipline as secondary aids. Śaṅkara was stricter, designating *jñāna*—the study of philosophy and the attainment of knowledge of the *brahman*—as the only way. Like him, Plotinus taught that philosophy and mystical experience comprised the way; moral discipline was regarded as a necessary aid or precondition but not the actual channel. He, like Śaṅkara, denigrated ceremonial types of piety.

Porphyry was very different on this point. More a non-dualist than Plotinus in most ways, he rejected the soul's embodiment as "an illusion of thought" (cf. *avidyā*), and taught that the enlightened soul merges completely with the One in an act of "non-comprehensive comprehension."[6] Yet his approach to practice was more populist. Whereas philosophy, he conceded, was the primary instrument for educated people, for others he felt forms of ritual piety could be more appropriate. This is a common view in later Hinduism, too, where the path of knowledge (*jñāna*) is said to be for the few and the path of works (*karma*), combined with devotion (*bhakti*), for the many. Ramānuja, for example, taught that *jñāna* was second in importance to virtue, ritual, and devotional-love practices such as images and songs. Among the Neoplatonists, the same range of opinions is found. Iamblichus taught that for all people the path of theurgy, or ritual magic, was of paramount importance, and philosophy secondary.

The religious myth of the divine soul lost in appearances of mortality and needing to find its way home survived through Platonism and Neoplatonism to become the basis of Gnosticism, the mystery religions, and later European occultism. The eclectic popular philosophy surrounding this myth in the Roman imperial period may have provided the ideological framework for the Hermetic Books and Gnosticism. Through Philo and other channels both in Egypt and Palestine, this popular or eclectic form of Platonism-Pythagoreanism seems likely to have passed into the Hebrew tradition and participated in shaping the Kabbalah. It survives still (through the mediation of the Kabbalistic and Hermetic books in the Renaissance) as the basis of western occultism.

The Occultizing of Neoplatonism

The occult tradition arose as an offshoot of late Middle Platonism, yet was largely rejected by Plotinus, who attempted to revert to an earlier age of Greek philosophy. In the next generation the occult tradition reacted upon Plotinian Neoplatonism and altered it drastically. Its input into Neoplatonism came through Neopythagoreanism, which included ascetics and miracle workers alongside number mystics such as

Nicomachus of Gerasa (fl. c. 150 A.D.), who identified the Hellenic gods with numbers and influenced Iamblichus and Proclus. Proclus indeed felt that he was a reincarnation of Nicomachus.[7]

Another source from which theurgic practices seem to have entered late Neoplatonism was *The Chaldean Oracles*, a book written in Greek hexameters in the reign of Marcus Aurelius by one "Julianus," who claimed to have been divinely inspired. This book presents a complex hierarchical pantheon of deities from many cultures and offers "a clear-cut way of salvation through theurgic ritual."[8] The approach was carefully separate from common magic; it was "magic applied to a religious purpose and resting on a supposed revelation of a religious character. Whereas vulgar magic used names and formulae of religious origin to profane ends, theurgy used the procedures of vulgar magic to a religious end."[9] This definition could describe tantric practices, too. Whether or not Plotinus was familiar with *The Chaldean Oracles* is a disputed point, but if he was, he rejected its claims. For Plotinus, theurgy could effect changes in the world of Nature, but could not reach higher than the level of Soul—it could have no effect on the unchanging intelligible realm or the transcendent One. Magic, a type of causality, had the limits of the causal realm.

After Plotinus's death Porphyry introduced *The Chaldean Oracles* into Neoplatonism. Plotinus was right, he said, that philosophy-plus-contemplation (*theōria*) comprised the best means for the philosopher to approach union with the One, but the path of theurgy, he felt, was better for those who could not aspire that high; they could pacify their lower faculties through theurgy, thus allowing them to turn their attention to higher things through the path of contemplation (*theōria*).

Iamblichus went even farther in this direction. In his view the path of theurgy was the highest path for everyone, philosopher or not. He denounces Plotinus's path as mere thought:

> It is not thought that links the theurgist with the gods: else what should hinder the theoretical philosopher from enjoying theurgic union with them? The case is not so. Theurgic union is attained only by the efficacy of the unspeakable *acts*, performed in the appropriate manner, acts which are beyond all comprehension, and by the potency of the unutterable symbols which are comprehended only by the gods.[10]

Iamblichus, and Proclus after him, were nevertheless avid metaphysicians and gave first authority among all scriptures to Plato's *Parmenides*.

Porphyry's distinction between the higher path of *theōria* and the lower path of *theurgia* equates with the distinction between *jñānamarga*, the path of knowledge, and *bhaktimarga*, the path of religious observances, in Hinduism. Both tantrism and theurgy emphasize acts and symbols. The theurgists' allegiance to the *Parmenides*, the most dialectical and negative-thinking of all the Platonic dialogues, equates with the Tibetan tantrists' allegiance to the Mādhyamika dialectic as an esoteric doctrine of which tantric rituals are considered exoteric expressions.

The Maṇḍala Visualization

It is not certain exactly what Plotinus meant by the word *theōria*. Iamblichus, in the passage just quoted, seems to have regarded it as a form of discursive theorizing. It may, on the other hand, have meant something more like "meditation." This is not a possibility that scholars of Neoplatonism credit. One such scholar has written, for example: "There are [in Plotinian Neoplatonism] (no) methods of prayer or meditation or devices for concentrating and liberating the mind such as are used by both theistic (Christian and Moslem) and non-theistic (Vedāntin and Buddhist) mystics."[11] But this statement is definitely not correct; in fact, it seems almost willfully wrong. Plotinus repeatedly speaks in terms that suggest Indian and Tibetan meditation practices. The most striking passage is this:

> Let us, then, make a mental picture of our universe: each member shall remain what it is, distinctly apart; yet all is to form, as far as possible, a complete unity so that whatever comes into view, say the outer orb of the heavens, shall bring immediately with it the vision, on the one plane, of the sun and of all the stars, with earth and sea and all living things as if exhibited upon a transparent globe.
>
> Bring this vision actually before your sight, so that there shall be in your mind the gleaming representation of a sphere, a picture holding all the things of the universe moving or in repose or (as in reality) some at rest, some in motion. Keep this sphere before you, and from it imagine another, a sphere stripped of magnitude and of spatial differences; cast out your inborn sense of Matter, taking care not merely to attenuate it: call on God, maker of the sphere whose image you now hold, and pray Him to enter. And may He come bringing His own Universe with all the gods that dwell in it—He who is the one God and all the gods, where each is all, blending into a unity, distinct in powers but all one god in virtue of that one divine power of many facets. (*Enn.* V.8.9)

Plotinus's instruction to his students has almost exact parallels in tantric practices, where "the characteristic . . . method of meditation is visualization."[12] The tantric aspirant is instructed to work on the detailed and clear visualization of a *maṇḍala*, a "magic circle" which is "above all, a map of the cosmos."[13] "It is the whole universe in its essential plan, in its process of emanation and of reabsorption."[14] Or, as Plotinus said, "a picture of the universe . . . the sun, the stars, the earth and sea and all living things as if exhibited upon a transparent globe." The tantric aspirant is instructed to practice until the visualized *maṇḍala* becomes clear, sharp, and stable in his mind. As Plotinus says: "Bring this vision actually before your sight, so that there shall be in your mind the gleaming representation of a sphere . . . Keep this sphere before you . . ." When the tantric aspirant has attained a stable visualization, he is instructed to invoke the presence of a deity into the *maṇḍala*; when the deity enters the *maṇḍala*, it has the effect of unifying or integrating the inner spirit of the visualizer. He becomes identical with the deity and with the *maṇḍala*—that is, with the All. As Plotinus says: "Call on God, maker of the sphere whose image you now hold, and pray him to enter (it). And may He come bringing His own universe . . . where each is all, blending into a unity . . ." Plotinus seems to be instructing his students in a tantric practice in which (as Wayman says of the Indian Buddhist Tantras), "the maṇḍala circle (of deities) is taken as the means . . . this shows *devata-yoga* (yoga of the deities) . . ."[15]

Plotinus wanted his students to visualize the circular cosmos or maṇḍala, but it is not clear how much of their time he directed them to devote to developing the necessary concentration to do so. Despite the denials by some, there is evidence suggesting formal meditation practice in Plotinus's school, directed by Plotinus himself, perhaps as part of his instructions in *theōria*, literally "seeing." Perhaps it is here that the influence of Indian yogins in Alexandria registered itself on this philosopher who was sufficiently interested to actually set out on the long and arduous overland journey to India.

Porphyry says that Plotinus had his major mystical experiences only three times; so in the following passage Plotinus must be talking about something else—something very much like a regular meditation practice:

> Often I escape from my body and awake to myself. Turning away from all other things, I behold a marvellous beauty within the inward parts of myself . . . But after this repose in the divine being I descend again from intelligence to reflective thought. (*Enn.* IV.8.1)

Plotinus also gives his students what sounds like advice or instructions on meditation, in addition to the visualization practice quoted above. Like certain passages in Plato's *Phaedo*, Plotinus's advice parallels the stages of meditation as set down in the *Yoga Sūtras* of Patañjali. He advises the student to "turn away from the things that are present," as Patañjali advises beginning with a "withdrawal from sense objects" (*pratyāhāra*). Plotinus's student is to turn inward and "dismiss" discursive thought processes (VI.7.35), as Patañjali recounts the stages of *dhyāna*, or turning within, and *samādhi*, or dismissal of discursive thought processes. When Plotinus speaks of a sudden shock, unforeseeable and independent of the will, with which the soul passes beyond Mind, he parallels later descriptions of the sudden onset of *satori* in Zen meditation and of the highest *samādhis* in Hindu yoga. Finally, Plotinus speaks of union with the One in terms that closely parallel the yogic descriptions of *nirvikalpa samādhi*.

The *Yoga Sūtras* of Patañjali distinguish two types of advanced mystical experience. *Savikalpa samādhi* is a trance state with form, in which the mind, though out of its usual mode, is still relating to an object of some kind. This type includes theistic mystical experiences. The form regarded as higher in Patañjali's tradition is called *nirvikalpa samādhi*, a trance state without form (perhaps it is similar to what in the Buddhist tradition is called *nirodha*, cessation of mental activity). Plotinus's descriptions of his own mystical experiences suggest they were sometimes of the one type, sometimes of the other. He refers to them as the mode of separation and the mode of identity.

> At the first stage, that of separation, a man is aware of self; but retreating inwards, he becomes possessor of all; he puts sense away behind him in dread of the separated life and becomes one in the Divine . . . The novice must hold himself constantly under some image of the Divine Being and seek in the light of a clear conception; knowing thus, in a deep conviction, whither he is going—into what a sublimity he penetrates—he must give himself forthwith to the inner and, radiant with the Divine Intellections (with which he is now one), be no longer the seer, but, as that place has made him, the seen.
>
> Still, we will be told, he cannot be in beauty and yet fail to see it. The very contrary: to see the divine as something external is to be outside of it; to become it is to be most truly in beauty; since sight deals with the external, there can here be no vision unless in the sense of identification with the object . . .
>
> We have told how this vision is to be procured, whether by the mode of separation or in identity . . . (*Enn.* V.8.11–12)

Plotinus's distinction between the two modes parallels Patañjali's. There is an interesting echo of both in the experiences of the nineteenth-century Hindu mystic Ramakrishna. He describes *samādhi* of the formed type in which he, as a devotional mystic, seemed to be relating directly to the mother-goddess, and other, formless *samādhis* in which "a man no longer feels the existence of his ego . . . The 'I' which may be likened to a salt doll, melts in the Ocean of (the) Absolute and becomes one with It. Not the slightest trace of distinction is left."[16] Plotinus seems to have passed in some way through a similar yoga.[17]

The Pantheon

Iamblichus's theurgic Neoplatonism drew heavily on *The Chaldean Oracles* and introduced into the system of levels many deities unknown even to that text. Julian the Apostate, who referred to himself as a follower of "the divine Iamblichus," had a shrine room with icons of gods from many cultures. The mysteries of Isis, Serapis, Mithra and other imported deities were combined with Hellenic deities and ideas to form a kind of vast maṇḍala—or totality—of symbols uniting the stages and forces of the universe at all levels. The leading god of this polyglot pantheon was Helios/Apollo, in three aspects: as transcendent head of the Ideas, as center of the "knowing gods" (*theoi noeroi*) who are engaged in contemplation of the Ideas, and as the visible sun in Nature. Roundabout him were ranked other gods making up the number 360, an ancient Near Eastern number of cosmic fullness. "Such *maṇḍalas* or *yantras*," a scholar writes of Indian Tantra, "were at once . . . ritual and meditational supports, and models of and for microcosmic, mesocosmic, and macrocosmic reality, in which color, number, direction, divine name . . . etc., were so many simultaneous proofs for the coherence of the world system they charted . . ."[18]

Among this number Hermes and Aphrodite are known as the "solar cooperators" who beget the hermaphroditic Attis, intermediary between the above and the below. Symbolically, Attis is the solar rays, on which souls descend from and reascend to the heights of Being. The souls make this passage in an attenuated form which later, in theosophy, is called the "astral body," and which may already have been known to Plato, and behind him to the Egyptians, as the stellar body, the body of light referred to in the *Book of the Dead*, and so on.

In this complex cult of hundreds of deities, the importance which tantric sects tend to lay on worship of the female is evident. Worship of the Phrygian Mother of the Gods was prescribed, and the Platonic World Soul of the *Timaeus* was hypostasized as Hecate, the goddess of magic and transformation. In Indian tantrism the emphasis on female forms of deity and their incorporation by the practitioner seems to point to "a special vigour of mother-right prevalent in India since pre-Vedic days . . ." This is associated with the village or low-caste social setting of the early Tantras, since "the matriarchal cultural elements could not be stamped out from lives of the masses,"[19] despite the fact that, being omitted from the written record until the social elevation of the Tantras, they are invisible in terms of the record. Something similar could be said of the Pelasgian, probably matrilineal substrate on which the Indo-European Greeks erected a male-dominant superstructure. "The main feature of the Tantras is the higher standard to which they have raised womanhood . . . women, as manifestations of the great world cause, are entitled to respect and even to veneration . . . a woman is Śakti incarnate, and there is no doubt that she is Brahman . . ."[20] The survival of this earlier (pre-Indo-European?) substrate in Greece as in India, and its revival under the impact of similarly ancient Near Eastern practices at the time when, as Juvenal said, "Orontes flowed into Tiber," seems more than likely.

"Theurgy" means "the god work," or "making god." It involves the devotional worship of a chosen deity which the worshipper is in a sense to become. In tantric practice also an *iṣṭadevatā*, or personal deity, is the center of each worshipper's devotional practice. In both cases the goal is to incorporate the personal deity, to become it in some sense. "Since ultimately," a tantric scholar writes of that tradition, "our identity with . . . the divine power is incontestable," we should have "a firm belief that through our perseverance in patterning ourselves after the god's form, speech and mood our temporal activities become significant and . . . ultimately the god's essence is realized by us."[21]

In theurgy, again, the worship of deities involves the use of symbols, sometimes herbs or stones which, on the theory of correspondence, are regarded as the locations of the god's immanent presence—engraved gems or magical vowels or words or divine names which could be uttered after ritual purifications or worshipped enclosed in statues. The Neoplatonic use of sacred vowels and names corresponds closely to the tantric emphasis on divine names and mantras. The tantric mantra is often only a single vowel, or a divine name or a brief formula. Tantric mantras and theurgic spells are both regarded as, in the words of Iamblichus, "beyond all comprehension . . . unutterable . . . comprehended only by the gods."

Along with the visualization of maṇḍalas and the repetition of mantras, both traditions involve the use of god-icons which are stated to be alive, or inhabited by the god. Iamblichus, in his work *On Images*, insisted that "idols are divine and filled with the divine presence."[22] In the same way, tantric texts speak of the chosen personal god (Tibetan *yidam*) "entering into" the icon or the mantra. Then the worshipper is in "the *samādhi* in which the Buddha is present, stationed face to face."[23] After the god has entered into it, drawn by ritual purifications and invocations, the icon or sacred sound is effective for magical purposes, though in both traditions the adept is advised not to avail himself of these powers except for inner spiritual growth.

The prescribed ritual practice is intended to effect transformation in the inner consciousness of a human self through use of powers inherent in nature. Tantrism is defined as "an inner mental-spiritual growth which is expressed in ritual."[24] In both traditions this progress effected through working with symbols and their powers is said to lead ultimately to the highest realization of nonduality. Its practitioners in both traditions become saints and semidivine gurus, as Iamblichus was to Julian. Iamblichus, by the end of his days, was said, in return for his troubles, to be able to conjure up "luminous phantoms of Hecate." In occult terminology, he enters or conjures beings from the astral plane. Tantric practice has the same idea, the summoning of deities being a central ritual practice. Theurgy, finally, is said to lead the practitioner to freedom from *Heimarmene*, or fate, as tantric practices lead to freedom from *karma*.

The Historical Situation

The occult aspect of Neoplatonism is not much discussed in modern scholarship. But its general similarity with the Indian and Tibetan practices known as tantric cannot be denied. The diffusion situation is obscure and, in a way, surprising. The earliest known tantric texts are currently being dated to sometime before the seventh century A.D.—though dates as early as the third century have been advocated.[25] Still, insofar as tantrism (like theurgy) represented a revival and reinterpretation of ancient ritual practices, some of its elements may be presumed to have existed long before the texts. If influence were to be posited, it would most likely be from the Near East into both Greece and India.[26] But it is not necessary to posit influence. It is possible that there were such deep inherent linkages between Greek and Indian thought from an early date that the two traditions went on producing like forms to the end of antiquity.

Notes to Chapter Twenty-Four

1. Sententia 31 in *Porphyrii Sententiae ad Intelligibilia Ducentes*, ed. Erich Lamberz (Leipzig: Teubner, 1975), p. 21. One could also compare this view with the interpenetration of *svabhāvas* in the Hua Yen school.

2. P. Hadot, "Fragments d'un commentaire de Porphyre sur le Parmenide," *Revue des Études Grecques* 74 (1961): 410–438.

3. This similarity has been remarked before, by R. T. Wallis, *Neoplatonism* (London: Duckworth, 1972), p. 107.

4. Debiprasad Chattopadhyaya, *Lokāyata, a Study in Ancient Indian Materialism* (New Delhi: People's Publishing House, 1959); Narendra Nath Bhattacarya, *History of the Tantric Religion* (Delhi: Manohar Publishers, 1992), especially pp. 9–34.

5. Alex Wayman, *The Buddhist Tantras: Light on Indo-Tibetan Esotericism*, Buddhist Tradition Series 9 (Delhi: Motilal Banarsidass, 1973), p. 15. Bhattacarya says more loosely that it "was composed evidently before the 7th century A.D." (*History of the Tantric Religion*, p. 61).

6. Wallis, *Neoplatonism*, p. 114, on the Hadot fragments.

7. Which recalls the *tulku* tradition in Tibetan tantrism, wherein an important spiritual teacher will be reborn repeatedly as other important teachers.

8. Wallis, *Neoplatonism*, pp. 106–107.

9. E. R. Dodds, *The Greeks and the Irrational* (Berkeley and Los Angeles: University of California Press, 1951), p. 291.

10. Iamblichus, *De Mysteriis* (96.13 Parthey), quoted by Dodds, *The Greeks and the Irrational*, p. 287.

11. A. H. Armstrong, "Plotinus," *The Cambridge History of Later Greek and Early Medieval Philosophy*, ed. Arthur H. Armstrong (Cambridge: Cambridge University Press, 1967), p. 260.

12. John Blofeld, *The Tantric Mysticism of Tibet* (New York: E. P. Dutton, 1970), p. 83.

13. Giuseppe Tucci, *The Theory and Practice of the Maṇḍala* (New York: Samuel Weiser, 1970), p. 23.

14. Ibid.

15. Wayman, *The Buddhist Tantras*, p. 5.

16. Swami Nikhilananda, trans., *The Gospel of Sri Ramakrishna*, abridged edition (New York: Ramakrishna-Vivekananda Center, 1970), p. 208–209.

17. That a practice of or like meditation continued after Plotinus into Late Neoplatonism is suggested by Damascius's statement that his teacher Isidorus was "unwilling to worship images but preferred to approach directly the gods that are concealed within—not in temple sanctuaries but in the hidden depths of knowledge" (quoted by Lloyd, "The Later Neoplatonists," *The Cambridge History of Later Greek and Early Medieval Philosophy*, p. 313).

18. David Gordon White, *The Alchemical Body: Siddha Traditions in Medieval India* (Chicago: University of Chicago Press, 1996), p. 78.

19. Bhattacarya, *History of the Tantric Religion*, p. 116.

20. Ibid., p. 108.

21. Herbert Guenther, *Buddhist Philosophy in Theory and Practice* (Baltimore, Maryland: Penguin, 1972), p. 187.

22. Dodds, *The Greeks and the Irrational*, p. 294.

23. Alec Wayman, *Untying the Knots in Buddhism: Selected Essays*, Buddhist Tradition Series 28 (Delhi: Motilal Banarsidass, 1997), p. 403.

24. Guenther, *Buddhist Philosophy in Theory and Practice*, p. 155.

25. For example, Tuc̣ci (*ap.* Eliade, *Yoga*, p. 400); Bhattacarya dates the *Guhyasamāja Tantra* "about the fifth or sixth century A.D." (*History of Sakta Religion*, p. 93).

26. Wayman claims "there is a suggestion of Greco-Roman tie-ups with the Buddhist tantras" (*The Buddhist Tantras*, p. 210). He has in mind, primarily, a correlation of the Buddhist idea of the five *skandhas* with Greco-Roman traditions about the locations of the various cognitive and perceptual functions in the human body. "In assessing Greek transmissions to India," he notes, "these need not be attributed to Greeks alone, because around the beginning of the Christian era many Greco-Roman ideas circulated in Central Asia and were carried by miscellaneous peoples . . . During this period," he notes, "two systems of Roman astronomy were circulated in India" (*The Buddhist Tantras*, pp. 22–23).

Chapter Twenty-Five

The Ethics of Imperturbability

Some ethical systems have regarded certain acts as good or evil in themselves; others have held that the nature of the act has to be complemented by a certain state of mind in order to have ethical significance; still others have regarded states of mind themselves as the ethical material, regardless of the acts that may be performed.

An example of the first type is Jainism. To a Jain, to kill is ethically negative (which is to say, karmically disadvantageous) regardless of whether the act is or is not voluntary. Along with its other archaic features, Jainism in this respect resembles so-called "primitive" systems based on ideas of taboo and pollution.

An example of the second type is Buddhism. To a Buddhist, to kill is karmically disadvantageous only if it is voluntary. Both the nature of the act and the voluntary state of mind are relevant to its ethical value. The ethical systems of the monotheistic religions—Zoroastrianism, Judaism, Christianity, and Islam—are generally of this type.

In the western tradition the third approach is least familiar: The same act performed with one's mind in one posture may be good, and with one's mind in another posture, evil. The ethical systems enunciated by philosophers in both ancient Greece and ancient India were mostly of this type.

The agreement of the Greek and Indian traditions on this point has been obscured by the fact that the Greek tradition was largely clouded over by the Judeo-Christian; it has been convenient for western cultures to forget the fact that the ethical attitude espoused by most of the Greek philosophers of whom we have knowledge was inimical to the Judeo-Christian type of ethics.

Imperturbability, Two Approaches

Both Indian and Greek philosophers held the highest ethical good to be an attitude which regards with the same emotion or valuation those events which are to one's personal worldly advantage—such as pleasures and fulfilled intentions—and those which are not—such as pains and frustrated intentions. Various terms are used for this mental stance, from the Greek *ataraxia* to the Sanskrit *upekṣā*, both of which may be translated as "imperturbability." The ethics of imperturbability involves an attempt to get one's mind beyond the fluctuations of pleasure and pain. There are two approaches, one transcendentalist, the other naturalistic.

To attain such an attitude is to disengage oneself from the ordinary patterns of motivation. In some contexts the disengagement is prescribed in order to promote a transcendentalist motivation. Sensations are considered unreal in comparison with some hypersensual realm; the goal is to become "dead to this world" (impassive, impartial, equanimous, indifferent) in order to gain access to higher Being. This transcendentalist approach is found in Platonism and Neoplatonism, the Vedānta, and most schools of Mahāyāna Buddhism.

In other contexts, such as Theravāda Buddhism and Epicureanism, this-worldly experience is accepted as what is given to deal with. Imperturbability is advised not in hopes of attaining a transcendental viewpoint but on naturalistic grounds, in response to the uncontrollability of experience.

"Medical Philosophy"

On the one hand, imperturbability might not seem a natural posture since, as Epicurus points out, animals of all species, as soon as they are born, proceed to seek pleasure and withdraw from pain. On the other hand, imperturbability may in fact seem natural, due to its being in harmony with the fact that many things are out of one's control. To achieve the transition from the first standpoint to the second involves techniques of reprogramming that represent an overlap between philosophy and therapy.

In the Greek tradition, the "idea that *logos* is to illnesses of the soul as medical treatment is to illnesses of the body" is found as early as Homer. Indeed, the connection between the two fields may be much older, extending back into realms of Paleolithic shamanism that can no longer be clearly seen. As Eliade says, "The principal function of the shaman in Central and North Asia is magical healing." He speaks of the shaman's function in terms of "disease" and "treatment," "illness" and "cure."[1] A shaman's healing function seems to have been closely bound up with his account of the world and the individual's place in it, both before and after death. This account was his "logos," which may have begun in mythology but culminated in philosophy. Pindar and Aeschylus both recognize the connection, and some of the pre-Socratics featured it, above all Empedocles (who says his poem provides "*pharmaka* (drugs) for human ills" [frs. 111, 112]),[2] Pythagoras (who seems to have participated in medical research), and Democritus (who "first really developed the [medical] analogy at length in a clearly philosophical context").[3] "Throughout antiquity," says Frede, "the relation between philosophy and medicine was very close."[4] Burnet writes that "it is impossible to understand the history of philosophy . . . without keeping the history of medicine constantly in view."[5] Another scholar uses the terms "'medical' argument" and "medical philosophy" in connection with the Hellenistic schools.[6]

"The idea that philosophers . . . are like doctors," she writes, "and can cure diseases of the soul, is a Hellenistic commonplace."[7] The Greek Skeptics regarded themselves as doctors who "wish to cure by argument (*logos*) the opinions of the dogmatists" (Sextus, *OP* III.280–281). They choose different arguments for different opinions, as medical doctors "have remedies which differ" for different cases (ibid.).

Epicurus also presented himself as a physician showing the way to eliminate suffering:

> Just as there is no profit in medicine if it does not expel disease from the body, so there is no profit in philosophy if it does not expel disease from the mind. (*Sent. Vat.* LIV)

And:

> Vain is the word of a philosopher which heals not the suffering of man. (*Ap.* Porph. *Ad Marc.* 31; Us. 221)

The connection is more than a metaphor. Empedocles was a medical doctor, Pythagoras and Democritus were both experts in the medicine of their day. "At first," Celsus wrote, "the science of healing was supposed to be part of philosophy" (*Prooem.* 6). These "deep" "connections between medicine and philosophy"[8] were persistent. At a later date, two examples of philosopher-physicians were Sextus Empiricus and Galen, both of whom wrote philosophical as well as medical treatises—not to mention Alcmaeon of Croton (fl. 480), Diocles of Carystus (c. 350), Erasistratus (c. 260), Herophilus (c. 260), Heraclides of Tarentum (c. 100), Thessalus of Trales (c. 50 A.D.), Theodas and Medodotus (both c. 150 A.D.), all of whom wrote works, no longer extant, on both medicine and philosophy. As Aristotle said, "the most refined philosophers of nature end up by discussing the principles of medicine" (*De Resp.* 480b28–30)[9]. The idea that philosophy is medicine for a sick soul persists through the Roman Empire (Dio Chrysostom, a Cynic teacher of the second century A.D., described himself as a doctor "who cures mental ill-health")[10] and may be seen as extending all the way forward to the era of, say, Cornelius Agrippa and Montaigne.

In India also the medical view of philosophy appeared, especially in the records of Buddhism. Candrakīrti saw the medical analogy in terms like those of the Pyrrhonists—opinions are the disease, critical philosophy the cure:

> Emptiness is not a property, or universal mark, of entities . . . it is a mere medicine, a means of escape from all fixed convictions. (*Prasannapadā* 12)[11]

Again like the Pyrrhonist Sextus Empiricus, the *Lotus Sūtra* discusses the way the Buddhist teachers choose different arguments for different opinions. "As the king of medicine or the great king of medicine, they discriminate the phases of a disease, know well the properties of medicines, dispense medicines according to the disease, and make people take them."[12] Mixing arguments as a physician mixes medicines, "they remove the fever of the passions of life."[13] The idea endured as Buddhism passed from culture to culture; the Chinese philosopher Chi Tsang, for example, wrote:

> The idea of non-existence is presented primarily to handle the disease of the concept of existence. If the disease disappears, the useless medicine is also discarded.[14]

This conception of its role gave philosophy in both India and Greece a weighty responsibility and an urgent involvement in the human community. Like Buddhism, "The Hellenistic philosophical schools in Greece and Rome . . . all conceived of philosophy as a way of addressing the most painful problems of human life." Their prescription was radical surgery: "These philosophers do not simply analyze the emotions, they also urge, for the most part, their removal from human life."[15]

The Early Period in Greece

In the Greek tradition the therapeutic approach to philosophy is especially associated with the schools of the Hellenistic period—Epicureanism, Stoicism, and Skepticism—which emphasized the ethics of imperturbability from secular or nontranscendentalist positions. Because of this emphasis, these schools are often called philosophies of retreat—since they retreat from the tumult of conflicting opinions and impulses, which arises from the unpredictable alternation of pleasure and pain. These schools are often contrasted with earlier eras of Greek thought which supposedly did not feature the idea of retreating—but in fact the ethics of imperturbability was characteristic of Greek philosophy at all periods.

The "retreat" into imperturbability was implied already in the monistic systems of the Milesians and in the monism of the Upaniṣads: If all things are of one substance then they are of one value; nothing is particularly more to be sought or avoided than anything else, and hence an attitude of detachment or imperturbability toward phenomena is appropriate. This ethical attitude cannot be explicitly documented for the Milesians, due to the paucity of their texts and ancient testimonia, but their great inheritor Heraclitus (who "was a moralist as well as a metaphysician")[16] speaks overtly to this point. In fragment 102, for example, he writes: "To God, all things are beautiful, good and just; but men have assumed some things to be unjust, others just." The distinctionless or imperturbable attitude is held to be higher than the ordinary dualistic attitude which deals in distinctions and preferences. Other Heraclitean fragments suggest that humans are to emulate God in this impartiality. Fragment 78, for example, declares that "human nature has no power of understanding; but the divine nature has it." That man is expected to "grow" into divine knowledge is suggested by fragment 79: "Man is called childish compared with divinity, just as a boy compared with a man." Heraclitus anticipates the Hellenistic schools in his suggestion that the control of passion and desire (see, e.g., frs. 85, 110) is the means to the godlike impartiality which he seems elsewhere to equate with the "wisdom" of knowing how to live "according to nature" (fr. 112), that is, without rejecting any phenomena which naturally arise.

Parmenides' Way of Truth disallows ontological distinctions and may have disallowed the ordinary responses that naïve realism brings with it, such as avoidance and pursuit. Since everyday things do not really exist, their avoidance or pursuit is the pursuit or avoidance of a phantom. Parmenides endorses a distinction between higher and lower types of awareness which corresponds to Heraclitus's distinction between divine and human knowledge: The higher awareness, according to Parmenides, is beyond distinctions, the lower awareness is made up entirely of unreal distinctions. The attempt to live by this credo involves cultivation of a standpoint beyond the fluctuation of pleasure and pain.

Pythagorean cultic practices involved elements of taboo—for example, the so-called *acusmata*, such as the abstinence from beans or the prohibition against touching a white rooster (DK 58C3). But the overall ethical attitude inculcated in the sect seems to have been one of detachment or imperturbability. Heraclides Ponticus attributes to Pythagoras the parable of the Olympic games, in which three types of humanity are distinguished, those who go to the games to compete, those who go to sell things, and those who go simply to observe; the last category is declared to be the best (*ap.* Cicero, *Tusc.*, V.3.8). The philosophical standpoint, in other words, is not interested in profit but in observation and analysis.

Democritus

Democritus "came to be regarded, in the Hellenistic period, as something of an ethical pioneer, and was regarded as having adumbrated an ethical theory which Hellenistic thinkers took to be primitive, but recognizably like their own."[17] Like Parmenides, he taught higher and lower truths; the lower is the natural standpoint, which accepts sensa as given; the higher is the knowledge that sensa are not ultimately real. Democritus seems to have recommended imperturbability in order to withdraw the mind from the uncritical belief in the reality of sensa.

Democritus described this ideal negatively, as a turning away from, rather than a turning toward.

> One should choose not every pleasure, but only that concerned with the beautiful. (Fr. 207)
>
> The brave man is not only he who overcomes the enemy, but he who is stronger than pleasures. Some men are masters of cities, but are enslaved to women. (Fr. 214)

Several Democritean fragments lie in the background of Epicurean ethics. Fragment 210, for example, ("A rich table is provided by luck, a sufficient one by wisdom") suggests that, since the fulfillment of desires is out of one's control, they put one at the mercy of chance; one should instead develop an attitude of indifference so whatever chance provides will seem sufficient. In addition, fragments 211 ("Moderation multiplies pleasures, and increases pleasure") and 223 ("The things needed by the body are available to all without toil and trouble. But the things which require toil and trouble and which make life disagreeable are not desired by the body but by the ill-constitution of the mind") suggest that Epicurus derived major ethical attitudes from Democritus along with atomism. Democritus describes the ethical goal as *athambia*, for which the Liddel-Scott-Jones lexicon gives "imperturbability." In addition Stobaeus attributes to Democritus the term *ataraxia* which would become basic to both Epicurus and the Pyrrhonists.[18]

Plato

In Plato's works the naturalistic approach is featured in the early dialogues, in which Socrates demonstrates imperturbability in several scenes, from his standing all night in the snow, and his remaining chaste through a night of temptation, both told in the *Symposium*, to his imperturbable death in the *Phaedo*. Socrates, in fact, became the primary saint of the ethics of imperturbability in later Greek philosophy, the model on whom the Cynic and Stoic *sophoi*, or wise men, are based.

In addition Plato features the transcendental approach in the middle dialogues, where he makes a distinction between the natural standpoint, which he regards as a kind of *doxa* or delusion, and a higher or transcendent standpoint. For the sake of perceiving the transcendent aspect of reality a disengagement from the natural standpoint must take place. This stance is explained in the *Phaedo* (79), where wisdom is said to consist of communion with the invariable, and in order to commune with the invariable one's attention must be withdrawn from the variable, including value-distinctions based on the changing proportions of pleasure and pain. This withdrawal leads to a higher level where pleasure and pain are resolved in imperturbability: Wisdom, as Socrates says, makes all things conduce to one's happiness, not just the things one enjoys but the things which make one suffer also (*Meno* 88c). This wisdom which makes all experiences acceptable *is* virtue, that is, it is the ethical goal (*Meno* 89a). It is sometimes identified by the term *sōphrosyne*, roughly "temperance," which in the middle dialogues means the power to control one's pleasures and desires (*Symp.* 196c, *Rep.* 430e); this control of one's responses to pleasure and pain is glossed in turn as "mastery of oneself," *engkrateia heautou*, a quality embodied by Socrates and later made much of by the Cynics as *autarkeia*, "self rule," a condition in which the appetitive faculty is ruled by the rational.

Plato's Orphism sometimes draws him into the area of the ethical taboo, as in the *Phaedo*'s insistence (114e) that the virtuous man will avoid pleasure (and cf. *Rep.* VI.485e); but often the element of ascesis seems only propaideutic, and elsewhere we find the roots of Epicurus's later doctrine of rational pleasure, for example in the distinctions between necessary and unnecessary pleasures in the *Republic* (561a, 572c, 581e) and pure and impure pleasures in the *Philebus* (52d ff.). Unlike the Orphic taboo, Plato's theory does not really require the eradication of pleasure, only its guidance by reason. On the one hand, passionate personal desires fasten the soul to the body and its variable senses, making it impossible for it to gain transcendent and invariable knowledge (*Phaedo* 83c ff.); yet, on the other, the appetitive nature has great strength which, when it is under rational control, can be used by the soul (as in the allegories of the charioteer [*Phaedr.* 246 ff., 253 ff.] and the shepherd [*Rep.* 440d]). Once reason is in charge of the appetites there is nothing inherently evil about them.

Aristotle, the Model for Hellenistic Ethics

Among Greek philosophers Aristotle is one of the rare exceptions who do not recommend imperturbability; in fact, that ideal conflicts directly with his view that engagement in life's processes and relationships should involve full feeling. Aristotle does not subscribe to the ideal of the *sophos* exemplified by Socrates.[19] He does not recommend that his students attempt to extirpate the passions, and for this "Peripatetics [were] sharply attacked by Hellenistic thinkers, who view the Aristotelian position as a cowardly halfway measure that fails to address the most urgent human problems."[20]

Yet certain aspects of Aristotle's ethics became foundational for the Hellenistic schools, which aimed "to rewrite and update Aristotle's ethics in an explicitly developmental form."[21] These include his insistence, based on Plato, that "all types of desire are responsive to reasoning and teaching"[22] and his correlative belief that emotions represent assent to unspoken propositions. "He describes the emotions as closely bound up with judgments, and therefore as capable of being modified by the modification of judgment";[23] "in other words, what is stressed is the fact that it is the way things are seen by the agent, not the fact of the matter, that is instrumental in getting emotions going."[24] Both Plato and Aristotle enunciated as a leading reason for the cultivation of imperturbability that one should not rely on "items that he or she does not fully control."[25] Emotions, since they usually involve such reliance, "are based on . . . beliefs about the worth of externals that will be regarded [in the Hellenistic schools] as both false and irrational."[26]

Finally Aristotle's concept of the *hexis* or habit system—"a settled disposition of character, acquired gradually by persistence in . . . practice"[27]—was basic to the Hellenistic thinkers. Aristotle stresses "the difficulty of changing one's disposition once it is developed," and thus focuses "on development of the young more than conversion of the mature."[28] The challenge is so formidable because "the beliefs that ground the emotions are bound up with one another"[29] so that the appeal to any emotion will engage the entire disposition, and in order to change a single element of one's ethical makeup one might have to change the whole arrangement. Solving this problem might be said to be the principal goal of both the Stoic and Epicurean ethical systems.

Aristotle's axiology is naturalistic in that the ethical goal for him is happiness in this world. His view still retains a remnant of the Orphic myth of the soul, but the soul's fate has been cut loose from the control of human actions: The active intellect (which Aristotle retained from the Orphic concept of the soul) disposes itself in the same way after the death of the body, regardless of one's merit or lack of it.

Hellenic and Hellenistic

Many scholars have felt that Greek philosophy underwent an abrupt break at the transition between the Hellenic and Hellenistic periods. They see the physics of the Hellenistic schools as firmly based on the pre-Socratic, Platonic, and Peripatetic traditions, but the ethics of the later schools as disturbingly new and un-Greek. Greeks, they feel, being healthy outgoing westerners, do not define happiness negatively—as, for example, an absence of emotional engagement—and do not advise withdrawal from the world to obtain it. Thus the ideal of *ataraxia*, or imperturbability, taught by both Pyrrhon and Epicurus, they find either an import from the East or a sign of declining life-force in Greece itself, or both.[30]

But in fact it is easy to see in the early period all the elements later foregrounded in the Hellenistic "philosophies of retreat." It is not a difference in content that occurs at the time of Zeno and Epicurus, but only of emphasis. In the early period first physics then logic seemed more important than ethics, but in the Hellenistic period ethics became of primary importance, though it did not basically alter its message, which remained imperturbability. In Plato's assertion that the wisdom which leads to happiness is the knowledge of what one does and does not know (*Charm.* 167a sq.), one can see the germ of Pyrrhon's eudaimonistic skepticism. In Heraclitus's statement that the restraining of impulse is difficult but necessary to the soul's health lies the source of the Stoic emphasis on intervening in the mental process that leads from sensation to action. And in Democritean *athambia* is found the root of Epicurus's *ataraxia*. Most Greek philosophies, like most Indian philosophies, were, in their ethics anyway, philosophies of retreat.

The Transcendental Approach in India

In the case of India it is not controversial that the ideal of imperturbability dominated ethical systems of all periods. As in Greece, the early monistic systems clearly implied it; the Upaniṣadic phrases "*iti, iti*" and "*neti, neti*," for example, encapsulate the dogma that since everything is *brahman* (if *brahman* is viewed as immanent), everything is to be affirmed; whereas, since nothing is *brahman* (if *brahman* is viewed as transcendent), nothing is to be affirmed. In either case, there is no opening left for dualistic judgments based on personal advantage, or *ārtha*. As in Plato, the quelling of desire is enjoined for the sake of a totalized awareness; this higher knowledge (*parāvidyā*) is said to transcend all distinctions which belong to lower knowledge (*aparāvidyā*), and the philosopher, to attain this higher knowledge, must leave them behind, at least passionally. The higher knowledge is monistic; it is that "by which the Immutable is known," according to the opening passage of the *Muṇḍaka Upaniṣad*. The lower knowledge, in contrast, is dualistic or pluralistic; it includes (the passage of the *Muṇḍaka Upaniṣad* continues) knowledge of the Vedas and of the six academic "accessories" to the study of the Vedas, "phonetics, ritual, grammar, etymology, metrics, and astronomy." The proper attitude in the face of dualistic experience is to be spiritually monistic, through the influence of *virāj* or transcendent intelligence, which has been described as "the bridge that leads . . . from the Manifest to the Unmanifest."[31] The virtues of self-control and tranquility, under a number of names, are of primary importance (see e.g. *CU* III.17; *TU* I.9.1).

In Jainism, also, self-renunciation and the quelling of the passions are enjoined on the basis of a transcendentalist agenda. Austerity promotes the hope of separation from the body and attainment of a higher station in the universe. *Śauca*, "indifference towards the sweets of life,"[32] is developed to attack desire, much as *tapas*, or "asceticism," attacks aversion. As with Plato, Parmenides, Pythagoras, and other pre-Socratic idealists, so with Yājñavalkya, Sanatkumāra, Pippalāda and other Upaniṣadic contemplatives, what was sought was "communion with the invariable," and indifference toward the variable was seen as a necessary condition.

The Sāṇkhya philosophy enshrines the same principle, aiming at the complete separation of the soul from the concerns of the individual self and its body. As in Parmenides, what is needed is "a fundamental change in the basic orientation of a man," toward a "consciousness emptied of all . . . distinction."[33] In the later, Yogācāra schools of Buddhism, this transcendentalist ethic of imperturbability is found again (as it is, in a parallel chronology, in the Neoplatonic schools of the Roman Empire). The Prasaṇgika Mādhyamika school may also have belonged in this group, as does the Advaita Vedānta.[34]

The Naturalistic Approach in India: Cārvākas and Ājīvikas

Generally a naturalistic ethics might be expected to exhibit a sense-based theory of knowledge; an empirical doctrine of causality; a model of human mental processes based on empirical observation of them; an acceptance of a naturalistic value system which holds that the goal of human action is to make the best, in terms of happiness, of a given situation; and a pragmatically tested strategy for adapting one's mental processes to the given conditions of experience.

The Cārvāka system contained several of these elements. Only sense perception was accepted as a valid means to knowledge. The mind was not regarded as separate from the causality to which the body was subject. Psychic life was conceived as an epiphenomenon of the commingling of physical elements. No afterlife, hence no transcendent condition of reward or punishment, was hypothesized. The ethics was eudaimonistic, stressing happiness within the world given by the senses.

The Cārvāka doctrine of causality, however, invoked a dogma that was not susceptible to naturalistic testing—an absolute determinism that applies to mental life as much as physical. On this view a human is, as Kalupahana says, "an automaton."[35] There is little that one can do to alter his or her mental process anymore than his or her physical constitution; reflections on powerlessness are recommended in order to cease striving and promote tranquility, but no detailed psychology seems to be involved. Practitioners are encouraged to pursue pleasure and wealth rather than karmic release or a happy afterlife—apparently "an unmitigated selfish outlook on life"[36]—but not without an element of calculus. The early Cārvāka belief seems to have been that the aggressive pursuit of sense pleasures will lead, due to conditions beyond one's control, to frustration. Hence, the Cārvāka lifestyle (like the Epicurean) was austere, and the mental trait regarded as essential for happiness was detachment or tranquility.

In the Ājīvika system, *niyati*, or Natural Determinism,[37] was regarded as nearly absolute. Human exertion was denied to have any effect. There is neither moral responsibility nor hedonic calculus; pain and pleasure come as they come; human effort cannot affect the situation one way or another. Nevertheless, the Ājīvikas seem to have encouraged asceticism as a means of cultivating detachment from events, since it was impossible to control them. Like the Cynics, Ājīvikas repudiated education and speculation as pointless and frustrating, and attempted to return to the state of biological nature, going altogether naked and homeless.[38] The shared ideas of the Cārvākas and Ājīvikas parallel the thought of their near contemporary Democritus, who also taught that the soul is a by-product of combined material elements, that natural causality amounted to complete determinism (fr. A39), that tranquility in the midst of phenomena was the moral end, and that an afterlife is not involved in human prospects.

Early Buddhism 1: Naturalistic Theory of Knowledge

Early Buddhism recognized only sense-experience and inductive inference as valid sources of knowledge. In the *Sabba Sutta*, the Buddha, when asked what the universe, or "everything" (*sabba*) consisted of, replied that "everything" meant the six senses (eye, ear, tongue, nose, skin, mind) and their appropriate types of sense objects (*S.* IV.15). He went on to say that the positing of other things than these as reals could lead "only to vexation and worry, because any such thing would be *beyond the sphere of experience* (*avisaya*)."[39]

Another famous passage describes the connection between "vexation and worry" on the one hand and, on the other, the belief system that goes beyond the sphere of experience:

> Depending on the visual organ and the visible objects, O brethren, arises visual consciousness; the meeting together of these three is contact; because of contact arises feeling. What one feels, one recognizes or identifies; what one recognizes or identifies, one thinks and has emotions about; what one thinks or has emotions about one becomes preoccupied with. What one is preoccupied with, due to that, concepts . . . assail him in regard to visible objects cognizable by the visual organ in the past, the future and the present. (*M.* I.111–112)[40]

Being "preoccupied" or "obsessed" with something contributes to repetition and habit formation. This preoccupation or obsession is *prapañca*, "thought proliferation," the tendency to spin out one's thoughts farther and farther from their base in sense experience; it is this which is declared the root of human problems. *A priori* deductionism is not only not a valid source of knowledge, it is actually a cause of suffering.

Early Buddhism 2: Naturalistic Doctrine of Causality

The Buddha declared causality to be real, or objective—not a subjective fabrication or projection of the mind—and to involve no supernatural or transcendent elements. Furthermore, in his view it is regular, unvarying, and inevitable; there need be no hope or fear of miraculous or heavenly interventions; the prisoners of a situation of causality must learn to use it to their advantage. Fortunately this is possible, since causality is conditionality, not outright determinism. Among the factors participating in the causal process are some which human effort can direct. The knowledge of the causal process and of the extent and type of influence which can be exerted upon it *is* the *dharma*: "He who perceives causation perceives the *dhamma*" (*M.* I.262 ff.; *S.* II.28).

The result of understanding causality is "the attainment of perfect happiness (*parama sukha*) arising from the absence of craving or attachment."[41] Imperturbability, in other words, is perfect happiness. Suffering results from a belief system which does not accord with the facts of causality, leading to patterns of desire and aversion which will often be frustrated. This approach is in line with Plato's assertion, in the

Charmides, that *sōphrosyne* consists in knowing what we know and what we do not know. If we understand causality then we know what is possible to us; we are not in danger of desiring what is impossible and being frustrated.

Causality has three "direct corollaries."[42] The first is impermanence, the governing principle of experience; as "everything in this universe comes within the framework of causality,"[43] everything in the universe is impermanent. Human nature has certain instincts or dispositions which must take cognizance of this, such as the desire to live and the aversion to dying, the desire for lasting pleasure and the aversion to pain.[44] The will is constantly involved in strategies to implement these dispositions or instincts; it is the use of ineffective strategies which causes suffering. Strategies are ineffective if they take cognizance only of the instincts, and not of the conditions within which they must operate. Ineffective strategies establish themselves as habitual belief systems (*hexeis*, in Aristotle's terminology) which are primarily based on wishful thinking.

The knowledge of impermanence can counteract and correct an ineffectual belief system by eliminating the element of wishful thinking. Impermanence means that expectations of lasting pleasure, life, happiness, relationships, and so on, will sooner or later be frustrated, so such expectations are guarantees of suffering (*duḥkha*). All experiences, when depended upon in this way, are turned into suffering either now or in the future. The adoption of a strategy which has been cleared of wishful thinking (what we do not know) and brought into line with the facts of causality (what we do know) will minimize suffering and frustration. Such a strategy must be based on a naturalistic ethics, a naturalistic psychology, and an empirical understanding of the causal processes of the mind, in order to find the points at which it is possible to tamper with them. Such tampering can be effective with much repetition, as Aristotle had said concerning the project of changing a *hexis*. In Buddhism, as for Aristotle, "the only remedy is for bad or wrong habits of action, speech, and thought to be gradually replaced by good and correct habits until the latter become as spontaneous as the former are now."[45]

Early Buddhism 3: Naturalistic Ethics

Like Epicurus, the Buddha of the Nikāyas and Āgamas held it as an inductive generalization that the human personality has a natural disposition to avoid suffering and attain pleasure. He taught a naturalistic ethic in which the goal is not the attainment of a supernatural or transempirical state, but the empirical fulfillment of natural dispositions. Thus Buddhist ethics is a therapy concerned with pleasure and pain, rather than a morality, which would be concerned with good and evil. This character has been found also in the ethical systems of the Hellenistic period, which have been described as "therapies of desire."[46]

The fundamental ethical distinction of early Buddhism, in line with its therapeutic intent, is between wholesome (*kusala*) and unwholesome (*akusala*) actions. Actions are not in themselves either good or evil; they are good or evil in a utilitarian sense, in regard to their consequences:

> Whatever action, bodily, verbal, or mental, leads to suffering for oneself, for others, or for both, that action is bad (*akusalam*). Whatever action, bodily, verbal, or mental, does not lead to suffering for oneself, for others, or for both, that action is good (*kusalam*). (*M.* I.414 ff.)[47]

On this view, if an action has consequences only for oneself, then one's own happiness is the only criterion. The early Buddhists were criticized by some of their contemporaries on the grounds that this doctrine was selfish and hedonistic. But a Buddhist apologist might reply that the objection neglects the hard facts of causality. As in Cārvāka calculus, Buddhism held that a thoughtless grasping at sense pleasures will lead to frustration because, as Plato pointed out, one is not really in control, so some will not be attained at all, and others, though attained, will not last.

Thus unhappiness is to be avoided not primarily by the seeking of specific pleasures, but by the "pacification (*vūpasama)*of craving and desires."[48] Through reflecting on the causal patterns of the mental processes which lead either to craving and aversion on the one hand or to the pacification of craving and aversion on the other, one may gain distance from a naïvely hedonistic disposition. Then strategies may be implemented for interrupting the process which binds one to wishful thinking and conceptual proliferation (*prapañca*).

"The saint," as Kalupahana writes, "although he has experienced all of the impressions coming through the senses, is able to prevent the generation of attachment (*rāga*) or aversion (*paṭigha*), because these impressions are properly understood through insight (*paṇṇa*) and because he has mastery of the psychic process. Although these impressions produce their respective feeling, pleasurable or painful, the saint is unmoved by them. It is as if he were able to jam the brakes without much effort."[49] It is this ability to "jam the brakes" that requires more specific definition.

Early Buddhism 4: Naturalistic Psychology

The process whereby sensation leads to or is converted into action is mapped out in the doctrine of the five categories of psychic experience, the five "groups" or "aggregates" (Skt. *skandhas*, Pali *khandas*) which are the stages along the way from sensation to action.

At the beginning of the process, a sensation occurs through contact between a sensum and a sense; at this stage there is consciousness of the sensation, but it has not yet been classified or reacted to. Contact is followed instantaneously by a hedonic feeling (*vedanā*) of pain, pleasure, or neutrality; the primacy of hedonic feeling in guiding human motivation is illustrated by the fact that *vedanā* is the first reaction to contact, occurring even before the recognition of the sensation as this or that. Even before the subject has begun to classify or identify the experience or object, he has already felt pleasure or pain or neutrality with regard to it.[50] Recognition or identification of the sensum occurs at the third stage (Skt. *saṃjñā*, Pali *saññā*).[51] could as well be called "recognition." As distinct from the sensation itself, it is "the active noting of that sensation, and the recognition of it" as this or that.[52] As Potter says, "The term . . . strongly suggests the presence of linguistic aspects";[53] it implies that moment when one connects a sensation with a word. *Saṃjñā* is followed by the fourth stage (Skt. *saṃskāra*, Pali *sankhāra)*, in which the combination of hedonic feeling (*vedanā*) and conceptual identification (*saṃjñā*) takes the form of an emotional response or reaction. *Saṃskāra* is also translated as "conditioning factors," since it is this stage which produces *karma*, or karmic conditioning, which is only generated by voluntary behavior. Thus "the *nikāyas* define *samkhāras* primarily in terms of will or volition (*cetanā*) . . . *samkhāras* are presented as conditioning factors conceived of as active volition forces."[54] This phase of the mental process may be called "reaction," "impulse," "reactive impulse," "reaction association," "emotional involvement," and so on. It is here that "wholesome" and "unwholesome" factors enter the process, bringing karmic formation with them; the cognitive faculty, having classified the sensum, then relates it to other past and (hoped for or feared) future sensa, bringing into play emotional patterns and behavioral habits based on them. Here conceptual proliferation (*prapañca*), activated by emotion, enters and has free rein unless the subject has developed some means to rein it in or head it off. It is at this stage that a flood of associations and responses occurs. Craving produces a kind of mental fever that distorts further conceptualization, often very subtly. Out of the tremors a reaction forms and begins to unfold itself in time. Thus, in a process that seems mechanical, a moment of sense contact leads, through hedonic response, conceptual identification, emotional association, and impulse, to a new *karma*-producing act. The fifth aggregate (Skt. *vijñāna*, Pali *viññāna*), is the accompanying consciousness, which is found in conjunction with each of the first four stages.[55]

Early Buddhism 5: Strategies for Interrupting Mental Process

If the process initiated by a sense contact is uninterrupted, it will proceed automatically through the four stages and the person will, like the Cārvāka at the mercy of determinism, be an automaton. But the Buddha was not a determinist; despite the momentum of factors keeping the process on course, the "person" still has sufficient free will to intervene and possibly interrupt the process. The question is what stage to intervene at, and how to intervene. The early stages—contact and hedonic feeling—are more or less automatic; the brakes cannot be jammed there. Furthermore, at the end of the process, when the reaction impulse is underway and the endless stream of obsessive wishful thinking has the mind in its grip, one may be passive and helpless—"acting out." It is usually too late to intervene at that stage of the process. It is the point where the energy turns around from going inward, into the person, and starts to proceed outward, into the world—the boundary between recognition (*samjñā*) and reaction (*saṃskāra*)—that is most susceptible to interruption.

As one scholar remarks, "[T]his rudimentary categorization of experience [the five *skandhas*] was eventually expanded dramatically in the Abhidharma literature in an attempt to analyze minutely and exhaustively the various possible moments of consciousness."[56] In that literature the doctrine of five *skandhas* is presented in terms of "mind-moments" or extremely brief consciousness-events.

A "course-of-cognition" (*vīthi*) is instigated when a contact (*phassa*) between a sense-object and a sense-organ occurs, and lasts for seventeen mind-moments, including the moment of the contact.[57] In between courses of cognition the consciousness is maintained in the *bhavanga* state, a minimal level of consciousness that is rendered in English as "the undercurrent subconsciousness"[58] or the "subconscious life-continuum."[59] This is very near the "passive state of mind," or sleep. It is consciousness but at such a low level of intensity that it seems that nothing is happening except that the life-continuity is being maintained.

The series of seventeen mind-moments begins with moment one, the "past *bhavanga*," a quieted consciousness from which the last course of cognition has just passed away. At moment two, the moment of "vibrating *bhavanga*," some sense contact approaches and the *bhavanga* begins to vibrate or awaken. At moment three, the arrest *bhavanga*, the arrest factor arises and holds the *bhavanga* ready to receive the sense contact. In moment four, "sense-door consciousness," the sense door opens. At moment five the sense-contact occurs. At moment six the "receiving consciousness" receives it. At moment seven the "investigating consciousness" examines it. At moment eight the "determining consciousness" ascertains whether or not the contact is of sufficient weight or momentum to topple over into the next mind-moment, which will bring it into the realm of impulsion; this "weight" means primarily how much memory association the contact brings after it, and whether the memory associations are emotionally volatile or not. As a commentator explains it: It's as if you are riding along in a car and have glimpses of passersby; if you receive a weak impression of one passerby and do not recognize him or her, there will likely be no reaction-association; but if you recognize a person and reactions arise from memory associations, then the impact of the contact is strong enough to carry the process on to moment nine.[60] In moments nine through fifteen, seven moments of impulsion or reaction formation arise; these are the moments which are conditioned by past *karma* and which themselves condition future *karma*. Actions may or may not rise from these impulse moments, but emotional entanglements are activated and reinforced by them, so new *karma* is created in any case. In moments sixteen and seventeen, consciousness registers the experience, like an aftertaste, as it is passing away. At moment eighteen, the *bhavanga* or undercurrent consciousness returns.

Moments one through seven are mechanical and cannot be voluntarily interrupted or intercepted. But moment eight has some uncertainty in it; if the impetus of the stimulus is sufficiently strong, it will tip over into impulsion; if it is not sufficiently strong, it will fall back and not result in impulsion. That is a mechanical matter. But in addition, at this moment of uncertainty—and decreasingly in the following seven moments—it is also possible for volition to intercede. Some of the reactive impulses which arise in the impulsion moments are wholesome (i.e., karmically favorable) and some unwholesome. It is possible to influence the process toward either the wholesome or the unwholesome through the intervention of *prajñā* or "wisdom."[61] Wisdom is achieved through a process of "mental development" which involves both mindfulness (the ability to scrutinize the mental process closely and accurately) and discursive reflection, which can rearrange the mental disposition so as to incline it toward the wholesome.

Mindfulness (Skt. *smṛti*, Pali *sati*) is the introspective correlate of the extrospective attitude of the scientist or researcher; it means looking at or attending to one's own mental processes as constantly and objectively as possible, with as little interpretation and evaluation and as much "dry white light" (in Francis Bacon's phrase) as possible. Mindfulness is said to be obscured, in the natural attitude of the unreformed sufferer, by confusion or cloudiness of mind (*moha*). It can be strengthened to break free of *moha* by concentration practices on the one hand and philosophical reflections on the other. Concentration practices increase the ability to maintain attention on the chosen object (in this case the ongoing sensation-to-impulse process). In addition, reflection on the Dharma, that is, the nature of things, the pattern of causality, will stimulate countervailing impulses (*kusala saṃskāra*) to the blind clinging and condemning of the mind sunk in wishful thinking. "Attachment (*rāga*) and aversion or repulsion (*paṭigha*) that one develops toward things of the world are . . . due to ignorance of the nature of existence."[62] The mind which has reflected deeply on impermanence will present countervailing impulses to those unwholesome impulses which are based on the expectation of permanent satisfaction or the fear of permanent dissatisfaction; here are the brakes; when they are jammed on by these counterimpulses, the *saṃskāra* process will not continue to the point of obsession. The generation of new *karma* will be held to a minimum.

Once the process is visible to mindfulness, it is increasingly difficult for the ineffective strategies to continue. Their existence was sustained by the cloak of *moha*, or cloudiness of mind, which made it possible for them to be mistaken for effective strategies. Once *moha* has been replaced by mindfulness, the ineffective strategies will begin to evaporate; they will be seen as leading to pain rather than pleasure, and the natural disposition to avoid pain will cause one naturally to avoid the ineffective strategy.[63] "By the development of insight the normal process of perception is changed."[64] Or, rather, the process which leads from sensation through recognition and impulse to action is guided into a more realistically hedonistic direction.

The condition of mind which results from this alteration in mental process is characterized by stability or steadiness (*thitata*). The steadied mind no longer runs this way in pursuit of unobtainable pleasures or that way in flight from inescapable pains. It is no longer thrown about by the impermanence of the *vedanās*. Gain and loss, pleasure and pain, good and ill repute, and so on, are experienced with the same feeling tone, that is, with equanimity, imperturbability, steadiness, and so on.

> He whose mind is not overwhelmed when in contact with worldly phenomena is freed from sorrow, taintless and secure. (*SN* 268)

This and other passages suggest that the state of mental steadiness was an early definition of nirvāṇa. Later Buddhist groups assigned more transcendental meanings to nirvāṇa.

Some Analogues in Plato and Aristotle

In the Greek tradition the motif of equanimity was embodied above all by Socrates. His students, including Plato, sought to give the psychology of imperturbability more detail and, like many Indian thinkers, focused on the process of pleasure and its habituation. Plato, whatever his transcendental motives, was an early theorist of naturalistic psychology and developed an account of the process leading from sensation to action which is remarkably parallel to that of early Buddhism.

In the *Timaeus*, Plato speaks of the process of bondage:

> Now, when the souls be implanted in bodies by necessity and be always gaining or losing some part of their bodily substance, then, in the first place, it would be necessary that they should all have in them one and the same faculty of sensation, arising out of irresistible contacts; in the second place, they must have love, in which pleasure and pain mingle—also fear and anger and the emotions which are akin or opposite to them. If they conquered these they would live righteously, and if they were conquered by them, unrighteously. (*Tim.* 42a ff.)[65]

The components of the process are much the same as in the Buddhist version: There is a sense contact (*phassa*), a hedonic feeling (*vedanā*), and an emotional reaction (*saṃskāra*); in addition the "faculty of sensation" seems likely to comprise an identification (*samjñā*). The order, however, is not entirely clear. The hedonic feeling may accompany the sense contact or the emotional reaction, or both. In either case the hedonic feeling is not described as a separate stage in the process; clearly it occurs in conjunction with the fourth stage, *vedanā* and *saṃskāra* mingling together as emotional reactions bring pleasure and/or pain with them from memory associations; in addition the hedonic feeling or *vedanā* may accompany the first stage of contact or the vaguely indicated "recognition" phase. In either case, the combination of emotional reaction (*saṃskāra*) with pleasure and/or pain (*vedanā*) is explosive and can culminate in actions. When the emotional response to the recognition is overcome, says Plato, one is able to live virtuously, which is to say, with rational oversight of one's desire system.[66] As in the Buddhist view, this is the stage at which emotions flood in around the recognition of the sensation and acts of pursuit or avoidance arise in an automatic and mechanical way:

> When a man is carried away by enjoyment or distracted by pain, in his immoderate haste to grasp the one or to escape from the other he can neither see nor hear aright; he is in a frenzy and his capacity for reasoning is then at its lowest. (*Tim.* 86c)

But for Plato, who mentions the possibility of getting free of the process, as for the Buddha, it is evidently possible to intervene. Plato calls the faculty which has the ability to intervene *phronēsis*, which is frequently translated by the somewhat vague term "wisdom"; the concept seems roughly similar to the Buddhist term (Skt. *prajñā*, Pali *paṇṇa)* which is usually translated the same way. But in Greek ethical thought from Plato to Epicurus it is closer to the more specific term, "mindfulness" (Skt. *smṛti*, Pali *sati*). It is through mindfulness that one can perceive the mental process in sufficient detail to make intervention possible. Similarly *phronēsis*, says Epicurus, "patiently searches out the motives for every act of grasping and fleeing, and banishes those beliefs through which the greatest tumult enters the mind" (*ap*. D.L. X.129–132). Epicurus adds in the *Letter to Menoeceus* (132) that "all the other virtues have come by nature from *phronēsis*"—much as in *abhidharma* they all arise from mindfulness. Through *phronēsis* the chain of impulse and action can be interrupted and, to some extent, guided. Plato is not clear about where and how to interrupt the sequence, though it is the emotional reactions, evidently, which must be "conquered" by *phronēsis*; that is, in terms of the Buddhist aggregates, it is the arising of the phase of reaction formation (*saṃskāra*) where, as in the Buddhist system, the intervention of mindfulness should be aimed.

In this passage of the *Timaeus* (42a) lies the germ of the various Hellenistic systems which, focusing on the same process, attempt to clarify the techniques for interrupting the chain at the crucial point where the feelings of pleasure and pain, with cognitive identification overlaid on them, unleash the storm of emotions which produce reaction formations.

Aristotle, like Plato, Buddha, and Epicurus, focused on the pleasure-pain aspect of experience as the lynchpin of ethical reality and on imperturbability as the solution:

> It is by reason of pleasures and pains that men become bad, by pursuing and avoiding these . . . Hence some even define the virtues as certain states of impassivity (*apatheia*) and rest. (*NE* 1104b24)

Aristotle's system, which followed on Plato's and was to a large extent the source of the Stoic and Epicurean systems, begins with Plato's naturalistic starting point:

> Anything painful is an object of avoidance and anything pleasant is an object of pursuit. (*De Motu Animal.* 701b–c)

As in early Buddhism and in Plato's system, the process is set going by sense perception (including the mind sense):

> The animal is moved and walks from desire or purpose, when some alteration has been caused as the result of sensation or imagination. (*De Motu Animal.* 701a4–6)

The process continues through a number of stages which are much like the five "aggregates" of the Buddhists:

> A man thinks he ought to go, and goes, practically at the same time, unless something else hinders him. For the affections fittingly prepare the organic parts, the desire prepares the affections, and the imagination prepares the desire, while the imagination is due to thought or sensation. (*De Motu Animal.* 702a10–21)[67]

The stages then are: (1) sensation or sense-perception (*aisthesis*), which is equivalent to contact (*phassa*) in the Buddhist model; (2) mental picture (*phantasia*) or identification, which seems to be accompanied by hedonic feeling, since at the next moment it leads to desire; thus, this stage is equivalent to *saṃjñā* (recognition) and *vedanā* (hedonic feeling) as one or experienced together;[68] (3) desire (*orexis*), which is equivalent to *saṃskāra* or impulse in the Buddhist list, is aroused by the hedonic quality and defined by the recognition or identification; (4) this combination of conceptual identification and hedonic feeling produces emotions (*pathē*). So as Aristotle's *phantasia* seems to combine two of the Buddhist stages (*saṃjñā* and *vedanā*), the fourth stage in the Buddhist reckoning, *saṃskāra*, is analyzed into two: first a desire-or-aversion response (*orexis*) to the pleasure-or-pain *vedanā*, then the multitude of emotional associations (*pathē*).

As Aristotle describes the process there seems to be no discontinuity in it, no fissure where he recommends a strategy of interference. The overwhelming emphasis he places on the *hexis*, or formed disposition, diminishes the prominence of the element of voluntary choice. It is true that the action must be caused by an *orexis*, or desire, but this desire is not a free decision. It is produced mechanically by the combination of the external stimulus with the established disposition (*hexis*) of the individual. At an early stage of personal development, before the hexis is fixed by habituation (*ēthos*), some deliberate formative influence can be exercised upon it, whether by oneself or by others, such as parents and teachers. "States of character," says Aristotle, "are formed from similar activities":

> It is by building that people become builders and by playing an instrument that they become musicians . . . It is by doing just actions that we become just . . . states come about as a result of similar activities. (*NE* 1103a14-b25)[69]

Repetition of actions imposed in childhood does most of the *hexis*-formation. Each individual has voluntarily participated at an early stage in the formation of his *hexis*, and thus is ultimately responsible for any actions produced through it, however mechanically (see *NE* 1114a3ff.), but it is not clear that one can interfere in the *hexis* after it has developed to a certain point. In the *Nicomachean Ethics* (1114a12–21, 1137a4–9) it seems that "when character has once been established it cannot be changed at will."[70] Sometimes the point is softened as in a later passage of the same work: "It is hard, if not impossible, to remove by argument [i.e., by philosophy] the traits that have long since been incorporated in the character" (*NE* 1179b16–17).[71] The psychē involves "a non-rational element capable of responding to reason,"[72] but also capable of responding to other types of persuasion; if reason gets to it at an early age through a parent or a teacher, well and good; if not, the connections that wire the *hexis* are made anyway, by other ambient forces, and are likely to remain in place despite subsequent rational persuasion.[73]

In the *De Anima* (432b26–433a1) Aristotle seems to leave room for interference or voluntary guidance of the process:

> Even when the mind does think of an affective object [one which might serve as a trigger for action], it does not at once give orders to avoid or pursue. For instance, it often thinks of something that provokes fear or pleasure, but does not give the command to be afraid though the pulse-rate increases or, if it is a case of pleasure, something else [the penis].

Again, evidently, the fissure or discontinuity where the sequence might turn either way is said to lie between the phase of recognition-with-hedonic-feeling and the phase of emotional-response or impulse-reaction. But for Aristotle the route of intervention does not seem likely to succeed, as the *hexis* has been bound together by early pleasure-pain conditioning:

> Moral virtue is a matter of pleasures and pains; it is for the sake of pleasure that we do what is bad, and because of pain we fail to do what is good. Hence we must be brought up from youth, as Plato, says, to feel pleasure and pain about the right objects; that is right education. (*NE* 1104b8–13)

The point is that the mind commands responses according to its habituated disposition, not with a decision made freely for each specific case. Aristotle does, in a handful of passages, seem to believe in a faculty of choice (*prohairesis*) which has some autonomy from the *hexis*, but not much. Fundamentally it is not a free choice in most cases: The mind chooses responses according to its disposition, that is, through a habitual choice; and once the habit, or disposition, is firmly fixed, it seems more or less unchangeable. So no decision is really free or uncaused; all are determined by past events.

Here, as in the Cārvāka and Ājīvika naturalistic psychologies, causality in mental events is so strong as to overshadow the concept of free will. It is primarily this ethical system which influenced both Epicurus and the Stoics, who attempted to mitigate its determinism by insisting that the disposition could in fact be changed at any time in life by certain techniques. Both systems paralleled the *abhidharma* approach. The Stoic ethics, in fact, has been declared[74] more like that of early Buddhism than any other western system; what is less commonly known is that Epicureanism may be even more like early Buddhism than Stoicism is.

Epicureanism 1: Introduction

Epicurus studied first under Pamphilus the Platonist, then under Nausiphanes of Teos, a Democritean. It is also reported that he associated with Pyrrhon after the latter's return from the East. The Platonist imprint passed on by Pamphilus did not last for Epicurus, who wrote polemics against the transcendentalist tradition of the Platonists—but not against Aristotle, from whom he adopted a good deal. Evidently it was Nausiphanes who won him away from the pursuit of eidetic metaphysics. Nausiphanes was, like Democritus, a naturalist. He taught that knowledge depends on observation and inductive inference. In ethics, also, he followed Democritus, teaching the ideal of *akataplēxia* (DK 75B3), "undisturbedness," "imperturbability," evidently based on the *athambia* (and *ataraxia* if Stobaeus is correct) of Democritus. Epicurus was to derive from Democritus, through Nausiphanes, his atomism, his ethics of imperturbability (his favorite term for it being *ataraxia*), his phenomenalistic theory of knowledge, and his materialism. On one point, however, Epicurus disliked the Democritean doctrine and gave it a Platonic reform. He felt Democritus's system lacked ethical basis because of its determinism, and wanted to reinsert the Platonic free-will ethics. It seems, nevertheless, to have been primarily the ethics of Aristotle that was his model, the norm, as it were, from which he reacted in designing his own reform of Democritus.[75] By perhaps 310 B.C. Epicurus's system was complete, and in 306 he founded a school in Athens where he taught until his death in 271.

Epicureanism 2: Naturalistic Theory of Knowledge

Epicurus held that speculation divorced from experience was not only fruitless but harmful; he set out to demystify his tradition by the "wholesale substituting of naturalistic explanations for the traditional superstitions."[76] Similarly, early Buddhism, as Warder put it, "attacked old superstitions and sought knowledge of nature, knowledge which we may characterize as scientific on account of its basis of perception, inference, verification."[77]

Epicurus taught that perception never errs, that "all sensations are true" (D.L.X.31–32)—much as Democritus had said, "The appearance is the truth." Cicero testified that "Epicurus places the criterion of reality in the senses" (*De Fin.* I.22). In doing so he is as outspoken and absolute as the Buddha in the *Sabba Sutta* saying that "everything" consists of the six types of sense contacts. An Epicurean articulation of the point says similarly, "[M]an has nothing left if sensations are removed from him" (Cicero, *De Fin.* I.29).[78]

Error arises, then, not from perceptions but from their interpretation. Inductive generalizations based directly on perceptions are valid up to a point, but *a priori* conclusions—deductive or revealed—are rejected. Epicurean practice involves carefully distinguishing between a percept in itself and the interpretive or associative material that may have clustered around it in the mind:

> The wise do not disturb themselves with empty words, but look simply at the facts of experience. (D.L. X.152)

For Epicurus, as for the Buddha of the Nikayas, the given experience is the ultimate fact which nothing can discredit; he gives the point a special dialectical twist:

> Reason cannot refute sensation since it is only valid when it is based on sensation; and one sensation cannot refute another since all sensations are equal [i.e. factual]. (D.L. X.32)
>
> In natural science one must be ruled by the appearances themselves, not by empty axioms and law-making. (D.L. X.87)

By remembering the primacy of empirical facts, one avoids "being carried into the realm of the unintelligible" (D.L. X.87) as were, for example, Platonists and others who strove against the appearances.

> If you fight against the plain facts of experience, you will never attain peace of mind. (D.L. X.96)
>
> Our life has not now any place for irrational belief and groundless imaginings, since we are to live free from trouble. (D.L. X.87)

Epicurus's belief that conceptual proliferation (Greek *kenodoxia*, empty opinion) is the source of most human suffering recalls the Buddhist doctrine of *prapañca*—the drive toward conceptual proliferation which is identified in many early Buddhist texts as a principal root of mental disquietude.

Epicurus cautioned against the forming of conclusions before verification (*epimarturēsis*) through empirical research had been completed:

> Falsehood and error always depend upon the intrusion of opinion before a point has been confirmed or contradicted evidentially. (D.L. X.50)

The Buddha similarly warned against "the tendency toward proliferation in the realm of concepts," "the spreading out, expansion, and diffusiveness" of the untrained thought process, "the tendency of the worldling's imagination to break loose and run riot."[79] Like the Buddha rejecting the *avyākrta*, or questions which are not to be answered, and like the rejection of education for its own sake by Zen and other sects of Buddhism, Epicurus advised his followers to "Abandon all *paideia*" (D.L. X.6), following the Cynics in attacking Platonic mathematics and dialectics.[80]

The accumulation of sensations leads to *prolēpseis*, "preconceptions" or "general concepts," which function as a further criterion.[81] *Prolēpseis* include linguistic categories—for example, the general concept "man" by which specific perceptions of men are classified—and also basic patterns of behavior which have been developed by conditioning and repetition. They have in the latter case some resemblance to Aristotle's "dispositions." (Furley, attempting to provide a physical atomistic model for Epicurus's psychology, calls them "durable patterns of motion" in the atoms of the psyche.)[82]

Epicureanism 3: Naturalistic Doctrine of Causality

Epicurus, like the Buddha of the Nikāyas, stressed inductively derived concepts of causality which eliminate supernatural forces from the account. In both cases it was believed that a knowledge of natural causation would eliminate groundless fears and superstitions, as well as make clear the way to alter one's own behavior patterns. Epicurus said he found serenity in natural science, which has as its content "knowledge about causality" (D.L. X.78). From the knowledge of causality, in other words, arises peace of mind. As Strodach says, "To know the causes of things and to know that these are wholly natural is to banish groundless fears of a god or gods who work in unsearchable ways; and the conquest of such fear represents a marked diminution of human pain and suffering and hence is an essential ingredient of the good life."[83] Similarly, Kalupahana says, "The essence of the Buddha's enlightenment . . . consist[ed] of the realization of . . . causal uniformity." And: "The realization that every occurrence is a causal occurrence is said to clear the mind of all doubts."[84] Says Epicurus:

> Happiness is bound up with causal knowledge. (D.L. X.78)

And the Buddha:

> He who sees causality sees the *dhamma*. (*M.* I.190–191)

The purpose of the study of causality, says Epicurus, is "mental composure and self-reliance" (D.L. X.85). And Kalupahana, speaking of early Buddhism: "Knowledge of causality should go hand in hand with restraint of the senses."[85]

Both Epicurus and the Buddha of the Nikāyas taught a causality which was complete. "Every event whatsoever has a prior cause," says Strodach of Epicurus's system.[86] And Kalupahana, speaking of Buddhism: "The causal process is operative in all spheres."[87] Yet each wished this causality to be less than absolute determinism, in order to give meaning to efforts to reform behavior—for it was above all the causality of mental processes, and thus the methods to guide them, which were at issue.

Epicureanism 4: Naturalistic Psychology

The view of the Cārvākas and Democritus has been mentioned before, to the effect that consciousness is an epiphenomenon of matter which arises under certain conditions and which, when those conditions end, disappears. In early Buddhism similarly,

Kalupahana says, "Consciousness is dependent on a physical personality."[88] Still, it is true that for the Buddha there was a small part of the personality which survived the death of the body and transmigrated directly into the next (the "rebirth consciousness"), and that the doctrine of *karma* also implies something surviving at least through its effect. Epicurus was more extreme. For him, as for the Cārvākas, life and consciousness are temporary by-products of certain atomic combinations (D.L. X.64). Nature is "a nonintelligent system of atoms that incidentally and accidentally produced minds."[89] There is no afterlife of any kind nor any possibility that there could be one, since there is even less of a self than the not-self doctrine of the early Buddhist texts allows.

As in the early Buddhist model and Plato, Epicurus reduces all sensation to the model of touch: the contact between a sensum and a sense organ. A floating film of atoms enters a sense organ and stirs its atoms to a similar kind of motion. Like the authors of the Nikayas and *abhidharma*, Epicurus regarded the mind as a sixth sense which, like the other five, operates by touch or contact. Thoughts and imaginings are atomic clusters received from the ambience by the mind organ, which is itself atomic, and in which the sensum sets up a movement which is thought. This thought-movement takes place, as in the *abhidharma* version, in a series of atomic moments. These are indivisible and imperceptible units of time a huge number of which are unseen within each big-body moment and which define the "speed of thought." In each of these moments, according to scholarly opinion, a single movement of thought takes place, though most of these never reach our awareness.[90] The authors of the *abhidharma* are held to have perceived this minim through a microscopic time perception attained in deep concentration. Epicurus, in contrast, may have deduced it, partly, perhaps, with an eye toward the elegance of a fully atomic system.

The process whereby sensation leads to emotional activity is viewed by Epicurus much as by the Buddhists. But whereas the *abhidharma* divides the process into four stages—contact, pleasure/pain tonality, recognition/classification, reaction-association/impulse—Epicurus collapses two of the stages into one, recognizing a total of three. In Epicurus's version (as in Plato's), an *epibolē*, or contact, is followed by a *phantasia*, or mental image or presentation, which is immediately accompanied by a tonality of pleasure or pain; the *phantasia* stage, then, is equivalent, in the Buddhist schema, to the stages of hedonic feeling (*vedanā*) and recognition (*samjñā*) at once. Like Aristotle, Epicurus compresses into one complex event the two events separated out, in the Buddhist version, as pleasure/pain feeling and recognition/imaging. The *phantasia*, in Epicurus's model, is followed by reaction-associations (impulses of craving or shunning, depending on the pleasure/pain tonality of the event), and these reactions are determined by earlier conditioning—including, in the case of Buddhism, conditioning from earlier lives—until steps have been taken to redirect them—that is, to rearrange the *hexis*.

Epicureanism 5: Naturalistic Ethics

Epicureanism has been described as "a peace of mind technique"[91] and a therapy.[92] Epicurus himself regarded it this way. His concern was for human happiness, which meant to him "the absence of pain in the body and anxiety in the mind" (D.L. X.131).

> The magnitude of pleasure [in his view] reaches its limit in the removal of all pain. (D.L. X.140)

Plato, in the *Philebus* (31d) had already presented the quietistic theory that pleasure is the ending of pain. Pain, he wrote, is a disturbance of the natural equilibrium of a thing; when the pain goes, the restoration of that natural state *is* the experience of pleasure. Once that state has been restored, a rather neutral feeling ensues which also is experienced as a type of happiness. Aristotle similarly taught that the natural unobstructed continuance of an organism as itself (or in its own way) *is* pleasure or happiness.[93] The Buddha also spoke of the goal of life not as the attainment of positive pleasures so much as the cessation of unnecessary pains.

Both Epicurus and the Buddha regarded the pain-pleasure experience as the central problem of life. Both concluded, through an inductive generalization based on human behavior, that the natural purpose of life is the termination of suffering (which both sometimes referred to misleadingly as the attainment of bliss). According to Epicurus:

> The end of all our actions is to be free from pain and anxiety and when once we have attained all this, the tempest of the soul is laid. (D.L. X.128)

Both warned their listeners not to be distracted from this goal. Epicurus was as radical on this point as the Buddha of the *Sutta Nipāta*:

> I spit on the beautiful and those who pointlessly respect it when it produces no pleasure. (*Ap.* Ath. XII.547a)
>
> Beauty and the virtues are to be honoured if they provide pleasure, but if they do not, we must say goodbye to them. (*Ap.* Ath. XII.546f)

The fact that both the Buddha and Epicurus espoused the doctrine of personal happiness, caused them to be represented by their antagonists as simple-minded hedonists. It seems that the word *hēdonē* in Epicurus should not be translated "pleasure" but something like "joy" or "serenity."[94] What Epicurus means is not simply positive sense-pleasure, Buddhist *sukha*, though it may include this. It is a more quietist concept, which holds *ataraxia*, imperturbability, as the highest delight. It derives from Aristotle's statement:

> Pleasure is found more in rest than in movement. (*NE* 1154b27)

Pleasure in rest is perfect, not subject to change, and is god's kind of pleasure. Pleasure in motion is sensual pleasure, the kind that is the object of most human striving; since it is transient it is regarded as a poor foundation for happiness.

Epicurus, characteristically bringing the subject down to earth, distinguished between kinetic and static pleasures, a distinction apparently based on Aristotle and going back to an above-mentioned passage of the *Philebus* (31d). Static pleasure is the godlike state of absence of pain. It is based upon the development of what Strodach calls "a Buddha-like tranquility," a mental imperturbability (*ataraxia*) which is so strong that it outweighs the vicissitudes of the body. It is this state, the general elimination or diminution of suffering, which is the *hēdonē* recommended by Epicurus. Thus Epicurus's brand of "hedonism" should hardly be so called at all. Probably he used the term "pleasure" for his moral end because it was such a key term in the philosophical discourse of his time. Yet *ataraxia*, tranquility or imperturbability, as in Pyrrhonism, was the more accurate formulation of his ideal. As Long and Sedley say, "Although freedom from bodily pain and freedom from mental disturbance jointly constitute the Epicurean good, the superiority of mental pleasure . . . makes freedom from mental disturbance (*ataraxia*), or tranquillity, the supreme hallmark of Epicurean happiness."[95]

The happiness of tranquility is like the mental state of a god, whose natural condition is stable, as opposed to the immediacy of grasped-at pleasures which come and go.

> Happiness is a twofold notion: the highest, such as god enjoys, which is incapable of increase; and the happiness which is capable of addition and subtraction of pleasures. (D.L. X.121)

The basic guiding principle for behavior, then, should be to pursue the most efficient strategy for diminishing suffering and promoting the negatively defined states of *ataraxia*, nonanxiety, and *aponia*, nonpain. This is a utilitarian ethic like that of early Buddhism, not an ethic of virtue: It is pleasure/pain, not good/evil, which is the governing dichotomy. "Strictly speaking there is no concept of moral obligation or of moral evil in Epicureanism."[96] What produces unhappiness is evil, what produces the absence of unhappiness is good. Compare the Buddhist teaching (quoted above) called the Mirror of the *Dharma*:

> Whatever action . . . leads to suffering for oneself or others or for both, that action is bad (*akusalam*). Whatever action . . . does not lead to suffering . . . is good (*kusalam*). (*M.* I.414)

The passage goes on to analyze humans into four categories: those who torment (1) themselves, (2) others, (3) themselves and others, and (4) neither themselves nor others—these last being the enlightened.[97] Epicurus arrived at this same formulation (for example at *Sent. Vat.* LXXIX and *KD* 1):

> He who has attained *ataraxia* torments neither himself nor another.

An immoral act is one that will cause pain to oneself or others. Epicurus, like the Buddha of the *Kālāma Sutta*, advises his listeners to determine on the basis of their own experience the results of actions, and to construct a quietistic hedonic calculus.

> It is our duty [says Epicurus] to judge all such cases by measuring pleasures against pains, with a view to their respective assets and liabilities. (D.L. X.130)

In fact, both the Buddha and Epicurus, like more recent utilitarians, teach an ethic of self-interest. Both agree that if one is willing to accept the painful consequences of, for example, unjust acts, there is no other reason to hold back from them. In the Buddha's view, karmic consequences in future lives are to be figured into the hedonic calculus. Epicurus, abjuring afterlife and its suggestions of self, teaches that one should fear revenge and punishment in this life.

This attitude leads Buddha to formulate the Middle Way, between simple (uncalculated) hedonism on the one hand and asceticism on the other; the Buddha, after a period of hedonism and a period of austerities, decided either approach was an impediment, and commenced a diet of frugal nourishment. Similarly Epicurus says:

> There is also a limit in simple living. He who fails to heed this limit falls into an error as great as that of the man who gives way to extravagance. (*Sent. Vat.* LXIII)

Theoretically, then, there is nothing inherently wrong with kinetic pleasures. The *sophos*, like the ordinary man, need not abjure them when they come along. Still, Epicurus, like the Buddha, was wary of the active seeking of them, which can involve proportions hard for the calculus to contain:

No pleasure is in itself evil, but the things which produce certain pleasures entail annoyances many times greater than the pleasures themselves. (D.L. X.141)[98]

Epicureanism 6: Strategies for Reforming the Mental Process

Epicurus, in the meager extant works, does not deal intensively with the process whereby sensation leads to action. He was, as Annas says, "comparatively uninterested in impulse as a phenomenon in its own right." In his works "there is nothing to compare with the careful Stoic treatment of *hormē*."[99] His view on these points must to an extent be reconstructed from texts only obliquely concerned with it, supplemented by passages in Lucretius (especially IV.881–891) and Philodemus. "Epicurus is . . . silent as to any mechanism whereby we could get from images striking the soul to content that can be interpreted and acted on."[100] He does however make prominent use of Aristotle's idea of the fixed or established disposition (*hexis*) at this juncture, regarding action as "the product of the world's impinging on an agent who already has a character and reactive capabilities of a certain kind."[101]

In Epicurus's reconstructed sequence, first an atomic film carrying an image impinges on the atomic surface of the sense organ, as in the Buddhist *phassa* or contact stage of the five *skandhas*. The mind then produces a responding image, or *phantasia*, which is not merely a copy of the received image but also involves a hedonic value (or *pathos*) and one or more preconceptions (or *prolēpseis*) derived from accumulated memory of previous experiences; these "general concepts" bring language with them, and this aspect of the *phantasia* phase equates to *saṃjñā* or identification in the system of *skandhas*, which also involves translating the sensation into a linguistic sign. The *abhidharma* account attempts to deal with each factor in isolation in its moment of arising, while the less time-precise Greek analysis sees two or three factors arising together, conditioning each other even as they arise. Through its hedonic component, this complex movement also includes the stage of *vedanā* which is separate in the Buddhist formulation. It is here that the direction of the culminating impulse or *hormē* begins to be formed. Every sensation, including every thought, is said to be accompanied by either pleasure or pain, and "it is by means of these that acts of choice and aversion are decided upon" (D.L. X. 34). They are "Nature's Go and Stop signals,"[102] waiting for the emerging impulse to receive definition. In the third stage, the impulse becomes complete. The mental image with verbal identification and hedonic value interacts with the established disposition (*hexis* or *diathesis*) to produce a belief (*doxa*) about the mental image which focuses[103] the energy of the pleasure-pain feeling into an emotion or impulse. This complex and subtle analysis corresponds to the *saṃskāra* phase of the five *skandhas*. Finally, the faculty of action takes over, imparting motion to the atoms of the body.

It is the element of belief (*doxa*) which opens the way for error, since the belief can be either accurate or false—and not only false but, according to Epicurus, harmful. Once established, harmful opinions become hard to avoid. The disposition (*hexis*) is formed by past habit formation and mechanically expresses itself as a set of implicit beliefs (*doxai*). According to Aristotle, "It is hard, if not impossible, to remove by argument the traits that have long since been incorporated in the character" (1179b4–17).[104] But Epicurus, unlike Aristotle, seems to have taught that these formed dispositions can be willfully changed. At least, he recommended philosophizing at all ages:

> To say either that the time is not yet ripe for philosophizing, or that the time for philosophizing has gone by, is like saying that the time for happiness either has not arrived or is no more. So both young and old must philosophize . . . (*Ep. Men.* 122)

Epicurus implies that the mental disposition, or *hexis*, can be changed at any age. The desired change is a reformation of one's belief system to bring it into accord with the doctrines of the calculus. As Sextus Empiricus put it, "Epicurus used to say that philosophy is an activity which by arguments and discussions brings about the happy life."[105]

The "beliefs" which in Epicurus's view cause suffering are to be compared, in Buddhism, to the beliefs in a self, in permanence, and in the obtaining of personal satisfaction, which are to be counteracted by reflection on and positivistic observation of the Three Marks, impermanence (*anicca*), unsatisfactoriness (*duḥkha*), and absence of selfhood (*anatta*). Epicurus similarly attacks the belief in a soul (self) and the belief that either pleasant or painful conditions can be made permanent; another belief which he, like the Buddha, attacked was the deterministic idea that established mental dispositions are unchangeable.

According to Epicurus's atomistic physics, ideas impart their characteristic motions to the atoms of the psyche. Foolish opinions which create unrest, such as self and permanence, are motions which have become virtually autonomous and self-sustaining due to their long repetition in childhood and after. By deliberately entertaining contrary ideas for a long time every day, one may set up counteracting atomic motions which in time will replace the old. Epicurus enjoined daily memorization and repetition on his students. The *Key Doctrines* (*Kuriai Doxai*) and the doctrinal epitomes contained in the three *Letters* were to be studied and repeated in this way. At the end of the *Letter to Menoeceus*, Epicurus says, "Practice these things and things similar to these night and day, saying them to yourself and to someone similar to yourself" (that is, another Epicurean student). Epicurus recommends that his followers read and reread his basic works constantly, committing them to memory; the memorization of the Buddhist Sūtras held a comparable place in early Buddhist mind-training.

Epicurus regarded four reflections as especially important and called them the *Tetrapharmaka*, "The Four Medicines": (1) reflection on the fact that the gods can do nothing either for or against one; (2) that since there is no enduring sentience or self, death is of no importance; (3) that good (pleasure) is easily attainable; and (4) that evil (pain) is easily endurable. With shifts in articulation, these correspond loosely to the Buddhist Three Marks.

For Epicurus, equal in importance to the forming of new opinions through reflection and repetition is an investigative attention to one's own mental processes, an activity related to the Buddhist technique of mindfulness:

> It is necessary [says Epicurus] to pay constant attention to one's pain and pleasure process as it works in the present moment. (D.L. X.82)

This constant attention to one's own hedonic process and the mental process that deals with it suggests an introspective examination of minute mental events that goes beyond mere reflection, somewhat as in the Buddhist practice of mindfulness but perhaps without the intensifying effect of concentration practices.

Other techniques are suggested to nudge the student's *hexis* into motion. The "confession," for example, seems to have been a therapeutic interview in which the student set forth for the teacher his or her passional attachments, inviting the teacher's subversive dialectical responses to them. Here, in sharp distinction to Aristotle, it was believed that factors established in the disposition can in fact be altered through argument and reflection combined with mindful observation and analysis. In addition

Epicurus recommends behavioral modification techniques such as the temporary reversing of one's habitual patterns of activity in hopes of opening a crack in them. If, for example, one feels addicted to overeating or luxurious eating, one should embark on a temporary period of extreme austerity in eating. Before long one will be aware that his addiction was not a physical fact but an opinion and that it is not necessary to be bound by it. A new *hexis* will be forming. The formation of a new *hexis* equates, in the Buddhist system of five aggregates, to the reformation of the set of *saṃskāras*, or reaction formations, which similarly are a disposition arranged by repeated conditioning.

The Consequences of Epicurean Hedonism

Epicurus's so-called hedonism, finally, leads to a rather austere way of life. Like the Buddha, he stressed the hard facts of things as they empirically are, against the soft facts of one's wishes and preferences. Events are to be regarded as things not within our control (D.L. X.135), and therefore the *sophos* must "confront adversity" (D.L. X.21).

Epicurus withdrew from public life and lived in relative seclusion with his listeners, ate no meat, drank no wine, and was probably celibate. Yet he spoke of techniques for "condensing pleasures" in order to maximize the enjoyment of the simple life, primarily involving the application of mindfulness, for example, chewing one's food "mindfully" (*epilemōs*).[106]

Epicurus's followers, like the Buddha's, came to live with him—not so much "in the garden" as "on the farm." This retreat from the world was fairly traditional in Greek philosophy as in Indian. Heraclitus frequented the wilds. Socrates and Plato both abstained from political careers. In Epicurus's view this withdrawal contributed to restraint of the senses and detachment from goals and values.

Like Buddhist communities, these retreat groups resembled religious establishments ("cults" in present-day parlance), while not being based on religious beliefs. As Buddhism rejects Vedic ritual and prayer, so Epicurus rejects ritual:

> True religion is rather the power to contemplate nature with a quiet mind. (Lucr. V.1203)

Prayer also is rejected on the basis of the need for self reliance:

> It is pointless for a man to pray for what he can provide himself, namely, happiness. (*Sent. Vat.* LXV)

Both Siddartha and Epicurus accepted the existence of gods, but declared them irrelevant to human life, and postulated the existence of a huge number of world-systems. Their grounds, however, were different. Siddartha claimed to have perceived these "facts" empirically by means of ESP developed through intense concentration practices. Epicurus taught them on the ground that they are wholesome doctrines, and at times justified them by deduction, a method which usually he abjured.

Both Buddhism and Epicureanism, despite their rejection of religious values and practices, carried with them something of the religious significance of healing cults, magnified into worldwide missionary scale. Epicurus, like the Buddha, was not so much a philosopher as "the founder of a movement for the emancipation of the ordinary man,"[107] and it is not out of the question "to claim world significance for the Epicurean movement"[108]—as for the Buddhist.

Like Buddhism, Epicureanism spread widely, new garden communities springing up in various cities, planted by Epicurean missionaries. These were organized around lineages of teachers who had heard the master, and members of each community swore obedience to the Epicurean scriptures—similar to the studying of the Sūtras in Buddhist communities. The history of these Epicurean communities covers seven hundred years. During his lifetime, Epicurus kept in touch with the foreign communities by long doctrinal letters which are precursors of St. Paul's Epistles to distant Christian communities.

As in Buddhism, the Master came to be increasingly venerated and several hundred years after his death was more or less deified. The Buddha had left unanswered the question of the sage's afterlife, perhaps fearing a loss of motivation among the followers if he flatly denied it. It was not long before his successors were filling that silence with more and more exalted forms of deification. Epicurus, however, had left no room whatever for an afterlife. His followers, making the best of it, had to content themselves with attributing to him the "godlike" status of an epochal hero, or, in slightly later terms, a messiah. The doctrine that the Wise were like gods went all the way back to Orphic roots, where it had been held literally true. Lucretius repeats it but more as a figure of speech: "If I am to suit my language to the majesty of his revelations, he was a god" (V.98). In fact, what Epicurus had accomplished, according to Lucretius, surpassed not only the exploits of Heracles, but even the gift of wheat by Ceres and of wine by Dionysus. He had hurled the gods from their thrones, demonstrating his greater power.

> [He was] a savior of the race, the first mortal to have lifted mankind from its religious debasement and to have brought it into the light of truth . . . He wandered in spirit through the limitless cosmos and returned a conqueror, to tell us what can and what cannot come to pass and how each thing's natural power is hedged by a limit deep within. Thus religion in its turn lies prostrate, ground beneath our feet, and his victory exalts us to the skies. (Lucr. I.62–101)

The Hīnayāna Buddha was represented iconographically by footprints—indicating that he had gone but had left (in the Sūtras) the markings of the path. Similarly, Lucretius says:

> I follow after you, O Epicurus, ornament of Greece, and pliantly set my feet in the tracks you have already printed. (Lucr. III.3–4)

Both Buddhism and Epicureanism were criticized for lack of a social conscience; and both made more or less the same answer (the answer later given by the Utilitarians), that enlightened self-interest is the most socially useful ethic. Says Epicurus:

> The just man is the least disturbed by passion, the unjust man the most highly disturbed. (*KD* 17, D.L. X.144)

Society would be most improved, then, by the development of *ataraxia* in its individual citizens. Epicurus taught a missionary zeal based on the (originally Cynic) concept of brotherly love:

> Love goes dancing round the world bidding us all awake and pass on the salutation of blessedness. (*Sent. Vat.* III)

"Blessedness," *to makarion*, is *hēdonē/ataraxia*. Attitudes of nonaggression were also cultivated:

> There is no need for actions which involve competition. (*KD* 21)

The concept of Love (*philia*), in fact, figures large in Epicurean axiology.

> The noble nature devotes itself to wisdom and love, of which the first is a mortal god, the second immortal. (*Sent. Vat.* LXXVIII)

Since the gods spend their time in friendly intercourse, Love is an "immortal" virtue. When wisdom, the mortal virtue, has tamed the aggression in one—when one no longer causes suffering to oneself or others—then one is ready, like the gods, to enjoy *philia*. The life of the devotees in the garden was to be dominated by *philia*; mythologically, it represented a return to the Golden Age before strife entered the garden. The *sophos* himself will be so imperturbable that he "will be the same asleep or awake" (D.L. X.121) and so, being in need of nothing, will be better at giving than receiving.

Epicureanism was "the only missionary philosophy produced by the Greeks."[109] It spread widely in the Near East, Italy, and North Africa, some communities surviving into the fourth century A.D. Diogenes Laertius says its followers could not be counted, "even by whole cities." It is known that in the second century A.D. the town of Amastris on the Black Sea was largely Epicurean in tone. Cicero remarks that Epicureanism "had a sensational influence not upon Greece and Italy alone, but also upon the whole barbarian world" (*De Fin.* II.15.49). As the "court philosophy" of the Antiochids in the second century B.C., it exerted enormous influence in Syria and Palestine. In Epicurus's own school in Athens, the custom, established by the master, was for each leader to appoint his successor, a lineage which went on for twenty-five generations or more. It was finally, it seems, its near atheism—its denial (like Buddha's) of Divine Providence, and its emphasis on self-reliance—that did it in. As Christian piety advanced, there was less and less room for a creed which openly ridiculed the adherents of religions. By the end of the fourth century A.D. there are no more references to Epicureanism as a living force.

Stoicism 1: Introduction

Whereas Epicurus's teacher was Nausiphanes, and through him Democritus, Zeno of Citium was formed primarily by Crates the Cynic, and through him Diogenes and Socrates. This difference in sources may account for the ancient impression that there was more contrast between the schools than one feels today. In antiquity—and still somewhat today—Stoicism was often regarded as the great antagonist of Epicureanism, though in comparison with a worldview which is radically different (such as the Judeo-Christian) the two seem remarkably alike. Chrysippus is said to have devoted his life to a demolition of Epicurus's doctrines. Yet the later Stoics, including Seneca, Musonius Rufus, Epictetus, and Marcus Aurelius, seem to have recognized the sympathy between the two points of view and to have actively syncretized them. The Stoic emperor Marcus Aurelius gave state salaries to the heads of all Epicurean schools. Zeno, like his ultimate model Socrates, expressed concern for religion and the state, while Epicurus, following Democritus, did not. This difference does not penetrate deeply into the content of the teachings, yet nevertheless it gave to Stoicism, throughout antiquity, an air of respectability that Epicureanism lacked. In any case, Stoicism observes the same basic structure of empiricism, causality, and interruption of the psychological process for eudaimonistic ends which dominates both early Buddhism and Epicureanism.

Stoicism 2: Naturalistic Theory of Knowledge

Like Epicurus, Zeno of Citium and his successors taught that all knowledge consists of knowledge of particulars, that is, all knowledge is empirically based, and inductive inferences from empirical data are preferred to deductive ones (though the latter sometimes occur). From sense perception arises memory, and from remembered perceptions general concepts are induced, called *prolēpseis* (a term seemingly borrowed from Epicurus). Both Epicurus and the Stoics had difficulty establishing a method for distinguishing objective perceptions from subjective ones; Epicurus spoke of *enargeiai*, or surpassingly clear perceptions, which are to be the basis of ontological distinctions, and this seems to be preserved to some extent in the Stoic *phantasia kataleptikē*, the cataleptic impression, or the impression which takes hold of the subject in such a way that it cannot be denied. Less rigorously empirical than the Epicureans, the Stoics admitted a wide range of *prolēpseis* which were not directly sense-based but derived by a variety of logical processes from sense-based concepts. This does not nullify, though it may weaken somewhat, the basic naturalism of the Stoic position, which holds that no mental activity is conceivable without sensory input.

Stoicism 3: Naturalistic Doctrine of Causality

Like the Epicurean (and the Buddhist), the Stoic denies acausal events and also denies causality from outside of nature. Says Chrysippus:

> No single event, not even the smallest, can take place otherwise than in accordance with universal Nature and its *logos*. (*SVF* II.937)

And Alexander of Aphrodisias:

> There neither exists nor occurs anything uncaused in the cosmos. (*SVF* II.991)

Cicero brings out the implications for scientific inquiry:

> If there were a man whose soul could discern the links that join each cause with every other cause, then surely he would never be mistaken in any prediction he might make. (*De Div.* I.127)

Stoicism 4: Naturalistic Psychology

In their discussions of the self or soul the Stoics maintained a materialistic and causal point of view while making concessions to the old Orphic supernaturalism as it was retained in a weakened form by Aristotle. The soul is, like everything real, corporeal; it exists only in conjunction with the body.[110] But though it is material, its substance is not gross matter; rather, it is of the quintessence, or ether, the divine fire of the universe from which the soul in Plato's view also was formed—along with Aristotle's Prime Mover and active intellect. (A residual trace of this cult of the soul may remain in Epicurus's nearly mystical "nameless" atoms which make up the most sensitive part of the soul and are the smallest and finest atoms in the universe)[111].

The Stoic account of the process which leads from sensation to action is, like Epicurus's, based primarily on Aristotle's *Nicomachean Ethics* and *De Motu Animalium* (with Plato in the more distant background), but—again like Epicurus's version—with avenues opened up toward revision of the *hexis*. It also bears a strong similarity to the process as described in early Buddhism. At the first stage, again, occurs sensation (*aisthesis*) resulting from contact of an object with a sense organ. The second stage, like Aristotle's and Epicurus's, combines the *vedanā* and *saṃjñā* stages of the Buddhist model: A *phantasia*, image or presentation, arises in the mind, already bearing a tonality of pain or pleasure; this pain or pleasure aspect gives initial directionality to an emerging impulse (*hormē*) of either grasping or shunning (either *orexis*, a stretching out toward, or *ekklisis*, a leaning away from). In the third stage, the *orexis* or *ekklisis* will be decided in its overall directionality and also articulated in its nuances of texture, urgency, and ambiguity by the *hexis* or formed disposition, which in the Stoic view contains a stock of general conceptions, or *prolēpseis*.[112] These are formed by generalizing from the data of experience, and are "immediately activated when a sense-impression is received."[113] Thus far, the model is not so different from Aristotle's; but in addition the Stoics posit a factor of free will or choice (*hairesis*) which has the power to either assent to or dissent from the impulse.[114] In this model the prohaeretic faculty has more autonomy than in Aristotle's. It can intervene in the sensation-to-action sequence at the point of the *hormē* or impulse, the phase equivalent to *saṃskāra* in the Buddhist description of the process.

For the Stoics, then, actions rise from a psychological process which may appear to be automatic—the arising of impulsive actions from the collaboration of pleasure/pain with early conditioning (the *hexis* or disposition)—but which in fact contains a more or less concealed element of free will. This hidden force, the *prohairesis*, can be uncovered by self-study and brought into an ascendancy over one's activities. That is the achievement of the *sophos*.

Stoicism 5: The Naturalistic Ethics

The Stoic sense of ethical values was derived closely from the Cynic and featured the Cynic ideals of *apatheia*, "nonreactiveness," and *autarkeia*, "self-rule." Again there is a pronounced similarity with Epicurus, who taught that since events are outside of one's control one's emotions should be outside of *their* control.

According to the Stoic concept of cosmic harmony, the ethical end is to bring one's patterns of desire and aversion into harmony with the actual flow of events which are outside our control, or with nature. "Living in agreement with nature is the end," said Zeno, and Chrysippus added, "for our own natures are parts of the nature of the whole" (D.L. VII.87–88). One should desire the things which actually do happen, and should not desire the things which do not actually happen. To desire things which do not happen, or hate things which do happen, is regarded as actually sinful: It represents a perverse personal willfulness which goes against natural harmony. An inclination to position oneself in conflict with nature amounts to a *pathos* or passion, which "could be properly located as a subdivision of 'impulses' . . ."[115] As Stobaeus says (II.88.8), "They say that passion is impulse which is excessive and disobedient to the dictates of reason, or a movement of soul which is irrational and contrary to nature."[116] The goal of ethical philosophy must be to bring personal preferences and aversions into harmony with those of the ruling principle of the universe, variously called "Zeus," "Reason" (*Logos*), and "Nature." As Cleanthes wrote in his "Hymn to Zeus," "Zeus leads the willing person, the unwilling he drags." One must develop an ability to block personal impulses when the order of Nature displays other preferences. At such a moment one needs the qualities of imperturbability and mental detachment from the *hormē* and its infectious spirit of enthusiasm. For this detachment the Stoics used the term *apatheia*, nonemotional response, adopted from the Cynic tradition.[117]

The Cynics taught that certain qualities (such as self-reliance) are virtuous, others (such as lack of self-reliance) are vicious. All other qualities are indifferent (*adiaphora*). So far the Stoic view agrees with the Cynics. But the Cynics seem to have taught that there is absolutely no preference among the things which are indifferent. In that area one may follow personal preferences absolutely, so long as one does not let go of basic detachment or self-reliance; if one's personal preference on an indifferent matter be frustrated, one must be ready to be apathetic, indifferent, nonreactive—otherwise one loses hold of virtue, which consists in not losing one's balance by either grasping or withdrawing.

If one tends to lose hold of virtue/imperturbability through the attraction of one category of experience more than any other, then this area of experience may take on the appearance of a different moral value than the others. One teacher might recommend avoiding this area. Another might recommend emphasizing one's work on it. Yet another might insist that no distinctions of that sort be made.

Zeno seems to have been involved in this discussion and to have introduced distinctions into the class of "indifferents"—or rather, to have introduced an additional class of "secondary" preferreds and condemneds. Some "indifferents," he taught, though they do not actually embody self-reliance and imperturbability, may nevertheless allow the development of these traits and thus are "preferred indifferents"; others may be specially conducive to loss of imperturbability, and thus are "avoided indifferents." A Cynic might have regarded this innovation as regressive. Having won freedom from the compulsive moralism of Plato and other "gods," Zeno had proceeded to give back part of the ground won, by dividing and limiting it with new prescriptions and proscriptions.[118] This controversy surfaced between Zeno and his disciple Ariston of Chios, who wanted to return to the more tough-minded categories of the Cynics:

> Ariston of Chios . . . said that the end is to live a life of indifference to what is between virtue and vice and not to admit any distinction whatever in things of this kind, but to behave identically to all of them. (D.L. VII.162)

Zeno, or possibly Chrysippus, introduced yet another distinction within the "indifferent" class, that of appropriate and inappropriate actions (making, finally, seven categories of actions: virtuous, preferred, appropriate, indifferent, inappropriate, avoided, vicious). The distinction between appropriate and inappropriate actions is again one which the Cynics rejected. It was primarily a concession to social stability, a concern of the Stoics which the Cynics did not share. For a Stoic, to help one's brother when he needs it, regardless of his behavior toward one, is appropriate; for a Cynic one's brother is no different from any other person.

But the Stoic compromise on this matter should not be exaggerated. The dispute is parallel to differences in approaches taken by Buddhist teachers. Some advise developing imperturbability through the exclusive application of mindfulness, a direct confrontation with consciousness with no selection of situations; others advise selection of situations as an aid for the development of imperturbability. The distinction is related to the Buddhist distinction between sudden and gradual enlightenment, which was also an issue between the Cynics, who stressed suddenness, and the Stoics, who had a more lenient approach to practice. For the Stoics, in fact, as for Buddhists of various schools and periods, the development of wisdom seemed so difficult and protracted that there was a real question whether any genuine *sophoi* or wise men existed in the world.

Cynicism is a doctrine too radically individualistic to provide a philosophical basis for a stable ongoing society. Zeno wanted to preserve the essential virtue of Cynic tough-mindedness—its relentless and uncompromising cultivation of imperturbability—while taming other aspects of the doctrine in order to make it socially useful. Not everyone could be expected to attain the degree of freedom and imperturbability embodied by Diogenes. Zeno himself, if we are to believe Diogenes Laertius, did attain a comparable freedom, but did not expect it of everyone. Society, in his view, should be guided by a few individuals who have attained real *apatheia* and *autarkeia* (the echo of Plato's philosopher-kings may show the influence of Polemon), while the great masses would be encouraged to develop these qualities as much as they could. On the Stoic view the individual could go all the way, to the extent of "jamming the brakes" for supposedly involuntary functions like breathing and pumping blood, if he or she should so decide, and persevere in the decision. A lesser hero must learn to intervene in the process of impulse where he or she can, and may be helped in this effort by certain principles of self-protection and avoidance of temptation which the *sophos* will no longer need. Concepts such as preferred and appropriate are for this purpose.

The selection of a preferred action does not commit one to an emotional clinging to the results of the action (which would be a *pathos*). It is the *selection* which is preferred; the outcome is still indifferent. One might choose to try to save somebody's life, but if one failed, one should feel neither anger at the frustration of one's intent, nor pity for the person who died.

> The virtuous man, having done everything in his power [to bring about a certain end], does not feel pity or regret [if his efforts fail]. (*SVF* III.450–2)
>
> When desire and aversion are under your own control, what more is there to care for? (Epict. *Disc.* II.2.6)
>
> Enable my mind to adapt itself to whatever comes. (Epict. *Disc.* II.2.21)

The purpose of this development of *apatheia* is, as in Buddhism and Epicureanism, essentially eudaimonistic—its purpose is to minimize suffering. For Stoics, again as for Buddhists and Epicureans, happiness means primarily tranquility or equanimity, not the ebb and flow of kinetic pleasures. Seneca writes:

> What is a happy life? Peacefulness and constant tranquility. (*Ep.* 92.3)[119]

And Epictetus:

> What is the goal of virtue? Serenity. (I.4.5–6)

For "serenity," in this passage, Epictetus does not use a negative term such as *ataraxia*, but the positive term, *euroia*, harking back to Democritus's *euthumia*. *Euroia* literally means "well-flowingness" and relates to many eastern ethical terms such as the *Tao Te King*'s "water principle," the *Anābhogacaryā*, or life free from conscious strivings, of the *Laṅkāvatāra Sūtra*,[120] and indeed to "emptiness" or "nonobstructedness" when used as psychological or ethical terms. It relates to Plato and Aristotle's idea that the unobstructed continuance of an organism *is* happiness, and is to be equated with Epicurus's static pleasure.

Epictetus's many formulations of this principle are roughly parallel to the Buddhist Four Noble Truths. The First Noble Truth defines suffering as either not getting what one wants or getting what one does not want. Similarly Epictetus says:

> Show me how you stand in regard to desire and aversion, whether you do not fail to get what you wish, or do not fall into what you do not wish. (*Disc.* II.1.31)

Like Siddhārtha, Epictetus focuses above all on the problem of having one's will out of tune with events which are out of one's control. That suffering is caused but not absolutely determined, and hence, that its causation can be stymied—the Second and Third Noble Truths—are also basic principles for the Stoics.

Stoicism 6: Strategies for Interrupting Mental Process

The Stoic psychology was written primarily by Chrysippus, virtually all of whose works have perished. There is, consequently, considerable uncertainty about many of the details, especially the apparently complex nature of that stage of the process which Chrysippus called the *hormē* or impulse.

Every human deed and thought, in the Stoic view, is preceded by an act of assent (or the withholding of assent, which is referred to as dissent). This assent "will be a product of character and habit and one's past up to that point"[121]—in other words, it will arise, as for Aristotle, from an interaction of the immediate perception with one's *hexis* or established disposition. The act of assent or dissent happens so fast that it is seldom noticed. In order to gain rational control of one's impulses it is necessary to identify and isolate this fleeting mental act, to foreground it as an object of study because it is the area in which free will can be exercised: This is where the brakes are. "Impulses [*hormai*] are the origins of action," Plutarch said (*Anim. An. corp.* 501C). "Humans, however," as Annas points out, "have a choice as to whether and how they react to stimuli."[122] "Epictetus lays constant stress on our ability to accept or reject appearances."[123] Diogenes Laertius also refers to "nonprecipitancy (*aproptōsia*) [which] is knowledge of when one should assent, and when not . . ." (D.L. VII.46). "Origen [speaks of reason] choosing between impulses; Clement tells us that reason helps us to discriminate among appearances and not be carried away by them."[124] By Epictetus's day several pairs of terms for assent and dissent were used interchangeably: In addition to *orexis* and *ekklisis*—the stretching one's arms toward something or leaning away from it—*hormē* and *aphhormē*—mean the surging of one's energies and intentions toward or away from something (both pairs of terms being based on Plato's observation that a desire is a "movement of the soul" toward or away from an object).

The process culminating in the *hormē*, as described by Chrysippus, was three-staged, as with Aristotle and Epicurus, rather than four-staged, as in the *abhidharma*: first, *aisthesis* or sensation (i.e., *phassa* or contact); second, *phantasia* or mental imprint left by the sensation, which is directly accompanied by pleasure or pain (i.e., *saṃjñā* or recognition along with *vedanā* or hedonic feeling); and third, the *hormē* or impulse (i.e., *saṃskāra* or emotional reaction). In this version of the process it seems that there are either two or three moments of assent: First, there is assent to the identification of the sensation in the second stage; in the propositional linguistic mode that goes back to Aristotle and is still used by the Stoics, that assent takes the form of a conversation within oneself: "Yes, that is a plausible identification; I assent to it," or "No, that is an implausible identification; I decline it." In addition, still in stage two, if the *phantasia* is not hedonically neutral but accompanied by either pleasure or pain, it may be that another assent is needed, to the leaning toward or withdrawing from that must occur as soon as the pleasure or pain does. This affective assent or dissent—"Yes, I will bend in the direction this pleasure or pain is inducing," or "No, I will not"—amounts to an early forecast of the assent or dissent to the approaching *hormē*. Finally, when the stage of the *hormē* proper arrives, there is the crucial moment of assent to it. This is the only assent traditionally recognized in the process, but if the doctrine of the assent is fully carried out, it seems that at least one act of assent or dissent, and perhaps two such acts, are already in effect by the time the third stage—the impulsive or hormetic stage proper—arrives.

Another way of stating this is that when a *phantasia* comes equipped with either pain or pleasure, what is involved is not merely an assent but an assent-plus-impulse. There is an assent to the facticity of the *phantasia* plus a second assent to the pleasure. This second assent, since it involves a desire, becomes an assent-with-impulse or an assent-with-desire-or-aversion, just as the presentation was not merely a presentation but a presentation-with-pleasure-or-pain. Seen in succession, there are five elements involved in the second or *phantasia* stage: First there is the *phantasia* or presentation, then (2) the assent to the reliability of the presentation; meanwhile, along with the presentation comes (3) a feeling of pleasure or pain, and this is followed by (4) an impulse toward or away from the pleasure or pain which in turn is followed by (5) an act of assent to or dissent from the impulse. It is not at all certain how Chrysippus and his successors systematized this, but modern scholars have leaned toward the view that there are plain presentations and feeling-toned or affective presentations, and also, corresponding to them—plain assents and assents-with-impulse.[125]

As there are different aspects to the *phantasia* in stage two, so there are different types of *hormai* to respond to them in stage three. The simplest *hormē* involves just the assent or dissent to the impulse; but as the *hexis* gets stirred up and its associated memories and conceptions cluster round the *hormē*, each bringing with it a hedonic response of its own independent of the hedonic response to the original presentation, the *hormē* gets complex and layered; like any moment of desire it may be ambiguous or even inwardly contradictory. The complex impulse may be experienced in stages, first the impulse, then the basic assent or dissent, then the associative strings of memories and conceptions, each with its secondary hedonic accompaniments. The third or hormetic stage may become a psychological composite far more nuanced than a simple act of reaching toward or leaning away.

The relationship between *samjñā*, recognition/identification, and *vedanā*, hedonic feeling, was treated as one of successive stages in the *abhidharma*, but as complex simultaneous single events by the Greek philosophers. It may be that the Greek thinkers had not concentrated as deeply on concrete observation of the processes: To them, events following one another with eye-blink rapidity seemed simultaneous. The *abhidharma*, in contrast, is traditionally said to have been empirically researched by meditators on whom prolonged concentration exercises have bestowed a slow-motion apprehension of the passage of psychological events, and who can discern the different stages at a level of detail so minute as to be microscopic. There is no indication that any of the Greek philosophers went through the specialized discipline necessary to develop this acuteness. Still, as Nyanaponika Thera noted, "cautious and intelligent use . . . of one's own introspective observations . . . though far from infallible, may well lead to important and reliable conclusions."[126] Whether the Hellenistic philosophers meditated or not, their self-observation was sensitive and accurate, as is showed by the fact that they describe the process virtually identically with the *abhidharma* except for a tendency to see as aspects of a single complex stage what the *abhidharma* sees more minutely as successive simple stages.

Like Aristotle, the Stoics held that several parts of the *hormetic* process were determined by the *hexis*. First, the experience of pleasure and pain is dictated by the *hexis*. It may be that all humans take pleasure in eating when hungry, but it is also true that some are disposed to take pleasure in fasting and others not. In this sense, the pleasure or pain component of the *phantasia* is not autonomous and automatic, but at least partially dependent on the acquired *hexis*. Secondly, the mere assent to the plausibility of the identification will in some cases be affected by the *hexis*: If one person has been taught as a child that centaurs do not exist, and another that they do, their respective *hexeis* will enforce on the first a tendency to withhold assent when confronted with a presentation of a centaur, and on the other a tendency to give assent. The *hexis* equates roughly with the mass of *saṃskāras* or ingrained mental and emotional reactions in the fourth aggregate of the Buddhist sequence. The most important role of the *hexis* is the effect it has on the third stage, when it is time to give assent to the impulse or *hormē*, preparing the way for it to be acted out. "There is no doubt that the Stoics held that the assent was determined by the nature of the fixed disposition."[127] The question, then, as in Epicurean psychology, is whether or not the *hexis* can be altered deliberately after a certain age.

Aristotle distinguished between the formative years, in which the *hexis* is taking shape, and the fixed years, in which it can no longer be changed. Yet he does not fix this boundary, and certain passages of the *Nicomachean Ethics* imply that a middle-aged person may still be formative.[128] Chrysippus seems to have believed that it is always possible to change one's *hexis* with the right techniques. In an infant, in his view, the impulses are all natural and healthy. But in time they grow dangerous unless restrained or interrupted somehow; to protect the child when he is endangered by the unquestioned nature of his impulses, adults present him with a set of beliefs which pervert the naturalness of the *hormetic* faculty. These may develop into *pathē*, disadvantageous impulses which are so strong as to be absolutely irresistible to the untrained mind: obsessions, compulsions, complexes, character defects.

The one tool which can avail against the *pathē* is reason or explanation (*logos*); *logos* here is quite close to Sanskrit terms like *prajñā*, which also indicates the ability to cut through habitual confusions and delusions and forestall the unhealthy impulses that arise from them. According to Chrysippus, at some point in one's development, "Reason supervenes as the craftsman, or technician, of impulse" (D.L. VII.86).

Until reason "supervenes as the craftsman of impulse," the *hormetic* process is more or less mechanical. The influence of adults has ingrained the ability to intervene in the impulse in certain cases, but that is a restraint enforced by reward-punishment conditioning, and little exercise of reason is involved in its calculus. Potentially, however, reason may develop the ability to supervene on impulse to any extent whatever. Many will not pursue its intervention beyond a primitive egocentric calculus. Some few may pursue it as far as the ability to intervene voluntarily in breathing or blood-pumping. The degree of rational control over the *hormetic* process which an individual has gained constitutes his or her ethical status; this degree of rational control is absolutely the central issue in Stoic ethics, as it is in a number of other Greek schools, such as Plato's, Aristotle's, and Epicurus's and in early Buddhism. Those who have not taken control of the *hormetic* impulse are robots or programmed machines, acting out their program (*hexis*) permanently. The unique power of reason is the ability to reprogram oneself. Cicero reports a five-stage model of the process, perhaps derived from Chrysippus, which is based on an increasing accumulation of "selection" impulses: (1) first are infantile prerational impulses where selection is based only on pleasure and pain; (2) then early exercise of socially oriented selection occurs under parental and other influences, without strong involvement of reason yet; this may be the stage with which selection-development ceases for many; but (3) for one exposed to philosophy, there may supervene some conscious application to the task of selecting impulses that will be in harmony with reason (nature); (4) in a lifetime devoted to this task, the continuous performance of this process of selection will conduce to the development of (5) virtue, understood as approaching natural selection at all times (*De Fin.* III.20–21). Theoretically, stages three to five—which comprise a willed programming of oneself—can effect a transition from one *hexis* to another which contradicts it.

The Stoics, especially Chrysippus, were deeply engaged in the analysis of logic and language, and Chrysippus, like Aristotle, taught that emotional acts of assent represent assent to actual propositions, though the latter might not be consciously articulated. If the proposition that is assented to is contrary to reason, the assent-with-impulse may become a *pathos*, or neurotic reaction, for assent to such a proposition leads to action that is contrary to nature. If assent to false propositions is eliminated, *pathē*, which only occur in association with them, will also be eliminated. Hence the great Stoic interest in logic: The elimination of assent to irrational propositions will straighten out the *hexis*, or character, by liberating it from *pathē*, or neurotic reactions. One's emotional patterns, then, are the surface manifestations of an underlying propositional system to which one long ago gave assent. One grieves at the death of a member of one's family because: (1) as a child, one was told that the death of a family member was an evil and (2) one assented to this view and (3) incorporated it into one's *hexis*, where it was held in abeyance, until (4) the presentation of a death in the family actually occurs, whereupon (5) one grieves, because one has long ago decided that one would grieve at that time and because (6) one still assents to that earlier decision. Epictetus focuses on the voluntariness of *decision*, whether made in the past, or ratified in the present. He insists that "the hormetic faculty is within the realm of choice" (*Disc.* I.1.2), and suggests more or less the same techniques suggested by Epicurus and the early Buddhists: mindful inspection of the mental process combined with reflections on causality. Through maintaining focus on the experience of sensation being converted into impulse, one begins to catch glimpses of the subliminally made decisions or assents involved. First, the crudest of these can be seen, then briefer, subtler, or more hidden ones. The anecdote of Zeno's death by stopping his breath, regardless of its historicity, implies the doctrine that the decision process went so deep as to be involved in every breath one takes. This is a level of decision-making that is so deeply hidden and so quick to transpire that few can expect to see it, even when looking closely. But in this tradition seeing the decision-making process at any level is regarded as useful; when one sees it happening one might be able to intervene in it—but not before (somewhat along the lines of Socrates saying that no one would do wrong if he knew he was doing wrong).

This practice of introspection, according to Epictetus, is to be guided by reflections which involve redescribing and visualization.

> If you have a favorite piece of china don't think of it as that: think of it just as a jug. Then you will not be upset if it gets broken. If you have a wife, don't think about her as that: think of her just as a person (a someone). Then you won't be upset if she dies. (*Ench.* 3)

Epictetus goes on to argue that nothing outside of one's own body is in one's power, and in fact, not even that body itself, which may become ill or die without one's willing it. Only the faculty of giving or withholding assent to impulse is in one's power: Only the ability to be imperturbable (*Diss.* I.1). Impermanence is declared to apply to everything, like causality. Epictetus said:

> That which has become must also perish. (*Disc.* II.5.12–13)

The Buddha's last words, on his deathbed, were recorded as more or less the same:

> All things that have come together must also come apart. (*D.* XVI.6.8)

The Academic-Skeptic Carneades is credited with virtually the same last words:

> Nature which puts things together also will take them apart. (D.L. IV.64)

Techniques such as visualizations and reflections on the obstacles to gratification are supposed to increase one's ability to interfere with impulses. This intervention, in turn, weakens the existing *hexis*, or habit-system, and at the same time, reprograms it. Like Locke's sock, it gradually becomes a new habit system or disposition. The *sophos* is one whose *hexis* has been brought into harmony with whatever happens. This situation is understood as the ability to live without unnecessary sufferings. "The wise man feels pleasures and pains; what he does not feel are those pleasures and pains which are [the result of] mistaken judgments."[129]

Epictetus and Seneca both state the general principle:

> It is not things themselves that disturb people, but their opinions about the things . . . It is the part of an untrained person to blame others when he feels badly; to blame himself is the action of one whose training has begun. To blame no one is the part of one whose training is complete. (*Ench.* 5)
>
> All our pains hang on opinions . . . Opinion is what we are sad for. Each of us is as wretched as he believes. (Seneca, *Ep.* 78.13)

The effectiveness of such approaches is measured by their ability to interrupt the staged process from sensation to emotion to action.

The Pyrrhonist technique of suspension, or *epochē*, may seem to interrupt the process at an earlier stage than the Stoic technique. Sextus, in effect, advises not only withholding assent to the affective predicate—the impulse of desire or avoidance that the *phantasia* gives rise to—but also withholding primary assent in every case to the veracity of the *phantasia* itself, that is, to the existential proposition it implies. A problem with this position, from the Stoic point of view, is the loss of motivation that might ensue on complete suspension or *epochē*. Cicero, expressing the Stoic point of view, says:

> Those . . . who say that nothing can be grasped tear out the very tools or equipment of life, or rather they actually ruin the foundations of the whole of life and rob the living being itself of the mind which gives it life . . . (*Academica* II.31)[130]

The Stoics were more action-oriented—they wanted to rule, as Plato had wanted also—and accordingly, "did not budge from the thesis . . . that infallible knowledge of the world is possible."[131]

The Later History of Stoicism

In Seneca's day—the first century A.D.—Greco-Roman culture was characterized by both the mystery religions and the naturalistic therapeutic cults—Stoicism, Epicureanism, and Skepticism. Around that time, there is evidence of a revival of Cynicism and, accompanying it, a reform of Stoicism along Cynic lines. Roman Stoics deemphasized the complex conceptual system of the Chrysippan Stoa and reemphasized the practical ethical teaching of the Cynics and Zeno. This New Stoa became a significant source of action in the tumultuous Roman politics of the late Republic and the early Empire. At the same time the Stoics made their ethical ideal less forbidding by emphasizing the concept of gradual progress rather than the condition of infallible perfection which was its theoretical end. As in Buddhism after its first centuries, the idea arose that the fully enlightened sage was rare to the point of being almost mythical.

Two candidates for the status of *sophos* illustrate the universal appeal the doctrine could exercise: the slave Epictetus and the emperor Marcus Aurelius, both second century A.D. It was surprising for an emperor to be a serious student of a school which had made its mark in the Roman tradition by its advocacy of republican values such as self-reliance and self-determination; and it was prestigious for the Stoics that, as a modern author wrote, "the sovereign of the whole known world . . . professed Stoicism and lived as a Stoic."[132] Indeed, so deeply identified with that tradition was Marcus Aurelius that he even wrote a Stoic book of some significance.

One might compare Aśoka's momentous conversion to Buddhism in the third century B.C. The difference lies in the fact that Aśoka stood near the beginning of Buddhist history, and Marcus Aurelius was close to the end of the Stoic. By the close of his century it was already losing its appeal, as lack of the genuine political participation that had invigorated Roman Stoicism for centuries led to a steady spiritualization of imperial culture; Stoicism's materialism put it at a disadvantage to resurgent Platonism, the Mystery religions, and emerging Christianity. In the third century A.D. Stoicism ceased operating as an autonomous school and more or less disappeared until the remaining record of it struck a chord in Renaissance humanists more than a thousand years later.

It endured for a while, however, in foreign milieux to which it diffused widely as it was carried to the far reaches of the empire by itinerant teachers. The Christian fathers Clement and Tertullian were both influenced by Seneca and recommended the control of emotions and impulses as a part of Christian spirituality. Traces of Epictetus have been found in Arabic texts of several centuries later. Tamil literature in south India seems to show not only a somewhat kindred spirit with the Stoa but actual Stoic influences from the Roman trading colonies that were wealthy and influential in the Tamil country.

The Diffusion Question

The comparison at the center of this chapter—between the Buddhist five *skandhas* on the one hand and the ethical psychologies of Epicureanism and Stoicism on the other—shows stunningly similar investigative introspections which may or may not have been carried out independently of one another. Still, there is no strong reason for either proposing or denying historical diffusion in regard to this material. In the Hellenistic and early Roman imperial periods, the Greco-Roman presence in India was widespread, thriving, and specially connected with Buddhism. Certain moods of inquiry and certain specific ideas and lines of thought may have been in the air commonly in the mixed mercantile communities of Greeks, Romans, Indo-Aryans, Tamils, Kushans, and others. In the Parthian period a Stoic teacher named Archedamus founded in Seleucia a Stoic school with succession. Susa was renowned as a center for the teaching of Greek philosophy. In Bactria and India, also, it is likely that elements of Pyrrhonism, Epicureanism, Stoicism, Śaivism, Theravāda, Mahāyāna, Vedānta, Sāṃkhya, and other strains of philosophical thought mingled with Mediterranean and Indian grammatical theorizing, astronomical arithmetic, algebraic and geometrical investigations, and—the bottom line of the whole thriving hybrid cultural mélange—mercantile trade. The mechanisms of diffusion, in whatever direction, were clearly in place, but there is no crucial detail that requires invoking them.

Scholarly Shadings

Prejudices about the nature of Greek culture in general have shaded the understanding of the Hellenistic schools. Long, for example, says, "Epicureanism was always an inward-looking movement in antiquity, and under the later empire it probably flourished more in the eastern provinces than the Roman west."[133] The connection between the two clauses implies that it is "eastern"—even, in fact, nonwestern—to be "inward-looking." Long proceeds to declare that Pyrrhonism also must be denied the status of a truly western way of thinking: "Sextus's detailed presentation of skeptical arguments and his criticism of the dogmatists implies a conception of philosophy which was very different from the moralizing pre-occupation of Roman writers."[134] So Sextus also must be expressing an eastern attitude. But in fact, the evidence of their writings suggests that the classical Greeks and Romans may have been as well-equipped for introspection as for action and as ready for skeptical argument as for proofs. Stoicism found a more congenial home in the western empire—and also in the Christian milieu—than did either Epicureanism or Pyrrhonism; but this need not suggest that Epicureanism and Pyrrhonism were felt to be nonnative to that region. It might better be explained by the fact that Stoics were willing to mouth both patriotic and religious pieties, and neither Epicureans nor Skeptics were. It was their public concern with Divine Providence, Soul, and Justice that endeared the Stoics to rulers and bishops. The Epicureans and Pyrrhonists, who openly rejected such concepts, have received a less favorable press from their day till our own. How could respectable rulers and prelates accept the Epicurean idea that justice and virtue were epiphenomena of pleasure? Or the Pyrrhonist refusal to make even that much of an assertion?

A stereotype related to the idea that Greeks were extraverted and Indians introverted holds that Greeks were optimistic and Indians pessimistic. But the traditional folk wisdom of archaic Greece was anything but optimistic. "Call no man happy," ran a Greek folk saying in the age of the Seven Sages, "until he is dead." Homer asserts that human life has twice as much pain in it as pleasure, while Theravādin Buddhist tradition, on the other hand, claims to know that human life has slightly more pleasure in it than pain.

It has recently been claimed[135] that the Greeks did not characteristically describe happiness negatively and that therefore the type of formulation found in Epicurus's *ataraxia* must have come into Greece from Indian by way of Pyrrhon. But the view that negative ethical terminology was un-Greek seems far from obvious. Aristotle had referred to Greek thinkers for whom *apatheia* was the goal, and Democritus had used the terms *athambia* and quite possibly the term *ataraxia* also. Other terms for happiness prominent in Greek philosophy include *akataplēxia*, inability to be amazed or frightened (Nausiphanes); *apatheia*, inability to be distressed (Speusippus, Diogenes); *aphasia*, nonspeech (Sextus); *arrepsia*, inability to be put off balance (Pyrrhon?, Sextus); and *aponia*, nonlabor (Epicurus).

Another questionable cliché about East and West lies behind Radkakrishnan's observation, "If the Greek origin of European philosophy has made it more intellectual, in the East the emphasis has been on the unrest of the soul rather than on metaphysical curiosity."[136] But surely the Hellenistic philosophers, at least, were as concerned with "the unrest of the soul" as were the Indians in any period. In fact, as early as the pre-Socratics Greek philosophy emphasized the development of equanimity, which was implied in the early monistic systems and made explicit by Democritus, the Buddha's chief rival as first expounder of a naturalistic psychology and ethics.[137]

Notes to Chapter Twenty-Five

1. Mircea Eliade, *Shamanism: Archaic Techniques of Ecstasy*, Bollingen Series 76 (Princeton, New Jersey: Princeton University Press, 1964), p. 215.

2. On Empedocles and medicine see M. R. Wright, ed., *Empedocles: The Extant Fragments* (New Haven, Connecticut, and London: Yale University Press, 1981), pp. 9–14.

3. Martha C. Nussbaum, *The Therapy of Desire: Theory and Practice in Hellenistic Ethics* (Princeton, New Jersey: Princeton University Press, 1994), p. 51.

4. Michael Frede, *Essays in Ancient Philosophy* (Minneapolis: University of Minnesota Press, 1987), p. 225.

5. John Burnet, *Early Greek Philosophy* (Cleveland, Ohio, and New York: World Publishing Company, 1964), p. 201, n. 4.

6. Nussbaum, *Therapy of Desire*, pp. 16 and 35.

7. Ibid., p. 246.

8. R. J. Hankinson, *The Sceptics* (London and New York: Routledge, 1995), p. 225.

9. Quoted by Michael Frede, "Philosophy and Medicine in Antiquity," in *Essays in Ancient Philosophy*, p. 228.

10. A. A. Long, *Hellenistic Philosophy* (London: Duckworth, 1974), p. 234.

11. Quoted by Edward Conze, trans., *The Large Sūtra on the Perfect Wisdom* by Maitreyanatha (Berkeley, California, and Los Angeles: University of California Press, 1975), p. 144, n. 4.

12. Bruno Kato et al., trans., *The Threefold Lotus Sūtra* (Tokyo: Kosei Publishing Co., 1975), p. 5.

13. Ibid., p. 4.

14. Wing-Tsit Chan, ed., *A Source Book in Chinese Philosophy* (Princeton, New Jersey: Princeton University Press, 1963), p. 366.

15. Nussbaum, *Therapy of Desire*, pp. 3 and 41.

16. Jonathan Barnes, *The Presocratic Philosophers*, The Arguments of the Philosophers (London and New York: Routledge, 1982), p. 127.

17. Julia Annas, *The Morality of Happiness* (New York: Oxford University Press, 1993), p. 18.

18. The attribution is rejected by some, who argue that, though *athambia* and *euthumia* (another Democritean ethical term) are both poetic words, *ataraxia* is not. (See, for example, Everard Flintoff, "Pyrrho and India," *Phronēsis* 25 [1980] pp. 95–96.) But this distinction seems insignificant: *ataraxia* and *ataraktos* are used by Hippocrates and thus were part of literate Greek in Democritus's time. That the polymath Democritus may have read technical texts by medical writers and indeed writers of all kinds is not the least surprising. Furthermore, Ibycus uses *athambes* (*PMG* 286.11) and Pindar *euthumia* (*I.* I.63).

19. Nussbaum, *Therapy of Desire*, p. 93.

20. Ibid., p. 78.

21. Annas, *The Morality of Happiness*, p. 148.

22. Nussbaum, *The Therapy of Desire*, p. 82.

23. Ibid., p. 97.

24. Ibid., pp. 85–86.

25. Ibid., p. 91.

26. Ibid., p. 93.

27. A. H. Armstrong, *An Introduction to Ancient Philosophy* (n.c.: Littlefield, Adams and Company, 1981), p. 102.

28. Annas, *The Morality of Happiness*, pp. 58, 55 n. 19.

29. Nussbaum, *Therapy of Desire*, p. 92.

30. For a recent and vigorous expression of this position see Flintoff, "Pyrrho and India," pp. 88–108.

31. Rohit Mehta, *The Call of the Upaniṣads* (Delhi: Motilal Banarsidass, 1996), p. 290.

32. Walter Schubring, *The Doctrine of the Jainas* (Delhi: Motilal Banarsidass, 1962), p. 305.

33. Gerald J. Lawson, *Clàssical Sāṅkhya* (Delhi: Motilal Banarsidass, 1979), p. 205.

34. These are very ancient traditions; indeed, for two of them claims of Bronze Age origins have been made. (For apparent connections between Indus Valley culture and the Jain tradition, see Thomas McEvilley, "An Archeology of Yoga," *Res: Anthropology and Aesthetics* 1 (1981), and "Approaches to the Question of the Antiquity of Jainism," *Jinamañjari: International Journal of Contemporary Jaina Reflections*, vol. 13, no. 1 (1996). For an implied argument that Sāṇkhya goes back to that period see Alain Daniélou, *While the Gods Play: Shaiva Oracles and Predictions on the Cycles of History and the Destiny of Mankind* [Rochester, Vermont: Inner Traditions International, 1991].) The idea that indifference leads to wisdom may derive in part from the shamanic idea that austerity buys power.

35. David Kalupahana, *Buddhist Philosophy: A Historical Analysis* (Honolulu: University of Hawaii Press, 1975), p. 12.

36. P. C. Devanji, "Naturalism in Greek and Indian Philosophies," *Journal of the Oriental Institute* 4 (Baroda, 1954–55), p. 172.

37. For this capitalized phrase see David Kalupahana, *Causality: The Central Philosophy of Buddhism* (Honolulu: University of Hawaii Press, 1975), p. 38.

38. A. L. Basham, *History and Doctrine of the Ājīvikas: A Vanished Indian Religion* (London: Luzac, 1951), pp. 107 ff.

39. Kalupahana, *Buddhist Philosophy*, p. 24.

40. For a discussion of this passage see Bhikku Nanananda, *Concept and Reality in Early Buddhist Thought* (Kandy, Sri Lanka: Buddhist Publication Society, 1971).. In this case I have intervened in Nanananda's translation, which employed the word "perceive" where I say "recognize or identify," the word "reasons" where I say "think and have emotions about," and the word "obsessed" where I say "preoccupied."

41. Kalupahana, *Buddhist Philosophy*, p. 33.

42. Ibid., p. 36.

43. Ibid., p. 30.

44. Ibid., p. 38.

45. Nyanaponika Thera, *Abhidhamma Studies: Buddhist Explorations of Consciousness and Time*, ed. with intro. by Bhikku Bodhi (Boston: Wisdom Publications, in collaboration with the Buddhist Publication Society, Kandy, Sri Lanka, 1998), p. 10.

46. Nussbaum, *Therapy of Desire*.

47. Kalupahana, *Buddhist Philosophy*, p. 62.

48. Ibid., p. 60.

49. Ibid., p. 77.

50. Since a basic human disposition is desire for pleasure and aversion to pain, the experience of *vedanā* is already a potentially reactive one. Ego-identification could begin at this point, as the subject, driven into irrational projection by the feeling of pleasure or pain, begins to identify the feeling, and the experience which brings it, as "mine." Thus the recognition stage—*samjñā*—will already be distorted by craving or avoidance. Caring begins, clinging and condemning take hold, and so on—even before the mind has moved to classify or attach a name to the experience. But this type of reaction to the sensory stimulus is usually attributed to the later phase, *saṃskāra*, and the foreshadowing of it at the *vedanā* stage is not specified in the texts.

51. Karl H. Potter ("A Few Early Abhidharma Categories," in *Encyclopedia of Indian Philosophies*, vol. 7, *Abhidharma Buddhism to 150 A.D.*, ed. Potter et. al. [Delhi: Motilal Banarsidass, 1996], p. 128), translates *samjñā* as "(conceptual) identification"; in "Vibhanga," ibid., p. 166, he calls it "identification"; Noble Ross Reat, "The Historical Buddha and His Teachings," ibid., p. 41, calls it "conceptual identification." *samjñā* used to be regularly translated "perception" (for example in Nyanatiloka's *Buddhist Dictionary* [Kandy, Sri Lanka: Buddhist Publication Society, 1980]), a word which in English usage is linked to the concept "sensation," which is not directly relevant to *samjñā*.

52. R. M. Gethin, "The Five *Khandas*: their treatment in the *nikāyas* and early Abhidhamma," *Journal of Indian Philosophy* 14 (1986): 36.

53. Potter, "A Few Early Abhidharma Categories," p. 128.

54. Gethin, "The Five Khandas," p. 37.

55. The fifth "aggregate," *vijñāna* or consciousness, may be regarded as present because it accompanies each of the previous three stages. In addition it seems to be included in the list for two other reasons: (1) ". . . consciousness is that type of factor the stream of which persists beyond bodily demise. It is evidently this stream that maintains individual identity through the intermediate state and on into the next life." Thus the factor of consciousness is necessary to comport with the Buddhist doctrine of reincarnation with no soul; and (2) the Abhidharma texts say that even in the highest states of meditation *vijñāna* is present to maintain the grounding in the psyche of the individual who is meditating. In both these cases the presence of consciousness is required purely by itself, with no accompanying factors of any kind; the fifth *khanda* fills this need (Potter, "A Few Early Abhidharmic Categories," p. 130).

56. Reat, "The Historical Buddha and His Teachings," pp. 41–42.

57. U Kyaw Min, *Buddhist Abhidhamma* (Union City, California: Heian International, 1987), p. 23. According to Nyaniponika Thera, "the unit of one moment of consciousness is metaphorically defined as 'the billionth part of a flash of lightning'" (*Abhidamma Studies*, p. 100). How is such a brief event to be perceived? The series of sixteen or seventeen moments making up a "course of cognition" (as U Kyaw Min calls it) or a "serial process" (as Nyanaponika Thera calls it) repeats itself "in order to bring about the result of a complete perception such as we are actually aware of" if the evaluation by greed and so on at the *samskāra* stage "impresses a strong mark" (Nyanaponika Thera, *Abhidhamma Studies*, p. 107). If it has not made a strong mark it is not consciously noted except for cases when "the exceedingly short-lived processes in the world of the mind become cognizable . . . with the help of . . . a mind sharpened by methodical meditative training" (ibid., p. 6). Such cognition is "delicate mental microscopy" (ibid., p. 7).

58. U Kyaw Min, *Buddhist Abhidhamma*, p. 15.

59. Thera, *Abhidhamma Studies*, p. 128 n. 54.

60. Ibid., p. 25.

61. The changing of an immoral [unwholesome] to moral [wholesome] consciousness comes when the mind, after mental development, uses wisdom to change the moral direction of consciousness," ibid., p. 24.

62. Ibid., p. 71.

63. "[T]ransformations of character, conduct, ideas, and ideals are made possible" through "the five spiritual faculties," which are dominated and kept in line by the faculty of mindfulness (Thera, *Abhidamma Studies*, p. 62). It is likely that these faculties intervene at the point where the third stage (*samjñā*) gives way to the fourth (*saṃskāra*), pointing the energy toward a wholesome *saṃskāra* rather than an unwholesome one. In addition the faculties of "good consciousness" (*sobhana-citta*) include the property of pliancy that "is the capacity of the intellectual faculties to learn and to unlearn ever anew, to be benefitted by experience. It [pliancy] allows one to discard inveterate habits and prejudices pertaining to thought, emotion, and behavior" (ibid., p. 73). It is this quality of pliancy that saves the *hexis* or disposition from the rigidity that Aristotle feared in it.

64. Ibid., p. 73.

65. I have slightly revised Jowett's translation (B. Jowett, *The Dialogues of Plato* [New York: Random House, 1920], p. 23), using "contact" for "impression" and "emotions" for "feelings," to bring it into line with the terms used here.

66. Terence Irwin, *Plato's Ethics* (New York and Oxford: Oxford University Press, 1995), discusses the relation between reason and desire on p. 208. Basically, reason is able to interfere in a nonrational desire, somewhat as the "spiritual faculties" in Buddhism are able to interfere in the *samskāra* stage.

67. Trans. E. S. Forster in *Aristotle: Parts of Animals, Movement of Animals, Progression of Animals*, Loeb Classical Library (Cambridge, Massachusetts: Harvard University Press, and London: William Heinemann, 1937), pp. 461, 467.

68. *Phantasia* is usually translated "mental picture," which means conceptual recognition or identification of the phenomenon involved in the contact or sense-perception. But Nussbaum argues that it means simply "the phenomenon"—that is, the recognition of the phenomenon directly without the intercession of a "mental picture" (Nussbaum, *Therapy of Desire*, p. 291, n. 13).

69. Trans. Annas, *The Morality of Happiness*, p. 57.

70. Sir David Ross, *Aristotle* (London: Methuen, 1949), p. 201.

71. Trans. Sarah Broadie, *Ethics with Aristotle* (New York: Oxford University Press, 1991), p. 67.

72. Ibid., p. 64.

73. Ibid., pp. 64–65.

74. Dale Riepe, *The Naturalistic Tradition in Indian Thought* (Seattle: University of Washington Press, 1961), p. 151.

75. See Philip Merlan, *Studies in Epicurus and Aristotle* (Wiesbaden: Otto Harrassowitz, 1960), and David J. Furley, *Two Studies in the Greek Atomists* (Princeton, New Jersey: Princeton University Press, 1967), for Aristotelian influence on Epicurus.

76. George K. Strodach, *The Philosophy of Epicurus* (Chicago: Northwestern University Press, 1963), p. 95.

77. See A. K. Warder, "Early Buddhism and Other Contemporary Systems," *Bulletin of the School of Oriental and African Studies* 18 (1956): 57; and compare K. N. Jayatilleke, *Early Buddhist Theory of Knowledge* (London: George Allen and Unwin, 1963), p. 464.

78. Trans. A. A. Long and D. N. Sedley, *The Hellenistic Philosophers*, vol. 1, *Translations of the Principal Sources with Philosophical Commentary* (Cambridge: Cambridge University Press, 1987), p. 112.

79. Bhikku Nanananda, *Concept and Reality in Early Buddhist Thought* (Kandy, Sri Lanka: Buddhist Publication Society, 1971), pp. 3–4.

80. Epicurus's empiricism (like the Buddha's) was not perfect. He argues on *a priori* grounds, for example, against the infinity of the universe and other points not normally accessible to verification (D.L. X.41–42). Still, in the *Letter to Pythocles*, he advises that if one cannot distinguish a true model from a false, because empirical evidence on the point is not available, one should put the matter on hold till it can be evidentially resolved (D.L. X.87).

81. John M. Rist, *Epicurus: An Introduction* (Cambridge: Cambridge University Press, 1972), p. 26, calls them "general concepts."

82. Furley, *Two Studies in Greek Atomists*, p. 200. I cannot agree with DeWitt's interpretation of the *prolēpseis* as "innate ideas," on the basis of which he interprets Epicurus as an intuitionist rather than an empiricist. See Norman W. DeWitt, *Epicurus and His Philosophy* (Minneapolis: University of Minnesota Press, 1954), pp. 122, 136.

83. Strodach, *The Philosophy of Epicurus*, p. 14.

84. Kalupahana, *Causality*, pp. 107, 89.

85. Ibid., p. 137.

86. Strodach, *The Philosophy of Epicurus*, p. 13.

87. Kalupahana, *Causality*, p. 140.

88. Ibid., p. 117.

89. Strodach, *The Philosophy of Epicurus*, p. 56.

90. See Furley, *Two Studies in Greek Atomists*, p. 211, and pt. 1, ch. 8; and Rist, *Epicurus*, pp. 47, 59, 66, etc.; the chief extant ancient sources are D.L. X.47–48 and Lucr. IV.7–8.

91. Strodach, *The Philosophy of Epicurus*, p. 95.

92. Nussbaum, *Therapies of Desire*.

93. *NE* 1153a12–15: "Pleasure is the unimpeded activity of the natural state" (*anempodistos energeia tes kata phusin hexeos*). In *Magna Moralia* (1205b6–7) he says that pleasure is the restoration from an unnatural to a natural state (*he de hēdonē esti katastasis ek tou para phusin eis phusin hekastoi ten heautou*).

94. Merlan, *Studies in Epicurus and Aristotle*, pp. 18–19, compares the German term *Freude*.

95. Long and Sedley, *Hellenistic Philosophers*, vol. 1, p. 124.

96. Rist, *Epicurus*, p. 125.

97. See Kalupahana, *Buddhist Philosophy*, p. 62.

98. Here is how the calculus, with its implicit assumption of rational proportions, is summed up by Epicurus:

> Pleasure is the starting point of every choice and of every aversion, and to it we come back, inasmuch as we make feeling (pleasure/pain) the rule by which to judge of every good thing. And since pleasure is our first and native good, for that reason we do not choose every pleasure whatever, but pass over pleasures if greater pain is their consequence to us. And we regard many pains as superior to pleasures when a greater pleasure arises for us after we have put up with pains over a long time. Therefore although every pleasure on account of its natural affinity to us is good, not every pleasure is to be chosen; similarly, though every pain is bad, not every pain is naturally always to be avoided. It is proper to evaluate these things by a calculation and consideration of advantages and disadvantages . . . We regard independence of outward things as a great good, not so as in all cases to use little, but so as to be contented with little if we have not much. To habituate one's self to simple and healthy fare . . . renders us fearless of fortune. When we say then that pleasure is the end and aim, we do not mean the pleasures of the prodigal or the pleasures of sensuality . . . By pleasure we mean the absence of pain in the body [*aponia*] and of anxiety in the mind [*ataraxia*]. It is not an unbroken round of drinking parties and sexual adventures . . . which produces a happy life. It is sober reasoning which patiently searches out the motives for every act of grasping and fleeing, and banishes those beliefs [*doxas*] through which the greatest tumult enters the mind. For all this the beginning and greatest help is prudence [*phronēsis*]. Wherefore prudence is a more precious thing even than philosophy. From it spring all the other virtues. (D.L. X.129–132)

But as others have observed, Epicurus was not a thoroughgoing calculist, as the calculus did not apply to static pleasures, which are the main goal of his program. The calculus is thus of a secondary importance, a way to regulate the kinetic pleasures that may lead one to the state of static pleasure—somewhat like Aristotle's transition from an unnatural to a natural state.

99. Julia Annas, *Hellenistic Philosophy of Mind* (Berkeley, California: University of California Press, 1992), p. 176.

100. Ibid., p. 177. For a discussion of the deficiencies of Epicurus's theory of the impulse, at least as it appears in the extant works, see ibid., pp. 176–178.

101. Ibid., p. 180.

102. DeWitt, *Epicurus and His Philosophy*, p. 122.

103. See Annas, *Hellenistic Philosophy of Mind*, p. 191, for this "focusing."

104. Trans. Broadie, *Ethics with Aristotle*, p. 67.

105. Trans. Long and Sedley, *The Hellenistic Philosophers*, vol. 1, p. 156.

106. See Rist, *Epicurus*, p. 114, n. 4.

107. Benjamin Farrington, *The Faith of Epicurus* (London: Weidenfeld and Nicolson, 1967), p. 133.

108. Ibid., p. 108.

109. DeWitt, *Epicurus and His Philosophy*, p. 329.

110. In Epictetus's discourse on "things which are not our own," he argues that even our bodies are not "our own" and that we therefore must learn not to cling to them. The tradition of the philosophy of change originating with Heraclitus had involved the rejection of a permanent essence; Epictetus modulates from impermanence into the question of control: It is unhealthy (because an invitation to suffering) to identify as one's self anything which cannot be controlled by one; and one ultimately can control only one's selection of assents and dissents. The Buddha taught the same doctrine:

> The body, *bhikkus*, is not-self. Were the body self, the body would not be subject to disease, and it would be possible in the case of the body to command: "Let my body be thus, let not my body be thus." But because the body is not-self, therefore the body is subject to disease, and it is not possible to command: "Let my body be thus, let not my body be thus."...
>
> "What think you, *bhikkus*: is the body static or subject to growth, decay and death?"
>
> —"Subject to growth, decay and death, Lord."
>
> "But is that which is subject to growth, decay, and death painful or pleasant?"
>
> —"Painful, Lord."
>
> "Is it fit to consider what is subject to growth, decay and death, what is painful and impermanent, as 'Mine,' 'I Myself'?"
>
> —"Certainly not, Lord."
>
> (*Samyutta Nikāya* III, *Khandha-samyutta*, 59)

111. It is worth briefly comparing Epicurus's "nameless" atoms with the "hidden" or "unknown" force, *adṛṣṭa*, in Vaiśeṣika atomism. "The nameless kind of atom," says Annas, "is the only purely theoretical entity in Epicureanism" (*Hellenistic Philosophy of Mind*, p. 139.) The same may be said of the *adṛṣṭa* in the Vaiśeṣika system. The nameless element "animates and directs the body" (ibid., p. 140), as the *adṛṣṭa* is the cause that begins the motion of the whole universe of atoms in the Vaiśeṣika system. These special atoms should also be compared with "karmic matter" in both Orphism and Jainism. In all three cases it seems as if a spiritual entity were introduced in a somewhat awkward disguise into a physicalist position in the metaphysics.

The residual element of Orphic transcendentalism in the Stoic model of the soul is expressed with unusual frankness by Seneca, who calls the body the "prison" of the soul (*Ep.* 65.16, 25ff.), declares that the soul longs to escape from it (*Ep.* 78.10 and 79.10–11), and says that the soul escapes from the body as from "a foul and stinking womb" (*Ep.* 102.27–28) (Annas, *Hellenistic Philosophy of Mind*, p. 55, n. 46).

112. Zeno felt that judgments are without emotion, Chrysippus that "judgments must have some kind of emotional coloring" (J. M. Rist, *Stoic Philosophy* [Cambridge: Cambridge University Press, 1969], pp. 30, 34–35).

113. Long and Sedley, *The Hellenistic Philosophers*, vol. 1, p. 240.

114. Rist says, "All human activities without any exceptions whatever involve some degree of assent. A totally non-voluntary act is an impossibility" (*Stoic Philosophy*, p. 42). Seneca, for example, says "impulse never exists without the mind's assent" (*De Ira* II.4 [Long and Sedley, *The Hellenistic Philosophers*, vol. 1, p. 419]). But one might wonder about the phrase "all human activities without any exceptions." Extant Stoic sources do not seem to make clear where voluntary actions give way to involuntary: Is it true for example that an act of assent is made to each beat of the heart and each breath? Zeno seems to have agreed with the yogis of India that even those bodily functions usually regarded as involuntary involve a voluntary assent, however hidden, which can be rescinded by an exercise of free will. According to the tradition (D.L. VII.28) he died by voluntarily stopping his breath (which one yoga teacher has described as an advanced feat of *prāṇāyāma*).

115. Long and Sedley, *The Hellenistic Philosophers*, vol. 1, p. 346.

116. Ibid., p. 410.

117. Rist argues that the Cynic and Stoic uses of this word were different. The Cynic *apatheia*, he argues, meant actual emotionlessness, while the Stoic *apatheia* meant a certain kind of rational guidance or control or selection of emotions. (See Rist, *Stoic Philosophy*, p. 72; and "The Stoic Concept of Detachment," in *The Stoics*, ed. J. M. Rist [Berkeley, California, and Los Angeles: University of California Press, 1978], p. 260.) I am not convinced by his claim that the Cynics held absolute unfeelingness to be the ideal (Diogenes enjoyed sex, and Crates advocated *philanthropia* or compassion). But the Stoic view of *apatheia*, at least, is fairly clear.

118. See C. O. Brink, "Oikeiosis and Oikeiotes: Theophrastus and Zeno on Nature and Moral Theory," *Phronēsis* 1 (1955): 12–145, for the suggestion that Zeno was influenced in this compromise of Cynic principles by the Academician Polemon. Both Cynics and Epicureans attacked the Academy as the stronghold of reactionary thought.

119. Trans. Long and Sedley, *The Hellenistic Philosophers*, vol. 1, p. 396.

120. Daisetz T. Suzuki, *Studies in the Laṅkāvatāra Sūtra* (London: Routledge and Kegan Paul, 1930), p. 379.

121. Annas, *Hellenistic Philosophy of Mind*, p. 81.

122. Ibid., p. 89.

123. Ibid., p. 81, n. 20.

124. Ibid., p. 93.

125. See, for example, Annas, *Hellenistic Philosophy of Mind*, pp. 97–98. Annas and I use the related terms "impulse" and "assent" somewhat differently.

Most modern accounts of the process fail to realize the complexity of the *hormē*. Bréhier and Long, for example, both reduce the process to representation, assent to objectivity of representation, and inclination toward or away from object. This implies that every act of mental assent involves an impulse, which does not seem to be what the Stoics meant. Lloyd is closer when he speaks of affective predicates, and Ressor also, who notes that Stobaeus distinguishes two types of *hormē*, the assent, and the assent-plus-movement. The first applies only to the question of truth; the second is an acting out. Stobaeus also preserves the parallel distinction between the plain *phantasia* and the hormetic *phantasia*, the latter triggering a response, the former merely a noting or brief focusing on (*SVF* III.169). (See Bréhier, *The Hellenistic and Roman Age*, p. 55; A. A. Long, *Hellenistic Philosophy* [London: Duckworth, 1974], pp. 126ff.; Margaret E. Ressor, "Necessity and Fate in Stoic Philosophy," in *The Stoics*, ed. Rist, p. 188; A. C. Lloyd, "Emotion and Decision in Stoic Psychology," ibid., pp. 233–247; Charlotte L. Stough, "Stoic Determinism and Moral Responsibility," ibid., pp. 203–230.) The distinction corresponds, in the *abhidharma* psychology, to the distinction between the unfolding of the process when the *vedanā* is neutral, on the one hand, and, on the other, when it is not. Both the classification of the sensum (*saṃjñā*) and the type of reaction-association (*saṃskāra*) are affected. In the Chrysippan system too the presence of accompanying pleasure or pain may have an effect not merely on the impulse but even on the assent to objectivity, that assent being more easily given to a pleasant presentation than to a painful one.

126. Nyanaponika Thera, *Abhidhamma Studies*, p. 7.

127. Ressor, "Necessity and Fate in Stoic Philosophy," p. 191.

128. See especially Rist, *Stoic Philosophy*, ch. 1.

129. Rist, *Stoic Philosophy*, p. 52.

130. Trans. Long and Sedley, *The Hellenistic Philosophers*, vol. 1, p. 247.

131. Ibid., p. 249.

132. Pohlenze, *La Stoa*, 2.11; quoted by Giovanni Reale, *A History of Ancient Philosophy*, vol. 4, *The Imperial Age*, trans. John R. Catan (Albany, New York: State University of New York Press, 1990), p. 101.

133. Long, *Hellenistic Philosophy*, p. 236.

134. Ibid., p. 237.

135. Flintoff, "Pyrrho and India."

136. Sarvepalli Radhakrishnan, "On Philosophical Synthesis," *Philosophy East and West* 1 (1951): 4.

137. Among modern psychological systems the closest parallels to the ancient therapy of intervention in the impulse-system are not to be found in psychoanalysis but in certain roughly behavioral therapies. The so-called "rational-emotive therapy" developed by Alfred Ellis on the basis of the Stoic system of Posidonius, for example, bears many resemblances to the ancient systems' reviewed in this chapter (See Alfred Ellis, "Rational-emotive Therapy" in *Current Psychotherapies*, ed. R. Cosini [Itasca, Illinois: F. E. Peacock, 1979]; Charles Zastrow, "Conceptualizing and Changing the Self from a Rational Therapy Perspective," in *Changing the Self: Philosophies, Techniques, and Experiences*, ed. Thomas M. Brinthaupt and Richard P. Lipka [Albany, New York: State University of New York Press, 1994]). Various Greek elements can be recognized here, from Aristotle's concept of the *hexis*, or habit formation, to Posidonius's understanding of the emotion as a verbal proposition translated into feeling-tone; along with these elements a general parallel to early Buddhist psychology can be discerned. This approach in particular, the Buddhist *abhidharmic* approach, is even more closely assumed as subtext by Daniel Goleman in *Emotional Intelligence* (New York: Bantam Books, 1995). Goleman (who previously wrote on Buddhist meditation) often seems to formulate mental process on the model of the five *skandhas*. "The first step," he writes of interfering intentionally in undesired emotional states, "is self-awareness, catching the worrisome episodes as near their beginning as possible—ideally, as soon as or just after the fleeting catastrophic image triggers the worry-anxiety cycle" (ibid., p. 68). "Self-awareness" is Pali *sati*, usually translated mindfulness, which is presented here as called up by a dangerous *sañña*, or perception, in hopes of forestalling its tendency to call up a *sankhāra*, or emotional response, of "worry-anxiety."

Afterword

Remarks toward a Conclusion

Ultimately the preceding twenty-five chapters must stand by themselves. They constitute the argument which I undertook to present. The meaning of that argument is obvious and needs no final clinching statement to underline its point. Still, if only to give this book a rounded shape with a sense of closure, some additional remarks seem called for. These remarks will summon up again the context of postcolonial discourse that was introduced in the foreword, with attention to how the long unfolding of this argument has affected it.

An earlier chapter explains the title, *The Shape of Ancient Thought*, as a reference to the cyclicity which was prominent in cultural attitudes throughout the Neolithic and Bronze Ages and still permeated Early Iron Age cogitations, though often in a more abstract than mythic way. Another aspect of the shape is historical, having to do with two massive transfers of ideas or methods of thinking, first from India into Greece in the pre-Socratic period and again from Greece back into India in the Hellenistic; this double or reciprocal movement is another aspect of circularity to the shape. While the comparison of Indian and Greek thinkers may have clarified some scholarly problems on both sides, a special intensity clings around those periods of actual interchange.

Upaniṣadic influences on the pre-Socratics seem likely to have included monistic solutions to the Problem of the One and the Many, the doctrine of the transformation of the elements into one another, at least the ethical aspect of the reincarnation doctrine associated with it, and elements or aspects of the doctrine of the cosmic cycle; at the same time Jain influences were entering Greece through the Orphic community. Since the ideas in question remained fundamental elements of Greek thought for a thousand years, it is time to acknowledge that one of the major strains of Greek thought was Indian-influenced—that it might even be called the Indianized or Greco-Indian lineage.

In the later period the presence of Greek colonists in India who remained in touch with the Mediterranean, and later the continual intrusion of Greco-Roman merchant ships, created a situation in which Mediterranean cultural elements were carried to India. The principal diffusion wave that took place in this period seems to have been the transmission of Hellenic-Hellenistic logical and dialectical traditions to Indian schools which had been protodialectical before.

Would the Greeks, without Indian influence, have generated the doctrines of monism and ethical reincarnationism? Would Indian thinkers, without Greek influence, have systematized the dialectic in the mode originated by Zeno, or the syllogism in a mode similar to that of Philodemus? There is no reason to think the answer to either question should be affirmative.

Issues of Turf

Still, from the point of view of either a Hellenist or an Indologist, one can imagine the enormity of these claims. Within the academic departments where the Greek and Latin classics are custodialized, the fragments of the pre-Socratics occupy the pinnacle of a hierarchy of texts. They are the Ur-fountainhead of the western tradition from the archaic period of ancient Greece right through to the present—with a major lapse in the so-called Christian millennium. From this font, ultimately, arose the Renaissance, the Enlightenment, Modernism, and post-Modernism. The corpus of the pre-Socratics is arguably the crown of the Greek heritage as it has survived: In terms of cultural prestige among western classicists, nothing is quite its equal—not the tragedians, not Plato, not the historians. What western cultural savants might find most irksome about the conclusions of this book is that an intrusion of significant formative influence from a nonwestern culture is being posited at that point in particular. It is hard to imagine a more traumatic rearrangement of the pieces with which classics scholars make their moves upon the board.

From the Indologist's point of view—especially the Buddhologist's—an equally fundamental rearrangement is being proposed. Within Buddhist scholarship the dialectical formalization that is first found in the texts of Nāgārjuna and Āryadeva is placed at the very top of the hierarchy of texts, as are the pre-Socratics in western classicism. Nāgārjuna's dialectical formulation of the doctrine of emptiness is regarded as comprising the second turning of the wheel of the law, the beginnings of the Mahāyāna, and throughout the long history of the Mahāyāna schools—from Vasubandhu to Tzong-ka-pa and Dogen—it has been regarded as the crowning monument of systematic thought. The Hindu tradition from Śaṅkara to Radhakrishnan is equally based on it. Now it is proposed that it is the product of a Hellenistic dialectical manual transposed into the terms of Indian discourse.

These two radical conclusions are indicated by the evidence, but nevertheless might find a hard time being accepted by experts in their respective fields.

Mirror Images, Slightly Distorted

In terms of all similarities—with or without claims of diffusion—the most striking fact is that there is no major feature of one tradition that cannot be found in the other. In response to the nineteenth-century imperialist view that the western tradition is logical, the eastern mystical, this investigation has shown that every mystical element in Indian thought can be found in Greek thought too, and every rational element in Greek thought can be found in Indian.[1]

Various ways have been found to dismiss the similarities that have been recognized in the past. Nakamura, for example, argues that with such a diverse population, with languages and dialects "said to be of more than 700 varieties," India is bound to have a "variegated and multiform civilization" and a philosophical culture that is "extremely complex" and "cannot be summarized in a single frame of reference." As a result, "the various opposing types of world-view which confront each other in western philosophy or Chinese thought can be found [there] in almost identical form."[2] Without disagreeing with his general point, one might focus on the ambiguity of the phrase "almost identical." There's a place where one draws the line between a purely coincidental similarity, a similarity brought about by particular loaded circumstances (such as a common inheritance), and a borrowing or diffusion event. Nakamura's position just quoted would suggest that all Greek-Indian similarities are purely coincidental. To account for such similarities no factor would be needed except the complexity of the cultures involved, greater complexity increasing the probability of coincidental similarities.

But when such a similarity holds good in detail, the researcher has to be alert to the possibility of diffusion. In the case of the particular form of the doctrine of the transformation of elements found in Heraclitus and the *Maitrī Upaniṣad*, for example, if one looks for conditions in the Greek tradition that would account for it plausibly, one does not find them. But one does find them in the Indian tradition, and one also finds ample historical opportunity for the diffusion event to have taken place. In the case of the Mādhyamika dialectic the same applies: It is an anomaly in the Indian tradition, perfectly normal in the Greek one, and the historical apparatus for the diffusion transfer is neatly in place. In the cases of the fourfold negation and the rope-snake, wood-fire, and fire-smoke exempla, any one of them might easily have arisen in two settings independently; but when all three of them have done so, in conjunction with detailed parallels in the forms of argumentation, it becomes harder to account for and the reasonable step is to look around for the possibility of diffusion from one setting to the other. Random similarities that arise from the complexity and fecundity of different cultures cannot be expected to have overall cogency and systematic coherence.

Merely to note that every type of thought on the Greek side is also found on the Indian, and vice versa, does not, however, consider the emphases. What was found to be prominent, even dominant, in one culture, may occur as a minor feature of the other. Despite their multitude of detailed similarities, in terms of these proportions and emphases Indian and Greek cultures were indeed different. It is these differences which were exaggerated by scholars of the colonial era and hardened into the unwarranted East vs. West dichotomies that cast "the East as some shadowy, threatening 'other' with which the West is in sharp conflict."[3] One such dichotomy dealt with the two cultures' relationship to the concept of history.

History and Timelessness

In the Hegelian Modernist view, history is regarded as the story of progress. Hegel himself, and many western scholars in his tradition, believed that progress characterizes western civilization but not others. Whereas western nations had the mandate of continual change for the better built into them, nonwestern cultures supposedly remained "ahistorical"; they lacked the inner mandate to pursue change up to an ultimate consummation which would represent the final triumph of civilization and history.

The full weight of this judgment consists of the fact that, on the Hegelian view, the non-western ahistorical cultures were not simply out of touch with issues of social improvement—they were out of touch with universal Spirit. On this view history begins with the fragmentation of Spirit and runs its course as the gradual reestablishing of Spirit's wholeness; history is Spirit's macrocosmic form of the Orphic quest for a return to full selfhood. In saying that the non-western world is ahistorical, then,

Hegel is saying that it is out of touch with Spirit. Far from being closer to Spirit, traditional cultures, on this view, have lost touch with it altogether. They have forgotten their true nature and are not doing the work that is necessary to regain it. Timelessness is not really the proper domain of Spirit, at least not until its quest for return to fully aware selfhood is completed. Instead, time, understood as history, is the proper domain of Spirit so long as it is engaged in its quest. Hegel divided things into culture, or Work, on the one hand, and nature, or Madness, on the other. "Timeless" Asia was supposed to be on the Madness side of things.

This attitude about history and timelessness was an "Orientalist" element in early western Indology. In the early nineteenth century, for example, the influential French missionary J.-A. Dubois argued that "in science, arts, and manufactures, they [the Indians] have remained stationary at the point where they were two or three thousand years ago."[4] The British author James Mill, a few years later (1817), remarked that from the time of the invasion of Alexander the Great to that of the invasion of the British, Indian "manners, society, and knowledge" . . . "presented a very uniform appearance."[5] Indians were, as Max Müller put it, "a people . . . never destined to act a prominent part in the history of the world."[6] Colebrooke agrees, focusing the issue on the competition between Greece and India in the European mind of his day: "Not only were the genius and characteristics of the two peoples widely different, but Greece had no Vedas. There was no stagnant period in its history, such as marked the institution of castes and the establishment of Brahminical ascendancy."[7] In 1908 Risley confidently referred to India as "a land where all things are always the same . . ."[8] More recently, Peter van der Veer, commenting on this position, noted that "the myth of India's timelessness was not invented by western Orientalists but by the Brahmanic tradition in India itself, in its use of 'the timeless . . . Vedas' . . . to legitimate practices that in reality depended largely on the historical and regional contexts in which they were produced."[9]

An odd situation emerges. India, which has seemed to many to be the most spiritually committed of civilizations, is declared to be out of touch with Spirit, even to be retarding Spirit's advance by its own inertia. Civilizations that change rapidly are declared to be more spiritual than those that remain themselves, because the reconstitution of the fullness of Spirit is regarded not as a present fact but as a future goal; those cultures that hurry toward it, casting off their misconceived cultural identities as quickly as they can, are the more spiritual.

This question of the rate of cultural change has been a prominent part of the "competition" between Greece and India in the minds of modern scholars. As Conger wrote, "The Greeks, to be Greeks, must have shown originality."[10] Originality, in other words, was an aspect of the very essence of "Greekness" or the "Greek miracle." Yet India is supposed to be just the opposite—a culture that stayed the same, sublimely indifferent to the call for change and development, for thousands of years. Understandably, some scholars have regarded this idea as a symptom of "colonial Indology." Yet there is something to be said for the view that history has developed at different rates in different cultural settings.

In the case of the dialectic in Greece and India, for example, it appears that the step-by-step linked-problems-and-solutions development went much faster in Greece than in India, though both traditions in time incorporated the whole milieu of stratagems. Surely one of the reasons is, as Colebrooke observed, that "Greece had no Vedas." In India the link between philosophy and established religion was solider than in Greece; in that situation traditions of thought had all the inertia of myths or dogmas making them less malleable.

In another example, it is said of the Vaiśeṣika atomists and dialecticians that they "fought . . . for the atomic theory and sought to develop it against the relentless tirade of the idealists through the ages for a period extending over about 1500 years."[11] But fifteen hundred years is an awfully long time for the same argument to go on in more or less the same terms with the same modes of argumentation. The forms of argument that were effective in this debate in the third and fourth centuries A.D. were still being used, with very minor adjustments, in the seventeenth century. In Greece the same range of arguments appeared in less than a century.

The same chronological disparity can be seen in the debate about universals; in Greece it began with Pythagoras and Socrates and culminated with Aristotle a century or two later. In India the same ground was covered in something between eight and fifteen centuries—depending on whether Kaṇāda and the *Vaiśeṣika Sūtras* are dated to the second century A.D. or to the sixth century B.C. or somewhere in between. Udayana (c. 1000 A.D.) and Aparārkadeva (c. 1100 A.D.) were still engaged in the refinement of Kaṇāda's theory which had been crystallized at least a millennium earlier.

Though the Greeks "had no Vedas," Europe during the Christian millennium had its "Vedas" firmly in place and maintained a pace at least as slow as the Indian, in terms of intellectual innovation, for close to a thousand years. Both Hinduism and Christianity, as religions that believe their rituals and dogmas embody eternal truth, are wary of change. Since a past doctrine was, in its day, regarded as absolute truth, it cannot simply be discarded without tacitly denouncing past teachers and creating problems about the whole credibility of the school: If it had once strayed, what is to guarantee that it has ever regained its grip on the truth? Thus in India *astika* texts from the *Nyāya Sūtras* to the *Brahma Sūtras* were layered accumulations of different ideas which had arisen over centuries, newer ideas often appearing side by side with the older ones they had been intended to replace.

So it does indeed seem that cultural and intellectual change took place more rapidly in Greece than in India. But it is not obvious, today, how a value judgment on this situation should be made. There may be a misplaced emphasis in the discourse surrounding this issue—or several misplaced emphases.

For one thing, the West's self-congratulatory claim of progress is not very old. Gordon Childe, in *What Happened in History*, observed that the material conditions of life did not change significantly from the Early Bronze Age to the Industrial Revolution of the nineteenth century.[12] Only in two periods of its long history—the Greek period from about 600–300 B.C. and the Modern period since the Enlightenment (with its promulgation of democratic constitutions, an autonomous middle class, and the goal of perfection attained through social engineering), the Industrial Revolution (with its suggestion of social perfection aided by technology), and the revolution in physics early in this century (with its promise of unimaginable power for whatever purpose)—can the West claim to be conspicuously progressive. And indeed its "progressiveness" has come very close to destroying the world as it careened on its course. This "progress" may not be something the rest of the world should covet.

Rethinking Time and Timelessness

Modernism was essentially the conviction that history is instilled inwardly with a force of progress which will be effectuated by a kind of vanguard class of "World Historical" individuals, and that these individuals live primarily in the West. The West therefore is the natural-born leader of the world. That this attitude permeated western Indology in the nineteenth century and the first half of the twentieth—that is, the high colonial period—is beyond doubt. But Chakrabarti's *Colonial Indology* was published in 1995, not 1945. And clearly the mainstreams of western scholarly thought about history and its subheadings—art history, the history of philosophy, and so on—have changed in the intervening half century. In fact, beyond the scholarly realm, in cultural arenas in general, even popular culture, the Modernist view of history as History has lost force and had its hierarchies reversed. Terms such as post-Modern and posthistorical, though perhaps overstated, express that reversal.

Still, it is beyond doubt that many western Indologists did for a long time hold the view that Chakrabarti criticizes them for, so much so that it developed into an "internal Orientalism" in which the colonized adopt the views of the colonizer—much what Gandhi called "English rule without the Englishman."[13] As in the psychological process described by Albert Memmi in *The Colonizer and the Colonized*, this stage of internalized Orientalism is apt to be followed by a stage of appropriating the colonizers' claims by the colonized. Some Indian scholars, for example, insist that India *has* in fact embodied the force of progress, or History, as much as the West has. Bibin Chandra Pal, for example, expressing displeasure with the Orientalizing attitudes of western scholars, complains that "neither Max Müller nor any other European Orientalist has been . . . able to grasp the truth that age after age, and epoch after epoch, there have been evolution and progress in India as elsewhere."[14] Part of Lal's claim is well taken, that "age after age . . . there [has] been evolution . . . in India . . ." But whether this evolution should be called "progress" in the western sense of the term, and whether the phrase "as elsewhere" truly applies, are both less certain. Nothing quite like the cultural change that led to Modernism and modernity in the West has ever happened elsewhere. That is why Heidegger and Husserl and some other western thinkers have claimed that modernity and westernization are one and the same, that there can be no modernity without westernization, that western modernity has gone beyond the scale of previous cultural changes and has created a new reality sharply demarcated from the old. Still, these thinkers seem to exaggerate the necessity of the connection between where an event has happened and where it might or could happen.

In any case, in the writings of Indian thinkers such as Lal the mantle of progress, which much of the post-Modern West has now turned its back on, is being claimed by the East for itself. But the colonized may be appropriating to themselves a previous value of the colonizers that has now become a thing of little value—or at least a thing of the past. Many westerners nowadays would say that if Indian scholars want credit for cultural progress they are welcome to it. The fact that previously colonized peoples still lay claim to the mistakes of the colonizers is not flattering to them. It implies that Europe's castoff follies are good enough for them. Even aside from that problem, there may be an error in thinking involved.

Pre-Modernism, Modernism, and Post-Modernism

Some Indian scholars feel, when westerners say that India has never exhibited exactly that exotic flora which is called Modernism, that they are denigrating India as *pre*-Modern, which is taken to mean primitive. But the situation is not that simple.

In the last generation or so, during which Modernism has lost much of its credibility in the West—though many nonwestern cultures still covet the privilege of entering it—two options arose to replace the discredited ideology. Neo-pre-Modernism (or pre-Modern revivalism) is an attempt to reestablish channels of connection with pre-Modernist cultures which were supposedly more harmonious, more communal, more feminine, and closer to nature than Modernist ones. Many in both Europe and America who were exhausted spiritually by the ordeals of Modernism—individualism, patriarchy, and technology—turned to this option as to a more spiritual and refreshing world. The fact that certain of the values of Modernism, such as individualism and the cult of innovation, had to be forsaken in this move did not seem to involve too serious a loss. This was the age of the flower-child movement, the dropout hippie communes, the counterculture, the Summer of Love that was supposed to last forever. This was also the period when young westerners in enormous numbers went to India seeking a mystical, goddess-based, supposedly nonpatriarchal culture, where "the link of life with the archaic, the contact with the profoundly mysterious and ancient coherence of existence had not been torn apart—the placenta had not yet cut loose."[15]

Clearly, though European imperial authors may have looked down on India as pre-Modern, the value-situation has changed; for at least a generation now many westerners have envied India its elements of pre-Modernism, regarding it as a superior way of life. Indian authors such as Chakrabarti are trying to right the intellectual wrongs that an earlier generation of westerners did to their tradition, though the western attitudes in question are for the most part long over. To Indians who are striving for Modernism the intrusion of dropouts from western Modernism seeking pre-Modernism in India may be unwelcome. But it is nonetheless meaningful that since sometime in the 1960s many western cultural workers and intellectuals have regarded India, not the West, as the superior culture.

The second option that arose when Modernism vacated its seat of authority might be called post-Modernism proper. The essential difference is that the neo-pre-Modernist is willing to relinquish the package of ideas which has been called the Enlightenment and to live with the pretense that Modernism never even happened. The post-Modernist, on the other hand, is not willing to give up the basic Enlightenment package. While stunned by the hideously destructive consequences of Modernism on the world scene—colonialism, patriarchalism, racism, world war, holocaust, environmental pollution, and the hegemony of international corporations—he or she is nonetheless unwilling to jettison the Enlightenment package altogether and evacuate Modernism of all claim to social good.

Still, post-Modernism does relinquish the use of the concept of truth for purposes of power, and with it ideas of the hierarchization of cultures, which it tends to relativize rather than hierarchize. In this regard Indian culture might be regarded as not pre-Modern but post-Modern. There are problems to attributing cultural relativism to India, since Hinduism tends to posit absolutes, one of which is the caste system. Still, the coexistence of a half dozen different religions and philosophies, and at least that many ethnicities, looks culturally relativized in comparison with Christian and Muslim cultures in the West. As an Indian journalist writes, "We are all minorities in India . . . pluralism emerges from the very nature of the country."[16] The situation in which every group is a minority is the opposite of the Modernist situation, in which dominance and centrality were firmly in place and rigidly controlled. India with its many ethnic, cultural, and religious groups, its many ways of life and lifestyle differences, seems to have moved from pre-Modernism to post-Modernism without ever having been Modern. Certain of the groups or traditions involved in the mélange might be regarded as pre-Modern, but taken together as a vast cultural pastiche, they look not pre- but post-Modern. India, thus, may be regarded as both pre-Modern and post-Modern, with occasional forces within it (such as the Bombay Progressives in the realm of art history) seeking to penetrate directly into Modernism.

Mysticism and Critical Analysis

In the Greek tradition it is the monistic systems that seem to carry Indian influence; in the Indian tradition it is the formalization of dialectic and logic that seems to represent Greek influence. So in effect this study could be construed as giving the prize in mystical affirmation to India and in critical analysis to Greece—not unlike the prejudices of the colonial era. But in fact, the situation is not a simple dichotomy. These two ancient cultures were not purely and simply one thing or the other; both were complex and multidirectional, and the differences between them are not a matter of absolutely contrary natures but of relocated emphases. Indian thinkers from a very early period demonstrated as acute a capacity for critical analysis as the Greeks, but in somewhat different ways. Pāṇini's *Aṣṭādhyāyī* is a meticulously thorough analytical description of Sanskrit grammar, especially word-formation, at an earlier date than any Greek thinker had produced such a work about language. Plotinus, on the other side, was as unambiguous a mystic as any Indian thinker, not only in terms of the transcendental ambitions of his thought but of his personal experiences of what Patañjali calls *nirvikalpa samādhi*. Neither mystical nor analytical intelligence is limited to one side.

As Debiprasad Chattopadhyaya said, "Some of the ancient Indians were as serious about [constructing scientific concepts for the investigation of physical phenomena] as were some of the ancient Greeks," yet this fact has been neglected due to "the lopsided emphasis on the world-denying tendency of Advaita Vedānta and on the mysticism associated with yoga practices."[17] As a result, "natural science and science-oriented philosophical thought is left to the prerogative of the west, and there grew a rather distorted view of Indian cultural heritage." He notes that Stcherbatsky, "as late as 1922," characterized Indian thought as "enveloped in the mist of oriental fantasy." Even scholars who "consciously strive to overcome Europo-centrism," he goes on, remain unaware of "India's contribution to the general fund of scientific ideas in the ancient period,"[18] which include impressive accomplishments in geometry (the *Sulva Sūtras* and other works), astronomy (the *Jyotisha Vedanga* and other works), cosmological mathematics, massive agricultural irrigation projects, medical theory and practice, siegecraft and warcraft, mechanical devices and automata, and so on.[19]

In the Greek tradition the "mathematical" dialectic—as in Zeno's arguments—arose in connection with atomism, and in India too there was a special emphasis on deconstructive argumentation in connection with the atomist tradition. Even representatives of schools that are primarily known for logic and the syllogism learned how to wield confidently the ancient dialectical apparatus. The tradition of commentaries on the *Nyāya Sūtras*—especially Vātsyāyana (c. 300 A.D.), Uddyotakara (c. 635 A.D.), Vacaspati (840 A.D.), and Uddayana (984 A.D.)—was one of the strongest carriers of this mode of thought. The dialectic has a stronger polemical bent, through its emphasis on the *reductio* or negative argument, and ironically, the *Nyāya Sūtras*, the great Indian text on the syllogism, was defended not primarily through syllogistic logic but through dialectical reductions.

In both traditions the tough-minded rational-scientific argumentation clustering around the problems of atomism caused conflict with religious authority. In Greece a sign of this tension is the prosecution of the philosopher Anaxagoras for impiety in Athens sometime in the period 450–430 B.C.[20] On the other side, "the Nyāya-Vaiśeṣika [who were] unique in not having any religious affiliation . . . were best suited to follow a scientific line of thought [and] fought . . . for the atomic theory . . . against the relentless tirade of the idealists . . ."[21] In the process, the Naiyāyikas became masters of the dialectic. It seems that the dialectic arose in India later than in Greece, and probably diffused thither from Greece, but still, the fact remains that Indian thinkers developed the whole arsenal of dialectical arguments and were anything but averse to it. One scholar speaks of "the extraordinary appreciation that the Greeks had for . . . eristic-dialectical virtuosity . . ."[22] But Indian thinkers shared this appreciation and were as given to virtuoso demonstrations of it as were the Eleatic and neo-Eleatic schools, and others, in Greece.

The Exclusion of India from the History of Philosophy

In the West the distinctions mentioned here have been treated as simple and absolute dichotomies: history vs. timelessness, critical analysis vs. mysticism. Because of its longstanding connection with religion, and the particularly overpowering presence of Hinduism, Indian thought has often been regarded in the West as something other than—and implicitly less than—philosophy, something that lacks the autonomy and abstraction of pure philosophy. It may be true, as Zeller wrote, that "the Greeks themselves were inclined from early times . . . to grant the peoples of the Orient . . . that they had a share in the origination of their philosophy," and that the ancient Greeks, in Halbfass's words, showed "readiness to accept the possibility of a philosophical partnership, of debate and instruction, in what is foreign, specifically Indian," but still their successors in modern Europe, as Halbfass points out, tended toward "the exclusion of India from the history of philosophy."[23] "There is still," says one scholar, "reluctance in the [western] academic world to take traditional Asian thought seriously."[24] Or, as another succinctly put it, "Philosophy speaks Greek and only Greek."[25]

The high opinion of Indian thought in early nineteenth century Europe was reversed steadily until, by the early twentieth century, it became usual to omit India altogether from the history of philosophy or dismiss it with a phrase or two which relegated its thought to the domain of the primitive or of religion. Even at the height of Romantic Orientalism this tendency was dimly present. Friedrich Schlegel's famous book of 1808, for example, is titled *Über die Sprache und Weisheit der Indier* (*On the Language and Wisdom of the Indians*). Regardless of the author's respect for the Indian tradition, it remains true that "wisdom" is not the same as "philosophy." It is something more primal or archetypal. One might refer to the wisdom of animals, but not to their philosophy. One might refer to the wisdom of nature—but not to its philosophy. Wisdom means something more instinctual than philosophy, less rigorous and systematic—in sum, less rational. "Wisdom" may as easily belong on the nature or Madness side of Hegel's dichotomy as the culture or Work side. India was classified in Hegel's theory of history as ahistorical, and although an ahistorical society cannot have philosophy in the Hegelian sense, it can have wisdom. Wisdom is always the same, it does not evolve or follow a path of progress; it is not engaged in history. It is timeless and ahistorical. Hegel's separation of culture from nature, and of history from the ahistorical, is paralleled by his separation of philosophy from religion. On these dichotomies is based "his conviction that Europe, by unfolding the 'actual,' 'real' philosophy committed to the spirit of free science, had essentially surpassed the Orient."[26]

So great was the influence of this position for a time that it became normal to exclude India, and indeed all of Asia, from the history of philosophy. Asia, it seemed, had not yet realized the reality of the individual, his rights and responsibilities, and instead still spoke of archetypes, as in the mythological utterances of the Bronze Age.

This tendency to exclude India from the history of philosophy had already occurred in antiquity. Diogenes Laertius began his doxography by questioning whether philosophy had originated in Greece or among the barbarians of the East, and concluded that Asia did not have philosophy per se. His work, first translated into Latin in 1431, at once exerted enormous influence.

The idea of the history of philosophy developed within the seventeenth and eighteenth century quest for a universal history.[27] One such attempt in the field of philosophy concluded that "[t]he beginning of the history of philosophy may thus be found among the Greeks, or more precisely, at that moment when a greater degree of reason developed from the culture of fantasy . . . and research into basic principles began. This took place during the time of Thales."[28] This idea, which goes back to Diogenes Laertius, maintained its preeminence till Bertrand Russell's succinct assertion: "Philosophy begins with Thales."[29] Another nineteenth-century historian of philosophy implies the racial view inherent in the colonial ideology when he says, "Philosophy is the fruit of the Hellenic spirit."[30] Thales's "spirit of philosophical research," that author continues, "which has been transmitted from the Greeks to more recent peoples via a variety of channels, is that which, in its different schools, forms, and effects, comprises the compass of the history of philosophy." This view derived, in modern times, from the Cartesian school, which generally held that "the methodologically ordered and progressive activity of reason first occurred among the Greeks," and did not reappear again until postscholastic European philosophy.[31] This was bad news for the "Orient": "No Asian people . . . has lifted itself to the heights of free human contemplation from which philosophy issues," a nineteenth-century scholar observed.[32] The fact that Thales' basic insights seem to have been made earlier in the Upaniṣads was either not noticed or neglected by agenda. Edward Zeller blithely insisted: "We do not need to search for any foreign sources: the philosophical science of the Greeks may be completely explained by recalling the spirit, the devices, and the educational status of the Hellenic tribes."[33] Citations of such assertions could go on almost endlessly. In the nineteenth century the Romantic Orientalist reverence for the Upaniṣads was gradually replaced by the Hellenocentric view that better supported the colonial project. The nineteenth-century German historian of philosophy Rixner, who early in his life extolled the Upaniṣads as the "original source of true knowledge," later called them "ancient mythical and phantastical monistic speculations by a kind of reasoning that has not yet come of age or ripened to understanding, not to mention attained the status of science."[34]

"Ancient philosophy is essentially Greek philosophy," wrote a contemporary of his. "That which the mind of . . . the Orient has aspired to . . . has remained more or less at the stage of the primeval phantasies of the peoples." Another: "Just as its name, so philosophy itself is originally Greek." Another: "It is the distinguishing peculiarity of the Greeks, that they were the only people of the ancient world who were prompted to assume a scientific attitude in explaining the mysteries which surrounded them."

Another: "No one now will suggest that Greek philosophy came from India, and indeed everything points to the conclusion that Indian philosophy came from the Greeks."[35] The Oriental Renaissance was over. The enthusiasm of the Romantic era was dissolving into the increasingly rigorous and constricted perspective of modern philology.

As modern philology advanced it ceased to believe in what the seventeenth-century Islamic scholar Darah Shukoh, referring to the message of the Upaniṣads, had called "the Great Secret."[36] Philology became increasingly specialized, and grand inclusive concepts came to seem wishful and old-fashioned. Under the influence of historical linguistics the idea of universal history came to seem naïve. Just as one language family could not be used to gain insight into another, but each had to be studied separately, on its own terms, so, it seemed, with philosophy. Increasingly in the nineteenth century historians of culture in general and philosophy in particular distanced themselves from the impulse toward universality. There was no "Great Secret," there were only lots of little secrets. Windleband, Zeller, and many others, became convinced that "there was no room for sweeping world-historical assessments and speculative comparisons."[37] The history of philosophy began to be confined in the array of tightly separate categories which have caused the most fundamental of historical questions—the relationship between Greek and Indian philosophies—to remain uninvestigated until this time.

Acknowledgment of India as a Participant in the History of Philosophy

So our tradition, since it began to become aware of India and its philosophies, has proposed two polar attitudes toward them. First, in the period of Romantic Orientalism typified by Friedrich Schlegel, India was proclaimed the primal font of wisdom; this view was strengthened by the translation into French by Anquetil Dupperon in 1801–02 of the fifty Upaniṣads that Darah Shukoh had translated into Persian in 1657 under the title *Sirr-i Akbar* (*The Great Secret*). The *Oupnek'hat*, as Anquetil called it, came to be seen as the very essence of that font, the "original source of true knowledge," as Rixner called it.[38] Secondly, at a somewhat later period, Europe came to see India as prephilosophical; even its reputation for primal "wisdom" was degraded as texts such as the Upaniṣads came to seem "mythical and phantastical speculations."

Since the end of colonialism in India, western attitudes toward Indian philosophy have become less defensive. Western dictionaries of philosophy now (since the 1960s) contain at least an overview article on Indian philosophy and usually a series of more focused articles on specific concepts or schools. Bochenski included a treatment of Indian logic in his *History of Formal Logic* (1961); Jaspers gave a chapter of *The Great Philosophers* (1957)to Nāgārjuna.[39] Two recent works on "world philosophies" have shown a consciously post-Modernist or multicultural perspective. One gives about the same number of pages to India (40) and Greece (53); the Greek corpus is, however, much smaller, and the other more proportionally gives 55 pages to ancient Greece and 95 pages to India.[40]

The Indian Miracle

When the so-called "method" of comparative philosophy originated, in the context of the Romantic search for origins or archetypes, its purpose was conceived as finding an ultimate or Ur-philosophy that lay behind all particular philosophies—a single Great

Secret, as it were. Methodologically the idea seems much like Socrates' method of looking for the meaning of a word by seeking what is common in its various usages. In the cases of ancient India and Greece the Ur-philosophy would seem to lie semi-hidden but implicit in the prephilosophical texts of the Bronze Age Near East.

I have been as concerned with a search for historical connections as for an ultimate source; this book is as much a diffusionist study as a comparativist one. Though typological comparisons may reveal something about the possibilities for thought in a particular age, the present study would not, at least to its author's mind, seem as alive without the lure of concrete historical contacts and influences. If Indian and Greek philosophies were historically interactive and partially formative upon one another, it would seem a mere cultural or ethnic prejudice to exclude Indian thought from that history of philosophy of which Greek thought is supposedly both the source and the central event.

In terms of the priority issue, assuming that the chronologies conventionally used for Indian philosophies are more or less correct, the Upaniṣads seem to precede Parmenides in monism, and to have directly influenced Heraclitus's view of the process of nature; Jain atomism and Cārvāka materialism would seem to precede Democritus (though not by much). On the other side Parmenides and Zeno formalized dialectic and Aristotle formalized logic well before Indian thinkers. One might say that India established the content of philosophy, and Greece pioneered its method and form.

In terms of the issue of priority, the amazing thing is how close in time the two cultural developments are, each preceding in some ways and following in others. The most likely or at least obvious explanation of the amazing contemporaneity is that both derived from the ancient Near East at about the same time. Was the ancient Near East, then, as in this century so many have said, the "original source of true knowledge"? Tempting though the simplicity of the idea of the "nuclear Near East" may be, de Santillana and von Dechend, McClain, and others, have shown that much of the "wisdom" of the Bronze Age must already have been developed in the Neolithic and Chalcolithic periods.

The contacts and influences presented in this study go part way toward bridging a gap which our thinkers have tended to regard as unbridgeable. H.-G. Gadamer, for example, writes: "Although . . . the research in Eastern philosophy has made further advances . . . what can be considered established is only the negative insight that our own basic concepts, which were coined by the Greeks, alter the essence of what is foreign."[41] Obviously, the attitudes of one culture are liable to be misinterpreted somewhat in another. Still, Gadamer implies a hard-and-fast dichotomy between Greek and Indian that does not seem justified. What if some of the "basic concepts, which were coined by the Greeks" were not, strictly speaking, "coined by the Greeks" but by the Indians, who passed them on to the Greeks? Such may be the case with philosophical monism, substance monism, atomism, elemental transformation, and more. Further, many of the "basic concepts" which, according to Gadamer, "were coined by the Greeks" may have been inherited by both Greeks and Indians from Near Eastern sources; this clearly applies to the idea of the cosmic cycle and its accompanying number mysticism, to the monism of the *pantheos*, and perhaps to re-incarnationism or something like it. The absolute dichotomy which Gadamer and so many others draw between the Greek and the Indian needs to be reconsidered. It seems to have too much of that desire of the West to define itself by demarcating itself off from the East.

This cavil is not in the least to deny that the Greeks performed what the western world has traditionally called a "miracle"—but the scope of that miracle needs some demarcation. It seems clear that the Greeks cracked the code of the dialectic—the dichotomy-and-dilemma with reduction by infinite regress, circularity, and contradiction—and the logic of the syllogism. This is an accomplishment that easily stands alongside the "phantastical monistic speculations" of the Upaniṣads as a primal font of civilization—the more so in that it does not seem to have derived from Bronze Age Near Eastern precedents, which the Upaniṣads may to some extent have done. But the philosophical (not prephilosophical) accomplishments of India also amount to a "miracle" of civilization—an Indian miracle to stand alongside the Greek one.

Notes to Afterword

1. This overlap, however, does not include the practice of yoga, which seems a distinctively Indian accomplishment though much of its theory is present somewhere or other in the Greek tradition.

2. Hajime Nakamura, *A History of Early Vedānta Philosophy* (Delhi: Motilal Banarsidass, 1989), p. 1.

3. J. J. Clarke, *Oriental Enlightenment: The Encounter between Asian and Western Thought* (London and New York: Routledge, 1997), p. 4.

4. Quoted by Dilip K. Chakrabarti, *Colonial Indology: Sociopolitics of the Ancient Indian Past* (Delhi: Munshiram Monoharlal, 1997), pp. 87–88.

5. Quoted ibid., p. 91.

6. F. M. Müller, *Chips from a German Workshop*, vol. 1 (London: Longmans, Green and Co., 1867), p. 66; quoted by Chakrabarti, *Colonial Indology*, p. 99.

7. Sir T. E. Colebrooke, *Life of H. T. Colebrooke* (London: Trubner and Co., 1873), p. 370.

8. Quoted by Chakrabarti, *Colonial Indology*, p. 122.

9. Peter van der Veer, "The Foreign Hand: Orientalist Discourse in Sociology and Communalism," in Carol A. Breckenridge and Peter van der Veer, eds., *Orientalism and the Postcolonial Predicament: Perspectives on South Asia*, New Cultural Studies Series (Philadelphia: University of Pennsylvania Press, 1993), p. 27.

10. George P. Conger, "Did India Influence Early Greek Philosophies?" *Philosophy East and West* 2 (1952): 115.

11. Mrinalkanti Gangopadhyaya, *Indian Atomism, History and Sources* (Atlantic Highlands, New Jersey: Humanities Press, 1981), p. 54.

12. Gordon Childe, *What Happened in History* (Harmondsworth and Baltimore, Maryland: Penguin, 1942), p. 91–92 and elsewhere.

13. Breckenridge and van der Veer, *Orientalism and the Postcolonial Predicament*, p. 11 and elsewhere; for the Gandhi quotation, p. 190.

14. Quoted by Chakrabarti, *Colonial Indology*, p. 6.

15. A. Leslie Willson, *A Mythical Image: The Ideal of India in German Romanticism* (Durham, North Carolina: Duke University Press), 1964, p. 114.

16. Shashi Tharoor, cited in the *New York Post*, August 17, 1997, editorial, p. 48.

17. Debiprasad Chattopadhyaya, "Editorial Note," in Gangopadhyaya, *Indian Atomism, History and Sources*, p. v.

18. Ibid., p. vii. Nevertheless, it is difficult to arrive at reliable information on this point. One still, for example, reads the old saw that "the world owes the zero and the decimal system to the

Indians" (Wilhelm Halbfass, *India and Europe: An Essay in Understanding* [Albany, New York: State University of New York Press, 1988], p. 31). But according to Neugebauer the Babylonians had the zero, or placeholder, which they represented by a dash (Otto Neugebauer, *The Exact Sciences in Antiquity* [Providence, Rhode Island: Brown University Press, 1957]). This came into Greece where Claudius Ptolemy replaced the dash by the circle, representing the letter omicron, the first letter of the word *ouden*, "nothing"; the zero means "there is nothing in this space." This symbol, along with the concept, seems to have passed into India by one of several routes, whence it returned into Christian Europe, which had demolished all such knowledge, by way of Islamic civilization. And decimality surely was present in the Pythagorean system.

19. For a brief summary see H. J. J. Winter, "Science," in *A Cultural History of India*, ed. A. L. Basham (Delhi: Oxford University Press, 1997), pp. 141–161.

20. For discussion of the problems of this dating see G. S. Kirk, J. E. Raven, and M. Schofield, *The Presocratic Philosophers* (Cambridge: Cambridge University Press, 1973), pp. 353–355.

21. Gangopadhyaya, *Indian Atomism, History and Sources*, p. 54.

22. Giovanni Reale, *A History of Ancient Philosophy*, vol. 1, *The Systems of the Hellenistic Age*, trans. John R. Catan (Albany: State University of New York Press, 1985), p. 54.

23. For Zeller and Halbfass see Foreword, notes 40 and 41. The section that follows here is especially indebted to Wilhelm Halbfass, *India and Europe*, pp. 145–159.

24. Clarke, *Oriental Enlightenment*, p. 5.

25. Quoted ibid., p. 18, citing Simon Critcheley, "Black Socrates? Questioning the Philosophic Tradition," *Radical Philosophy*, 69 (1995): 18

26. Halbfass., *India and Europe*, p. 146.

27. See ibid., pp. 147 ff., for numerous examples.

28. W. G. Tenneman, *Gründriss der Geschichte der Philosophie*, (Leipzig: J. A. Barth, 1820), p. 10, trans. Halbfass, *India and Europe*, pp. 149–150.

29. Bertrand Russell, *A History of Western Philosophy* (New York: Simon and Schuster, 1945), p. 3.

30. F. Michelis, quoted by Halbfass, *India and Europe*, p. 152.

31. Ibid., p. 150.

32. F. Michelis, quoted ibid., p. 182.

33. Edward Zeller, *Die Philosophie der Griechen in ihrer geschichtlichen Entwicklung*, vol. 1 (Hildesheim: Georg Olms Verlag, 1953), p. 41.

34. Quoted by Halbfass, *India and Europe*, pp. 151–152.

35. For quotations in this paragraph, see ibid., pp. 153–154.

36. Ibid., p. 34.

37. Ibid., p. 155.

38. As Halbfass has noted (ibid., p. 35), the Oupnek'hat's subsequent influence, by way of Anquetil's Latin version, on Schopenhauer extends its lineage through three ages and strengthens its claim to be the "original font."

39. Karl Jaspers, *Die Grössen Philosophen* (Munich: R. Piper, 1957).

40. David E. Cooper, *World Philosphies: An Historical Introduction* (Oxford: Blackwell, 1996); Randall Collins, *The Sociology of Philosophies: A Global Theory of Intellectual Change* (Cambridge, Massachusetts: Harvard University Press, 1998).

41. Preface to W. Dilthey, *Gründriss der allgemeinen Geschichte der Philosophie* (Frankfurt: Klostermann, 1949), p. 18, note.

Appendix A

The Aryans

The traditional western view of the Indo-Aryans is that they were an Indo-European-speaking people from outside South Asia who entered India around the time of, or shortly after, the collapse of the urban system of the Indus Valley culture and either contributed to that collapse by military invasion or took control of the area after the collapse. Recently this long-standing view has been vigorously questioned, primarily but not exclusively by Indian scholars who have been regarded by some western scholars as influenced by nationalistic motives.

An extreme position is maintained by Kalyanaraman. "It is erroneous," he says, "to suggest that the Aryans ever came to India from an alien territory. The people who called themselves Aryan . . . were autochthonous to the region which is now known as Punjab, Afghanistan, Sind and Kashmir."[1] In his view the Aryans composed the *Ṛg Veda* at least two thousand years before civilization appeared in Sumer and Egypt, whither it was brought by Aryan colonists from India. The Sumerians were "an Indian race, which passed . . . into the valley of the Two Rivers" after having developed in the Indus Valley the culture and writing system which would be adapted by the Babylonians.[2] Finally he identifies India as "the original . . . fountain source" of civilization, which was created by the Aryans.[3] To the West, the Phoenicians, the Persians, the Greeks, and, to the East, the civilizations of Tibet, Southeast Asia, the Oceanic islands, and the pre-Columbian New World were, on this view, all founded by the Indo-Aryans in their "almost riotously unimpeded progress."[4] The nationalistic root of such claims is stated overtly by Kalyanaraman when he says, "The *raison d'etre* of the *Aryatarangini* lies in the historical injustice which has been done . . . by Western historians . . ."[5]

Similarly, Shrikant Talageri, according to two supporters of his position, "has pointed out [that] there is now persuasive evidence from diverse sources pointing to India as the original home of Indo-European speakers who migrated to the west and northwest in prehistoric times. This is the exact reverse of the Aryan-invasion theory."[6] The "persuasive evidence" for such a view may seem to be tortured out of almost nothing, as the view itself seems more a postcolonial reversal—a type of self-recovering move in which a previously colonized people reverses the value structures imposed on them by the colonizers—than an attempt to objectively confront such evidence as there is.

Often a scholar of a previously colonized culture feels justified in such a maneuver by the previous wrongs of the colonizer. It is hard to deny, for example, that the British archeologist Mortimer Wheeler exaggerated the importance of limited signs of violence in Mohenjo-daro in order to convince himself and others that he was dealing with a site of Aryan conquest. Thus authors like Kalyanaraman and Talageri feel justified in righting an obviously skewed balance by making an opposite case. They and others who take what Allchin calls "the conservative Indian position" on such matters seem to feel that they are fighting the war of independence from the British Empire all over again on the level of intellect and scholarly construction. Their cultural history has been appropriated at many levels by foreigners, and they are fighting level by level to take it back. Western scholars are seen as "denying any voice to 'Orientals' in the Western apprehension of what they are about . . ."[7] These Indian nationalistic scholars may be seen as failing in "the necessity for members of an academic community to struggle constantly for critical distance on their own work,"[8] but after all, they are emotionally engaged in a war of liberation. In denying what often seems transparently obvious to the western scholar they are denying that "scholarship . . . as privileged ground for understanding between cultures [is] a universalist ideal that is firmly grounded in the liberal tradition of the West."[9] That claim to a scholarly "privileged ground" is a part of the distorted mirror image of itself that the West sees in the world as a whole.

There are few today, in East or West, who would wholeheartedly defend the idea that the Indus civilization was ended by an Aryan Invasion, which has been displaced in most people's thought by factors of climatic change, such as the drying up of the Sarasvati River, as cause for the abandonment of the Harappan centers. But the issue of the origin of the Aryans is still very much contested. What once appeared to be a scholarly consensus about the origin of the Indo-European peoples in the area north of the Black and Caspian Seas has been seriously challenged by the view of some western scholars that the Indo-European homeland was south rather than north of the Caucasus, in the area of eastern Anatolia, Armenia, Azerbaijan, and environs.[10] But even in that case, northwest India is still seen as one of several places that the variously migrating Indo-European groups later settled in after wandering from the vaguely located homeland.

Yet on the revisionist Indian view, which goes much farther, the Indo-Europeans were a branch of the Vedic Indians rather than the other way around; the whole vast Indo-European migration system, then, originated from what was previously regarded as one of its particular sites. In view of what Chakrabarti calls "colonial Indology," the claim is made that western scholars reversed the order of things so that a nonwhite culture would not seem to be the origin of the whole network of Indo-European centers of civilization. Romila Thapar, an Indian historian who is reviled by some Indian scholars for her acquiescence to many western points of view, calls the view that the Indo-European peoples originated in northwest India simply "a false theory."[11] Allchin distinguishes between "the conservative Indian view which regards the Aryans and their languages as indigenous to South Asia . . ." and "the view of western philologists that the Indo-Aryan languages were carried to South Asia around the middle of the second millennium B.C., as part of the much wider dispersal of Indo-European languages."[12] He states that he himself maintains a clear commitment to the latter view, which must be based primarily on linguistic evidence since western scholars do not feel they have located the archeological homeland. Thapar again shows her westernizing tendency when she asserts that "the linguistic evidence of the Vedic Sanskrit supports the coming into India of an Indo-European language from Iran but does not support the notion that India was the homeland of the Aryan-speaking people."[13]

Indeed, the tendency of western Indologists for two hundred years now to rely on philological evidence is much criticized by those who maintain "the conservative Indian view." Rajaram and Frawley, revisionist authors who are connected with the Aurobindo Center in Pondicherry, quote Aurobindo himself to the effect that philology is a "petty conjectural pseudo-science,"[14] and from the point of view of Indian revisionist authors evidences such as changes in climate and river course constitute harder evidence.

A scholar who is ambiguously placed in regard to this breach between western and Indian scholarship is George Erdosy, who on the Aryan issue inclines toward the "conservative" view, suggesting that the Aryan invasions might have been a fiction devised by a dominant Indian group "to enhance their prestige by creating a fictitious foreign ancestry for themselves"—a position held earlier by Shaffer.[15] Erdosy goes on to assert that "[t]he view that they were indigenous to South Asia" explains certain problems in the Indo-European record, such as lack of West- or Central-Asian parallels.[16] Others have frequently pointed to another problem in the record, namely that the *Ṛg Veda*, though it deals with battles and perhaps an invasion, does not suggest a migration, as of a people who have arrived in a new land after long journey.[17]

So if the Aryans were indigenous to South Asia, where did they live in the Vedic period, and when was that period? According to Rajaram and Frawley, "the probability ,[is] that (Harappan) civilization in the Indus Valley (ca. 3000–1900) actually represents the declining stages of a civilization centered in the Sarasvati Valley. [This civilization] is . . . post-Vedic."[18] The South Asia–indigenous Aryans, in other words, lived in the Harappan region from some time before 3000 B.C., and that early period was in fact the Vedic age. The Indus Valley culture was a later phase of the Vedic civilization rather than a predecessor phase which was replaced by the culture of the Vedic Aryans.

Erdosy's view supports the even more extreme position of Talageri to the effect that the movement of the early dynasties—"during and even before, the composition of the majority of hymns of the *Ṛg Veda*"[19]—went from East to West rather than the reverse, as western archeologists have concluded.[20] This is part of the larger theory that the Aryans, native to India, moved from India to the West, thus carrying their lineage finally into Europe. Talageri "claims that many of the ancient Europeans are descendants of Indians who were driven out of India in a series of campaigns" by other Indians.[21] These campaigns are vaguely reconstructed from elements of Indian tradition which westerners have generally regarded as mythological, such as the so-called Battle of Ten Kings, which is arbitrarily placed around 3730 B.C. The Iranians, Persians, Parthians, Celts, Greeks—indeed, "nearly all the ancient Indo-Europeans" "he traces to India."[22] He even traces specific individuals, such as Zoroaster, back to India, whence, supposedly, the prophet emigrated under military pressure as early as the third or early second millennium B.C. In seeking arguments to support these revisions such authors argue that the Purāṇas were far earlier than the Vedas, reversing another basic conclusion of western scholarship. "[O]verwhelming evidence," write Rajaram and Frawley without enumerating it, "suggests a layer of civilization before the rise of Egypt, Mesopotamia, and the Indus-Sarasvati Valleys. The Indo-Europeans were part of this ancient layer. . . . Its heartland was the region from the Indus to the Ganga. The *Ṛg Veda* is a living remnant of it."[23] Vedic India thus precedes the ancient Near East as the "cradle of civilization," and the *Ṛg Veda* extends much farther back into antiquity than western linguists had believed.

This fabulous construction more or less reverses all the relevant conclusions of western scholarship. On this view, for example, the language of the Indus Valley seals must be an Indo-European language, a later derivation of Vedic, yet, as Allchin points out, "[N]early all the scholarly attempts to pinpoint the language of the Indus seal inscriptions agree (with one to two exceptions) that the evidence points to its being structurally ancestral to Dravidian."[24] This whole pan-Indian or Indocentric construction may be viewed as a postcolonial reversal—a turning of the tables on the British conquerors by Indian scholars who reverse their assumptions and conclusions, in effect taking Indian history back into their own hands. Unfortunately, if those hands seem willful in their handling of the evidence, the reversal will only tend to reinforce the colonists' self-righteous sense that there was a real need for them to take charge in the first place.

Notes to Appendix A

1. A. Kalyanaraman, *Aryatarangini: The Saga of the Indo-Aryans*, vol. 1 (Bombay: Asia Publishing House, 1969), p. 21.

2. Ibid., p. 96.

3. Ibid., p. iii.

4. Ibid., p. i.

5. Ibid., vol. 2, p. vii.

6. Navaratna S. Rajaram and David Frawley, *Vedic 'Aryans' and the Origins of Civilization* (Quebec: W. H. Press, 1995), p. 4.

7. Charles Hallisey, "Roads Taken and Not Taken in the Study of Theravada Buddhism," in *Curators of the Buddha: The Study of Buddhism Under Colonialism*, ed. Donald S. Lopez Jr. (Chicago and London: University of Chicago Press, 1995), p. 32.

8. Ibid., p. 31.

9. Stanley K. Abe, "Inside the Wonder House: Buddhist Art and the West," in *Curators of the Buddha*, ed. Donald S. Lopez Jr., p. 67.

10. This view has been "powerfully advocated," as M. L. West says (*The East Face of Helicon: West Asiatic Elements in Greek Poetry and Myth*, [Oxford: Clarendon Press, 1997], p. 1, n. 2) by Robert Drews, in *The Coming of the Greeks: Indo-European Conquests in the Aegean and the Near East* (Princeton, New Jersey: Princeton University Press, 1988). I agree with West (*The East Face of Helicon*) that Colin Renfrew's countersuggestion which associates the spread of agriculture with the Indo-Europeans and thus sees them on the scene in Greece and elsewhere as early as 6500 B.C. "ignores" much evidence, "has found few if any adherents," and does not amount to a "serious alternative to the orthodox view."

11. Romila Thapar, "The Perennial Aryans," *Seminar* 400 12 (1992): 23–24.

12. F. R. Allchin, ed., *The Archaeology of Early Historic South Asia: The Emergence of Cities and States* (Cambridge: Cambridge University Press, 1995), p. 41.

13. Thapar, "The Perennial Aryans," p. 20.

14. Quoted by Rajaram and Frawley, *Vedic 'Aryans,'* p. x.

15. George Erdosy, "The Prelude to Urbanization: Ethnicity and the Rise of Late Vedic Chiefdoms," *Archaeology of Early Historic South Asia*, ed. F. R. Allchin, p. 90, with a reference to J. G. Shaffer, "The Indo-Aryan Invasions: Cultural Myth and Archaeological Reality," in *The People of South Asia*, ed. J. R. Lukacs (New York and London: Plenum Press, 1984).

16. Erdosy, ibid., p. 91.

17. This is not, however, a problem on the view of Drews (*The Coming of the Greeks*), who regards the Aryan appearance in India not as the culmination of a long migration but as a sudden lightning-like takeover made possible by the technology of chariot warfare.

18. Rajaram and Frawley, *Vedic 'Aryans,'* p. 59.

19. Shrikant G.Talageri, *The Aryan Invasion Theory: A Reappraisal* (New Delhi: Aditya Prakashan, 1993), p. 297.

20. See, for example, George Erdosy, in *Archaeology of Early Historic South India*, ed. F. R. Allchin, p. 81: "[W]hile the number of Early Iron Age sites in some areas of the Indo-Gangetic divide show a decline from late Harappan levels, the number of sites in the Ganga valley increases dramatically, showing an eastward shift of power that continued up to the time of the Mauryas."

21. Rajaram and Frawley, *Vedic 'Aryans,'* p. 125.

22. Ibid., p. 126.

23. Ibid. p. 129.

24. Allchin, *The Archaeology of Early Historic South Asia*, p. 46.

Appendix B

The Aryan Invasion

Allchin notes that "there is a fashionable tendency these days to dismiss 'Aryan invasions' as mere myths, the aberrations of 'Diffusionist' thinking."[1] His tone, calling the dismissal merely "fashionable," implies he still believes in the invasion, or anyway does not believe there is enough reason to thoroughly dismiss it. Yet elsewhere, in contrast, he asserts bluntly: "It is unlikely that there was any single migration, let alone 'invasion,'"[2] in effect taking the "fashionable" view himself. And yet in another passage he describes the Aryans as conquerors, mentioning "the picture which we have from the material record of the Indo-Aryans as a mobile and warlike aristocracy."[3] And still again, after remarking that the people of the Cemetery H culture seem likely to have been Indo-Aryans, he declares: "[T]here appears to be a good case for seeing in the Cemetery H culture the presence of an element of foreign intruders who have dominated the existing population . . ."[4] Elsewhere he opines that "the Indo-Aryan speakers accorded themselves an elite role," raising echoes of Colin Renfrew's concept of "elite dominance."[5] It is true that in these remarks Allchin is not talking about the Aryan Invasion per se, as conceived, say, by Wheeler, but a later smaller version of it; the Harappan urban system has already crumbled or begun to crumble, and it is its late Cemetery H remnant that the Aryan "warlike aristocracy" conquers and dominates. Still it is evidently difficult for an Englishman of the colonial generation to fully withdraw his belief-system from the Invasion. Compromising somewhat, Allchin declares a "clear assumption" that Indo-Aryan languages were brought into India from without, but notes that this "is unlikely to have constituted an invasion or invasions."[6] What emerges from these shifting positions is a compromise which might endure, rejecting the full-scale Aryan Invasion, yet keeping the Aryans as intruders from Central Asia who establish a position of dominance over what is left.

So in response to both a revised appraisal of the Harappan evidence and a nationalistic backlash among Indian scholars, the Aryan Invasion is being reconceived as an Aryan Migration. On this view it would have been a version of the *Völkerwanderungen* made familiar from the later Germanic migrations—"driving their herds before them," as Breasted imagined such a mass movement, "with their families in rough carts drawn by horses . . ."[7] According to Diakonoff, "[T]he main tribal mass . . . moved along on foot with its cattle, probably accompanied by heavy carts.

Pastoral tribes . . . in time exhaust the steppe within the region they inhabit and are thus continually compelled to resettle in new places."[8] Thus the Indo-European dialects spread from the homeland "more by a process of osmosis than by mass replacement of whole populations . . . [in] a real migration, probably a slow migration . . . unmounted herdsmen practising subsidiary agriculture . . ."[9] Diakonoff regards it as probable that, by the time the Indo-Aryans were on their way into northwest India, "the tribal aristocracy began to use war-chariots,"[10] though the masses of people trudged along behind them with their carts. The Indo-European movements, he says, "must not be seen as victorious expeditions of conquerors," but as migrations of "pastoral agriculturalists over the spring grass in the course of a number of generations."[11] This tendency to deemphasize the charioteering and the aspect of conquest—especially in the case of Indo-European movements into northwest India—and to emphasize the aspect of peaceful pastoral migration has been intensified recently by Hindu nationalist sentiment.

But here and there, still more recently, the scholarly feeling has showed signs of turning back toward the nineteenth-century idea of the fierce Indo-European warrior class and the elite dominance theory of their method of conquest. "It is time," says Robert Drews, "to put the PIE speakers back in their chariots."[12] His reexamination of both linguistic and archeological evidence leads him to a redating of both charioteering and Indo-European conquests to about 1600 B.C. "All the Indo-European movements of the Bronze Age that we *know* about are takeovers, date no earlier than ca. 1600 B.C., and are associated with chariot warfare."[13] There is, he insists, "reason for reviving the old notion that the Indo-European 'invasions' were in fact conquests by charioteering people" who constituted "an international elite."[14] This is especially true, he argues, for "the Aryans of India," for whom "charioteering was an obsession."[15] Various evidences suggest to Drews that the Aryan Invasion of northwest India did not take place overland across the Hindu Kush but by the sea route through the Persian Gulf and the Indian Ocean which Mesopotamian merchants had used since the late third millennium.[16] Still, by Drews' dating, the Aryan Invasion would have come in the sixteenth century B.C., seemingly after the abandonment of the major cities of the Indus civilization for nonmilitary reasons, and thus would not have involved a conquest of urban-based armies but of a less concentrated rural population. The last word has not been said on all this.

Notes to Appendix B

1. F. R. Allchin, *The Archaeology of Early Historic South Asia: The Emergence of Cities and States* (Cambridge: Cambridge University Press, 1995), p. 45. He cites Shaffer, "The Indo-Aryan Invasions."

2. Ibid., p. 47.

3. Ibid., p. 48.

4. Ibid., p. 49.

5. Ibid., p. 53. Renfrew, *Archaeology and Language: The Puzzle of Indo-European Origins* (London: Jonathon Cape, 1987).

6. Allchin, *The Archeology of Early Historic South Asia*, p. 44.

7. J. H. Breasted, *Ancient Times: A History of the Early World* (Boston: Ginn and Co., 1916), p. 174.

8. I. M. Diakonoff, in *Cambridge History of Iran*, vol. 2 (Cambridge: Cambridge University Press, 1985), p. 49.

9. Ibid.

10. Ibid.

11. Ibid., vol. 1, p. 46.

12. Robert Drews, *The Coming of the Greeks: Indo-European Conquests in the Aegean and the Near East* (Princeton: Princeton University Press, 1988), p. 148.

13. Ibid., p. 153.

14. Ibid., pp. 152, 179.

15. Ibid., p. 155.

16. Ibid., pp. 182–184. This hypothesis is based on recent attempts to situate the homeland of the Proto-Indo-Europeans in Armenia. "With Mitanni and southern Mesopotamia taken over soon after 1600 B.C., the next most attractive target may have been the rich Indus Valley far to the east. Those Aryans who were too slow off the mark to carve out a domain closer to home may very well have embarked their horses and chariots and sailed to India" (p. 184). On linguistic grounds Oswald Szemerenyi had observed that "we must assume that part at least of the later Indians also lived for a time in, or on the fringes of, Mesopotamia" (cited at p. 184, n. 63).

Appendix C

Black Athena and Western Xenophobia

Martin Bernal, in the first volume of his *Black Athena*,[1] argued that in the nineteenth century the various academic fields that deal with the Greek and Latin classics—archeology and philology above all—were concerned not to allow Semitic influence on the ancient Greeks. He seems clearly to have been right about that, and the tendency, as he correctly averred, maintained its momentum well into the twentieth century. But Bernal's feeling that anti-Semitism was still a dominant concern of western classicists as late as 1985, when he was writing, seems exaggerated. T. B. L. Webster's demonstrations of Near Eastern—mostly Semitic—influences on Homer were considered risqué in the 1950s,[2] but that was a long time ago in terms of cultural attitudes, and they have not been so regarded for about forty years—quite a long time for an attitudinal change to not be noticed by a scholar.

Bernal's belief that western classicism featured anti-Semitism until 1985 is exaggerated. But while the issue of Semitic influence is no longer controversial, suggestions of influence even farther afield in terms of both geography and ethnicity are still regarded as unacceptable. The community of classics scholars who have accepted West Semitic input into their subject matter, however grudgingly, may still not be anywhere near accepting Central Asian or East Asian or South Asian influence from a nonwhite people.

Bernal, in his second volume, claimed black African influence on Greek philosophy—a claim long made by Afrocentric scholars.[3] It now seems, after the controversy over his work has settled down somewhat, that the ambitions of Bernal's second volume have not been successfully carried out. While his first volume's analysis of earlier periods of anti-Semitic attitude in regard to ancient Near Eastern culture may remain valuable, his attempt, in volume 2, to derive Greek philosophy from Africa seems so glaringly unsupported by evidence that it is likely to pass without leaving a trace.

But in a negative sense there *will* be a ripple. Like the diffusionist extravagances of Elliot-Smith a century ago, the Quixotic tilting of Bernal's second volume is in danger of giving the whole comparative enterprise a bad name once more. One contemporary scholar refers to "that comparative compulsion" in western Indological studies, as if there were something pathological about it.[4]

Notes to Appendix C

1. Martin Bernal, *Black Athena: The Afroasiatic Roots of Classical Civilization*, vol. 1, *The Fabrication of Ancient Greek 1785–1985* (New Brunswick, New Jersey: Rutgers University Press, 1987).

2. For example, T. B. L. Webster, *From Mycenae to Homer* (New York: W. W. Norton, 1964 [1958]). Chakrabarti, *Colonial Indology*, p. 52, writes: "From our point of view a more important issue is to know how the concept of ancient Greece came to be divested of all postulates of Egyptian and Phoenician influences." He is evidently thinking of *Black Athena*. What neither Bernal nor Chakrabarti acknowledges is that since the 1950s at the latest ancient Greece has not been "divested of all [such] postulates." It is commonplace and uncontroversial, for example, to see Egyptian influence on archaic Greek sculpture and on the development of Greek temple architecture; it is, now, also commonplace to recognize Ugaritic and other "Phoenician" influences on early Greek literature.

3. The classic text is George G. M. James, *Stolen Legacy: Greek Philosophy Is Stolen Egyptian Philosophy* (Newport News, Virginia: United Brothers Communications Systems, 1954); also Cheik Anta Diop, *Civilization or Barbarism: An Authentic Anthropology* (Brooklyn, New York: Lawrence Hill Books, 1991), pp. 337–358. The idea goes back at least to the writings of Marcus Garvey.

4. Andrew P. Tuck, *Comparative Philosophy and the Philosophy of Scholarship: On the Western Interpretation of Nagarjuna* (New York and Oxford: Oxford University Press, 1990), p. 8. Another Indologist, when I mentioned some Greek-Indian topics, replied simply, "I don't like comparative studies."

Appendix D

The Golden Thigh

The tendency which the Pythagoras material has to spread out in a web of connections, none seeming like an end-point, may be illustrated by what Burkert calls "the most remarkable detail of the Pythagoras legend, his golden thigh."[1] "Antiquity," Burkert goes on, "understood this as a sign of divinity, but we find no explanation of just how this is so."[2] "A scholium on Lucian tells us that the thigh of Pythagoras was imprinted with the image of Apollo . . . But why precisely the thigh?"[3] Scholars have tended to connect this detail with myths of dismemberment, which in turn are interpreted as remnants of shamanic legend and rite. Burkert notes rightly that "the myths tell over and over of the favorite of the Great Mother being wounded in the thigh, as also of the thigh wounds of those who attempt to make their way into the underworld. Only he who bears the sign can descend into the pit with impunity."[4] Yet still, his question—"Why precisely the thigh?"—remains unanswered.

A comparison of mythological motifs points simultaneously toward the Bronze Age high cultures of the ancient Near East for an answer—and toward India. To begin with Egypt, in the coronation rite known as the Ramesseum drama a ritual combat occurs in which Horus, the son of Osiris (who represents the dead pharaoh) fights Osiris's enemy, Set, who represents a false pretender to the throne. Horus, victorious, wrests off Set's testicles and grafts them onto himself.[5] In terms of the myth as a whole he has not stolen Set's genitals but regained his own—as a surrogate for his father, Osiris. At an earlier stage of the myth, Set had dismembered Osiris, and when the dead god's body was recomposed by the sorceress goddess Isis, the genital organ was found to be missing. Within a primitive fertility milieu it might seem that Set has deprived Osiris of his genital in order to deprive him of kingship, that sexual potency, as in so many cases recorded by J. G. Frazer in *The Golden Bough*, was specially associated with kingship and that the king, without it, must be replaced.

In any case, after his fight with Set, but in the same ceremony, Horus hands the thighbone of a sacrificed ram to his father, who is symbolically present, and says, "Behold, I plucked the thighbone from yon Set."[6] Yet it was not Set's thighbone but his testicles that were taken from him. At this point in the ceremony, the thigh seems to have become a disguised or surrogate genital.

In the Sumero-Akkadian *Epic of Gilgamesh* something similar is found, though more heavily disguised. Ishtar, the goddess of sexuality, has propositioned Gilgamesh. He has refused to become her lover, declaring that her lovers all become her sacrificial victims. Angered, she sends a champion called the Bull of Heaven to fight Gilgamesh and his male friend Enkidu because of their rejection of sexuality. When Gilgamesh and Enkidu dispatch the Bull of Heaven, Enkidu throws the beast's right thigh in Ishtar's face as a gesture of insolence.[7] Ishtar's response is to gather "the votaries, the pleasure-lasses and the temple harlots" around the bull's thigh to lament.

This is clearly a fertility motif. When the figure who represents male fertility and hegemony dies or disappears, as in the Babylonian Tammuz liturgies, the temple harlots and votaries of Ishtar lament the event. It is not simply his death that is lamented, it is his loss of fertility. They lament because, deprived of its fertile lord, the land goes barren. The lamentation over the bull's thigh is in effect a lamentation for his fertility or sexuality. Once more the thigh seems a surrogate phallus. The scene is reminiscent of the moment in Egyptian myth when Isis and her maidens lament the loss of Osiris's phallus and attempt to revive it, as Ishtar and her votaries may hope to revive the bull's "thigh."

This motif is found repeatedly in the world's fertility myths. Aphrodite's lover Adonis was wounded in the thigh by a boar's tusk, thereby setting up the lamentation of the bereaved sex goddess (Hdt. I.34–45). It surfaces again in the Grail legends, where, according to Chretien de Troyes, the Grail king, Amfortas, is wounded in the thigh, causing the earth to fall barren; but according to Wolfram von Eschenbach's version, the wound is in the genitals. The displacement of genital to thigh occurs frequently in the Grail myths. When Gawain, in the *Quest of the Holy Grail*, is nearly seduced by a woman, he stabs himself in the thigh to take care of the problem in the future.

Other occurrences of the motif are found in India in the *Vairāgya Sataka* of Bhartrihari,[8] where the Ganges River is drunk dry by the Rishi Jahnu, who thereafter releases it through his "thigh." Greek myths which fall into this group include the myth that, when the fetus Dionysus's mother was incinerated by a lightning bolt, Zeus, the infant's father, rescued the six months' fetus from the ashes and incubated him in his thigh for three months, then delivering him (Apollodorus, III.4, Ap. Rh. IV.1137). The same motif is found in India again in Harivamsa's story of the offspring of the sage Aurva, "born from the thigh"; he produced from his "thigh" the flame that would burn up the world at the age's end.[9] Again, Indra has an adulterous affair and his son from it, Kutsa Aurava, is born from his thigh.[10] Such myths represent an attempt by the male to take over or lay claim to the power center of the female, her birth-giving ability. The web runs back to India again when Pliny says that the myth of the birth of Liber (Dionysus) from the thigh of Zeus originated in Nysa, a possibly legendary Greek colony in India (*NH* VI.79).

If this reading of the mythologem is correct, then the thigh wound which, as Burkert noted, allows the visitor to enter Hell, is a symbolic castration wound indicating that this individual no longer has the power to create life, and therefore may suitably enter the land of the dead.

Alongside the story of Pythagoras's golden thigh, Greek lore preserves the story that King Midas of Lydia, who was involved in many minor fertility myths, had a golden thigh, and the story told by Diogenes Laertius (VIII.73) that Empedocles, "as he was going in a carriage to Messene to attend some festival, fell and broke his thigh."

(Similarly in the *Mahābhārata* I [2] 180, one encounters "the rancorous Prince Duryodhana, whose thighs have been broken.") Midas's case may be connected with the cult of the Great Mother, common in his area, in which at the burial of an initiate "the 'dedicated' member of the body was covered with a gold plate" (Prudentius, *Perist.* X.1076 ff.).

Pythagoras's case is more complex and should be connected with the fact that his thigh was also said to be imprinted with the image of Apollo. Among the Greeks gold was regarded, as Sappho says, as an incorruptible metal, a metal which did not rust and hence was associated with immortality and deity. To attribute a golden genital to Pythagoras is to suggest that he is outside of the cycle of birth and death, no longer subject to ordinary desires and impulses, his energy that of an immortal. Hence it was reasonable to say, as the scholiast on Lucian said, that Pythagoras's thigh was imprinted with the image of Apollo. Apollo, the god of transcendence, represented the state beyond birth and death. Pythagoras's golden "thigh" was a mark of the tradition that he was a type of being in between human and divine.

Notes to Appendix D

1. Walter Burkert, *Lore and Science in Ancient Pythagoreanism* (Cambridge, Massachusetts: Harvard University Press, 1972), p. 159.

2. Ibid.

3. Ibid., n. 215.

4. Ibid., p. 160.

5. Theodor H. Gaster, *Thespis: Ritual, Myth and Drama in the Ancient Near East*, new and revised edition (Garden City, New York: Doubleday, 1961), p. 391.

6. Ibid., p. 397.

7. James B. Pritchard, ed., *Ancient Near Eastern Texts Relating to the Old Testament* (Princeton, New Jersey: Princeton University Press, 1955), p. 85.

8. *Vairāgya Sataka* of Bhartrihari, trans. Swami Madhavananda (Calcutta: Advaita Asharama, 1971), p. 45.

9. John Dowson, *A Classical Dictionary of Hindu Mythology; and Religion, Geography, History and Literature*, 8th ed. (London: Routledge and Kegan Paul, 1953), pp. 32 ff.

10. Arthur B. Keith, *The Religion and Philosophy of the Veda and Upaniṣads*, vol. 2, Harvard Oriental Series 31 and 32 (Cambridge, Massachusetts: Harvard University Press, 1925), p. 470.

Appendix E

Philosophy and Grammar

In the *Ṛg Veda* and the Upaniṣads language was worshipped as the goddess Vāc, from whom both those bodies of texts are said to have been born. Among some of the Greek philosophers, similarly, Logos, "word" or "speech," means "the governing principle of the universe," a law "universal and all-pervading." This usage may have been current as early as Heraclitus, and in any case was common from the fourth century onward. Both cultures may have been purveying a Late Bronze Age cult of language which can be seen in Egyptian, Persian, and other Near Eastern traditions.[1]

But subsequently the two cultures developed the theme of language somewhat differently. The idea of language became steadily secularized in the Greek tradition and steadily sacralized in the Indian. Early Indian grammarians were motivated in part by an anxiety to maintain the efficacy of the Vedic rite by guaranteeing the integrity of its text, the pronunciation of each word, and the meanings involved. If the rite were performed with an incorrect text, an unrecognizable pronunciation, or without understanding of its meaning, it would be ineffectual. The apparently earlier development of grammatical thought in India than in Greece may speculatively be connected with the social function it was performing. Study of Sanskrit was a way of fortifying the Vedic rite and with it the social privilege of the Aryan community. "In the ancient hymns of the *Ṛg Veda* semitechnical vocabulary was already developed to deal with such linguistic matters as grammar, poetic creation, inspiration, illumination, and so on."[2] This discipline now seems to begin with Pāṇini, but "Pāṇini refers to ten earlier authorities, most of them presumably grammarians."[3]

Pāṇini's date is uncertain. Nakamura feels that his multiple references to the Greeks means he must have written after the Alexandrian invasion—therefore in the late fourth century at the earliest.[4] Many scholars, however, feel that the digamma in his formation Yavanes/Iawones indicates a considerably earlier date, before the disappearance of digamma from Greek—that is, the fifth century at the latest. Most scholars recently have dated Pāṇini to the fifth century without arguing the point.[5] Pāṇini's major work *Aṣṭādhyāyī*, then, may have been as early as the grammatical observations of Protagoras, which were seemingly far more primitive, or he may have been a contemporary of the early Stoic grammarians. In either case he seems well in advance of the Greeks.

Pāṇini was primarily concerned with the formation of Sanskrit words, though in his discussion of them he managed to present a more or less complete grammar of Vedic and classical Sanskrit. Though Pāṇini was no doubt aware of the religious associations the Vedic language carried with it, still his *Aṣṭādhyāyī* is a work of secular scholarship.

Pāṇini's great commentator Patañjali—commonly dated to the second century B.C.—shows the increasing interpenetration of grammatical studies and religious philosophy. The first book of his *Mahābhāṣya*, or Great Commentary, on Pāṇini's *Aṣṭādhyāyī*, was comprised mainly of philosophical thinking with a transcendentalist Hindu point of view. In keeping with the revealed status of the *Ṛg Veda*, for example, "[a] linguistic item is considered [by Patañjali] eternal and not capable of being newly produced."[6] Language was created by the gods and not by humans; as such it is not malleable by human intervention. This is a view of language related to the so-called mantric view which developed from the Vedic cult; the metric hymns of the Vedas themselves were known as mantras—eternal and creative metaphysical entities in verbal form—and a derivative view was later held by the tantric sects, that various sacred syllables incarnate divine powers and are responsible for creating and maintaining the world of form.

This tendency is even more prominent by the time of Bhartrihari in the fifth century A.D. It was he "who led grammar into philosophy proper by making a case for *vyākaraṇa* [grammatical theory] as a *darśana*, a view about ultimate things, eventually about liberation."[7] Here too the eternalist metaphysical view of language is in effect. It is basic to Bhartrihari's view that "the linguistic units are permanent," and that "language is innate and without a beginning"[8]—that is, it is eternal in the way metaphysical entities are said to be.

Bhartrihari is essentially in the Vedāntic tradition. Much of his thought is modeled on the Upaniṣads and in turn influenced Śaṅkara. In the first verse of his *Vākyapadīya* he equated the Absolute, or Brahman, with Language, or Śabda. The *Ṛg Veda* had already equated language with Brahman, using the name Vāc. As language is eternal truth, and the Vedas are the essential expression of language, "the Vedic seers are not considered to be composers of the hymns but rather the 'seers' of eternal truth."[9] The Vedas as eternal truth are for Bhartrihari the Śabda Brahman—the absolute as language. Through its appearance as the Vedas, Śabda Brahman creates the universe and its cycles. Language is like a divine spirit "descending and embodying itself in phenomena . . ."[10] As language contains the names of all things, so, when it becomes ontologically reified through its *śakti*, all those things exist empirically too.

The seer of the truth is not merely one who has studied grammar but also one who has prepared himself through the proper yoga. This *Śabdapūrvayoga*, or yoga of the word, is, according to Bhartrihari, "the door leading to liberation (I.14)." It begins with the down-to-earth purification of one's everyday language from grammatically incorrect forms. This seemingly inconsequential point has two purposes. First, since language is eternal and unchanging, the speaker who changes it by speaking incorrectly is straying from a fixed, eternal code. Moreover, since language represents eternal truth, and that truth is embodied in the Vedas, the speaker who wanders from this eternal truth is threatening the Vedas and the religion and society which are based on them. If language is changed it will no longer be the language of the Vedas, and the society whose hieratic language is not Vedic will lose Vedic accreditation. The compact by which the gods entrusted this society with the Vedas will have been broken. Secondly, it was held that acts of speaking incorrectly leave traces that obscure the vision of the truth—the Vedas, or the Śabda Brahman. Repeated use of proper grammar gradually cleanses the mind of these traces. This stage is followed by breathing practices and mantric recitation, which further cleanse the mind of past traces.

The most essential and most difficult requirement is the "suppression of sequence,"[11] meaning, in terms of language, word order, but also the sequencing of thoughts. This is not unlike what Patañjali in the *Yoga Sūtras* called the suppression of mental fluctuations. Finally the mind is quieted and the intuitive experience of Śabda Brahman can ensue, which brings with it *mokṣa* or release from the cycle of reincarnations. "[B]y practicing the Vedas, the vast darkness is removed . . ."[12]

Bhartrihari's religion of language, or yoga of the word, did not, however, refer to language generically. It was strictly the language of the Vedas and Upaniṣads—that is, Sanskrit—which was worshipped. In addition to being the language of the Vedas, Sanskrit was also the language of the ruling class—the Aryans and Aryanized groups—and the exclusivity of their language represented also the exclusivity of their privilege. The worship of the Sanskrit language, in other words, became a tool of dominance. Noncaste (non-Aryan) Indians were regarded by Aryans as unclean and subhuman—and that low status was represented by the fact that they did not use the Sanskrit language. The *Manavadharmaśastra* decrees that if a noncaste Indian shall have accidentally seen the performance of a Vedic rite the Aryans should pour molten lead into his eyes. Similar feelings would have been provoked by the use of Sanskrit by a non-Aryan Indian.

The attitude was much the same toward foreigners, who did not natively speak Sanskrit, the language of the gods. Foreigners, like non-Aryan Indians, were regarded as inherently degraded, lower than the Aryan in ways that could never be remedied because they were metaphysically permanent, like the nature of one's soul.

In the classical age of Hinduism, from the early centuries A.D. through the Gupta period, Hindu xenophobia or exclusivity increased steadily; Bhartrihari's new form of the religion of the Sanskrit language—still based on the Vedic worship of Vāc but reconceived in terms of the new Hinduism with ideas from Vedānta liberally included—was an expression both of Sanskrit's unquestioned cultural hegemony in the Middle Ages and of the Hindu community's aversion to having contact with peoples who were not sanctified by being native speakers of it.

In Greece, meanwhile, the idea of language was becoming increasingly secularized. The concept of *logos* started, with Heraclitus, as a deity, but to the Stoics it was a secular concept whose principal meanings were "reason" and "speech." It was still regarded as fundamental to philosophy, but not in a theological so much as a technological way. As Chrysippus put it: "Philosophy . . . is the discipline concerned with reason (*logos*)."[13]

Philosophers in the fifth century B.C. began to show special interest in the mechanics of how their language worked. Protagoras, for example, "distinguished the three genders" (Aristotle, *Rhet.* 1407b 6).[14] This seems an elementary thing, but may never have been articulated before, at least in the context of philosophy. In the fourth century Plato worked on etymology in the *Cratylus* and Aristotle on declensions in the *De Interpretatione*. Subsequently "it was the Stoics . . . who first formulated traditional grammar,"[15] beginning with "their doctrine of the cases of the noun and their verbal tense system."[16] Gradually this process of piecemeal decoding developed into the discipline of grammar, especially in the writings of the Stoics, above all Chrysippus. From being treated under the heading of "Diction" as a subheading of "Dialectic," grammar gradually became a separate discipline.

The period of this development was also characterized by an increasing secularization of language, an increasing separation of it from religious types of thought. The Stoics, for example, "preferred . . . a very plain language." "[They] may . . . have been impressed by the idea that it was in ordinary rather than in highly refined language [that] reason articulated itself, and that, hence, a study of ordinary language was philosophically much more relevant."[17]

At the same time that grammatical studies were developing within the context of philosophy, the Greek language gradually lost its cultural value as defining a certain community, even as the grip of Sanskrit on Indo-Aryan identity was tightening. As late as the fourth century B.C. there was a sense that the Greek language belonged to a certain ethnic group. Theoreticians of linguistics regarded "Hellenism" as the primary stylistic criterion. "Aristotle . . . said (*Rhet.* 3.5 [1407a 19–20]) that Hellenism is the principle of diction. . . . Dionysius of Halicarnassus . . . says that the other virtues are of no use if they are not accompanied by this primary virtue (*Ad Pompeium* 3)."[18] This was a criterion which obviously tended to exclude foreigners, though one could learn linguistic "Hellenism," which wasn't, like Sanskritism, a matter of birthright. Hellenism was never identified with blood and soil to the extent of Sanskrit in Hindu culture. To begin with it was just a matter of a certain style of speaking and writing; lacking it might make one less of a cosmopolitan sophisticate, but would not render one subhuman.

And in fact the elevation of the virtue of "Hellenism" did not survive the immersive contact with other cultures. After the Alexandrian conquest of West and South Asia, Greek was deliberately simplified and converted into a language for foreigners—the *koinē* or common dialect. While Aryan Indians were jealously guarding their language and keeping it safe from the profanation of being spoken by non-Aryans, the Greeks were literally giving their language to foreign peoples, even making a new form that was especially tailored for them. At about the time Bhartrihari's religion of hypostasized Sanskrit was formulated in India, the Greek grammatical tradition culminated in Apollonius Dyscolus's various works in the second century A.D. and Priscian's *Institutiones* in the sixth, modern-style descriptive grammars dealing with sound, word-formation, and syntax, and assuming a vocabulary of concepts including the parts of speech and the "accidents" such as gender, number, case, mood, and tense.[19]

India, as well as Greece, provides a contrast with Bhartrihari's transcendentalist view of language. In the age of the *nāstika* religions—traditionally the sixth century B.C.—religious and philosophical pluralism reigned in India. Ājīvikism, Jainism, Buddhism, Upanisadism, Vedic ritualism, Cārvāka materialism, and various brands of Skepticism coexisted. There was no absolutely dominant denomination that could make everyone else feel like an outsider. In the following period, the Mauryan Empire, Buddhism was the leading religion, and the possibility of being considered an outsider to Vedism was not a threat. At that time Buddhism, as it rejected the Vedas, also rejected—or at least neglected—Sanskrit. The native language of the Buddha is unknown, though it is presumed to have been a Middle Indic dialect related to Sanskrit, the Prākrits, Pali, and other Indo-European dialects of north India. When he started teaching, the Buddha adopted the principle of teaching in the native language of his listeners—the exact opposite of Hinduism's desire to exclude non-Sanskrit-speakers from their tradition and their lore. The Buddha seems to have taught primarily in four languages, including Magadhi, the language of Magadha where his royal patron Bimbisāra lived, and three related languages that occurred natively in the regions of his annual sojourning and teaching. These versions of the teachings have all been lost, preempted by the translation into Pali, another related dialect or language of north India. Several centuries later, during the period of the rise of Hinduism to hegemony, the canon was translated into Sanskrit, though it did not exercise a presence in that form comparable to the Pali and, later, the Tibetan and Chinese. Japanese, Burmese, English, and many other linguistic embodiments of the Buddhist canon followed as it traveled from culture to culture. Buddhism, like Hellenism, after a time aimed itself specifically at foreign cultures and attempted to present itself to them in useful forms.

Meanwhile in the early centuries A.D. Hinduism was putting itself together as a major unified religion, reconciling components as varied as Vedic Vaisnavism and Dravidian Śaiva Tantrism. By the Gupta period Hinduism's dominance was unquestioned and that is when Bhartrihari's full-blown religion of Sanskrit was formulated. By the sixth and seventh centuries Vedāntic Hinduism had incorporated so much from Mādhyamika and Yogacara Buddhism as to render them marginal.

The Vedic religion in its original Aryan form had exercised a more exclusive appeal. Mature Hinduism included countless elements of non-Aryan, non-Vedic doctrine, mythology, yoga, ritual, philosophy, and magic. Chronologically, the late blossoming of Hinduism in relation to Greek culture, which was virtually at its end, can account to some extent for the countermovements of the two cultural trajectories. As Greece was becoming secularized, a vast religion was sweeping all of India. This also has been grist for the mill of colonial Indology.

Notes to Appendix E

1. W. K. C. Guthrie, *History of Greek Philosophy*, vol. 1 (Cambridge: Cambridge University Press, 1962), pp. 419–422. M. L. West (*Early Greek Philosophy and the Orient* [Oxford: Clarendon Press, 1971], pp. 124–129) argues against this use in Heraclitus.

2. Harold G. Coward and K. Kunjunni Raja, "Introduction to the Philosophy of the Grammarians," in *Encyclopedia of Indian Philosophies*, vol. 5, *The Philosophy of the Grammarians*, ed. Coward and Raja (Princeton, New Jersey: Princeton University Press, 1990), p. 33.

3. Ibid., p. 111.

4. Hajime Nakamura, *A History of Early Vedānta Philosophy* (Delhi: Motilal Banarsidass, 1989), p. 33, n. 24.

5. K. Kunjunni Raja, "Philosophical Elements in Pāṇini's Aṣṭādhyāyī," *The Philosophy of the Grammarians*, ed. Coward and Raja, p. 111.

6. K. Kunjunni Raja, "Philosophical Elements in Patañjali's *Mahābhāṣya*," in ibid., p. 116.

7. Coward and Raja, "Introduction to the Philosophy of the Grammarians," p. 18.

8. Ashok Aklujkar, "Brief Analysis [of Bhartrihạri]," *The Philosophy of the Grammarians*, ed. Coward and Raja, pp. 123, 124.

9. Coward and Raja, "Introduction to the Philosophy of the Grammarians," p. 35.

10. Ibid., p. 35.

11. Ibid., p. 47.

12. Ibid., p. 49.

13. Michael Frede, "Principles of Stoic Grammar," *Essays in Ancient Philosophy* (Minneapolis: University of Minnesota Press, 1987), p. 327.

14. See ibid., p. 339.

15. Ibid., p. 302.

16. Ibid., p. 304.

17. Ibid., pp. 321, 320.

18. Ibid., p. 310.

19. See Frede, "The Origins of Traditional Grammar," ibid., p. 338.

List of Works Cited

Abe, Stanley K. "Inside the Wonder House: Buddhist Art and the West." In *Curators of the Buddha: The Study of Buddhism under Colonialism*. Edited by Donald S. Lopez Jr. Chicago and London: University of Chicago Press, 1995.

Ackrill, J. L. "Zwei Aristotelische Frühschriften über die Ideenlehre." *Mind* 61 (1952): 102-113.

Adam, J. *The Republic of Plato*. 2 vols. Cambridge: Cambridge University Press, 1926 and 1929.

Afnán, Ruhi M. *Zoroaster's Influence on Anaxagoras, the Greek Tragedians, and Socrates*. New York: Philosophical Library, 1969.

——. *Zoroaster's Influence on Greek Thought*. New York: Philosophical Library, 1965.

Agrawal, D. P., and Dilip K. Chakrabarti, editors. *Essays in Indian Protohistory*. Delhi: B. R. Publishing Co., 1979.

Agrawala, V. S. "Some Foreign Words in the Ancient Sanskrit Literature." *Indian Historical Quarterly* 27 (1951).

Aiyar, K. Narayanasvami. *Thirty Minor Upanisads*. El Reno, Oklahoma: Santarasa Publications, 1980.

Aklujkar, Ashok. "Brief Analysis [of Bhartrihari]." In *Encyclopedia of Indian Philosophy*. Vol. 5, *The Philosophy of the Grammarians*. Edited by Harold G. Coward and K. Kunjunni Raja. Princeton, New Jersey: Princeton University Press, 1990, pp. 122–172.

Allan, John, Sir T. Wolseley Haig, and H. H. Dodwell, *The Cambridge Shorter History of India*. Edited by H. H. Dodwell. New York: Macmillan; Cambridge: Cambridge University Press, 1934.

Allchin, Bridget, and Raymond Allchin. *The Birth of Indian Civilization*. Baltimore, Maryland: Penguin, 1968.

Allchin, Raymond, editor. *The Archeology of Early Historic South Asia:* The Emergence of Cities and States. Cambridge: Cambridge University Press, 1995.

Allchin, Raymond, et. al., editors. *Gandhāran Art in Context: East-West Exchanges at the Crossroads of Asia*. New Delhi: Regency, 1997.

Allegro, John. *The Sacred Mushroom and the Cross*. New York: Doubleday, 1971.

Anacker, Stefan. "Major Schools of the Mahāyāna: Yogācāra." *In Buddhism: A Modern Perspective*. Edited by Charles S. Prebish. University Park, Pennsylvania, and London: Pennsylvania State University Press, 1978, pp. 97–101.

Annas, Julia. *Hellenistic Philosophy of Mind*. Berkeley, California: University of California Press, 1986.

——. *The Morality of Happiness*. New York: Oxford University Press, 1993.

Anton, John Peter, and George L. Kustas, editors. Essays in *Ancient Greek Philosophy*. Albany, New York: State University of New York Press, 1972.

Armstrong, Arthur H. *An Introduction to Ancient Philosophy*. N.c.: Littlefield, Adams and Company, 1983.

——. *The Architecture of the Intelligible Universe in the Philosophy of Plotinus: An Analytical and Historical Study*. Cambridge: Cambridge University Press, 1940.

——. "Plotinus." *The Cambridge History of Later Greek and Early Medieval Philosophy*. Edited by Arthur H. Armstrong, pp. 195–270.

——, editor. *The Cambridge History of Later Greek and Early Medieval Philosophy*. London: Cambridge University Press, 1967.

Arnou, René. *Le désir de dieu dans la philosophie de Plotin*. 2nd edition. Rome: Presses de la Université Gregorienne, 1967.

Arrian. *The Campaigns of Alexander*. Translated by Aubrey de Selincourt with introduction and notes by J. R. Hamilton. London: Penguin, 1971.

Asthana, Shashi. "Indus-Mesopotamia Trade: Nature of Trade and Structural Analysis of Operative System." In *Essays in Indian Protohistory*. Edited by D. P. Agrawal and Dilip K. Chakrabarti. Delhi: B. R. Publishing Co., 1979, pp. 31–43.

Avalon, Arthur (Sir John G. Woodroffe), translator. *Hymn to Kālī*. Madras: Ganesh and Co., 1965.

——, translator. *Tantra of the Great Liberation (Mahanirvāṇa Tantra)*. New York: Dover, 1972.

Ayer, A. J. *The Problem of Knowledge*. New York: Penguin, 1977.

Bailey, Cyril. *The Greek Atomists and Epicurus*. Oxford: Clarendon Press, 1928.

Ballard, Edward G. *Socratic Ignorance: An Essay in Platonic Self-knowledge*. The Hague: Nijhoff, 1965.

Barnes, Jonathon. *The Presocratic Philosophers*. The Arguments of the Philosophers. London and New York: Routledge, 1982.

Barrett, William, editor. *Zen Buddhism: Selected Writings of D. T. Suzuki*. Garden City, NewYork: Doubleday, Anchor Books, 1956.

——"Zen in the West." *Zen Buddhism: Selected Writings of D. T. Suzuki*. Garden City, NewYork: Doubleday, Anchor Books, 1956, pp. VII-XX.

Barua, Benimadhab. *A History of Pre-Buddhistic Indian Philosophy*. Delhi: Motilal Banarsidass, 1981.

——. *Prolegomena to a History of Buddhist Philosophy*. Calcutta: University of Calcutta Press, 1981.

——. "The Background to the Rise of Buddhism." In *Studies in History of Buddhism*. Edited by A. K. Narain. Delhi: B. R. Publishing Co., 1980, pp. 13–32.

Basham, A. L., editor. *A Cultural History of India*. Delhi: Oxford University Press, 1997.

——. *History and Doctrine of the Ājīvikas: A Vanished Indian Religion*. London: Luzac, 1951.

Batchelor, Stephen. *The Awakening of the West: The Encounter of Buddhism and Western Culture*. Berkeley, California: Parallax Press, 1994.

——, and Robert A. F. Thurman. "Reincarnation: A Debate." *Tricycle: The Buddhist Review* 6, no. 4 (1997): 24–29.

Benn, A. W. *History of Ancient Philosophy*. New York: Putnam, 1912.

Bernal, Martin. *Black Athena: The Afroasiatic Roots of Classical Civilization*. Vol. 1, *The Fabrication of Ancient Greece 1785–1985*. New Brunswick, New Jersey: Rutgers University Press, 1987.

Bertschinger, Richard. *The Secret of Everlasting Life: The First Translation of the Ancient Chinese Text on Immortality*. Shaftesbury, Dorset: Element, 1994.

Bevan, E. R. "Alexander the Great." *The Cambridge History of India*. Vol. 1, *Ancient India*. Edited by Edward J. Rapson. Cambridge: Cambridge University Press, 1922, pp. 345–385.

Bhagat, M. G. *Ancient Indian Asceticism*. Delhi: Munshiram Manoharlal, 1976.

Bhandarkar, Devadatta Ramakrishna. *Some Aspects of Ancient Indian Culture*. Sir William Meyer Lectures 1938–1939. Madras: University of Madras, 1940.

Bhattacharjee, Sukumari. *Literature in the Vedic Age*. Vol. 1, *The Saṁhitās*. Bagchi Indological Series 3. Calcutta: K. P. Bagchi and Company, 1984.

Bhattacarya, Sachhidananda. *Select Aśokan Epigraphs*. Calcutta: Mukhopadhyay, 1960.

Bhattacharya, Kamaleswar. *The Dialectical Method of Nāgārjuna*. Delhi: Motilal Banarsidass, 1978.

Bhattacharyya, Narendra Nath. *History of Śakta Religion*. New Delhi: Munshiram Manoharlal, 1974.

——. *History of the Tantric Religion: A Historical, Ritualistic and Philosophical Study*. Delhi: Manohar, 1982.

Bhattacharyya, Vidhushekhara. *The Basic Conception of Buddhism*. Adharchandra Mookerjee Lectures 1932. Calcutta: University of Calcutta, 1934.

Bidez, Joseph. *Eos; ou, Platon et l'Orient*. Brussels: M. Hayez, Imprimeur de la Academie Royale de Belgique, 1945.

Jim Bigwood, "Ctesias as Historian." *Phoenix* 32 (1978): 36–39.

Black, Jeremy, and Anthony Green. *Gods, Demons and Symbols of Ancient Mesopotamia: An Illustrated Dictionary*. Austin, Texas: University of Texas Press, 1995.

Blofeld, John. *The Tantric Mysticism of Tibet*. New York: E. P. Dutton, 1970.

——, translator. *The Zen Teaching of Huang Po*. New York: Grove Press, 1958.

——, translator. *The Zen Teaching of Hui Hai*. New York: Samuel Weiser, 1972.

Bloomfield, Maurice. *The Life and Stories of the Jaina Savior Parsvanatha*. Baltimore, Maryland: Johns Hopkins Press, 1919.

——. *The Religion of the Veda, The Ancient Religion of India (from Ṛg-Veda to Upaniṣads)*. New York: AMS Press, 1969.

Bochenski, Innotentius M. *A History of Formal Logic*. Translated and edited by Ivo Thomas. Notre Dame, Indiana: University of Notre Dame Press, 1961.

Bongard-Levin, G. M. *Ancient Indian Civilization*. Delhi: Gulab Vazirani for Arnold-Heinemann Publishers, 1985.

Bonwick, James. *Egyptian Belief and Modern Thought*. London: C. K. Paul and Co., 1878.

Bosworth, A. B. *Alexander and the East: The Tragedy of Triumph*. Oxford: Clarendon Press, 1996.

——. *Conquest and Empire: The Reign of Alexander the Great*. Cambridge: Cambridge University Press, 1988.

Bottero, Jean. *Mespotamia: Writing, Reasoning, and the Gods*. Translated by Zainab Bahrani and Mac Van De Mieroop. Chicago: University of Chicago Press, 1992.

Brahmananda, Swami. *The Philosophy of Sage Yājñavalkya*. Rishikesh: Shivanandanagar/Divine Life Society, 1981.

Breasted, James Henry. *Ancient Times: A History of the Early World*. Boston: Ginn and Co., 1916.

Breckenridge, Carol A. and Peter van der Veer, editors. *Orientalism and the Postcolonial Predicament: Perspectives on South Asia*. New Cultural Studies Series. Philadelphia: University of Pennsylvania Press, 1993.

Bréhier, Émile. *The History of Philosophy: The Hellenistic and Roman Age*. Chicago: University of Chicago Press, 1965.

——. *The Philosophy of Plotinus*. Translated by Joseph Thomas. Chicago: University of Chicago Press, 1958.

Breloer, B., and F. Boemer, editors. *Fontes historiae religionum Indicarum*. Bonn: Ludovicum Röhrscheid, 1939 (*Fontes Historiae religionum*, fasc. 7).

Brink, C. O. "Oikeiosis and Oikeiotes: Theophrastus and Zeno on Nature and Moral Theory." *Phronesis* 1 (1955): 12–145.

Brisson, Luc. "Premises, Consequences, and Legacy of an Esotericist Interpretation of Plato." *Ancient Philosophy* 15 (1995): 117–134.

Broadie, Sarah. *Ethics with Aristotle*. New York: Oxford University Press, 1991.

Brochard, Victor C. L. *Les sceptiques grecs*. Paris: Impr. Nationale, 1887.

Brumbaugh, Robert S. *The Philosophers of Greece*. New York: Crowell, 1964.

Budge, E. A. Wallis. *Amulets and Talismans*. New York: Collier Books, 1970.

——. translator. *The Egyptian Book of the Dead (The Papyrus of Ani)*. New York: Dover, 1967.

——. *Gods of the Egyptians*. 2 vols. New York: Dover, 1969.

Bühler, Georg, translator and commentator. *The Laws of Manu*, translated with extracts from seven commentaries. Sacred Books of the East 25. New York: Dover Publications, 1969.

Buren, E. Douglas van. *Symbols of the Gods in Mesopotamian Art*. Rome: Pontificium Institutum Biblicum, 1945.

Burkert, Walter. *Lore and Science in Ancient Pythagoreanism*. Cambridge, Mass.: Harvard University Press, 1972.

——. *The Orientalizing Revolution: Near Eastern Influence on Greek Culture in the Early Archaic Age*. Translated by Margaret E. Pinder and Walter Burkert. Revealing Antiquity 5. Cambridge, Massachusetts, and London: Harvard University Press, 1992.

Burn, A. R. "Persia and the Greeks." In *The Cambridge History of Iran*. Vol. 2, *The Median and Achaemenian Periods*. Edited by Ilya Gershevitch. Cambridge: Cambridge University Press, 1985.

Burnet, John. *Early Greek Philosophy*. Cleveland and New York: World Publishing Company, 1964.
——. "Sceptics." In *Encyclopaedia of Religion and Ethics*. Edited by James Hastings. Edinburgh: T. and T. Clark; New York: C. Scribner's Sons, 1908–27.
Burnyeat, Myles. "Can the Skeptic Live His Skepticism?" *In Doubt and Dogmatism: Studies in Hellenistic Epistemology*. Edited by M. Schofield, M. Burnyeat, and J. Barnes. Oxford: Clarendon; New York: Oxford University Press, 1979.
Burstein, S. *The Babyloniaca of Berossus*. Sources from the Ancient Near East 5. Malibu, California: Undena, 1978.
Bury, R. G., translator. *Sextus Empiricus*. 4 vols. Loeb Classical Library. Cambridge, Massachusetts: Harvard University Press, 1933–1949.
Butterworth, Edric A. S. *The Tree at the Navel of the Earth*. Berlin: Walter de Gruyter and Co., 1970.
Cameron, Alister. *The Pythagorean Background of the Theory of Recollection*. Menasha, Wisconsin: George Banta Publishing Co., 1938.
Campbell, Joseph. *The Masks of God: Oriental Mythology*. New York: Viking Press, 1962.
Cannon, Garland. *Oriental Jones*. London: Asia Publishing House, 1964.
Cary, M., and E. H. Warmington. *The Ancient Explorers*. Baltimore, Maryland: Penguin, 1963.
Casson, Lionel. *The Ancient Mariners: Seafarers and Sea Fighters of the Mediterranean in Ancient Times*. Princeton, New Jersey: Princeton University Press, 1991.
——. *Travel in the Ancient World*. London: George Allen and Unwin, 1974.
Chadwick, John. *The Decipherment of Linear B*. New York: Random House, 1958.
Chakrabarti, Dilip K. *Colonial Indology: Sociopolitics of the Ancient Indian Past*. Delhi: Munshiram Monoharlal, 1997.
——. "India and West Asia, An Alternative Approach." *Man and Environment* 1: 33–34.
——. "'Long Barrel Cylinder' Beads and the Issue of Pre-Sargonic Contact between the Harappan Civilization and Mesopotamia." In *Harappan Civilization: A Contemporary Perspective*. Edited by Gregory Possehl. New Delhi: Oxford and IBH Publishing Co. in collaboration with American Institute of Indian Studies, 1992, pp. 265–270.
——. "Origin of the Indus Civilization: Theories and Problems." In *Frontiers of the Indus Civilization*. Edited by B. B. Lal and S. P. Gupta. New Delhi: Books and Books, 1984, pp. 43–50.
——. *The Logic of Gotama*. Monographs of the Society for Asian and Comparative Philosophy 5. Honolulu: University Press of Hawaii, 1977.
Chakrabarti, Kumar, editor. *Pāśupata Sūtram with Panchārtha-Bhāṣya of Kaundinya*. Calcutta: Academie Publishers, 1970.
Chakraberty, Chandra. *An Interpretation of Ancient Hindu Medicine*. Delhi: Low Price Publications, 1997.
Chakraborti, Haripada. *Asceticism in Ancient India*. Calcutta: Punthi Pustak, 1973.
Chan, Wing-Tsit, compiler and translator. *A Source Book in Chinese Philosophy*. Princeton, New Jersey: Princeton University Press, 1963.
Chanda, Ramaprasad. "Sind Five Thousand Years Ago." *Modern Review* (August 1932): 159–169.
——. *The Buddhist Teaching of Totality*. University Park, Pennsylvania, and London: Pennsylvania State University Press, 1974.
Chang, Garma C. C. *Teachings of Tibetan Yoga*. New Hyde Park, New York: University Books, 1963.
Chapple, Christopher. *Karma and Creativity*. Albany, New York: State University of New York Press, 1986.
Charlesworth, Martin P. *Trade Routes and Commerce of the Roman Empire*. Cambridge: Cambridge University Press, 1924.
Charpentier, Jarl. "Ājīvika." *Journal of the Royal Asiatic Society* (1913): 669–673.
Chatterjee, Asir Kumar. *A Comprehensive History of Jainism*. Calcutta: Firma KLM, 1978.
Chatterji, S. K. "Race Movements and Prehistoric Culture." In *The Vedic Age*. Edited by R. C. Majumdar. London: George Allen and Unwin, 1951, pp. 141–168.
Chattopadhyaya, Debiprasad. "Editorial Note." In Mrinalkanti Gangopadhyaya, *Indian Atomism: History and Sources*. Atlantic Highlands, New Jersey: Humanities Press, 1980, pp. v–vii.

———. *Indian Philosophy: A Popular Introduction*. Delhi: People's Publishing House, 1964.
———. *Lokāyata: A Study in Ancient Indian Materialism*. New Delhi: People's Publishing House, 1959.
Chaudhuri, Nirad C. *Hinduism: A Religion to Live By*. Delhi: Oxford University Press, 1979.
Cheng, Chung-ying. "Nature and Function of Skepticism in Chinese Philosophy." *Philosophy East and West* 27 (1977): 137–154.
Cherniss, Harold F. *Aristotle's Criticism of Plato and the Academy*. New York: Russell and Russell, 1962.
———. *The Riddle of the Early Academy*. Berkeley and Los Angeles: University of California Press, 1945.
Childe, V. Gordon. "The Indus Civilization." *Antiquity* 11 (1937): 351.
———. *What Happened in History*. Harmondsworth, Middlesex, and Baltimore, Maryland: Penguin, 1942.
Chowdhury, Paramesh. *Indian Origin of the Chinese Nation: An Unconventional Challenging Theory about the Origin of the Chinese*. Calcutta: Dasgupta and Co., 1990.
Cilento, Vincenzo. *Antologia Plotiniana*. Bari: N.p., 1970.
Clarke, J. J. *Oriental Enlightenment: The Encounter between Asian and Western Thought*. London and New York: Routledge, 1994.
Colebrooke, Sir T. E. *Life of H. T. Colebrooke*. London: Trubner and Co., 1873.
Collins, Randall. *The Sociology of Philosophies: A Global Theory of Intellectual Change*. Cambridge, Massachusetts: Harvard University Press, 1998.
Conger, George P. "Did India Influence Greek Philosophy?" *Philosophy East and West* 2 (1952): 102–128.
———, editor. *D. T. Suzuki on Indian Mahāyāna Buddhism*. New York: Harper and Row, 1968.
Conze, Edward. *Buddhism: Its Essence and Development*. New York: Peter Smith, 1959.
———, editor. *Buddhist Texts through the Ages*. New York: Harper and Row, 1964.
———. *Buddhist Thought in India*. London: George Allen and Unwin, 1962.
———. *Buddhist Wisdom Books*. London: George Allen and Unwin, 1958.
———, translator. *The Large Sūtra on Perfect Wisdom*, by Maitreyanatha. Berkeley, California, and Los Angeles: University of California Press, 1975.
———. *The Prajñāpāramitā Literature*. The Hague: Mouton, 1960.
———. *Selected Sayings from the Perfection of Wisdom*. London: Buddhist Society, 1955.
———, translator. *The Short Prajñāpāramitā Texts*. London: Luzac, 1973.
———. *Thirty Years of Buddhist Studies*. London: Bruno Cassirer, 1967.
Cook, J. M. *The Greeks in Ionia and the East*. New York: Praeger Books, 1963.
———. *The Persian Empire*. New York: Schocken Books, 1983.
Cooper, David E. *World Philosophy: An Historical Introduction*. Oxford: Blackwell, 1996.
Cornford, Francis M. *Before and After Socrates*. Cambridge: Cambridge University Press, 1932.
———. *From Religion to Philosophy: A Study in the Origins of Western Speculation*. New York: Harper and Row, 1957.
———. "Mathematics and Dialectic in the *Republic* VI–VII." *Mind* n.s. 41 (1932): 37–52, 173–190.
———, translator and commentator. *Plato's Cosmology: The Timaeus of Plato*. International Library of Psychology, Philosophy and Scientific Method. London: K. Paul, Trench, Trubner and Co.; New York: Harcourt Brace Jovanovich, 1973.
———. *Principium Sapientiae: The Origins of Greek Philosophical Thought*. Cambridge: Cambridge University Press, 1952.
Coward, Harold G., and K. Kunjunni Raja, editors. *Encyclopedia of Indian Philosophy*. Vol. 5, *The Philosophy of the Grammarians*. Princeton, New Jersey: Princeton University Press, 1990.
Crombie, I. M. *Plato on Knowledge and Reality*. Vol. 2, *An Examination of Plato's Doctrines*. New York: Humanities Press, 1963.
Cullican, William. *The Medes and the Persians*. Ancient People and Places 2. London: Thames and Hudson, 1965.
Cumont, Franz. *Astrology and Religion among the Greeks and Romans*. New York: Dover Publications, 1960.
Cuvier, George Leopold. *Cuvier's Animal Kingdom*. London: William S. Orr, 1811.
Dandamaev, Muhammad A., and Vladimir G. Lukonin. *The Culture and Social Institutions of Ancient Iran*. Translated by Philip L. Kohl. Cambridge: Cambridge University Press, 1989.

Daniel, Glyn. *The First Civilizations*. New York: Thomas Y. Crowell, 1968.

Daniélou, Alain. *Hindu Polytheism*. Bollingen Series 73. New York: Pantheon Books, 1964.

——. *Śiva and Dionysus*. Translated by K. F. Hurry. London and The Hague: East-West Publications, 1982, and Rochester, Vermont: Inner Traditions, 1984.

——. *While the Gods Play: Shaiva Oracles and Predictions on the Cycles of History and the Destiny of Mankind*. Rochester, Vermont: Inner Traditions International, 1991.

Darmesteter, James, translator. *The Vendidad*. Part 1 of The *Zend-Avesta*. Sacred Books of the East 4. Delhi: Motilal Banarsidass, 1980.

Dasgupta, Shashi Bhusan. *Introduction to Tantric Buddhism*. Berkeley, California: Shambhala, 1974.

——. *Obscure Religious Cults*. Calcutta: Firma KLM, 1976.

Dasgupta, Surendranath. *History of Indian Philosophy*. 5 vols. Delhi: Motilal Barnarsidass, 1975.

Daye, Douglas D. "Major Schools of the Mahāyāna: Mādhyamika." In *Buddhism: A Modern Perspective*. Edited by Charles Prebish. University Park, Pennsylvania, and London: Pennsylvania State University Press, 1975.

Deichgraber, K. "Hymnische Elements in der philosophischen Prose der Vorsokratiker." *Philologus* 88 (1933): 347–442.

DeLacy, Estelle A. "Meaning and Methodology in Hellenistic Philosophy." *Philosophical Review* 47 (1938): 406–409.

DeLacy, Phillip H. "*ou mallon* and the Antecedents of Ancient Skepticism." *Phronēsis* 3 (1958): 59–71.

DeLacy, Phillip H., and Estelle A. DeLacy. *Philodemus: On Methods of Inference*. Philological Monographs 10. Philadelphia: American Philological Association, 1941.

De Nicolas, Antonio T. *Avatara: The Humanization of Philosophy through the Bhagavad Gita*. New York: Nicolas Hay, Ltd., 1976.

——. *Meditations through the Ṛg Veda: Four Dimensional Man*. Boulder, Colorado, and London: Shambhala, 1978.

De Selincourt, Aubrey, translator. *Herodotus: The Histories*. Baltimore, Maryland: Penguin, 1954.

Deussen, Paul. *The Philosophy of the Upaniṣads*. New York: Dover Publications, 1966.

Devanji, P. C. "Naturalism in Greek and Indian Philosophies." *Journal of the Oriental Institute* 4 (1954–1955): 162–175.

DeVogel, Cornelia J. *Philosophia*. Philosophical Texts and Studies 19. Assen: van Gorcum, 1970.

DeWitt, Norman W. *Epicurus and His Philosophy*. Minneapolis: University of Minnesota Press, 1954.

Dhavalikar, M. K. *Indian Protohistory*. New Delhi: Books and Books, 1997.

Diakonoff, M. "Media." *Cambridge History of Iran*. Vol. 2, *The Median and Achaemenian Periods*. Edited by Ilya Gershevitch. Cambridge: Cambridge University Press, 1985, pp. 36–148.

Diels, Hermann, editor. *Poetarum Philosophorum Fragmenta*. In *Poetarum Graecorum Fragmenta*. Edited by U. von Wilamowitz-Moellendorf. Fasc. 3, part 1. Berlin, 1901.

——, editor. *Die Fragmente der Vorsokratiker*. 3 vols. Revised by W. Kranz. Dublin and Zurich: Weidman, 1969.

Dilthey, W. *Gründriss der allgemeinen Geschichte der Philosophie*. Frankfurt: Klostermann, 1949.

Diop, Cheik Anta. *Civilization or Barbarism: An Authentic Anthropology*. Brooklyn, New York: Lawrence Hill Books, 1991.

Di Santillana, Giorgio. *Prologue to Parmenides*. Cincinnati, Ohio: University of Cincinnati, 1964.

——, and Hertha Von Dechend, *Hamlet's Mill*. Boston: David R. Godine, 1977.

Dodds, E. R. *The Greeks and the Irrational*. Berkeley, California, and Los Angeles: University of California Press, 1951.

Dowson, John. *A Classical Dictionary of Hindu Mythology and Religion; Geography, History, and Literature*. 8th edition. London: Routledge and Kegan Paul, 1953.

Drews, Robert. *The Coming of the Greeks: Indo-European Conquests in the Aegean and the Near East*. Princeton, New Jersey: Princeton University Press, 1988.

——. *The End of the Bronze Age: Changes in Warfare and the Catastrophe ca. 1200 B.C.* Princeton, New Jersey: Princeton University Press, 1993.

Duchesme-Guillemin, J. "Persische Weisheit in Griechischen Gewande?" *Harvard Theological Review* 49 (1956).

Dudley, Donald R. *A History of Cynicism*. London: Methuen and Company, 1937.

Dumont, Jean-Paul. *Le scepticisme et le phenomène, essai sur la signification et les origines du pyrrhonisme*. Paris: J. Vrin, 1972.

Dupree, Louis. *Afghanistan*. Karachi: Oxford University Press, 1997.

Dyczkowski, Mark S. G. *The Canon of the Śaivagama and the Kubjika Tantras of the Western Kaula Tradition*. Albany, New York: State University of New York Press, 1988.

Ebert, Theodor. "A Pre-Socratic Philosopher behind the *Phaedrus*: Empedocles." *Revue de philosophie ancienne* 11, no. 2 (1993).

Edgerton, Franklin. *The Beginnings of Indian Philosophy*. Cambridge, Massachusetts: Harvard University Press, 1970.

Eisenberg, Jerome M. "Glyptic Art of the Ancient Near East: 'A Seal upon My Heart,' Part 1." *Minerva, The International Review of Ancient Art and Archeology* (May/June 1988); "Part 2." Ibid. (July/August 1988).

Eliade, Mircea, editor. *Encyclopedia of Religion*. 16 vols. New York: Macmillan, 1987.

——. *Shamanism: Archaic Techniques of Ecstasy*. Bollingen Series 76. Translated by Willard R. Trask. Princeton, New Jersey: Princeton University Press, 1964.

——. *Yoga: Immortality and Freedom*. Bollingen Series 56. Translated by Willard R. Trask. New York: Princeton University Press, 1969.

——. *Zalmoxis: The Vanishing God*. Translated by Willard R. Trask. Chicago: University of Chicago Press, 1972.

Ellis, Alfred. "Rational-Emotive Therapy." In *Current Psychotherapies*. Edited by R. Cosini. 2nd edition. Itasca, Illinois.: F. E. Peacock, 1979.

Empson, William. *Seven Types of Ambiguity*. Baltimore: Penguin, 1962.

Erdosy, George, editor. *The Indo-Aryans of South Asia: Language, Material Culture and Ethnicity*. Indian Philology and South Asian Studies 1. Berlin and New York: Walter deGruyter, 1995.

——. "The Prelude to Urbanization: Ethnicity and the Rise of Late Vedic Chieftans." In *The Archeology of Early Historic South Asia: The Emergence of Cities and States*. Edited by F. R. Allchin. Cambridge: Cambridge University Press, 1995, pp. 75–98.

Erman, Adolf, editor and translator. *The Ancient Egyptians, a Sourcebook of their Writings*. New York: Harper and Row, 1966.

Facheux, R. F. *Une vieille cité indienne près de Pondicherry, Virapatnam*. Pondicherry, 1945.

Faddegon, Barend. *The Vaiśeṣika System Described with the Help of the Oldest Texts*. Nieuwe Reeks, Deel 18, no. 2. Amsterdam: Afdeeling Letterkunde, 1918.

Fagles, Robert, translator. *The Iliad*. Introduction and notes by Bernard Knox. New York: Penguin, 1990.

Fairservis, Walter A. Jr. *The Roots of Ancient India: The Archaeology of Early Indian Civilization*. New York: Macmillan, 1971.

Farmer, Henry G. "The Music of Ancient Egypt." In *New Oxford History of Music*. Vol. 1, *Ancient and Oriental Music*. Edited by Egon Wellesz. London and New York: Oxford University Press, 1969, pp. 255–282.

——. "The Music of Ancient Mesopotamia." In *New Oxford History of Music*. Vol. 1, *Ancient and Oriental Music*. Edited by Egon Wellesz. London and New York: Oxford University Press, 1969, pp. 228–254.

——. *The Faith of Epicurus*. London: Weidenfeld and Nicolson, 1967.

Farrington, Benjamin. *Greek Science: Its Meaning for Us*. Baltimore: Penguin, 1961.

Faulkner, Raymond O., translator. *The Ancient Egyptian Book of the Dead*. Edited by Carol Andrews. New York: Macmillan, 1985.

Festugière, André-Marie J. *Contemplation et vie contemplative selon Platon*. Paris: J. Vrin, 1950.

——. "Platon et l'Orient." *Revue de Philologie* 21 (1947): 5–45.

——. "Trois Rencontres entre la Grèce et l'Inde." *Revue de l'histoire des religions* 125 (1942–1943): 32–57.

Feuerstein, Georg, Subhash Kak, and David Frawley. "A New View of Ancient India." *Yoga Journal* (1992): 64–69, 100–102.

——. *In Search of the Cradle of Civilization: New Light on Ancient India*. Wheaton Illinois, and Madras: Quest Books, 1995.

Filliozat, J. "Graeco-Aramaic Inscription of Aśoka Near Kandahar." *Ep. Ind.* 34 (1961–1962): 1–8.

——. "La doctrine des brahmanes d'après saint Hippolyte." *Revue de l'Histoire des Religions* 130 (1945): 56–91.

——. *Les relations exterieures de l'Inde*, 1. Pondicherry: Institut francais d'indologie, 1956.

Findlay, J. N. *Plato: The Written and Unwritten Doctrines*. London: Routledge and Kegan Paul, 1974.

Fisher, Louis. *Gandhi*. New York: New American Library, 1954.

Fleet, John F. "Śiva as Lakulīṣa." *Journal of the Royal Asiatic Society* (1907): 419–426.

Flintoff, Everard. "Pyrrho and India." *Phronēsis* 25 (1980): 88–108.

Foucher, Alfred C. A. *L'art gréco-bouddhique de Gandhāra, étude sur les origines de l'influence classique dans l'art bouddhique de l'Inde et de l'Extrême-Orient*. Publications de l'École Française d'Extrême-Orient, vols. 5 and 6. Paris: E. Leroux, 1905–1914.

Fränkel, Hermann. "Xenophanes' Empiricism and His Critique of Knowledge (B 34)." In *The Presocratics*. Edited by Alexander P. D. Mourelatos. Garden City, N. Y.: Doubleday, Anchor Books, 1974, pp. 118–131.

Frankfort, Henri. *Cylinder Seals*. London: Gregg Press, 1965.

——. *Kingship and the Gods, a Study of Ancient Near Eastern Religion and the Integration of Society and Nature*. Chicago: University of Chicago Press, 1948.

Fraser, P. M. "The Son of Aristonax at Kandahar." *Afghan Studies* 2 (1979): 9–21.

Frauwallner, Erich. *History of Indian Philosophy*. 2 vols. Translated by V. M. Bedekar. Delhi: Motilal Banarsidass, 1973.

Frazer, J. G. *The Golden Bough: A Study in Magic and Religion*. Abridged edition. New York: Macmillan, 1943.

Frede, Michael. *Essays in Ancient Philosophy*. Minneapolis: University of Minnesota Press, 1987.

——. "The Origins of Traditional Grammar." In Michael Frede, *Essays in Ancient Philosophy*. Minneapolis: University of Minnesota Press, 1987, pp. 338–362.

——. "Principles of Stoic Grammar." In Michael Frede, *Essays in Ancient Philosophy*. Minneapolis: University of Minnesota Press, 1987, pp. 301–337.

Freeman, Kathleen. *Ancilla to the Presocratic Philosophers*. Cambridge, Massachusetts: Harvard University Press, 1970.

Frenkian, A. M. "Sextus Empiricus and Indian Logic." *Philosophical Quarterly* (India) 30, no. 2 (1957): 115–126.

Freud, Sigmund. *Beyond the Pleasure Principle*. Translated by James Strachey. New York and London: W. W. Norton, 1961.

Friedlander, Paul. *Plato*. 3 vols. Bollingen Series 59. Translated by Hans Meyerhoff. New York: Princeton University Press, 1958.

Fritz, Kurt von. "The Philosophical Passage in the Seventh Platonic Letter and the Problem of Plato's 'Esoteric Philosophy.'" In *Essays in Ancient Greek Philosophy*. Edited by John Peter Anton and George L. Kustas. Albany, New York: State University of New York Press, 1972, pp. 408–447.

Frye, Richard N. *The Heritage of Persia*. London: Wiedenfeld and Nicolson, 1962.

Fuller, J. F. C. *The Generalship of Alexander the Great*. Ware, Hartfordshire: Wordsworth Editions, 1998.

Furley, David J. *Two Studies in the Greek Atomists*. Princeton, New Jersey: Princeton University Press, 1967.

Gadd, C. J. "Seals of Ancient Indian Style Found at Ur." *Proceedings of the British Academy* 18 (1932): 191–210.

Gaiser, Konrad. *Platons ungeschreibene Lehre, Studien zur systematischen und geschichtlichen Begrundung der Wissenschaften in der Platonischen Schule*. Stuttgart: E. Klett, 1963.

Gangadean, Ashok Kumar. "Formal Ontology and the Dialectical Transformation of Consciousness." *Philosophy East and West* 29 (1979): 21–48.

Gangopadhyaya, Mrinalkanti. *Indian Atomism, History and Sources.* Atlantic Highlands, New Jersey: Humanities Press, 1980.

Garner, Dick. "Skepticism, Ordinary Language, and Zen Buddhism." *Philosophy East and West* 27 (1977): 165–181.

Gaster, Theodor Herzl. *Thespis: Ritual, Myth and Drama in the Ancient Near East.* New and revised edition. Garden City, New York: Doubleday, 1961.

Gershevitch, Ilya, editor. *The Cambridge History of Iran.* Vol. 2, *The Median and Achaemenian Periods.* Cambridge: Cambridge University Press, 1985.

Gethin, R. M. "The Five *Khandas*: Their Treatment in the *Nikāyas* and Early Abhidhamma." *Journal of Indian Philosophy* 14 (1986): 35–54.

Gimbutas, Maria. "The Beginning of the Bronze Age in Europe and the Indo-Europeans: 3500–2500 B.C." *Journal of Indo-European Studies* 1 (1973): 163–214.

——. "The First Wave of Eurasian Steppe Pastoralists into Copper Age Europe." *Journal of Indo-European Studies* 13 (1985): 185–202.

——. *The Goddesses and Gods of Old Europe, 6500–3500 B.C.: Myths and Cult Images.* New and updated edition. London: Thames and Hudson, 1982.

Gladow, Rupert. *Origin of the Zodiac.* New York: Castle Books, 1968.

Glasenapp, Helmuth von. "Indian and Western Metaphysics." *Philosophy East and West* 3 (1953): 223–231.

Gleason, H. A. Jr. *An Introduction to Descriptive Linguistics.* Revised edition. New York: Holt, Rinehart and Winston, 1961.

Godolphin, Francis R. B., editor. *The Greek Historians.* New York: Random House, 1942.

Godwin, Jocelyn. *Mystery Religions in the Ancient World.* San Francisco: Harper and Row, 1981.

Goetze, A. "Persische Weisheit in griechischen Gewande." *Zeitschrift für Indologie und Iranistik* 2 (1923): 60–98, 167–177.

Goff, Beatrice M. *The Symbols of Prehistoric Mesopotamia.* New Haven, Connecticut: Yale University Press, 1963.

Gold, Jeffrey. "Plato in the Light of Yoga." *Philosophy East and West* 46 (1996): 17–32.

Goleman, Daniel. *Emotional Intelligence.* New York: Bantam, 1995.

Gomez, Luis O. "Proto-Mādhyamika in the Pali Canon." *Philosophy East and West* 26 (1976): 137–166.

Gomperz, Theodor. *The Greek Thinkers: A History of Ancient Philosophy*, 4 vols. London: John Murray, 1920.

Gonda, J. "Zur Frage nach dem Ursprung und Wesen des indischen Dramas." *Acta Orientalia, Ediderunt Societates Orientales Batava Danica Norvegica* 19 (1943): 329–453.

Gonzalez, Francisco. *The Third Way: New Directions in Platonic Studies.* Lanham, Maryland: Rowman and Littlefield, 1995.

Gordon, D. H. *The Prehistoric Background of Indian Culture.* Bombay: Bulabhai Memorial Institute, 1960.

Gospel of Sri Ramakrishna. Abridged edition. New York: Ramakrishna-Vivekananda Center, 1970.

Green, Peter. *Alexander of Macedon, 356–323 B.C., A Historical Biography.* Berkeley, California; Los Angeles; London: University of California Press, 1991.

Greenlees, Duncan. *The Gospel of Zarathustra.* Adyar, Madras: Theosophical Publishing House, 1951.

Grene, David, and Richmond Lattimore, editors. *Euripides II.* In *The Complete Greek Tragedies*, vol. 6. New York: Random House, 1956.

Grenfell, B. P., A. S. Hunt, et al., editors. *The Oxyrhynchus Papyri I ff.* London: Egypt Exploration Society, 1898–1998.

Griffith, Ralph T. H. *The Hymns of the Ṛg Veda.* Benares: E. J. Lazarus and Co., 1896.

Grousset, René. *The Empire of the Steppes: A History of Central Asia.* Translated by Naomi Walford. New Brunswick, New Jersey: Rutgers University Press, 1970.

Grube, George M. A., editor and translator. *A Greek Critic: Demetrius on Style*, by Demetrius of Phaleron. *The Phoenix, Journal of the Classical Association of Canada*, supplementary vol. 4. Toronto: University of Toronto Press, 1961.

——. *Plato's Thought.* Boston: Beacon Press, 1968.

Guenther, Herbert V. *Buddhist Philosophy in Theory and Practice*. Baltimore: Penguin, 1972.

——, translator. "Long-chen-pa, 'The Natural Freedom of Mind.'" *Crystal Mirror, Journal of the Nyngma Meditation Center* 4 (1974): 113–146.

Gulley, Norman. *The Philosophy of Socrates*. London: Macmillan, and New York: St. Martin's Press, 1968.

Gupta, S. N. "The Nature of Inference in Indian Logic." *Mind* 6 (1895): 159–174.

Gupta, S. P. *The Indus-Saraswati Civilization: Origins, Problems, and Issues*. Delhi: Pratibha Prakashan, 1996.

Guruge, Ananda W. P. "Buddhist Tradition and Aśokan Inscriptions." In *King Aśoka and Buddhism: Historical and Literary Studies*. Edited by Anuradha Seneviratna. Kandy, Sri Lanka: Buddhist Publication Society, 1994, pp. 27–66.

Guthrie, William K. C. *A History of Greek Philosophy*. 6 vols. Cambridge: Cambridge University Press, 1965–1981. Vol. 1, *The Earlier Presocratics and the Pythagoreans*, 1971. Vol. 2, *The Presocratic Tradition from Parmenides to Democritus*, 1965. Vol. 3, *The Fifth-Century Enlightenment*, 1969. Vol. 4, *Plato, The Man and His Dialogues: Earlier Period*, 1975. Vol. 5, *The Later Plato and the Academy*, *1978*. Vol. 6, *Aristotle, An Encounter, 1981*.

——. *Orpheus and Greek Religion, a Study of the Orphic Movement*. New York: Norton, 1966.

——. *Socrates*. Cambridge: Cambridge University Press, 1971.

Hackforth, R. *Plato's Phaedrus Translated with an Introduction and Commentary*. Cambridge: Cambridge University Press, 1952.

Hadas, Moses. *Hellenistic Culture: Fusion and Diffusion*. New York: W. W. Norton, 1972.

Hadot, P. "Fragments d'un commentaire de Porphyre sur le Parmenide." *Revue des Études Grècques* 74 (1961): 410–438.

Hakeda, Y. S. *The Awakening of Faith*. New York: Columbia University Press, 1967.

Halbfass, Wilhelm. *India and Europe: An Essay in Understanding*. Albany, New York: State University of New York Press, 1988.

Hall, T. C. "Asceticism, Introduction." *Encyclopaedia of Religion and Ethics*, vol. 2. Edited by James Hastings. Edinburgh: T. and T. Clark; New York: C Scribner's Sons, 1908–1927, pp. 63–69.

Hallade, M. *Gandhāran Art of North India*. New York: Abrams, 1968.

Hallissey, Charles. "Roads Taken and Not Taken in the Study of Theravāda Buddhism." In *Curators of the Buddha: The Study of Buddhism under Colonialism*. Edited by Donald S. Lopez Jr. Chicago and London: University of Chicago Press, 1995, pp. 31–62.

Hamilton, Edith, and Huntington Cairns, editors. *The Collected Dialogues of Plato*. Bollingen series 71. New York: Pantheon Books, 1963.

——. *Alexander the Great: King, Commander and Statesman*. London: Duckworth, Bristol Classical Press, 1980.

Hammond, N. G. L. *A History of Greece to 322 B.C.* Oxford: Oxford University Press, 1959.

——. *The Genius of Alexander the Great*. London: Duckworth, 1997.

Hankinson, R. J. *The Skeptics*. London and New York: Routledge, 1995.

Hardy, Robert S. *Eastern Monachism*. London: Partridge and Oakey, 1850.

Harrington, S. P. M. "Early Indus Script." *Archeology* (1999).

Harris, R. Baine, editor. *Neoplatonism and Indian Thought*. Norfolk, Virginia: International Center for Neoplatonic Studies, 1982.

Harris, Marvin. *Our Kind: Who We Are, Where We Came From, Where We Are Going*. New York: Harper and Row, 1989.

Harrison, Jane Ellen. *Prolegomena to the Study of Greek Religion*. 3rd edition. New York: Meridian Books, 1966.

Hastings James, editor. *Encyclopaedia of Religion and Ethics*. Edinburgh: T. and T. Clark; New York: C. Scribner's Sons, 1908–1927.

Hauer, Jakob W. *Der Yoga, ein indischer Weg zum Selbst: kritisch-positive Dastellung nach den indischen Quellen, mit einer Ubersetzung der massgeblichen Texte*. Stuttgart: W. Kohlhammer, 1958.

Hawley, D. S. "L'Inde de Voltaire." In *Studies on Voltaire and the Eighteenth Century*, vol. 120. Banbury: Voltaire Foundation, 1974, pp. 139–178.

Head, Joseph, and S. L. Cranston. *Reincarnation in World Thought*. New York: Julian Press, 1977.

Heath, Thomas L. *A Manual of Greek Mathematics*. New York: Dover, 1963.

Hermanns, Matthias. *Schamanen-Pseudoschamanen, Erlöser und Heilbringer: Einer vergleichende Studie religiöser Urphänomene*. 3 vols. Wiesbaden: Franz Steiner Verlag, 1970.

Herodotus. *The Histories*. Translated with introduction by Aubrey de Selincourt. Baltimore, Maryland: Penguin, 1954.

Hicks, Harry H., and Robert N. Anderson. "Analysis of an Indo-European Vedic Aryan Head—4th Millennium B.C." *Journal of Indo-European Studies* 18 (1990): 435–446.

Hilprecht, H. V. *The Babylonian Expedition of the University of Pennsylvania, Series A, Cuneiform Texts*, vol. 20, part 1. Philadelphia: University of Pennsylvania, University Museum, 1906.

Hinnels, John R. *Persian Mythology*. London: Hamlyn, 1973.

Hiriyana, M. *Outlines of Indian Philosophy*. New York: Macmillan, 1932.

Hooke, Sidney H. *Babylonian and Assyrian Religion*. Norman, Oklahoma: University of Oklahoma Press, 1963.

Hopkins, Jeffrey. *Meditation on Emptiness*. Boston: Wisdom Publications, 1996.

Hopkirk, Kathleen. *A Traveller's Companion to Central Asia*. London: John Murray, 1993.

Hopkirk, Peter. *Foreign Devils on the Silk Road: The Search for the Lost Cities and Treasures of Chinese Central Asia*. Oxford: Oxford University Press, 1980.

Hopper, Vincent. *Medieval Number Symbolism*. New York: Columbia University Press, 1938.

Hourani, George F. *Arab Seafaring in the Indian Ocean in Ancient and Early Medieval Times*. Revised and expanded by John Carswell. Princeton, New Jersey: Princeton University Press, 1995.

Hubbard, Jamie, and Paul L. Swanson, editors. *Pruning the Bodhi Tree: The Storm Over Critical Buddhism*. Nanzan Library of Asian Religion and Culture. Honolulu: University of Hawaii Press, 1997.

Humbach, H. "The Aramaic Aśoka Inscription from Taxila." *Journal of Central Asia* 1, no. 2 (1978): 87–98.

Hume, David. *Essays and Treatises on Several Subjects*. Edinburgh: Bill and Bradfute, 1817.

Hume, Robert E., translator. *The Thirteen Principal Upaniṣads*. 2nd edition, revised. Madras: Oxford University Press, 1949.

Huntington, C. W. Jr. *The Emptiness of Emptiness: An Introduction to Early Indian Mādhyamika*. Honolulu: University of Hawaii Press, 1989.

Huxley, Aldous. *The Perennial Philosophy*. New York: Harper and Row, 1970.

Huxley, George. *The Interaction of Greek and Babylonian Astronomy*. Belfast: Queen's University, 1964.

Inada, Kenneth K. *Nāgārjuna: A Translation of His Mūlamadhyamikakārikā with an Introductory Essay*. Tokyo: Hokuseido Press, 1970.

Ingalls, Daniel H. "Cynics and Pāśupatas: The Seeking of Dishonor." *Harvard Theological Review* 55 (1962): 281–298.

Inge, William R. *Christian Mysticism; Considered in Eight Lectures Delivered before the University of Oxford*. 6th edition. London: Methuen, 1925.

———. *The Philosophy of Plotinus*. 2 vols. Gifford Lectures 1917-1918. 3rd edition. New York: Greenwood Press, 1968.

Ions, Veronica. *Indian Mythology*. London: Paul Hamlyn, 1967.

Irwin, Terence. *Plato's Ethics*. New York and Oxford: Oxford University Press, 1995.

Jackson, Abraham V. W. *Zoroastrian Studies, the Iranian Religion and Various Monographs*. New York: AMS Press, 1965.

———. "Indian Atomism." In *Studies in the History of Indian Philosophy*. 3 vols. Edited by Debiprasad Chattopadhyaya. Calcutta: K. P. Bagchi and Company, 1978, pp. 132–145.

Jacobi, Hermann. *Jaina Sūtras*. Sacred Books of the East 22. Oxford: Clarendon, 1884.

Jacobson, Jerome, editor. *Studies in the Archeology of India and Pakistan*. New Delhi: Oxford and IBH Publishing Co, and American Institute of Indian Studies, 1986.

Jacobsen, Thorkild. *Treasures of Darkness*. New Haven: Yale University Press, 1975.

Jacoby, F., editor, *Die Fragmente der Griechischen Historiker*. Berlin: Weidmann, 1923–58.

Jaeger, Werner W. *Aristoteles, Grundlegung einer Geschichte seiner Entwicklung*. Berlin: Weidman, 1923.

——. *Paideia: The Ideals of Greek Culture*. 2 vols. Translated by Gilbert Highet. New York: Oxford University Press, 1965.

——. *The Theology of the Early Greek Philosophers*. Translated by Edward S. Robinson. Gifford Lectures 1936. Oxford: Clarendon Press, 1947.

Jain, Amar Sing. "Path of Mokṣa According to Kundakunda." *Jinamañjari: International Journal of Contemporary Jaina Reflections* 18, no. 2 (1998): 21–24.

Jaini, Padmanabh S. "On the *Sarvajñātva* of Mahāvīra and the Buddha." In *Buddhist Studies in Honour of I. B. Horner*. Edited by L. Cousins, A. Kunst, and K. R. Norman. Dordrecht: D. Reel, 1974.

——. *The Jaina Path of Purification*. Delhi: Motilal Banarsidass, 1998.

James, George G. M. *Stolen Legacy: Greek Philosophy Is Stolen Egyptian Philosophy*. Newport News, Virginia: United Brothers Communications Systems, 1954.

Jarrige, Jean-Francois. "Excavations at Mehrgarh: Their Significance for Understanding the Background of the Harappan Civilization." In *Harappan Civilization*. Edited by Gregory Possehl. New Delhi: Oxford and IBH Publishing Co., 1982.

——, and Richard H. Meadow. "The Antecedents of Civilization in the Indus Valley." *Scientific American* 243 (1980): 122–133

Jash, Pranabananda. *History of Śaivism*. Calcutta: Roy and Chaudhury, 1974.

Jaspers, Karl. *Die Grössen Philosophen*. Munich: R. Piper, 1957.

——. *The Message of the Buddha*. New York: Macmillan, 1974.

Jayatilleke, K. N. *Early Buddhist Theory of Knowledge*. London: George Allen and Unwin, 1963.

Joël, Carl. *Der Echte und der Xenophontische Sokrates*. 2 vols. Berlin, 1893–1901.

Johnston, E. H. "Two Notes on Ptolemy's Geography of India." *Journal of the Royal Asiatic Society* (1941): 208–222.

Jones, Horace L., translator. *The Geography of Strabo*. 8 vols. Based in part upon the unfinished version of John Robert Sitlington Sterrett. Loeb Classical Library. Cambridge, Massachusetts: Harvard University Press, 1917–1933.

Jones, Richard H. "The Nature and Function of Nāgārjuna's Arguments." *Philosophy East and West* 28 (1978): 485–502.

Jones, Rufus M. "Liberalism in the Mystical Tradition." In *Liberal Theology, an Appraisal: Essays in Honor of Eugene William Lyman*. Edited by David E. Roberts and Henry P. van Dusen. New York: C. Scribner's Sons, 1942, pp. 121–136.

Jones, Sir William. *Works*. London: J. Hatchard, 1807.

——, translator. *The Dialogues of Plato*. New York: Random House, 1920.

Jowett, Benjamin, translator. *Plato's Republic*. New York: Random House, n.d.

——, translator. *Protagoras*, by Plato. Edited by Gregory Vlastos. Library of Liberal Arts 59. New York: Liberal Arts Press, 1956.

Jung, Carl G. *Symbols of Transformation*. Bollingen Series 20. Princeton, New Jesey: Princeton University Press, 1956.

Kahn, Charles H. *Anaximander and the Origins of Greek Cosmology*. New York: Columbia University Press, 1960.

——. *The Art and Thought of Heraclitus*. Cambridge: Cambridge University Press, 1979.

——. *The Astronomical Code of the Ṛg Veda*. New Delhi: Aditya Prakashan, 1994.

Kak, Subhash. "A Frequency Analysis of the Indus Script." *Cryptologia* 12, no. 3 (1988): 129–143.

——. "The Indus Maṇḍala and the Indo-Aryans." In *Dr. S. R. Rao's 70th Birthday Felicitation Volume*, 1992, pp. 1–19.

Kalupahana, David J. "A Buddhist Tract on Empiricism." *Philosophy East and West* 19 (1969): 65–67.

——. *Buddhist Philosophy, A Historical Analysis*. Honolulu: University of Hawaii Press, 1976.

——. *Causality: The Central Philosophy of Buddhism*. Honolulu: University of Hawaii Press, 1975.

——. *A History of Buddhist Philosophy: Continuities and Discontinuities*. Honolulu: University of Hawaii Press, 1992.

——. *Nāgārjuna: The Philosophy of the Middle Way*. Albany: State University of New York Press, 1986.

Kalyanaramn, A. *Aryatarangini: The Saga of the Indo-Aryans*. 2 vols. Bombay: Asia Publishing House, 1969.

Kato, Bruno, et al., translators. *The Threefold Lotus Sūtra*. Tokyo: Kosei Publishing Co., 1975.

Keith, Arthur B. *Buddhist Philosophy*. Oxford: Clarendon, 1923.

——. *Indian Logic and Atomism*. Oxford: Clarendon, 1921.

——. *The Religion and Philosophy of the Veda and Upaniṣads*. Cambridge, Massachusetts: Harvard University Press, 1925.

——. *The Sanskrit Drama, Its Origin, Development, Theory, and Practice*. Oxford: Oxford University Press, 1924.

Kern, H. *Saddharma-puṇḍarīka or the Lotus of the True Law*. Sacred Books of the East 21. New York: Dover, 1963.

Khamit-Kush, Indus. *What They Never Told You In History Class*. New York: Luxxor Publications, 1983.

Kirk, Geoffrey S., editor. *Heraclitus: The Cosmic Fragments*. Cambridge: Cambridge University Press, 1954.

——, and J. E. Raven. *The Presocratic Philosophers: A Critical History with a Selection of Texts*. Cambridge: Cambridge University Press, 1973.

——, J. E. Raven, and M. Schofield. *The Presocratic Philosophers: A Critical History with a Selection of Texts*. 2nd edition. Cambridge: Cambridge University Press, 1983.

Kneale, W., and M. Kneale. *The Development of Logic*. Oxford: Oxford University Press, 1962.

Kornfield, Jack. *Living Buddhist Masters*. Santa Cruz, California: Unity Press, 1977.

Kosambi, Damodar Dharmanand. *Ancient India: A History of Its Culture and Civilization*. New York: Random House, Pantheon Books, 1965.

——. *An Introduction to the Study of Indian History*. Bombay: Popular Prakash, 1975.

Krämer, Hans J. *Arete bei Platon und Aristoteles: Zum Wesen und zur Geschichte der platonischen Ontologie*. Heidelberg: C. Winter, 1959.

Kramer, Samuel Noah. *Enmerkar and the Lord of Aratta*. University Park, Pennsylvania: University of Pennsylvania Museum Monographs, 1952.

——. "The Indus Civilization and Dilmun: the Sumerian Paradise Land." In *Ancient Cities of the Indus*. Edited by Gregory Possehl. New Delhi: Vikas Publishing House, 1979, pp. 168–173.

Kramrisch, Stella. *The Presence of Śiva*. Princeton, New Jersey: Princeton University Press, 1981.

Krishna, Daya. *Indian Philosophy: A Counter Perspective*. Delhi: Oxford University Press, 1991.

Kulke, Hermann, and Dietmar Rothermund. *A History of India*. 3rd edition. London and New York: Routledge, 1998.

Kuhrt, Amelie, and Susan Sherwin-White, editors. *Hellenism in the East: The Interaction of Greek and Non-Greek Civilizations from Syria to Central Asia after Alexander*. London: Duckworth, 1987.

Lacombe, Olivier. "Note sur Plotin et la pensée indienne." *Annuaire de l'École Pratique des Hautes Études, Section des Sciences Religieuses* (1950–1951).

Lal, B. B., and S. P. Gupta, editors. *Frontiers of the Indus Civilization*. Delhi: Books and Books, 1984.

Lamberg-Karlovsky, C. C. "Sumer, Elam and the Indus: Three Urban Processes Equal One Structure." In *Harappan Civilization: A Contemporary Perspective*. Edited by Gregory Possehl. New Delhi: Oxford and IBH Publishing Co. in collaboration with American Institute of Indian Studies, 1992, pp. 61–67.

Lamberg, Erich, editor. *Porphyrii Sententiae ad Intelligibilia Ducentes*. Leipzig: Teubner, 1975.

Lamotte, Etienne. "Early Relations between India and the West, Part 1." *Buddhist Studies Review* 5, no. 2 (1988).

——. "Early Relations between India and the West, Conclusion." *Buddhist Studies Review* 6, no. 1. (1989).

——. *Histoire du Boudhisme Indien*. Louvain: Université Catholique de Louvain, 1958.

——. "Sur la formation du Mahāyāna." *Asiatica* (1954).

Latham, R. E. *Lucretius: The Nature of the Universe*. Baltimore, Maryland: Penguin, 1951.

Lattimore, Richmond, translator. *Hecuba*. In *The Complete Greek Tragedies: Euripedes II*. Edited by David Grene and Richmond Lattimore. Chicago: University of Chicago Press, 1958.

Lawson, Gerald J. *Classical Sāṅkhya*. Delhi: Motilal Banarsidass, 1979.

Lee, H. D. P. *Zeno of Elea*. Cambridge Classical Studies 1. Cambridge: Cambridge University Press, 1936.

Levi, Sylvain. "Alexander and Alexandria in Indian Literature." *Indian Historical Quarterly* 12 (1936): 121–133.

——. *La Doctrine du Sacrifice dans les Brāhmaṇas*. 2nd edition. Bibliotheque de l'École des Hautes Études, Section des Sciences Religieuses 73. Paris: Presses Universitaires de France, 1966.

Levy, G. Rachel. "The Oriental Origin of Herakles." *Journal of Hellenic Studies* 54 (1934): 40–53.

Liddell, Henry G., Robert Scott, and Henry Stuart Jones, editors. *Greek-English Lexicon*. Oxford: Clarendon, 1966.

Linforth, Ivan M. *The Arts of Orpheus*. Berkeley, California, and Los Angeles: University of California Press, 1941.

Littleton, C. S. *The New Comparative Mythology*. Berkeley, California, and Los Angeles: University of California Press, 1982.

Lloyd, A. C. "Emotion and Decision in Stoic Psychology." In *The Stoics*. Edited by John M. Rist. Berkeley and Los Angeles: University of California Press, 1978, pp. 233–247.

——. "The Later Neoplatonists." In *The Cambridge History of Later Greek and Early Medieval Philosophy*. Edited by Arthur H. Armstrong. Cambridge: Cambridge University Press, 1967, pp. 272–330.

Lloyd, Alan B. *Herodotus Book II-Commentary*. 3 vols. Leiden: Brill, 1988.

Lobel, Edgar, and Denys Page, editors. *Poetarum Lesbiorum Fragmenta*. N.p., n.d.

Long, A. A. "Empedocles' Cosmic Cycle in the 'Sixties.'" In *The Presocratics: A Collection of Critical Essays*. Edited by Alexander P. D. Mourelatos. Garden City, New York: Doubleday, Anchor Books, 1974, pp. 397–425.

——. *Hellenistic Philosophy: Stoics, Epicureans, Skeptics*, 2nd edition. London: Duckworth, 1974. Berkeley, California: University of California Press, 1986.

——, and D. N. Sedley, editors. *The Hellenistic Philosophers*. Vol. 1, *Translations of the Principal Sources with Philosophical Commentary*. Cambridge: Cambridge University Press, 1987.

Long, Herbert Strainge. "A Study of the Doctrine of Metempsychōsis in Greece from Pythagoras to Plato." Unpublished Ph. D. dissertation, Princeton University, 1943.

Long-Chen-Pa. "Sems-nyid rang-grol (The Natural Freedom of Mind)." Translated and commented on by Herbert V. Guenther. *Crystal Mirror: Journal of the Tibetan Nyingma Meditation Center* 4 (1975): 113–146.

Longrigg, James. *Greek Medicine from the Heroic to the Hellenistic Age: A Source Book*. London: Duckworth, 1998.

Lopez, Donald S. Jr., editor. *Curators of the Buddha: The Study of Buddhism Under Colonialism*. Chicago and London: University of Chicago Press, 1995.

Lorenzen, David N. *The Kāpālikas and Kālamukhas: Two Lost Śaivite Sects*. New Delhi: Thomson Press (India), 1972.

Luk, Charles [Lu K'uan-yü], translator and editor. *Ch'an and Zen Teaching. First Series*. Berkeley, California: Shambala, 1970.

——, translator. *The Surangama Sūtra*. London: Rider and Co., 1973.

Lukacs, John R., editor. *The People of South Asia*. New York: Plenum, 1984.

Lusthaus, Dan. "Critical Buddhism and Returning to the Sources." In *Pruning the Bodhi Tree: The Storm Over Critical Buddhism*. Edited by Jamie Hubbard and Paul L. Swanson. Nanzan Library of Asian Religion and Culture. Honolulu: University of Hawaii Press, 1997, pp. 30–55.

MacDermot, Violet. *The Cult of the Seer in the Ancient Middle East*. London: Wellcome Institute of the History of Medicine, 1971.

MacDonald, George. "The Hellenic Kingdoms of Syria, Bactria and Parthia." *The Cambridge History of India*. Vol. 1, *Ancient India*. Edited by E. J. Rapson. Cambridge: Cambridge University Press, 1922, pp. 427–466.

MacKay, Ernest J. H. *Further Excavations at Mohenjo Daro, Carried Out by the Government of India between 1927 and 1931*. 2 vols. New Delhi: Indological Book Corporation, 1938.

——. *The Indus Civilization*. London: Luzac, 1913.

MacKenna, Stephen, translator. *The Enneads*, by Plotinus. 2nd edition. Revised by B. S. Page. New York: Pantheon Books, 1957.

McClain, Ernest G. *The Myth of Invariance: The Origins of the Gods, Mathematics and Music from the Ṛg Veda to Plato*. New York: Nicolas Hays, 1976.

McCrindle, John W. *Ancient India as Described in Classical Literature*. Westminster: Archibald Constable, 1901.

——. *The Commerce and Navigation of the Erythraean Sea and Ancient India as Described by Ktesias the Knidian*. Amsterdam: Philosophical Press, 1973.

McDermott, James P. "Karma and Rebirth in Early Buddhism." In *Karma and Rebirth in Classical Indian Traditions*. Edited by Wendy Doniger O'Flaherty. Berkeley, California: University of California Press, 1980, pp. 165–197.

McEvilley, Thomas . "Approaches to the Question of the Antiquity of Jainism." *Jinamañjari: International Journal of Contemporary Jaina Reflections*. Brahmi Society Publications 13, no. 1 (1996): 6–21.

——. "An Archeology of Yoga." *Res: Anthropology and Aesthetics* 1 (1981): 44–77.

——. "The Common Air: Contemporary Art in India." *Artforum* (Summer 1986): 106–115.

——. "Early Greek Philosophy and Mādhyamika," *Philosophy East and West* 31 (1981): 141–164.

——. *Fusion: West African Artists at the Venice Biennale*. New York: Museum for African Art, and Munich: Prestel, 1993.

——. "Here Comes Everybody." In *From Beyond the Pale: Art and Artists at the Edge of Consensus*. Dublin: Irish Museum of Modern Art, 1994.

——. "Penelope's Night Work: Negative Thinking in Greek Philosophy." *Krisis* 2 (1984): 41–58.

——. "Plotinus and Vijñānavāda Buddhism," *Philosophy East and West* 30 (1980): 181–193.

——. "Pyrrhonism and Mādhyamika," *Philosophy East and West* 32 (1982): 3–35.

——. "Sappho, Fragment 2." *Phoenix* 26 (1972): 323–333.

——. "The Spinal Serpent," *Res: Anthropology and Aesthetics* 24 (Autumn, 1993).

McKeon, Richard, editor. *The Basic Works of Aristotle*. New York: Random House, 1941.

Madhavananda, Swami, translator. *Vairāgya Śataka*, by Bhartrihari. Calcutta: Advaita Aśrama, 1971.

Maharshi, Ramana. *The Spiritual Teachings of Ramana Maharshi*. Berkeley, California: Shambhala Publications, 1972.

Mahoney, William K. *The Artful Universe: An Introduction to the Vedic Religious Imagination*. Albany, New York: State University of New York Press, 1998.

Majumdar, Ramesh Chandra, editor. *The History and Culture of the Indian People*. Vol. 1, *The Vedic Age*. London: George Allen and Unwin, 1951. Vol. 2, *The Age of Imperial Unity*. London: George Allen and Unwin, 1953.

——. "India and the Western World." *Age of Imperial Unity*. Edited by R. C. Majumdar, pp. 611–633.

Malherbe, A. J., editor. *The Cynic Epistles: A Study Edition*. Missoula, Montana: Scholars Press, 1977.

Mallory, J. P. *In Search of the Indo-Europeans: Language, Archeology and Myth*. London: Thames and Hudson, 1989.

Manu. *The Laws of Manu*. Translated by Georg Bühler with extracts from seven commentaries. Sacred Books of the East 25. New York: Dover, 1969.

Marcovich, M. Review of West, *Early Greek Philosophy and the Orient*. *Gnomon* 47, no. 4 (1975): 324–325.

Marlow, A. N. "Hinduism and Buddhism in Greek Philosophy." *Philosophy East and West* 4 (1954): 3–38.

Marshack, Alexander. *Roots of Civilization*. London: Weidenfeld and Nicolson, 1972.

——. *The Buddhist Art of Gandhāra*. Cambridge: Cambridge University Press, 1960.

Marshall, Sir John H. *Mohenjo-Daro and the Indus Civilization*. 3 vols. London: A. Probsthain, 1931.

Marshall, Lorna. "!Kung Bushmen Religious Beliefs." *Africa* 32 (1962): 221–252.

Mates, Benson. *Stoic Logic*. Publications in Philosophy. Berkeley, California: University of California, 1953.

Matics, Marion L. *Entering the Path of Enlightenment*. New York: Macmillan, 1970.

Maziarz, Edward A., and Thomas Greenwood. *Greek Mathematical Philosophy*. New York: Frederick Ungar Publishing Co., 1968.

Meiggs, R., and D. M. Lewis. *A Selection of Greek Historical Inscriptions*. Oxford: Clarendon Press, 1969.

Mehta, M. L. *Outline of Jaina Philosophy*. Bangalore: Jain Mission Society, 1954.

Mehta, Rohit. *The Call of the Upaniṣads* Delhi: Motilal Banarsidass, 1996.

Mercer, Samuel A. B. *The Tell El-Amarna Tablets*. Toronto: Macmillan Co. of Canada, 1939.

Merlan, Philip. *Studies in Epicurus and Aristotle*. Wiesbaden: Otto Harrassowitz, 1960.

Mellaart, James. *Earliest Civilizations of the Near East*. New York: McGraw-Hill, 1978.

Meuli, Karl. "Scythica." *Hermes* 70 (1935): 121–176.

Michalowski, Kazimierz. *Great Sculptures of Ancient Egypt*. New York: William Morrow, 1978.

Min, U Kya. *Buddhist Abhidhamma*. Union City, California: Heian International, 1987.

Mishra, Umisha. *Conception of Matter According to Nyāya-Vaiśeṣika*. Allahabad: M. N. Pendeyattre Allahabad Press, 1936.

Mitchell, Larkin. "Earliest Egyptian Glyphs." *Archeology* (1999): 28–29.

Mitchell, Stephen, editor. *Dropping Ashes on the Buddha: The Teaching of Zen Master Seung Sahn*. New York: Grove Press, 1976.

Mitra, Kalipada. "Magic and Miracle in Jaina Literature." *Indian Historical Quarterly* 15 (1939).

Miura, Isshy, and Ruth F. Sasaki. *The Zen Koan*. New York: Harcourt, Brace and Co., 1965.

Mookerji, R. "Candragupta and the Maurya Empire." *The Age of Imperial Unity*. Edited by R. C. Majumdar, pp. 54–70.

Moron, Eleanor. *Angkor Wat: Meaning Through Measurement*. Ann Arbor, 1974. Facsimile.

Mourelatos, Alexander P. D., editor. *The Presocratics: A Collection of Critical Essays*. Garden City, New York: Doubleday, Anchor Books, 1974.

Müller, Friedrich Max. *Chips from a German Workshop*. London: Longmans, Green and Co., 1867.

——. *The Six Systems of Indian Philosophy*. London: Longmans, Green and Co., 1919.

Murray, Margaret. *The Splendour that Was Egypt*. New York: Philosophical Library, 1949.

Murti, T. R. V. *The Central Philosophy of Buddhism*. London: George Allen and Unwin, 1974.

Naess, Arne. *Scepticism*. Oslo: Universitetsforlaget, 1968.

Nakamura, Hajime. *A History of Early Vedānta Philosophy*. Delhi: Motilal Banarsidass, 1989.

——. *Indian Buddhism: A Survey with Bibliographical Notes*. Delhi: Motilal Banarsidass, 1996.

Nanamoli, Bhikku, translator. *Visuddhi Magga* (*The Path of Purification*). Kandy, Sri Lanka: Buddhist Publication Society, n.d.

Nanananda, Bhikku. *Concept and Reality in Early Buddhist Thought*. Kandy, Sri Lanka: Buddhist Publication Society, 1971.

——. *The Indo-Greeks*. Oxford: Clarendon, 1957.

Narain, A. K., editor. *Studies in History of Buddhism*. Delhi: B. R. Publishing Co., 1980.

Nath, Pran. "The Script on the Indus Valley Seals." *Indian Historical Quarterly* 7, supplement, pp. 1–52.

Nauck, A., editor. *Tragicorum Graecorum Fragmenta*. Leipzig: Teubner, 1889.

Needham, Joseph, et al. *Science and Civilization in China*. 6 vols. Cambridge: Cambridge University Press, 1954–1988.

Neugebauer, Otto. *The Exact Sciences in Antiquity*. Providence, Rhode Island: Brown University Press, 1957.

Nicolas, Antonio T. de. *Avatara: The Humanization of Philosophy through the Bhagavad Gita*. New York: Nicolas Hay, Ltd., 1976.

——. *Meditations through the Ṛg Veda: Four Dimensional Man*. Boulder, Colorado, and London: Shambhala, 1978.

Nikhilananda, Swami, translator. *The Gospel of Sri Ramakrishna*. Abridged edition. New York: Ramakrishna-Vivekananda Center, 1970.

Nilsson, Martin P. *A History of Greek Religion*. New York: W. W. Norton, 1964.

——. *The Minoan-Mycenaean Religion and Its Survival in Greek Religion*. Lund: C. W. K. Gleerup, 1927.

Nissen, Hans J. *The Early History of the Ancient Near East 9000-2000 B.C.* Translated by Elizabeth Lutzeier, with Kenneth J. Northcott. Chicago: University of Chicago Press, 1988.

Norman, K. R. "Notes on the Greek Version of Aśoka's Twelfth and Thirteenth Rock Edicts." *Journal of the Royal Asiatic Society*, Part 2 (1972): 111–118.

Nussbaum, Martha. *Therapy of Desire: Theory and Practice in Hellenistic Ethics*. Princeton, New Jersey: Princeton University Press, 1994.

Nustamandy, Chaibi. "The Impact of Hellenised Bactria on Gandhāran Art." in *Gandhāran Art in Context*. Edited by Raymond Allchin et al. New Delhi: Regency, 1977, pp. 17–27.

Nyberg, Harri. "The Problem of the Aryans and Soma: The Botanical Evidence." In *Indo-Aryans of Ancient South Asia: Language, Material Culture, and Ethnicity*. Edited by George Erdosy. Berlin and New York: Walter de Gruyter, 1995, pp. 382–406.

Obeyesekera, Gananath. "The Rebirth Eschatology and Its Transformations: A Contribution to the Sociology of Early Buddhism." In *Karma and Rebirth in Classical Indian Traditions*. Edited by Wendy Doniger O'Flaherty. Berkeley, California: University of California Press, 1980, pp. 137–164.

O'Brien, Elmer, translator. *The Essential Plotinus*. New York: New American Library, Mentor Books, 1964.

O'Brien, John Maxwell. *Alexander the Great: The Invisible Enemy*. London and New York: Routledge, 1992.

O'Flaherty, Wendy Doniger editor. *Karma and Rebirth in Classical Indian Traditions*. Berkeley, California: University of California Press, 1980.

Oldenberg, Hermann. *The Religion of the Veda*. Translated by Shridar B. Shrotri. Delhi: Motilal Banarsidass, 1988.

Olmstead, A. T. *History of the Persian Empire*. Chicago: University of Chicago Press, 1948.

O'Meara, John J. "Indian Wisdom and Porphyry's Search for a Universal Way." In *Neoplatonism and Indian Thought*. Edited by R. Baine Harris. Norfolk, Virginia: International Center for Neoplatonic Studies, 1982, pp. 5–25.

Onians, Richard B. *The Origins of European Thought about the Body, the Mind, the Soul, the World, Time, and Fate*. Cambridge: Cambridge University Press, 1989.

Oppenheim, Leo A. "Analysis of an Assyrian Ritual (KAR 139)." *History of Religions* 5 (1965–1966): 250–265.

——. "The Seafaring Merchants of Ur." In *Ancient Cities of the Indus*. Edited by Gregory Possehl. New Delhi: Vikas Publishing House, 1979, pp. 155–163.

Padmarajiah, Y. J. *A Comparative Study of the Jaina Theories of Reality and Knowledge*. Bombay: Jain Shitya Viks Mandal, 1963.

Page, Denys, editor. *Poetae Melici Graeci*. Oxford: Clarendon Press, 1962.

Palmer, George Herbert, translator. *The Odyssey of Homer*. Cambridge, Massachusetts: Houghton Mifflin Company, 1949.

Palmer, Leonard. *The Greek Language*. Norman, Oklahoma: University of Oklahoma Press, 1980.

Parke, H. W. "The Massacre of the Branchidae." *Journal of Hellenic Studies* 105 (1985): 59–68.

Parker, DeWitt H., editor. *Schopenhauer, Selections*. New York: Charles Scribner's Sons, 1956.

Parpola, Asko. *Deciphering the Indus Script*. Cambridge: Cambridge University Press, 1994.

——. "The Problem of the Indus Script." In *Essays in Indian Protohistory*. Edited by D. P. Agrawal and Dilip K. Chakrabarti. Delhi: B. R. Publishing Co., 1979, pp. 163–186,

Parpola, Simo, Asko Parpola, and Robert H. Brunswig Jr. "The Meluhha Village: Evidence of Acculturation of Harappan Traders in Late Third Millennium Mesopotamia." *Journal of the Economic and Social History of the Orient* 20 (1977): 129–165.

Parrot, Andre. *Sumer, the Dawn of Art*. New York: Golden Press, 1961.

Patrick, Mary M. *Greek Skeptics*. New York: Columbia University Press, 1969.

Pauly, A., G. Wissowa, and W. Kroll, editors. *Real-Encyclopädie der classischen Altertumswissenschaft*. Stuttgart, 1894–1980.

Pericles, Georges. *Barbarian Asia and the Greek Experience: From the Archaic Period to the Age of Xenophon*. Baltimore: Johns Hopkins University Press, 1994.

Petrie, Sir William M. F. *Personal Religion in Egypt before Christianity*. Harper's Library of Living Thought. London: Harper and Brothers, 1909.

Philip, J. A. *Pythagoras and Early Pythagoreanism*. Toronto: University of Toronto Press, 1966.

Piggot, Stuart. *Prehistoric India*. Baltimore, Maryland: Penguin, 1950.

Pingree, David. *The Yavanajātaka of Sphujidhvaja.* 2 vols. Cambridge, Massachusetts: Harvard University Press, 1978.

Possehl, Gregory. "African Millets in South Asian Prehistory." In *Studies in the Archeology of India and Pakistan.* Edited by Jerome Jacobson. New Delhi: Oxford and IBH Publishing Co, and American Institute of Indian Studies, 1986, pp. 237–252.

——, editor. *Ancient Cities of the Indus.* New Delhi: Vikas Publishing House Pvt. Ltd., 1979.

——, editor. *Harappan Civilization: A Contemporary Perspective.* New Delhi: Oxford and IBH Publishing Co. in collaboration with American Institute of Indian Studies, 1992.

——. *Indus Age: The Writing System.* New Delhi and Calcutta: Oxford and IBH Publishing Co., 1996.

Potter, Karl H. "A Few Early Abhidharma Categories." In *Encyclopedia of Indian Philosophies.* Vol. 7, *Abhidharma Buddhism to 150 A.D.* Edited by Karl H. Potter et. al. Delhi: Motilal Banarsidass, 1996, pp. 121–136.

——. *Encyclopedia of Indian Philosophies.* Vol. 2, *Indian Metaphysics and Epistemology: The Tradition of Nyāya-Vaiśeṣika up to Gangesa.* Princeton, New Jersey: Princeton University Press, 1977.

——, et al., editors. *Abhidharma Buddhism to 150 A. D.* Vol. 7, *Encyclopedia of Indian Philosophies.* Delhi: Motilal Banarsidass, 1996.

Poussin, L. de la Vallée. *The Way to Nirvāṇa.* Cambridge: Cambridge University Press, 1917.

Prebish, Charles, editor. *Buddhism: A Modern Perspective.* University Park, Pennsylvania, and London: Pennsylvania State University Press, 1975.

Priaulx, Osmond de Beauvoir. *The Indian Travels of Apollonius of Tyana and the Indian Embassies to Rome.* London: Quaritch, 1873.

Price, A. F., and Wong Mou-Lam. *The Diamond Sūtra and the Sūtra of Hui Neng.* Berkeley, California: Shambhala, 1969.

Pritchard, James B., editor. *Ancient Near Eastern Texts Relating to the Old Testament.* Princeton, New Jersey: Princeton University Press, 1955.

Puri, B. N. *Buddhism in Central Asia.* Delhi: Motilal Banarsidass, 1987.

Quintus Curtius Rufus. *The History of Alexander.* Translated by John Yardley with introduction and notes by Waldemar Heckel. London: Penguin, 1984.

——. *The Brahmā Sūtra: The Philosophy of Spiritual Life.* London: George Allen and Unwin, 1960.

Radhakrishnan, Sarvepalli, editor. *History of Philosophy, Eastern and Western.* 2 vols. London: George Allen and Unwin, 1952–1953.

——. *Indian Philosophy.* 2 vols. London and New York: George Allen and Unwin, 1971.

——. "On Philosophical Synthesis." *Philosophy East and West* 1 (1951): 4.

——,translator and editor. *The Principal Upanisads.* London: George Allen and Unwin, 1969.

——, and Charles A. Moore, editors. *A Source Book in Indian Philosophy.* Princeton, New Jersey: Princeton University Press, 1957.

Raja, K. Kunjunni. "Philosophical Elements in Patañjali's Mahābhāṣya." In *The Philosophy of the Grammarians.* Edited by Harold G. Coward and K. Kunjunni Raja. Princeton, New Jersey: Princeton University Press, 1990, pp. 115–119.

Rajaram, Navaratna S., and David Frawley. *Vedic 'Aryans' and the Origins of Civilization.* Quebec: W. H. Press, 1995.

Rampuria, S. C. *The Cult of Ahiṃsā: A Jain View-Point.* Calcutta: Sri Jain Swetamber Terapanthi Mahasabha, 1947.

Ranada, R. D. "Presocratics." *History of Philosophy Eastern and Western,* vol. 2. Edited by Sarvepalli Radhakrishnan. London: George Allen and Unwin, 1953.

Randle, Henry N. *Indian Logic in the Early Schools.* Oxford: Oxford University Press, 1930.

Rank, Otto. *Myth of the Birth of the Hero.* New York: Vintage Books, 1959.

Rapson, Edward J., editor. *The Cambridge History of India.* Vol. 1, *Ancient India.* Cambridge: Cambridge University Press, 1922.

Raven, J. E. *Plato's Thought in the Making.* Cambridge: Cambridge University Press, 1965.

Rawlinson, H. G. "Foreign Influence in the Civilization of Ancient India, 900 B.C.–400 A.D." *Journal of the Royal Asiatic Society* (1908–1913): 217–238.

——. *India: A Short Cultural History*. London: Cresset Press, 1965.

——. *Intercourse between India and the Western World from the Earliest Times to the Fall of Rome*. 2nd edition. Cambridge: Cambridge University Press, 1926.

Ray, Nikar Ranjan. "Sculpture." *Age of Imperial Unity*. Edited by R. C. Majumdar, pp. 506–527.

Reale, Giovanni. *A History of Ancient Philosophy*. Vol. 1, *From the Origins to Socrates*. Translated by John R. Catan. Albany, New York: State University of New York Press, 1987. Vol. 3, *The Systems of the Hellenistic Age*. Translated by John R. Catan. Albany, New York: State University of New York Press, 1985. Vol. 4, *The Imperial Age*. Translated by John R. Catan. Albany, New York: State University of New York Press, 1990.

Reat, Noble Ross. *Buddhism: A History*. Berkeley, California: Asian Humanities Press, 1994.

——. "The Historical Buddha and His Teachings." In *Abhidharma Buddhism to 150 A.D.* Edited by Karl H. Potter et al. Delhi: Motilal Banarsidass, 1996, pp. 3–58.

Reitzenstein, Richard, and Hans H. Schaeder. *Studien zum antiken Synkretismus*. Studien der Bibliothek Warburg 7. Leipzig: B. G. Teubner, 1926.

Renfrew, Colin. *Archaeology and Language: The Puzzle of Indo-European Origins*. New York: Cambridge University Press, and London: Jonathan Cape, 1987.

Reps, Paul. *Zen Flesh, Zen Bones*. Garden City, New York: Doubleday/Anchor, n.d.

Ressor, Margaret E. "Necessity and Fate in Stoic Philosophy." In *The Stoics*. Edited by John M. Rist. Berkeley and Los Angeles: University of California Press, 1978, pp. 187–201.

Rhys-Davids, T. W. "Asceticism." In *Encyclopaedia of Religion and Ethics*, vol. 2. Edited by James Hastings. Edinburgh: T. and T. Clark; New York: C. Scribner's Sons, 1908-1927, p. 96 ff.

——, translator. *The Questions of King Milinda*. Sacred Books of the East 35 and 36. New York: Dover, 1963.

Riepe, Dale. *The Naturalistic Tradition in Indian Thought*. Seattle: University of Washington Press, 1961.

Rist, John M. *Epicurus, An Introduction*. Cambridge: Cambridge University Press, 1972.

——. *Plotinus: The Road to Reality*. Cambridge: Cambridge University Press, 1967.

——. *Stoic Philosophy*. Cambridge: Cambridge University Press, 1969.

——, editor. *The Stoics*. Berkeley and Los Angeles: University of California Press, 1978.

Robin, Leon. *Pyrrhon et le scepticisme grèc*. Les Grandes Philosophies. Paris: Presses Universitaires de France, 1944.

Robinson, Richard. *Plato's Earlier Dialectic*. Ithaca, New York: Cornell University Press, 1941.

——. "Elenchus." In *The Philosophy of Socrates, A Collection of Critical Essays*. Edited by Gregory Vlastos. Garden City, New York: Doubleday, 1971.

Robinson, Richard H. *Early Mādhyamika in India and China*. Delhi: Motilal Banarsidass, 1976.

——, and Willard L. Johnson. *The Buddhist Religion: A Historical Survey*. 4th edition. Belmont, California: Wadsworth Publishing Company, 1997.

Rodier, David F. T. "Meditative States in the Abhidharma and in Pseudo-Dionysius." In *Neoplatonism and Indian Thought*. Edited by R. Baine Harris. Norfolk, Virginia: International Center for Neoplatonic Studies, 1982, pp. 121–136.

Rogers, Arthur K. *The Socratic Problem*. New York: Russell and Russell, 1971.

Rogers, Benjamin B. *Aristophanes*. 3 vols. Loeb Classical Library. Cambridge, Massachusetts: Harvard University Press, 1961–1963.

Rohde, Erwin. "Die Religion der Griechen." In *Kleine Schriften*. 2 vols. Hildesheim: Georg Olms Verlag, 1969.

——. *Psychē: The Cult of Souls and Belief in Immortality among the Greeks*. Translated by W. B. Hillis. London: Kegan, Paul, Trench, Trubner and Co., 1925.

Roheim, Geza. *The Eternal Ones of the Dream*. New York: International Universities Press, 1969.

Romm, James S. *The Edges of the Earth in Ancient Thought: Geography, Exploration, and Fiction*. Princeton, New Jersey: Princeton University Press, 1992.

Ross, W. D. *Aristotle*. London: Methuen, University Paperbacks, 1964.

Rowland, Benjamin. *The Art and Architecture of India*. 3rd edition. Baltimore, Maryland: Penguin, 1970.

Rowlands, Michael, Morgens Larsen, and Kristian Kristiansen, editors. *Centre and Periphery in the Ancient World*. Cambridge: Cambridge University Press, 1987.

Ruben, Walter. *Geschichte der Indischen Philosophie*. Berlin: Deutsches Verlag der Wissenschaften, 1954.

Runciman, W. G. *Plato's Later Epistemology*. Cambridge: Cambridge University Press, 1962.

Russell, Bertrand. *A History of Western Philosophy*. New York: Simon and Schuster, 1945.

——. *The Autobiography of Bertrand Russell: The Middle years, 1914–1944*. New York: Bantam Books, 1969.

Sadakata, Akira. *Buddhist Cosmology, Philosophy and Origins*. Translated by Gaynor Sekimori with a foreword by Hajime Nakamura. Tokyo: Kosei Publishing Co., 1997.

Saddhatissa, Hammalawa. "Foreward." In *The Debate of King Milinda*. Translated and edited by Bhikku Pesala. Abridged edition. Delhi: Motilal Banarsidass, 1991, p. VII.

——, translator. *The Sutta Nipāta*. London: Curzon Press, Ltd., 1976.

Said, Edward. *Orientalism*. New York: Random House, 1979.

Salomon, Richard. *Ancient Buddhist Scrolls from Gandhāra: The British Library Kharoṣṭhī Fragments*. Seattle: University of Washington Press, 1999.

Sandys, Sir John E., translator. *The Odes of Pindar, Including the Principal Fragments*. Loeb Classical Library. Cambridge, Massachusetts: Harvard University Press, 1919.

Santillana, Giorgio de. *Prologue to Parmenides*. Cincinnati, Ohio: University of Cincinnati, 1964.

——. *The Origins of Scientific Thought from Anaximander to Proclus, 600 B. C. -500 A. D.* New York: New American Library, Mentor Books, 1961.

——, and Hertha von Dechend. *Hamlet's Mill*: Boston: David R. Godine, 1977.

Sastri, K. N. *New Light on the Indus Civilization*. 2 vols. Delhi: Atma Ram and Sons, 1965.

Sauneron, Serge. *The Priests of Ancient Egypt*. Translated by Ann Morrissett. New York: Grove Press, 1980.

Sayre, Farrand. *Diogenes of Sinope: A Study of Greek Cynicism*. Baltimore, Maryland: J. H. Furst Co., 1938.

Schenkeveld, D. M. *Studies in Demetrius "On Style."* Amsterdam: A. Hakkert, 1964.

Schlegel, Friedrich. *Über die Sprache und Weisheit der Indier*. In History of Linguistics Series. Vol. 4, *18th and 19th Century German Linguistics*. London: Routledge/Thoemmes Press, 1995.

Schlumberger, Daniel, and Emil Benveniste. "A New Greek Inscription of Aśoka at Kandahar." *Ep. Ind.* 38 (1965–1966): 193–200.

——, Louis Robert, Andre Dupont-Sommer, and Emil Benveniste. "Une bilingue grec-araméenne d'Aśoka." *Journal Asiatique* (1958): 1–48.

Schmandt-Besserat, Denise. *Before Writing*. Vol. 1, *From Counting to Cuneiform*. Austin, Texas: University of Texas Press, 1992.

———. "From Tokens to Tablets: A Re-evaluation of the So-called 'Numerical Tablets.'" *Visible Language* 15 (1981): 321–344.

Schneider, Marius. "Primitive Music." In *New Oxford History of Music*. Vol. 1, *Ancient and Oriental Music*. Edited by Egon Wellesz. London and New York: Oxford University Press, 1969, pp. 1–82.

Schofield, M., M. Burnyeat, and J. Barnes, editors. *Doubt and Dogmatism: Studies in Hellenistic Philosophy*. Oxford: Clarendon Press, and New York: Oxford University Press, 1979.

Schubring, Walter. *The Doctrine of the Jainas*. Delhi: Motilal Banarsidass, 1962.

Schwab, Raymond. *The Oriental Renaissance: Europe's Rediscovery of India and the East, 1680-1880*. Translated by Gene Patterson-Black and Victor Reinking. New York: Columbia University Press, 1984.

Schwyzer, H. R. "Plotinos" In *Paulys Realencyclopadie der classischen Altertumswissenschaft* 21 (1951): 471–592.

Sedlar, Jean W. *India and the Greek World: A Study in the Transmission of Culture*. Totowa, New Jersey: Rowman and Littlefield, 1980.

Seneviratna, Anuradha, editor. *King Aśoka and Buddhism: Historical and Literary Studies*. Kandy, Sri Lanka: Buddhist Publication Society, 1994.

Shaffer, Jim G. "The Indo-Aryan Invasions: Cultural Myth and Archeological Reality." In *The People of South Asia*. Edited by John R. Lukacs. New York: Plenum, 1984, pp. 77–90.

——, and Diana A. Lichtenstein. "The Concepts of 'Cultural Tradition' and 'Paleoethnicity' in South Asian Archeology." In *Indo-Aryans of Ancient South Asia: Language, Material Culture, and Ethnicity*. Edited by George Erdosy. Berlin and New York: Walter de Gruyter, 1995, pp. 126–154.

Sharma, I. C. *Ethical Philosophies of India*. Edited and revised by Stanley M. Duagert. New York: Harper and Row, 1970.

——. "The Plotinian One and the Concept of Paramapuruṣa in the Bhagavadgīta" In *Neoplatonism and Indian Thought*. Edited by R. Baine Harris. Norfolk, Virginia: International Center for Neoplatonic Studies, 1982, pp. 87–100.

Shastri, Indra Chandra. "Jainism and the Way to Spiritual Realization." In *Aspects of Jainism*, reprints from *The Aryan Path*. Bangalore: Jain Mission Society, 1955.

Shekhar, I. *Sanskrit Drama, Its Origin and Decline*. Leiden: Brill, 1960.

Shelley, Percy Bysshe. *Hellas*. London: Reeves and Turner, 1886.

Sherrat, Andrew. "Fata Morgana: Illusion and Reality in Greek-Barbarian Relations". *Cambridge Archeological Journal* 5.1 (April 1995): 139–153.

Shivananda, Swami. *Kuṇḍalinī Yoga*. Shivanandanagar, India: Yoga-Vedānta Forest Academy, 1971.

Siderits, Mark, and J. Dervin O'Brien. "Zeno and Nāgārjuna on Motion." *Philosophy East and West* 26 (1976): 281–301.

Silberman, Neil Asher. *Between Past and Present: Archeology and Nationalism in the Modern Middle East*. New York: Henry Holt and Company, 1989.

Simpson, William. "The Buddhist Praying Wheel." *Journal of the Royal Asiatic Society* (1898): 873–875.

Singh, Jaideva. Introduction to *The Conception of Buddhist Nirvāṇa*, by Theodore Stcherbatsky. Delhi: Motilal Banarsidass, 1978.

Sinh, Pancham, translator. *The Haṭha Yoga Pradipika*. New Delhi: Munshiram Manoharlal, 1980.

Sinnige, Theodorus G. *Matter and Infinity in the Presocratic Schools and Plato*. Philosophical Texts and Studies 17. Assen: van Gorcum, 1971.

Sircar, D. S. *Studies in the Religious Life of Ancient and Medieval India*. Delhi: Motilal Banarsidass, 1971.

Smart, Ninian. *Doctrine and Argument in Indian Philosophy*. London: George Allen and Unwin, 1964.

Snell, Daniel C. *Life in the Ancient Near East, 3100–332 B.C.* New Haven: Yale University Press, 1997.

Snowden, Frank M. Jr. *Before Color Prejudice: The Ancient View of Blacks*. Cambridge, Massachusetts: Harvard University Press, 1983.

Soper, A. C. "The Roman Style in Gandhāra." *American Journal of Archeology* 55 (1951): 301–319.

Spiritual Teachings of Ramana Maharshi. Berkeley, California: Shambhala, 1972.

Spivak, Gayatri. *The Post-colonial Critic: Interviews, Strategies, Dialogues*. Edited by Sarah Harasym. New York and London: Routledge, 1990.

Sprung, Mervyn, translator. *Lucid Exposition of the Middle Way: The Essential Chapters from the Prasannapadā of Candrakīrti*. Boulder, Colorado: Prajñā Press, 1979.

——, editor. *The Problem of Two Truths in Buddhism and Vedānta*. Dordrecht and Boston: D. Reidel, 1973.

Srinivasan, Doris. "Gandhāran Textiles: A Local Craft with Western Connections." In *Gandhāran Art in Context: East-West Exchanges at the Crossroads of Asia*. Edited by Raymond Allchin et al, pp. 95–117.

Śrinivasiengar [Srinivasa-Aiyangar], C. N. *The History of Ancient Indian Mathematics*. Calcutta: World Press, 1967.

Staal, J. Fritz. *Advaita and Neoplatonism*. Madras: University of Madras, 1961.

——. *Exploring Mysticism*. Berkeley and Los Angeles: University of California Press, 1975.

——. "Parmenides and Indian Thought." *Philosophical Quarterly* (India) 28 (1955), pp. 81–106.

Stcherbatsky, Theodore. *Buddhist Logic*. 2 vols. New York: Dover, 1962.

——. *The Central Conception of Buddhism*. Delhi: Motilal Banarsidass, 1970.

——. *The Conception of Buddhist Nirvāṇa*. Leningrad: Academy of Sciences of the USSR, 1927; The Hague: Mouton, 1965; Delhi: Motilal Banarsidass, 1978.

Stevenson, Alice M. *The Heart of Jainism*. Religious Quest of India. London: Oxford University Press, 1915.

Stevenson, Ian. *Twenty Cases Suggestive of Reincarnation*. 2nd edition, revised and enlarged. Charlottesville: University Press of Virginia, 1974.

Stokes, Michael C. *One and Many in Presocratic Philosophy*. Cambridge, Massachusetts: Harvard University Press, 1971.

——, translator. *The Greek Alexander Romance*. London: Penguin, 1991.

Stoneman, Richard, translator and editor. *Legends of Alexander the Great*. London: J. M. Dent, 1994.

Story, Francis. *Rebirth as Doctrine and Experience, Essays and Case Studies*. Introduction by Ian Stevenson, M.D. Kandy, Sri Lanka: Buddhist Publication Society, 1975.

Streng, Frederick J. *Emptiness: A Study in Religious Meaning*. Nashville, Tennessee, and New York: Abingdon Press, 1967.

Stough, Charlotte L. *Greek Skepticism: A Study in Epistemology*. Berkeley, California, and Los Angeles: University of California Press, 1969.

——. "The Process of Ultimate Transformation in Nāgārjuna's Mādhyamika." *The Eastern Buddhist* n.s. 11, no. 2 (1978): 12–32.

——. "The Significance of Pratītyasamutpāda for Understanding the Relationship Between Saṃvṛti and Paramārthasatya in Nāgārjuna." In *The Problem of Two Truths in Buddhism and Vedānta*. Edited by Mervyn Sprung. Dordrecht and Boston: D. Reidel, 1973, pp. 27–39.

——. "Stoic Determinism and Moral Responsibility." In *The Stoics*. Edited by John M. Rist. Berkeley, California, and Los Angeles: University of California Press, 1978, pp. 203–230.

Strodach, George K. *The Philosophy of Epicurus*. Chicago: Northwestern University Press, 1963.

Sutcliffe, F. E., translator. *Descartes: Discourse on Method and the Meditations*. Harmondsworth and Baltimore, Maryland: Penguin, 1968.

Suzuki, Daisetz T. "The Basis of Buddhist Philosophy." In *D. T. Suzuki on Indian Mahāyāna Buddhism*. Edited by Edward Conze. New York: Harper and Row, 1968, pp. 227–250.

——. "Existentialism, Pragmatism and Zen." In *Zen Buddhism, Selected Writings of D. T. Suzuki*. Edited by William Barrett. Garden City, New York: Doubleday, 1956, pp. 259–275.

——. "The Gandavyuha." In *D. T. Suzuki on Indian Mahāyāna Buddhism*. Edited by Edward Conze. New York: Harper and Row, 1968, pp. 147–226.

——, translator. *The Laṅkāvatāra Sūtra*. London: Routledge and Kegan Paul, 1932.

——. *Studies in the Laṅkāvatāra Sūtra*. London: Routledge and Kegan Paul, 1930.

——. *D. T. Suzuki on Indian Mahāyāna Buddhism*. Edited by Edward Conze. New York: Harper and Row, 1968.

——. *Zen Buddhism, Selected Writings of D. T. Suzuki*. Edited by William Barrett. Garden City, New York: Doubleday, 1956.

Swearer, Donald K., editor. *Toward the Truth*, by Buddhadāsa. Philadelphia: Westminster Press, 1971.

Szabo, A. "Eleatica." *Acta Antiqua Academiae Scientiarum Hungaricae* 3 (1955): 67–103.

——. "Wie is die Mathematik zu einer deduktiven Wissenschaft geworden?" *Acta Antiqua Academiae Scientiarum Hungaricae* 4 (1956): 109–152.

Takakusu, Junjiro. *The Essentials of Buddhist Philosophy*. 3rd edition. Edited by Wing-Tsit Chan and Charles A. Moore. Delhi: Motilal Banarsidass, 1975.

Talageri, Shrikant G. *The Aryan Invasion Theory: A Reappraisal*. New Delhi: Aditya Prakashan, 1993.

Taran, Leonardo. *Parmenides*. Princeton, New Jersey: Princeton University Press, 1965.

Tarn, W. W. *Alexander the Great*. 2 vols. Cambridge: Cambridge University Press, 1948–1950.

——. *The Greeks in Bactria and India*. Cambridge: Cambridge University Press, 1951.

Taylor, A. E., translator. *Plato, Timaeus, and Critias*. Oxford: Clarendon Press, 1929.

Taylor, Timothy. "The Gundestrup Cauldron." *Scientific American* (March 1992): 84–89.

Tenneman, W. G. *Gründriss der Geschichte der Philosophie*. 3rd edition. Leipzig: J. A. Barth, 1820.

Thani-Nayagam, X. S. "Indian Thought and Roman Stoicism." *Tamil Culture* 10, no. 3 (1963), pp. 1–36.

Thapar, Romila. *Aśoka and the Decline of the Mauryas.* Oxford: Oxford University Press, 1961.

——. "Epigraphic Evidence and Some Indo-Hellenistic Contacts during the Mauryan Period." In *Indological Studies: Prof. D. C. Sicar Commemoration Volume.* Edited by S.K. Maity and Upendra Thakur. New Delhi: Shakti Malik, Abhinav Publications, 1987, pp. 15–20.

——. *Interpreting Early India.* Delhi: Oxford University Press, 1993.

Thera, Nyanaponika. *Abhidhamma Studies: Buddhist Explorations of Consciousness and Time.* Edited with an introduction by Bhikkhu Bodhi. Boston: Wisdom Publications, in collaboration with the Buddhist Publication Society, Kandy, Sri Lanka, 1998.

——. *The Heart of Buddhist Meditation.* New York: Samuel Weiser, 1973.

——. *The Power of Mindfulness.* San Francisco: Unity Press, 1972.

Thibaut, G. *Mathematics in the Making in Ancient India.* Reprints of *On the Sulvasūtras and Baudhyayana Sulva Sūtra.* Edited with introduction by Deviprasad Chattopadhyaya. Calcutta: K. P. Bagchi, 1974.

Thomas, Edward J. *The History of Buddhist Thought.* 2nd edition. New York: Barnes and Noble, 1951.

——. *The Life of Buddha as Legend and History.* London: Routledge and Kegan Paul, 1949.

Thomson, George. *Studies in Ancient Greek Society: The Prehistoric Aegean.* New York: Citadel Press, 1965.

Thurman, Robert A. F. *The Central Philosophy of Tibet: A Study and Translation of Jey Tsong Khapa's* Essence of True Eloquence. Princeton: Princeton University Press, 1984.

Trevor-Roper, Hugh. *The Rise of Christian Europe: The Middle Years.* London: Thames and Hudson, 1965.

Tripathi, C. L. "Influence of Indian Philosophy on Neoplatonism." In *Neoplatonism and Indian Thought.* Edited by R. Baine Harris. Norfolk, Virginia: International Center for Neoplatonic Studies, 1982, pp. 273–292.

Trouillard, Jean. "Le neoplatonisme." *Encyclopédia de la Pléiade.* Vol. 1, *Histoire de la philosophie.* Paris: Gallimard, 1969, pp. 886–935.

Trungpa, Chogyam. "Remarks on the Tradition of Mindfulness." *Gāruda* 4 (1976).

Tuana, Nancy, editor. *Feminist Interpretations of Plato.* University Park, Pennsylvania: University of Pennsylvania Press, 1994.

Tucci, Giuseppe, editor and translator. *Pre-Dinnaga Buddhist Texts on Logic from Chinese Sources.* Baroda: Oriental Institute, 1929.

——, translator. "The *Ratnāvalī* of Nāgārjuna." *Journal of the Royal Asiatic Society* (1934): 307–325.

——. *The Theory and Practice of the Maṇḍala.* New York: Samuel Weiser, 1970.

Tuck, Andrew. *Comparative Philosophy and the Philosophy of Scholarship: On the Western Interpretation of Nāgārjuna.* New York and Oxford: Oxford University Press, 1990.

Tull, Herman W. *The Vedic Origins of Karma: Cosmos as Man in Ancient Indian Myth and Ritual.* SUNY Series in Hindu Studies. Albany, New York: State University of New York Press, 1989.

Tyagisananda, Swami, editor and commentator. *Narada Bhakti Sūtras.* Madras: Sri Ramakrishna Math, 1972.

Ui, H. *The Vaiśeṣika Philosophy.* Varanasi: Chowkhamba Sanskrit Series Office, 1962.

Uno, Atusi. "A Study of Syādvāda." in *Jinamañjari: International Journal of Contemporary Jaina Reflections* 18, no. 2 (1998): 14–24.

Usener, H., editor. *Epicurea (Epistula, Fragmenta, Sententiae)*, Leipzig, 1887.

Valle Poussin, Louis de la. *Abhidharmakośabhāṣyam by Louis de la Vallee Poussin.* 4 vols. Translated by Leo M. Pruden. Berkeley, California: Asian Humanities Press, 1988–1990.

Van Buren, E. Douglas. *Symbols of the Gods in Mesopotamian Art.* Rome: Pontificium Institutum Biblicum, 1945.

Van der Veer, Peter. "The Foreign Hand: Orientalist Discourse in Sociology and Communalism." In *Orientalism and the Post-Colonial Predicament: Perspectives on South Asia.* Edited by Carol A. Breckenridge and Peter van der Veer. New Cultural Studies Series. Philadelphia: University of Pennsylvania Press, 1933, pp. 23–44.

Von Arnim, H., editor. *Stoicorum Veterum Fragmenta.* 4 vols. Leipzig: Teubner, 1924.

Von Fritz, Kurt. "The Philosophical Passage in the Seventh Platonic Letter and the Problem of Plato's 'Esoteric Philosophy.'" In *Essays in Ancient Greek Philosophy.* Edited by John Peter Anton and George L. Kustas. Albany, New York: State University of New York Press, 1972.

Von Glasenapp, Helmuth. "Indian and Western Metaphysics." *Philosophy East and West* 3 (1963): 223–231.

Von Soden, Wolfram. *The Ancient Orient: An Introduction to the Study of the Ancient Near East.* Translated by Donald G. Schley. Grand Rapids, Michigan: William R. Eerdmans, 1994.

Vasu, Rai Bahadur Srisa Chandra, translator. *Śiva Saṁhitā*. New Delhi: Munshiram Manoharlal, 1979.

Verdu, Alfonzo. *Dialectical Aspects in Buddhist Thought.* Lawrence: University of Kansas, Center for East Asian Studies, 1974.

Vidyabhusana, Satis Chandra. "Influence of Aristotle on the Development of the Syllogism in Indian Logic." *Journal of the Royal Asiatic Society* (1918): 469–488.

——, translator. *The Nyāya Sūtras of Gotama*. New Delhi: Munshiram Manoharlal, 1975.

Vishnudevananda, Swami. *The Complete Illustrated Book of Yoga*. New York: Julian Press, 1960.

Visvader, John. "The Use of Paradox in Uroboric Philosophies." *Philosophy East and West* 28 (1978): 455–467.

Vlastos, Gregory, editor. *Protagoras*, by Plato. Library of Liberal Arts 59. Translated by B. Jowett. New York: Liberal Arts Press, 1956.

——. Review of *Arete bei Platon and Aristoteles*, by Hans J. Krämer. *Gnomon* 35, Heft 7 (1963): 641–655.

——. *Studies in Greek Philosophy*. Vol. 1, *The Presocratics*. Vol. 2, *Socrates, Plato, and Their Tradition.* Edited by Daniel W. Graham. Princeton, New Jersey: Princeton University Press, 1995.

——. "Zeno of Elea." *The Encyclopedia of Philosophy* Vol. 8. Edited by Paul Edwards. New York: Macmillan, 1967, pp. 369–379.

Vogel, Cornelia J. de. *Philosophia*. Philosophical Texts and Studies 19. Assen: van Gorcum, 1970.

Wallis, Richard T. "Phraseology and Imagery in Plotinus and Indian Thought." In *Neoplatonism and Indian Thought*. Edited by R. Baine Harris. Norfolk, Virginia: International Center for Neoplatonic Studies, 1982, pp. 101–120.

——. *Neoplatonism*. London: Duckworth, 1972.

Warder, A. K. "Early Buddhism and Other Contemporary Systems." *Bulletin of the School of Oriental and African Studies* 18 (1956).

——. "Foreword." In Fumimoro Watanabe, *Philosophy and Its Development in the Nikāyas and Abhidhamma.* Delhi: Motilal Banarsidass, 1983.

——. *Indian Buddhism*. Delhi: Motilal Banarsidass, 1970.

Warmington, E. H. *The Commerce between the Roman Empire and India.* Cambridge: Cambridge University Press, 1928.

Warren, Henry C. *Buddhism in Translation*. New York: Atheneum, 1977.

Wasson, R. Gordon. *Soma: Divine Mushroom of Immortality*. NC: Harcourt Brace Jovanovich, n.d.

Watanabe, Fumimoro. *Philosophy and Its Development in the Nikāyas and Abhidhamma.* Delhi: Motilal Banarsidass, 1983.

Wayman, Alex. *The Buddhist Tantras: Light on Indo-Tibetan Esotericism.* Buddhist Traditions Series, 9. Delhi: Motilal Banarsidass, 1973.

——. *Untying the Knots in Buddhism: Selected Essays.* Buddhist Tradition Series, 28. Delhi: Motilal Banarsidass, 1997.

Weber, Max. *The Religions of India*. New York: Free Press, 1958.

Webster, T. B. L. *From Mycenae to Homer*. New York: W. W. Norton, 1964.

Wellesz, Egon, editor. *Ancient and Oriental Music. New Oxford History of Music*, Vol. 1. London and New York: Oxford University Press, 1969.

West, M. L. *Early Greek Philosophy and the Orient*. Oxford: Clarendon Press, 1971.

——. *The East Face of Helicon: West Asiatic Elements in Greek Poetry and Myth.* Oxford: Clarendon Press, 1997.

——. *The Orphic Poems*. Oxford: Clarendon Press, 1983.

Wheeler, Mortimer. "Arikamedu: An Indo-Roman Trading Station in the East Coast of India." *Ancient India* 2 (1947): 17–124.

——. *Civilizations of the Indus and Beyond*. London: Thames and Hudson, 1966.

——. *Early India and Pakistan*. London: Thames and Hudson, 1960.

——. *Flames over Persepolis*. New York: William Morrow, 1968.

——. *The Indus Civilization*. 3rd edition. Supplement to the Cambridge History of India. Cambridge: Cambridge University Press, 1968.

——. *Rome Beyond the Imperial Frontiers*. London: Bell, 1954.

White, David Gordon. *The Alchemical Body: Siddha Traditions in Medieval India*. Chicago: University of Chicago Press, 1996.

Whitman, Cedric H. *Homer and the Heroic Tradition*. New York: W. W. Norton, 1958.

Wilford, John Noble. "Who Began Writing? Many Theories, Few Answers." *The New York Times*, April 6, 1999.

Wilcken, Ulrich. *Alexander the Great*. Translated by G. C. Richards. Notes and introduction by E. N. Borza. New York: W. W. Norton, 1967.

Wile, Douglas. *Art of the Bedchamber: The Chinese Sexual Yoga Classics Including Women's Solo Meditation Texts*. Albany, New York: State University of New York Press, 1992.

Wilkinson, Sir John G., *The Manners and Customs of the Ancient Egyptians*. New edition, revised and corrected by Samuel Birch. London: J. Murray, 1878.

Williams, C. A. S. *Outlines of Chinese Symbolism and Art Motives*. Shanghai: Kelly and Walsh, 1932.

Willson, A. Leslie. *A Mythical Image: The Ideal of India in German Romanticism*. Durham, North Carolina: Duke University Press, 1964.

Willson, Martin. *Rebirth and the Western Buddhist*. London: Wisdom Publications, 1987.

——. *The Blue and Brown Books*. Oxford: Basil Blackwell, 1958.

Wittgenstein, Ludwig. *Philosophical Investigations*. 3rd edition. New York: Macmillan, 1968.

——. *Tractatus Logico-Philosophicus*. Translated by C.K Ogden. London: Routledge and Kegan Paul, 1922.

Witzel, Michael. "Early Indian History: Linguistic and Textual Parameters." In *The Indo-Aryans of South Asia: Language, Material Culture and Ethnicity*. Edited by George Erdosy, pp. 85–125.

Wolters, Albert M. "A Survey of Modern Scholarly Opinion on Plotinus and Indian Thought." In *Neoplatonism and Indian Thought*. Edited by R. Baine Harris. Norfolk, Virginia: International Center for Neoplatonic Studies, 1982, pp. 293–308.

Woodcock, George. *The Greeks in India*. London: Faber and Faber, 1966.

Woolley, C. Leonard. *Ur of the Chaldees: A Record of Seven Years of Excavation*. Harmondsworth: Penguin, 1929.

Wright, M. R. *Empedocles: The Extant Fragments*. New Haven and London: Yale University Press, 1981.

Yardley, John, translator. *Quintus Curtius Rufus: The History of Alexander*. London: Penguin, 1984.

Zaehner, Robert C. *The Dawn and Twilight of Zoroastrianism*. London: Widenfeld and Nicolson, 1961.

——. *Teachings of the Magi*. New York: Oxford University Press, 1976.

Zakbar, Louis V. "Herodotus and the Egyptian Idea of Immortality." *Journal of Near Eastern Studies* 22 (1963): pp. 57–63.

Zastrow, Charles. "Conceptualizing and Changing the Self from a Rational Therapy Perspective." In *Changing the Self: Philosophies, Techniques and Experiences*. Edited by Thomas M. Brinthaupt and Richard P. Lipka. Albany, New York: State University of New York Press, 1994.

Ziegler, K., and R. Keydell. "Orphische Dichtung." In Pauly, Wissowa, editors. *Real-Encylcopädie*. p. 1385.

Zeller, E. *Die Philosophie der Griechen in ihrer geschichtlichen Entwicklung*. Hildesheim: Georg Olms Verlag, 1963.

——. *Outlines of the History of Greek Philosophy*. 13th edition. New York: Dover Publications, 1980.

——. *Socrates and the Socratic Schools*. New York: Russell, 1962.

Zimmer, Heinrich. *Art of Indian Asia*. Bollingen Series 39. 2 vols. Princeton, New Jersey: Princeton University Press, 1955.

——. *Myths and Symbols in Indian Art and Civilization*. New York: Harper and Row, 1962.

——. *Philosophies of India*. Bollingen Series 26. Princeton, New Jersey: Princeton University Press, 1969.

Zuntz, Gunther. *Persephone*. Oxford: Oxford University Press, 1971.

Index

Abaris, 102, 269
Abhayarājakumāra Sutta, 414
abhidharma, 167, 168, 355, 374–375, 378, 390, 414–415, 503, 572, 583*n*25, 609, 611, 614, 617, 627, 636*n*55, 640*n*125, 641*n*137
absence, 529–531, 532, 538*n*44
Absolute. *See* Being; One
absolutism, 300, 585
  dialectical, 421, 428, 433, 437, 470
  metaphysical, 335, 337, 416
  transcendental, 340, 434, 452
abstinence, 182–184, 269
Academicians, 540
Achaemenids, 125–126, 213, 359
acoustics, 80, 281
  cosmic cycle and, 81–88
  instruments and, 85–87
  Orphic music and, 202
  Pythagoreans and, 47–48, 81–83, 84, 85, 86, 87–88, 330
  scales in, 83, 86
  Sumerian music and, 85–86, 87
action
  (Buddhist) sensation to, 605–608
  (Epicurean) sensation to, 614
  (Greek) sensation to, 608–611
  (Stoic) sensation to, 622–623
  wholesome/unwholesome, 604, 605, 616, 639*n*98
ad infinitum, 461, 463, 465
Adapa, 263, 292*n*151
adiaphora (in-difference), 624. *See also* non-difference
Aditi, 32
Adonis, 670
Advaita Vedānta, 58, 165, 170, 336, 391, 445*n*6, 499, 508*n3* 0, 520, 557, 585–586, 602, 649
Aenesidemus, 450–451
  Nāgārjuna and, 503–505
Aeschylus, 596
Afghanistan, 1, 657. *See also* Bactria
Africa, 220
afterlife, 602
  immortality of, 132–135
  Jain, 201
  no, 320, 328, 334
  not as human prospect, 602–603
  one myth for three (Greek/Egptian/Indian) culture's afterlife and, 135–138
  parinirvāṇa, final body and, 344–345
  path of, 135–138, 154*n*186
  Plato, 345
  pneuma/prāṇa and, 546
  rebirth in, 129–130
  reincarnation and, 112–113, 115, 275, 345, 478
  repayment/punishment and, 108–109, 135, 199
  return of dead and, 118–119, 131, 135, 148*n*81
  two paths of, 42–43, 274–275, 304–305
Āgamas, 604
ages, 68–69, 71–72, 78, 166
Agni, 29, 63*n*35, 90, 301
ahimsā, 182, 201, 202, 229, 232, 268, 269
air, 34–35, 46, 301, 302, 306, 331, 541
  as soul, 34–35, 545
air. *See also* breath
aither, 301, 304, 305, 306, 308
ajīva, 345
Ājīvikas, 107, 139, 202, 225, 231, 276, 284, 337. *See also* Cynics; Gosāla; Pāśupata; Seeking of Dishonor
  atomism, 317–318, 319, 344
  austerities of, 232–233, 278, 443, 602–603
  determinism and, 278, 296*n*242, 326, 327–328, 436
  elements and, 304, 305
  imperturbability, ethics and, 602–603, 611
  Jain schism with, 277–278, 296*n*242
  Ningizzida and, 271–273
  as non-Vedic, 519
  Seeking of Dishonor for, 204, 226–229
  shaman/powers of, 266, 267, 269, 271–273, 277, 295*n*237, 343
  Vedas denied by, 327
ākāśa (space), 164, 301, 304, 308, 525
Akkadian(s), 266, 283
  iconography, 247, 250
  Indian trade with, 240–243
  language, Vedas and, 4, 11, 26, 29, 32, 61, 112m, 257–258, 275, 285, 302
  Sumerians and, 244, 285, 302
Albinus, 581
Alcmaeon, 210, 211, 330
Alexander (the Great), 12, 13, 14, 21*n*68, 258, 282, 283, 349, 495, xxiii–xxiv, xxv, xxxii*n*38, xxxii*n*55
  death of, 356, 379
  democracy sanctioned by, 363
  as drama fan, 386
  Indian expedition/conquest by, 350, 352–355, 362, 379, 381, 443–444, 450, 491, 495, 501, 520, 675
  motives/effects of, 355–357, 363, 366, 379, 3543
Alexander of Aphrodisias, 426, 447*n*26
Alexander Romance, 387–388
Alexandria(s), 358, 360, 361–363, 366, 368, 371, 383
ambition, 167, 182, 185, 186
Ameinias, 52
Ammonius, 551
Amon-Re, 24–25, 26, 32, 134, 259, 268
amṛta, 263

analogy. *See also* images
fire, wood, smoke and, 462–463, 498, 511–512
Naiyāyika, 512–515
phantom, 555
rope, snake, 498–499
syllogism use of, 511–512
Anatolia, 3, 5
anatta (not self), 168, 431
Anaxagoras, 311, 316, 323*n*2
atomism, mind separate from matter, by, 313–314, 315, 321–322, 327, 331, 650
infinity of, 311–314, 576
interpenetrated infinity, the One and, 312, 313, 315
rejection of cosmic cycle/reincarnation by, 314–315
Anaxarchus, 450, 451, 491–492, 494–495, 520
Anaximander, 45, 51, 53, 65*n*54, 111, 121, 125, 281, 327
atomism, pluralism and, 305, 306, 314
cosmic cycle, time and, 73
Indian monism, infinite/brahman and, 30–33, 35, 74
separating opposites by, 31, 34
Anaxmenes, 59, 74, 111, 121, 305, 311, 541
condensing, rarefying by, 34, 40, 306–307, 314, 327
Indian monism and, 33–35
anekāntavāda (indeterminacy), 335–337
anicca (impermanence), 168, 431
animal imitations, 230–232, 262, 278
anthropomorphism, 49. *See also* macranthropy
Antisthenes, 183, 196*n*31, 233, 236*n*60, 315, 420, 438–439, 443, 444
Anu, 263, 264, 265
apatheia (noninvolvement), 420, 439, 443, 444, 452, 623, 625, 632, 633, 640*n*117
apeirōn (unlimited), 31–32
aphasia (nonspeech), 420, 453, 456, 457, 458, 633
Aphrodite, 55–56, 591
Apollo, 90, 110, 388, 390, 670
appetites, 167, 182, 185–186, 189, 208
Aquarian Age, 78
Aramaic, 13, 373, 374
Āraṇyakas, 113–114, 407
Arcesilaus, 453–454
archeology, 271
Alexandrias and Indian, 381, 383
autonomist/minimalist study of, xxvi, xxxiii*n*58
colonial, xxvi
Hellenism, India and, 500–501
Indus Valley and, 244, 259, 360
as means for subjugation, xxv
multiculturalism in Persian artifacts and, 9
Archilochus, 325
architecture, 361–362, 386
Argonauts, 81, 105
arhats (saints), 502
Aries, Age of, 81
Aristotle, xvi, 46, 170–171, 203, 210, 427, 438, 580, 623, 626, 628, 632. *See also* Peripatetics
active intellect of, 586
the Arrow and, 424
belief systems for, 604
chance of, 331
comparison to, xxvii
cosmic cycle and Great Year of, 73–74
dialectic and, 433
domination of one society over another by, xviii, 351, 356
dualism and, 37
elements and, 306
ethics, imperturbability and, 600–601, 604, 609–611
exhalation of soul-stuff, 41
happiness/pleasure for, 615, 625, 638*n*93, 639*n*98
logic/syllogism of, 408, 422, 435–436, 496, 510, 511, 519–536, 653
"no more formula" cancellation of, 451
numbers, metaphysics and, 160–161, 319
on Plato, 158
pluralism and, 157, 300
Prime Matter of, 31, 46
Prime Mover of, 535, 560, 570, 622
psychology for, 534–535
reincarnation and, 92
self-knowing mind for, 559, 568, 570, 574
semen and, 211
on Thales, 28–29
universals of, 511, 512, 527–528, 646
universe, cosmic sphericity and, 51–52, 53
Xenophanes and, 64*n*48
arithmetic. *See* mathematics
arrepsia, 420
art
Gandhāran, 374, 388–390, 401*n*207
Greek art diffused through Persian empire and, 9–10
Greek influence on Chinese, 371
Greek influence on Indian, xxi, xxiv, xxv, 9, 365, 371, 374, 389
Gupta, 390
Near East influence on Greek, 6, 14
Āryadeva, 406, 425, 499, 503, 514, 643
Aryan(s), 19*n*4
assimilation of, 276–277, 279–280, 285
as autochthonous, 657–660, 661*n*10, 663
Buddhism and, 280, 297*n*246
constraints, patriarchy and, 276, 286, 586
cremation of, 277
Dravidian and, 19*n*4, 112, 126, 229, 258, 277, 289*n*71
iconography and, 257–258
idealism, 229, 276–277, 286, 302–303
invasion, xxv, xxvi, 289*n*71, 657, 658, 659, 662*n*17, 663–664, 665*n*16
lifestyles established by, 279, 286
Mesopotamia and, 258
migration, not conquest, by, 663–664, 665*n*16
into northwest India, 1 96*n*88
Rg Veda, 188, 257, 657
shamans/asceticism and, 276–277, 279, 295*n*231
trade with, 350
tradition, 112, 116, 674
Vedic, 559
Vratyas and, 274
as white, xix, xx
āsanas, 219, 268, 285
Asaṅga, 514
ascetic communities, 80, 91, 107, 233, 268. *See also* brotherhood
Cynic, 232–233, 439–440
dropout, 321
Jain/Ājīvikas, 225, 278, 334, 342, 405, 549, 602
Orphic, 27, 321
Stoic, 546–547
Vratyas and, 274
yogic, Vedic, 8, 10, 17–18, 22*n*95, 99–100, 141–142, 558
asceticism, xvi, 36, 67, 182–184, 186, 269, 302, 432, 502,
of dishonor, 226–230
ethics, imperturbability and, 595, 602–603, 616
reform of, 279
reincarnation release and, 278, 279
shaman, 276, 278, 558
Asia, Central, 233, 244, 257, 286, 298*n*267, 349, 350, 352, 359, 360, 370–371, 372, 373, 379, 381, 389, 394*n*26, 663, 666, 676
Asia, Western, 275, 286, 362, 389, 659, 666, 676
Aśoka Maurya, 17–18, 204
buddhism of, 360, 368–369, 373, 374, 375, 500, 631
Greeks and, 360–361, 367–370, 382, 397*n*96
aśrama, 279
assent, 627, 629, 640*n*114, 640*n*125

Assyrian empire, 4, 5, 6, 7, 8, 10–11, 14, 239, 257, 265, 268
āstika sect, 327
astrology, 266, 385
  Chaldean, 171–172, 176*n*47
astronomy, 6, 20*n*22, 45, 281, 282, 327, 365, 432
  Chaldean, 171–172, 176*n*47
  cosmic cycle and, 77–79, 80, 87, 88–89, 96*n*66
  India, Greece, post/Alexandrian/Roman period and, 384–386, 502, 513
  Mesopotamian, 23–24, 28, 31, 32, 47, 48, 52, 53, 70, 77–79
  numerology of, 88–89, 96*n*88, 140, 586
asuras, 257, 276
Aśvins, 3
ataraxia (imperturbability), 420, 432, 453, 454, 455, 457, 479, 493, 601, 615–616, 620, 632, 634*n*18, 638*n*98
Atharva Veda, 188, 260, 586
  afterlife, reincarnation and, 112–113, 115, 275
  creation, destruction and, 70
  dating of, 60
  elements and, 302
  Near East (Akkadian) influence in, 4, 11, 26, 29, 32, 61, 112, 115, 257–258, 289*n*71
  numerology of, 89
  Vratyas and, 274
atheism, 333, 337, 341, 621
Atlantis, 202–203
ātman, 317, 455
  brahman, 558–560, 563–564
  as Cosmic Self (universal subject), 27, 33, 49, 50, 101, 138, 165, 185, 543, 547, 559
  knowledge of, 100
atomism, 34, 311, 337, 523
  Anaxagoras and, 313–315, 327, 331, 650
  atoms, soul and, 318, 319
  Buddhist, 324*n*28
  Cārvāka/Lokāyata, 320, 334, 337, 344, 345, 653
  Democritus and, 311, 315, 316–317, 318, 319, 320, 331, 334, 429, 443, 513, 599, 611
  dialectical, 406
  Epicurean, 520, 622, 639*n*111
  finite (matter) as infinitely divisible and, 312, 313, 319–320
  Greek, 315–317, 318, 327, 331–333, 424–426, 447*n*25
  Indian, 317–321, 324*n*28, 344
  Indian before Greek, 318, 320–321
  Jain, 198–199, 203, 317–320, 519–520, 525, 527, 653
  Kaṇāda and, 524
  Milesian, 306, 307, 327
  Nyāya-Vaiśeṣika, 319, 324*n*28, 510, 515, 517*n*1
  plurality *vs.*, 424–426
  point monad and, 319, 519, 520
  psychē and, 618
  senses and, 316–317, 318, 331–332, 334, 534
  skeptism/subjectivity *vs.*, 451
  Upaniṣads, 318–319
  Vaiśeṣika, 425, 519–520, 535–536, 539*n*51, 639*n*111, 646
Atrahasis, 262
attachment *(raga)*, 605, 607
Attic, 351–352
Attis, 591
austerity, 182–184, 229, 232–233, 257–258, 268, 278, 279, 286, 439–440, 443, 558, 587, 635*n*34. *See also tapas*
  rejection of, 279, 280
Australoid, Proto, 285, 286, 297*n*265
autarkeia (self-rule), 439, 443, 444, 600, 623, 625
Avataṃsaka. See Hua Yen
avatarism, 130–131
Āyurveda, 15

ba, 127–128, 132–133
Babylonia, 3, 5, 7, 11, 14, 16, 21*n*49, 25, 31, 45, 80, 87, 282, 283
  sacred number of, 75, 76, 78, 87, 96*n*66
Bactria, 4, 6, 8, 11, 14, 21*n*68, 258, 632
  Greek, 350, 354, 358–364, 366, 370–372, 373, 376–379, 388, 398*n*114, 399n136, 500
Bādarāyana, 566*n*15
barbarian, 351, 352, 356, 364, 376, 391, 512, xxii
Battle of Ten Kings, 659
Beauty, 185, 188, 208
becoming, 460–461, 530
Being. *See also* Brahman; Infinite; Sameness and Difference
  absolute, pure, 58, 59, 60, 123, 162, 170, 301, 333, 427, 433, 525, 529, 541, 555, 566*n*20, 575, 590
  experience and, 53, 164
  middle position, (being/non-being) and, 456–458, 459, 467, 469, 580
  non-Being and, 53–54, 57, 58, 59, 69, 158, 160, 163, 164, 174*n*13, 307, 312, 314, 315–316, 318, 339, 407–408, 415, 420, 421, 426–427, 431, 434, 436, 456, 464, 530, 531, 553, 555, 569, 574, 580–581, 585–586
  not non-Being and, 316, 427, 530
  One beyond, 164
  Real, 179, 184, 185, 189
  regression/emanation to, 561, 563, 569, 571, 575
  soul and, 163
  stars and, 172
  three levels of, 572
  trisvabhāva (three modes of), 568, 571–573, 582*n*5
  Unity and, 159
Berossus, 76
Bhāgavad Gita, 58, 257, 542–543
Bhāgavati Sūtra, 58, 267, 277
Bhartrihari, 673–674, 675, 676
Bhāskara, 551, 553, 554, 557
Bhattacarya, 586, 593*n*5
bhāvanga (subconscious life-continuum), 606–607
Bhavaviveka, 421–422, 446*n*7
bhedābheda (difference/nondifference), 557, 559, 568, 580
bios, 178
Black Athena, 666–667
Black Sea, 443, 449n70, 658
bliss, 562, 615
bodhisattva, 168–169, 275, 388, 440, 442, 579
body
  mind and dualism with, 128–129, 197–198, 200–201, 205*n*8
  not as self, 639*n*110
  soul and, 107, 110–111, 562, 564, 603, 622, 639*nn*110–111
Book of Dead, The, 129–130, 132–134, 135–137, 153*n*171, 153*nn*162–167, 154*n*175, 154*n*192, 154*nn*188–189, 155*n*194, 155*nn*197–199, 525, 563, 591
Brahmā Sūtra, 551–552, 554, 555, 556, 557–559, 563, 566*n*15, 646
Brahmajāla Sutta, 410
brahman, xxvii
  absolute, 555, 557
  ātman (self), 558–560, 563–564
  becoming *vs.* "already is," 558–560
  as beginning and ending, 34
  language as, 673
  as neuter, 30, 32
  nirguṇa and saguṇa, 51, 542, 556*n*20, 586
  nondual knowledge of, 558–561
  prāṇa and, 543, 545

reincarnation, freedom and knowledge of, 100–101, 138, 559–560, 567*n*29
Supreme, 559
as unity underlying all things, 30, 164, 555, 556, 559–561, 601
women and, 591
Brāhmaṇas, 42, 113–114, 230, 407
brahmātman, 558–560, 563–564
Brahmins, 166–167, 225, 258, 492, 494
activities of, 391
aśramas of, 279
caste system and, 297*n*246
culturalization of, 279–280
mokṣa (liberation), caste system and, 133
priest, 42
ritual practice and, 42–43, 114
Vratyas and, 274
brahmodya, 408–409
Branchidae, 354, 359, 360
breath, 34–35, 46, 138, 541, 629, 640*n*112. *See also pneuma; prāṇa*
Brihaspati, 334, 409
British. *See also* West
colonialism, xxii–xxiii, xxiv, 648
questioning India's dominance by, xix
Bronze Age, 1, 11, 24, 25, 26, 28, 46, 49, 56, 60, 72, 76, 81, 84, 88, 91, 101, 128, 130, 140, 216, 225, 237–239, 246, 251, 259, 267, 268, 269, 275, 276, 284, 286, 306, 321, 386, 635*n*34, 642, 664, 672
cosmology of, 301
mythology of, 28, 281, 314, 326, 327, 651, 668
rituals of, 587
synthesis of philosophy/mathematics in, 281, 646
trade route of, 238*m*, 239–240
brotherhood, 45, 104, 105, 110, 620–621. *See also* Pythagorean thought; sect
cult of, 118, 119, 151*n*131, 210, 225–226, 229, 231, 234*n*12, 265, 271–272, 275, 284, 321, 500, 598, 619–620, 673
secrecy in, 80, 91, 158, 178
Buddha, 38, 89, 140, 406, 443, 479–480. *See also* Siddhārtha
atheism of, 337, 341
background of, 265–266, 297*n*246, 551, 619–620, 675
birth of, 391
dating of, xxvi, 426
deification of, 620
dialogues of, 412–414
extrasensory perception of, 341–344, 348*n*65
eye, 482–483
impermanence, transcending duality and, 479–480
pragmatism, 339
questions not answered and, 339
as rationalist/empiricist, 339–340
rejection of magic by, 267, 280
self knowledge essential for, 38, 338, 343, 551
suffering, happiness and, 615
teaching language of, 675–676
Buddha Maitreya, 387–388
Buddhism, 139, 141, 178, 230, 321, 488*n*56, 492. *See also* emptiness; Mādhyamika; tantra; Vijñānavāda Buddhism
abhidharma of, 167, 168, 355, 374–375, 378, 390, 414–415, 572, 583*n*25, 609, 611, 614, 617, 627, 636*n*55, 640*n*125, 641*n*137
Aryan culturalization and, 280, 297*n*246
Aśoka, Mauryas and, 360–361, 367–370, 373, 397*n*96, 500, 631
atomism of, 324*n*28
bodhisattva, 168–169, 275, 388, 440, 442, 579
body and, 639*n*110
causality, ethics, imperturbability and, 603–604
Chinese, 572, 573–574, 577, 578, 580, 582*n*8, 597
consciousness' levels in, 572–573
conversion/missionary of, 360–361, 366, 368–370, 372–376, 378, 382, 389, 392, 631
crypto, 470, 549
denial of self/soul in, 128, 129, 152*n*145, 589, 636*n*55
detachment/enlightenment for, 439, 441, 456, 469, 478, 613
dharma, Ideas, and, 166–167, 175*n*30, 206*n*17
double truth of, 474–475, 494
elements and, 303–304
emptiness of emptiness in, 469, 470–471
ethics, imperturbability and, 534, 595–596, 602–611, 612, 625–626, 614, 615–616
Four Noble Truths of, 332, 481, 509*n*64, 625–626
fullness-emptiness, 38, 406, 431
Gandhāran, 372–376, 378, 379, 390
Greeks and, 372–379, 382–383, 392, 448n49, 500–501, 503–504
hedonism and, 619–621
Hīnayāna, 486*n*12, 620
humanism and, 337, 344
iconography of, 249–250, 259
Ideas, order and, 206*n*17
impermanence of, 332, 338–339, 340, 453
Indo-Greeks, Menander and, 374–379, 382, 383
knowledge theory, imperturbability and, 604
Mādhyamika (Middle Way), 168, 170, 406, 409, 412, 416, 420, 421–444, 453, 454–484, 486*n*10, 486*n*12, 492, 494, 497, 499–505, 520, 588, 602, 676
Mahāyāna, 168–169, 179, 215, 228, 315, 372, 374, 387, 388, 390, 439, 486*n*10, 502, 503–504, 572, 573, 575, 576–579, 580, 585, 596
medicine and, 596–597
mental process interruption and early, 606–608, 609–611, 617–618, 627
between middle and negation, 456–458
middle position, being/non-being and, 456–458, 459, 467, 469, 473, 488*n*63, 616
mometariness of, 336
naturalism of, 337–344, 347*n*38, 602–608
naturalistic ethics of early, 603, 604–605
Nikāyas, 409–410, 411, 519, 604, 612, 613, 614
nirodha (mental activity cessation) in, 590
nirvāṇa of, 168, 169, 192, 266, 344–345, 442, 459, 475, 477–484, 504, 608
noble silence of, 405, 426, 431, 439
openness to foreigners by, 360–361
perception of senses for, 338, 343–344
perpetual flux of, 320
Platonic monism parallel to, 165, 166, 167–168
Plotinus and three levels of, 572–573
psychology, imperturbability and, 415, 605–606, 614, 623, 641*n*137
ranking of, 277
reincarnation for, 341, 348*n*51
rejection of austerity/rituals/Veda in, 280, 327, 519, 619, 675
skepticism and, 411–413, 503
suffering and, 332, 338, 339, 615
syllogism of, 513
Theravāda, 478, 483, 596, 632

three-level ontology
(*trisvabhāva*) of, 568, 571–573, 582*n*5
Tibetan, 504–505, 509*n*64, 586, 588, 589, 592, 593*n*7, 676
truths of, 332, 474–475, 481, 494, 509*n*64, 625–626
Vijñānavāda (consciousness-only school) of, 568, 571–572, 572–573, 582*n*5
yoga and, 582*n*5
Yogācāra, 602, 676
bull, 265, 271, 273
iconography, 251, 252, 256
Byzantine, 103

calendar, Indian, 385
Candragupta, 357, 360, 362, 366–367, 371
Candrakīrti, 421–422, 434, 453, 459, 461, 469, 470, 477, 479, 484, 499, 503, 504, 528, 530
cannibalism, 231
Carneades, 454, 485*n*10, 498, 503, 630
Carthaginians, 351
Cārvākas, 409
(materialist) atomism, 320, 334, 337, 344, 345, 613–614, 653, 675
naturalistic ethics, imperturbability and, 602–603, 611
Vedas denied by, 327–328
caste, 133, 238, 297*n*246, 352, 500, 586
Hindu and Plato's system of, xxi, 166–167
catastrophe, the, 4–5
categories
combine to become facts, 523, 526, 527, 528
linguistic-metaphysical nature of, 522–523, 538*n*23
listings of, 511, 521
catuṣkoṭi (negations), 495
causality, 530, 532–534, 539*nn*50–51
absolute determinism of, 602
dharma and, 603, 697
dialectic against, 459–463, 468
naturalistic doctrine of, 603–604, 613, 622
celibacy, 99–100, 182, 185, 186, 201, 269, 276, 391, 619
ceremony, *See* ritual practice
cakras, 209–210, 211, 212, 215, 222*n*16, 270
Chaldean astronomy, 171–172, 176*n*47, 407
Chaldean Oracles, 588, 591
Ch'an, 441, 450, 468, 476, 478
Chattopadhyaya, 586
ch'i, 214
Chi Tsang, 597
China, 214, 242, 301, 350, 358, 360, 371, 376, 389, 644
Buddhism, 572–574, 577, 578, 580, 582*n*8, 597, 676
China. *See also* Tibet
Chi-tsang, 467
Christianity, 69, 76–77, 341, 541, 549, 566*n*28, 589, 620, 621
mind/body dualism in, 128–129
Plotinus and, 550
polemicists of, 391
spirituality/ethics in, 595, 621, 631, 646
Chrysippus, 497, 540, 542, 545, 621, 622, 623, 626, 628, 629, 640*n*112, 640*n*125, 674
Cicero, 454, 485*n*9, 622, 628, 630
city
abandonment of development of, 243–244, 257
development of, 238, 241–245, 246, 281, 285, 379
Greek (*poleis*) development of (conquered), 354–355, 356, 359, 360–364, 366, 385, 395*n*52
structure of (*polis*), 361, 363, 386
urban state of, 261, 262, 360–363
waning of (*polis*), 512
civilization
Western *vs.* Eastern progress for, 644–647
civilization, first
date of writing and, 246
India as birthplace of, xvii, xxv, 658–660
Indus-Mesopotamia trade and, 238–242, 246
Near East and Indus Valley, 237–238
new developments of cities/writing in, 242–245
Sumero-Dravians and, 245–246
Cleanthes, 543, 545, 623
clothing, 274
cognition, 189, 192, 328–329, 439, 441, 606
colonialism, xviii
British, xxii–xxiii
education of non-Westerns by, xxii
Greek, 364–366, xx, xxi, xxii, xxiii–xxiv
Mesopotamian, 238, 242
Mesopotamians/Sumerians ideas and, 238, 242
supremacy of Europeans in, xviii, xxii, xxv, xxxi*n*16, 644, 647
two types of, xxii–xxiv
colors, 48
comparison. *See* philosophy, comparison of Greek and Indian
condensation/rarefaction, 34, 40, 306–307, 314, 327
Confession, Negative, 133–134
Conger, George P., xxvii–xxviii
conjunctions, 531–532
consciousness (*vijñāna*), 320, 580
as basis, 570
as being/universe, 570–571, 577
bhāvanga (subconscious life-continuum), 606–607
Buddhist schools of, 568, 571–572
course of cognition and, 606, 636*n*57
denial of, 328, 331, 334
determining, 606
as epiphenomenon of matter, 613–614
higher, 188, 192, 473, 477–479
individual *vs.* higher unity, 557–558
layers/levels of, 89, 562–563, 568, 572–573, 598
moment-to-moment, 482–483
moral, 607, 636*n*61
pneuma/prāṇa as, 544, 546
senses and, 605–606, 636*n*55
storehouse (*ālayavijñāna, pariniṣpanna*), 572–574, 576
wakefulness of, 571
contemplation, 569, 570–571, 581, 588, 591
contradiction, 452, 453, 496
law of, 37, 53, 54, 403, 404, 408, 427, 435, 436, 475–476, 489*n*70
conventions, essences *vs.*, 451, 452
cosmic cycle, 142, 282, 567*n*29, 642
acoustical account of, 81–88, 95*n*64
astronomical account of, 77–79
background of, 67–68
different "Ages" of, 68–69, 71–72, 78, 166
exact repetition of, 72
general parallelism of Indian/Greek thought in, 68–70, 90–91
Great Year of, 70–72, 73–74, 75, 78
Greek, 71–74
Indian, 70–72, 73
Jain, 71
linear view of time, 70
Love/Hate, 68–69, 71, 315, 318, 569
numerology and, 70, 76–77, 83–84, 87, 88–90
reincarnation and, 92, 117
rejection of, 314
reservations on parallelism of Indian/Greek thought in, 90–91
round shape of, 91–92
Sumerian (arithmetic) influence on, 74–77, 90–91
unwritten evidence for, 79–81
Cosmic Person, 158

dance of, 555
Egypt and, 24–25; 59
Greece and, 27–28, 46
India and, 26–27, 555
Jain, 284
macranthropy and, 25–28, 32, 46, 112, 164, 258, 285, 543, 546, 555
Mesopotamia and, 25–26
Pythagorean, 46–47, 545
unlimited *(apeirōn)*, 31–32
Vratyas and, 275
cosmogony, 23, 59, 81, 319, 331
water and, 29–30, 74
cosmology, 81, 569
Heraclitean, 41, 44
Indian, 29–30, 70, 88, 302–303, 463–464, 541–542
monism, theism and, 542
Stoic, 540–541, 567*n*29
cosmopolis, 352, 356
Crates, 439, 440, 443, 475, 540, 621, 640*n*117
Cratylus, 430–431
cremation, 277
Ctesius, 349
cult. *See* brotherhood
culture
Greek impact on Indian, 358–360, 395*n*52, 395*nn*54–55
Greek-Asian colonial, 363–366
nature *vs.*, 351
currency
Greek, 360, 371, 379, 381, 396*n*76
Roman, 513
Cynics, 183, 236*n*60, 261, 294*n*196, 346, 352, 356, 493, 540, 541. *See also* Ājīvikas; Pāśupata
animal imitations of, 230–232
austerities of, 232–233, 439–440, 443
canon lacking, 441–442
dialectic and, 420, 431, 437–444, 475, 477
Diogenian, 17
ethics, imperturbability and, 599, 600, 623–625, 640*n*117
goal of, 439, 452
Jains and, 443
Mādhyamika (Middle Way) and, 437–444
practices of, 440–443, 613, 620, 624
Seeking of Dishonor and, 229
shamanism and, 449*n*70
Zen and, 441–443
Cyrus, 6, 7, 11, 14, 15, 16, 125, 349

daimon, 163, 169, 181, 183
dakṣiṇā, 42
Darius, 6, 7–8, 9–10, 11–12, 14, 15, 16, 124, 125
darśana, 178
Death, Holy, 201
debates, 409
decad, 160–161
deduction, 511
Demetrius, 371, 378
Demiurge, 161, 164, 260, 575
Democedes, 16, 18, 204, 210, 211–213
democracy, 363, xxii
Democritus, 73, 212, 333, 349, 382, 444, 492, 520, 621
atomism, pluralism and, 311, 315, 316–317, 318, 319, 320, 331, 334, 429, 443, 513, 599, 611
conventions *vs.* essences for, 451, 452
dialectic and, 415, 420, 428, 432
ethics, impermanence and, 332
ethics, medicine, imperturbability and, 596, 597, 598–599, 601, 611, 613, 634*n*18
fourfold negation and, 496–497
materialism *(physiologoi)* and, 326, 603
non-difference of, 451, 452, 493–494
Plato's censoring of, 491–492, 494
demonstration, 471
deporation, Persian/Assyrian, 8
Descartes, 180–181
desire, 208, 332, 604, 606, 608, 610, 626. *See also orexis*
control of, 600, 628–629
freedom from, 481, 482, 598, 599
reincarnation and, 100–102, 108–109, 118
destruction, 70, 74, 81, 463–464, 531
detachment, 184, 332, 439–440, 442; 482–483. *See also apatheia* (noninvolvement), senses, withdrawal from
determinism, 278, 296*n*242, 326, 327–328, 334, 436, 602–603, 611
devas, 257, 276
devotion, 587
dhammas, 415
dhāraṇā, 180, 272
dharma, 337, 467, 504
causality and, 603, 607, 616
Ideas and, 167–168, 175*n*30
mirror of, 338
release from, 471, 478
three marks of, 168
Wheel of, 486*n*12, 503
Dharma Śāstra, 163
dharmadhātu (infinite interpenetration), 576–579
Dharmaraksita, 369–370, 374–375, 378
dhyāna, 180
dialectic, 186, 189, 311, 313, 337, 613, 674. *See also* identity, partial
absolutist, 421, 428, 433, 437, 479
ancient logicians *vs.*, 403
anti-linguistic aspect of, 420
breakdown of tribal beliefs by, 405
against causality, 459–463, 468, 498
cleansing of soul by, 199
Cynics and, 420, 431, 437–444
deconstructivist, 403, 428, 455
development of, 646–647, 649–650, 653
Eleatics, Mādhyamikas and, 422–428, 447*nn*25–26
Eleatics, Plato and, 423, 435, 438
empiricism and, 500
equanimity and, 420–421
fifth-century, 430–431
fire, wood and, 462–463, 498
formal, 405, 500, 503
fourfold negation and, 495–497
illusion's imagery and, 498–499
Indian proto, 406–414, 421, 428, 499–505, 501, 645–646, 649
job of, 422
language and, 674–675
logic and, 421–422, 476, 477
Lokāyatika/Lokāyata, 406, 410
Mādhyamika (Buddhist), 406, 409, 412, 420, 421–444, 451–452, 459–466, 468, 469–477, 478–479, 482–484, 494, 497, 499–505, 520
mathematical, 426, 427
meaning/structure of, 403–404, 417*nn*1–2
Megarian, 434–436, 437
motives of, 420–421
mystical intuition/ transcendence after, 420, 421, 445*n*7
Nāgārjuna, Greeks, Aenesidemus and, 499–505
Nāgārjuna and, 406, 409, 412, 415, 416, 419–420, 423, 428, 430, 431, 434, 436–437, 445*n*6, 446*n*7, 458, 494, 499–505, 643
negative, 437, 438, 441, 495–497
Nyāya Sūtras and, 406, 408–414
Parmenides and, 407–408, 415–416, 420, 421–423, 431, 432, 438, 460, 461, 464, 499–500, 653
phenomenalist, 421, 429, 437
Plato and, 416, 432–434
pre-Alexander Greek, 414–415

Pyrrhonic/Skeptic, 451–452, 459–466, 468, 469–477, 482–484
Pyrrhon's teachers and, 493–495
reductio ad absurdum in, 420, 423, 427, 446*n*17, 459, 515
sophistic movement, Indian skepticism and, 428–430
on three levels, 458
total, 416
transformational, 482
as uroboric/self-destroying path, 451–452, 469–473
Zeno and, 416, 417n2, 426, 427, 429, 430, 431, 447*nn*25–26, 461, 649, 653
dichotomy-and-dilemma structure in, 404, 406, 408, 409, 413–414, 415, 416, 422–424, 427, 430, 431, 433, 434, 437, 459, 493, 653
Diffusionist theory, xx
Dighanakha Sutta, 413, 429, 431, 438
Dignāga, 510, 515
dilemma, 414, 416
Diodorus, 436
Diodotus, 370
Diogenes, 17, 230–233, 236*n*60, 356, 438, 439, 441, 443, 444, 448*n*49, 450, 491, 625, 633, 640*n*117, 669
Diogenes Laertius, 450, 454, 456, 468, 483, 492, 493, 620, 626, 651
Dioscuri, 3
Dionysus, 118, 120, 126, 130, 133, 148*n*77, 212, 367, 390, 669
disjunctions, 532
discourse, 477
disposition. *See hexis*
devas, 257
divine telekinesis, 50
Dodds, E.R., xvi–xvii
Dogmatism, 479
dokein/doxa (illusion), 54–55, 134, 169–170, 300, 316, 521
dokos, 50–51, 52, 54–55
dompteur, 281
doxa (belief), 617
drama
India, Greece, post/Alexandrian/Roman period and, 386–388, 401*n*199
Dravidian(s), 19*n*4, 112, 115, 126, 141, 258, 277, 286, 297*n*265, 660
Sumero, 245–246, 257, 283
dravya, 178
dreaming, with gods, 266–267
drugs, 262, 263, 271, 286, 295*n*31, 367
dualism, 37, 52, 55, 56. *See also* Advaita Vedānta
absolute unity beyond, 560, 561, 574
gate, 57
Jain, 197–198, 205*n*8
mind/body, 128–129, 197–198, 205*n*8
non-dualism and, 552–554, 556–558, 592, 601
Orphico-Pythagoraean, 128, 162
Plato and, 158, 197–198, 326
reincarnation and, 122–123
soul, body, matter, 562, 564, 603
transcending of, 479–480
Zorastrian and Sāṃkhya, xxviii, 122, 171
duḥkha (suffering), 168
dyad, 161–162

eagle, 262, 263
iconography of, 216, 247, 262, 269–270
earth, 301, 303
Edenic age, 72
education
colonialism and non-Western, xxii
Greek (paideia), xxii, xxiii, xxiv, 351, 355, 359, 361, 363–364, 651
higher, 354–355, 394*n*28
rejection of, 603, 613
Egypt, 80, 86, 87, 246, 672. *See Also The Book of Dead*
afterlife and, 115, 116–117, 131–138
Black Athena and, 666–667
the *Book of Dead* and, 129–130
cosmic person in, 24–25, 31
diffusionist theory of, xx
first civilization and, 238, 242
Greeks and, 5, 282
iconography, India and, 251, 258–260, 269–270, 271
India trade routes with, 350, 383–384
kuṇḍalinī and, 213–214, 269–271, 298*n*267
mythology of, 257, 259, 302, 668
"one and many problem in, 24, 46, 301
pharaoh, avatarism and, 130–131
reincarnation and, 126–142, 152*n*148, 156*n*209, 260
shamans/priests for, 264, 268–274, 284
soul, body and, 116, 128–130
theurgy of, 591
yoga and, 268–274, 285, 298*n*267
ekstasis, 584n38
Elean-Eretian school, 437, 477
Eleatics, 45, 49, 58, 64*n*48, 68, 80, 105, 110, 157, 311, 312, 316, 331, 524
Being, non-Being and, 530
dialectic, Mādhyamikas and, 422–428, 446*n*17, 461, 463, 650
dialectic, Plato and, 423, 435, 438
monism of, 49, 52, 307, 315
sophists and, 428–429
elements, 38, 40, 123, 124, 142, 157. *See also* illusion
air, 34–35, 46, 301, 302, 306, 331, 541, 545
ākāśa/aither, 301, 304, 305, 306, 308, 525, 541
Chinese, 301
earth, 301, 303, 313–314, 525
as the Few, 68, 301
fifth, 301, 307–308, 525
fire, 38, 40–43, 63*n*35, 77, 90, 121, 136, 301, 304–305, 306, 313–314, 462, 520, 525, 541, 545
four, 301, 305, 306, 307, 326, 337, 345, 524–525
Greek doctrine of, 305–309, 311, 314
Indian doctrine of, 301–305, 308–309
materialism and, 301, 306
opposites and, 306
relationship of, 303–304, 307, 313, 320, 324*n*28, 327
seven, 304
six, 520, 614
of soul, 202
three, 318
transcendence/disappearance of, 345
two fire doctrine of, 304–305
water, 29–30, 301, 302, 303, 313–314, 327, 331, 407, 525
elenchus (test), 432, 433, 439, 476, 493, 520, 524
elephant iconography, 256
emanations, 585–586. *See also* regression
emotions, 600, 608, 609, 623, 628–629, 636*n*50, 606, 635*n*40. *See also pathos; saṃskāras; vedanā*
Empedocles, 18, 67, 163, 179, 193, 526, 669
atomism, pluralism and, 314, 315, 316
cosmic cycle of, 68, 73, 162, 314
death of, 107, 201–202
elements and, 305–307, 308, 311, 313, 520, 524–525
medicine and, 596, 597
naturalism and, 330–331
One and Many problem and, 45, 58, 157, 307, 312
Orphism, reincarnation and, 106–107, 127, 132–133, 563
physiology of, 212

reincarnation and, 68, 99, 102, 104, 106–107, 109, 111, 113, 135, 139, 140, 145*n*32, 178, 201–202
as shaman, 15, 67–68, 107
empiricism, 326, 331–333, 339–340, 638*n*82
of Buddha, 339–341
dialectic and, 500
inductive, 512–513, 516
radical, 338
for science, 330, 333
verification process of, 340–341, 612
emptiness, 38, 406, 431, 434, 441, 466–467, 469–471, 472, 483, 493, 509*n*64, 538*n*44, 643
energy. *See Śakti*
engkephalos (cerebral-spinal fluid), 212–213
Enkidu, 669
enlightenment, 378, 439
Buddhism, detachment and, 439, 441, 456, 469, 478, 613
embyro of, 169
fertility heroes and, 275
full, 277, 502
Hindu, 547
middle position for, 456–457
mind and, 169, 343, 478
in the moment in, 442, 482
non-ego for, 547
prāṇa and, 544–545
premeations of, 575–576, 585, 586
shortcut/direct path to, 441–442, 443
stages for, 14–15, 267
Stoics and, 546–547
Epictetus, 621, 625, 626, 629, 630, 631, 640*n*110
Epicureanism, 602
atomism of, 520, 618, 622, 639*n*111
causality for, 613
ethics, imperturbability and, 596, 597–598, 599, 600, 601, 609, 611–618, 631, 632
hedonism, missionary qualities and, 619–621
knowledge theory for, 612–613
lifestyle of, 602
mental process reformation in, 617–619
naturalistic ethics of, 614–617
naturalistic psychology for, 613–614
syllogism of, 441, 451, 511–516, 520
"the Four Medicines" of, 618
therapy of, 618–619, 641*n*137
Epicurus, 320, 333, 334, 338, 501, 513, 600, 601, 609, 611, 619, 622, 623, 629, 633
Epiphanius, 46
epistemology
ontology, Plotinus and, 569–571, 572–573
epochē (suspension), 454, 456, 457, 471, 473, 479, 481, 483, 484, 630
equanimity, 420–421
Eratosthenes, 356, 357
eros, 208, 257, 376
error, 162
eschatology, 111, 112, 123, 146*n*41
essence(s), 455, 467
conventions *vs.*, 451, 452
unchanging, 459–460
essentialism/eternalism, 475
Etana, 262–263
ethics. *See also* Platonic ethics
Buddhist, 534, 595–596, 602–608
Cynic, 439–440
Democritus, impermanence and, 332
equanimity and, 420–421
forms of, 595
Jainism and, 201, 534, 595
mystical experience as path above, 587
Orphism and, 201
Stoic, 542–543
Vaśeṣika, 534
ethics, imperturbability of
Ājīvikas, Carvakas and naturalist approach to, 601–602
Aristotle, Hellenistic ethics and, 600–601, 609–611
Democritus and, 332, 598–599, 601
diffuse of Greek and Buddhist ideas for, 631–633
early Buddhist interrupting mental process and, 606–608, 609–611, 617–618, 627
early Buddhist naturalistic approach to, 595–596, 602, 604–605, 614, 615–619, 625–626
early Buddhist naturalistic doctrine of causality and, 603–604
early Buddhist naturalistic psychology and, 605–606, 614, 623, 641*n*137
early Buddhist naturalistic theory of knowledge and, 604
early Greek, 595, 597–598, 601, 609
Epicurean hedonism and, 619–621
Epicurean naturalistic approach to, 614–617
Epicurean naturalistic doctrine of causality and, 613
Epicurean naturalistic psychology and, 613–614
Epicurean naturalistic theory of knowledge and, 612–613
Epicurean reforming mental process and, 617–619
Indian transcendental approach to, 601–602
medical philosophy of, 596–597
naturalistic approach to, 596–601, 602–619
Plato and, 599–600, 601, 608–609
Stoic interrupting mental process and, 626–630, 640*n*125
Stoic later history and, 631
Stoic naturalistic approach to, 623–626
Stoic naturalistic doctrine of causality and, 622
Stoic naturalistic psychology and, 622–623
Stoic naturalistic theory of knowledge for, 622
transcendental approach to, 595–596, 599–600, 601–602, 608
Eubuleides, 435, 475, 501
Eucleides, 434–435
Eudemus, 358, 426, 580
Eudoxus, 171–172, 212, 382
eunuch, 359
Euripides, 99, 119, 203, 275, 386–387
Europe. *See West*
Euthydemids, 370–372, 376–378, 387, 398*n*114, 399*n*136
Euthydemus, 416, 429, 435
evanishment, 560–561, 566*n*28
Excluded Middle, Law of, 403, 404, 407, 412, 415, 419, 421, 430, 436, 437, 455, 460, 461, 463, 469, 489*n*70
rejection of, 458, 464, 470, 472–473, 474, 476
exhalation, 41–42
experience (perception) *See also* empiricism
to action, 605
to (Aristotle/Greek) action, 608–611
to (Buddhist) action, 605–608
to (Epicurean) action, 614
to (Stoic) action, 622–623
Being and, 53, 59
beyond, 603
categorization of, 606–607, 636*n*57
cut off from mind by philosophy, 458
error, interpretation and, 612
knowledge from, 330, 340, 450, 471, 602, 612
phenomenally real, 455, 474, 494
poiema, mind and, 581
extrasensory perception, 328, 341–344, 348*n*65. *See also* siddhis

Fa Hsiang, 574
Fa Tsang, 578, 580
facts, 523, 526, 527, 538
fasting, 269, 278
fate, of love, 542, 543
fertility, 229, 273, 275, 276, 280, 285, 286, 669
finite, infinite *vs.*, 314–315, 576, 580
fire, 38, 40–43, 63*n*35, 77, 90, 121, 136, 301, 302, 304–305, 306, 545. *See also* Agni; elements
  Heraclitus and, 38, 40, 42–43, 121, 306, 307, 541, 545
  Path of Gods and, 42–43
  serpent and, 270
  smoke and, 498, 511, 513–515
  two paths of, 304–305
  and universal destruction, 70, 74
  wood, smoke, causality and, 462–463, 498, 511
five, 301
Five Fires, Doctrine of, 35, 40–41, 44, 115, 121, 304, 308
flood, 283
flying, 263–264
form, 530
four, 88, 301, 305, 306, 307
free will, 140, 278, 296n242, 322, 326, 327, 331, 436, 567*n29*, 606, 611, 640*n*114
funeral process, 277, 295*n*236

game, pure intellectual, 188
Gandhāra bias, xxi, xxiv, xxv
Gandhāran(s), 60, 66*n*68
  art, 374, 388–390, 401*n*207
  Buddhism, 372–376, 378–379, 390, 502
Ganges Valley, 113, 146*n*50, 405, 660, 662*n*20, 669
Genesis, Book of, 76–77, 257, 270, 313
genus, 527–528, 544
geometry, 23–24, 28
Gilgamesh, 262, 264, 271, 272, 274, 281, 669
Gnosticism, xxvii, 587
God. *See also* monism
  mind of, 575
  nameless/transcendent value of, 25, 259, 313, 458
  nonphysical, 534
  Stoic, 541–542
god(s), 259, 260, 263, 264, 265, 272, 273, 294*n*208, 301, 302, 305–306. *See also* *pantheos*; Osiris; *specific gods*
  active/inactive, 166, 175*n*23
  all things of full of, 327
  creation of language by, 673
  denial of, 329, 333, 334, 341, 344
  as devas/asuras, 257
  dreaming as communication with, 266–267
  Egyptian, 130–135, 668
  female, 591
  forgetful, 577
  Giants (materialists) *vs.* (noumenalists), 325, 415–416, 420, 428
  Greek, 591, 669
  knowing, 591
  as lower levels, 165
  path of, 42–43, 274
  realms of, 586
  sex, 669
  soul, reincarnation and, 105–108, 136–137
  soul, sun (heaven) and, 128–129, 131–132, 157
  (liberated) soul as, 563
  soul as exited, 155*n*204, 163, 183, 201–202
  war of, 133
  world, 164
goddess, 55–57, 257, 258, 275
gold plates, 105–107, 136, 137, 145*n*28
Golden Age, 68, 71, 108
Golden Lion, 578
Golden Thigh, 668–670
Good, 189, 434, 447*n*36
Gorgias (of Leontini), 416, 420, 426–430, 434, 438, 458, 460, 501, 564
  rejection of, 521
Gosāla, 138–139, 140, 141, 225, 227–228, 230, 231, 232, 277–278, 295*n*238, 406
  determinism and, 278, 296*n*242, 334
  reincarnation and, 278, 296*n*242
  as shaman, 266, 267, 278–279
Gotama, 406, 511, 514, 515, 516
grammar
  categories and, 522, 538*n*23
  philosophy and, 672–676
  Stoics and, 674
Great Secret, 652, 653
Great Wheel, 91
Great Year, 70–72, 73–74, 75, 78
Greece
  afterlife and, 135–136, 138, 154*n*186
  art of diffused through Persian empire, 9–10
  colonialism of, xxiii–xxiv
  currency of, 360, 371, 379, 381, 396*n*76
  Cynics of, 229–233
  education (paideia) of, xxii, xxiii, xxiv, 351, 355, 359, 361, 363–364
  India's colonization by, xx, xxi, xxii
  kuṇḍalinī and, 210–213
  Magian (Persian) hypothesis and, 121–122, 123, 124–126, 149*n*92, 149*n*95
  mysticism of, 171
  non-racism of, xxiii, xxiv
  Orphism, reincarnation and, 104–111
  parthenogenesis of, xxvii, 260
  Persia, reincarnation and, 121–122
  Persian wars with, 349, 351, 355–356
  reincarnation appearance in, 102–104, 111, 117–118, 148*n*71
  reincarnation doctrine in, 45, 98–103, 103–111, 128–129, 132–135, 138, 140–142
  shamans and, 268
  shared Attic (koinē), 351–352, 515, 586
  as West's guiding light, xx
Greece, post/Alexandrian, post/Socratic period, 353*m*, 405. *See also* Hellenization; philosophers; philosophy, comparison of Greek and Indian; Yavanas; yoga
  aftermath of Alexander's conquests of, xxiii–xxiv, 357–358
  Alexander's expedition/conquest to India and, 352–355, 379
  Alexander's motives/effects of conquests of, 352–355
  architecture of, 361–362
  art, India and, 388–390, 401*n207*
  Aśoka, Buddhism, Mauryas and, 360–361, 367–370, 373, 382, 397*n*96
  astronomy, India and, 384–386, 502, 513
  Bactrian Greek (Euthydemids) Indian conquests and, 370–372, 399*n*136
  barbarians and, 351, 352, 356, 364, 391, 512, xxii
  Buddhism, Greeks and, 372–379, 382–383, 392, 448n49, 500–501, 503–504
  city/state *(poleis)* development of conquered lands and, 354–355, 356, 359, 360–364, 366, 395*n*52
  colonial culture in Asia of, 363–366
  cosmopolitan tendencies of, 350–352, 355
  dialectic and, 432–444
  drama/literature, India and, 386–388, 401*n*199
  ethics, imperturbability, and, 599–601
  Greek books in Indian language in, 350
  Greek's settlement/culture/philosophy, influence on India by, 95*n*52, 358–360, 395*nn*54–55, 500–505, 514–516, 520, 536, 580–581, 592, 631–632, 642–643

Indian influence on, 443–444, 491–492, 494, 495, 499, 502–505, 540, 549–551, 565*n*12, 580–581, 592, 632–633, 641–642
Indian knowledge in, 390–392
Indo-Greeks, Menander and, 376–379, 502–503
inscriptions of, 350–360, 362, 363, 368, 397*n*100
merchants of, 350, 351
sea trade for, 379–383, 383*m*
trade routes of, 350, 352, 360, 393*n*8, 443–444, 449*n*68
Wars of Successors and, 358, 367
Greece, pre-Socratic period
acoustics, cosmic cycle and, 81–83, 84–88
Anaximenes, Indian monism and, 33–35
astronomy (Mesopotamian) in, 11–12, 13–14, 21*n*68
atomism and, 315–317, 318, 327, 331–333, 344–345
Black Athena, Egypt and, 666–667
chronological consideration of, 59–61
cosmic cycle, astronomy and, 77–79
cosmic cycle, unwritten evidence and, 79–82
cosmic cycle parallelism with Indian thought and, 68–74, 90–91
cosmic person and, 27–28
Dark Age and, 5, 17, 23
development of, 59, 61, 321
dialectic and, 415–416, 422–431
Egyptian influence on, 282
elements of, 305–309
ethics, imperturbability, and, 597–599
Greek, Indian language influence in Persian empire in, 12–13
Heraclitean monism, Indian thought and, 36–44
Indian before Greek atomism and, 318, 320–321
Indian intermixing/influence with, 10, 11–12, 13–14, 21*n*68, 122, 443–444, 491–492, 642
medical profession diffusion in, 15–16, 17, 18
Mesopotamian influence on, 282
name-and-form (idea-complex) and, 57–59*n*
Near-East influence on, 3–5, 282
numerology, cosmic cycle and, 88–90
orientalizing period of, 5–6
Parmenidean monism, Indian thought and, 52–55
Persian empire influence on, 6–7, 10, 349
philosophical Goddess and, 55–57
pluralism, atomism and, 315–317, 320–321
Pythagorean monism, Indian thought and, 44–48
seers/yogis' wandering in, 10, 16–18
sexagesimal arithmetic, cosmic cycle and, 74–75, 77–79, 87, 88, 89, 90
workers imported and deported and, 8–9
Xenophanean monism, Indian thought and, 48–52
Greek (language)
commonness of, 365
Indian language influenced by, 365–366, 395*n*55
Sanskrit and, xviii, xx, xxii, xxx*n*13, 381, 387, 502
Gudea, 266, 271
Gudea Vase, Cylinders, 90, 219, 244, 270
gunas, 167, 178, 182, 186
Gupta, 164, 676
art, 390
guru
direct teaching of, 158, 171, 442–443, 450, 471, 551
reincarnation freedom with, 551
Guthrie, W.K.C., xvi–xvii, xxviii

habit (belief) system, 600, 604, 610–611. *See also hexis*
Hades, 305
Hall of Double Truth and Right, 133–135, 137
Hall of Mirrors, 578
happiness, 412, 415, 452
as absence of pain, 614, 632
detachment for, 602
knowledge and, 338, 599, 600, 601, 613
natural/unnatural, 615, 625, 638*n*93, 638*n*98
of tranquillity, 615–616
as virtue, 444
Harappans, 238, 241, 242, 243, 246, 258, 281, 405, 662*n*20, 663
Hate, Age of, 68, 71, 202, 315, 318
Heart Sūtra, 453, 478, 481
heaven, 116, 117, 148*n*71, 199, 202, 328
Heavenly Twins, 3
hedonism, 328. *See also vedanā*
consequences of Epicurean, 619–621
imperturbability, perception, feelings and, 605, 608, 610, 615, 616, 627
utilitarian, 332, 338, 339
Hegel, Georg Wilhelm Friedrich, 56, 505, 644, 650, xxi, xxv, xxvii
hēgemonikon (soul of Zeus), 546, 547
Heliocles, 372
hell, 116, 117, 148*n*71, 199, 328
Hellenization
aftermath of Alexander and, 358
Alexander's expeditions/conquests into India and, 352–354
Aristotelian schools of, 600–601
city/state *(poleis)* development of, 354–355, 356, 359, 360–364, 366, 395*n*52
ethics of, 600–601
homonoia (common mind) of, 352, 355–356, 357
language and, 675
process of, 351–352, 363–366, 500–501, 642
hepatoscopy, 17
Heracles, 230, 273, 294*n*196
Heraclitus, 18, 107, 178, 203, 210, 306, 330, 430–431, 448*n*49, 467, 496, 531, 541, 554, 575
background of, 36, 44, 170, 619
bright and dark exhalations of, 43–44
change (flux) of things and, 36–37, 40, 158–159, 160, 162, 320
cosmic cycle and, 73
ethics, medicine, imperturbability and, 598, 602
fire and, 38, 40, 42–43, 121, 306, 307, 541, 545
Laws of Thought, rejection by, 37, 54
monism, Indian thought and, 36–44
Orphism, reincarnation and, 110–111, 121, 127
Platonic monism and, 158–159, 168, 531
Upaniṣads and, 38–44
Hermes, 591
Hermetic Books, 587
Hermotimus, 102
Herodotus, 16, 203, 268, 282, 283, 305, 333, 350, 359, 390
reincarnation and, 118–119, 126–129, 130, 135, 138–139, 155*n*205, 156*n*209
Heroes, Age of, 72
Hesiod, 57, 60, 69, 72, 106, 212, 213, 237, 305
Orphism, reincarnation and, 108–110, 113
Hestia, 56–57
hexis (disposition/habit), 600, 604, 606, 610–611, 617–619, 623, 627, 628, 629, 630, 641*n*137
Hīnayānism, 486*n*12, 620

Hinduism, 258, 503, 646, 676
blossoming of, 676
castes, Plato and, xxi, 166–167
cosmology, Stoics and, 541
enlightenment of, 547
philosophy mixed with, 177, 478, 650
Platonic monism to, 164–167
prāna of, 544, 546
Puranic, 163–164
Pythagoreanism and, 165
reincarnation synthesis with, 115–117
serpent iconography in, 259
spiritual advancement for, 558
tantra of, 586
unchanging ground of, 320
Vedāntic tendencies of, 164, 336–337, 555, 676
Hippasus, 46
Hippocratics, 330, 634*n*18
Hiraṇyagarbha, 164, 302
history
Indian exclusion from history of philosophy and, 650–652
modernist, 646–648, xxi
post-modernist, 648–649
pre-modernist, 644–646, 648
Homer, 60–61, 212–213, 237, 326, 386–387, 452
homonoia (common mind), 352, 355–356, 357
hormē (culminating impulse), 617, 623, 626, 628
Horus, 668
Hsuan Tsang, 580
Hua Yen (Avatamsaka), 573, 574, 577, 578–579, 580, 585
Hui Hai, 478, 482
humanism
Buddhist, 337, 344
Greek secular, 325–327
naturalism and, 325
Hydra seal, 270–271, 294*n*196
hypothesis, 432–434

Iamblichus, 552, 585–586, 588, 591
iconography, 224*n*55, 225, 232
Akkadian, 247, 250
Aryan community and, 257–258
Buddhist, 249–250, 259
bull, 251, 252, 256
eagle, 216, 247, 262, 269–270
Egypt, India and, 251, 258–260, 269–270, 271
elephant, 256
heraldic flanking in, 247, 249–250
Hydra seal, 270–271, 294*n*196
Indus, 241–242, 247, 250, 252–256, 258, 271
Jain, 250
lion/tiger, 249, 251, 255
Mesopotamian, 242, 246, 249, 250, 251, 252–253, 255, 256, 259, 281, 285, 286, 291*n*113
Near East, Indus influence on, 246–60
Near East influence on Greek, 6, 14
Pārśva, 271–272, 278
Persian, 255
priest-king and other figures of, 250–256
serpent, 216–217, 219, 224*nn*55–56, 247, 259, 268–270, 272–273, 274, 275, 285, 294*n*206
Sumerian, 216–218, 242, 247, 250, 251–252, 253, 254, 256, 258, 260, 281, 291*n*106, 294*n*200, 294*n*206
tree, 247, 251, 270, 271, 291*n*104
yogic, 252–253, 254
Idea(s), 494
of Beauty, 185, 188, 208
contained in soul, 165–166
dharma and, 167–168, 175*n*30
forms/levels of, 161–162
of Good, 189, 434, 447*n*36
mind and (unchanging), 195*n*30, 554, 561, 563, 568, 575, 576–577, 578
naturalism and, 325, 591
One and, 168
Theory of, 68, 160, 161, 167–168, 174*n*13, 175*n*30, 195*n*30, 432, 433, 576, 581
idea-complex, 57–59
idealism, 520
Aryan, 229, 276–277, 286, 302–303
Buddhist, 572
Greek, 602, 650
mentalist, 569, 571
radical, 582*n*5
transcendental, 330
Vedic, 602
identity
law of, 37, 54, 403, 417*n*1, 430, 460
(denial of) partial, 420–430, 434–435, 437
ignorance, 453, 498, 554, 557, 572–573, 574, 585
Iliad, xxv, 305
illusion, 50–51, 54–55, 56, 134, 142, 167, 169–170, 257, 300, 316, 318, 439–440, 442, 467, 469, 474, 521, 552–553, 554, 555, 558, 574. *See also dokein/doxa*; *māyāvada*; *parikalpita; typhos*
imagery (ropes/snakes) of, 498–499, 576
mind, soul and, 575, 586, 587
source of, 572–573, 575
transparency and, 579
images, 498–499, 514, 569, 578–579, 668–669
rope, snake, 498–499
immanentalism, 122, 552–553
immortality, 208, 223*n*53, 262, 263, 271
imperialism, xx, 238
race and, xviii–xix
impermanence, 332, 338–339, 340, 431, 451, 452, 453, 480, 604, 607, 630
imperturbability, 420, 432, 453, 454, 456, 457, 479, 483, 493. *See also ataraxia*
Ājīvika, Carvaka naturalist approach to ethics and, 601–602
Aristotle, Hellenistic ethics and, 600–601, 609–611
Democritus and, 598–599
diffusing of Greek and Buddhist ethics and, 631–633
early Buddhist naturalistic approach to ethics and, 595–596, 604–605, 612, 614, 615–619, 635–626
early Buddhist naturalistic doctrine of causality, ethics and, 603–604
early Buddhist naturalistic psychology, ethics and, 605–606, 614, 623, 641*n*137
early Buddhist naturalistic theory of knowledge, ethics and, 604
early Buddhist's interrupting mental process, ethics and, 606–608, 609–611, 617–618, 627
early Greek, 595, 597–598, 601, 609
Epicurean hedonism consequences and, 619–621
Epicurean naturalistic approach to ethics and, 614–617
Epicurean naturalistic doctrine of causality and, 613
Epicurean naturalistic psychology and, 613–614
Epicurean naturalistic theory of knowledge and, 612–613
Epicurean's reforming mental process and, 617–619
Indian transcendental approach to, 601–602
medical philosophy of, 596–597
Nāgārjuna, nirvāna and, 478–479, 482–484
naturalistic approach to, 596–601, 602–619, 622–626, 631
Plato, Socrates and, 599–600, 601, 608–609
Skepticism, nirvāṇa and, 478–484
Stoic later history and, 631

Stoic naturalistic approach to ethics and, 623–626
Stoic naturalistic doctrine of causality and, 622
Stoic naturalistic psychology and, 622–623
Stoic naturalistic theory of knowledge for, 622
Stoic's interrupting mental process and, 626–630, 640*n*125
transcendental approach to, 595–596, 599–600, 601–602, 608
impulse, 627, 628–630, 640*n*125
See hormē
incarnation(s), 118
soul and, 165, xvi
Indefinite Dyad, 161, 188
indeterminacy *(aoristia)*, 335–337, 458, 471, 486
India
as birthplace of civilization, xvii, xxv, 658–660
commonness of Greece and, xxi
dating of history/philosophy of, xxvi
Greek influence on art in, xxi, xxiv, xxv, 9, 274, 365, 371
iconography, Egypt and, 251, 258–260, 269–270, 271
Mesopotamian influence on, 215–219
nationalism of, xxviii
nonviolence and, 99–100
Roman trade with, 381–383
as source of West, 658–660
India, post/Alexandrian, post/Socratic period. *See also* philosophers; philosophy, comparison of Greek and Indian; yoga
aftermath of Alexander's conquests of, 357–358
Alexander's expedition/conquest of India and, 352–355, 362, 379, 381, 443–444, 450, 491, 495, 501, 520
art, Greece and, 388–390, 401*n*207
Aśoka, Buddhism, Mauryas and, 360–361, 367–370, 373, 397*n*96
astronomy, Greece and, 384–386, 502, 513
Bactrian Greek (Euthydemids) conquest of, 370–372, 399*n*136
Buddhism, Greeks and, 372–376
city/state *(poleis)* development of (conquered), 354–355, 356, 359, 360–364, 366, 395*n*52
dialectic and, 432–444, 491–505
drama/literature, Greece and, 386–388, 401*n*199
Greek and Roman knowledge of, 390–392
Greek books in Indian language in, 350
Greek colonial culture in, xx, xxi, xxii, 364–366
Greek influence of language in, 365–366
Greek's settlement/culture/philosophy influence on, 358–360, 395*n*52, 395*nn*54–55, 500–505, 514–515, 516, 520, 536, 580–581, 592, 632–634, 642–643
Indian influence on Greeks in, 443–444, 491–492, 494, 495, 499, 502–505, 540, 549–551, 565*n*12, 580–581, 592, 632–633
Indian skepticism, sophism, dialectic and, 428–430
Indo-Greeks, Menander and, 376–379
lack of dialectic text from, 501
Plotinus and, 549–551
sea trade for, 379–384, 383*m*
trade routes of, 350, 350*n*8, 352, 443–444, 449*n*68, 501
India, pre-Alexandrian, pre-Socratic period. *See also* Aryans; Brahman; Indus Valley; philosophy, comparison of Greek and Indian
acoustics, cosmic cycle and, 83–84, 86, 88, 95*n*64
Anaximander, Indian monism, infinite/brahman and, 30–33, 35
Anaximenes, Indian monism and, 33–35
atomism, pluralism and, 317–321, 324*n*28, 344–345
Being, non-Being and, 53–54, 57, 58
chronological consideration of, 59–61, 657
cosmic cycle, astronomy and, 78
cosmic cycle parallelism with Greece and, 68–72, 73–74, 90–91
cosmic person in, 26–27, 284, 285
creation and, 29–30
development of, 321, 649, 654
dialectic before logic in, 406
(proto) dialectic of, 406–414, 416, 421–428, 430–431
elements doctrine of, 301–305, 308–309
Greece/Persia influence by yogi of, 8, 10
Greek, Indian language influence in Persian empire in, 12–13
Greek descriptions of, 349–350
Greek influence of language in, xviii, xx, xxii, xxx*n*13, 395*n*55
Greeks influenced by, 443–444, 505
Greeks intermixing in, 13–14, 21*n*68, 122, 443–444, 505
Heraclitean monism, Indian thought and, 36–44
iconography, 241–242, 247, 250, 252–256, 258, 271
iconography, Near East, and, 246–256, 269–270, 271
Indian before Greek atomism and, 318, 320–321
lack of writing history in antiquity by, 7
medical profession diffusion in, 15–16, 17, 19
meetings of Greeks and, 10, 11–12, 122
Mesopotamian influence on, 3–5, 238–242, 245–246, 281–288, 298*n*267
monism and, 30–35, 61
name-and-form (nāmarūpa) and, 57–59
Near-East influence of, 3–5, 281–288, 298*n*267
numerology, cosmic cycle and, 88–90
Parmenidean monism, Indian thought and, 52–55
Persian empire influence/trade on, 6–8, 10–11, 258, 283
philosophical Goddess and, 56–57
priest-king, other iconographic figures and, 250–256
Pythagorean monism, Indian thought and, 48
religious orthodoxy evolution slow in, 59, 61
seers' wandering of, 10, 16–18, 22*n*95
sexagesimal arithmetic, cosmic cycle and, 75–79, 88, 90
shamans and, 263, 265–280
Sumeria affected by, 657
Sumerian influence on, 238, 240–242, 246, 281–288
Sumero-Dravidian from, 245–246, 257, 283
Thales, Indian thought and, 28–30
workers/soldiers in Persian empire in, 9, 10
Xenophanean monism, Indian thought and, 48–52
Indian thought. *See also* philosophy, comparison of Greek and Indian; yoga
afterlife and, 135, 137–138, 154*n*186
as artificial construct, xxxii*n*55
China, Taoism and, 214

cosmology of, 29–30, 70, 88, 302–303, 463–464, 541–542
Europe uncomfortable with, 582*n*3
exclusion from history of philosophy for, 644–647, 650–652
history of philosophy participant by, 652–654
kuṇḍalinī, 209–216, 219
Magian (Persian) hypothesis and, 121–122, 123, 124–126, 149*n*92, 149*n*95
Pāśupatas, Ājīvikism and, 225–229
Persia, reincarnation and, 121–122
Platonic monism and, 163–171
prāna and, 34–35, 209, 214, 301, 543–545
pre-modernism to post-modernism in, 647–649
reincarnation doctrine of in, 98–103, 112–117, 128–129, 132–142, 146*n*50, 148*n*71
Stoics and, 540–547
Upanisadic-Vedāntic tradition, Neoplatonism and, 549–564
indifference, 599, 601, 624, 635*n*34, 640*n*112. *See also* *adiaphora*
individual. *See* self
Indo-European languages, 658
noun/verb separation in, 3
Sanskrit and, xix, 372
Indo-Europeans, 185, 289
dating of, 1, 3, 657, 661*n*10
kuṇḍalinī and, 213, 214
migration, not conquest, by, 663–664
Near-East influence on, 3–5
Indo-Greeks, 360, 370–372, 374, 375–376, 386, 395*n*52, 406, 500–501
indology, colonial, xxiv–xxvi
Indo-Scythians, 374–375
Indra, 259, 263
induction, 511, 512, 513, 516
Indus Valley, 352, 372, 586, 659–660. *See also* Veda
city development (indigenous) in, 238, 241–243, 246, 257, 285
collapse of, 289*n*71
iconography, 241–242, 247, 250, 252–256, 258, 271
Indian merchants influence on Mesopotamian trade with, 240
Indus-Saraswati civilization and, 243
Mesopotamian influence/trade with, 238–242, 245–246, 281–288, 298*n*267
Mesopotamians/Sumerians colonizing/ideas for, 238, 242
Middle Vedic culture, Mesopotamia and, 283–284
no Sumerian merchants living in, 240
Proto-Australoid peoples and, 285, 286, 297*n*265
shamans, asceticism, and culturalization in, 275–276, 279–280
Sumeria affected by, 657
Sumerian influence on, 238, 240–242, 246, 281–288
Sumero-Dravidians from, 245–246, 257, 283
writing from, 242, 243–244, 246, 247
Industrial Revolution, 646
Infinite
Anaxagoras, 311–314, 576
Anaximander, 31–33, 35
finite (matter) as divisible by, 312, 313, 319–320
finite *vs.*, 314–315, 576, 580
interpenetration, 576–579
in number, 312
as pair of opposites, 31
Plotinus, totality and, 566*n*28, 576–579
infinite regress . *See also regressus ad infinitum*
intellect, 534–535, 559, 561, 586
primal intellection and, 560–561
interlocutor, 422, 426, 435, 475, 477
Ionians, 36, 45, 48, 52, 73, 125, 325, 329, 362, 395*n*55
Iran, 350, 366, 372
Iris, 668
Iron Age, 61, 72, 110, 141, 142, 275, 642, 662*n*20
logic, philosophy making in, 281, 301, 560
irrationalism. *See* rationalism
Ishtar, 669
Islam, 69, 341, 541, 589, 595
Īśvara, 164
Īśvara praṇidhāna (endurance/devotion), 542, 543

Jahnu, 669
Jainism, 71, 89, 100, 103, 107, 126, 139, 141, 142, 178, 205*n*8, 227, 312, 355. *See also* Ājīvikas; Mahāvīra
ascetic communities of, 225, 278, 334, 342, 549
atomism of, 198–199, 203, 317–320, 519–520, 525, 527, 653
austerities of, 232, 257, 278, 443, 602
clothing and, 274
contradictions of, 203
Cosmic Person in, 284
Cynics and, 443
Digambara, 228
dreaming power in, 266–267
elements and, 304, 305
ethics of, 201, 534, 595, 602
gods denied by, 334
heavens/hells of, 199
iconography of, 250
imperturbability, ethics and, 595, 602
indeterminacy (*anekāntavāda*) of, 335–337
Jambudvipa and, 202–203
karmic dirt of soul and, 198–200, 203, 639*n*111
logic of, 495–496
mind cleansed in, 478
naturalism of, 334–337
Ningizzida and, 271–273
as non-Vedic, 327, 519
nonviolence of, 100, 201, 229, 232, 268, 269, 278, 280, 595
Orphism and, 157, 163, 165, 183, 308, 319, 535, 576, 581
Orphism influenced by (missionary), 197, 199, 204, 233, 272, 298*n*267, 642
Plato and, 197–204
reincarnation and, 201–202, 260, 278, 296*n*242, 344
relativism and, 334–335, 337, 405, 411, 413
schism with Ājīvikas, 277–278, 296*n*242
in-a-sense doctrine (*syādvāda*) of, 335–337
serpent and, 272
shaman/powers of, 266, 267, 269, 271–273, 277, 295*n*237, 342
skepticism and, 411
soul/mind/body dualism of, 197–198
soul's release/escape for, 200–201, 327
suicide in, 278–279
Jayatilleke, 337, 342
jiva (little self), 345, 547
jivanmukta, 102
Judaism, 69, 76–77, 259, 541, 587, 595, 666
Jung, Carl, 59

Kabbalah, 587
Kala, 260
Kālāma Sutta, 339, 340, 616
Kālī, 56
kalpa, 69, 74, 166, 250
Kalpa Sutta, 342–343
Kalupahana, 613, 614
Kaṇāda, 519, 521–524, 526, 646
Kārikā, 459
karma, vii, 122, 171, 178, 227, 328, 341, 348*n*51. *See also* actions
black magic and, 228, 230
consequences of, 614, 616
devotion and, 587
efficacy (denied) for, 327, 328

forcing of, 232
good, 114, 115, 147*n*67
magic, dreams and, 267
matter (dirt) of, 198–200, 203, 308, 639*n*111
new, 605, 607
path of, 587
purification for, 268, 269, 534
reincarnation and, 113–114, 115, 147*n*64, 342, 558, 562–563, 567*n*29, 614
release from, 558, 563, 567*n*29, 602
rituals and, 113–114, 147*n*64
Seeking of Dishonor and, 228
senses and, 267
stages of, 103
tantric freedom from, 592
transferring of, 228
yoga and, 542–543
katharsis, 99
kevala, 272
Kharoṣṭhī script, 372–376, 390
Khyber Pass, 350, 354, 360, 372
king(s)
purification of, 265
ritual sacrifices for, 262
sacred, 263, 264–266, 267
shamans for, 262–263
King Midas, 669
knowledge, 433, 572
absolute (beyond), 574
from convention, 199
divine *vs.* human, 598
from (sense) experience, 330, 340, 450, 471, 602, 612
freedom from, 100–101, 115–116
happiness and, 338, 599, 600, 601, 613
higher, 601
intellectual *vs.* practical, 192–193
mystical (Platonic), 187–189
nondual *(brahman)*, 558–561, 587
opinion *vs.*, 159
path to (attaining) *(jñāna)*, 169–170, 587
as seeing, 191–192, 330
self, 184–193, 199, 338, 343, 383, 450, 471, 475, 551, 558–560, 570, 601
soul and, 187, 190–191
spirituality, philosophy and East/West, 177–178
of true nature, 199
unhypothesized, 439
koinē, 351–352, 515, 586
Krishna, 263, 543
krita, 39
kṣatriya, 42, 114, 115, 142, 166–167, 265, 279, 297*n*246
kuṇḍalinī. *See also nāḍīs, cakras*
Africa and, 220
awakening of, 270
Egypt and, 213–214, 269–271, 285, 298*n*267
from India to Greece, 211–213, 285, 298*n*267
Indian history and, 209–210, 213–216, 219, 298*n*267
Mesopotamian influence on, 215–219, 285–286, 298*n*267
Near East influence on, 213, 298*n*267
Ningizzida, yoga and, 269–271, 285, 298*n*267
occult vascular system and, 209, 215, 217, 259, 298*n*267
Plato's parallel to, 208–209, 210–212
proto-Indo-European influence on, 213, 214
semen, body fluids and, 124, 208–209, 210, 212, 215, 222*nn*28–29
serpent power and, 209, 213, 216–217, 219, 222*n*31, 224*nn*55–56, 258, 270–271, 285
Taoist parallel to, 214–215
yoga, 209–210, 214, 259, 260, 269–273, 285–286
kurtash, 8
Kushans, 374–375, 379, 381, 386
kusula. See action

Lakulīśa, 225–226, 228, 230, 233
language(s), 643, 663). *See also* linguistics
Akkadian, 4, 11, 26, 29, 61
Aramaic, 13, 373, 374
birth of, 57
Buddha's teaching in local, 675–676
common dialect *(koinē)* for Greek (Attic), 351–352, 515, 586
Eleatic/Mādhyamika critique of, 428, 430
Gandhāri, 372–374
gods creation of, 673
Greek and Sanskrit, xviii, xx, xxii, xxx*n*13, 381, 399*n*137, 502, 508*n*43, 595, 652
Greek influence on Indian, 365–366, 395*n*55
Indo-European, xix, 3, 372, 658
Iranian, 366, 659
metaphysical view of, 673
negation, criticism of, 477, 494
Pali, 342, 372, 376, 399*n*137
Persia influenced by Greek and Indian, 12–13
Prākrit dialect, 164, 372
realism and isomorphism, 493–494, 522
Rg Veda and, 672, 673
Sanskrit, xix, xviii, 387, 401*n*199, 439, 453, 458, 649, 652, 659, 672–676
Sumerian, 245
Laṅkāvatāra Sūtra, 572–573, 574, 625
Laws of Thought. *See also* Contradiction, Law of; Excluded Middle, Law of;
Identity, Law of, 37, 53, 54, 403–404, 417*n*1, 430
rejection of, 54, 475–477
Leucippus
atomism of, 311, 315–316, 317, 318, 320, 321, 331
Being, non-Being and, 316
ideas, language and, 494
liberation, 563. *See also mokṣa*
linguistics, 629
descriptive, xix
dialectic and, 420
gender in, 32
grammar, categories and, 522, 538*n*23, 672–676
hierarchization of, xix–xxii
reification in, 57–58, 438, 494, 522, 523, 532
semantic realism and, 512
suffering and, 478
lion/tiger iconography, 249, 251, 255
literature
India, Greece, post/Alexandrian/Roman period and, 386–388
Tamil, 502, 508*n*43, 631
logic, 446*n*17, 489n70. *See also* reason; Laws of Thought; syllogism
Aristotelian, 408, 422, 435–436, 496, 510, 513, 519–536, 653
dialectic and, 421–422, 476, 477
Eubuleides' (Megarian), 435–436
formal Indian, 414–415
Jain, 495–496
mathematical, 437
meaning/structure of, 403–404, 417*n*2
in philosophy, 46–47, 54, 68, 190, 282
propositional, 436, 437
Stoic, 435, 496, 512, 513, 514
logos, 596, 628, 674
Lokāyata ("This Worldly") atomism, 276, 320
Lokāyatika, 276, 320, 406, 409, 410, 412, 429
love, 184, 439, 444, 564
brotherly, 620–621
cosmic cycle of hate/strife and, 68–69, 71, 315, 318, 569
devotion, 542, 543
of fate, 542, 543
Love, Age of, 68, 71, 73, 315, 318
Lucretius, 320, 333, 334, 345, 620
luminaries, 41, 57
lunacy, 226–227, 230, 261
lyre, 67, 86, xvi

Macedonians, 354, 356, 357, 366, 394n24
Macranthropus, 24, 27, 34, 60, 543, 546. *See also* cosmic person
macranthropy, 25–28, 32, 46, 49, 164, 258, 285
Madhva, 549
Madhya-loka, 202
Mādhyamika (Middle Way), 168, 170, 602, 676. *See also* emptiness
  background of, 419–420
  Cynics and, 437–444
  definition of, 455
  dialectic and, 406, 409, 412, 416, 420, 421–444, 451–452, 459–466, 468, 469–477, 478–480, 482–484, 494, 497, 499–505, 520, 588
  dialectic, Eleatic and, 422–428
  double truth of, 474–475
  Elean-Eretrians and, 437
  enlightenment for, 478
  goal of, 456–459, 478
  imperturbability in, 493
  language and, 428
  Law of Excluded Middle and, 455, 460, 461, 463, 489*n*70
  Laws of Thought breached by, 475–477
  Megarians and, 434–437
  middle position, being/non-being and, 456–458, 459, 467, 469, 473, 488*n*63, 580
  negation (fourfold) in, 441, 452, 453, 495, 497
  nirvāna of, 168, 169, 192, 266, 344–345, 442, 459, 475, 477–484
  Nyāya-Vaśeṣika *vs.*, 514–515
  Plato and, 431–434
  Prasangika (dialectic) *vs.* Svātantrika (syllogistic) schools of, 421–422
  Pyrrhonism/Skepticism and, 453, 454–484, 486*n*10, 486*n*12, 492, 498–499
  regressus ad infinitum in, 466
  relational existence, Pyrrhonism and, 466–469
  Sophists, Indian skepticism and, 428–430
  uroboric/self-destroying path and, 469–473
Magdalenian period, 284
magic, 588
  Buddha's rejection of, 267, 280, 337
  dreams, karma and, 267
  karmic black, 228, 230
  naturalism and, 325, 341
  religion, theurgy and, 586, 587, 591
  sexual, 229
  shaman, powers and, 103, 231, 263–264, 267, 279–280, 285
Mahābhārata, 225, 263, 266, 274, 279, 409
  Greeks and, 387, xxv
Mahākammavibhaṅga Sutta, 342
Mahāmatras, 17
Mahāmudra, 478
Mahāparinibbana Sūtra, 168
Mahāvamsa, 369–370
Mahāvīra, 100, 103, 138, 139, 141, 204, 227, 230, 250, 267, 269, 271–272, 274, 277–280, 283, 297*n*246, 336, 406, 411
  free will and, 140, 278, 296n242
  omniscience of, 342–343, 344
Mahāyāna, 168–169, 179, 215, 228, 315, 372, 374, 387, 388, 390, 439, 486*n*10, 502, 503–04, 585, 643
  The Awakening of Mahāyāna Faith and, 572, 573, 575, 577, 581
  dharmadhātu (infinite interpenetration) in, 576–579
  ethics, imperturbability and, 596
Māluṅkyaputta Sutta, 339
manas (mind), 523, 534
maṇḍalas, 588–589, 591, 592
Manu, 71, 72, 75, 79, 99, 260, 269, 283
Marcus Aurelius, 621, 631
marriage alliance, 367, 370
massacre, 354, 356, 357
Master Argument, 436–437
materialism, 301, 306, 311, 319, 325, 415–416, 420, 428, 653, 676. *See also* naturalism
  atomism in, 327
  Milesian, 327
  secular, 325
  Stoic, 631
mathematics, 6, 46, 158, 162, 281, 282–283, 429, 432, 433, 566*n*28, 638*n*98
  dialectic and, 426, 427, 613
  logic and, 437
  metaphysics of, 160–161, 162, 190, 575
  numerology and, 46–47, 157, 160
  sexagesimal, 74–79, 82, 84, 87, 88, 90–91, 140
  worship of numbers and, 46–47, 171, 175*n*42
  "zero" for, 656*n*18
matriarchal society, 276, 669
matter, 524–525, 570, 589
  mind separate from, 313–314, 315, 321–322
  Prime, 31, 46
  soul, mind and, 562, 564, 566, 571
mauna, 179, 269
Mauryan empire, 353, 360–361, 371, 405, 502, 659, 662*n*20. *See also* Aśoka Maurya
  founding of, 357–358, 366–367
  Greek marriage alliance with, 367
  possible Greek conquest of, 370–372, 376
māyāvāda (illusion), 50–51, 54–55, 56, 134, 169–170, 257, 300, 316, 552–553, 555, 558, 573
Medes, 11, 124, 125, 151*n*125
medicine, 209, 619
  Empirical, 451, 513–514
  Indian, 15, 222*n*28
  of longevity/immortality, 223*n*53
  philosophy and, 596–597
  pre-Alexandrian period of, 15–16, 17, 18, 211–212, 545, 596–597
  Sicilian, 211–212
  Skeptic, 209, 470, 479
meditation. *See also* contemplation; *pratyāhāra; samādhi*
  Neoplatonism, Upaniṣadic-Vedāntic traditions and, 547, 555, 558
  Neoplatonism, Vijñānavāda Buddhism and, 583*n*25, 584*n*38, 588–589
  Neoplatonism and tantric, 588–590, 593*n*17
  in yoga, 180–182, 285, 341–342, 590
Megarian school, 434–436, 437, 438, 471, 477, 493, 494, 496, 497, 501, 512
memorization, 618
memory, 136–138, 154*n*193, 163, 183, 184, 206*n*18
  soul and, 105–107, 145*n*32, 563–564, 577, 581, 586
Menander, 376–379, 387, 439, 502–503
Menedemus, 437
mental picture. *See phantasia*
mentalist-idealist, 569, 571
mercenaries
  Greek, 5, 8, 10, 13, 21*n*68, 349, 358, 360
  Indian, 10, 11
Mesopotamia, 4–5, 17, 86, 87, 154*n*193, 156*n*209. *See also* Sumerians
  astronomy of, 23–24, 28, 31, 32, 47–48, 52, 53, 70, 77–79, 88
  city development in, 238, 241–245, 261, 281
  colonizing of Indus Valley by, 238, 242
  cosmic cycle and, 70, 77–79, 87–91, 88, 286
  cosmic person in, 25–26, 39

development of social system/philosophy for, 281
Greek influence on, 363–364
Greeks influenced by, 4–5, 282
iconography of, 242, 246, 249, 250, 251, 252–253, 255, 256, 259, 281, 286, 291*n*113
ideas of civilization for Indus Valley from, 238
Indus merchants influence on, 240
Indus Valley trade with, 238–242, 246, 664, 665*n*16
kuṇḍalinī and, 215–219, 257, 285–286, 298*n*267
mythology of, 257, 262, 264, 272, 281, 286, 294n208
no Mesopotamian merchants living in Indus from, 240
numerology and, 87–90, 140, 157
priests of, 281, 284
scorpion and, 242
shamans and, 262–268, 270–271, 294*n*190
state mechanism of, 261, 262
Sumerian arrival in, 245–246, 283
water of life/death of, 136, 154*n*193
writing of, 246
metaphysics, 311, 522, 529, 554, 576
absolutism in, 335, 337, 416
deductive thinking and, 512
idealist, 582*n*5
language and, 673
of mathematics, 160–161, 162, 190, 575
negative (dialectic) thinking and, 415–416, 421, 432
real, 532, 535
Vaśeṣika, 534, 535, 536
metempsychōsis, 127, 145*n*20, 148*n*79
Middle Way. *See also* Mādhyamika
Milesians, 35, 36, 306, 307, 326–327, 328, 331, 598
Miletus, 10, 23, 28, 30, 35, 36, 49, 59–60, 121, 354, 360
Milindapañha, 390
Mill, John Stuart, 511
mind. *See also nous*; *paratantra*
beyond, 561
cessation of activity of, 559, 561, 590
cleansed, 478
cloudiness *(moha)* of, 607–608
creation of world through, 570, 572
cut off from experience by philosophy, 458
as dependent being, 572–573
dualism of body and, 128–129, 197–198, 200–201, 205*n*8
enlightenment and, 169, 343, 478
First, 581
as goal, 579–580, 584*n*38
Higher Soul and, 569, 570, 582*n*1, 585
Idea and, 195*n*30, 554, 561, 563, 568, 575, 576–577, 578
Ideal, 174*n*13
illusion and, 575, 586
as interpenetrated subject/object, 568, 569, 570
Lower Soul and, 573, 585
as *manas*, 523, 534, 562
as material, 523
matter separate from, 313–314, 315, 321–322
mental process interruption, imperturbability, and, 606–611, 626–630, 640*n*125
mental process reformation, imperturbability and, 617–619
as middle realm, 574–575, 579
mindfulness of, 607–608, 609, 618, 629, 637*n*63, 641*n*137
moral consciousness and, 607, 636*n*61
One and, 579, 580, 584*n*38, 585–586
providential, 542
Second, 581
self-knowing, 559, 568, 570, 574
senses and, 427–428, 468, 559, 561
as sixth sense, 614
soul/self and, 534, 555, 566*n*20, 570, 572–573
speech, suffering and, 478
super, 542
three qualities of, 167, 186, 562
as transcendent deity, 315
transformation doctrine for, 555
unchanging nature of, 195*n*30
unity-in-multiplicity of, 568, 570
universal, 163, 541, 554, 560–561, 563–564, 568, 571, 575, 577, 579–580, 581
upper and lower, 568
withdrawal from senses by, 179–180, 478, 599
minimalism, xxvi
Mithraism, 149*n*95, 151*n*131
modernism
history and, xxi, 646–647
pre-modernism, post-modernism and, 647–649
modus tollens, 404, 410, 423, 459
mokṣa (liberation), 115–116, 133, 178, 328, 341, 567*n*29
moment, living for, 442, 472, 477, 481–483, 566*n*28
monism, 24, 27, 300. *See also* Platonic monism
abandonment of, 157
asceticism and, 269
change/process and, 36–37, 40, 158–159
Cosmic Person in, 158
cultic/number/math in, 46, 48
development of, 649, 654
Eleatic, 49, 52, 307, 315
Heraclitean, 36–44
Indian, 28–35, 325, 581
Indian (Upaniṣadic), 30–33, 37, 649, 654
macranthropic, 25–28, 158, 285
material, 28–29, 30, 34, 52, 60, 61, 65*n*54
mathematical, 158
Mesopotamian, 285
Milesian, 35, 36, 307
monotheism *vs.*, 64*n*48
neuter concept of, 30, 32
Parmenidean, 52–55, 321
Pythagorean, 44–48
reincarnation and, 122–123
Stoic, 540, 542
subjectivist, 49–51
substrate, 28–29, 30, 31, 46, 51, 158, 162, 578, 581
transcendental, 52, 158
unqualified, 585
Xenophanean, 48–52, 53, 61, 65*n*54
Zoroastrianism and, 122–123, 124
motion/rest, 425–426, 436–437, 463, 464–465, 466
Mount Meru, 202
mūlabandhāsana, 274, 280, 297*n*265
multiplicity, 570, 579
Muni, 257, 263, 264, 277, 279
music. *See* acoustics
Music of the Spheres, 47, 81, 86, 87, 308, 429
Musonius Rufus, 621
mysticism, 300, 341. *See also* shamans
critical analysis *vs.*, 649–650
dialectic and, 420, 421, 445*n*7
direct experience of, 177, 551, 590
kuṇḍalinī and, 209–211
occult for, 587–588
as path, not ethics, 587
mythology
Bronze Age, 28, 281, 301, 325, 327, 651, 668
Egyptian, 257, 259, 302, 668
of fertility, 669
formations of, 29, 31, 32
Mesopotamian, 257, 262, 264, 272, 294*n*208
naturalism *vs.*, 325–326, 329, 331
one myth for three (Greek/Egyptian/Indian) cultures in, 135–138
Orphic, 131–135, 157, 197

Proto-Australoid peoples and, 285, 286, 297*n*265, 302–303
Sumero-Akkadian, 284
unity, 321
Vedic, 257, 259, 263, 302

nādis, 209, 211–212, 215, 219, 270
Nāgārjuna, 383. *See also* emptiness; Mādhyamika (Middle Way)
analogy/imagery of illusion (ropes/snakes) for, 498–499, 514
dating/background of, 455, 486*n*14, 499, 503
dialectic and, 406, 409, 412, 415, 416, 419–420, 423, 428, 430, 431, 434, 436–437, 445*n*6, 446*n*7, 458, 494, 499–505, 643
dialectic of causality for, 459–463, 468, 498
double truth of, 474–475
fourfold negations of, 495
Greeks, Aenesidemus and, 499–505
infinite divisibility, not continuum of, 423–424, 464
laws of thought breached by, 475, 477
negations of, 441, 452, 453, 495, 643
nirvāṇa, imperturbability and, 478–479, 482–484
Pyrrhonism and, 435, 453
refutations of, 455, 456, 475
regressus ad infinitum and, 466
relational existence and, 466–469
Sextus Empiricus's parallelism to, 455, 459, 461–488
substance-attribute relationship and, 436–437
uroboric/self-destroying path and, 469–473, 488*n*63
world unchanging and, 464–465
Nāgasena, 377–378
Naiyāyika, 406, 408, 498, 507*n*20, 510, 650
analogy in syllogism of, 513–515
Epicurean parallels to, syllogism of 512–513
five-limbs of, syllogism of, 511, 515–516
structure of syllogism of, 510–511, 536
Nakamura, 566*n*15, 643, 672
nakedness, 257, 273–274, 277, 279, 492, 549, 550, 603
name-and-form (nāmarūpa), 58
nāstika sect, 327–328
Nataputta, 419
nationalism, 356
nation/state
tribal transition to, 405
urban aspect of, 261, 262, 360–363
naturalism. *See also* materialism; phenomenalism
Ājīvikas, 602–603
appearance *vs.* Being, 332–333
Buddhist, 337–344
Cārvāka, 602–603
characteristics of, 325
Democritean lineage of, 325–334
empiricism/observation for, 330–331, 335
Greek, 325–327, 328–334, 344–345, 595–599, 600–601, 608–611, 611–619, 622–626, 631
hedonism and, 328
Indian, 327, 328–329, 332, 334–345, 602–611
Jain, 334–337
Milesian, 326–327
vs. mythology, 325–326, 329, 331
nature and, 541, 543, 586, 588, 622
pluralism and, 316, 319
Pythagoras theologos and, 328–329
religion *vs.*, 319, 333
skepticism, Xenophanes, 319–320
superstition *vs.*, 334
Nausiphanes, 611, 621, 632
naya/nayavāda, 335–336
Near East, 4, 11, 14, 16, 26, 29, 32, 61, 112, 115, 213
Aryan community and, 257–258
first civilization and, 237–246
iconography issues, Indus Valley and, 246–260
Indus Valley and, 237–238
Indus-Mesopotamia trade and, 238–242, 246
Mesopotamian/Sumerian influence on Indus Valley and, 238–242, 281–288, 298*n*267
new developments, civilization and, 242–245
shamans, Indus Valley and, 260–275, 280
Sumero-Dravians and, 245–246
negations, 417*n*1, 433–434, 438, 441, 452, 453, 454, 469–473, 475, 477, 538*n*44, 649
fourfold, 475, 495–497, 506*n*8
negative theology, 553–554
Neolithic age, 56, 81, 82, 84, 90, 91, 97n91, 215, 243, 262, 275, 281, 284, 286, 642, 653
Neoplatonism, 326, 349, 391, 512. *See also* Plotinus
absolute One by, 568, 569, 570, 572, 573
consciousness layers for, 562–563, 569, 571
contemplation for, 570–571, 588
epistemology/ontology of, 569–571, 572–573, 577
ethics, imperturbability and, 596, 602
goal of, 579–580
historical considerations for, 580–581
Idea, mind and, 554, 561, 563, 568, 575, 576–577
individual, the All and, 562–564, 568
infinity, totality and, 566*n*28, 576–579
knowing the One by, 558, 560–561
meditation and, 547, 555, 558, 583*n*25, 584*n*38, 588–589, 588–590
mind *(nous)* and, 554, 561, 563, 568, 570, 572, 573–574, 574–575, 576–577, 579
non-dualism, Many and, 554–556
One and Many problem and, 552–554, 566*n*28, 568, 576, 579, 581
paradoxical formulations of, 556–557
Plotinus, India and, 549–551, 565*n*12
regressions/emanations of Being by, 561, 563, 569, 571, 575–576, 583*n*25, 585–586
ritual practices for, 591–592
social situations of, 586–587
soul for, 569, 570, 572
tantra and, 585–592
three-level ontology of, 560, 562, 568–569, 570–571, 572, 580–581
universe model of, 571
Upaniṣadic-Vedāntic tradition and, 549–564, 551–552, 571–572
Vijñānavāda Buddhism and, 568, 571–581, 582*n*5, 584*n*38
visualizations for, 588–590, 592
Neopythagoreanism, 452, 569, 580
Net of Indra, 578
Nicomachus, 588
nihilism, 473, 474–475, 504
Nikāyas, 409–410, 411, 519, 604, 612, 613, 614
Nimbarka, 553, 557
Ningizzida temple, 219
Ājīvika-Jain tradition and, 271–273
kuṇḍalinī yoga and, 269–271
nakedness and, 273–274
Nirvāṇa, 168, 169, 192, 266, 344–345, 442, 459, 475, 477–484, 504, 608
niyativāda, 436–437
non-being/existence, 529–530, 564. *See also* Being

non-difference/difference, 439, 450–451, 452, 453, 456, 493–494, 553, 554, 557, 559, 568. *See also bhedābheda*; Sameness and Difference
noninvolvement. *See apatheia*
nonviolence, 100, 182, 201, 202, 229, 232, 268, 269, 278, 280, 595, 620
noumenalism, 325, 415–416, 420, 428, 437–438, 494, 508*n*37, 528
nous (mind), 574–575, 579
ntum, 220
Numenius, 570, 581
numerology, 70, 76–77, 83–84, 84–85, 87, 88–90, 150*n*111, 157, 160, 270–271, 282
  worship of, 46–47, 171, 175*n*42, 586
Nyāya Sūtras, 319, 514, 516
  background of, 406, 519, 646
  as inductive logic, 511
  structure of syllogism of, 408–414, 425, 515, 649
Nyāya-Vaśeṣika, 528, 539*n*53
  atomism of, 319, 324*n*28, 510, 515, 517*n*1, 539*n*51, 650
  Mādhyamika (Middle Way) *vs.*, 514–515
  non-Vedic aspect of, 515, 519
Nysa, 359–360

occult, 587–588
Odyssey, XXV, 15, 16, 81
omniscience, 342–343, 344, 348*n*65
One
  absolute/immobile, 159, 568, 569, 570, 572, 573, 580
  beyond Being, 164, 580
  Few to Many from, 162, 164, 301
  as goal, 579, 584*n*38
  Ideas and, 168, 188
  knowledge of, 190
  magic no effect on, 588
  mind and, 579, 580, 584*n*38, 585–586
  Neoplatonism investigated by, 552–554
  self-canceling formulas of, 452
  self-knowledge aspect of, 570
  sex, immortality and, 208
  soul and, 585
  two aspects of, 159–160
  Unity and, 157, 159, 160, 164, 561
  Universal Mind co-existence with, 563, 568, 571
One and Many, Problem of, 142–143. *See also* monism; Platonic monism
  Anaximander, Indian monism, infinite/brahman and, 30–33, 35
  Anaximenes, Indian monism and, 33–35
  annihilation of Many in, 36
  astronomy and geometry influence on, 23–24
  Being, non-Being and, 53–54, 57, 58, 158, 160, 426–427
  change (of things) and, 36–37, 40, 53, 158–159, 160, 301
  chronological consideration of, 59–61
  cosmic cycle and, 69
  Egyptian cosmic person in, 24–25, 301
  Empedocles, logic and, 68, 157, 301, 311
  the Few and, 68, 157, 300–301
  Greek cosmic person in, 27–28
  Heraclitean monism, Indian thought and, 36–44
  Indian cosmic person in, 26–27
  macranthropic monism and, 28–29
  material monism and, 28–29
  māyāvāda (illusion) of Many and, 50–51
  Mesopotamian cosmic person in, 25–26
  Mesopotamian/Egyptian thought in, 24
  name-and-form (idea-complex) and, 57–59
  One as form and formless, unchanging and, 50–51, 53–54, 301, 568
  One as universal subject/object and, 49
  Parmenidean monism, Indian thought and, 52–55, 157, 301, 426
  philosophical Goddess and, 55–57
  Plato and, 157
  Plotinus and, 552–556, 557, 566*n*28, 568, 576, 579, 581
  Pythagorean monism, Indian thought and, 44–48, 157, 160
  restoring balance of, 36–37
  as single cyclical (time) process, 68
  Thales, Indian thought and, 28–30
  Xenophanean monism, Indian thought and, 48–52
  Yājñavalkya and, 50–51, 59, 60, 170, 408, 421, 552
Onesicritus and, 491, 502, 540
ontology and, 161, 312, 338, 427, 458, 459, 463, 489n70
  epistemology, Plotinus and, 569–571, 572–573
  gradational, 157
  Indo-European languages and, 3
  logic and, 54
  mentalist-idealist *vs.* ontic in, 569
  senses, *syādvāda* and, 336, 337
  three-level *vs.* two-level in, 560, 562, 568
  universality of relation as, 469
  wholeness and, 467
opinion, 477, 500, 603, 605, 612
oral tradition, 79–80, 158, 173*n*7, 284
orexis (desire), 610, 623, 626
organs , 211, 222*n*16
Orientalism, xviii, 645, 647
  India as source of civilization by, xix–xx
  Renaissance, 652, xvii, xx
  Romantic,xix, 650, 651–652
Original Moment, 55
original sin, 81
origination, 431, 531. *See also* destruction
ornaments, 251, 253, 291*n*106
Orpheus, 104–105, 171, 202
Orpheus's lyre, 67, xvi
Orphism, xvii; 17, 18, 39, 40, 60–61, 67, 163, 190, 206*n*33, 477, 478, 565*n*12, 600
  brotherhood of, 27, 105, 145*n*22, 145*n*28, 204, 261, 321, 405
  cosmic cycle and, 71–72, 576
  dualism of, 128, 200–201
  Empedocles, reincarnation, 106–107, 127, 201–202
  ethics of, 201
  gold plates and, 105–107, 136, 137, 145*n*28
  Heraclitus, reincarnation and, 110–111, 121, 127
  Hesiod, reincarnation and, 108–110
  Jainism and, 157, 163, 165, 183, 308, 319, 344, 535, 576, 581
  Jain influence on, 197, 199, 203–204, 233, 272, 298*n*267, 642
  karmic dirt of soul and, 198–199, 639*n*11
  kuṇḍalinī and, 272
  myth of, 131–135, 157, 197, 576, 577, 600–601
  Parmenides, reincarnation and, 111
  Pindar, reincarnation and, 107–108, 109, 110, 115, 127
  Plato, reincarnation and, 101, 102, 108–110, 127, 145*n*22, 534
  Plato, monism and, 169
  polytheism of, 162, 163
  recollection of soul in, 105–107, 145*n*32, 563–564, 577
  reincarnation in, xvi, 41, 45, 99, 101, 102, 104–106, 106–111, 120, 127, 131–135, 140, 142, 145*n*28, 155*n*205, 162, 199, 344
  semen and, 210
  soul, punishment in human body and, 105, 106, 132, 162
  soul, transcendence and, 197, 558, 561, 563, 600–601

soul's destiny with, 203
Osiris, 130–135, 138, 213, 259, 271, 668, 669
Ovidian chaos, 31

padārtha (categories), 521–522
paideia (education), xxii, xxiii, xxiv, 351, 355, 359, 361, 363–364, 613
pain
(aponia) non, 616, 638*n*98
pleasure and, 440, 493, 520, 524, 595, 596, 599, 604, 605, 608, 609, 614–615, 630, 636*n*50
Pakhuda Kaccayana, 317–318, 320, 520
Paleolithic age, 56, 84, 97n91, 231, 262, 275
Pali, 342, 372, 376, 641*n*137, 675, 676
Suttas, 410, 414, 421, 495
pañca-makāra (5 *M*'s), 276
Pāṇini, 671–672
pantheism, 24, 25, 39, 61, 64*n*48, 260, 269, 279, 541, 555
pantheos (meta-deity), 24, 27, 49, 653
body of, 25–26, 34
mental qualities of, 32
paradox, 189–193, 451–452, 465, 475, 476, 477, 564, 580
in Neoplatonism and Upanisads 556–557
of Yājñavalkya, 475, 553, 557
Paramahaṃsas, 227
Parameṣṭhin, Prajāpati, 407
paratantra (mind), 572, 574–575, 577, 579, 580
parikalpita (ignorance/illusion), 572–573, 574, 577
parinamavāda (transformation doctrine), 553–554
parinirvāṇa (body/death), 344–345
parinispanna (storehouse consciousness), 572, 573–574, 576
Parmenides, 18, 36–37, 50, 51, 56, 64*n*52, 193, 305, 312, 315, 466, 505, 549, 569, 571, 602
background of, 52, 67, 170, 192
Being, non-Being and, 53, 58, 59, 158, 159, 160, 162, 169, 307, 314, 316, 318, 320, 333, 339, 407–408, 415–416, 420, 421–423, 426, 427, 433, 434, 443, 460, 464, 469, 525, 531, 553–554, 555, 564, 569, 580–581, 585–586
birth of language and, 57–58
dialectic and, 407–408, 415–416, 420, 421–423, 431, 432, 438, 460, 461, 464, 499–500, 653
higher/lower awareness for, 598
logic, sense and, 37, 54–55, 68, 162, 330
monism, Indian thought and, 52–55, 65*n*56
Orphism, reincarnation and, 111
particulars for, 520
philosophical Goddess and, 57
Platonic monism and, 159–160, 169
Pārśva, 271–272, 277–278, 279, 283–284, 297*n*246
Parthia, 370
Parthian Empire, 350
particulars, 511, 520, 527–529, 577
passivities, 524
Pāśupata. *See also* Ājīvikas; Cynics
animal imitations and, 230–231
black magic karma and, 228
cult of, 225–226
"seeking of dishonor" and, 225–227, 228
Pāṭaliputra, 370–371, 375, 398*n*114
Patañjali, 166, 179–180, 182–183, 184–185, 188, 192, 264, 551, 580, 590, 673
Path(s)
of Fathers, 42–44, 116, 274
of Gods, 42–43, 116, 274
Two, 115–116, 121, 150*n*112, 304–305, 308
pathos (pathē), 623, 625, 628, 629
patrilinealism, 276, 669
pēlon, 199
perception. *See* experience
Perfect Wisdom. *See also* *Prajñāpāramitā Sūtras*
Peripatetics, 437, 541, 551
categories of, 511, 521–524, 538*n*23
causality of, 532–534, 539*n*50
doctrine of privation of, 530
facts in, 523, 526, 527, 528
historical aspects of, 535–536
matter for, 524–525
mind, soul and, 534–535
particulars in, 511, 520, 527–529
passivities, affections for, 524
potentiality of, 529–531
relations/conjunctions in, 531–532
substance-attribute relationship of, 523, 526–527
summing up of, 535–536
time, space and, 525–526
universals of, 511, 512, 527–528
Vaśeṣikas and, 520–536
Persian empire, 2*m*, 672
afterlife and, 113
Greece invaded by, 10
Greek and Indian medicine in, 15–16
Greek art diffused through, 9–10
Greek mercenaries of, 5, 8, 10, 13, 21*n*68, 349
Greek workers/artists in, 349, 364
Greeks, pre-Alexander and, 359–360
iconography, 255
imported (Greek) workers and deportation in, 7–9
Indian and Greek languages influence on, 12–13
Indian relationship to, 7–8, 10–11, 258, 283, 298*n*267, 360, 395*n*55
Indian thought "robbed" by, 126
kuṇḍalinī, India and, 211, 213
Magian (Persian) hypothesis and, 121–122, 123, 124–126, 127, 149*n*92, 149*n*95, 151*n*131
medical profession diffusion in, 15–16, 17, 18
meetings of Greeks/Indians in, 11–12, 122
multiculturalism in, 9–10, 11
Platonic monism, Eudoxus and, 171–172
reincarnation and, 121–122, 123, 125–126, 127, 142, 171
religious tolerance in, 9–10, 16–18, 125–126, 151*n*131
sanctuary for Greeks, Indians in, 6–7
wars of, 349, 351, 355–356, 379
before Zoroaster, 123–124, 150*nn*111–112
Zoroastrianism and, xxviii, 9–10, 69, 122–126, 149*n*95
Phaedo, 437
phantasia (mental picture), 610, 614, 617, 623, 626–627, 630, 631, 637*n*68, 640*n*125
pharaoh, 130–133
phassa (sense contact), 606, 608, 610, 626
phenomenalism, 311, 316, 317, 325, 332, 333, 338, 421, 429, 437–438, 445*n*7, 492. *See also* materialism
arguments against, 463
composite *vs.* simple, 439
experiences as real in, 455, 474, 494
linguistics and, 438
noumenalism *vs.*, 437–438, 494, 508*n*37, 514, 528
as truth, 452, 474
without mental picture, 610, 617*n*68
Pherecydes, 103–104, 121, 124, 170–171, 204, 260, 306, 307, 327, 382
Philo, 451, 493, 575, 587

Philodemus, 512, 513, 514, 516
philology, xviii, 652, 658
philosopher(s)
  comparison of East/West, xxvii, 177–178, 300
  Greek contact with Indian, 355, 382, 385, 391, 393*nn*1–2, 440, 443–444, 449*n*71, 450, 491–492, 494, 495, 540, 549–551, 632
  naked, 492, 549, 550
  platonic monism, bodhisattva and, 168–169, 551
  psychology of Greek and Indian, 632–633
  reincarnation and prince, prophet and, 99–100, 106, 130–131, 132–133
  release from wheel of cycling (reincarnation) by, 166, 178, 190
  self knowledge (as teaching) of, 186–190, 200–201, 383, 450, 471, 551
philosophy, 3
  colonial comparative, xxvi–xxvii
  contemplation plus, 588
  cosmogony as preparation for, 23
  cutting mind off from experience, 458
  development of, 281
  grammar and, 672–676
  happiness as goal of, 452
  medicine and, 16, 22*n*82, 596–597
  as tranquil attitude, 493, 494
philosophy, comparison of Greek and Indian, xvii, xxi–xxii, xxvii–xxviii
  almost mirror image in, 643–644
  Indian exclusion from history of philosophy and, 644–647, 650–652
  Indian participant of history of philosophy for, 652–654
  mysticism, critical analysis and, 649–650
  pre-modernism, modernism, and post-modernism in, 647–649
  Western *vs.* Eastern civilization progress and, 644–647, 650
Phoenicians, 4, 5, 104
phronēsis, 609
physiologoi (matter), 326, 327, 328
Piaget, Jean, 571
Pindar, 210, 596
  reincarnation, Orphism and, 107–108, 109, 110, 115, 127, 128
Pipalāda
  imperturbability, indifference and, 602
Plato, 16, 28, 56, 80, 149*n*92, 315, 319, 378, 475, 482, 505, 554, 587, 612, 625, xvi, xvii
  absolute Being and, 58, 568, 580
  acoustics and, 84, 87
  Atlantis, Jambudvipa and, 202–203
  atomism, soul's matter and, 198–200, 203
  background of, 157
  cosmic cycle and, 73–74, 75
  Degrees-of-Reality theory of, 157
  Democritus's censoring by, 491–492, 494
  dialectic of, 416, 432–434, 435, 438
  dualism of, 158, 197–198, 326
  Eleatics and, 423, 435, 438
  eros, spine, soul fluid and, 208–209
  Giants (materialists) *vs.* Gods (noumenalists) in, 325, 415–416, 420, 428, 438
  Good and, 189, 434
  Indian philosophers and, 393*n*2
  Jainism and, 197–204
  kuṇḍalinī and, 208–212
  Mādhyamika (Middle Way) and, 431–434
  marriage number of, 150*n*111
  naturalism and, 326, 329, 337
  negation and, 496
  occult vascular system and, 209
  One and Many problem and, 157, 568
  paradox in, 452
  particulars for, 520
  phenomenalism and, 438–439
  philosopher-kings of, 625
  pleasure, pain and, 615
  pluralism and, 157
  recollection doctrine of, 157
  reincarnation, Orphism and, 101, 102, 108–110, 118, 127, 145*n*22, 534
  reincarnation and, 99, 178, 182, 190, 198
  soul and, 128, 132, 135, 154*n*187, 197–198, 208
  soul's destination and escape for, 200–201
  supersensible world of, 197
  unity principle of, 157
  universals/abstractions of, 521, 523, 528, 529, 532, 586
  universe sphericity and, 51, 53, 165
  World Soul of, 165, 169, 208, 541
Platonic ethics, 611. *See also* yoga
  abstinence/austerity and, 182–184, 195n30
  consciousness and, 188
  contemplative silence and, 178–179
  control of senses in, 185–186
  daimon and, 181, 183
  imperturbability and, 596, 599–600, 601, 602, 605, 608–609
  ladder of self knowledge in, 184–185
  lifestyle, balance and, 183–184, 186
  meditation *vs.* reason and, 180–181
  mystical, higher knowledge in, 186–189, 192
  self knowledge in, 184–185, 190–192
  Socrates' paradoxes of, 189–193
  three qualities of self in, 185–186
  withdrawal (of soul from senses) in, 179–181, 182–183, 185, 195*n*30, 332
Platonic monism
  astrology and, 171–172
  Being of, 158–159, 162, 163, 164, 170, 174*n*13, 430, 467, 569
  Buddhist parallel to, 165, 167–169
  Heraclitus and, 158–159
  Hindu parallel to, 164–167
  historical situation of, 170–171
  Ideas (Theory) and, 68, 160, 161, 167–168, 174*n*13, 175*n*30, 195*n*30, 576, 581
  imprisoned god, soul and, 163
  offspring of One and the Other and, 160–162
  One, the Other and, 159–160
  One, Unity and, 157, 159, 160, 164, 434, 554
  One-and-Many groupings and, 157, 162, 430
  One-Few-Many structure and, 157, 162–163
  oral teaching of, 158, 173*n*7
  Parmenides as father for, 159–160, 170
  Persian issues, Eudoxus and, 171–172
  Pythagoreans and, 170–171
  Sameness and Difference and, 160, 164, 167, 175*n*13
  synthesis of, 162–163
  tripartite soul for, 167, 182, 185, 203
Platonism, Middle, 580, 581, 587
pleasure, 184, 185, 196n31, 497, 524. *See also* happiness
  natural/unnatural, 615, 638*n*93, 638*n*98
  pain and, 440, 493, 520, 595, 596, 604, 605, 609, 615, 617, 627, 630, 636*n*50, 638*n*98
  pursuing of, 328, 332, 602, 604, 638*n*98
  rational, 600
Plotinus, 182, 187, 311, 416, 419, 434, 452, 491, 503

absolute One by, 568, 569, 570, 572, 573
  Christianity and, 550
  consciousness layers for, 562–563, 569, 571
  contemplation for, 570–571, 588
  epistemology/ontology of, 569–571, 572–573, 577
  free will for, 567*n*29
  goal of, 579–580
  historical considerations for, 580–581
  Idea, mind and, 554, 561, 563, 568, 575, 576–577
  India and, 549–551
  individual, the All and, 562–564, 568
  infinity, totality and, 566*n*28, 576–579
  knowing the One by, 558, 560–561
  meditation and, 588–590
  mind *(nous)* and, 554, 561, 563, 568, 570, 572, 573–574, 574–575, 576–577, 579
  non-dualism, Many and, 554–556
  One and Many problem and, 552–554, 557, 566*n*28, 568, 576, 579, 581
  Plato's influence on, 550, 565*n*12
  regression/emanations of Being by, 561, 563, 569, 571, 575–576, 583*n*25, 585–586
  reincarnation and, 562, 567*n*29
  soul for, 569, 570, 572
  tantra and, 585–587, 588–590
  teaching style of, 551
  three-level ontology of, 560, 562, 568–569, 570–571, 572, 580–581
  three-level's of Buddhism and, 572–573
  universe model of, 571
  Upaniṣadic-Vedāntic tradition and, 549–564, 551–552, 571–572, 581
  Vijñānavāda Buddhism and, 568, 571–581, 582*n*5, 584*n*38
  visualizations for, 588–590
pluralism
  Anaxagoras and, 311–314, 323*n*2
  Aristotle and, 157, 300
  atomism *vs.*, 424–426
  finite *vs.* infinite and, 314–315
  Greek atomism and, 315–317, 320–321
  Indian atomism and, 317–321, 324*n*28
  Indian before Greek atomism and, 318, 320–321
  naturalistic, 316, 319
  Zeno and, 316, 319
Plutarch, 109, 356–357, 377, 442, 451, 626
pneuma (breath), 543, 545–546
poetry, 14, 108, 110, 306, 326, 508*n*43
point monad, 319, 519, 520
Polemon, 182, 540, 625
polis/poleis. See city
politics, 45, 104, 352, 361
  pantheism and, 24
polygamy, 397*n*96
polytheism, 24, 55, 61, 124, 162, 163, 301
  dismissing of, 49
  Indian, 29, 558, 559
Porphyry, 98, 102, 104, 391, 550, 551, 552, 554, 584*n*38, 587
  theurgy of, 588
  two-level (nondual) model of, 585, 587
Poseidon, 305
Posidonius, 543
positive doctrines, 455, 469
potentiality . *See also Śakti* , 436–437, 464, 529–531
prajñā (wisdom), 189, 192, 439, 441, 628
Prajñāpāramitā Sūtras (Perfect Wisdom), 39, 419, 439, 451, 454–455, 457, 475, 476, 477, 486*n*12, 492, 493, 500, 501, 503, 508*n*37
Prākrit, 164, 372, 376, 555
pralaya, 541, 542
prāṇa, 34–35, 209, 214, 301, 543–545
  consciousness, soul and, 545–546, 562
  pneuma and, 545–546
prapañca (thought proliferation), 477, 500, 603, 605, 612
Prasaṅgika, 456
Praśastapāda, 528, 531, 532, 539*n*51
pratyāhāra, 166, 179–180, 185, 590
Precession (of the Equinoxes), 78–79, 80, 81, 82–83, 85, 89, 91, 157
preconceptions. *See also prolepseis*
priesthood, 42, 264, 267, 268–274, 281, 284, 325, 328. *See also* brotherhood
primal intellection, 560–561
Prime Mover, 535, 560, 570, 622
privation, 529–530
Proclus, 588
prolepseis (preconceptions), 613, 617, 622, 623
proof, 471–472
Protagoras, 332–333, 415, 416, 420, 429, 430, 432, 438, 451, 496, 672
psychology, 415, 534–535, 577, 632–633
  Buddhist, 415, 605–606, 608, 613–614, 641*n*137
  Epicurean, 613–615
  Stoic, 622–623, 641*n*137
Ptah, 24, 29, 134, 259, 268
Ptolemies, 379
Ptolemy, 83, 351, 367, 379, 381, 383–384, 390, 656*n*18
punishment
  in heavens and hells, 116, 117, 148n71, 199, 202
  in human body for soul, 105, 106
Purāṇas, 163–164, 228, 542, 543, 567*n*29, 659
purification, 131–135, 179, 190, 193, 198–199
  by fasting, 269, 278
  for karma, 268, 269, 534
  of king, 265
  by ritual, 269, 591
Puruṣasūkta, 27, 260
Purusa, 164
Purva Mimamsa, 165
Pyrrhon (of Elis)
  background of, 450, 452, 550, 601, 611, 632
  dialectic and, 411, 418*n*15, 419, 420, 444
  sayings of, 451
  teachers of, 493–495
Pyrrhonism, 488*n*56, 491, 599. *See also* Skepticism
  Aenesidemus and, 499–505
  background of, 449*n*71, 450–451, 491–492, 506*n*3
  dialectic of, 416, 431, 451–452, 459–466, 468, 469–477, 482–484, 501
  foreign input unlikely in, 499
  goal of, 456–459
  imperturbability, ethics and, 599, 601, 630, 632–633
  Mādhyamika (Middle Way) and, 453, 454–484, 486*n*10, 486*n*12, 492, 498–499
  negative terms and, 453, 459
  non-difference and, 439, 450–451, 452, 453
  relational existence critique for, 459, 466–469
  second/third academies and, 453–454
  Stoics *vs.*, 454, 470, 471
  syllogism of, 513
Pythagorean thought, 16, 18, 149n92, 326, 415, 426, 505, 541, 549, 554, 565*n*12, 587, 646
  acoustics and, 47–48, 81–83, 84, 85, 86, 87–88, 330
  atomism of, 447*n*25
  background/contemplative activity of, 45, 103, 107, 170–171, 178–179, 182, 193, 283, 315, 328, 382
  brotherhood of, 45, 80, 158, 170–171, 178–179, 181–182, 210, 261, 265, 284, 405, 598, 668

cosmic organism, breath/air and, 46–47, 53, 545
dualism of, 128, 162
exact repetition of cosmic cycle by, 72
fifth element of, 308
golden thigh story of, 668, 669–670
Hinduism and, 165
imperturbability, ethics, medicine and, 596, 597, 602
kuṇḍalinī and, 210, 211–212
metempsychōsis of, 145*n*20
monism, Indian thought and, 44–48
Music of the Spheres by, 47, 81, 86, 429
point monad and, 319, 519
Pythagorean comma and, 82–83, 85, 91
Pythagorean Theorem of, 85, 90
qualities of Being of, 52, 314
reincarnation and, 45, 100, 102, 104, 119, 155*n*205, 178
science, math, numerology and, 45–48, 157, 160, 162, 330, 433, 575, 586, 656*n*18
theologoi of, 328–329

race
Caucasian *vs.* nonwhite, xviii–xix, xxii, xxiii, xxvii
non-racism of Greece with, xxiii, xxiv
rajas, 167, 182, 186
Ramana Maharshi, 470
Ramānuja, 164, 542, 543, 549, 551, 552, 554, 555, 587
Rāmāyana, xxv, 229
rationalism
irrationalism *vs.*, 300, 331, 341, 600, 636*n*50, xvii, xviii, xxi, xxviii
self-canceling/uroboric formulas and, 451–452
Re. *See* Amon-Re
reaction . *See samskāra*
realism, semantic, 512
reanimation, 226, 229, 296*n*242
reason, 167, 180–181, 182, 185, 186, 610, 612, 674. *See also* logic; *logos*
appetites/desires controlled by, 600, 628–629
theory of, 409
wisdom and, 185, 189, 600
recognition. *See samjñā*
reductio ad absurdum, 420, 423, 427, 446*n*17, 459, 515, 649, 654
refutation, 433–434, 451, 455, 456, 475
regression, 561, 563, 569, 571, 575–576, 583*n*25
regressus ad infinitum, 403, 420, 423, 424, 425, 426, 437, 459, 464, 466, 467
reincarnation, 45, 294*n*208, 337. *See also* metempsychōsis; soul
Achaemenid religious policy and, 125–126
afterlife, return of dead and, 118–119, 129, 131, 148*n*81
afterlife and, 112–113, 115, 275, 345
afterlife's repayment/judgment and, 108–109, 133–138
animalistic/naturalistic relationship to, 99, 112–113, 115, 116, 117, 147n70, 202
to another person, 588
Āranyakas, Brāhmaṇas and, 113–114
asceticism and release from, 278, 279
avatarism of pharaoh and, 130–131
the *Book of Dead* and, 129–130, 132–134, 135–137
Buddhism and, 341, 348*n*51
cosmic cycle and, 92, 117
desire and, 100–101, 108–109, 118
determinism in, 278, 296*n*242, 327
development *vs.* appearance of concept of, 103–104, 111, 117–118, 141–143, 148*n*71
distinctiveness of Indian and Greek, 98–99, 111, 117
Egypt and, 126–142, 152*n*149, 156*n*209, 260
Empedocles and, 68, 99, 102, 104, 106–107, 109, 111, 113, 127, 132–133, 135, 139, 140, 145*n*32, 178, 201–202
features of, 142–143
forgetfulness and, 105
formulae of, 98
free will with, 140, 278, 296*n*242
freedom through knowledge from, 100–101, 115–116, 551
Greece and, 45, 98–103, 103–111, 128–129, 132–135, 138, 140–142
Heraclitus and, 110–111, 121, 127, 178
Herodotus and, 118–119, 126–129, 130, 135, 138–139
Hesiod, Orphism and, 108–110, 113
India and, 98–103, 112–117, 128–129, 132–142, 146*n*50
Jain, 201–202, 260, 278, 296*n*242, 345
karma and, 113–114, 115, 116, 147*n*64, 147n67, 147*n*67, 342, 558, 614
Magian (Persian) hypothesis of, 121–122, 123, 124–126, 127, 149*n*92, 149*n*95, 151*n*131
mechanistic aspect of, 138–139
memory and, 105–107, 136–138, 145n32, 154*n*193, 183, 206*n*18, 563–564, 577, 581
mind/body dualism and, 128–129
monism, dualism and, 122–123
moral behavior effect on, 99–100, 106, 107, 113, 115, 141–142, 147*n*67
nearly perfected soul in last, 15
negative aspect of, 99
no soul and, 636*n*55
number years and, 107, 109, 138–139
numerology and, 139–140
one myth for three (Greek/Egptian/Indian) cultures' afterlife and, 135–138
Orphic myth and, 131–135
Orphism and, 41, 45, 99, 101, 102, 104–106, 106–111, 131–135, 145*n*22, 155*n*205, 344, xvi
Parmenides, Orphism and, 111
Persian religion before Zoroaster and, 123–124, 150*nn*111–112
Pherecydes and, 103–104, 121, 124
philosopher and release from, 166, 178
Pindar, Orphism and, 107–108, 109, 110, 115, 127
Plato and, 99, 101, 102, 108–110, 127, 128, 145*n*22, 178, 182, 190
prince, prophet highest in, 99–100, 106, 130–131, 132–133
Pythagorean, 45, 100, 102, 104, 119, 128, 155*n*205
reanimation and, 226, 229
rejection of, 314
ritual practice and, 101, 105, 113, 155*n*205
ritual (taboo) violations and, 113–114
self denied and, 128, 129, 152*n*145
shamanism and, 102–103, 105, 118, 120–121, 130
shape changing *vs.*, 120, 131
soul, punishment, memory loss and, 105–106
soul released from, 101–103, 115, 128–129, 135, 154*n*187, 562, 567*n*29, 580, 586
Thracian hypothesis of, 118–121, 148*n*83

tripartite doctrine of, 101, 118, 120, 122, 124, 126, 135, 138, 142, 157, 580
Two Paths (knowledge and rituals) and, 115–116
Uddālaka and, 115, 138, 141
Upaniṣads and, 100–102, 112, 114–115, 121, 129, 132, 138, 140, 141, 142
Vaśeṣikas and, 534
Vedas, afterlife and, 112–113, 137–138
Vratyas and, 274–275
Yājñavalkya and, 100–101, 102, 114–115, 124–125, 138, 140, 141, 183
yoga and, 140, 278, 285, 296*n*242
relational existence, 466–469, 471
relativism, 333, 487*n*36
critique of, 466–469
cultural (human), 49, 333, 428
emptiness of, 466
Jain, 334–335, 337, 405, 411, 413
Sophistic, 429, 443, 450, 451
religion
astral, 171–172
Bon, 586
Indian philosophy mixed with, 177, 478, 650
magic and, 586, 587
nāstika, 675
naturalism *vs*., 319, 333
Neolithic/Bronze age, 284
suicide and, 107
Sumerian, 216–218
tolerance of, 9–10, 13, 16–18
Zen and apprehension/intuition of, 489*n*70
rest. *See* motion/rest
revelation, 339
Revelations, Book of, 77
Rhea, 57
Ṛg Veda, 38, 77, 86, 124, 263, 269, 277, 302, 410, 415, 543, 552
acoustics and, 83
Aryans and, 188, 257
Being, Non-Being and, 408, 555
creation and, 29–30, 70
dating of, 60–61, 289*n*71, 657, 659, 660
eschatology, reincarnation and, 112, 114
language and, 672, 673
macranthropic hymns in, 26
Near East influence in, 4
sacrifice in, 407
ritual/rite(s), 110, 261, 500, 587, 668
blood, 229, 231
Brahmanical, 42–43, 114
Bronze Age, 587
human sacrifice, 262
karma and, 113–114, 147*n*64
naturalism *vs*., 325, 334
Orphic, 203
purification, 269, 591
reincarnation and, 101, 105, 113–114, 155*n*205
rejection of, 619
of sacrifices, 42–43, 407, 408–410, 558
secrecy of, 284
sexual, 229, 264, 275, 669
syncretism, 264, 275
theurgic, 588
Vedic, 325, 327, 334, 407, 408–410, 558, 619, 672, 674, 675
road, trunk, 350
Roman empire, 351, 370, 380*m*, 388, 512, 515, 520
art, India and, 388–390, 401*n*207
book-burnings in, 391
currency of, 513
Indian trade with, 381–383, 501, 550, 581
knowledge of India in, 390–392
persecution in, 391–392
Stoicism and, 631
theurgy, tantra and, 586, 594*n*26
wars in, 350
ropes, 498–499
Rosetta Stone, xx

Sabba Sutta, 338, 429, 603, 612
śabda (hearing), 516
sacrifice
human, 262
interiorization of, 42–43
Vedic, 407, 408–410, 558
saint. *See* seers
Śaiva, 229, 230, 257, 274, 276, 280, 542
Śakas, 374–375, 379, 385, 386
samādhi (transcendence), 166, 180, 182, 187, 590
sāmānya, 178
Sameness and Difference, 160, 164, 167, 174*n*13, 314
samjñā (recognition), 608, 610, 614, 617, 623, 627
Sāṃkhya, xxviii
saṃskāra (emotional reaction), 605, 608, 609, 610, 619, 623, 626, 628, 636*n*57, 637*n*63, 637*n*66
samvara, 267
samvaya (inherence), 267, 531–532
Sanatkumāra, 30, 602
Sandaka Sutta, 339
Sañjaya, Belaṭṭhiputta, 411–412, 418*n*15, 419, 426, 427, 492
Śaṅkara, 58, 164, 170, 409, 503, 525, 542, 549, 551, 553–554, 557–558, 587, 602
Sāṅkhya, 530–531, 539*n*50
Sanskrit
commonness of Greek, Latin and, xviii, xx, xxx*n*13, 387
drama, 387, 401*n*199
as Indo-European language, xix, 652
language of, xviii, 439, 453, 458, 649, 672–676
Śāntideva, 228, 425, 427, 440, 462, 468, 481
Sargonid trade, pre, 241, 263
Śatapatha Brāhmaṇa, 77, 112, 113, 114, 116, 278, 283, 544
sattva (purity), 167, 182, 186
scapegoat, 227, 286
Schlegel, Friedrich, xix, xx
Schopenhauer, Arthur, xix, xx, xxxi*n*21
science, 35, 45–46, 79, 480, 649–650, 651
empiricism for, 330, 333
insights for, 521
mindfulness for, 607
Pythagorean, 45–46
Scylax, 8, 11, 14, 20*n*27, 100, 349
secrecy, 80, 91, 158, 170, 178, 182, 284
sect, *astika or nāstika*, 327–328
Seeking of Dishonor, 204, 226–229
seers, 546–547, 599, 605, 624, 630, 673
children, abstinence and, 186
pre-Alexandrian period wandering by, 16–18, 22*n*95, 204
Seleucus, 350, 352, 358, 359, 361, 362, 363, 364, 367, 370, 371, 379
self. *See also* ātman
awareness, 641*n*137
disappearing of little into great, 557–558
divinity of, 561
great, 557
knowledge, 184–193, 193, 199, 338, 343, 383, 450, 471, 475, 558–560, 570
liberation of, 115–116
little (*jīva/* individual), 345, 547, 557
not, 168, 431, 522
proof of, 522–523
reincarnation and denial of, 128, 129, 152*n*145
rule, 439, 443, 444, 600, 623
soul and co-existence of, 560, 563
three qualities of, 185–186
universal, unchanging, 132, 199, 459, 557
self-immolation, 443
self-nature, 451, 455, 458, 466–469, 472
semeia (sign), 513–514
semen, 208–209, 210, 212, 213, 214, 215, 222*n*28, 222*n*35, 555
Seneca, 190, 621, 630, 631, 639*n*111, 640*n*114
sense contact. *See phassa*
senses, 185, 612. *See also* experience; imperturbability; phenomenalism; pleasure; *syādvāda*

to action (Buddhist), 605–608
to action (Epicurean), 614
to action (Plato/Aristotle), 608–611
to action (Stoic), 622–623
atomism and, 316–317, 318, 331–332, 334, 534
Buddhist perception of, 338, 343–344
consciousness, 605–606, 636*n*55
controlling from, 186, 605, 628–629
extrasensory cognitions and, 328, 341
karma and, 267
lifting above (beyond), 432, 558
logic and, 37, 54–55, 68, 162, 330
the mind and, 427–428, 468
naturalism and, 325, 329–330
sixth, 614
soul and, 190–191
spiritual (faculties), 637*n*63, 637*n*66
syādvāda and, 335–337
withdrawal from, 166, 179–181, 182–183, 185, 482–483, 493, 539*n*53, 559, 561, 590, 596, 599, 602–603

serpent, 89, 257, 259, 262, 294*n*196
iconography, 216–217, 219, 224*nn*55–56, 247, 259, 268–270, 272–273, 274, 275, 285, 294*n*206
kuṇḍalinī and, 209, 213, 216–217, 219, 222*n*31, 258, 270–271

Set, 668

seven, 88–89, 270–271, 273, 275, 284

sex, 212, 213, 228, 276, 285, 669. *See also* celibacy; fertility; matriarchial society; tantra
abstinence from, 182, 184
constraints on, 276
immortality, One and, 208
mythology and, 669–670
for procreation, 208, 268
rituals, 229, 264, 276

Sextus Empiricus, 326, 329, 385, 416, 419, 420, 422, 439, 450–451, 618, 630, 633
dating of, 455, 486*n*14, 499
dialectic of, 401, 499, 501
dialectic of causality for, 459–463, 498
double truth of, 474–475
fourfold negations of, 495–497
imagery of illusion (ropes/snakes) for, 498–499
laws of thought breached by, 477
medicine and, 596, 597
Nāgārjuna's parallelism to, 455, 459, 461–488
nirvāna, imperturbability and, 478–484, 630
regressus ad infinitum and, 466
relativity, skepticism and, 467–469
Skeptism of, 450–451, 454–456, 458, 485*n*9
syllogism of, 513–514
uroboric/self-destroying path and, 469–473, 488*n*54

Śakti (energy), 56, 530, 554

shaman(s), 15–16, 67, 79–80, 171, 197, 230–231, 233, 668. *See also* occult; magic; mysticism
Adapa as, 263, 292*n*151
Ājīvikism-Jainism and, 266, 267, 269, 271–273, 277, 279, 295*n*237
Aryan/non-Aryan, 257–258, 276, 279, 286, 295*n*295
asceticism for, 275–276, 278, 279–280, 635*n*34
Black Sea/Cynics, 449*n*70
direct teaching of, 158, 171
Dravidian, 286
drugs and, 262–263, 271, 286, 295*n*231
Egyptian, 264, 268–274
fertility cult, yoga and, 275, 285
flying and, 263–264
Gosāla and, 266, 267, 278
Greek, 268
king's sacredness for, 263, 264–266, 267
kuṇḍalinī yoga and, 269–271, 285–286, 294*n*190, 298*n*267
lunatics and, 261
magic, powers and, 103, 263–264, 267, 279–280, 285, 286
medicine of, 596
Mesopotamian, 262–268, 270–271, 294*n*190
nakedness and, 273–274, 277
Ningizzida temple and, 269–274
oneiromancy, dreams and, 266–267
priesthood and, 261, 262, 265, 267–268
Proto-Australoid peoples and, 285, 286, 297*n*265
reform from, 279
reincarnation and, 102–103, 105, 118, 120–121, 130
Sumerian, 262–265, 267
taboo and, 265, 268, 269
Uttanka and, 263
village, 260–261
Vratyas and, 274–275
yoga, Vedic and, 268–274, 286, 558
Zu and, 263–264

shape changing, 120, 131

She Lun, 574

Siddhārtha, 103, 107, 140, 141, 265, 279, 332, 411, 412, 413, 429, 435, 625

siddhis. *See also* shaman, 103, 280

sign, 513–514

silence, 178–179, 257, 269, 444, 453, 457, 477. *See also* *aphasia*
noble, 405, 426, 431, 439
wisdom from, 471

Simplicius, 31, 306, 312, 447*n*26

Śiva, 219, 225, 228, 230, 259, 274, 500, 555

Skambha (Substrate), 32–33, 34

skandhas, 605, 606, 617, 641*n*137

Skepticism, 311, 317, 378, 422, 453, 485*n*2, 580. *See also* Pyrrhonism
about essences, 455
background of, 450–451
causality dialectic of, 459–463, 468–469
dialectic of, 451–452, 459–466, 468, 469–477, 482–484
double truth of, 474–475
ethics, medicine, imperturbability and, 596, 597–598, 599, 631, 632
fourfold negations of, 495
goal of, 456–459
Law of Excluded Middle and, 455, 460, 461, 463, 489*n*70
laws of thought breached by, 475–477
middle position, being/non-being and, 456–458, 459, 467, 469
negation, criticism of language in, 477, 494
nirvāṇa, imperturbability and, 478–484
Protagoras, 429
regressus ad infinitum, 466
relational existence critique for, 459, 466–469
Stoics *vs.*, 454, 470, 471–472
suspension of, 454, 456, 457, 471, 473, 479, 481
uroboric/self-destroying path and, 469–473, 488*n*54

skepticism, 326, 334, 343, 416
Buddhist, 411–413, 503
Indian, 405, 406, 407, 410–412, 415, 418*n*16, 428–430
Jain, 410–413
Xenophanes, naturalism and, 319–320

slaves
in Greco-Roman world, xxiii
Persian, 8

sleep, 571
smoke, 439, 498, 511, 513–515
  Path of Fathers and, 42–44
snakes, 498–499
Socotra, 379
Socrates, xxvi, 158, 162, 167, 169, 170, 206*n*33, 233, 355–356, 497, 621, 629
  Beauty and, 185, 188
  daimon, meditation and, 181, 183, 184
  death of, 201, 230, 434
  elenchus (trial) of, 432, 433, 439
  ethics, imperturbability and, 599
  ignorance and, 453
  irony of, 170
  on knowledge from foreign nations, 172, 351
  ladder for (spiritual growth for), 184–185
  lifestyle of, 183
  paradoxes of, 189–193
  persuasion/dialectic of, 378, 416, 422, 432–433, 493
  purification of mind/soul and, 179, 190, 193
  (dialectic) schools of, 434–444
  self knowledge (as teaching) for, 191–193, 338, 343, 450, 551
  yogi talk with, 10
sophism, 334
  Indian, 502
Sophists, 317, 351, 415, 443, 450
  Eleatics and, 428–429
  Indian skepticism, dialectic and, 428–430
  relativism and, 429, 443, 450
sophos, 600, 616, 623, 630, 631
sorcery, 231
soul, 205*n*8. *See also* afterlife
  afterlife and, 116–117, 131–136, 138–139, 230
  air, *pneuma/prāna* and, 34–35, 545–546
  body, matter and dualism with, 197–198, 200–201, 562, 564, 603, 622, 639*nn*110–111
  body alive and buried alive nature of, 107, 110–111
  Christianity and, 165
  co-existence of self and, 560, 563
  dead, 112, 130, 134
  denial of, 128, 129, 152*n*145, 589, 636*n*55
  desire of, 108–109
  destination of, 200
  destiny of, 203
  disappearing of little into great, 557–558, 563
  Doctrine of Five Fires and, 40–41
  dualism of body and, 197–198
  dynamic continuum of, 1562
  Egyptian, 117, 128–130, 132
  from elements, 320, 326
  elements of, 202
  elements produced from, 326
  exhalation of, 41–42
  of exited god, 155*n*204, 163, 183, 201–202
  food, dying again, re-birth and, 113
  gods, Spring of Memory and, 105–106, 108, 136–137, 146n38, 154n193
  heaven and body separate from, 117, 128–130, 131–132
  Higher, 208, 569, 570, 582*n*1, 585, 588
  hypernoetic, 561
  Ideas contained in, 165–166
  immaterial, 128, 198, 200, 318
  immortality/universalness of, 107, 110, 132, 134–135, 139, 163, 200, 344, 523, 542
  incarnations and, 165, xvi
  individuality even with, 557–558, 562
  judgment/confession/ purification of, 131–135
  karmic matter (dirt) of, 198–200, 203, 308, 318, 319, 639*n*111
  knowledge and, 187, 190–191
  Lower, 208, 569, 570, 573, 585
  magic no effect on Higher, 588
  material, 318
  memory, recollection and, 105–107, 145*n*32, 563–564, 577, 581, 586
  mind and, 534, 555, 566*n*20, 571
  no, 328, 334
  omniscience of, 344
  One and, 585
  path of, 135–136, 154*n*186
  primal crime/ancient wrong of, 133
  punishment in human body for, 105, 106, 132, 133, 157
  purification of, 131–135, 179, 190, 193, 198–199
  re-entering living shaman, 120
  reincarnation and denial of, 128, 129, 152*n*145
  reincarnation and release of, 102–103, 115, 128–129, 135, 154*n*187, 198, 200–201, 567*n*29, 580
  senses and, 190–191
  sublevels of, 569
  sun god (heaven) and, 128–129, 131–132
  time purification (million of years) and, 132
  tripartite, 167, 182, 185, 203
  unity-and-multiplicity in, 569, 570
  wandering of, 199–200
  withdrawal of, 179–180
  World, 165, 169, 208, 541, 555, 556, 562, 569
space, 164, 578. *See also ākāśa*
  time, 423–424, 446*nn*18–19, 465–466, 523, 525–526
species, 527–528
speech, 477, 478
sperm. *See* semen
Speusippus, 444, 580
sphericity, 51, 53, 91, 165, 202, 525
spirit, immaterial, 128, 198
spirituality
  ladder for, 14–185
  philosophy, knowledge and, 177–178
Spring of Memory, 105–106, 108, 109, 136–137, 146n38, 154n193
Śrīdhara, 531
state
  mechanism of, 261, 262, 285, 325
  world government and, 352, 355–356
steadiness *(thitata)*, 608
Stilpo, 435, 437, 540
Stoics (Stoa), 72, 73, 79, 149*n*92, 157, 222*n*28, 229, 352, 355, 356, 441, 454, 580, 672
  background of, 540, 621
  causality, ethics, imperturbability and, 622
  cosmology of, 540–541, 567*n*29, 623
  dialectic and, 420, 496–497, 501, 515
  disjunctum, 496–497, 515
  enlightenment and, 546–547
  ethics, medicine, imperturbability and, 542–543, 597–598, 599, 611, 623–626
  grammar of, 674
  Indian thought and, 540–547
  later history and, 631
  logic of, 435, 496, 512, 513, 514
  mental process interruption and, 626–630, 640*n*114, 640*n*117, 640*n*125
  naturalistic theory of knowledge for, 622
  pneuma/prāṇa and, 543–546
  psychology, ethics, imperturbability and, 622–623
  Pyrrhonism/Skepticism *vs.*, 443, 454, 485*n*10
  religion and, 543, 586
  Skepticism *vs.*, 454, 470–472
Strabo, 390–391, 440
strange accident, 434, 448*n*40
Strife (separation), Age of, 68, 73
subjectivism, 333, 405, 429, 451
subjectivity/objectivity, 570–571, 575–576, 577, 579, 580
substance-attribute relationship, 436–437, 523, 526–527
substrate, 23–33, 28–29, 30, 31, 46, 51, 158, 162, 530
suchness, 575, 577
suffering, 332, 338, 339, 340, 440, 478, 481, 603–604, 612, 615, 625, 639n110

suicide, 107, 229, 278–279
Sulva Sūtras, 77, 90, 96*n*88
Sumerian(s), 3, 11, 70, 237. *See also* Mesopotamia
  Akkadians and, 244, 285, 302
  arrival in Mesopotamia of, 245–246, 283
  calendar of, 78
  cosmic cycle, arithmetic and, 74–79, 82, 84, 87, 88, 89, 90, 140, 165
  cults of, 284
  Dravidians and, 245–246, 283
  iconography, religion and, 216–218, 219, 242, 247, 250, 251–252, 253, 254, 256, 258, 260, 281, 291*n*106, 294*n*200, 294*n*206
  India influence by, 238, 240–242, 246, 281–288
  Indians before, 657
  kuṇḍalinī and, 215–219, 285–286, 298*n*267
  lion swastika, 219
  music and, 85–87, 95*n*64
  origination of, 245–246, 290*n*77
  Renaissance, 241
  shamans, 262–265, 267
  trade with Indus Valley, 240–241
  Vedic poets teaching of, 86, 95*n*64
  writing of, 243–244
śūnyata (emptiness), 469, 471
supernatural, 325–326, 333, 334, 341
  rejection of, 325, 329
superpowers. *See* extrasensory perception; shaman; *siddhis*
Susa, 243–244, 350, 363, 386, 632
suspension, 454, 456, 457, 471, 473, 479, 481, 483, 484, 630
Sutta. See also specific Sutta
Sutta Nipāta, 338, 412–413, 419, 438, 440, 456, 494, 500, 501, 615
svabhāva (self-nature/being), 451, 455, 458, 466, 572, 580
swastika, 219
syādvāda (in-a-sense doctrine), 335–337, 411, 495
syllogism, 403–404, 417*n*2, 649
  analogy for, 511, 512, 513–515
  Aristotelian, 408, 510–511, 513
  Buddhist, 513
  deductive, 511
  Empirical Medical Writers and, 451, 513–514
  Epicurean, 512–516
  Indian dialectic before, 406
  inductive, 511, 512, 513, 516
  John Stuart Mill and, 511
  Mādhyamika (Svātantrika), 421–422
  modus tollens, 404, 410, 423, 459
  Naiyāyika, 406, 408, 498, 507*n*20, 511–513
  Nyāya Sūtras structure of, 408–414, 425, 515, 649
  Peripatetic, 511, 512
  Pyrrhonist, 513
  Stoic, 435, 496, 512, 513, 514
synchronicity, 59

taboo(s)
  reincarnation and, 113–114
  shaman/priest and, 265, 268, 269
tamas, 167, 182, 186
tantra, 214, 257, 274, 280, 286, 673, 676
  cosmology of, 585
  historical situation for, 592, 594*n*25
  left-hand, 229, 276, 586
  maṇḍala visualizations and, 588–589, 591
  meditation and, 588–590, 593*n*17
  Neoplatonism and, 585–592
  occultizing of, 587–588
  pañca-makāra (5 *M*'s) of, 276
  personal god and, 591–592
  right-hand, 276
  ritual practices for, 587, 591–592
  social situations of, 586–587
  theurgy and, 586–587, 588, 591–592
  Tibetan, 586, 588, 589, 592, 593*n*7
  Vedāntization of, 586–587
Taoism, 450
  kuṇḍalinī and, 214–215
tapas, 182, 183, 268, 270, 279, 558, 602
tarka-śāstra, 409
Taxila, 354–355, 362, 367, 372, 376, 394*n*28, 396*n*76, 491, 492, 500, 502
teaching, direct, 158, 171, 186–190, 200–201, 383, 442–443, 450, 471, 551
teleology, supernatural, 325–326, 333, 334, 341
temperance, 600–601
temples, 267–268, 270–274
test, *See elenchus*
tetractys, 160–161, 165
Thales, 72, 103, 281, 306, 313, 651
  One and Many and, 23, 28–31, 59, 407
  physiologoi (materialism) and, 326–327
theism
  nontheism and, 589
  Stoic, 541–542
theologoi, 326, 328
therapy, 618–619, 641*n*137
Theravāda Buddhism, 478, 483, 586, 632
theurgy
  meaning of, 591–592
  tantra and, 586–587, 588, 592
thought. *See* Laws of Thought, 37, 53, 54, 403–404
Thrace, 197, 233, 298*n*267
  reincarnation and, 118–121, 130, 148*n*83, 197
Tibet
  Buddhism of, 504–505, 509*n*64, 676
  tantra of, 586, 588, 589, 592, 593*n*7
Tient-t'ai, 574
time, 142. *See also cosmic cycle*
  cycling of, 259–260, 283, 294*n*208, 567*n*29
  Indian *vs.* Greek, 644–647
  linear view of, 70, 117
  space, 423–424, 446*nn*18–19, 465–466, 523, 525–526
Timon (of Phlius), 452, 453–455, 501
Titans, 133
tranquil attitude, 493, 494, 615–616
transcendence (transcendentalism), 453, 458, 675. *See also samādhi*
  absolutist, 340, 434, 452
  after dialectic, 420, 421, 445*n*7
  of duality, 479–480
  of elements, 345
  God, name and, 25, 259, 313, 458
  imperturbability, ethics and, 595–596, 599–600, 601–602, 608
  monism and, 52, 158
  Orphism, soul and, 197, 558, 561, 563
transformation doctrine, 553–554
transmigration, 42
tree iconography, 247, 251, 270, 271, 291*n*104
tribal beliefs. *See also* gods, denial of
  breakdown of, 405, 429
  unified, 406
trisvabhāva (three modes of being), 568, 571–573, 580, 582*n*5
Troy, xxv
truth(s), 477, 506*n*3
  double, 474–475, 494
  eternal, 646
  four noble, 332, 481, 509*n*64, 625–626
  language reification as, 494
  from propositions, 514
Tu channel, 215
Tu Shun, 578
typhos (illusion), 439–440, 444, 467, 469, 474

Ubaid, 245–246
Udāna, 344–345
Udayana, 528, 539*n*50
Uddālaka
  atomism of, 317, 327, 330

(proto) dialectic of, 407, 410, 415. 423
matter infinitely divisible by, 312–313
One and Many Problem and, 30, 32, 40, 41, 58, 60, 66*n*68, 407–408, 423, 436
reincarnation and, 115, 138, 141
Uddyotakara, 520, 649
undefinableness, 25, 259, 313, 453, 458
Unity. *See* One
Universal Mind, 163, 541, 554, 560–561, 563–564, 571, 575, 577
universal order, 24, 47–48, 577
universals, 538*n*36
Aristotle, 511, 512, 527–528, 646
Plato, 521, 523, 528, 529, 532
Vaśeṣikas, 527–528, 646
universe
as consciousness, 570–571, 575–576
spherical, 51–52, 53, 165, 525
Upaniṣads, 70, 89, 99, 261, 285, 297*n*246, 315, 320, 325, 337, 342, 410, 475, 541, 571, 651 . *See also* Vedic tradition
afterlife and, 135–136, 154*n*186
Aitareya, 27, 303
atomism , 318–319
Brahmā, 209–210
Bṛhadāraṇyaka, 40, 43, 49, 50, 51, 58, 60, 100–101, 112, 302, 304, 318, 408, 543, 553, 555, 559, 561, 563
Chāndogya, 35, 39, 40, 41, 42, 43, 58, 60, 99, 101, 112, 115, 136, 147*n*67, 165, 166, 179, 209, 303, 304, 312, 317, 334, 543–544, 555, 557, 561, 601
dating of, 60, 125
Dhyānabindu, 210
Doctrine of Five Fires and, 35, 40–41, 44, 115, 121
elements and, 302–304, 307, 308–309
Great Secret of, 652, 653
Hansa, 210
Heraclitus and, 38–43
individual (self), the All *(brahman)* and, 562–564, 567*n*29
Īśa, 556
Katha, 38, 50, 185, 190–191, 559, 561, 562, 563
Kauṣitaki, 40, 135, 137
Kena, 258, 475, 560
knowing the One in, 557–560
knowledge's path of, 169–170, 554–556, 558–559, 587, 601, 602, 651
kuṇḍalinī and, 209–210, 211
Māṇḍukya, 566*n*15
Maitrayani, 138
Maitri, 209, 260, 549, 560
monism of, 30–33, 35, 37, 164, 651, 654
Muṇḍaka, 192, 557, 558, 559, 601
Nādabindu, 499
Neoplatonism and, 549–564, 551–552, 571–572, 581
non-dualism, Many and, 554–556, 558
old, 566*n*15
One and Many and, 552–554, 556, 642
paradoxical formulations of, 556–557
Praśna, 209
reincarnation and, 100–102, 112, 114–115, 121, 129, 132, 138, 140, 141–142, 178
self knowledge in, 190–191
Shandilya, 210
Śvetāśvatara, 70–71, 185, 303, 304, 555, 567*n*29
Taittirīya, 303, 304, 308, 549, 562
Two Paths and, 115–116, 121, 150*n*112
two-level ontology of, 560, 562, 568
Xenophanes and, 49–50, 65*n*54
yoga and, 179, 185, 188
Ur, 240–241, 250, 252, 291*n*106, 422, 464, 643, 652–653
urbanization. *See* city
uroboric (self-destroying) formulas, 451–452, 469–472
Uruk, 245, 246, 250, 262, 281, 283
Uttanka, 263

Vāc, 672, 673
Vacaspati, 528, 649
Vairocana Tower, 578, 579
Vaśeṣika Sūtras, 178, 425, 519, 523
Vaśeṣikas. *See also Nyāya-Vaśesika*
absence in, 529–531, 532, 538*n*44
atomism of, 425, 519–520, 527, 535–536, 539*n*51, 646
categories of, 521–524, 527
causality in, 532–534, 539*nn*50–51
elements for, 524–525
Empedocles and, 520, 524–525. 526
ethics, 534
facts in, 523, 526, 527, 528
historical aspects of, 535–536
infima species of, 527–528
inherence relations in, 531–532
Jain atomism and, 519–520, 525, 527, 535
matter for, 524–525
metaphysics of, 534, 535, 536
particulars in, 520, 527–528
Peripatetics and, 520–536
reincarnation and, 534
soul, mind and, 534–535
substance-attribute relationship of, 526–527, 538*n*25
summing up of, 535–536
time, space and, 525–526
universals in, 527–528, 646
yoga and, 535, 539*n*53
Vaiṣṇavism, 164, 676
Vasubandhu, 425, 572, 573–574, 577, 580, 583*n*25, 585, 643
Vātsyāyana, 516, 520, 531, 539*n*51, 647
Vātulatantra, 226
Veda(s), 558 . *See also Atharva Veda; Ṛg Veda; Yajur Veda*
afterlife, reincarnation and, 112–113, 137–138, 141
dating of, 60–61, 289*n*71, 657, 659
mythology of, 257, 259, 263, 302
as oldest Indo-European document, xix
rejection of, 280, 327, 519, 619, 675
ritual/rite of, 325, 327, 334, 407, 408–409, 558, 619, 672, 674f, 675
vedanā (hedonic feeling), 605, 608, 610, 614, 617, 623, 626, 627
Vedānta, 164, 336–337, 478, 589
Advaita (nondualistic), 58, 165, 170, 336, 391, 445*n*6, 499, 508*n*30, 520, 542, 585–586, 602, 649
early, 165
ethics, imperturbability and, 596
two-level ontology of, 560, 562, 568
Vedic period
Aryans and, 658
late, 269, 285, 661*n*15
middle, 116, 258, 259, 274, 276, 279, 283–284, 285
Vedic tradition. *See also* asceticism; reincarnation
historic *vs.* ahistoric, 644–646
individual (self), the All *(brahman)* and, 562–564, 567*n*29
knowing the One in, 557–560
language importance in, 672–674
Neoplatonism, 549–564, 551–552, 571–572, 581
non-dualism, Many and, 554–556, 558
One and Many and, 552–554, 556
paradoxical formulations of, 556–557
of sacrifice, 407, 408–410, 558
as source of Western culture, 658–660, xvii, xxv
tantra and, 586–587

vegetarianism, 36, 45, 98, 99–100, 106, 201, 268, 391, 443
vidyā (knowledge), 189, 560, 601
Vijñānavāda Buddhism, 568, 571–572, 582*n*5
  dharmadhātu (infinite interpenetration) of, 572–573
  goal of, 579–580
  historical considerations for, 580–581
  levels of consciousness of, 572–573
  Neoplatonism and, 568, 571–581, 582*n*5, 584*n*38
  paratantra (mind) for, 572, 574–575, 577, 579, 580
  parikalpita (ignorance/illusion) for, 572–573, 574, 577
  parinispanna (storehouse consciousness) for, 572, 573–574, 576
  premeations of (enlightenment/nonenlightenment) for, 575–576
vikalpa (model), 421, 432, 474
Vimaṃsaka Sutta, 341
virgin birth, 391
virtue, 439–440, 600
viśiṣṭādvaitin (nondualist), 552
Viṣṇu, 263, 542, 555, 557
Viṣṇu Purāṇa, 39
visualizations, 588–590, 592, 629–630
Visvanatha, 531
Voltaire, Francois, xvii
Vratya, 257, 264, 274–275
Vritra, 259

water, 136, 301, 302, 303, 331
  cosmogony and, 29–30, 59, 313, 327, 407
  memory and spring of, 105–106, 108, 136–137, 146*n*38, 154*n*193
West. *See also* colonialism
  East *vs.*, civilization progress of, 644–647
  Greece as guiding light of, xx
  India as source of, 658–660
  self-knowledge quest by, xix
West, M.L., 13–14, 39, 121–122, 123–126, 145*n*28, 149*n*92, xxviii
wheel
  of Dharma, 486*n*12, 503
  Great, 91
  release from, 166, 178, 190, 278
wisdom, 189, 192, 439, 477, 579. *See also prajñā* ; seers
  cognition of, 189, 192, 439, 441
  happiness, virtue and, 599, 601
  indifference with, 599, 601, 635*n*34
  mental development, reflection for, 607
  with nature, 598
  perfect, 433
  primal, 652, 650
  reason and, 185, 189
  as silence, 471
  transfer of, 442–443
Wisdom Eye, 168, 169, 170, 192, 433
wise men. *See* seers
Wittgenstein, Ludwig, 452, 470, 488*n*56
word, the, 259, 672, 673–674
world government/view, 352, 364
  World Soul, 165, 169, 208, 541, 555, 556, 562, 569
worry, 603, 635*n*40, 641*n*137. *See also prapañca*
writing
  Chalcolitic, 245
  city development and, 243–244
  cuneiform, 243, 246
  development of, 246–247
  Indus (Harappan), 242, 243–244, 246, 247, 281
  Kharoṣṭhī, 372–376, 390
  Mesopotamian, 246
  Sumerian, 243–244
  Susa and, 243–244

Xeniades, 431
Xenocrates, 540, 572, 580–581
Xenophanes, 105, 111
  cosmic cycle of, 73, 74
  monism, Indian thought and, 48–52, 53, 61, 65*n*54
  as monist *vs.* monotheist, 64
  One, unchanging Being, dokos and, 50–51, 53
  skepticism, naturalism and, 319–320
Xenophon, 171, 183
  sacrifice in, 407

Yājñavalkya, 283
  (proto) dialectic, 408, 410, 415, 421, 434
  imperturbability, ethics and, 602
  One and Many problem and, 50–51, 59, 60, 170, 408, 421, 552
  One with *brahman* by, 555, 557, 560–561
  paradox of, 475, 553, 557
  reincarnation and, 100–101, 102, 114–115, 124–125, 138, 140, 141, 183, 275
Yajur Veda, 278–279
Yavanajātaka, 385
Yavanas, 382, 383, 385–386, 387, 502
Yavaneśvara, 385
yoga, 166, 337, 377, 580. *See also* ascetic communities; austerity; enlightenment; Patañjali; seers
  abstinence/austerity in, 182–183, 229, 232–233, 257–258, 268, 278–280, 640*n*114
  āsanas (postures), 219, 268, 285
  ascetic communities for, 8, 10, 17–18, 22*n*95, 99–100, 141–142
  clothing and, 274
  contemplative silence and, 178–179, 269
  detachment in, 184, 640*n*114
  development of, 285–286, 655*n*1
  difficult postures and, 229, 274, 280, 297*n*265, 391
  Egyptian, 268–274, 285, 298*n*267
  fertility cult and, 275
  flying, 263–264
  Greeks and, 355, 382, 385, 391, 393*nn*1–2, 438, 440, 443–444, 449*n*71, 450, 491–492, 494, 495, 540
  hatha, 210, 219, 268
  higher knowledge, consciousness and, 188–189
  iconography, 252–253, 254
  jñāna, 169–170
  karma, 542–543
  kuṇḍalinī, 209–210, 214, 259, 260, 269–273, 298*n*267
  meditation in, 180–182, 285, 341–342, 390
  Ningizzida and kuṇḍalinī, 269–271
  prāna and, 544–545
  purification through, 268
  rāja, 86
  reincarnation and, 140, 278, 285, 296*n*242
  Śaiva, 229, 230, 257, 274
  self knowledge through, 185, 190–192
  sexual, 214
  shamans and, 268–274, 286, 649
  stages for enlightenment in, 184–185, 192
  Stoics and, 547
  sun-gazing, 391
  tantric, 214–215, 257, 590
  Vaśesikas and, 535, 539*n*53
  withdrawal from senses in, 179–181, 182–183, 539*n*53
  of the word, 673–674
Yoga Sūtras, 179, 185, 580, 590
Yogācāra Buddhism, 602, 676
yugas, 71, 76, 83

Zalmoxis, 118–119
Zen
  Great Doubt of, 483
  koan discourse of, 477
  Law of Excluded Middle and, 476

practice of, 431, 441–442, 478, 479, 481–482, 580, 590, 613
religious apprehension/ intuition of, 475–476, 478, 489*n*70
Zeno, 352, 355, 356, 454, 464, 524, 564, 622, 623, 625, 631, 640*n*118
background of, 546, 621, 629, 640*n*114
dialectic and, 416, 417*n*2, 426, 427, 429, 430, 431, 447*nn*25–26, 461, 649, 653
Dichotomy of, 423–424
indifference and, 624, 640*n*112
infinite divisibility continuum of, 423–424, 464, 493, 519, 601, 622
paradoxes of, 465, 475
plurality and, 313, 314, 315, 319, 426
Stoics and, 540, 545, 546
Zeus, 60–61, 104, 148*n*78, 305, 306, 326, 331, 541–543, 545–547, 623, 669
Zoroastrianism, xxviii, 9–10, 69, 122–123, 124–126, 171, 541, 595, 659
Zurvanism, 151*n*131